Donald S. Schen
1964 -5

The National Experience

A HISTORY OF THE UNITED STATES

HARCOURT, BRACE & WORLD, INC.

New York · Burlingame

The National Experience

John M. Blum   YALE UNIVERSITY

Bruce Catton   EDITOR, *American Heritage*

Edmund S. Morgan   YALE UNIVERSITY

Arthur M. Schlesinger, Jr.   HARVARD UNIVERSITY

Kenneth M. Stampp   UNIVERSITY OF CALIFORNIA, BERKELEY

C. Vann Woodward   YALE UNIVERSITY

MAPS BY HARRY SCOTT

Library of Congress Catalog Card Number: 63–11175

Printed in the United States of America

Preface

Men make history. Their ideas and their hopes, their goals and contrivances for reaching those goals, shape all experience, past and present. The Indians, the first Americans, had to decide, by deliberation or by default, how to use the continent and its extraordinary resources. So have the successors of the Indians and the children of those successors—the early European settlers, the English colonists, the men and women of the new United States, and the generations that have followed them. Each generation has committed the nation to a complex of policies, some the product of thought and debate, others of habit or inadvertence, still others of calculated or undiscerning indifference. As the nation has grown, as its population has diversified, its economy matured, and its responsibilities multiplied, questions of national policy have become more difficult to understand, but no more troubling. It took long thought and hard debate to settle the issues of independence, of democratic reform, of expansion, of slavery, of union itself, of control of private economic power, of resistance to totalitarianism across two oceans. All these issues and many more have made up the national experience.

This book endeavors to recount and explain that experience. It examines both the aspirations (often contradictory among themselves) and the achievements (often less grand than the best hopes) of the American people. It examines, too, the ideas, the institutions, and the processes that fed hope and affected achievement. It focuses on the decisions, positive and negative, that reflected national goals and directed national purposes, and consequently it focuses continually on the men who made those decisions, the men who made history. The book emphasizes public policy, but the history of public policy perforce demands continuing discussion of the whole culture that influenced it.

The authors of this book believe that a history emphasizing public policy, so conceived, reveals the fabric and experience of the past more completely than does any other kind of history. They believe, too, that an emphasis on questions of public policy provides the most useful introduction to the history of the United States. In the light of those convictions they have agreed on the focus of this book, on its organization, and on the selection and interpretation of the data it contains. The structure of the separate parts and chapters is now chronological, now topical, depending on the form that seemed most suitable for the explanation of the period or the subject under discussion. The increasing complexity of public issues in the recent past, moreover, has persuaded the authors to devote half of this volume to the period since Reconstruction, indeed more than a third to the twentieth century.

The authors have elected, furthermore, to

confine their work to one volume so as to permit instructors to make generous supplementary assignments from the abundance of excellent monographs, biographies, and "problems" books now readily and inexpensively available. Just as there are clear interpretations of the past in those books, so are there in this, for the authors without exception find meaning in history and feel obliged to say what they see; the truth cannot lie halfway between right and wrong. The authors also believe that, especially for the beginning student of history, literature is better read than read about. Consequently, in commenting on belles-lettres and the other arts, they have consciously stressed those expressions and aspects of the arts relevant to an understanding of public policy. Finally, they have arranged to choose the illustrations and the boxed selections from contemporary and other sources in order to enhance and supplement not only the text but its particular focus.

This is a collaborative book in which each of the six contributors has ordinarily written about a period in which he is a specialist. Yet each has also executed the general purpose of the whole book. Each section of the book has been read and criticized by several of the contributors, of whom one, John M. Blum, helped to edit the entire book. It has profited from the careful attention and advice of several friends. But not even a collaboration as easy and agreeable as this one has been can erase the individuality of the collaborators. Each section of this book displays the particular intellectual and literary style of its contributor; each contributor has been permitted, indeed urged, to remain himself. The ultimate as well as the original responsibility for prose, for historical accuracy, and for interpretation remains that of the author (in one case the authors) of each section of this book: Edmund S. Morgan, Chapters 1–6; Kenneth M. Stampp, Chapters 7–12; John M. Blum and Bruce Catton, together, Chapters 13–14; C. Vann Woodward, Chapters 16–21; John M. Blum, Chapters 15, 22–27, and the sections of Chapter 32 dealing with the period since January 1961; and Arthur M. Schlesinger, Jr., Chapters 28–33.

JOHN M. BLUM

New Haven, Connecticut

A Note

On the Suggestions for Additional Readings

The lists of suggested readings following each chapter of this book are obviously and intentionally selective. They are obviously so because a reasonably complete bibliography of American history would fill a volume larger than this one. They are intentionally so because the authors of the various chapters have tried only to suggest to students those stimulating and useful works that they might profitably and enjoyably explore while studying this text. Consequently each list of suggested readings points to a relatively few significant and well-written books, and each list attempts to emphasize, in so far as possible, books available in inexpensive, paperback editions—books whose titles are marked by an asterisk.

Use of the suggested readings, then, permits a student to begin to range through the rich literature of American history, but interested and energetic students will want to go beyond the lists. They will profit from the bibliographies in many of the works described briefly in this text, especially from the excellent bibliographies in the volumes of the New American Nation Series (Harper), edited by R. Morris and H. Commager. They should also consult the card catalogues in the libraries of their colleges and the invaluable bibliography in the *Harvard Guide to American History* (Belknap). For critical comments about the titles they find, they should go on, when they can, to the reviews in such learned journals as the *American Historical Review,* the *Mississippi Valley Historical Review,* the *Journal of Southern History,* and the *William and Mary Quarterly.*

Those students who want to acquire libraries of their own and who want also to economize by purchasing paperback editions will find the availability of titles in paperbacks at best uncertain. Every few months new titles are published and other titles go out of print. For the most recent information about paperbacks, students should consult the handy guide, *Paperbound Books in Print* (Bowker), which appears quarterly.

The reading lists refer to very few articles, not because articles are unimportant, but because they are often rather inaccessible to undergraduates. There are, however, some useful collections of important, selected articles on American history, such as D. H. Sheehan, ed., *The Making of American History,* 2 vols. (Dryden, 1954), and Sidney Fine and G. S. Brown, eds., *The American Past,* 2 vols. (Macmillan, 1961). Other valuable articles appear in the various pamphlets of the Amherst Series, *Problems in American Civilization* (Heath).

Contemporary documents add depth and excitement to the study of history, as the selections that appear throughout this text suggest. These documents, too, are often inaccessible to students, but, again, there are some helpful collections, including the following:

H. S. Commager and Allan Nevins, *The Heritage of America* (Heath, 1949)

R. N. Current and J. A. Garraty, *Words That Made American History,* 2 vols. (Little, Brown, 1962)

Oscar Handlin, ed., *Readings in American History* (Knopf, 1957)

Richard Hofstadter, *Great Issues in American History,* 2 vols. (Vintage, 1958)

Marvin Meyers *et al., Sources of the American Republic* (Scott, Foresman, 1960)

S. E. Morison, *An Hour of American History* (Beacon, 1960)

Social Sciences I staff, U. of Chicago, *The People Shall Judge,* 2 vols. (U. of Chicago, 1949)

So also, various excellent books organize contemporary and other materials around sundry historical problems, as in Leonard Levy and Merrill Peterson, *Major Crises in American History,* 2 vols. (Harcourt, Brace & World, 1962).

The problems books, documents books, and collections of articles will whet the appetite of engaged students for further reading in the fields of their interest. They can serve in their way, then, as can the lists of suggested readings in this volume, as avenues leading to the adventures of the mind and the development of the understanding that American history affords.

Contents

CHAPTER **31**

The Cold War 730

CHAPTER **32**

The Eisenhower Years 759

Maps

The National Experience

1

Making Use
of a New World

Exploration

The First Americans The first American was an immigrant. Although anthropologists disagree about where man first appeared on earth, no one claims the honor for the Western Hemisphere, which had probably never been seen by human eyes until twenty or thirty thousand years ago. Presumably the earliest immigrant came by way of the Bering Straits and was followed by hundreds, perhaps thousands, more who trickled slowly southward, spreading out across North America and funneling through Mexico into Central and South America, venturing across the water to the Caribbean islands and perhaps much farther, to the South Pacific. The immigration may have gone on for centuries, and it probably included people from various parts of Asia, Africa, and Europe.

For these early arrivals America was no melting pot. The people we lump together as Indians, or Amerinds, were divided into hundreds of tribes, enormously varied in physical appearance, language, and civilization. Those who made their homes south of the present United States were unquestionably the most numerous and the most skillful in exploiting their territory. They were the inventors of Indian corn (maize), as efficient a method of transforming earth into food as man has ever devised. Corn is a hybrid so complex that botanists are still not certain from what wild plant or plants the Indians developed it. The early inhabitants of Mexico and South America were skilled in other ways too: they built great cities of stone, richly carved and ornamented. They knew enough mathematics and astronomy to construct a calendar that required no leap year and to predict eclipses of the sun. And they knew enough political science to construct strong governments under which they worked out an advanced division of labor.

By contrast, the Indians who lived north of Mexico were primitive. They made less effective use of the land, and it supported far fewer of them, probably not many more than a million in the present area of the United States. They grew some corn and other vegetables but also relied on nuts and berries, game and fish, and starved when these were unavailable. In parts of the Southeast they organized governments with real authority, the Powhatan Confederacy in Virginia and the Creek Confederacy in the Gulf Plains. But most often they joined together only loosely in tribes or clans under leaders or chiefs whose authority was merely nominal. They had dignity in abundance, self-reliance, and self-control—it was rare for an Indian to show anger or even to raise his voice. Indeed they were so self-reliant, so individualistic, that even in war it was apt to be every man for himself; and in peace they could not achieve the cooperation and organization, the division of labor, needed to make the most of the country's resources, or to defend it against strangers better organized than they.

3

The Rise of Kings and Commerce

These strangers began to arrive shortly after 1492. There had been earlier visitors in the eleventh century, when some wandering Norsemen from Iceland, led by Leif Ericsson, spent a winter in what they called Vinland, probably somewhere in New England or Nova Scotia. A few years later other Icelanders attempted to establish a settlement. But the Norsemen had no real need for this vast continent and went home without leaving any perceptible mark on it.

If Columbus had sailed when the Norsemen did, his voyages would probably have had as little effect as theirs on the course of history. By 1492, however, Europeans were ready for new worlds. During the intervening centuries two important historical developments had prepared them. The first was the rise of a large merchant class hungry for foreign trade. Spices, dyestuffs, and textiles from India and the Far East traveled overland by slow, expensive caravan through Asia, or partly by sail through the Red Sea or the Persian Gulf, passing from one dealer to another along the way until they finally reached the market places of Europe. The prices people were willing to pay for these exotic imports were enough to send fifteenth-century sailors in search of sea routes to the source of the treasures. A direct sea route would permit importation in greater volume at less expense and would net the importer a huge profit.

Portugal took the lead in maritime exploration with a new type of vessel, the caravel—faster, more maneuverable, more seaworthy than any formerly known. Portuguese explorers, encouraged by their kings and by Prince Henry the Navigator (1394–1460), discovered the Azores and pushed their caravels farther and farther south along the coast of Africa. In 1488 Bartholomeu Diaz rounded the Cape of Good Hope. Ten years later Vasco da Gama reached India.

The rise of kings, supporting and supported by the simultaneous rise of merchants, was the second great development that prepared Europeans to use a new world. At the time of Leif Ericsson's voyage Europe was divided into tiny principalities, usually owing nominal al-

Christopher Columbus:
A man with a mission.

legiance to a king but actually dominated by local magnates who levied tolls on all trade passing through their territories. Even towns and cities tended to be autonomous, bristling with local regulations designed to discourage trade with the outside world. The rise of kings meant the reorganization of society into larger units, into national states more wealthy and more powerful than any one of the towns or cities or principalities of which they were composed. A state organized under a king had the power and resources to cut through the strangling web of local trade barriers, to sponsor exploration for new lands to trade with, and even to seize the lands and their riches when the natives were not strong enough to resist.

During most of the fifteenth century Portugal far outran the rest of Europe in pursuit of foreign trade and of new lands to conquer. Other countries were still too troubled by domestic feuds and foreign wars to offer much competition. The first to emerge as a serious rival was Portugal's neighbor, Spain. And as luck had it, Spain was also first to find America and first to find a use for it.

Columbus and the Spaniards   Christopher Columbus, the son of a Genoese weaver, was a man with a mission. He wanted to reach the Orient by sailing west, and he was convinced that the distance was no more than three or four thousand miles. Columbus was wrong, and when he tried to sell his idea, the experts told him so. The experts had known for centuries that the world was round, but they had a much better notion of its size than Columbus did. The king of Portugal would have none of his scheme, and neither would anyone else until Queen Isabella of Spain, who was not an expert, decided to take a chance. In the very year when the consolidation of the Spanish monarchy was completed by the conquest of Granada from the Moors, she persuaded her husband, Ferdinand II, to pay for an expedition of three ships and to give Columbus authority, under Spain, over any lands he might discover on the way.

Armed with this commission and with a letter to the emperor of China, Columbus made his magnificent mistake. He failed to deliver the letter but found America (so named after his death for a later explorer, Amerigo Vespucci), at the island of San Salvador, on October 12, 1492. From here he threaded his way through the other Bahamas to Cuba and Hispaniola. By March 15, 1493, he was back in Spain. In succeeding years he explored the rest of the Caribbean area, still looking for China and Japan. Though he did not find them, he did find gold; and everyone in Europe knew what to do with that.

But for the gold, Europeans would probably have looked upon America as a mere obstacle on the route to the Orient. Even after Ferdinand Magellan carried out Columbus' original intention by sailing around the tip of South

Voyages of Columbus

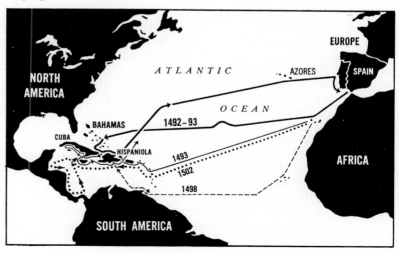

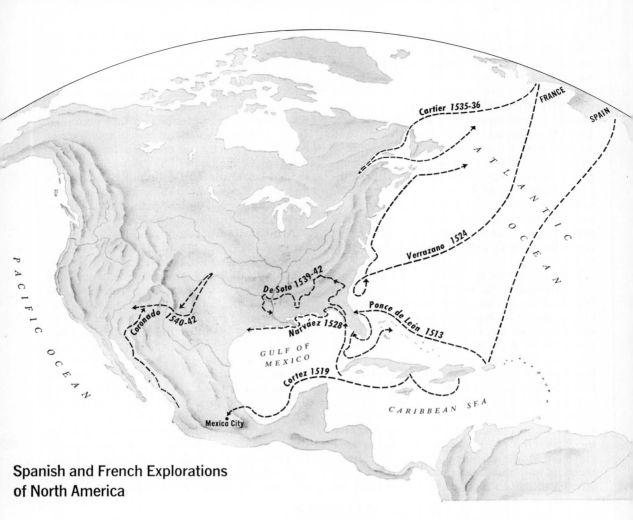

Spanish and French Explorations
of North America

America (1519–22), explorers continued for two centuries to probe hopefully up American rivers in search of the Pacific. But the Spaniards recognized at once that Columbus' substitute for China might have advantages surpassing the original. With approval of Pope Alexander VI they joined the Portuguese in the Treaty of Tordesillas (1494), dividing the New World by a line drawn north and south, 370 leagues west of the Cape Verde Islands (between the present forty-sixth and forty-seventh meridians of longitude): Spain was to get everything she found to the west of the line, Portugal everything to the east. Thereafter Spaniards swarmed over the Caribbean islands and on to the mainland of North and South America.

In numbers the invaders were few—not many Spaniards cared to leave home—but they were courageous, unscrupulous, and tough. They wanted gold, and they were ready to take what the natives had and make them dig for more. The Indians were no match for them. The Spaniards killed or enslaved wherever they went, and slavery was only a slower form of killing. After working the Caribbean natives to death, they brought in Negro slaves purchased from the Portuguese. The Negroes died too, but the Spaniards got their gold, shiploads of it.

On the mainland, where the Indians were more numerous, small armies led by private adventurers, the conquistadores, subdued whole countries. Hernando Cortez with 550 men conquered the Aztecs in Mexico—and took their gold (1519–21). Francisco Pizarro conquered the Incas of Peru—and took their gold and silver (1531–35). Where people were more plentiful than gold, the Spaniards used them to grow or gather things as good as gold. Organizing the natives as serfs in *encomiendas*, under Spanish overlords, they produced sugar, indigo, foodstuffs to feed the workers in the mines, and plants that Europeans valued for their alleged medicinal properties. The supposed cure for any disease in the sixteenth century was likely to be a plant, and several American plants gained so high a reputation that Europe bought them by the shipload— sassafras, sarsaparilla, guaiacum—all thought to be sovereign cures for syphilis.

The Spaniards had other uses for the people of America. The invaders made wives of the Indian women, and the resolute bands of priests and friars who accompanied the conquistadores were eager for Indian souls. Rivaling the *encomiendas* were the missions, communities in which the Church directed the bodies as well as the souls of the converts. Some were little better than slave camps; others resembled Utopian communities.

North of Mexico the Spaniards found little to interest them. Ponce de León cruised along the shores of the Florida peninsula in 1513, and Panfilo de Narváez and Hernando de Soto both explored the western side of the peninsula and the Gulf Plains before the middle of the sixteenth century. But there was no visible gold about and both expeditions marched on across the continent to Mexico without finding anything on the way that made them want to stay. In a futile search for seven legendary cities of gold, Francisco Vásquez de Coronado circled through present Arizona, New Mexico, Texas, Oklahoma, and Kansas (1540–42). He too thought the country not worth taking and returned to Mexico. During the second half of the sixteenth century the Spaniards did establish a fort at St. Augustine, Florida (1565), and extended missions northward to Port Royal (South Carolina) and for a few years even to the Chesapeake Bay region. By the end of the century they had begun to plant missions and *encomiendas* in present New Mexico and Arizona. In the seventeenth century they moved into Texas and in the eighteenth into California. But long before this the force of the Spanish thrust had spent itself, and other countries were ready to make use of the empty and idle American continent.

The Europeans in North America   Columbus never saw the shores of North America, nor do we know what European was the first to do so. Perhaps other sailors had happened on it just as the Norsemen had. There may even have been fishermen walking the streets of St. Malo or Bristol or Plymouth who could have told Columbus of a distant coast where pines were tall and codfish plentiful. If so, no chronicler set down their discoveries until in 1497 John Cabot, like Columbus a Genoese, sailed west for the king of England and returned to report a new land. Henry VII gave Cabot £10 and an annuity of £20. Cabot undertook another voyage the next year, but he and other Europeans thought of the new land as a barrier, not an opportunity.

In 1524 the king of France, Francis I, sent a Florentine navigator, Giovanni da Verrazano, along the Atlantic coast from North Carolina to Nova Scotia in search of a passage through the barrier to the Pacific. Ten years later he sent Jacques Cartier on the same errand. Cartier, encouraged by the promisingly large entrance of the St. Lawrence River, sailed inland as far as the first rapids before giving up. He was sufficiently impressed by the surrounding country, however, to attempt a settlement there in 1541. Since Spain had found riches in the southern continent, it seemed reasonable to expect them in the north as well. When Canadian gold proved to be fool's gold, Canadian diamonds quartz, and Canadian winters terrible, the colonists returned home, and France forgot about North America for the rest of the century.

The first people to find a lasting use for the continent were summer people, who liked the fishing there. Every spring in the ports of France, England, Portugal, and Spain fishermen piled aboard their precarious craft and headed for the Grand Banks, where the continental shelf of North America lies submerged at a depth that codfish find congenial. They set up docks and drying stages ashore and assembled knocked-down dories and other small boats carried in the holds of their ships. They killed a few auks or netted some minnows for bait, rowed far out to the deeper waters, and fished all day with hand lines. Each night they brought in their catch to be dried, salted, and packed for sale in the markets of Europe. Caring little for the doings of their remote monarchs, they lived together in little international communities in Newfoundland and Nova Scotia—sleeping aboard their ships or in rough cabins ashore, planting gardens, and visiting one another of an evening—until the approach of winter sent them and the cod to friendlier climates. None of them seems to have contemplated a permanent residence.

As the years passed, more and more Europeans sailed west to cruise along the coasts of North America, catching its codfish, prying into bays and rivers, kidnaping an occasional Indian to show off at home. Gradually they became aware that the country had more to offer than fish and pine trees. Behind the coast lay rivers and lakes teeming with beaver, otter, and other fur-bearing animals, which the Indians were adept at trapping. When Indian and European met, the Indian was quick to recognize. The furs he offered in exchange brought a good price in Europe, especially beaver, which was turned into felt for hats.

Early in the seventeenth century the French, the Dutch, and the Swedes all set up permanent fur-trading posts in America. The great French explorer Samuel de Champlain, after reconnoitering the New England coast and the St. Lawrence region, founded Quebec in 1608. Henry Hudson, an Englishman working for a Dutch company, in 1609 sailed up the river he named for himself; the Dutch planted trading posts there in 1624, on the Delaware River in 1623, and on the Connecticut River in 1633. A Swedish company also maintained posts on the Delaware from 1638 until the Dutch seized them in 1655.

The French and the Dutch came to trade with the Indians, not to subjugate them. Neither in New France nor in New Netherland, as their settlements were called, did the Indian become a slave. Instead he lived on in his customary manner, roaming the woods he had roamed before, though trapping beaver in unaccustomed numbers. Contact with the Europeans inevitably meant new things for him: guns, hatchets, sharper rivalry with other tribes, a weakening of tribal customs, Christianity, comfort, progress, deadly drinks, deadlier diseases. But the continent was still his. In the course of time both the French and the Dutch did try to transform their trading posts into larger settlements of Europeans, who would supplant rather than suppress the Indian, but this was only after the English had arrived on the scene to show the world at last how North America could best be used.

Tudor England and the New World

Before England could turn her interests to America at all, before her merchants could support expensive and dangerous overseas expeditions, she had to experience the same political consolidation under a powerful king that Spain and Portugal had undergone a century earlier. Henry VII, who sent John Cabot to America in 1497, began the job; his son Henry VIII and his granddaughter Elizabeth I finished it. In the process they transformed England from a Catholic country into a Protestant one, a fact that would affect profoundly the land which Cabot found.

Henry VIII and the Reformation Soon after Martin Luther launched the Reformation, which split the monolithic west-European Church into Protestant and Roman Catholic segments, Luther's teachings reached England. Perhaps no Englishman was less receptive to them than the king, Henry VIII, who demonstrated his devotion to Rome by writing a book against the German heretic. The pope rewarded Henry by conferring on him the title "Defender of the Faith."

Before many years passed Henry found himself, if no friendlier to Luther, a good deal less friendly to the pope. Henry was the most powerful king England had ever known, so powerful that no baron or lesser local potentate could oppose him. Only one set of men in England dared challenge his authority: the priests and bishops, the monks and abbots, who acknowledged a higher power than Henry not only in the heavens but on earth, in Rome. Moreover, the Church owned about one-fourth of England and collected a yearly income of more than £320,000, much of it from the rent of lands owned by monasteries. When Henry needed funds to meet the cost of England's new and growing governmental machinery, the wealth of the monasteries inevitably caught his eye. In 1539 he found an opportunity to lay hold of it.

In 1509 Henry had married Catherine of Aragon, daughter of Ferdinand and Isabella, and in twenty years she bore him no son who lived. Henry desperately wanted an heir, and besides he had grown tired of Catherine. In 1529 he asked the pope for a divorce. When the pope refused, Henry defied him, married Anne Boleyn, severed England's ties with Rome, made himself head of the English Church—and in 1539 confiscated the monastic lands.

The Results of Henry's Break with Rome Although Henry never showed the slightest interest in the New World, his divorce and his defiance of the pope had enormous consequences for both England and America.

The first and simplest consequence was that his new wife bore him a daughter, Elizabeth, who was to become England's greatest monarch. Elizabeth became queen in 1558 and ruled for forty-four glorious years—years in which Englishmen triumphed on land, at sea, and in the human spirit. Under her direction England became strong enough to begin the building of a North American empire.

Second, by divorcing his Spanish queen Henry touched off over a hundred years of intermittent hostility with Spain. Spain, the spearhead of Catholicism and the headquarters of the Inquisition, gradually became synonymous in Protestant England with antichrist. Englishmen attacked the Spaniard most successfully at sea not only by outright war but by privateering against Spanish shipping. The English privateers (or sea dogs, as they came to be called) resembled the earlier conquistadores in their daring, toughness, unscrupulousness, and flair for the spectacular and heroic. But the sea dogs operated on sea rather than on land, scouring the Atlantic for homeward-bound Spanish vessels laden with gold and silver from the New World. Under Queen Elizabeth privateering against Spain reached its height and drew England's attention to the riches of America.

Third, Henry's break with Rome gave impetus to a Protestant movement in England that had been covertly under way for some years. Its adherents interpreted Henry's de-

fiance of the pope as a total repudiation of Roman hierarchy, ritual, and doctrine. Henry himself would have been content to serve as England's pope without substantially altering the internal organization or doctrines of the Church. But he could not wholly control the forces he had unleashed. The ideas of Luther and of the French reformer John Calvin became increasingly popular during the next 125 years; and, as their numbers grew, the extreme Calvinists—the Puritans—became increasingly discontent with the incomplete reformation of the English church. Many of them would come to America with a view to completing the Reformation there.

Finally, Henry's confiscation of the monasteries set off a train of unexpected events that indirectly provided still more Englishmen willing to people a new world. Henry, not content with the income from the lands he had confiscated, began to sell them; succeeding monarchs continued the process, selling other royal lands as well. They were led to do so partly by a steady rise in prices during the sixteenth and seventeenth centuries (the so-called Price Revolution) that was induced or accelerated by the flow of Spanish gold from America. Other people felt the pinch, especially landlords whose rents were usually fixed by custom and were unalterable. They too began selling land to make ends meet. Inevitably the turnover of so much real estate had widespread repercussions: in some places rich men got richer and poor men poorer, while in other areas the rich were getting poor and the poor rich. The sale of monastic lands was certainly not wholly responsible for this upheaval, but it was a first step in the chain of events that destroyed the social and economic security of large numbers of Englishmen and helped to make the fortunes of others, especially the merchants. Whoever lost from the rise of prices and the sale of lands, it was not they. As the sixteenth century wore on, they accumulated more and more capital, enough to finance costly overseas expeditions, while men who lost their homes or fortunes began to think of regaining them, perhaps in another part of the world.

Gilbert Finds a New Use for America The historical developments which were set in motion by Henry VIII's break with

Rome became significant for America only gradually. After the voyage of John Cabot in 1497, Englishmen showed very little interest in the New World until 1576 when the Cathay Company (Cathay was another name for China) was formed to trade with China by way of North America. The company sent Martin Frobisher to find a way through the continent. He probed the northern waters and found Baffin Land and Frobisher's Bay, where glittering gold-colored rocks diverted his attention from further search. With the usual captive Indian and a case of ore samples, he hurried back to England. The assayers declared that the ore was indeed gold, and he returned to North America for more. When the two hundred tons he brought back turned out to be iron pyrites, the Cathay Company folded up. For years thereafter Englishmen with capital to invest were wary of risking it in America.

Although the Cathay Company had planned to establish a small permanent settlement in America, it was intended to serve merely as a supply station for voyages to the Orient. The first Englishman, probably the first European, to have a glimmering of the continent's colonial future was a soldier of fortune named Humphrey Gilbert. Gilbert had served the queen in Ireland, where his skill in exterminating the natives won him a knighthood. While there he concocted a scheme for settling Ireland with Englishmen. But North America was a larger Ireland. Englishmen planted there could exploit the natives (the counterpart of the wild Irish), forestall Spanish settlement, catch codfish, and search for a passage to the Pacific (Gilbert wrote a tract in 1576 to prove that there must be one). When the passage was found, they could supply ships passing through. What was more immediately attractive, an American colony would serve as a base from which sea dogs could raid the Spanish treasure fleets that sailed every year from the Caribbean. In every way America was more attractive than Ireland.

Gilbert, impelled by greed and chauvinism, had great vision: he was the first to see America as a place for Englishmen to live. In 1578 he induced Queen Elizabeth to grant him a charter empowering him to discover and take possession of North American lands not claimed by any other Christian monarch. Within six years he was supposed to settle a colony over which he would exercise absolute authority provided he made no laws contrary to the Christian faith, and provided he gave the queen one-fifth of the gold and silver he mined (a provision generally inserted by subsequent monarchs in such charters).

Gilbert made two attempts to found his colony. The first attempt, in 1578, is a mystery. No one knows where he went or what he found, but there is a strong suspicion that he went not far and found a number of ships not his own—in short, that piracy, for the moment, proved more attractive than colonization.

Gilbert's second attempt, in 1583, was a larger undertaking, for by this time he had managed to sell his idea to other Englishmen: noblemen who felt the pressure of inflated prices and the loss of lands and power their fathers had had; merchants who scented opportunities for trade in the new land; discontented religious minorities, privateers, pirates, paupers, and fools. Drawing men and money from these divergent sources, Gilbert was able to equip an expedition. One ship he owned himself. Another he stole from a pirate just before departing, and took her along, pirate crew and all. Three more ships were contributed by enthusiastic backers. He got under way in June 1583, with 260 prospective settlers, including many craftsmen. Apparently they were ill supplied, and one ship had to turn back for lack of provisions. The pirate ship had no such trouble: she simply plundered another vessel encountered along the way.

In August the expedition reached Newfoundland, where Gilbert came upon a sizable international community of summer fishermen. He probably did not intend to establish his colony this far north (though it should be remembered that Newfoundland is south of England), but he made a great ceremony of taking possession of the settlement. The fishermen humored him and even agreed to pay rent for their fishing stages. They probably calculated, rightly, that no one would come to collect it.

After two weeks in Newfoundland, the men on one of the ships decided they had had enough of America and sailed for home. Gil-

English Explorations of the New World

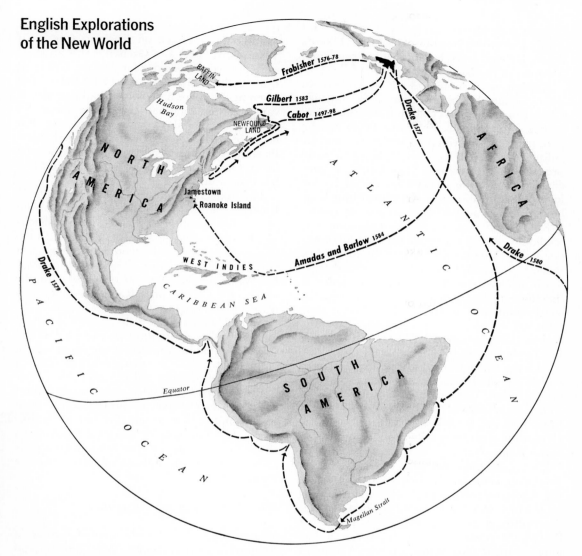

bert, with the other three, cruised southward, filled with enthusiasm by the splendor of the uninhabited coast. He lost another ship on a reef, with all the eighty men aboard, and shortly thereafter was obliged to turn the two remaining ships back to England for supplies. But his spirits were still high, and he talked expansively to his comrades about his plans for the following year and the £10,000 he was going to borrow from the queen. In mid-ocean they ran into an alarmingly heavy sea, but Gilbert demonstrated his nonchalance by sitting on the afterdeck of his small vessel reading a book. At one point he shouted across to a friend in the other ship: "We are as near to heaven by sea as by land." That night, as the others watched, the lights of his vessel went out. No more was ever heard of the man who first envisaged England's American empire.

Raleigh and Roanoke   Although Gilbert's ventures accomplished nothing concrete, he had stirred the imagination of other Englishmen: the kind of men who backed him would back other expeditions to the New World. Before his last voyage, he had enlisted the talents of his younger half-brother, Sir Walter Raleigh. Raleigh equaled Gilbert in daring and exceeded him in polish. He was a favorite with Queen Elizabeth, who gave him nearly everything he asked for. After Gilbert's death, Raleigh asked her for a charter to found a colony in the New World.

Raleigh was, as interested as Gilbert in piracy against Spanish treasure fleets, but like Gilbert he wanted his colony to be more than a base of operations. From the beginning he planned it as a permanent settlement and he enlisted his friend Richard Hakluyt to write propaganda persuading Englishmen to emigrate. Hakluyt too became fascinated by the idea of colonization and developed into England's greatest advocate of overseas expansion.

Raleigh got his charter in 1584 and immediately sent out a reconnoitering force under Philip Amadas and Arthur Barlow. They made their landfall a couple of thousand miles south of Newfoundland—perhaps in order to be closer to the Spaniards—and explored the coast south of Chesapeake Bay. When they returned with glowing descriptions of the region, Raleigh named it Virginia in honor of Elizabeth the Virgin Queen.

In 1585 Raleigh fitted out an expedition to settle Roanoke Island, near the present boundary between Virginia and North Carolina. The group, under the command of Ralph Lane, included John White, an artist; Thomas Cavendish, who later sailed round the world; and Thomas Hariot, a noted mathematician. White made some excellent drawings of the American Indians, the best executed during the whole colonial period; Hariot took notes from which he later prepared the first detailed description of any part of the present United States. The settlers themselves, instead of digging in, spent their time searching Virginia's rivers unsuccessfully for the Pacific, and her shores unsuccessfully for gold. In June 1586, when Sir Francis Drake called to visit them after searching successfully for gold in the holds of Spanish ships, they all climbed aboard with him and went home.

Raleigh tried again the next year, 1587, sending 120 persons under the command of John White. White spent a month getting the new Roanoke settlement started and then returned to England for supplies, leaving his daughter, her husband, and their new-born child with the settlers. A supply fleet commanded by Sir Richard Grenville was pre-

pared, but the Spaniards chose this moment for an all-out attack on England (the great Spanish Armada) and Grenville and his ships were pressed into service for defense. Not until 1590 could White sail back to Roanoke, and when he got there his colonists had completely vanished. Someone had carved the name of a neighboring island, CROATOAN, on a post. But no trace of the colonists was ever found there. Presumably, hostile Indians had overwhelmed them, but to this day no real clue to their fate has been found.

The sixteenth century closed without an English colony in North America. Raleigh turned his attention to South America. Richard Hakluyt sang the praises of England's explorers and published accounts of their great voyages in *The Principal Navigations of the English Nation* (1589). But no one else with the vision of a Gilbert or a Raleigh stepped forward to lead Englishmen to new homes.

Actually Gilbert and Raleigh were as wrong, in their way, as Columbus. He expected to find China and found America. They expected not only to settle North America but to make a profit out of it. They failed, and even if their settlements had succeeded there would almost certainly have been no profit, unless from piracy. But they were not the last to be mistaken. In 1606 another group of Englishmen risked their money, and lost it, in an enterprise from which in the fullness of time grew the United States.

The Founding of Virginia

While Elizabeth reigned, men of daring in England enjoyed risking their money and their lives for her by attacking Spain. Her successor, James I, was so different from the great queen that he has always suffered by comparison. Elizabeth knew everything about power, and kept her own counsel. James knew everything about everything and told everybody. One of the things he knew was that the war with Spain had gone on long enough. In 1604, the year after his accession, he made a peace that lasted twenty years.

James was probably right in ending the war, but Englishmen did not love him for it, especially after he told them that raids on Spanish shipping must cease. During the six-

Indians of the Virginia area, as seen by John White.

teenth century the line between legitimate privateering and piracy had been left conveniently thin, and hijacked Spanish gold had poured into England. Francis Drake alone picked up $200 million worth of loot from Spanish ships he met during his dramatic voyage around the globe (1577–80). Elizabeth knighted Drake for his exploits and cheerfully collected a share of the profits. But James foreswore such profits for his subjects as well as himself. As a result, men with spare lives and money began to think again about getting gold where the Spaniards got it. Efforts to find it in North America had thus far been unsuccessful, but no one had tried very hard. Even if no gold was found, the continent might hold other things of value. After the Roanoke venture of 1586, Thomas Hariot had described some promising native commodities, including sassafras, which was

selling at high prices in London. And piracy itself, now that the king had pledged his protection to Spanish shipping, might still be carried on from a base out of royal reach on the other side of the Atlantic. And so the tantalizing possibility of riches from America again lured Englishmen to try to plant a colony there.

Jamestown   In 1606 a number of men joined to petition the king for authority to establish colonies in America. Most of them were merchants, and merchants had discovered a means of undertaking large and dangerous enterprises without risking financial ruin. Their scheme was the joint-stock company, in which participants profited or suffered in proportion to the number of shares they purchased. By investing modestly in a number of companies a man would gain only modest profits from successful ventures, but he would

Virginia and New England Land Grants

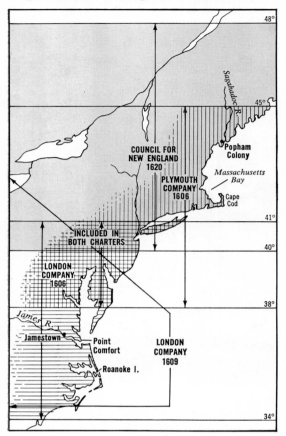

also avoid heavy losses from unsuccessful ones. In this way, through many small contributions, it was possible to accumulate the large amounts of capital necessary for undertakings that were beyond the range of private fortunes. The joint-stock company became the principal instrument of England's overseas expansion.

The men who petitioned the king in 1606 were divided into two groups, one from London, the other from Plymouth; and the king gave them a charter incorporating two companies for the colonization of North America: the Virginia Company of Plymouth was to operate in the northern part of the continent, and the Virginia Company of London in the southern part. The companies planned to send out settlers who would agree to relinquish the fruits of their labors to the investors for the first seven years; after that the settlers could enrich themselves. Anyone willing to pay his own passage was free to begin getting rich at once.

Both companies got off to a quick start. The Plymouth group dispatched an exploratory expedition in 1606, and in 1607 founded a colony at the mouth of the Sagadahoc River in Maine. The colony survived only one winter. The Virginia Company of London, in December 1606, sent over its first settlers, a hundred men and four boys crammed aboard three small ships, the *Susan Constant*, the *Godspeed*, and the *Discovery*. In May 1607 they sailed up a river they called the James and landed on a peninsula they called Jamestown. Swampy and forested, the site was well situated for defense but a haven for malaria-carrying mosquitoes. The colonists made almost every possible mistake in their new environment, but they also corrected their mistakes; and they had the vision, the courage, or the foolhardiness to stick it out.

Their first big problem was leadership. In the charter granting authority to settle the colony the king had retained authority to govern the colony himself, and he exercised it through a council sitting in England. This council in turn acted through another sitting in Virginia. The Virginia council consisted of seven men with a president who presided over its meetings but who had no authority to give orders of his own and no power to enforce orders transmitted from the king's council in England. Government by council proved to be no government at all. The members of the council in the colony quarreled with one another, and the colonists, undisciplined and disorganized, neglected the elementary tasks of plowing, planting, and building.

Fortunately one man had the nerve to take command. John Smith, twenty-seven years old, of humble background but no humility, was not popular with the other members of the council, all men of greater age, importance, and indecision. Smith had spent four years fighting the Turks in Hungary, where he had been captured, sold into slavery, and rescued by fair maidens. In Virginia, by his own account, when the other members of the council proved fools, knaves, or cowards he took control of the colony, explored it, mapped it, overawed the Indians (and was again rescued

C.Smith taketh the King of Pamavnkee priſoner 1608

John Smith had the nerve to take command.

by a maiden, Pocahontas), and obtained from them the corn that kept the settlers from starving. He stopped the disorganized scramble for gold, built fortifications, planted Indian corn, and cut a cargo of cedar wood to send back to the investors as the first tangible evidence of the colony's worth. He later told about it with such relish for his own role that readers ever since have suspected his veracity. Nevertheless, wherever his account can be checked, it holds up. Moreover, he prepared a surprisingly accurate map of the region—a map that could only have been the product of first-hand observation.

In London, however, the armchair colo-nizers were not pleased. Smith, they heard, was unkind to the Indians. He had failed to find either gold or the Pacific Ocean. And some of the other members of the Virginia council, returning to the mother country, de-scribed his leadership as tyranny. The com-pany did recognize, however, that the colony needed stronger direction. In 1609 it obtained a new royal charter establishing a new govern-ing council (resident in London) composed entirely of company members and empowered to appoint an all-powerful governor or gover-nors in the colony. The council decided on a single governor who should choose a council of Virginians to advise him. To prevent a repetition of the colony's earlier squabbles over leadership and to ensure that the governor's council understood that its function was limited to advice, the London council specified that the Virginia councilors "shall not have, single nor together, anie bindinge or negative voice or power." The post of governor went not to Smith but to a nobleman, Lord De La Warr.

Under the new charter the company launched an elaborate campaign to sell Virginia to the English public. With the proceeds of stock sold at £12 10s. a share, it fitted out a fleet of nine vessels to carry some six hundred emigrants. Some were servants who had agreed to work for the company for seven years in return for their passage. The rest paid their own way (passage was worth about £6) and received a share of stock as a bonus. All would work together until 1616, at which time the servants would be freed, the profits would be divided among the shareholders both in England and in America, and every shareholder would receive at least a hundred acres of land.

The expedition set sail from Plymouth in June 1609. Though one of the ships was wrecked at Bermuda, at least four hundred settlers reached Virginia that summer. Unfortunately Lord De La Warr was not among them. His departure from England had been delayed, and his substitute, Sir Thomas Gates, was on the ship lost at Bermuda. John Smith, injured in a gunpowder explosion, returned to England in the fall of 1609 and from then until the arrival of Governor Thomas Dale in 1611 the colony was without effective government and fell into worse disorder than before. Men starved; fortifications fell to ruins; at one point the entire colony had embarked, prepared to abandon the settlement, when a relief ship arrived. After 1611, Governor Dale and Governor Samuel Argall, who succeeded him, imposed rigorous disciplinary laws and resumed the course set by John Smith. Once again the colonists began to plant corn, erect and repair fortifications, and build houses. The settlement spread up the shores of the James River; women began to arrive; and gradually life in Virginia, though still arduous, became more normal.

But the men who left England for Virginia wanted more than corn bread and a place to

By the end of the sixteenth century people were smoking for the fun of it.

lay their heads. To them survival was a means to an end, and they kept looking for a way to wealth, a way to live better in Virginia than they had in England. Since they had found no gold or silver, they had to find some other commodity of high value that they could produce in sufficient quantity and with sufficient ease to make the long voyage to English or European markets worthwhile. They tried cedar. They tried sassafras. But the market for both was quickly satisfied. The directors of the company had high hopes at different times for wines, silk, iron, tar. But in 1612, though they were not at once aware of it, the Virginians discovered their future—in smoke.

Tobacco was native to America. The Indians had taught the Spaniards to use it, and the Spaniards had taught the rest of Europe. At first it was valued only as a medicine, said to cure any disease afflicting a man from the waist up. But by the end of the sixteenth century people were smoking for the fun of it, much to the distress of those who knew better, including King James, and much to the joy of Spanish tobacco merchants. The Indians of Virginia smoked a native variety, coarse and unpalatable. John Rolfe, who later gained greater fame by marrying Pocahontas, in 1612 tried planting the West Indian species, just as other settlers were experimenting with other

Spanish products. The West Indian variety grew extraordinarily well in Virginia, but it did not smoke as well as when grown in the tropics and it consequently brought a lower price. It was nevertheless by far the most profitable commodity Virginia had yet been made to yield. The settlers turned enthusiastically to tobacco culture, and by 1617 were able to ship twenty thousand pounds to England.

The Virginia Company's Great Effort The stockholders of the Virginia Company were pleased to have their faltering confidence in the colony reconfirmed by the promising shipments of tobacco. Hitherto they had received nothing but a few tons of sassafras, cedar, and other trifles in return for an investment of approximately £50,000. In fact, when they sat down to divide up their profits in 1616, they had found nothing to divide except the land itself, and to many of them it hardly seemed worth dividing. Moreover, most of the servants they had sent over to work for the company had served out their time and become free to work for themselves. To hire more men to produce so little would be to throw good money after bad.

Although the colonists' success with tobacco rekindled the expectations of the investors, they did not suppose that the colony could prosper with that product alone. But if Virginia could grow tobacco there must be other things it could produce too. They must keep the settlers experimenting until the right products were found, and then everyone could sit back and reap the profits of perseverance. While this new burst of enthusiasm was upon them, the members of the Virginia Company decided to revitalize and expand their venture by means of a reform program which they inaugurated in 1618 under the leadership of Sir Edwin Sandys, a prominent figure in the English House of Commons. The program contained four points designed to entice more adventurers (investors), more planters (settlers), and more servants:

1. By overhauling its land policies the company made both investment and emigration more profitable. Henceforth anyone who paid for the passage of a man to Virginia, himself or anyone else, received a "headright" of fifty acres. A wealthy individual investor could send

over servants to cultivate headright lands for him as a private plantation. Less wealthy investors could pool their funds and send over servants to cultivate their headright lands as a joint enterprise. The sponsors acquired joint ownership of fifty acres of land for each man sent and received an agreed percentage of the profit from the crops; the servants worked for an agreed number of years in return for their passage and a percentage of the profits. These joint enterprises were known as "particular plantations." The Virginia Company itself sent over more servants who worked on company lands for seven years and received half of whatever profit their labor produced. Anyone who owned headright lands paid the company an annual "quitrent" of a shilling per fifty acres. Thus the company, with almost unlimited acreage at its disposal, ensured that it would gain a perpetual income from rents. For the original investors and colonists there was a land bonus. To the hundred acres of land free of rent that had already been given to shareholders, both adventurers and planters, the company added the promise of another hundred acres as soon as the first grant had been "sufficiently peopled." The original servants, who had already served out their terms, were encouraged to remain in Virginia by the grant of a hundred acres apiece, but had to pay the company an annual quitrent of two shillings on it.

2. To make life in Virginia more like life in England the company relaxed the severity of its discipline and assured actual and potential settlers that henceforth the colony would be governed by English law and that the colonists would have the rights of Englishmen.

3. Even more important, the company decided to give the settlers a voice in the management of the colony. The planters were allowed to elect representatives to an assembly which would provide the company with badly needed advice. The company retained a veto on the assembly's actions, but the assembly was promised an eventual veto on the company's actions.

4. The final point in the new program called for an all-out effort to diversify the colony's activities. The company itself took responsibility for sending over various craftsmen: vintners, ironworkers, brick-makers, glass-

blowers. Somewhere among these skills, it was hoped, would be the right ones to give Virginia a healthy and profitable economy of which tobacco-growing would be only one part.

For five years and more, new settlers streamed into the colony. By the end of 1618 the population, which was only 400 in April of that year, had risen to 1000. Between 1618 and 1624, about 4000 more arrived. To judge by the number of ships landing passengers in Virginia, the colony was a success. To judge by the number of graves dug there, it was not. In spite of the heavy immigration the population in 1624 stood at only 1275. Some of the settlers had doubtless returned to England, but for most of them the colony had been a death-trap. Sandys (who never set foot in Virginia) had sent shipload after shipload of men without supplies. Ill-fed, ill-clothed, and ill-housed, they sickened and died. In 1622 the Indians rose up and killed 347.

Sandys was also in trouble in England, for he had managed to antagonize the old leaders of the company by charging them with defalcation and by interfering with a pirate ship in which some of them had invested—piracy was not one of the new occupations Sandys had envisaged for the colonists. In 1624, at the request of the old leaders, James I appointed a commission to investigate the company. The commissioners reported such shocking neglect of the settlers that James dissolved the company and resumed control of the colony himself.

Thus ended the Virginia Company of Lon-

don. At the cost of several thousand lives and perhaps a hundred thousand pounds, it had established some twelve hundred Englishmen in America. The price was high, but the colony was there to stay.

In the cultivation of tobacco the Virginians had found a way to use America. And in spite of all efforts to turn them to other occupations, they persisted in growing tobacco. They demonstrated, indeed, a certain headstrongness that England was to find characteristic of Englishmen living in America. In 1619 (before any other permanent English settlement had even been launched) Virginians met in their first representative assembly and, though the assembly's stated function was merely advisory, they passed their first laws. When James I took control of the colony in 1624 he did not renew the company's request that the colonists furnish advice through a representative assembly; nor did his son Charles I, who became king in 1625. Charles was having enough difficulties with his own Parliament in England. But the governors he appointed found it impossible to rule Virginia without the help of Virginians. Though Charles refused them recognition until 1639, annual assemblies of representatives began making laws again in 1629 and have been doing so ever since.

The Founding of New England

James I stopped the Virginia Company, but not the flow of Englishmen to America. The social, religious, and economic forces that had made their appearance in the time of Henry VIII were still at work, upsetting the lives of an increasing number of people. Prices were still rising; lands were changing hands; and sheep were grazing where men once drove their plows. To make matters worse, a depression settled over the woolen industry in the 1620's and lasted through the next decade. The land seemed "weary of her inhabitants," and the new king made it seem wearier by levying taxes without the consent of Parliament and by repressive measures against religious dissenters. The result was the Great Migration, in which perhaps as many as fifty thousand people left for the New World. The exodus lasted until 1640, when Englishmen began to see a more hopeful future for their own country. By that year Virginia's population had risen to eight thousand; Maryland had been founded and peopled; and so had the Bermudas, Barbados, St. Kitts, and other West Indian islands. About twenty thousand of the emigrants came to that northern part of Virginia now called New England.

After the failure of its Sagadahoc settlement in 1608, the Virginia Company of Plymouth had shown only sporadic interest in its territory. The company's most important action was to send Captain John Smith to explore the country in 1614; Smith named the place New England and first described its attractions. But his backers were not sufficiently impressed or not sufficiently affluent to support him in attempts to colonize it, and in 1620 they surrendered their rights to a more distinguished group of forty men who were impressed with New England but not with Smith.

The new group, including a duke, two marquises, six earls, a viscount, three barons, and nineteen knights, were moved by Humphrey Gilbert's old dream of organizing feudal estates on a grand scale. Led by Sir Ferdinando Gorges, a Devonshire man who had also been the leading spirit of the Plymouth group, they gained from the king a charter establishing them as the Council for New England and granting them proprietary and governmental rights over the whole area from the fortieth to the forty-eighth parallel of latitude and from the Atlantic to the Pacific. In addition they were to have a monopoly of fishing in the offshore waters.

Cut up forty ways, the region would have provided each member of the council with a huge estate, a whole new England larger than the old. But the future of New England was to be less grand than gritty. In the very month in which the Council for New England was created, a band of humble but determined men and women put ashore below Cape Cod and began to use the country in their own way. Their way was called Puritanism.

Puritanism Puritanism has come to mean prudishness, cruelty, fanaticism, superstition, Philistinism, and hypocrisy. Actually, the Puritans who settled New England had no greater share of these human qualities than did their contemporaries or their descendants. What they did possess in stronger measure than other men was John Calvin's belief that God is omnipotent and good and that men are evil and helpless, predestined before they are born either to salvation or to eternal torment. Critics of this doctrine of predestination have always charged that it leads to moral indifference: if a man's present behavior does not affect his future salvation, why be good? But the facts belie the criticism: those who accept Calvin's doctrine have always outdone their neighbors in efforts to follow God's commandments as given in the Bible. The Puritan, knowing his efforts to be futile, nevertheless took a holy joy in them. They made him feel close to God's transcendent purpose. They also helped to ease his agonizing concern over whether he was headed for heaven or hell. Even though good behavior could not alter a man's predestined fate, it was observable that religious conversion (a personal experience by which God let a saved man know he was saved) often befell those who did try to live godly lives. Moreover, conversion manifested itself outwardly in renewed and intensified efforts to obey God's commands. A man's striving might thus be a sign that he either was or would be saved.

Not content with his own striving, the Puritan also felt responsible for his fellow men. Indeed he was certain that any society which failed to honor God by punishing infractions of His commands would meet with His sudden wrath, not in the next world but here and now. Governments, he thought, existed for the purpose of enforcing obedience to God.

The Puritan's ideas of what God required were less rigorous than many people have supposed. God did *not* require that men wear drab clothes, live in drab houses, or drink water when something stronger was available. He *did* require that they refrain from drunkenness, theft, murder, adultery, and breaches of the Sabbath. Puritans were vastly uneasy about the English government's indifference to these evils. They were even more concerned because the Church of England—supported by the government—retained corrupt practices inherited from Rome and not sanctioned by God in the Bible. They thought the Church should abolish bishops and ecclesiastical courts and such other relics of Catholicism as kneeling and the use of priestly vestments and altars.

Puritans all agreed on what was wrong with the English Church, but they disagreed on how to make it right. Though they all relied on the Bible for guidance, they extracted different opinions from it about how God wanted His churches to be run. The group that settled New England were Congregationalists, and they differed from the other principal group of Puritans, the Presbyterians, in two beliefs: first, that there should be no general church organization with authority over individual churches; second, that a church should admit to membership only those who gave visible evidence of their Christian beliefs. Persons who openly flouted the laws of God should be excluded or expelled. Congregationalists wanted to change the structure and practices of the Church to conform with these beliefs.

Their dissatisfaction with the Church of England inevitably led them to the problem of all reformers: whether to remain inside a corrupt institution and try to reform it from within, or to separate from it and start a pure new one. In 1583 an early congregational leader, Robert Browne, advocated the latter course in a pamphlet appropriately titled *Reformation without Tarrying for any.* His followers, known as Separatists, deserted the English Church to meet in little churches of their own—of necessity in secret because the government did not acknowledge or permit any church other than the established one. But most Congregationalists were not Separatists. They preferred to stay within the Church of England and await the opportunity for reform.

The Pilgrims   The men and women who began the settlement of New England at Plymouth in 1620 were Separatists, part of a group that originated in 1607 at the village of Scrooby in Nottinghamshire. The English government did not look with favor on Separatists. Under Elizabeth two had been executed and many more imprisoned for long periods. Although the members of the Scrooby group were not seriously molested, they were distressed by the hostility of the government and the contempt of their neighbors. In 1608–09 they made their way, not without many hardships, to Holland, where the Dutch were known to be more tolerant. But as the years passed in Leyden they were still unhappy: their children were turning into Dutchmen; the only work they could get was day labor, poorly paid; and the weak among them were being tempted by the other religions that flourished under Dutch tolerance. They thought of Virginia, a place where they might remain Englishmen and work for themselves, a place isolated from contagious heretical religions and far enough from government control so that they could have a church of their own design.

Since they were poor people, without funds to finance their passage, they proposed to set up a "particular plantation" in Virginia for a group of English merchants. As in other such ventures, they would work together for seven years as a community and then the profits would be divided between them and their sponsors. They evidently intended to establish themselves some distance north of the other settlements (the claims of the Virginia Company extended as far north as the present site of New York City) and at one point even considered seeking a grant from the Council for New England, which was then being formed. In the end 102 persons boarded the *Mayflower*, bound for Virginia. But after making their landfall at Cape Cod and exploring the coast, they decided to stay. In late December 1620 they began a settlement which they named Plymouth after the English port from which they had embarked.

These "Pilgrims," as Americans have come to call them, were as poorly equipped in everything but courage as any group that ever landed in America. They had guns but knew little about shooting. They planned to become fishermen but knew nothing about fishing. They expected to settle in Virginia but landed in New England without enough supplies to last the winter. Like their predecessors and contemporaries in Virginia, many of them sickened and died. But the living stuck it out and justified their own estimate of themselves: three years earlier they had written to the men they hoped would sponsor their emigration, "It is not with us as with other men, whom small things can discourage, or small discontentments cause to wish themselves at home again." Since New England was outside the jurisdiction of Virginia's government, the Pilgrims established a government of their own by the "*Mayflower* Compact," which forty-one adult males subscribed before going ashore. For governor they elected John Carver; and upon his death in 1621 they chose William Bradford, who recorded the colony's struggles in an eloquent history and was re-elected nearly every year from 1621 to his death in 1657. Under his leadership the Pilgrims liquidated their debt to the English merchants (who had failed to send them the supplies they expected) and established a self-supporting community.

The Pilgrim settlement was important as a demonstration that men could live in New England. It remained, however, a small and humble community, attracting few immigrants. The great Puritan exodus did not begin until ten years after the landing of the Pilgrims. It engulfed, but did not greatly expand, the Plymouth colony.

The Massachusetts Bay Company

While the Pilgrims went their way outside the Church of England first in Holland and then in America, other Congregational Puritans continued the struggle to reform the church from within. While James I reigned, the struggle did not seem hopeless. Although James scolded them, and even married his son to a Catholic princess, he did not "harry them out of the land," as he once threatened to do. If he had tried, they would have had enough strength in Parliament to stop him. But when Charles I became king in 1625, he quarreled incessantly with Parliament and finally announced in 1629 that he intended to rule henceforth without it. At the same time he befriended a group of aspiring churchmen who were as eager to suppress Puritanism as the Puritans were to make it prevail. Under the leadership of William Laud, whom Charles made bishop of London in 1628 and archbishop of Canterbury in 1633, these friends of the king deprived Puritan ministers of their pulpits and moved the Church of England ever closer to Rome in its ceremonies, vestments, and doctrines.

As the prospects of reform grew dim and the sins of the land grew heavy, the Puritans feared that God was preparing England for some great purging catastrophe. In despair and hope they too turned their thoughts to America, where they might escape God's wrath, worship in purity, and gather strength for future victory.

In 1628 a number of prominent congregational Puritans bought their way into a commercial company that was being organized in London. Called the New England Company, it took over the rights of a defunct group, the Dorchester Adventurers, which in 1623 had tried to plant a farming and fishing settlement at Cape Ann. From the Council for New England, the new company obtained a charter authorizing settlement in the area known as Massachusetts Bay, to the north of Plymouth. A year later, on March 4, 1629, the New England Company reorganized as the Massachusetts Bay Company under a new charter obtained directly from the king.

In the shuffle the Puritan stockholders

gained control of the company, and they had something more than commerce in mind. The royal charter bestowed on the company full authority to govern its own territory, and made no mention of where company meetings were to be held. In 1629 the Puritans simply voted to transfer the company to Massachusetts. This meant that if Puritan company members emigrated, they would have full control of the government under which they would live. Thus in one bold stroke the Puritans won for themselves the opportunity to do in Massachusetts what Puritans for nearly a century had been yearning to do in England.

To act as governor, the company elected a solid Puritan squire, John Winthrop of Groton Manor, Suffolk. He and perhaps a dozen other company members, all Puritans, crossed the ocean in 1630, accompanied by a thousand like-minded men and women, who preferred a wilderness governed by Puritans to a civilized land governed by Charles I. Before the year was over they had planted settlements around Massachusetts Bay at Dorchester, Roxbury, Watertown, Newtown (Cambridge), Charlestown, and Boston. During the next ten years,

Governor of a Puritan republic: John Winthrop.

as Charles ruled without Parliament and Laud grew increasingly powerful, fifteen or twenty thousand more followed and their towns stretched out in all directions.

Winthrop and the handful of other company members had authority from the king's charter to govern this whole body of settlers. But Winthrop and his friends wanted a broader base for their government. And so, shortly after their arrival in New England, they transformed the Massachusetts Bay Company from a trading company into a commonwealth. In 1631 they admitted more than a hundred adult males as members or "freemen" of the company eligible to vote at its meetings. The term "freeman" in seventeenth-century England generally meant a voting member of a business corporation or an incorporated city or borough. In America the word came to mean a man who had the right to vote for representatives to the assembly in his colony. In Massachusetts, when the company and colony were blended, the freemen of the company became the freemen of the colony. The increase in their numbers did not remove the colony from Puritan control, because most of the new freemen (who must have been a majority of the heads of families then in the colony) were probably Puritans; moreover, it was specified

---

Massachusetts: A Contented View

I prayse God, we haue many occasions of comfort heer, and doe hope, that our dayes of Affliction will soon haue an ende, and that the Lord will doe vs more goode in the ende, then we could haue expected, that will abundantly recompence for all the trouble we haue endured. yet we may not looke at great thinges heer, it is enough that we shall haue heaven, though we should passe through hell to it. we heer enjoye God and Jesus Christ, is not this enough? What would we haue more? I thanke God, I like so well to be heer, as I doe not repent my comminge.... I neuer fared better in my life, neuer slept better, neuer had more contente of minde, which comes meerly of the Lordes good hande, for we haue not the like meanes of these comforts heer which we had in England, but the Lord is allsufficient, blessed be his holy name, if he please, he can still vphold vs in this estate, but if he shall see good to make vs partakers with others in more Affliction, his will be doone, he is our God, and may dispose of vs as he sees good.

From John Winthrop, Letter to His Wife, 1630.

that, in the future, members of Puritan congregational churches (and only such) should be eligible to become freemen.

The charter, which had envisaged only a trading company with limited membership, provided that company members assemble as a "General Court" four times a year to make laws. Between the meetings of the General Court a governor (or his second in command, a deputy governor) and a council of eighteen "assistants," elected annually, were to manage the company. When Winthrop and his associates opened the company to all church members, they foresaw that the number of freemen would soon become too large to operate effectively as a legislature; and they decided to leave lawmaking to the council of assistants, who were still to be elected annually by all the freemen. But in 1634 the freemen insisted that the lawmaking powers assigned to them by the charter be delegated to "deputies" elected from each settlement. Henceforth the General Court consisted of the governor, the deputy governor, the executive council of assistants, and a body of deputies or representatives, all elected annually by the freemen. Since the company had power to govern the colony, this General Court was in reality both the legislature and the supreme court of the colony. Here, in truth, was a self-governing commonwealth, a Puritan republic.

Puritan New England The freedom to do as they pleased posed many new problems to men who had not hitherto wielded the powers of government. Reformers and idealists are notoriously prone to dissipate their energies wrangling with one another. And there were disagreements in New England, though not so numerous or severe as has sometimes been suggested. The New England Puritans agreed on a great deal. They wanted congregational churches. They did not want bishops, church courts, or hierarchy. They wanted a government that would take seriously its obligation to enforce God's commandments and to support pure religion. Accordingly they confined suffrage to church members and levied taxes to pay ministers' salaries. But, contrary to common assumption, they did not want their clergy to take any hand in government. For a minister to exercise temporal au-

thority of any kind seemed to the Puritans a dangerous step toward Roman Catholicism. Compared to the clergy of England and Europe the New England minister, though highly influential, had little authority even within his own church. He taught, prayed, preached, and admonished; he commanded respect—else he lost his job—but he did not rule his church. Admissions to membership, censures, pardons, and excommunications were all decided by vote of the church members.

Neither the leaders of the Massachusetts Bay Colony nor the great majority of settlers were Separatists. Though they organized their own churches in the congregational manner, they took pains to affirm their love and friendship for the churches of England. Some even thought that the churches of Rome were not beyond redemption. But among the thousands who stepped ashore at Boston every year were substantial numbers of Separatists and other extremists, full of zeal and eloquence, full of impatience with anyone who disagreed with

---

Massachusetts: A Hungry View

her cam ouer xxv passeingares and thare cume backe agayn fouer skore and od parsones and as maney more wolld a cume if thay had whare withe all to bringe them hom.... We may liue if we haue suppleyes euerey yere from ould eingland other weyse we can not subeseiste I maye as I will worck hard sete an ackorne of eindey wheat and if we do not set it withe fishe and that will cost xxs and if we set it witheought fishe thay shall haue but a por crope so father I pray consedre of my cause for her will be but a uerey por beinge and no beinge withe ought Louinge father youer helpe withe prouisseyones from ould eingland I had thought to a cam home in theis sheipe for my prouisseyones ware all moste all spente but that I humbley thanck you for youer gret loue and kindnes in sendinge me s[o]me prouissyones or elles i sholld and myne a bine halef famiuyshed but now I will if it plese god that I haue my hellthe I will plant what corne I can and if prouisseyones be no cheper betwein theis and mychellmes and that I do not her from you what I wase beste to do I purpose to c[o]me hom at myckellmes

From John Pond, Letter to His Father, 1631.

them. John Winthrop, whom the freemen elected governor year after year during most of his life, was good at turning away wrath and directing zeal to constructive ends. But during the three years from 1634 to 1637, when lesser men sat in the governor's chair, Massachusetts all but succumbed to the denunciations of a brilliant, saintlike, intractable man and a brilliant, proud, magnetic woman.

Roger Williams, who arrived in 1631, was a Separatist. He wanted everyone to repudiate the wicked churches of England. Moreover, he insisted that the royal charter of Massachusetts contained a lie (in claiming that England first discovered the region); that the king had had no right to grant the charter in the first place without first purchasing the land from the natives. If word got back to England that the Massachusetts government allowed the expression of such subversive ideas, the king might be prompted to take control of the colony and end the Puritan republic. Williams also tried to persuade people that no government had authority over religious matters, not even the right to punish breaches of the Sabbath. In a community which believed that the prime purpose of government was to enforce God's commandments, this was pure sedition.

Williams was a man whom everyone loved on sight; even John Winthrop became his good friend. But he propagated his inflammatory ideas so insistently, first as assistant to the minister and then as minister of the church at Salem, that the colony was endangered and the government finally felt obliged to banish him in 1636. He went to Rhode Island, where he was joined by those who believed him. There, while retaining his conviction that the state had no authority over religious matters, he gradually shed his other extreme views and lived out a long and useful life as the spiritual guide of the new colony.

Scarcely had Williams been banished when a new threat to the civil and religious security of Massachusetts appeared: Anne Hutchinson, the wife of a merchant whom Winthrop described as "a man of a very mild temper and weak parts, and wholly guided by his wife." An amateur theologian, Mrs. Hutchinson took to elucidating her minister's Sunday sermons in informal gatherings of her neighbors. As the circle of her listeners steadily widened, her discourses became more original, for her keen and imaginative mind could not be contained within the standard doctrines of Puritanism. Starting from the accepted principle that God grants salvation without regard to human merit, she denied (what other Puritans affirmed) that good conduct could be a sign of salvation and affirmed (what other Puritans denied) that the Holy Spirit in the hearts of true believers relieved them of responsibility to obey the laws of God. So, at least, her enemies charged, and she gave substance to the accusation by asserting that all the New England ministers except her favorite John Cotton and her brother-in-law John Wheelwright were preaching unsound doctrines. By emphasizing morality, she said, they were deluding their congregations into the false assumption that good deeds would get them into heaven. The accusation was hotly denied by the clergymen, and Mrs. Hutchinson herself protested that she had intended no insult. But a host of devoted Bostonians hung on every word she uttered and refused to conceal their contempt for everyone else. The colony split into hostile camps, and finally Mrs. Hutchinson was brought before the authorities. After they had cross-examined her for two days, she made the mistake of claiming that she had received an immediate revelation from God. To Puritan ears, this was blasphemy. So Mrs. Hutchinson too was banished and went to Rhode Island, which thus became the refuge for Puritans with too much originality.

After Charles I was forced to resummon Parliament in 1640, Roger Williams applied to that body (which was overwhelmingly Puritan) for a charter for his colony. The charter, granted in 1644, gave the Rhode Islanders a government much like that of the colony from which they had been expelled: they elected annually a representative assembly, a council of assistants, and a governor (at first called a president), but they did not confine suffrage to church members or collect taxes to support the clergy. In 1663 the existing government was confirmed by a royal charter that also guaranteed the "liberty in religious concernments" which had been the colony's distinction from the beginning.

Meanwhile another part of New England was filling up with Puritans who differed from those of Massachusetts only in their desire for more elbow room. In 1636 Thomas Hooker, the minister of Newtown (Cambridge), led an exodus overland to the fertile Connecticut Valley, where the small garrison of a Dutch trading post at Fort Hope (Hartford) was unable to prevent them from settling. They formed a government by a simple agreement among themselves (called the "Fundamental Orders"). The model, once again, was Massachusetts (but suffrage was not confined to church members), and again the existing arrangement was confirmed by royal charter (1662). The charter also joined to Connecticut the colony of New Haven, initiated in 1638 by a group of Londoners who could find no lands in Massachusetts to suit them.

The settlers of New Haven, beginning with a good supply of capital, had been disappointed in their expectations of a thriving commerce; but they had succeeded in establishing a somewhat stricter government than existed elsewhere in New England, and they were not altogether happy about the union with Connecticut.

There was nevertheless no serious difference between New Haven and the rest of New England. In New Haven as in Plymouth, Massachusetts, Rhode Island, and Connecticut, the population was predominantly Puritan. Puritans directed public policy and the only serious resistance came from other Puritans. Although some of the inhabitants may have been indifferent or hostile to Puritanism, they were never strong enough or discontented enough to challenge Puritan control.

Settlers who wanted nothing more from the New World than an opportunity to make their fortunes or to live more comfortably than in England had little reason to object to Puritan control anyway. The government frowned on private cupidity when it threatened the public welfare, but Puritans saw no virtue in poverty. They had not traveled three thousand miles simply to starve in a holier manner than in England. They were building a society for all the world to copy, a "city upon a hill," and they meant it to be a success, economically as well as religiously.

So long as the Great Migration lasted, the colonists prospered by selling cattle and provisions to the newcomers each year. When the Migration ended in 1640, New England had its first depression. The settlers looked hard for some native product they could sell to the outside world. Fortunately for them, they found no single product such as the Virginians' tobacco, and they consequently developed a more balanced and more prosperous economy. They caught fish, raised corn and wheat, bred cattle, cut lumber, and built ships. Before many years had passed, New England vessels were prowling the Caribbean and the Mediterranean, peddling their assorted wares, transporting other people's, and bringing home the profits to the city on the hill. By mid-century New England had laid down its economic as well as its religious foundations.

Proprietary Ventures

During the years that Puritans were building their republics in New England, nonpuritans were trying to establish private domains there and elsewhere. Three years after the Pilgrims landed, Sir Ferdinando Gorges, the most active member of the Council for New England, had backed a settlement at Wessagusset (Weymouth) in the Massachusetts Bay region, but it broke up after a year. Its failure discouraged the rest of the council from further efforts, and they apparently raised no serious objections in 1628 when the earl of Warwick, president of the council, took it upon himself to grant the Puritans permission to settle the Bay area. In 1637 the Council for New England finally dissolved, leaving behind a host of shadowy claims. Only one claim was perfected: that of Ferdinando Gorges to the region north of the Merrimac River. Gorges divided the area with another would-be New England lord, John Mason, and in 1639 obtained a separate royal charter for his own share. He died in 1647, with no feudal retainers in his New World barony except a few hardy fishermen who pledged allegiance to no one. Massachusetts annexed the whole region in 1651.

The king authorized other ambitious gentlemen to colonize Newfoundland, Nova Scotia, and the Carolinas, but to no effect. The first English nobleman to realize the aristocrat's dream of founding a New World domain for his family was George Calvert, Lord Baltimore. A notable figure in the court of James I,

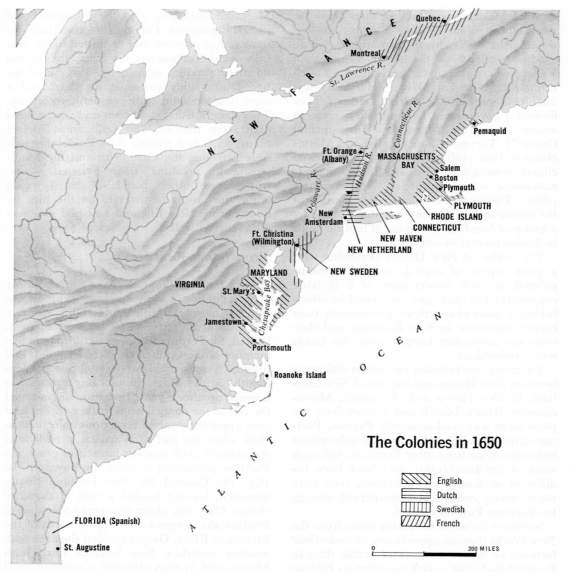

The Colonies in 1650

English
Dutch
Swedish
French

0   200 MILES

(Map labels: Quebec, Montreal, St. Lawrence R., NEW FRANCE, Connecticut R., Pemaquid, Ft. Orange (Albany), Hudson R., MASSACHUSETTS BAY, Salem, Boston, Plymouth, Delaware R., New Amsterdam, PLYMOUTH, RHODE ISLAND, CONNECTICUT, NEW HAVEN, Ft. Christina (Wilmington), NEW NETHERLAND, NEW SWEDEN, MARYLAND, VIRGINIA, St. Mary's, Chesapeake Bay, Jamestown, Portsmouth, ATLANTIC OCEAN, Roanoke Island, FLORIDA (Spanish), St. Augustine)

Calvert had become interested in America first as a member of the Virginia Company and later as a member of the Council for New England. In 1620 he purchased rights in southeastern Newfoundland from another noble dreamer and started a settlement there. When he visited the place himself, he found "that from the middle of October to the middst of May there is a sadd face of wynter upon all this land." Deciding to leave Newfoundland to the fishermen, he asked the king for a grant farther south. The charter, which

was in the making when Calvert died in 1632, was finally issued to his son Cecilius. It conveyed to him ten million acres on Chesapeake Bay, where the Calvert family was to have complete powers of government. The colony was to be called Maryland, in honor of the queen of Charles I.

The name was appropriate, for both the queen and the Calverts were Catholics. Maryland was to be a feudal seignory and at the same time a religious refuge. As a feudal seignory it came nearer to success than any other attempted in America. Though the Calverts did not live there, they governed the colony (sometimes through a younger son), owned all the public lands, granted small estates or "manors" to their friends, and collected rents from the settlers. Because Virginia, Plymouth, and Massachusetts lent a hand, the settlers of Maryland were spared the early days of starvation that had been suffered by other colonists. Tobacco grew as readily in Maryland as in Virginia, and the two colonies became identical in economic pursuits and interests.

As a religious refuge Maryland also succeeded. Although official hostility to Catholicism had relaxed in England under Charles, Catholics were still required by law to take oaths and to attend religious services that conflicted with their beliefs. In Maryland they would be free to worship as they chose, and so would other Christians. As it turned out, more Puritans came to the colony than Catholics. The Calverts welcomed both, and from the time of the first settlement in 1634 tried to prevent either group from oppressing the other. When the Jesuits threatened to become too powerful, Baltimore, in 1641, forbade them to hold land in Maryland. The Puritans were harder to handle, especially after 1640 when

their friends gained the upper hand in England, but Baltimore did his best to restrain them. By the terms of his charter he was obliged to obtain the consent of the "freemen" (presumably in this case the term meant all adult males not bound as servants) to all legislation. As the population increased, the freemen deputed a few individuals to act for them in this matter, and thus arose a representative assembly similar to those which developed in the other colonies. This assembly in 1649 consented to the famous Maryland Toleration Act, securing freedom of worship to all Christians, whether Protestant or Catholic, who believed in the Trinity. The Calverts upheld the act through successive generations and thus made their colony a model of what the rest of America was to become.

By the middle of the seventeenth century England had seeded North America. Many more immigrants were to come, from England and elsewhere, but the future was already visible on the coasts of New England and of Chesapeake Bay. Englishmen had moved in, and whether they favored toleration, as in Maryland and Rhode Island, or intolerance, as in Massachusetts, whether they caught fish or grew tobacco, the continent was effectively theirs.

SUGGESTIONS FOR READING   A good account of the American Indians before the coming of the white man is Kenneth MacGowan, *Early Man in the New World* * (1950). Clark Wissler, *Indians of the United States: Four Centuries of Their History and Culture* (1940), is more comprehensive.

Anyone interested in the age of exploration should give his first attention to S. E. Morison's great biography of Columbus, *Admiral of the Ocean Sea* (1942). For the later explorations, J. B. Brebner, *The Explorers of North America, 1492–1806* * (1933), is both authoritative and well written. On the English voyages there is no substitute for Richard Hakluyt's collection of first-hand accounts, *The Principall Navigations, Voiages, and Discoveries of the English Nation* (1589, 1599), reprinted in Everyman's Library (*Hakluyt's Voyages*, 8 vols.). Hakluyt's work has been carried on in the voluminous publications of the Hakluyt Society. Among these, see especially the volumes edited by D. B. Quinn, *Voyages and Colonising Enterprises of Sir Humphrey Gilbert*, 2 vols. (1940), and *The Roanoke Voyages, 1584–1590*, 2 vols. (1955). A full account of methods of navigation in this period is D. W. Waters, *The Art of Navigation in England in Elizabethan and Early Stuart Times* (1958).

The English Reformation is ably discussed in M. M. Knappen, *Tudor Puritanism* (1939); Maurice Powicke, *The Reformation in England* * (1941); and C. H. and Katherine George, *The Protestant Mind of the English Reformation* (1961). For social conditions in sixteenth- and seventeenth-century England, R. H. Tawney, *The Agrarian Problem in the Sixteenth Century* (1912), and *Religion and the Rise of Capitalism* * (1926), are both important, as is "The Rise of the Gentry, 1558–1640," *Economic History Review*, XI (1941), 1–38. This article started a

* Available in a paperback edition.

lively controversy among historians as to whether the gentry were rising or falling in the sixteenth and early seventeenth centuries. The controversy is summarized and continued in J. H. Hexter, "Storm over the Gentry," *Encounter*, May (1958), 22–34. This and several other penetrating essays by Professor Hexter are reprinted in *Reappraisals in History* (1961). Mildred Campbell, *The English Yeoman under Elizabeth and the Early Stuarts* (1942), is fully documented and has met with no serious challenge. The best account of English political and legal institutions is Wallace Notestein, *The English People on the Eve of Colonization, 1603–1630* (1954).

On the first permanent English settlements in America, the most convenient and the most authoritative account is C. M. Andrews, *The Colonial Period of American History*, Vols. I–III (1934–37). For the Southern colonies this should be supplemented by W. F. Craven, *The Southern Colonies in the Seventeenth Century* (1949). Captain John Smith tells his own story in *Travels and Works of Captain John Smith*, 2 vols. (1910), ed. by Edward Arber and A. G. Bradley. A sympathetic modern biography is Bradford Smith, *Captain John Smith: His Life and Legend* (1953). W. F. Craven, *The Dissolution of the Virginia Company* (1932), is a masterful study of the internal divisions that impaired the company's efforts in America.

The New England Puritans have been subjected to the scrutiny of historians, sympathetic and unsympathetic, from the time the settlers first stepped ashore. William Bradford, the governor of the Plymouth Colony, told the story of the Pilgrims in *Of Plymouth Plantation*, an American classic that can best be read in S. E. Morison's edition (1952). In his *Journal*, Governor John Winthrop did for Massachusetts Bay what Bradford did for Plymouth. The best edition is that of James Savage, 2 vols. (1853), but this is hard to come by. The only edition in print is the modernized and expurgated one of J. K. Hosmer, 2 vols. (1908). For a contrast with Bradford and Winthrop read Thomas Morton, *New English Canaan* (1637, 1883).

In the nineteenth century J. G. Palfrey, *History of New England*, 5 vols. (1858–90), praised the Puritans excessively, while Brooks Adams, *The Emancipation of Massachusetts*, condemned them excessively. In the twentieth century J. T. Adams again attacked them, in *The Founding of New England* (1921), while S. E. Morison defended them in *Builders of the Bay Colony* (1930), which is by all odds the best introduction to the history of New England. Morison continued his study of the Puritans in his monumental works on Harvard, *The Founding of Harvard College* (1935) and *Harvard in the Seventeenth Century*, 2 vols. (1936), and in a briefer study, *The Puritan Pronaos* (1936), reprinted as *The Intellectual Life of Colonial New England* * (1956).

New England Puritanism is also the subject of the most profound study of intellectual history yet written by an American, Perry Miller, *The New England Mind: The Seventeenth Century* * (1939) and *The New England Mind: From Colony to Province* * (1953). These volumes were preceded by his briefer study, *Orthodoxy in Massachusetts, 1630–1650* * (1933), the subject of which falls chronologically between the two. Miller explores other aspects of New England history in a brilliant collection of essays, *Errand into the Wilderness* (1956).

Puritan domestic life is examined in E. S. Morgan, *The Puritan Family* (1944). The conduct of church affairs is treated in Ola Winslow, *Meetinghouse Hill* (1952), and in Emil Oberholzer, Jr., *Delinquent Saints* (1956).

The best study of early New England economic history is Bernard Bailyn, *The New England Merchants in the Seventeenth Century* (1955). E. S. Morgan has dealt with some of the political problems faced by the founders of Massachusetts in *The Puritan Dilemma: The Story of John Winthrop* (1958). Later Puritan problems as exemplified in the Winthrop family are treated in R. S. Dunn, *Puritans and Yankees: The Winthrop Dynasty of New England* (1962). G. L. Haskins, *Law and Authority in Early Massachusetts* (1960), describes political and social as well as legal institutions.

* Available in a paperback edition.

2

The Pattern of Empire

The first settlements in America, which cost Englishmen dearly in lives and money, cost the English government nothing. But in authorizing settlement the government did expect to gain something more than an outlet for disgruntled Puritans and adventurous fortune-seekers. Every European government, from the sixteenth century through the eighteenth, followed an economic policy which has been known since 1776, when Adam Smith coined the word, as mercantilism.

Mercantilism

Mercantilism meant that the state directed all economic activities within its borders, subordinating private profit to public good. In particular the government sought to increase national wealth by discouraging imports and encouraging exports. The English government let Englishmen go to America because it was persuaded that their presence there would further this end.

Long before the settlement of Jamestown, Richard Hakluyt had explained how the mother country could profit from American colonies: they would furnish England with supplies such as lumber, tar, and hemp, which she was buying from other countries, and they would offer a market for the woolens which were England's principal export. "It behooves this realm," Hakluyt wrote in 1584, "if it mean . . . not negligently and sleepingly to slide into beggary, to foresee and plant [a colony] at Norumbega [a name for northern North America] or some like place, were it not for anything else but for the hope of the sale of our wool." What England wanted from America was what Hakluyt said she would get: a market for her woolen cloth and other manufactures and a source of supply for raw materials that she had to import from other countries.

What England wanted was not incompatible with what the settlers wanted. North America was full of valuable natural resources and short of people. The most profitable activity for the settlers was therefore the extraction of resources that required a minimum of labor— lumber, for example, or iron or furs. It would be unprofitable for them to make things whose value came primarily from the labor that went into them—fine furniture, for example, or clothing, or wrought iron. England, on the other hand, was full of people and short of the raw materials that America possessed in such abundance; so her interests lay the other way round. It would be mutually advantageous for the colonies to buy manufactures from the mother country and for the mother country to buy raw materials from the colonies.

The British Empire in America was based on this compatibility of interests. But while the interests were compatible, they required guidance to make them coincide. Left to themselves, the colonies might peddle their produce in France or Holland instead of England and take home French textiles instead of English, or they might produce materials not needed in England. In order to make the system work, it was necessary for the mother country to maintain continuous supervision and control over the economic activities of the settlers just as she did over the activities of Englishmen at home. The English government never doubted its right to exercise such control, but was slow to develop consistent directives or effective machinery for carrying them out.

England's Imperial Delay In the early years, before the colonies began to fulfill Hakluyt's glowing predictions, economic regulation probably did not seem urgent. Although the English government in 1621 ordered all Virginia tobacco to be brought to England, the order was not enforced, perhaps because English authorities considered it a mixed blessing for the nation to have its own private supply of smoke. But other regulations, adopted from time to time, also went unenforced. One reason was distance. Three thousand miles of water made a formidable barrier in the seventeenth century—not the water but

---

The Use of America: Mercantilism

And in reguard his Majesties Plantations beyond the Seas are enhabited and peopled by his Subjects of this His Kingdome of England, For the maintaining a greater correspondence and kindnesse betweene them and keepeing them in a firmer dependance upon it, and rendring them yet more beneficiall and advantagious unto it in the farther Imployment and Encrease of English Shipping and Seamen, vent of English Woollen and other Manufactures and Commodities rendring the Navigation to and from the same more safe and cheape, and makeing this Kingdome a Staple not onely of the Comodities of those Plantations but alsoe of the Commodities of other Countryes and Places for the supplying of them, and it being the usage of other Nations to keepe their Trade to themselves, Be it enacted ... that ... noe Commoditie of the Growth Production or Manufacture of Europe shall be imported into any ... Place to His Majestic belonging, ... but what shall be bona fide and without fraud laden and shipped in England Wales ... and in English built Shipping,... and which shall be carried directly thence to the said Lands.

From *The Second Navigation Act*, 1663.

---

the miles. Until the coming of the railroad, it was much faster and easier to travel long distances by water than by land. If the colonies had been separated from England by three thousand miles of land, control would have been impossible. Even over water three thousand miles was space enough in which to lose messages, orders, and interest.

A more serious obstacle to English control than either the distance or the seeming unimportance of the colonies was politics. During the seventeenth century, when most of her American colonies were founded, England was torn by a struggle for power between king and Parliament. In the 1630's King Charles I ruled without Parliament, but by 1640 he needed it to pay his bills. He called it, dismissed it, called it again, and then found that he could not dismiss it any more. In 1642 the members raised an army to make war on him; in 1649 they cut off his head, and for eleven years England had no king. In his place, from 1649 to 1658, stood Oliver Cromwell, the soldier who had defeated him.

When Charles II, son of the old king, was placed on the throne in 1660, the acts of the preceding eleven years were declared null and void. But Charles had the good sense to realize that English kings henceforth must work with Parliament or not at all. His brother and successor, James II, had no sense, and within three years of his accession in 1685 he had to flee the country. Parliament quietly replaced him with William and Mary in the bloodless Revolution of 1688. After 1688 the king was still no cipher in government, but everyone understood that he was subordinate to Parliament.

All but one (Georgia) of the thirteen colonies that later became the United States were founded before 1688, during the years when the ultimate location of sovereignty in England was uncertain. They were all founded under authority of the king, and their relationship to Parliament remained ambiguous. Parliament sometimes passed legislation affecting them, but even after 1688 it did not do so regularly. Yet if the king had denied the authority of Parliament in the colonies, Parliament would doubtless have brought him up short.

Distance, indifference, and the uncertain

location of authority in England conspired to delay the development of a consistent and continuous colonial policy. From the founding of Virginia in 1607 until the middle of the seventeenth century the colonies interested king and Parliament only as a minor prize in the contest for sovereignty. In 1633, when Charles I was trying to rule without Parliament, he appointed a commission headed by Archbishop Laud to govern the colonies. But the commissioners were too busy in England to do anything about America. During the English civil wars of the 1640's, Parliament and king both claimed authority over the colonies, but neither was able to exercise it.

Oliver Cromwell was the first ruler of England sure enough of his position at home to think seriously about fitting the colonies into a general imperial scheme. In 1650 and 1651 he secured legislation to keep foreign shipping out of the colonies. He also planned a great expan-

Charles II, King of England, 1660–85.

sion of the empire in the Caribbean, and tried to persuade New Englanders to move to the West Indies, where the cultivation of sugar and other tropical products promised rich rewards. But his legislation against foreign shipping led to war with the uncooperative Dutch; his large military and naval expedition to the West Indies in 1655 captured only Jamaica; and his powers of persuasion proved insufficient to lure New Englanders from their rocky soil; they suspected, perhaps, that Puritanism would not work well in the tropics.

The Navigation Acts When Charles II came to the throne in 1660, the colonies, in spite of Cromwell's failures, had grown enough to require attention. Virginia and Maryland were exporting over seven million pounds of tobacco yearly, much of which never reached England, and New England harbored a group of merchants whose ships were already familiar in the markets of the world. English merchants, awakened to the potentialities of colonial trade, pressed the government for measures to prevent the profits from leaking into the pockets of foreign rivals. What they wanted was not merely to exclude foreign shipping from the colonies (as Cromwell had attempted in the acts of 1650 and 1651) but to direct colonial trade into channels profitable to the mother country. King and Parliament, in the first flush of Restoration harmony, agreed on two acts to take care of the matter.

These so-called Navigation Acts (1660 and 1663) were modified from time to time during the ensuing century, but their basic principles remained the same: (1) they forbade all trade with the colonies except in ships owned and constructed there or in England and manned by crews of which at least three-quarters of the men were English or colonial; (2) they forbade the transportation *from* the colonies *to* any place except England or another English colony of certain "enumerated commodities," namely sugar, cotton, indigo, dyewoods, ginger, and tobacco; and (3) they forbade the transportation of European goods *to* the colonies *from* any place except England.

Subsequent modification of the Navigation Acts consisted mainly of additions to the list of enumerated commodities (rice in 1704, naval stores in 1705, copper and furs in 1721) or specific limitations on, or encouragement of, colonial products. The act of 1705 that enumerated naval stores (pitch, tar, turpentine, masts, spars) also placed bounties on their production. The Wool Act (1699) forbade export from the colonies of certain textiles manufactured there. The Hat Act (1732) forbade export of colonial-made hats. The Iron Act (1750) removed all duties on English imports of colonial pig and bar iron (thus encouraging their production) but forbade the erection of any new colonial iron mills for manufacturing raw iron into finished products.

The Navigation Acts were ostensibly intended to ensure that the mother country would benefit from the economic activities of the colonies. But in passing the original acts and in modifying them over the years, Parliament was not immune to the wishes of special groups. Adam Smith, in coining the very name "mercantilism," was charging that English policies were dictated by merchants at the expense of the rest of the community. And indeed particular acts were often opposed by one group as much as they were favored by another. The Iron Act, for example, represented a victory of English iron manufacturers over English iron miners and smelters; and in 1733 the Molasses Act, which placed a heavy duty on foreign molasses imported into North America, was a victory for one group of colonists, the West Indian sugar planters, over another, the rum-distilling colonists of New England.

Besides serving such private interests, and besides subordinating colonial trade to English, the Navigation Acts aimed at increasing the revenue of the English government, at least indirectly. Although the acts of 1660 and 1663 levied no taxes, the government from the beginning had collected duties in England on imports from the colonies. By requiring enumerated commodities to be brought only to England, the government expected to step up the importation of taxable goods. The expectation was not unrealistic. Revenue obtained from duties on tobacco imports alone amounted in the 1660's to £100,000 a year, as much as the planters themselves made from the crop.

The Navigation Acts transformed the hopeful predictions of Hakluyt into specific legislation which told the colonists what they could and could not make, where and how they could trade. But the colonies were still three thousand miles from the lawmakers. If England was to receive the full benefit of the acts, they had to be enforced against foreign nations on the one hand and refractory colonists on the other.

The Dutch   The principal foreign threat to England's emerging mercantilist empire in the seventeenth century came from the Dutch. This was their century; they seemed on the way to running the world. After shaking off Spanish domination, they built the largest merchant fleet ever known. Dutch captains nosed out rival vessels everywhere, took over most of the Portuguese empire in the East Indies, opened trade with Japan. Dutch privateers led the pack in raiding Spanish treasure fleets. Dutch merchants controlled the lumber trade from the Baltic and made Amsterdam the sawmill of Europe. Dutch fishermen domi-

New Amsterdam, 1653.

nated the North Sea. Dutch textile workers finished and resold woolen cloth imported raw from England. When England tried to stop the export and save the valuable finishing process for her own workers, the Dutch simply boycotted English cloth, and depression settled over the whole English woolen industry. This was the century of Rembrandt, Vermeer, Hals, Hobbema, DeHooch, the century of Huygens and Spinoza. Man for man, no people has ever matched the seventeenth-century achievement of the Dutch.

In North America the Dutch had not extended themselves with the vigor they showed elsewhere, probably because North America offered fewer prospects of immediate reward. Nevertheless, Dutch ships every year appeared in Virginia's great rivers to carry tobacco to Holland instead of England. Dutch textiles were sold in the shops of Boston. And the region that the Dutch had chosen for their settlements and trading posts in North America was strategically and economically the most important on the continent. The Hudson

River commanded access to the interior by the only water-level route through the Appalachian Mountains. From the Hudson, it was possible to reach the Mississippi Valley along the Mohawk River Valley (or with greater difficulty by Lake George, Lake Champlain, and the St. Lawrence). Economically the Hudson River was the principal outlet of the fur trade south of the St. Lawrence; strategically it was an avenue along which an ambitious nation could strike for control of the inner continent. The Dutch were not that ambitious, but they did find New Netherland a convenient base from which to attack the Spaniards, drain off the continent's fur supply, and collect profit from England's settlements to the north and south.

When Charles II set about enforcing the Navigation Acts, he took care of the Dutch problem in North America in the simplest possible way. He made a gift of the Dutch territories to his brother James, the duke of York. To the seemingly formidable task of delivering the gift he assigned four commissioners, with four frigates and four hundred men. The commissioners arrived in 1664, a time when the Dutch settlers had been demoralized by arbitrary and incompetent governors. To everyone's surprise, the colony surrendered without resistance, and the commissioners took possession for the duke of the entire region from Maryland to Connecticut.

The Dutch in Holland, already at odds with England, declared war and continued to violate the Navigation Acts wherever willing colonists and the absence of the British navy made it possible. In the long run, the problem of enforcement could not be solved by foreign war but only by effective administrative machinery within the colonies themselves. That problem became at once more difficult and more urgent as a new burst of colonizing activity increased the dimensions of the empire.

The Restoration Colonies

The colonies founded in the second half of the seventeenth century were "proprietary," that is, they were founded by proprietors who exercised government over them and initially owned all the land in them. The proprietors, generally friends or relatives of the king, hoped to grow rich from the sale of their lands and from the annual fees, or "quitrents" (usually a shilling per fifty acres), that they charged the settlers. They kept the quitrents low enough so as not to deter prospective immigrants, but high enough to guarantee themselves a tidy permanent income when the colony should be fully populated.

The new colonies all resembled Maryland in their proprietary origin (see p. 26); they differed from Maryland and the other old colonies in the sources from which they drew their actual settlers: comparatively few came directly from England. Some were on the spot already, like the Dutch and Swedish settlers in New Netherland. More came from Scotland, Ireland, Wales, France, and Germany. Still more came from America itself, men who had grown discontented for one reason or another with the part of the New World they already occupied and who wanted to try a new place.

This search for greener pastures was to become one of the abiding characteristics of American life. Once uprooted, a man might wander long before he found a spot where he could remain content. After a few months or years in a new home, one morning he would turn his back on surroundings that had scarcely become familiar and be off to the promised land beyond the horizon. His children too might never put down the kind of roots that held Europeans to the family farm or village. The Great Migration that ended in England in 1640 never quite ended in America.

From this restless breed of men the new proprietors hoped to draw tenants for their feudal domains. Tenants less likely to pay feudal rents would have been hard to find, but that fact was not immediately apparent.

New York   The most important of the new colonies was New York, whose settlers and problems the duke of York had inherited from the Dutch. New Netherland had been primarily a series of trading posts, located at Fort Orange (Albany), Esopus (Kingston), and New Amsterdam (New York) on the Hudson, and at Swaanendael, Fort Nassau, and Fort Casimir on the Delaware. But in several areas settlement was already more advanced. The merchants of New Amsterdam, for example, were much more than mere Indian traders, and their business supported a sizable and diversified community. In the Hudson Valley a number of well-to-do Dutchmen had tried to found agricultural settlements, known as patroonships, of the very kind that English proprietors were hoping to establish. One of these, belonging to Kiliaen Van Rensselaer, had approached success. Though Rensselaer himself had gained little profit from it, his tenants still occupied the lands. On Manhattan, on the western end of Long Island, and in the lower Hudson Valley there were a few villages of Dutch farmers; and in eastern Long Island a number of New England Puritans had transplanted themselves and their way of life. The Dutch, finding them difficult to cope with, had left them much to themselves.

The Dutch West India Company had governed these sprawling settlements through a director general. Of the men who held the post, Wouter Van Twiller (1633–38) and Willem Kieft (1638–47) had been disastrously foolish; and Peter Stuyvesant (1647–64), who surrendered the colony to the English, was little better. All had governed without benefit of a popular assembly. English rule brought no immediate changes, except in the quality of the governors. The terms of surrender confirmed the old settlers in their property rights. The duke of York, by the charter which conveyed the area to him, was given full authority to govern as he saw fit. Since the duke had no fondness for representative assemblies, he appointed a governor to rule in the same manner as the old director general.

Though the Dutch were not happy about rule by Englishmen, they submitted peacefully to the governors James sent: Richard Nicolls (1664–68), Francis Lovelace (1668–73), Edmund Andros (1674–81), and Thomas Dongan (1683–88). The New Englanders on Long Island were less docile. They showed the familiar unfriendliness of Englishmen toward governments not of their own choosing. Governor Nicolls tried to appease them at the outset by compiling a special set of laws for them, drawn in part from the New England laws which they presumably liked. This code, known as the Duke's Laws, was presented to a meeting of representatives from seventeen towns in 1665, but the meeting was not allowed to alter or add to it. The inhabitants accepted it but not gratefully. During the ensuing years they objected continually to paying taxes without representation and, instead of being happy about their rescue from the Dutch, complained that they were now "inslav'd under an Arbitrary Power."

Perhaps because of the noisy discontent of these New Englanders, New York attracted comparatively few new settlers. There was consequently little profit from rents for the duke of York. His governors told him of the demand for a representative assembly and hinted that the colony might be easier to govern with one than without. In 1683 he gave way, and on October 17 the first assembly was held at New York with seventeen representatives elected from the various areas of the duke's propriety. One of the assembly's first actions was to pass a Charter of Liberties stating the civil and political rights of the inhabitants. Though this received the duke's assent, he repudiated it in 1686, after New York had been transformed from a proprietary

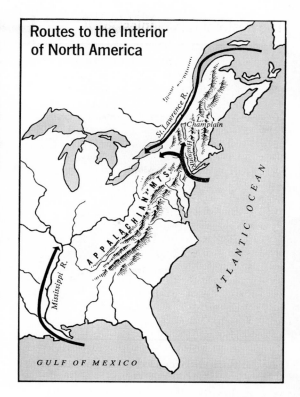

Routes to the Interior of North America

to a royal colony by his accession (1685) to the throne of England as James II.

New Jersey   New York in 1685 was not as large as New Netherland had been. Three and a half months after receiving his grant of the area, James had transferred the part later called New Jersey to two friends: John, Lord Berkeley, a privy councillor much interested in naval affairs, and Sir George Carteret, vice-chamberlain of the royal household and treasurer of the navy (James himself was Lord High Admiral, in charge of the navy). There followed a comedy of errors that was never entirely straightened out.

James' governor in New York, Richard Nicolls, did not learn of the transfer to Berkeley and Carteret until after he had himself granted lands in the New Jersey region to a number of New England Puritans from eastern Long Island. Nicolls, who was anxious to get the land settled and producing revenue, offered the Puritans the right to govern themselves through their own assembly. They in turn agreed to pay quitrents to James. Nicolls actually had no authority to offer such terms,

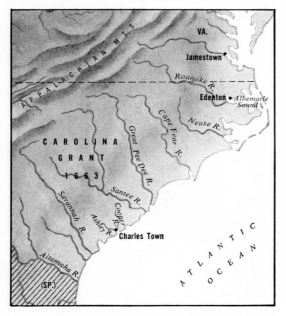

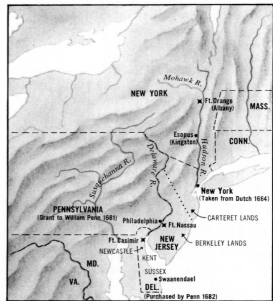

but the Puritans accepted them and moved in.

When Berkeley and Carteret gained possession, they too offered liberal terms to settlers. They too wanted quitrents and promised a representative assembly to make laws. More Puritans, this time from New Haven, accepted the offer and moved in.

James, in transferring New Jersey to Berkeley and Carteret, gave them only property rights over the colony. His own governmental authority was not transferable. Berkeley and Carteret therefore had no authority either to hold a representative assembly or to appoint a governor. Yet they did both, and neither James nor his brother the king objected.

But the cantankerous transplanted New Englanders, who had accepted grants from Nicolls, did object. They held their own assembly and refused to accept the authority of the government established by the proprietors. The vehemence of their protests and their carelessness in paying rents were not diminished by subsequent developments. Berkeley and Carteret divided the province in two in 1674. Berkeley, who had taken the western half, sold it that same year to a Quaker, who resold shares to other Quakers. In 1680, after Carteret died, the eastern half, where both

groups of Puritans were located, was sold at auction to another group of Quakers. The fact that the proprietors were now Quakers did not endear them or their government to the Puritan settlers. The Puritans continued to protest until the English government awoke to the fact that the government of New Jersey rested on a false assumption of power by the original proprietors. In 1702 East and West New Jersey were united as a royal colony with a single representative assembly and with the proprietors retaining only their property rights. To this day the public lands of New Jersey belong to two boards of proprietors inheriting their rights from Berkeley and Carteret.

The Carolinas Before Berkeley and Carteret received the grant of New Jersey, they had already become involved with several highly placed friends in a project for another colony in the region directly south of Virginia, known as Carolina. The moving spirit in this enterprise was probably Sir John Colleton, an old royalist soldier. After Charles I lost his head in 1649, Colleton had gone to Barbados. There he found that the Great Migration had deposited thousands of hopeful immigrants, who had carved the island into small farms. After 1640, however, as sugar gradually became the dominant crop, the land was absorbed into ever-larger plantations worked by increasing numbers of imported Negro slaves. Most of the settlers had been squeezed off their farms and were now ready to move to the continent, where land was more plentiful.

When Colleton returned to England in 1660, he realized that this ready-made population for a new colony lay waiting, and he was probably already interested in the Carolina region. In London he met Sir William Berkeley, brother of John and royal governor of Virginia (1641–52 and 1660–77). Berkeley knew that the Virginians had occupied much of their own tidewater land and were ready to expand down the coast into Carolina. Before long, Berkeley and Colleton had assembled a blue-ribbon board of would-be proprietors for the new colony. Besides themselves there were Berkeley's brother John; Sir George Carteret; Anthony Ashley Cooper, later earl of Shaftesbury; George Monck, duke of Albemarle (who had engineered Charles II's return to the throne); William, earl of Craven; and Edward Hyde, earl of Clarendon. To such men the king could not say no even though they were asking for the whole area extending from the present Atlantic border of the states of North Carolina, South Carolina, and Georgia westward to the Pacific.

The proprietors received the territory by royal charter on March 24, 1663, and they moved at once to fill it with footloose farmers from Virginia, New England, and Barbados. From the beginning they proposed two distinct centers for settlement. The region of Albemarle Sound, in the northernmost part of their grant, was already sparsely occupied by settlers who had drifted in from Virginia. The proprietors gave them a governor in 1664; a popularly elected assembly met for the first time by June 1665. At the end of the century this colony of North Carolina had a population of four or five thousand engaged in subsistence farming and tobacco culture. They shipped a million pounds of tobacco a year, in shallow-draft vessels sent to Albemarle Sound by enterprising New England merchants.

Farther south, where the Cape Fear River offered a better harbor than did Albemarle Sound, the proprietors intended to plant a second colony. New Englanders had already tried living here without authorization from England but had pulled out after tacking up a sign at the mouth of the river, warning future settlers that the country was not worth occupying. This may have been an early piece of Yankee shrewdness, for the proprietors found a continuing interest in the region among New Englanders. Not enough, however, to induce many Puritans to move there and pay quitrents to absentee proprietors (there were no quitrents in New England). The first authorized colonists were mainly Barbadians who came in 1665 and dispersed in 1667—to Virginia, to the Albemarle region, to New England, or back to Barbados. A successful settlement, sponsored primarily by Anthony Ashley Cooper, was finally made farther south. Well equipped with provisions, an expedition set out from England in 1669 and picked up reinforcements at Barbados and other islands en route. The settlers located themselves at first on the south bank of the Ashley River about twenty-five miles from the sea. In 1680 they moved to the present site of Charleston (called Charles Town until 1783), where, as later Carolinians would have it, the Ashley and Cooper Rivers join to form the Atlantic Ocean.

The proprietors had provided the settlers with a constitution designed to strike a balance between aristocracy and democracy. Drafted presumably by Cooper's secretary, John Locke, the Fundamental Constitutions of Carolina were based more on the political philosophy of James Harrington than on the philosophy for which Locke himself was to become famous (see p. 65). Harrington believed that the structure of government should match the distribution of property among the governed. The proprietors proposed to people three-fifths of their property with ordinary settlers (who would pay an annual quitrent) and to keep the rest in seigneurial and manorial estates for a hereditary nobility. The government was to consist of a governor appointed by the proprietors and a legislature in which the upper house would represent the nobility, the lower the commoners. The upper house was to have the sole right to initiate legislation (another idea of Harrington's).

The settlers of South Carolina, by accretions

of Barbadians, French Huguenots, New Englanders, Englishmen, Scots, and Negro slaves, increased to eight or ten thousand by the end of the century. Having discovered that rice grew well in the area, they cultivated it extensively in plantations around Charles Town. Beyond the plantations, frontiersmen outflanked the Appalachian Mountains, pushed back Spanish missions, and penetrated the interior of the continent to open a brisk trade with the Indians in deerskins and in slaves captured from other tribes. Charles Town grew into a city, the only one in the South. In spite of hurricanes, Indian attacks, and internal quarrels, South Carolina succeeded.

The Fundamental Constitutions did not. As in other colonies, the representative assembly —the lower house of the legislature—was impatient of restrictions: it claimed and took the right to initiate legislation, quarreled with the governor and the upper house, and generally got its way. By 1700 the Fundamental Constitutions were a dead letter, and proprietary rule was faltering. In 1719 a rebellion in Charles Town overthrew the last proprietary governor, and two years later a provisional royal government was organized in the colony. The proprietors finally surrendered their

William Penn: Enemy of royal prerogative.

charter in 1729, and royal governments were provided for both North and South Carolina, each with a governor and council appointed by the king and an assembly elected by the landowners.

William Penn's Holy Experiment   The last English colony to be founded in the seventeenth century was also the private property of a friend of the king. It would be hard to imagine a more unlikely friend for Charles II than William Penn, Quaker, commoner, and enemy of royal prerogative. The association, a tribute to breadth of character in both men, began in the career of Penn's father, who was no Quaker. William Penn the elder started life as an ordinary seaman and by sheer ability worked his way to the rank of admiral. He was in charge of naval operations in Cromwell's grandiose expedition to the West Indies. When the expedition captured nothing but Jamaica, the admiral retired in disgrace to Ireland, where he remained until Charles II took the throne.

Disgrace under Cromwell was no bar to preferment under Charles. Admiral Penn was on hand to see the new king crowned in 1660 and took the occasion to present his son, then aged sixteen. In the ensuing years, while the father headed the navy office under the duke of York, young Penn did the things that sons of gentlemen were expected to do. It was conventional that he should attend Oxford and almost conventional that he be expelled after two years and sent on the grand tour of the Continent by a worried father. It was conventional too that he should spend some time at the Inns of Court studying law, but without becoming a barrister. As he reached maturity, Penn had the standard qualifications of a young courtier: high spirits, ready wit, skill as a swordsman. He cut a dashing figure at the court of the king. But he had one quality that was not quite conventional, one that kings, courtiers, and fathers of young gentlemen have often found embarrassing: he took ideas seriously.

What was worse, the ideas he took most seriously were of the most embarrassing kind: radical, lower-class, faintly ridiculous. The Quakers (later called Friends) had initially been the lunatic fringe of the Puritan movement. They heard voices; they insulted their betters; they appeared naked in church. One of them, James Nayler, thought he was Jesus Christ and entered the city of Bristol riding on an ass, with his admirers singing holy, holy, holy before him.

The authorities dealt with Nayler: they bored his tongue with a hot iron, cut off his ears, and branded his forehead with the letter *B* for blasphemer—thereby demonstrating what might have happened to Christ if he *had* reappeared. Respectable Englishmen thought that madmen like Nayler were typical of Quakerism. But by the 1660's Quakers had shaken free of these eccentricities and were challenging the world by practicing what they preached.

What they preached was not far different from what other Christians had always preached. What others had variously called conscience, revelation, or saving grace, Quakers called the Inner Light. The Inner Light, they said, glowed in every man. He had only to live by it in order to be saved. Quakers tried to live by it.

All Christians believed that humility was a virtue. But the Quakers studiously, almost fanatically, avoided pride and the institutions that pride erected: they wore conspicuously plain and out-of-date clothes; they refused to honor one another—or anyone else—by bowing or kneeling or taking off their hats, or by using the second person plural when addressing an individual (ultimately they forgot the nominative and used only "thee"). All Christians professed brotherly love. But the Quakers refused to make war. They also refused to give or take oaths, partly because the imposition of an oath implied distrust of one's fellow men.

Ideas of this kind first attacked William Penn as a student at Oxford and may have been responsible for his expulsion. One reason for the grand tour was to get them out of his head and something more fashionable into it. The tour worked, too, but only until Penn encountered a Quaker named Thomas Loe, whom he may have known earlier. In 1667 Samuel Pepys, a diarist who worked in the navy office, recorded the sad fact that Sir William Penn's son was "a Quaker again, or some very melancholy thing."

From this time forward, Penn was Quakerism's most energetic and effective supporter. He knew enough theology to argue with priests, enough law to argue with judges. He was so friendly with the king that no one dared ignore him, and he had such courage that he never allowed his friendship to weaken his arguments against the king's policies. He fought not only for Quakerism but for the right of all Englishmen to worship as they pleased and to run their own government.

The "golden days of good King Charles" were nevertheless hard times for Quakers. The Anglican Church was doing its best to limit and control dissent. Quakers, because they refused to hold their meetings in secret, spent more time in jail than other dissenters. Penn joined with other Quakers in the purchase of New Jersey, which for a time served as a Quaker refuge. But eastern New Jersey was full of Puritans, always unfriendly to Quakers, and western New Jersey had poor soil. Penn heard that the land across the Delaware was better and that no one was there but wild Indians, who would be easier to live with than English bishops or New Jersey Puritans. The king owed him £16,000, a debt contracted to his father (who died in 1670) for back pay and loans to the royal exchequer. In 1680 Penn asked the king for the land and, after many protests from the king's advisers, got it. Charles named it Pennsylvania after the admiral. In addition, Penn later bought from the duke of York the region that is now the state of Delaware, which was already populated by a few Dutch and Swedish settlers.

According to the terms of his charter, issued in March 1681, Penn was specifically required to enforce the Navigation Acts, to submit laws to the king for approval, to allow appeals to the king from Pennsylvania courts, and to provide an Anglican minister whenever twenty or more colonists asked for one. He was also required to obtain the approval of the freeholders (the male owners of land) for any laws that he imposed. Otherwise he had a free hand to govern the colony as he saw fit.

Penn saw fit to govern in a manner that he hoped would demonstrate the virtues of Quakerism and of political liberty. Though, like other proprietors, he hoped to profit from his colony by quitrents on land, his primary purpose was to conduct a holy experiment in popular government and Christian living. He served as governor when in the province and appointed a deputy when absent, but neither for himself nor for his deputy did he retain extensive powers. The people, he made plain in a statement issued a month after he received the charter, "would be allowed to shape their own laws." In the Frame of Government that he worked out to embody this principle, Penn placed the entire legislative power in a council and an assembly, both elected by the freeholders. The council, the more powerful of the two bodies, had the sole right to initiate legislation.

Attracted by the prospect of good land and free government, English, Irish, Welsh, Dutch, and German Quakers flocked to the colony, which prospered from the start and attracted many non-Quakers as well, partly because Penn advertised the advantages of his colony in pamphlets that were circulated widely. Penn himself went to the colony in 1682 but had to return to England in less than two years to defend his southern boundary in a legal dispute with Lord Baltimore. The dispute was not fully settled until the 1760's when Charles

---

Religious Liberty
in Pennsylvania

First. Because no people can be truly happy, though under the greatest enjoyment of civil liberties, if abridged of the freedom of their consciences as to their religious profession and worship; and Almighty God being the only Lord of conscience,... I do hereby grant and declare that no person or persons inhabiting in this province or territories, who shall confess and acknowledge one Almighty God, the creator, upholder, and ruler of the world, and profess him or themselves obliged to live quietly under the civil government, shall be in any case molested or prejudiced ... because of his or their conscientious persuasion or practice, nor be compelled to frequent or maintain any religious worship, place, or ministry contrary to his or their mind, or to do or suffer any other act or thing contrary to their religious persuasion. And that all persons who also profess to believe in Jesus Christ the Saviour of the world shall be capable ... to serve this government in any capacity,... he or they solemnly promising, when lawfully required, allegiance to the king as sovereign, and fidelity to the proprietor and governor.

From the Pennsylvania Charter of Privileges, 1701.

Mason and Jeremiah Dixon surveyed their famous line. Litigation, losses, and revolution kept Penn in England for fifteen years. During that time his friend King Charles died and his friend the duke of York ascended the throne, only to flee from it in 1688.

In Pennsylvania, Quakerism in power fulfilled many but not all of Penn's anticipations. It brought religious peace (other sects found complete freedom), economic prosperity, and political quarrels. Although the council, where power was concentrated, was elected by the same people as the assembly, just as the United States Senate and House of Representatives are today, the assemblymen acted as though their lack of the right to initiate legislation was a denial of popular rights. The council and the assembly joined in attacking the governors whom Penn sent over, even though the executive power in Pennsylvania was weaker than in any other colony. It is true that Penn, who could never believe ill of any man, often sent incompetent, or at least inappropriate, governors, such as the old Cromwellian soldier, John Blackwell. Blackwell left the province saying that Quakers prayed for their neighbors on Sundays and preyed on them the other six days of the week.

After the fall of James II, Penn was for a while suspect in England because of their longstanding friendship. His province was temporarily taken from him and, from 1692 to 1694, was under a royal government which gave the assembly the right to initiate legislation. Upon recovering the colony, Penn recognized that right, but by then the assembly was in pursuit of still larger powers. In 1699 he finally returned to the province and told the members of the assembly, since they did not like his plan of government, to draft one of their own. They did so, eliminating the legislative authority of the council altogether (it retained only the function of advising the governor), and leaving the proprietor with only the ownership of ungranted land and a veto power over legislation, which was normally exercised through his appointed governor.

The new plan, known as the Charter of Liberties, was established in 1701, with Penn's approval, by an act of the assembly. Pennsylvania thus became the only colony with a unicameral legislature. The same Charter of Liberties gave the counties of Newcastle, Sussex, and Kent (later the state of Delaware) a separate representative assembly, though they retained the same governor as Pennsylvania. In 1701 Penn returned to England, where the brotherly love that had founded Pennsylvania eventually landed him in prison for debts incurred by dishonest agents whom he had trusted. No quitrents arrived from Pennsylvania to extricate him. He died in 1718.

Problems of Enforcement

The settlement of Pennsylvania completed English occupation of the Atlantic coast from Spanish Florida to French Canada. All the colonies had been founded under authority of the king, but without his active participation or financial support. The government of each had been uniquely shaped by the varying purposes of the founders and settlers, not by an over-all imperial policy. When, with the Navigation Acts, the king and his Parliament proposed to apply an imperial policy to America, they found that most of the machinery of colonial government by which the acts might have been enforced lay beyond their immediate control. Only in Virginia (through the royally appointed governor and council) did England have a voice in colonial government.

Even as the Navigation Acts were passed, Charles II was furthering this dispersion of power. In 1662 he gave Rhode Island a royal charter (to replace a similar Parliamentary charter of 1644), authorizing the settlers to choose their own governmental officers. In 1663 he gave a charter with the same privilege to Connecticut (including New Haven, which would have preferred a separate charter). By these charters and by those granted to the duke of York, the Carolina proprietors, and William Penn, Charles, perhaps thoughtlessly, distributed authority that might have been used to enforce imperial policies.

At the same time he strengthened another element in colonial government that would make imperial control difficult. In each of his charters, except the one given to the duke of York, he required the consent of the settlers

to local legislation. The requirement was met by popularly elected representative assemblies such as already existed in the older colonies. Assemblies had demonstrated their usefulness: to operate effectively, a colonial government had to obtain the advice and cooperation of the actual settlers, especially where they were Englishmen used to taking a hand in politics. But the assemblies had also demonstrated a truculence, not unlike that of Parliament in England, which promised trouble for policies imposed from above. Nowhere was the threat greater than in New England.

Recalcitrant Colonists New England, of all the regions in the empire, fitted least well into the mercantilist scheme of supplying needed raw materials to the mother country. She had nothing in quantity that the mother country wanted and little except fish that anybody else wanted. Since furs from the interior of the continent came out by way of the Hudson or the St. Lawrence, the New England fur trade lasted only until the local animals had been depleted. Lumber and lumber products, such as pitch and tar, were a minor resource. But mostly New England grew rocks, and even these contained no valuable minerals or ores. As a result New Englanders went

---

Religious Covenant in Massachusetts

Who must have liberty to sit downe in this Commonwealth and enjoy the liberties thereof is not our place to determine, but the Magistrates who are the rulers and governours of the Commonwealth, and of all persons within the same. And as for acknowledging a company to be a sister Church, that shall set up, and practice another forme of Church Discipline, being otherwise in some measure, as you say, approveable, we conceive the companie that shall so doe, shall not be approveable therein. For the Discipline appointed by Jesus Christ for his Churches is not arbitrary, that one Church may set up and practice one forme, and another another forme, as each one shall please, but is one and the same for all Churches.... And if that Discipline which we here practice, be (as we are perswaded of it) the same which Christ hath appointed, and therefore unalterable, we see not how another can be lawfull.

From Richard Mather, *Church Government and Church Covenant*, 1643.

New Englanders away from home: John Greenwood's "Sea Captains at Surinam."

into the business of distributing what the rest of the world produced. In trading freely wherever the best price was offered, they competed all too successfully with the merchants of the mother country.

They could still have carried on a successful trade in obedience to the Navigation Acts, but disobedience was more profitable. The merchant who bought French silks and laces in France and carried them directly to Boston could undersell one who bought the same goods in England, because English prices included the extra cost of English duties and of transportation from France to England. The same advantage accrued to a merchant or captain who illegally carried enumerated commodities, such as sugar or tobacco, directly from the colonies to Europe.

New Englanders, therefore, had good economic reasons for resisting or evading directions from England. And, as was often the case in New England, economic interest coincided with religious interest. The New Englanders were Puritans, and they had come to New England to live as Puritans. Charles II, whatever else he may have been, was notoriously not a

Puritan. New Englanders consequently looked with suspicion on his government and were wary of any move to bring them under its control. Their fathers had struck this kind of defensive attitude almost as soon as they set foot in New England. According to Governor Winthrop, the Puritans had "hastened" their fortifications in 1633 when they heard that Charles I had appointed a commission under Archbishop Laud to govern them. Fortunately the fortifications did not have to be manned against the archbishop. Thereafter New Englanders had easily withstood the half-hearted efforts at control made by Parliament and by Oliver Cromwell. When Charles II came to the throne, they still had their royal charter intact and did not hesitate to remind the new king of the privileges granted by his father (even though they were secretly harboring the men who had passed the death sentence on Charles I).

Charles II knew that New England was full of Puritans, whom he abhorred, and that Massachusetts in particular had passed laws which did not fully satisfy the requirement, stated in her charter (as in other colonial charters), that all laws conform to those of England. In 1662 he sent a letter commanding revisions. The assembly ignored it. And so, in 1664, when Charles sent his commission of four to capture New Netherland from the Dutch, he assigned them the additional task of investigating New England. They were empowered to adjust boundaries, hear appeals from colonial courts, redress grievances against colonial governments, and report to the king on how well New England was obeying the Navigation Acts.

The commissioners, who went to New England fresh from their triumph over the Dutch, made a discovery that was to be repeated often in the history of the British Empire: England could govern Dutchmen (and Frenchmen, Spaniards, Egyptians, Indians, and Chinese) more easily than it could govern Englishmen. The commissioners were treated well enough in Rhode Island, Connecticut, and Plymouth, all of which were looking for improvements in their boundaries. Plymouth had no charter and perhaps hoped to get one by good behavior. But when the commissioners appeared in Boston, they met with a reception the coolness of which has seldom been matched even in that city. The officers of government referred them to the charter of 1629 and ostentatiously refused to recognize their authority. A herald appeared before the house where the commissioners were staying and, after a blast from his trumpet, in the name of the king formally forbade anyone to appear before them. Frustrated at every turn, they went back to England to report that the Massachusetts government was making no effort to enforce the Navigation Acts. They also recommended to the king that he revoke the Massachusetts charter, a suggestion echoed by every royal official to visit the colony in the next twenty years.

The king could not revoke the charter at will. It was a contract, binding both grantor and grantee. But the terms required that Massachusetts make no laws contrary to those of England. If it could be shown that Massachusetts had done so, a court of law would declare the charter void and the king would recover all governmental powers.

After the experience of his commissioners, Charles decided to continue the investigation in England and demanded that Massachusetts send agents to account for its behavior. The General Court (as the Massachusetts assembly was called) sent masts for the king's navy, money for the sufferers in the great fire of London, provisions for the fleet, but no agents. The leaders of Massachusetts knew that many of their laws did violate England's, especially their laws about religion. It was precisely these laws that they wished to keep, even more than they wished to escape the Navigation Acts. So they tried every means to avoid a showdown, relying heavily on distance to support them in one delaying action after another. For ten years they got away with it and grew ever more prosperous and powerful.

In England the king paid only sporadic attention to them and made no effective move against them. But Parliament, in 1673, passed an act to make smuggling to foreign countries less profitable. It levied export duties, known as "plantations duties," on any enumerated commodity shipped to another colony instead of to England. Now, if a shipper pretended to be taking tobacco from Virginia to Boston but took it instead to Holland, he would already have paid a tax equivalent to that levied in England and he would be unable to sell his cargo in Holland at a price much lower than that of tobacco reshipped legitimately from England. The act of 1673 made smuggling more difficult but did not stop it. As before, the most persistent evaders were the New Englanders, and the governors of other colonies complained that the example of Massachusetts undermined their own attempts to enforce the Navigation Acts.

The main reason for Charles II's failure to act decisively against Massachusetts during these years was that he had no administrative body devoted primarily to colonial affairs. At last, in 1675, he appointed a special committee of the Privy Council known as the Lords of Trade, which set about pulling together the strings of empire. The members quickly realized that England could not rely on the colonial governments to enforce her policies. She must have her own means of enforcement in the colonies. The first step, the Lords of Trade decided, was for the king to take a hand in governing them.

The earliest opportunity came in New

Hampshire, into which Massachusetts had extended her authority beyond the boundaries set by her charter. Robert Mason, who had inherited a claim to the region from the Council for New England, complained to the king about this encroachment, and in 1679 Charles took New Hampshire away from Massachusetts and gave it a royal government. Massachusetts was in danger of losing Maine as well, after an English court had declared her title to that area invalid. But Massachusetts managed to purchase the title of the counter-claimant, Ferdinando Gorges (heir of the original Ferdinando), before the king could act.

The Lords of Trade took over Charles' fight against the Massachusetts charter by renewing the demand that the colony send agents to London. The General Court finally did so, but it gave them no authority to answer the questions the Lords wanted answered. The Lords insisted that the Massachusetts government enforce the Navigation Acts. The General Court, hardened by thirty years of ignoring and defying orders from England, loftily retorted that it was legally endowed by the king's own charter with full powers to govern the province and that therefore Parliament had no authority to pass laws affecting Massachusetts. But in order to avoid a head-on collision, the General Court formally ordered enforcement of the Navigation Acts. Without waiting to see if Massachusetts would actually carry out the order, the Lords sent an imperial customs officer, Edward Randolph, to do the job; the General Court refused to recognize his commission, set up its own customs office, and imprisoned the deputies appointed by Randolph. The Lords demanded that Massachusetts show cause why its charter should not be revoked; again the General Court sent agents with insufficient powers and inadequate answers. In 1683 legal proceedings were begun, and in 1684 the charter was revoked. In 1685 the duke of York became King James II.

The Dominion of New England The accession of James II, which made New York a royal colony, together with the revocation of the Massachusetts charter, cleared the way for a scheme the Lords of Trade had long had in mind: a reconstruction of the American empire from New Jersey northward. The scheme shows that they had identified clearly the immediate sources of trouble; it also shows that they had learned little about political realities either in England or America. They proposed to place New Jersey, New York, Connecticut, Rhode Island, Plymouth, Massachusetts, New Hampshire, and Maine under one governor. And in this whole area, to be called the Dominion of New England, there would be no troublesome representative assembly. The royally appointed governor would be assisted by a council whose members would also be appointed by the king. It apparently did not occur to their lordships that the people, deprived of any share in their own government, might prove more troublesome than the assemblies had been.

When news reached Boston that the Massachusetts charter had been revoked, men talked of resistance, as their fathers had fifty years before when threatened with the rule of Archbishop Laud. But their fathers had never been put to the test and had had less to lose in ships, houses, and money than the Bostonians of 1685. Boston was no longer a mere beachhead on an unsettled coast. It was a prosperous city of some 7,000 people with a fleet rivaling that of any English city except London. Most Bostonians held to the faith of their fathers, but they and other New Englanders were perhaps a little more prosperous than Puritan. They allowed their General Court to be dissolved and submitted reluctantly to the interim government of a council appointed by the king. In 1686, when Sir Edmund Andros arrived to establish the Dominion of New England, he faced hard looks and sullen words but no manned fortifications. Although the charters of Rhode Island and Connecticut had not been revoked, Andros extended his government over them without difficulty and in 1688 completed his domain by taking over New York and New Jersey, which he ruled thereafter through a lieutenant-governor. In each colony he dissolved the assembly.

Andros was not a happy choice to inaugurate the new system. An administrator of proved ability, he had already served successfully as governor of New York and would, in the years ahead, serve as governor of Virginia. But the present task called for diplomacy and tact as well as administrative skill. A blunt, outspoken

The Dominion of New England

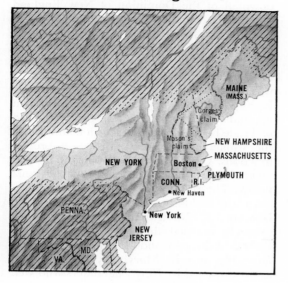

man, Andros made decisions more easily than he made friends. He and the Lords of Trade believed, not without reason, that in order to establish imperial authority in New England the grip of the Puritan leaders must be broken and room made for a party of moderation. But it would have required a man of moderate temper and winning ways to organize and lead such a party.

The Lords of Trade, encouraged by the reports of Edward Randolph, supposed that the Puritans were a minority, and that the majority of the population would welcome their fall and gladly step in line behind a royal governor. Nothing could have been further from the truth. Enemies of the old government were few, and Andros, by following the instructions of his superiors in England, succeeded in alienating what few there were. He levied taxes for the support of government, necessarily without the consent of a representative assembly. When the inhabitants objected and pleaded their rights as Englishmen, he told them they had no rights. Massachusetts had parceled out lands to individuals through the agency of incorporated towns; Andros maintained that the Massachusetts Bay Company had no authority to create corporations and that all titles to land granted by towns were therefore invalid. Anyone who wanted to own

the land that he or his fathers had carved out of the wilderness must ask for a new deed from the governor, pay a fee for it, and agree to pay quitrents ever after.

Andros, with the help of customs officers sent from England, enforced the Navigation Acts, and Randolph later claimed that this was the real cause of opposition to him. But the fact was that the Lords of Trade, in their zeal to establish imperial authority, had assigned Andros an impossible task. They required him to violate long-established rights and privileges, and, without the support of an army, a police force, or a political party, to rule arbitrarily over a people who for more than fifty years had ruled themselves. Whether Puritan, non-Puritan, or anti-Puritan they could not be expected to like it. As Andros spelled out the dimensions of his immense authority, they began to have second thoughts about the wisdom of their submission.

The Revolution of 1688 Fortunately for New England, the rule of Andros coincided with the reign of James II. Although James could not dispense with Parliament as he had with the New England assemblies, he made it appear that he would have liked to. By exercising his power of pardon he effectively suspended the operation of many Parliamentary enactments. He was, besides, a Catholic and made no secret of it. The political patience of Englishmen was as thin in old as in New England. In 1688 they welcomed William of Orange and chased James out of the country.

In Boston the Puritans did not wait for the fall of James to liquidate the Dominion of New England. After they had heard of William's landing in England, but before they had learned of his success in ousting James, they carried out a tidy, bloodless revolution of their own. Spurred by rumors that Andros and James were plotting to hand New England over to the pope, the inhabitants of Boston seized and imprisoned the governor and his council, restored the old government, and waited to hear how William was faring in England. The colony's most eminent minister, Increase Mather, had gone to London the year before to plead the colony's cause against Andros. Mather did his best to persuade the new monarchs, William and Mary, that the Dominion of New England was part and parcel of James' tyrannical policies in England, and that the Glorious Revolution ought to include a glorious restitution of the Massachusetts charter. William gave orders for the recall of Andros and authorized Massachusetts to proceed temporarily under her old government, but he refused to restore the charter until he and his advisers should have time to investigate the situation.

Plymouth, Rhode Island, and Connecticut quietly resumed their old governments, and New Jersey returned to anarchy. But New York had its own revolution, which was not entirely bloodless. Andros' lieutenant-governor there, Francis Nicholson, was left in an anomalous position as the appointee of a deposed officer who was in turn the appointee of a deposed king. Nicholson was, besides, young and inexperienced. When rumors of popish plots alarmed the population, he did nothing to quiet them.

At the end of May 1689 a party of local militia seized the fort which commanded New York harbor and took control of the government. The party was led by Jacob Leisler, a successful German immigrant who had married into a prominent Dutch family. After Nicholson departed for England in June 1689, a meeting of delegates from different parts of the province chose a committee of safety, which in turn named Leisler as commander in chief of the province. Leisler proclaimed the accession of William, and when ambiguously addressed letters arrived from the new king authorizing a continuation of government, Leisler claimed them.

Basing his authority on the letters, Leisler governed the colony arbitrarily but effectively for nearly two years. New York, thinly settled by people of differing nationalities and religions living in widely differing circumstances, was a long way from political maturity. To maintain order, Leisler had to rely heavily on his followers among the militia. When King William finally got around to appointing a regular governor in 1691, Leisler hesitated before surrendering authority to him and thereby gave the new appointee the pretext for an accusation of treason. Leisler and his son-in-law, Jacob Milborne, were convicted and hanged on May 16, 1691. Four years later Parliament reversed the sentence.

The Reorganization of 1696 The downfall of the Dominion of New England, together with the revolution in England, brought to a halt the efforts to consolidate the empire. After William mounted the throne, he was kept busy defending England in war against France and trying to shore up what was left of the royal prerogative. The new men he appointed to the Privy Council were unfamiliar with colonial problems, and the Lords of Trade had been turned into a committee of the whole, charged with new and broader functions. Once again nobody in the government devoted himself exclusively to colonial policy. The result was seven years of neglect.

In the colonies merchants and shippers ignored the Navigation Acts, and pirates brazenly pursued their prey in and out of harbors. Edward Randolph, now trying to enforce the acts in Maryland, found himself again thwarted by New Englanders who were buying tobacco from the planters and taking it to Scotland instead of England. Though Scotland had the same king as England, the two countries remained separate until 1707. Under the Navigation Acts, Scotland, like nations on the Continent, was excluded from the benefits of trade with England's colonies.

Scottish competition for the tobacco trade raised such a howl of protest from English merchants that the king and Parliament were driven to act. In 1696, guided by Edward Randolph, Parliament in one extensive enactment constructed machinery for enforcing the Navigation Acts. Henceforth the governors of all colonies, whether royal, proprietary, or corporate (Rhode Island and Connecticut), were to take an oath to enforce the acts. Failure to do so meant forfeiture of office. In place of the occasional peripatetic customs officer, a regular customs service subject to the English Treasury department was established in each colony. The customs officers were authorized to take out "writs of assistants" from local courts entitling them to open buildings by force in search of smuggled goods. The officers were also empowered to prosecute violators of the Navigation Acts in admiralty courts, which the Privy Council ordered to be established in the colonies. Admiralty courts operated without juries, and it was hoped that the judges would give short shrift to smugglers.

While Parliament was passing this measure, it also considered, and then rejected, a bill to create a council of trade and plantations to develop and administer colonial policy. The Privy Council, which had already planned a similar body, now swung into action to keep control of colonial policy under the king. In May 1696, by royal order, a new bureau was established to replace the old Lords of Trade. The Lords Commissioners of Trade and Plantations, as it was called, or more simply the Board of Trade, resembled a national chamber of commerce. It was appointed by the king and was charged to furnish him with information and advice on all colonial matters. Although the board included some members of the Privy Council, ex officio, the eight working members were not councillors and had no authority to issue orders. Their function was purely advisory. But since they constituted the only body directly concerned with the colonies, their advice was seldom ignored.

Although the king retained control of colonial policy and administration, the circumstances of William's accession affected the kind of control that he and his successors were able to exert in the colonies. After the unhappy experience with James II, Parliament would have looked with suspicion on any move by the king to do away with a representative assembly, even in America. Parliament did not object, however, to the introduction of royal governors in colonies that had not formerly had them. Nor was there serious objection from the settlers, for in almost every case the advent of royal government relieved an intolerable internal situation, just as it had in Virginia in 1624. Maryland was converted to royal government in 1689, after a local rebellion against the proprietor. (It returned to proprietary government in 1715 after the fourth Lord Baltimore turned Anglican.) And, as we have seen, New Jersey, became a royal colony in 1702 (see p. 36), South Carolina and North Carolina in 1729 (see p. 38). In the new charter that William granted Massachusetts in 1691 (which incorporated Plymouth and Maine as parts of Massachusetts), the king retained power to appoint the governor. Thus most of the colonies reverted eventually to the king.

Wherever a royal government was introduced, the king gained more direct control over his subjects. He appointed the governor and he appointed the governor's council (except in Massachusetts). Although in each royal colony a representative assembly of freeholders retained legislative authority, the governor's council served as the upper house of the legislature, and its approval was necessary before any act passed by the lower house became law. Even an act passed by both houses was subject to veto by the governor, and even an act approved by the governor might be disallowed by the king. During the eighteenth century, usually on the advice of the Board of Trade, some 5½ per cent of the acts passed by colonial assemblies were disallowed by the king, though no act of Parliament was ever vetoed after 1708. Moreover, in the eyes of the mother country the king's instructions to his governors were supposed to bind the assembly as well as the governor. But in spite of royal theories, the popularly elected lower house of the assembly became in practice the most powerful branch of government in every colony. It enjoyed sole authority to levy taxes, and by threatening to withhold them it was often able to get its own way against both king and governor.

The Old Colonial System   Of the three agencies England now had for enforcement of the Navigation Acts, the admiralty courts proved unable to exercise jurisdiction because of ambiguities in the act of 1696; the customs service was ill-paid and susceptible to bribes and could not operate effectively without the support of the local government. England's control of her colonies depended most heavily on the success of her royal governors in working with the colonial assemblies. Since every legislative act required the assent of both the governor and the assembly, the needs of neither the mother country nor the colonies could be satisfied if the two parties refused to cooperate.

Thus in the last analysis the Old Colonial System (embodied in the Navigation Acts and in the act of 1696) rested on the harmony of English and colonial interests. Although occasional discord developed, especially at points of contact between royal governors and assemblies, and although smugglers often escaped the law, the harmony was real and the system worked. Enriched by her colonies, England grew to be the world's most powerful nation. And protected by England, the American colonies grew, each in its own style, toward a new way of life.

SUGGESTIONS FOR READING

Eli Heckscher in *Mercantilism*, 2 vols. (1935), sets the economic policies of the seventeenth and eighteenth centuries in historical perspective and thus furnishes the best introduction to an understanding of the Navigation Acts. For the acts themselves and the thinking behind them, the pioneering works of G. L. Beer are still valuable: *The Origins of the British Colonial System* (1908) and *The Old Colonial System*, 2 vols. (1912). On the administration and interpretation of the acts, see L. A. Harper, *The English Navigation Laws* (1939), and C. M. Andrews, *The Colonial Period of American History*, Vol. IV (1938). Special aspects of British policy are well treated in Curtis Nettels, *The Money Supply of the American Colonies Before 1720* (1934), and A. C. Bining, *British Regulation of the Colonial Iron Industry* (1933).

On New Netherland and on the Restoration colonies the best general work is again C. M. Andrews, *The Colonial Period of American History*, Vols. II and III. T. J. Wertenbaker, *The Founding of American Civilization: The Middle Colonies* (1938), stresses social and cultural history. J. E. Pomfret has untangled much of New Jersey's early history in *The Province of West New Jersey, 1609–1702* (1956). The most important single work on the early history of the Carolinas is Verner Crane, *The Southern Frontier, 1670–1732* * (1929, 1956). On the Fundamental Constitutions, see H. F. Russell Smith, *Harrington and His Oceana* (1914).

There is no definitive biography of William Penn, but Bonamy Dobrée, *William Penn, Quaker and Pioneer* (1932), is adequate; and F. B. Tolles and E. G. Alderfer have edited a selection of Penn's writings in *The Witness of William Penn* (1957). Rufus Jones, *Quakers in the American Colonies* (1911), is a standard work, but see also F. B. Tolles's eloquent essays in *Quakers and the Atlantic Culture* (1960), and his *James Logan and the Culture of Provincial America* (1957).

Efforts of England to enforce the Navigation Acts are dealt with in Michael Hall, *Edward Randolph and the American Colonies* (1960). Viola Barnes, *The Dominion of New England* (1923), is the classic account of that episode, exonerating Andros of blame. Kenneth Murdock, *Increase Mather* (1925), treats fully of Mather's role in seeking the overthrow of the dominion and in securing a new charter for Massachusetts. J. R. Reich, *Leisler's Rebellion: A Study of Democracy in New York, 1664–1720* (1953), discusses long-range causes and effects.

On the reorganization of colonial administration in 1696, see again C. M. Andrews, *Colonial Period of American History*, Vol. IV, and Peter Laslett, "John Locke, the Great Recoinage, and the Origins of the Board of Trade: 1695–1698," *William and Mary Quarterly*, 3rd series, XIV (1957), 370–402. The standard works on the Board of Trade are O. M. Dickerson, *American Colonial Government, 1696–1765* (1912), and A. H. Basye, *The Lords Commissioners of Trade and Plantations, 1748–1782* (1925). On the activities of the Board in securing the disallowance of colonial acts of legislation, see E. B. Russell, *The Review of American Colonial Legislation by the King in Council* (1915). The role of colonial governors in administering British policy is the subject of L. W. Labaree, *Royal Government in America: A Study of the British Colonial System Before 1783* (1930). Finally, Lawrence Gipson, in a monumental work of which ten volumes have appeared, surveys *The British Empire Before the American Revolution* (1936–   ).

* Available in a paperback edition.

3

The First American
Way of Life

Americans moving across their continent
have faced three questions again and
again: how to live, how to live with one another, how to live with the outside world.
They first learned how to live by tobacco, rice,
furs, fish. England told them, in the Navigation Acts, how they must live with the outside
world. How did they live with one another?

A few simply did not. When the Puritans
explored Boston harbor, they came upon an
Englishman at Beacon Hill living alone among
the blueberries. William Blackstone was company enough for himself. After the Puritans
moved in, he moved out. For nearly three
centuries the continent afforded room for men
like Blackstone, American hermits who felt
crowded when they could see the smoke from
their neighbor's campfire.

Patterns of Existence

Most Americans have been more gregarious.
They have asked *how*, rather than whether, to
live together, and they have answered partly
from the heritage of ideas and institutions carried from Europe, partly from their own ideas
and experience. Each generation has solved
the problem a little differently from the preceding one, but the first settlers, moving from
an old established world to an empty new one,
had the biggest problem and made the biggest
change. Many of them came to America primarily for a chance to live together in a new

and, hopefully, a better way. All of them had
to adapt ideas made in Europe to experience
made in America. The results differed from
time to time and from place to place. But before the end of the colonial period most Americans were living together in one of four distinct
patterns: the southern plantation, the New
England town, the loose collection of individual farms, or the coastal city.

The Plantation   Plantations developed
in colonies where the majority of the people
lived by growing a single crop: tobacco in Virginia and Maryland, rice or indigo in South
Carolina, sugar in the West Indies. Originally
"planter" meant simply a settler, and "plantation" a settlement—Jamestown was the London Company's plantation. Gradually the
name came to be attached to individual holdings. The size of a plantation in this sense
depended on the number of servants the
planter brought with him. Under the headright system he got fifty acres per man; if he
prospered, he could import more men and get
more land. In Virginia, where the system
began, fortunes fluctuated rapidly for the first
two or three generations, and those who accumulated large tracts were seldom able to
retain them. But in the long run free land, low
tobacco prices, and a supply of cheap labor
favored the development of the large working
estate to which we now apply the name
"plantation."

At the outset, in 1617, the price of tobacco

The Tidewater and the Piedmont

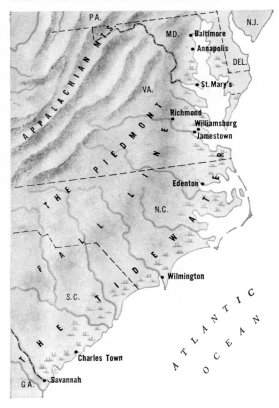

in Virginia was three shillings a pound; it dropped to less than a shilling in the 1630's and thereafter seldom rose above twopence. But the low price of tobacco was balanced by the low cost of labor. Servants (bound by contract or custom to serve without pay for up to seven years) could be bought for fifteen to twenty pounds in the seventeenth century; in addition to growing enough corn to feed themselves, they could produce one thousand to two thousand pounds of tobacco in a year, worth eight to sixteen pounds sterling. Thus the man who could buy servants (and claim fifty acres of land for each of them) could expect a handsome return on his investment.

Methods of cultivation also favored the large plantation. Since tobacco exhausted the soil in three or four years, the tobacco grower divided his land into three parts: one where he grew tobacco, one where he had grown it, and one where he would grow it. In order to continue in operation, a plantation had to be much larger than the area under cultivation at any one time.

It had also to be properly located. The tidewater lands of Virginia and Maryland were cut by great rivers and bays up which ocean-going ships made their way to collect the tobacco at wharves only a stone's throw from where much of it was grown. The grower who had to pay the cost of carting his crop from the interior to a ship lost much of his profit along the way. Successful planters bought more and more land adjoining the water, and here the great plantations grew.

They grew slowly in the seventeenth century, when servants arriving each year from England were the main source of labor. As the diminishing supply of unappropriated river land and the falling price of tobacco reduced the ordinary man's prospect of success, fewer and fewer Englishmen were willing to give seven years of their lives, or even a shorter span, in return for passage to Virginia. But by the end of the century a cheaper and more lasting form of labor had become available.

The first Africans reached Virginia in 1619, and during the next half-century a few more were imported from time to time. There is some evidence that they were at first treated like other servants and freed after a term of years. But perpetual slavery, unknown in England, was no novelty in America. The Spaniards had practiced it to the south for more than a century, and in the English colonies Indians who made unsuccessful war on the settlers usually ended up as slaves. The theory was that the lives of captives taken in just wars belonged to the captors, and history records no war acknowledged by the victors to have been unjust. Although Africans may not have grasped the rationale, they knew that slave traders waited in ships off their coasts, eager to buy the losers in tribal wars.

As time went on, an increasing number of losers became Americans. Traders began bringing them to Virginia and Maryland in quantity toward the end of the seventeenth century. By then the colonists had passed laws differentiating Negroes from other servants. While the courts protected white servants from abuse, they left Negroes almost entirely at the mercy of their masters. Slaves had to serve for life, and so did their children and grand-children forever.

Slavery is the crudest way that men have devised for living together. Cruelty was essential to it, but cruelty was mitigated by the owner's need to keep his slaves, like his cattle, healthy and by the human intimacy that often grew up between master and slave. What life held for a slave depended on where he lived. On the West Indian sugar plantations slavery meant being worked to death: the life expectancy of a freshly imported field hand was only about seven years. But growing tobacco, rice, or indigo in the mainland colonies was less arduous; here a slave could do his work and raise a family at the same time, so that when he died he left a whole brood of new workers to take his place.

Slavery offered the plantation-owner a permanent solution to his labor problem and a larger profit on his crop. A slave cost more than a servant—from twenty to thirty pounds in the first half of the eighteenth century—but the investment could be recovered by resale, it brought a yearly return, and it appreciated in value by the simple process of human reproduction.

In every American colony slavery was sanctioned by law. And in the colonies with large plantations—Virginia, Maryland, and South Carolina—half or more of the population was enslaved to part of the other half by the middle of the eighteenth century. Slaves who belonged to small farmers often worked side by side with their owners in the fields, but probably the majority lived on plantations where they worked in gangs ranging from ten to a hundred under the direction of the owner or his overseer. Since the largest effective unit of tobacco production was a thousand acres (including uncleared and exhausted land), few colonial plantations outside the West Indies had as many as a hundred slaves. A smaller area, with no more than thirty slaves, was the most efficient unit for rice. If a planter had more land and men, he divided them into two or more plantations, living on one and hiring overseers to manage the others until he was ready to turn them over to his children.

The large-scale plantation was a community in itself. At the center lay a great house, often facing the river and surrounded by trees and shrubs. Arranged symmetrically around it were attendant buildings: laundry, smoke-house, kitchen, and perhaps a schoolhouse, where a hired tutor taught the planter's children. At some distance lay the barns and the cabins of the slaves, with little plots of ground where they could work evenings and Sundays growing vegetables and raising chickens to piece out their meager rations. They might even be permitted to sell any surplus for pocket money.

In addition to field hands, the community included a small army of household slaves and skilled artisans—carpenter, blacksmith, tailor, cobbler—who might be either indentured white servants (bound by a contract to serve a specific number of years) or slaves educated for the purpose. With its own permanent labor force and with ready access to ocean-going ships, the riverside plantation needed little from its neighbors. What could not be made on the premises was imported directly from London.

And yet the planter and his family were not isolated. The river was a highway to the world by which he kept in touch not only with London but with other planters. His children often went to stay for several weeks at other plantations, and his own home was seldom without guests. Sometimes he gave a ball for friends who came from miles around and stayed for three or four days. Or he might attend the House of Burgesses (the representative assembly) in Williamsburg and take the family with him. Over a glass at the Raleigh Tavern he could arrange to marry his daughter to another planter's son, and the two fathers would haggle over who should give what to set the young couple up on their own plantation. So common was matchmaking of this sort that by the middle of the eighteenth century most Virginia planters could call each other cousin. In South Carolina, young people met and matches were made when planters left their steaming rice fields during the summer months for the sea breezes of Charles Town.

Not all Southerners lived on plantations. Probably the majority of the free population, even in the plantation colonies, consisted of small farmers with holdings well back from the river banks. Here they worked like any

A community in itself: A tidewater plantation.

slave, but they worked for themselves. It was the great planter, however, who dominated the society, buying and marketing the small farmers' surplus crops, sometimes renting them their lands, often commanding their votes. It was the planter who sat in the House of Burgesses, in the county court, in the vestry of the church. Here and in the management of his plantation he learned to deal with men both free and unfree. And the ships that arrived at his wharf brought him regular news of the way men were dealing with one another across the water. Though he lived from the forced labor of slaves, he was no barbarian. When the time came, he showed that slavery had not blinded him to the meaning of freedom.

The New England Town   Rivers, tobacco, and slavery made the plantation. Puritanism and past experience made the New England town, an institution which also appeared in the parts of New York and New Jersey that were settled by New Englanders.

The past experience of New Englanders (as of other English colonists) included at least three English types of community: the borough, the village, and the parish.

The English borough was a town that normally possessed a charter of incorporation from the king entitling it to send two members to Parliament and to exercise a degree of local governmental independence. The "freemen" (or "burgesses") of the borough, usually a very small proportion of the population, elected the members of Parliament as well as a mayor or a set of aldermen to handle local affairs. In many boroughs the aldermen had become so powerful that they bypassed the freemen and filled vacancies in their ranks by themselves.

The English village was not a formal political institution like the borough. It was simply a cluster of houses inhabited by men and women who cultivated the adjoining lands according to customs prescribed by earlier generations. All the village's arable land was laid out in three or four large fields, and every householder had strips of land scattered through all of them. Each man worked his own strips but they were not fenced off from those of his neighbors; and everyone worked together at plowing (and subsequently at sowing, tilling, and harvesting) one field before moving on to the next. Thus every man would get part of his crop early, part of it late. By the time the settlers left England, this "open-field" system was giving way to individual farms, but it still existed in many places.

Every Englishman, whether he lived in a borough or a village, belonged to a parish. Originally the parish was simply the area served by a single church, but it had gradually taken on, outside the boroughs, many of the functions of local government. In most villages a "vestry" made up of some ten or twenty of the more substantial inhabitants exercised the powers of the parish or chose two or three "churchwardens" to do so. The churchwardens or vestrymen not only maintained the church and managed its property, but provided for the poor, required fathers to support their children, levied taxes, and sometimes acted as a kind of grand jury.

In creating their towns New Englanders drew something from the parish, the village, and the borough; but they also rejected parts of this institutional heritage because of their Puritan ideas about how men ought to live with one another. Puritans generally "gathered" a church before, or about the same time as, they established a town. The two usually covered the same territory, as was true of the English village and parish. But in New England the church and its officers were entirely distinct from the town and its officers. The church owned no property, not even a church building. People worshiped in a meetinghouse which was owned by the town and used for any community meeting. It was not regarded as sacred. Nor did the church exercise any temporal, political powers. There was no vestry and no churchwarden. The church might elect "ruling elders" to reprimand erring members or to report them to the church, but neither elders nor church enjoyed coercive authority. The church was a spiritual association; its severest penalty was excommunication, which could be pronounced only by

unanimous vote of the members. Excommunication deprived a man of his church membership but carried no civil or political disabilities. Once a church assumed temporal powers, Puritans believed, it was on the wicked road to Rome. In New England, therefore, they assigned to the town both the duties of local government performed in the English borough by the mayor and aldermen, and the secular duties exercised in the English parish by church officers.

New England towns and their governments were created under the authority of the colony's General Court (the legislature). A group of men, perhaps already gathered in a church, approached the court and requested a tract of land, usually adjoining some established town. If the court approved, it had the area surveyed and then named the applicants as "proprietors" of the town of Concord, Sudbury, or whatever name they chose. The proprietors then moved to their new home and laid out the land in a pattern similar to that of an English village. Every man got a house lot in the center of town, where space was also set aside for a meetinghouse and perhaps for a school. Each man also received one or more parcels of arable land, a parcel of meadow for pasturage, and a parcel of woodland for fuel, all located in different parts of the town. In a few cases there seems to have been an attempt (quickly abandoned) to practice the open-field system. When the land of a town was originally apportioned, most of it was left undivided to meet the anticipated growth in population. The undistributed land, or commons, belonged to the proprietors jointly until they converted it into their private property through subsequent land divisions. A new settler moving into town might buy land from a proprietor's private holdings or might be granted or sold parts of the commons, but he did not become a proprietor: he did not share in the ownership of the remaining commons.

The power of the proprietors was limited to control over the commons; government of the town rested in a town meeting, in which they had no greater voice than other inhabitants. The town meeting acted on matters that intimately concerned the inhabitants: constructing and repairing roads, building a meetinghouse, hiring a schoolmaster, or de-

New England town meeting.

lation inside the existing towns, the proprietors often became a minority and an extraordinary demand arose for the distribution of the common lands to unpropertied residents. In the resulting conflict between the economic power of the proprietors and the political power of the town meeting, political power usually won.

With the return of peace the frontier began to move again. By this time colonial governments had come to realize that their unoccupied lands were a potential source of public revenue. In creating new towns they did not give the proprietorship to prospective settlers but sold it to groups of investors, assembled for the sole purpose of buying it. These men sold land to settlers, reserving large sections to be divided among themselves as population and land values rose. In western Massachusetts a set of investors known locally as the Connecticut River Gods owned proprietary shares in many different towns and accumulated large private holdings at every division of the commons.

The new towns of the interior were somewhat different in character from the old towns of the coastal areas. For one thing, the houses were set farther apart. Each resident, instead of living close to the meetinghouse with his holdings scattered about the countryside, was likely to have all his land in one piece. He rubbed elbows less often with his neighbors and did not know them as intimately as his father had known his.

Still the New England town remained in the eighteenth century, as in the seventeenth, a closely knit community. On Sunday everyone gathered in the meetinghouse, where the position of a man's pew indicated his place in the community and whether he must be addressed as "Mister," as "Goodman," or by no title at all. In general, the closer he sat to the pulpit, the higher his social rank. But proximity to God's minister was no sign of proximity to God. Though the law required that everyone attend church, only a minority of the town's inhabitants were "members," and membership in itself carried no social prestige. A slave might belong and a gentleman not. During the eighteenth century church membership became increasingly feminine, with women outnumbering men by more than two to one.

ciding whether hogs should be fenced into pens or fenced out of gardens. The meeting also elected representatives to the colonial assembly and town officials of all kinds, including "selectmen," who administered the rules made by the meeting. There was some attempt in early Massachusetts to confine voting in town meetings to the freemen, who it will be remembered had to be church members. After 1648, however, and probably before then in many towns, all free adult males were allowed to vote on all questions except the choice of representatives. Until 1685, these continued to be elected only by the freemen.

In the early years of a town's existence there was no conflict of interest between town meeting and proprietors, because all or most of the free adult males were also proprietors. But from 1676 to 1713, when a series of French and Indian wars dammed up the expanding popu-

Members or not, New Englanders went to church, were taxed for the minister's salary, and had a voice in selecting him.

The men of the town met not only at church and town meeting but on training day when the militia exercised. In frontier settlements, under constant threat of Indian attack, this was a serious business; in the older coastal towns it was likely to require more rum than gunpowder. Rum and hard cider lubricated most community activities in New England, whether marrying or burying, raising a meetinghouse or bringing home a harvest. The tavern, originally intended for the convenience of travelers, became another meeting place where men of the neighborhood bent an elbow of an evening and where, according to John Adams, "vicious habits, bastards, and legislators" were frequently begotten.

In tavern, school, and church, at town meeting and militia drill, the New Englander measured out the distance between himself and his fellow man. The distance was small, but it was enough to give him an independence of spirit for which he became famous. For those who needed more room, America offered another way of life.

The Farm   In the colonies from New England southward, the average American lived a lonely life. He made his living from the land, as his fathers had done in Europe. But in the great emptiness of the New World, sheer space separated him from his neighbors in a way that few Europeans knew. His farm might run to several hundred acres and might lie miles from any other occupied land, because settlers, whenever they could, chose lands that supported a stand of hardwood. These, they thought, were most fertile.

Hardwood meant hard work in clearing the land, but many farmers simplified the task by girdling trees at the base to kill them, planting crops between the lifeless trunks, and then disposing of the trunks as they rotted away. This technique was probably brought to America by Finnish immigrants who settled along the Delaware River. They had first tried life in the forests of Sweden and had there learned to girdle trees and to build log cabins. The first English settlers, better sawyers than axmen, had built their houses with hand-sawed boards. But succeeding generations copied the

Finns. By the eighteenth century American farmers built log cabins and put up frame houses only after they had achieved a measure of prosperity.

Though most farmers owned the land they cleared and cultivated, farm tenancy became common in some areas where the soil was fertile enough to support both a landlord and a tenant. In New York's Hudson Valley, for example, landlords exacted high rents and feudal services. In Virginia's tidewater, tenants took farms and even plantations as sharecroppers, paying the owner a proportion of the crop as rent. Even in the uncleared back country it was not always easy for a farmer to obtain title to land in the most fertile areas, because speculators often acquired such lands in advance of actual settlers. By the eighteenth century the headright system (practiced earlier in most of the colonies south of New England) had become a mere form. A speculator could obtain title to as much land as he could afford simply by paying a fee (usually five shillings per hundred acres) to the colony's secretary or land office. Later he could rent the land to a bona-fide settler or else sell it for a good deal more than he had paid. Not all speculators were rich men. Many farmers, tradesmen, and even parsons invested their small earnings in real estate, for everyone knew that land values would rise as population increased, and everyone could see that population was increasing rapidly.

Most of the increase came from the natural growth of the old stock. In spite of the heavy toll taken by smallpox and diphtheria, scarlet fever and yellow fever, families were large. Then in the eighteenth century a new flood of settlers, mainly from northern Ireland and Germany, entered the colonies. After landing in the New World, usually at Philadelphia, they traveled west to the Appalachian valleys and spilled down into the hinterland of Maryland, Virginia, and the Carolinas. The Scotch-Irish, America's most formidable frontiersmen, led the advance. Germans, in the rear, tidied up the lush valleys into checkerboards of wheat and corn and rye.

At crossroads in the farming areas, storekeepers traded hardware, clothing, and gossip for crops. But there was no real community, no local nucleus of political, social, and religious life. Even the churches responded slowly to the needs of the farmer. In colonies where the Anglican Church was supported by taxation (New York, Maryland, Virginia, and the Carolinas) it organized parishes to keep pace with the westward advance, but they were too large in area to serve the widely scattered farmers, many of whom were not Anglicans anyhow. The parish had been designed for more densely populated areas, where enough people to support a minister lived within Sunday traveling distance of his sermons. By the eighteenth century some denominations, especially Presbyterians and Methodists, were sending itinerant missionaries through the back country. Now the people could hold at least an occasional service, sometimes under a tree, sometimes in a courthouse, sometimes in a church built for the purpose. The circuit-riders, as the missionaries were called, often encountered families whose children had never seen a minister.

In the absence of village or town, colonial farmers relied heavily on a looser and larger community, the county. Every colony was divided into counties, and everywhere the county court was an important arm of government. Even in New England the county judges (appointed as elsewhere by the colonial governments) decided administrative as well as judicial questions, questions as important as where to build new roads. Outside New England, the county court took over the duties of the town and sometimes of the parish. Besides trying cases, both civil and criminal, it might record wills and deeds, take charge of orphans and the poor, register births, marriages, and deaths, collect taxes, license taverns, authorize the establishment of ferries, and pay bounties for wolves' heads. On days when the court was in session, usually once a month, farmers from near and far would gather to sue one another for small sums, to exercise in the militia, to elect a representative to the colony's assembly, or simply to watch the proceedings, learn the news, and share talk and a bottle with distant neighbors.

The thinness of community life put a heavy burden on the family. Everywhere during the colonial period the family fulfilled many more functions than it does today, but among farmers it was everything—factory, church, school,

hospital, and tavern. Unless a man held especially rich land and had ready access to a market, his crops went to feed his family, with little left over for sale. He and his wife had to make everything they could not buy, which might be most of their clothing and furniture. Without a school, they had to teach their children to read; without a church, to worship at home; without a tavern, to entertain passing strangers; without a doctor, to care for their sick. Children were plentiful and made more hands to do the endless work. Some might take over the farm as their parents grew old, but most of them would eventually leave to carve new farms out of the empty land.

The farmer, isolated from his neighbors and living a self-sufficient life within his own family, was the typical eighteenth-century American—even the townsman of western New England resembled him. But as farmers spread out through the interior, a significant minority of Americans piled up in five cities and several large towns along the coast.

The City   The colonial farmer riding into a city for the first time left a road that was only a ribbon of stumps and mud and came upon streets of gravel or cobblestones, where a bewildering activity surrounded him. Swine roamed everywhere, feeding in the refuse; drovers herded sheep and cattle to the butchers. Elegant carriages rolled impatiently behind lumbering wagons as great packs of barking dogs worried the horses. Sailors reeled out of taverns, and over the roofs of the houses could be seen the swaying masts and spars of their ships. The farmer had been told that the city was a nursery of vice and prodigality. He now saw that it was so. Every shop had wares to catch his eye: exquisite fabrics, delicate chinaware, silver buckles, looking glasses, and other imported luxuries that never reached the crossroads store. Putting up at the tavern, he found himself drinking too much rum. And there were willing girls, he heard, who had lost their virtue and would be glad to help him lose his. Usually he returned to the farm to warn his children as he had been warned. He seldom understood that the vice of the city, if not its prodigality, was mainly for transients like himself. Permanent residents had work to do.

The key men in the community were the

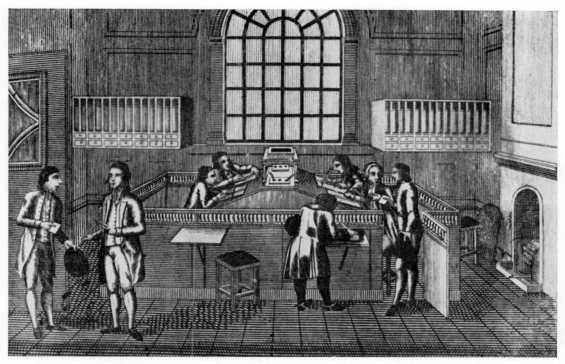
Without the merchants, there would have been no cities.

merchants, for colonial cities were built on trade. Merchants bought corn, wheat, cattle, and horses from thousands of farms and fish from hundreds of fishermen and shipped them to the West Indies. The planters there could not waste their valuable sugar lands growing corn, but they needed food for their slaves and horses to turn their sugar mills. Colonial merchants supplied them and brought back molasses, a by-product of sugar-making. Distilleries turned it into rum, much of which the merchants shipped off to exchange for slaves on the coast of Africa or to help fishermen fight back the icy winds of the North Atlantic. The merchants also bought beaver and deerskins from Indian traders, and huge pine trunks from lumbermen to send to England for masts. From England they brought back woolens and hardware, which the mother country made better and cheaper than the colonists could. Without the merchants there would have been no cities.

Many of the other city-dwellers depended on the merchants for a living. Besides the rum-distillers, there were shipwrights who turned out ships at a lower price than English ones. Workers in ropewalks and sail lofts rigged them. Instrument-makers fitted them with quadrants, telescopes, and clocks. Retail traders helped to distribute the goods imported from abroad. Millers ground wheat and corn into flour, and coopers built barrels to ship it in.

But cities accumulate people by a magic of their own, and many colonists found jobs that had no direct connection with the overseas trade. Schoolmasters were better trained and more plentiful than in the country. Dancing masters taught ladies and gentlemen the newest steps; stay-makers laced them into the newest shapes. Barbers cut their hair; wig-makers put it on again. And dozens of skilled craftsmen offered American-made copies of the latest English fashions in wearing apparel, furniture, and houses.

For all the glamour and excitement of their environment, city-dwellers had problems that other Americans had not yet faced: city opulence bred thieves and vice of all kinds; city filth necessitated sewers and sanitation laws; city traffic required paved streets and lights; and the city's closely packed wooden houses and shops invited fires that might, and repeatedly did, destroy vast areas. To cope with these problems citizens relied both on voluntary associations, such as fire companies, and on their city governments. Boston and Newport were governed by selectmen and town meetings, New York (after 1731) by a popularly elected city corporation. In all three, city officials, under direct control of the citizens, were responsive to their needs. In Philadelphia and Charles Town, on the other hand, the citizens had no voice in their local government. Philadelphia was badly governed by a self-perpetuating closed corporation, and Charles Town just as badly by the South Carolina assembly.

By contemporary standards these were all substantial cities. Though small compared with London, by the middle of the eighteenth century they were larger than most English cities. Boston, which reached seventeen thousand in 1740, was at that time the largest, but it had already begun a decline that lasted for the rest of the colonial period. In the seventeenth century it had served as the shipping center for most of the mainland colonies, and it continued to serve as New England's major port. But other New England towns were cutting into its business, most notably Newport, which grew to urban dimensions in the eighteenth century.

New York City was the natural outlet and supply point for farmers in the Hudson Valley and adjoining regions of Connecticut and New Jersey; Philadelphia served not only Pennsylvania and the Delaware Valley and Bay but also the Southern back country. From the Carolinas, Virginia, and Maryland, farmers drove their wagons and cattle north along the great Appalachian valleys to the Philadelphia market. Although Baltimore began to drain off some of this trade after about 1750, Philadelphia continued to grow so rapidly that by 1776, with forty thousand people, it was probably second only to London in the English-speaking world. South of Baltimore the tobacco planters dealt directly with London and needed no cities; but in South Carolina

the rice and indigo planters shipped their produce by way of Charles Town, as did the Indian traders who trekked around the southern limit of the Appalachians and brought deerskins from the lower Mississippi Valley.

Overseas trade gave city-dwellers and plantation-owners communication with the larger world that was denied to most other Americans, and for that matter to most Englishmen and Europeans. Boston and Philadelphia, with hundreds of ships coming and going, were in closer contact with London than many English cities were. The ships carried ideas as well as goods, and colonial cities were as well equipped to distribute one as the other. Every city had at least one newspaper by the middle of the eighteenth century, with every issue devoted largely to news from England and Europe. Through the columns of the newspapers and through the books imported from abroad and sometimes reprinted locally, the city man found his way out of the seventeenth century into the eighteenth. Gradually he learned to make rationality a test of all things, to look upon revealed religion with a degree of skepticism, to cherish tolerance and shun persecution, and to expect from the progress of science (or philosophy, as he called it) what his ancestors had expected only from God. From the city such ideas filtered into the countryside. Although the cities held less than 5 per cent of the colonial population, it was the best informed and most influential 5 per cent.

The Emerging American Mind

Before the middle of the eighteenth century Americans had little occasion to think of themselves as a distinct people. They had no opportunity at all to act as one. There was no American government, no single political organization in which all the colonies joined to manage their common concerns. There was not even a wish for such an organization except among a few eccentric individuals. America, to the people who lived in it, was still a geographical region, not a frame of mind.

Asked for his nationality, the average American in 1750 would have said English or British. In spite of substantial numbers of Dutch,

Germans, and Scotch-Irish, Englishmen and English institutions prevailed in every colony, and most colonists spoke of England as home even though they had never been there. Yet none of their institutions was quite like its English counterpart; the heritage of English ideas that went with the institutions was so rich and varied that Americans were able to select and develop those that best suited their situation and forget others that meanwhile were growing prominent in the mother country. Some of the differences were local: the New England town, for example, and the Puritanism that went with it, set New Englanders off not only from Englishmen but from Virginians. But some ideas, institutions, and attitudes became common in all the colonies and remained uncommon in England. Although American Englishmen were not yet aware that they shared these "Americanisms" with one another or that Englishmen at home did not share them, many of the characteristic ideas and attitudes that later distinguished American nationalism were already present by mid-century.

Responsible Representative Government Englishmen brought with them to the New World the political ideas that still give English and American government a close resemblance. But Americans very early developed conceptions of representative government that differed from those prevailing in England during the colonial period. Representative government in England originated in the Middle Ages when the king called for men to advise him. They were chosen by their neighbors and informed the king of his subjects' wishes. Eventually their advice became so compelling that the king could not reject it, and the representatives of the people, organized as the House of Commons, became the most powerful branch of the English government.

At first the House of Commons consisted of representatives from each county, or "shire," and from selected boroughs. Over the centuries many of these boroughs became ghost towns with only a handful of inhabitants, and great towns sprang up where none had existed before. Yet the old boroughs continued to send members to Parliament and the new towns sent none. Moreover, only a fraction of the English population participated in the election of county representatives. In order to vote, a man had to own property that would, if rented, yield him at least forty shillings yearly. Few could meet the test. A number of Englishmen thought the situation absurd and said so. But nothing was done to improve it; in fact, a theory was devised to justify it. A member of the House of Commons, it was said, did not represent the people who chose him. Instead he represented the whole country and was not responsible to any particular constituency. Not all Englishmen could vote for representatives, but all were "virtually" represented by every member of the House of Commons.

Colonial assemblies were far more representative than the House of Commons. Although every colony had property qualifications for voting, probably the great majority of adult white males owned enough land to meet them. In apportioning representation, New England colonies gave every town the right to send delegates to the assembly. Outside New England, the unit of representation was usually the county. The political organization of new counties and the extension of representation seldom kept pace with the rapid advance of settlement westward, but nowhere was representation so uneven or irrational as in England.

The American colonist knew nothing of "virtual" representation; to him representation was a means of acquainting the government with his needs and demands and with the amount and method of taxation he could most easily bear. A colonial assemblyman was supposed to be the agent of the people who chose him. In the large counties, of course, it was seldom possible, except on election day, for voters to gather in one place and express their opinions. But elections came every two or three years (annually in New England and Pennsylvania), and a representative was unlikely to stray far from his constituents' wishes in so short a time. In New England, where town meetings could be called any time, people often gathered to tell their delegate how to vote on a particular issue. He was supposed to look after their interests first, those of the colony second.

In America, therefore, representative government meant something different from what it did in England. Government existed to do a job, and it must be kept responsible to its employers. While "virtual" representatives in Parliament created offices whose only purpose was to enrich the men who filled them, colonial assemblymen, watched closely by their constituents, had comparatively little opportunity to dip into the public purse.

Clergy and Laity   Americans looked on their clergymen as they did on their elected representatives. They wanted the clergy to serve, not rule, them. The attitude had its roots in the English Reformation, and most Englishmen were sufficiently Protestant to share it in some degree; English Dissenters shared it wholeheartedly. But the Anglican Church held great powers in England: it was the only church supported by state taxation; during much of the colonial period only its members could hold public office; and its bishops enjoyed an authority that reached far beyond the realm of the spirit. As ex officio members of the House of Lords they voted on every act of Parliament, and as presiding judges in courts with jurisdiction over probate of wills and breaches of morality they could impose sentence of excommunication on offenders. Since excommunication cut a man off from political rights and from intercourse with his neighbors, it could mean economic ruin as well as social ostracism. An offender could get the sentence lifted only by paying a heavy fee.

In the colonies churchmen had no such powers. Except in Rhode Island, Delaware, Pennsylvania, and New Jersey the assemblies did levy taxes in support of churches, favoring the Congregational churches in New England, the Anglican elsewhere. But this was the only connection between church and state that most Americans would tolerate. The Massachusetts rule that only church members could vote had ended with the revocation of the colony's charter in 1685.

In New England the old Puritan hostility to clerical authority persisted into the eighteenth century. Ministers were influential and highly respected; a few were even elected as representatives to colonial assemblies. But no minister enjoyed temporal authority by virtue of being a minister.

The Anglicans in America also kept their clergymen on short leash. Because England never sent a bishop to the colonies (and without a bishop there could be no ecclesiastical court), the Anglican Church lost most of its temporal powers when it was transplanted to America. In the Northern colonies, Anglicans, who were a small minority of the population, repeatedly asked for a bishop—much to the annoyance of Congregationalists and Presbyterians. In the Southern colonies, where the Anglican Church was the established church, its members were cool to the proposal. The Southerners, acting through their vestries, ran their churches and hired and fired their ministers almost as independently as any New England Puritan congregation. The minister, unless he had been ordained, could be dismissed at any time. But only a bishop could ordain, and with the nearest bishop three thousand miles away in England, few ministers obtained ordination.

Probably one reason for the failure of the Anglican Church to send a bishop was the fear of resistance from non-Anglicans, who multiplied rapidly during the eighteenth century. Besides Congregationalists and Presbyterians, there were Baptists, Quakers, Dutch Reformed, Lutherans, Mennonites, and a host of minor sects. This diversity of religious groups, each growing as population grew, made it increasingly difficult for any one of them to dominate the rest, and made the extension of religious authority in America ever more unlikely. Even in New England, where the Congregationalists remained a majority, they ceased after the seventeenth century to persecute Quakers and allowed persons of other denominations to support their own ministers through public taxation.

Religious Developments   In the 1740's the number of religious groups was expanded by a rash of schisms which followed a religious revival. The Great Awakening was touched off in 1741 by a traveling English preacher who combined Calvinism and showmanship. George Whitefield, only twenty-seven at the time, was not a gifted theologian. But he had perfected a technique of preaching that brought remarkable results: he frightened his audience by depicting in vivid detail the pain awaiting sinners in Hell. He dramatized the scene for them, playing all the parts himself. Now he was an angry God booming out fearful judgments, now a damned soul weeping in

George Whitefield: The Great Awakener.

brought religious experiences to thousands of people in every rank of society. One of its staunchest defenders was Jonathan Edwards, minister of Northampton, Massachusetts, who had himself inspired a local revival in 1735. Edwards was the most talented theologian America ever produced. He preached a stricter Calvinism than New England had ever heard, and he recast Calvinist doctrines to give a primary place to the emotions. He particularly emphasized the emotional impact of an omnipotent God on impotent man. Both conviction and conversion, Edwards insisted, were such overwhelming emotional experiences that the human frame could scarcely contain them. If occasionally a man fell to the ground or cried out in the grip of such powerful experiences, this was no reason to doubt that the spirit of God was the moving cause. Edwards' theology commanded respect in Europe as well as America and furnished the Awakening with an intellectual foundation that Whitefield could not have provided.

But not everyone agreed with Edwards. Many ministers thought that the new method of preaching provoked more hysteria than holiness. They were offended by the itinerant preachers who entered their churches unbidden and wrung from a hitherto sane congregation a chorus of shrieks and groans and hallelujahs. After listening to an itinerant, people sometimes decided their own minister was worthless, and the most enthusiastic followers of the Awakening deserted their old churches to form new ones with more rigorous doctrines and standards of admission.

Once the shrieking had subsided, it became apparent that the Awakening had seriously undermined the position of the clergy. In every denomination, but especially in the Calvinist ones, ministers had been forced to take sides in favor of the revival (New Light) or against it (Old Light). The Old Lights were shocked by the sight of ignorant men screaming damnation and of masses of people wallowing in terror or ecstasy. Nor were they comforted by the less exuberant expressions of piety that followed. "Nay han't it been common," asked the Boston minister Charles Chauncy, "in some Parts of the Land, and among some Sorts of People, to express their religious Joy, by singing through the Streets,

anguish. He strained to bring his audience to the point of hysterical despair. He wanted them to writhe in agony, for he had found that thorough "conviction"—of their own sinfulness, helplessness, and utter dependence on Christ for salvation—was usually followed by "conversion," the feeling that they actually had been saved. As Whitefield journeyed from the Carolinas to New England, preaching indoors and out, Sundays and weekdays, he wrought conversions by the hundreds, among old and young, rich and poor, educated and ignorant.

His technique, requiring only a flair for the dramatic, was not hard to imitate. In his wake other self-appointed messengers of Christ traveled about the country, outdoing him in the sound and fury of their preaching. Gilbert Tennent, a Pennsylvania Presbyterian, made a specialty of laughing loud and long at sinners in the throes of conviction. James Davenport, an itinerant Congregationalist, was at his best at night, when smoking torches revealed him half naked, jumping up and down to stamp on the devil.

In spite of these excesses, the Awakening

Jonathan Edwards: The most talented theologian America ever produced.

and in Ferry Boats?" The Old Lights, having set themselves against such emotional "enthusiasm," prided themselves on a cool rationality. In this mood they re-examined Calvinist dogma and found it wanting. It was absurd, Chauncy decided, that men should suffer eternally by divine predestination: a rational God would allow some merit in human effort. The Old Lights took the road that led ultimately to Unitarianism, Universalism, and deism, to a world in which there was little need either for Christ or for clergymen. Not many Americans went the whole length of that road in the eighteenth century, but many of the best educated traveled it for some distance.

The New Lights undermined the position of the clergy in a more indirect manner. They began by teaching congregations to be bold in judging ministers. Itinerant preachers often pronounced local ministers unregenerate and made much of the idea that a minister could not be God's instrument in bringing salvation to others unless he himself was saved. With this principle in mind, the New Lights in a church did not hesitate to interrogate the minister and then declare him saved or damned. The minister's learning, which had once won him respect, suddenly became a handicap, for many itinerants, uneducated and uneducable, dismissed religious erudition as an impediment to saving grace.

Ironically, in the decades that followed the Great Awakening, the New Light clergy of New England outran their congregations in learned pursuit of Edwards' Calvinist theology. Edwards was not easily understood at best, but his disciples drew out his doctrines in subtle elaborations that scarcely anyone understood but themselves. The New Divinity it was called, and among many bright young men of the day it became the prevailing intellectual fashion. Entering the ministry, they uttered its complexities in sermons addressed more to one another than to their audience. The passionate preaching of the Awakening was forgotten, and the New Divinity grew into a recondite game for clergymen.

Congregations reacted with the boldness they had been taught by deserting the preachers who seemed to have deserted them. By the third quarter of the eighteenth century New England had been infiltrated by Presbyterians, Baptists, Anglicans, Universalists, and other denominations, and a man could shop around for a preacher and a religion that suited him. Samuel Hopkins, leading exponent of the New Divinity, preached away most of his congregation at Great Barrington, Massachusetts. He found another at Newport, Rhode Island, only to see it too dwindle under the impact of his incomprehensible sermons. An American minister was expected to serve his people. When they thought he was failing to do so, they dismissed him or left him.

Education   If the American colonist stood in no awe of his ministers and government officials, it was because the workings of state and church held no mysteries for him. He understood them better than the average European, not only because he had a large share in operating them but because he was better educated. Europeans were fond of picturing Americans as children of nature who learned wisdom from the trees and flowers but not from books. Actually, in spite of their

Massachusetts: The Schools

It being one chief project of that old deluder, Satan, to keep men from the knowledge of the Scriptures, as in former times by keeping them in an unknown tongue, so in these latter times by persuading from the use of tongues, that so at least the true sense and meaning of the original might be clouded by false glosses of saint-seeming deceivers, that learning may not be buried in the grave of our fathers in the church and commonwealth, the Lord assisting our endeavors.

It is therefore ordered, that every township in this jurisdiction, after the Lord hath increased them to the number of fifty householders, shall then forthwith appoint one within their town to teach all such children as shall resort to him to write and read, whose wages shall be paid either by the parents or masters of such children, or by the inhabitants in general, by way of supply, as the major part of those that order the prudentials of the town shall appoint; provided those that send their children be not oppressed by paying much more than they can have them taught for in other towns; and it is further ordered that where any town shall increase to the number of 100 families or householders, they shall set up a grammar school, the master thereof being able to instruct youth so far as they may be fitted for the university, provided that if any town neglect the performance hereof above one year, that every such town shall pay £5 to the next school till they shall perform this order.

From Massachusetts School Law, 1647.

---

wilderness life, or perhaps because of it, colonial Americans were a bookish lot.

Most of them were Protestants, and Protestants believed that religious truth was incomprehensible to the man who did not read the Scriptures for himself. They wanted to read; they wanted their children to read. And their desire was sharpened by the sight of the real children of nature, the Indians, naked, savage, and ignorant. In Massachusetts the law directed every town of fifty families to maintain a schoolmaster, and other New England colonies had similar requirements. The laws were not always enforced, but the rate of literacy (compared to that of England or Europe) was high throughout the colonies and especially high in New England.

By the middle of the eighteenth century nearly every colony had at least one printing

Massachusetts: The College

After God had carried us safe to *New-England,* and wee had builded our houses, provided necessaries for our livelihood, rear'd convenient places for Gods worship, and setled the Civill Government: One of the next things we longed for, and looked after was to advance Learning and perpetuate it to Posterity; dreading to leave an illiterate Ministery to the Churches, when our present Ministers shall lie in the Dust. And as wee were thinking and consulting how to effect this great Work; it pleased God to stir up the heart of one Mr. *Harvard* (a godly Gentleman, and a lover of Learning, there living amongst us) to give the one halfe of his Estate (it being in all about 1700.£.) towards the erecting of a Colledge, and all his Library: after him another gave 300.£. others after them cast in more, and the publique hand of the State added the rest: the Colledge was, by common consent, appointed to be at *Cambridge,* (a place very pleasant and accommode) and is called (according to the name of the first founder) *Harvard Colledge.*

From *New Englands First Fruits,* 1643.

---

press, and the printer usually produced a weekly newspaper, devoted mainly to news from abroad and from other colonies—everybody knew the local news—and to literary and political essays and verse, much of which was culled from English newspapers. The printers also turned out broadsides, almanacs, pamphlets, and books. Though the clergy were the most prolific colonial authors and sermons the most popular reading matter, local political issues were often discussed in print. There were even some efforts at verse. The best of these, the meditative poems of Edward Taylor, minister of Westfield, Massachusetts, were not published until the present century, but colonial readers bought another minister's versified account of the Last Judgment (*The Day of Doom* by Michael Wigglesworth) in such numbers that it went through five editions between 1662 and 1701.

The colonists made early provision for higher education. In 1636, only six years after the Puritans came to Massachusetts, they founded the college that later took the name of its first benefactor, John Harvard. Although the founders' purpose was to furnish the colony with a learned ministry, Harvard was no mere theological seminary. From the beginning its students followed the traditional curriculum of the liberal arts taught in European universities: they studied grammar (Latin, Greek, and Hebrew), rhetoric, logic, mathematics, astronomy, physics, metaphysics, and moral philosophy. Only once a week, on Saturdays, did they turn to theology. Those who intended to become ministers received their professional training after they graduated, not before. But many Harvard graduates, the majority after the seventeenth century, went into professions other than the ministry.

The same was true of most other colonial colleges: William and Mary, chartered in 1693, remained for some years little more than a grammar school, but Yale (1701) offered a program similar to Harvard's, and so did Princeton (1746), Rutgers (1766), Pennsylvania (1755), Columbia (1754), and Brown (1764). It was not simply the children of the well-to-do who attended these colleges. Tuition rates were low, and every class contained boys fresh from the farm. Education even at the college level was widely diffused by comparison with England.

The fact that New Englanders fell victims to hysteria over witchcraft has often been cited as evidence of the shallowness of their education. How could educated people be so superstitious? The answer is that educated people everywhere believed in witchcraft. In 1692 twenty persons were hanged as witches in Massachusetts, and hundreds more had been accused when the ministers' objections to the unfairness of the trials induced the government to stop them. No subsequent execution for witchcraft is recorded in America, but in Europe thousands were executed in the seventeenth century and the executions continued into the eighteenth.

The Enlightenment The ideas that conquered man's belief in witchcraft were originated, not by Americans, but by a succession of Europeans who had the imagination and daring to take the measure of God's world for themselves. During the sixteenth and seventeenth centuries Copernicus, Galileo, and Kepler had studied the motions of the planets and accumulated evidence to show that they rotated around the sun. Sir Isaac Newton, building on their work, discovered the laws of motion, the "natural laws" by which God governed the movement of the planets. He also studied light and learned to break it into its different colors and to bend it with mirrors and lenses. Newton's success convinced his contemporaries that human reason was capable of exploring the universe and of ascertaining by observation and experiment the principles by which God governed it. Men who had been taught that reason was a feeble instrument, all but destroyed by Adam's original sin, now turned inquiring eyes on the world around them. They wanted to measure everything, to see how the world worked.

In looking so closely at God's world, men inevitably formed a new image of God himself. Where He had formerly been an arbitrary monarch, who glorified himself in the damnation of sinners and the salvation of saints, He now became a divine craftsman, whose glory lay in his craftsmanship, a celestial watchmaker whose intricate and orderly handiwork lay everywhere visible to the eyes that reason directed toward it. The new God appeared more reasonable than the old, but also more

---

The Enlightenment: Freedom of Religion

I retain a sincere Affection for my Mother College & wish it in my Power to contribute to her Prosperity and Reputation. The People this Way have conceived a very unhappy Idea of it, as a Nursery of bigotted Presbyterianism, & that all free Inquiry is as much extirpated & kept out of it, as from any of the popish Seminaries.... Different men indeed object from different Motives, some from the Love of Orthodoxy & some from the Hatred of it, & some from the generous sentiments of that generous & equal Liberty for which Protestants & Dissenters have made so noble a stand. It is true with this Liberty Error may be introduced; but turn the Tables the propagation of Truth may be extinguished. Deism has got such Head in this Age of Licentious Liberty, that it would be in vain to try to stop it by hiding the Deistical Writings: and the only Way left to conquer & demolish it, is to come forth into the open Field and dispute the Matter on even Footing.... *Truth* & this alone being *our* Aim in fact, open, frank & generous we shall avoid the very Appearance of Evil.

From Ezra Stiles, Letter to Thomas Clap, president of Yale, 1759.

---

remote and indifferent, a watchmaker who wound up his universe and then left it to run itself. He seemed, in fact, so reasonable that some men decided He was reason itself, or at least that reason was an adequate substitute for Him.

Though few went this far, the eighteenth century earned the title of the Age of Reason. And the English philosopher John Locke furnished the century with a theory about reason that gradually won acceptance and further encouraged the pursuit of experiment and observation. In *An Essay concerning Human Understanding* (1690) Locke concluded that the human mind at birth was not the repository of any innate ideas placed there by the Creator. Rather, it was a complete blank, and only gradually accumulated knowledge from the experiences of the five senses attached to it. He who would grow in knowledge, therefore, must devote himself not simply to books, perhaps not even to the Bible, nor to abstract contemplation, but to seeing, hearing, feeling, tasting—in a word, to observation and experiment.

Man himself was a fair subject for scrutiny, and Locke turned his attention to the relations of men to one another. He decided that God had provided natural laws to make the human world run as smoothly as the physical world; but the enforcement of these natural laws of society God had left to men. In two *Treatises* on civil government (published in 1689 and 1690 but written earlier) Locke explained that men had voluntarily left the free state of nature (in which they were born and originally lived) and had, by mutual agreement, instituted civil government for the purpose of enforcing natural laws. The most important natural law was that no man should take away the life, liberty, or property of another (these were "natural rights" of man). A government that failed to protect life, liberty, and property lost its reason for existence and deserved to be altered or overthrown by the people it governed.

Reason led Locke to condemn absolute government, whether in church or state. It led others to advocate free trade, free speech, free thought. Together, Locke and Newton gave men confidence that all the world's evils as well as its mysteries would yield to the persistent application of human reason.

This confidence in reason, which animated the European philosophers of the eighteenth century, came to be known as the Enlightenment. Although the Enlightenment originated in Europe, its doctrines penetrated society more widely in America. Students in American colleges learned Newton's physics and Locke's psychology. Ministers, whether Old Light or New, adapted their theology to the new ideas and welcomed the discoveries of reason as an aid to revelation, a means to improve their understanding of God's creation. Politicians cited Locke to support their arguments (see Chapters 4 and 5). Gentlemen formed clubs to discuss philosophy. Men awakened to the newness of the New World and turned amateur scientists; they described American plants and animals and made astronomical observations of the American skies to swell the growing body of scientific information that might provide answers to the limitless questions reason could now ask. In Boston the Reverend Cotton Mather and Dr. Zabdiel Boylston demonstrated by experiment the efficacy of inoculation against smallpox. In Philadelphia David Rittenhouse built the first American orrery, a mechanical model that reproduced the motions of the solar system.

Even the common man, who never himself read Locke or Newton, was receptive to their philosophy. To the European peasant, following the footsteps of his ancestors, unable to read or write, with no voice in church or state, the Enlightenment meant little. But the ordinary American colonist had constantly to apply his reason to new situations, whether in field or forest, church or state. The Enlightenment made a virtue of his necessity and encouraged him to lift his voice against unreasonableness wherever he met it.

It is perhaps no accident that the man who best exemplified the Enlightenment both to his countrymen and to foreigners was not only an American but an American who came from the ranks of common men and never lost touch with them. Benjamin Franklin (1706–90) was born in Boston, made his fortune in Philadelphia, and then spent much of the remainder of his life in England and France on political missions for the American people. His genius brought him success in everything

The Enlightenment:
A Free Press

Printers are educated in the Belief, that when Men differ in Opinion, both Sides ought equally to have the Advantage of being heard by the Publick; and that when Truth and Error have fair Play, the former is always an overmatch for the latter: Hence they chearfully serve all contending Writers that pay them well, without regarding on which side they are of the Question in Dispute....

That it is unreasonable to imagine Printers approve of every thing they print, and to censure them on any particular thing accordingly; since in the way of their Business they print such great variety of things opposite and contradictory. It is likewise as unreasonable what some assert, "That Printers ought not to print any Thing but what they approve;" since if all of that Business should make such a Resolution, and abide by it, an End would thereby be put to Free Writing, and the World would afterwards have nothing to read but what happen'd to be the Opinions of Printers.

From Benjamin Franklin, "Apology for Printers," 1731.

Franklin: Arch-American.

he tried, whether it was running a Philadelphia newspaper in his youth or wooing the ladies of Paris in his old age. The Enlightenment sang the praises of intellectual freedom; Franklin as a printer defended his right to publish what he pleased. The Enlightenment called for freedom of trade; Franklin worked as a diplomat to achieve that freedom. The Enlightenment encouraged scientific experiment. Franklin made significant observations on a wide variety of scientific subjects (from ocean currents to the theory of heat); he was a prolific inventor (a stove, a clock, a musical instrument); and, as one of the first experimenters with electricity, he made important contributions to both the theory of the subject (positive and negative current) and to its application (lightning rods).

As a son of the Enlightenment, Franklin was at home anywhere in the world, yet everywhere men recognized him as a typical American. Even without the fur cap he wore to emphasize it, no one could miss his American style, his down-to-earth insistence on doing things his own way and finding out for himself. Franklin's insistence on results in everything he undertook accorded with his coun-

trymen's insistence that their governments and churches perform what was expected of them.

Social Mobility   In describing America for Europeans, Franklin advised no one to go there unless he had more to recommend him than high birth, for Americans, he said, "do not inquire concerning a Stranger, *What is he?* but, *What can he do?*" Franklin wrote these words after the period we are considering—probably in 1782. But by mid-century it had already become clear that birth meant less in America than in Europe.

Europeans learned at an early age that God made men unequal. To some He gave riches beyond measure, to others nothing. The land on which European peasants worked was, in a sense, theirs; but it also belonged to their superiors, who did not labor on it but received rents and services from those who did. Riches brought dignity. It might take more than one generation for a wealthy family to climb to the top of the social ladder, but once there its members enjoyed the security of a title— count, duke, earl, marquis—that passed in perpetuity from father to son. Riches and dignity brought power, and men who had neither must do the bidding of those who had both.

In Europe, men of title generally had a voice in government. In England, even though the House of Commons became the dominant branch of Parliament, its members were drawn from the higher ranks of English society, and they could still pass no law without the consent of the highest ranks, assembled in the House of Lords.

Although eighteenth-century Americans were taught that God assigned men to different ranks in society, the idea did not have quite the same meaning as in Europe. The American could see plainly that merchants and planters had more wealth and dignity than other men. But the social ladder was both shorter and shakier in America than in Europe. Since huge tracts of land were unclaimed and unsettled, it was not hard for an enterprising man to gain possession of all he needed. Except for slaves, no large class of men worked for other men. And those who did enjoyed a higher status than they would have in England, because labor was scarce, and hired workers were paid accordingly. Everyone knew that the servant bound to his master for a set term would in time be free and might himself become wealthy. At the foot of the ladder, then, free Americans who worked with their hands enjoyed a higher position than European peasants or artisans. At the top of the ladder, the greatest American aristocrats had no titles and would have ranked in England below any member of the House of Lords.

Without the security of a title, American families had difficulty in staying at the top. Hard work and good luck made a man rich; hard work and bad luck made him poor again. And while wealth inevitably brought power, the rich had no place of their own in government. Generally the governor's council, whether popularly elected or appointed by the king, was selected from their number. But no American could claim a seat in the council simply by virtue of his social position. Nor could he expect to retain either government office or social rank indefinitely. Mobility, not nobility, dominated society in America.

In a number of ways, then, the eighteenth-century American differed from the Englishman or the European. He was better educated and therefore less in awe of his superiors, who were in any case not far above him. He had

The Extension of Settlement, 1660-1760

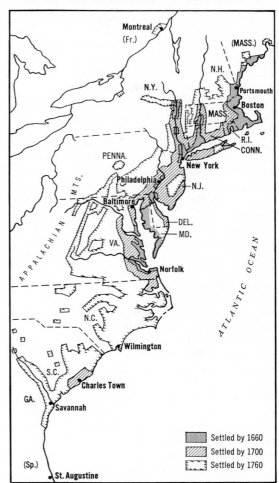

Settled by 1660
Settled by 1700
Settled by 1760

more control over his government and over his clergymen. Unless he was a slave—the exception to most statements about Americans before 1863—he had a greater opportunity to mold his own life. He used whatever tools might serve him to do it, whether ax, plow, rifle, or vote; and he got results, from governments as well as from forest and field. He did not yet know it, but he was becoming a new kind of man.

The Contest for the Continent

America was the growing tip of Europe. The European population did not begin its own spectacular growth until after the middle of the eighteenth century. Meanwhile Europe grew in America, where population doubled every twenty-five years.

American ways of living together had been designed for growth: the plantation with its reserve of unused and uncleared land, the New England town with its undivided commons, the farm surrounded by forest. But population rapidly outgrew existing communities and Americans thrust steadily westward until they came up against other peoples who were uninterested in sharing American ways of living together. Indians, Frenchmen, and Spaniards preferred their own ways, and the contest with these rivals for the continent was one of the persistent facts of life for colonial Americans.

Indian Warfare   The Indians of eastern North America were slow to perceive that their way of life was incompatible with that of the English. They often sold their land or gave it away without realizing that it would no longer be theirs too. They used the land mainly for hunting, and were willing to let the English hunt on it with them. But Englishmen taking possession cut the trees, drove out the game, and evicted the Indians. Before the Indians realized what was happening, they were outnumbered.

They could probably have done nothing to stem the English advance anyhow. Except when supported and organized by Europeans, Indians were not formidable military opponents. Superior woodsmanship gave them some advantage, especially when they were armed with the white man's weapons, and they posed a constant threat to the isolated frontier farmer. But they were too independent, too incorrigibly individualistic, to submit for long to military discipline. They might gather for a surprise assault, but they could not stick together long enough to take advantage of their success.

The colonists, if not more warlike, were better armed, better organized, and more systematic about killing. Indians of the Powhatan Confederacy in Virginia massacred 347 settlers in a surprise attack in 1622 (Indian victories in American history are generally known as massacres), but from that time on the Virginians pursued a policy of extermination that gradually eliminated the Indian menace in the

tidewater area. In 1637 the Puritans broke the power of the most dangerous New England tribe, the Pequots. An army led by John Mason surprised their main village at night, set fire to it, and shot men, women, and children as they ran to escape the flames. Thereafter New England suffered no serious Indian attack until 1676, when the Wampanoag chieftain Philip undertook a war that lasted longer than usual but ended with the usual result.

By this time the English had driven most of the seaboard tribes to inland regions already occupied by other Indians, who fought the retreating Indians as well as the advancing English. Virginia, which for many years had been living at peace with the broken remnant of the Powhatan Confederacy, was invaded by displaced Susquehannocks from the north. In September 1675, when a party of Virginia militia on a peace mission murdered the chiefs who had come to negotiate, the Susquehannocks retaliated with a raid that killed thirty-six Virginians.

The new Indian menace caught Virginia at a bad time. Tobacco prices had been low too long, and tobacco farmers were poor and short-tempered. Eastern Virginians had been free of Indians too long, and they did not recognize the danger or know how to meet it. The once-popular governor William Berkeley and the House of Burgesses had been in office too long (Berkeley had not called an election since 1661), and the government had lost touch with the people. When Berkeley and the Burgesses, who were mainly easterners, proposed to combat the Indian invasion by erecting a series of costly forts, the back country was indignant. Frontiersmen wanted dead Indians now, not more taxes for useless forts next year. In Charles City County a gathering of farmers and planters asked Nathaniel Bacon, a newcomer who had recently been appointed to the governor's council, to lead them in collecting Indian scalps.

During the months that followed, the Virginians battled with one another more often than with the Indians. Bacon, young and headstrong, demanded that the governor commission him to fight the Indians; Berkeley, old and headstrong, declared him a rebel. For six months the two men struggled for mastery of the colony. Initially Bacon attracted a large

Major Indian Tribes in the East

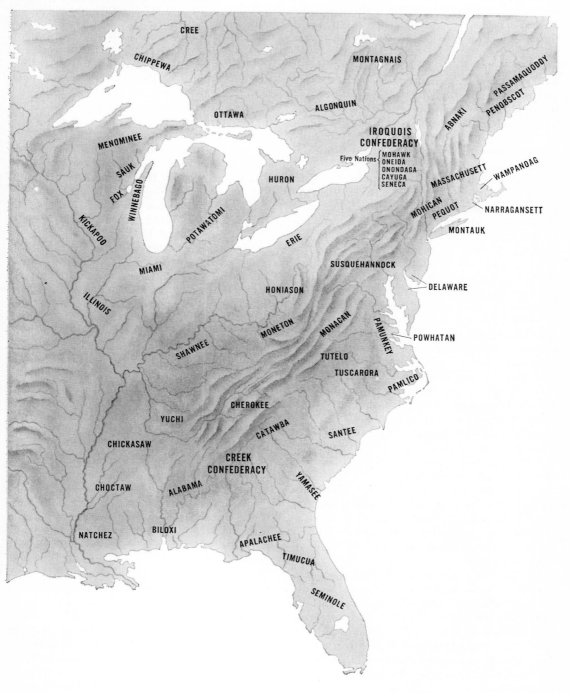

CREE

CHIPPEWA

MONTAGNAIS

OTTAWA

ALGONQUIN

PASSAMAQUODDY

PENOBSCOT

MENOMINEE

ABNAKI

IROQUOIS
CONFEDERACY

Five Nations { MOHAWK
ONEIDA
ONONDAGA
CAYUGA
SENECA

SAUK

FOX

WINNEBAGO

HURON

MASSACHUSETT

WAMPANOAG

MOHICAN

PEQUOT

NARRAGANSETT

KICKAPOO

POTAWATOMI

ERIE

MONTAUK

MIAMI

SUSQUEHANNOCK

ILLINOIS

HONIASON

DELAWARE

MONETON

MONACAN

PAMUNKEY

POWHATAN

SHAWNEE

TUTELO

TUSCARORA

PAMLICO

CHEROKEE

YUCHI

CATAWBA

SANTEE

CHICKASAW

CREEK
CONFEDERACY

YAMASEE

CHOCTAW

ALABAMA

NATCHEZ

BILOXI

APALACHEE

TIMUCUA

SEMINOLE

following among the depressed and discontented of all classes, and for a time he controlled most of Virginia except the Eastern Shore. After he died of a fever in September 1676, his men carried on without him for a time. But Berkeley had recovered his authority by January 1677, when royal commissioners arrived from England to investigate the conflict and relieve him of office. In the course of the struggle Bacon and his men killed a number of peaceful Pamunkey Indians; the Susquehannocks escaped but ceased to bother the colony.

Rivalry with France and Spain   After 1676 the surviving Indians east of the Appalachians were too few in number to menace the English settlers. But those farther west, led by the French, stood ready to halt English expansion at the mountains. Frenchmen in Canada, from the time of Champlain's founding of Quebec in 1608, had taken an acquisitive interest in the interior of North America. Missionaries in search of souls and *coureurs de bois* in search of furs traveled up and down the Mississippi and through the wilderness of its eastern tributaries. The *coureurs* were as good woodsmen as the Indians and as casual with their lives as the old English sea dogs. One of them, Louis Jolliet, together with the Jesuit Father Marquette, descended the Mississippi to the Arkansas as early as 1673. Robert Cavelier, Sieur de la Salle, reached the mouth of the Mississippi in 1682, and seventeen years later the French took possession of Louisiana by planting a settlement at Biloxi. In 1702 they started another one at Mobile. They also set up forts and trading posts in the Illinois country at Kaskaskia, Cahokia, and Vincennes, way stations between the St. Lawrence and the Mississippi, the two main arteries into the heart of North America.

In the competition for Indian furs, the French worked under a handicap, because French craftsmen could not supply, as cheaply as the English did, the textiles and hardware that the Indians demanded in exchange. But in spite of the better bargains offered by the English, the Frenchman did a better job of winning the Indians' friendship. Instead of evicting them from their land, he lived in their wigwams, married their daughters, and taught them to like Catholicism and hate the English.

The French government during the seventeenth century did not appreciate the exploits of its wandering subjects. In 1663 the king had taken New France from a French trading company, and thereafter the colony was governed by royal decrees (executed through a governor and an intendant, with no representative assembly). The king consistently discouraged the activities of the *coureurs*. He rejected, for example, the scheme of two *coureurs*, Pierre Radisson and Médart Chouart, Sieur de Groseilliers, who proposed a trading company to reach the northern fur supply by sea instead of by land; as a result, in 1672 they formed the Hudson's Bay Company in England instead of France.

Louis XIV was not interested in the wastes of Hudson Bay. Guided by his great minister Colbert, he wanted New France to be populated with hard-working, docile farmers. He sent women to entice the wild *coureurs* into a more settled life; he placed a bounty on large families. He forbade all but a few privileged individuals to engage in the fur trade. He even enlisted the Church in the cause: men who left their farms without permission were liable to excommunication. But all Louis' efforts produced only a meager scattering of agricultural settlements in Nova Scotia, along the St. Lawrence River, and later in Louisiana and in the Illinois country. Immigrants were few, and the total population remained small, no more than fifty or sixty thousand by the middle of the eighteenth century.

That so small and scattered a population could be in any way formidable to the million and a half English colonists was owing to the fact that the government's decrees against the *coureurs* had not been enforced. It is doubtful that they could have been; but some of the governors of Canada, notably Count Frontenac (who governed during most of the period from 1672 to 1698), perceived the strategic importance of what the *coureurs* were doing and disregarded instructions to halt them. Whenever France went to war with England, the *coureurs* led their Indian friends in raids on outlying English settlements in New England and New York. The English protected themselves by an uneasy alliance with the Iroquois. The Iroquois controlled the Mohawk Valley, which, in combination with the Hudson Valley, Lake George, and Lake Champlain, was the only

French Penetration of North America

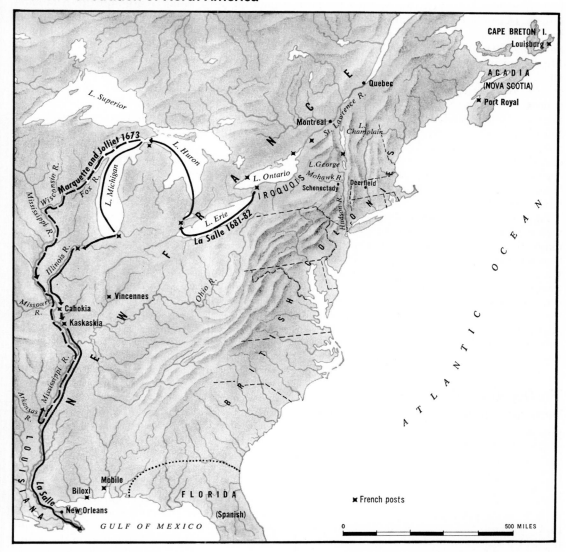

easy invasion route through the mountains from New England to the Carolinas.

From 1689 to 1713 warfare between England and France was almost continuous, in the War of the League of Augsburg (1689–97) and the War of the Spanish Succession (1702–13), known in the colonies as King William's War and Queen Anne's War. At this time neither France nor England considered America worth the expenditure of royal troops. But the settlers, aware of how much was at stake, carried on their own warfare. The French sent their Indians to raid Schenectady and Deerfield and the thinly populated villages in Maine. The New Englanders in turn captured Port Royal in Nova Scotia in 1690, saw it returned to France at the Peace of Ryswick in 1697, and recaptured it in 1710. The Treaty of Utrecht in 1713, besides recognizing England's claim to Hudson Bay, gave her Nova Scotia with its population of more than a thousand French farmers; it left Cape Breton Island, unpopulated but strategically located at the mouth of the St. Lawrence, to the French.

In the south, where the Appalachian barrier ended, both sides had carried on their warfare largely through Indians. South Carolina fur traders rivaled the French in their skillful handling of Indian tribes. Ranging as far as the Mississippi in search of deerskins, they gradually gained the allegiance of the Yamasee and of most of the tribes forming the great Creek confederacy of the Southeast. With Indian assistance they pushed back the Spaniards in Florida and threatened the French in Louisiana. Two years after Queen Anne's War ended, however, the Creeks and Yamasee turned and attacked their allies. But for the loyalty of the Cherokee, South Carolina might have suffered disaster.

After their assault failed, the Creeks moved westward to the Chattahoochee and the Yamasee southward, mostly to the vicinity of the Spanish fort at St. Augustine, thus relieving the English settlers of immediate danger. But the territory vacated by the Indians now offered the French and Spanish an undefended route by which to attack the Carolinians. Spain had always claimed this area as part of Florida, by right of prior discovery and occupation. She now threatened to recover it. The English at-

tempted to forestall Spanish occupation by planting Fort King George on the Altamaha River in 1721. After the fort proved ineffective against Indian raids and had to be abandoned, England turned to a more familiar method of holding the territory. Forts and missions and Indian diplomacy were a Spanish and French specialty. The English way of occupying America had always been to live in it, and in 1732 Englishmen prepared to move their homes into the area deserted by the Creeks and Yamasee.

The Founding of Georgia   During the quarter-century of peace following the Treaty of Utrecht, the population of the English colonies passed the million mark. The expansion took place east of the mountains, within the bounds of the old colonies. But one new colony, Georgia, was organized in the exposed region of South Carolina.

Like most of the original colonies, Georgia was founded for two purposes, one worldly and realistic, the other altruistic and hopeful. In order to defend her southern flank in America, England needed settlers. At the same time, an English gentleman with military experience and philanthropic motives wanted to do something for the poor. General James Oglethorpe, while serving on a Parliamentary committee, had looked into the appalling condition of debtors jailed by their creditors. Since they could do nothing in jail to work off their debts, they might linger there for years, until they were incapable of working at all.

General Oglethorpe organized other philanthropic gentlemen to seek a charter for a colony in which debtors and other unfortunate but deserving paupers might rehabilitate themselves. The English government was glad to get people out of jail and into the firing line on the southern frontier of the Carolinas, but it did not propose to let them get out of hand. In 1732 the government gave Oglethorpe and his friends a charter granting them authority as trustees for twenty-one years, after which the colony would revert to the king.

The trustees collected enough capital to get the enterprise off to a strong start. The area had been pictured in English tracts as a paradise compared to which the Garden of Eden was "at most but equal," and settlers eager to pay their own way appeared from Scotland, Ger-

The Departure of the Creeks and Yamasee and the Founding of Georgia

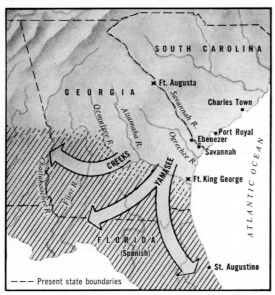

--- Present state boundaries

Philanthropists at work. "Trustees of Georgia," by William Verelst. London, 1734–35.

many, and New England as well as from England. The trustees gave them their blessing and rounded up deserving debtors to go with them. In Georgia, Oglethorpe himself saw that each man got fifty acres of land (those who paid their own way might get up to five hundred acres), tools to work it with, and enough supplies for the first year.

The trustees did their best to bar sin and temptation from the new paradise. To keep the rehabilitated debtor sober they forbade rum. To keep him industrious they forbade slavery. To ensure his livelihood they forbade land sales without their permission. But the zeal was only on the part of the trustees. Georgia proved after all to be somewhat less attractive than paradise, and the Georgians thought they de-

served at least the compensation of sinning like other men. In 1751 the trustees conceded defeat, allowed slavery and rum, and in 1752, a year before their charter expired, turned their fallen colony over to the king.

The colony's more worldly purpose was better realized, for Georgia had begun to serve as a very effective buffer. When England and Spain fought the War of Jenkins' Ear (1739–42) over English infiltration and Spanish atrocities in the Caribbean, Oglethorpe led the Georgians in campaigns against Florida and held off a Spanish invasion.

After the European conflict broadened into the War of the Austrian Succession (1740–48), known in the colonies as King George's War, the action shifted to the northern colonies.

There New Englanders got up an expedition under William Pepperell, a merchant from Maine, to attack the French fortress of Louisburg on Cape Breton Island. The colonists' capture of Louisburg was England's only real success on any front during the war, and it enabled her to go to the peace table with a make-weight to set against French conquests in the Austrian Netherlands. Although the Treaty of Aix-la-Chapelle (1748) restored the status quo and thus gave Louisburg back to France, its capture had focused the attention of both countries on the increasing strength and importance of England's American subjects.

They were a million and a half now and growing steadily. The advance guard of settlement—speculators, fur traders, and explorers —were already probing the mountain passes and eyeing the rich bottom lands of the Ohio. France had no settlers to occupy those lands, but she did have men to fight for them. If the English grew any further, she was prepared to make it hurt as never before. The English grew.

SUGGESTIONS FOR READING In many ways the most challenging problem of American history has been to discover in colonial America those institutions, attitudes, and events that found fruition in the later American way of life. George Bancroft first made the attempt on a large scale in his *History of the United States*, 10 vols. (1834–74), in which he saw divine providence guiding the colonists toward independence. F. J. Turner searched for the answer along the frontier in *The Frontier in American History* (1920), and V. L. Parrington traced a conflict between the common man and the would-be aristocrat in *The Colonial Mind* * (1927). These men were giants, and their works are too lightly dismissed today. More recent attempts to discern the abiding meaning of the colonial past are Max Savelle, *Seeds of Liberty* (1948); Clinton Rossiter, *Seedtime of the Republic* [Part I: *The First American Revolution* *] (1953); and D. J. Boorstin, *The Americans: The Colonial Experience* (1958).

The origins of the plantation system in Virginia are traced in T. J. Wertenbaker, *The Planters of Colonial Virginia* (1922), which argues that the seventeenth century was the heyday of the yeoman farmer and that neither slavery nor the large plantation was common before the eighteenth century. The servants who supplied the colonial labor force, both North and South, before the rise of slavery are the subject of A. E. Smith, *Colonists in Bondage* (1947). Oscar and Mary Handlin, "The Origins of the Southern Labor System," *William and Mary Quarterly*, 3rd series, VII (1950), 199 ff., reprinted in Oscar Handlin, *Race and Nationality in American Life* * (1957), traces the origin and development of slavery. The Handlins are challenged by Carl Degler in "Slavery and the Genesis of American Race Prejudice," *Comparative Studies in Society and History*, II (1959–60), 49–66.

The best over-all account of plantation agriculture is L. C. Gray, *History of Agriculture in the Southern United States to 1860*, 2 vols. (1933). On the Virginia plantation in the mid-eighteenth century, Louis Morton, *Robert Carter of Nomini Hall* (1941), offers a close-up view. L. B. Wright, *The First Gentleman of Virginia* (1940), does the same for a number of earlier planters. On domestic life in the South see E. S. Morgan, *Virginians at Home* (1952), and Julia Spruill, *Women's Life and Work in the Southern Colonies* (1938). Carl Bridenbaugh, *Myths and Realities: Societies of the Colonial South* (1952), challenges many conventional ideas about Southern culture. On the other side, see L. B. Wright, *The Cultural Life of the American Colonies* (1957), for intellectual activities in all the colonies.

The origin of the New England town was a lively subject of discussion among nineteenth-century historians, but the twentieth century has shown little interest in it. The best general discussion of the English institutions from which the town derived will be found in Wallace Notestein, *The English People on the Eve of Colonization* (1954). R. H. Akagi, *The Town Proprietors of New England* (1924), is still valuable. That it needs revision, however, is evident

* Available in a paperback edition.

from Charles Grant's study of a single Connecticut town in *Democracy in the Connecticut Frontier Town of Kent* (1961). Much valuable information about town affairs is contained in Ola Winslow, *Meetinghouse Hill* (1952).

There is no good study of the American farm in the colonial period, but the anonymous *American Husbandry* (1775; reprinted 1939, H. J. Carman, ed.), offers a wealth of information.

On the colonial cities the works of Carl Bridenbaugh are unique and outstanding: *Cities in the Wilderness, 1625-1742* (1938); *Cities in Revolt, 1743-1776* (1955); *The Colonial Craftsman* (1950); and, with Jessica Bridenbaugh, *Rebels and Gentlemen* (1942). The last is a study of Philadelphia in the age of Franklin.

The rise of American representative government is dealt with in L. W. Labaree, *Royal Government in America* (1930). R. E. Brown, in *Middle-Class Democracy and the Revolution in Massachusetts* (1955), argues convincingly that most adult males in colonial Massachusetts had the right to vote and that all districts of the state were equitably represented. A more general survey of the franchise in the colonies is Chilton Williamson, *American Suffrage: From Property to Democracy, 1760-1860* (1960).

W. W. Sweet, *Religion in Colonial America* (1942), is more concerned with church history than with religion itself. On the Great Awakening, see E. S. Gaustad, *The Great Awakening in New England* (1957); L. J. Trinterud, *The Forming of an American Tradition* (1949); and W. M. Gewehr, *The Great Awakening in Virginia* (1930). Ola Winslow, *Jonathan Edwards* * (1940), is the best biography; Perry Miller, *Jonathan Edwards* * (1949), is a brilliant interpretation of Edwards' thought. Joseph Haroutunian, *Piety Versus Moralism* (1932), traces the development of Edwards' theology in the New Divinity, while Conrad Wright, *The Beginnings of Unitarianism in America* (1955), shows how a liberal theology developed among the opponents of the Awakening. E. S. Morgan, *The Gentle Puritan: A Life of Ezra Stiles* (1962), shows the influence of the Enlightenment on an orthodox New England minister. The best biographies of Benjamin Franklin are Carl Van Doren, *Benjamin Franklin* (1941), and V. W. Crane, *Benjamin Franklin and a Rising People* (1954).

Bernard Bailyn, *Education in the Forming of American Society* * (1960), surveys the literature on a subject that has not been fully treated by recent historians. The history of Harvard College through the seventeenth century, written by a master, is S. E. Morison, *The Founding of Harvard College* (1935) and *Harvard College in the Seventeenth Century*, 2 vols. (1936). Robert Middlekauff, *Ancients and Axioms* (1963), is the best study of secondary education.

Francis Parkman made a study of the conflict between England and France in North America his life work, and all his writings are worth careful reading. More recently, George Hunt, *The Wars of the Iroquois* * (1940), challenges some of Parkman's views, and A. W. Trelease, *Indian Affairs in Colonial New York: The Seventeenth Century* (1960), offers still another interpretation. Wilcomb Washburn, *The Governor and the Rebel* (1957), sees Bacon's Rebellion as the result of frontiersmen's desire for Indian lands.

* Available in a paperback edition.

4

The Second Discovery of America

England had joined the War of the Austrian Succession in order to prevent France from gobbling up the Austrian empire and thus destroying the European balance of power. The Peace of Aix-la-Chapelle, which ended the war in 1748, was recognized everywhere in Europe as more a truce than a treaty. It restored the balance but left French ambition unsatisfied and French power unbroken. Having been obliged to give up her conquests in the Austrian Netherlands in order to recover Louisburg, France set about to ensure that her position in America would be stronger in the next war. Not only did she refortify Louisburg, but in a more ominous move she sent her agents along the western slope of the Appalachians to build forts, to cement alliances with the Indians, to claim the region for the king of France.

Contest for Empire

The Albany Congress　The English Board of Trade and the Privy Council, in order to bolster the loyalty of their own allies, called on the colonies from Virginia northward to send representatives to a meeting with the Iroquois at Albany. Virginia and New Jersey ignored the summons, but in June 1754 nineteen delegates from New Hampshire, Massachusetts, Connecticut, Rhode Island, Pennsylvania, and Maryland together with the lieutenant-governor of New York and four gentlemen of his council rode into Albany to confer with Iroquois chieftains who had slipped down the Mohawk Valley in response to a similar summons. As the Iroquois listened, the white men went through the formalities that Indians demanded in all negotiations: the grandiloquent declarations of esteem, the ceremonial presentation of gifts—scarlet coats, silver buttons, axes, scissors, guns. But the Iroquois had just been watching the French at work on fortifications in the interior, and they found English talk and English gifts less impressive than French action. They departed with the gifts but without offering the hoped-for assurance that they would help when the fighting began.

While in Albany the twenty-three colonial delegates discussed a scheme that had been talked of before: the formation of a permanent intercolonial union to conduct Indian relations. Benjamin Franklin, as he rode north from Philadelphia, had worked out the heads of a plan which he presented at the beginning of the congress. By the time the congress ended, the delegates had agreed to propose to the colonial assemblies a grand council with authority over matters of defense, westward expansion, and Indian relations. The council would handle purchases of land from friendly Indians and the planting of new settlements. It would raise armies and build forts and warships. And it would pay its own expenses by levying taxes. Its presiding officer, appointed by the king, would have veto power over all its actions.

When the plan reached the assemblies, their reaction was cool—some rejected it, others ignored it. Experience had shown them that the power to tax was father to every other governmental power. They often used it to get their own way in legislative conflicts with royal governors, and they did not propose to share it with any intercolonial council. Nor did they wish to be deprived of the chance to beat their neighbors in the race for Indian lands.

The assemblies' rejection of the Albany plan spared the English government the embarrassment of having to veto it. England wanted a unified direction of Indian affairs, not a permanent colonial union that might prove more difficult to deal with than the separate assemblies. Failure of the plan suggested that she need not worry about a union: the assemblies were apparently more uncooperative in dealing with one another than with England. No one stopped to think that Indian relations and western policy had always been the most divisive issues in colonial politics. How to use the unsettled land in the West and how to deal with its Indian inhabitants were questions that divided coast from interior, farmer from fur trader, merchant from landowner, colony from colony. On other questions the colonists were more united than either they or England knew.

English Defeats   As the gentlemen at Albany were conducting their elaborate and unsuccessful courtship of the Iroquois, a younger gentleman was already firing on the French in the Ohio country. Virginia, instead of sending delegates to Albany, had sent a twenty-two-year-old colonel of the militia, George Washington, to help construct a fort at the forks of the Ohio (where the Monongahela and Allegheny rivers join). When Washington arrived in the Ohio country, the French were already in possession of the forks and hard at work on their own Fort Duquesne. He built a crude stockade, which he called Fort Necessity, at Great Meadows, fifty miles south, but was obliged to surrender it to a superior French force on July 3, 1754. Then the French let Washington march his men home to report that the land over the mountains belonged to France.

Washington's defeat was bad news to his fellow Virginians, for many reasons: as Eng-

The Ohio Country

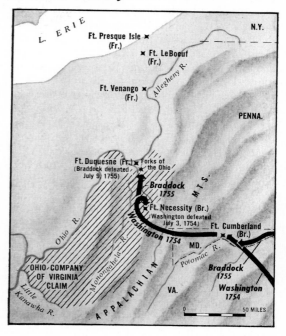

lishmen they disliked Frenchmen; as Protestants they disliked Catholics; as Virginians they disliked anybody who invaded their empire. On the basis of their 1609 charter Virginians claimed all land to the west and northwest of their colony, and they were jealous of encroachments on their territory whether by France or by other colonies. Reluctance to admit that other colonies should have any voice in dealing with the great Virginian West may have been one reason for Virginia's absence from the Albany Congress.

One group of Virginians in particular regarded the Ohio country as private property. In 1747 a number of prominent planters, including George Washington's brothers, Lawrence and Augustine, and Robert Dinwiddie, then surveyor general of the customs, had organized the Ohio Company to trade with the western Indians and to speculate in western lands. In 1749, with the approval of the Privy Council, the government of Virginia gave the company 200,000 acres between the Monongahela and the Great Kanawha rivers, and followed this by other grants of western lands to other speculators. By 1751, when Robert Dinwiddie became governor, many Virginians were looking to the lands of the trans-Appalachian west to make their fortunes.

Dinwiddie had arranged Washington's expedition in order to hold the Ohio Valley for England, for Virginia, and for the Ohio Company. Upon Washington's return, it was apparent that the job was too big for either the Ohio Company or Virginia, and Dinwiddie signaled for help from England. Although officially England and France remained at peace, the home government recognized that the new war was beginning, and it dispatched General Edward Braddock with two regiments.

Braddock, arriving in Virginia early in 1755, expected to increase his force by a large number of colonists and Indians and then to march on Fort Duquesne and teach the French that the Ohio Valley belonged to England. But Virginia had no wilderness diplomats to furnish the general with Indian braves. South Carolina could have delivered them, but Virginians were wary of letting Carolinians into the affairs of the Ohio country. Some Pennsylvania fur traders showed up with their own Indian friends, who executed an impressive war dance for the general but disappeared when it came time to march. In the end, Braddock set off with only eight Indians and about 1200 colonial militia to supplement his 1500 regulars. He took them successfully over the mountains, along with enough cannon to pound Fort Duquesne to dust. But as they were approaching the fort on July 9 the French surprised them and turned the march into a disastrous rout. Braddock himself was fatally wounded, and 976 of his men were killed or wounded.

The Indians of the area concluded that the English were finished, and for the next two years it looked as though they were. The colonists, despite their numerical strength, seemed more interested in scoring against each other than in defeating the French; and the English government was occupied with its European involvements. England gave Governor William Shirley of Massachusetts the title of commander in chief, but left him to collect most of his men and money from the colonists. Shirley was an able man, the most popular of the royal governors, but his abilities were no match for the jealous intrigues of the other governors, the

recalcitrance of the colonial assemblies, or the fire power of the French. While the assemblies dallied over raising troops, Shirley's ill-supported expeditions in 1755 against Fort Niagara and Crown Point both failed, but he did manage to build Fort William Henry at the southern end of Lake George.

Fear that France might try to regain Nova Scotia (or Acadia) led the British government in 1755 to deport several thousand French inhabitants from the province. The Acadians had lived under English rule since 1713, but they had never lost their affection for France and conscientiously passed it on to their children. Governor Shirley, recognizing that in case of a French invasion they were likely to side with the enemy, had suggested their deportation as early as 1747. In 1755 the British dispersed them through the other English colonies instead of sending them off to Canada, where they would have augmented the French forces. The circumstances of the deportations were inevitably cruel, and the treatment of the refugees by the English colonists was unnecessarily cruel. But Nova Scotia was made more secure.

In 1756, after gaining the support of Prussia, England finally resolved on a full-scale conflict and declared war. The declaration did nothing to break her losing streak, for immediately the French defeated the English fleet in the Mediterranean and captured Minorca. In America a new commander in chief, Lord Loudoun, was given military authority over the colonial governors in order to unite the colonies in their own defense. But the colonial assemblies, holding fast the purse strings, regarded Loudoun's authority with suspicion and complied only casually with his requests for men and supplies. Nor did he achieve success with the troops, regular or colonial, that he did get. Shortly after he assumed command, the French captured Fort Oswego; in the following year they took the new Fort William Henry.

Victory under Pitt   In 1757 the English at last found a statesman to bring their real strength into play. William Pitt had never doubted England's need for him. "I am sure," he said, "that I can save the country, and that no one else can." Pitt's assurance rested on a view of the war and of England's imperial future unlike that of earlier leaders. Hitherto the

The War in the North, 1758-60

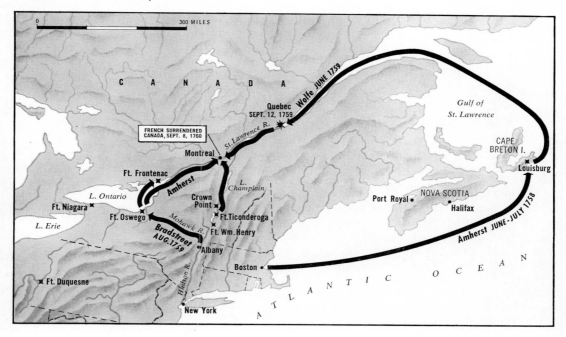

war in America had been regarded as an incidental part of a traditional European war. The fighting would hopefully facilitate the continued expansion of colonial population, but English statesmen weighed American victories and defeats on a European scale, for their effect on the balance of power. When Pitt took office, English policy underwent a radical change. Pitt's object was not simply to reduce French power in the European balance or to facilitate colonial expansion. He proposed instead to make England master of all North America and perhaps of the rest of the world too.

In Pitt's vision of empire Europe loomed less large than America and India. Accordingly he paid Frederick of Prussia to wage the European war and threw England's weight into a campaign of violent aggression abroad. Territory was his object, and he dipped into the national treasury with a lavish hand to pay the men who would seize it for him. Rather than waste time bickering with colonial assemblies over the cost, he promised them reimbursement for all their expenses in raising troops. The national debt went soaring, but so did colonial enlistments.

To drive France from the New World, Pitt needed not only men and money but military talent. He got it, as statesmen frequently have, by jumping young men over the heads of their elders. His greatest find was a gangly, hollow-chested boy of thirty, with a receding chin and a vile temper. James Wolfe was a prig and a martinet, but Pitt sensed his talent. Pitt also promoted Lieutenant-Colonel Jeffrey Amherst, who at the age of forty had been in the army twenty-two years without ever holding an independent command, to the rank of major general and put him in charge of a large-scale expedition against Louisburg. With Wolfe supervising the landing operations, Amherst took the fortress on July 26, 1758, giving England her first great victory of the war.

The capture of Louisburg destroyed French power at the mouth of the St. Lawrence and jeopardized communications between New and old France. A month later Lieutenant-Colonel John Bradstreet captured Fort Frontenac, which guarded the other end of the St. Lawrence on the shores of Lake Ontario. Now the French in Canada were cut off from the Mississippi Valley and had to give up Fort Duquesne,

The British taking Quebec, September 13, 1759.

which the British renamed Fort Pitt (later Pittsburgh).

At last Pitt was ready for his grand strategy, a pincers move on Quebec and Montreal, with troops approaching from the north by the St. Lawrence and from the south by the Hudson River, Lake George, and Lake Champlain. Amherst was to operate from the south, Wolfe from the north. Wolfe sailed up the St. Lawrence with nine thousand men and on September 12, 1759, made a surprise night attack up one of the steep gullies in the cliffs that protect Quebec. In the battle that then took place on the Plains of Abraham the British were victorious but both Wolfe and the able French commander, the marquis de Montcalm, received fatal wounds.

With the capture of Quebec, English victory in North America was only a matter of time. The French immediately laid siege to the city, but, when spring opened the ice-choked river and a British fleet appeared, the French withdrew. During the late summer, the expected troops from the south and a force from Quebec converged on Montreal for the final campaign.

On September 8, 1760, the French gave up the city and all Canada with it. The war did not end until 1763, but in its final phases the action shifted from North America to the Caribbean, India, and the Philippines, as England plucked the overseas empires of her European rivals.

George III   Six weeks after the fall of Montreal, King George II died. Between them, George II and his father, George I, had ruled England since 1714, when the latter had been summoned to the throne from the quiet German principality of Hanover. Neither was distinguished in intelligence or character, but George II was the more energetic and enjoyed leading the army, which knew him affectionately as the Little Captain. Though George II took an active part in selecting his ministers, the English government during his reign and his father's fell more and more into the hands of a powerful group of private families. They called themselves Whigs, in memory of the Revolution of 1688, from which they liked to date their ascendancy. Though they made an occasional bow to the principles of liberty, there was nothing very revolutionary about them. Comfortable and wealthy, they entered politics to get wealthier and organized small groups or factions to juggle the spoils of government office.

George II outlived his eldest son Frederick (who died in 1751 of a blow from a tennis ball), and George III, who ascended the throne in 1760, was the old king's grandson. At twenty-two George III had a mind, such as it was, of his own and no intention of letting the great Whig families run *his* government. Under the tutelage of a Scottish peer, the earl of Bute, he had learned to dislike vice, to distrust talent, and to love patriotism, barley water, and the earl of Bute. As a Scot, Bute had no seat in the House of Lords, and as a lord he was disqualified from the House of Commons. But the new king did not hesitate to give him at once a place in the inner "Cabinet Council," which was taking the place of the larger Privy Council in conducting the executive branch of government. Together, George and the earl of Bute set about reforming the wicked ways of English politics.

The politicians shared neither the king's aversion to vice nor his fondness for Bute, and they were not interested in reform. Lacking any party organization, they could not present a united front against the king, but he and they both knew that he could not run the government without their help, and they made him pay dearly for it. For ten years George appointed and dismissed members of the council at a bewildering rate. Ministers responsible for colonial affairs came and went and came again as the king sparred with politicians over issues that usually had nothing to do with the colonies. Consequently, English colonial policy in this crucial decade was inconsistent and incoherent, not to say capricious.

When George took the throne, Pitt was running the war and the government. Trouble broke out almost immediately. Tormented by gout, hobbling about on crutches, Pitt snapped at everyone who disagreed with him and did not gladly suffer the many fools he had to deal with. The politicians liked him as little as they liked Bute. With the fall of Canada and the subsequent British successes in the rest of the world, they were ready to make peace with France and rid themselves of the tyranny of this ailing genius.

George III King of England, 1760–1820.

Pitt was ready for peace too, provided he could strip France of all her overseas possessions. France, however, though defeated abroad, was still a formidable power in Europe and was courting the support of Spain. Pitt, hearing of the negotiations, stopped talking peace and demanded instead that England declare war at once against Spain—Pitt always preferred to attack. No one had dared oppose Pitt while England was underdog in the war with France. But he had made England strong enough to do without him and now his colleagues would not agree to take on a new enemy. When he could not have his way, Pitt resigned the ministry.

The Peace of Paris   With Pitt's resignation in 1761, the king's "dearest friend" became the leading figure in the council and the most unpopular man in England. Bute did not enjoy either role and retired from politics in 1763, but not until he had presided at Paris over the treaty that ended England's most successful war. The momentum of victory generated under Pitt carried the country through the final year of war without him. As he had foreseen, England ultimately had to add Spain to her list of enemies, but after crushing defeats at Manila and Havana Spain was ready to call halt. When Bute made peace in 1763, he took the whole of North America east of the Mississippi (Florida from Spain, Canada from France), and also took back Minorca, carved up the French possessions in India, and extricated England from her commitments in Germany. But Bute was schooled in the traditional diplomacy of balancing European powers against one another and he was unmoved by Pitt's imperial ambitions. He gave Cuba and the Philippines back to Spain and let France give Louisiana to Spain. He returned Guadeloupe and Martinique to France and allowed her to keep the two tiny islands of St. Pierre and Miquelon as fishing bases.

Pitt was outraged by Bute's liberality toward France and Spain, and some of the colonists shared his view. But most Englishmen, both in England itself and in the colonies, welcomed the treaty even while they denounced its maker and glorified Pitt. For the colonists it meant the end of a threat that had been hanging over them for as long as anyone could remember. Now as their children grew up and went looking for new homes, they could trek over the mountains into the lush Ohio Valley, into bluegrass lands they would name Kentucky and Tennessee, into the prairies of the Illinois country. The Indians, without the French to organize and direct them, could offer

North America in 1763

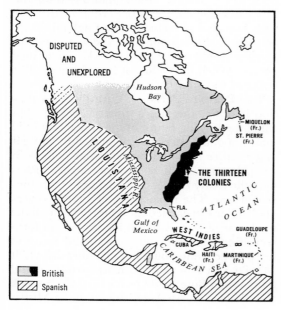

■ British
▨ Spanish

no serious obstacle to the settlement of the interior by Englishmen.

A New Empire and New Ideas

In England men looked with pride at their new territories. America was still the growing tip of Europe, and the conquest of New France conjured up the vision of a Mississippi Valley filled with men who spoke English and talked familiarly of a small island across the ocean as "home." Englishmen had been the first to think of America as a place to live in. Now their perception was rewarded with an empire that promised to cover the continent.

The Question of Imperial Authority With the coming of peace a few men sensed that the government of the empire again needed overhauling, for it was clearly inadequate for a population of two million about to advance into the immense interior of North America. Several colonial governors, who had seen America at first hand, wrote urgently on the subject. From Massachusetts, for example, Francis Bernard warned his superiors in England that this was "the proper and critical time to reform the American governments upon a general, constitutional, firm, and durable plan; and if it is not done now, it will probably every day grow more difficult, till at last it becomes impracticable."

Bernard's sense of urgency was justified. Most of the colonies had been founded before the supremacy of Parliament in England had been firmly established. Even after the question of supremacy was settled Parliament concerned itself little with them. But now that America had grown important to England, Parliament would be giving it more attention. That attention (as Bernard foresaw) might not be welcomed by the colonies; for, since the time of their founding, they had regularly dealt with the mother country through the king, his councils, his governors. Before Parliament began making laws for them or levying taxes on them it needed to establish its own authority over them by reorganizing their governments.

Bernard thought that all the colonial governments should be given identical constitutions by act of Parliament, with governors appointed by the king. He recognized that the colonists, like other Englishmen, expected a share in

Government:
A Royal Governor's View

They who claim exemption from acts of Parliament by virtue of their rights as Englishmen, should consider that it is impossible the rights of English subjects should be the same, in every respect, in all parts of the dominions. It is one of their rights as English subjects, to be governed by laws made by persons, in whose election they have, from time to time, a voice; they remove from the kingdom, where, perhaps, they were in the full exercise of this right, to the plantations, where it cannot be exercised, or where the exercise of it would be of no benefit to them. Does it follow that the government, by their removal from one part of the dominions to another, loses its authority over that part to which they remove, and that they are freed from the subjection they were under before; or do they expect that government should relinquish its authority because they cannot enjoy this particular right? Will it not rather be said, that by this, their voluntary removal, they have relinquished for a time at least, one of the rights of an English subject, which they might, if they pleased, have continued to enjoy, and may again enjoy, whensoever they will return to the place where it can be exercised?

From Governor Thomas Hutchinson, Speech to the Council and House of Representatives of Massachusetts, 1773.

Government:
A Colonial Legislature's View

When English subjects remove from the kingdom to the plantations,... their right [of representation] ... will travel with them through all the colonies, wherein a Legislature, similar to that of the kingdom, is established. And therefore, in this respect, and, we suppose, in all other essential respects, it is not impossible the rights of English subjects should be the same in all parts of the dominions, under a like form of Legislature.

This right of representation, is so essential and indisputable, in regard of all laws for levying taxes, that a people under any form of government, destitute of it, is destitute of freedom: of that degree of freedom, for the preservation of which, government was instituted; and without which, government degenerates into despotism. It cannot, therefore, be given up, or taken away, without making a breach in the essential rights of nature.

From the Answer of the Council to the Speech of Governor Hutchinson, 1773.

their government, and he suggested that they be represented in Parliament. He did not think that they had any right to such representation but he felt that it would be good politics to give them a voice in the decisions that Parliament would doubtless be making about them.

Francis Bernard was an ambitious man, and his superiors probably smiled at his advice. They realized that the empire needed repair, but Bernard's far-reaching plans seemed prompted as much by a desire for promotion as by the actual needs of the situation. And at the moment more immediate and pressing problems demanded their attention. For the next thirteen years a succession of short-sighted politicians and an industriously dull king kept their minds on a succession of immediate and pressing problems. By so doing, they inadvertently and unintentionally taught the colonists that Americans had more in common with one another than with Englishmen.

Trouble in the West   After the war England decided to station several thousand troops permanently in America. So much blood and money had been spent winning the continent that it seemed only proper to guard it, and the presence of troops would discourage France from trying to regain her losses. Almost at once the troops were called into action, not against France but against her former allies, the Indians, for whom the coming of peace presaged another westward surge of English colonists. In an effort to halt the English advance, northern Indians sparked by the Ottawa chieftain Pontiac attacked on a wide front from Detroit to western Pennsylvania in the spring of 1763. Since the British troops were not well located to protect the frontiers, the outlying settlers suffered heavily before the attacks could be stopped.

Pontiac's Rebellion had the divisive effect that western problems usually produced among Americans. Easterners were reluctant to take it seriously. Westerners blamed the easterners for the loss of farms and the death of wives, husbands, children, and friends. In western Pennsylvania a group of outraged pioneers known as the Paxton boys fell upon a village of peaceful Indians, massacred them, and marched on

The Proclamation Line of 1763

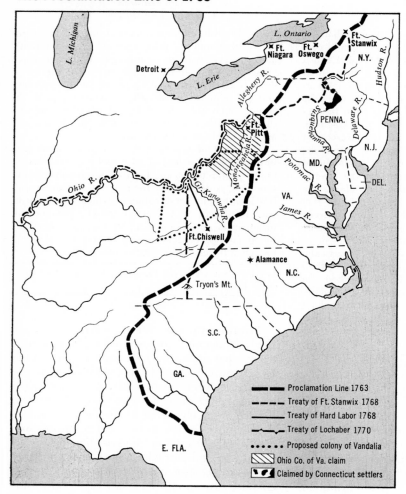

Legend:
- ▬ ▬ ▬ Proclamation Line 1763
- ‒ ‒ ‒ Treaty of Ft. Stanwix 1768
- ——— Treaty of Hard Labor 1768
- —⌐—⌐— Treaty of Lochaber 1770
- • • • • • Proposed colony of Vandalia
- ⧄ Ohio Co. of Va. claim
- ▨ Claimed by Connecticut settlers

Philadelphia to get some action out of the government. They were halted by the Philadelphians, who evidently feared other Pennsylvanians more than Indians.

English statesmen could easily conclude that the Americans were a hopelessly uncooperative and cowardly lot, unwilling to help each other and unable to protect themselves against savages. During the preceding French and Indian War British officers had sent back disparaging reports of colonial troops. General Wolfe himself had characterized his four companies of American rangers at Quebec as "the worst soldiers in the Universe." Now once again, it seemed, the colonists had demonstrated their

weakness—and England proceeded to demonstrate hers.

When Bute took the Mississippi Valley from France and returned the islands of Guadeloupe and Martinique, the decision was widely justified on the grounds that the valley was potentially more valuable than the West Indies. But if its potential was to be realized, the area would have to be settled and exploited by Englishmen, not kept as a giant game preserve. British politicians recognized this fact, but most of them saw no need to hurry settlers into the great emptiness beyond the mountains, where they would be less accessible to British control. Moreover, westward expansion would aggravate the most pressing colonial problem—the Indian resistance. While their troops crushed Pontiac's warriors, the politicians drafted a solution to the problem of Indian warfare: keep the colonists out of Indian territory. They had the king issue a proclamation forbidding settlement beyond the crest of the Appalachian Mountains and advising settlers in search of homes to go to Nova Scotia or Florida, for which England now provided colonial governments.

The proclamation had little effect on American westward expansion, for the colonists took little notice of it. But it showed that the British were incapable of grasping the desperate speed of American growth. They thought they could take their time about developing the West, that they could deflect the expanding population by issuing a proclamation.

George Grenville's Search for Revenue While the king was erecting his paper fence along the crest of the Appalachians, one of his ministers was occupied with a matter closer to home, the enormous national debt that England had piled up in acquiring Canada and the Mississippi Valley. George Grenville, First Lord of the Treasury, knew his pounds, shillings, and pence. With the end of the French and Indian War and the retirement of Bute, the king turned to him as the man best qualified to put England's finances in order. Grenville was not impressed with a continent full of naked savages, impecunious Frenchmen, and wild beaver; he was impressed with a national debt that had doubled since 1754; and he was still more impressed with the cost of keeping troops under arms to protect England's new possessions. He did not question the need for the troops. That was beyond his concern. But he had to find the money to pay them, as well as the money to pay the interest on the national debt.

Soon after he took office in April 1763 Grenville came upon a remarkable fact: the American customs service was costing the government nearly £8,000 a year in salaries but was collecting less than £2,000 in duties. Everyone knew that the colonists were importing large quantities of molasses from the French West Indies, on which the Molasses Act of 1733 required them to pay a duty of sixpence a gallon. Obviously they were evading the duty. In

October 1763 Grenville issued a sharp directive for its collection and ordered the British navy to patrol American waters for smugglers.

Grenville had another grievance against the colonists: they alleviated their perpetual currency shortage (resulting from their unfavorable balance of trade with the mother country) by issuing paper money. Although the money served an essential purpose and showed little depreciation in most colonies, its value was well below that of silver, and English creditors feared that the colonists might attempt to pay their English debts with it. As a result of complaints by creditors, the New England colonies had been forbidden in 1751 to make their paper money legal tender. By the Currency Act of April 1764, Grenville extended the prohibition to all the colonies.

In the same month Grenville directed through Parliament an act (later known as the Sugar Act) revising American customs duties and regulations. With good reason he reduced the duty on foreign molasses from sixpence a gallon to threepence. The purpose of the original levy had been to induce the colonists to buy their molasses from the British West Indies, where they could get it duty-free (though higher priced). But colonial rum-distillers needed far more molasses than the British sugar-planters could supply. More was obtainable from the French islands; but the distillers could not afford to pay the sixpence duty and still sell their rum at a competitive price. So the colonial importers simply bribed the customs officials (from a half-penny to a penny and a half per gallon) not to collect the duty. Grenville accepted the fact that the sixpence duty was too high, but he believed that the merchants would not be ruined by paying a threepence duty instead of a bribe.

The Sugar Act also imposed new duties on colonial imports of sugar, indigo, coffee, pimento, wine, and textiles. To discourage smuggling, it required that elaborate official papers be filed for every ship entering or leaving a colonial port. Finally, it provided that violators of the customs regulations could be tried in admiralty courts which operated under royally appointed judges acting without juries (in the common-law courts juries made up of local residents were inclined to sympathize with offenders). The colonists had been subject to such an enactment since 1696, but ambiguities in it had often enabled smugglers to avoid admiralty jurisdiction.

The stated purpose of the Sugar Act was to help defray the expenses England would incur in protecting her new American possessions. Grenville did not expect to raise the whole amount from the colonists, but he did expect more than the new duties were likely to yield; and in introducing the bill for the Sugar Act to Parliament he announced that he might soon levy a "stamp" tax on the colonies.

There was nothing novel in the idea of stamp taxes. Englishmen at home had been paying them ever since the reign of King William, and there had already been suggestions that Parliament impose such taxes on the colonies. Massachusetts had even tried a stamp tax of her own in 1755. By February 1765 Grenville had completed his study of taxable items being used in the colonies and was ready to introduce his Stamp Act to Parliament. It called for taxes on every type of legal document and on newspapers, almanacs, playing cards, and dice (all of which had to bear a stamp, signifying that the tax was paid). As in the case of the Sugar Act, violators would be prosecuted in admiralty courts. A few members of Parliament raised objections to taxing the colonists. Colonel Isaac Barré, who had served under Wolfe in North America, warned that the Americans would resist. But the act passed both houses and was signed by the king on March 22, 1765, to take effect November 1.

In May 1765 Grenville put through a third measure, the Quartering Act, to help support English troops in America. This act provided that any colony in which troops were stationed must furnish them with living quarters and with fire, candles, vinegar, salt, bedding, and beer, cider, or rum.

Colonial Suspicions The colonists were stunned by Grenville's actions. In 1763 colonial merchants felt sure that his order calling for the strict collection of molasses duties would ruin the rum trade and the whole New England economy with it. Nor did they welcome the reduction in duties provided by the Sugar Act, for they believed that even a threepence duty would drive their rum out of the market. Moreover, the act established customs procedures so strict and complicated that all kinds of trade would be hampered. The currency restriction made matters still worse. With silver in short supply and with paper money no longer legal tender, merchants had no medium of exchange and were sometimes reduced to barter. When economic depression followed the acts, Americans blamed Grenville.

But the most shocking aspect of Grenville's measures was that they seemed to embody a new policy—a deliberate aim to disinherit the colonists by denying them the rights of Englishmen. The Americans believed that it was their right as Englishmen not to be taxed except by their own elected representatives; but Parliament had taxed them directly in the Stamp Act, indirectly in the Sugar Act and the Quartering Act. They believed that it was their right as Englishmen to be tried by a jury of their peers; but Parliament had made infringement of the Sugar and Stamp Acts punishable in admiralty courts. These courts were objectionable not only because they violated the right to trial by jury but also because they put the burden of proof on the defendant, assuming that he was guilty until he proved himself innocent. Furthermore, in England admiralty courts tried only cases arising on the high seas. By giving the courts a wider jurisdiction in the colonies, the Sugar and Stamp Acts suggested that England thought Americans not entitled to rights long recognized in the mother country.

Further evidence of some sinister design seemed apparent in the announced purpose of the acts: to support troops in America. Why, the colonists wondered, did England want to keep armed soldiers in their midst? The troops had helped, to be sure, in crushing Pontiac's Rebellion. But protection against Indians was patently not the purpose of keeping them in America. Before 1754, while the French were sending their Indian allies to attack the colonists from Maine to Carolina, England had maintained scarcely any military garrison in America. Now, with the danger gone, with the French crushed and the Spaniards pushed beyond the Mississippi, she insisted on keeping several thousand men on hand. Why? Perhaps, it was whispered, England intended to use the army not to protect but to suppress the colonists. There is no evidence of any such intention, but it was easy to believe that one existed.

Colonial Convictions   The British statesmen who started Americans talking of standing armies, taxation without representation, and trials without juries would have done well to consider the origin and history of the colonies. New England and many other parts of America had been founded by Puritans who carried to America the ideas that shortly led to Oliver Cromwell's commonwealth in England. After that commonwealth ended with the restoration of the monarchy in 1660, many more dissenters joined the exodus to America, and their descendants could talk of Hampden and Pym and other heroes of the struggle against Charles I with a familiarity that might have struck some Englishmen as quaint. Though loyal to the House of Hanover, the colonists admired much in the writings of James Harrington, the advocate of republican govern-

---

Taxation: An American View

An Exemption from the Burthen of ungranted, involuntary Taxes, must be the grand Principle of every free State.... The People of this Colony, inspired by the Genius of their Mother Country, nobly disdain the thought of claiming that Exemption as *a Privilege.*—They found it on a Basis more honourable, solid and stable; they challenge it, and glory in it as their Right. That Right their Ancestors enjoyed in *Great-Britain* and *Ireland;* their Descendants returning to those Kingdoms, enjoy it again: And that it may be exercised by his Majesty's Subjects at Home, and justly denied to those who submitted to Poverty, Barbarian Wars, Loss of Blood, Loss of Money, personal Fatigues, and ten Thousand unutterable Hardships, to enlarge the Trade, Wealth, and Dominion of the Nation; or, to speak with the most unexceptionable Modesty, that when *as Subjects,* all have equal Merit; a Fatal, nay the most odious Discrimination should nevertheless be made between them, no Sophistry can recommend to the Sober, impartial Decision of common Sense.

From the New York Petition to the House of Commons, October 18, 1764.

---

ment, of Algernon Sidney, and of John Locke.

Locke no Englishman found quaint. In affirming the natural right of a people to alter their government (see p. 65), he had provided his countrymen with an intellectual justification for their long contest to gain ascendancy over their kings. All Englishmen believed that the course of their history had been a struggle to achieve a government which would protect their lives, liberty, and property. They believed that they had at last achieved such a government with the overthrow of James II in 1688 and the establishment of the House of Hanover in 1714. The colonists shared this belief, and they were proud to be members of the nation whose government stood foremost in the world in protecting the natural rights of its subjects.

Like other Englishmen the colonists regarded the representative nature of English government as the most important guarantee of continued protection. They rejoiced in Parliament's supremacy in England and in the supremacy of their own assemblies in America. In each the elected representatives of the people guarded the rights of Englishmen, and the most precious right they guarded was the right of property, without which neither life nor liberty could be secure. Since the power to tax was a power to take away property, no man could call himself free if he was taxed without his own consent, given either personally or by his representative. The right to be taxed in this way, and in no other, was a hard-won principle of the British constitution. In England only the representative branch of Parliament, the House of Commons, could initiate tax bills; and in the colonies the representative assemblies claimed the same exclusive privilege. It therefore seemed monstrous to Americans that, in the Sugar Act and the Stamp Act, Parliament, a body in which they had no representative, had presumed to tax them. If Parliament could levy these taxes it could levy others. Once the precedent was set, the colonists would be as badly off as England had been before the rise of Parliament. They would, ironically, be oppressed by the very body that had rescued England from the same kind of tyranny.

As the colonists measured acts of Parliament against their own ideas of right, they faced the question that Governor Bernard had wished to settle earlier, the question of Parliament's authority in America. Their decision was different from Bernard's. Parliament, they believed, had some right to legislate for them; but it had no right to tax them. It was the central legislative body for matters of common concern to the entire empire, and as such it could regulate their commerce, even by imposing duties to discourage certain kinds of trade which it believed prejudicial to the good of the empire as a whole. But it had no right to levy duties to raise money; such duties were taxes, and Parliament had no right to tax the colonies in any manner. Its members could not grant the property of people whom they did not represent.

The American colonists in 1764 and 1765 were remarkably unanimous in adopting this distinction between taxation and legislation. They began to affirm it in pamphlets and newspaper articles as soon as the Sugar Act was passed. New York and Virginia expressed it officially in petitions to Parliament. By the time the Stamp Act was passed, people in every colony were discussing the limits of Parliament's authority, and during the summer

and fall of 1765 colonial assemblies passed resolutions setting forth those limits.

The Stamp Act Crisis   The Stamp Act was to go into effect on November 1. In the May session of the Virginia assembly, Patrick Henry, a young lawyer, presented a series of resolutions declaring that only the House of Burgesses had the right to tax Virginians. The Burgesses adopted the resolutions but rejected some additional ones calling for outright resistance if England should try to collect the stamp tax. The other colonial assemblies rapidly followed Virginia's example, modeling their own resolutions on hers. Although the newspapers had printed Henry's rejected resolutions as though they had actually been passed, thus creating the impression that Virginia had acted more radically than was the case, nevertheless most of the other assemblies stopped where Virginia did, with a simple denial of Parliament's right to tax the colonies.

In addition to the resolutions of their individual assemblies, the colonies prepared a joint statement of their position. In June, before the colonial consensus had become apparent, Massachusetts proposed that all the colonies send delegates to a general meeting for the purpose of concerting their opposition to parliamentary taxes. Nine assemblies complied: in October 1765 the Stamp Act Congress met at New York. After avowing "all due subordination" to Parliament, the delegates resolved that colonial subordination did not include acceptance of Parliamentary taxation or of admiralty courts operating beyond their traditional limits. They also sent petitions to king and Parliament demanding repeal of the Sugar and Stamp Acts.

In objecting to taxation by Parliament, the colonists believed that they had common sense, natural law, and the British constitution all on their side. It was common sense that they already contributed to the wealth of the mother country by submitting to the Navigation Acts. If a more direct contribution was required, it ought to be made by the colonists' own representatives who alone could know, as the Virginia resolves said, "what Taxes the People are able to bear, or the easiest Method of raising them, and must themselves be affected by every Tax laid on the People." If the members of Parliament could establish their authority to tax the colonies, they would have an all but irresistible motive to shift their own burdens and those of their constituents to America. Every penny collected in the colonies would be a penny less to take from English pockets. It was common sense that such a situation spelled tyranny.

It was also a violation of the British constitution and of the laws of nature by which every free people should be governed. The people's right to be taxed only by their own representatives was "the grand Principle of every free State . . . the natural Right of Mankind," proclaimed the members of the New York assembly. The Massachusetts assembly, in the same vein, announced that "there are certain essential Rights of the British Constitution of Government, which are founded in the Law of God and Nature, and are the common Rights of Mankind." Among those rights was "That no man can justly take the Property of another without his Consent."

Besides informing Parliament and posterity of what was right, the colonists took practical steps to see that right prevailed. Merchants in New York, Philadelphia, and Boston agreed to stop importing British goods, hoping by economic pressure to enlist British merchants and manufacturers against the Stamp Act. Other Americans, too impatient to wait for repeal, were determined to prevent the Stamp Act from taking effect. On the night of August 14, a Boston mob stormed the house of Andrew Oliver, the local stamp distributor. They broke the doors and windows and roamed through the house calling for the owner's head. Oliver resigned his office the next day. Stamp distributors in other colonies hastened to follow Oliver's example. Mobs helped those who hesitated to make up their mind. On November 1, when the Stamp Act was scheduled to go into effect, there was no one to distribute the stamps.

In every colony the violence which forced the resignation of the distributors had been carefully engineered by a group of conspirators. These men now organized under the name of Sons of Liberty and prepared to resist "to the last extremity" any efforts to enforce the Stamp Act. They had learned from John Locke that a people could alter or overthrow a government that exceeded its authority; and

they repeated Locke's precepts to their countrymen in resolves, like those adopted at New London on December 10, 1765, declaring that "the People have a Right to reassume the exercise of that Authority which by Nature they had, before they delegated it to Individuals."

The total overthrow of government did not prove necessary. For a few weeks after November 1, people in most colonies simply refrained from doing any business that required stamps. Then newspapers began to appear without them. By threatening mob action, the Sons of Liberty soon persuaded judges to try cases and customs officers to clear ships with unstamped bonds and clearance papers. In less than three months the Stamp Act had been effectively nullified.

English response to colonial defiance was not what it might have been had Grenville remained in power. George III, for reasons that had nothing to do with the colonies, dismissed Grenville in July 1765, and in his place named the marquis of Rockingham as first minister. Rockingham and the men he brought into the administration with him had opposed the Stamp Act in the first place and wanted nothing more than to escape the embarrassment of trying to enforce it. English merchants, stung by the American boycott, reinforced Rockingham's determination to wipe the act off the books, and he enthusiastically favored a repeal bill in Parliament.

But the spate of resolutions and riots in the colonies made repeal difficult. Most members of Parliament were reluctant to back down, especially after William Pitt, with his usual tactlessness, publicly rejoiced at American resistance and endorsed the colonists' definition of the limits of Parliament's authority. Taxation, he said, was "no part of the governing or legislative power." Other members were baffled by the distinction between taxation and legislation. Grenville declared it absurd. But in March 1766 Parliament repealed the act after first passing a Declaratory Act which deliberately skirted the distinction and simply affirmed the authority of Parliament to "make laws and statutes of sufficient force and validity to bind the colonies and people of America, . . . in all cases whatsoever." Precisely what that meant Americans were to find out later.

For the moment they rejoiced in the end of the contest that had led them to the brink of war with the mother country. Repeal of the Stamp Act seemed to signalize a return to the Old Colonial System under which England and her colonies had alike enjoyed freedom, prosperity, and harmony. Now they could take up once again the position of leadership in world trade that they had won together.

Colonial Discoveries Nevertheless, as the colonists joined their English friends in celebrating repeal, they could reflect on their discoveries of the preceding two years. They had already found out more than England could have wished. A decade earlier, when the Albany Congress proposed a union against a danger in the west, they had unanimously declined. This time, when the danger came from the east, they had spontaneously joined to boycott British goods, to prevent the distribution of stamps, to define the limits of Parliament's authority. Indian tomahawks and French guns had revealed nothing but discord; the threat of tyranny had revealed fundamental agreement. The definition of Parliament's authority that the Stamp Act Congress had formulated was no compromise measure reluctantly agreed to under the pressure of circumstance. The congress merely reiterated principles already familiar in newspapers and pamphlets, principles that the colonial assemblies themselves had embodied in their resolutions. It nevertheless surprised the Americans to find themselves agreeing so readily. "The Colonies until now were ever at variance and foolishly jealous of each other," Joseph Warren of Massachusetts wrote to a friend, "they are now . . . united . . . nor will they soon forget the weight which this close union gives them."

In defending their rights the colonists also discovered that the ideas which united them and which they thought inherent in the British constitution were not shared by most Englishmen. Men in England had denied not only the colonists' distinction between taxation and legislation but also their conception of representation. At the outset of the tax controversy Grenville and his backers, admitting that Englishmen had a right to representation in the body that governed them, had claimed that the colonists *were* represented—not actually but virtually. A member of Parliament, Grenville

maintained, represented not only the men who elected him, but the whole empire. The concept of virtual representation was widely accepted in England, but it was nonsense to Americans who thought that a representative should be directly responsible to his constituents. By Grenville's reasoning, they said, Parliament could equally well claim an authority to tax the whole world.

Although a few suggestions had been made, like Governor Bernard's, that England should allow the colonies to send representatives to Parliament, the colonists did not take to the idea. It would be impractical, they thought, because of the great distance. Colonial representatives in London would lose contact with their constituents; it would cost too much to send them back and forth and to pay for their keep; they would be corrupted by the metropolis. But most important, there would be too few of them to have any real effect on the decisions of empire, yet their presence could be used to justify Parliamentary taxation of America.

These objections were serious, but not insuperable had either England or the colonies wanted to resolve them. But the plain fact was that the colonists did not want representation in Parliament. Perhaps they were unconsciously influenced by a new attitude which had been taking shape in the colonial mind but which few men yet recognized. England, by treating the colonists differently from Englishmen at home, was teaching them what she should have done her best to conceal: that they actually *were* different, and perhaps even wanted to be.

Though England had no way of knowing it, the men in whom this attitude first took hold included several of extraordinary ability. In Massachusetts three emerged as leaders of the opposition to Parliamentary taxation: James Otis, Samuel Adams, and John Adams. Otis, a lawyer, was volatile, unpredictable, and unbalanced, but powerful in argument and very influential among the people of Boston. Samuel Adams, a failure at everything else he tried, was a brilliant politician, gifted in organizing popular support for any measure. In the years to come, as Otis became more erratic and finally went insane, Adams would become the virtual dictator of Boston, against whom royal governors would write home in helpless expostulation. John Adams, whose gifts were more those of a statesman than of a politician, was as ardent as his cousin Samuel in hostility to Parliament. He despised everyone who sought political office by royal appointment, and searched out opportunities to advance the interests of America and Americans.

In Virginia the Stamp Act had alerted another trio of men whose names would likewise become unpleasantly familiar to Englishmen. Patrick Henry, as eloquent and almost as erratic as James Otis, gained instant fame by sponsoring Virginia's resolutions against the Stamp Act. George Washington, known to at least a few outside Virginia for his service in the late war, was more given to actions than to resolutions. He was at the House of Burgesses and may have voted for Henry's resolutions, but his thoughts went more toward home manufactures and new crops as a means of shaking off America's economic dependence on Great Britain. Thomas Jefferson, a twenty-two-year-old law student, was too young for politics in 1765. But he stood at the door of the House of Burgesses and listened to Henry's "torrents of sublime eloquence." Later Jefferson would show a certain eloquence himself.

Townshend's Folly   The repeal of the Stamp Act set the bells ringing in England and America. But the marquis of Rockingham, who had engineered the happy event, found himself unable to please either king or Parliament. In July 1766 he went the way of Grenville, and George III gave the government once again to William Pitt, now earl of Chatham. Unfortunately, bad health made Pitt a mere figurehead, and the new government fell under the influence of the volatile and irresponsible Chancellor of the Exchequer, Charles Townshend.

In taking up the search for revenue, Townshend, like Grenville, looked to the colonies. Fastening on their reviving trade as the likeliest source of new income, he persuaded Parliament in 1767 to pass a series of ill-considered acts levying duties on colonial imports of lead, paint, paper, glass, and tea. Since these items could be legally imported only from England, the new taxes would actually discourage purchases from the mother country and encourage the manufacture of taxable goods in the colo-

Samuel Adams: A brilliant politician.

nies, thus violating every principle that British economic policy had hitherto supported. The taxes also violated the colonists' expressed views on the limits of Parliament's authority.

The colonial assemblies were at this time registering their unabated disapproval of parliamentary taxes by resisting Grenville's Quartering Act, which they regarded as a form of taxation. To demonstrate their own superior authority, they voted to supply only part of the provisions that the act specified. Townshend nevertheless believed that the colonists were becoming more amenable to taxation, especially to taxes on trade, because they were paying the duty on molasses. In 1766 the duty had been reduced to a penny a gallon, which approximated the cost of a bribe; it had also been extended to include molasses of British production. This new duty was clearly a tax and not a regulation of trade. Encouraged by the colonists' seeming compliance, Townshend decided that, if he but acted boldly, he could now settle the question of Parliament's authority in America for good and all.

To cow the assemblies into obeying the Quartering Act, he made an example of New York, one of the principal offenders: in 1767, at his bidding, Parliament declared all acts of the New York assembly to be void until the colony furnished full supplies for the troops quartered there. To ensure collection of his new taxes on trade and of older regulatory duties as well, Townshend directed a reorganization of the American customs service. Hitherto customs officers throughout the empire had been under the administration of a board of commissioners located in England. From now on a special board of commissioners for America would reside in Boston, the center alike of colonial smuggling and of open resistance to taxation.

Americans did greet the Townshend acts less violently than they had the Stamp Act, but they soon made it clear that they were just as determined as ever to rid themselves of Parliamentary taxation. The New York assembly was hailed everywhere for its resistance to the Quartering Act. Once again newspapers and pamphlets cited the British constitution and the laws of nature. Once again the representative assemblies, stiffened by a circular letter from Massachusetts, denied the authority of Parliament to tax the colonies. Once again merchants joined in nonimportation agreements, and violators received visits from the Sons of Liberty.

The new customs commissioners were as unpopular as the new duties. They were regarded as superfluous bureaucrats sent by a corrupt ministry to fatten on the toil of Americans. And, it was feared, they were only the first of many to come; soon the colonist would have to support as many functionless officeholders as the taxpayer in England did.

The commissioners lost no time in exceeding everyone's worst expectations. The procedures prescribed by the Sugar Act were immensely complicated, and it was easy for a merchant to make an unintentional mistake in carrying them out. By insisting on technicalities, an unscrupulous commissioner could usually find a pretext for seizing a ship and its cargo of goods. Rather than take the risk, most merchants were willing to grease the commissioners' palms. Anyone who refused to play the game was likely to have his ship condemned in an admiralty court: unless he could prove that he had fulfilled every provision of the law, the court would order his ship and cargo sold. One third of the proceeds went to the English Treasury, one third to the governor of the colony, and one third to the customs officers prosecuting the case.

The officers had nothing to lose—except perhaps their lives. Even that danger was reduced when the commissioners persuaded the authorities in England to provide special protection against the hazards of their occupation. In September 1768 two companies of troops were sent to Boston.

England's readiness to send the troops indicated how far her relations with the colonies had deteriorated and what caliber of men had taken over the empire. In 1768 Lord Hillsborough had just been made Secretary of State for the Colonies, a post created to handle the increasingly complex colonial business. His decision to send the troops to Boston may have sprung from ignorance of the situation there, but it was one of a series of blunders that prompted Benjamin Franklin to characterize his conduct in office as "perverse and senseless."

The English troops landed in Boston without trouble. Samuel Adams had called for resistance. But the Massachusetts assembly was under suspension for refusing to rescind its circular letter against the Townshend Acts, and the extralegal convention which Adams organized in its place was unwilling to act on his radical demand.

The presence of the soldiers in Boston nevertheless spelled tyranny to Americans everywhere and showed again that England regarded Americans as not quite Englishmen. The soldiers themselves contributed to the impression by their arrogance. Even during the French and Indian War, when British and

British troops on the Boston Common.

colonial troops were fighting side by side, the regulars had never disguised their contempt for the Americans. Now the feeling was returned with interest.

For a year and a half the soldiers lived in Boston, suffering icy stares, open taunts, and all the subtle harassments the citizens could devise. Hostility was steadily aggravated by the inflammatory speeches and publications of the indefatigable Samuel Adams on the one side and by the rapacity of the customs commissioners on the other. But there was no real violence until March 5, 1770. On that day a crowd of boys looking for trouble found it in front of the Boston customhouse. They jeered the ten soldiers who stood guard before it, pelted them with snowballs, dared them to fire. The soldiers did fire, and so did some of the customs men from the windows of the building. Eleven of the unarmed rioters were hit, five of them fatally. The massacre, as the Bostonians

called it, roused such hostility to the troops that Lieutenant-Governor Thomas Hutchinson ordered them to Castle Island in the harbor. There they sat for the next four years.

Meanwhile a movement to repeal Charles Townshend's taxes was growing in England. Townshend died shortly after his acts were passed, and almost at once Englishmen began to realize that the Townshend duties were a mistake. Even without the pressure of colonial nonimportation agreements, English merchants would have protested against taxes that encouraged colonial manufacturing. Many members of the king's council favored outright repeal of the duties, but once again the government was reluctant to back down in the face of colonial defiance. The new Chancellor of the Exchequer, Lord North, who took office January 31, 1770, suggested that all the duties that encouraged colonial manufactures be repealed, and that only the duty on tea, which could not be grown in America, be retained. Since Americans were inordinately fond of tea, they were importing substantial quantities of it in spite of the duty. By keeping the duty in force, England would preserve an annual revenue of ten or twelve thousand pounds and would also sustain her authority.

Parliament adopted North's solution, and the king was pleased. North was the kind of politician George had been looking for—a plodding, dogged, industrious man, neither a fool nor a genius, much like the king himself. For the next twelve years he remained at the head of the government.

Toward Independence

North's repeal of all the Townshend duties except the one on tea was well calculated. In England it mollified both the merchants and the Parliamentary critics of the administration. In America it brought a wave of good feeling for the mother country, comparable to that following repeal of the Stamp Act. The Sons of Liberty met defeat when they demanded per severance in the boycott of British goods until the tax on tea should be repealed. Merchants began importing, and trade boomed. Royal governors reported that only a factious few continued to object to British policies.

Discord and Concord As good will toward the mother country rose, the recent harmony among the colonists themselves gave way to new quarrels, from which England concluded, too hastily, that American unity was a fiction. Anglicans in the northern colonies petitioned for the appointment of an American bishop; most Anglicans in the southern colonies opposed such an appointment; Congregationalists and Presbyterians everywhere were horrified at the prospect but were unable to cement an effective union amongst themselves to work against it.

The West was also causing trouble again. In both North and South Carolina settlers in the back country complained that the assembly was dominated by easterners, that its taxes were too high, that its officials were corrupt, that it had failed to extend county organization in the West. In 1771 a large force of westerners calling themselves Regulators rose against the tax collectors of North Carolina.

An army of easterners defeated them easily at the Battle of Alamance, but the clash left the back-country men with an enduring hatred of the East.

In other colonies disputes arose over the control of western lands. Connecticut claimed land on the Susquehanna River in northeastern Pennsylvania and even organized a county there. In England Connecticut agents pressed for official recognition of their claim and Pennsylvania agents for its rejection. Meanwhile Pennsylvanians and Virginians were squabbling over lands in the Ohio Valley.

England still adhered to the land policy outlined in the Proclamation of 1763—namely, that a boundary line should be maintained between settlers and Indians. But now, instead of following the crest of the Appalachians, the line was set farther west by treaties with various Indian tribes (the most important with the Iroquois at Fort Stanwix in 1768). Americans, however, were still competing vigorously for land beyond the line. A group of speculators from the middle colonies kept agents in England lobbying for the creation of a colony to be known as Vandalia south of the Ohio River. The site of the proposed colony was in territory claimed by Virginia, and the speculators of the Ohio Company angrily protested the scheme. Hillsborough heeded the Virginians and refused to authorize the new colony.

To British politicians all these disagreements seemed more serious than they were, and colonial good will toward England seemed stronger than it was. The good will, though real, rested on the hope that Parliament was retreating from its new policies. American hostility to those policies was by no means extinguished, nor was it likely to be, so long as customs commissioners sat in Boston, the British navy patrolled American waters, and admiralty courts condemned American vessels without jury trial. Men like Samuel Adams were able to keep the colonists talking about colonial rights and Parliamentary tyranny by seeing to it that every new affront committed by the British was given wide publicity in the newspapers. And then, in 1772, at Adams' instigation the towns of Massachusetts appointed committees to formulate statements of American rights and grievances and to correspond with one another on the subject. From

Massachusetts the idea spread through the rest of New England; and in 1773, as a result of the *Gaspee* affair, it was taken up on an inter-colonial basis.

The *Gaspee* was a British naval vessel which, in 1772, patrolled Narragansett Bay and inflicted daily outrages upon the inhabitants: her commander seized small boats engaged in local traffic; her sailors cut orchards for firewood and helped themselves to livestock. When the *Gaspee* ran aground on one of her missions, the people of Providence came out after dark and burned her. It was a daring action and not the first of its kind. England decided to make an example of the colony. Suspecting that Rhode Island courts would make no serious effort to uncover the culprits, she appointed a special commission to investigate the incident. But Rhode Islanders would give no helpful testimony and the commissioners never discovered the guilty parties.

The *Gaspee* commission attracted attention throughout America. Because it bypassed the Rhode Island courts, the colonists regarded it as an infringement of common-law procedures and consequently of the rights of Englishmen. In Virginia the assembly felt incited to establish a committee of correspondence for the whole colony (Patrick Henry was a member) and to propose that each of the other colonies appoint a committee of its own. When the proposal was accepted, Americans gained the machinery for coordinating their views and actions on any question affecting their common interests.

The Intolerable Acts   While men like Adams and Henry were laying the foundations of American union, Lord North was worrying over another immediate and pressing problem. England had left the administration of her empire in the East largely in the hands of a giant trading corporation, the East India Company; and the company was in serious financial trouble. After bringing it under more direct supervision of the British government, Lord North secured legislation to increase the company's profits from tea-drinking Americans.

The Tea Act of May 1773 relieved the company of various taxes in England and empowered it to export tea directly from its English warehouses to America, where it would be distributed by company agents. Hitherto the company had been required to sell its tea only to English merchants; they sold it to American merchants, who in turn sold it to retailers. By eliminating the middlemen's profits and the company's taxes, North hoped to lower tea prices in America so sharply that the colonists would step up their purchases and put the East India Company back on its feet. The Americans would still have to pay the tax imposed by the Townshend Act, but even so they would be able to buy tea cheaper than ever before.

North, it soon became apparent, had misjudged the colonists. By the Tea Act he lost whatever ground he had won in America by repealing the other Townshend duties. Merchants who had been importing tea themselves resented being shut out of the competitive market by a powerful privileged company. Even the consumers, who would have benefited by the act, were hostile to it. Political leaders warned that the scheme was a trap to make Americans accept Parliamentary taxation. When the first shipments from London arrived in colonial ports, angry citizens forced the ships to return without unloading or stored the tea in warehouses from which no East India man dared remove it. In Boston, where Governor Hutchinson ruled that the ships could not depart without unloading their cargoes, Samuel Adams and his friends pitched the tea into the harbor.

Lord North, who had had enough trouble with Boston, decided to punish the town with another demonstration of authority. Assisted by a new Secretary of State for the Colonies, Lord Dartmouth (Hillsborough had resigned in August 1772), he drafted the Boston Port Act, which ordered the port closed to shipping until the town made restitution for the tea. Parliament readily passed the act. North and Dartmouth might have been willing to stop there, but their fellow ministers insisted on proving Parliament's authority with three more acts (1774).

The Massachusetts Government Act altered the old constitution established by the charter of 1691 (see p. 47): henceforth the governor's council would be appointed by the king (rather than elected by the assembly) and town meetings would be held only once a year except by express permission of the governor. The Ad-

The Quebec Act, 1774

Quebec 1763-74   Quebec after 1774

ministration of Justice Act provided that any government or customs officer indicted for murder could be tried in England, beyond the control of local juries. A New Quartering Act authorized the quartering of troops within a town (instead of in the barracks provided by a colony) whenever their commanding officer thought it desirable. To underline the meaning of this act the British troops, with heavy reinforcements, were brought back into Boston from the fort in the harbor; and General Thomas Gage, the commander in chief of all the North American troops, was sent to act also as governor of the colony.

The colonists promptly dubbed these new measures the Intolerable Acts. They were followed by the Quebec Act, which had no punitive intention but which the colonists thought as outrageous as the others. Canada, since its acquisition in 1763, had been provisionally in the hands of a military governor; the Quebec Act gave the province a permanent government with no representative assembly, established French civil law, and offered special protection to the Catholic Church. Although Canada as a French colony had never had a representative assembly, Americans thought it ominous that Parliament had failed to establish one now that it was an English colony. It disturbed them even more that the Act ignored colonial territorial claims by annexing the whole region west of the Appalachians and north of the Ohio to the province of Quebec. Now when settlers moved west they would have to live under Canada's autocratic government.

The Quebec Act and the Intolerable Acts

were not the result of hasty or capricious decisions. The Quebec Act had been drafted only after lengthy discussions with officials who had been in Canada, and the Intolerable Acts incorporated certain changes that had often been recommended by royal governors and customs officers. The redesigning of the Massachusetts government in particular was a long-awaited assertion of Parliament's authority over colonial governments. It came, however, as Governor Bernard had feared it would, too late. By subjecting Massachusetts to direct Parliamentary control and by backing up that control with an army, Lord North and his colleagues thought they could teach Americans to respect the supremacy of Parliament. But the lesson the colonists learned was that the supremacy of Parliament meant an end to the power of their own representative assemblies and courts, an end to the right to trial by jury, an end to every political principle they held dear.

The committees of correspondence went into action immediately. Boston had once been known, and not loved, throughout the colonies for the hard bargaining of its merchants and the riotous behavior of its inhabitants. Now the town received universal admiration and sympathy. It was deluged with gifts of rice from the Carolinas, flour from Pennsylvania, and pledges of support from everywhere. To help carry out the pledges and to coordinate action against the Intolerable Acts, the committees of correspondence arranged for an intercolonial congress to meet in September.

The First Continental Congress Fifty-five delegates from twelve colonies (Canada, Florida, and Georgia sent none) assembled at Philadelphia in September 1774. As soon as the sessions began, it became apparent that the Southerners and the New Englanders had more radical ideas about what should be done than did the moderates from Pennsylvania and New York. Samuel Adams of Boston presented a set of resolutions that had just been passed by a convention in Suffolk County, Massachusetts, recommending outright resistance to the Intolerable Acts. The congress adopted these Suffolk Resolves and went on to adopt a nonimportation, nonexportation, and nonconsumption agreement, called "The Association," against trade of any kind with Great

Britain, Ireland, and the West Indies.

Joseph Galloway of Pennsylvania, speaking for the moderates, countered with a plan for imperial reorganization which he wanted the Congress to present to the king and Parliament. Galloway's plan called for a grand council of the colonies along the lines projected at the Albany Congress (see p. 76). Enactments of the council would be subject to Parliamentary review and veto; acts of Parliament affecting the colonies would likewise have to receive the approval of the grand council. But Galloway could not quite persuade the delegates to subordinate their union to Parliament. In the years since the Stamp Act crisis they had had time and provocation to think further about their relationship to that body.

In 1765 the colonists had categorically denied that Parliament had the authority to tax them; and they had acquiesced in its general legislative authority over the whole empire, mentioning specifically only trade regulation and amendment of the common law as examples of what kind of legislation they thought acceptable. Apart from an unexpanded stipulation in some of their resolutions that Parliament should not alter their "internal polity" they had not defined the limits of Parliament's legislative authority over them.

Since 1765 many of them had decided that Parliament had no more right to make laws concerning them than it did to tax them. This idea had few adherents until the punishment of the New York assembly, the *Gaspee* commission, and the Intolerable Acts clearly demonstrated that Parliament could destroy men's rights as readily by legislation as by taxation. Thereafter the idea spread rapidly. Benjamin Franklin adopted it privately as early as 1766, and Samuel Adams led the Massachusetts assembly in affirming it to Governor Hutchinson in 1773. In the summer of 1774 prospective members of Congress could read powerful demonstrations of it in two pamphlets. In *Considerations on the . . . Authority of the British Parliament*, James Wilson, a Pennsylvania lawyer, pointed out that all the familiar arguments against parliamentary taxation applied equally well against parliamentary legislation. Jefferson took the same position in *A Summary View of the Rights of British America*.

Neither Jefferson nor Wilson was present at the First Continental Congress, but enough of the delegates agreed with them to defeat Galloway's plan by one vote. The radicals were unable, however, to bring this bloc to repudiate all colonial ties with Parliament. Of those who were no longer willing to admit that Parliament had any authority in the colonies, some still believed that it should be allowed to regulate colonial trade as a just compensation for the British navy's protection of colonial shipping. When the delegates came to framing a statement of colonial rights and grievances, John Adams finally got them to compromise on a series of resolutions which denied that Parliament had any authority over the colonies, but agreed—as a matter of fairness and expediency—to submit to its acts for regulation of trade.

The congress was inviting Parliament to return to the same supervisory role it had exercised in the colonies before 1763. Had Parliament been willing to do so, the breach, instead of widening, might have closed. The earl of Chatham (William Pitt) and Edmund Burke both recognized the opportunity but neither could muster more than a few votes for proposals to repeal the Intolerable Acts and renounce American taxation. Lord North, however, did secure passage in February 1775 of what he regarded as a conciliatory measure proposing that the colonists tax themselves "for contributing their proportion to the common defence." The proposal gave no indication of how much each colony's "proportion" might be, and it ignored the other issues raised by the Intolerable Acts and by the declarations of the Continental Congress.

But English statesmen were not sanguine about the future. Most of them were convinced that Samuel Adams and his tribe were leading the colonists toward independence and that the march could be halted only by more forceful demonstrations of Parliamentary supremacy. The session which passed Lord North's conciliatory act also passed an act requiring New England to trade only with the mother country and the British West Indies and excluding New Englanders from the Newfoundland fisheries. At the same time the ministry took steps to prevent exportation of arms and ammunition to the colonies. Even the king expected the worst. "The New England Governments are in a State of Rebellion," he had told Lord North in November 1774. "Blows," he added, "must decide whether they are to be subject to this Country or Independent."

England clearly anticipated war, but her leaders had no conception of the size of the enemy. In spite of the increasingly obvious signs of colonial unity Lord North and his colleagues persisted in regarding the enemy as Massachusetts alone. General Gage, sitting uneasily in the governor's chair in Massachusetts, did his best to disillusion them. The Americans, he reported, were as ready for blows as the English; to enforce Parliament's authority he would need twenty thousand men. Until England was prepared to send that many, he said, it would be well to suspend the Intolerable Acts.

George III thought Gage's dispatches absurd; Lord North turned from them to ask Parliament for a reduction in the size of Britain's armed forces. Gage was allowed about thirty-five hundred.

From Lexington to Bunker Hill The general knew from his informers that the colonial militia were assembling arms and ammunition at strategic points. In Portsmouth, New Hampshire, they carried off a hundred barrels of powder belonging to the crown. Gage did not dare detach any part of his small force to recover the royal gunpowder, but occasionally he marched sizable columns for a few miles into the country around Boston hoping by this show of strength to overawe incipient rebels. On April 14 he received instructions from Lord Dartmouth to take the offensive against the rebellious colonists, and

on April 19 he sent seven hundred men to Concord to seize a supply of arms reportedly stored there.

Although the force got started in the dark of early morning, the tolling of alarm bells and the firing of signal guns showed that its errand was no secret. Anticipating trouble, the commanding officer sent back for reinforcements but ordered six companies under Major John Pitcairn to proceed. At Lexington, Pitcairn found colonial militia drawn up on the village green. At his command, they began to disperse. Then suddenly a shot rang out. Whether British or American, musket or pistol, accidental or deliberate, was not apparent; but when they heard the shot, the British soldiers fired a volley into the departing militiamen, killing eight of them and wounding ten.

This episode delayed the troops for only fifteen minutes, and by eight o'clock they were entering Concord. The Americans had already removed most of the military stores they had assembled there, but the British burned a few gun carriages and repulsed a group of militiamen who tried to drive them off. Two colonials and three British were killed in the skirmish. By noon the "battles" of Lexington and Concord were over and the British troops started back to Boston.

Now a real battle began, a battle unlike any the troops had ever seen. Colonial militiamen for miles around had been alerted by a system of riders organized for just such an emergency, and the seven hundred British regulars were obliged to run a gauntlet of fire from three or four thousand Americans. At Lexington the returning troops were joined by nine hundred reinforcements, but still the Americans fired from rock and tree at the massed target of moving redcoats.

The total casualties on both sides were not large: the British lost 73 killed, 174 wounded, and 26 missing; the Americans, 49 killed and 39 wounded. But Gage's worst fears had been justified: his offensive had turned into a rout. That night, as haggard British soldiers dragged themselves into Boston, watch fires dotted the landscape around the city: militia were beginning to move in from all over New England. Boston was already under siege by a people who had no proper army, no system of command, no regular government.

Lexington and Concord, April 19, 1775

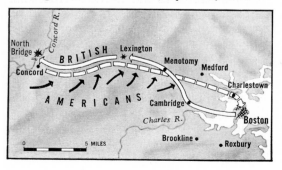

Boston and Charlestown, June 17, 1775

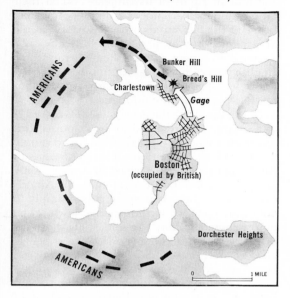

On June 17, less than two months later, Gage found how tightly he was held. Reinforced by sea with eleven hundred troops and three major generals (William Howe, John Burgoyne, and Henry Clinton), he decided to roll back the siege. On the night of June 16, the Americans, forewarned of his plans, marched twelve hundred men to Breed's Hill (just south of Bunker Hill, from which the ensuing action, for no good reason, received its name), overlooking Boston from the north. By morning, when four hundred more joined them, they had dug a formidable redoubt.

That afternoon General Howe set out with twenty-two hundred men to displace the rebels from their position. Since Breed's Hill was on a peninsula, Howe could have cut the Americans off by landing a force at their rear. Instead, he launched a frontal assault. The Americans inside the redoubt held their fire as the enemy, firing regularly and harmlessly, marched coolly up the hill. When the Americans finally returned the fire, the British went down in rows.

Howe regrouped his forces and tried again, with the same result. But now the Americans were low on ammunition, and the British regulars, reinforced by six hundred men, finally forced the redoubt with bayonets. The Ameri-

cans, clubbing their muskets, retreated slowly, leaving 140 of their men dead, 271 wounded, and 30 captured. Howe's victory had cost him 226 killed and 828 wounded. Another such victory, wrote Clinton ruefully, "would have ruined us." It had now been demonstrated beyond dispute that Americans with guns were dangerous men. The British never again underestimated the men they were fighting.

One People   While sixteen thousand colonial militia pinned down the British forces in Boston, other Americans were taking the necessary steps to support the war. Royal governors everywhere watched their authority collapse, as surely as Gage's had collapsed outside Boston. A few tried to organize loyalist support to combat the rebellion, but sooner or later they all gave up and fled to the safety of British warships. The colonial assemblies, which had hitherto met under royal authorization, now gathered as extralegal provincial congresses and began to act as independent governments, raising troops and issuing forbidden paper money to pay them. The transition in government presented no serious difficulty because the representatives to the provincial congresses were for the most part former assemblymen and they simply carried on with their usual business.

A more extraordinary task faced the delegates who, in May 1775, assembled at Philadelphia for the Second Continental Congress (which had been arranged by the First Congress). Previous intercolonial meetings, the Albany Congress, the Stamp Act Congress, and the First Continental Congress, had devoted themselves to hammering out agreements of principle. But by the time the Second Congress met, the colonists were already deeply committed to common principles and a common cause. Fighting had just begun and the delegates, instead of conducting another debating council, found themselves conducting America's first central government: they assumed responsibility for the provincial militia besieging Boston, ordered their transformation into a Continental Army, named George Washington as commander, issued paper money to support the troops, and appointed a committee to negotiate with foreign countries.

Although in taking these actions the Congress assumed many of the powers of an independent government, the members still did not intend to establish an independent nation. Repudiation of Parliament was not repudiation of England, and they did not see why Englishmen in America and in England should not retain their brotherhood in loyalty to a common king. In July they laid their cause at the feet of the king with a petition asking him personally to promote repeal of the oppressive measures. Significantly they placed the blame for those measures on the ministry—"those artful and cruel enemies who abuse your royal confidence and authority for the purpose of effecting our destruction." They issued at the same time a "Declaration of the causes and necessity for taking up arms," in which they explained that they were "reduced to the alternative of choosing an unconditional submission to the tyranny of irritated ministers, or resistance by force." In choosing resistance, they said, they had no "ambitious designs of separating from Great Britain, and establishing independent states." As soon as England acknowledged their rights, they would lay down their arms.

Although some Americans had already begun to think of independence, the declarations of the congress were made in good faith. Even at this date the repeal of the Intolerable Acts and the restriction of Parliamentary legislation to the regulation of trade might have kept the colonists in the empire. They still thought of their rights as the rights of Englishmen, and of their union as a means of protecting those rights. But George III and Lord North were bent on subjecting the colonists to a Parliament in which they elected no representative. The king did not answer their petition; Parliament did, however, answer their "declaration"—by voting to send twenty-five thousand more troops against them. The addition would bring British military strength in America to forty thousand. In August the king issued a proclamation declaring the colonies in a state of rebellion, and in December Parliament passed an act outlawing all their trade and subjecting their ships and goods to confiscation.

Each British action weakened the colonists' emotional attachment to England. The principal ingredient in their national feeling had been admiration for the British form of government, which better than any other guaranteed the human rights of its subjects. When their admiration for Parliament crumbled, they had fastened the last shreds of their loyalty on the king alone. But he had enthusiastically supported Parliament against them. If the whole English government was determined to destroy the rights of its subjects, then it was a dubious privilege to be an Englishman.

In January 1776 the new image of George III as a tyrant was presented to the colonists with biting eloquence in a publication called simply *Common Sense*. The author, Thomas Paine, an Englishman who had arrived in America only in 1774, argued that it was foolish for Americans to stake their lives and fortunes simply to obtain a repeal of Parliamentary laws. "The object contended for," he said, "ought always to bear some just proportion to the expence. . . . Dearly, dearly, do we pay for the repeal of the acts, if that is all we fight for." Common sense forbade that Americans should remain loyal to a king who sanctioned the spilling of their blood. In fact monarchy itself was an absurdity, a form of government that had laid the world in blood and ashes. "Of more worth," declared Paine, "is one honest man to society and in the sight of God, than all the crowned ruffians that ever lived." Here Paine struck a responsive chord. Since the days of Cromwell republican government had never ceased to have its devotees both in Great Britain and in America, and the old distrust of kings had never entirely died out. The colonists' very devotion to the House of Hanover was in part an expression of this distrust, an oblique way of denouncing the House of Stuart (which the Hanovers had replaced) and affirming the right of a people to change kings. By calling on Americans to cast off kings altogether, Thomas Paine kindled a latent enthusiasm for republican government.

In the six months that followed the publication of *Common Sense*, sentiment in favor of independence and republicanism grew rapidly. Many who hoped that George III would save American liberty had been convinced by Paine that no king could help them. Many who had considered independence impossible to attain now began to change their minds. Ever since Lexington, American forces throughout the colonies had been fighting the

British with heartening success in one engagement after another. And as men thought beyond the mere repeal of Parliamentary laws, they began to cut their ties with England and England's king. The provincial congress of South Carolina established a republican constitution in March, and in May the Rhode Island congress repealed the law requiring allegiance to the king. North Carolina in April and Virginia in May instructed their delegates in the Continental Congress to vote for independence.

The Continental Congress with representatives from thirteen colonies (delegates from Georgia had arrived in September, 1775) was itself behaving more and more like an independent national government. In March it authorized privateering against British ships. In April it forbade the further importation of slaves and declared other trade open to all the world except Great Britain. In May, urged by John Adams, it even recommended that any member colonies who had not already done so should suppress all vestiges of royal authority within their borders and establish governments resting on popular consent.

By this time Adams and many other delegates from New England and the Southern colonies were prepared to make an outright declaration of independence. They were restrained only by the reluctant rebels of the middle colonies. Although virtually the whole Congress had by now concluded that Parliament had no constitutional authority at all in America, some Americans still felt bound to England by a lingering loyalty to the king and a sentimental attachment to the English people. By the end of June both feelings had worn too thin to sustain the weight of continuing war. On July 2, the Congress finally agreed to a motion which had been introduced by Richard Henry Lee of Virginia nearly a month before: "That these United Colonies are, and of right ought to be free and independent states." Thomas Jefferson, assisted by Franklin and John Adams, expanded the resolution into the famous declaration which was adopted on July 4.

Jefferson's declaration was an eloquent application of the ideas made familiar by John Locke and by a century and a half of American experience. It affirmed the origin of government in the consent of the governed, its obligation to protect natural rights, and the duty of a people to alter or abolish a government which failed to fulfill its obligation. That the British government had failed was demonstrated by a long list of misdeeds. These were attributed not to Parliament, whose authority the colonists had already denied, but to the king, the only remaining link between the colonies and England. Every grievance suffered by Americans since 1763 was laid at his door. The indictment was not altogether realistic, but it effectively expressed the American rejection not only of George III but of monarchy itself. Embedded in the preamble was evidence that the colonists had learned the lesson that England had taught: "When in the course of human events, it becomes necessary for one people to dissolve the political bands which have connected them with another. . . ." Englishmen were "another" people; and the colonists, who twenty-two years before had rejected the union proposed at Albany, now spoke of themselves as "one people."

SUGGESTIONS FOR READING The period covered by this chapter was first treated in the grand manner by George Bancroft in Vols. IV–VII of his *History of the United States*, 10 vols. (1834–74); Bancroft is still grand reading. Although subsequent historians have been able to correct him on many points, few if any have matched him in literary gifts or in comprehensive knowledge of the sources. Where Bancroft measured events against the future of the United States, G. L. Beer, in *British Colonial Policy, 1754–1765* (1907), viewed the French and Indian War from a British point of view. Lawrence Gipson follows Beer in *The British Empire Before the American Revolution* (1936–   ). Volumes V–VIII deal with the French and Indian War, which Professor Gipson has renamed "The Great War for the Empire." The first two volumes of Douglas Freeman, *George Washington*, 7 vols. (1949–57), cover Washington's role in the war. Stanley Pargellis, *Lord Loudoun in North America* (1933), is important for its treatment of the problem of command.

The understanding of British politics in the 1760's and 1770's has been considerably altered since Bancroft's time. The older views were well expressed in G. O. Trevelyan's magnificently written *The American Revolution*, 4 vols. (1898–1907), and *The Early History of Charles James Fox* (1901). L. B. Namier, in *The Structure of Politics at the Accession of George III*, 2 vols. (1929), and *England in the Age of the American Revolution* (1930), showed that the party system assumed by Trevelyan did not yet exist and that George III was a better monarch than anyone had supposed. More recently, Herbert Butterfield, *George III and the Historians* (1959), argues that the older views were not quite so mistaken as Namier and his followers thought them to be. A valuable study of the radical political tradition in England is Caroline Robbins, *The Eighteenth-Century Commonwealthman* (1959).

Clarence Alvord, *The Mississippi Valley in British Politics*, 2 vols. (1916), is a classic study of British policy toward the American West. This should be supplemented by T. P. Abernethy, *Western Lands and the American Revolution* (1937), and J. M. Sosin, *Whitehall and the Wilderness: The Middle West in British Colonial Policy, 1760–1775* (1961).

Perhaps the best introduction to the multitude of books on the origins of the Revolution is C. M. Andrews, *The Colonial Background of the American Revolution* * (1924). A good one-volume account of the events from 1763 to 1776 is J. C. Miller, *Origins of the American Revolution* (1943). Bernhard Knollenberg, *Origin of the American Revolution, 1759–1766* (1960), stresses the variety of causes that irritated Americans in those years. O. M. Dickerson, *The Navigation Acts and the American Revolution* (1951), argues that the Navigation Acts were not a cause of the Revolution but that the creation in 1767 of an American Board of Customs Commissioners resulted in widespread "customs racketeering," which dissolved the cement of empire. A. M. Schlesinger, *The Colonial Merchants and the American Revolution* (1917), shows how the merchants initially took the lead in opposition to England but became wary as popular feeling seemed to threaten their own position.

Several books discuss the political and constitutional principles developed by the colonists before 1776. E. S. and H. M. Morgan, *The Stamp Act Crisis: Prologue to Revolution* (1953), describes the events and ideas of the years 1764–66; and E. S. Morgan, *Prologue to Revolution: Sources and Documents on the Stamp Act Crisis* * (1959), reprints many of the resolutions, petitions, newspaper articles, and pamphlets in which the colonists expressed their views. Later development of colonial opinion is treated in Carl Becker, *The Declaration of Independence* * (1922), and R. G. Adams, *The Political Ideas of the American Revolution* * (1922). C. H. McIlwain, *The American Revolution* * (1923), argues that the colonists' interpretation of the British Constitution was well grounded in historical precedent; but R. L. Schuyler, *Parliament and the British Empire* (1929), challenges McIlwain.

A number of able books describe the internal developments within different colonies in the years preceding independence. Robert Brown, *Middle-Class Democracy and the Revolution in Massachusetts* (1955), stresses the absence of internal class conflict, but R. J. Taylor finds more evidence of such conflict in the West in *Western Massachusetts in the Revolution* (1954). A good close-up of Boston is found in two biographies: J. C. Miller, *Sam Adams: Pioneer in Propaganda* (1936), and Esther Forbes, *Paul Revere and the World He Lived In* (1942). David Lovejoy, *Rhode Island Politics and the American Revolution* (1958), traces political divisions and shows that all sides in Rhode Island were united against the British. Carl Becker, *The History of Political Parties in the Province of New York, 1760–1776* * (1909), shows that in New York the Revolution was a contest not only about home rule but also about "who should rule at home." Similar studies for other states are Theodore Thayer, *Pennsylvania Politics and the Growth of Democracy, 1740–1776* (1954); C. A. Barker, *The Background of the Revolution in Maryland* (1940); H. J. Eckenrode, *The Revolution in Virginia* (1916); Carl Bridenbaugh, *Seat of Empire* (1950); and Oscar Zeichner, *Connecticut's Years of Controversy* (1950).

* Available in a paperback edition.

5

An American People

Although the colonists had moved slowly and reluctantly toward declaring independence, once the deed was done most of them had no regrets. There were, of course, loyalists, many of whom left for Canada. Of those who remained, some were ready to fight their countrymen for their king—some, but never enough to win. There were also men indifferent to who ruled them and willing to sell supplies to either side, depending on the price offered. But in every colony that joined in the Declaration of Independence, the patriots were sufficiently numerous, vociferous, and aggressive to outweigh the loyalists and the indifferent. Once the royal governments collapsed, it proved impossible to revive British authority except in the immediate vicinity of British guns.

The Winning of Independence

The Rebel Army   Perhaps because they could overawe the loyalists, the patriots counted too easily on doing the same to the British armies. After the rout on April 19 and the slaughter on June 17 (see pp. 98 and 99), they were inclined to believe that their militia could handle any force the British sent against them. George Washington knew better: the men encamped around Boston did have spirit, courage, and marksmanship, but they were not an army. To make them into one was Washington's first concern after taking command at Cambridge on July 3, 1775.

It was not simply a matter of instruction

and training in the art of war. Militia units had to be reorganized under a corps of officers appointed from above. In the process, many of the old officers lost rank and stalked off in disgust. Furthermore, the militia who had come to besiege Boston were used to electing their own officers and were touchy about taking orders from higher up. They were also used to short terms of service (for a local emergency or a particular campaign) and eager to get home to their crops. Wherever the enemy appeared, Americans from miles around would turn out to fight him; but they did not want to join the army. To join the army was to desert one's family for danger, discomfort, and disease hundreds of miles from home. The pay was low, and no pension system existed to compensate a man or his family for the loss of life or limb. It therefore took all of Washington's diplomacy and tact to persuade ten thousand militiamen to enlist until the end of 1776 as regular soldiers in the Continental army. In addition the provincial governments supplied him with about seven thousand short-term militiamen.

The total was much smaller than Washington had hoped for. Throughout the war Congress was able to provide him with an ample army of men on paper. But men with arms, legs, heads, and guns remained in short supply. Since Congress had no power either to raise money or to draft men, it was dependent on requisitions to the states for both; and when the states lagged in supplying their assigned

Major Campaigns of the Revolutionary War

Circled numbers ① are keyed to detail maps in the pages which follow. The following symbols are used to designate American and British forces:

◀━━━ American advance
◀▬▬▬▬ American retreat
⬅══ British advance
▭▭⟹ British retreat

quotas, Congress could do nothing to coerce them. Supplies were as hard to come by as men; Washington had to spend much of his time pleading for both and to fight the war with an army that was constantly in danger of dissolution.

The new army's first venture away from Boston began while Boston was still under siege, before independence was declared. In May 1775 militia under Ethan Allen and Benedict Arnold had captured Fort Ticonderoga without resistance and had gone on to take Crown Point (see map inset, p. 108). General Richard Montgomery moved up from Lake Champlain with a small force to capture Montreal on November 13, 1775. He then pushed on toward Quebec to meet Colonel Benedict Arnold, who was bringing more troops through the Maine woods. The Congress had invited the people of Canada to join their union, and though the Canadians had failed to respond, some reports suggested that they would welcome an invading army. In any case, it was desirable to strike at the British in Quebec and Montreal in order to forestall an attack from that direction. After a grueling winter march, the effective forces that converged on Quebec amounted to only a thousand men, and the Canadians showed no disposition to help them. They besieged the city through the winter, but smallpox, hunger, cold, and an unsuccessful assault so thinned their ranks that in the spring they retreated to Ticonderoga. The colonists made no further military effort to draw Canada into their union.

In the South the Americans fared better when Josiah Martin, the royal governor of North Carolina, tried to hold the colony with the help of loyalists. On February 27, 1776, at Moore's Creek Bridge, eleven hundred militia overwhelmingly defeated sixteen hundred loyalists and captured a welcome fifteen thousand pounds in cash. Four months later, when Generals Henry Clinton and Charles, Lord Cornwallis, and Admiral Sir Peter Parker arrived off Charles Town, South Carolina, with fifty ships and an army of three thousand men, few loyalists showed up to greet them. Attempting to enter Charles Town harbor on June 28, they were met by deadly fire from a seemingly impregnable fort constructed of palmetto logs and dirt. After a ten-hour duel the British withdrew and left Charles Town alone for the next four years.

In Massachusetts Washington had meanwhile built a force strong enough to close in on Boston. He began by occupying and fortifying Dorchester Heights, which overlooked the city on the south as Breed's Hill did on the north. This time the British did not try to storm the hills. Instead, on March 17, 1776, they departed by sea for Halifax, Nova Scotia, taking over a thousand loyalists with them.

A few months after the British evacuation of Boston, when Americans declared their independence, they appeared to be in a strong position. Although they were challenging the

world's greatest military and naval power and had failed to win Canada to their cause, they had overpowered the British army in the march from Concord, withstood its assaults at Breed's Hill, forced its withdrawal from Boston, and fought off the British navy at Charles Town. But the British war machine, always a slow starter, was now grinding into action. Parliament had authorized an army of fifty-five thousand, and, when recruitment lagged in England, the government hired thirty thousand German mercenaries, seventeen of them from Hesse-Cassel (hence the name Hessians).

The British plan was to split the colonies in two by occupying New York. General William Howe and his brother, Admiral Richard Howe, were given command. They would move on New York City by sea from Halifax; another force would descend from Canada by way of Lake Champlain and the Hudson River. Once they had taken New York and thus cut off communications and reinforcements between the rebels in the north and

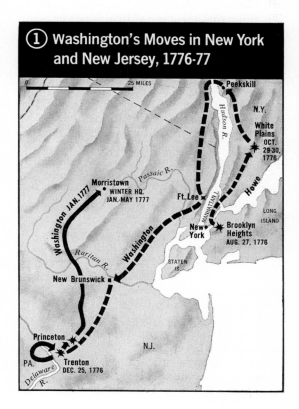

① Washington's Moves in New York and New Jersey, 1776-77

those in the south, the British could deal with each separately.

The Howes were authorized to end the war as soon as the colonists submitted. Hoping to end it before they began, they addressed a conciliatory letter to "George Washington, Esq." (thus ignoring his military status). But General Washington was not receiving letters for George Washington, Esq., letters that denied American independence even in the address. The Howes therefore proceeded according to plan. On August 12, 1776, they arrived in New York harbor with thirty-two thousand troops and ten thousand seamen (the city's normal population was twenty-five thousand) aboard four hundred transports and thirty warships. Ten days later twenty thousand of the troops landed on Long Island near Brooklyn.

Washington had twenty-three thousand men in the New York area, but most of them were inexperienced local militia. When Howe, with plenty of men to spare, launched both frontal and flank attacks, Washington was forced to withdraw to Manhattan with heavy losses. Thinking that this taste of British power might have chastened the Americans, Howe offered to confer about a settlement before any more blows were struck. Congress sent Franklin, John Adams, and Edward Rutledge to deal with him, but the resulting conference broke off when it turned out, as Washington had suspected, that Howe was empowered to negotiate only with submissive colonists, not with the proud representatives of an independent nation. In September the British drove Washington off Manhattan Island; and by November the Continental army, depleted by captures and desertions, was in full retreat across New Jersey.

Washington crossed the Delaware River into Pennsylvania on December 7. Now, with the river between him and the enemy, he planned his next move. The outlook was bleak. While pursuing him across New Jersey, the British had been able simultaneously to send a large force to Rhode Island, where on December 8 they occupied Newport. Washington's force was down to fewer than eight thousand effective fighting men, all of them dispirited, exhausted, ready to quit. By the end of the month all but fifteen hundred would have

completed their term of enlistment, and with winter coming on they would sling their packs, head for home, and let someone else fight the war. While he still had them, Washington attacked. On the night of December 25, 1776, in high, freezing winds, he shuttled his men back across the river, marched them nine miles to Trenton, and caught the enemy asleep and befuddled. With a loss of only four men he took nine hundred prisoners. A few days later at Princeton he dealt the British another smashing blow, and they pulled back to New Brunswick for the winter. The brilliant reversal so cheered the troops that Washington was able to persuade many of them to re-enlist. With spirits high again, the army moved into winter quarters at Morristown.

General Howe, contemplating the reverses that Washington had dealt him, had difficulty making up his mind about what to do when spring should come. After changing plans several times he finally decided to storm the rebel capital of Philadelphia, which, like New York, contained a large loyalist population. In July he took fifteen thousand men by sea from New York to the head of Chesapeake Bay. From there they marched north toward Philadelphia, the Hessians helping themselves to food, furniture, and women along the way. Washington intercepted them at Brandywine Creek; but, as on Long Island, Howe won the pitched battle and entered Philadelphia on September 26, 1777. When Washington challenged him a week later at Germantown, where most of the British troops were quartered, Howe again was victorious.

These defeats were inevitably discouraging for the colonists, but actually Howe's success was hollow. Though he had captured America's largest cities and repeatedly defeated her generals, he had captured no armies and he controlled only a small portion of American territory. And to the north of him disaster was brewing. General John Burgoyne, a vain, witty, and silly man, had been authorized by the high command in England to mount an expedition for a march south from Canada by the Lake Champlain route. He set out from Fort St. John's in June with four thousand British, three thousand Germans, fourteen hundred Indians, and a pleasing mistress to cheer him along. Everything went swimmingly

Battle of Princeton, January 3, 1777.

for a time. But on August 16 a force of New Hampshire militia under John Stark caught a British detachment at Bennington, killed over two hundred, and took seven hundred prisoners. As Burgoyne advanced he ran into more traps. His Indians, quick to sense what was coming, quietly left him. American forces, under Horatio Gates and Benedict Arnold, gathered ever stronger before him, and each time they clashed Burgoyne lost several hundred more men. On October 17, 1777, he finally surrendered at Saratoga.

The French Alliance Saratoga was one of the turning points of history, but not because it turned back any threat to the American armies. Burgoyne's march, if successful, would have signified little in a military sense; his surrender did not seriously reduce the British margin of superiority in troops and equipment. Saratoga had its great effect, not in New York or Philadelphia, but in London and Paris.

In London a complacent Parliament began to sense the possibility that England might lose the war. Better make peace, the ministry decided, and authorized a commission headed by Lord Carlisle to offer the Americans virtually everything they had previously demanded: renunciation of Parliamentary taxation, repeal of the Intolerable Acts, and suspension of every other objectionable act passed since 1763. Two years earlier such concessions would probably have kept the colonies within the empire. But by now the rebels found independence exhilarating. England's eagerness to have them back merely furnished them with the final weapon they needed to make their independence last: the recognition and assistance of France.

From the outset the Americans had been hoping for help from England's traditional enemy, and on November 29, 1775, Congress had appointed a secret committee to seek

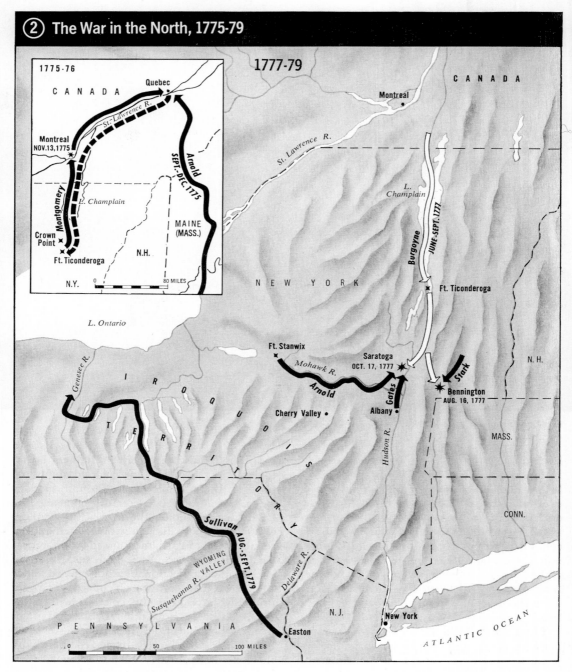

1775-76

1777-79

CANADA

Quebec

St. Lawrence R.

Montreal
NOV. 13, 1775

Arnold
SEPT.-DEC. 1775

Montgomery

L. Champlain

Crown
Point ✕

Ft. Ticonderoga

MAINE
(MASS.)

N.H.

N.Y.

0   80 MILES

CANADA

Montreal •

St. Lawrence R.

L.
Champlain

Burgoyne
JUNE-SEPT. 1777

Ft. Ticonderoga ✕

L. Ontario

NEW   YORK

N. H.

Genesee R.

I   R   O   Q   U   O   I   S

Ft. Stanwix ✕

Mohawk R.

Arnold

Saratoga
OCT. 17, 1777 ✸

Stark

Gates

Bennington
AUG. 16, 1777 ✸

Cherry Valley •

Albany •

T   E   R   R   I   T   O   R   Y

MASS.

CONN.

Sullivan
AUG.-SEPT. 1779

Hudson R.

WYOMING
VALLEY

Susquehanna R.

Delaware R.

N. J.

New York •

ATLANTIC OCEAN

P   E   N   N   S   Y   L   V   A   N   I   A

Easton •

0   50   100 MILES

foreign aid. Louis XVI, delighted by the rebellion of England's colonies, had sent Achard de Bonvouloir to observe the situation in America. With Bonvouloir's encouragement the committee dispatched Silas Deane, a shrewd and sophisticated Yankee, to negotiate with France. Deane arrived in Paris on July 7, 1776, to find that the French foreign minister, the comte de Vergennes, had already persuaded the king to help the American rebellion with a million livres worth of munitions and supplies. Furthermore, Spain had matched the amount. The goods were to be dispensed secretly through a fake trading company run by Pierre Beaumarchais (author of *The Barber of Seville*). They were Deane's for the asking, though whether as a gift or as a loan remained uncertain.

Deane's negotiations took place before news of the Declaration of Independence reached France, when secret assistance was all the Americans dared ask for. Once the Declaration had been announced, they hoped that France would recognize their independence and offer open assistance. To help Deane push these more ambitious requests, Congress sent Arthur Lee, who had been serving as a secret observer in London, and Benjamin Franklin, who arrived from Philadelphia in December 1776. The three men constituted a commission with power to make treaties of amity and commerce.

The French at this time envisaged America as an Arcadia peopled by noble savages and almost equally noble farmers, rich in nature's wisdom; Franklin, seeing what was expected, donned his fur cap and played the role to the hilt. Completely enchanted, the Parisians showered the arch-American with favors, but Vergennes and his royal master remained cautious. Besides furnishing supplies to the colonists they sometimes allowed American privateers the use of French harbors. They hesitated, however, to join in open war on England when the British armies, with the capture of New York, appeared to be winning.

As American military fortunes declined, Congress instructed the commissioners to go beyond their request for French assistance and to seek the deeper commitment of an alliance. All Franklin's charm was insufficient to win it. Vergennes wanted Spain by his side before he took on the British lion, and Spain was unwilling. Spain feared even to give open assistance to the Americans lest she encourage her own colonies to revolt.

When news of Saratoga reached Paris on December 3, 1777, Vergennes perceived at once that the American victory might produce a conciliatory temper in England, and the last thing he wanted was to see the rebellious colonies reconciled to the mother country. Franklin played on his fears, and Vergennes sent frantic messages to Spain. When Spain remained immovable, he finally told the commissioners that France was ready to enter into a treaty of commerce and amity and a treaty of alliance with the Americans. He indeed required an alliance before entering the war, in order to prevent the United States from mak-

British view of the battle of Saratoga.

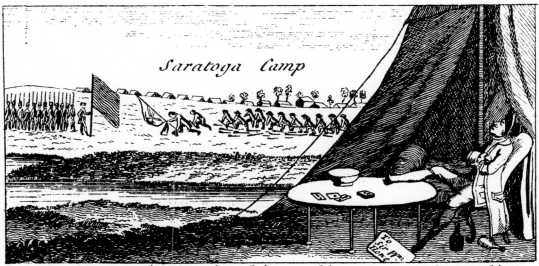

The Generals in America doing nothing, or worse than nothing.

Franklin played the role to the hilt.

ing peace before England was humbled.

The terms of the alliance, signed on February 6, 1778, were all that the United States could have wished for. The stated purpose of both parties was to maintain the independence of the United States. In case of war between France and England (which the signing of the treaty made inevitable), neither France nor the United States was to make peace without the consent of the other. France renounced all future claims to English territory on the continent of North America and agreed that any such territory captured in the war would go to the United States. These generous terms were less the result of American diplomatic skill than of French determination to weaken England and French distaste for further colonizing in the New World.

Even before the alliance the Americans had depended heavily on aid from France. The victory at Saratoga, for example, would have been impossible without French supplies. And French financial support helped to bolster American credit at a time when Congress, with no authority to tax, was financing the war with money begged from the states or manufactured by the printing presses. With the signing of the alliance the hopes of the Americans soared, for France was the first nation to recognize them as "one people," and she had the military and naval power to make that recognition meaningful.

From Saratoga to Yorktown   After the battle of Saratoga the British fought a cautious war, their dreams of easy victory gone. Howe, snug in Philadelphia during the winter of 1777–78, did not even try to attack Washington's wretched forces, who were starving and freezing in their winter quarters at nearby Valley Forge. In the spring Howe was replaced by Sir Henry Clinton, who was to prove somewhat less languid though no bolder. The spring of 1778 also brought France's entry into the war and American refusal of the Carlisle Commission's peace overtures (see p. 109). Uncertain of where France would throw her weight, the British high command decided to play safe and ordered Clinton to withdraw from Philadelphia to New York. There he should plan a major campaign in the South, where—according to the strategists—loyalists would lend a decisive hand.

At Valley Forge, as mild weather came on, Washington's forces thawed out and were drilled with Prussian precision by Baron Friedrich von Steuben, an idealist from the Old World who had come to help usher in the independence of the New. By June he and a good supply of provisions had restored the haggard men into a hard and maneuverable army. When Clinton pulled out of Philadelphia to march across New Jersey to New York, Washington kept pace with him on a parallel route and watched for a chance to strike. But the only opportunity that came (the battle of Monmouth Courthouse on June 28) was badly bungled by General Charles Lee, and the main body of Clinton's troops arrived safely in New York.

While the British and American armies were marching across New Jersey, the first French forces arrived in America—Vice-Admiral the comte d'Estaing with seventeen ships and four thousand troops. Washington proposed to use them in recovering Newport, and planned an assault with D'Estaing in charge of naval operations and with General John Sullivan and a French volunteer, the marquis de Lafayette, handling the French and American troops. But in August, just before the assault was to begin, a storm scattered and damaged the French fleet, and the land forces, which had already dug into battle positions, were forced to withdraw when reinforcements arrived from Clinton. D'Estaing took his ships to Boston to refit and, in November 1778, sailed south to protect the French West Indies.

The departure of D'Estaing was a serious disappointment to Washington, for the Americans had no means of their own to combat the British navy. It offered deadly support to British land troops along the coast, and it

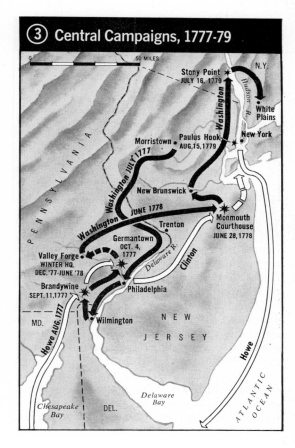

③ Central Campaigns, 1777-79

regularly sent raiding parties to devastate towns far from any army. Though the Americans commissioned hundreds of privateers (probably over two thousand in all), which rendered invaluable service in disrupting the merchant shipping, communications, and supply lines of the enemy, the privateers were no more a navy than the militia were an army; they were simply not up to engaging British warships in a sustained action.

The Congress had tried to create a navy, but could scrape together the money for only a few ships, which were no match for the royal navy. Nevertheless, one of them, commanded by the unpopular but unsinkable John Paul Jones, carried the war to the British Isles. Jones raided coastal towns and seized British ships. With French assistance he hoped to do much more. But the French navy preferred to fight its own war. In the only significant engagement in which American and French

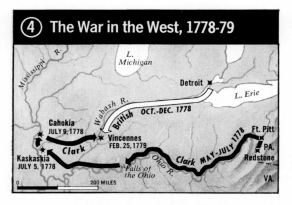

④ The War in the West, 1778-79

vessels fought side by side under his command (off Flamborough Head in the North Sea, September 1779) Jones got little help from his supporting force. He lost his flagship, the *Bonhomme Richard*, but not before he had boarded and captured the fifty-gun British *Serapis*.

Unfortunately there were not enough Joneses to divert the British navy from North America; and Clinton kept most of his troops near the coast within reach of naval assistance. Without naval assistance of his own Washington dared not risk an all-out assault on the British army, and after following it from New Jersey to New York he had camped outside the city and waited for the French fleet to return or to draw the British ships to other waters. For a year and a half he waited while the fighting was carried on mostly by small forces remote from New York, the strategic center. During the summer and fall of 1778 the British sent a force of loyalists and Iroquois warriors to massacre settlers in the Wyoming Valley of Pennsylvania (July 3 to 6) and in the Cherry Valley of New York (November 11). In December a British expeditionary force landed in Georgia and easily subdued the small population, many of whom were loyalists. Savannah fell on December 29, and the province reverted to British rule. Meanwhile, George Rogers Clark, a twenty-five-year-old Virginian, took a handful of men to the Illinois country and by the end of February 1779 had captured Cahokia, Kaskaskia, and Vincennes for the Americans. When summer came, General Sullivan marched four thousand men against the Iroquois and broke their power forever, while the troops around New York City scored a

few minor morale-building victories against local British garrisons (at Stony Point on July 16, 1779, and at Paulus Hook on August 15, 1779). In the fall of 1779 all prospect of French naval support disappeared when D'Estaing took his fleet from the West Indies back to France.

Encouraged by the recapture of Georgia, Clinton now went ahead with the southern campaign he had been ordered to conduct. Leaving an army equal to Washington's to hold New York, he pulled his troops out of Newport (thus freeing New England of all British troops) and, in December 1779, sailed with an expeditionary force of over eight thousand for Charles Town, South Carolina. He took it on May 12, 1780, along with its defending general, Benjamin Lincoln, and his entire force of fifty-five hundred men. The Carolinas now lay open to a British sweep. But Clinton was still cautious. Departing for New York on June 8, he left Cornwallis in command, with instructions not to fan out beyond South Carolina. If the British forces were spread too thin they might not be able to hold what they had gained. But the British winning streak was not yet over. On August 16,

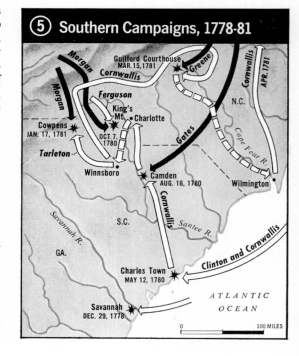

⑤ Southern Campaigns, 1778-81

1780, near Camden Cornwallis intercepted and routed over three thousand men under General Horatio Gates who were coming to the defense of South Carolina. Washington sent General Nathanael Greene, his ablest commander, to pick up the pieces.

In December, when Greene reached Charlotte, North Carolina, to assume command of the southern forces, he found less than two thousand men, poorly equipped and without supplies. With the assistance of Daniel Morgan, a Virginia rifleman, Greene built a mobile fighting unit, which owed much to the Southern militiamen who appeared whenever a fight was in the offing. A group of these tough campaigners had already demonstrated their worth before Greene arrived by capturing a British force atop King's Mountain in North Carolina (October 7, 1780). Greene and Morgan lured Cornwallis into trap after trap, chewing off a bit of his force here and a bit there (notably at Hannah's Cowpens on the Broad River, January 17, 1781, and at Guilford Courthouse, March 15).

In April 1781 the two generals turned their backs on each other: Greene headed south to pick off more British outposts in South Carolina and Georgia, while Cornwallis, disregarding his instructions from Clinton, set out to conquer Virginia. By July Greene had pushed the British in Georgia back to Savannah and in South Carolina back to Charles Town; Cornwallis had run through Virginia and had settled at Portsmouth, from which he later moved to Yorktown. Portsmouth and Yorktown both lay on the seacoast, the only safe place for a British army in America; but the coast would remain safe only so long as the British navy commanded the sea. Without naval support Cornwallis could be cut off from his own forces in Charles Town and Savannah and from Clinton's forces in the north.

In New York Clinton still looked out at Washington's waiting army and Washington still waited for the French navy. The French had sent five thousand land troops under the comte de Rochambeau to occupy Newport in July 1780, but the eleven warships that accompanied them under the comte de Barras had been promptly bottled up inside the harbor by a superior British fleet.

In May 1781 Washington's patience was

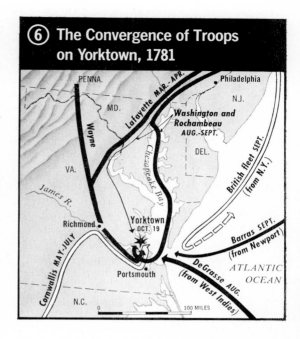

⑥ The Convergence of Troops on Yorktown, 1781

finally rewarded by news that Admiral de Grasse with twenty warships was sailing from France for the West Indies and would detach part of his force to assist a campaign on the mainland. In conference with Rochambeau Washington decided that this was his opportunity to close in on New York. But on August 14 word arrived that De Grasse was heading for the Chesapeake with his whole fleet; he would, however, be able to stay only a short time. Washington immediately decided to give up the planned New York campaign and to dash south for a try at Cornwallis. Leaving behind a part of his troops to fool Clinton, he marched the rest to the head of Chesapeake Bay and placed them aboard transports for the last leg of the journey. Barras meanwhile had managed to slip out of Newport and was sailing south loaded with siege guns. When the British naval squadrons discovered what was going on, they hurried to the Chesapeake to drive off Barras and De Grasse but found themselves outnumbered and outgunned. French naval power was at last decisive. Back went the British fleet to New York, and Washington with fifty-seven hundred Continentals, thirty-one hundred militia, and seven thousand French began to close in on Yorktown. On October 19, when

Washington and his generals at Yorktown.

a relief expedition was already under way from New York, Cornwallis gave up. With the bands playing "The World Turned Upside Down," seven thousand British troops marched out of Yorktown and stacked their arms in surrender.

Peace   Yorktown was as much a French as an American victory. And because the war too was a French war, it could not end at Yorktown. France was ready for peace but encumbered by a commitment to Spain. Vergennes, upon concluding the treaty of alliance with the United States on February 6, 1778, had continued his efforts to bring Spain into the war; he finally succeeded after agreeing not to stop fighting until Spain had won Gibraltar from England. Since the United States had agreed not to make peace without French consent, Americans were indirectly bound to await the capture of Gibraltar also. Spain, on the other hand, refused to recognize the independence of the United States, and after entering the war on June 21, 1779, accorded only a devious and frosty tolerance to the American cause. Once she had seized the thinly held territory of West Florida (a former Spanish possession) from the British, she confined herself mainly to blockading Gibraltar.

After the defeat at Yorktown, most Englishmen were ready to give up the struggle for the colonies even though George III was bent on continuing it. On March 20, 1782, Lord North was forced from office, and the king was obliged to accept a ministry favorable to peace, which immediately sent agents to get in touch with American commissioners in France.

Congress had first formulated American war aims in August 1779, when it optimistically sent John Adams to France as minister plenipotentiary. Adams was then forbidden to enter into any peace negotiations with Great Britain unless she first recognized the United States as a sovereign, free, and independent state. After that recognition had been granted, he was to insist on certain boundaries for the new nation: the Mississippi on the west, the thirty-first parallel and the Flint and St. Mary's rivers on the south, and roughly the present boundary on the north.

In June 1781 the French ambassador to the United States, the Chevalier de la Luzerne, persuaded Congress to revise its arrangements for making peace. John Adams was replaced as sole negotiator by a five-man commission consisting of himself, John Jay (minister to Spain), Franklin (minister to France), Henry Laurens (designated as minister to the Netherlands but captured by the British en route and held in the Tower of London), and Thomas Jefferson (who was unable to go and dropped from the commission). The commissioners' instructions were weak: they were still to insist on British recognition of American independence before undertaking peace negotiations, but they were free to accept any settlement "as circumstances may direct and as the state of the belligerent and the disposition of the mediating powers may direct." What was worse, they must do nothing without the knowledge and concurrence of the French, and indeed must be governed by their advice and opinion.

These instructions put the commissioners under the direction of Vergennes, a position none of them relished. When secret information reached them that he would not support the American demand for prior recognition of independence, and that his secretary, Rayneval, had secretly encouraged the British to think of a boundary well to the east of the Mississippi, with Spain and England dividing up the territory between, they decided they would do better to negotiate with the British separately rather than to sit down at the peace table under French direction. Violating their instructions, they negotiated with British representatives without insisting on advance recognition of independence, and they did not keep Vergennes informed of what they were doing. Nor did they get all they wanted in the negotiations. Franklin, who had hoped to acquire Canada as a fourteenth state and to secure trading privileges in the Empire, got neither.

Nevertheless, by playing on British desires to destroy the American alliance with France, the commissioners were able to secure both recognition of independence and the boundaries prescribed in John Adams' original instructions. In preliminary articles signed on November 30, 1782, they presented this diplomatic triumph to Vergennes as an accomplished fact. Actually there had been no violation of the alliance, for the treaty based on the articles was not to go into effect until France and England had concluded a treaty of their own. The commissioners' coup enabled Vergennes to exert pressure on Spain to give up the fight for Gibraltar, and in the end she settled for East and West Florida and Minorca. The final treaties were signed at Paris on September 3, 1783, and the last British troops left New York on November 25. The Declaration of Independence was at last a description, not a wish.

The Experimental Period

At Lexington, Concord, and Bunker Hill Americans had fought against Parliamentary taxation. After July 2, 1776, they had fought for independence, though in the beginning probably few of them had any clear idea of what independence would mean besides the end of British tyranny. Between 1776 and 1789 they explored the possibilities of their new freedom. These thirteen years may be considered the Experimental Period in American history, the time when Americans were trying their wings, discovering their nationality. They formulated ideas and ideals that had been only half articulate before, and they found ways and means to put their ideas and ideals into practice. During this period the Americanisms discussed earlier (see Chapter 3) underwent further development and some of them were transformed from characteristic attitudes into national principles.

The Fruition of Americanisms American ideas about the separation of church and state and about education advanced less rapidly during the Experimental Period than did political and social concepts. But the assumption that widespread education was desirable did show itself in a revival of schooling, which had lapsed during the war, and in the proliferation of new educational institutions, most of of them private. Many academies were founded (especially in New England) to furnish instruction at the secondary level, and sometimes beyond, to both boys and girls. And the number of colleges in the United States

North America in 1783

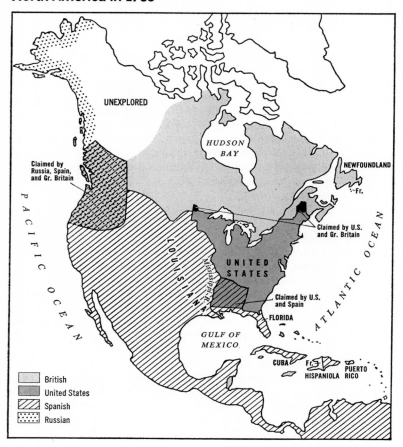

UNEXPLORED

HUDSON BAY

NEWFOUNDLAND

Fr.

Claimed by Russia, Spain, and Gr. Britain

PACIFIC OCEAN

LOUISIANA

Mississippi R.

UNITED STATES

Claimed by U.S. and Gr. Britain

ATLANTIC OCEAN

Claimed by U.S. and Spain

FLORIDA

GULF OF MEXICO

CUBA

Fr.

HISPANIOLA

PUERTO RICO

British

United States

Spanish

Russian

doubled: in 1776 there were nine; by 1789 as many more had been opened or chartered; and every state but Delaware had at least one in operation or being organized. Writers in newspapers and pamphlets argued about what kind of education was best suited to Americans. Many demanded that it be made more practical, and new textbooks reoriented traditional subjects like arithmetic and grammar in this direction.

The colonists' wariness of allowing their clergy a hand in government gave rise to a greater separation of church and state. Though most states continued to levy taxes in support of the Protestant religion, the Anglican Church lost the exclusive claims to that support which it had enjoyed in the Southern colonies. Under all the state constitutions a man could at least specify which Protestant church his taxes should support. And in Virginia the principle of complete separation of church and state received its finest expression in an act drafted by Thomas Jefferson and adopted by the Virginia legislature in 1786. Beginning with the assertion that "Almighty God hath created the mind free," the act provided that "no man shall be compelled to frequent or support any religious worship, place, or ministry whatsoever."

Jefferson was also author of the phrase which translated social mobility into an American principle. By declaring on July 4, 1776, that "all men are created equal," the United States committed itself to a doctrine that was to prove the world's most powerful lever for social and political change. The declaration was intended simply to justify the colonists' withdrawal from the mother country, which had refused to treat them as the equals of Englishmen. But no great imagination was required to discern wider implications in Jefferson's axiomatic statement of human equality.

Its relevance to Negro slavery was inescapable. As soon as Americans complained that British taxation would reduce them to slavery, they began to feel uneasy about their own enslavement of Africans; they even foreswore the slave trade in their nonimportation agreements. In the Experimental Period most of the states, Southern as well as Northern, forbade the further importation of slaves, and the Northern states passed laws for the eventual liberation of those already within their borders. Massachusetts seems to have rid herself of the institution by judicial decision: her constitution, echoing the Declaration of Independence, stated that "all men are born free and equal," and her courts interpreted the phrase literally. With the coming of peace newspaper articles warned that Americans had won only partial freedom; as one writer, who signed himself "Vox Africanorum," put it, "Thousands are yet groaning under their chains; slavery and oppression are not yet banished [from] the land." Though appeals of this kind led many men to free their slaves even in the South, slavery there continued and grew in strength while simultaneously the doctrine of equality was growing elsewhere, until at last the one could not exist beside the other.

The doctrine of equality was as hostile to aristocracy as to slavery. Having got along without a titled nobility for a century and a half, Americans were determined to continue without one and looked suspiciously at anything that smacked of special privilege. States forbade their citizens to accept titles from foreign nations. And when officers of the Continental army formed the Society of the Cincinnati in 1783, they met with a storm of protest from critics who feared that the association might become the nucleus of an aristocracy. In Connecticut even a medical society, seeking to raise the standards of the profession by licensing practitioners, was at first denied a charter because its members were to be chosen for life and might thus become a privileged order.

The Revolutionary War itself had an equalizing effect on property: wealthy merchants had lost heavily from the British blockade of commerce, while many a poor farmer had prospered in selling his produce to the armies. Wartime finance, with its reliance on steadily inflating paper currency, favored debtors (who were most often farmers) at the expense of creditors. The confiscation and sale of loyalists' lands and the abolition of primogeniture (the inheritance of a man's entire estate by his eldest son) by the state governments likewise contributed to a more equal distribution of property by breaking up some of the larger concentrations of wealth. By the time the war ended many Americans regarded equality of property as a goal in itself. When economic depression struck in the 1780's, legislators in some states sponsored bills favoring debtors, on the grounds that republican government required a general equality of property.

The emerging doctrine of equality can also be detected in the reform of voting laws. Although property qualifications had disfranchised only a small minority in most colonies (because most Americans owned property) and though there had been few complaints, every state but Massachusetts reduced the amount of property required for voting. There remained, nevertheless, a strong belief that political rights should be confined to property-holders. Only two states, Georgia and Pennsylvania, opened the franchise to all taxpayers. And in most states there were higher property qualifications for holding office than for voting. In the eighteenth century it was assumed that a man without property had no reason to participate in government either by voting or by holding office. According to Locke the purpose of government was to protect property, so a man without any was thought to have little stake in society. Moreover, only property could free a man from the control of employers or landlords. Without property a man was not a free agent and could not be trusted with authority or even with a voice in the selection of those who were to wield it. Hence the concern already noted for the maintenance of a wide distribution of property. If America were to become like Europe, with a

Crèvecœur on the American

I wish I could be acquainted with the feelings and thoughts which must agitate the heart and present themselves to the mind of an enlightened Englishman, when he first lands on this continent.... If he travels through our rural districts he views not the hostile castle, and the haughty mansion, contrasted with the clay-built hut and miserable cabin, where cattle and men help to keep each other warm, and dwell in meanness, smoke, and indigence. A pleasing uniformity of decent competence appears throughout our habitations. The meanest of our loghouses is a dry and comfortable habitation. Lawyer or merchant are the fairest titles our towns afford; that of a farmer is the only appellation of the rural inhabitants of our country. It must take some time ere he can reconcile himself to our dictionary, which is but short in words of dignity, and names of honour.... We have no princes, for whom we toil, starve, and bleed: we are the most perfect society now existing in the world.

From Michel Guillaume Jean de Crèvecœur, "What Is an American?" *Letters from an American Farmer,* 1782.

mass of propertyless workers and peasants, liberty would fall with equality; and authority, concentrated in the hands of a few, would turn into tyranny.

Authority in the hands of the many, of the people, was the essential characteristic of a republic; and with independence colonial insistence on responsible representative government turned into a conscious pursuit of republicanism. Although nothing in the Declaration of Independence had precluded the possibility of monarchy, Americans took it for granted that the new states would be republics. After severing their ties with England, Connecticut and Rhode Island, which in effect were republics already, simply continued the governments defined by their old charters. In other colonies the provincial congress which replaced the representative assembly (often with the same membership) acted without formal authority until independence was declared. Then, sooner or later, it drafted a written constitution establishing and defining a new government, usually similar in structure to the old one but more responsible to the people.

Since the colonial representative assembly (or lower house) had always been the branch of government most directly dependent on the people, the state constitutions gave the greatest powers to the lower houses of the new legislatures. In some states the lower house chose both the upper house and the governor. Only Pennsylvania, which had had a unicameral legislature since 1701, actually did without an upper house or a governor, but everywhere they had less authority than their colonial counterparts.

Determination that the government should be the servant of the people and not their master also prompted the inclusion of bills of rights in most of the state constitutions. The Virginia Bill of Rights began by asserting that "all men are by nature equally free and independent, and have certain inherent rights, of which, when they enter into a state of society, they cannot by any compact deprive or divest their posterity." It then enumerated the rights that lay beyond the reach of government, such as freedom of religion and of the press and the right to trial by jury.

In most states, after the provincial congress had drafted and approved a constitution, it went into effect without being submitted to a popular vote. But Massachusetts (the last state to adopt a constitution) elected a special convention to draft hers and submitted its work to direct vote by the people. Once it had been ratified in 1780, it could be changed only by another popularly elected convention called for that specific purpose. This was a step which other states had groped for but never quite reached. The purpose of writing out a constitution was to set limits to government by a fundamental law, embodying the will of the people. British jurists had often maintained that the unwritten British Constitution, consisting of traditions and customs, was superior to government, but custom and tradition had failed to protect the colonists from what they regarded as tyranny by the British government. They wanted something in black and white by which to measure any departure by their own governments from the proper limits of authority. They began to get what they wanted when their provincial congresses wrote and adopted state constitutions. But keen observers soon noted a flaw in this procedure: as the town of Concord pointed out in 1776, a constitution adopted by a legislative body could be altered or abolished by the same body and thus would constitute no protection against legislative tyranny. The device of a special convention and popular ratification elevated the constitution above the legislature and made it easier for the other branches of government to nullify unconstitutional legislation. The courts, for example, could and would refuse to enforce any law that violated the constitution. The Massachusetts invention of the constitutional convention was so widely admired by other Americans that subsequent constitution-making in America followed the Massachusetts method.

Building a National Government   The same insistence on responsible government that resulted in written constitutions and constitutional conventions operated for a long time against the creation of an effective national government. Americans, like other men of the eighteenth century, believed that republican government was not adaptable to large areas. In a large republic the central legislature must inevitably sit so remote from most of its constituents that it would eventually escape their control and thus cease to be republican. On the other hand, a small republic could never survive in a world of aggressive large nations. There was only one way, it was thought, to overcome these difficulties: a number of small republics might join in a federation and exert their united power for specific purposes.

Americans had formed such a federation in 1774 in the Continental Congress, and after independence the Congress had continued to exercise governmental powers for the whole nation. It was composed of delegates (usually several from each state) appointed annually by the state legislatures. Each state had one vote, which was determined by the majority of its delegates (if they were evenly divided the state's vote was lost).

In the absence of a more effective central organization, the Congress served a useful purpose. But it existed only by common consent, and from the beginning the members felt the need for a more binding union. As Americans joined against a common enemy and became aware of their shared principles and beliefs, their feeling of nationality grew stronger. Something more than an unstable succession of congresses was necessary to embody this sentiment and to demonstrate to other nations that the United States was not a mere diplomatic alliance. Congress accordingly, in the intervals between dealing with the everyday problems of the war, often discussed the formation of a permanent national government. As early as July 12, 1776, a committee had brought in the draft of a constitution, but acceptance had foundered on how expenses and voting power should be apportioned among the states, and on the old question of Western policy. This earliest proposal would have given considerable governmental authority to a national legislature; but as the state governments became more firmly entrenched, they grew increasingly reluctant to surrender any part of their power to a central body.

On November 17, 1777, Congress finally agreed on a constitution to be presented to the state legislatures for approval or rejection. The Articles of Confederation provided for a congress like the existing one. Each state, whatever its size, was still to have only one

---

Monroe on the American

You desire information whether it is the intention of Congress to extend their foreign appointments. At present I believe it is not. The idea seems to prevail that secretarys of legation are absolutely useless. the motive or cause which originally gave birth to the office in Europe does not apply here. there a nobleman held the office in quality of his rank in the court, tho' destitute of the necessary talents to discharge its duties, in consequence of which it became necessary to appoint a person who did and annex him to the legation. but with us this is not the case. we shall appoint the man, the minister, in consideration of his talents only. why it hath been adopted at all, arose from a ridiculous and servile limitation of the usages of Europe in the first instances and the last from a cause wh. I cannot explain to you out of cypher. The only argument in favor of it is, it will teach young men to form ministers themselves, yet I doubt whether this is not rather visionary than real, for I question much whether service in our different publick offices will not be equally or more instructive.

From James Monroe, Letter to William Short, 1786.

vote, to be cast, as before, by delegates appointed by the state legislatures; each state (by taxing itself) was to contribute to the common expenses according to the value of its lands; none was to be deprived of its Western lands for the benefit of the United States; and each was to retain its "sovereignty, freedom and independence, and every power, jurisdiction, and right," not expressly delegated to Congress. Congress was permitted to decide on war or peace, appoint military and naval officers, requisition the states for men and money, send and receive ambassadors, enter into treaties and alliances, establish a post office, coin money, borrow money or issue paper money on the credit of the United States, fix weights and measures, regulate Indian affairs, and settle disputes between states.

Although the states found much to object to in the Articles of Confederation the need to give permanent form to the union moved all but Maryland to accept it by 1779. Maryland's refusal, though probably prompted by narrow, partisan, and pecuniary motives, forced the settlement of a problem which might have wrecked the union—the problem of Western lands.

The West had always been a divisive force, as Bacon's Rebellion, the failure of the Albany Congress, and the Regulator movement all testified. Even more serious trouble lay ahead. Colonial assemblies from Pennsylvania southward had failed to extend full representation to their Western regions as population increased there. Pennsylvania remedied the inequality in her state constitution, but Virginia and the Carolinas did not, and the result was Western resentment against the Eastern-dominated state governments.

Concurrent with these internal disputes the state governments quarreled with one another about the West. The Revolution had dissolved their ties to England but not their territorial boundaries, which had been fixed by royal charters. By their charters, Georgia, the Carolinas, Virginia, Connecticut, and Massachusetts extended to the Pacific Ocean, while Maryland, Delaware, Pennsylvania, New Jersey, and Rhode Island were limited to a few hundred miles on the seacoast. The "landless" states wanted Congress to take control of unoccupied Western lands and restrict the West-

ern boundaries of the "landed" states. The landed states resisted any such proposal and squabbled with one another over their conflicting charters. Virginia, whose charter was the oldest, could claim most of the West all to herself. The people of every state, when they looked west, found reason for jealousy or distrust of their neighbors.

The problem was aggravated by land speculation. Before the war, speculators from Pennsylvania, Maryland, and New Jersey (all landless states) had purchased land from the Indians and sought authorization from the king to establish a new colony (Vandalia) in the Ohio Valley. Though bitterly opposed by Virginia's Ohio Company, they had been on the verge of success when the Revolution upset their plans. Now they argued that Congress had inherited the king's authority over all unoccupied lands; and, supported by their state governments, they pressed Congress to recognize their claims. The landed states had fought them off by including in the Articles of Confederation a guarantee that no state should be deprived of territory for the benefit of the United States. But Maryland stubbornly refused to approve the articles as long as the proposed union lacked control over Western lands. Without her the union was stalled, for it was not to go into effect until unanimously approved.

Maryland could produce better arguments than the mere greed of her land speculators. The landed states, she pointed out, would be able to command such an abundant source of revenue by selling their Western lands that their citizens would pay few or no taxes. People from the landless states would consequently move to the landed ones. Maryland, next door to the leviathan Virginia, would be depopulated.

In Virginia the sentiment for union was strong, and some patriots wanted to give up the state's Western territory, which they thought was too large for a single republican government anyhow. Rather than jeopardize republicanism in Virginia, they preferred to see new states formed in the West and joined to the old ones by the Articles of Confederation. Thomas Jefferson accordingly led Virginia (on January 2, 1781) to offer Congress her claims to all lands north of the Ohio. The

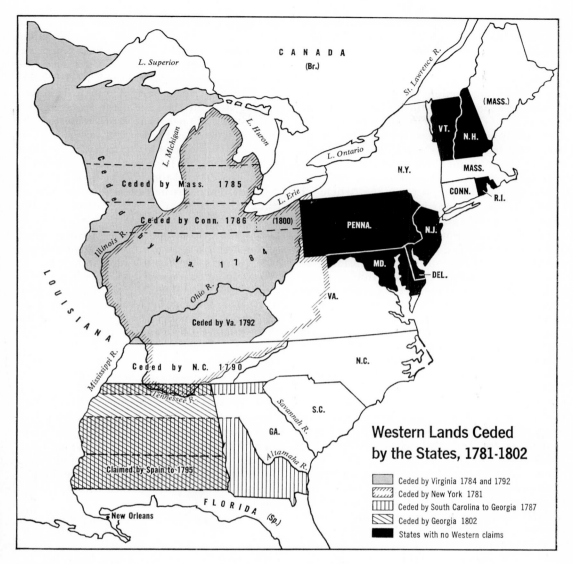

C A N A D A
(Br.)

L. Superior

L. Michigan

L. Huron

St. Lawrence R.

L. Ontario

L. Erie

Ceded by Mass. 1785

Ceded by Conn. 1786   (1800)

Illinois R.

Ceded by Va. 1784

Ohio R.

Ceded by Va. 1792

L O U I S I A N A

Mississippi R.

Ceded by N.C. 1790

Tennessee R.

Savannah R.

Claimed by Spain to 1795

GA.

Altamaha R.

New Orleans

F L O R I D A (Sp.)

(MASS.)

VT.   N.H.

N.Y.

MASS.

CONN.

R.I.

PENNA.

N.J.

MD.

DEL.

VA.

N.C.

S.C.

Western Lands Ceded by the States, 1781-1802

(light shade)	Ceded by Virginia 1784 and 1792
(diagonal hatch)	Ceded by New York 1781
(vertical hatch)	Ceded by South Carolina to Georgia 1787
(cross hatch)	Ceded by Georgia 1802
(black)	States with no Western claims

transfer was contingent on a number of conditions which in effect canceled speculative claims to the region and required that the land be divided into "distinct republican States" which should ultimately be admitted to the union on equal terms with the old ones. When Virginia's cession was made known, Maryland capitulated (though the speculators still tried to block her) and approved the Articles of Confederation in February 1781. New York had already ceded her shadowy Western claims, and the other landed states eventually followed the example that she and Virginia had set (Georgia held out until 1802).

Congress under the Confederation   In the Articles of Confederation the American people got what most of them at that time wanted. Having just suffered from the power of a distant British government, they were wary of allowing much authority to their own central government. They gave Congress no power to enact laws; it could only pass resolutions or make recommendations. They gave it no power to levy taxes; instead it must ask the states for funds. In fact Congress was allowed less authority than the colonists had once acknowledged in Parliament: Congress did not even have the right to regulate trade. The disadvantages of such a powerless central government soon became apparent.

After the coming of peace diminished the urgency of united action, the states became increasingly enamored of their own power and increasingly casual, even contemptuous, in their relations to Congress, ignoring its resolutions, refusing to fill its requisitions for funds, sending inferior men to represent them or sometimes none at all. Congress was unable to cope with the situation because the Articles of Confederation had provided it with no means to enforce obedience. The weakness of the national government made the years from 1783 to 1789, in the phrase of one historian, the "Critical Period" of American history.

A man elected to Congress during these years might arrive at the meeting place on the appointed day and find a dozen or more delegates like himself eager to proceed to business. But the Articles of Confederation required that each state be represented by at least two delegates, and that the representatives of at least seven states be present to make a quorum. Unless more than seven states were represented, every decision had to be unanimous; and the assent of nine states was necessary in most matters having to do with war and peace (including treaties) and with appropriating money. Because the states were often slow about appointing delegates and the delegates themselves slow in taking up their duties, the first arrivals at a session sometimes had to wait several weeks before enough members were present to transact business. Even after a session was organized, it led a precarious existence; for if one or two delegates fell sick, the rest might have to twiddle their thumbs until more arrived or the sick got well.

Each delegate was elected for a one-year term and was prohibited from serving for more than three years in six. As a result, the membership of Congress was constantly shifting. The government was further handicapped by the failure of the Articles of Confederation to provide a regular executive department. Congress exercised executive powers through special commissions and committees and achieved a degree of continuity by appointing three secretaries to manage crucial executive mat-

ters. Benjamin Lincoln, the first Secretary of War, served until 1783. After his resignation the office was vacant until Henry Knox was appointed in 1785. Knox served as long as the Articles of Confederation lasted. Robert Morris, the Superintendent of Finance, stayed until 1784; but then his office reverted to a committee of Congress. Robert Livingston, the first Secretary for Foreign Affairs, lasted less than two years; after his resignation the office was vacant until John Jay was appointed in 1784. Jay retained the office until 1789.

These officers struggled to give the United States the appearance of a government. But Congress, pursuing its intermittent existence, belied the appearance. Even when it could scrape together a quorum it had no permanent headquarters or capitol. A mutiny in the Philadelphia barracks frightened it out of that city in 1783, and thereafter the delegates wandered from Princeton to Annapolis to Trenton to New York—talking endlessly about where they should settle permanently. Shortly after they began their travels, Oliver Ellsworth, a congressman from Connecticut, observed dryly, "It will soon be of very little consequence where Congress go, if they are not made respectable as well as responsible, which can never be done without giving them a power to perform engagements as well as make them." Congress, in short, had responsibility without power. It could recommend endlessly but no one either inside or outside the United States paid much attention to what it recommended.

The impotence of Congress made the United States a beggar in the eyes of the world. During the Revolution, Congress had boldly capitalized on popular enthusiasm for the cause of independence by printing paper money, but the money had become worthless before the war's end. Congress had also begged money and supplies from France, but after the peace France preferred to keep her ally poor and humble. Dutch bankers, with more vision than many Americans, did continue to lend. But when Congress turned to the states for funds or for the power to levy a 5 per cent tariff on imports, the states turned the beggar down. The power to levy tariffs would have required the unanimous approval of the states, and each time it was proposed (in 1781 and

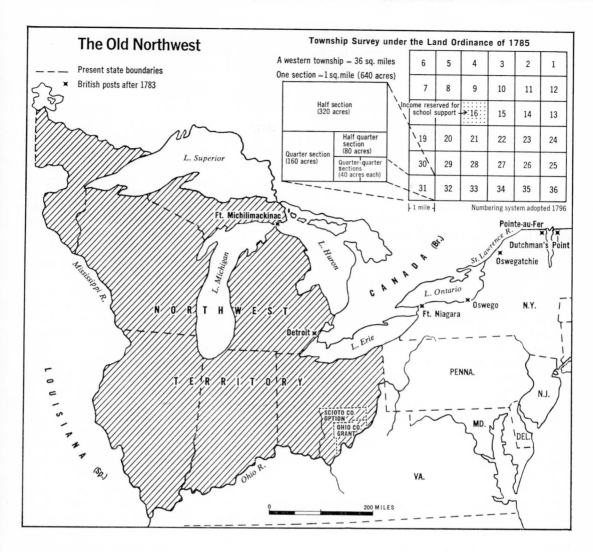

The Old Northwest

- - - - Present state boundaries
× British posts after 1783

Township Survey under the Land Ordinance of 1785

A western township = 36 sq. miles
One section = 1 sq. mile (640 acres)

Half section (320 acres)

Quarter section (160 acres)

Half quarter section (80 acres)

Quarter-quarter sections (40 acres each)

6	5	4	3	2	1
7	8	9	10	11	12
Income reserved for school support → 16			15	14	13
19	20	21	22	23	24
30	29	28	27	26	25
31	32	33	34	35	36

├ 1 mile ┤   Numbering system adopted 1796

L. Superior

Ft. Michilimackinac

L. Michigan

L. Huron

CANADA (Br.)

St. Lawrence R.

Pointe-au-Fer
Dutchman's Point
Oswegatchie

L. Ontario

Oswego

Ft. Niagara

N.Y.

Mississippi R.

N O R T H W E S T

Detroit

L. Erie

PENNA.

N.J.

L O U I S I A N A (Sp.)

T E R R I T O R Y

SCIOTO CO. OPTION
OHIO CO. GRANT

MD.

DEL.

VA.

Ohio R.

0   200 MILES

again in 1783) at least one state refused; and the others insisted on conditions that would have made the power meaningless anyhow.

The one area in which the United States enjoyed at least the appearance of power was the wilderness north of the Ohio River, a region thinly populated by squatters, Indians, and Frenchmen. When Virginia offered to cede the area in 1781, Congress had been prevented from taking any formal action to accept it because of pressure from speculators who objected to the terms attached to the cession. Early in 1784, when Virginia renewed the offer, Congress was stalled for lack of a quorum. But by March 1 enough members were present to act favorably, and the United States gained formal authority over the Northwest.

Now Congress might begin to raise the funds it needed by selling land in the newly acquired territory. On April 23 the delegates passed an ordinance, drafted by Thomas Jefferson, which fulfilled the terms of Virginia's cession. It divided the territory into states each of which was to be admitted into the Union on equal terms with the existing states as soon as its free population equaled any of theirs. Until then the inhabitants could govern themselves according to the constitution and laws of any of the existing states.

To prepare for the sale of lands to individuals, Congress passed an ordinance in 1785 providing that the Northwest be surveyed into townships six miles square along lines running east-west and north-south. Each township was divided into thirty-six lots one mile square (640 acres). A lot (later called a section) was the smallest unit that could be purchased, and neither a township nor a lot was to be sold for less than a dollar an acre in specie. To speed up the transformation of the national domain into hard cash, land offices were to be established in all the states.

Surveying and the settlement of Indian claims proceeded slowly. Before the lands were ready for public sale, a group of ambitious and not very scrupulous speculators from New England came to Congress with a proposition. Calling themselves, like an earlier group, the Ohio Company, they offered to buy a million and a half acres for which they would pay in currency so depreciated that the price amounted to less than ten cents an acre in specie. Presumptuous as the offer was, the United States needed the money desperately, and Congress decided to accept it. The Ohio Company also agreed to take an option on five million additional acres, to be turned over to a subsidiary company known as the Scioto Company. By no coincidence, this company included several congressmen.

To oblige the Ohio Company, Congress passed a new ordinance for governing the Northwest. Jefferson's ordinance of 1784 had never gone into operation, because the area as yet contained no authorized settlers. It did, however, contain many squatters who had helped themselves to public lands and stoutly resisted eviction. Because of the difficulty anticipated in establishing property rights against squatters, and because of the frontier's reputation for violence and disorder, many Easterners believed that congressional rule would be more appropriate than self-government during the initial years of settlement. Accordingly, the Northwest Ordinance of 1787 provided for a period during which a governor, a secretary, and a court of three judges, all appointed by Congress, would hold full powers. Once the population had reached five thousand free adult males, a representative legislature would be established, but none of its actions would

be valid without the approval of the governor who would still be appointed by Congress. The legislature could send a representative to Congress, but he would have no vote. The whole area was to be divided into not fewer than three or more than five territories, each of which would be admitted to the Union on equal terms with the existing states when it attained a population of sixty thousand. Slavery was forbidden throughout the area; no person was to be "molested" for his religious beliefs or mode of worship; and "schools and the means of education" were to be encouraged. Though the ordinance did not say how the encouragement was to be effected, the Land Ordinance of 1785 had already reserved one lot in each township "for the maintenance of public schools."

The Northwest Ordinance, if less liberal than the one drafted by Jefferson, nevertheless established for the United States a Western policy that embodied the most cherished American principles. Though the ordinance applied to only a part of the West, it set a precedent that guided the territorial expansion of the nation until the end of the nineteenth century.

National Humiliation   One serious obstacle stood in the way of Congress' noble aspirations for the American West: the United States held only a tenuous grip on the area. England had never completely evacuated the Northwest nor had Spain recognized American possession of any territory south of the Ohio. As the weakness and poverty of the new nation grew more apparent, European statesmen intrigued to push its western boundary back to the Appalachians.

When England made peace in 1783, she was not fully persuaded—nor was the rest of Europe—that the United States would last. While the king officially proclaimed the treaty and commanded his subjects to comply with it, his ministers sent secret orders to the governor general of Canada to retain Britain's trading posts and military garrisons in the Northwest. The United States, with its own armies disbanded and the French forces gone, was in no position to compel the British to withdraw. To excuse their continued occupation of the posts, the British charged that the Americans had violated the treaty.

Again the weakness of the national government was to blame. The treaty required that neither side make laws impeding the collection of private debts contracted before the war, and it required that Congress "earnestly recommend" to the states the restoration of confiscated loyalist property. Congress did recommend the restitution, and the fact that the states did not follow the recommendation was not really a violation of the treaty. But when they passed laws impeding the collection of British debts, the states violated the treaty as surely as England did in keeping troops on American territory. Congress was as helpless to prevent one violation as the other. It sent John Adams to England as American minister; and he protested the British garrisons with characteristic Adams vigor, but in vain, for England knew that no American troops stood behind him.

England showed her contempt for the government of her former colonies by failing to establish a legation in the United States to match the American legation in London. More ominously she dickered with the influential Allen brothers, Ethan and Levi, for help in acquiring Vermont. Claimed by both New Hampshire and New York, Vermont had asserted its independence of both and applied for statehood. Congress was reluctant to antagonize either claimant by admitting Vermont into the Union, and there was danger that the Vermonters might attach themselves to Canada (Vermont was not admitted until 1791).

In the Southwest, Spain was grasping for the area that later became the states of Kentucky and Tennessee. Americans were moving into it at such a rate that by 1790 it contained more than a hundred thousand of them, but their presence was hardly a guarantee of permanent American possession. Barred by the mountains from trade with the East, the settlers relied on the Mississippi River to float their produce to market at New Orleans. New Orleans belonged to Spain, and so did the lower Mississippi. The Spaniards had gained Louisiana in 1763, the Floridas in 1783; and they maintained forts on the west bank of the Mississippi as far north as St. Louis, on the east bank as far as the present site of Memphis. Anyone who wanted to use the river had to do business with Spain.

Although commercial exports from the Southwest were still meager, everyone in the region was expecting future prosperity through the Mississippi trade. Spain was well aware of that expectation. In 1784 she closed the river to navigation by Americans and waited for the settlers to abandon their feeble Congress for the solid commercial advantage of Spanish citizenship. For a time it seemed that the settlers might do just that, for they were far from pleased with the way Eastern Americans were treating them. In 1772, by the Watauga Compact, pioneers in the Tennessee area had formed a government of their own which lasted until 1776, when North Carolina organized them into Washington County. In 1784, after her land speculators had established claims to the most valuable land, North Carolina ceded the region to Congress in order to avoid the expense of protecting it from the Indians. The next year she changed her mind and decided to take it back. Meanwhile, the settlers had resumed their own government as the independent state of Franklin and had asked to be admitted to the Union. When Congress failed to act on their request and North Carolina tried to regain possession, many settlers grew disgusted and began to look favorably toward Spain. In Kentucky, the western region of Virginia, there was a similar secessionist movement, and a similar flirtation with Spain threatened to disrupt the Union.

As the Southwest began to draw away from the United States, Spain in 1785 sent Don Diego de Gardoqui to wring from Congress a formal recognition of her exclusive control over the Mississippi. Congress instructed its Secretary of Foreign Affairs, John Jay, to insist in his negotiations with Gardoqui on the right of Americans to navigate the Mississippi through Spanish territory. There was no support for that right in international law or practice, and Americans claimed no such right over the St. Lawrence. Moreover, they had no means to enforce their claim. Nevertheless, Gardoqui refrained from taking advantage of Jay's weak position and made what seemed a generous proposal. He agreed to recognize American territorial rights as far south as the old border of British West Florida and as far west as the Mississippi, and to give American merchants a few trading privileges in Spain. In return, he asked only that the United States agree to give up navigation of the Mississippi for twenty-five years. The offer was attractive to Easterners. Jay was ready to accept, and so was a majority in Congress. But ratification of a treaty required the approval of nine states, and the five Southern states would not agree to it. Now the shrewdness of Gardoqui's calculations became apparent; for though the treaty failed, Spain still gained an advantage: the willingness of the Northern states to give up the Mississippi further weakened the Southwest's attachment to the Union.

While Gardoqui led Jay into alienating the Westerners, the Spanish governor of Louisiana, Esteban Rodríguez Miró, was wooing them with bribes and privileges. General James Wilkinson, a veteran of the Revolutionary War and a consummate double-dealer, took a trip to New Orleans in 1787. While there, he took a secret oath of allegiance to Spain in return for trading concessions. The following year he accepted a Spanish pension, with the understanding that he would lead his neighbors in the Tennessee region to repudiate the United States. Wilkinson was not the only Southwestern traitor. Daniel Boone, James Robertson, and John Sevier all accepted Spanish gold. Instead of doing what they were paid to do, however, they cheerfully deceived both sides while they waited to see what was going to happen. If, as seemed likely, the United States should break up, they were ready to learn Spanish.

The United States had troubles even in the Mediterranean. For years European countries had been protecting their Mediterranean shipping from pirates by paying an annual tribute to the rulers of Morocco, Algiers, Tripoli, and Tunis. As long as American ships carried the British flag, they were safe; but after 1776, when they began to fly the Stars and Stripes, pirates swarmed out upon them. The captured American captains and crews were put on the auction block and sold as slaves. Congress bought protection from Morocco in 1787, but had neither money nor guns to stop the other African pirates.

Nor were pirates the only difficulty to beset American trade. Though American merchants during the Revolution had looked forward to expanding their business throughout the world, the development of new commercial connections was slow and the immediate fruit of independence was not expansion but contraction of trade. With the coming of peace, American customers demanded the British textiles and other manufactures to which they had been accustomed. English merchants gladly supplied them in return for American tobacco and raw materials; but when American merchants tried to re-enter their prewar markets in Canada and the West Indies, they found every British port closed to them. In response to the merchants' demand for retaliatory action against British trade, each state adopted different measures, and the total effect was negligible. Congress, with no authority to regulate trade, was helpless. It instructed John Adams to ask England for a commercial treaty, but he was no more successful in this than in pressing for the evacuation of British garrisons in the Northwest.

The Crisis of American Nationality

Many Americans found the impotence of the national government intolerable. The Revolution had widened their vision beyond the affairs of town or county or colony and had taught them to think, as Alexander Hamilton put it, "continentally." They knew that the only way to solve the difficulties of the United States was to strengthen the national government—they had known it before the ink was dry on the Articles of Confederation. Now, as the weakness of the government became more and more embarrassing, they spoke out ever more loudly.

Thinking Continentally The Americans had had plenty of practice in making and breaking governments. Their usual method had been to call an extralegal convention—like the Stamp Act Congress or the Continental Congress or the provincial congresses that replaced the royal governments. Conventions were also summoned whenever the people of a state or region wanted to achieve a public purpose for which their regular government had proved inadequate. Several interstate conventions had met during the war in an effort to regulate prices. Connecticut held a convention in 1783 to protest the founding of the Society of the Cincinnati and the granting of extra pay to army officers. And, as we have seen, Massachusetts called a convention to draft a state constitution.

It was only natural, then, for men who had begun to think "continentally" to turn to a convention for the purpose of strengthening the continental government. As early as 1784 they had talked of it, but at that time public sentiment was overwhelmingly against it. The opposition did not arise from a deficiency of national patriotism or from too much local patriotism. Nationalism, which has proved the most lively—and deadly—force in the modern world, attached itself in America to the Union rather than to the states. Thomas Paine, in his first publication after the peace, wrote: "I ever feel myself hurt when I hear the Union, the great palladium of our liberty and safety, the least irreverently spoken of. . . . Our citizenship in the United States is our national character. Our citizenship in any particular state is only our local distinction."

This sentiment was echoed by statesmen, poets, painters, and schoolmasters. George Washington, the nation's hero, was a great Virginian but a greater American. "We are known by no other character among nations," he declared in 1783, "than as the United States." Connecticut during the 1780's produced a host of brilliant young men who celebrated in literature and art not their own state but America. John Trumbull depicted the great events of the American Revolution in a series of historical paintings. Joel Barlow attempted an American epic in *The Vision of Columbus*. Noah Webster wrote schoolbooks designed to teach American English. Jedidiah Morse published an *American Geography*. And Ezra Stiles, the president of Yale, preached of *The United States Elevated to Glory and Honor*. Some authors, to be sure, wrote the history of their own states (Jefferson, for example, published his *Notes on the State of Virginia* in 1785), but the local pride they exhibited was different in kind from the national pride that was evident throughout the Union.

Yet however proud of their country's past and confident of its future, Americans needed leadership and a government capable of elevating the United States to the glory and honor they wanted for it. National policy was drifting, and continental-minded men warned that the nation faced collapse or conquest if its government were not strengthened. But their appeals met stout resistance from people who feared that a stronger government might become aristocratic or tyrannical; it might threaten the principles that brought the Union into being—the principles of equality and of responsible, republican government. In 1785, for example, when the legislature of Massachusetts proposed a general convention to strengthen the national government, her delegates in Congress objected. Would-be aristocrats, they argued, would use such a convention to establish a government based on special privilege, loaded with lucrative positions for themselves, and bolstered by a standing army.

Because of such sentiments on the part of honest and patriotic men, a national constitutional convention, though often talked of, had failed to materialize. By 1786, however, Americans had become so impatient with British trade restrictions and conflicting state laws that they arranged for an interstate meeting at Annapolis, Maryland, to consider the extension of national authority to the regulation of commerce. The first delegates to arrive at Annapolis told each other that the contemplated revision of the national government was insufficient; those from New Jersey had even been instructed to ask for a general overhaul of the Articles of Confederation. When representatives from five states had convened, though more were on the way, they drew up a proposal to Congress and the several states and dissolved the convention. What they proposed was another convention the next year at Philadelphia for the larger purpose of making "the constitution of the Federal Government adequate to the exigencies of the Union."

The message reached the states along with some alarming news from Massachusetts. In the summer of 1786 the citizens in the economically depressed western part of the state had called a number of local conventions to demand changes in the state government: they objected to the state senate (the upper house of the legislature) as a needless expense and an aristocratic influence; they objected to the heavy taxation of land; and they objected to the high fees charged by lawyers and county courts. After the conventions had voiced their protests and adjourned, mobs prevented the county courts from sitting; and during the winter of 1786–87, some two thousand western farmers rose in armed rebellion under the leadership of Daniel Shays, a veteran of the Revolutionary War.

Though Shays's Rebellion was easily quelled by the loyal militia of Massachusetts, it alarmed Americans in every part of the United States. Other states too had depressed areas and discontented debtors; it was widely feared that the whole country might be teetering on the edge of anarchy. This might be only the beginning of a series of uprisings to intimidate the courts and state legislatures everywhere. One incident in the rebellion dramatically emphasized the weakness of the national government: a United States arsenal at Springfield had been threatened by the rebels, and there was no United States army to protect it or to come to the aid of the militia had they been unable to stop the rebellion.

By threatening law and order, Shays's Rebellion threatened property: the closing of the courts in western Massachusetts had halted mortgage foreclosures and all suits for the collection of debts. Property was also endangered from other directions. In several states, the coming of peace had brought no end to the flood of paper money that inflated values and defrauded creditors. Rhode Island made it illegal for a man to refuse the state's worthless paper money as payment for debts owed him.

Even before Shays's Rebellion people were saying that something must be done about this undermining of property rights. It would be a mockery of the national purpose if Americans who had undertaken a revolution to defend property should themselves destroy property through irresponsible government. After the shock of Shays's Rebellion every state but Rhode Island agreed to send delegates to Philadelphia to revise the Articles of Confederation.

The Great Convention   The United States in the Revolutionary period produced six men of indisputable greatness: Franklin, Washington, Jefferson, Madison, Hamilton, and John Adams. Four of them—Franklin, Washington, Madison, and Hamilton—were among the fifty-five delegates sent by the state governments to the convention that met in Philadelphia from May 25 to September 17, 1787. Jefferson and Adams would doubtless have been there too if they had not been representing the United States in Europe, for the convention was an extraordinary assemblage of talent. The delegates had a wealth of experience and tradition to draw upon: the heritage of British political and constitutional ideas stretching back to Magna Carta and beyond; the experience of five generations of colonists in representative assemblies, town meetings, and county courts; the searching debates about authority that preceded the Declaration of Independence; the drafting of state constitutions; the running of state governments and of a rudimentary national government. In no period of American history could a group have been gathered with more sophistication in political thought or with more practical experience in the construction and reconstruction of governments.

Almost without exception the delegates were men who thought continentally; and they were eager for a central government that would preserve and embody the national feeling that had grown out of the Revolution, a government that would be respected at home and abroad. The only way to achieve that end, they believed, was to give the central government more authority than Congress had been allowed. It must be able to levy taxes so that it could support itself and not be starved into impotence. It must be able to regulate commerce so as to bargain effectively with foreign nations. It must offer better protection to private property than the existing national or state governments did. And it must have coercive powers to enforce its decrees.

The delegates, while agreeing on these objectives, realized that two obstacles stood in the way of attaining them. The first was the fear of the American people that a national government, if given enough power to do its job, would quickly seize more than enough, that it would fall into the hands of a select group of wealthy and clever men who would use it to their own advantage and to the disadvantage of ordinary men. The American people would not accept an effective central government unless they could be sure of controlling it.

The second obstacle was rivalry among the

states. Each state feared that a strong national government might give unfair advantage to the others. For example, it might levy taxes that would injure one state and benefit another. Fortunately quarrels over the West were momentarily at a minimum because of Virginia's renunciation of claims to the Northwest, and because the status of future states in the territory was determined by Congress (in the Northwest Ordinance) while the convention was sitting. The convention itself, after preliminary debates, skirted the knotty question of whether new states should be equal to old and decided simply that "New States may be admitted by the Congress into this Union."

But another form of state rivalry could not be bypassed and threatened to deadlock the convention: in a national government composed of states, how was representation to be apportioned? Under the Articles of Confederation, each state, no matter what its size, had one vote in Congress (this manner of voting was also followed in the convention). Such an arrangement gave undue advantage to the citizens of small states: 68,000 Rhode Islanders had the same influence on decisions as 747,000 Virginians. The large states would not be satisfied with any national government in which their influence was not at least approximately commensurate with their size. But the small states believed that, unless they retained an equal vote, the large states would be able to advance their own interests at the expense of the small states.

When the convention opened, Edmund Randolph of Virginia presented a plan, drafted by his colleague James Madison, that was designed to overcome both the fears of the people and the fears of the states. Madison, who at thirty-six was the most astute political thinker of his day, perceived that what the small states took for a problem was partly an illusion: the people of a small state did not necessarily have different interests from those of a large state. There was a serious, though not irreconcilable, difference between the economic interests of the Southern states and those of New England, but there was no serious difference between the interests, say, of the people in Pennsylvania and those in Delaware. Madison proposed, therefore, to rest the government on the people rather than on the state governments and to make representation in the national government proportionate to population.

To keep the government from seizing more power than it was assigned, Madison proposed to divide it into different branches which would check and balance one another: a two-house legislature, an independent executive, and an independent judiciary. Each would have specific functions and would see to it that the others did not overstep their bounds. Thus the most distant constituent in America would have guardians within the government itself watching to make sure that it did not get out of hand. The Americans had already endorsed the principle of separation of powers in their state governments, but their discussions of national government had revolved around the granting of further powers to the existing unicameral Congress. As soon as Madison proposed a separation of powers in the national government itself, many of the fears about its escaping control were dispelled. Pierce Butler, a delegate for South Carolina, said that "he had opposed the grant of powers to Congress heretofore, because the whole power was vested in one body. The proposed distribution of the powers into different bodies changed the case, and would induce him to go great lengths."

The delegates spent two weeks revising Madison's plan and working out its details, without altering its basic structure. They decided, among other things, that members of the lower house of the legislature should be popularly elected and those of the upper house appointed by the state legislatures. And they agreed that representation in both houses should be according to population. Then on June 15 William Paterson of New Jersey suddenly came up with a new plan calling for a continuation of the existing unicameral Congress with increased powers, but with each state retaining its equal vote. Paterson and his supporters would allow Congress the power to tax, to regulate trade, and to enforce its own decrees, but they wanted the national government to remain what it had been, an assembly of the states, not of the people, its members chosen by the state governments, not by popular election. Paterson's plan was rejected, but the small-state delegations had rallied to it and finally threatened to bolt the convention unless each state were given an equal vote in at least one house of the national legislature. To pacify them, the other members of the convention agreed on July 16 that all the states would have equal representation in the upper house, but to this concession they attached several provisions: representation in the lower house and direct taxation would be apportioned according to population, with five slaves to be considered the equivalent of three free men; all bills for raising or spending money would originate in the lower house; a census would be taken every ten years. The last two provisions had not been discussed earlier, but the convention had agreed on the others before the Paterson plan was introduced.

Once they had made this Great Compromise (which was actually a concession to the illusions of the small states) there was no longer any serious danger that the delegates would fail in their attempt to strengthen the national government. They had started out in substantial agreement about what must be done, and they had overcome, in large measure at least, both the rivalry of the states and the fear of tyranny. They still argued about many things: an executive (one or more? elected by the people, by Congress, or by the state legislatures? elected how often?), slavery, trade duties, the ratio of representation, terms of office, and more. But these were details, and, within three and a half months of assembling, the convention had finished drafting the new Constitution.

The Constitution provided for a national government with authority to collect taxes, make treaties with foreign countries, maintain an army and a navy, coin and borrow money, regulate commerce among the states and with foreign nations, and make any laws necessary to carry its powers into execution. The United States Constitution and all the treaties and laws made under it were to be the supreme law of the land, superior to state laws and binding on state courts. Moreover, the federal government would have its own executive and its own courts to enforce its treaties, Constitution, and laws, and to settle disputes between states. As a last resort it could call on the militia for help.

The national legislature or Congress was to consist of an upper house, or Senate, and a House of Representatives. Each state was to have two senators, both appointed by the state legislature for six-year terms, and one representative for every thirty thousand persons, to be popularly elected for a two-year term by the same persons who were qualified to vote for members of "the most numerous branch of the State Legislature." The executive, known as the President, was to be elected every four years by an electoral "college" to which each state might appoint (in any way its legislature prescribed) as many members as the total of its representatives and senators in Congress. It was intended, of course, that the members of this body should exercise their own discretion in selecting the best man in the country. The man who received the second largest number of votes became the Vice-President, who was to preside over the Senate.

The Constitution hedged both the federal and the state governments with specific prohibitions. To protect private property, it forbade the state governments to pass laws impairing the obligation of contracts, or to coin money, issue paper money, or make anything but gold and silver legal tender in payment of debts. To prevent the states from encroaching on the sphere of the federal government, it forbade them to make treaties, levy import or export duties, or engage in war unless actually invaded. Conversely the states were protected by clauses prohibiting the federal government from levying direct taxes except in proportion to population, from levying export taxes at all (a protection for the tobacco and rice exporters of the South), and from restricting immigration "or Importation of such Persons as any of the States now existing shall think proper to admit" before the year 1808 (a protection for the slave trade until that time). Republicanism and individual rights were protected by clauses forbidding either the states or the federal government to grant titles of nobility, or to pass bills of attainder or ex post facto laws. And the federal government could not make any religious test a qualification for public office nor suspend the writ of habeas corpus "unless when in Cases of Rebellion or Invasion the public Safety may require it."

Apart from these prohibitions, the Constitution did not contain any guarantee of individual rights such as freedom of speech or religion, or trial by jury. In the last days of the convention Elbridge Gerry of Massachusetts and George Mason of Virginia proposed that this omission be corrected, but their colleagues rejected the suggestion as unnecessary on the grounds that the Constitution defined and limited the powers of the national government to specified actions and that the state constitutions already contained bills of rights. But in case experience should prove this or any other of their decisions to be unwise, the convention provided a means of correction: the Constitution could be amended if two-thirds of both houses of Congress and three-fourths of the state legislatures agreed. The convention adjourned on September 17, after sending a copy of its work to Congress for transmission to the states.

Ratification The Constitution drafted at Philadelphia was the greatest creative triumph of the Experimental Period, and it showed how much its authors had learned during those experimental years. After the war the initial reaction against monarchy and aristocracy had led Americans to create state governments with feeble executives and ineffective upper houses; the new Constitution proposed a powerful executive and a senate equal in power to the House of Representatives. The Articles of Confederation had created a national government controlled by the state governments and having no direct relation to the individual citizen; the new Constitution proposed a national government independent of the state governments, with a House of Representatives elected directly by the people of the United States and with federal courts acting directly on them. The Articles of Confederation had placed the national government in the hands of a single congress of delegates and provided it with little authority; the new Constitution split up the national government to prevent abuses and gave it real authority.

The members of the Philadelphia Convention had been empowered only to revise the Articles of Confederation. Actually, they had drawn up a completely new government to take the place of the debating society that Congress had become. Knowing that their ambitious plan would meet opposition, and unwilling to have it defeated by the stubbornness of a few states, the delegates boldly proposed

that as soon as nine states had accepted the new Constitution it should go into effect among those nine (revisions of the Articles of Confederation required unanimous approval). The convention also proposed the revolutionary technique of bypassing the state legislatures, where power-hungry state politicians and pressure groups might exert an influence as pernicious as the speculators had exerted against ratification of the Articles of Confederation. In each state the people would elect a special convention to judge the new constitution. The state government would issue the call for the ratifying convention but would have no part in accepting or rejecting the Constitution. The new national government, if adopted, would thus be authorized directly by the people; its power would derive from them.

The prestige of its authors, especially Washington and Franklin, as well as its intrinsic merits assured the Constitution a hearing. But its adoption was not at all certain. Several members of the convention, including the influential Edmund Randolph, had refused to sign the completed document. When it reached Congress, Richard Henry Lee took an immediate dislike to it. Why, he asked, should Congress approve its own dissolution? Why should nine states be allowed to withdraw from the Confederation to form a new and dangerously powerful government? Before transmitting the document to the states, Lee proposed at least the insertion of a bill of rights.

Lee's proposal was defeated by what he termed "a coalition of monarchy men, military men, aristocrats and drones whose noise, impudence and zeal exceeds all belief." When the Constitution reached the American people, many reacted as Lee had. But in every state the legislature eventually, if sometimes reluctantly, issued the necessary call for a popular ratifying convention.

The opponents of the Constitution were moved less by a desire to perpetuate the superiority of the state governments than by the old fear that a strong national government would escape from popular control and become oppressive. The system of checks and balances, they felt, was not adequate insurance against tyranny. The House of Representatives was too small to represent so many people.

A Case Against Ratification

Something must be done to preserve your liberty and mine. The Confederation, this same despised government, merits, in my opinion, the highest encomium. It carried us through a long and dangerous war; it rendered us victorious in that bloody conflict with a powerful nation; it has secured us a territory greater than any European monarch possesses: and shall a government which has been thus strong and vigorous, be accused of imbecility, and abandoned for want of energy?...

When the American spirit was in its youth, the language of America was different: liberty, sir, was then the primary object.... We drew the spirit of liberty from our British ancestors: by that spirit we have triumphed over every difficulty. But now, sir, the American spirit, assisted by the ropes and chains of consolidation, is about to convert this country into a powerful and mighty empire. If you make the citizens of this country agree to become the subjects of one great consolidated empire of America, your government will not have sufficient energy to keep them together. Such a government is incompatible with the genius of republicanism.

From a Speech by Patrick Henry at the Virginia Ratifying Convention, 1788.

And the failure to include a bill of rights seemed an ominous indication of the direction the national government would take. Madison had argued at the convention, and now wrote in the newspapers, to persuade people that there were no grounds for the long-accepted notion that a large republic would fall into tyranny. In a large republic there would be so many different groups with such varied and opposing interests that they would be unable to submerge their differences and combine into a tyrannical majority. The danger of a tyrannical coalition was far greater in a small republic, Madison pointed out, because of the fewer divergent interests and the greater ease of communication.

The supporters of the Constitution were generally more aggressive than their opponents, and sometimes their tactics were unworthy of their cause. In Pennsylvania they pushed through the call for a convention after the legislature had voted to adjourn; they rounded up a quorum only by forcibly detaining two members. Everywhere they campaigned with a vigor and invective born of urgency. This, they felt, was the crisis of American nationality. If the Constitution failed of adoption, the Union might be doomed.

Opposition to the Constitution was generally weakest in the small states, which would have more than their share of power in the new government. But the Federalists, as the supporters of the Constitution called themselves, knew that it was imperative to win over the four largest states: Massachusetts, Pennsylvania, New York, and Virginia. For any one of them to abstain would imperil the success of the new government. Pennsylvania, in spite of determined opposition, fell in line first, on December 12, 1787. Massachusetts ratified on February 6, 1788, by a narrow majority, which included several anti-Federalist delegates. They had been persuaded to change their position after John Hancock proposed that ratification be accompanied by a recommendation for a bill of rights.

A Case for Ratification

Among the numerous advantages promised by a well-constructed Union, none deserves to be more accurately developed than its tendency to break and control the violence of faction. The friend of popular governments never finds himself so much alarmed for their character and fate as when he contemplates their propensity to this dangerous vice. He will not fail, therefore, to set a due value on any plan which, without violating the principles to which he is attached, provides a proper cure for it....

The influence of factious leaders may kindle a flame within their particular States, but will be unable to spread a general conflagration through the other States. A religious sect may degenerate into a political faction in a part of the Confederacy; but the variety of sects dispersed over the entire face of it must secure the national councils against any danger from that source. A rage for paper money, for an abolition of debts, for an equal division of property, or for any other improper or wicked project, will be less apt to pervade the whole body of the Union than a particular member of it; in the same proportion as such a malady is more likely to taint a particular county or district than an entire State.

In the extent and proper structure of the Union, therefore, we behold a republican remedy for the diseases most incident to republican government.

From James Madison, *The Federalist*, No. 10, 1787.

In Virginia the opposition, led by Patrick Henry, was weakened when Edmund Randolph swung back in favor of adoption. The state accepted the Constitution by a vote of eighty-nine to seventy-nine on June 26. Meanwhile every other state but New York, North Carolina, and Rhode Island had voted for ratification. Several had, like Massachusetts, included recommendations for amendments. In New York Alexander Hamilton, John Jay, and James Madison had campaigned for the Constitution in an impressive series of newspaper articles, known as the *Federalist* papers. Though these were perhaps the most searching discussion of the Constitution ever written, they did not prevent the election of a hostile ratifying convention. Only after news of Virginia's decision reached New York was Hamilton able to persuade a small majority to follow suit on July 26. North Carolina did not ratify until November 21, 1789; Rhode Island not until May 29, 1790. But the rest of the country did not wait for them. As soon as the four big states had given their assent, Congress arranged for its own demise by ordering national elections for January 1789.

The United States was at last to have a government that would embody on a national scale the American principle of responsible representative government. The world had said that republican government was impossible for a country the size of the United States, that only a federation of republics or a powerful monarchy or aristocracy could extend so wide. But vision, daring, and experience created a new kind of republic, a federation that would be more than a federation, a government that would remain responsible to the people though its territory and population expanded tenfold, a union in which the people would be joined not as citizens of rival states but as a nation of equals.

SUGGESTIONS FOR READING

Two good introductions to the military history of the Revolution are Howard Peckham, *The War for Independence* * (1958), and Willard Wallace, *Appeal to Arms* (1951). J. R. Alden, *The American Revolution* (1954), also concentrates on military history. The standard account of naval operations is G. W. Allen, *Naval History of the American Revolution*, 2 vols. (1913), but for the exploits of John Paul Jones, see S. E. Morison, *John Paul Jones: A Sailor's Biography* (1959). T. G. Frothingham, *Washington, Commander in Chief* (1930), assesses the general's military genius, but a more complete, day-by-day account is D. S. Freeman, *George Washington*, 7 vols. (1948–57). The story of the war as seen by participants is told, with extensive quotations, by G. F. Scheer and H. F. Rankin in *Rebels and Redcoats* * (1957).

The classic account of the diplomacy of the Revolution is S. F. Bemis, *The Diplomacy of the American Revolution* * (1935, 1957). On the loyalists, see C. H. Van Tyne, *The Loyalists in the American Revolution* (1902). Clarence Ver Steeg, *Robert Morris* (1954), deals largely with the financing of the Revolution. A more extensive study is E. J. Ferguson, *The Power of the Purse: A History of American Public Finance, 1776–1790* (1961).

Since 1909, when Carl Becker offered his opinion that the Revolution, in New York at least, was a contest about who should rule at home, many historians have addressed themselves to the effect of the Revolution on social conflicts within the participating states. J. F. Jameson, *The American Revolution Considered as a Social Movement* * (1926), argued that the Revolution acted as a leveling movement in the direction of greater democracy and accelerated social change. Studies of individual states in the period from 1776 to 1789 do not all bear out this contention. For example, Richard McCormick, *Experiment in Independence: New Jersey in the Critical Period, 1781–1789* (1950), finds little evidence of class conflict, but E. W. Spaulding, *New York in the Critical Period* (1932), finds a good deal, as does Staughton Lynd, "Who Should Rule at Home? Dutchess County, New York, in the American Revolution," *William and Mary Quarterly*, 3rd series, XVIII (1961), 330–59. Robert Brown, *Middle-Class Democracy and the Revolution in Massachusetts* (1955), argues that there was little democratizing of Massachusetts during the Revolution because Massachusetts already had democratic government, with the vast majority of adult males enjoying the right to vote. Chilton

* Available in a paperback edition.

Williamson, *American Suffrage from Property to Democracy, 1760–1860* (1960), finds that the majority of males in most colonies had the right to vote but that the majority became larger during the Revolution as a result of reductions in the property qualifications. E. S. Morgan, *The Birth of the Republic* * (1957), emphasizes the growth of common principles rather than conflicts among Americans of the period 1763–89.

John Fiske, *The Critical Period of American History, 1783–1789* (1883), painted a black picture of the United States under the Articles of Confederation and told of the nation's rescue by the Constitution of 1787. Merrill Jensen, in *The Articles of Confederation* * (1940) and *The New Nation* (1950), sought to redeem the reputation of the Articles, which he saw as a true embodiment of the principles of the Declaration of Independence. Edmund Burnett, *The Continental Congress* (1941), covers the activities of Congress before and after adoption of the Articles. Irving Brant, *James Madison the Nationalist, 1780–1787* (1948), gives a view of the period through the eyes of one of America's most perceptive statesmen.

Most modern accounts of the Constitutional Convention take their point of departure from Charles Beard, whose *Economic Interpretation of the Constitution* * (1913) exercised a powerful influence. Beard maintained that the authors of the Constitution had invested heavily in public securities and sought to bolster the national government in order to gain protection for the economic interests of their own class. In recent years Beard's thesis has been attacked and all but demolished in Robert Brown, *Charles Beard and the Constitution* (1956), and Forrest McDonald, *We the People: The Economic Origins of the Constitution* (1958). Max Farrand, *The Framing of the Constitution of the United States* * (1913), is a good account of the Convention itself, but there is no substitute for the records of the Convention and of the debates in it, which are published in Max Farrand, ed., *Records of the Federal Convention of 1787*, 4 vols. (1911–37), and C. C. Tansill, ed., *Documents Illustrative of the Formation of the Union of the United States* (1927).

* Available in a paperback edition.

6

The Establishment
of National Institutions

In adopting the Constitution, Americans gave the United States a permanent and effective government. But the men who drafted the Constitution were well aware that they had left many details undecided, and that the first officers of the new government would have a greater opportunity than their successors to determine what the United States should be and become.

Launching the New Government

Fortunately many of the leaders of the Philadelphia Convention were eager to finish the job they had begun. Franklin was too old now to do more than give his blessing, but most of the nation's other great men repaired to New York in 1789 to launch the new government and help shape its institutions. There had never been any question about the candidate for President: Washington's election was unanimous and unopposed. His progress from Mount Vernon to New York was marked by a succession of triumphal arches, cheering spectators, and pretty girls strewing his path with flowers and offering him crowns of laurel. He bore it all with his usual dignity. Though he would rather have stayed at home, he was excited by the opportunity to give stature to the nation he had done so much to create.

The Vice-President, John Adams, who had just returned from England, was a more complicated man, vain enough to invite laughter, but so quick, so keen, so talented in every way

that no one dared laugh. Benjamin Franklin had once said of him that he was "always an honest man, often a wise one, but sometimes, and in some things, absolutely out of his senses." Adams soon found that the vice-presidency carried little prestige or power, and an Adams could not be comfortable without a good deal of both. During Washington's administration the Vice-President set the pattern for future holders of the office by keeping himself in the background.

More influential in the first years of the new government was James Madison, the young Virginian who had played so large a role at Philadelphia. Madison's old political opponent, Patrick Henry—a powerful figure in the Virginia legislature—had succeeded in preventing his election to the Senate, but his neighbors had elected him to the House of Representatives. There, in spite of his lack of humor, his small frame and unimposing appearance, he quickly became the dominant figure. In the early months he was also Washington's principal adviser.

Madison, like many Americans who had lived through the Revolution, was passionately interested in the art of government. So were his two friends, Thomas Jefferson and Alexander Hamilton, both of whom Washington also called on for advice and assistance. Hamilton, the younger of the two, was perhaps the more brilliant; certainly he had the greater genius as an administrator. But he was also the more ambitious, both for the United States

Where united colonies became United States: The State House (Independence Hall), Philadelphia.

and for himself. Jefferson was interested in government because he was interested in human beings, of whom he thought well. The new government, he believed, was going to be a good thing for them, but he remained less committed to it than to them.

Jefferson, Madison, and Washington were the ultimate justification of the eighteenth-century Virginia plantation. Aristocrats to the core, living from the forced labor of slaves, they had the time, energy, and vision to see beyond slavery, beyond the plantation, beyond Virginia, to think continentally and even more to think humanely.

A Strong Executive   In this galaxy of leaders, Washington was at once the most limited and the strongest. His strength came not only from the fact that he had earned the unbounded confidence of the people, but from his simplicity of mind. As commanding general of the Revolutionary armies, he had devoted himself wholly to winning the war. As President of the United States he devoted himself with equal singleness of purpose, equal de-

tachment, and equal success to making the new government respected at home and abroad.

The biggest part of the job, Washington felt, was to establish respect for his own office. In the first flush of republican revulsion from England, Americans had identified executive power with hereditary, irresponsible monarchy, and they had accordingly neglected or suppressed it in their new governments. Most of the state constitutions had made the executive the creature of the legislature; the Articles of Confederation had provided for no real executive. The Constitutional Convention had rectified that error by creating the office of President and assigning extensive powers to it: command of the army and navy, responsibility for foreign negotiations, and authority to appoint other governmental officers. Some of the powers were to be shared with the Senate, but the line of demarcation between the executive and legislative branches was not clear. It was up to him, Washington believed, to establish the extent of executive power and to organize the office so that future Presidents would be able to keep it strong.

Simply by taking office Washington went a long way toward achieving this end, for his own immense prestige could not fail to lend weight to any position he accepted. But he took pains to surround himself with more of the trappings of honor than he allowed himself at Mount Vernon. When he rode abroad it was on a white horse, with a leopard-skin saddlecloth edged in gold, or in an elegant coach pulled by six cream-colored horses. He rented one of the most sumptuous mansions in New York and stationed powdered lackeys at the door. He held "levees" in the manner of European monarchs, passing among the assembled dignitaries to give each a brief moment of the presidential presence.

Some of Washington's associates thought this was going too far; others could not get enough of it. After the President's inauguration on April 30, 1789, his admirers in Congress had brought on a heated debate by proposing to address a formal congratulatory message to "His Highness the President of the United States and Protector of their Liberties." John Adams and Richard Henry Lee argued strenuously that some such title was needed to testify to the President's eminence, especially for the edification of the foreigners for whom he would personify the United States. The idea horrified ardent republicans, and James Madison carried the majority with him when he proposed that the message be addressed simply to "George Washington, President of the United States."

By eliminating ostentatious titles Madison had no intention of minimizing the executive office. He had written most of the President's inaugural address as well as the Congressional reply to it. In the first crucial months of the new government his was the hand that guided President and Congress alike in the legislation that organized the executive office and gave it the strength the President sought.

Though the Constitutional Convention had not directly provided for any executive departments, it clearly envisaged them in stating that the President should have power to call for the opinions of the principal officer in each such department. One of the first acts of the new government was to pass laws establishing the departments of the Treasury, State, and War, which, together with the offices of Attorney General and Postmaster General, were the only executive departments under Washington.

Had Washington and Madison been less insistent on executive independence, these departments might have formed the nucleus of a Cabinet responsible to the legislative branch, as in the emerging British system. Such a development was prevented when Madison persuaded the House of Representatives, against considerable opposition, that the heads of departments, though appointed by the President with the consent of the Senate, should be subject to removal by the President alone.

Washington's first appointments to the new offices included Jefferson at State and Hamilton at the Treasury. His other choices were less distinguished: Henry Knox as Secretary of War and Edmund Randolph as Attorney General. Washington did not regard his secretaries as a team or Cabinet that must act collectively. Rather, he thought of them as assistants, and in the first years they held no regular meetings. The President might refer decisions to them when he was absent from the seat of government, and he expected them to take the initiative in developing plans within their own fields of responsibility. But he kept the reins in his own hands. Executive decisions were his decisions.

Legislative decisions were not. Washington made only very general suggestions for legislation and scrupulously refrained from disclosing his views on specific measures being considered by Congress. He was extremely reluctant to use his veto power and did so only twice during his presidency. It was his business, he believed, to administer the laws, not to make them. Consequently, while he established the authority and independence of executive action within the range allowed by the Constitution he took no active part in the formation of public policy by legislation.

In the absence of presidential initiative, three men guided Congress: Madison, Hamilton, and Jefferson. For the first five months Madison had the job to himself, for no other member of Congress combined the requisite political talents with the imagination that the new situation demanded. Hamilton acquired a position of leadership by his appointment to the Treasury on September 11, 1789, because in creating that department Congress had provided for a close connection between the Secretary and the legislature. At Madison's insistence, Congress had authorized the secretary to prepare plans for collecting revenue and sustaining public credit and to present them to the House of Representatives, which under the Constitution had the sole right to initiate money bills. Washington approved Hamilton's active participation in the affairs of the House for, though he refrained from legislative matters himself, he did not think it necessary or desirable that his department heads should do so.

Jefferson did not accept the Secretaryship of State until January 1790, and did not arrive in New York until two months later. His office was less closely connected with legislative affairs than Hamilton's. Moreover, while Hamilton ran the Treasury pretty much by himself, Washington took an active part in the management of foreign affairs and frequently overruled his Secretary of State. Nevertheless, Jefferson's close friendship and alliance with Madison gave him considerable influence in Congress.

The Bill of Rights   In ratifying the Constitution, six states had suggested amendments to specify the popular rights that the government must never invade. Many of the legislators who had been elected to the first Congress under the new Constitution arrived in New York prepared to carry out the suggestions. Although Madison had opposed a bill of rights both before and during ratification, when it became clear to him that the people of the United States were determined to have one he decided to draft it himself.

Madison had initially opposed a bill of rights for two reasons: First, he thought that declarations of popular rights, while useful against a monarch, would be ineffective against a republican government, in which the people themselves were ultimately the lawgivers. Second, he feared that any explicit statement of rights would prove too narrow and might be used to limit freedom instead of limiting authority: a wayward government might construe the specified rights as the only rights of the people. The debates over ratification had introduced another ground for fear: many advocates of amendment, including some members of Congress, wanted to reduce the authority of the federal government in relation to that of the state governments. In order to forestall amendments that might weaken the new government or ones that might undermine American freedom, Madison wanted to frame the bill of rights himself.

From the proposals he first presented to Congress in June 1789 there emerged the first ten amendments to the Constitution, which were ratified by the necessary number of states in December 1791. Known as the Bill of Rights, the amendments protected freedom of religion, of speech, and of the press, and the right to assemble, to petition the government, to bear arms, to be tried by a jury, and to enjoy other procedural safeguards of the law (see p. 818). They forbade general warrants, excessive bail, cruel or unusual punishments, and the quartering of troops in private houses.

To prevent the government from ever claiming that the people had no rights except those specifically listed, the ninth amendment provided that "The enumeration in the Constitution of certain rights shall not be construed to deny or disparage others retained by the people." The tenth amendment reassured the state governments about their relationship to the federal government by affirming, "The powers not delegated to the United States by the Constitution, nor prohibited by it to the States, are reserved to the States respectively, or to the people."

Madison fought hard for his amendments, because in preparing them he had convinced himself that a bill of rights might be more effective than he had originally supposed. If a republican legislature proved hard to control, specific prohibitions would at least form a rallying point around which popular resistance could gather. The amendments would also assist the executive and judiciary branches in checking the legislature, for the amendments would be part of the Constitution, which every officer of government must swear to uphold. Even the state governments might be brought into action to resist encroachments, a thought that recurred some years later to Madison and Jefferson alike (see p. 157).

While Madison guided the Bill of Rights through Congress, the Senate passed a judiciary bill establishing the Supreme Court and thirteen inferior district courts. When the bill came to the House of Representatives, some members wanted to eliminate the provision for district courts and leave the everyday enforcement of federal laws to the state courts. But Madison persuaded the majority that the states could not be trusted in the matter. The Judiciary Act of 1789 as finally passed established thirteen district courts and three circuit courts with both concurrent and appellate jurisdiction. It also explicitly provided that the Supreme Court should review decisions of state courts and nullify state laws which violated the United States Constitution or the laws and treaties made under it.

The Shaping of Domestic Policy

By adopting a Bill of Rights and by establishing federal courts to uphold the Constitution, Americans completed the work of the Constitutional Convention and made secure the inheritance that the preceding generation had won for them. The next pressing problem was to recover the nation's economic credit.

National Credit and National Debt   At the Constitutional Convention it had been understood that the new government would levy taxes to pay not only its own expenses but the debts of the old government. The debts were the debts of the nation, regardless of which government contracted them. On July 4, 1789, Congress established customs duties on all imports and two weeks later placed a tonnage duty on all shipping, with high rates for foreign vessels, low ones for American. When Alexander Hamilton took office at the Treasury, it became his task to apply the income from these duties to the national debt.

Hamilton found that the United States owed $54,124,464.56, including interest. It was widely assumed that the amount would be scaled down, at least the amount owing to creditors who were themselves citizens of the United States. Much of the domestic debt was in the form of certificates which had been either issued as pay to soldiers during the Revolution or bought by patriotic citizens to

Alexander Hamilton: Architect of the national economy.

further the war effort. But by now most of the certificates were held by speculators or merchants who had secured them at a considerable discount when the credit of the government fell and hard times forced the owners to sell. The restoration of national credit, it seemed to many Americans, did not require payment at face value to men who had themselves discounted that value. Hamilton thought otherwise. In his "Report on Public Credit," presented to Congress on January 14, 1790, he proposed to fund the entire national debt, both foreign and domestic, at its face value. Existing certificates of indebtedness would be redeemed by interest-bearing government bonds worth the original value plus the unpaid interest, calculated at 4 per cent.

The very boldness of the proposal won acclaim, and there was no real opposition to the full payment of the nation's obligations. The only question—and a large one—was who should be paid. On this question Madison and Hamilton came to a parting of the ways.

Hamilton insisted that payments be made to whoever held the certificates. Many of his associates, including members of Congress, had known that his report would contain such a recommendation and had begun buying up certificates wherever they could be found. Madison, shocked by the scramble, rose in the House of Representatives to offer an alternative to Hamilton's scheme. There were, he said, four kinds of creditors who held or had held the certificates: (1) original holders who still held them, (2) original holders who had sold them at less than face value, (3) present holders who had bought them from someone other than the government, and (4) intermediate holders, who had bought them and sold them. The first group, Madison agreed, should be paid in full. The fourth group, he agreed, should be paid nothing. But he did not agree that full value should be paid to the third group and that nothing should be paid to the second. Instead, he proposed that the third group, which included the speculators, be paid the highest market value that the certificates had formerly commanded (fifty cents on the dollar) and that the difference between this amount and the face value be paid to the second group, the Revolutionary soldiers and patriots who had been obliged to part with the certificates at less than face value because of the government's inability to maintain its credit.

Madison's plan would not have reduced by a penny the amount paid by the government. In fact, Madison proposed to pay the original interest rate of 6 per cent, instead of the 4 per cent advocated by Hamilton. But Madison's plan would have offered partial compensation to the original certificate-holders instead of giving a bonus to speculators. Unhappily for Madison, and not by accident, the speculators included many members of Congress, who did not hesitate to wrap their own shady transactions in the national honor. Men who had agents combing the country for certificates stood on the floors of Congress and denounced Madison's proposal as an attempt to make the government evade its just obligations. Madison, hitherto the master of Congress, now saw his motion defeated in the House of Representatives by a vote of thirteen to thirty-six.

Before bringing Hamilton's funding scheme to a vote, Congress took up an even more controversial matter, which Hamilton had also recommended in his report: the assumption by the national government of debts owed by the state governments. Such a move was not necessary to sustain national credit, and many supporters of the funding measure failed to see the point of it. Gouverneur Morris, a stanch conservative, was in London when he heard of the scheme and wrote back in puzzlement: "To assume the payment of what the States owe, merely because they owe it, seems to my capacity not more rational, than to assume the debts of corporations, or of individuals." Senator Robert Morris of Pennsylvania, to whom the letter was written, had other views. "By God," he said, "it must be done."

The crucial difference between Gouverneur Morris and Robert Morris was that one was in England and the other in America. Robert, like other speculators in America, had an opportunity to take advantage of assumption before it became a fact. During the Revolutionary War the states, like the national government, had borrowed money by issuing securities. Many of these state securities had since depreciated even more than national ones. Speculators, including congressmen, now rushed to buy them. And with the prospect of making fortunes they lined up behind the assumption of state debts as they did behind the funding of the national debt.

But there was more opposition to assumption than to funding because Hamilton's proposition contained no allowance for states that had already paid a large proportion of their debt. These included Virginia, Maryland, Pennsylvania, and North Carolina. The largest debts were owed by Massachusetts and South Carolina. As a result, the people of Virginia, for instance, having been taxed by their own state government to pay off its debt, would be taxed again by the federal government to help pay off the debts of Massachusetts and South Carolina.

The inequity of the scheme enabled Madison to muster a small majority against it on a test vote in the House. But he did not dare to push his advantage, because the speculative interests threatened to vote against funding unless they got assumption as well. Much as he disliked Hamilton's funding plan, Madison knew that the rejection of funding altogether would mean the total destruction of national credit and possibly of the national government itself.

Both funding and assumption were still undecided when Jefferson arrived to take up his duties as Secretary of State. Hamilton approached him to arrange a bargain with Madison. Congress had been arguing for some time about whether the national capital should be permanently located at New York, Philadelphia, Baltimore, or at a site on the Potomac River. Hamilton suggested that his speculators would deliver Northern votes for the Potomac site favored by Virginia, with a ten-year interim period at Philadelphia, provided Virginia and Pennsylvania would furnish enough votes to pass assumption. Convinced that funding could not pass without assumption and that without funding the nation faced catastrophe, Madison consented to supply the votes if Hamilton made some allowance for states that had already paid a large part of their debts. The bargain was fulfilled in July 1790 when Congress agreed to assumption, funding, and the ultimate location of the capital on the Potomac.

The fact that the two sides had been able to reach a compromise was heartening, but the line of division was ominous: Hamilton spoke for the merchants and creditors of the North, who would benefit enormously from funding and assumption, because they had accumulated most of the government's certificates of indebtedness; Madison and Jefferson spoke for the planters and farmers of the South, whose taxes would flow steadily north to pay the debt. The differing interests of North and South, which Madison had already perceived in 1787, were beginning to affect national policy.

The Hamiltonian Program   Hamilton's victory, for it amounted to that, was not simply a successful swindle. The speculative frenzy set off by his measures was a calculated part of one of the boldest programs ever envisaged for the development of the nation and the nation's economy. Hamilton believed that the future of the United States depended on a large-scale expansion of industry and commerce. The suspension of imports from England during the war had forced the growth of manufacturing in America; and the production of hardware and textiles had continued in some measure afterward. To effect the kind of growth that Hamilton wanted the primary need was capital, capital in large quantities concentrated in the hands of men willing to risk investing it. By means of funding and assumption Hamilton created just such a group of wealthy entrepreneurs or, to use a less attractive word, profiteers. Hamilton was no profiteer himself—he was too interested in power to give much attention to his own finances. But he was well satisfied with the huge speculative profits that others reaped from his measures, for those profits meant capital for business investment. Moreover, funding and assumption, by restoring national credit, would make investment in American enterprises more attractive to foreign capital.

Hamilton's measures were prompted not merely by economic considerations but by his consistent determination to strengthen the national government and to overcome the centrifugal force of the state governments. He anticipated that all the capitalists created by funding and assumption would be eager to maintain the national credit and the national government, if only to protect their investments. By the same token, the assumption of state debts would deprive the state governments of such support. The national government, working hand in glove with powerful investors, would grow strong as industry and commerce grew.

Hamilton's scheme generated its own support. The opportunity to get rich easily and by methods not strictly illegal was more than congressmen could resist. Washington was disturbed by the rumor that "The funding of the debt has furnished effectual means of corrupting such a portion of the Legislature as turns the balance between the honest voters whichever way it is directed." Hamilton, who was doing the directing, assured the President that "there is not a member of the Legislature who can properly be called a stock-jobber or a paper-dealer. . . . As to improper speculations on measures depending before Congress, I believe never was any body of men freer from them." Washington believed him.

Hamilton's next objective was a national bank with capital supplied partly by the government and partly by private investors. But since the investors would be permitted to pay in government bonds for three-fourths of the bank stock they purchased, the bank's notes would rest very heavily on the national debt.

Hamilton's View
of the Good Society

It is now proper ... to enumerate the principal circumstances from which it may be inferred that manufacturing establishments not only occasion a positive augmentation of the produce and revenue of the society, but that they contribute essentially to rendering them greater than they could possibly be without such establishments. These circumstances are:

1. The division of labor.
2. An extension of the use of machinery.
3. Additional employment to classes of the community not ordinarily engaged in the business.
4. The promoting of emigration from foreign countries.
5. The furnishing greater scope for the diversity of talents and dispositions, which discriminate men from each other.
6. The affording a more ample and various field for enterprise.
7. The creating, in some instances, a new, and securing, in all, a more certain and steady demand for the surplus produce of the soil.

Each of these circumstances has a considerable influence upon the total mass of industrious effort in a community; together, they add to it a degree of energy and effect which is not easily conceived.

From Alexander Hamilton, "Report on Manufactures," 1791.

According to Hamilton, the national debt, if utilized in this way, could be a national advantage. In arguing for funding and assumption, he had emphasized the fact that where a national debt "is properly funded, and an object of established confidence, it answers most of the purposes of money." He intended to make it serve this purpose through the bank: notes issued by the bank would serve as a much needed medium of exchange (specie being scarce) and would greatly facilitate business and the accumulation of capital. Besides acting as a central exchange, the bank would handle government finances; and it would expedite borrowing both by the government and by individuals. Through this government-sponsored expansion of credit, the bond between private capital and the national government would be tightened.

When the bill to charter the bank came be-

fore the House early in February 1791, Madison attacked it with arguments he would not have used two years earlier. Before the adoption of the Constitution, he had argued strenuously that Congress should assume all the powers it needed to do its job. Under the new government he had hitherto taken a generous view of the extent of congressional authority. By now, however, he was thoroughly worried over the emerging shape of Hamilton's program and intent on stopping it. He argued that because the Constitution did not specifically empower Congress to issue charters of incorporation it had no right to do so. Hamilton answered that the Constitution empowered the government to do anything "necessary and proper" to carry out its assigned functions.

This was the first great debate over strict, as opposed to loose, interpretation of the Constitution. Congress readily accepted Hamilton's loose construction and passed the bill. Washington weighed the question more seriously, listening carefully to Madison and Jefferson as well as to Hamilton. Though he remained doubtful to the end, at the last minute, on February 25, 1791, he signed the bill. Hamilton's program moved ahead another step.

Having provided capital and credit Hamilton was now ready to direct the expansion of manufacturing. In December he presented to Congress his "Report on Manufactures," a scheme to make investment in industry attractive by means of protective tariffs and bounties. This time a combination of forces opposed him. Farmers and merchants preferred free competition to keep down the price of manufactures, and they feared retaliatory action by other countries against American agricultural exports. And almost everyone wondered whether the United States could afford a measure that would discourage importation, when the government's principal income came from import duties. To raise them to protective levels might reduce the volume of imports so drastically as to endanger the national credit. Moved by these considerations, Congress dealt Hamilton his first defeat by shelving his report.

Madison and Jefferson, who engineered the defeat, were both alarmed by the apparent intent of Hamilton's program. No one had done more than Madison to resuscitate and strengthen the central government a few years earlier at the Constitutional Convention, but in the Hamiltonian system he saw the beginnings of a national government so strong that it would endanger the individual liberties he had been trying to protect in the Bill of Rights. Jefferson, even more than Madison, was wary of governmental power. That government was best, he believed, which governed least.

To this distrust of government, Jefferson joined a dislike of cities and of the merchants and manufacturers who thrived in them. Farmers, he believed, enjoyed a greater virtue and a closer contact with their Maker than did the inhabitants of cities. From Paris he had written to Madison in 1787, "I think our governments will remain virtuous for many centuries; as long as they are chiefly agricultural. . . . When they get piled upon one another in large cities, as in Europe, they shall become corrupt as in Europe." Jefferson and Madison were both convinced that the federal government would have all the strength it needed and would be less likely to exceed its authority, if it depended not on an alliance with powerful creditors but on the support of the producing classes, the simple farmers and artisans who formed the bulk of the population. Opponents of the Constitution had feared that a strong central government would be manipulated to bring power and wealth to a few. Hamilton seemed bent on justifying their fears, which he and Madison had earlier joined to combat in the *Federalist* papers. Moreover, Hamilton's program was driving a wedge between the North, where capital and credit were accumulating, and the South, whose farmers and planters feared that the accumulation was at their expense. Almost all the stock in Hamilton's United States Bank was purchased by Northern and European creditors; and Hamilton made it plain that the bank was intended to assist the expansion of commerce and industry, not agriculture. He dismissed out of hand a proposal that the bank lend money to Southern planters on the security of tobacco warehouse receipts.

Thus within three years of the inauguration of the national government its leaders had reached a fundamental disagreement over its scope and policy. Washington stood above the quarrel, and both sides could still join in persuading him to accept another term of

---

Jefferson's View of the Good Society

Those who labor in the earth are the chosen people of God, if ever He had a chosen people, whose breasts He has made His peculiar deposit for substantial and genuine virtue. It is the focus in which he keeps alive that sacred fire, which otherwise might escape from the face of the earth. Corruption of morals in the mass of cultivators is a phenomenon of which no age nor nation has furnished an example. It is the mark set on those, who, not looking up to heaven, to their own soil and industry, as does the husbandman, for their subsistence, depend for it on casualties and caprice of customers. Dependence begets subservience and venality, suffocates the germ of virtue, and prepares fit tools for the designs of ambition. This, the natural progress and consequence of the arts, has sometimes perhaps been retarded by accidental circumstances; but, generally speaking, the proportion which the aggregate of the other classes of citizens bears in any State to that of its husbandmen, is the proportion of its unsound to its healthy parts.... While we have land to labor then, let us never wish to see our citizens occupied at a workbench, or twirling a distaff.... For the general operations of manufacture, let our workshops remain in Europe.

From Thomas Jefferson, *Notes on the State of Virginia,* 1782.

---

office when the national elections were held in 1792. But the gap between the views of Hamilton on the one hand and of Jefferson and Madison on the other was about as wide as constitutional government could stand. During Washington's second term the dissension spread from domestic policy to foreign affairs, with a growing bitterness that threatened to split the Union.

Foreign Affairs under Washington

The Constitution assigned to the President the conduct of relations with Europeans and Indians, and, where Washington gave Hamilton a free hand in developing financial policy and refused to meddle in congressional enactments of that policy, he gave Jefferson no such freedom as Secretary of State. He turned to Jefferson for advice, but he sought advice from other department heads as well. As foreign affairs assumed greater and greater complexity, he began the practice of calling together the Attorney General and the Secretaries of State, War, and the Treasury to discuss policy. During these meetings, from which grew the Cabinet as an institution, Jefferson and Hamilton again revealed their differing conceptions of the national welfare.

Jeffersonian Neutrality   The discord in foreign affairs first showed itself in 1790, when a threatened war between Spain and England offered the United States an opportunity to press American claims against both countries. Spain had seized three British vessels trading in Nootka Sound, Vancouver Island, which had been Spanish territory ever since its discovery. England demanded the return of the ships, reparation for damages, and recognition of British trading rights in the area. It seemed likely that Spain would fight rather than submit.

Washington's advisers all agreed that the United States should remain neutral in case of war, but they did not agree on what the United States should do if England decided to march troops through American territory in the Mississippi Valley in order to attack the Spaniards in Florida and Louisiana. Since Hamilton had just tied his funding program to duties on British trade, he was reluctant to do anything that might offend England. Jefferson wanted to keep both Spain and England guessing and make them both bid high for American neutrality.

As it happened, Spain gave in to the British ultimatum, and no war occurred. But another European war was clearly in the making, and mounting tensions in Europe generated a notable increase in the cordiality of European countries toward the United States. In 1791 England sent a minister plenipotentiary, George Hammond, to reside in Philadelphia; the United States in turn sent Thomas Pinckney to London. Full diplomatic relations had thus been established between England and the United States when war finally did break out in 1793 between England and France —and something close to war between Hamilton and Jefferson.

Thomas Jefferson, as American minister to France during the 1780's, had learned to admire French civilization and French people. Just before returning to the United States late

in 1789, he had witnessed the beginnings of their revolution, which, like most other Americans, he welcomed as a by-product of the spirit of '76. When he took up his post as Washington's Secretary of State, he brought with him a warm sympathy for the French and their cause, a sympathy that was not destroyed by the execution of Louis XVI in 1793 or by the reign of terror that followed.

Hamilton, by contrast, watched with horror as the French Revolution overturned the foundations of society, destroying monarchy and aristocracy, exalting democracy and demagogues. His horror mounted when the French Revolutionists launched the "war of all peoples against all kings," with England and Spain as primary targets. England, even under King George III, seemed to Hamilton a safer friend for Americans than republican France. Hamilton was moved not simply by his repugnance for the French Revolution but by the belief that, if the United States had to choose sides, England was more to be feared than France, simply because England had the stronger navy. American commerce was more vulnerable to English sailors than to French soldiers.

Hamilton agreed with Washington's other advisers that the United States should stay out of the war, but he wanted to use the crisis as an opportunity to scrap the French alliance. The treaties of 1778, he argued, had been made with the French monarchy and were no longer binding now that the monarchy had been overthrown. The United States should therefore declare its neutrality and refuse to receive the minister, Edmond Genêt, sent by the new French republic early in 1793.

Jefferson argued that the treaties had been made with the French nation and were still binding. He was as certain as Hamilton that the United States should stay out of the war, but wanted the country to do so without publicly announcing its intention. A declaration of neutrality would affront the French and would destroy the possibility of bargaining with the British, who still had troops stationed in the American Northwest and still withheld trading privileges in the empire. Washington decided the matter on April 22, 1793, by issuing a proclamation of neutrality addressed to American citizens only and not actually mentioning the word "neutrality." The treaties with France were not repudiated, and Citizen Genêt was accorded formal recognition. But the bargaining power that Jefferson valued was gone. Shortly afterward he announced that he would retire at the end of the year.

Genêt was a fool. From the moment of his arrival he assumed powers that no independent country could permit a foreign envoy: he commissioned American ships to sail as privateers under the French flag; he set up courts to condemn the ships they captured; he arranged an expedition of western frontiersmen to attack Spanish New Orleans. Jefferson tried hard to like him but gave up in disgust. Finally Washington demanded Genêt's recall.

While Genêt was losing friends for France, the British government was losing them for England. Under the terms of the French treaties and of the neutrality proclamation of 1793, Americans claimed the right as neutrals to carry noncontraband goods (including naval stores) to and from the ports of belligerents. France had lifted some of her mercantilist restrictions regulating trade with her West Indian islands, and American ships were swarming there to take advantage of the new opportunity. But England did not recognize the principle that "free ships make free goods." Instead she adhered to a rule of 1756 that trade which was closed in peacetime could not be opened in wartime. In December 1793, without warning, her naval vessels began seizing American ships trading with the French West Indies.

The seizures combined with an Indian episode in the Northwest to bring the United States, in spite of Hamilton, to the brink of war with England. The record of Washington's government in dealing with hostile Indians had not been good. He had arranged a treaty with Alexander McGillivray, the half-breed chieftain of the Creeks, but the Creeks had broken it as soon as it was made. He had sent General Josiah Harmar to crush the Miamis in Ohio, but they had crushed him. He had sent Arthur St. Clair with a much larger force in 1791, but St. Clair, like Braddock in 1755, had been surprised just short of his objective and completely routed. In February 1794, as General Anthony Wayne gathered a force to try again, the governor general of Canada, Lord Dorchester, made a speech to the Indians in which he in effect exhorted them to do their worst. Reports of the speech reached Congress along with news of the Caribbean seizures.

The House of Representatives was then debating whether restrictions against British commerce (suggested by Jefferson shortly before his resignation) might lead England to reduce her own restrictions against American commerce. News of the seizures precipitated an overwhelming demand for much stronger anti-British measures, to which Hamilton felt sure England would react by declaring war on the United States—if indeed the United States did not declare war first. The country was swept by war hysteria: volunteer defense companies sprang up. Mobs mistreated English seamen and tarred and feathered pro-British Americans. To prevent a plunge into actual warfare, Hamilton urged Washington to send a special mission to England. Hamilton seems to have thought of heading it himself, but Washington gave the job to Hamilton's alter ego, John Jay.

A Hamiltonian Treaty   John Jay had had abundant experience as a diplomat, but in the eyes of most Americans it had been unsuccessful experience. As envoy to Spain during the Revolution, he had failed to gain either alliance or recognition of American independence. As Secretary for Foreign Affairs under the Articles of Confederation, he had conducted the nearly disastrous negotiations with Gardoqui. In both cases failure arose less from lack of skill on his part than from the fact that the other side held all the cards. This time, with England engaged in a major European war, Jay was in a strong position to play the game that Jefferson had recommended all along: namely, to make England pay for continued American neutrality. Edmund Randolph, the new Secretary of State, agreed with the Jeffersonian strategy. He instructed Jay to consult with Russia, Sweden, and Denmark about the possibility of an armed-neutrality agreement in order to bring pressure on England to stop seizures of neutral shipping.

Once again, however, Jay found himself on the losing side through no fault of his own. Denmark and Sweden, which shared the American view of the rights of neutral ships, took the initiative, and just after Jay's departure for Europe the United States received an invitation from them to join in forming an alliance of neutrals. Randolph wanted to accept, for he felt that such backing would strengthen Jay's hand. But Hamilton persuaded Washington to decline, on the grounds that the alliance would jeopardize Jay's mission by antagonizing the British. Not content with rejecting the assistance of other neutrals, and eager to create a friendly climate of opinion in England, Hamilton weakened Jay's position still further by informing George Hammond, the British minister in America, of Washington's decision.

With this information to guide him, Lord Grenville, the British foreign minister, felt safe in conceding little. He promised again to surrender the Northwest posts—provided the United States permitted the continuation of the English fur trade with the Indians in the area; he promised recompense for the American ships that had been seized without warning in December 1793 in the Caribbean—provided the United States compensated British creditors for prerevolutionary debts whose collection had been impeded by state governments. He refused to compensate American slave-owners for slaves kidnapped or liberated by the British during the Revolution, and he refused to give any guarantee against the British navy's practice of stopping American vessels to impress alleged British subjects as seamen. Instead of stopping the seizure of neutral ships he required the United States to give up for twelve years her own view of neutral shipping rights. He consented to reciprocal trading rights between England and America but restricted American trade with the British West Indies to vessels of no more than seventy tons, and even these he allowed only in return for an American promise to ship no molasses, sugar, coffee, cocoa, or cotton from the islands or from the United States to any other part of the world. The only generosity he showed was at the expense of the Spanish: it was agreed that both British subjects and Americans should have the right to navigate the Mississippi through Spanish territory to the sea.

When the treaty containing these terms reached Washington on March 7, 1795, Hamilton was no longer at the Treasury. He had resigned at the end of January, a little more than a year after Jefferson, but he retained as much influence over the President out of office as in. His replacement, Oliver Wolcott, Jr., had been his assistant and continued to consult him on every important matter. Hamilton thought that the treaty was satisfactory and that failure to ratify it would mean war. Washington reluctantly agreed, but he could see that other Americans might not. To avoid a premature hardening of opposition, he tried to keep the terms secret until he could present the treaty for ratification at a special session of the Senate called for June 8. It was impossible. By the time the Senate met, rumors of the contents had produced wide public hostility, which increased as the details became known. Nevertheless, the senators, after striking out the clause regarding trade with the West Indies, accepted the treaty by the exact two-thirds majority required.

As the treaty came before Washington for his signature, the press was denouncing Jay, the treaty, the Senate, and even the President. Popular meetings in Boston, Philadelphia, New York, and other cities urged Washington to reject it. In the Cabinet everyone but Randolph urged him to sign. Dismayed by the public antagonism, Washington hesitated. In the meantime, the British minister handed to Oliver Wolcott some intercepted dispatches written by the French minister, Jean Fauchet. In them Fauchet, referring to some transactions with Randolph, seemed to imply that Randolph had turned over state secrets to him for money. Although the dispatches had nothing to do with the treaty, they discredited the only Cabinet member who opposed it. Washington signed the treaty, and, after confronting Randolph with the dispatches, refused his explanations and accepted his resignation.

The Winning of the West   Jay's Treaty was the low-water mark of foreign affairs under Washington. General Wayne had defeated the Indians of the Northwest at the Battle of Fallen Timbers (August 20, 1794) and had gone on to devastate their settlements. At the Treaty of Greenville (August 3, 1795) they gave up most of the territory that was to become the state of Ohio. In the next year the British at last honored their agreement to evacuate their posts in the Northwest.

Meanwhile, Spain had become fearful that

The Treaty of Greenville, 1795

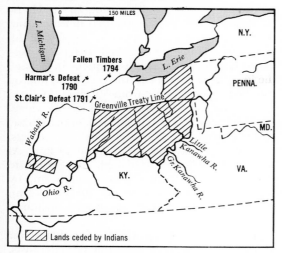

Lands ceded by Indians

the United States would throw her small weight on the British side in the precarious European balance. The clause about the Mississippi in Jay's Treaty suggested that England and the United States might be contemplating joint action against Louisiana. Taking advantage of this fear, the American envoy, Thomas Pinckney, who was sent to negotiate a treaty, won for the United States everything she had been seeking from Spain: free navi-

Pinckney's Treaty, 1795

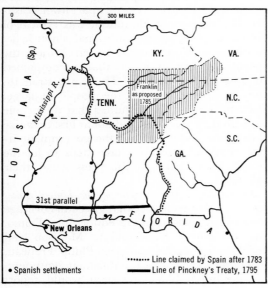

• Spanish settlements
•••••••• Line claimed by Spain after 1783
━━━━ Line of Pinckney's Treaty, 1795

gation of the Mississippi, permission for American traders to deposit goods for shipment at the mouth of the river, acknowledgment of the American southern boundary at the thirty-first parallel and the western boundary at the Mississippi, and an agreement by each country to prevent Indians within its territory from making incursions into the territory of the other.

The Senate accepted Pinckney's Treaty unanimously on March 3, 1796. With it the danger of secession in Kentucky and Tennessee (admitted to the Union in 1792 and 1796) disappeared; with the Mississippi open to trade, any attachment to Spain lost its charm for the Americans of the Southwest. Washington's foreign policy, which had begun in failure, ended in the final recognition by both Spain and Britain of United States sovereignty over the area first won from Britain in 1783.

Federalists Versus Republicans

Alexander Hamilton, by dictating domestic policy to Congress and foreign policy to the President, gave the national government its initial direction. Although Madison and Jefferson managed to modify some of his measures, in all essentials Hamilton prevailed. But in their efforts to defeat him, Madison and Jefferson set a pattern of political action that in ten years' time gave them control of the government and thereafter became the only way of gaining or keeping control. They started a political party.

The Republican Challenge The framers of the Constitution, Madison included, had not thought well of parties. "Faction" was the word generally used for party in the eighteenth century, and a faction meant, by Madison's own definition, a group of men organized to procure selfish advantages at the expense of the community. Denunciation of factions or parties was a standard ingredient in every discussion of politics in the eighteenth century, as safe and as platitudinous as denunciation of corruption and praise of honesty.

The parties of the time deserved denunciation. In the British House of Commons, and to some degree in the colonial assemblies, politicians had joined forces from time to time in order to make legal raids on the public purse.

New States 1791-96

VERMONT
1791

KENTUCKY
1792

TENNESSEE
1796

Because neither Madison nor Jefferson had any such end in view, they did not at first think of their opposition to Hamilton as constituting a party. Madison, to be sure, had a following in the House of Representatives and was an old hand at collecting votes in support of his measures. But in lining up opposition to indiscriminate funding and wholesale assumption, neither Jefferson nor Madison anticipated a continuing, organized opposition.

It was only as the full dimensions of Hamilton's program revealed themselves that the two men deliberately set out to gather and consolidate their strength against him inside the government and out. Jefferson was aware that Washington consulted Hamilton on every kind of measure, including matters which seemed to belong properly in the Department of State; in response, he tried to extend his own influence within the executive departments. Washington liked Jefferson, as did most of the other members of the presidential entourage. And yet Jefferson made little headway in his campaign. Though he succeeded in having the mint established under the State Department instead of the Treasury, his attempts to get the Post Office transferred to the State Department failed, and so did his efforts to get his friend Tench Coxe appointed as Comptrol-

ler, and Thomas Paine as Postmaster General.

Madison was more successful. In the House of Representatives he was often defeated, but every defeat strengthened the loyalty of his followers. Though he lacked Jefferson's personal charm and was not eloquent in debate, he knew how to work in the corridors; and on the floor his colleague from Virginia, William Giles, was an able spokesman of his views. John Beckley, the perennial clerk of the House, who seemed to know everybody's secrets, turned over valuable information to him. As the Madison forces hardened, they began to call themselves the republican interest, and by 1792 they even dared to say the republican party—a phrase which gradually acquired capital letters.

Their opponents, not considering themselves a party, appropriated the name of Federalists, which had been used earlier by the advocates of the Constitution of 1787. This maneuver identified the Republicans with the anti-Federalists of that period. Actually there was no connection. The leaders of the Republican party had supported the Constitution in 1787 and still did; the Federalists of the early 1790's were distinguished not by any special reverence for that document, but by a conception of the national welfare that included a permanent national debt, a national bank, and dependence on England.

Madison and Jefferson believed that the source of Federalist strength, apart from Washington's support of Hamilton, was typical of faction or party in the traditional sense: it lay in the corruption of congressmen through the speculative opportunities that accompanied funding and assumption. Their own strength, they believed, lay with the people at large. Perhaps because they assumed that the people were on their side, they did not at first organize their party except within the government itself; they did, however, take steps to let the people know, through the press, what their side was.

Before 1791 the *Gazette of the United States* was the only newspaper that gave full coverage to national politics, and its editor, John Fenno, was an ardent Hamiltonian. Madison and Jefferson persuaded the poet Philip Freneau, whom they knew to be republican in sentiment, to establish a newspaper that would report

State Rights
and Individual Liberty

Resolved, that the several states composing the United States of America, are not united on the principle of unlimited submission to their General Government; but that by compact under the style and title of a Constitution for the United States and of amendments thereto, they consituted a General Government for special purposes, delegated to that Government certain definite powers, reserving each state to itself, the residuary mass of right to their own self Government; and that whensoever the General Government assumes undelegated powers, its acts are unauthoritative, void, and are of no force: That to this compact each state acceded as a state, and is an integral party, its co-states forming as to itself, the other party: That the Government created by this compact was not made the exclusive or final judge of the extent of the powers delegated to itself; since that would have made its discretion, and not the constitution, the measure of its powers; but that as in all other cases of compact among parties having no common judge, each party has an equal right to judge for itself....

Resolved ... that no power over the freedom of religion, freedom of speech, or freedom of the press being delegated to the United States by the Constitution, nor prohibited by it to the states, all lawful powers respecting the same did of right remain, and were reserved to the states, or to the people: That thus ... the act of the Congress ... which does abridge the freedom of the press, is not law, but is altogether void and of no effect.

From Thomas Jefferson, *The Kentucky Resolutions*, 1798.

National Authority
and Individual Loyalty

The unity of government which constitutes you one people is also now dear to you. It is justly so; for it is a main pillar in the edifice of your real independence, the support of your tranquility at home; your peace abroad; of your safety; of your prosperity; of that very liberty which you so highly prize. But as it is easy to foresee, that from different causes and from different quarters, much pains will be taken, many artifices employed, to weaken in your minds the conviction of this truth; as this is the point in your political fortress against which the batteries of internal and external enemies will be most constantly and actively (though often covertly and insidiously) directed, it is of infinite moment, that you should properly estimate the immense value of your national Union to your collective and individual happiness....

To the efficacy and permanency of your union, a Government for the whole is indispensable.... This Government, the offspring of your own choice uninfluenced and unawed,... has a just claim to your confidence and your support. Respect for its authority, compliance with its laws, acquiescence in its measures, are duties enjoined by the fundamental maxims of true liberty....

Towards the preservation of your Government ... it is requisite, not only that you steadily discountenance irregular oppositions to its acknowledged authority, but also that you resist with care the spirit of innovation upon its principles however specious the pretexts.

From George Washington, *The Farewell Address*, 1796.

national issues from their point of view. On October 31, 1791, the first issue of the *National Gazette* was published, and the Republicans gained a medium for spreading attacks on the Hamiltonian program (some of them written by Madison) throughout the country.

At the same time spontaneous popular societies began to form that might have furnished the basis for Republican party organization at the local level. Admiration for the French Revolution and discontent with the government's evident bias in favor of England prompted the formation of these "Democratic Clubs," first in Pennsylvania and then all over the country. The clubs, which were imitations of the Jacobin societies in France, felt that they were continuing the tradition of the Sons

of Liberty of the 1760's and 1770's. They sympathized with the French Revolution and passed resolutions against the government's pro-British foreign policy; they supported the Republicans in Congress and in elections for Congress. But before Madison and his friends could capitalize on their support, the Federalists found an opportunity to discredit the clubs and capture a wide popular following for themselves.

The Federalist Response   The Federalist opportunity arose from a tax on whiskey, passed by Congress in 1791 to help pay the expenses of funding and assumption. The taxation of alcoholic beverages was peculiarly unpopular in the eighteenth century. A cider tax nearly caused rebellion in England in 1733,

President and general: Washington at the time of the Whiskey Rebellion.

and so did a rum tax in Massachusetts in 1754. By 1794 the federal excise tax on liquor did cause rebellion, or what looked like it, in Pennsylvania. Farmers in the western part of the state generally turned their surplus grain into whiskey, which could be transported over the mountains more easily than wheat and which brought a better price in the Eastern markets. But the profit was small, and there was much evasion of the tax. In July 1794 the United States marshal, summoning offenders to court, met with mass resistance.

The governor of the state, Thomas Mifflin, thought that the courts could handle the situation. But Washington, urged on by Hamilton, decided that the challenge to national authority called for military action, and in October he marched fifteen thousand militiamen to western Pennsylvania. No rebel fired a shot against him, and Washington returned to Philadelphia, leaving Hamilton to complete the arrest of the ringleaders.

When Congress assembled shortly after his return, Washington delivered an address that made clear his contempt for all organized opposition to the policies of the national government, whether from whiskey rebels, Democratic Clubs, or Republicans. Although there is no evidence that the clubs had anything to do with the rebellion, Washington had somehow got the notion that they had. In spite of the fact that the Constitution guaranteed the right to assemble, he rebuked the clubs as "self-created societies." Dismayed by his disapproval, many of them dissolved at once, and the rest expired within a year or two.

Washington's personal popularity was thus revealed as the strongest weapon in the Federalist arsenal. The Republicans were not fully aware of how strong it was or of how it could be used against them. Nor was Washington aware. He continued to regard himself as standing above party and seems never to have realized that as he came more and more to rely on Hamilton he was choosing sides in a party conflict. Hamilton did realize and used Washington's prestige to turn popular opinion against the Republicans.

When the President signed Jay's Treaty, in spite of popular meetings that urged him not to, the Republicans, instead of conceding defeat, carried the battle to the House of Representatives. Although the Constitution gave only the Senate the authority to approve or reject treaties, the House, under Madison's leadership, asserted its right to examine treaties before appropriating funds to implement them. On this basis, the House demanded copies of the papers which had passed to and from Jay during the negotiations. Washington, defending the integrity of the executive department, indignantly refused; Hamilton, by decrying the demand of the House as an insult to the President and a step toward war, soon had Congress flooded with petitions supporting the President. Republican efforts to secure counterpetitions were less successful, and Madison saw his majority dwindle to a minority. The House in the end supported the treaty.

The Election of 1796   When the Republicans attacked the treaty in the House of Representatives, they had an eye on the presidential election that was to take place later in the year. In the elections of 1788 and 1792 there had been no serious contest for the presidency. In 1796 it was probable, though not certain, that Washington would retire. If he did, the Republicans would have a chance to challenge Hamilton at the polls. But the Republican hope of unseating the Federalists received a strong setback when Madison's attack on the treaty foundered against Washington's popularity.

As the election approached, Washington gave the Federalists another advantage by delaying his decision to withdraw. The Republicans were wary of advancing any candidate of their own unless the still insuperable national hero was out of the race. It was understood that if Washington chose not to run, Adams would be the Federalist candidate; for Hamilton, though influential among politicians, did not have a wide enough popular following to assure election. For the same reason the Republicans had settled on Jefferson rather than Madison. In September Washington finally

announced his retirement and delivered a farewell address written by Hamilton. The address contained a strong warning against partiality for foreign countries on the one hand (i.e., for France) and against political parties on the other (i.e., the Republicans). Washington still refused to think of the Federalists as a party.

Having secured Washington's support for a Federalist successor, Hamilton set about substituting a more pliable candidate for the prickly, independent Adams. Because of Adams' popular following, Hamilton could not renounce him publicly, but he hoped to achieve his purpose by manipulating the electoral vote.

The maneuver was made possible by the peculiar constitutional provisions for electing the President. Each state could select its members for the electoral college in any manner it saw fit. Six did it by popular vote, nine by vote of the state legislature, and one, Massachusetts, by a combination of the two. Most candidates for the college announced beforehand for whom they would vote; but this practice was not universal, and the college as an institution retained some small measure of choice. Each elector cast two ballots, without specifying which man he preferred for President; the candidate who received the largest vote became President, and the candidate with the second largest vote became Vice-President. Since this was a system designed for a partyless government, complications arose when political parties appeared. If all the electors who favored the strongest party voted for both its candidates, a tie vote would result. In order to elect the party's preferred presidential candidate some electors must divert their second vote from the party's vice-presidential candidate to some other candidate. This could be dangerous: if too many votes were diverted from the party's vice-presidential candidate he might be left with fewer than the presidential candidate of the opposing party, who would then become Vice-President instead. There was also the possibility that if both parties wanted the same man for Vice-President, he might receive more votes than either presidential candidate and thus become President.

It was this latter possibility that led Hamilton to arrange for Adams' running mate on the Federalist ticket to be Thomas Pinckney of

South Carolina. Pinckney, who had just returned in triumph from his Spanish mission, enjoyed great popularity in the South, where the Republicans were strongest. Southerners would certainly give most of their votes to Jefferson, but they might be persuaded to designate Pinckney as second choice. If a substantial number of electors did so, the combined Federalist-Republican vote might be large enough to put Pinckney into the presidency.

But Hamilton was not the only one who knew the deficiencies of the electoral system. When the votes of the electoral college were cast, it appeared that his advocacy of Pinckney had failed. Adams' friends in Connecticut and New Hampshire, refusing to endanger his success, had all scattered their second votes, and the Southern Republicans had actually given Pinckney nothing. Even so, he had fifty-nine votes; but Adams with seventy-one became President and Jefferson with sixty-eight became Vice-President. Jefferson's running mate, Aaron Burr of New York, had only thirty.

Had the Federalist electors of Connecticut and New Hampshire given Pinckney their second votes, Hamilton's strategy could have succeeded. Pinckney would have tied Adams' vote, and tied presidential elections, according to the Constitution, were to be decided in the House of Representatives. There, with Jefferson out of the contest, Southern Republicans might have joined with Hamilton's forces to make Pinckney President. For Adams it was a bitter thing to have come so close to losing and to know that Alexander Hamilton was to blame.

The Presidency of John Adams

The new President was a man of conflicting emotions, ideas, and loyalties. Round of face and frame, he looked like an English country squire and often behaved like one, lashing out at those who crossed him as though he were lord of the manor. Yet he was sometimes remarkably patient when there was real cause for anger. Like Washington and Jefferson and George III, he loved the land and found high office uncongenial and inconvenient. Yet no man wanted the presidency more or would have found defeat more humiliating.

Adams had had a distinguished career during the Revolution, both in the Continental Congress and in negotiating the peace treaty. His political experience and his study of history had given him strong ideas about the proper form of government: liberty, he believed, could be preserved only where a strong executive presided over a legislature divided into two houses, the upper representing the wealthy and well born, the lower representing the people at large. This idea, expounded at length in his *Defence of the Constitutions of the United States* (1787), had influenced the Philadelphia Convention and had helped produce the strong executive office which Adams inherited from Washington. As President, Adams continued to think that the executive must stand above the other branches of government and mitigate differences between them.

The President and the Politicians Adams, like his contemporaries, spoke of political parties only to condemn them. Though he had been elected in a contest between parties, the circumstances were not such as to endear either side to him. The Republicans had branded him as a monarchist because of his openly avowed advocacy of a strong executive, while the Federalists had almost betrayed him for Thomas Pinckney.

In his inaugural address Adams did his best to minimize party differences. Answering for the first time the accusations that had been made against him during the campaign, he assured the Republicans that he did not want a monarchical or aristocratic or indeed any but a republican government. Lest anyone think him an enemy of the French alliance, so dear to Jefferson, he affirmed his personal esteem for the French nation, "formed in a residence of seven years, chiefly among them"; and his "sincere desire to preserve the friendship which has been so much for the honor and interest of both nations."

The Republicans were delighted. Newspaper editors who had been warning of the approach of tyranny suddenly discovered the President's "incorruptible integrity," his intelligence, his patriotism. Jefferson had always liked Adams. The two had become estranged in 1791 when one of Jefferson's friends published a private letter from him criticizing Adams' political writings. Before the inauguration they made it up and took rooms in the same Philadelphia boardinghouse. In assuming office as Vice-President, Jefferson hailed the man "whose talents and integrity have been known and revered by me through a long course of years."

The political backers of both men were suspicious of the new harmony and uneasy about the effect it might have on the party organizations they had been building. Before coming to Philadelphia, Jefferson had drafted an open and generous letter to Adams, declaring his pleasure in the outcome of the election. He had always served as a junior to Adams and would be glad to continue doing so. He sent the letter to Madison to deliver at his discretion. Madison thought it best not to: if made public, it might alienate Jefferson's supporters and embarrass him in a future contest. Jefferson himself avoided getting too close to the administration: the separation of powers, he decided, should prevent his sitting in the President's Cabinet.

Federalist leaders, equally cautious, were worried about Adams' charity toward the Republicans and pulled him up sharp when he proposed appointing Madison as special envoy to France. Adams, who had already told Jefferson of his intention, with some embarrassment withdrew the nomination when Oliver Wolcott, Jr., the Secretary of the Treasury, threatened to resign in protest. Thereafter relations between the President and the Vice-President cooled off, for the behavior of Adams seemed clearly to indicate that in spite of his good beginning he would not stand very far above party.

It might, in the end, have been better for Adams if he had used his famous temper on Wolcott. Since there was as yet no tradition requiring Cabinet officers to submit their resignations when a new President took office, Adams inherited the Cabinet that Washington left behind. And a sorry lot they were. Besides Wolcott at the Treasury, there was James McHenry in the War Department and Timothy Pickering at State. Hamilton, in suggesting McHenry's appointment to Washington, had said that "he would give no strength to the administration, but he would not disgrace the office." Three years later, Hamilton had to admit that "my friend McHenry is wholly insufficient for his place." Timothy Pickering had originally served as Postmaster, a position

John Adams: Always honest, often wise.

that strained his talents to their limits. When Randolph resigned, Washington gave Pickering the State Department temporarily, but was unable to persuade a more competent man to take the job.

Apart from their palpable mediocrity, the only thing that Wolcott, McHenry, and Pickering had in common was that they all took orders from Hamilton. Adams was too keen a man not to perceive the quality of their minds, but he did not realize that the advice they gave him came by mail from New York. Even had he known, he might have hesitated to drop them. They had been appointed by the great Washington, and it would have been brash for a President who had barely won the office to cashier the advisers whom the national hero had thought adequate. Even if Adams had let them go, he might have had difficulty replacing them. Cabinet officers received a salary of only three thousand dollars a year, and a man of talent who could earn much more in private business might be reluctant or unable to make the financial sacrifice, especially since there was as yet little prestige in any appointive office. Washington had kept second-rate men simply because he could not get first-rate ones.

Surrounded by incompetent advisers who remained loyal to a politician who had betrayed him, Adams could have preserved the strength of the executive department only by showing a resolute determination to make his own decisions. Instead, he spent much of his time at home in Quincy, Massachusetts, leaving the members of his Cabinet to deliberate by themselves. Consequently his administration drifted into policies with which he did not fully agree and from which he finally extricated it only at the expense of his political career.

The End of the French Alliance   In the opening months of his administration Adams' cordiality for France as for Jefferson cooled rapidly. During Washington's presidency the French government had become increasingly angered by the apparent partiality of its American ally for England. Although the commercial treaty of 1778 stated that the United States would give no nation greater trading privileges than it gave to France, Congress had never given France anything more than equality with other nations—and that only on paper. In operation, the laws that Congress passed consistently favored England. One clause of Jay's Treaty effectually guaranteed that England would be as favored as was France. The treaty had outraged France, and the French minister to America, Pierre Adet, had warned that his country would henceforth treat American ships "in the same manner as they suffer the English to treat them." Actually the French had already intercepted several American vessels bound for England and had impounded them in French harbors. Now France announced that she would no longer recognize the treaty principle that free ships made free goods, and that she would treat

American sailors serving on British ships as pirates. She went even further: she refused to have anything to do with the American minister, Charles Cotesworth Pinckney (brother of Thomas).

President Adams proposed to meet the crisis diplomatically by sending a three-man mission to France, the mission for which he had considered Madison. The members of his Cabinet were at first opposed not only to Madison but to any mission. Only after Hamilton cautioned them not to get too far ahead of public opinion did they fall in with Adams' plan. The commissioners appointed were the Virginia Federalist lawyer, John Marshall; the rejected minister to France, C. C. Pinckney; and an astute but unpredictable Massachusetts politician, Elbridge Gerry. To announce the mission the President called a special session of Congress in May and delivered a message that the Cabinet, speaking for Hamilton, had thought the only proper accompaniment to negotiations. It called for the strengthening of coastal defenses, the arming of merchant vessels, the completion of three frigates begun in 1794, and the establishment of a provisional army.

The message put an end to Republican sympathy for the President. Jefferson, the former advocate of bargaining from strength, now thought that the recommendations would be offensive to France and would make the mission's task impossible. As it turned out, neither American nor French belligerence but French corruption prevented the mission's success. The French minister of foreign affairs, Talleyrand, after keeping the envoys waiting for several weeks, informed them through three unaccredited go-betweens, known only as X, Y, and Z, that the price of negotiating would be $250,-000 for himself. The price of a treaty would be several million dollars for France. "Not a sixpence," said Pinckney, as he and Marshall departed, leaving Gerry to continue the futile conversations until he was ordered home.

When Adams reported the XYZ affair, incredulous Republicans in Congress demanded to see the commission's papers. Adams did not follow Washington's example in the case of the Jay's Treaty papers, probably because he knew that the record would fully sustain him. He turned the papers over, and Congress supported the President in retaliating against France by actions just short of war: The treaties of 1778 were repudiated. Commercial intercourse was suspended. American ships were authorized to seize French armed vessels, and for the next two years French and American ships fought an undeclared war on the high seas.

It would have been foolhardy to go such lengths without preparing for full-scale war. But the President and his advisers could not agree on the kind of preparation to make. The most ardent Federalists saw in the crisis an opportunity to strengthen themselves as well as the government at the expense of the Republicans. They wanted a large standing army, not merely to repel a French invasion but to overawe and if necessary to suppress their political opponents. Hamilton also dreamed of leading an army of conquest into Florida and Louisiana. Adams, while denouncing the French and their American friends, had a more realistic and more comprehensive view of the national interest. He thought it wise to keep a small army in readiness, but he discounted the possibility of a French invasion, and he had no ambition to rule by military force or to conquer territories peopled by Frenchmen and Spaniards. What the country really needed, he believed, was a navy to defend its commercial interests in the shifting tides of European conflict. To concentrate on an army would leave the United States no choice but to side always with the country whose navy dominated the seas, in other words, with England. Though Adams' own sympathies lay with England, he thought it was bad policy to let the safety of American commerce depend on the good will of any foreign country. Accordingly, in May 1798 he persuaded Congress to establish a Department of the Navy, with Benjamin Stoddert, a Maryland merchant, as Secretary. In Stoddert Adams gained his first loyal adviser in the Cabinet.

While Adams and Stoddert proceeded with the construction and commissioning of warships, the High Federalists, as the more extreme branch of the party came to be called, continued their build-up of the army, dragging the reluctant President with them, and levying heavy taxes to pay for it. Washington was persuaded to accept command again, and

Hamilton was eager to join him. Adams agreed to make Hamilton a general but refused at first to rank him above Henry Knox, Daniel Morgan, and Benjamin Lincoln, Hamilton's seniors in the Revolutionary army. Hamilton, perhaps with more than military ends in view, declined to play second fiddle to anyone but Washington and made his refusal a test of strength. When Washington, still willing to play Hamilton's game, joined the Cabinet in demanding that Hamilton be his second in command, Adams was forced to back down.

After this victory, the High Federalists pressed hard for a declaration of war against France. The harder they pressed, the more apparent it became that their aims were domestic rather than foreign. England's depredations against American shipping had continued unabated, while France, according to reports from Elbridge Gerry, had become far more conciliatory in response to the violent American reaction to the XYZ affair. Gerry was denounced by the Federalists upon his return in 1798, but he was courted by the Republicans and heeded by the President. George Logan, an ex-Quaker from Philadelphia who had conducted an unauthorized peace mission of his own, confirmed Gerry's view of the shift in France's attitude. Adams objected to private citizens meddling in the country's foreign relations and got the Logan Act passed to prevent it in the future, but he was impressed by what Logan told him. Similar reports were arriving from the President's son, John Quincy Adams, also in Europe, and from Rufus King, the American minister in London, and from William Vans Murray at The Hague. In January the President received from Murray a letter sent by Talleyrand to the French chargé at The Hague, specifically stating that an American envoy to France would "undoubtedly be received with the respect due to the representative of a free, independent and powerful nation."

Adams did not assume that Talleyrand's character had improved, but he suspected that American firmness had worked a change in French policy. To declare war now would be to lose all the advantages of neutrality, to sacrifice the national interest to party politics. Hamilton, Pickering, Wolcott, and their followers were all ready to make that sacrifice.

Adams was not, and he decided for once to be President. In February 1799, without consulting his Cabinet further, he sent to the Senate the nomination of William Vans Murray as minister to negotiate a new agreement with France.

Having done so, Adams went off to Quincy, leaving the High Federalists furious and frustrated. They tried delaying tactics, and they substituted a three-man commission for Murray, but they were unable to thwart Adams. When the commission consisting of Murray, Oliver Ellsworth (Chief Justice of the United States), and William R. Davie (former governor of North Carolina) arrived in France, they found Bonaparte in control. He was eager to line up a coalition of neutral nations against England and ready to renew Franco-American relations on terms advantageous to the United States. France was willing to declare the old treaties of 1778 void, thus formally freeing the United States of its only permanent alliance. France was also willing to accept again the principle of free-ships-free-goods and, on September 30, 1800, the negotiators signed a convention that put an end to French spoliation of American commerce. The President's declaration of independence from his Cabinet had thus saved his country from a needless war and gained it greater freedom on the seas.

The Alien and Sedition Laws   In sending the mission to France, John Adams had risen above party, as he believed a President should. But he never fully admitted, even to himself, how much he had been and still remained a member of the Federalist party. After his initial *rapprochement* with Jefferson had faded, his very devotion to the national interest and to the dignity of his office betrayed him, as it had Washington, into regarding himself and his supporters as impartial patriots and the Republican opposition as a criminal conspiracy.

After the disclosure of the XYZ affair, Adams had been deluged by addresses from groups of patriotic citizens declaring their readiness to fight the French. In his public replies he commended his correspondents and deplored the "few degraded or . . . deluded characters" who viewed the crisis differently. "These lovers of themselves," he announced, "who withdraw their confidence from their own Legislative Government, and place it on a foreign nation, or Domestic Faction, or both in alliance, deserve all our contempt and abhorrence." The references to Republicans were oblique but unmistakable. Even Hamilton thought the President might be pushing anti-Republican sentiment a little too far. But other Federalist leaders (without specific encouragement from either Adams or Hamilton) persuaded Congress to pass legislation designed to harass, if not destroy, the Republican opposition.

The Alien Acts, three in number, were passed in June and July 1798. One, the Alien Enemies Act, was a nonpartisan measure that simply provided for the restraint of enemy aliens in time of war. Since war was never declared against France, the act did not operate during Adams' presidency. The other two were partisan measures aimed against immigrants, who were widely suspected of being Republican in politics. The Naturalization Act required that an alien seeking citizenship must have resided for fourteen years in the United States, five of them in the state where naturalization was sought. The Alien Friends Act, which was to run for two years only, gave the President power to deport any alien whom he considered dangerous to the welfare of the country.

The Sedition Act, which was passed in July 1798, was one of the most repressive measures ever directed against political activity in the United States. It provided fines and imprisonment for persons unlawfully combining or conspiring "with intent to oppose any measure or measures of the government of the United States," or counseling or advising such opposition, or writing, printing, uttering, or publishing "any false, scandalous, and malicious writing or writings against the government of the United States, or the President of the United States, with intent to defame . . . or to bring them or either of them, into contempt or disrepute." The blatant political purpose of the act was admitted in the date when it was to expire: March 3, 1801, when the next President would be inaugurated. The act would last long enough to gag Republican criticism of the administration until the next election was safely over; it would expire soon enough to permit Federalist criticism in case the election brought in a Republican administration.

The first victim of the Sedition Act was Matthew Lyon, Republican representative from Vermont. On the floor of the House, Lyon and the Connecticut Federalist Roger Griswold had already engaged each other with canes, fire tongs, and spit. In the autumn following the passage of the Sedition Act, Lyon, who was up for re-election, directed his campaign against the Federalist party's conduct of the government. Although his attacks were returned measure for measure by his opponent, Lyon was indicted, convicted, and sentenced (by a Federalist judge) to four months in jail and a thousand-dollar fine. He was reelected while serving his jail sentence.

The Republicans were alarmed—and rightly so. The Alien and Sedition Acts demonstrated that the Federalists were prepared to abandon the principles of the Enlightenment, of the Revolution, and of the Constitution. When Madison sponsored the first amendments to the Constitution, he had recognized that they might one day have to be defended against an ambitious executive or legislature. He had suggested that the federal courts might protect them, but thus far the courts had shown a disposition to restrain the states more than the national government. They had declared a few state laws unconstitutional, and in the case of *Chisholm* v. *Georgia* (1793) the Supreme Court had awarded judgment against the state of Georgia in a suit brought by citizens of South Carolina. This affront to state sovereignty caused so many protests that an eleventh amendment to the Constitution was adopted to deny federal jurisdiction in suits brought against a state by foreigners or by citizens of another state.

The Eleventh Amendment, which was ratified in January 1798, was a direct blow at the federal courts, whose prestige was already at a low ebb. Men of high talents refused to serve on them. John Jay had resigned as Chief Justice of the United States in 1795 in order to run for the governorship of New York. The judges who remained and who presided at sedition trials had no more scruples about the constitutionality of the Alien and Sedition Acts than John Adams had had when he signed them.

Since there seemed to be no other way of protecting the Constitution from the Federalists, Madison and Jefferson turned to the state governments. With the election of Adams, Madison had retired temporarily from Congress and returned to Virginia. In the Virginia legislature, he now secured passage (December 24, 1798) of a series of resolutions affirming the authority of the states to judge the constitutionality of federal legislation and declaring the Alien and Sedition Acts unconstitutional.

Madison's resolutions did not go beyond the statement of unconstitutionality. But Vice-President Jefferson had framed another set, for the state of Kentucky (November 16, 1798), which declared the acts to be "void and of no force." When the other states declined to support Virginia and Kentucky, Kentucky reaffirmed in another set of resolutions (November 22, 1799) that "nullification" by the states was the proper remedy for unconstitutional actions by the federal government. But the other states still refused to follow suit and allowed the Alien and Sedition Acts to expire under their own terms. Though the resolutions of Kentucky and Virginia failed in their immediate object, they posed a question that would trouble the nation for many years to come. The Philadelphia Convention had not decided which was sovereign, state governments or national government, and the resolutions were a reminder that the question was still open.

The Election of 1800   The steadily declining fortunes of the Republicans convinced them that in order to survive they would have to build a national organization. As a result of the XYZ affair they had lost congressional seats in the elections of 1798; even Virginia, the Republican stronghold, had returned five "certain Federalists" and three moderates who leaned toward Federalism. With Jefferson directing party strategy, the Republicans resolved to do better in the next election. Following regional patterns of local government, they appointed county committees in the South and township committees in the North to instruct the voters about the vices of Federalists and the virtues of Republicans. The local committees were supervised by state committees, which in turn took their direction from a "caucus," or extralegal meeting of Republican congressmen at Marache's boardinghouse in Philadelphia. By now there were Republican newspapers scattered throughout the country, the most

The Election of 1800

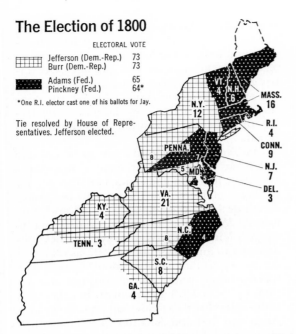

ELECTORAL VOTE

Jefferson (Dem.-Rep.)	73	
Burr (Dem.-Rep.)	73	
Adams (Fed.)	65	
Pinckney (Fed.)	64*	

*One R.I. elector cast one of his ballots for Jay.

Tie resolved by House of Representatives. Jefferson elected.

For all election maps in this book, the electoral vote will be given within each state. When a state's electoral vote is split, as were the votes of Pennsylvania, Maryland, and North Carolina in this election, the split will be shown with the number of electoral votes going to each candidate. The graphic presentation in such cases is not intended to indicate the geographic distribution of votes within the state.

prominent of which was Philadelphia's *Aurora*. The editors, defying the Sedition Act, charged the government with aristocratic and monarchical pretensions, and with levying heavy taxes to support an expensive navy, a standing army, and a corrupt funding system.

The charges struck home, for they were substantially correct. Armies and navies are always expensive, and in 1798 the Adams Administration had levied an extremely unpopular direct tax on houses, lands, and slaves to pay the rising costs. What was worse, in 1799 the army had been ordered into action to enforce collection of the tax, after a mob led by one John Fries released two tax-evaders from prison in Northampton County, Pennsylvania. Although the army, as in the case of the Whiskey Rebellion, could find no one to fight, the use of it lent support to Republican accusations of tyranny.

Federalist newspapers replied by calling Republicans the tools of the godless French. Federalist attorneys and judges made full use of the Sedition Act to silence Republican editors, but the wheels of the law did not turn rapidly enough to make more than a few martyrs. The Federalists also caucused at Philadelphia and tried to organize support at the local level. But their efforts were hampered by their own divisions. The rank and file of the party approved John Adams' peace mission to France, and would have been outraged by a proposal to support any other candidate for the presidency. The High Federalists, however, considered Adams a traitor. Pickering thought that the mission to France would "subvert the present administration and with them the government itself." Hamilton declared he would never again support Adams and even wrote a pamphlet attacking him.

In spite of the defection in his own camp, Adams made a strong bid for re-election. By the spring of 1800 it had become probable that he would take New England and New Jersey, that Jefferson (the inevitable Republican candidate) would win most of the South, and that a deadlock would neutralize Pennsylvania. New York and South Carolina, both uncertain, held the balance. In New York the legislature chose the presidential electors, and the state was so divided that the thirteen representatives from New York City held the balance of power in the legislature. In 1800 Aaron Burr, perhaps the Republicans' best working politician on the local level, was able to offer the city a slate of thirteen extremely influential and popular candidates for representative. They took the city by five hundred votes, thus assuring Republican control of the state legislature and of New York's electoral votes in the coming national contest.

New York City had hitherto been the private preserve of Alexander Hamilton, and the significance of his defeat was not lost on John Adams. The President knew that he had been right about the peace mission, regardless of party considerations; but he knew now that he was also right politically and that the High Federalists were wrong. After putting up with their insolence for three years, he had had enough. On May 6 he asked for and received McHenry's resignation from the War Department. On May 10 he asked for Pickering's; when Pickering refused, Adams simply discharged him.

While Adams was cutting loose from the High Federalists, the Republicans had decided that Aaron Burr would again make the best running mate for Jefferson. The Federalists' vice-presidential candidate was Charles Cotesworth Pinckney. Hamilton, who had been responsible for the choice, used the same strategy as in 1796: to throw support to a vice-presidential candidate in the hope that he would overtake both presidential candidates.

The outcome of the election was in doubt for some time, for electors were still chosen at different times and in different ways; but when the ballots were finally counted, Adams had sixty-five electoral votes, and Pinckney sixty-four. The Republican machine, working a little too well, had given Jefferson and Burr each seventy-three. It had been understood that Burr was the vice-presidential candidate, but no Republican elector had diverted one of his two ballots to preclude a tie. To prevent this situation from recurring, the twelfth amendment to the Constitution, adopted in 1804, required the electoral college to vote separately for President and for Vice-President. But in 1800, as directed by the Constitution, the choice between Jefferson and Burr was thrown to the House of Representatives, with each state allowed only one vote. Voting went on for a week through thirty-five ballots without the necessary nine-state majority being reached. Finally Hamilton, who considered Jefferson a lesser evil than Burr, persuaded some of the latter's supporters to cast blank ballots. Jefferson was declared elected.

Since Republican candidates for Congress were also victorious, the election of 1800 brought to an end the Federalist control of the national government. Nevertheless, the Federalists could look forward to a continuing influence: the United States judiciary, manned by Federalist appointees, enjoyed a lifetime tenure. The last acts of the Adams Administration made the most of this fact. A new judiciary act of February 27, 1801, created sixteen circuit courts; and Adams, instead of leaving the appointment of the new circuit judges to his successor, filled the offices with loyal Federalists. Even more significantly Adams in January 1801 appointed as Chief Justice of the United States John Marshall of Virginia, an ardent Federalist. Under Marshall the court was to rise to new heights of prestige and power, to the considerable annoyance of Marshall's fellow Virginian in the White House.

Jefferson liked to think of his election as the Revolution of 1800. But the election had been no landslide. John Adams had only six votes less than the winners. If he had taken either New York or South Carolina, he would have won; and he might have taken them had he parted sooner from the High Federalists. Actually John Adams' capture of the Federalist party marked as great a political change as Jefferson's triumph at the polls, a change possibly more crucial to the preservation of national unity. Hamiltonian policies, tied to urban business interests at home and to Great Britain abroad, had repeatedly threatened to divide the nation. By sending the mission to France and by repudiating Hamilton, Adams reduced the gap between Federalist and Republican views of the national interest. His action came too late to win an electoral majority for himself or his party, but it did ensure peace, not only between the United States and France, but between two groups of Americans who had drifted dangerously far apart.

SUGGESTIONS FOR READING   The period covered by this chapter is surveyed in more detail by J. C. Miller, in *The Federalist Era* (1960), and by Nathan Schachner, in *The Founding Fathers* * (1954), both of which are readable and reliable.

Leonard White, *The Federalists* (1948), assesses the achievements of the Washington and Adams administrations in establishing the bureaucratic machinery of national government. The political foundations of Federalist power are analyzed in Manning Dauer, *The Adams Federalists* (1953). In *The Economic Origins of Jeffersonian Democracy* (1915), Charles Beard saw the rise of the Republican party as a continuation of the small-farmer hostility to the

* Available in a paperback edition.

Constitution, which he had described in his *Economic Interpretation of the Constitution* * (1913). Joseph Charles, *The Origins of the American Party System* * (1956), denies that there was any such continuity. Noble Cunningham, *The Jeffersonian Republicans* (1957), describes the political organizing activities of the Republicans and is particularly good on the election of 1800.

Two aspects of political discontent during the 1790's are treated in E. P. Link, *Democratic-Republican Societies* (1942), and L. D. Baldwin, *The Whiskey Rebels* (1939). R. A. Rutland, *The Birth of the Bill of Rights* (1955), discusses the origins of the first ten amendments. L. W. Levy, *Legacy of Suppression* (1960), shows that the first amendment offered less firm protection for freedom of speech and the press than has generally been supposed. J. M. Smith, *Freedom's Fetters* (1956), is the most complete account of the Alien and Sedition Acts and their enforcement. Adrienne Koch and Harry Ammon, "The Virginia and Kentucky Resolutions," *William and Mary Quarterly*, 3rd series, V (1948), 145–76, is a good account of that subject.

Two important episodes in foreign relations during the Federalist decade have been definitively treated in S. F. Bemis, *Jay's Treaty* (1923) and *Pinckney's Treaty* * (1926, 1960). Felix Gilbert, *To the Farewell Address* (1961), discusses the intellectual origins of the attitudes that found classic expression in Washington's warning against alliances. Alexander DeConde, *Entangling Alliance* (1958), discusses American relations with France under Washington, as do L. M. Sears, *George Washington and the French Revolution* (1960), and Charles Hazen, *Contemporary American Opinion of the French Revolution* (1897).

So many men of large stature shared in the making of public policy during the 1790's that much of the history of the period has been written in the form of biography. D. S. Freeman, *George Washington*, 7 vols. (1948–57), is the most complete account; Vol. VII was written after Freeman's death by J. A. Carroll and M. W. Ashworth. J. C. Miller, *Alexander Hamilton: Portrait in Paradox* (1959), is the best biography of Hamilton. Irving Brant, *James Madison: Father of the Constitution, 1787–1800* (1950), the third volume of a six-volume study of Madison, contains a wealth of new information about the formation of the Republican party. Gilbert Chinard, *Honest John Adams* (1933), is a good biography, but the recent opening of the Adams family papers to scholars has resulted in the more informed study by C. Page Smith. Meanwhile Stephen Kurtz, *The Presidency of John Adams* * (1957), is particularly good on the election of 1796, and Zoltan Haraszti, *John Adams and the Prophets of Progress* (1952), is a delightful account of the comments Adams wrote in the margins of his books. Dumas Malone, *Jefferson and His Time*, in progress, 2 vols. (1948, 1952), covers Jefferson's career up to the beginning of the struggle with Hamilton. Claude Bowers, *Jefferson and Hamilton* (1936), is a lively account of the rivalry. A stimulating interpretation of Jefferson's thought is D. J. Boorstin, *The Lost World of Thomas Jefferson* * (1948). Good biographies of lesser figures are Frank Monaghan, *John Jay* (1935); F. B. Tolles, *George Logan* (1953); and George Dangerfield, *Chancellor Robert R. Livingston* (1960).

* Available in a paperback edition.

7

Jeffersonian Republicanism

For more than a <u>decade,</u> with mounting indignation, <u>Thomas Jefferson and his</u> <u>followers had been protesting against the trend</u> <u>of Federalist policies:</u> against <u>fiscal measures</u> that allegedly spawned a moneyed aristocracy and put an <u>unjust burden on the agrarian</u> "producing classes"; against the "monarchical aristocratical" tendencies of the federal bureaucracy; against the subversion of civil liberties; against "national consolidation" and encroachments on the rights of the states. Now, on March 4, 1801, the first Republican President was obliged to spell out a set of policies of his own. This, in broad outline, Jefferson accomplished in a brilliant inaugural address (the first to be delivered in the new capital on the banks of the Potomac) that affirmed his liberal democratic philosophy and his faith in the wisdom of the people.

Jefferson soothed jittery Federalists by assuring them that no Jacobin reign of terror would follow the "Revolution of 1800" and by inviting them to join Republicans "in common efforts for the common good." He cautioned Republicans that though the will of the majority must prevail, "the minority possess their equal rights, which equal law must protect." He reminded members of both parties that, in spite of the acrimonious campaign just past,

> every difference of opinion is not a difference of principle. We have called by different names brethren of the same principle. We are all Re-

publicans, we are all Federalists. If there be any among us who would wish to dissolve this Union or to change its republican form, let them stand undisturbed as monuments of the safety with which error of opinion may be tolerated where reason is left free to combat it.

Yet even as he tried to conciliate his political foes, Jefferson was stressing a difference between them and him, for Federalists did not share his confidence that reason ruled the minds of men.

Economy and Simplicity

The New Regime   The rustic simplicity and democratic manners that Jefferson thought proper for the leaders of an agrarian republic seemed appropriate in a crude, half-built capital city which lacked the social and cultural opportunities of Philadelphia. Though the President was a cultivated gentleman to the manner born, his plain informality was natural and uncontrived. Unlike his predecessors, he sent his annual messages to Congress to be read by a clerk, lest reading them in person should suggest that he was imitating the British monarch delivering his speech from the throne. Jefferson abandoned the elegant weekly presidential levees that had previously been such a delight to the capital's aristocracy. At his infrequent state dinners and receptions and in his dealings with the diplomatic corps he avoided anything that smacked of the pomp and pretentiousness of European courts. In the White House he lived simply and made himself accessible to countrymen who had business with him.

Although Jefferson believed in the sovereignty of the people and tended to romanticize the independent farmer, he did not assume that untrained men could handle the responsibilities of important administrative posts. He rejected the theory of government by a political élite, and yet the men in his Administration were of as high a caliber as their Federalist predecessors. Actually he discharged few Federalists from nonpolicy-making offices, and most of his new appointees were educated, talented, and experienced upper-class Republicans. James Madison, a Virginia aristocrat who had led the congressional fight against the Federalists, joined the new Administration as Secretary of State. Albert Gallatin of Pennsylvania, a gifted and devoted Jeffersonian, accepted the crucial office of Secretary of the Treasury. Three major appointments—those of Secretary of War, Attorney General, and Postmaster General—went to New Englanders, in order to strengthen the Republican party in the chief bastion of Federalism.

Republican Policies   Jefferson repudiated most of Hamilton's mercantilist theories in favor of a general policy of laissez faire. His ideal was "a wise and frugal Government, which shall restrain men from injuring one another . . . [and] leave them otherwise free to regulate their own pursuits of industry and improvement." The principal responsibilities of such a government, Jefferson explained, would be to honor the Bill of Rights, seek equal justice for all men, respect the rights of the states, "the surest bulwarks against antirepublican tendencies," and practice strict economy, "that labor may be lightly burthened."

But the Jefferson Administration soon discovered—as would future Administrations when political supremacy passed from one party to another—that it could reverse the actions and repudiate the commitments of its predecessor only at the risk of serious confusion. Republicans, therefore, thought it best not to tamper with some of Hamilton's economic measures. The Bank of the United States, for example, continued its operations undisturbed

until 1811, when its charter expired. By then many Republicans, including Madison and Gallatin, favored granting the Bank a new charter, a proposal that failed in each house of Congress by a single vote. Nor did the Republicans reverse Federalist measures for refunding the national debt, or for federal assumption of the Revolutionary debts of the states, or for encouraging American shipping.

Without changing his opinion about the primacy of agriculture, Jefferson as President developed a greater respect for other economic pursuits. In his first message to Congress he referred to manufacturing, commerce, and navigation, along with agriculture, as "the four pillars of our prosperity"; and he even suggested, though somewhat vaguely, that "within the limits of our constitutional powers" their protection from "casual embarrassments" might be "seasonably interposed."

The "Revolution of 1800" did not, however, lack substance, for the Republicans lost no time in disposing of some of the Federalists' pet measures. They refused, of course, to renew the Alien Act when it expired in 1801. They reduced the residence requirement for naturalization from fourteen years to five; once again America became, in Jefferson's words, an "asylum" for "oppressed humanity." The Sedition Act also expired in 1801, and Jefferson saw to it that those who had been imprisoned for violating it were freed and that all fines were refunded. The Republican Congress repealed the Judiciary Act of 1801 and abolished, as a needless extravagance, the new circuit judgeships that act had created. Thus, defeated ("lame duck") Federalists to whom Adams had given "midnight appointments" in the judicial branch lost their jobs; and the courts, as one Republican explained, ceased to be a "hospital for decayed politicians." The House of Representatives then turned on the Supreme Court and, in 1804, impeached Associate Justice Samuel Chase, an arch-Federalist who had used the bench as a political stump. But the Senate did not interpret Chase's offense as a misdemeanor within the meaning of the Constitution and refused to remove him. Henceforth, the Republicans had to rely on new appointments in their efforts to reform the federal courts.

The Jeffersonian revolution also wrought a

significant change in fiscal policy. There is a tendency for governments, the new President said, "to multiply offices . . . and to increase expense"—to leave to labor only a small portion of its earnings and to "consume the whole residue of what it was instituted to guard." Unlike Hamilton, Jefferson regarded a public debt and the accompanying interest charges as beneficial only to a small class of investors, and felt that it was a "mortal canker" on the rest of the community. With the able support of Secretary of the Treasury Gallatin, he strove to retire the whole public debt, which had grown to $83 million, at the earliest possible date—in sixteen years, according to the original plan. Since the excise tax had been repealed, the only way to retire the debt was through revenues from import duties and the sale of public lands, and through the most rigid government economy. To cut costs in the executive department Jefferson reduced the number of officers in the diplomatic corps and revenue service. He urged Congress to abolish other public offices, to replace wasteful general appropriations with grants of "specific sums to every specific purpose," and to hold the Treasury Department responsible for all funds spent.

Thomas Jefferson: Confident that reason ruled the minds of men.

Jefferson was convinced, too, that military and naval expenditures could be cut without jeopardizing national defense. America, he said, was fortunately "separated by nature and a wide ocean from the exterminating havoc" of the Old World and consequently needed no large standing army. For defense against invasion, the country should rely on "the body of neighboring citizens as formed into a militia." Accordingly, the regular army was reduced from four thousand to twenty-five hundred officers and men. Jefferson realized, however, that the state militia systems needed to be improved, and in 1808 the federal government began to take a hand in reorganizing them and in defraying part of the cost of arms and equipment. Moreover, in 1802 Jefferson was instrumental in establishing the United States Military Academy at West Point.

Turning to the navy, the new Administration proceeded to sell some ocean-going vessels, lay up others, and halt construction on still others; it discharged many Navy Department employees, reduced the number of officers and enlisted men, and abandoned the improvement of navy yards and dry docks. Shore defense was to be maintained by coastal fortifications and by a fleet of small, inexpensive gunboats serving as a kind of naval militia. This policy was designed, Jefferson explained, "merely for defensive operations," not to protect commerce or to establish the United States as a sea power. The quarreling European states would thus be kept "at a distance," and at little cost.

Here, in short, was Jefferson's formula for an agrarian utopia: simplicity, frugality, and "a government founded not on the fears and follies of man, but on his reason"—a government whose authority the ordinary citizen would scarcely feel. For a time all worked according to plan, and in his second annual message Jefferson congratulated Congress for the "pleasing circumstances . . . under which we meet." The United States had become a nation of peaceful, prosperous citizens "managing their own affairs in their own way and for their own use, unembarrassed by too much regulation, unoppressed by fiscal exactions."

Unfortunately, this idyllic picture of rustic innocence was but a brief and passing phase.

Ferment in the West

The Westward Movement   In his vision of America as the ideal republic, Jefferson projected upon the nation at large an image of the stable, mellow society of Virginia's rural gentry. This image, however, did not fit much of the rest of the country—not even the trans-Appalachian West in whose future Jefferson placed such confident hopes. In 1800 nearly a million settlers were living in the vast area between the Appalachians and the Mississippi River; a new land act that year encouraged others to come by offering land for sale in individual tracts of 320 acres and by permitting four-year credits with a down payment of 25 per cent. A revision of this law in 1804 reduced the minimum tract to 160 acres; thus, with public land selling at a minimum price of two dollars an acre, a buyer could obtain a farm for an initial payment of eighty dollars. This generous federal policy brought a steady tide of immigrants into the West, whose rich lands Jefferson thought would afford "room enough for our descendants to the thousandth and thousandth generation." As the forests were cleared and as farms and villages dotted the land, new states were created from time to time—Kentucky in 1792, Tennessee in 1796, and Ohio in 1803.

Most of the Westerners liked Jefferson's politics and found much in his philosophy that pleased them, but they had mixed feelings about his economics and scarcely understood his agrarian dream—in fact, they did much to destroy it. Jefferson's ideal of a stable, self-sufficient yeomanry free of the corrupting influences of commercialism was hardly the ideal of the traders and speculators who infested the West—or, for that matter, of many of the farmers. Soon after they arrived, most Westerners began to dream not of self-sufficiency but of cash crops, of outlets to markets, and of the comforts and luxuries of the East.

The Problem of Transportation   Between the Western settlers and their ambitions stood two major obstacles: the mountains, which cut them off from the East, and the French, who were taking over from Spain possession of New Orleans and the mouth of the Mississippi. Before Jefferson left office, he was to find solutions to both these problems—solutions that in the long run helped to undermine his original goal of a simple agrarian society. In 1806 Congress authorized the building of a road from Cumberland, Maryland, across the mountains to Wheeling, Virginia, as a government-financed "internal improvement." Jefferson approved the measure, even though, without the constitutional amendment he had urged, it required a stretching of federal power to do so. Construction on the Cumberland Road began in 1811 and was completed in 1818.

The second problem—navigation of the Mississippi River—forced Jefferson to take vigorous action which compromised not only his constitutional scruples but his fiscal policy, his foreign policy, and perhaps even his principles of public ethics. Since 1763 the mouth of the Mississippi and the immense territory of Louisiana, stretching westward to the Rockies, had been held by a declining and enfeebled Spain; and Spain, in Pinckney's Treaty of 1795, had opened the Mississippi to American navigation and granted Western flatboatmen

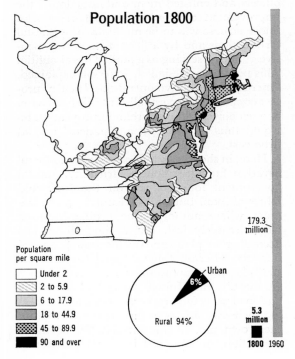

Population 1800

Population per square mile

☐	Under 2
▨	2 to 5.9
▦	6 to 17.9
▩	18 to 44.9
▨	45 to 89.9
■	90 and over

Urban 6%
Rural 94%

179.3 million

5.3 million

1800   1960

the right to deposit their cargoes at New Orleans for shipment abroad. This arrangement satisfied the Westerners, who saw in Spain no serious threat. But they were bound to react violently if Louisiana should fall into the hands of a stronger power, or if their river outlet should be cut off. As Madison explained: "The Mississippi is to them every thing. It is the Hudson, the Delaware, the Potomac, and all the navigable rivers of the Atlantic States, formed into one stream."

The Louisiana Purchase Soon after Jefferson became President two events shocked and angered the Western settlers. The first was the revelation that Napoleon, in the secret Treaty of San Ildefonso (1800), had negotiated the transfer of Louisiana from Spain to France (though formal possession by France was long

The Louisiana Purchase and Explorations of the Far West

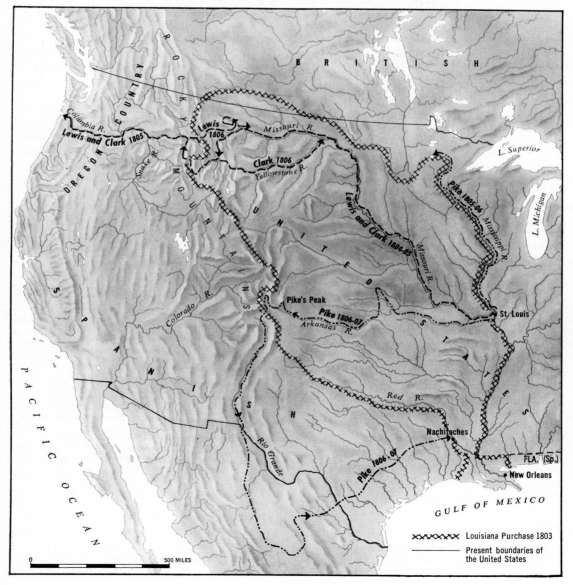

Jefferson:
On Assuming the Presidency

All, too, will bear in mind this sacred principle, that though the will of the majority is in all cases to prevail, that will to be rightful must be reasonable; that the minority possess their equal rights, which equal law must protect, and to violate would be oppression. Let us, then, fellow-citizens, unite with one heart and one mind. Let us restore to social intercourse that harmony and affection without which liberty and even life itself are but dreary things.... Every difference of opinion is not a difference of principle. We have called by different names brethren of the same principle. We are all Republicans, we are all Federalists. If there be any among us who would wish to dissolve this Union or to change its republican form, let them stand undisturbed as monuments of the safety with which error of opinion may be tolerated where reason is left free to combat it. I know, indeed, that some honest men fear that a republican government can not be strong, that this Government is not strong enough; but would the honest patriot, in the full tide of successful experiment, abandon a government which has so far kept us free and firm on the theoretic and visionary fear that this Government, the world's best hope, may by possibility want energy to preserve itself? I trust not. I believe this, on the contrary, the strongest Government on earth. I believe it the only one where every man, at the call of the law, would fly to the standard of the law, and would meet invasions of the public order as his own personal concern.

From Thomas Jefferson, First Inaugural Address, 1801.

delayed). The second was a proclamation by the Spanish intendant at New Orleans, on October 16, 1802, that the right of deposit was to be suspended. Taking this as a foretaste of Napoleon's future policy, indignant Westerners looked to Jefferson for support.

Alarmed, Jefferson feared for a time that Napoleon might force him to reconsider his basic foreign policy, perhaps even to abandon temporarily his opposition to "entangling alliances." The United States, he told Robert R. Livingston, the American minister in Paris, has always looked upon France as her "natural friend"; but there was

on the globe one single spot, the possessor of which is our natural and habitual enemy. It is New Orleans, through which the produce of

three-eighths of our territory must pass to market. . . . France placing herself in that door, assumes to us the attitude of defiance. The day that France takes possession of New Orleans . . . [we will be forced to] marry ourselves to the British fleet and nation.

To Congress he spoke of "the danger to which our peace would be perpetually exposed whilst so important a key to the commerce of the Western country remained under foreign power."

But before taking any drastic steps, Jefferson tried to negotiate peacefully with France. He instructed Livingston to offer to purchase New Orleans and West Florida; he obtained from Congress an appropriation of $2 million for vaguely defined expenses; and he sent James Monroe, who had the confidence of Westerners, as a special envoy to assist Livingston. Monroe arrived in Paris on April 12, 1803, two days after Talleyrand, negotiating for France, had startled Livingston by asking whether the United States would like to buy the whole of Louisiana! The two American diplomats, whose instructions were essentially to buy a city, hesitated, though only momentarily, before agreeing to buy an empire that would double the size of their country.

There were several reasons for Napoleon's decision to abandon his imperial ambitions in America and to concentrate on Europe. First, he suffered a major disaster when his troops failed to crush a slave insurrection, led by Toussaint L'Ouverture, in the French colony of Santo Domingo. Second, the Peace of Amiens of 1802 had really settled nothing, and a renewal of war between France and Great Britain seemed all but inevitable. Third, Napoleon needed money, and it was obviously wise to sell a province that the British navy could prevent France from occupying in any case. Finally, selling Louisiana to the United States would remove a source of friction and avoid an Anglo-American *rapprochement*. Accordingly, on April 11 Napoleon told one of his ministers: "I renounce Louisiana. It is not only New Orleans that I will cede, it is the whole colony without any reservation."

Livingston and Monroe soon decided that this was a poor time to quibble over the letter of their instructions. On April 30, 1803, after some higgling over price, they made the pur-

Jefferson:
On the Louisiana Purchase

Congress witnessed, at their last session, the extraordinary agitation produced in the public mind by the suspension of our right of deposit at the port of New Orleans.... Previous, however, to this period, we had not been unaware of the danger to which our peace would be perpetually exposed while so important a key to the commerce of the western country remained under foreign power. Difficulties, too, were presenting themselves as to the navigation of other streams, which arising within territories, pass through those adjacent. Propositions had, therefore, been authorized for obtaining, on fair conditions, the sovereignty of New Orleans, and of other possessions in that quarter interesting to our quiet....

The property and sovereignty of all Louisiana ... have on certain conditions been transferred to the United States.... While the property and sovereignty of the Mississippi and its waters secure an independent outlet for the produce of the Western States, and an uncontrolled navigation through their whole course, free from collision with other powers and the dangers to our peace from that source, the fertility of the country, its climate and extent, promise in due season important aids to our treasury, an ample provision for our posterity, and a wide-spread field for the blessings of freedom and equal laws. With the wisdom of Congress it will rest to take those ulterior measures which may be necessary for the immediate occupation and temporary government of the country; for its incorporation into our Union; for rendering the change of government a blessing to our newly-adopted brethren; for securing to them the rights of conscience and property; for confirming to the Indian inhabitants their occupancy and self-government, establishing friendly and commercial relations with them, and for ascertaining the geography of the country acquired.

From Thomas Jefferson, Third Annual Message to Congress, 1803.

chase for $15 million and a promise (written into the purchase treaty) to give citizenship and religious freedom to the Catholics residing in Louisiana. The boundaries of Louisiana were then only vaguely defined, and the treaty merely stated that they were to be the same as they had been when Spain possessed it. "You have made a noble bargain for yourselves," said the realistic Talleyrand, "and I suppose you will make the most of it." In later years the United States did precisely that.

Westerners were delighted with the terms of the treaty, and their devotion to Jefferson and confidence in the federal government grew correspondingly stronger. But New England Federalists, viewing the West as enemy territory, criticized Jefferson severely for accepting a treaty that was tainted with duplicity. In making the sale, they pointed out, Napoleon had violated the French constitution and a promise to Spain not to cede Louisiana to another power. Yet Jefferson approved the transaction knowing this to be the case—knowing, too, that the federal Constitution did not explicitly authorize the acquisition of new territory. Federalists also complained that the purchase of these worthless lands was a wasteful expenditure and meant a staggering addition to the public debt.

Jefferson was sensitive to such criticism, especially to the charge that he was exceeding the limits of the Constitution strictly construed. His first impulse was to urge an amendment to the Constitution expressly granting the power to acquire territory; but the amending process was painfully slow, and Livingston warned that Napoleon might have a change of heart. Moreover, some Republicans argued that the power to acquire territory might be *implied* from the power to make treaties. Such an argument could hardly have satisfied Jefferson, but he concluded that Congress would be wise to cast aside "metaphysical subtleties and . . . throw themselves on their country for doing for them unauthorized what we know they would have done for themselves, had they been in a situation to do it." Trusting that "the good sense of our country will correct the evil of [constitutional] construction when it shall produce evil effects," Jefferson submitted the treaty to the Senate.

During the debate Federalists and Republicans reversed their former positions on questions of constitutional interpretation—a few extreme Federalists even spoke of dissolving the Union. But the treaty was ratified by a vote of twenty-four to seven, and the House appropriated the money required to fulfill its terms. Thus the United States acquired the whole of the Mississippi River and its tributaries, some 828,000 square miles of territory, millions of acres of rich farmland, and a vast store of natural resources. Moreover, the purchase of Louisiana removed a major source of American concern about the internal politics of Europe; and, in the long run, it produced a basic shift in the national balance of political power. After the treaty was ratified, Jefferson seemed to forget quickly his anxieties about it —except to regret that Spanish West Florida had not been part of the bargain. Though for the present neither threats nor money—he tried both—could pry the Floridas loose from Spain, Jefferson was confident that it was America's destiny to obtain them, too, "and all in good time."

Western Exploration   On December 20, 1803, just a few weeks after France had taken formal possession of Louisiana from Spain, the French prefect at New Orleans turned the lower part of the territory over to the United States. The transfer of the upper part was delayed until the spring of 1804, when, at St. Louis, Meriwether Lewis, Jefferson's private secretary, accepted it in behalf of the United States. But Lewis was not there for that specific purpose; in fact, his presence was the result of presidential plans that antedated the Louisiana Purchase.

In January 1803 Congress had secretly appropriated money for an expedition to explore the upper reaches of the Missouri River and from there westward to the Pacific— though none of this territory at the time belonged to the United States. The expedition, which Jefferson had been trying to promote for many years, had several purposes. The President assured the Spanish minister that it would "have no other view than the advancement of geography"; and, to be sure, his scientific curiosity about the great unexplored interior was genuine. Lewis and his fellow explorer, William Clark (a brother of George Rogers Clark), were instructed to make astronomical observations, to study the flora and fauna, and to compile the fullest possible records. But they were to be alert to more practical matters, too, especially trading opportunities and mineral deposits. Moreover, Jefferson was fully aware that explorations had diplomatic value when nations laid claims to unsettled lands.

The Lewis and Clark expedition, which took more than two years to complete, was a remarkable success. The party of forty-five men ascended the Missouri River to the Great Falls, crossed the Rockies, and descended the Snake and Columbia Rivers to the Pacific. The explorers brought back with them an enormously expanded factual knowledge of Western North America (first made available to the public when their journals were published in 1814), a large botanical collection, information of value to American fur traders, and a strengthened foundation for an American claim to the Oregon country. This was only one of several Western explorations that Jefferson promoted. Two others were led by Zebulon Pike: one in 1805 up the Mississippi River in search of its source, and a second in 1806 up the Arkansas River to the Rockies in what is now Colorado. All of them combined the scientific and practical interests that Jefferson himself personified.

Political Complications

Even though Jefferson accommodated his political and economic principles to some of the realities of American life, he never managed to appease the more ardent Northern Federalists. Hamilton publicly described the Administration as composed of "indolent and temporizing rulers, who love to loll in the lap of epicurean ease, and seem to imagine that to govern well, is to amuse the wondering multitude with sagacious aphorisms and oracular sayings." On the other hand, some Republicans, notably the uncompromising staterighters of Virginia, felt that Jefferson had moved too far toward Federalism. His good friend John Taylor observed with dismay that "Federalism . . . has gained a new footing, by being taken into partnership with republicanism." Jefferson's most persistent Virginia critic was the brilliant but erratic John Randolph of Roanoke, who would tolerate not the slightest deviation from the principles of the Kentucky Resolutions of 1798 (see p. 157). After grumbling about several measures backed by the Administration, Randolph broke with Jefferson over a proposal to use federal funds to settle the claims of certain land speculators organized into the so-called Yazoo Land Companies. These speculators had corruptly obtained a large grant from the

Georgia legislature before the state, in 1802, ceded its Western lands to the federal government. Jefferson's desire to facilitate the transfer by compensating the Yazoo claimants, even though many of them were Northern speculators and their claims were tainted with fraud, drove Randolph's small faction of Republicans into open rebellion. The Randolph "Tertium Quids," as they were called, blocked the settlement of the Yazoo claims for many years and tormented Jefferson with accusations of apostasy.

Meanwhile, Vice-President Aaron Burr, who had lost all influence in Republican councils after the disputed election of 1800 (see p. 159), seemed ready for almost any reckless maneuver that might improve his political fortunes. By 1804 he was willing to accept the support of the Federalists in his campaign for the governorship of New York. Some of the more irresponsible Federalists, especially the "Essex Junto" in Massachusetts and the "River Gods" in Connecticut, had been toying with a scheme to unite New York and New England in an independent Northern confederacy; and now they hoped to enlist the services of Burr. But Hamilton exposed and denounced the plot and played a major role in Burr's defeat in New York. The enraged Burr then challenged his old New York rival to a duel, in which Hamilton, on July 11, 1804, was mortally wounded. In the presidential election of that year, Jefferson and his new running mate, George Clinton of New York, crushed the discredited Federalists. Charles Cotesworth Pinckney, the Federalist candidate, carried only Connecticut and Delaware.

The talented Burr had wrecked a promising political career by overreaching himself; he now courted final disaster by involving himself in a quixotic intrigue whose exact nature was obscured in a maze of conflicting reports. The British minister had heard that for a half-million dollars Burr would separate the Western part of the United States from the East; the Spanish minister had heard that he planned to establish a buffer state between Louisiana and Mexico; others had heard that he planned to conquer Mexico and establish an empire. Whatever his scheme was, Burr won the support of two confederates: General James Wilkinson, who commanded the American troops in Louisiana and had a greater taste for conspiracy than Burr; and Harman Blennerhassett, a wealthy Irish exile who lived on an island in the upper Ohio River. In the summer of 1806 Burr and some sixty men on thirteen flatboats departed from Blennerhassett's Island and floated down the Ohio and Mississippi for some unknown purpose to some nameless glory.

The enterprise collapsed when General Wilkinson shifted sides and sent Jefferson a report that Burr was plotting treason. On Jefferson's orders the fleeing Burr was caught and taken to Richmond where, in 1807, he was indicted. In the curious trial that followed, Jefferson seemed determined to get a conviction whether or not the evidence warranted it; and the presiding judge, John Marshall, a Federalist, seemed as interested in discrediting Jefferson as in giving Burr justice. In the end Burr was acquitted, for the case against him did not fulfill the terms of the Constitution's definition of treason. According to the Constitution, treason consists in "levying war" against the United States or in "adhering to their enemies, giving them aid and comfort." A conviction for treason requires "the testimony of two witnesses to the same overt act." In his charge to the jury, Marshall insisted that the witnesses must have directly implicated Burr in a specific warlike act, not just loosely in a conspiracy. Since the witnesses had failed to do this, Marshall's charge prepared the way for Burr's acquittal. It also set an important precedent that made convictions for treason extremely difficult and indictments rare.

Trouble on the High Seas

War and American Trade   When Jefferson became President in 1801, he was determined that the United States would pursue its destiny free from "entangling alliances" and from the wars and diplomatic duplicity of the Old World. Yet he found himself entangled in world affairs throughout most of his second Administration, and he left office with the country fast approaching total involvement. The abrogation of the French alliance in 1800, it appeared, did not mean that America had closed the door on Europe.

Since she exported foodstuffs and raw materials, imported foreign manufactured goods, and sent merchant ships to distant ports, America was bound to be affected by the course of international politics and the state of the world economy.

Even during Jefferson's first Administration the Barbary pirates, operating from bases on the coast of North Africa, had provoked the pacifistic President into surprisingly vigorous action. For many years these corsairs had been harrying American vessels and forcing the federal government, like the governments of Europe, to buy immunity by paying tribute to the rulers of Morocco, Algiers, Tunis, and Tripoli. To Jefferson this costly and humiliating practice was intolerable, and in 1801 he dispatched a naval squadron to the Mediterranean. For several years the United States was engaged in virtual war with Tripoli, until the Pasha, in 1805, was obliged to make a satisfactory peace. Tribute payments to other Barbary states, however, did not cease altogether until 1816.

The Tripolitan War, though a minor affair, had forced Jefferson to modify his naval policy. But the resumption of hostilities between Great Britain and France in 1803—a conflict that raged without interruption for the next eleven years—provided a far more strenuous test of the President's pacifism. In a larger sense, it was a test of how much the American people were ready to endure and sacrifice to remain at peace, for peace has its price as well as war. As Jefferson warned Congress, with "the flames of war lighted up again in Europe, . . . the nations pursuing peace will not be exempt from all evil." To him the price was not too great, and he thanked "that kind Providence which . . . guarded us from hastily entering into the sanguinary contest and left us only to look on and to pity its ravages." America's sole interest and desire, he said, would be "to cultivate the friendship of the belligerent nations by every act of justice and of innocent kindness." Of them he would ask only respect for the rights to which American vessels and citizens were entitled as neutrals under international law. Since American friendship and trade were useful to them, Jefferson was certain that "it can not be the interest of any to assail us, nor ours to disturb them."

While Jefferson professed confidence in his country's capacity to bring "collisions of interest to the umpirage of reason rather than force," the European belligerents were locked in a conflict whose stakes seemed to justify any means that promised ultimate victory. In 1805 Napoleon's smashing victory over the armies of Austria and Russia at Austerlitz made him for the time master of much of the European continent, while Lord Nelson's decisive defeat of the French and Spanish fleets at the Battle of Trafalgar gave Britain control of the high seas. Thereafter, in a savage war of attrition, neither antagonist showed much concern for the rights of neutrals or the punctilios of international law. Both rained blows on American shipping interests and insults on sensitive patriots.

Trouble began in 1805 when a British court ruled that goods from the French West Indies bound for Europe on American vessels, even though shipped by way of the United States, were subject to seizure. When the commercial provisions of Jay's Treaty of 1794 expired in 1807 and American diplomats were unable to negotiate a new agreement satisfactory to Jefferson, British interference with American shipping increased. Meanwhile Napoleon had developed a program of economic warfare; his so-called Continental System, elaborated in his Berlin Decree of 1806 and Milan Decree of 1807, closed the European ports under his control to British goods and stated that neutral ships complying with British trade regulations would be confiscated. The British government retaliated with a series of Orders in Council, the most important of which proclaimed a blockade of the ports of France and of the nations under her control. Thereafter American ships bound for western Europe risked seizure by one or the other of the belligerents, depending on whose rules they flouted. In the three years prior to 1807 the British seized at least a thousand American merchantmen and the French half that many.

To Americans the most grievous British wrong was the revival and vigorous application of the centuries-old system of impressment, by which the Royal Navy procured its man power. In enforcing the system British warships stopped American merchantmen on the high seas to search for deserters; they took off

British-born sailors who had become Americans by naturalization; and in the process they heedlessly impressed an unknown number of native-born Americans as well. The issue reached a crisis in June 1807, when the British frigate *Leopard* overhauled the United States frigate *Chesapeake* within sight of the Virginia coast and demanded the right to search her for deserters. When the commander of the unprepared *Chesapeake* refused, the *Leopard* fired three broadsides that killed three Americans and wounded eighteen others. The crippled *Chesapeake* submitted to the seizure of four deserters and then returned to Norfolk. This humiliation of an American frigate so infuriated both Federalists and Republicans that, judging from the tone of the press and the speeches of politicians, the country seemed ready to unite behind a war policy. But Jefferson asked for less: he ordered British warships out of American waters and demanded reparations and an apology.

The Embargo   Jefferson asked something of Americans, too. He called for a supreme effort, not to win a war, but to achieve what he considered the nobler goal of keeping the country at peace. He believed that denying the belligerents the benefits of American trade would cause them so much distress that they would abandon their encroachments on American neutral rights. For this purpose, and to avoid further provocative incidents, Jefferson proposed a policy that he had long cherished as an alternative to war, a policy he described as "peaceable coercion." On December 22, 1807, in response to his urgent plea, Congress passed the Embargo Act, which stopped the export of American goods and prohibited all ships from clearing American ports for foreign ports. This act, in effect, required shipowners to abandon their risky but extremely profitable wartime trade, and obliged planters and farmers to give up their rich European export market.

Jefferson asked for a greater sacrifice than most Americans seemed ready to make. Angry New England merchants, preferring risks and insults to commercial stagnation, denounced the embargo as an unconstitutional expansion of federal power. Many of them defiantly engaged in an illicit trade which severe enforcement measures could not altogether suppress.

Some again hinted at secession. Among them was Federalist Senator Timothy Pickering of Massachusetts, who described Jefferson as capable of almost any "nefarious act" and called on the states to resist "the usurpations of the general government." The agricultural interest was equally distressed when farm commodities began to accumulate at the ports and prices declined. John Randolph's assaults on the Administration matched those of the Federalists.

Eventually Congress yielded to overwhelming pressure and passed an act repealing the embargo. On March 1, 1809, a disappointed Jefferson signed it. That "peaceable coercion" lacked the needed public support should not obscure the fact that it had in fact kept the country at peace; moreover, there is reason to believe that, given time, the embargo might even have wrung concessions from the British.

"Nature intended me for the more tranquil pursuits of science by rendering them my supreme delight," wrote the weary Jefferson at the close of his second Administration. Retirement was a welcome relief not only from the vicissitudes of domestic politics, in which he counted more successes than failures, but from the trials of international affairs, in which he suffered his greatest defeat.

The Decision for War

By declining to run for re-election in 1808, Jefferson helped to establish the two-term tradition; but he also set the precedent by which a retiring President intervened in the selection of his successor. Jefferson won the Republican nomination for his friend and political collaborator, Secretary of State James Madison. Though the Federalists, who again nominated Charles Cotesworth Pinckney, regained control of New England and increased their strength in the new Congress, Madison won by a decisive majority of 122 to 47 in the electoral college. His inaugural address reflected the changing conditions of the past eight years, especially in its concern for the promotion of commerce and industry; but in spirit it was still a thoroughly Jeffersonian document which endorsed the domestic and foreign policies of his predecessor. Few Presidents have brought to the White House such

James Madison: A greater man than President.

rich experience in public life as did Madison; none, save John Adams, was so profound a student of political philosophy. Yet, though Madison had contributed much to the formulation of Republican doctrine and had never been Jefferson's mere pliant tool, the scholarly Virginian lacked Jefferson's political acumen and administrative skill.

The Failure of Diplomacy   The overshadowing problem confronting the new President and Congress was the continuing European holocaust, which still created difficult situations for neutrals. Although the embargo had been repealed, the policy of "peaceable coercion" persisted in less drastic forms. The Madison Administration blundered badly in applying it, however. The first substitute for the embargo was a Nonintercourse Act, passed in 1809, which re-established trade with all nations except Great Britain and France so long as the latter continued to enforce their obnoxious orders and decrees. This act encouraged the British government to try negotiation. David Erskine, the friendly and sympathetic British minister, concluded an

agreement that was highly satisfactory to the United States, though he violated his instructions in doing so. On June 10, 1809, the delighted President renewed trade with Great Britain without waiting for the agreement to be approved in London, and hundreds of American ships cleared their home ports for the first time in many months. Unfortunately the British government repudiated the Erskine "treaty" as soon as it arrived and recalled its too-generous minister. Madison then proclaimed the restoration of nonintercourse, and Anglo-American relations worsened.

On May 1, 1810, nonintercourse gave way to a new policy incorporated in a curious measure called Macon's Bill Number 2. This bill restored trade with both Great Britain and France but threatened to resume nonintercourse with either of them whenever the other agreed to respect America's neutral rights. Now it was Napoleon's turn to try some shifty diplomacy. Proclaiming his love for Americans and his concern for their prosperity, he announced that on November 1, 1810, the French commercial restrictions would be repealed—but he attached conditions that made his promise almost meaningless. Madison fell into Napoleon's trap and on February 2, 1811, re-established nonintercourse with Britain, though, in fact, the French continued to seize American ships. Unable to get Britain to repeal her Orders in Council, Madison recalled the American minister, William Pinkney, and thus virtually severed diplomatic relations.

Ironically, a few months later the policy of "peaceable coercion" won a striking victory. On June 16, 1812, beset by an economic crisis at home, the British foreign minister announced the immediate suspension of the Orders in Council (though not impressment). But the announcement came too late. On June 1 Madison had asked for a declaration of war against Great Britain, and Congress soon complied: the House on June 4 by a vote of seventy-nine to forty-nine, the Senate on June 18 by a vote of nineteen to thirteen.

The Motives of the "War Hawks"   The geographical distribution of the vote for and against war raises some difficult questions about its causes. In the House, Pennsylvania and the Southern and frontier states, including Vermont, voted sixty-five to fifteen for war;

New York, New Jersey, and the New England maritime states voted fourteen to thirty-four against. The Federalist commercial interests, though directly affected by British impressment and interference with American shipping on the high seas, nevertheless considered war with Great Britain the ultimate folly. War would be more devastating to their trade than the Orders in Council had been—and the blow would be dealt by their own government. Moreover, to them Britain was not only a profitable market but the defender of conservatism, stability, and order against the obscenities of Napoleonic France. Sharing these views with the Federalists was a handful of Republicans representing Southern coastal districts. John Randolph, a severe critic of the war policy, urged Republicans to live up to their principles of economy and retrenchment and not to become "infatuated with standing armies, loans, taxes, navies, and war."

An able and highly articulate group opposed the declaration of war, but the majority seemed to support it. Although the center of this majority was in the agricultural South and West, rather than in New England, neutral rights and impressment were important issues in the decision to go to war. The grievances which Madison stressed in his war message were "the injuries and indignities which have been heaped upon our country"—the British actions "hostile to the United States as an independent and neutral nation." Patriotic Southerners and Westerners felt these insults keenly and resented the implicit unwillingness of the British to concede the reality of American independence. According to one Kentuckian, "we must now oppose the farther encroachments of Great Britain by war, or formally annul the Declaration of our Independence, and acknowledge ourselves her devoted colonies." Neutral rights involved economic interests, too; as Madison explained, British policy struck not only at commerce but at agriculture as well. By closing European markets to American staples, the British threatened the prosperity of farmers and planters who lived hundreds of miles from the sea and might never have seen an ocean-going vessel. "The interests of agriculture and commerce are inseparable," said Representative Langdon Cheves of South Carolina.

In the Congress that voted for war there was a remarkable little band of youthful Republicans from the Southern and Western states. Some of them had taken their seats for the first time in November 1811 and had at once begun to badger the President and harangue their colleagues with appeals for war. They managed to elect Henry Clay of Kentucky Speaker of the House; and Clay in turn gave important committee assignments to the young "War Hawks"—among them, Richard M. Johnson of Kentucky, Felix Grundy of Tennessee, and John C. Calhoun of South Carolina. These second-generation Republicans were critical of the pacifistic measures of Jefferson and Madison; indifferent to the state-rights political tradition embodied in the Resolutions of 1798; nationalistic to a degree exceeding the Federalists in their prime; and eager for geographic expansion and economic growth, with none of the anxieties that Jefferson sometimes seemed to feel. To them war was, to be sure, a means of redressing intolerable wrongs too long endured, a way of asserting America's power. But it was also an opportunity to capitalize again on Europe's strife and to gain some of the tangible things that their constituents coveted, especially more land.

The insatiable agrarian demand for land was one of the impelling forces behind the War Hawks. The American frontier was not advancing in a slow, orderly manner, with contiguous tracts of the public domain successively opened for sale and then compactly settled. Rather, farmers and speculators rushed into new areas, often before Indian claims were cleared and surveys completed, and sought out the most fertile parcels. With such an abundance of good land, few buyers were interested in land of second- or third-rate quality. Hence, the government was under constant pressure to open additional tracts even before those already open had been properly settled.

An unfortunate consequence of this planless expansion was that the Western Indians were being cajoled into making treaties whose terms they rarely comprehended, treaties by which they surrendered more and more of their hunting grounds. Jefferson's hope of incorporating the Indians in the body politic—of introducing among them "the implements and the practice of husbandry and of the household arts"—never had a chance to materialize. The white invasion was too swift; moreover, the Westerners preferred simply to drive the Indians farther and farther west. In the Ohio Valley alone, during the first decade of the nineteenth century, the Indians had been obliged to cede more than a hundred million acres of land. In 1809, Governor William Henry Harrison, of Indiana Territory, negotiated the last of a series of cessions under particularly dubious circumstances, bargaining with the demoralized remnants of several tribes for nearly three million acres in the lower Wabash Valley. The Indians realized that if they were ever to make a stand east of the Mississippi, it would have to be now.

At this crucial time two Shawnees of uncommon ability, Tecumseh and his brother "the Prophet," managed to unite the tribes east of the Mississippi for resistance against further white encroachments. Tecumseh supplied political leadership, while the Prophet provided spiritual inspiration and a call for moral regeneration. Together they organized an efficient Indian confederation supported by braves determined to preserve their lands and uncorrupted by the white man's proffered gifts of liquor. Terror spread along the frontier. In the summer of 1811, when Tecumseh went south to bid for the support of the Creeks, Governor Harrison decided to take advantage of his absence. He advanced with a force of a thousand men to the outskirts of Prophetstown, the chief Indian settlement on the Wabash River near the mouth of Tippecanoe Creek. There, on November 7, after repelling an Indian attack, his men destroyed the town. The Battle of Tippecanoe marked the beginning of a long and savage Indian war and was directly related to the American declaration of war on Great Britain.

In his war message Madison expressed an opinion held by the majority of Westerners: that the Indians had been receiving arms and encouragement from the British in Canada. The War Hawks were certain of it. "I can have no doubt of the influence of British agents in keeping up Indian hostility" and of encouraging them "to murder our citizens," cried Richard M. Johnson of Kentucky. Felix

Grundy of Tennessee agreed, adding, moreover, that there would be no peace on the frontier until the British were driven out of Canada. "We shall drive the British from our continent," Grundy affirmed; "they will no longer have an opportunity of intriguing with our Indian neighbors. . . . That nation will lose her Canadian trade, and, by having no resting place in this country, her means of annoying us will be diminished." To Westerners, the rich lands of Upper Canada were not the least of the prizes to be won in a successful war with the British. "Agrarian cupidity, not maritime rights, urges the war," was the acid comment of John Randolph. In Congress he had "heard but one word—like the whip-poor-will, but one eternal monotonous tone—Canada! Canada! Canada!"

There was in fact a second tone—Florida—which for Southerners provided the harmony. East and West Florida were still in the possession of Spain, Great Britain's ally, and their conquest might well be another reward of a war policy. They contained fertile cotton lands, and through them flowed the navigable rivers of the Mississippi Territory. As early as 1810, Madison, in collusion with American settlers, had seized a portion of West Florida; but nothing short of the whole of the Floridas would now satisfy the expansionists of the Southwest.

In a letter summarizing the causes of the war, Andrew Jackson mentioned neutral rights, impressment, national vindication, Indian pacification, and the desire for territorial conquest. He then condensed all these motives into two phrases: "to seek some indemnity for past injuries, some security against future aggression." Jackson seems to have reflected the sentiment of the majority in the Southern and Western states, and in the presidential election of 1812 they, along with Pennsylvania and Vermont, endorsed the war policy by giving their electoral votes to Madison. De Witt Clinton of New York, the candidate of the Federalists and peace Republicans, carried the rest of the New England and Middle states.

Madison's rather narrow margin in the electoral college (128 to 89—the shift of one state, Pennsylvania, could have changed the result), together with the bitter resentment of the commercial centers, meant that the country went to war dangerously divided. No patriot, wrote a Boston editor, "conceives it his duty to shed his blood for Bonaparte, for Madison or Jefferson, and that Host of Ruffians in Congress." New England Federalists wanted no part of "Mr. Madison's War."

The War of 1812

National Unpreparedness The War Hawks were convinced that the war could be won with little effort and a minimum of sacrifice. Henry Clay announced that "the militia of Kentucky alone are competent to place Montreal and Upper Canada at your feet." His friends in Congress must have believed him, for they led into war a country that was internally divided and hopelessly unprepared. As war approached, the Madison Administration loyally adhered to Jefferson's gunboat policy and continued to neglect the regular navy; even in his message to Congress of November 1811 Madison made no recommendation for naval expansion. The following January two-thirds of the Representatives who were to vote for war five months later helped to defeat a modest proposal to add ten frigates to the navy. During the debate on this measure, Richard M. Johnson of Kentucky, one of the War Hawks, vowed that he would not vote a penny for a naval force "destined to entail upon this happy Government perpetual taxes and a perpetually increasing public debt."

Congress made no effort to increase American naval power until months after the outbreak of war, and the new forty-four-gun frigates and seventy-four-gun ships of the line then provided for were not ready for action until the war had ended. Indeed the United States had an ocean-going navy of only sixteen vessels fit for service with which to challenge the world's foremost sea power, whose warships were numbered in the hundreds. The American navy had the advantage of a talented, well-trained group of officers but suffered from a serious shortage of experienced seamen. It had no real fleet organization, each ship operating more or less as an independent unit. Moreover, since most of the ships were expected to function as commerce raiders, the question of naval strategy seemed superfluous.

But the War Hawks, after all, were thinking primarily of a land war, not of challenging Britain's naval supremacy. With Florida weakly defended, with less than five thousand British troops in Canada, and with war raging in Europe, the odds seemed to favor the Americans. Had the United States trained, equipped, and put in the field an army of only fifty thousand men—no serious strain on the country's resources—it might have conquered Canada and Florida with relative ease. Congressional action seemed adequate enough: it authorized an expansion of the small regular army by the recruitment of twenty-five thousand five-year volunteers; provided for the raising of an additional fifty thousand one-year volunteers; and made repeated calls on the state militias, which numbered, on paper, some seven hundred thousand men.

Even in the regions most enthusiastic for war, however, Americans were reluctant to abandon their civilian pursuits; neither coercion nor persuasion, such as offers of cash bounties and land grants, had much effect. Never during the war did the army number more than thirty-five thousand men, and even this small force was poorly trained and unimaginatively commanded by overage veterans of the Revolution and incompetent militia officers. Militiamen, moreover, generally felt that their duty was limited to state defense, and some refused to leave their states for operations across the frontier.

Congress, including the War Hawks, hesitated to adopt the fiscal measures demanded by a war policy. Eventually Congress doubled tariff rates and levied a new excise tax, a stamp tax, and a direct tax on the states, but these unpopular measures brought the government little revenue until near the end of the war. It authorized loans, but the Treasury Department managed to market the bulk of about $80 million in securities only at a discount and at high interest rates. Since most New England capitalists opposed the war, and since the Bank of the United States had been abolished in 1811, Secretary of the Treasury Gallatin had to rely on state banks which were poorly equipped to handle business of this sort. In short, the whole configuration of Republican policy over the past decade had been designed

The War of 1812: Northern Campaigns, 1812-14

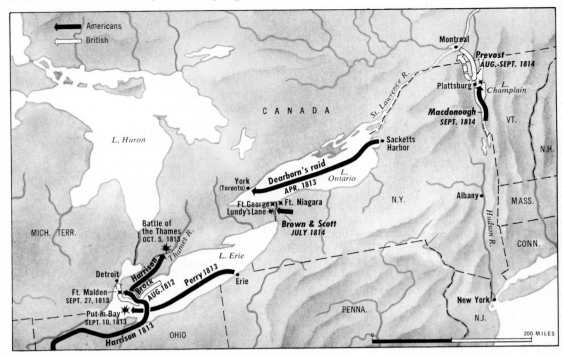

for a simple agrarian nation at peace with the world; the War Hawks, in effect, attempted to apply Jeffersonian means to a non-Jeffersonian end. In so doing, they barely escaped national disaster.

The Military Campaigns   Plans for the conquest of Canada (which Southern Republicans, incidentally, had never viewed with much enthusiasm) ended in a complete fiasco. Effective strategy called for a concentration of forces in an attack on Montreal, whose fall would have cut British communications along the St. Lawrence and the Great Lakes and made the British position in Upper Canada untenable. But, in response to the Western demand for protection from Tecumseh's Indian confederation, the nation's forces were diffused. As a result, the military campaign of 1812 was a feeble, poorly planned, uncoordinated attempt to invade Canada at three separate points. General William Hull marched an army from Detroit toward the British garrison at Malden. But, doubting the wisdom of an invasion before winning control

of Lake Erie, and hearing that Tecumseh and his warriors had joined the British, Hull soon lost his nerve and returned to Detroit. There, on August 6, a brilliant British commander, General Isaac Brock, surrounded Hull's army and forced him to surrender without firing a shot. A second invasion across the Niagara River culminated in defeat and surrender when New York militiamen refused to enter Canada to reinforce their countrymen. Finally, General Henry Dearborn led an advance along Lake Champlain toward Montreal. When he reached the Canadian border he found that his militiamen would not cross it, and was obliged to march back to Plattsburg. So ended the land campaigns of 1812. If they had made no conquests and won no glory, at least they had cost few lives.

Things went little better the next year. Canadians astonished their would-be "liberators" by vigorously supporting British efforts to drive the invaders out. Two events, however, enabled the Americans to recover lost ground on the Northwest frontier and all but eliminate the danger of another British offensive there. The first was Captain Oliver Hazard Perry's notable victory at Put-in-Bay on Lake Erie, September 10, 1813. When Perry reported, "We have met the enemy and they are ours," he gave the Americans control of the Great Lakes and made the British position at Detroit hopeless. The second event was General Harrison's victory over the retreating British at the Battle of the Thames, October 5, 1813. Here the great Indian leader Tecumseh was killed; with his death the Indian confederacy collapsed and the Northwest frontier was secure. But the conquest of Canada was as remote as ever.

By 1814 the Americans were striving desperately to prevent the British from invading their land and, perhaps, taking a slice of it. With the defeat of Napoleon and his exile to Elba, the British were able for the first time to turn their undivided attention to the American war and to send some of their best troops across the Atlantic. Their plan was to harass the cities on the Atlantic coast with amphibious operations while launching invasions at three points: Niagara, Lake Champlain, and New Orleans.

The most ambitious coastal attack was a thrust up Chesapeake Bay culminating in the capture of Washington on August 24. As the President and other Administration officials fled, the British burned the Capitol, the White House, and other public buildings. Having avenged an earlier American raid on York (Toronto) with this crowning humiliation, the British withdrew. The military significance of the raid was negligible, but it underscored the utter failure of the War Hawks' ambitious schemes.

The British invasion plans, however, seriously miscarried, for by 1814 the Americans had found some vigorous young officers and no longer had to rely on untrained, undisciplined militia units. The projected British offensive at Niagara was thwarted by the aggressive operations of General Jacob Brown and his able young subordinate, Winfield Scott. The Battle of Lundy's Lane, near Niagara Falls, on July 25, was itself indecisive, but it ended the British invasion threat from that position.

"We have met the enemy": Battle on Lake Erie, 1813.

The War of 1812: Southwestern Campaigns, 1813-15

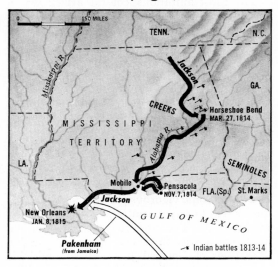

In August a powerful force of British veterans, commanded by Sir George Prevost, advanced toward Lake Champlain with the apparent purpose of cutting off the New England states from the rest of the Union. Early in September Prevost paused before the strong American fortifications at Plattsburg to await the outcome of a bitter duel between British and American flotillas on Lake Champlain. On September 11 Captain Thomas Macdonough's American fleet won a decisive victory, forcing Prevost to abandon his campaign and retire to Canada. Clearly, the war on the Canadian frontier had reached a stalemate.

The final campaign took place in the Southwest. Here Andrew Jackson of Tennessee, an authentic self-trained military genius, somehow managed to make soldiers out of militiamen and to furnish them with supplies. Jackson had already smashed the military power of the Southwestern Indians by defeating the Creeks at the Battle of Horseshoe Bend, on March 27, 1814, and had also forced them to cede some of their richest lands in Mississippi Territory. Next he captured and destroyed Pensacola in Spanish Florida to prevent the British from using it as a base, and then marched his army to New Orleans to meet the invaders. Placing his men behind

earthworks and bales of cotton, he awaited the attack of eight thousand seasoned British troops commanded by Sir Edward Pakenham. Contemptuous of Jackson's motley army of militiamen, sailors, and pirates, Pakenham, on January 8, 1815, led his men in tight formation in a rash frontal assault. American rifles and artillery raked the British columns with a deadly fire. Before the British withdrew, the Americans had killed their commander and inflicted more than two thousand casualties, while suffering little more than a dozen of their own. The Battle of New Orleans was the last engagement of the war—in fact, it was fought two weeks after a treaty of peace had been signed. But it helped sweeten the bitter taste of the defeats and disappointments of the past two and a half years, and it launched Andrew Jackson, the Hero of New Orleans, on his dazzling career.

On the high seas in the early months of the war the tiny American navy won a series of stunning victories in single-ship engagements, bolstering public morale during the disasters in the Canadian frontier. The most spectacular of these victories were those of the American frigate *Constitution* (Old Ironsides) over the British frigates *Guerrière* and *Java*, and of the *United States* over the *Macedonian*. These successes shocked the British public, which had heard the American navy described as a "few fir-built frigates, manned by a handful of bastards and outlaws"; but they constituted no real challenge to British naval supremacy, nor did they have any great strategic significance.

By 1813 most of the American men-of-war were bottled up in their home ports by an effective British blockade, and by the end of the war only the *Constitution* and a few smaller vessels were still at sea. American cruisers and privateers continued to prey on British commerce and altogether captured more than a thousand merchantmen. These commerce raiders were a costly annoyance to the British but fell far short of seriously crippling her overseas trade or disrupting her economy. The decisive fact of the naval war was the British blockade of the American coast, which dealt an almost mortal blow to the American carrying trade. In 1814 exports and imports fell to less than 10 per cent of what they had

Victory at New Orleans: Occasion for capital rejoicing.

been in the peak year of 1807. Flour exports declined from 1,443,000 barrels in 1812 to 193,000 barrels in 1814. The blockade was equally disastrous to American interstate commerce, most of which still moved along coastal waterways. Francis Wayland described the devastating impact of the blockade on the whole economy: "Our harbors were blockaded; communications coastwise between our ports were cut off; our ships were rotting in every creek and cove where they could find a place of security; our immense annual products were mouldering in our warehouses; the sources of profitable labor were dried up." If the land war was a stalemate, the war on the high seas culminated in a British victory that was well-nigh complete. Floating in the wreckage was Jefferson's gunboat policy.

Disaffection in New England   This is what antiwar Federalists in the Northeast had

anticipated—what Josiah Quincy of Massachusetts had in mind when he said, "This war, the measures which preceded it, and the mode of carrying it on, are all undeniably southern and western policy, not the policy of the commercial states." Feeling betrayed by their own government, convinced that the Madison Administration had deliberately set about to destroy their political and economic power, New England Federalists throughout the war regarded the Republican politicians in Washington, not the British, as their mortal enemies. And, having regained political control of all the New England states, they were in a position to translate their angry polemics into defiant deeds.

Federalist governors contested federal calls on the state militias, insisting that their proper function was to repel invasion, not to invade foreign territory. Federalists discouraged voluntary enlistments; and when Congress debated a militia draft, they defended state sovereignty against national tyranny. "Where is it written in the Constitution," asked Daniel Webster, a young congressman from New Hampshire, "that you may take children from their parents, and parents from their children, and compel them to fight the battles of any war in which the folly or the wickedness of government may engage it?" Federalists resisted tax measures and boycotted government loans. According to a Boston editor, "any man who lends money to the government at the present time will forfeit all claim to common honesty." Meanwhile, New Englanders defiantly continued to trade with Canada and even furnished supplies to the British fleet. The more extreme dissenters favored either a separate peace and the withdrawal of New England from the war, or else secession from the Union.

In 1814 British depredations along the New England coast and the belief that the federal government would do nothing to check them precipitated a serious political crisis. In October the Massachusetts legislature called for a convention of the New England states, asserting that the federal Constitution "has failed to secure to this commonwealth, and as they believe, to the Eastern sections of this Union, those equal rights and benefits which are the greatest objects of its formation." Twenty-six delegates, most of them from Massachusetts, Connecticut, and Rhode Island, assembled in Hartford on December 15 and deliberated secretly for nearly three weeks. A few reckless men, such as Timothy Pickering, were ready to take desperate measures; but the moderates, led by Harrison Gray Otis, gained control and adopted a final report that was relatively mild.

The report began with a gloomy account of the evils the country had endured under the "withering influence" of the Republicans. The Jeffersonians, it claimed, had debauched the civil service; destroyed "the balance of power which existed among the original states" by creating new Western states; and entertained a "visionary and superficial theory in regard to commerce, accompanied by a real hatred but a feigned regard to its interests." As a remedy for these grievances the Hartford report demanded a series of constitutional amendments abolishing the three-fifths compromise, requiring a two-thirds vote of both houses of Congress to declare war and to admit new states, prohibiting embargoes lasting for more than sixty days, excluding the foreign-born from federal offices, limiting the President to one term, and prohibiting the election of two successive Presidents from the same state. If these demands were ignored and the war continued, the report recommended that another convention be called and given "such powers and instructions as the exigency of a crisis so momentous may require."

When representatives from the Hartford Convention arrived in Washington with their ultimatum, they found the capital rejoicing over Jackson's victory at New Orleans and over the signing of a treaty of peace. Under the circumstances their complaints seemed pointless, and their demands were ignored. But the Hartford Convention was remembered; to nationalists it symbolized the disloyalty, the narrow, selfish provincialism, of Federalism. Consequently, the Federalist party itself was one of the casualties of the War of 1812.

Oddly enough, New England, in spite of her political disaffection, was the only region that profited materially from the war. Since the British blockade was not enforced along her coast until 1814, she received the bulk of foreign imports. Gold from the rest of the country flowed to her banks, which were thus able to maintain specie payments while other banks were forced to suspend payments. Above all, the war gave an immense impetus to New England manufacturing; between 1810 and 1814 the number of cotton spindles in the area increased sixfold. A war that was launched in part to acquire more land for the agrarians of the Northwest and South ended without an acre of new territory but with hundreds of thousands of spindles whirling in New England factories.

Peace Negotiations

The Treaty of Ghent   Almost from the start of this curious conflict there had been talk of peace. As early as September 1812 the czar of Russia, anxious that the British give their full attention to Napoleon, offered to act as mediator. President Madison responded favorably and, early in 1813, sent Albert Gallatin and James A. Bayard to work with John Quincy Adams, the American ambassador in St. Petersburg. The British declined the Russian offer—Russia could not be trusted to support the British position on neutral rights —but soon indicated a willingness to negotiate directly with the Americans. This, too, was acceptable to Madison, though he did not hear of the suggestion until January 1814. He then appointed Henry Clay and Jonathan Russell to join the three commissioners already in Europe, and in August negotiations began in the city of Ghent.

The British diplomats, an unimpressive group, were under the strict control of the Foreign Office in London. The Americans, superior in talent, had received from their government broader powers and greater freedom to negotiate. But they found it difficult to agree among themselves on matters of policy, and during the tedious months of negotiation their personal relations sometimes became tense. Adams' colleagues found him an irritating companion, and Adams, in turn, took a dim view of them, especially of Clay with his taste for cards and late hours. "They sit after dinner and drink bad wine and smoke cigars, which neither suits my habits nor my health, and absorbs time which I cannot spare," wrote the austere New Englander. Gallatin turned out to be the chief peacemaker not only in dealings with the British but also with his own colleagues.

Had the two delegations adhered to their initial instructions, the negotiations would have been brief and the result complete failure. The Americans were to insist that the British abandon impressment, agree to respect international law in setting up blockades, and pay indemnity for their illegal seizure of American ships. The British, anticipating decisive military victories in the campaigns of 1814, presented a list of terms that would have jeopardized the sovereignty and future growth of the United States. They demanded territorial cessions in northern New York and Maine, the surrender of American control of the Great Lakes, the creation of an autonomous Indian buffer state south of the Great Lakes, the right to navigate the Mississippi River,

and the relinquishment of American fishing rights off the coasts of Newfoundland and Labrador. The Americans made it clear that if the British insisted on these terms the war would continue. "Our negotiations may be considered at an end," wrote Gallatin to his government.

But the British did not insist. News of Macdonough's victory on Lake Champlain and Prevost's retreat from Plattsburg drastically changed the military picture, and the Duke of Wellington, when consulted by the British ministry, argued that failure to gain control of the Great Lakes made the British demands unreasonable. "I confess," he said, "that I think you have no right, from the state of the war, to demand any concession of territory from America." British merchants and manufacturers, eager to resume trade with the United States, favored an end to hostilities. The tax-burdened British public, too, had had enough of war.

As negotiations proceeded, the diplomats dropped one demand after another and eventually agreed to a peace treaty that settled nothing but simply restored the *status quo ante bellum*. The Treaty of Ghent, signed on December 24, 1814, was silent on impressment and neutral rights, boundaries and fisheries, trade and indemnities—although it referred some of these questions to joint commissions for future settlement. In submitting the treaty to the Senate for ratification, Madison claimed no victory. "The late war," he said with more than a little ambiguity, "has been waged with a success which is the natural result of the wisdom of the legislative councils, of the patriotism of the people, of the public spirit of the militia, and of the valor of the military and naval forces of the country." As Adams described the document, "Nothing was adjusted, nothing was settled—nothing in substance but an indefinite suspension of hostilities was agreed to." Clay, though he signed it, described it as a "damned bad treaty."

Nevertheless, Americans looked back on the war with pride and satisfaction. That the British had yielded nothing on neutral rights or impressment could be overlooked, because these issues lost their significance when the war ended in Europe. In the selective memories of patriots the military defeats, the bungling of

Boundary Treaties, 1818-19

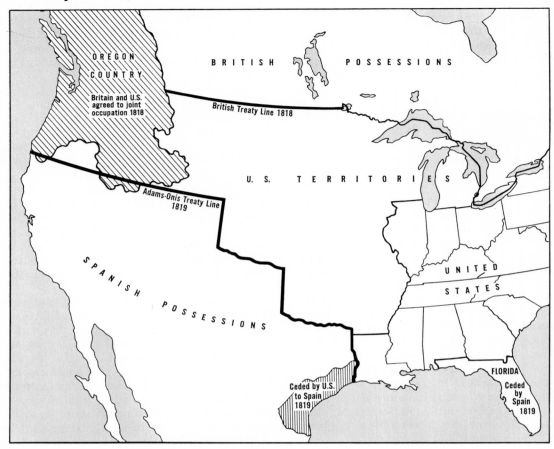

the Canadian campaigns, and British supremacy on the high seas faded into insignificance; the early exploits of American frigates and privateers, Perry's victory on Lake Erie, and, best of all, Jackson's victory at New Orleans were remembered vividly as the crucial events of the war. The very fact that no territory had been lost—that the British had abandoned their extreme demands—contributed to this myth of military success. Moreover, the death of Tecumseh, the collapse of the Indian confederation, and the destruction of Indian military power east of the Mississippi meant that at least one purpose of the war had been fully achieved. Finally, the rise of manufacturing made the country more self-sufficient, and the preservation of their threatened independence gave the Americans a greater

feeling of national identity than ever before. As Gallatin observed: "The war has renewed and reinstated the national feelings and character which the Revolution had given. . . . The people now have more general objects of attachment. . . . They are more Americans; they feel and act more as a nation."

Postwar Settlements   Though memories of the war were to keep alive an undercurrent of Anglo-American hostility for many years, several specific issues that might have caused trouble were resolved soon after the stalemate at Ghent. In 1815 a commercial treaty removed most of the restrictions on Anglo-American trade (except with the British West Indies). An agreement of 1817, signed by Richard Rush, the Acting Secretary of State, and Charles Bagot, the British minister, provided for naval disarmament on the Great Lakes. Though either side could terminate it on six months' notice, the Rush-Bagot Agreement became a permanent policy and eventually was applied to the land frontier as well. Another agreement the following year reopened the coasts of Newfoundland and Labrador to American fishermen, established the forty-ninth parallel as the northern boundary of the Louisiana Purchase from the Lake of the Woods to the Rocky Mountains, and provided for a joint occupation of Oregon for the next ten years. Neither the British nor the Americans could have guessed it then, but these postwar negotiations, rather than the War of 1812, were to set the pattern for subsequent Anglo-American relations.

Another long-standing source of diplomatic friction was removed when Spain finally agreed to give up the Floridas. Internally weak and rapidly losing her once great empire in South and Central America, Spain maintained only a tenuous hold on the Floridas. Her feeble garrison was unable to control the Seminole Indians or to prevent white outlaws and runaway slaves from using the region as a sanctuary. In 1818 Andrew Jackson, giving the broadest possible interpretation to vague instructions from his government, led a military force into the Floridas to punish the Seminoles for depredations along the American frontier. In the process he seized St. Marks and Pensacola, deposed the Spanish governor, and raised the American flag; he also arrested two British subjects for inciting the Indians, tried them by court-martial, and executed them. At home Jackson's high-handed conduct added to his popularity, but it immensely complicated matters for Secretary of State John Quincy Adams, who had been negotiating with the Spanish minister, Luis de Onís.

Making the best of a bad situation, Adams brazened his way through. He not only refused to apologize for Jackson's behavior but threw responsibility on the Spanish for failing to preserve order in the Floridas. Spain, he insisted, must either govern the provinces efficiently or cede them to the United States, for they had become "a derelict, open to the occupancy of every enemy, civilized or savage, of the United States, and serving no other earthly purpose than as a post of annoyance to them." This was a challenge that the Spanish were in no position to accept, and in 1819 the Adams-Onís Treaty arranged for the transfer of the Floridas to the United States. In exchange, the American government agreed to assume payment of $5 million worth of claims that American citizens held against the Spanish government. Ratification of the treaty was delayed for two years, but in 1821 Jackson triumphantly reentered Florida Territory as the first American governor.

Those who had moral sensibilities about the rough tactics of Jackson and Adams soothed their conscience with the argument that since the Floridas were contiguous to American territory Providence intended that America should have them. A later generation would call this argument "Manifest Destiny." Even so, the age of the Jeffersonians, who believed in man's reason and disliked the cynicism of the Old World, was closing on a slightly sour note.

SUGGESTIONS FOR READING

Jefferson in Power

Jefferson's political philosophy has had an enduring influence on American thought; it is analyzed sympathetically in Adrienne Koch, *The Philosophy of Thomas Jefferson* (1943). Its historical significance is treated in C. M. Wiltse, *The Jeffersonian Tradition in American Democracy* * (1935), and in Merrill Peterson, *The Jefferson Image in the American Mind* * (1960). The best completed biography of Jefferson is Nathan Schachner, *Thomas Jefferson: A Biography*, 2 vols. (1951). Two earlier biographies, A. J. Nock, *Thomas Jefferson* * (1926), and Gilbert Chinard, *Thomas Jefferson, The Apostle of Americanism* * (1929), are still valuable. The contributions of Jefferson's two ablest lieutenants can be studied in three works of genuine distinction: Adrienne Koch, *Jefferson and Madison: The Great Collaboration* (1950),

* Available in a paperback edition.

Irving Brant, *James Madison: Secretary of State, 1800–1809* (1953), and Raymond Walters, *Albert Gallatin: Jeffersonian, Financier and Diplomat* (1957).

A brilliant analysis of the Republican era, in spite of its hostility to Jefferson and Madison, is Henry Adams, *History of the United States During the Administrations of Jefferson and Madison*, 9 vols. (1889–91). The balance is more than redressed in C. G. Bower's vivid but partisan account, *Jefferson in Power* (1936). In many ways the most satisfactory studies of the era are Edward Channing, *The Jeffersonian System* (1906), and Vol. IV of his *A History of the United States*, 6 vols. (1905–25). An expert analysis of Republican administrative organization is provided in L. D. White, *The Jeffersonians: A Study in Administrative History, 1801–1829* (1951).

An unfriendly biography of John Randolph, Jefferson's chief Republican critic, is Henry Adams, *John Randolph* (1882); a sympathetic analysis of his ideas is Russell Kirk, *Randolph of Roanoke: A Study in Conservative Thought* (1951). The case for Aaron Burr is presented in Nathan Schachner, *Aaron Burr: A Biography* * (1937); the case against him, in T. P. Abernethy, *The Burr Conspiracy* (1954).

Foreign Policy and the War of 1812

The two most useful works on the Louisiana Purchase are E. W. Lyon, *Louisiana in French Diplomacy, 1759–1804* (1934), and, by the same author, *The Man Who Sold Louisiana: The Life of François Barbé-Marbois* (1942). Two earlier books should also be consulted: J. K. Hosmer, *History of the Louisiana Purchase* (1902), and F. A. Ogg, *The Opening of the Mississippi* (1904). The best accounts of the conflict with the Barbary pirates are G. W. Allen, *Our Navy and the Barbary Corsairs* (1905), and R. W. Irwin, *Diplomatic Relations of the United States with the Barbary Powers* (1931).

Several excellent works are available on the problems of American neutrality. A good place to begin is with Irving Brant's study of Madison as Secretary of State, mentioned above, and with the same author's *James Madison: The President, 1809–1812* (1956). Outstanding monographs include W. W. Jennings, *The American Embargo* (1921); J. F. Zimmerman, *Impressment of American Seamen* (1925); L. M. Sears, *Jefferson and the Embargo* (1927); Harry Bernstein, *Origins of Inter-American Interest, 1700–1812* (1945); and Bradford Perkins, *First Rapprochement: England and the United States, 1795–1805* (1955).

The view that the War of 1812 was caused by Western and Southern expansionism and fear of the Indians is developed in J. W. Pratt, *Expansionists of 1812* (1925). The case for neutral rights as the fundamental cause of the war is presented in A. L. Burt, *The United States, Great Britain, and British North America from the Revolution to the Peace after the War of 1812* (1940). The careers of two of the leading War Hawks can be studied in Bernard Mayo, *Henry Clay: Spokesman of the New West* (1937), and C. M. Wiltse, *John C. Calhoun: Nationalist, 1782–1828* (1944).

The best general account of the War of 1812 is F. F. Beirne, *The War of 1812* (1949). A. T. Mahan, *Sea Power in Its Relation to the War of 1812*, 2 vols. (1919), is the classic study of the naval war. Marquis James, *Andrew Jackson: The Border Captain* * (1933), provides an absorbing account of the campaigns in the Southwest. An excellent analysis of the peace negotiations is in S. F. Bemis, *John Quincy Adams and the Foundations of American Foreign Policy* (1949). Federalist disaffection is treated perceptively in George Dangerfield, *The Era of Good Feelings* (1952), and S. E. Morison, *The Life and Letters of Harrison Gray Otis*, 2 vols. (1913).

* Available in a paperback edition.

8

Nationalism and
Economic Expansion

One might have expected the War Hawks to be discredited by their failure to capture Canada and their general mishandling of military affairs. But at the end of the War of 1812 the Republican party, with the young nationalists at the helm, was still firmly in power. Though the record of Madison's wartime Administration was somewhat less than brilliant, the country was still intact and flourishing. Farmers had regained their European markets, agricultural prices were good, and land values were rising. Settlers swarmed into the West, and within a few years after the Treaty of Ghent four new states—Indiana in 1816, Mississippi in 1817, Illinois in 1818, and Alabama in 1819—entered the Union. A new economic interest, manufacturing, was growing in importance and striving to expand at the rate it had achieved during the wartime dearth of British goods. Shipping, though it would never again dominate the economy of the Northeastern maritime states as it once had, gradually recovered from the blows the embargo and the war had dealt.

This vast land, with its burgeoning economy and its optimistic, nationalistic people (nine and a half million of them by 1820), was no longer the plain, uncomplicated Republic that Jefferson had once so much admired. Jefferson's party was changing with the country and now counted manufacturers, factory workers, and other urban groups, as well as farmers and planters, among those it had to serve. Henry Clay, John C. Calhoun, and John Quincy

Adams were impatient with the old-fashioned Virginia Republicans' emphasis on constitutionalism, state rights, and agrarianism. They had a vision of national growth, economic expansion, and social progress that required a more dynamic and imaginative government than had been contemplated in traditional Republican philosophy. Postwar Republicans still waged their political battles with Jeffersonian rhetoric, but the old creed had lost much of its substance. In 1801 Jefferson's remark that "We are all Republicans, we are all Federalists" was only a loose figure of speech; in 1816 it was almost a fact.

The Triumph of Neo-Federalism

The American System Circumstances had forced Madison, time after time, to compromise traditional Republicanism. In his seventh annual message to Congress, December 5, 1815, his surrender to the nationalists was well-nigh complete; Hamilton himself could hardly have composed a message that embraced orthodox Federalist doctrine more fully. In the name of national defense, Madison urged an expansion of the navy, a reorganization of the militia, and an enlargement of the Military Academy at West Point. Without a blush he recommended federal assumption of certain state debts incurred for militia expenses during the recent war. To establish a uniform national currency, he suggested that "a national bank will merit con-

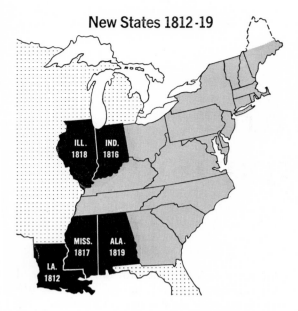

New States 1812-19

ILL.
1818

IND.
1816

MISS.
1817

ALA.
1819

LA.
1812

sideration." A federal tariff should provide industry with the protection that "is due to the enterprising citizens whose interests are now at stake." Finally, Madison urged Congress to finance such internal improvements as required "a national jurisdiction and national means," thus "binding more closely together the various parts of our extended confederacy."

Congressional leaders had few qualms about the program of neo-Federalism, and Henry Clay soon labeled it the "American System." The trouble with the prewar economy, thought Clay and his supporters, had been its dependence on the exchange of American raw materials for European manufactured goods, a dependence that exposed it to the whims of other powers and made it the victim of every international crisis. "Dame Commerce," said Clay, "is a flirting, flippant, noisy Jade and if we are governed by her fantasies, we shall never put off the muslins of India and the cloths of Europe." Hence the foundation of Clay's American System was a protective tariff to stimulate domestic manufacturing and to create an enlarged domestic market for the agricultural products of the South and West. Internal improvements, financed with tariff revenues, would encourage interstate commerce, and a national bank would provide the currency and accumulate the capital required

for economic growth. This nationalistic program, Clay believed, would bring to all sections of the country both prosperity and independence of the outside world.

The Tariff of 1816 The first postwar Congress, one of the most fruitful of the nineteenth century, took long strides toward the goal of an American System. By 1816 the Republican party numbered in its ranks a large cluster of interest groups, both urban and rural, clamoring for protective duties on foreign manufactured goods entering the American market. Leading the protectionists were those who had invested in New England textile mills and Pennsylvania iron-smelters when the embargo and war had choked off European supplies. Seconding them were the hemp-growers of Kentucky, the wool-growers of Ohio and Vermont, and an assortment of Southerners and Westerners who hoped either to promote industry or to expand their domestic market behind a tariff wall.

The cries of the protectionists increased when British exporters, seeking to dispose of surpluses accumulated during the war and to drive competing American manufacturers out of business, flooded the American market with low-priced goods. A member of Parliament suggested that British goods might even be sold at a loss for a time, in order "to stifle in the cradle those rising manufactures in the United States, which war has forced into existence, contrary to the natural course of things." Now the protectionists could claim that the British were plotting to wreck the American economy and could present their demand for a higher tariff as a plea for national economic survival. America's "infant industries" were fragile things, they said, requiring the tender care of the government while they grew to maturity.

Congress responded with the Tariff of 1816, the first fiscal measure specifically designed to provide protection as well as revenue. In the House the Western and Middle states gave the bill overwhelming support; New England divided seventeen to ten for it, the South twenty-three to thirty-four against. Webster and other Federalists, speaking for the shipping interests, opposed higher duties as an obstacle to foreign trade; John Randolph, like most Southerners, vowed that he would not "agree to lay a duty on the cultivator of the soil to encourage exotic manufactures." On the other hand, Calhoun, the South Carolina nationalist, hoped that the manufacturing interest would "at all times, and under every policy . . . be protected with due care." In 1816 a considerable minority in the South shared Calhoun's point of view; within a few years, as conditions and expectations changed, Southern support for the tariff—and for the American System in general—almost vanished.

The Second Bank of the United States Republican leaders, chastened by their fiscal experiences during the war, made their most dramatic surrender to Federalism when they revived both Hamilton's plan and his arguments for a national bank. When the first Bank of the United States perished in 1811, its business had fallen to the state-chartered banks; within five years the number of these banks had increased from 88 to 246, their issues of banknotes from $28 million to $68 million. Since most state-chartered banks did not maintain adequate specie reserves (gold and silver), their notes usually circulated at a discount. The bewildering variety of notes, their fluctuating value, and an epidemic of counterfeiting brought the country to the edge of fiscal chaos. The final blow came when the state banks, except those in New England, suspended specie payments altogether during the war—and showed no disposition to resume specie payments with the restoration of peace.

Meanwhile, the federal government lacked a safe depository for its funds, a reliable agency to transfer them from place to place, and adequate machinery to market securities when it needed to borrow. The absence of a uniform paper currency was a severe handicap to businessmen engaged in interstate commerce. Even some of the old Republican agrarians, though they opposed all banks that issued paper currency, favored chartering a new national bank as the lesser of two evils. Madison discarded his constitutional doubts and decided that the question had been settled "by repeated recognitions . . . of the validity of such an institution, in acts of the legislative, executive, and judicial branches of the government, accompanied by . . . a concurrence of the general will of the nation." Calhoun, taking a thoroughly nationalistic position, attacked the state banks for usurping the federal government's exclusive power to issue and regulate the country's currency. Clay, who had opposed rechartering the first Bank, confessed that he had not anticipated the evils its demise had caused.

In 1816 a bill to grant a twenty-year charter to a second Bank of the United States passed both houses of Congress over the opposition of state banking interests, Federalist partisans, and Virginia agrarians. The functions and structure of the second Bank were essentially the same as those of the first, except that its capital was increased from $10 million to $35 million. The federal government again held one-fifth of the stock, and the President appointed five of the twenty-five directors. The Bank's headquarters were to be in Philadelphia, but it could establish branches elsewhere. Its liabilities were not to exceed its capital, one-fifth of which must be in specie; and it was to report annually to the Treasury Department and open its books for periodic inspection. This powerful banking corporation could serve a number of useful purposes: it could assist the government in its fiscal business; it could regulate the state banks; and it could support business enterprise. But as the largest capitalistic institution in the country, depending as it did upon the government for special favors, the Bank was always in a vulnerable position. Should it lack responsible leadership, should federal control of its operations prove to be inadequate, the Bank might loom as a threat to democracy and as an instrument of economic tyranny.

Internal Improvements The War of 1812, by disrupting coastal shipping, had demonstrated the inadequacy of the country's internal transportation system for both interstate commerce and national defense. The landlocked West was the most persistent solicitor of federal funds for internal improvements; New England, suffering a loss of population and a decline of political strength, was the center of opposition. President Madison, stretching his constitutional scruples to support projects that were national in scope, approved appropriations for the continued building of the Cumberland (National) Road to Wheeling, which had been started in 1811. But he doubted that Congress had power to subsidize local roads and canals without an ap-

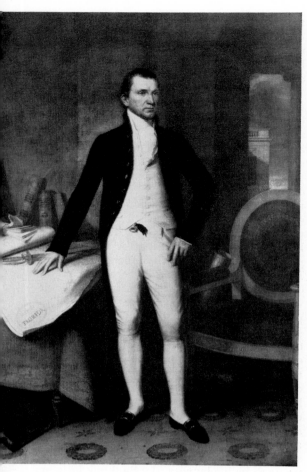

Monroe: A last nostalgic look.

The Era of Good Feelings Nearing the end of his second term, Madison supported another Virginian, his Secretary of State, James Monroe, to succeed him to the presidency. The Randolph Republicans preferred William H. Crawford of Georgia, and some Northern Republicans fretted about the long domination of their party by the "Virginia Dynasty." But Madison had his way, and Monroe won an easy victory over his Federalist opponent, Rufus King of New York. Four years later, with the Federalists too feeble even to run a candidate, Monroe was re-elected without opposition.* After a few more years of activity in scattered localities, the Federalist party was extinct. The party's war record, its failure to adjust to new conditions, its narrow particularism, and the Republican pirating of its program all contributed to its death.

James Monroe, a representative of the small-planter class of the Virginia piedmont, reached the presidency at the age of sixty-one after many years of devoted, though not brilliant, public service. Once the favorite of the Randolph "Quids" (see p. 169), Monroe continued to interpret the Constitution more narrowly than the nationalists in his party, especially when it came to internal improvements. He accepted the tariff and the banking legislation passed during Madison's last year in office, but while he was President the American System made only limited progress. Though he was less talented than his distinguished predecessors, Monroe's contemporaries found something solid and reassuring in this member of the Revolutionary generation. In Monroe, with his wig, his cocked hat, and his knee-length pantaloons, the postwar generation had a last nostalgic look at the eighteenth century.

The year of Monroe's inauguration, 1817, found the country in a complaisant mood. On a good-will tour that ultimately carried him into once-hostile New England, the new President saw everywhere abundant signs of national unity. His warm reception in Boston caused the *Columbian Centinel*, a Federalist paper, to speak of an "Era of Good Feelings," thus giving a popular label to Monroe's Administrations. Political factionalism was at a low ebb, and there was relative harmony among

propriate amendment to the Constitution. In 1817 Congress ignored his doubts and passed a bill to distribute among the states for local internal improvements a $1,500,000 bonus paid to the government by the Bank of the United States for its charter. For Madison this was going too far, and in one of his last presidential acts he vetoed the so-called bonus bill. Calhoun, disgusted with this narrow view of things, grumbled that the Constitution "was not intended as a thesis for the logician to exercise his ingenuity on; . . . it ought to be construed with plain good sense." But Madison's veto stalled this crucial phase of the American System. Local internal improvements remained, for the time being, the responsibility of the individual states and private enterprise.

* One elector from New Hampshire voted for John Quincy Adams.

sections. Above all, as Monroe observed in his first message to Congress, the country was in a "prosperous and happy condition. . . . The abundant fruits of the earth have filled it with plenty." The "Era of Good Feelings" lasted, however, only about two years—until the middle of Monroe's first Administration—when party strife and sectional bitterness suddenly revived, and the national prosperity came to an abrupt and shocking end.

John Marshall and the Supreme Court

Marshall's Role   In these postwar years still another Virginian played a key role in the formulation of public policy and in the molding of the American political structure. This was John Marshall, Chief Justice of the Supreme Court from 1801 to 1835, who gave the judicial branch of the government the prestige it had previously lacked and who, unlike most of his fellow Virginians, supported nationalistic measures with unqualified enthusiasm. Born in 1755, Marshall saw military service during the Revolution and then went home to become one of the most successful lawyers before the Richmond bar. In 1792 Jefferson, already suspicious of Marshall's politics, suggested to Madison that Marshall ought to be appointed a judge to keep him out of mischief. As it turned out, Jefferson understood his man—Marshall became a Federalist—but he could scarcely have been more mistaken about how to render him harmless. After a term in Congress and brief service as John Adams' Secretary of State, Marshall received his appointment as Chief Justice shortly before the last Federalist President left office. The Supreme Court, at least, would remain in Federalist hands!

In personal appearance and social intercourse Marshall impressed one as a plain, homespun democrat, for he was the most unpretentious of men, an amiable lover of sports and other simple pleasures. But underneath he was a resolute Federalist, suspicious of popular government and contemptuous of what he considered Jefferson's sentimental trust in the people. Marshall was in no sense a scholar or philosopher of the law; he lacked the patience for intensive study and the imagination for metaphysical speculation. But he had a keen

Marshall: A tough mind.

intelligence and a tough mind that readily discovered the logic of a case and swiftly drove to its core. According to Joseph Story, whom Madison made an Associate Justice in 1811, Marshall "examines the intricacies of a subject with calm and persevering circumspection and unravels its mysteries with irresistible acuteness." His personal magnetism and intellectual powers gave him enormous influence over his colleagues on the bench, including those appointed by Republicans. Marshall's domination of the Court is evident from the fact that during his thirty-four years as Chief Justice he wrote almost half the decisions and dissented from the majority opinion only eight times. Caring little for precedents, avoiding legal jargon, using crisp prose and careful reasoning, Marshall delivered a series of the most momentous decisions in American judicial history.

Judicial Review   Soon after assuming his new office, Marshall found an opportunity to pronounce a vigorous and, in the long run, decisive opinion on a matter of prime importance for a federal government based on a written constitution. While the Federalists were in power there had been a persistent but inconclusive debate over who was to decide when Congress had exceeded its delegated powers or encroached upon the rights of the states. Since the Constitution is not explicit on this point, the answer had to be found by inference rather than from the plain language of the document. Probably the majority of delegates to the Constitutional Convention had expected the Supreme Court to pass on the constitutionality of the acts of Congress, and Hamilton, in one of the articles in the *Federalist*, had upheld the principle of judicial review. Jeffersonian Republicans, however, had argued that the federal government was the agent of the sovereign states and that those who had created it must define its powers. The individual states, said Jefferson in the Kentucky Resolutions of 1798, would decide when the Constitution had been violated, as well as "the mode and measure of redress."

This is where things stood when, in 1803, Marshall gave the Court's decision in the case of *Marbury* v. *Madison*. Intrinsically of minor importance, this case related to a section of the Judiciary Act of 1789 which, according to Marshall, expanded the Court's original jurisdiction beyond what the Constitution intended it to be. "The question of whether an act repugnant to the constitution can become the law of the land, is a question deeply interesting to the United States," Marshall wrote. His answer to the question was clear: The wording of the Constitution establishes the principle "that a law repugnant to the constitution is void; and that courts, as well as other departments, are bound by that instrument." Moreover, "It is emphatically the province and duty of the judicial department to say what the law is. Those who apply the rule to particular cases must of necessity expound and interpret that rule."

Marbury v. *Madison* thus established a precedent for the Supreme Court to determine the constitutionality of congressional legislation and to act as the final authority on the meaning of the Constitution. This doctrine of judicial review has been challenged many times, but it has weathered all the storms and survives to this day. Having established the precedent, Marshall never again disallowed an act of Congress—more than a half-century passed before the Supreme Court exercised this power again. But Marshall frequently applied the positive side of judicial review—that is, he reviewed and *approved* congressional legislation as constitutional.

National Supremacy   As a nationalist Marshall was, in fact, eager to interpret the powers of Congress as broadly as possible and to assert the federal government's supremacy over the states. For example, in two important cases, *Martin* v. *Hunter's Lessee* (1816) and *Cohens* v. *Virginia* (1821), the Marshall Court affirmed the right to review and reverse decisions of state courts when they concerned issues arising under the federal Constitution. On thirteen occasions it voided state laws as violations of "the supreme law of the land." One of the most significant of these cases, *Gibbons* v. *Ogden* (1824), involved a New York law giving a steamboat company a monopoly of the business of carrying passengers on the Hudson River to New York City. In rejecting the law Marshall gave the term "commerce" an extremely broad definition and came close to saying that the power of Congress over interstate commerce is absolute. This power, he ruled, 'is complete in itself, may be exercised to its utmost extent, and acknowledges no limitations other than are prescribed in the constitution.''

But the Chief Justice expounded the nationalist doctrine most fully in the case of *McCulloch* v. *Maryland* (1819), which tested the constitutionality of the second Bank of the United States. Conceding that the Constitution does not explicitly grant Congress authority to charter a bank, Marshall insisted that Congress must have some discretion in exercising the powers it does possess. Surely the authority could be implied from the "necessary and proper" clause. Then Marshall made a classic statement of the doctrine of "loose construction": "Let the end be legitimate, let it be within the scope of the Constitution, and all means which are appropriate, which are plainly adapted to that end, which are not prohibited, but consist with the letter and spirit of the constitution, are constitutional." The nationalist advocates of the American System could scarcely have asked for a warmer endorsement.

John Marshall
on Judicial Review

If Congress remains at liberty to give this court appellate jurisdiction, where the constitution has declared their jurisdiction shall be original; and original jurisdiction where the constitution has declared it shall be appellate; the distribution of jurisdiction, made in the constitution, is form without substance....

The question whether an act repugnant to the constitution can become the law of the land, is a question deeply interesting to the United States; but, happily not of an intricacy proportioned to its interest....

The constitution is either a superior paramount law, unchangeable by ordinary means, or it is on a level with ordinary legislative acts, and, like other acts, is alterable when the legislature shall please to alter it.

If the former part of the alternative be true, then a legislative act contrary to the constitution is not law; if the latter part be true, then written constitutions are absurd attempts, on the part of the people, to limit a power in its own nature illimitable.

Certainly all those who have framed written constitutions contemplate them as forging the fundamental and paramount law of the nation, and consequently the theory of every such government must be that an act of the legislature repugnant to the Constitution is void.

From *Marbury* v. *Madison*, 1 Cr. 137, 1803.

Sanctity of Contracts   As a conservative defender of property rights, Marshall also sought to make the federal courts a sanctuary of the propertied classes whenever they were harassed by unfriendly state legislatures. He sympathized with creditors and entrepreneurs who considered contracts sacred and inviolable, and he admired the clause in the Constitution that prohibited states from "impairing the obligation of contracts." In the case of *Fletcher* v. *Peck* (1810), Marshall gave evidence of the extremes to which he would go to defend this principle. As we have seen (p. 169), the Georgia legislature, in 1795, had granted a large tract of Western land to the Yazoo Land Companies. The following year a new legislature, discovering bribery and fraud, repudiated the grant and thus provoked litigation that ultimately reached the Supreme Court. To Marshall the case was perfectly clear: the grant

John Marshall
on Contract

The term "contract" must be understood ... as intended to guard against a power of at least doubtful utility, the abuse of which had been extensively felt, and to restrain the legislature in future from violating the right of property. That anterior to the formation of the constitution, a course of legislation had prevailed in many, if not in all, of the states, which weakened the confidence of man in man, and embarrassed all transactions between individuals, by dispensing with a faithful performance of engagements. To correct this mischief, by restraining the power which produced it, the state legislatures were forbidden "to pass any law impairing the obligation of contracts," that is, of contracts respecting property, under which some ... individual could claim a right to something beneficial to himself....

This is plainly a contract ... made on a valuable consideration. It is a contract for the security and disposition of property. It is a contract on the faith of which real and personal estate has been conveyed to the corporation. It is then a contract within the letter of the constitution, and within its spirit also.

From *Dartmouth College* v. *Woodward*, 4 Wheat. 518, 1819.

---

of land was a binding contract, and the circumstances under which it was negotiated did not concern the Court. The withdrawal of the grant, therefore, was an unconstitutional violation of the obligation of contract.

Another case, *Dartmouth College* v. *Woodward* (1819), enabled Marshall to make an equally extreme application of the contract clause. The case originated in an attempt of the New Hampshire legislature to revise Dartmouth's charter, which dated back to colonial days, and to transform the college into a state institution. The trustees went to court and employed Daniel Webster, a Dartmouth alumnus, to represent them. Webster's sentimental plea in behalf of his alma mater brought tears to the eyes of the unsentimental Chief Justice, who ruled that a charter was a contract and could not be violated. This decision won praise from the promoters of business corporations, for it now appeared that their charters, once granted, could not be tampered with.

Some old-line Republicans believed that Marshall's decisions had dealt "a deadly blow to the sovereignty of the states." Judge Spencer

**Latin America
in the Early Nineteenth Century**

UNITED STATES

MEXICO
1821

GULF OF
MEXICO

SANTO DOMINGO
1821

CUBA

PUERTO
RICO

BR.
HONDURAS

HAITI
1804

CARIBBEAN SEA

BR. AND FR.

CENTRAL AMERICA
1821

VENEZUELA
1811

GUIANA

Br. Du. Fr.

COLOMBIA
1811

ECUADOR
1822

PERU
1821

BRAZIL
1822

BOLIVIA
1825

PARAGUAY
1811

CHILE
1818

ARGENTINA
1816

URUGUAY
1828

■ Countries under foreign control
1821 Date independence declared

Roane of Virginia sent angry dissenting opinions to the newspapers, and John Taylor waged a pamphlet war against the Supreme Court. To Jefferson the federal justices were a "corps of sappers and miners" steadily undercutting the powers of the states. "The Constitution," he wrote, "is a mere thing of wax in the hands of the judiciary, which they may twist and shape into any form they please." Yet, except for Marshall's interpretation of the contract clause (which later courts have modified), there was little in these decisions that the dominant element in the postwar Republican party really cared to criticize. Giving his blessing to the nationalistic trend of Republican legislation, Marshall used the Constitution as a flexible instrument adaptable to conditions that the Founding Fathers could never have anticipated. If judicial review was a usurpation, no majority in Congress ever agreed on any alternative to it. As for Marshall's defense of property rights, the Republicans could hardly be called enemies of property.

The Monroe Doctrine

Revolutions in Latin America   One of the most striking expressions of postwar American nationalism was in the field of foreign policy. While Spain was preoccupied with France during the Napoleonic wars, her South and Central American colonies had had a pleasant taste of freedom from her strict political and commercial control. Their appetite whetted, the colonies revolted and soon expelled the Portuguese from Brazil and the Spanish from all their American possessions, save Cuba and Puerto Rico. When,

in 1820, a revolution broke out in Spain and Portugal, all hope of recovering the lost colonies perished—unless other European powers could be induced to intervene.

To the people of the United States this was 1776 all over again. Henry Clay, a warm admirer of the Latin-American patriots, rejoiced at "the glorious spectacle of eighteen millions of people, struggling to burst their chains and to be free." When a modest commerce developed with South America, Clay, optimistic about its further expansion, incorporated Pan-American trade into his American System. Both justice and self-interest, thought

Clay, required quick recognition of the revolutionary governments.

After 1815 the State Department had pursued a policy of neutrality which recognized the revolutionists as belligerents and permitted them to purchase supplies in the United States; but a neutrality act of 1818 prohibited American citizens from serving in the rebel armies. Impatient with Secretary of State Adams' coolness toward the rebel cause, Clay introduced a resolution in the House giving the *de facto* governments of Latin America immediate recognition. The resolution alarmed Monroe and Adams, who feared that it would end the negotiations then in progress for the purchase of Florida, or even lead to war. After the President and Secretary of State exerted their influence against the resolution, the House finally voted it down. Recognition came in 1822 after the Florida negotiations had been completed and after the new governments in South America had shown themselves capable of maintaining their independence. To Clay this recognition was disgracefully late, but the United States was nevertheless the first nation to grant it.

The Fear of Foreign Intervention Granting recognition at that time was in fact a bold step. Thus far the British had refrained from establishing diplomatic relations with Latin America and had even indicated a willingness to see Spain re-establish her authority there. Moreover, the reactionary governments of Russia, Prussia, Austria, and France had formed an alliance pledged not only to preserve the *status quo* and to suppress liberalism but also to intervene in the internal affairs of any country that threatened the peace and security of Europe. Under this mandate Austria had invaded Italy and France had invaded Spain to liquidate revolutionary movements for which many Americans felt a deep sympathy. Perhaps the alliance would now apply its policy to the New World and assist Spain in the reconquest of her colonies. France, it was rumored, had an eye on Cuba as a reward for intervening in Spain; and Russia seemed intent on spreading her influence southward from Alaska along the Pacific Coast. Actually there was not much danger that any European power would intervene in Latin America without British support, and,

when Adams warned Russia that the Western Hemisphere was closed to further colonization, the two countries soon negotiated a satisfactory agreement. Nevertheless, the time seemed appropriate for formulating some kind of policy that would cover all contingencies.

By 1823 Great Britain, too, was ready to take a stronger stand. Her liberals resented the reactionary schemes of the continental alliance, and her merchants and manufacturers were determined to maintain the profitable markets they had established in Latin America. Accordingly, the British Foreign Minister, George Canning, approached the American minister in London, Richard Rush, with a proposal that their governments make a joint statement of policy. Canning told Rush that his government was now convinced that Spain could not recover her colonies and that recognition of their independence was only a matter of time. Great Britain had no designs on any of them, nor would she permit any portion of them to be transferred to another power. If the American government shared these feelings, Canning asked, "why should we hesitate mutually to confide them to each other; and to declare them in the face of the world?"

In October 1823 President Monroe had the British proposal before him and turned to the Republican elder statesmen for advice. Jefferson and Madison both supported his own inclination to accept it. An exception to the policy of nonentanglement in European politics was justified in order, as Jefferson explained, to bring British power into the scale of free government and to "emancipate a continent at one stroke." Oddly enough, it was a statesman from New England, the traditional center of pro-British sentiment, who objected most strenuously to accepting British leadership in the Western Hemisphere. Secretary of State Adams opposed any agreement by which the United States would, in effect, commit itself not to annex additional territory. With an eye on Texas and Cuba, Adams argued that "we should at least keep ourselves free to act as emergencies may arise." Moreover, he disliked a joint statement that would make the United States appear "to come in as a cockboat in the wake of the British man-of-war." After long discussion

James Madison:
Advice to Monroe

It appears ... that the success of France against Spain would be followed by an attempt of the Holy allies to reduce the revolutionized colonies of the latter to their former dependence.

The professions we have made to these neighbours, our sympathies with their liberties and independence, the deep interest we have in the most friendly relations with them, and the consequences threatened by a command of their resources by the Great Powers, confederated against the rights and reforms of which we have given so conspicuous and persuasive an example, all unite in calling for our efforts to defeat the meditated crusade. It is particularly fortunate that the policy of Great Britain, though guided by calculations different from ours, has presented a co-operation for an object the same with ours. With that co-operation we have nothing to fear from the rest of Europe, and with it the best assurance of success to our laudable views. There ought not, therefore, to be any backwardness ... in meeting her in the way she has proposed.

From James Madison, Letter to President Monroe, October 1823.

John Quincy Adams:
Advice to Monroe

We have no intention of seizing either Texas or Cuba. But the inhabitants of either or both of them may exercise their primitive rights, and solicit a union with us. They will certainly do no such thing to Great Britain.... Without entering now into the enquiry of the expediency of our annexing Texas or Cuba to our Union, we should at least keep ourselves free to act as emergencies arise and not tie ourselves down to any principle which might immediately afterwards be brought to bear against ourselves....

It would be more candid, as well as more dignified, to avow our principles explicitly to Russia and France, than to come in as a cock-boat in the wake of the British man-of-war....

The answer to be given to Baron Tuyll, the instructions to Mr. Rush relative to the proposals of Mr. Canning, those to Mr. Middleton at St. Petersburg, and those to the Minister who must be sent to France, must all be parts of a combined system of policy and adapted to each other.

From *Memoirs of John Quincy Adams*, November 7, 1823 (12 vols., 1874–77).

in the Cabinet, Adams noted with satisfaction that his position ''was acquiesced in on all sides.'' The President, it was agreed, would make a statement of *American* policy emphasizing the separateness of the Old World and the New.

The American Response   Monroe incorporated his famous doctrine rather unsystematically in his annual message to Congress on December 2, 1823, a message that dealt with many other topics as well. With some rearranging, the relevant passages run substantially as follows: First, wherever American sympathies may lie, it does not comport with American policy to intervene in the "internal concerns" or the wars of European powers when they involve matters only "relating to themselves." Second, the United States will not interfere with "existing colonies or dependencies" in the Western Hemisphere. Third, with the Latin-American governments "whose independence we have . . . acknowledged, we could not view any interposition for the purpose of oppressing them, or controlling in any other manner their destiny, by any European power in any other light than as the

manifestation of an unfriendly disposition toward the United States." Fourth, "the American continents, by the free and independent condition which they have assumed and maintain, are henceforth not to be considered as subjects for future colonization by any European powers." Finally, Monroe warned the autocrats of Europe that "we should consider any attempt on their part to extend their [political] system to any portion of this hemisphere as dangerous to our peace and safety." In brief, the essence of this nationalistic pronouncement was the concept of two worlds, each of which was to refrain from intervening in the internal affairs of the other.

Monroe and Adams, of course, were responsible for the precise phrasing of these principles, but they owed much to earlier Presidents and Secretaries of State. They had brought together the elements of an American foreign policy that had been gradually evolving since the Revolution. To European diplomats, for the young Republic to promulgate a policy that it lacked the power to enforce was a piece of presumptuous impertinence. Canning, who knew that British diplomacy and the British navy had been decisive in preventing continental powers from meddling in America, was particularly annoyed; he was aware that Monroe's unilateral statement could be invoked against Great Britain as well as against other nations. Yet, though the response of the American people was overwhelmingly favorable, within a few years the President's dramatic message was nearly forgotten. A generation later it would be rediscovered and identified as the Monroe Doctrine; and long thereafter it would be accepted as the authoritative and almost definitive statement of American foreign policy.

The Westward Movement

These displays of nationalism in domestic politics and foreign policy reflected the underlying optimism of the American people—their confidence in the destiny a kind Providence planned for them. To be sure, their nationalistic creed also embraced an awareness of their past: they had their nostalgic and sentimental side; they gloried in their traditions each Fourth of July; and they were deeply stirred when a Webster waxed eloquent upon the Constitution and the Founding Fathers. But most Americans would have agreed with Jefferson when he affirmed that he liked "the dreams of the future better than the history of the past." America was still primarily a promise: as Ralph Waldo Emerson rejoiced, it was "a country of beginnings, of projects, of designs, of expectations."

Advance of the Agricultural Frontier The prevailing confidence and optimism were rooted in a popular belief that man's potentialities were unlimited when he was free to develop them, and in the socioeconomic realities of nineteenth-century America. One of the most important of these realities was the virgin land—the seemingly unlimited space and inexhaustible resources that promised a life of greater dignity and abundance than Europe's common people had ever dreamed of. The West—the untapped wealth of the great interior stretching from the Appalachians to the Rockies—helped to give the future its rosy hue; and the West became one of the central interests of the American people in the decades after the Treaty of Ghent. The story of the westward movement of population is, in the main, the story of the expansion of American agriculture—of the development of new areas for wheat, corn, tobacco, cotton, and wool.

"Old America seems to be breaking up and moving westward," observed an English visitor in 1817 during the first spectacular wave of postwar migration. After falling off for a few years during the depression following the Panic of 1819 (see p. 208), the number of emigrants increased again and reached a peak in the 1830's. Whereas in 1810 only a seventh of the American people lived west of the Appalachians, by 1840 more than a third lived there. Below is a table showing population growth in the New Western states between 1810 and 1840:

	1810	1840
Ohio (1803)	230,760	1,519,467
Louisiana (1812)	76,556	352,411
Indiana (1816)	24,520	685,866
Mississippi (1817)	40,352	375,651
Illinois (1818)	12,282	476,183
Alabama (1819)		590,756
Missouri (1821)	20,845	383,702
Arkansas (1836)	1,062	97,574
Michigan (1837)	4,762	212,267

Some of the people who settled the great Mississippi Valley were recent immigrants from Europe, but most of them came from the older states. Kentuckians and Tennesseeans moved to the new cotton lands of the Southwest or crossed the Ohio River into the Northwest; migrants from New England and the Middle states generally settled in the Great Lakes region; and people from the South Atlantic states (the largest group of all) invaded southern Ohio, Indiana, and Illinois, as well as the Southwest. By and large those who moved west came from the lower middle classes and traveled with their few worldly possessions loaded on wagons or flatboats—or even on packhorses or pushcarts.

Factors Encouraging Migration Why were these hundreds of thousands of settlers—most of them farmers, some of them artisans—drawn away from the cleared fields and established cities and villages of the East? Apart from the fact that the West happened to be an inviting land of opportunity, certain characteristics of American society help to

A center of Western power: Cincinnati, 1838.

explain this remarkable migration. The European ancestors of the American people had lived century after century rooted to the same village or the same piece of land until some religious or political or economic crisis uprooted them and drove them across the Atlantic. Those who experienced this sharp and devastating break tended thereafter to lack the ties that had bound them and their ancestors to a single place. Moreover, in the relatively stratified European society men inherited the occupations and social status of their fathers, but in American society there was a less rigid class structure. Men changed occupations easily and believed that it was not only possible but almost a moral duty to improve their social and economic position. As a result, Americans were, as many European visitors observed, an inveterately restless, rootless, and ambitious people.

The Frenchman Alexis de Tocqueville, who published a remarkably penetrating study of American society after a tour in the early 1830's, was impressed with these traits. "In the United States," he wrote, "a man builds a house in which to spend his old age, and he sells it before the roof is on; . . . he brings a field into tillage and leaves other men to gather the crops; . . . he settles in a place, which he soon afterwards leaves to carry his changeable longings elsewhere." The reasons for this "strange unrest," Tocqueville believed, were, first, the American "taste for physical gratifications"; second, a social condition "in which neither laws nor customs retain any person in his place"; and, third, a pervasive belief that "all professions are open to all, and a man's own energies may place him at the top of any one of them." These social traits helped to produce the nomadic and daring frontiersmen who kept pushing westward beyond the fringes of settlement, as well as the less adventurous immigrants who followed them across the mountains in search of new homes, material success, and a better life.

Transportation to the West, about 1840

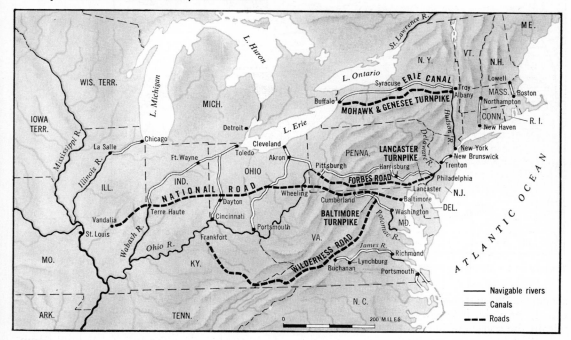

The West had plenty of attractions for a people conditioned to appreciate them. The alluvial river bottoms, the fecund soils of the rolling forest lands, and the black loams of the prairies were tempting to New England farmers working their rocky, sterile acres and to Southeastern farmers plagued with soil exhaustion. The Indian menace east of the Mississippi was now substantially reduced; after 1815 the helpless tribes made a succession of treaties ceding lands which the government surveyed and put up for sale. In 1820 a new land law ended the credit system but reduced the minimum tract for individual sales to eighty acres and the minimum price to $1.25.* Now it was possible for a man to buy a farm for $100, and the continued proliferation of state banks made it relatively easy for those without cash to negotiate loans in paper money. Western farmers borrowed with the confident expectation that the expanding economy would keep farm prices high, thus making it easy to repay the loans when they fell due.

* New lands, however, were first put up at auction, and the best sold for a good deal more than the minimum price.

Transportation was becoming less of a problem for those who wished to move west and for those who had farm surpluses to send east. Though the Western rivers were still the chief arteries, several turnpikes were now feeding them at crucial points. Financed by private corporations that charged tolls, most of the turnpikes were built to connect Eastern cities, but a few were designed to serve the New West. By the 1820's migrants could follow the Baltimore Turnpike to Cumberland, Maryland, and then the National Road to Wheeling (a decade later, to Vandalia, Illinois); the Lancaster Turnpike and Forbes Road to Pittsburgh; or the Mohawk and Genesee Turnpike to Lake Erie.

Two developments brought an end to the era of turnpikes and started a transportation revolution that had a profound impact on the New West. First came the steamboat. In 1811, four years after Robert Fulton's *Clermont* made its celebrated voyage up the Hudson River, Nicholas J. Roosevelt launched the steam-powered *New Orleans* at Pittsburgh and sent it on a successful voyage down the Ohio and Mississippi. A witness found it an awesome

Tollgate on the Baltimore-Reistertown Road.

spectacle: "a boat moving without appearance of sail, oar, pole, or any manual labor—moving within the secrets of her own mechanism and propelled by power undiscoverable." Within twenty years some two hundred steamboats were plying the Western waters and had superseded all other craft in the carrying of passengers and freight.

Next came the Erie Canal, which spanned the 350 miles between the Great Lakes and the Hudson River. With the support of Governor De Witt Clinton and funds from the New York legislature, construction began in 1817 and was completed in 1825. The project's immediate success (tolls enabled the state to recover the cost within seven years) launched the country into the Canal Age. New York's rivals, such as Philadelphia and Baltimore, strove to tap the West with their own canal systems, but with less success; Ohio and Indiana built canals to connect the Ohio River with the Great Lakes. Between 1815 and 1840 (after which construction declined), various states invested about $125 million in three thousand miles of canals. By the 1830's the country had a complete water route from New York City to New Orleans. By then, however, a new marvel, the railroad, promised an even more dazzling answer to the West's transportation needs (see p. 297).

Life on the Frontier   Only hope could make bearable the hardships of a farmer getting his start in this crude Western country. The propaganda literature of the land speculators abounds in descriptions of the salubrious climate, the health-giving waters, the ease with which one could make the land bloom, and the increasing comforts of civilization. The realities, for some years at least, were quite different. To clear a piece of land for cultivation—girdling the trees to kill them, cutting the branches and rolling the logs into great piles to burn, grubbing out the stumps, and breaking the root-infested ground with primitive plows—meant backbreaking labor for pioneer families. Disease and death hung over the Western settlements; trained doctors were scarce, and the only resort was to home remedies or the patent-medicine panaceas of itinerant quacks. Malaria, dysentery, pneumonia, smallpox, yellow fever, cholera, and dietary deficiencies took a heavy toll; travelers often commented on the pale and sickly appearance of Westerners. Living in primitive lean-tos or floorless cabins, surviving on a diet mainly of corn and salt pork, making their own clothing from homespun and deerskin, enduring the almost unmitigated bleakness of frontier life, these pioneers would have been hard-put to discover the Arcadian quality that

Excavation at Lockport on the Erie Canal.

some romanticists see in their agrarian society. A prospective migrant to Illinois warned his family: "What awaits you in this region, which, as of now, is not much better than a wilderness, is a life full of hardships, want and toil. By this choice we shall close ourselves off from the rest of the world for many years."

But the settlers looked beyond the ordeal of these early years, and eventually better times did come. Life softened for them as schools and churches were built, as neighbors became less remote, and as the growing villages and county seats acquired printing presses and newspapers and began to offer social diversions to the surrounding countryfolk. These cultural amenities, the modest comforts earned from subsistence agriculture, and the feeling of independence derived from owning and cultivating a small piece of land, were the ultimate rewards of many who made their homes in the Western wilderness.

For many others, however, this was not enough. The more ambitious Westerners, if they came to farm, thought of agriculture as a business enterprise and of themselves as small capitalists producing for the market. Moreover, to those who invaded the West in search of wealth, farming was only one way—and perhaps the slowest—to gain their end. Along with the yeomen came the frontier boomers, the speculators in real estate to whom land was simply a commodity to be bought and sold for a profit. The greatest rewards in the West were not always earned by industrious and thrifty farmers; they were often won by shrewd operators who knew how to exploit the vagaries of federal land policy or to buy favors at the local land offices. A long chapter in the history of the New West belongs to the land companies —one of the earliest forms of large-scale American business enterprise—whose agents spied out the best tracts, bought them at public auction, and then sold them at higher prices to authentic settlers.

Other Westerners engaged in the fascinating business of promoting towns at strategic trading sites. Many of these wilderness metropolises never materialized, and often the giddy purchasers of unseen town plots wound up with a "business block" knee-deep in swamp water. But important urban centers, such as Cincinnati, Cleveland, Detroit, Indianapolis, and Chicago, did grow with amazing speed. To them came not only promoters and speculators but men with capital to invest in banking, commerce, and manufacturing. Surprisingly early these cities became the centers of Western political and economic power, and of Western culture when it pushed out its first tender shoots.

The Significance of the Frontier   What impact did the New West make on American society? Not much in the way of political innovation, for state and local government in the West was for the most part modeled after the East. Apparently the forces generating the trend toward increased political democracy in these years were as much Eastern as they were Western. Socially and culturally the West was dependent on the East and again showed a greater tendency to copy than to innovate. This was natural enough, for those who moved West were less often critical of the fundamental structure of Eastern society than dissatisfied with their position in it.

But the impact of the New West was not insignificant. Because of its lack of local traditions, its interior position, and its need for protection and improved transportation, the West was the most nationalistic section of the country. Certainly the problems that settlers faced on a raw frontier encouraged them to develop to a high degree such qualities as individualism and resourcefulness. By stripping Eastern and European civilization down to its fundamentals, Westerners exposed some of its shams and discarded some of its superficialities. Though the West did not produce a society of social and economic equals, it did give added emphasis to the notion that all artificial barriers to advancement must be removed—that all must have an equal chance to make their way in the world. Moreover, the West showed uncommon respect for the man who, starting

with little, achieved success in the competitive struggle.

Above all, the New West was America's treasure house of unused land and untapped resources. It was a major, though not exclusive, factor in producing the social mobility, economic expansion, and steadily rising standard of living from which all white Americans profited more or less. When the historian Frederick Jackson Turner, near the end of the nineteenth century, called his colleagues' attention to the significance of the frontier in American history, he perhaps claimed too much. But there is some truth in his assertion that "this expansion westward with its new opportunities" accounted for the "fluidity of American life." These Western wilds, Turner wrote, "constituted the richest free gift that was ever spread out before civilized man."

Slavery and the Cotton Kingdom

Southern Expansion   The migration into Alabama, Mississippi, and Louisiana was, as we have seen, a part of the westward movement; and the great majority of the early settlers were pioneer farmers, mostly from Virginia and the Carolinas, who endured the same hardships and cherished the same ambitions as those who settled north of the Ohio River. They engaged in subsistence farming to begin with, and many of them never managed to produce more than occasional small surpluses for the market. But enterprising farmers in the Southwest knew that cotton-planters in the South Carolina and Georgia piedmont had been making fortunes ever since Eli Whitney, in 1793, invented a gin that efficiently separated the seeds from the lint of upland, or short-staple, cotton. Since cotton prices before 1837 seldom fell below fifteen cents a pound and often rose much higher, those who obtained suitable land soon devoted at least part of their time to cotton cultivation. Eventually a fortunate few established large plantations on the rich, silt-loamed prairies of the Alabama-Mississippi Black Belt, or on the bottom lands of the Mississippi and Yazoo delta. These great cotton-planters, together with the rice-planters of coastal South Carolina and Georgia and the sugar-planters of Louisiana, developed agriculture to the highest levels of

Agricultural Regions of the South

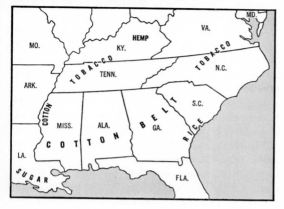

efficiency, complexity, and commercialization to be found anywhere in nineteenth-century America.

Within two decades after the War of 1812 the booming Gulf states were ceasing to be part of the New West, as Ohio, Indiana, and Illinois continued to be. Instead, they became increasingly identified with the Old South, even though they differed socially from Virginia and the Carolinas in many significant ways. Their identification with the South Atlantic states came at a time when Southerners were becoming more, rather than less, conscious of their special sectional problems and interests.

The Survival of Slavery   What was it that made the Old South unique? Not physical isolation, for it lacked natural frontiers separating it from the rest of the country; nor geographic and climatic uniformity, for it had great diversity of soils, topography, mean temperatures, growing seasons, and average rainfalls. Not a difference in population origins, for the South, like the North, was originally settled by middle- and lower-class people; nor contrasts in religion or political philosophy, for here, too, the similarities outweighed the differences. Not even the economies of North and South were altogether unlike, for, although Northerners invested relatively more capital in manufacturing and commerce, the majority of the white people of both sections were independent yeoman farmers who worked their own lands. By far the most important difference was the presence

and survival in the South of Negro slavery, which Southerners themselves called their "peculiar institution." It was slavery, with all its ramifications, that eventually gave the Old South its identity and Southerners their feeling of separateness from the rest of the Union.

In the eighteenth century, of course, Southern slavery had not been a peculiar institution, for it existed in the Northern colonies and throughout the Western Hemisphere. During or soon after the Revolution, however, the Northern states abolished it; and in the first half of the nineteenth century slaves gained their freedom in most of Central and South America. Many Southerners of Washington's and Jefferson's generation also were critical of slavery; as late as the 1820's there were numerous emancipation societies in the Upper South that carried on a discreet but steady agitation. In Virginia, in the late eighteenth and early nineteenth centuries, a prolonged agricultural depression resulting from low tobacco prices and soil exhaustion led some to believe, or hope, that slavery would soon die. In August 1831 Southampton County, Virginia, was the scene of the South's bloodiest slave insurrection, led by a bondsman named Nat Turner, in which sixty whites and scores of Negroes (including Turner) were killed. This event precipitated an earnest debate in the Virginia legislature the following January during which various legislators denounced slavery as a social canker, an economic blight, and a moral evil, and demanded a program of gradual emancipation. But the Virginia emancipationists, like those in other Southern states, were defeated; and soon after 1832 Southern critics were either silenced or driven into exile.

Southern slavery, then, did not die of natural causes; it did not even decline. Instead, with the rise of the Cotton Kingdom and the eventual improvement of agriculture in the seaboard states, it flourished and seemed to have the vitality to survive indefinitely. Since the federal Constitution recognized slavery as a local institution within the jurisdiction of individual states, Southerners saw nothing to prevent them from introducing it into the Southwest. Some moved there with their Negroes, while others stayed behind and operated new plantations as absentee owners.

Still others took advantage of high slave prices resulting from the labor shortage in the Southwest and sold a portion of their Negroes to professional traders who took them to the busy markets in New Orleans and Natchez. There at the slave auctions the self-made men of the Cotton Kingdom, some of whom had started with no slaves at all, purchased "prime field hands" to work their growing estates.

So it was that Negro slaves became an important element in the migration to the Southwest and played a major role in clearing the land for cultivation. By 1840 almost half the population of Alabama and Louisiana and more than half the population of Mississippi (by now the leading cotton-producing state) consisted of Negro slaves. Yet at all times nearly three-fourths of the white families in the South as a whole held no slaves and depended on their own labor alone. Moreover, the great majority of slaveholders owned just a few slaves; as late as 1860 only ten thousand Southern families belonged to the planter aristocracy operating large estates with slave gangs numbering more than fifty.

Why did Southern slavery survive far into the nineteenth century? Not because Negroes were natural slaves; nor because white labor could not adjust to the Southern climate and successfully cultivate the Southern crops; nor because the Negroes' health was not adversely affected by living in the malarial swamps, where most of the cotton, sugar, and rice plantations were located. The reasons why the South clung so tenaciously to slavery are to be found in the fears, ambitions, and aspirations of Southern white men.

By the nineteenth century the South's peculiar institution was two hundred years old, and to abolish it would have brought painful changes in long-established habits and attitudes. Those who would destroy slavery, warned a Georgian, "would have to wade knee-deep in blood"; indeed, slavery is "so intimately . . . mingled with our social conditions that it would be impossible to eradicate it." To some, who thought that Negroes were naturally shiftless and immoral, slavery was a system of controlling an inferior race. To nonslaveholders slavery symbolized their link with the privileged caste of white men and the Negroes' social and legal subordination. "Now suppose they was free," explained a poor Southern farmer to a Northern visitor, "you see they'd all think themselves as good as we." To the master class the possession of slaves brought great prestige, for in the South the ownership of a plantation worked by slave labor was the sign of success and high social position.

But, above all, slavery survived because it was an efficient and profitable labor system and because it represented an enormous investment of Southern capital. Slavery, of course, did not make every master a rich man, nor did every master strive to wring the last ounce of profit from his toiling bondsmen. Nevertheless, most slaveholders earned good returns on their investments—and this accounts for the generally heavy demand for slaves and for their high price in the market. The system, moreover, was highly adaptable. Slaves were employed not only in agriculture and as domestics, but also as skilled artisans, as laborers in construction gangs, and as workers in iron foundries, textile mills, and tobacco factories. In short, the master class had no compelling economic reason for wanting to abolish slavery.

The Nature of Slavery   In governing their bondsmen most masters were neither inordinately cruel nor remarkably indulgent; they simply dealt with their human property in the manner they deemed necessary to make the system work. They bought and sold slaves, used them as security for loans, and divided them among heirs. In these transactions husbands were often separated from their wives and children from their mothers, for state laws gave slave marriages no recognition. Except for the deliberate killing or maiming of a slave, the master's power to administer physical punishment was virtually unlimited, and planters could delegate this power to white overseers employed to manage their estates. Most slaveholders used the whip for "moderate correction" only when they believed it essential to maintain discipline; but an element of cruelty was inseparable from slavery, as even many of its defenders recognized. Some slaves fell into the hands of brutal masters, or of men who were corrupted by the power the institution conferred upon them. Since a Negro was unable to give testimony against a white man, the justice he received in court was, at the best, very eccentric.

The average slave's standard of living was near the subsistence level. He lived on a diet mainly of corn and pork, adequate in bulk but unbalanced and monotonous; he wore coarse, skimpy clothing made from some variety of cheap "Negro cloth"; and he lived in a cabin that was too often drafty, cramped, and scantily furnished. His labor routine kept him at work from dawn to dusk. By nineteenth-century standards, he was not often worked excessively, but a long day of hard toil was usually exacted from him. The slave was most in danger of being overworked to the detriment of his health on the large cotton and sugar plantations managed by overseers.

One cannot pretend to know all that being a slave meant to the Negroes; one certainly must be cautious about assuming that they accepted slavery as their natural lot. No doubt they made certain psychological adaptations to their condition; no doubt they enjoyed the occasional holidays and simple pleasures that most masters permitted them; no doubt their untrained intellects seldom dwelt on freedom as a philosophical abstraction. But to conclude from this that they had no idea of the meaning of freedom, no comprehension of its practical advantages, no desire to obtain it, would be quite unwarranted. The evidence of their submission and obeisance suggests not so much contentment as the superior power of the white caste and the effectiveness of its elaborate techniques of control. The swift and ruthless suppression of Nat Turner's followers drove home to the slaves the futility of organized rebellion. But it did not deter some of the bolder ones from less spectacular forms of protest. Of these, running away was among the most common—and certainly the most irksome to the master class.

White men paid a high price for slavery: artisans and yeoman farmers suffered from the competition of cheap slave labor; most white Southerners were more or less distressed by the obvious paradox of slavery in a Republic whose moral commitment was to individual freedom and natural rights; and all were bedeviled by a nagging fear of slave rebellions, a fear that is endemic wherever bondage exists. But the Negro paid an even higher price. Apart from his exposure to cruelty and his meager rewards, slavery afforded him little opportunity for cultural advancement. It gave him some vocational training, indoctrinated him with a crude form of Christianity which provided emotional release more than spiritual nourishment, and exposed him to some of the external forms of white civilization. But slavery also made the Negro family unstable, encouraged sexual promiscuity, and exposed Negro women to the lust of white men. It robbed the Negro of his manhood, encouraged infantile and irresponsible behavior, and put a premium on docility. In short, slavery deprived a whole race of the chance to develop its potentialities and of the freedom that white men treasured so highly.

Missouri and the Issue of Slavery Expansion Eventually the South's peculiar institution was to have a tragic impact upon the whole nation, and a few intimations of this impact were evident even in the early years. Slavery was a topic of debate at the Constitutional Convention of 1787, and just what would happen to it under the new Constitution was a subject of inquiry at Southern ratifying conventions. The compromise by which Southerners obtained congressional representation for three-fifths of their slaves (see p. 130) provoked repeated complaints, especially from New England. Antislavery Northerners frequently resisted enforcement of the Fugitive Slave Act of 1793, which enabled Southern masters to recover runaways in the free states. In the Deep South some doubted the wisdom of a federal law that closed the African slave trade on January 1, 1808, and the law was often flagrantly violated thereafter.

But these were minor irritants compared to the succession of crises generated by the steady march of slavery into the Southwest. Before 1820 five additional slave states (Kentucky, Tennessee, Louisiana, Mississippi, and Alabama) had been admitted to the Union; these increased the total number to eleven, which, as it happened, were balanced by eleven free states. The resulting political equilibrium in the Senate was threatened, however, when the territory of Missouri, settled mostly by proslavery Kentuckians and Tennesseans, petitioned for admission to statehood. In February 1819 a House committee reported an enabling

The Missouri Compromise, 1820

OREGON COUNTRY

SPANISH POSSESSIONS

UNORGANIZED TERR.

MICHIGAN TERR.

admitted as free state 1820 — MAINE

VT. N.H. MASS.

N.Y.

R.I. CONN.

PENNA.

N.J.

DEL.

MD.

admitted as slave state 1821 — MISSOURI

ILL. IND. OHIO

VA.

KY.

N.C.

36°30′N.

TENN.

S.C.

ARKANSAS TERR.

MISS. ALA. GA.

LA.

FLORIDA TERR.

Free
Slave

act; but Representative James Tallmadge, Jr., a Republican from New York, proposed an amendment to prohibit the introduction of additional slaves into Missouri and to provide gradual emancipation for those already there. The Tallmadge Amendment passed the House on a sectional vote but was defeated in the Senate. When neither chamber would yield, slavery's critics and defenders plunged into an ill-tempered debate that showed the existence of a deep sectional wedge.

Much of the Missouri debate revolved around constitutional issues. Southerners, especially Virginians, insisting that new states had the same sovereign rights as the old, denied that Congress could make the abolition of slavery a condition of admission. Northerners claimed that the Founding Fathers had thought of slavery as a temporary institution and had not intended that it should spread into the Western territories. In the heat of the debate angry Southerners accused Federalists of deliberately fomenting a crisis in order to win popular support in the North and revive their dying party. Jefferson, who strongly opposed the Tallmadge Amendment, was convinced that the Federalist leader Rufus King was "ready to risk the Union for any

chance of restoring his party to power and wriggling himself to the head of it." Northern opposition to slavery expansion, wrote Charles Pinckney of South Carolina, "sprang from the love of power, and the never ceasing wish to regain the honors and offices of the government."

No doubt political advantage and sectional power—the North already had a substantial majority in the House—were basic ingredients of the Missouri controversy. But the crisis might have looked less portentous had this been all there was to it. Tallmadge himself appeared to have no crass political motive; rather, he seems to have acted from a conviction that slavery was a moral evil which should not be permitted to spread. So did many others whose humanitarian impulses were aroused by the apparent vitality of Southern slavery. According to a resolution of the Pennsylvania legislature, to admit Missouri as a slave state would be to open "a new and steady market for the lawless venders of human flesh"; it would be a "covenant with crime, contrary to duty, to God, and to the fathers of the Republic." Never before had the peculiar institution been so severely attacked—and so vigorously defended—on moral grounds as it was during the Missouri debate.

The basic issue was not resolved on this occasion; it was simply postponed by a compromise in whose passage Henry Clay played a leading role. In 1821 Congress finally agreed to admit Missouri as a slave state, but it preserved the balance by admitting Maine as a free state. It divided the remaining territory acquired in the Louisiana Purchase along the line 36'30° north latitude. North of that line, except for Missouri, slavery was "forever prohibited."

The Missouri crisis made some Americans apprehensive about the future of the federal Union. John Quincy Adams foresaw the possibility of a political realignment along sectional lines, "threatening in its progress the emancipation of all . . . [Southern] slaves, threatening in its immediate effect that Southern domination which has swayed the Union for the last twenty years." Tallmadge, said a Georgia congressman, had "kindled a fire which all the waters of the ocean can not put out, which seas of blood can only extinguish." And Jefferson, showing hardly a glimmer of his earlier antislavery sentiments, poured his indignation on Northerners for opening this sensitive issue. "All, I fear, do not see the speck on our horizon which is to burst on us as a tornado, sooner or later. The line of division lately marked out between different portions of our confederacy is such as will never, I fear, be obliterated." Writing thus in 1821, Jefferson had, in effect, formulated the doctrine of the "irrepressible conflict."

Even in an era of nationalism and expansion, then, slavery hung like a menacing shadow over the young Republic. And in the South the conflict between slavery, which Southerners would not abolish, and the American liberal tradition, which they claimed as their birthright, created tensions that were ultimately to become unbearable.

Another Frontier: Industry and Technology

Beginnings of the Factory System   The western edge of settlement was not the only frontier that attracted Americans and promised a future of increased abundance. Since the War of 1812 growing numbers had been drawn to the thriving towns and cities of the New England and Middle Atlantic states. Here lived the men who pioneered in the development of large and intricate forms of business enterprise and in the application of science and technology to the twin goals of lightening the burdens of labor and multiplying the comforts of human life. These pioneers of the American Industrial Revolution gradually rendered obsolete the system of household manufacturing that had been almost universal in colonial days. In a sense the Industrial Revolution, in America as in Europe, was merely an acceleration of technological changes that had no clear beginning and as yet have no foreseeable end. It involved the development and increasing use of power-driven machines in industrial production, the location of these machines in factories that tended to grow in size and complexity, and the distribution of their products in ever-widening mass markets. American industrial technology was in part copied from England and in part an indigenous outgrowth of the genius of American scientists, inventors, skilled mechanics, and entrepreneurs. Nowhere in Europe did environmental problems provide such incentives for mechanical innovations; nowhere was there a society so viable and so free from the sort of hampering traditions that impede technological change.

What the pioneers in technology accomplished lacked the romance and drama of the Western frontiersman's elemental struggle for survival. Yet their work was equally vital to national growth and expansion, and its long-run social and economic consequences were, if anything, greater. In the field of transportation, for example, the builders of turnpikes experimented with various kinds of road-surfacing and with truss-type and suspension bridges; engineers on the Erie Canal designed new excavating equipment and developed a special cement for use in its eighty-eight locks; and Henry M. Shreve, among others, built flat-hulled steamboats of shallow draft especially adapted to service on the Western rivers. Meanwhile, a patent act adopted by Congress in 1790 (revised in 1793) encouraged numerous men to pursue fame and fortune through the improvement or invention of devices useful to mankind. As Hamilton claimed in his report on manufactures, there did seem to exist "in the genius of the people of this country, a peculiar aptitude for mechanical improvements."

The factory system in the United States had its beginnings during the presidency of Washington. In 1790 Samuel Slater, an English immigrant who knew the secrets of English textile machinery, built a cotton-spinning mill at Pawtucket, Rhode Island, for the merchant Moses Brown. This first successful American factory contained seventy-two spindles tended by nine children, and its machinery was soon harnessed to water power. After years of slow and faltering growth, Jefferson's embargo and the War of 1812 gave the American cotton textile industry a chance to become a significant part of the national economy. By the end of the war cotton factories were counted in the hundreds, most of them in New England; the number of spindles in operation approximated 130,000, and by 1840 the number exceeded two million. In these years of expansion constant improvements were made in the machinery for carding the raw cotton and for spinning it into yarn and thread; after 1814 the power loom brought weaving as well as spinning into the factory system.

From cotton textiles the factory spread to other industries. In 1793, at Byfield, Massachusetts, John and Arthur Schofield, who came to the United States from Yorkshire, England, built the first factory to manufacture woolens. War in Europe, a series of improvements in carding, napping, and shearing machines, and the introduction of water power soon placed the American woolens industry on a secure foundation. Meanwhile, merchant capitalists were taking the manufacture of shoes out of the cobblers' shops and into the homes of semi-skilled workers who specialized in making a single part of the finished product. Eventually, when the shoe industry began to be mechanized, the workers were brought into factories where their role changed from that of craftsmen to tenders of machines. Similarly, in the iron industry Pennsylvania's furnaces and rolling mills were fast supplanting the small local forges and blacksmith shops.

In 1804 Oliver Evans of Philadelphia, one of the most remarkable pioneers of American technology, developed a high-pressure steam engine that was adaptable to a great variety of industrial purposes. Within a few years it was being used not only in steam navigation but to run sawmills, flour mills, and printing presses—and, in 1828, steam power replaced water power at the Slater cotton mills. Evans also experimented with the techniques of mass production and built the first completely mechanized flour mill. In 1798 Eli Whitney applied these techniques to the manufacture of guns and conceived the idea of interchangeable parts. He taught his workers to make identical parts from metal molds, or "gigs"; now guns could be assembled in a fraction of the time required by a skilled gunsmith. Whitney then introduced his system in the clock industry, and Connecticut manufacturers were soon mass-producing inexpensive clocks for a national market.

To build a factory equipped with expensive machinery run by steam or water power required more capital than the average individual entrepreneur could obtain. As a result, business partnerships increased in number, but the ultimate answer to this financial problem was the corporation. Chartered under state laws, corporations could accumulate capital from numerous small investors; and the stockholders enjoyed "limited liability"—that is, they were financially responsible for the corporation's debts only to the extent of their investment. Used first by bankers and the builders of turnpikes, bridges, and other internal improvements, the corporate form spread to manufacturing, expecially textiles, after the War of 1812. In 1813 a group of wealthy merchants known as the "Boston Associates," including Francis Cabot Lowell, Nathan Appleton, and Patrick Tracy Jackson, formed the Boston Manufacturing Company in Waltham, Massachusetts. With capital exceeding a half-million dollars and an efficient managerial staff, these men built the first integrated textile factory that performed every operation from the carding of the raw cotton to the weaving of the cloth with power looms. A decade later the "Boston Associates" shifted the center of their activities to Lowell, "the Manchester of America," where they chartered the Merrimack Manufacturing Company. During the 1820's and 1830's they chartered additional companies in Massachusetts and New Hampshire, until they and their imitators had made the manufacturing corporation an entrenched economic institution.

In other areas, too, the American economy began to show the effects of advancing technology. Eastern merchants used improved transportation and marketing techniques to compete for the trade of the hinterland, with New York merchants rapidly outstripping their rivals. The New York group siphoned much of the Western trade through the Great Lakes and Erie Canal and captured most of the cotton trade between the South and Europe. The skill of Yankee shipbuilders and the initiative of New York merchants combined to improve transatlantic service for passengers and cargo. The New York packet lines, beginning with the Black Ball Line in 1818, were the first to post sailing dates and observe them regardless of weather. The sleek vessels in this service were built for speed and maximum cargo; they were, said an English reporter, "probably the finest and fastest sailing vessels in the world . . . , beautifully modeled and of the best workmanship." The whaling industry, concentrated at New Bedford and Nantucket Island, Massachusetts, was also more highly organized after the War of 1812 than before, because the depletion of the Atlantic supply necessitated long, expensive voyages to the Pacific. Still another sign of the new era was John Jacob Astor's American Fur Company, a million-dollar corporation chartered in New York in 1808. Until the 1830's, when the fur supply of the Northwest began to near exhaustion, Astor used efficient organization and ruthless methods to destroy his weaker competitors and to lay the foundation for the first great American fortune.

As mechanical devices played an increasingly important part in the lives of the American people, applied science began to invade the precincts of American education. A network of mechanics' institutes, beginning with one in Boston in 1795, spread through American cities to train men in the mechanical arts. When President Madison, like his predecessors, urged the founding of a national university, he stressed its potential value as a "temple of science" to diffuse "useful knowledge." Nothing came of this, but several private colleges soon added applied science to their cur-

ricula. At Harvard, in 1814, Dr. Jacob Bigelow began to lecture on "The Elements of Technology" and tried to awaken his students to the possibilities of this exciting frontier. At Yale, Benjamin Silliman brought a similar message not only to his students but to a wider audience through his *American Journal of Science*, founded in 1818, and through his enormously popular public lectures. In 1825 Rensselaer Polytechnic Institute, the first of its genre, opened its doors at Troy, New York, "for the purpose of instructing persons who may choose to apply themselves in the application of science to the common purposes of life."

If newspapers and periodicals accurately reflected public opinion, the American people were proud of their technological achievements and fascinated by the many useful products of applied science. The promise of a rising standard of living encouraged them to rationalize agriculture, to build great internal improvements, to mechanize industry, and to widen commercial horizons. Looking back at the half-century of economic growth since independence, Tocqueville concluded that "no people in the world had made such rapid progress in trade and manufactures as the Americans; they constitute at the present day the second maritime nation in the world"; their manufacturing makes "great and daily advances"; "the greatest undertakings and speculations are executed without difficulty. . . . The Americans arrived but as yesterday on the territory which they inhabit, and they have already changed the whole order of nature for their own advantage."

Capital and Labor   Yet, while they found the promises of the Industrial Revolution irresistible, many Americans were at the same time a little uneasy about what had been happening to their society since industry got a foothold. Carrying with them into the new age the assumptions of a simple agrarian society, they watched apprehensively the paper-money speculations, the growth of cities, and the movement of young people from the land to the factory. They wondered whether the American tradition was somehow being betrayed, whether the craving for material success was undermining their morals and compromising their virtue. To be sure, these fears were still rather vague and sporadic, for in the 1820's and 1830's the cities and the factories were not very large, and the urban-industrial population was a small fraction of the whole. But the trend was clear.

A particularly conspicuous consequence of the factories and machines was the emergence of two new social classes. The first were the industrial capitalists, whom the agrarian gentry regarded as vulgarly ambitious and dangerously powerful. With their wealth they burrowed their way into government, made politicians their vassals, and, as James Fenimore Cooper complained, substituted their "fluctuating expedients for the high principles of natural justice." Industrialists operated in mysterious ways through corporations, those cold, impersonal institutions "having neither a body to be kicked nor a soul to be damned." The second new social class were the factory workers, the hirelings who tended machines for a weekly wage and had no personal contact with either owners or ultimate consumers. They were recruited from the farms and, increasingly by the 1830's, from among newly arrived immigrants. Less and less the non-agricultural "laboring population" meant the village artisans and mechanics; more and more it meant the miners, construction gangs, and urban factory employees.

Thanks to a chronic labor shortage, workingmen's wages and living conditions were far better in America than in Europe. Visitors to Lowell often commented on the attention that the "Boston Associates" gave to the welfare of the young women who worked in their mills. The "Lowell girls" lived in comfortable boardinghouses built by the company; their morals were strictly supervised; and they were provided with recreational facilities, educational opportunities, and religious instruction. They published their own monthly magazine, the *Lowell Offering*, "as a repository of original articles, written by females employed in the mills." After a visit to Lowell, Charles Dickens reported that he had seen "no face that bore an unhealthy or an unhappy look." According to Anthony Trollope, Lowell was "the realization of a commercial utopia" where the women were "taken in, as it were, to a philanthropical manufacturing college."

But industrial paternalism soon declined in the Lowell mills as professional managers fought competitors by cutting costs and making increased use of immigrant labor. Even in the 1830's the working day at Lowell was thirteen hours in summer and from sunrise to sunset in winter. Another visitor had a less happy report about conditions among the women employees: "The great mass wear out their health, spirits, and morals without becoming one whit better off than when they commenced labor." Children under sixteen, who constituted two-fifths of the labor force in New England textile mills, worked twelve or more hours a day. Real wages declined; in 1830 it was estimated that some twenty thousand of the lowest-paid women in Eastern cities worked sixteen hours a day for $1.25 a week. The callousness of the factory system in a laissez-faire economy began to be reflected, too, in the crowded dwellings of drab factory towns.

Such conditions produced disturbing social fissures and a greater awareness of class interests and class identity than had been the case before the rise of the factory. When workingmen tried to improve their status through united action, unprecedented tensions developed in the relations between labor and capital. In the 1790's the carpenters, printers, and cordwainers had begun to organize in several cities; in the early nineteenth century other skilled trades followed their example. The next step was the formation of city federations of craft unions, six of which united, in 1834, to form a short-lived National Trades' Union. Strikes for higher wages usually failed, first, because labor organizations were still weak and inexperienced, and, second, because state courts usually treated strikes as criminal conspiracies under common law. Turning briefly to political action in the 1820's, workingmen's parties, especially in New York and Philadelphia, agitated for free public education, shorter working hours, and other social reforms to aid the laboring class. Distressed by such novel phenomena as trade unions and workingmen's parties, some conservatives might well have recalled Jefferson's pessimistic predictions about the evil consequences of industrialization.

Economic Crisis   The Panic of 1819 introduced America to still another hazard of a commercial-industrial economy. The emergence of the modern business cycle—the rhythmic rotation of booms, panics, and depressions

—was so mystifying that many contemporaries turned to the supernatural for an explanation. An angry deity, they said, periodically brought hard times to punish man for his moral delinquencies—extravagance, speculation, and greed. This first modern panic followed several years of postwar prosperity. With cotton selling at thirty-three cents a pound and wheat at two dollars a bushel, land speculation financed by the state banks became a national disease. Meanwhile, the Bank of the United States caught the spirit of the times and extended credit generously to speculators and business promoters in both the East and the West.

At length an accumulation of adverse economic forces brought these flush times to a sudden halt. First came a decline in the European demand for American agricultural products, especially cotton, then a shrinking of the market for textiles. Early in 1819 the Bank of the United States, now under new and more conservative management, began to call in its loans and to exert pressure on the state banks to redeem their notes with specie. The Bank's attempt to save itself from its own recent follies was the immediate cause of a financial panic that forced many state banks to close their doors. In the subsequent depression thousands of farmers saw their lands sold at public auc-tion to satisfy the claims of creditors; numerous speculators and business promoters forfeited property to the Bank of the United States for failing to repay their loans. In the Eastern cities a half-million workers lost their jobs when factories closed or curtailed their operations.

By the mid-twenties prosperity had returned, but not before the panic and depression had created bitter feelings that were reflected in national politics. Many accused the Bank of the United States of coldly sacrificing thousands of innocent victims to protect the selfish interests of its wealthy stockholders. Thereafter much of the anxiety about the new order was focused on the monopolistic Bank, the most powerful of the "soulless" corporations. Senator Thomas Hart Benton of Missouri pictured the Bank as a ruthless "money power" to which the Western cities were enslaved: "They may be devoured by it at any moment. They are in the jaws of the monster! A lump of butter in the mouth of a dog! One gulp, one swallow, and all is gone!"

The ground had been prepared for the growth of the Jacksonian movement, which, in a strange way, benefited from both the acquisitive impulses that the new order had aroused in the American people and the lingering doubts they felt about its results.

| SUGGESTIONS FOR READING | Postwar Nationalism |

George Dangerfield, *The Era of Good Feelings* (1952), is a superb book covering the period from the War of 1812 to the election of Andrew Jackson as President. Two older works that are still worth consulting are K. C. Babcock, *Rise of American Nationality* (1906), and F. J. Turner, *Rise of the New West* (1906). The period may also be studied through several excellent biographies of Republican leaders: W. P. Cresson, *James Monroe* (1946); C. M. Wiltse, *John C. Calhoun: Nationalist, 1782–1828* (1944); G. G. Van Deusen, *The Life of Henry Clay* (1937); and Clement Eaton, *Henry Clay and the Art of American Politics* (1957). Sympathetic and authoritative accounts of the chartering of the Second Bank of the United States and its role in the American economy are R. C. H. Catterall, *The Second Bank of the United States* (1903), and Bray Hammond, *Banks and Politics in America from the Revolution to the Civil War* (1957).

The role of the Supreme Court in the Marshall era is treated fully in A. J. Beveridge's distinguished biography of the great Chief Justice, *The Life of John Marshall*, 4 vols. (1916–19). Some of the best of the briefer studies are E. S. Corwin, *John Marshall and the Constitution* (1919); Charles Warren, Vol. I of *The Supreme Court in United States History*, 2 vols. (1937); and C. G. Haines, *The Role of the Supreme Court in American Government and Politics, 1789–1835* (1944). E. T. Mudge, *The Social Philosophy of John Taylor of Caroline: A Study in Jeffersonian Democracy* (1939), presents the view of one of Marshall's ablest contemporary critics.

The most authoritative book on the Monroe Doctrine is A. P. Whitaker, *The United States and the Independence of Latin America, 1800–1830* (1941). Three other excellent monographs are Dexter Perkins, *The Monroe Doctrine, 1823–1826* (1927); E. H. Tatum, *The United States and Europe, 1815–1823* (1936); and C. C. Griffin, *The United States and the Disruption of the Spanish Empire* (1937). Two fine biographies should also be consulted: J. H. Powell, *Richard Rush: Republican Diplomat, 1780–1859* (1942), and S. F. Bemis, *John Quincy Adams and the Foundations of American Foreign Policy* (1949).

The Westward Movement

General histories of the westward movement with useful chapters on the period following the War of 1812 are R. E. Riegel, *America Moves West* (1947); R. A. Billington, *Westward Expansion* (1949); and T. D. Clark, *Frontier America* (1959). The classic statement of the importance of the West to the whole of American society is in F. J. Turner, *The Frontier in American History* (1920). The best study of public land policy in the West is R. M. Robbins, *Our Landed Heritage: The Public Domain* * (1942). Agricultural development in the Northwest is traced in P. W. Bidwell and J. I. Falconer, *History of Agriculture in the Northern United States, 1620–1860* (1925); in the Southwest in L. C. Gray, *History of Agriculture in the Southern United States to 1860*, 2 vols. (1933). It can be studied comprehensively in P. W. Gates, *The Farmer's Age* (1960). The importance of urban development in the West, long neglected, is stressed in R. C. Wade, *The Urban Frontier* (1959). R. C. Buley, *The Old Northwest: Pioneer Period, 1815–1840*, 2 vols. (1950), provides an exhaustive study of social conditions in the West.

Three general studies of transportation are rich in detail on efforts to deal with this problem in the West: Seymour Dunbar, *A History of American Travel*, 4 vols. (1915); B. H. Meyer, C. E. MacGill, and others, *History of Transportation in the United States before 1860* (1917); and G. R. Taylor, *The Transportation Revolution 1815–1860* (1951). L. C. Hunter, *Steamboats on the Western Rivers* (1949), is a classic. Two other valuable studies are P. D. Jordan, *The National Road* (1948), and L. D. Baldwin, *The Keelboat Age on Western Waters* (1941).

The Old South and Slavery

The best surveys of the Old South are Clement Eaton, *A History of the Old South* (1949), and F. B. Simkins, *A History of the South* (1953). There is a brilliant essay on the Old South in the first section of W. J. Cash, *The Mind of the South* * (1941). U. B. Phillips, *Life and Labor in the Old South* (1929), is a somewhat sentimental description of life on the plantations. F. L. Owsley, *Plain Folk of the Old South* (1949), deals with the life of the nonslaveholders, whom Phillips almost ignored. An indispensable book, based on extensive travels in the South in the 1850's, is F. L. Olmsted, *The Cotton Kingdom* (1861). A new edition of Olmsted, edited by A. M. Schlesinger, was published in 1953.

Slavery may be studied from several perspectives in U. B. Phillips, *American Negro Slavery* (1919); K. M. Stampp, *The Peculiar Institution* (1956); and Stanley Elkins, *Slavery: A Problem in American Institutional and Intellectual Life* (1959). One of the best of the many books on special aspects of slavery is Frederic Bancroft, *Slave-Trading in the Old South* (1931). The best study of the Missouri Compromise is Glover Moore, *The Missouri Controversy* (1953).

Industry and Technology

Several surveys of American economic history have good sections on the beginnings of industrialization, among them, F. A. Shannon, *America's Economic Growth* (rev. ed., 1951); E. C. Kirkland, *A History of American Economic Life* (rev. ed., 1951); and H. U. Faulkner, *American Economic History* (rev. ed., 1954). Useful specialized surveys are V. S. Clark, *History of Manufactures in the United States*, 3 vols. (1928), and J. W. Oliver, *History of American Technology* (1956). Books especially valuable for their interpretations are Roger Burlingame,

* Available in a paperback edition.

The March of the Iron Men (1938); L. M. Hacker, *The Triumph of American Capitalism* (1940); T. C. Cochran and William Miller, *The Age of Enterprise* (1942); and Jeannette Mirsky and Allan Nevins, *The World of Eli Whitney* (1952).

Two outstanding studies of the early textile industry are A. H. Cole, *The American Wool Manufacture*, 2 vols. (1926), and C. F. Ware, *The Early New England Cotton Manufacture* (1931). The beginnings of the corporation can be studied in E. M. Dodd, *American Business Corporations until 1860* (1954). The best treatment of the early labor movement is in J. R. Commons and others, Vol. I of *History of Labor in the United States*, 4 vols. (1918–35).

* Available in a paperback edition.

9

Politics for the Common Man

The rapid economic growth and social change that followed the War of 1812 soon began to influence the nation's political life. In the 1820's, after the death of the Federalists (see p. 188), the Republican party split to form two new parties: the Democrats and the National Republicans (renamed the Whigs in the 1830's). The control of public affairs then became less exclusively the business of select groups of prudent gentlemen than it had been before. The Democratic party, under the leadership of Andrew Jackson, made skillful appeals to the fears and aspirations of the common man; but the Whig party, under the leadership of Clay and Webster, also made an effective bid for mass support and became equally adept in the use of new political tactics. The politics of the Jacksonian era was enlivened by bitterly fought presidential contests, by disputes over who were the friends and who the enemies of the people, by ill-tempered conflicts between nationalists and state righters, and by a heightened sectionalism. Political wars were waged with intense fervor, and each faction predicted that the victory of its rival would bring disaster to the nation. Although the heated rhetoric of political partisans cannot be taken at face value, these party battles did in fact involve basic issues of public policy.

The New Democracy

The Rise of the Common Man   The Jacksonian era, it has been claimed, marked the "rise of the common man." But precisely how did he rise? One way, of course, was for an ambitious and energetic young man to take advantage of the tempting opportunities to achieve material success in his fluid and thriving society. With economic affluence he would, more than likely, soon gain social prestige and political influence as well. This was the road followed by numerous men who began with modest means—in effect, they emerged from the ranks of common men and pushed their way into the ranks of the élite, as Jackson himself did.

But if this is what is meant by the rise of the common man, there would be nothing remarkable about the Jacksonian era. For in this sense common men had been rising ever since the colonial period. We have seen that most of the people who came to America had few worldly possessions and no social prestige. Here they found cheap land and rich resources, neither a feudal tradition nor an aristocracy of birth; in short, unprecedented opportunities to accumulate wealth were open to those who wished to make a career of accumulating it. The fact that America had a class of wealthy merchants and landowners by the end of the eighteenth century indicates that success had already rewarded the enterprise of many. In the years of prosperity and expansion after the War of 1812, common men continued to flourish and rise by engaging in manufacturing in New England, or by speculating in land in the West, or by growing cotton with slave labor in Alabama and Mississippi. And some common men would continue to rise by piling up riches long after the Jacksonian era had come to a close.

But the great majority of common men, in this era as in those that preceded and followed it, neither grew rich nor rose to high social position. Instead they managed only to make a more or less comfortable living and continued to be common men. So the social mobility in Jackson's America was not unique; nor was it the means by which the *average* common man enhanced his prestige. To be sure, a major goal of the Jacksonians was to remove obstacles to success and to provide equal opportunities for all to prosper materially. But the special significance of the postwar years was that the power and influence of the common man increased while he *remained* a common man. The base of American democracy was broadened to give him a greater voice in politics without his first having to achieve uncommon economic success. Then, for the first time, politicians were obliged to square their goals with the desires and tailor their rhetoric to the tastes of a mass of ordinary voters. More than ever before, they celebrated the sovereign people's moral virtue and common-sense wisdom. "Never for a moment believe," said Jackson, "that the great body of the citizens . . . can deliberately intend to do wrong."

Democratic Reforms   This was not the beginning of American democracy, only its expansion; nor was the expansion initiated by President Jackson, for the trend had been evident long before. This impulse came in part from the newly settled West, where conditions of life encouraged a spirit of equalitarianism; but it also came from the cities of the East, where middle-class reformers and spokesmen for urban artisans demanded that government be not only *for* the people but *of* and *by* the people as well. Armed with the Declaration of Independence and the doctrine of natural rights, they argued that they were seeking no radical innovations but merely harmonizing political practices with the principles on which the nation was founded. Restrictions on the popular will, insisted one reformer, "arose from British precedents." Moreover, America was safe for political democracy because there were no mass poverty, no sharp class lines, and no need for ambitious men to remake society

before they could advance in it. Indeed, conservative property-holders could yield, if sometimes grudgingly, to the democratic upsurge without fearing that they were paving the way to their own destruction.

When, for example, political reformers urged the removal of property restrictions on the suffrage, they invariably stressed the argument that no one would be hurt. A delegate to the New York constitutional convention of 1821 agreed that if manhood suffrage would in fact impair the rights of property "this would be a fatal objection." But this was not the case: "Will not our laws continue the same? Will not the administration of justice continue the same? And if so, how is private property to suffer?" Unlike Europeans, said another delegate, "We have no different estates, having different interests, necessary to be guarded from encroachments. . . . We are all of the same estate—all commoners."

The best-remembered protest against manhood suffrage was that of Chancellor James Kent, a New York Federalist. Though Kent warned of the "tendency in the poor to covet and to share the plunder of the rich," he did not advocate the rule of a small aristocracy of large property-holders. Rather, he accepted the election of the governor and the lower house of the state legislature by manhood suffrage and asked only that the upper house be chosen by owners of freehold estates worth at least $250. In defending his position he sounded more like a Jeffersonian than a champion of a capitalist plutocracy, for he spoke of the "freeholders of moderate possessions" as the "safest guardians of property and the laws." Like Jefferson, Kent feared "the crowds of dependents connected with great manufacturing and commercial establishments, and the motley and undefinable population of crowded ports." In large cities like New York, "one master capitalist with his one hundred apprentices, and journeymen, and agents, and dependents will bear down at the polls an equal number of farmers of small estates who cannot safely unite for their common defense." Another New York conservative professed "great veneration for the opinions of Mr. Jefferson," quoted his view that cities are "ulcers on the body politic," and expressed fear that manhood suffrage "would occasion political demoralization, and ultimately overthrow our government." But these conservatives frightened few and went down to overwhelming defeat.

Indeed, it is remarkable how easily the reformers carried the day—how feeble the resistance of the conservatives proved to be. The constitutions of the new Western states provided for white manhood suffrage, or at least enfranchised all taxpayers, which was almost the same thing. The Eastern states had originally restricted the suffrage to property-holders, and in some of them this restriction doubtless disenfranchised many adult males. But one by one they gave way, until the last of them, Virginia and North Carolina, adopted manhood suffrage in the 1850's. Only in Rhode Island did the reformers have to resort to violence—in the so-called Dorr Rebellion—but even there, by 1843, the conservatives had surrendered.

Manhood suffrage alone, however, had only a minor impact on American politics until the mass of qualified voters began to take a personal interest in it. Since the Revolution, a large proportion of the voters had been apathetic; save for an occasional state election, they turned out in limited numbers and seemed willing to accept the leadership of a small political élite. But with the end of the Virginia Dynasty in 1825 and the formation of vigorous new political parties, attendance at the polls began to rise. When Jackson was elected President in 1828, 56 per cent of the adult white males voted, which was more than double the percentage of 1824; and in 1840, 78 per cent of them voted. Since no state yet had the secret ballot, ordinary voters were still subject to the influence of powerful neighbors. Nevertheless, an increasing number paid less deference to the gentry and became more independent in exercising their political rights.

Another democratic reform gave the common man a more direct role in the selection of the President. From the time of Jefferson, Federalists and Republicans had named their candidates in secret congressional caucuses. This system was used for the last time in 1824; by 1832 "King Caucus" had given way to the national nominating convention, which in theory gave the party rank and file a voice in choosing candidates. Meanwhile, one state after another transferred the election of presidential electors from the legislature to the voters, and by 1832 only South Carolina adhered to the old system. The states also made an increasing number of state offices elective rather than appointive. Finally, the idea of a trained—and therefore, presumably, aristocratic—civil service was repudiated so that common men could aspire to state and federal offices as a reward for faithful party service. "To the victors belong the spoils" was the slogan of the New York Jacksonians; and in its day the "spoils system" appeared to be another step toward the democratization of American politics. The anti-Jacksonians were critical of this debasing of the civil service, but when they came to power they found the system irresistible and used it with equal enthusiasm.

"The day of the multitude is now dawned," observed a Jacksonian politician who saw the rise of the common man as one of the most notable achievements of his generation. As voters and as office-holders ordinary citizens now had a part in the shaping of public policy.

John Quincy Adams and National Republicanism

The Election of 1824   As the end of his second term approached, President Monroe tried to name his own successor, as both Jefferson and Madison had done. He chose William H. Crawford, his Secretary of the Treasury, a Virginian by birth though a resident of Georgia, and a state-rights representative of the planter class. A sparsely attended congressional caucus nominated Crawford as the official Republican candidate. But this time there were other ambitious politicians in the field—all professed Republicans—whose supporters repudiated the caucus system as undemocratic and won endorsements for their candidates from state legislatures and mass meetings. Crawford's competitors included John Quincy Adams, the talented Secretary of State, a nationalist, and the favorite of New England; Henry Clay, Speaker of the House, champion of the American System, and a man of captivating charm; and Andrew Jackson, a military hero with wide popular appeal, though at the time with rather vague political views. With four competing candidates, each attracting

The Election of 1824

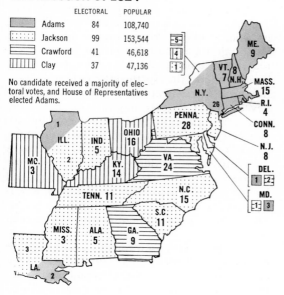

	ELECTORAL	POPULAR
Adams	84	108,740
Jackson	99	153,544
Crawford	41	46,618
Clay	37	47,136

No candidate received a majority of electoral votes, and House of Representatives elected Adams.

somewhat different sections and interests, the Republican party quickly disintegrated as a national political organization.

In the election Jackson won a plurality of the popular vote and ninety-nine electoral votes; he had substantial support everywhere except in New England. Adams' eighty-four electoral votes came chiefly from New York and New England, Crawford's forty-one from the Southeast, and Clay's thirty-seven from the Northwest.* Since none of the four polled a majority in the electoral college, the choice had to be made by the House of Representatives from among the three leading candidates, with the congressional delegation from each state casting one vote. Clay, who had come in fourth, was thus eliminated from the competition, and a serious illness had put Crawford out of the running. The choice was between Adams and Jackson.

Clay, because of his power in the House and his control over the three states he had carried, could swing the election either way. Jackson's friends approached Clay and argued that their man had the stronger claim, because he had polled the largest popular vote; and the Kentucky legislature instructed Clay to support the Hero of New Orleans. But Clay not

* Calhoun easily won election as Vice-President.

only feared Jackson as a formidable competitor in Western politics, but doubted that he was qualified to be President—doubted, too, that he would support the American System. Adams, meanwhile, was tortured by a conflict between his ambition to be President and his distaste for the political higgling that was required to win the prize. Eventually his ambition triumphed: he made the necessary promises and had an interview with Clay that seemed to satisfy the President-maker and win his support. Adams and Clay were as different as two men could be, and their personal relations had been far from cordial; but Adams was still the logical man for Clay to favor, because he shared Clay's views on public policy. Accordingly, when the House voted on February 9, 1825, Adams, with Clay's backing, won a clear majority on the first ballot (Adams thirteen, Jackson seven, Crawford four).

When President Adams appointed Clay Secretary of State, the disappointed Jacksonians immediately detected a shocking case of political jobbery. Adams, they claimed, had purchased Clay's support by giving him the post from which he could best hope to succeed to the presidency. It was, said John Randolph, an alliance "of the puritan and the black-leg." The nation's political virtue, wrote an angry Jacksonian editor, had died "of poison administered by the assassin hands of John Quincy Adams, the usurper, and Henry Clay." For the next three years the enemies of the Adams Administration charged that "bargain and corruption" had betrayed the plain will of the people. Though Adams doubtless had reached a political understanding with Clay, he had in fact made no corrupt bargain. But neither man ever successfully refuted the accusation. Jackson resigned his seat in the Senate, the Tennessee legislature again nominated him for the presidency, and the political campaign of 1828 was under way almost as soon as Adams was settled in the White House.

The Adams Administration   Adams' term as President was a tragic episode in an otherwise brilliant public career, which included service as a diplomat, as Secretary of State, and in later years as a congressman from Massachusetts. Unfortunately the superb talents of this son of John Adams did not include the adroitness, tact, and personal warmth es-

John Quincy Adams: Scrupulous nationalist.

sential to presidential leadership, and as a result he met with a series of political disasters. This was all the more unfortunate because Adams represented a point of view on the federal government's role in the national economy, and on its responsibilities to the states and the people, that deserved to be considered on its own merits.

The new President was an enthusiastic champion of national economic growth, especially of commercial and manufacturing expansion, and looked benevolently upon the new capitalistic enterprises that were spawned by the Industrial Revolution. He was, moreover, as he made clear in his first annual message, a nationalist who believed that the Constitution gave the federal government ample power to direct and encourage this growth and to undertake numerous projects "for the common good." Adams spoke in support of the American System with as much fervor as Clay, especially when he urged the use of federal funds for internal improvements. Citing the National Road as a precedent, he asked: "To how many thousands of our countrymen has it proved a benefit? To what single individual has it ever proved an injury?" After the retirement of the public debt he would use the proceeds

from the sale of public lands for roads and canals to facilitate communication "between distant regions and multitudes of men." More, he would build a great national university at Washington for "moral, political, and intellectual improvement," finance explorations of the interior and of the Northwest coast, and establish an astronomical observatory. Adams believed that Congress might even pass laws designed to promote "the elegant arts, the advancement of literature, and the progress of the sciences." Congress would, in fact, betray a sacred trust by not doing so; nor should it use as an excuse for inaction "that we are palsied by the will of our constituents." The time was ripe for action, said Adams confidently, for "the spirit of improvement is abroad upon this earth."

But these very sentiments prompted his critics to assail him as a tyrant and an aristocrat. Crawford found them "replete with doctrines which I hold to be unconstitutional." Jefferson accused Adams of seeking to establish "a single and splendid government of an aristocracy . . . riding and ruling over the plundered ploughman and beggared yeomanry." Congress responded to the President's proposals with little enthusiasm—even his friends thought he had gone too far—and after the congressional election of 1826 his enemies had full control of the Senate and the House. Appropriations for internal improvements far surpassed those provided during previous administrations but fell short by a great deal of Adams' grand design. A new tariff, enacted in 1828, sponsored by both Administration and anti-Administration congressmen from the Middle and Western states, was not the judicious measure he had called for. The bill was poorly drawn, and because of its concessions to the extreme protectionists the Southern cotton interest called it the "tariff of abominations." Yet Adams signed it.

Somehow his good intentions always seemed to lead him to personal disaster. He conscientiously repudiated a fraudulent Indian treaty, by which the Creeks were to be shorn of all their lands in Georgia, and ordered the negotiation of a new one. But his scrupulous concern for the rights of Indians irritated both Southerners and Westerners. Worse, when the governor of Georgia defied the federal government and threatened to take jurisdiction over the disputed lands, Adams flouted the principle of state rights: he warned that it was the President's duty to vindicate federal authority "by all the force committed for that purpose to his charge." Even in foreign affairs, in spite of Adams' rich experience, the Administration failed to achieve its goals. In 1826, chiefly for partisan reasons, Congress obstructed Clay's attempt to send delegates to a conference at Panama in order to strengthen ties with Latin America. Adams also failed to persuade the British to open their West Indian islands to American trade. And at home, while his foes continued their unmerciful attack, Adams further weakened his position by refusing to use the patronage weapon in his own defense. Many hostile politicians continued to hold office in his Administration—including Postmaster General John McLean, whose appointment policy seemed to be to reward the President's enemies and punish his friends.

The Triumph of the Jacksonians

Adams realized that his chances for re-election in 1828 were slim; "the base and profligate combination" of his critics, he wrote bitterly, would probably succeed in defeating him. During the past three years the anti-Administration forces had rallied around Andrew Jackson. Included in this heterogeneous group were those who disliked the nationalistic American System, or who had been alienated by the President's inept handling of public affairs and public relations. Though political divisions did not follow clear occupational lines, the Jacksonians included a large proportion of the planters and farmers in the South and West, small entrepreneurs in all parts of the country, and artisans and factory workers in the towns and cities. What strength remained to Adams was concentrated in the Northeast, mostly in New England. Thinking it proper to remain aloof from electioneering, the President gave little help to those who ran his campaign. But his lieutenants were no match in any case for the able and hard-hitting Jacksonian leaders, among whom were three senators: Martin Van Buren of New York, Thomas Hart Benton of Missouri, and John H. Eaton of Tennessee; and three newspapermen: Amos Kendall and Francis Preston Blair of Kentucky, and Isaac Hill of New Hampshire. These men and their

Jackson: Commanding Democrat.

associates skillfully exploited the fears and prejudices as well as the ideals of the mass electorate.

In the background of the campaign were a number of specific public policy issues: the tariff, internal improvements, banking, land policy, and at the local level the question of bankruptcy laws and debtor relief laws. But the politicians and party editors were usually vague on these issues, first, because they feared to divide their friends and hoped to win over the doubtful, and, second, because they found other kinds of appeal that seemed better calculated to win votes. In a campaign that revolved largely around personalities, few political leaders showed much respect for the intelligence of the American electorate.

Jacksonians described the election as a contest between democracy and aristocracy. Old Hickory was a man of the people who had their interests at heart. Adams was a monarchist, an enemy of the people, a parasite who had lived off the taxpayers all his life, the head of a band of rascally office-holders, an extravagant waster of public funds for his own pleasure, and the darling of the old Federalists. Voters were also reminded of the "corrupt bargain" of 1825 and of the need to vindicate the will of the people.

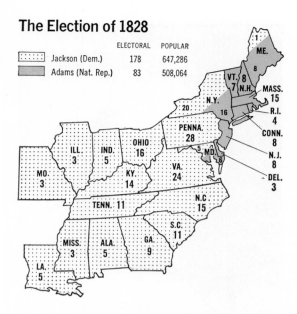

The Election of 1828

	ELECTORAL	POPULAR
::::: Jackson (Dem.)	178	647,286
▓▓ Adams (Nat. Rep.)	83	508,064

Friends of Adams retaliated by describing Jackson as an inexperienced, hot-tempered incompetent—a demagogue having no program and totally unfitted for the responsibilities of the presidency. At a still lower level campaign leaders resorted to mud-slinging and character assassination.

Somehow, in spite of these unedifying exchanges, most of those who voted came to the conclusion that Jackson would better protect the interests of the people against special privilege. Though scarcely more than half of the adult males went to the polls, they gave Jackson a substantial popular majority: 647,286 to 508,064. The electoral vote was 178 to 83, with Adams carrying only New England, New Jersey, Maryland, and Delaware. Observing the boisterous celebration in Washington on the day of Jackson's inauguration, men with different perspectives came to different conclusions. Some saw the start of the reign of King Mob, others the triumph of the common man. Webster observed dryly, "People have come five hundred miles to see General Jackson, and they really seem to think that the country has been rescued from some dreadful danger."

Jacksonian Democracy

The New President Andrew Jackson was a controversial figure in his own day and has been one ever since. This may be explained in part by the complexity of the man, in part by the divergent goals of those who supported him, and in part by the fact that he soon became not only a man but an abstraction—a symbol and a myth. Jackson's original appeal was not as an experienced statesman with a clear-cut program but as a nationally popular figure who embodied numerous American virtues and towered above the ranks of "mere" politicians. To some his election represented a victory for the nationalistic West, to others a victory for the state-rights South, and to still others a victory for those everywhere who would dislodge entrenched privilege from positions of power.

Above all, Jackson's victory was interpreted as a vindication of the common man. Born in poverty to Scotch-Irish immigrant parents in the Carolina back country, lacking formal schooling, he had moved to Tennessee and made his own way as a lawyer, land speculator, and planter. He was the first President who did not come from a well-established American family in comfortable circumstances. Jackson was, in fact, the first President to embody the American success story in its most romantic form: from a log cabin to the White House. This does not mean, however, that he was at the time of his election still a crude and simple frontiersman, as his political enemies described him. For he had already held several public offices; he had accumulated lands and slaves and lived in a mansion, "The Hermitage," near Nashville; and he had been allied with affluent speculators and creditors in Tennessee politics. In fact, Jackson had entered the ranks of the gentry of the Southwest and with advancing years had become increasingly mellow and perhaps a little pompous. A visitor who met him after his inauguration reported that he had seen dukes, and princes, and kings, "but none of such elegance and courtliness of manners, and of so commanding presence, as were possessed by General Jackson."

Nevertheless, Jackson was closer to the people than any of his predecessors had been, and his view of himself as their special defender was not a mere demagogic pose. As the one officer of the federal government chosen in a truly national election, he felt that he was in a position of peculiar responsibility. He was not intimidated by congressmen, whose acts, he felt, were too often controlled by small, selfish groups of powerful constituents, and he used his veto power more freely than had any previous President. Nor would Jackson agree that the Supreme Court had the final word on matters of constitutional interpretation, for he believed that the President's oath bound him to support the Constitution "as he understands it, and not as it is understood by others." The decisions of the Court were entitled "to have only such influence as the force of their reasoning may deserve." Beyond being governed by the dictates of his own judgment, Jackson professed to know of no tribunal to which a public man "can appeal with greater advantage or more propriety than the judgment of the people."

As the guardian of the people's interests, Jackson promised to use his appointive power to "reform" the civil service and to make it more responsive to the public will. He would discharge all "unfaithful or incompetent" office-holders who had acquired a "habit of looking with indifference upon the public interest," or who had come to regard their offices "as a species of property" and "a means of promoting individual interests." Long tenure in the civil service, he said, was corrupting; a rotation of civil servants every four years would force them to "go back to making a living as other people do." Jackson saw little to be gained from long incumbency, for in general the duties were "so plain and simple that men of intelligence may readily qualify themselves for their performance; and I can not but believe that more is lost by the long continuance of men in office than is generally to be gained by their experience."

Jackson thus elevated the spoils system to a democratic principle, though its practical purpose was to reward loyal party workers with public offices. His rejection of an experienced civil service was not a major disaster in an age when the functions of government were relatively few and uncomplicated; but it did nothing to encourage efficiency or to increase the devotion of office-holders to the public interest. One Democrat observed with dismay that "office-seeking and office-getting was becoming a regular business, where impudence triumphed over worth." Clay indignantly described the "lank, lean, famished" Jacksonians

who descended on Washington in 1829 with the cry: "Give us bread! Give us treasury pap! Give us our reward!" But Clay and other critics exaggerated the thoroughness with which Jackson applied his principle. In practice he left 80 per cent of the office-holders undisturbed during his eight years as President, and at least a few of the removals were not for political reasons but for dereliction of duty. Though Jackson used the spoils system more freely than his predecessors, subsequent administrations used it with far less restraint than he.

In selecting heads of departments Jackson drew on the various regions and factions that had elected him. But save for Van Buren, who became Secretary of State, the men he appointed were an undistinguished lot, and he never consulted them as an organized group of Cabinet advisers. Instead he counseled informally with a shifting group of men in whom he had confidence, among them the shrewd, talented, ambitious Van Buren; the Second Auditor of the Treasury, Major William B. Lewis of Tennessee, who lived with Jackson in the White House; Francis Preston Blair of Kentucky, who came to Washington to edit the Washington *Globe* as an Administration organ; Isaac Hill, editor of the New Hampshire *Patriot;* and the Fourth Auditor of the Treasury, Amos Kendall, a man of great influence who helped Jackson prepare many of his state papers. This so-called Kitchen Cabinet, which was not a Cabinet in any formal sense, played an important role in the development of Administration policies and ideas.

The Jacksonian Philosophy   Much of what may be called the ideology of Jacksonian Democracy can be found in the President's inaugural addresses, annual messages to Congress, and veto messages. The Jacksonians lived in a vastly more complex society than had Jefferson, and they favored the advances in political democracy that individual states had since achieved. Yet they were strikingly traditional and conservative on most questions of public policy. In a sense, John Quincy Adams had endorsed a more radical program for national economic growth and social progress with the aid of a vigorous federal government. Adams' call for government action was in sharp contrast to Jackson's warning: "To suppose that because our government has been instituted for the benefit of the people it must therefore have the power to do whatever may seem to conduce to the public good is an error into which even honest minds are too apt to fall." Jackson repeatedly emphasized that the federal government was one of limited powers and cautioned against "overstrained constructions" of the Constitution. He would guard against "all encroachments upon the legitimate sphere of State sovereignty."

Federal intervention in the affairs of the people, Jackson believed, usually came in the form of special favors to influential minorities or of encouragement to monopolistic corporations. There would always be distinctions in society, he conceded, as a result of "superior industry, economy, and virtue, . . . but when the laws undertake to add to these natural and just advantages artificial distinctions, to grant titles, gratuities, and exclusive privileges, to make the rich richer and the potent more powerful, the humble members of society— the farmers, mechanics, the laborers—who have neither the time nor the means of securing like favors to themselves, have a right to complain of the injustice of their Government."

As an exponent of laissez faire, Jackson promised to reduce the government "to that simple machine which the Constitution created." Experience had vindicated the Founding Fathers in their decision to withhold "the power to regulate the great mass of the business and concerns of the people" and to leave them to "free enterprise . . . aided by the State sovereignties." The people would find happiness not in a "splendid government . . . but in a plain system, void of pomp, protecting all and granting favors to none, dispensing its blessings, like the dews of Heaven, unseen and unfelt save in the freshness and beauty they contribute to produce."

Some Jacksonians favored this formula of state sovereignty, strict construction, and laissez faire because they hoped for a return to old-fashioned Jeffersonianism. On numerous occasions Jackson, unlike Adams with his enthusiasm for economic and social progress, looked back wistfully to the simpler, and presumably purer, young republic of Jefferson's day. He praised "the examples of public virtue left by my illustrious predecessors"; he suggested that

it was "time to pause in our career to review our principles"; and he expressed a desire "to revive and perpetuate those habits of economy and simplicity which are so congenial to the character of republicans." Like Jefferson, Jackson idealized an agrarian society. He described the agricultural interest as "superior in importance" to all others and the cultivators of the soil as the "best part" of the population. "Independent farmers are everywhere the basis of society and true friends of liberty."

But the agrarian ideal was already hopelessly out of date. Reducing the government's role in the economy made it harder for favored groups to win special privileges, but it also gave free rein to irresponsible entrepreneurs in a period of frantic economic activity. At best, Jackson's followers had mixed feelings about his conception of the ideal society. Many of them doubtless shared his nostalgia, but few could resist the temptations of their age. Indeed, more often than not they liked Jackson because, in one way or another, they expected him to help them get ahead in the world—and it was not Jefferson's world that interested them.

Indians, Internal Improvements, and Public Lands

Indian Removals   After his inauguration in 1829, Jackson faced a problem that nearly every President in American history has faced: that of holding together the disparate groups that elected him. The Democratic party of Jackson's day was, as the two major parties have always been, an unstable coalition of men from many regions with differing needs and interests. In so far as voters had favored Jackson over Adams for rational reasons, they preferred what they believed would be his stand on most, but seldom all, of the issues that concerned them. Moreover, the Democrats were loosely organized at the national level, and party discipline was correspondingly lax. Not even the Democratic majority in Congress shared Jackson's view on every issue, and it seldom voted as a unit. Those who differed with the President on questions of secondary importance might rebel momentarily but still remain in the party and continue their general support of the Administration. But those who differed with him on a crucial issue might break away entirely and join the opposition party. This is what actually happened to many of the men who had supported Jackson in 1828, while some of his original opponents turned to him because of his stand on one or another major issue.

Indian policy caused the President relatively little political trouble, because his critics were a minority of humanitarians concentrated in the Northeast, most of them already affiliated with the anti-Jackson party. Jackson, to the delight of land-hungry Southerners and Westerners, vigorously enforced a plan, favored by both Monroe and Adams and approved by Congress, to remove all the Indian tribes to lands west of the Mississippi. Removal would be better for the Indians themselves, said Jackson, because they were not only unhappy living among the whites but threatened with extinction. "Doubtless it will be painful to leave the graves of their fathers," he conceded, but we need only "open the eyes of those children of the forest to their true condition" to make them appreciate the "humanity and justice" of removal. "Rightly considered," Jackson concluded, "the policy of the General Government toward the red man is not only liberal, but generous."

These unctuous words covered a policy that was callous in its conception and often brutal in its execution. Most of the tribes were more or less coerced into signing removal treaties; usually the lands they received in the West were inferior to those they gave up; the migrations themselves were poorly planned and caused much suffering; and in some cases the Indians were literally driven from their old homes by military force. Only a few tribes put up organized resistance. In 1832 about a thousand Sac and Fox Indians, led by Chief Black Hawk, defiantly returned to Illinois, but militiamen and army regulars easily drove them back across the Mississippi. This so-called Black Hawk War was hardly more than a skirmish, but the resistance of the Seminoles in Florida was a good deal more formidable. In 1835 many of them, led by Chief Osceola and supported by scores of runaway slaves, rose in rebellion and thus began a costly war that dragged on into the 1840's. The highly civilized Cherokees of Georgia, on the other hand, tried resistance through legal action. When the government of Georgia refused to recognize their autonomy and threatened to seize their lands, the Cherokees took their case to the Supreme Court and won a favorable decision. Marshall's opinion for the Court majority was that Georgia had no jurisdiction over the Cherokees and no claim to their lands. But Georgia officials simply ignored the decision, and the President refused to enforce it. At length the Cherokees had to leave, too, and when Jackson retired from office he counted the near completion of Indian removals as one of his major achievements.

The Maysville Veto   On another issue, internal improvements, Jackson was bound to antagonize either his friends in the West who favored federal support, or his friends in the South and in New York and Pennsylvania who opposed it. He gave a full statement of his position in 1830 when he vetoed a bill to subsidize the construction of a sixty-mile road from Maysville on the Ohio River to Lexington, Kentucky. In this veto message as well as in other state papers, apparently in part because of the influence of Van Buren, he opposed in principle federal spending for internal improvements of any kind. But, like Madison and Monroe, Jackson insisted that if such appropriations were to be made without a constitutional amendment, they must be for projects that were national and not local in character. The Maysville Road, he protested, had "no connection with any established system of improvements; is exclusively within the limits of a State, . . . and even as far as the State is interested . . . [it gives] partial instead of general advantage."

Federal appropriations for such purposes, Jackson feared, would bring corruption and wasteful spending; they would lead to a consolidated government with powers so vast as to endanger the liberties of the people. It would be far better for the government, after the public debt was retired, to distribute its surplus revenues among the states and permit them to manage their own internal improvements. Yet, in spite of these views, Jackson did not veto all the internal improvement bills that Congress passed, not even all that were for local projects. At most it can be said that his Maysville veto checked the acceleration of such appropriations. But this was enough to give the National Republicans an issue which they exploited effectively in the West where the need for improved transportation determined the political affiliations of many voters.

Land Policy   On the question of public land policy Jackson redeemed himself somewhat in the West. In general, Westerners wanted the government to encourage the rapid settlement of unoccupied lands by offering generous terms rather than to seek maximum revenue for the federal treasury. With this in mind, Senator Thomas Hart Benton of Missouri advocated a gradual reduction of the minimum price of public lands of inferior quality from $1.25 to fifty cents an acre, after which any lands still unsold might be given free to actual settlers. Another favorite scheme of Westerners was to permit "squatters"—that is, men who had settled on the public domain before the land was surveyed and offered for sale—to purchase the land they had improved at the minimum price. Neither the first of these schemes (called "graduation") nor the second (called "pre-emption") was enacted into law during Jackson's Administration, but the President clearly shared the Western point of view. In his message to Congress in 1832 he urged that "the public lands shall cease as soon as practicable to be a source of revenue." To give everyone a chance to obtain a freehold, land should be sold to settlers in small tracts at a price barely sufficient to cover the cost of surveys and clearing Indian titles. More, Jackson recommended that each new state be given that portion of the public domain that lay within its boundaries.

Easterners, especially the manufacturers, hoped to slow down the westward movement and the resulting depletion of the labor supply. They strongly opposed both graduation and pre-emption and even looked with favor on a proposal to stop temporarily the survey and sale of new Western lands. Henry Clay, seeking a plan that would satisfy all sections, suggested that rather than giving public lands to individual Western states the proceeds from the sale of the lands should be distributed among all the states, to be used as each saw fit. In 1833 Congress passed such a bill, but the President vetoed it. Land policy was thus an unsettled issue when Jackson left office, but the position he had taken weakened him politically among the industrial interests of the East.

The Tariff and Nullification

Disaffection in South Carolina   Jackson favored a fiscal policy which, in its broad outlines, was consistent with old-fashioned Republican principles: he promised rigid economy and a swift reduction of the public debt in order to "counteract that tendency to public and private profligacy" encouraged by large federal expenditures. But on one critical issue, the tariff, he wavered. Some of his early statements gave aid and comfort to the protectionists—for example, in his first inaugural address he endorsed protective duties on all products "that may be found essential to our national independence." As Southern opposition increased, however, Jackson's position began to change. By 1832 he advocated a tariff designed primarily to provide the government with revenue, one that would give only "temporary and, generally, incidental protection"; and he warned manufacturers not to expect the people to "continue permanently to pay high taxes for their benefit." This shift in favor of tariff reduction antagonized the Northern protectionists. Yet when South Carolina defied federal authority to force a reduction of duties, Jackson firmly denounced her and thereby alienated many Southerners who believed in free trade and extreme state rights.

Though the tariff was never a clear-cut sectional issue, protectionist sentiment was concentrated in the North and free-trade sentiment was concentrated in the South. By the 1820's most Southerners, especially the cotton-growers, were convinced that the protective tariff was a discriminatory tax—designed, according to a public meeting in Charleston, to elevate the manufacturing interest "to an undue influence and importance" and thus to benefit "one class of citizens at the expense of every other class." Clay's American System, Southerners believed, gave no advantage to the South, because the South had built few factories and because it exported two-thirds of its cotton crop to European markets. Southern exports paid for most of the country's imports, and the federal government supported itself chiefly by taxing this exchange. Hence

Southerners complained that they were paying more than their share of federal taxes; and, to make matters worse, much of the income from the tariff was spent on internal improvements, mostly in the North. In short, the tariff was a peculiar tax on Southern farmers and planters, a tax that raised the price of everything they consumed and the cost of everything they produced. Such an arrangement, Southerners soon concluded, was unconstitutional. They agreed that the Constitution had empowered Congress to levy duties on imports, but the purpose was to provide the government with revenue, not to protect industry.

These were the opinions of cotton-growers everywhere, but nowhere were they so strongly held as in South Carolina. Facing the competition of the new cotton states of the Southwest, South Carolinians, especially in the eastern Low Country, found production costs on their worn lands relatively high and their crop yield per acre and their profit margin correspondingly low. Charleston's commercial interest was languishing, and the state's population had almost stopped growing as farmers moved out in search of better land. Economic adversity caused political unrest, and soon South Carolinians had oversimplified the cause of their plight. Not soil exhaustion, not the competition of the Southwest, but the high tariff, they said, was responsible for their troubles. And they looked suspiciously at their leading politician, John C. Calhoun, who had supported the tariff of 1816 (see p. 187) and still in the early 1820's gave evidence of being a protectionist. To have a political future in his state Calhoun had no choice but to revise his views; to advance his ambitions in national politics he had to find some remedy that would satisfy the South without alienating all his friends in the North and West. He faced this challenge while he was still Vice-President under Adams, and faced it even more after the passage of the high tariff of 1828 while he was seeking re-election with Jackson.

Calhoun and State Interposition By then Calhoun had changed his mind and adopted the Southern position that the protective tariff was not only discriminatory but unconstitutional as well. Now, in 1828, he proposed a remedy in an essay entitled *The South Carolina Exposition and Protest*, which the state legislature published without revealing the name of its author. This document indicated that Calhoun had abandoned much of his earlier nationalism and that he had become a conservative spokesman for the Southern planter class. From his new state-rights position he found the way by which a numerical minority, such as the South, could protect itself from obnoxious legislation adopted by the majority. His solution was the doctrine of nullification, or state "interposition," which he offered as a procedure less drastic than a dissolution of the Union. It was his hope that this remedy would find approval in other sections and thus enable him to protect the interests of the South and to continue his pursuit of the presidency.

Calhoun was an able student of political theory and a skillful logician. The premises on which he based his doctrine of nullification, however, were not altogether original, for he borrowed much from Madison's and Jefferson's Virginia and Kentucky Resolutions of 1798 (see p. 157). As they had, Calhoun argued that before 1787 the states had been completely sovereign and that in framing and ratifying the new Constitution they had not given up their sovereignty. Rather, they as the "principals" had merely formed a "compact" and created the federal government as their "agent" to execute it. This agent had only limited powers, and the sovereign states, not the Supreme Court, were the judges of what powers had been delegated to it.

From these premises Calhoun concluded that if Congress exceeded its delegated powers by enacting, say, a protective tariff, any one of the states might interpose state authority to block enforcement of the law. To accomplish this the people of a state would elect delegates to a state convention; if the convention decided that the act in question was unconstitutional, it would declare the act null and void within the state's boundaries. Congress might then choose between acquiescing in nullification or proposing a constitutional amendment specifically granting to the government the desired power. Thus whenever a single state challenged the constitutionality of an act of Congress, the cumbersome amending process, requiring ratification by three-fourths of the states, would be the government's only recourse. This system, thought Calhoun, would

Hayne:
The Nature of the Union

The measures of the Federal Government have, it is true, prostrated [South Carolina's] interests, and will soon involve the whole south in irretrievable ruin. But even this evil, great as it is, is not the chief ground of our complaints. It is the principle involved in the contest—a principle which, substituting the discretion of Congress for the limitations of the constitution, brings the States and the people to the feet of the federal government, and leaves them nothing they can call their own. Sir, if, the measures of the Federal Government were less oppressive, we should still strive against this usurpation. The south is acting on a principle she has always held sacred—resistance to unauthorized taxation.... Sir, if acting on these high motives, if, animated by that ardent love of liberty which has always been the most prominent trait in the Southern character, we should be hurried beyond the bounds of a cold and calculating prudence, who is there, with one noble and generous sentiment in his bosom, that would not be disposed, in the language of Burke, to exclaim, "You must pardon something to the spirit of liberty."?

From Robert Y. Hayne, Speech in the United States Senate, January 21, 1830.

provide a sufficient safeguard for the interests of the minority South. True democracy, he said, was not the rule of an absolute, or numerical, majority, for such a majority could ride roughshod over the rights of minorities. Instead, he proposed rule by the "concurrent" majority, with the people of each state having a veto over federal legislation. Minority rights would thereby be protected, and only legislation beneficial to all sections would be enacted.

Calhoun's ingenious system had a full review in the United States Senate early in 1830 during a debate that began over public land policy but soon centered on the nature of the federal Union. Robert Y. Hayne of South Carolina and Daniel Webster of Massachusetts, both brilliant orators, were the chief contestants, while Vice-President Calhoun listened carefully as presiding officer of the Senate. Hayne explained and defended the doctrine of nullification, enumerated his section's grievances, appealed to the West to join the South in resisting the avarice of the Northeast,

and reminded New Englanders that they themselves had toyed with both nullification and secession during the War of 1812. Webster, now an intense nationalist, denied that the Constitution was a mere compact to be interpreted as individual states might please. The people, not the states, had created it, and the Supreme Court was the proper authority to settle disputes over its meaning. Nor was the federal government simply an agent of the states; in exercising its powers it was sovereign and acted directly on the people. "It is," he said, "the people's Constitution, the people's government, made for the people, made by the people, and answerable to the people." The Union was not a voluntary federation of sovereign states; it was intended to be perpetual, and any attempt to dismember it would be treasonable and would lead to civil war. There may have been flaws in Webster's logic and in his history, but he understood better than Hayne the direction of events and the views of the majority. The South sympathized with Hayne's expression of its grievances, but outside South Carolina few Southerners showed much sympathy for his remedy.

The cold response of Congress to the doctrine of nullification disappointed Calhoun, but the response of President Jackson produced a major crisis in Calhoun's political career. Jackson had a deep respect for the rights of the states, and he was now convinced that Southerners had reason to complain about the existing tariff; but to talk of nullification or secession, as South Carolinians did, was another matter. Soon after the Webster-Hayne debate, at a public banquet, Jackson rose, looked squarely at Calhoun, and proposed his famous toast: "Our *Federal* Union—*It must be preserved.*" This incident was only one of numerous signs of a growing rift between the President and the Vice-President, a rift that Secretary of State Van Buren encouraged in his effort to supersede Calhoun as Jackson's successor to the presidency. Even a petty social tiff among Administration wives contributed to Calhoun's downfall. Mrs. Calhoun, a South Carolina aristocrat, snubbed the wife of the Secretary of War, Peggy Eaton, the attractive daughter of a Washington tavern-keeper. Jackson had no patience with this kind of snobbery, and Van Buren, a widower, made it clear that he shared the irritated President's admiration for Mrs. Eaton. Meanwhile, Calhoun's enemies let Jackson know that back in 1818, Calhoun, as Secretary of War, had denounced Jackson for his high-handed invasion of Florida. Explanations were offered and rejected. In 1831 there was a Cabinet reorganization, and Calhoun's friends were forced out of the Administration. Van Buren was now Jackson's candidate to succeed him, and Calhoun found himself pushed more and more out of his role of national leadership into the position of chief defender of the South.

The Nullification Crisis   The doctrine of nullification was put to the test in 1832, when Congress passed a new tariff bill which conceded little to the Southern demand for lower duties. After Jackson signed the bill, South Carolina's congressmen sent an address to their constituents stating that "all hope for relief from Congress is irrecoverably gone," and Calhoun now openly announced his support of nullification. The nullifiers won control of the South Carolina legislature, and when it met in October it ordered the election of delegates to a state convention. On November 24, 1832, the convention, by an overwhelming majority, adopted an ordinance which pronounced the tariffs of 1828 and 1832 "unauthorized by the Constitution" and therefore "null, void, and no law, nor binding upon this State, its officers or citizens." The ordinance prohibited state or federal officers from enforcing the tariff laws after February 1, 1833, forbade appeals to federal courts, and warned that any federal attempt to coerce the state would force South Carolina to secede from the Union. At this juncture Hayne resigned from the Senate to become governor of South Carolina, and Calhoun resigned as Vice-President to take Hayne's place and lead the fight on the Senate floor. The tariff issue had precipitated a serious national crisis.

But South Carolina's position was an uncomfortable one, for no other Southern state was prepared at that time to approve of her radical action. And the angry President reacted vigorously: he threatened to hang Calhoun, he sent a warship and revenue cutters to Charleston harbor, and he announced his readiness to take the field personally in case of a clash of arms. In a proclamation to the

---

Webster:
The Nature of the Union

If the government of the United States be the agent of the state governments, then they may control it, provided they can agree in the manner of controlling it; if it be the agent of the people, then the people alone can control it, restrain it, modify, or reform it…. The people of the United States have declared that this Constitution shall be the supreme law. We must either admit the proposition or dispute their authority. The states are, unquestionably, sovereign so far as their sovereignty is not affected by this supreme law. But the state legislatures, as political bodies, however sovereign, are yet not sovereign over the people…. So far as the people have restrained state sovereignty, by the expression of their will, in the Constitution of the United States, so far, it must be admitted, state sovereignty is effectually controlled…. The fact is that the people of the United States have chosen to impose control on state sovereignties. There are those, doubtless, who wish they had been left without restraint; but the Constitution has ordered the matter differently.

From Daniel Webster, Second Reply to Hayne, January 26, 1830.

---

people of South Carolina, Jackson endorsed Webster's position on the nature of the Union and warned them of the serious consequences of their action. Nullification, he said, was "incompatible with the existence of the Union, contradicted expressly by the letter of the Constitution, unauthorized by its spirit, inconsistent with every principle on which it was founded, and destructive of the great objective for which it was formed." As President he had no choice but to see that the laws of the United States were executed.

Tension increased when the legislature of South Carolina defiantly replied that Jackson's views were "erroneous and dangerous" and that the state would "repel force by force, . . . and maintain its liberty at all hazards." It increased further when Congress considered a "force bill" authorizing the President, if necessary, to use the army and navy to enforce the laws. Yet Jackson hoped to avoid violence except as a last resort, and South Carolina politicians, feeling their isolation, were eager to find a way to escape from their predicament without losing face. At length Henry Clay came forward with a compromise tariff, the details of which he worked out in consultation with Calhoun. It provided that tariff schedules would be gradually reduced over a period of nine years, until by 1842 no duty would exceed 20 per cent. On March 1, 1833, Congress passed both the compromise tariff and the force bill, and Jackson signed them. On March 15, the South Carolina convention accepted the compromise and withdrew its nullification of the tariff; but, yielding nothing in principle, it solemnly declared the force bill null and void. Since the crisis had passed, Jackson had the good sense to overlook this final petulant gesture by the Palmetto State.

Though Jackson irritated both the uncompromising protectionists and the state-rights followers of Calhoun, nationalists in subsequent sectional crises remembered him fondly for his bold action against the nullifiers. At the same time, even though most Southerners rejected nullification, the fight over the tariff made them more conscious than ever before of their minority position. Looking back at the tariff crisis, Chancellor Harper of South Carolina was pessimistic about the future:

> It is useless and impracticable to disguise the fact that the South is a permanent minority, and that there is a *sectional* majority against it—a majority of different views and interests and little common sympathy. . . . We are divided into slave-holding and non-slave-holding states; and . . . this is the broad and marked distinction that must separate us at last.

The Bank War

Criticism of the Bank Before the controversy over the tariff and nullification had been resolved, Congress and the Administration were engaged in an equally bitter dispute over whether the charter of the Bank of the United States should be renewed when it expired in 1836. Jackson had been hostile to the Bank long before he became President, criticized it repeatedly during his first term in office, made it a basic issue in his campaign for a second term, and gave it so much attention after his re-election that he seemed almost obsessed with a desire to destroy it. To many Jacksonians the Bank was by far the most crucial problem, for it went to the very heart of their philosophy; and Jackson himself doubt-

less counted his ultimate victory over "the Monster" as his greatest single accomplishment. To his critics, however, the destruction of the Bank was a major blunder in public policy, a singularly irresponsible exercise of presidential power which did incalculable harm to the country. The merits of the two positions still remain a subject of lively historical debate.

After a shaky start this powerful financial institution had settled down to become, in the decade after the Panic of 1819, a conservative, prosperous, and reasonably responsible business enterprise. Since 1822, the president of the Bank had been Nicholas Biddle, an aristocratic, cultivated, and talented Philadelphian whose acumen as a banker was unfortunately matched by his ineptitude in dealing with politicians. Many of his admiring contemporaries credited him with developing the Bank and its twenty-nine branches into an effective regulator of the expanding American economy. The Bank marketed government bonds and served as a reliable depository for government funds; it was an important source of credit for the business community; its bank notes provided the country with a sound paper currency; and it exerted a restraining influence on the state banks by forcing them to back their notes with adequate specie reserves. The source of its power was its control of one-fifth of the bank notes and one-third of the bank deposits and specie of the country.

But it was in part the Bank's possession of this vast economic power that made it so vulnerable politically. Many Jacksonians had not forgotten its seemingly selfish behavior during the Panic of 1819 (see p. 209), and they believed that democracy was in peril when so much power was concentrated in a single corporation. During the 1820's Biddle ran the Bank with considerable restraint, but he tactlessly admitted to a congressional committee that most state banks might have been "destroyed by an exertion of the powers of the [United States] Bank." Moreover, its influence over the national economy was not subjected to sufficient government control. Senator Benton complained that it was to this privileged monopoly that "the Federal Government, the State Governments, and great cities, must, of necessity, apply, for every loan which their

Defense of the Bank

The national bank, though not properly a *political* institution, is one of the most important and valuable instruments that are used in the practical administration of the government.... As the fiscal agent of the executive, it has exhibited a remarkable intelligence, efficiency, energy, and above all, INDEPENDENCE. This ... has been its real crime. As the regulator of the currency, it has furnished the country with a safe, convenient and copious circulating medium, and prevented the mischiefs that would otherwise result from the insecurity of the local banks. As a mere institution for loaning money, it has been ... the Providence of the less wealthy sections of the Union.... Through its dealings in exchange at home and abroad, the bank has materially facilitated the operations of our foreign and domestic trade. The important advantages which have thus been derived from this institution have been unattended by any countervailing evil. As its term advanced, and its officers acquired additional experience, it has been constantly gaining on the public favor.

From the Boston *Daily Advertiser*, September 1832.

exigencies may demand." The danger seemed all the greater because so many influential politicians and editors were indebted to the Bank for loans. Webster was not only a heavy borrower but was on the Bank's payroll as a legal counsel. "I believe my retainer has not been renewed or *refreshed* as usual," he once wrote to Biddle. "If it be wished that my relation to the Bank should be continued, it may be well to send me the usual retainer." As a result, Biddle's enemies accused him of corrupting the nation's political life.

Thus, by the time Jackson became President the Bank had incurred the hatred of numerous groups for either practical or ideological reasons. Curiously, it antagonized both those who favored "soft money" (more state bank notes) and those who favored "hard money" (only gold and silver coins). The former included some state banking interests, land speculators, and small entrepreneurs who felt that their needs were best served by an abundant paper currency. The latter included Eastern workingmen who resented receiving their wages in paper of uncertain value, and Westerners, such as Senator Benton, who considered any currency other than gold and silver dishonest.

The hard-money men were hostile to banks of any kind, state or national, that issued bank notes, and tended to look upon banking as a parasitic enterprise. Among them was Jackson, who once told Biddle, "I do not dislike your Bank any more than all banks." By using gold and silver in ordinary business transactions, he told Congress, the country would avoid "those fluctuations in the standard of value which render uncertain the reward of labor."

Veto of the Bank Bill   Jackson's first two messages to Congress left little doubt that he would veto any bill to recharter the Bank. In his first message, in December 1829, he affirmed that "both the constitutionality and the expediency of the law creating this bank are well questioned by a large portion of our fellow-citizens." A year later he again pointed to the dangers posed by the Bank as it was then organized. If a national bank were

Death of the Bank

The Bank of the United States ... enjoys ... a monopoly of ... favor and support, and, as a necessary consequence, almost a monopoly of the foreign and domestic exchange. The powers, privileges, and favors bestowed upon it in the original charter, by increasing the value of the stock far above its par value, operated as a gratuity of many millions to the stockholders....

The modifications of the existing charter proposed by this act are not such, in my view, as make it consistent with the rights of the States or the liberties of the people.... All the objectionable principles of the existing corporation, and most of its odious features, are retained without alleviation.... Already is almost a third of the stock in foreign hands and not represented in elections. It is constantly passing out of the country, and this act will accelerate its departure. The entire control of the institution would necessarily fall into the hands of a few citizen stockholders....

If we can not at once ... make our Government what it ought to be, we can at least take a stand against all new grants of monopolies and exclusive privileges, against any prostitution of our Government to the advancement of the few at the expense of the many, and in favor of compromise and gradual reform in our code of laws and system of political economy.

From Andrew Jackson, Veto of the Bank Bill, July 1832.

needed, he suggested that it be established as a branch of the Treasury Department, to act simply as a bank of deposit without power to issue notes, make loans, or acquire property. Such a bank, "having no stockholders, debtors, or property," would raise no constitutional objections. That the constitutionality of the present Bank had already been affirmed by the Supreme Court was to Jackson irrelevant. "I have read the opinion of John Marshall," he said, "and could not agree with him."

In Biddle's campaign to save the Bank, he could not avoid getting deeply involved in national politics. He had started as a Jeffersonian Republican and had tried to appease Jackson by appointing some of his supporters to directorships of the branch banks. But Jackson's hostility drove Biddle into the camp of the opposition, and Biddle's loans to congressmen became increasingly motivated by politics. At length, in 1832, he took the advice of Clay and Webster and applied for a new charter, though the old one would not expire for four more years. Clay assured Biddle that Congress would pass the bill, and he was ready to make a presidential veto an issue in the coming campaign. The bill to recharter the Bank, amended to meet some of Jackson's objections, easily passed both houses of Congress with the support of a substantial minority of the Democrats. Jackson accepted the challenge. "The Bank," he told Van Buren, "is trying to kill me, but I will kill it."

Jackson's veto message, a powerful political document, maintained that the Bank was unconstitutional in spite of the changes in its charter and described the dangers of "such a concentration of power in the hands of a few men irresponsible to the people." Much of the stock was held by foreigners, "and the residue is held by a few hundred of our own citizens, chiefly of the richest class." Their demands for "grants of monopolies and special privileges" had "arrayed section against section, interest against interest, and man against man, in a fearful commotion which threatens to shake the foundations of the Union." Webster bitterly denounced the President for executive usurpation and for seeking "to inflame the poor against the rich," but the veto stood and became a central issue in the presidential election of 1832. Indeed, Clay, Biddle, and the Na-

tional Republicans helped to make it so by giving the veto message wide circulation, mistakenly thinking that it would serve to discredit Jackson. Whatever the weaknesses of its reasoning, however it may have exposed Jackson's limitations as a student of money and banking, the election showed that Jackson knew how to reach the ordinary voter better than they.

Jackson Vindicated   The campaign of 1832 was notable not only for its vindication of Jackson but for two political innovations: the appearance of the first American third party, the Anti-Masonic party, and the holding of the first national nominating conventions. The new party, like so many third parties, focused on a single issue: opposition to secret societies, especially the Society of Freemasons. The party's strength was concentrated in the rural districts of New England and the Middle states, where its supporters objected to the secrecy, exclusiveness, and allegedly undemocratic character of these societies. In 1826 William Morgan of Batavia, New York, a former Mason who was about to publish an exposure of the secrets of Freemasonry, suddenly vanished, and rumors spread that members of the society had murdered him. The resulting popular indignation eventually took the form of a political movement designed to drive the "grand kings" of Freemasonry out of public office. In September 1831 the Anti-Masonic party held a national convention at Baltimore and nominated William Wirt of Maryland for President, the first candidate to be selected in this fashion. The new party, in spite of its democratic assaults on a presumably privileged group, was essentially anti-Jacksonian—Jackson was himself a Mason—and in a short time most of its leaders joined the National Republicans.

Wirt hoped to win the nomination of the National Republicans, too, but in December 1831 this party held its own convention in Baltimore and nominated Henry Clay for President and John Sargeant of Pennsylvania for Vice-President. Its national platform attacked Jackson for abusing the patronage and the veto power, endorsed Clay's American System, and boldly demanded the rechartering of the Bank. The Democrats also met in Baltimore, in May 1832, but Jackson had already been renominated by numerous local conventions, and a party platform seemed superfluous. All that remained was to nominate a candidate for Vice-President, and Jackson saw to it that his choice, Van Buren, was selected. Jackson was then at the peak of his popularity, and with Wirt taking votes away from Clay the outcome of the campaign was never in doubt. Jackson won by a comfortable majority in the popular vote, and in the electoral college he polled 219 votes to Clay's 49. Wirt carried only Vermont, while the disaffected leaders of South Carolina gave their state to John Floyd of Virginia. To Jackson the significance of the election was clear: he had been given a mandate to press his war against the Bank of the United States until this "Hydra of corruption" had been destroyed.

The Bank Destroyed   Nicholas Biddle was not yet ready to surrender. "This worthy President," he said, "thinks that because he has scalped Indians and imprisoned judges, he is to have his way with the Bank. He is mistaken." So the battle went on, and in its final phase the friends and enemies of the Bank fought so recklessly that they impaired the stability of the entire American economy.

Jackson refused to wait for the Bank's charter to expire, for he feared that Biddle might still use its political and economic power to buy a new charter from Congress. Soon after the election Jackson decided to deprive the Bank of federal support for its financial operations by ceasing to use it as a depository for government funds. He justified his decision on the grounds of the Bank's "misconduct"—its attempt to influence the outcome of the election by playing on "the distress of some and the fear of others." Jackson had to get rid of two uncooperative Secretaries of the Treasury before he found a man in complete sympathy with his scheme: Roger B. Taney, the former Attorney General. The gradual removal of federal funds from the Bank was accomplished simply by paying government expenses from the existing deposits and by refusing to place current revenues in its vaults. These revenues were now distributed among numerous state banks—eventually, eighty-nine of them— which critics called "pet banks." The use of state banks of varying degrees of soundness was, as Jackson himself admitted, an unsatis-

factory expedient subject to strong political pressures.

Jackson's enemies struck back hard. In the Senate Clay mustered a majority in 1834 to pass a resolution censuring the President for removing the deposits and thus assuming power "not conferred by the constitution and the laws." Not until 1837 were indignant Jacksonians able to get this partisan resolution expunged from the Senate record. Meanwhile, as federal deposits diminished, Biddle began calling in the Bank's loans and contracting credit, in part to protect himself and in part as a deliberate means of creating economic distress in order to force the government to return the deposits and renew the charter. The resulting credit shortage caused unemployment and business failures and brought delegations of businessmen to Washington to petition for relief. But the angry President told them to "go to Biddle." "I never will restore the deposits," he vowed, "I never will recharter the United States Bank, or sign a charter for any other bank, so long as my name is Andrew Jackson." At length the businessmen turned against Biddle and forced him to relax his credit policy, but not before he had managed to increase his unpopularity and thus to destroy even the faint hope that a drastically revised federal charter could be obtained. In 1836 Biddle received a charter from the state of Pennsylvania which enabled the Bank to continue in business until 1841, when, because of the economic depression and unwise speculations, it was finally forced to close its doors.

The Bank war was over, and Jackson's victory was complete. The anti-Jacksonians fumed at his highhanded tactics; they spoke indignantly of the "reign of King Andrew I"; they renamed themselves the "Whigs" in imitation of the British party which, in the eighteenth century, had sought to reduce the power of the monarch; and they formed a loose coalition of those who opposed the Administration. In 1836, in their extremity, they held no national convention and drew up no platform; party strategists decided to run not one but three presidential candidates: Webster to appeal to New England, Hugh Lawson White of Tennessee to appeal to the South, and General William Henry Harrison of Ohio to appeal to the West. The Whigs hoped thus to throw the

Martin Van Buren: "The Little Magician."

Yorker of Dutch descent was a self-made man from a rural family of modest means. After a successful law career which gave him financial independence, Van Buren turned to state politics and soon became the leader of an efficient Republican machine called the Albany Regency; following the presidential campaign of 1824, he linked his political fortunes with Jackson's and rose with him as a faithful advocate of his principles. But Van Buren was a pale copy of his chief: he lacked Jackson's forcefulness and popular appeal and had to rely on his tact and his skill in the management of men. Unfortunately neither these talents nor the Jacksonian philosophy enabled him to cope with the serious economic problems that beset the nation while he was President. Jackson was fortunate to have left office when he did, for within two months the country plunged into a panic and depression whose intensity was attributable at least in part to the policies of his Administration. Van Buren thus had the misfortune of being remembered as a "depression President."

After the brief "Biddle panic" of 1833–34, the country enjoyed a period of glorious prosperity and unprecedented economic expansion. Manufacturers and merchants flourished; planters found a seemingly limitless market for cotton at good prices; Western farmers enjoyed flush times; speculators drove up land prices and, between 1834 and 1836, were responsible for a fivefold increase in government land sales; and the states and private entrepreneurs (often with state support) undertook ambitious canal and railroad projects. Funds were made available by British capitalists, who invested in both private and state securities, and by the multiplying state banks, which expanded note issues and liberalized loan policies once they had been freed from the control of Biddle's Bank. Between 1829 and 1837 the number of state banks more than doubled, their note issues trebled, and their loans quadrupled. In an economically "underdeveloped" country with a rapidly growing population, much of this business activity was healthy. But some of it was reckless and speculative—and the economy now lacked even the modest check that the Bank of the United States had exercised. The Jackson Administration, besides trying to divorce government from business,

election into the House of Representatives where they might unite behind a single candidate. The Democrats held a convention at Baltimore, dutifully nominated Van Buren, and presented him on Jackson's record without a formal platform. After a dull campaign, Van Buren won by a slim majority in the popular vote and by 170 electoral votes to 124 for his several opponents.

Panic and Depression

Economic Crisis   Jackson remained in Washington to witness Van Buren's inauguration, and Benton observed dryly that "the rising was eclipsed by the setting sun." It was not easy to follow the dynamic Jackson into the presidency, not even for Van Buren, whose political adroitness had earned him the title of "the Little Magician." Like Jackson, this New had adopted fiscal policies that intensified the crisis when it came.

First, as Jackson himself observed, the deposit of federal funds in numerous "pet banks" tended to multiply state-chartered banks and "had a great agency in producing a spirit of wild speculation." Many state banks, especially in the West where they were almost unregulated, indulged in "wildcat financiering" by failing to maintain adequate specie reserves for their note issues and by making loans without demanding adequate collateral. Speculators borrowed paper of dubious value from Western banks and gave it to the government land offices for new lands; the government in turn deposited the paper in the "pet banks," which made the money available again for further speculation. This was a happy situation for those who favored "soft money," but it distressed the "hard-money" men who, as Benton said, had not joined "in putting down the paper currency of a national bank in order to put up a paper currency of a thousand local banks." Jackson shared this point of view and, in July 1836, suddenly intervened with his so-called Specie Circular. In the future, he ordered, the federal land offices would accept only gold and silver in payment for public lands. This was a severe blow to the speculators, and for a time land sales almost ceased and inflated land prices dropped precipitately.

Next, the Congress, with Jackson's approval, gave an enormous stimulus to costly internal-improvement projects launched by the states. In 1836, with the federal government out of debt and with a surplus of almost $40 million, an act provided that beginning on January 1, 1837, the surplus above $5 million was to be distributed among the states in proportion to population in four quarterly installments. Many states, assuming that they would receive a similar subsidy each year and ignoring the fact that the federal funds were intended to be only a loan, immediately designed ambitious projects that exceeded the limits of their own resources. At the same time, the act deprived the "pet banks" of the bulk of their federal deposits and, in consequence, obliged them to call in their loans from private borrowers.

But there were causes other than federal fiscal policy for the economic crisis. In the years of prosperity and free spending imports of luxury goods increased, the balance of trade was upset, and specie flowed out of the country. Hard times in Great Britain caused the demand for cotton to decline and the support of British investors to be withdrawn. Business conditions in the United States had been deteriorating for some months, but the real panic began in May 1837, when New York banks, soon followed by banks in the rest of the country, suspended specie payments. In the economic shakedown that followed, banks and business houses failed by the hundreds, factories closed and unemployment mounted, farm prices and land values collapsed, internal improvement projects were abandoned, and some states either stopped payments on their debts or repudiated them outright. The most feverish activity was among lawyers and auctioneers who arranged the foreclosure sales of farms, plantations, and urban business properties. One of the most severe depressions in American history followed, and full recovery did not come until the middle of the 1840's.

The Independent Treasury Understanding of the causes of business cycles had advanced very little since the depression following the Panic of 1819—President Van Buren attributed the present crisis to "overbanking" and "overtrading." The idea that government might give assistance to distressed farmers, workers, and businessmen was not yet seriously considered. In so far as the government did react to the crisis, it adopted fiscal policies that served to deepen the deflation and heighten economic distress. Distribution of funds to the states for internal improvements was stopped, federal spending was curtailed, and the President concentrated on getting the government out of debt. Van Buren also rejected pleas for the withdrawal of the Specie Circular and continued the hard-money policy of his predecessor; he scorned the argument that the crisis justified the chartering of a new national bank. He thus identified himself with the radical, or "Locofoco," * wing of his party —the extreme hard-money, antibank, anti-

* "Locofoco" was a popular name for the newly invented friction matches. The radical Democrats once carried "locofocos" to a party meeting, because they feared that the conservatives would try to break it up by turning off the gas lights. This incident explains how the Locofocos got their name.

monopoly faction that was especially strong among workingmen and reformers in his own state of New York.

The chief aim of the Locofocos was to divorce the federal government from banking altogether by denying all private banks the use of federal deposits. Van Buren urged such a step repeatedly, and finally, in 1840, Congress passed the Independent Treasury Act. This act authorized the establishment of subtreasuries in various cities where government funds could be placed in vaults for safekeeping. Although this system insured the government from loss, it was highly deflationary, because it deprived the banks of funds which could have been used for private loans.

Banking was now entirely in the hands of the states. A few, notably New York and the New England states, managed to establish reasonably satisfactory and responsible state banking systems; a couple of Western states adopted the Locofoco philosophy and for a time abolished banking altogether. In many states the Jacksonians established "free banking" systems, which enabled promoters to secure a bank charter without a special act of the legislature. Free banking and so-called general incorporation laws were important aspects of Jacksonian Democracy at the state level. By eliminating the need for small entrepreneurs to have political influence in order to obtain state charters, these laws were expected to provide equal opportunities for all.

The Election of 1840   As the presidential campaign of 1840 approached, the country was still deep in economic depression; the Democrats were bound to lose the support of many voters who would express their discontent by turning against the party in power. The Democratic national convention at Baltimore was a gloomy affair. The delegates renominated Van Buren unanimously, but with restrained enthusiasm, and adopted a platform reaffirming the party position on state rights, banking, internal improvements, and the Independent Treasury. The Democrats were on the defensive throughout the campaign.

The Whigs, however, were in an optimistic mood when their convention assembled at Harrisburg, Pennsylvania. Having been branded the enemies of the common man, a party of aristocrats and monopolists, having

The Election of 1840

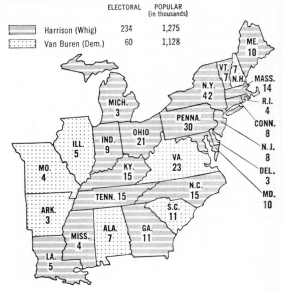

	ELECTORAL	POPULAR (in thousands)
Harrison (Whig)	234	1,275
Van Buren (Dem.)	60	1,128

endured a succession of humiliating defeats, they now looked forward to giving the Democrats some of their own medicine. They had already attributed the depression to Democratic fiscal measures, charged that the Independent Treasury scheme was a callous attempt of the government to protect itself without regard for the welfare of the country, and accused Van Buren of indifference to the suffering of the people. Now, having learned much from the tactics of their enemies and from their own mistakes, they prepared to out-Jackson the Jacksonians in a bid for popular support. The Whigs passed over Clay in favor of a military hero: William Henry Harrison of Ohio, who had defeated the Indians at the Battle of Tippecanoe and the British at the Battle of the Thames. With an eye on the South, they nominated John Tyler of Virginia, a conservative, state-rights Whig, for the vice-presidency. They adopted no platform, for the campaign they planned was to have little relevance to concrete issues.

The Democrats were guilty of much low-level electioneering, but their campaign seemed almost dignified compared to the antics of the Whigs. Though Harrison was descended from an aristocratic Virginia family and lived as an Ohio country gentleman in a sixteen-room mansion, the Whigs transformed "Old Tippecanoe" into a simple frontier farmer and man of the people. When a blundering Democratic editor sneered that Harrison would be satisfied to retire to a log cabin with a barrel of hard cider, the Whigs happily accepted the statement as true. They praised his simple tastes, made log cabins and cider barrels their party symbols, and boasted of their own log-cabin backgrounds. (Webster apologized for not having been born in one.) The Whigs described Van Buren as a squanderer of public funds on lavish entertainment, a man of expensive aristocratic tastes who fancied fine wines, ate from gold plates, and effeminately scented his whiskers with cologne. They dazzled the voters with boisterous mass

meetings, barbecues, and torchlight processions; they nicknamed Van Buren "Martin Van Ruin" and "Sweet Sandy Whiskers"; they promised to cleanse the civil service of corruption and to restore prosperity; and they chanted their campaign slogans: "Tippecanoe and Tyler too" and "Van, Van is a used-up man." If this was the way to win democratic elections, the Whigs proved that they had mastered the technique as well as their opponents.

The voters responded by turning out in larger numbers than in any previous presidential election—even Jackson had not attracted so large a proportion to the polls. Harrison's popular majority was small, but he won overwhelmingly in the electoral college: 234 votes

Philadelphia: "Tippecanoe and Tyler too," 1840.

to 60 for Van Buren. After twelve years of Democratic supremacy, the Whigs were to have their turn.

The Supreme Court under Taney   But the Democrats, like the Federalists in 1801, retained a firm hold on the third branch of the federal government: the judiciary. While he was President, Jackson had appointed six new Associate Justices to the Supreme Court, all of them stanch Democrats; and when Chief Justice Marshall died in 1835, Jackson had selected Roger B. Taney, a state-rights agrarian, to replace him. Jacksonians thus controlled seven of the nine positions on the Court, and conservatives such as Webster feared an irresponsible and radical new departure from the constitutional doctrines laid down by Marshall. Actually, though the Taney Court modified Marshall's opinions on the rights of corporations and the sanctity of contracts, the main corpus of his decisions remained almost intact. Even the doctrine of judicial review went unchallenged. Indeed, it was used in several important cases to throw out state and (on one occasion) federal legislation that a majority on the Court found to be unconstitutional.

The chief departure from the extreme nationalism of Marshall was the new Court's tendency to give the states greater power to regulate corporations. This change is best illustrated in the case of *Charles River Bridge* v. *Warren Bridge* (1837). The issue was whether the state of Massachusetts, having given a charter to the Charles River Bridge Company to build and operate a toll bridge, could now grant a charter to a second company to build and operate another and competing bridge. The first company contended that this would constitute a breach of contract, but the Court disagreed and held that the rights of corporations are subordinate to the interests of the community—"that the community also have rights, and that the happiness and well-being of every citizen depends on their faithful preservation." The Court thus provided an admirable statement of several of the basic goals of Jacksonian Democracy: encouragement to new entrepreneurs, an attack on special privilege and entrenched "monopoly," and the promotion of the happiness and welfare of all the people.

Tyler and Paralysis

The Whig Disaster   The Whigs had barely organized their first Administration when disaster struck, and within less than a year the party was so torn by factionalism that it produced not a period of progress along the lines of Whig principles but a period of almost complete political stalemate. Harrison seemed to favor the goals of the American System and to be ready to accept guidance from Clay and Webster—he made Webster Secretary of State and gave most of the other Cabinet posts to followers of Clay—but a month after his inauguration the sixty-eight-year-old President died of pneumonia. Thus, for the first time, the Vice-President rose to the presidency. Unfortunately for the Whigs, John Tyler represented the Southern planters who opposed nearly everything the Whig majority hoped to accomplish. This Virginia aristocrat had once been a Democrat but had broken with Jackson over nullification and the removal of federal deposits from Biddle's Bank. He drifted over to the Whigs because they were dominated by affluent men of high social status, and because he opposed the radical, Locofoco tendencies of the Democracy under Jackson and Van Buren. But although Tyler was considered a political friend of Clay's, he made it clear that the imperious Kentuckian was not going to run his Administration, and none of his messages showed any sympathy for Clay's views on banking, tariffs, or internal improvements.

Clay, however, confidently planned a legislative program that would at last put his American System into full operation. In 1841 he introduced a bill to distribute the proceeds from the sale of public lands among the states for internal improvements. In a bid for Western support, this bill also contained a provision for pre-emption, which would permit squatters on the public domain to purchase 160 acres of the land they had improved at the minimum price of $1.25 an acre when the land was put up for sale. To get his bill adopted, Clay had to agree that distribution would cease if tariff schedules were increased. A year later, in 1842, the Whigs tried to raise the tariff without repealing distribution. But a presidential veto forced them to give up distribution in order to get the increase in duties for which manufacturers were clamoring. Tyler then reluctantly approved the tariff of 1842 to solve the government's need for more revenue, though it restored the level of duties provided in the tariff of 1832. The new tariff was virtually the only Whig achievement—Tyler not only forced the abandonment of distribution but vetoed internal improvement bills with essentially the same arguments that Jackson had used.

The final disappointment came when Clay and the majority of Whigs attempted to establish a third Bank of the United States. Tyler approved the repeal of the Independent Treasury Act, but it was well known that he would not accept a new system of national banking in its place. Hence the Whigs tried to disguise their purpose by using other names. First they provided for the creation of a "Fiscal Bank," but Tyler was not deceived and vetoed the bill; then they proposed the chartering of a "Fiscal Corporation," only to be thwarted by another presidential veto. With that, national banking ceased to be a serious issue in national politics for two decades. The angry Whigs in Congress formally read Tyler out of the party, the Cabinet resigned (except Webster, who was involved in diplomatic negotiations with the British), and Clay gave up his seat in the Senate to try again for the presidency. After making a fiasco of the Whig victory, Tyler and his conservative Southern allies began to drift back to the Democratic party, where, in subsequent years, they would challenge the Jacksonians for control.

Foreign Affairs under Tyler   The political paralysis at home did not prevent the Tyler Administration from solving several problems in the country's foreign relations. Jackson, in spite of his blunt tactics, had already disposed of two issues that had survived the negotiations following the War of 1812: he managed to persuade the British to permit American merchants to trade with their West Indian Islands; and he made a satisfactory settlement of claims against France for damages inflicted on American shipping during the Napoleonic wars. But new sources of friction in Anglo-American relations had begun to appear during the 1830's and had reached serious proportions by the time Tyler became President. The traditional undercurrent of hostility, heightened by British travelers who made disparaging comments on American culture and by local politicians bidding for the Irish vote, made it dangerous to permit disagreements to go unsettled.

Trouble began in 1837 when an insurrection broke out in the eastern provinces of Canada. Though many Americans hoped the uprising might ultimately lead to annexation, the British suppressed it with relative ease. But while it was in progress Americans along the frontier aided the rebels and afterward gave the defeated rebel leaders refuge. When raids across the border continued from American bases on the Niagara River, Canadian officials one night impetuously crossed the river, killed one American, and burned an American steamer, the *Caroline*, which had been carrying supplies to the rebels. In spite of growing tension, the British government ignored the American demand for reparations and an apology. Then, in 1840, a Canadian named Alexander McLeod was arrested in New York on suspicion of being a member of the party that had attacked the *Caroline;* he was brought to trial for murder and arson. The British government responded with a vigorous protest: it assumed responsibility for the attack on the *Caroline* and warned that McLeod's conviction would have serious consequences. Fortunately McLeod established an alibi and was acquitted, much to the relief of the State Department.

Meanwhile, a long-standing controversy over the Maine boundary flared up when, in 1838, American and Canadian lumberjacks battled for possession of part of a disputed area along the Aroostook River. Another dispute grew out of a British request that its naval patrols along the west coast of Africa be permitted to stop and search ships flying the American flag to determine whether they were engaging in the slave trade. This request revived memories of British practices during the Napoleonic wars, and the American government would not agree to it. Finally, in 1841, a group of slaves being transported from Virginia to New Orleans on the American brig *Creole* mutinied and sailed to Nassau, where British officials freed them. Prodded by angry Southerners, Secretary of State Webster demanded that the slaves be returned, but the British refused.

The Webster-Ashburton Treaty, 1842

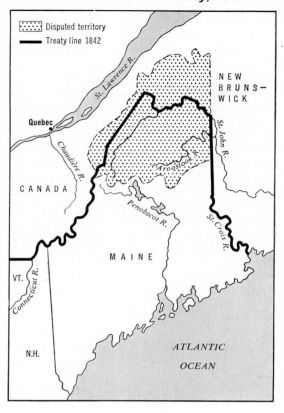

Disputed territory
Treaty line 1842

St. Lawrence R.

NEW BRUNS-WICK

Quebec

St. John R.

Chaudière R.

Aroostook R.

CANADA

Penobscot R.

St. Croix R.

MAINE

VT.

Connecticut R.

N.H.

ATLANTIC OCEAN

At this point a new British government decided that the time had come for negotiations and sent Lord Ashburton to Washington as a special envoy. Ashburton was a happy choice, for he was friendly to the United States and a man of infinite tact; moreover, he had met Webster in England, and the two men liked each other. Neither was an experienced professional diplomat, but both were in a conciliatory mood, and their patient and highly informal negotiations culminated in the important Webster-Ashburton Treaty of 1842.

Except for Oregon, which remained under joint occupation, the treaty settled all border controversies by awarding seven-twelfths of the disputed territory along the Maine boundary to the United States and by making minor adjustments around Lake Champlain and between Lake Superior and the Lake of the Woods. The treaty also included an agreement for the mutual extradition of fugitives accused of any of seven major crimes. As for the slave trade, the United States did not agree to British search of her vessels but did agree to maintain a squadron off the African coast to apprehend slavers flying the American flag. Neither the *Caroline* nor the *Creole* affair was dealt with in the treaty, but Ashburton disposed of them through an exchange of notes which Webster chose to accept as satisfactory. With regard to the *Caroline* affair, Ashburton simply expressed regret "that some explanation and apology for this occurrence was not immediately made." In the case of the *Creole*, the slaves were not to be returned, but he promised that in the future there would be no "officious interference" with American vessels forced to enter British ports by "violence or accident."

Webster, after concluding these negotiations and seeing the treaty ratified by both governments, followed the example of the other Whigs and resigned from Tyler's Cabinet. Thereafter the Tyler Administration, disrupted and lacking congressional support, looked rather futile in the face of an increasingly powerful drive for the moral reform of American society. This drive would have a shattering effect on both national parties and, eventually, on the federal Union itself. In the critical years ahead, disheartened patriots would remember the strength and firmness of Andrew Jackson with growing admiration. As the country moved from crisis to crisis, the cry that would be heard with increasing frequency was "Oh, for an hour of Old Hickory."

SUGGESTIONS FOR READING   The Advance of Democracy

The most perceptive contemporary analysis of the workings of American democracy in the Jacksonian era is Alexis de Tocqueville, *Democracy in America*,* 2 vols. (1945). Moisei Ostrogorski, *Democracy and the Organization of Political Parties*, 2 vols. (1902), is the best

* Available in a paperback edition.

general work on the democratization of American politics. The advance of democracy in two important states can be studied in D. R. Fox, *The Decline of Aristocracy in the Politics of New York* (1919), and A. B. Darling, *Political Changes in Massachusetts, 1824–1848* (1925). The standard work on the extension of the suffrage is K. H. Porter, *A History of the Suffrage in the United States* (1918).

The disputed election of 1824, as well as the goals and misfortunes of the Adams Administration, are described with rich detail in George Dangerfield, *The Era of Good Feelings* (1952). Two biographies are essential for an understanding of these years: G. G. Van Deusen, *The Life of Henry Clay* (1937), and S. F. Bemis, *John Quincy Adams and the Union* (1956). A fascinating personal record of Adams' presidency can be found in C. F. Adams, ed., *The Memoirs of John Quincy Adams*, 12 vols. (1874–77).

The Age of Jackson

A good recent survey of Jacksonian Democracy, based on modern scholarship, is G. G. Van Deusen, *The Jacksonian Era* (1959). C. G. Bowers, *Party Battles of the Jackson Period* (1922), is a highly partisan, pro-Jackson account. Marquis James, *Andrew Jackson: Portrait of a President* * (1937), is a sympathetic and lucid biography of the presidential years. Two of Jackson's strongest supporters in Congress are the subjects of distinguished biographies: C. G. Sellers, Jr., *James K. Polk: Jacksonian, 1795–1843* (1957); W. N. Chambers, *Old Bullion Benton: Senator from the West* (1956); and E. B. Smith, *Magnificent Missourian: The Life of Thomas Hart Benton* (1958). There are also excellent biographies of two of the key figures in the Jackson Administration: C. B. Swisher, *Roger B. Taney* (1936), and W. B. Hatcher, *Edward Livingston: Jeffersonian Republican and Jacksonian Democrat* (1940). An authoritative study of administrative organization is L. D. White, *The Jacksonians: A Study in Administrative History, 1829–1861* (1954). The growth of the spoils system is traced in C. R. Fish, *The Civil Service and the Patronage* (1905).

The meaning of Jacksonian Democracy is still the subject of an animated controversy. The following books, all of them of major importance, provide a sample of the various ways in which Jacksonian Democracy can be viewed: A. M. Schlesinger, Jr., *The Age of Jackson* * (1945); T. P. Abernethy, *From Frontier to Plantation in Tennessee* (1932); Richard Hofstadter, *The American Political Tradition* * (1948); J. W. Ward, *Andrew Jackson: Symbol for an Age* * (1955); Joseph Dorfman, *The Economic Mind in American Civilization*, 3 vols. (1946–49); Marvin Meyers, *The Jacksonian Persuasion* * (1957); and H. C. Syrett, *Andrew Jackson: His Contribution to the American Tradition* (1953).

All the above volumes are concerned with Jackson's views on banking and are important to a study of the controversy over the Second Bank of the United States. But the key work on this topic is Bray Hammond, *Banks and Politics in America from the Revolution to the Civil War* (1957). Two other works merit consultation: R. C. H. Catterall, *The Second Bank of the United States* (1903), and W. B. Smith, *Economic Aspects of the Second Bank of the United States* (1953). The best possible case for Nicholas Biddle is presented in T. P. Govan, *Nicholas Biddle: Nationalist and Public Banker* (1959).

The tragedy of Indian removals is the subject of Angie Debo, *The Road to Disappearance: A History of the Creek Indians* (1941), and Grant Foreman, *Indian Removal: The Emigration of the Five Civilized Tribes* (1932). Land policy in the Jacksonian era is treated fully in R. G. Wellington, *The Political and Sectional Influence of the Public Lands, 1828–1842* (1914), and R. M. Robbins, *Our Landed Heritage: The Public Domain* * (1942).

The Nullification Controversy

C. S. Sydnor, *The Development of Southern Sectionalism, 1819–1848* (1948), provides a good analysis of the nullification crisis in the broad setting of Southern history. Three important

* Available in a paperback edition.

monographs should also be consulted: D. F. Houston, *A Critical Study of Nullification in South Carolina* (1896); C. S. Boucher, *The Nullification Controversy in South Carolina* (1916); and Frederic Bancroft, *Calhoun and the South Carolina Nullification Movement* (1928).

Calhoun's ideas can be studied in a collection of his writings edited by R. K. Crallé: *Works of J. C. Calhoun*, 6 vols. (1851–55). A. O. Spain, *The Political Theory of John C. Calhoun* (1951), provides a detailed analysis. The essay on Calhoun in Richard Hofstadter, *The American Political Tradition* * (1948), is a brilliant critique. Two biographies are also helpful: C. M. Wiltse, *John C. Calhoun: Nullifier, 1829–1839* (1949), and M. L. Coit, *John C. Calhoun: American Portrait* * (1950).

Depression and the Whig Interlude

The best available biographical studies of Van Buren are Holmes Alexander, *The American Talleyrand* (1935), and R. V. Remini, *Martin Van Buren and the Making of the Democratic Party* (1959). These should be supplemented by Van Buren's relatively candid account of his own life: *The Autobiography of Martin Van Buren*, edited by J. C. Fitzpatrick (1920). The best studies of the panic and depression are R. C. McGrane, *The Panic of 1837* (1924), and W. B. Smith and A. H. Cole, *Fluctuations in American Business, 1790–1860* (1935).

The origin and growth of the Whig party are traced in detail in three monographs: A. C. Cole, *The Whig Party in the South* (1913); E. M. Carroll, *Origins of the Whig Party* (1925); and G. R. Poage, *Henry Clay and the Whig Party* (1936). Three biographies of Whig leaders also need to be consulted: the biography of Clay by Van Deusen, cited above; C. M. Fuess, *Daniel Webster* 2 vols. (1930); and R. N. Current, *Daniel Webster and the Rise of National Conservatism* (1955). R. G. Gunderson, *The Log-Cabin Campaign* (1957), is a brisk account of the election of 1840. The Tyler Administration is treated competently in O. D. Lambert, *Presidential Politics in the United States, 1841–1844* (1936), and O. P. Chitwood, *John Tyler: Champion of the Old South* (1939). A. B. Corey, *The Crisis of 1830–1842 in Canadian-American Relations* (1941), and J. B. Brebner, *North Atlantic Triangle* (1945), are good monographs on foreign policy under Tyler.

* Available in a paperback edition.

10

An Era of Reform

Many nineteenth-century Americans believed that the destiny of their country concerned not only themselves but all mankind. In America's congenial environment man would reveal his capacity to govern himself, to live in harmony with the laws of God's universe, and to eradicate social injustice; he would build an ideal society led by righteous men motivated by disinterested benevolence. In achieving these noble goals America would serve as a model for the rest of the world. To fail would be to betray a sacred trust.

This belief in a divine mission, together with a nagging awareness of their shortcomings, made Americans inordinately sensitive to criticism from European visitors. Tocqueville noted that their "irritable patriotism" caused them to take offense at any comment that was even mildly unfavorable. Outsiders could not speak freely, without risking resentment, "of anything at all except, perhaps, the climate and the soil; and even then Americans will be found ready to defend both as if they had co-operated in producing them."

But if Americans regarded criticism by outsiders as impertinent, they periodically displayed an ample capacity for self-criticism. For they knew that their society had not yet achieved that state of near-perfection toward which so many of them hopefully aimed. Though they cherished an optimistic belief that a benign Providence made progress inevitable, improvements did not always come fast enough to satisfy them, and they sometimes

tried to give Providence a helping hand. "We could not retard the great forward movement of Humanity if we would," wrote Horace Greeley, editor of the New York *Tribune*, "but each of us may decide for himself whether to share in the glory of promoting it or incur the shame of having looked coldly and indifferently on."

In the 1820's movements for moral uplift and social reform began to attract people who were unwilling to compromise with evil and were impatient with the slow pace of progress. The causes they championed were by no means peculiarly American—British reformers influenced reformers across the Atlantic—but there was a millennial quality about the American crusades that was unique. Theodore Parker, a distinguished Boston clergyman, described the aims of the reformers who kept the country in a turmoil for a whole generation: They looked to a society

> full of industry and abundance, full of wisdom, virtue, and the poetry of life; a state with unity among all, with freedom for each; a church without tyranny, a society without ignorance, want, or crime, a state without oppression; yes, a world with no war among the nations to consume the work of their hands, and no restrictive policy to hinder the welfare of mankind.

The goals of this perfectionist program, the reformers believed, were not only attainable but could be achieved without violent upheaval. There existed in America, one of them explained, "abundant elements for progress, and a field of action comparatively free from those obstacles which so impede reform elsewhere." Other countries might have to resort to violence in order to overthrow tyranny, but here "the better course of effecting reform by moral and intellectual means is more trustingly expected." The proper agencies of reform were the churches and benevolent societies, rather than revolutionary movements or even political parties. To be sure, some clergymen frowned on the crusaders, but many of them thought it their proper function to help realize the promise of American life by advancing the cause of reform.

The Religious Background

The Decline of Orthodox Calvinism Tocqueville believed that there was "no country in the world where the Christian religion retains a greater influence over the souls of men than in America." Certainly the Americans of the first half of the nineteenth century were still deeply religious, and the church was still a powerful force in their lives. But the various Protestant sects, especially those which had been based on Calvinist theology, had gone through some critical times during the century since the Great Awakening and Jonathan Edwards' stout defense of orthodoxy. By the start of the nineteenth century many of the Puritan dogmas— predestination, infant damnation, and the total depravity of man—had already been rejected, or at least qualified, by a more liberal theology that replaced Calvin's God of wrath with a benevolent God of love. The conservatives fought back: they admonished the faithful to "guard against the insidious encroachments of innovation—that evil and beguiling spirit which is now stalking to and fro in the earth, seeking whom it may devour." But this was no more than a rear-guard action.

Even in the eighteenth century certain heresies had begun to trouble the minds of a few New England clergymen: Arminianism, which raised doubts about some of the tenets of Calvinism and eventually became the theology of the Methodists; Arianism, which questioned the divinity of Christ; and Socinianism, which rejected both the Trinity and predestination. These early challenges were fortified by the rationalism of the Enlightenment and the more optimistic view of human nature expressed by the philosophers of the American and French Revolutions. Respect for the dignity of the individual, confidence in man's capacity to improve himself, and belief in the idea of progress led to a decline in otherworldliness and a growing interest in temporal affairs. Life on earth, according to this new view, was not a mere preparation for the hereafter, at best a kind of winnowing of the saved from the damned; rather, it had its own beauty and value.

These intellectual trends caused orthodox Calvinism to give way to a theology that was at once more rational and more humanistic. Many leaders of the Revolutionary generation, such as Jefferson and Franklin, withdrew from the established churches and became deists. Deism, which originated in Europe in the early eighteenth century, rejected the Trinity, the divinity of Christ, the idea of original sin, and the Bible as divine revelation. It held that God had created the universe but had then withdrawn to let it run by natural laws. The humanistic implications of deism were evident in Thomas Paine's *The Age of Reason*: "I believe in the equality of man, and I believe that religious duties consist in doing justice, loving mercy, and endeavoring to make our fellow creatures happy." Paine accepted the creed of no church; indeed, he described the established churches as "human inventions set up to terrify and enslave mankind and monopolize power and profit." But few intellectuals were prepared to carry rationalism this far, and most church leaders saw no difference between deism and atheism.

Unitarianism In the long run those who worked for a liberalized theology within the churches had a broader influence than the freethinkers who deserted organized Christianity entirely. These liberalizers rebelled especially against the deterministic Calvinist doctrine of salvation only for the elect in favor of the more hopeful doctrine of free will and salvation open to all. The revolt against traditional Calvinism produced several new sects, including the Universalists and Campbellites (Disciples of Christ), and a division of the Presbyterians into Old and New Lights. But

William Ellery Channing: The adoration of goodness.

the largest and most influential of the organized religious groups produced by eighteenth-century rationalism and humanism was the Unitarian Church. An offshoot of Congregationalism, it appealed chiefly to the better-educated and more affluent descendants of the New England Puritans. It showed its greatest vitality and grew most vigorously in the early decades of the nineteenth century. Unitarians, as their name indicates, did not believe in the Trinity—Jesus was mortal, the founder of a great religion but not the son of God. They denied that man was conceived in sin or that he was totally depraved; rather, he was by nature good. God was a merciful and loving Father, not a vindictive and arbitrary deity who predestined the mass of mankind to damnation. Unitarians were skeptical of fine-spun theological systems and urged each individual to search the Scriptures for truth. And once he had found it, he must not pervert it into dogma to be imposed on others. Instead, Unitarians preached tolerance of differences among sincerely devout men.

William Ellery Channing (1780–1842), pastor of the Federal Street Church in Boston, was the most eminent Unitarian clergyman of the early nineteenth century. Channing stressed the primary responsibility of man to his own conscience and helped to link the liberal Unitarian creed with humanitarianism. To him the essence of religion was "the adoration of goodness." Since he believed in the excellence of man and denied original sin, Channing found the doctrine of atonement preposterous—it was as if "the Creator, in order to pardon his own children, had erected a gallows in the centre of the universe, and had publicly executed upon it . . . an Infinite Being, the partaker of his own Supreme Divinity." Channing supported humanitarian reform, "because I have learned the essential equality of men before the common Father, . . . because I see in him a great nature, the divine image, and vast capacities." In Channing, Unitarianism found its ideal leader, for he balanced its rationalism and tolerance with humanistic warmth and active concern for the welfare of mankind.

The Transcendentalists   In the course of time, however, Unitarianism began to crystallize into a new orthodoxy. The church's well-fed members, though more reasonable and tolerant than their Puritan ancestors, became at least as smug; though given to philanthropy, they were free to pursue individual gain with far less restraint. Unitarianism struck a growing number of New England intellectuals as distressingly cold, formal, and passionless, and its communicants as more concerned with material than with spiritual well-being. Moreover, eighteenth-century rationalism, the foundation of Unitarianism, was succumbing to a romantic movement that was associated with the German philosophers Immanuel Kant and Georg Wilhelm Friedrich Hegel, and with the British men of letters Samuel Coleridge, Thomas Carlyle, and William Wordsworth. The romanticists rejected experience and pure reason as the keys to truth and substituted for them intuition, or spiritual insight, which they believed gave man knowledge that he could not derive through his senses.

During the 1830's, a small group of intellectuals living in and around Concord, Massachusetts, met at the home of the former Unitarian minister, Ralph Waldo Emerson, to exchange ideas about philosophy and theology.

In addition to Emerson, this distinguished group included, at one time or another, clergymen such as Theodore Parker, George Ripley, and James Freeman Clark; literary figures such as Henry Thoreau, Amos Bronson Alcott, Nathaniel Hawthorne, and Orestes Brownson; and talented women such as Margaret Fuller and Elizabeth Peabody. The Concord neighbors of this little band of idealists, in good-natured amusement, began to refer to them as the Transcendental Club. The members of the club were appalled by the crass materialism of a country preoccupied with economic development and were concerned that spiritual progress was not keeping pace. They were too individualistic and too hostile to institutional restraints to start a church of their own, but the philosophy of transcendentalism was shot through with theological implications. It was clearly an outgrowth of Puritanism and Unitarianism (with a touch of Quakerism and oriental mysticism) as well as of romanticism.

The transcendentalists, like the Unitarians, rejected Calvinist dogma and hopefully believed in man's essential goodness and in a God of love. But their idealism was warm and affirmative, not the bland concoction of "pale negations" that Emerson found so unsatisfying in Unitarianism. As Theodore Parker explained, transcendentalists held that man has "faculties which give him ideas and intuitions which transcend sensational experience; ideas whose origin is not from sensation, nor their proof from sensation." The mind of man "is not a smooth tablet on which sensation writes its experience, but is a living principle which of itself originates ideas." Moreover, God dwells in every man, and human nature, therefore, is not simply excellent but divine. Since the transcendentalists discovered no evil in the mind of man and had faith in his intuitive knowledge of right and justice, they urged everyone to follow his conscience even if he was thus driven to defy church or state. "To know what is right," said Parker, "I need not ask what is the current practice, what say the Revised Statutes, what said holy men of old, but what says conscience? what, God?" The transcendental belief that God, or the Over-

soul, permeated both matter and spirit, that man had in him a spark of divinity, and that his potentialities were limitless had several consequences. It led to a celebration of individualism and self-reliance and to an admiration of men who had the strength and confidence to strike out on their own. It produced, too, a rather naïve faith that in the long run everything would turn out well. As Emerson wrote: "An eternal beneficent necessity is always bringing things right. . . . The league between virtue and nature engages all things to assume a hostile front to vice."

But although the transcendentalists were optimists, they did not ignore the shortcomings of American society or wait complacently for an inevitable progress to produce the remedies. Instead, they were severe critics of governments, laws, social institutions, and debasing commercialism—whatever prevented man from realizing his full potential. "Their quarrel with every man they meet," said Emerson, "is not with his kind, but with his degree." Hence the transcendentalists, though they were not given to organizing or joining reform societies, nonetheless contributed to the intellectual climate of reform. Emerson asked, "What is man born for but to be a Reformer, a Re-

Emerson, Hawthorne, and Thoreau:
A hostile front to vice.

maker of what man has made; a renouncer of lies; a restorer of truth and good, imitating that great Nature which embosoms us all, and which sleeps no moment on an old past, but every hour repairs herself, yielding to us every morning a new day, and with every pulsation a new life?''

The Protestant Sects and Revivalism
If Unitarianism was too cold, transcendentalism was too intellectual (and perhaps too cheerful) to attract a large following. Most Americans remained in the Congregational, Presbyterian, Baptist, and Methodist churches or joined one of the numerous evangelical sects that proliferated in the nineteenth century. Even at the popular level, however, the hard tenets of orthodox Calvinism began to soften. Devout Protestants continued to believe in man's sinful condition, but they accepted the doctrine of a benevolent God who offered all men the chance of salvation through the experience of spiritual conversion and through faith. Moreover, the material opportunities that lay before Americans in a growing and flourishing society discouraged otherworldliness and tempted them to expect virtue to be rewarded on earth as well as in heaven.

Even so, much of orthodoxy still survived in the religion of the common man. In his cosmology, the Copernican revolution in astronomy notwithstanding, the earth was still the center of the universe; and God continued to be actively and intimately involved in the affairs of man. The ordinary churchgoer still believed in the Trinity, in the Bible as divine revelation, and in a literal heaven and hell. He might doubt man's total depravity, but he could never accept the transcendentalist's extreme optimism about human nature. For the reality of evil in the world was too manifest, human frailty in the face of temptation too obvious. The continued prevalence of endemic and epidemic diseases, and the resulting short life expectancy and high infant mortality, made the average man acutely conscious, sometimes almost obsessed, with the imminence of death. This awareness helps explain the persistence of a measure of gloom and pessimism in his outlook on life; it intensified his religious fervor and turned him to the church for solace.

With few exceptions, notably the Quakers, the various Protestant sects actively proselytized those who were seeking comfort and salvation. Some sects had greater success than others. After the Revolution the Protestant

Episcopal Church, formerly the Anglican Church, was discredited by the fact that much of its clergy had been Loyalist; it grew only slowly, appealing mostly to well-to-do Eastern conservatives. The Congregationalists of New England lost members to the Unitarians. In the newly settled regions of the West they joined with the Presbyterians, in 1801, to adopt a Plan of Union, by which they agreed to establish united churches which might select either Congregational or Presbyterian ministers. In the long run the Plan of Union benefited the Presbyterians, because most of the united churches entered their fold. Although the Presbyterians thus experienced a considerable growth, they were far surpassed by two other Protestant denominations. One of these, the Baptists, had phenomenal success with their system of autonomous congregations and with an untrained, uneducated clergy that spoke the language of the common man. Their ministers brought a primitive but passionate message of hell-fire for sinners and redemption for those who experienced conversion and admitted God into their souls. The second, and most successful of all, were the Methodists, each of whose itinerant ministers rode a circuit of several congregations in the scattered settlements of the West and preached an equally simple Christianity.

After the Great Awakening of the mid-eighteenth century, revivalism became a periodic phenomenon. During these interludes of religious enthusiasm Presbyterians, Baptists, and Methodists won new converts by the thousands. In the course of the Second Awakening, which began around 1800, the religious frenzy spread with increasing intensity from east to west. An innovation of this revival was the camp meeting, which brought crowds together for several days of uninterrupted preaching and prayers. Under the emotional influence of exhorters who called for repentance, many experienced conversion. Since the battle with Satan was often violent, a familiar spectacle at the camp meetings was the jumping, shouting, and moaning of tortured souls. When the battle had been won and Satan put to rout, as one witness observed, "hundreds were prostrate upon the earth before the Lord."

The 1820's witnessed still another period of revivalism, but this time many of its leaders combined a desire to save souls with an active interest in social reform. The greatest preacher of this revival was the Reverend Charles G. Finney, who gathered his first harvest of converts from the fertile soil of upstate New York, a land of transplanted New Englanders. Finney preached not only salvation through faith but the importance of good works and the obligation of the churches to take "right ground . . . on all the subjects of practical morality which come up for decision from time to time." To him original sin was a "deep-seated but voluntary . . . self-interest. . . . All sin consists in selfishness; and all holiness or virtue, in disinterested benevolence." Salvation was not the end but the beginning of life—a life of useful work and benevolent activity. Since Finney's doctrine, as one contemporary observed, encouraged mankind "to *work* as well as to *believe*," Finney became a powerful influence for social reform. In addition to winning the support of many established preachers, he sent out a remarkable group of young converts to advance his work, notably Theodore Dwight Weld, who went into the West to preach and to advance the cause of moral reform.

In 1830 Finney brought his revival to New York City, which he regarded as carrying the Gospel into the precincts of hell itself. Here he met two remarkable brothers, Arthur and Lewis Tappan, wealthy merchants and pious men who were already devoting most of their energy and fortunes to philanthropy. The Tappans welcomed Finney and organized an Association of Gentlemen to give financial support to both his religious and reform work. Lewis Tappan, once a Unitarian, had become dissatisfied with that faith and had moved not toward transcendentalism but back to evangelical Protestantism. He had concluded, he explained, that the Unitarians "did not, in an equal degree, consider themselves as stewards, and their property as consecrated to the cause of Christianity; and that they were deficient in a devotional frame of mind."

Religion thus encouraged reform in two different but parallel trends. First, the transcendentalists celebrated the divinity of man and called on him to trust his conscience in his quest for right and justice. Thoreau wrote: "It is not desirable to cultivate a respect for the law, so much as for the right. The only obligation which I have a right to assume is to do

at any time what I think right." Second, the evangelical Protestantism of the revivalists made good works a manifestation of holiness and of the experience of conversion, and reform a vital function of the churches. "And what is to reform mankind but the truth?" asked Finney. "And who shall present the truth if not the church and the ministry? Away with the idea that Christians can remain neutral and keep still, and yet enjoy the approbation and blessing of God."

The Movement for Reform

The Nature of the Movement William Ellery Channing observed that one of the remarkable circumstances of his age was "the energy with which the principle of combination, or of action by joint forces, by associated numbers, is manifesting itself. It may be said, without much exaggeration, that everything is done now by Societies. . . . You can scarcely name an object for which some institution has not been formed." Though the benevolent societies were numerous, there was a considerable overlapping of both leaders and members. Active reformers tended to be attracted to several causes, and the same names appeared repeatedly among the directors of the various reform organizations.

The reformers, for a variety of reasons, were severely criticized by their conservative contemporaries, and have been treated unsympathetically by some historians as well. In the first place, as a leading reformer himself noted, there is a "tendency of every reform to surround itself with a fringe of the unreasonable and half-cracked"; and the reformers had within their ranks a full quota of cranks whose bizarre crusades exposed the whole movement to ridicule. Some devoted their energies to stopping the wearing of corsets; others to food fads, such as the eating of whole-wheat bread; and still others to the "science" of phrenology. Reformers were accused, too, of being more concerned with denouncing evil than with advancing constructive remedies. Their movement, it has been said, was a vehicle for righteous men to assert their righteousness—for teetotalers to deplore the use of alcohol, and for the virtuous to denounce immorality. Moreover, as Emerson complained, many of them were "narrow, self-pleasing, conceited men" given to petty bickering and "personal and party heats." They often exhibited an uncompromising inflexibility that made them unattractive as human beings and ineffective in striving toward their own goals.

From the perspective of the twentieth century, these reformers have also been criticized for their naïve optimism about human nature and for their confidence that social problems could be solved simply by exposing them and by appealing to the innate goodness in man. In addition, most of them were blind to the problems of urban factory workers. Reform leaders usually came from the old middle-class families of rural and small-town New England; their social backgrounds and economic assumptions made them singularly insensitive to conditions in the growing industrial centers—or prone to blame the plight of the workingman on his use of liquor and tobacco. Indeed, it has been suggested that in a sense they were themselves victims of the Industrial Revolution. Belonging to families that in the past had been accustomed to social recognition and leadership in public affairs, they were now losing status and being displaced by the rising merchants and manufacturers. Presumably the discontent provoked by their loss of prestige found an outlet in movements for reform. This psychological interpretation can be neither proved nor disproved, but the dislocations of a period of economic growth and social change undoubtedly contributed to the reform impulse.

Though the shortcomings of the reformers were real enough, the whole crusade cannot be written off as an enterprise of impractical, shortsighted cranks and neurotics. There were in the ranks of reform many dedicated men and women who demonstrated a keen understanding of some of the social problems of their day. Their goals were noble, their accomplishments far from negligible. If the reformers were a trial to their friends it was in part because their work, by its very nature, forced them to "disregard the peace and proprieties of the social world." Each reformer seemed to bear a burden of personal guilt for the evils in his society and felt driven to do something to eliminate them. This sense of individual responsibility, which can easily be lost in a mass society,

was in itself a thing of inestimable value.

Treatment of Criminals and the Insane Humane and sensitive men and women who investigated the care of paupers, criminals, and the insane in their own communities found an ample field for reform. These social derelicts, the victims of public ignorance or indifference, were treated almost as they had been in the Middle Ages. In atrocious jails and dungeons young offenders were thrown together with hardened criminals and the violently insane; in neglected almshouses idiots and the destitute were left to the mercy of low-paid, untrained attendants. Humanitarians managed at least to start the painfully slow process of providing prisons with better physical accommodations. With their more enlightened approach to penology, they urged, with some success, that the community concentrate on reforming, rather than punishing, criminals. Meanwhile, the states, one by one, responded to the new spirit by abolishing several vestiges of primitive justice: the imprisonment of debtors, public floggings, and public executions.

Since little was known about the causes of insanity, or about therapy, society provided almost no mental hospitals; the insane were either cared for by relatives or committed to jails and almshouses. Among those who took an interest in the treatment of the insane, Dorothea Dix, a Boston schoolmistress, was the most active advocate of state-supported mental hospitals and of experiments in therapy. In 1841 she launched her crusade by investigating the condition of the insane in her own state. Two years later, she presented the legislature with an eloquent but factual memorial which described "the present state of insane persons confined in this Commonwealth, in cages, closets, cellars, stalls, pens! Chained, naked, beaten with rods, and lashed into obedience." Until her death in 1887 she worked with tireless patience to arouse public officials throughout the country, and her sincerity and command of the facts won her considerable success.

Temperance Concern for criminals, paupers, and the insane was intimately related to another goal of the reform movement: temperance. It was commonly believed that excessive drinking was a basic cause for the condition of these unfortunates, as well as for the poverty that plagued city workers. Temperance, therefore, would not merely redeem the individual sinner but would advance the whole program of social reform. That drunkenness was a genuine problem there can be no doubt, for this was an age of heavy drinking in which the per capita consumption of whiskey, hard cider, and rum was staggering. The temperance movement began with the formation of numerous local societies which, in 1826, combined to form a national organization, the American Society for the Promotion of Temperance. Some leaders merely preached moderation in the use of liquor, but others sought converts who would pledge total abstinence. Some relied on the voluntary decisions of individuals; others urged the use of the coercive power of state governments. In 1846 Maine passed the first prohibition law; within the next decade a dozen other Northern and Western states followed Maine's example, but most of these laws remained in force for only a few years. At its height the temperance movement resembled a religious revival; its flavor is suggested by a stanza from one of its popular songs, "One Glass More":

> Stay, mortal, stay! nor heedless thus
>   Thy sure destruction seal;
> Within that cup there lurks a curse,
>   Which all who drink shall feel.
> Disease and death forever nigh,
>   Stand ready at the door,
> And eager wait to hear the cry—
>   "O give me one glass more!"

Women's Rights Women took a special interest in temperance, but when they tried to participate actively in this or other reform movements they confronted a wall of prejudice and the rebuff that woman's place was in the home. American men characteristically treated women with deference, but few would accept them as equals. Woman's inferiority was sanctioned by laws recognizing the husband as the dominant figure in the family and even giving him control over the property his wife brought to the marriage. Except for female seminaries where the daughters of the well-to-do could learn the social graces, schools were closed to girls. Women were excluded from the professions. They could neither vote nor hold public office. Indeed, it was considered unfeminine for them even to speak in public places or to offer prayers in church. In 1840 a group of American women, including Elizabeth Cady Stanton and Lucretia Mott, went as delegates to a World Antislavery Convention in London, but they were denied the right to participate. This and similar experiences provoked a women's rights movement which became at once an integral part of the general reform crusade and a divisive issue among male reformers, some of whom favored and some of whom opposed permitting women to join their organizations.

In 1848 the first Women's Rights Convention was held at Seneca Falls, New York. Here the delegates adopted a statement which paraphrased the Declaration of Independence and proclaimed that "all men and women are created equal." The history of mankind, it said, "is a history of repeated injuries and usurpations on the part of man toward woman, having in direct object the establishment of an absolute tyranny over her." After listing women's specific grievances, the statement closed with a demand that women "have immediate admission to all the rights and privileges which belong to them as citizens of the United States."

In the years before the Civil War, the women of the United States did make some limited gains. A few states gave married women control over their own property, and everywhere one profession, elementary education, was opened to them. They secured admission to a few high schools and normal schools, and in 1833 Oberlin College became the first coeducational institution of higher learning. But most important was the example set by a courageous group of women who defied prejudice and played an active and constructive role in public affairs. Dorothea Dix, as we have seen, contributed to improved treatment of the insane; Dr. Elizabeth Blackwell won distinction as a physician; Margaret Fuller for a time edited the transcendentalist journal, *The Dial*, and then served as literary editor of the New York *Tribune;* Emma Willard campaigned for educational reform; Lucy Stone was a popular lecturer as well as a crusader for equal suffrage; and a small host of women, notably Frances Wright, Elizabeth Cady Stanton, and Lucretia Mott, worked to abolish slavery. Most men (and more than a few women) sneered at these "unsexed" women, citing Mrs. Amelia Bloomer's wearing of pantalettes as evidence of where it would all end. But the feminists had effectively challenged the myth that women were physically and intellectually unfitted for any useful activity outside the home.

Education   The reform movement revealed its debt to Jacksonian Democracy, and the reformers their concern for the welfare of the common man, in the crusade for free, tax-supported public education. In the early nineteenth century, except in Massachusetts, the children of the poor obtained their elementary education at home or in church or charity schools, and the children of the rich in private schools or from tutors. The lack of public support, together with the fact that most teaching was done by low-paid, untrained young men who regarded it as a temporary occupation, left a mass of people, both urban and rural, in a state of semiliteracy. In the two decades after 1830 the crucial battle to establish public responsibility for elementary education was fought and won, though in many states it took much longer for the idea to be translated into reality.

Opposition came from those who considered education a private concern, from taxpayers who objected to paying for the education of other people's children, and from religious groups that maintained their own schools. Support came from practical men in an increasingly commercial society where more and more occupations required the ability to read, write, and cipher. It came, too, from those who believed that mass education was essential to a political system based on manhood suffrage. Further support came from those who viewed public education as a means of providing the common man with better opportunities to advance. They hoped thus to achieve a more general diffusion of property ownership and a softening of class lines. In 1848, Horace Mann, in one of his celebrated reports as secretary of the Massachusetts Board of Education, noted the alarming contrasts of wealth and poverty in his state; he maintained that "nothing but Universal Education can counterwork this tendency to the domination of capital and the servility of labor." Educate

the workingman, and he will improve his position and acquire property, for "such a thing never did happen, and never can happen, as that an intelligent and practical body of men should be permanently poor." Education, Mann concluded, "is the great equalizer of the conditions of men—the balance wheel of the social machinery. . . . It does better than to disarm the poor of their hostility toward the rich; it prevents being poor." The city workers themselves made state-supported education one of their prime demands. A resolution adopted by the mechanics of Philadelphia in 1830 declared "that there can be no real liberty without a wide diffusion of real intelligence; . . . that until means of equal instruction shall be equally secured to all, liberty is but an unmeaning word, and equality an empty shadow."

By the 1850's the states were committed to making tax-supported public education available to all without the stigma of charity. Some of the states had already passed laws requiring local communities to establish elementary schools, and most of the others had at least required that when schools were established they must admit all children, not just those able to pay tuition. One of the decisive battles was fought in Pennsylvania, where in 1834 a state school law was passed. But opposition to the law was so formidable that the legislature seemed ready to repeal it in favor of one providing free education only for the poor. After a bitter struggle, the law was saved largely through the efforts of a young Whig legislator, Thaddeus Stevens, whose brilliant defense of free education carried the day. Similar battles were fought and won in other states. As a result, outside the South, where the movement was impeded by rural conditions and the indifference of the planter class, a steadily growing number of children found free public schools available to them.

But this was only the beginning, for compulsory-attendance laws had not yet been passed, school terms were short, the curriculum was thin, and teaching methods were still based on rote memorization and corporal punishment. Massachusetts led the way in remedying these conditions in 1837 by establishing a state Board of Education, with Horace Mann as secretary. Mann had devoted many years to teaching and the study of education, and during his eleven years as secretary his annual reports made him the most influential man in the public-school movement. In Massachusetts he did much to improve the curriculum and teaching methods, lengthen the school year, raise teachers' salaries, establish the first state-supported normal school for teacher training, and organize a state association of teachers. Other states appointed their own boards or superintendents of education who tried, with varying degrees of success, to achieve similar reforms.

For most American children formal education ceased after a few years in an elementary school. Secondary education was limited to those who could afford to pay the tuition to a private academy, where, in preparation for college, they took courses in mathematics, rhetoric, and the classics. In 1827 Massachusetts passed a law requiring every town of five hundred or more families to set up a public high school, and the other New England states soon followed suit. But as late as 1860 there were only slightly more than three hundred public high schools in the United States, with almost a third of them in Massachusetts and only a scattering in the South and West.

In higher education, which was less influenced by reform, the most notable development was the proliferation of private denominational colleges throughout the country. In the two decades between 1830 and 1850 about eighty of these colleges were founded. Most of them had poor endowments, small student bodies, and incompetent faculties; but every village seemed determined to have a college, and every religious sect seemed determined to have a network of colleges to train its clergy and indoctrinate its youth. The idea of state-supported institutions of higher learning was an old one, and four states (Vermont, North Carolina, Georgia, and Tennessee) chartered them in the late eighteenth century. The first one actually to win academic distinction, however, was the University of Virginia, which opened its doors in 1825. By the 1850's numerous state universities, most of them in the South and West, had been founded, but few were more than small colleges limping along on slender budgets. Both state and private colleges offered a traditional liberal-arts curricu-

lum which stressed Latin, Greek, science, mathematics, moral philosophy, and political economy. True universities in the European sense, with professional schools, graduate teaching, and emphasis on scholarly research, did not emerge until after the Civil War. Too many colleges were founded during these years, and few of them had the libraries and scholars they needed to become centers of creative intellectual life. The idea of academic freedom, moreover, had few defenders, and countless instructors fell victim to the political and sectarian controversies of the age.

Since the colleges served only a tiny fraction of the population, the mass of adults with a thirst for learning searched for other and more accessible avenues to cultural advancement. The "penny press," which began in 1833 when the New York *Sun* went on sale at a penny a copy, put newspapers within the reach of everyone and served up a mixed fare of sensationalism, news, and essays on practical and scientific subjects. Hundreds of magazines catered to all tastes, but the best of them offered essays, poetry, and fiction by the most distinguished European and American writers. This was an era of organized efforts for self-improvement, and most communities had their debating societies, literary societies, and library associations. The lyceum movement, a nationally organized program of adult education initiated in 1826 by a New Englander, Josiah Holbrook, was the most ambitious of these enterprises. The original plan was to encourage local lyceums to assemble libraries, study scientific subjects, and form discussion groups, but most of them soon concentrated on lecture courses. Though many a fraud and charlatan managed to get on the lyceum lecture circuit, men of letters such as Emerson and Charles Dickens, scientists such as Harvard's Louis Agassiz, and a host of reformers made the program a useful instrument of mass education.

The Peace Movement   Reformers not content with the piecemeal alleviation of domestic social ills turned to more ambitious projects, such as the cause of world peace. Remembering the dreadful suffering and waste of the Napoleonic wars, some reformers were attracted to the pacifist principles of the Quakers, or at least hoped to find nonviolent ways of settling international disputes. Local peace societies, which had begun to appear soon after the War of 1812, united in 1828 to form the American Peace Society. William Ladd, the Maine merchant who founded the national organization, proposed the formation of a Congress of Nations to interpret international law and a Court of Nations to apply it. Most peace men, however, distinguished between the use of force for aggressive and for defensive purposes and condemned only the former. In 1838 the peace movement split when the "ultraists," headed by Henry Clark Wright and William Lloyd Garrison, formed a Non-Resistance Society committed to oppose violence even in self-defense. Their constitution denounced military service, forceful resistance to tyranny, capital punishment, and actions at law for civil damages. This millennial program was designed to put Christian precepts into immediate action—to prepare the way "for the full manifestation of the reign of Christ on earth." It would secure "the reconciliation and salvation of a warring and lost world."

Communitarianism　　Other perfectionists worked for the complete regeneration of society by building model communities which they hoped would form the nuclei of a better social order. Early communitarian projects

had been undertaken by several small religious sects, such as the Shakers, with the goal of achieving holiness through a form of Christian communism. In 1825 Robert Owen, a Scottish textile manufacturer and philanthropist, established the first significant nonreligious communitarian enterprise at New Harmony, Indiana. Owen hoped to abolish poverty and crime through cooperative labor and the collective ownership of property, but within two years New Harmony proved an economic failure. Communitarianism reached its peak during the 1840's when the ideas of the French reformer, Charles Fourier, were embraced by many transcendentalists and popularized by his chief American champion, Albert Brisbane. The transcendentalists were attracted by Fourier's optimistic view of human nature, his goal of social harmony, and his plan of voluntary associations, or "phalanxes," free of governmental intervention. Association, explained the idealistic Brisbane, offered "the means of effecting peaceably and in the interest of all classes, a complete transformation in the social condition of the world." The successful establishment of only one association, he believed, would inspire men to form others. At last the movement would become universal, and there would emerge "a true Social and Po-

New Harmony, 1831.

litical Order in the place of the old and false one." Of the many phalanxes that briefly put Fourier's ideas into practice, the best remembered was Brook Farm near Boston, founded in 1841 by George Ripley. Until its abandonment in 1847 a number of transcendentalists repaired to it, as Ripley explained, "to prepare a society of liberal, intelligent, and cultivated persons" who could lead "a more simple and wholesome life, than can be led amidst the pressures of our competitive institutions."

Young Nathaniel Hawthorne was one of the transcendentalists who went to Brook Farm, but he left with doubts about the divinity of man and a conviction that the reformers did not understand the true source of evil in the world. "The heart, the heart," he wrote, "there was the little yet boundless sphere wherein existed the original wrong of which the crime and misery of this outward world were merely types." His caution to the perfectionists is perhaps more understandable to our generation than it was to his: "The progress of the world, at every step, leaves some evil or wrong on the path behind it, which the unrest of mankind, or their own set purpose, could never have found the way to rectify."

The Crusade Against Slavery

The Beginnings of Abolitionism In Boston on January 1, 1831, William Lloyd Garrison began publishing a weekly newspaper, *The Liberator*, dedicated to the immediate abolition of Southern Negro slavery without compensation to the masters. This event did not mark the beginning of the crusade against slavery, however, for organized activity, especially among the Quakers, dated back to the eighteenth century. Pressure from antislavery groups had already achieved the abolition of slavery in the Northern states, and in the 1820's a manumission movement in the Upper·South had called for gradual, compensated emancipation with colonization of the free Negroes in Africa. Benjamin Lundy, a New Jersey Quaker, organized local societies in Kentucky, Tennessee, North Carolina, and Virginia and at the same time edited an antislavery newspaper, *The Genius of Universal Emancipation*, in Baltimore. Garrison got his start writing for Lundy's paper, but he was a man of

William Lloyd Garrison: Harsh as truth.

different temperament who brought a new stridency and militancy to the attack. He set the tone for his crusade in the prospectus printed in the first issue of *The Liberator*:

I *will* be as harsh as truth, and as uncompromising as justice. On this subject, I do not wish to think, or speak, or write with moderation. . . . I am in earnest—I will not equivocate—I will not excuse—I will not retreat a single inch—AND I WILL BE HEARD.

In 1832 Garrison organized the New England Antislavery Society, and a year later helped to establish a national organization, the American Antislavery Society. During the next few years abolitionist agents were busy establishing local societies, until by 1840 a network of some two thousand of them with nearly two hundred thousand members stretched across the North. To many, Garrison was the embodiment of abolitionism, and the angry response of the South to his harsh words kept him in the public eye. But he was more an editor and publicist than a leader and tactician, and the movement soon grew too large for him to control. Other abolitionists were at least as important as Garrison: Wendell Phillips in New England, Gerrit Smith and the Tappans in New York, and Theodore Dwight Weld in the West. At length, in 1840, resentment against Garrison, disagreement over his effort to admit women to full participation, and differences over program caused a split in abolitionist ranks and led to the withdrawal of the anti-Garrisonians from the American Antislavery Society to form a society of their own. Thereafter abolitionism was only loosely organized at the national level, and the real force of the crusade came from the state and local groups.

By the end of the 1830's, for several reasons, abolitionism had become the most popular cause of the whole reform movement. Most of the reformers had come to agree that slavery was the greatest social evil in the way of the nation's moral regeneration. To prove its wickedness, the abolitionists dwelt on the cruelties of slavery, for they were always less interested in presenting a balanced picture than in winning converts. Slavery provided them with plenty of illustrations of cruelty. In 1839 Theodore Dwight Weld published a powerful abolitionist tract, *Slavery As It Is*, which was simply a documented compilation of incidents reported in Southern newspapers and court records. The Southern states made themselves especially vulnerable to criticism by failing to eliminate the system's worst abuses: its physical cruelty, its lack of legal recognition of slave marriages, the separation of children from their parents, and the callous practices of the interstate slave-traders.

Abolitionism also attracted Northern reformers because the Southern manumission societies had failed to accomplish their purpose; slavery, it appeared, would never be destroyed without intervention by the North. It no longer appeared to be a weak and declining institution that could be left to die a natural death; instead it was flourishing and spreading westward into new territories and states. The reformers were shocked by the Southerners' growing tendency to regard slavery as a desirable and permanent institution and by their increasingly harsh treatment of native Southern critics. One reformer expressed his dismay at "the sentiments openly expressed by the southern newspapers, that slavery is not an evil . . . [and] that it is criminal toward the South . . . to indulge even a hope that the chains of the captive may some day or other, no matter how remote the time, be broken." Moreover, the reformers were acutely conscious of the hypocrisy of America's posing as a model of liberal institutions while remaining one of the last countries in the western world to tolerate human bondage. Finally, the success of British abolitionists in securing emancipation in the British West Indies (1833) stimulated the reformers to undertake a similar crusade in America.

Abolitionist Tactics The tactics of the abolitionists were determined by their assumptions about human nature, by their belief in the power of truth, and by the political structure within which they had to operate. They were confronted with the problem that the federal Congress, unlike the British Parliament, had no constitutional power to interfere with slavery. At the same time, the pacifism of most abolitionists discouraged the use of force. In its statement of principles, the New England Antislavery Society affirmed that "we will not operate on the existing relations of society by other than peaceful and lawful means, and that we will give no countenance to violence or insurrection." Abolitionists, therefore, relied on "moral suasion." Their first goal was to persuade slaveholders that slavery was both a sin and a denial of the "unalienable rights" with which, according to the Declaration of Independence, all men are endowed. When the abolitionists failed to impress the slaveholders, when they found it nearly impossible to carry their message into the South, they turned to building up antislavery opinion in the North. Their propaganda hammered relentlessly at their central argument: every person of full age and sane mind has a right to freedom unless convicted of a crime; "mere difference of complexion is no reason why any man should be deprived of any of his natural rights"; "man cannot, consistently with reason, religion, and the eternal and immutable principles of justice, be the property of man"; "whoever retains his fellow-man in bondage is guilty of a grievous wrong." Abolitionists sometimes spoke of the alleged economic waste of slavery, but their indictment was chiefly moral and religious.

Whether moral suasion might be supplemented by some form of political action was a question on which abolitionists differed. Garrison's nonresistance principles turned him against government as an instrument of force and therefore against involvement in politics. Moreover, he viewed the political parties as tools of the slaveholders, the Union as their protector, and the Constitution as a proslavery document (in his words, "a covenant with death and an agreement with hell"). Most abolitionists, however, though recognizing that Congress could not touch slavery in the states, believed that some things might be accomplished through political action—for example, the abolition of slavery in the District of Columbia, the outlawing of the interstate slave trade, and the exclusion of slavery from federal territories. Hence they took an active part in politics and put pressure on congressional candidates to take antislavery positions. In 1840 a group of political abolitionists organized the Liberty party and nominated James G. Birney for the presidency, but the small vote the party attracted in this and subsequent elections indicated that most abolitionists preferred to operate through existing parties. With the growth of political abolitionism there was a notable decline in pacifist sentiment, and the sectional conflict of the 1850's prepared many abolitionists to turn from moral suasion to force as the ultimate remedy.

Another issue that divided abolitionists was the proper interpretation of the term "immediate emancipation." Abolitionists were, by definition, "immediatists"—slaveholding was a sin, and moral men could not advocate abandoning it gradually. To the Garrisonians immediate emancipation meant exactly what the term implied: slavery should be totally eradicated at once. But the majority of abolitionists took what they considered to be a more realistic position. They believed that the actual implementation of emancipation might take a little time, because there would probably have to be a period of transition while the Negroes were being prepared for their new status as freemen. Their definition of immediatism, therefore, was a program of emancipation "promptly commenced" but "gradually accomplished." Even Garrison once admitted privately that though he demanded immediate abolition, "it will, alas, be gradual abolition in the end. We have never said that slavery would

be overthrown by a single blow: that it ought to be, we shall always contend." But the theoretical immediatism to which abolitionists were committed strengthened the conviction of indignant Southerners that they were reckless incendiaries seeking to bring ruin upon the South.

During the 1830's most Northerners, too, regarded the abolitionists as irresponsible fanatics, and antislavery meetings were frequently broken up by violence. In 1834 a mob invaded Lewis Tappan's house and destroyed the furnishings; in 1835 a Boston mob treated Garrison so roughly that authorities took him to jail for his own protection; and in 1837 a mob in Alton, Illinois, murdered Elijah Lovejoy, an abolitionist editor. Northern businessmen, viewing antislavery agitation as a threat to their profitable trade with the South, more than once joined or encouraged the mobs. Race prejudice was nearly as intense in the North as in the South, and Northern free Negroes were subjected to many forms of discrimination. They were excluded from most trades and professions and forced into menial occupations; they were barred from the public schools or sent to segregated schools; they were assigned segregated seats in white churches and on public transportation; they were denied the ballot except in four New England states and in New York (where they had to meet a property qualification not required of whites); and they were prohibited from settling in several Western states. Even some of the abolitionists were unable to free themselves entirely from the prevailing prejudice and shrank from personal contacts with Negroes; but as a group their racial attitudes were so liberal that their contemporaries often denounced them as "nigger-lovers."

A Broadening Appeal Though abolitionists had only limited success in reducing Northern prejudice against Negroes, the growing sectional tension of the 1840's and 1850's caused Northerners to listen more sympathetically to what they had to say about the evils of slavery. Eventually abolitionist agitation helped to persuade the great majority of Northerners that slavery was morally wrong and therefore could not be accepted as a permanent institution. This agitation also produced an image of slaveholders as undemocratic, arrogant, immoral, cruel. The slave-holders and their political henchmen, said the abolitionists, formed a sinister "Slave Power" that ruled the South and conspired to rule the entire Union in order to destroy freedom. Theodore Parker described the Slave Power as

> the blight of this nation, the curse of the North and the curse of the South. . . . It confounds your politics. It has silenced your ablest men. It has muzzled the pulpit, and stifled the press. It has robbed three million men of what is dearer than life; it has kept back the welfare of seventeen million more.

Meanwhile, as the abolitionists braved mobs to defend freedom of assembly and of the press, they began to win admiration as champions of civil liberties not only for Negroes but for white men. They aroused sympathy when Southern mobs broke into post offices to seize and destroy packages of antislavery pamphlets, for now the right of minority groups to disseminate their ideas through the mails seemed to be at stake. In 1836, when the abolitionists deluged Congress with petitions urging the abolition of slavery in the District of Columbia, Southerners forced through the House a so-called gag rule which provided that petitions relating to slavery were to be laid on the table without being printed, referred to committee, or debated. Until the repeal of the gag rule in 1844, abolitionists stood as defenders of another sacred liberty: the right of petition.

Most Northerners also sympathized with the more or less systematic efforts of abolitionists to assist fugitive slaves to freedom along the routes of the "underground railroad." Few could help but feel compassion for the pathetic fugitive seeking his own liberty, and even a Negrophobe might resent the activities of the professional slave-catchers who roamed the free states. In 1842 an important case (*Prigg* v. *Pennsylvania*) involving the constitutionality of the fugitive slave act of 1793 came before the Supreme Court. Though the Court ruled that the act was constitutional, it conceded that a state might prohibit its own officers from helping to enforce it. Thereafter a number of states, under pressure from the abolitionists, adopted "personal liberty laws" which withheld assistance in the capture of fugitives.

On one issue—whether slavery should be introduced into new territories and states—the abolitionists eventually gained overwhelming Northern support. Northerners continued to agree that the Constitution prevented federal interference with slavery in the Southern states, but by the 1850's they were strongly of the opinion that slavery ought to be confined to its present limits. Often this sentiment sprang less from sympathy for the Negro than from a determination of free white farmers to keep slaveholders out of the territories they coveted. But the abolitionist indictment of slavery proved a handy weapon for them to use against Southern expansionists.

In one fundamental respect the abolitionist crusade was a failure. Since it did not convert the slaveholders, it never achieved its original goal: peaceful abolition through the triumph of truth over evil. But in another respect the crusade was a success. Though it was launched by pacifists, by 1861 abolitionism had armed the Northern population morally for the terrible struggle that lay ahead.

The Proslavery Argument

Slavery a Positive Good   In January 1837 Senator John C. Calhoun boldly took a position toward which many Southerners had been drifting:

> I hold that in the present state of civilization, where two races of different origin, and distinguished by color and other physical differences, as well as intellectual, are brought together, the relation now existing in the slaveholding states between the two is, instead of an evil, a good—a positive good.

There would be no more apologies—no concessions that slavery was at best a necessary evil—as Southern dialecticians spun out the arguments affirming the benign qualities of their peculiar institution. Never before had the justification of human bondage been presented with so much moral fervor and in such elaborate detail as in the ante-bellum South. Indeed the proslavery argument was one of the most impressive products of its intellectual life. Southern poets, theologians, moral philosophers, social theorists, jurists, and scientists combined their talents to uphold slavery and denounce heresy and radicalism.

This body of proslavery literature is significant not only because it was one of the principal contributions of Southern men of letters but because it was a rare expression in nineteenth-century America of deep pessimism about human nature, of doubt about the liberal tradition, and of skepticism about progress. One Southerner wrote with sarcasm:

No word in the English language is so much used as the dissyllable *progress*. In America we use it so much, that we have made a verb of it. This is an age of progress—a country of progress—a people of progress. Progress is synonymous with enlightenment, and he who falls into the rear rank, is considered recreant to the cause of civilization.

And yet, insisted another Southerner, "it cannot be denied that we must still look to antiquity for the noblest deeds and grandest thoughts that illustrate the race of men." Romanticism, which found expression in the North in the reform movement and in a remarkable burst of literary productivity, found expression in the South in a cult of chivalry and in the identification of the planter class with traditional aristocratic values.

The Nature of the Defense Since the average slaveholder was highly religious, a theological defense of slavery was fully developed and almost invariably incorporated in the numerous treatises on the subject. Out

"Sun of Intellectual light & liberty, stand ye still, in Masterly inactivity, that the Nation of Carolina may continue to hold Negroes & plant Cotton till the day of Judgment!"

Calhoun on slavery.

JOSHUA, COMMANDING THE SUN TO STAND STILL.

The negro slaves of the South are the happiest, and, in some sense, the freest people in the world. The children and the aged and infirm work not at all, and yet have all the comforts and necessaries of life provided for them. They enjoy liberty, because they are oppressed neither by care nor labor. The women do little hard work, and are protected from the despotism of their husbands by their masters. The negro men and stout boys work, on the average, in good weather, not more than nine hours a day.... Besides, they have their Sabbaths and holidays. White men, with so much of license and liberty, would die of ennui; but negroes luxuriate in corporeal and mental repose. With their faces upturned to the sun, they can sleep at any hour; and quiet sleep is the greatest of human enjoyments.... The free laborer must work or starve. He is more of a slave than the negro, because he works longer and harder for less allowance than the slave, and has no holiday, because the cares of life with him begin when its labors end. He has no liberty, and not a single right.

From George Fitzhugh, *Cannibals All!* 1857.

of the mass of scriptural arguments, three were of crucial importance. The first identified the Negroes as the descendants of Canaan, the son of Ham, of whom Noah said, "Cursed be Canaan; a servant of servants shall he be unto his brethren." The second pointed to Mosaic law, which authorized the Jews to make bondsmen "of the heathen that are round about you." The third noted that neither the prophets of the Old Testament nor Christ and his apostles ever condemned slavery. Rather, they repeatedly admonished servants to obey their masters and to submit to their earthly lot. The proper role of the church, therefore, was to bring spiritual salvation to the slaves and to urge benevolence on their masters.

Turning to history, the defenders argued that slavery had always existed in some form and that it had been the foundation of all the great civilizations of antiquity. Aristotle, whose thought permeates the proslavery argument, taught that in every organized society the men of superior talents would become masters over those of inferior talents. Slavery thus enabled a class to emerge that could devote its genius to art, literature, and other in-

tellectual pursuits. "It is a common remark," wrote George Fitzhugh of Virginia, "that the grand and lasting architectural structures of antiquity were the results of slavery."

Since Southern slaves were descended from Africans, proof that Africans were innately inferior to whites would presumably provide conclusive justification for the peculiar institution. By a curious combination of comparative anatomy and the pseudo-science of phrenology Southern ethnologists attributed to Negroes certain distinct physical and psychic traits which suggested their inferiority to the whites. In the Negro, claimed a Georgia doctor, "the animal parts of the brain preponderate over the moral and intellectual," which explains why he is "deficient in reason, judgment and forecast . . . thoughtless of the future, and contented and happy in the enjoyment of the mere animal pleasures of the present moment." The inevitable conclusion was that "nothing but arbitrary power can restrain the excesses of his animal nature: for he has not the power within himself." These and other alleged racial diversities established the master-slave relationship between whites and Negroes as a natural condition, its abo-

The slaves in the United States are treated with barbarous inhumanity;... they are overworked, underfed, wretchedly clad and lodged, and have insufficient sleep;... they are often made to wear round their necks iron collars armed with prongs, to drag heavy chains and weights at their feet while working in the field ...; they are often kept confined in the stocks day and night for weeks together, made to wear gags in their mouths for hours or days, have some of their front teeth torn out or broken off, that they may be easily detected when they run away;... they are frequently flogged with terrible severity, have red pepper rubbed into their lacerated flesh, and hot brine, spirits of turpentine, &c., poured over the gashes to increase the torture;... they are often stripped naked, their backs and limbs cut with knives, bruised and mangled by scores and hundreds of blows with the paddle, and terribly torn by the claws of cats, drawn over them by their tormentors.

From Theodore Dwight Weld, *Slavery As It Is,* 1839.

lition a profound disaster to both.

Belief in the Negro's inferiority led to the conclusion that the affirmations of the Declaration of Independence, the provisions of state bills of rights, and the benefits of citizenship did not and were not intended to apply to him. More, in its extreme form, the proslavery argument brought under attack the whole eighteenth-century philosophy of natural rights. Borrowing heavily from Edmund Burke and Thomas Carlyle, proslavery writers idealized a stable society in which men fell naturally into social gradations and enjoyed liberty only to the extent to which they could use it wisely. "It is a great and dangerous error to suppose that all people are equally entitled to liberty," said John C. Calhoun. Liberty had to be earned; it was "a reward reserved for the intelligent, the patriotic, the virtuous and deserving." Society must have a class "to perform the drudgery of life," affirmed James H. Hammond of South Carolina, a class "requiring but a low order of intellect," a class that "constitutes the very mud-sill of society." Boldly accepting a principle that Jefferson had passionately denied, George Fitzhugh proclaimed that "some were born with saddles on their backs, and others booted and spurred to ride them—and the riding does them good."

The South had found in slavery, argued its defenders, a way to avoid the dangers to order and property posed by the laboring classes in free society. Slavery served as a conservative bulwark against all the radical isms that threatened the North with revolution. "There are two kinds of labor, hireling labor and slave labor," explained a writer in the Charleston *Courier*. "The task of each is the same—continued hard work. The promised reward of each is the same also—subsistence." In the North and in Europe the hirelings were discontented; they clamored for change, for "communism, socialism, the organization of labor." In the South the slaves were "orderly and efficient," and society had within it no element of disharmony. "It is the only condition of society in which labor and capital are associated on a large scale in which their interests are combined and not in conflict. Every plantation is an organized community . . . where *all work*, where *each member gets subsistence and a home*." Slavery, in short, was a practical form of socialism.

In every respect, said Southern apologists, the slaves were better off than so-called free laborers. They were happy and contented, because they were well treated, well fed, well housed, and well clothed; they were cared for in childhood, in old age, and in times of sickness. The free labor system, which left the worker to shift for himself, was far more cruel and heartless. "I may say with truth," said Calhoun, "that in few countries so much is left to the share of the laborer, and so little exacted from him." Indeed, wrote a Virginian, "a merrier being does not exist on the face of the globe, than the Negro slave of the United States."

The endorsement of such ideas in the South at a time when a great reform movement was agitating the North produced an ideological conflict between the sections that threatened the survival of the Union. Slavery was no longer open to discussion in the South, and slaveholders intensely resented its denunciation on moral grounds in the North. Not even the two largest Protestant churches were able to bear the strain, and the slavery issue led to a split along sectional lines—the Methodists in 1844, the Baptists in 1845. Eventually the national political parties would also disintegrate, and thus another major institutional tie would be broken. Abolitionists and proslavery polemicists had raised a moral issue— the right and wrong of slavery—that stubbornly resisted the best efforts of a generation of able politicians and statesmen to resolve.

SUGGESTIONS FOR READING

Religion

The surveys of American cultural and intellectual history devote much space to religion in the first half of the nineteenth century. One of the earliest and most spirited of them, V. L. Parrington, *Main Currents in American Thought*,* 3 vols. (1927–30), though dated, is still decidedly worth reading. Among the good recent surveys are M. E. Curti, *The Growth*

* Available in a paperback edition.

of *American Thought* (rev. ed., 1951); R. H. Gabriel, *The Course of American Democratic Thought* (rev. ed., 1956); and Harvey Wish, *Society and Thought in Early America* (1950). Several useful general studies of American religion are available, among them W. W. Sweet, *The Story of Religion in America* (1920); H. K. Rowe, *The History of Religion in the United States* (1924); W. L. Sperry, *Religion in America* (1946); and J. W. Smith and A. L. Jamison, eds., *Religion in American Life*, 4 vols. (1961); Vol. III has not been completed. Alexis de Tocqueville, *Democracy in America*,* 2 vols. (1945), makes some interesting comments about religion and the American people.

The revolt against orthodox Calvinism can be traced in H. M. Morais, *Deism in Eighteenth Century America* (1934); Albert Post, *Popular Free Thought in America* (1943); Conrad Wright, *The Beginnings of Unitarianism in America* (1955); G. W. Cooke, *Unitarianism in America* (1902); and D. P. Edgell, *William Ellery Channing* (1955). Transcendentalism is examined in the surveys of American intellectual history cited above, and in two distinguished works on American literature covering this period: V. W. Brooks, *The Flowering of New England, 1815–1865* * (1936), and F. O. Matthiessen, *American Renaissance* (1941). Three other books worth consulting are: O. B. Frothingham, *Transcendentalism in New England* * (1876); H. C. Goddard, *New England Transcendentalism* (1908); and H. W. Schneider, *History of American Philosophy* (1946). There are good biographies of several transcendentalist leaders: H. S. Commager, *Theodore Parker: Yankee Crusader* * (1936); A. M. Schlesinger, Jr., *Orestes A. Brownson: A Pilgrim's Progress* (1939); J. W. Krutch, *Henry David Thoreau* (1948); and R. L. Lusk, *The Life of Ralph Waldo Emerson* (1949). Perry Miller, *The Transcendentalists* * (1950), is an excellent collection of transcendentalist writings.

A good survey of Protestant revivalism is W. W. Sweet, *Revivalism in America* (1944). Much valuable detail is added in W. R. Cross, *The Burned-Over District* (1950); C. A. Johnson, *The Frontier Camp Meeting* (1955); and B. A. Weisberger, *They Gathered at the River* (1958). Two important books tie revivalism to the reform movement: C. C. Cole, Jr., *The Social Ideals of the Northern Evangelists, 1826–1860* (1954), and T. L. Smith, *Revivalism and Social Reform in Mid-Nineteenth Century America* (1957).

Reform

A. A. Ekirch, *The Idea of Progress in America, 1815–1860* (1944), is a critical analysis of one of the reformers' basic assumptions. A. M. Schlesinger, *The American as Reformer* (1950), is a perceptive introduction to the reform movement. The best general treatment is A. F. Tyler, *Freedom's Ferment: Phases of American Social History to 1860* (1944). Other useful books are: C. R. Fish, *The Rise of the Common Man, 1830–1850* (1927); Meade Minnigerode, *The Fabulous Forties, 1840–1850* (1924); E. D. Branch, *The Sentimental Years, 1836–1860* (1934); and R. E. Riegel, *Young America, 1830–1840* (1949).

In the vast literature on specific reforms, the following are among the best: Blake McKelvey, *American Prisons: A Study in American Social History Prior to 1915* (1936); H. E. Marshall, *Dorothea Dix: Forgotten Samaritan* (1937); J. A. Krout, *The Origins of Prohibition* (1925); Paul Monroe, *The Founding of the American Public School System* (1940); L. H. Tharp, *Until Victory: Horace Mann and Mary Peabody* (1953); Carl Bode, *The American Lyceum* (1956); M. E. Curti, *The American Peace Crusade* (1929); and A. E. Bestor, Jr., *Backwoods Utopias: The Sectarian and Owenite Phases of Communitarian Socialism in America, 1663–1829* (1950).

Abolition and Proslavery

An exhaustive and highly sympathetic study of every aspect of abolitionism is D. L. Dumond, *Antislavery* (1961). Excellent brief surveys are available in Allan Nevins, *Ordeal of the Union*, 2 vols. (1947), and Louis Filler, *The Crusade Against Slavery* (1960). G. H. Barnes, *The Anti-slavery Impulse, 1833–1844* (1933), is a pioneer work that stresses the role of Theodore Dwight Weld at the expense of Garrison. Lawrence Lader, *The Bold Brahmins* (1961),

* Available in a paperback edition.

is a vivid, anecdotal account of the antislavery crusade in New England. An important facet of abolitionism is examined in R. B. Nye, *Fettered Freedom: Civil Liberties and the Slavery Controversy, 1830–1860* (1949). Two stimulating essays on the nature of the movement are in David Donald, *Lincoln Reconsidered: Essays on the Civil War Era* * (1956), and Stanley Elkins, *Slavery: A Problem in American Institutional and Intellectual Life* (1959).

Among the best biographies of abolitionist leaders are R. V. Harlow, *Gerrit Smith: Philanthropist and Reformer* (1939); B. P. Thomas, *Theodore Weld: Crusader for Freedom* (1950); Ralph Korngold, *Two Friends of Man: The Story of William Lloyd Garrison and Wendell Phillips* (1950); R. B. Nye, *William Lloyd Garrison and the Humanitarian Reformers* (1955); Oscar Sherwin, *Prophet of Liberty: The Life and Times of Wendell Phillips* (1958); and Betty Fladeland, *James Gillespie Birney: Slaveholder to Abolitionist* (1955). There is a good essay on Wendell Phillips in Richard Hofstadter, *The American Political Tradition* * (1948).

W. S. Jenkins, *Pro-Slavery Thought in the Old South* (1935), is a comprehensive analysis of the proslavery argument. Harvey Wish, *George Fitzhugh: Propagandist of the Old South* (1943), is an excellent biography of a leading defender of slavery. A special aspect of proslavery thought is analyzed by Richard Hofstadter in his essay on Calhoun in *The American Political Tradition*, cited above.

* Available in a paperback edition.

11

Expansion
and Sectional Crisis

The acquisition of Louisiana and Florida in the early nineteenth century temporarily quieted the American urge for geographic expansion. Feeling secure from foreign intervention, and satisfied that there was ample space for a growing population, most Americans who moved west in the 1820's and 1830's were content to take up the vacant lands in their already immense country. They occupied the unsettled regions of Mississippi, Missouri, and Illinois and poured into new territories that soon would become states: Arkansas (1836), Michigan (1837), Florida (1845), Iowa (1846), and Wisconsin (1848). The vast area beyond Missouri and Arkansas, stretching out to the Rocky Mountains, was then of no interest to the westward-moving settlers. Because explorers reported that the land was too arid for farming, cartographers labeled it the "Great American Desert" and white Americans made of it a "permanent" gift to the Indians. There was quite room enough for white men to the east of this "Indian Country."

Or so it seemed until the 1840's, when the impulse to expand suddenly stirred anew. Actually, few Americans had ever assumed that the boundaries of the United States would stand forever unchanged, though it is surprising that the desire for more territory revived so soon. Some Americans pressed expansion more aggressively than others, but few challenged the idea that Providence had destined their country to continued growth. Expansion in itself was not a serious issue. But

it had a vexatious consequence: it raised the touchy question of whether slavery should be permitted to spread into the territories that were acquired. Much of the controversy recently generated by proslavery and antislavery propagandists began to center on this problem, and by the end of the 1840's it had precipitated a national crisis. In 1850, after months of bitter debate, a compromise was painfully constructed—a makeshift arrangement that settled nothing but somehow held the Union together for another decade.

Westward to the Pacific

Manifest Destiny   The reasons for the revived interest in territorial expansion were several. The first and most obvious was that the American people, with their sense of mission, were sorely tempted by the boundless tracts of unsettled or sparsely settled land lying just beyond the borders of their country. All through the 1820's and 1830's American fur trappers, in their search for beaver streams, had been blazing trails, searching out passes through the mountains, and ranging over the fertile valleys of the Far West. The publicity they gave to the region beyond the "Great American Desert" at once strengthened the myth of the West as a land of romance and adventure and aroused interest in its agricultural possibilities. A second reason was a growing desire to develop trade with the Far East, and the belief, as one expansionist politician expressed it, that along the valley of the Columbia River "lies the North American road to India." Many Eastern businessmen began to look covetously at the three best natural harbors on the Pacific Coast, at San Diego, San Francisco, and Puget Sound. A third reason—and the one that probably explains the rebirth of expansionism at this precise time—was renewed fear of foreign intervention in lands bordering the United States, especially of British activity in Texas, California, and Oregon. Once again freedom and republican institutions in North America seemed threatened by the aggressive meddling of Europeans.

The expansionist drive was further strengthened by a mystical and romantic concept which, though hardly new, now received an attractive label. In 1845 a New York editor wrote exuberantly that it was America's "manifest destiny to overspread and to possess the whole of the continent which Providence has given us for the development of the great experiment of liberty and federated self-government entrusted to us." This doctrine of Manifest Destiny, quickly taken up by the press and politicians, was in part the kind of rationalization that nationalists everywhere have used to justify imperialist expansion. Nationalists invariably celebrate the superiority of their own culture and insist that their conquests are merely the fulfillment of a divine mission impelled by forces beyond human control. So did Americans when they spoke of their Manifest Destiny, and editors and stump speakers often advocated expansion in terms so extravagant as to make the United States sound like a nation of swashbucklers. "Make way, I say, for the young American Buffalo," shouted a New Jersey politician, "he has not yet got land enough."

But running through the boasts and the threats was a thread of idealism that tied expansion to America's supposed mission to serve as a model of political democracy. Expansion in these terms was simply a means of "extending the area of freedom," to quote a popular phrase of the day. America's destiny was not merely to teach by precept but to bring more land and more people under the nation's jurisdiction—in short, to spread its democratic institutions over the entire North American continent. Thus, as one politician explained, America would become "a vast theatre on which to work out the grand experiment of Republican government, under the auspices of the Anglo-Saxon race."

Texas The first area outside the United States to which settlers moved in substantial numbers was Texas. Many Westerners had been disappointed when the national government, in the Florida purchase treaty of 1819, accepted the Sabine River as a southwestern boundary, thereby surrendering whatever vague claim the government might have had to Texas as part of the Louisiana purchase. Mexico, after winning her independence from Spain in 1822, twice rejected American offers to buy this sparsely settled province; but during the 1820's she welcomed Americans who would submit to her jurisdiction and abide by her laws. Among the promoters of settlement, the first and most successful was Stephen F. Austin, who obtained a huge land grant from Mexico and planted a flourishing colony on the banks of the Brazos River. Most of the immigrants were Southern yeoman farmers and small slaveholders who were attracted by the rich lands suitable for cotton culture and available for a few cents an acre. By 1830 eastern Texas had been occupied by nearly twenty thousand whites and a thousand Negro slaves from the United States.

The Mexican government soon had cause to regret its hospitality, for the American settlers had no intention of giving their allegiance to a nation whose culture was so different from their own. Among numerous sources of friction, one of the most irritating was the fact that Texas did not have its own state government but remained a part of the state of Coahuila, whose legislature the Mexicans controlled. Moreover, the Americans were suspicious of Mexican land titles, which were unlike those they had been used to in the United States. In 1830 the mounting tension had prompted the Mexican government to make a drastic switch in policy: it prohibited further emigration from the United States, stopped the importation of slaves, placed heavy duties on American goods, and dispatched troops to the frontier to see that these laws were enforced. The final blow came when General Santa Anna, who had seized political power in

Mexico, not only repudiated his promise to give Texas separate statehood but nearly abolished the nation's federal system.

To the Texans the parallel between British oppression under George III and Mexican oppression under Santa Anna was clear, and revolution was the obvious and justifiable remedy. For a short time they pretended to be fighting in defense of the old Mexican constitution, but on March 2, 1836, they declared their independence. The struggle was brief. Santa Anna moved into Texas with a large army and won a few minor skirmishes, the most notable being the extermination of a small garrison of Texans at the Alamo mission in San Antonio. But on April 21, 1836, at the Battle of San Jacinto, an army commanded by General Sam Houston decisively defeated the Mexicans and took Santa Anna prisoner. Santa Anna was forced to sign a treaty recognizing Texan independence; and though Mexico later denounced the treaty as having been signed under duress, she made no further attempt to re-establish her authority. The new Republic of Texas then framed a constitution, but in September 1836, when the voters ratified it, they also indicated overwhelming support for annexation to the United States. President Houston forthwith began negotiations with the government at Washington, first for recognition and then for annexation.

American volunteers and supplies had contributed to the Texans' victory over Santa Anna, and proannexation sentiment was strong, especially in the South and West. But opposition to the admission of another slave state began to grow among Whigs and abolitionists in the Northeast. Some practical Whig politicians feared that annexation would lead to war with Mexico and objected that it would increase the South's power to block legislation favorable to Northern economic interests. Abolitionists charged that the settlement of Texas, the revolution, and the movement for annexation were all parts of a slaveholders' plot to enlarge their empire and open new markets for the vendors of human flesh. Texas thus became an issue between the critics and the defenders of slavery.

President Jackson was an ardent annexationist, but he acted cautiously lest he impair Van Buren's chances of winning the presidential election of 1836. Jackson even delayed recognition of Texan independence until the eve of his retirement from office, and Van Buren refused to recommend annexation during his term as President. Rebuffed by the United States, Texas in 1838 turned to Europe for recognition and aid; her leaders began to talk boldly of creating a nation that would expand to the Pacific and rival the United States in size and strength. This was a pleasing prospect to the British who saw in Texas a buffer to American expansion, a threat to the American cotton monopoly, and a promising new market. Moreover, British abolitionists hoped to persuade the Texans to abolish slavery and prove that cotton could be produced with free labor. As Texan leaders doubtless expected, British interest in their affairs alarmed the United States government, and the talk of abolition angered the slaveholders of the South.

These developments spurred President Tyler to reopen negotiations with Texas, and he worked vigorously to get a treaty of annexation before his term expired. By April 1844 Tyler's new Secretary of State, John C. Calhoun, had secured the desired treaty, and it was submitted to the Senate for ratification. Unfortunately Calhoun also sent a note to the British government concerning its interest in Texas, in which he defended slavery as a positive good and thus strengthened the abolitionist claim that annexation would be the culmination of a proslavery plot. This, along with the continued anxiety about war with Mexico, doomed the treaty; only sixteen senators voted for it, while thirty-five voted against. Annexation was again delayed, and Texas became an issue in the approaching presidential election.

The Santa Fe Trade   Meanwhile, a resourceful group of small entrepreneurs had aroused American interest in another of Mexico's remote provinces: New Mexico. The Spanish outpost at Santa Fe, planted in the seventeenth century, was hundreds of miles from the nearest Mexican settlements, and Spain's rigid trade restrictions had long deprived it of supplies from the United States. In the 1820's, however, the independent Mexican government had opened the Santa Fe trade to Americans. Every spring for the

Spanish church at the Santa Fe mission.

next two decades petty merchants assembled their wagons at Independence, Missouri, for the long journey along the Santa Fe Trail. Few merchants engaged in the trade—usually not many more than a hundred—but they always found a highly profitable market for their goods. In 1844, to the dismay of the traders, bad feeling generated by the Texas question caused Santa Anna again to exclude Americans from Santa Fe. By then, however, the trade had enlarged the American vision of Manifest Destiny to encompass New Mexico. Though few of the traders had actually settled in Santa Fe, they had opened a route into the Far West, had demonstrated that heavily laden wagons could cross the plains, and had developed a system of organized caravans for protection against the Indians. Another sparsely settled territory seemed ripe for

American plucking.

Oregon   Far to the northwest, in Oregon country, during the 1830's and early 1840's, merchants, fur trappers, and missionaries were awakening Americans to the potentialities of still another area, one to which the United States had a solid, though not exclusive, claim. That claim was based on the voyages of Boston merchants to the Oregon coast to buy furs from the Indians in the late eighteenth century; on Captain Robert Gray's discovery of the mouth of the Columbia River in 1792; on the explorations of the Lewis and Clark expedition between 1804 and 1806; and on the founding of Astoria on the Columbia River in 1811 by John Jacob Astor's Pacific Fur Company. In addition, the United States had acquired the French claim to Oregon in the Louisiana purchase treaty of 1803 and the

Spanish claim in the Florida purchase treaty of 1819. But the British claim was at least as good as the American. Sir Francis Drake, the British insisted, had discovered the Oregon coast in 1579; Captain James Cook and Captain George Vancouver had visited it again in the eighteenth century; and Alexander Mackenzie had made the first overland trip to Oregon in 1793 as an agent of British fur-trading interests. Moreover, by a treaty of 1825, the British had acquired the Russian claim to Oregon. Thus the Americans and British were the sole claimants to a huge territory bounded on the south by the forty-second parallel, on the north by the line of 54° 40', on the east by the Rocky Mountains, and on the west by the Pacific Ocean.

In the early nineteenth century, though neither the British nor the Americans claimed the whole of Oregon, they were unable to agree on a line of division. On several occasions the United States proposed an extension of the forty-ninth parallel to the Pacific, while the British suggested that the line follow the Columbia River from the forty-ninth parallel to its mouth. In 1818 the two countries postponed the settlement of this question and agreed to leave Oregon "free and open" to the citizens of both for a period of ten years. In 1827 they extended the agreement indefinitely, with the proviso that either country could terminate it on a year's notice. There the matter rested until the 1840's.

For many years Americans showed little interest in Oregon, and British fur traders had the area largely to themselves. After 1821 the Hudson's Bay Company monopolized the fur trade, establishing its headquarters at Fort Vancouver on the north bank of the Columbia and sending Dr. John McLoughlin there to serve as its chief factor. For more than twenty years McLoughlin gave Oregon the only government it had; he was scrupulously fair in dealing with the Indians, and under his efficient direction the company flourished. In the 1830's, however, agents of the Hudson's Bay Company operating in the Rockies began to encounter fierce and ruthless competitors: the intrepid Mountain Men who hunted beaver skins for the Rocky Mountain Fur Company directed by Thomas Fitzpatrick, James Bridger, and Milton Sublette. The Mountain

Men, along with the agents of Astor's American Fur Company, were the advance guard of American overland penetration of Oregon.

Efforts by several Eastern promoters to stimulate American migration to Oregon in the 1820's and 1830's ended in failure. But the impulse for settlement soon came from another source. In 1833 an Eastern religious periodical published a report that the Indians of the Oregon country were eager for instruction in the Christian faith. In response to this report (which had little substance to it) the Methodists sent the Reverend Jason Lee, who established a mission in the fertile Willamette Valley; the Presbyterians sent the Reverend Marcus Whitman, who was active farther east, near Fort Walla Walla; and the Catholics sent Father Pierre Jean de Smet, a Jesuit priest from St. Louis, who worked among the Indians in the Rockies. Dr. McLoughlin gave the missionaries a cordial welcome and much assistance, but the Indians showed little interest in the Gospel. Indeed, the religious work of

---

A Wagon Train

First, near the bank of the shining river, is a company of horsemen.... Then the wagons form a line three quarters of a mile in length.... Next comes a band of horses; two or three men or boys follow them, the docile and sagacious animals scarce needing this attention.... Not so with the large herd of horned beasts that bring up the rear; lazy, selfish and unsocial....

Nothing of the moving panorama, smooth and orderly as it appears, has more attractions for the eye than the vast square column in which all colors are mingled.... But the picture, in its grandeur, its wonderful mingling of colors and distinctness of detail, is forgotten in contemplation of the singular people who give it life and animation.... They have undertaken to perform, with slow moving oxen, a journey of two thousand miles. The way lies over trackless wastes, wide and deep rivers, rugged and lofty mountains, and is beset with hostile savages. Yet, whether it were a deep river with no tree upon its banks, a rugged defile where even a loose horse could not pass, a hill too steep for him to climb, or a threatened attack of an enemy, they are always found ready and equal to the occasion, and always conquerors.

From Jesse A. Applegate, *A Day with the Cow Column*, 1843.

Trails to the Far West

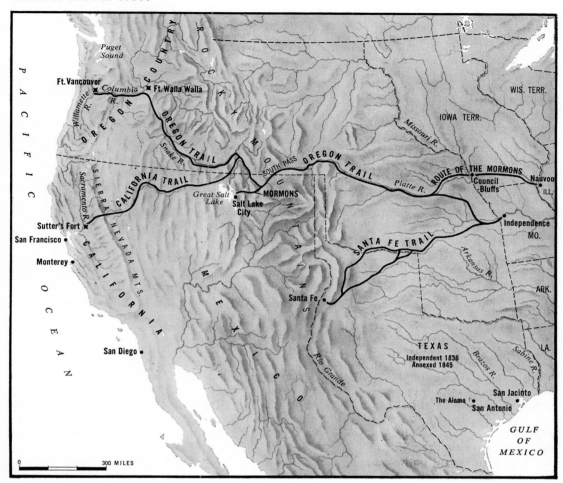

the missions proved to be less important than the publicity they gave to Oregon. Scores of missionary letters and reports filled with references to Oregon's fecund soil and salubrious climate found their way into the Eastern press.

As word spread that the Willamette Valley was a new Garden of Eden, the people of the Mississippi Valley began to catch the "Oregon fever." In the late 1830's a trickle of emigrants began to follow the Oregon Trail in quest of free virgin land; in 1841 the first substantial caravan of covered wagons made the two-thousand-mile journey; and by 1843 the movement to Oregon was taking on the dimensions of a mass migration. The Oregon Trail began at Independence, Missouri, ran northwest to

the Platte River, followed the Platte and its north fork into southern Wyoming, made an easy crossing of the Rockies at South Pass, followed the Snake River to a cutoff that led to the Columbia River, and then followed the Columbia to the Willamette Valley. By 1845 at least five thousand Americans had reached Oregon along this route; they had already formed a provisional government and were now demanding that the United States establish exclusive jurisdiction over them. Joint occupation was no longer a satisfactory formula, and a final settlement with the British could not be delayed much longer.

California   South of Oregon lay California, another of Mexico's remote provinces

San Francisco Harbor, 1847: Capacious enough to receive the navies of all the world.

and the fourth area in the Far West where Manifest Destiny seemed to beckon Americans. In the eighteenth century the Spanish, in order to strengthen their control over California and to convert the Indians to Christianity, had encouraged Franciscan friars to build a chain of missions along the coast from San Diego to San Francisco. The missions were highly successful both in their religious work and as large-scale agricultural enterprises; but in 1834 the Mexican government deprived them of their lands, and the mission system fell apart. Political chaos set in, under a succession of weak, inefficient, and often corrupt secular administrators. But the sparse Mexican population of approximately seven thousand settlers, most of them ranchers, still managed to live in easygoing comfort.

The first American contacts with California were made by merchant ships putting in along the coast for modest trading, and by whaleboats stopping for supplies. Now and then an American sailor deserted his ship and settled down; an occasional party of Mountain Men found their way to California on a trapping expedition; and by the 1830's a few merchants had come to trade with the Indians and Mexi-cans. Among the merchants was Thomas O. Larkin, who arrived at Monterey in 1832, built a flourishing trade, and worked tirelessly to promote American immigration to California. In the 1840's a few emigrants began to leave the Oregon Trail near the Snake River to follow the California Trail across the Nevada desert and the Sierra Nevada to the Sacramento River Valley. Invariably their goal was Sutter's Fort, the center of a private empire ruled by John A. Sutter, a German-born immigrant who had acquired Mexican citizenship and was a law unto himself. Sutter welcomed the Americans, furnished them with supplies, and helped them find land. By 1845 California was the home of about seven hundred Americans, almost none of whom expected to give up their American citizenship or to remain beyond the jurisdiction of their government very long.

The "California fever" had become almost as virulent as the "Oregon fever." Emigrants were attracted by the abundance of fertile, unoccupied land and by extravagant descriptions of California as "the richest, the most beautiful, and the healthiest country in the world." Eastern businessmen became increasingly interested in the commercial opportunities, and the American government coveted the harbors at San Diego and San Francisco—the latter was described as "capacious enough to receive the navies of all the world." Reports of British designs on California, though inaccurate, gave the matter a special urgency. In 1842 Commodore Thomas ap Catesby Jones, commander of the United States Pacific squadron, got the impression that his country had gone to war with Mexico and that British warships were moving toward California. He sailed into Monterey Bay, seized the city, ran up the American flag, and proclaimed the annexation of California to the United States. The embarrassed State Department disavowed Jones's act and made apologies to the Mexican government, but the incident was a clear sign of what the expansionists had in mind.

The Mormon Migration   One group of emigrants to the Far West had no interest in Manifest Destiny—indeed, they sought to escape the jurisdiction of the United States. These were the Mormons, who in 1847 crossed into Mexican territory and established a settlement in the isolated Great Salt Lake basin. The Mormon migration followed nearly two decades of persecution which had begun in the 1820's in western New York, where

Joseph Smith founded the sect. The "Church of Jesus Christ of Latter-Day Saints," as it was officially called, was based on miraculous revelations which Smith claimed to have received from God and which he incorporated in the Book of Mormon. From the beginning the Mormon Saints annoyed the "gentiles" about them with their close-knit communitarian social pattern, their thriving economic life, and their contempt for other religious sects. In their search for a Zion where they could escape this hostility and live in peace, they first moved from New York to Kirtland, Ohio, then to Missouri, then (in 1839) to Nauvoo, Illinois, where their numbers soon grew to fifteen thousand. In 1844, after five prosperous years, a new crisis developed when Smith received another revelation, this one justifying polygamy. The result was a schism in the Church, a rash of violence, and Smith's arrest and imprisonment. On June 27, 1844, an anti-Mormon mob took him from jail and murdered him. Once more the Mormons were obliged to abandon their homes and renew their wanderings.

Leadership now passed to Brigham Young, a brilliant, strong-willed man, who organized the most remarkable migration and settlement in the annals of the American West. In 1846 Young led almost the whole Mormon com-

Transformation of the land of the lizard: Salt Lake City, 1867.

munity across Iowa to the Council Bluffs on the Missouri River; the next year he sent the first band to the Salt Lake basin, which he had selected for the new Zion. No place could have appeared less promising; the first to arrive saw only "a broad and barren plain . . . a seemingly interminable waste of sagebrush . . . the paradise of the lizard, the cricket and the rattlesnake." But within a decade the Mormons, under the stern leadership of Young and the theocratic control of the Church, had transformed the landscape. Substituting cooperative labor for the individual effort of the typical pioneer, they built a splendid city and an efficient irrigation system with which they made the desert bloom. In the critical early years their economy benefited from the sale of supplies to emigrants passing through on their way to California. When their lands were annexed to the United States soon after they arrived, the Mormons tried first to organize their own state of "Deseret."

Failing, they acquiesced when Congress created the Territory of Utah. Even then, however, the Mormon Church continued to be the dominant political as well as religious force in the land of the Saints.

Polk and the Triumph of Manifest Destiny

The Election of Polk   The presidential election of 1844 exposed a variety of tensions that had been growing in American society in recent years. First, the long depression following the Panic of 1837 had kept alive issues of national policy concerning money, banking, and public lands, issues that sometimes divided labor and capital, sometimes farm and city. Second, the entrance of the abolitionist crusade into politics had given sectional differences a moral dimension that made compromise increasingly difficult to achieve. Third, the doctrine of Manifest Destiny was now reaching the height of its influence, and the drive for expansion to the Pacific was becoming an irresistible force. The complexity of these issues, all of which were more or less interrelated, sorely tried the national party system and led ultimately to a fragmentation of both the Whig and the Democratic organizations.

In 1844 Henry Clay and Martin Van Buren expected to receive the presidential nominations of their respective parties. They found the unsettled Texas question a source of embarrassment, because it had become involved in the slavery controversy. Hence they tried to eliminate it as a campaign issue by making separate but very similar statements (apparently after private consultation) opposing the annexation of Texas at that time without the consent of Mexico. The Whig convention unanimously nominated Clay and adopted a platform that avoided taking a stand either on Texas or on most other national issues. But the Democratic convention, where expansionist sentiment was stronger, denied Van Buren the nomination he coveted. Instead, the delegates chose James K. Polk of Tennessee, whose commitment to territorial expansion was clear and unqualified. To avoid the accusation of sectional favoritism, the Democratic platform cleverly united a demand for the admission of

Texas with a demand for the acquisition "of the whole of the Territory of Oregon." The platform also made the dubious assertion that the United States had a clear title to both. It followed, therefore, "that the re-occupation of Oregon and the re-annexation of Texas at the earliest practicable period are great American measures, which this convention recommends to the cordial support of the Democracy of the Union."

By combining the expansionist desires of South and West, the Democrats had found a winning formula. Throughout the campaign Manifest Destiny transcended all other issues, so much so that Clay began to shift his position on Texas. He would favor annexation after all if it could be accomplished without war and upon "just and fair terms." But this commitment still sounded halfhearted when compared with the spread-eagle oratory and aggressive slogans of the Democrats. Clay converted few of the expansionists but lost some antislavery votes to the Liberty party (see p. 253), especially in New York. In the election Polk won by a small plurality of thirty-eight thousand in the popular vote and by a margin of 170 to 105 in the electoral college.

Though Polk is remembered as the first "dark-horse" presidential candidate, the term is valid only in the sense that he had not been considered for the nomination before the Democratic convention. He was far from a political unknown in 1844. Born in North Carolina, he had moved to Tennessee as a young man and soon became a successful lawyer and planter. He entered politics as a Jacksonian Democrat and served seven terms in the House of Representatives (two as Speaker) and one term as governor of Tennessee. As President, Polk displayed neither extraordinary talent nor a striking personality, but by hard work and stubborn determination he had remarkable success in redeeming the pledges his party had made during the campaign. His inaugural address was unimaginative—a mere reiteration of the principles with which Jefferson and Jackson had been identified. Polk promised a passive domestic role for government "by abstaining from the exercise of doubtful or unauthorized implied powers."

Polk's Administration reflected both the continuing influence of Jacksonian principles on the Democratic party and the growing power of the South within the party. As a planter and slaveholder Polk shared the Southern hostility toward abolitionists; if they achieved their goal, he warned, "the dissolution of the Union . . . must speedily follow." He favored a low revenue tariff, and in 1846 his Secretary of the Treasury, Robert J. Walker of Mississippi, helped to frame such a measure, which Congress passed. The Walker Tariff delighted the South, but it angered Northern protectionists and increased their hostility to further strengthening the anti-protectionists by the admission of any more slave states. Polk shared Jackson's views on national banking and persuaded Congress to re-establish the Independent Treasury system, which it had abolished during the Tyler Administration. On two occasions, to the intense annoyance of Westerners in the Great Lakes region, he vetoed internal improvements bills. In short, Polk blocked every effort to revive the American System of Henry Clay and John Quincy Adams, and in his last message to Congress he devoted much space to attacking that system and celebrating its demise.

The Acquisition of Texas and Oregon Important as these domestic policies were, the Polk Administration's primary concern was with geographic expansion. The Texas question was the first to be disposed of, for Congress had virtually settled the matter shortly before Polk's inauguration. After the presidential election Tyler assured Congress that the verdict of the voters had been in favor of annexation, and he proposed now that the two houses accomplish it by a joint resolution. Annexation would thus require only a simple majority, rather than the two-thirds majority needed in the Senate to ratify a treaty. The introduction of a resolution for this purpose provoked a heated debate between proslavery and antislavery congressmen, but it finally passed the House by a vote of 120 to 98 and the Senate by a vote of 27 to 25. President Tyler signed the the joint resolution on March 1, 1845. Polk approved of this action, and within a few months Texas had accepted the terms of annexation. In December 1845 Texas was admitted to statehood.

The problem of Oregon was not so easily re-

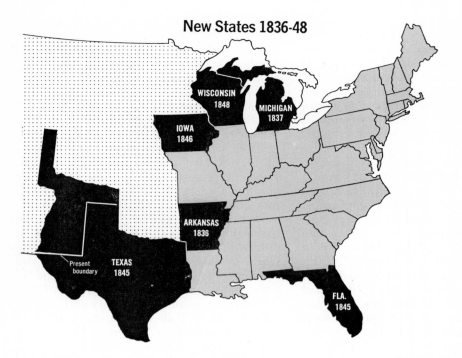

New States 1836-48

WISCONSIN 1848

MICHIGAN 1837

IOWA 1846

ARKANSAS 1836

Present boundary

TEXAS 1845

FLA. 1845

solved, for the Americans and British still had not agreed on a line of division. Indeed, the restless settlers in Oregon and the expansionists in the East were growing increasingly belligerent in their demand that the government make no division at all but, as the Democratic platform of 1844 had insisted, take the whole territory to its northern limits. Apparently ready for another war with the British, they repeated the slogans "All of Oregon or none," and "Fifty-four forty or fight." "We want thirty thousand rifles in the valley of the Oregon," cried Senator Benton of Missouri, "they will make all quiet there . . . and protect the American interests." In January 1845 the British government, realizing that continued joint occupation was impossible, proposed arbitration, but the State Department rejected the offer.

In referring to the Oregon question in his inaugural address, Polk seemed to stand firmly on his party's platform; it would be his duty, he said, "to assert and maintain by all constitutional means the right of the United States to that portion of our territory which lies beyond the Rocky Mountains. Our title to the country of the Oregon is 'clear and unquestionable,' and . . . those rights we are fully pre-

pared to maintain." Meanwhile, there was a good deal of irresponsible saber-rattling on both sides of the Atlantic, and the situation threatened to get out of hand.

But Polk did not want war with England at a time when there was danger of war with Mexico; accordingly, he soon decided to abandon the Democratic platform and try for a compromise. In July 1845 he notified the British minister in Washington, Richard Pakenham, that the United States was willing to renew its offer to divide Oregon along the forty-ninth parallel. Pakenham, without even consulting his government, rejected the offer and held firm to the earlier British demand for a division at the Columbia River. The indignant President then withdrew his offer, concluded that "the only way to treat John Bull was to look him straight in the eye," and decided to pursue "a bold and firm course." In his message to Congress that December, Polk recommended that the British government be given the year's notice required to end joint occupation. He also invoked the almost forgotten Monroe Doctrine to fortify his case: "it should be distinctly announced to the world as our settled policy that no future European colony or dominion shall with our consent be

The Oregon Controversy, 1818-46

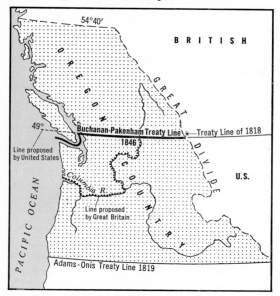

planted or established on any part of the North American continent." Once Congress had approved the termination of joint occupation of Oregon, the only remaining hope for a peaceful settlement seemed to be an offer of concessions on the part of the British.

Fortunately the British Foreign Office disapproved of Pakenham's blunt rejection of Polk's offer to compromise, for it did not believe that the disputed segment of Oregon between the Columbia River and the forty-ninth parallel was worth a war. Indeed, the flood of American settlers and the depletion of the fur resources had already prompted the Hudson's Bay Company to transfer its headquarters from Fort Vancouver on the Columbia northward to Fort Victoria on Vancouver Island. In June 1846 Secretary of State James Buchanan received from Pakenham the draft of a proposal to divide Oregon at the forty-ninth parallel but to retain for the British all of Vancouver Island and the right to navigate the Columbia River. Polk was at first inclined to reject the proposal, but he decided to submit it to the Senate and let that body assume responsibility for the decision.

After an angry debate the Senate advised acceptance; the treaty was signed on June 15 and the Senate ratified it by a vote of forty-one to fourteen. Most of the opposition came from Western Democrats who bitterly criticized Polk for backing down on the demand for the whole of Oregon. But most of the country was satisfied with the settlement, for the British, rather than the Americans, had given up their original claim. Eastern business interests had no taste for a war to secure the area north of the forty-ninth parallel; nor did the Southerners, whose interest in Oregon waned once Texas had been safely annexed. Besides, the United States was already at war with Mexico and had a richer prize in view.

War with Mexico

The Background   Among the causes of the war with Mexico were the inability of United States citizens to obtain compensation for claims against the Mexican government, the anger of Mexican patriots over American annexation of Texas, a dispute over the southern and western boundary of Texas, and the instability of the Mexican government which made negotiation with it difficult and irritating. But even more important was the determination of Polk (and of the expansionists generally) to obtain the provinces of New Mexico and California—with money if possible, by force if necessary. Though Mexico was far from blameless for the war that came— indeed, welcomed it—the central cause was nevertheless the readiness of Americans to resort to arms to fulfill their Manifest Destiny.

As soon as the United States annexed Texas, Mexico broke off diplomatic relations, thus closing the normal channels of negotiation. Yet there was need for negotiation, because Texas was not satisfied with its traditional southern boundary, which in Spanish days had been the Nueces River, but claimed instead the Rio Grande. Polk, convinced that the Texas claim was justified, ordered General Zachary Taylor to take fifteen hundred troops into the disputed area. By the summer of 1845, Taylor's small army was encamped at Corpus Christi on the Nueces River; in March of the following year it obeyed Polk's command and advanced to the Rio Grande. To Mexican patriots this act, following soon after what they considered the illegal seizure of Texas, was a further aggressive invasion of their territory, and the war spirit grew among them.

There was now little hope that Polk could persuade Mexico to give up California and New Mexico peacefully, but he decided to try none-the-less. In the fall of 1845 he explored the possibility of resuming diplomatic relations. When he learned that Mexico would receive an American commissioner to settle the Texas dispute, he appointed John Slidell of Louisiana as envoy extraordinary and minister plenipotentiary with authority to discuss not only Texas but California and New Mexico as well. Slidell was instructed to offer (1) the assumption by the United States of all claims of its citizens against Mexico if Mexico would accept the Rio Grande boundary; (2) $5 million for the rest of New Mexico west of the Rio Grande; and (3) as much as $25 million for California. Since the Mexican government needed money, and since its hold on these distant territories was weak, to Polk it seemed the course of wisdom for Mexico to sell.

When Slidell reached Mexico City on December 6, 1845, news about his purpose had already leaked out, and Mexican nationalists were furious at this brazen attempt to dismember their country. The existing government was collapsing, in part because of its alleged lack of firmness in dealing with the United States, and a new revolutionary government came to power pledged to uphold the national dignity. Neither the old nor the new government would receive Slidell. Mexico, he was reminded, had agreed only to receive a commissioner to negotiate on Texas, and until that question was settled there could be no regular diplomatic relations. The Slidell mission had failed. "Be assured," the angry diplomat wrote Polk, "that nothing is to be done with these people until they shall have been chastised."

Polk apparently agreed. On May 9, 1846, he told his Cabinet that the unpaid claims and the snubbing of Slidell would justify a declaration of war, and he began at once to prepare a war message to Congress. That evening news arrived that on April 25 Mexican troops had crossed the Rio Grande and engaged in a skirmish in which sixteen American soldiers had been killed or wounded. Polk hastily revised his war message and sent it to Congress on May 11. After reviewing recent relations between Mexico and the United States, his message concluded: "The cup of forbearance had been exhausted even before the recent information from the frontier. . . . But now, after reiterated menaces, Mexico has passed the boundary of the United States, has invaded our territory and shed American blood on the American soil." Therefore, "war exists, and, notwithstanding all our efforts to avoid it, exists by the act of Mexico herself." Two days later Congress passed a declaration of war, the Senate by a vote of 40 to 2, the House by a vote of 174 to 14. It then appropriated $10 million for war purposes and authorized the recruitment of an army of fifty thousand volunteers.

The country went to war somewhat less united than these votes in Congress indicated. Though most Whig politicians felt they had no choice but to support the military measures, they showed less enthusiasm for the conflict than the Democrats. War sentiment was strong in the Southwest, but it diminished to the east and north. Abolitionists and antislavery Whigs (who called themselves Conscience Whigs) denied that Polk had tried to avoid war and insisted that American blood had been shed not on American soil but on disputed soil which American troops should never have occupied. Senator Tom Corwin of Ohio accused Polk of involving the country in a war of aggression, and added bitterly: "If I were a Mexican, I would tell you, 'Have you not room in your own country to bury your dead men? If you come into mine, we will greet you with bloody hands and welcome you to hospitable graves.'" Abolitionists viewed the war as another attempt of the Slave Power to enhance its strength. In 1847 the Massachusetts legislature resolved that the war was "unconstitutionally commenced by the order of the President" and that it was being waged for the "dismemberment of Mexico" with "the triple object of extending slavery, of strengthening the slave power, and of obtaining the control of the free states." A new sectional crisis thus began to take shape almost as soon as the war commenced.

The Military Campaigns   In all probability the Mexicans entered the war with greater unity and enthusiasm than the Ameri-

The Mexican War, 1846-48

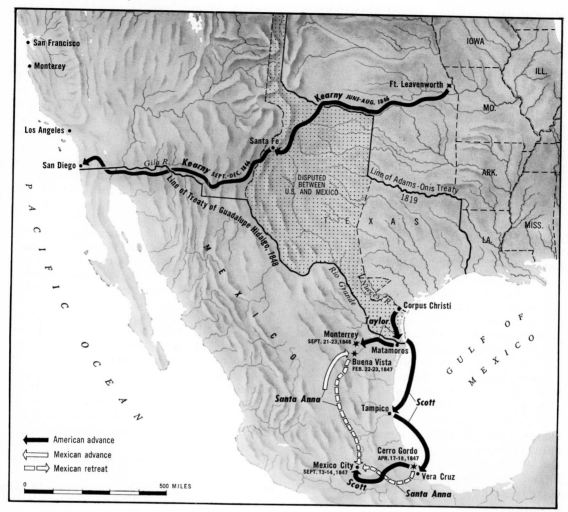

American advance
Mexican advance
Mexican retreat

0   500 MILES

cans. They had concluded that war was the only way to check Yankee aggression, and they were confident that their regular army, vastly superior in numbers to the American, could easily defeat the invaders. But the Mexicans were sadly deluded, for they did not take into account their outdated weapons, their limited supplies and inferior resources, and their oversupply of incompetent generals. The United States War Department was inefficient enough, but the Mexican was even more so. Though the United States had a regular army of less than eight thousand officers and men, it was able quickly to raise

a force of sixty thousand volunteers. With this man power, with superior equipment, and with at least one gifted military commander, General Winfield Scott, the Americans won the war with relative ease.

Polk, who planned the military operations himself, hoped that a few quick victories would persuade Mexico to make the desired territorial cessions. According to Senator Benton, Polk "wanted a small war, just large enough to require a treaty of peace." In the first of three major campaigns, General Taylor crossed the Rio Grande, captured Matamoros, and pushed on to Monterrey. There, in a severe battle

(September 21–23, 1846), Taylor defeated the Mexican garrison but permitted it to withdraw rather than surrender. Because of these early victories, "Old Rough and Ready," as Taylor's men affectionately called him, became a national hero, but he had betrayed limitations as a tactician and a tendency to be overcautious—serious flaws in a commanding officer. As a result, Polk lost confidence in him, took away half his army for a new offensive at Vera Cruz, and would have been content to let him remain idle for the rest of the war. But Santa Anna, who had regained power in Mexico, moved north to attack Taylor's weakened forces. At the Battle of Buena Vista (February 22–23, 1847) Taylor added to his national popularity by defeating Santa Anna and forcing him to return to Mexico City. This action ended the war in northern Mexico, but the decisive victories were still to be won elsewhere.

The second offensive was designed to bring the coveted Mexican provinces under American occupation before a peace treaty was negotiated. In the summer of 1846 a force of seventeen hundred men, commanded by Colonel Stephen W. Kearny, marched from Fort Leavenworth to Santa Fe and, on August 18, captured it without firing a shot. After proclaiming the annexation of New Mexico to the United States, Kearny sent part of his troops to join Taylor, left a small garrison at Santa Fe, and took the rest to California. There the American settlers, in the "Bear Flag Revolution," had already declared the independence of California; and Captain John C. Frémont, who had arrived earlier at the head of an exploring expedition, was in command of the rebels. Meanwhile, naval forces had landed at Monterey and raised the American flag. Hence, when Kearny arrived late in 1846 the only remaining task was to subdue scattered resistance to American authority in southern California. By January 1847 the United States had virtually undisputed possession of both New Mexico and California.

It took a third American campaign to force Mexico to accept these realities. In March 1847 an army commanded by General Scott landed near Vera Cruz, forced that city to surrender after an eighteen-day siege, and then began a slow and difficult advance toward Mexico City. Scott won a decisive victory over Santa Anna at Cerro Gordo (April 17–18, 1847), and by August he was on the high plateau before the Mexican capital. On September 14 American troops forced their way into the city, and soon after Mexico surrendered.

The Treaty of Guadalupe Hidalgo A new Mexican government was now ready to sign a treaty of peace. In anticipation of this outcome, Polk had sent Nicholas P. Trist, chief clerk in the State Department, along with Scott's army "to take advantage of circumstances, as they might arise to negotiate a peace." Trist was instructed to offer essentially the same terms that Slidell had offered. In November 1847, after a long and irritating delay, negotiations were about to begin when Trist received orders from the impatient President to return to Washington. But Trist, convinced that he was on the verge of getting all he had been sent for, decided to ignore his orders and enter into negotiations. On February 2, 1848, he signed the Treaty of Guadalupe Hidalgo, by which the United States obtained California, New Mexico, and the Rio Grande boundary for $15 million and the assumption of the claims of United States citizens against Mexico. Trist then hurried back to Washington, but he got no thanks from the President. Instead, Polk denounced him as an "impudent and unqualified scoundrel" for disobeying orders and dismissed him from his job.

But Polk could find no fault with the treaty and, notwithstanding "the exceptional conduct of Mr. Trist," decided to submit it to the Senate. By then some of the more rabid expansionists were asking why the United States should settle for only California and New Mexico. Why not take the whole of Mexico? As one partisan of Manifest Destiny asked, why "resign this beautiful country to the custody of the ignorant cowards and profligate ruffians who have ruled it for the last twenty-five years?" But after a volley of bombastic oratory, the Senate, on March 10, 1848, ratified the treaty by a vote of thirty-eight to fourteen. Thus, as one disgruntled Whig observed, the Mexican War ended with a peace "negotiated by an unauthorized agent, with an unacknowledged government, submitted by an accidental President to a dissatisfied Senate." Through it the United States gained possession of more than a half million square miles of territory.

Crisis and Compromise

The Issue of Slavery Expansion   On August 8, 1846, the House of Representatives had under consideration a bill appropriating $2 million to facilitate the acquisition of territory from Mexico when a peace treaty was negotiated. The bill appeared to be harmless enough until David Wilmot, a Jacksonian Democrat from Pennsylvania, rose to move an amendment making it "an express and fundamental condition" that "neither slavery nor involuntary servitude shall ever exist in any part of said territory." The "Wilmot Proviso," as the amendment was called, twice passed the House but each time failed in the Senate, and on numerous other occasions it was reintroduced and bitterly debated. During the next fifteen years the issue of the expansion of slavery, which had been a latent source of trouble ever since the Missouri controversy, was to drive a wedge ever deeper between North and South.

What personal motives Wilmot may have had for introducing his Proviso is of no great historical importance, because other Northern congressmen were prepared to offer similar proposals had not Wilmot acted first. The important question is whether the long and angry controversy over slavery expansion involved a genuine problem or was simply a flight from reality. Polk was the first of many contemporaries to denounce the Wilmot Proviso as "mischievous and foolish" and to accuse "Southern agitators and Northern fanatics" of raising a false issue merely for political advancement. He and other conservatives held that, since none of the territory acquired from Mexico was geographically suitable for plantation agriculture with slave labor, any legislation to exclude slavery from it would needlessly re-enact a "law of nature." From this, presumably, it followed that irresponsible demagogues were creating a great national crisis and endangering the Union over a mere abstraction.

By the end of the 1840's the Southern plantation system may well have reached its natural geographic limits within the existing boundaries of the United States, but it does not necessarily follow that the debate over slavery expansion was therefore meaningless. Though the politicians who had to deal with the problem may not have handled it well, many of them were convinced that the problem had substance to it. In the first place, not all Northerners and Southerners were sure that geography alone would keep slavery out of California and New Mexico. Some believed that even if the familiar plantation system could not be developed in these areas, slavery might still be introduced there in other forms of agriculture, as well as in industry and mining. In the second place, few Americans thought that their country's growth had stopped with the territory acquired in the Treaty of Guadalupe Hidalgo. There was a widespread conviction that at least Cuba would one day become part of the United States, and perhaps other Caribbean islands and Central America as well. In these tropical lands slavery would certainly not be a mere academic question. Indeed, much of the controversy over slavery expansion was waged with an eye on future annexations and on the precedent that laws excluding slavery from existing territories would provide.

Finally, and perhaps most important, the issue had meaning in terms of the moral positions of the two sections. The debate over slavery expansion was in reality an extension of the debate over slavery where it already existed. When Northerners with antislavery sentiments argued that it would be morally wrong to legalize slavery in New Mexico, they were by implication arguing that it was also morally wrong to tolerate it in Virginia. Southerners understood this perfectly well, which explains in part why they so vigorously opposed any move by Congress to prohibit slavery in territories where they knew it would never be established. For example, Southern congressmen delayed for two years (until 1848) the passage of a bill creating Oregon Territory, because the bill contained a clause excluding slavery.

Much of the debate over the Wilmot Proviso centered on the question of how much power the Constitution had given Congress to govern the territories. Antislavery Northerners cited the clause authorizing Congress to "make all needful rules and regulations respecting the Territory or other Property belonging to the United States." Until the 1840's, as Henry Clay observed, this clause had been accepted as giving Congress power over slavery in the territories "by the uniform interpretation and action of every department of our government, legislative, executive, and judicial." Moreover, the power had repeatedly been used. The First Congress had re-enacted the Ordinance of 1787, which prohibited slavery in the Northwest Territory; a later Congress had applied the same restriction to Illinois and Michigan Territories when they were created; and overwhelming majorities in the House and Senate had voted in 1820 to prohibit slavery in that portion of the Louisiana Purchase north of the line 36° 30′. After the Mexican War, when President Polk and many other Southern moderates suggested extending the Missouri Compromise line to the Pacific, they were in effect agreeing that Congress did have authority to regulate slavery in the territories.

Calhoun, however, led proslavery Southerners toward an extreme state-rights position similar to the stand that some Virginians had taken during the Missouri debates. In 1847 he introduced a series of resolutions in the Senate which asserted that the territories were the common property of all the states; that Congress had no power to deprive the citizens of any state of their right to migrate to the territories with their property, including slaves; and that only when a territory was ready for statehood could it constitutionally prohibit slavery. Calhoun's position, therefore, was that *all* the territories must be open to slavery—which made even the Missouri Compromise unconstitutional. Some of his supporters went a step further and insisted that it was the duty of Congress to *protect* slavery in the territories if necessary. This being the case, the Wilmot Proviso was, in the words of one Southern congressman, "treason to the Constitution," and its adoption would justify the secession of the South.

Between these two uncompromising antislavery and proslavery doctrines, a third doctrine, called "popular sovereignty," began to win the support of moderates in all sections but especially in the Old Northwest. With two Democratic senators, Lewis Cass of Michigan

and Stephen A. Douglas of Illinois, its chief advocates, popular sovereignty was designed in part to remove the explosive territorial question from the halls of Congress. Why not respect the American tradition of local self-government, these moderates asked, and permit the people who actually settled in a territory to decide the question of slavery for themselves? Congress could then organize new territories without reference to slavery. Southerners would escape the humiliation of congressional prohibition, while Northwestern farmers might hope that their numerical superiority over Southern slaveholders would enable them to win the territories for freedom.

The Election of 1848   Meanwhile, as the debate over the territorial question dragged on, California and New Mexico were left without government and the issue was injected into the presidential campaign of 1848. President Polk had failed to unite the Democrats behind his Administration, and as the election approached the party was torn by factionalism. Calhoun led a group of Southern-rights men unwilling to accept anything less than his extreme position on slavery expansion. Martin Van Buren commanded a faction of disaffected New York Democrats, called the "Barnburners" (presumably because they would burn the barn to get rid of the rats), who had thirsted for revenge ever since Polk defeated Van Buren for the presidential nomination in 1844. Throughout the North, especially in the Northeast, groups of free-soil Democrats endorsed the Wilmot Proviso. When the Democratic convention met in Baltimore, the party leaders, having decided that a Northern candidate was essential, threw the nomination to Lewis Cass of Michigan, a colorless old party wheel horse whose opposition to the Wilmot Proviso and support of popular sovereignty would appease the Southern moderates. The platform praised Polk for his territorial acquisitions and domestic policies but was silent on the slavery question. As a result, the Barnburners and pro-Wilmot delegates left the convention prepared for revolt.

The Whigs, meeting in Philadelphia, again staked their chances on a military hero, General Zachary Taylor. Born in Virginia and now a Louisiana slaveholder, Taylor was expected to reassure Southern Whigs who had grown uneasy about the antislavery sentiments of Northern Whigs. Old Rough and Ready had spent his whole career in the regular army; he had neither political principles nor political experience—and, indeed, had discovered only recently that he was a Whig ("but not an ultra Whig"). After nominating Taylor on the fourth ballot, the convention tried to avoid controversy by writing no platform at all. But this surrender to expediency was more than the Northern Conscience Whigs could bear. Many of them decided that rather than support a slaveholder whose views were unknown and who was uncommitted to a platform they would bolt their party.

Antislavery leaders saw in the disgruntled Van Buren Barnburners, free-soil Democrats, Conscience Whigs, and political abolitionists the elements of a powerful third party, one that would take a firm stand on the territorial question and make a broader appeal than the Liberty party had made in the past two elections. In August 1848 delegates representing all these groups met in Buffalo, organized the Free-Soil party, and nominated Van Buren for President and Charles Francis Adams (a Conscience Whig, the son of John Quincy Adams) for Vice-President. The platform bluntly demanded that slavery be excluded from the territories and opposed any additional concessions to the Slave Power. It supported federal appropriations for internal improvements and the passage of a "homestead act" giving actual settlers free farms from the public domain. In a concluding statement the platform summarized the principles of the new party as "Free Soil, Free Speech, Free Labor, and Free Men." Among the Free-Soilers were numerous self-seeking politicians, but the organization also reflected much of the idealism of the antislavery crusade.

In spite of the intensity of feeling about the territorial question, the campaign itself was unexciting, the voters apathetic. Taylor defeated Cass by a small plurality in the popular vote (1,360,967 to 1,222,342) and by a majority of 36 in the electoral college (163 to 127). The Free-Soil party failed to carry a single state, but its popular vote of 291,263 was impressive for a party organized less than three months before the election. A dozen Free-Soilers were elected to Congress, among

them Ohio's new senator, Salmon P. Chase.

Taylor and the Crisis   President Taylor was a man of honesty, integrity, and determination; he was capable of quick action, and he had a store of plain common sense. But these virtues were not sufficient to offset his limitations as chief executive in a time of crisis: his lack of training in politics and civil administration, his ignorance of public affairs —above all, his tendency to oversimplify complex problems. In a brief and vacuous inaugural address, he promised to devote his Administration "to the welfare of the whole country, and not to the support of any particular section or merely local interest." This pledge he tried conscientiously to fulfill; though he was a Southerner, he was a nationalist with no strong sectional loyalties.

When Taylor came into office, California and New Mexico, still lacking civil government, were being ruled by army officers directly responsible to the President. The settlers found this situation annoying under the best of circumstances, but it became intolerable soon after the discovery of gold in California. James Marshall had made the discovery in January 1848, along the American River about forty miles from Sutter's Fort; within six months San Francisco and other coastal towns were all but deserted as men rushed headlong to the "diggings" in the Sierra. By the end of 1848 the news had spread to the East, and during the next year some eighty thousand "forty-niners" came to California from the Mississippi Valley, from the Atlantic Coast, and from Europe, Asia, and Australia. Most of them followed the overland trails across the continent, others took the easier but more expensive route by ship around Cape Horn, and still others risked death by taking a short-cut through the jungles of Panama. The miners dreamed of fortunes in gold as they worked the beds of streams with picks, shovels, and wash-pans; a few struck it rich, but most of them gained only modest returns from their backbreaking labor and their months of discomfort in primitive mining camps. Much of the gold ultimately found its way into the pockets of merchants in San Francisco and Sacramento, who in effect mined the miners by selling them supplies at exorbitant prices.

By the end of 1849 California's population had grown to one hundred thousand, and in the absence of civil government crime and violence were endemic in the cities and mining camps. With military authorities unable to restore law and order, with Congress seemingly paralyzed by the slavery issue, President Taylor decided to take matters into his own hands. As he saw it, there was a simple solution to the problem that had bedeviled Congress ever since the introduction of the Wilmot Proviso. He proposed to avoid the territorial issue by encouraging California and New Mexico to frame constitutions and apply for immediate admission to the Union as states. Californians wasted no time in taking Taylor's advice; by October 1849 they had drafted and ratified a constitution prohibiting slavery, and soon after they elected state officers to whom the military gladly yielded its political authority. The people of New Mexico took more time, but by May 1850 they too had adopted a free-state constitution. Thus, when Congress met in December 1849, Taylor congratulated the country on the fact that the problem had been solved. All that remained was for Congress to admit California as a free state at once, and New Mexico as soon as it was ready.

The Compromise of 1850 Taylor had miscalculated. Rather than settling the matter, he helped precipitate one of the most bitter sectional debates in American history, one that carried the country dangerously close to disunion and civil war. Southerners denounced Taylor as an apostate and a tool of the abolitionists, while the followers of Calhoun vowed that they would break up the Union rather than see slavery excluded from California and New Mexico. Several other issues intensified the crisis: Texans and New Mexicans were on the verge of a private war over their common boundary; abolitionists were gaining Northern support for their demand that slavery be abolished in the District of Columbia; and Southerners were clamoring for a more effective fugitive slave law. Legislatures and mass meetings in both the North and the South adopted fiery resolutions, and violence threatened to break out in the halls of Congress. A Massachusetts convention of Democrats and Free-Soilers resolved that "we are opposed to slavery in every form and color, and in favor of freedom and free soil wherever man lives." Mississippi contributed to the atmosphere of crisis by issuing a call for a convention of the Southern states to meet at Nashville in June 1850. Many feared that the friends of Calhoun would use the convention to expedite Southern secession.

Moderates in both sections were convinced that nothing short of a comprehensive settlement of all outstanding issues could save the Union. And it was to Henry Clay, then in his seventy-third year and near the end of his long career, that lovers of the Union looked almost instinctively for a just and durable compromise. On January 29, 1850, Clay offered the Senate a series of resolutions which proposed (1) that California be admitted as a free state; (2) that territorial governments be provided for the rest of the Mexican cession without any restriction on slavery; (3) that Texas abandon its claim to the eastern portion of New Mexico; (4) that the federal government compensate Texas by assuming the public debt Texas had contracted before annexation; (5) that the use of the District of Columbia as a depot in the interstate slave trade be prohibited; (6) that slavery in the District of Columbia be abolished only with the consent of its residents and of the state of Maryland, and with compensation to the slaveholders; (7) that a new and more rigorous fugitive-slave act be adopted; and (8) that Congress declare that it had no power to interfere with the interstate slave trade. Among the many moderates who labored long and hard to secure the adoption of these compromise proposals, Stephen A. Douglas of Illinois was second only to Clay.

Congress debated the proposals for more than seven months, with the moderates under constant attack from both proslavery and antislavery opponents of compromise. Clay opened the memorable debate in February. For two days he spoke in defense of his measures and urged mutual concessions for the sake of the Union. He asked Northerners why they insisted on the Wilmot Proviso when they had a stronger force working for them: "You have got nature itself on your side." He warned Southerners that they would gain nothing and lose a great deal by secession—that secession was certain to lead to

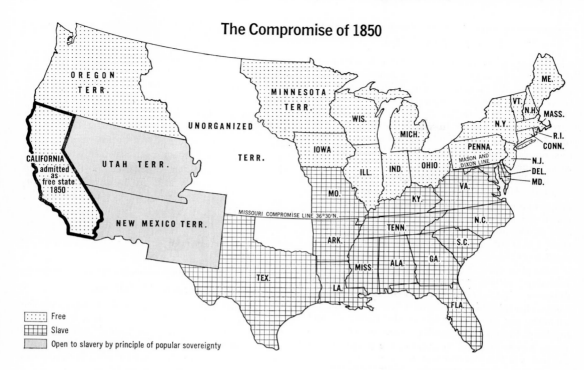

Free
Slave
Open to slavery by principle of popular sovereignty

civil war, "furious, bloody, implacable, exterminating." On March 4 John C. Calhoun, ill and close to death, listened to a colleague read his last address to the Senate. The present crisis, Calhoun insisted, was due to a breakdown of the old sectional equilibrium, to Northern aggression against the South, and to the destruction of the rights of the states and the creation of a consolidated government. Nothing could save the Union but an end of antislavery agitation, a faithful enforcement of the fugitive slave law, equal rights for the South in the territories, and a constitutional amendment restoring the balance between the two sections. If these points were not conceded, if the South were forced to choose between "submission or resistance," it would know how to act.

On March 7, three days after Calhoun had sounded his grim protest against Clay's compromise, Daniel Webster delivered the last great oration of his career. To the dismay of his antislavery constituents, he repudiated his free-soil sentiments and announced that he would speak "not as a Massachusetts man, not as a northern man, but as an American." Though Webster refuted Calhoun's charges

against the North, his speech was clearly an attempt to make the compromise palatable to his own section. He denounced antislavery agitation, urged Northerners not to insist on the Wilmot Proviso when slavery would not expand into the new territories in any case, called for an end to resistance to the fugitive slave act, and concluded with a tearful plea for the Union. Webster's speech immensely strengthened the forces of compromise, but for the remaining two years of his life antislavery men vilified him for his apostasy. Most of the Northern Conscience Whigs stood firm. Senator William H. Seward of New York spoke for them when he denounced compromise as "radically wrong and essentially vicious." There was only one way to end antislavery agitation, he said, and that was by "yielding to the progress of emancipation." In reply to Calhoun's constitutional defense of the right to carry slaves into the territories, Seward appealed to "a higher law than the Constitution," a divine law that intended these rich lands to be enjoyed by free men.

As the debate wore on and the House and Senate considered numerous variations of Clay's proposals, it became increasingly

1850: Daniel Webster

I wish to speak to-day, not as a Massachusetts man, nor as a northern man, but as an American, and a member of the Senate of the United States.... I speak to-day for the preservation of the Union. "Hear me for my cause"....

In the excited times in which we live, there is found to exist a state of crimination and recrimination between the North and South. There are lists of grievances produced by each....

I should much prefer to have heard, from every member of this floor, declarations of opinion that this Union could never be dissolved, than the declaration of opinion that in any case, under the pressure of circumstances, such a dissolution was possible. I hear with pain, and anguish, and distress, the word secession....

Instead of speaking of the possibility or utility of secession, instead of dwelling in these caverns of darkness ... let us come out into the light of day.... Let us cherish those hopes which belong to us.... Let us make our generation one of the strongest, and brightest links in that golden chain which is destined, I fully believe, to grapple the people of all the States to this Constitution, for ages to come.

From Daniel Webster, Seventh of March Speech, 1850.

evident that opinion in favor of a compromise of some kind was steadily building up in both North and South. Northern businessmen, frightened by the talk of secession, favored a compromise in order to protect their Southern trade and investments. The country had recovered from the depression of the 1840's, and practical men longed for a political peace so that they could make the most of a new era of prosperity and economic growth. The compromisers were further strengthened when the moderates won control of the Southern convention at Nashville and indicated that they were ready to accept a fair settlement. Now the most formidable obstacle to compromise was President Taylor, who bitterly resented Clay's rejection of the Administration's recommendations on New Mexico and California in favor of proposals of his own. The possibility of a presidential veto loomed until Taylor's sudden death on July 9 after an attack of cholera morbus. His successor, Vice-President Millard Fillmore, though a New York Whig of free-soil proclivities, immediately allied himself with Webster and

Clay and used his influence in favor of compromise.

Even then the adoption of a compromise was not easy. When Clay's major proposals had been combined in an "omnibus bill," they were threatened with defeat by a combination of Free-Soilers, antislavery Whigs, and Southern-rights men. But the moderates discovered that each of the measures might be enacted separately, for the moderates could then combine with those who opposed the compromise as a whole but favored individual parts of it. In the final weeks of the battle, Senator Douglas replaced the exhausted Clay as leader of the compromisers, and by September 1850 all the measures had been passed

1850: John C. Calhoun

The Union cannot ... be saved by eulogies on the Union, however splendid or numerous. The cry of "Union, Union, the glorious Union!" can no more prevent disunion than the cry of "Health, health, glorious health!" on the part of the physician, can save a patient lying dangerously ill....

How can the Union be saved? There is but one way by which it can with any certainty; and that is, by a full and final settlement, on the principle of justice, of all the questions at issue between the two sections....

But can this be done? Yes, easily; not by the weaker party, for it can of itself do nothing—not even protect itself—but by the stronger. The North has only to will it to accomplish it—to do justice by conceding to the South an equal right in the acquired territory, and to do her duty by causing the stipulations relative to fugitive slaves to be faithfully fulfilled—to cease the agitation of the slave question, and to provide for the insertion of a provision in the Constitution, by an amendment, which will restore to the South, in substance, the power she possessed of protecting herself before the equilibrium between the sections was destroyed by the action of this Government....

If you, who represent the stronger portion, cannot agree to settle them on the broad principle of justice and duty, say so; and let the States we both represent agree to separate and part in peace. If you are unwilling we should part in peace, tell us so; and we shall know what to do, when you reduce the question to submission or resistance.

From John C. Calhoun, Speech in the Senate, March 4, 1850.

Webster and Clay: They loved the Union.

and signed by President Fillmore. The Compromise of 1850 as it was finally adopted was essentially like the one Clay had proposed the January before: California was admitted as a free state; the territories of New Mexico and Utah were created from the rest of the Mexican cession, with no restriction on slavery; the Texas boundary was fixed as it exists today; Texas was paid $10 million from the federal treasury as compensation for yielding to New Mexico in their boundary dispute; slave-trading was prohibited in the District of Columbia; and a more severe fugitive-slave act replaced the old one of 1793.

The Aftermath

Public Reaction to the Compromise Few Northerners or Southerners were altogether satisfied with the Compromise of 1850, and some in each section spurned it as an unclean thing. Abolitionists and Free-Soilers refused to be bound by its terms and de-

nounced the Northern congressmen who had voted for it as unprincipled tools of the Slave Power. Emerson publicly declared that no man could obey the new fugitive slave law "without loss of self-respect and forfeiture of the name of a gentleman." In 1851 the Massachusetts legislature delivered a stern rebuke to Webster (who had joined Fillmore's Cabinet as Secretary of State) by electing Charles Sumner, a radical Free-Soiler and enemy of the compromise, to the United States Senate.

In the South, "fire-eaters" like Robert Barnwell Rhett of South Carolina and William L. Yancey of Alabama termed the compromise a fatal defeat for their section and called for drastic action. The position of the South in the Union was now hopeless, they said, and the proper remedy was immediate secession. In South Carolina the secessionists were defeated with the greatest difficulty, and then only because the "moderates" insisted that action be delayed until other Southern states were ready for independence. A state convention in Georgia adopted a series of resolutions, known as the Georgia Platform, which were probably an accurate expression of public opinion in the Deep South. These resolutions accepted the Compromise of 1850 but warned that Georgia would resist, "even (as a last resort) to a disruption of every tie which binds her to the Union," any act abolishing slavery in the District of Columbia, refusing to admit a slave state, excluding slavery from the territories, or repealing the fugitive slave law.

But most Americans in both sections, though doubting the wisdom of some provisions of the compromise, accepted it with great relief and hoped for a respite from sectional agitation. Mass meetings throughout the country celebrated its passage, and the merchants of New York City formed a Union Safety Committee to mobilize public opinion in its defense. Stephen A. Douglas announced that he had resolved "never to make another speech on the slavery question. . . . Let us cease agitating, stop the debate, and drop the subject." In his annual message of December 1850 President Fillmore told Congress that he regarded the compromise measures as "a final settlement of the dangerous and exciting subjects which they embraced." And forty-four congressmen of both parties signed a pledge to respect the terms of the compromise and never to support a candidate for public office who threatened to disturb it.

Franklin Pierce   The presidential election of 1852 gave further evidence of the widespread hope that the Compromise of 1850 would in fact be "a final settlement." The Democrats adopted a platform that endorsed the compromise without qualification and promised to resist "agitation of the slavery question, under whatever shape or color the attempt may be made." After many futile ballots the convention dropped the leading candidates—Douglas, Cass, and James Buchanan of Pennsylvania—and nominated another "dark horse," Franklin Pierce of New Hampshire. The Whig party, with its Northern and Southern wings now almost hopelessly divided, wrangled over a platform that unenthusiastically "acquiesced in" the compromise and therefore pleased almost no one. The convention rejected Fillmore and turned to another military hero, General Winfield Scott of

Virginia, whose friendship with Seward and whose failure to endorse the compromise made him suspect in the South. The election dealt a crushing blow to the Whig party—a blow from which it never recovered. Though Pierce's popular majority was not overwhelming, he carried twenty-seven states with 254 electoral votes, while Scott carried only four states with 42 electoral votes. The Barnburners had returned to the Democratic fold, and the Free-Soil party, with John P. Hale of New Hampshire as its candidate, polled only about half as many votes as it had four years earlier.

Pierce was a Jacksonian Democrat of amiable disposition, modest talent, and almost no capacity for executive leadership. His close ties with Southern Democrats, especially with Secretary of War Jefferson Davis, and his sympathy for their views on questions of public policy caused antislavery leaders to damn him as a "doughface"—"a northern man with southern principles." But his promise in his inaugural address that the provisions of the Compromise of 1850 would be "unhesitatingly carried into effect" suited the popular mood. In his first message to Congress in December 1853 Pierce rejoiced that the recent compromise had "given renewed vigor to our institutions and restored a sense of repose and security to the public mind." With the country prospering, with the sectional issues hopefully disposed of, some optimists went so far as to predict a new era of good feelings.

Surviving Sources of Friction   But even before Douglas reopened the territorial issue with his Kansas-Nebraska bill (see p. 306), there were abundant signs that the truce would be short. The disintegration of the Whig party after its defeat in 1852 snapped another of the ties holding the Union together. The admission of California had upset the sectional balance in the Senate—prior to 1850 there had been fifteen slave and fifteen free states—and the admission of several more free states could not be long delayed. The immigrants who poured into the United States during the 1840's and 1850's (see p. 293) shunned the South and thus further increased the North's numerical majority, and railroad-building and industrial expansion gave the North an accelerating economic supremacy. Now seces-

Population 1850

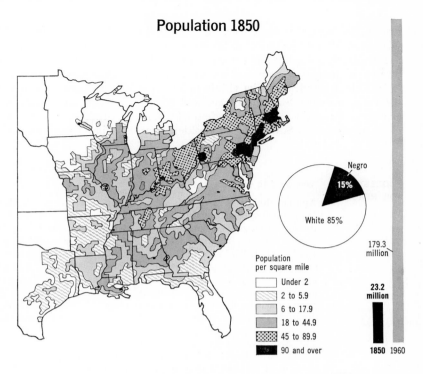

Negro 15%

White 85%

179.3 million

23.2 million

Population
per square mile

- ☐ Under 2
- ▨ 2 to 5.9
- ▥ 6 to 17.9
- ▦ 18 to 44.9
- ▧ 45 to 89.9
- ■ 90 and over

1850 1960

sionists could argue that the rights and interests of the minority South were at the mercy of a hostile and overbearing North.

To Southern-rights men the controversy that began at once over the enforcement of the new fugitive slave act proved their point. This was the provision of the Compromise of 1850 that Southerners regarded as their principal gain and that Northerners found most difficult to accept. It was a harsh measure that subjected alleged fugitives to summary hearings before federal commissioners without trial by jury or the right to testify in their own behalf. Since a commissioner received a fee of ten dollars if he ruled that a Negro prisoner was a slave but only five dollars if he ruled that the Negro was free, abolitionists charged that the commissioners were being bribed to collaborate with kidnapers who sought to sell free Negroes back into slavery. In the Northern strongholds of antislavery sentiment the new law simply could not be enforced; during the 1850's abolitionists executed a series of dramatic rescues of fugitives and sent them on to Canada and freedom. Moreover, various Northern states passed personal liberty laws which nullified the fugitive slave act or at least

interfered with its enforcement. This was an assertion of state rights and a form of nullification that Southerners scarcely appreciated.

Above all, the Compromise of 1850 could not stop the pens or quiet the voices of the abolitionists. Indeed, less than two years after the compromise was passed the most eloquent and influential appeal in behalf of the slave appeared in Harriet Beecher Stowe's justly celebrated novel, *Uncle Tom's Cabin.* Mrs. Stowe was the daughter of a New England clergyman, sister of seven others, and wife of still another. Her anger over the fugitive-slave act prompted her to declare: "I will write something. I will if I live." First published serially in an antislavery weekly, her novel appeared in book form in March 1852. By the end of the year, three hundred thousand copies had been sold. Thereafter the novel, together with its various adaptations for the stage, won thousands of converts to the antislavery cause. *Uncle Tom's Cabin* has more than a few flaws as a piece of literature: its situations are contrived; its dialogue is unreal; its slaves are romanticized. Mrs. Stowe knew almost nothing of slavery firsthand, but she understood clearly its tragic aspects; moreover, she had the wisdom to direct her moral indictment against the institution itself rather than against the Southern men and women who were caught in its toils. Indeed, the chief villain of her plot, the cruel overseer Simon Legree, was Northern-born. But these subtleties made the book no more attractive to Southern slaveholders than the cruder forms of abolitionist propaganda.

Slavery, then, still threatened the nation's peace and unity. On the eve of the Civil War Abraham Lincoln wrote to Alexander H. Stephens of Georgia: "You think slavery is right and ought to be extended, while we think it is *wrong* and ought to be restricted. That I suppose is the rub."

SUGGESTIONS FOR READING

Westward to the Pacific

Among the surveys of the westward movement, R. A. Billington, *Westward Expansion* (1949), is especially good on American penetration of the Far West. General coverage of the diplomacy of expansion is provided in S. F. Bemis, *A Diplomatic History of the United States* (rev. ed., 1955); T. A. Bailey, *A Diplomatic History of the American People* (6th ed., 1958); and J. W. Pratt, *A History of United States Foreign Policy* (1955). The best book dealing comprehensively with expansion in this period is R. A. Billington, *The Far Western Frontier, 1830–1860* (1956). N. A. Graebner, *Empire on the Pacific* (1955), stresses the desire for Pacific ports as a motive for expansion. A. K. Weinberg, *Manifest Destiny* (1935), is an excellent analysis of the ideology of expansionism. H. N. Smith, *Virgin Land** (1950), brilliantly discusses the place of the West in American literature and thought.

The two basic works on the American occupation of Texas are E. C. Barker, *Mexico and Texas, 1821–1835* (1928), and W. C. Binkley, *The Texas Revolution* (1952). A good popular account of the Santa Fe trade is R. L. Duffus, *The Santa Fe Trail* (1930). The best introductions to the fur trade of the Far West are H. M. Chittenden, *The American Fur Trade of the Far West*, 3 vols. (rev. ed., 1935); R. G. Cleland, *This Reckless Breed of Men: The Trappers and Fur Traders of the Southwest* (1950); and D. L. Morgan, *Jedediah Smith and the Opening of the West* (1953). Missionary activity in Oregon can be studied in two competent biographies: C. J. Brosnan, *Jason Lee: Prophet of the New Oregon* (1932), and C. M. Drury, *Marcus Whitman: M. D., Pioneer and Martyr* (1937). Two books on the overland trails, reliable and well written, are W. J. Ghent, *The Road to Oregon* (1929), and Jay Monaghan, *The Overland Trail* (1937). A superb contemporary account, Francis Parkman, *The California and Oregon Trail* (1849), is available in several modern editions under the title *The Oregon Trail.** The American occupation of Oregon is treated adequately in R. C. Clark, *History of the Willamette Valley, Oregon*, 3 vols. (1927), and O. O. Winther, *The Great Northwest* (1947). Early American interest in California is covered in two general histories: J. W. Caughey, *California* (1940), and R. G. Cleland, *From Wilderness to Empire: A History of California, 1542–1900* (1944). The best history of the Mormon settlement in the Salt Lake basin is Nels Anderson, *Desert Saints: The Mormon Frontier in Utah* (1942). F. M. Brodie, *No Man Knows My History: The Life of Joseph Smith* (1945), is an excellent biography. Preston Nibley, *Brigham Young: The Man and His Work* (1936), is warmly sympathetic.

Polk and the Triumph of Manifest Destiny

Polk's presidential years can be studied in E. I. McCormac, *James K. Polk* (1922), and in Allan Nevins, ed., *Polk: The Diary of a President, 1845–1849* (1952). A lively and readable introduction to the expansionism of the Polk era is Bernard De Voto, *The Year of Decision, 1846* (1943). Two books deal with negotiations for the annexation of Texas: J. H. Smith, *The Annexation of Texas* (1911), and J. W. Schmitz, *Texan Statecraft, 1836–1845* (1945). M. C. Jacobs, *Winning Oregon* (1938), is a good summary of the Oregon dispute and its settlement. The standard works on the background of the Mexican War are J. S. Reeves, *American Diplomacy under Tyler and Polk* (1907), and G. L. Rives, *The United States and Mexico, 1821–1848*, 2 vols. (1913).

* Available in a paperback edition.

The fullest and most authoritative work on the Mexican War is J. H. Smith, *The War with Mexico*, 2 vols. (1919). Three later books contribute few fresh interpretations but are brief and readable: A. H. Bill, *Rehearsal for Conflict: The War with Mexico, 1846–1848* (1947); R. S. Henry, *The Story of the Mexican War* (1950); and O. A. Singletary, *The Mexican War* (1960). The military campaigns are traced in two excellent biographies: C. W. Elliott, *Winfield Scott* (1937), and Holman Hamilton, *Zachary Taylor: Soldier of the Republic* (1941). Allan Nevins, *Frémont: Pathmarker of the West* (1955), is valuable for military operations in California.

Crisis and Compromise

Allan Nevins, *Ordeal of the Union*, 2 vols. (1947), contains a full, incisive, and well-written account of the issue of slavery expansion and of the Compromise of 1850. Other useful works include T. C. Smith, *The Liberty and Free-Soil Parties in the Northwest* (1897); J. M. White, *The Secession Movement in the United States, 1847–1852* (1916); R. H. Shryock, *Georgia and the Union in 1850* (1926); J. T. Carpenter, *The South as a Conscious Minority* (1930); and A. O. Craven, *The Growth of Southern Nationalism, 1848–1861* (1953). The election of 1848 and the Taylor Administration are treated thoroughly in two good biographies: Brainerd Dyer, *Zachary Taylor* (1946), and Holman Hamilton, *Zachary Taylor: Soldier in the White House* (1951).

Of the many books on the California gold rush, the following are among the best: R. W. Paul, *California Gold: The Beginning of Mining in the Far West* (1947); J. W. Caughey, *Gold Is the Cornerstone* (1948); O. C. Coy, *The Great Trek* (1931); A. B. Hulbert, *Forty-Niners* (1931); and J. H. Jackson, *Anybody's Gold: The Story of California's Mining Towns* (1941).

The sectional crisis and the Compromise of 1850 can be studied through the numerous biographies of national political leaders. Among the most useful are: C. B. Going, *David Wilmot, Free-Soiler* (1924); U. B. Phillips, *The Life of Robert Toombs* (1913); Frederic Bancroft, *The Life of William H. Seward*, 2 vols. (1900); F. B. Woodford, *Lewis Cass: The Last Jeffersonian* (1950); G. F. Milton, *The Eve of Conflict: Stephen A. Douglas and the Needless War* (1934); G. M. Capers, *Stephen A. Douglas: Defender of the Union* (1959); C. M. Fuess, *Daniel Webster*, 2 vols. (1930); R. N. Current, *Daniel Webster and the Rise of National Conservatism* (1955); G. G. Van Deusen, *The Life of Henry Clay* (1937) and *Thurlow Weed: Wizard of the Lobby* (1947); J. H. Parks, *John Bell of Tennessee* (1950); Rudolph Von Abele, *Alexander H. Stephens: A Biography* (1946); and C. M. Wiltse, *John C. Calhoun: Sectionalist, 1840–1850* (1951).

* Available in a paperback edition.

12

America at Mid-Century

From the Mexican War to the Civil War the major themes in the history of the United States were sectional conflict and national disintegration. But this period was also notable for its positive achievements, both for the burgeoning of the American economy and for the quality of American literature, unmatched until the 1920's. American writers had begun to heed Emerson's advice to stop imitating the "courtly muses of Europe" and to produce a distinctive literature of their own. The first of the earlier writers to win more than local recognition—Washington Irving and James Fenimore Cooper—had exploited American themes, but they had spent much of their lives abroad and had observed the conventions of Europe's men of letters. In the 1840's and 1850's, however, the essays of Emerson and Thoreau marked a turning away from Europe, a trend still more apparent in the novels of Nathaniel Hawthorne and Herman Melville and in the poetry of Walt Whitman. These writers gave this age of distinguished American literature its finest expression. Their masterpieces—Hawthorne's *The Scarlet Letter* (1850), Melville's *Moby Dick* (1851), Thoreau's *Walden* (1854), and the first edition of Whitman's *Leaves of Grass* (1855) —conveyed the best spirit of America at mid-century to a limited but appreciative audience of educated men and women. That audience, of course, has constantly grown, for the great works of the "American Renaissance" combine a nobility of expression and aspiration that

invigorates each successive generation of American readers.

The mass of Americans, however, were during the 1850's too busy with practical affairs to give much time to literature; they seldom thought about the philosophical questions that worried Hawthorne and Melville—the nature of man and the source of evil—for there was work to do. They were occupied with ships and railroads and machines and farm implements, with the settlement and development of the West, and with geographic expansion and Manifest Destiny. Stephen A. Douglas, energetic and tough-minded, idol of a bumptious element in the Democratic party that called itself Young America, cared little for literature, less for the moral issue of slavery. In the early 1850's Douglas struck a popular note when he urged his countrymen to forget the sectional quarrel and turn to the main business of building a prosperous and powerful nation. Young America was, to be sure, concerned about its soul, but it was concerned even more about getting things done.

Intimations of Imperialism

In his inaugural address President Pierce served notice that the acquisition of Oregon, California, and New Mexico was not the complete fulfillment of his country's Manifest Destiny. There were other areas that circumstances might force the United States to

The American Genius: Whitman

The genius of the United States is not best or most in its executives or legislatures, nor in its ambassadors or authors or colleges or churches or parlors, nor even in its newspapers or inventors ... but always most in the common people. Their manners, speech, dress, friendships—the freshness and candor of their physiognomy—the picturesque looseness of their carriage ... their deathless attachment to freedom—their aversion to anything indecorous or soft or mean—the practical acknowledgment of the citizens of one state by the citizens of all other states—the fierceness of their roused resentment—their curiosity and welcome of novelty—their self-esteem and wonderful sympathy—their susceptibility to a slight—the air they have of persons who never knew how it felt to stand in the presence of superiors—the fluency of their speech—their delight in music, the sure symptom of manly tenderness and native elegance of soul ... their good temper and open-handedness—the terrible significance of their elections—the President's taking off his hat to them not they to him—these too are unrhymed poetry. It awaits the gigantic and generous treatment worthy of it.

From Walt Whitman, Preface to *Leaves of Grass*, 1855.

The American Spirit: Hawthorne

"Are you a good little boy?" quoth I to Julian. "Yes," said he—"What are you good for?" asked I.—"Because I love all people," answered he. His mother will be in raptures with this response—a heavenly infant, powerless to do anything, but diffusing the richness of his pure love throughout the moral atmosphere, to make all mankind happier and better!!!!! Or perhaps he understood the question to mean for what reason he was good,—and meant to reply, that good deeds gushed forth from his heart of love, as the natural stream of such a fountain.

* * *

Julian, after picking up a handful of Autumnal red, maple-leaves, the other day:—"Look, father, here's a bunch of fire!"

* * *

In a grim, weird story, a figure of a gay, laughing, handsome youth, or young lady, all at once, in a natural, unconcerned way, takes off its face like a mask, and shows the grinning bare skeleton face beneath.

From Nathaniel Hawthorne, *American Notebooks*, 1851 and 1852.

---

acquire, and Pierce announced that his Administration would not shrink from further expansion because of "any timid forebodings of evil." In part he was expressing the continuing belief that eventually all or part of Canada and the rest of Mexico would be annexed to share the blessings of American democracy. But by mid-century some expansionists were looking beyond these adjacent territories to Cuba, Central America, and Hawaii, where commercial and strategic considerations fortified the hunger for land. This was a sign that Manifest Destiny might easily be converted into a doctrine of imperialism.

Cuba   The Spanish colony of Cuba, a land of slaves and plantations, interested Southerners who hoped to acquire it in order to increase their political and economic power. Cuba also attracted certain Northern commercial interests, especially a small but active group of business speculators in New York. Moreover, its proximity to Florida and its commanding position at the mouth of the Caribbean Sea and the Gulf of Mexico gave

it great strategic importance. The United States had always been apprehensive about the possibility that Cuba might pass from Spain to a stronger power. As early as 1810 President Madison had warned that his country "could not be a satisfied spectator" if Cuba were to fall to some European government "which might make a fulcrum of that position against the security and commerce of the United States."

Until the 1840's the chief aim of American diplomacy had been merely to keep Cuba out of the hands of Britain and France. After the Mexican War, however, proannexation sentiment became so strong that the government changed its policy. In 1848 James Buchanan, Polk's Secretary of State, instructed the American minister at Madrid to offer as much as $100 million for Cuba. The Spanish government responded with a cold refusal; indeed, the foreign minister vowed that he would sooner see the island sunk in the ocean than sold.

Failing to gain Cuba by diplomacy, some

expansionists (mostly Southerners) were ready to try force. In 1848 General Narciso López, a Venezuelan adventurer, appeared in New Orleans to find arms and recruits for a filibustering expedition against Cuba. The next year, in spite of federal attempts to stop him, López invaded the island with 250 volunteers, mostly Mexican War veterans, but Spanish troops quickly repulsed them. In 1851 López tried again with a force of 400 men, but once more he was defeated; this time Spanish authorities executed him and fifty other captives as pirates. Disappointed sympathizers in New Orleans retaliated by destroying the Spanish consulate, and the American and Spanish governments exchanged angry notes. Eventually the United States paid an indemnity for the damage committed by the New Orleans mob, and Spain pardoned the rest of the captured filibusters. But the government did not disavow its interest in Cuba; indeed, it rejected a British and French proposal for a tripartite agreement to assure the island's continued possession by Spain.

The Pierce Administration made the acquisition of Cuba one of its chief goals. It sent Pierre Soulé of Louisiana, a flamboyant French exile and ardent expansionist, as minister to Spain, and it gave him cause to believe that his mission was to acquire the island regardless of methods. Secretary of State William L. Marcy authorized Soulé to renew the attempt to purchase Cuba, this time for $130 million; failing in this, he might try to "detach" it from Spain by intrigue. Lacking the most elementary qualifications of a diplomat, the impetuous minister soon engaged in a bitter dispute with the Spanish government. In February 1854 an American merchant vessel, the *Black Warrior*, was seized at Havana for a technical violation of Spanish customs laws. Soulé promptly demanded a disavowal of the act and an indemnity; when he received no immediate reply, he renewed his demands in the form of a virtual ultimatum. The Spanish foreign minister simply ignored Soulé and negotiated a settlement directly with Washington and with the owners of the *Black Warrior*.

At this point Soulé might well have been replaced by a more skillful minister. Instead, Marcy showed no outward sign of disapproval and gave him an even more delicate assignment. Soulé was to confer with John Y. Mason, minister to France, and James Buchanan, minister to Great Britain, about methods of acquiring Cuba and of dealing with possible British and French opposition. In October 1854 the three ministers met for a few days at Ostend and then for a week at Aix-la-Chapelle. They sent their recommendations to the Secretary of State in a confidential memorandum, but its contents were soon known to the public —and the document itself was quite inaccurately named the Ostend Manifesto. Largely the work of Soulé, the memorandum declared that the United States would benefit from the possession of Cuba while Spain would be better off without it. Accordingly, it proposed that another effort be made to purchase the island. If Spain again refused to sell, the United States would have to consider whether Cuba was a threat to her internal peace. If it were found to be such a threat, "then by every law human and divine, we shall be justified in wresting it from Spain, if we possess the power."

The Ostend Manifesto delighted Southern expansionists and the Young America element in the Democratic party, and it played no small part in Buchanan's presidential nomination two years later. But the criticism from abroad and the indignation of antislavery Northerners forced the Pierce Administration to repudiate it. Marcy sent a strong rebuke to Soulé, and the shocked and humiliated minister resigned. But Cuba was not forgotten; the Democratic platform of 1856 favored annexation, and in three of his annual messages to Congress President Buchanan urged another attempt to purchase it. Cuba, however, had become a sectional issue, and further action was impossible.

Central America   For centuries men had dreamed of joining the Atlantic and Pacific by cutting a canal through Panama or Nicaragua, but the United States did not become seriously interested in the idea until after the Mexican War and the acquisition of California. In 1848 the need for faster communication between the East and the Far West led to the signing of a treaty with New Granada (Colombia), which gave the United States transit rights through Panama in exchange for a guarantee of New Granada's sovereignty over this isthmian province. By 1855 a group of American promoters had built a railroad across Panama; until the completion of the first transcontinental railroad in 1869, this was the easiest route to the Pacific coast.

Meanwhile, American diplomats, speculators, and adventurers had become deeply involved in the affairs of the small and politically unstable Republic of Nicaragua, which seemed as promising a site for a canal as Panama. Here, however, the Americans met a formidable competitor in Great Britain, whose world-wide trade, large navy, and extensive colonial possessions gave her a keen interest in an isthmian canal. Indeed, because of the enormous cost of such a project, many assumed that when a canal was built, British capitalists would finance and control it. The British government, watching American movements suspiciously, established a foothold at the mouth of the San Juan River (the probable eastern terminus of a Nicaraguan canal) and claimed a protectorate over the Mosquito Indians on the eastern coast of Nicaragua. This action alarmed the American government, and in the resulting diplomatic exchanges each country warned that it would not permit the other to have exclusive control over an isthmian canal. In 1850 the dispute was settled when Sir Henry Lytton Bulwer, the British minister to the United States, and John M. Clayton, President Taylor's Secretary of State, agreed to the terms of a treaty. It provided, first, that any canal built through Panama or Nicaragua was to be unfortified, neutral in time of war, and open to the ships of all countries on equal terms; second, that neither country was to colonize or establish dominion over any part of Central America.

The Clayton-Bulwer Treaty was ratified by the Senate and remained in force for the next half-century, but it was unpopular from the start. Expansionists disliked the commitment not to acquire territory in Central America, which meant, they said, that the United States had voluntarily applied the Monroe Doctrine against itself. This concession, together with the implicit recognition that Britain had equal interests in Central America, provoked critics to accuse Clayton of having been outwitted by Bulwer—Buchanan suggested that Clayton ought to be rewarded with elevation to the British peerage. Resentment increased when the British government maintained that the treaty applied only to the future and was not an obligation to abandon its existing protectorate over the eastern coast of Nicaragua. Impulsive Southern expansionists applauded when, in 1855, William Walker, a Tennesseean by birth, led a filibustering expedition into Nicaragua and seized control of her government. Walker was soon driven out, and when he tried to return in 1860 he was captured and executed.

In spite of the criticism, the Clayton-Bulwer Treaty was not a bad bargain for the United States, given the circumstances of the time. The British government removed one cause of complaint when in 1859 it voluntarily gave up its protectorate over the Mosquito Indians. Then and later the treaty avoided a race between the two countries for possessions in Central America. Above all, it assured the United States equal access to an isthmian canal at a time when she was in no position to ask for more.

Hawaii   Even before the acquisition of Oregon and California made the United States a Pacific power, some Americans had developed an interest in Hawaii. Merchantmen engaged in trade with the Far East, and whaling ships, had stopped there for supplies; by the 1830's missionaries had begun to arrive; others had come in search of land or commercial opportunities. In these early years there was little talk of annexation, but the government was uneasy about the intentions of the British and the French. In 1849, when France seemed ready to seize the islands, Secretary of State Clayton, though denying that the United States desired to establish her sovereignty over them, warned that she "could never with indifference allow them to pass under the dominion or exclusive control of any other power." The Pierce Administration, however, pursued a more aggressive policy; in 1854 Secretary of State Marcy negotiated a treaty of annexation with the Hawaiian government. But British protests and Senate opposition caused Pierce to drop the matter. Thereafter, until the 1880's, the United States seemed content merely to keep Hawaii free from foreign control.

The Gadsden Purchase The only tangible result of the various expansionist schemes of the 1850's was the purchase from Mexico of another slice of land in the Southwest. In 1853 the War Department made a survey of possible routes for a transcontinental railroad. The survey revealed that if a line were to be built westward from a Southern city it would probably have to enter Mexican territory south of the Gila River. Realizing that this would be an effective argument for a Northern route, Secretary of War Jefferson Davis persuaded President Pierce to send James Gadsden, a Southern railroad promoter, to negotiate with Mexico. When Gadsden arrived in Mexico City, he found Santa Anna back in power and in need of money. In 1854 they signed a treaty giving the United States a forty-five-thousand–square–mile strip of desert land below the Gila for $10 million. Except for Alaska, the Gadsden Purchase rounded out the continental frontiers of the United States.

International Trade

Europe American merchants and shipowners recovered only slowly from the disasters they had suffered during the War of 1812, and they were severely hurt again by the long depression following the Panic of 1837. By the mid-1840's, however, economic recovery and several other favorable developments combined to encourage a revival of foreign trade. The repeal of the British Corn Laws in 1846 opened a large market for American wheat; the passage of the low Walker Tariff the same year (followed by a still lower tariff in 1857) encouraged the flow of European manufactured goods to the United States; and a spectacular rise in immigration kept American ships filled to capacity on the homeward voyage. As a result, the combined value of American exports and imports increased from $222 million in 1840 to $318 million in 1850; during the next decade they more than doubled, to reach $687 million in 1860.

More than two-thirds of this commerce was with Europe, and the most valuable part of it was the exchange of American cotton, wheat, and flour for the products of British factories. In 1860 finished manufactured goods constituted only 10 per cent of United States exports,

but nearly half of her imports. As is typical of an agricultural country, the value of imports usually exceeded the value of exports—by $29 million in 1850. This unfavorable trade balance forced the United States to send a large part of the gold mined in California to Europe. Nevertheless, foreign trade was vital to the whole national economy. Though Americans still concentrated on their own internal development, they were bound to the outside world by important commercial ties.

China As late as 1860 scarcely more than 5 per cent of American trade was with Asia. Ever since the late eighteenth century, however, many New York and New England merchants had been dazzled by the profits they anticipated from the penetration of Far Eastern markets. As we have seen, their hope of developing this trade was related to the desire for ports on the Pacific Coast. By the early nineteenth century, American merchant ships were stopping in the Philippines, Java, and India, and in 1833 the United States signed a trade treaty with Siam. But the center of activity was at Canton, the one Chinese port open to foreigners, where furs were traded for tea, spices, and nankeens.

Though the United States government never took the initiative in wringing commercial concessions from China, it always capitalized on opportunities afforded by the encroachments of others. When Britain, after the Opium War of 1839–42, forced open several additional Chinese ports and gained various other advantages, American merchants demanded that their government intervene in their behalf. President Tyler responded by sending Caleb Cushing of Massachusetts, a man of rare diplomatic talent, to negotiate with China. In the Treaty of Wanghia (1844) Cushing won access to the ports that had been opened to the British; he established the right of extraterritoriality, which enabled resident Americans accused of crimes to be tried in American rather than Chinese courts; and he obtained a promise of "most favored nation" treatment for the United States, whereby privileges granted to other powers would also be granted to her. In subsequent years, as the British and French forced China to make further concessions, American merchants were thus able to claim similar rights. Since the United States merely asked to be given what others had seized by force, however, relations with China remained friendly.

Japan From the sixteenth century to the middle of the nineteenth century Japan's only contact with the outside world had been a limited trade with the Dutch East India Company through the port of Nagasaki. The military Shoguns, who dominated the weak emperors, had excluded foreign merchants, missionaries, and diplomats in order to preserve a feudal society. But during the 1840's some Americans began to take an interest in Japan. The Pacific whaling industry needed a treaty to assure proper treatment of shipwrecked sailors cast upon Japanese shores; merchants engaged in the China trade hoped to make Japan a port of call; and textile manufacturers were eager to exploit the Japanese market.

In 1852 pressure from these groups caused President Fillmore to send Commodore Matthew C. Perry to Japan with an imposing fleet of steam warships. Perry bore a letter and gifts to the emperor and an array of gadgets illustrating the wonders of western civilization. In July 1853 he arrived at Yedo Bay, insisted that his letter be delivered to the emperor, and promised to return in the spring. Perry made his second visit early in 1854 and found Japanese officials conciliatory and ready to negotiate. By combining vague threats of war with skillful diplomacy, he secured a treaty of friendship that opened two small ports to American trade, permitted the establishment of a consulate at one of them, guaranteed the safety of shipwrecked sailors, and gave the United States "most favored nation" treatment. Other Western powers soon negotiated their own treaties and forced Japan to open other ports and make additional concessions.

The State Department sent Townsend Harris, a brilliant diplomat, to Japan as the first American consul. Pointing to the fate of China under foreign domination, Harris assured Japan that the United States had no territorial ambitions and urged her to protect herself by modernizing and Westernizing under American guidance. "If you accept my proposals," he predicted, "Japan will become the England of the Orient." His case was persua-sive, and in 1858 he signed another treaty greatly enlarging the concessions that Perry had won. Ministers were now to be exchanged; American consuls could reside at the six ports then open to foreigners; American citizens could buy property and enjoy freedom of religion at the so-called "treaty ports"; and Japan could buy warships and merchantmen from the United States. In 1860 the first Japanese diplomatic delegation visited Washington, and soon thereafter Japan began to make rapid strides toward catching up with the modern world.

The Clipper Ships The recovery of American foreign trade was immensely aided by a series of dramatic changes in the design of the old three-masted packet ships (see p. 207), changes that produced a fleet of the swiftest and most beautiful sailing vessels ever to engage in ocean commerce. In 1845 the *Rainbow*, a 750-ton ship designed by John Griffith, a naval architect, was completed; it had a long, sleek hull with a concave bow, convex sides, and a rounded stern, and tall masts with an enormous spread of canvas. The launching of the *Rainbow*, a ship that incorporated the advances of several decades, marked the beginning of the era of the famed clipper ships.

Among the builders of clippers, Donald McKay, of Newburyport, Massachusetts, was the most sucessful; his yards produced scores of vessels, including the 1,783-ton *Flying Cloud*, the 2,421-ton *Sovereign of the Seas*, and the 4,000-ton *Great Republic*. Commanded by daring, hard-driving captains, these ships broke all records for speed. In 1851, on her maiden voyage, the *Flying Cloud* covered 374 miles in a day; then, on a voyage from New York to San Francisco, she made a run of 433 miles in a day to break her own record. The *Sovereign of the Seas* soon surpassed that with 495 miles in a day's run. Another clipper, the *Lightning*, set a record of thirteen and a half days for a voyage from New York to Liverpool; still another, the *Oriental*, set a record of eighty-one days for a voyage from New York to Hong Kong.

From the mid-1840's to the mid-1850's the clippers gave the United States a larger share of the world's carrying trade than ever before, a share that briefly promised to surpass the

The clipper "Flying Cloud": Triumph of American practical art.

British. The new ships and their masters took a commanding position in the commerce of both Europe and the Far East. But the most spectacular role of the clippers came in the early 1850's in the growing trade between the Atlantic coast and California. The older sailing vessels had taken more than five months to make the voyage around the Horn, whereas the clippers made it in three.

The era of the clipper ships, however, soon ended, for by the mid-1850's advances in technology were making them obsolete. The opening of the Panama Railroad in 1855 deprived them of the California trade, because cargoes could reach San Francisco along the shorter route in five weeks. Meanwhile the clippers were losing out in the competition with British ironclad steam vessels, which were less beautiful in design but superior in speed and cargo space. American steamship companies had only indifferent success in their rivalry with the British, who now recaptured much of the ocean commerce that they had lost to the clippers. Not until the First World

War would the United States again hold the position in the carrying trade that she enjoyed for a decade in the mid-nineteenth century.

Immigration

The Role of the Immigrant   Between 1830 and 1860 the population of the United States increased from 12,866,000 to 31,443,000. But in spite of this remarkable growth the country was still sparsely settled and short of man power. The factories needed more and more hands to tend the machines, and the limited supply and relatively high cost of labor retarded the rate of industrial expansion. Revived programs of internal improvements following the depression of the early 1840's created another heavy demand for workers. Above all, the supply of arable land still seemed to be inexhaustible, and the Western states and territories eagerly welcomed new settlers. Depression created temporary unemployment in the Eastern industrial centers, but most of the time before the Civil War there were not enough men and women to meet the labor requirements of cities and farms.

The man-power problem would have been even more acute had it not been for a sharp increase in European immigration to the United States beginning in the mid-1840's. Until then immigrants had been arriving at a slowly accelerating annual rate—8,385 in 1820, 23,322 in 1830, and 84,066 in 1840—but in the decade before 1840 fewer than 600,000 had crossed the Atlantic. In the following decade, however, immigration increased to 1,713,000, and during the 1850's to 2,598,000. Each year between 1850 and 1854 the number of immigrants exceeded 300,000, reaching a peak of 428,000 in 1854—a figure that would not be surpassed until the 1870's.

The overwhelming majority of immigrants still came from northern and western Europe. During the 1850's slightly more than 300,000 migrated from Great Britain, about 25,000 from the Scandinavian countries. But Germany and southern Ireland had now become the two principal sources. In addition to the usual incentives—technological unemployment, the lure of cheap land, and the vision of the United States as a country of opportunity, freedom, and social equality—several special conditions helped to bring in a tide of Irish and Germans. In Ireland the failure of the potato crop of 1845 began a succession of famine years that caused widespread misery and actual starvation. As a result, in the fifteen years after 1845 approximately a million and a half Irishmen, most of them in extreme poverty, crossed the Atlantic. In Germany the suppression of the liberal Revolution of 1848 brought many political refugees along with those who came in search of improved economic conditions. Between 1850 and 1860 nearly a million Germans arrived.

In the main these immigrants were not systematically recruited, and they were seldom subsidized by organized groups. The Mormon Church helped its converts, and an Irish Pioneer Emigration Fund, supported by British, Irish, and American leaders, paid the passage of a few. In addition, some immigrants helped friends or relatives to join them. But most came on their own. A minority of them were fairly well-to-do middle-class people whose motive for coming, according to one report, was "not want or oppression, but . . . a rage for speculation, or a desire to acquire wealth more rapidly." Usually, however, the immigrants were poor people who could afford to pay their way only because competing merchant ships, needing return cargoes, reduced fares to as low as thirty dollars. Immigrants were crowded into steerage quarters, where they suffered from poor food, inadequate sanitary facilities, and the ravages of smallpox, dysentery, and "ship fever."

Much of this immigrant stream poured into the country through New York, some of it through Boston, Philadelphia, Baltimore, and New Orleans. Since there was no public program to help these strangers find homes and jobs or to ease the difficult adjustment to a new environment, many of them at first had un-unhappy experiences. Until the state of New York, in 1855, gave immigrants some protection by establishing Castle Garden as a controlled landing place, they often fell victim to swindlers who cheated them with exorbitant charges for lodgings or transportation, or with false promises of employment. Because the Irish seldom had the means to become farmers, they congregated in the slums of New York and Boston and in the factory towns of New England. A much larger proportion of the Germans arrived with enough money to move to the Middle West, where they acquired farms or established business enterprises in cities such as Cincinnati, St. Louis, Chicago, and Milwaukee. Immigrants rarely settled in the South. Most of them debarked at Northern ports, but even those who arrived at New Orleans often took steamboats up the Mississippi to the free states. They were drawn north by their preference for the cooler climate, by their unwillingness to compete with slave labor, and, in the case of many Germans, by their opposition to slavery itself.

Though few immigrants found it easy to settle in a new land, though far too many lived in abject poverty in the cities of the East, in the long run most of them did manage to improve their economic lot, and their contributions to American society were incalculable. From the ranks of the immigrants in subsequent years came many of the country's distinguished leaders in politics, the professions, journalism, the fine arts, banking, industry, and transportation. The English and Germans augmented the short supply of skilled craftsmen; the Welsh and Cornish worked the coal mines of Pennsylvania and the lead mines of Missouri and Wisconsin; the Irish tended the machines in New England factories, built railroads, and dug canals; men and women from all the immigrant groups brought millions of acres of Western land under cultivation. Not the least of the immigrants' contributions was the richness and variety they gave to American society through the customs and amenities they brought with them from their old homes.

Nativism   Notwithstanding the value of the immigrants to a thinly settled country, their growing numbers began to alarm some Americans. By the 1850's aliens constituted half the population of New York City and outnumbered the native-born Americans in Chicago, Milwaukee, and St. Louis. Such conditions helped to produce the first nativist, or antiforeign, movement in American history, a movement that briefly exerted considerable influence in both state and national politics.

The causes of nativism were several. A few racists feared that the Celts from southern Ireland would pollute the old American stock, and that the United States would cease to be predominantly an Anglo-Saxon nation. Some criticized the Irish and Germans for their clannishness and for their tendency to preserve Old World customs and habits of dress. Others were distressed by the prevalence of crime and pauperism in the immigrant slums, resented the burden that alien indigents put on public funds and private charity, and accused European governments of deliberately exporting their "undesirables" to the United States. Native workingmen disliked the immigrants as economic competitors whose low standard of living threatened to depress wages. Southerners were unhappy to find them adding to the North's majority in population and congressional representation. Conservatives were concerned about the immigrants' political power, for many states permitted them to vote before they became naturalized citizens. Most immigrants supported the Democratic party as the party of the common man, and in the Eastern cities Democratic bosses used them to build political machines.

Though all these anxieties contributed to the nativist movement, the strongest force behind it was anti-Catholicism. In the early nineteenth century Roman Catholics were a small fraction of the population, but in the 1840's and 1850's nearly all of the Irish and many of the German immigrants were adherents of this faith. With the growth of the Catholic population, there was a corresponding increase in the number of Catholic priests and bishops, convents and monasteries, schools and colleges. Anti-Catholic sentiment among American Protestants was old and deep-rooted, having grown from a combination of bigotry and genuine disagreement over Christian doctrine. Frightened nativists viewed every Catholic immigrant as an agent of the pope sent to seize the government and destroy Protestantism. They believed the Church to be the ally of tyranny and reaction in Europe, the enemy of freedom and democracy in America. And their prejudices were confirmed by lurid accounts of immorality in the convents and among the priesthood.

Nativist agitation started in the 1830's. In New York the Reverend George Bourne edited an anti-Catholic weekly, *The Protestant*, while other clergymen organized a Protestant Association "to promote the principles of the Reformation" and to "unfold the true character of Popery." In 1834 Samuel F. B. Morse, portrait painter and promoter of the telegraph, published an influential anti-Catholic book, *A Foreign Conspiracy Against the Liberties of the United States*, that went through numerous editions. Urging Protestants to unite against the Catholic menace, Morse advocated stricter immigration laws to "stop this leak in the ship through which the muddy waters from without threaten to sink us." Nativists incited anti-Catholic riots, stoned Catholic institutions, and, in 1834, burned the Ursuline Convent School in Charlestown, Massachusetts.

During the 1840's, when Catholic immigrants began to arrive in large numbers, a bewildering array of secret nativist societies sprang up: the Sons of '76, the Sons of America, the Druids, the Order of United Americans, and many others. Early in the 1850's most of these groups united to form a powerful national organization, the Order of the Star Spangled Banner. Because members were sworn to secrecy and refused to answer questions about their aims and activities, they were usually called the Know-Nothings. It soon became evident, however, that their purposes were to defend Protestantism against Catholicism, to make immigration laws more restrictive, to increase the number of years required for naturalization, and to deprive aliens of the ballot.

Meanwhile, nativism had entered politics and had begun to score successes in local elections. After the presidential election of 1852, many former Whigs joined the movement as their own party disintegrated. Political nativism reached its peak in 1854 and 1855, when the Know-Nothings captured several state legislatures, elected numerous governors, and claimed the allegiance of at least seventy-five congressmen. Their most spectacular victory came in Massachusetts, where they controlled every state office and had an overwhelming majority in the legislature. In 1856 the nativists formed the American party, nominated Millard Fillmore for President, and polled about 25 per cent of the popular vote.

Thereafter, nativism rapidly declined. In Massachusetts most of the Know-Nothing legislators proved to be incompetent, and they were able to write almost none of their demands into law. Nationally the nativists soon lost their appeal as the country became increasingly absorbed in the conflict over slavery expansion—indeed, the American party itself split over this issue. Moreover, the religious bigotry and xenophobia of the Know-Nothings failed to destroy certain traditional American attitudes that soon began to reassert themselves: the belief in religious toleration, the idea of America as a refuge for the oppressed of the Old World, and a confidence that the United States could in time assimilate as many immigrants as came to her shores. Besides, nativism betrayed the Christian ideal of the brotherhood of man—as one critic observed, it "judges men by the accidents of their condition, instead of striving to find a common lot for all, with a common access to the blessings of life." Finally, nativist racism was refuted by another viewpoint, which held that the mixing of various nationalities was producing a new man, the American, superior to the old by the very fact of the mixing. As Herman Melville observed, "We are the heirs of all time, and with all nations we divide our inheritance."

"Mexicans shall rule America": Bigotry in Baltimore.

Economic Development

Domestic Commerce The flourishing American foreign trade of the mid-nineteenth century required the movement of huge quantities of bulky raw materials and foodstuffs to the seaports on the Atlantic and Gulf coasts, as well as the distribution of finished European goods to the markets of the interior. At the same time internal trade expanded as the population grew and as the economies of the various regions became increasingly specialized and interdependent. Much of this commerce continued to move along the country's excellent waterways. Coastal vessels carried cotton from Southern ports to New York and New England, while the glamorous Mississippi River steamboats carried more freight and passengers in the 1850's than ever before.

The paths of inland water transportation were rapidly changing, however, for the canals were diverting a growing amount of business from the rivers to the Great Lakes. The Miami and Erie Canal through Ohio, and the Wabash and Erie Canal through Indiana, both connected the Ohio River with Lake Erie at To-ledo, while the Illinois and Michigan Canal united the Mississippi and Illinois rivers with Lake Michigan at Chicago. As trade shifted to the Great Lakes and the Erie Canal, New York replaced New Orleans as the chief outlet for Western commodities destined for European markets, and young cities on the lakes outgrew the older cities on the rivers. In the 1830's Chicago had been a small village; by 1860 it had a population of 109,000.

Meanwhile, all forms of water transportation were beginning to face serious competition from the railroads. The principle of running cars on wooden or iron rails had long been in use in the British mining districts for hauling coal, but until the early nineteenth century men or animals had always provided the power. Experiments with steam engines began soon after 1800, and in 1820 John Stevens of New Jersey demonstrated a steam locomotive that successfully pulled a train of cars over a short piece of track. Five years later a small British line, the Stockton and Darlington, became the first commercial railroad to utilize steam power.

This development was enough to stimulate

West from Boston: A locomotive of the fifties on the Fitchburg line.

feverish activity in the cities of the Eastern United States, where merchants had been seeking a way to compete with New York for the trade of the interior. In 1828 construction began on the Baltimore and Ohio, and by 1830 a thirteen-mile segment was open for business. A year later the Mohawk and Hudson established service over sixteen miles of track between Albany and Schenectady. In 1833 South Carolina's 136-mile Charleston and Hamburg line was completed and became for a time the longest railroad in the world. Philadelphia soon had a rail connection with the coal fields of central Pennsylvania, Boston with Worcester and other interior New England cities. By 1840 these and other lines had a combined trackage of 2,818 miles; by 1850 the trackage had grown to 9,021 miles, and by 1860 to 30,-627 miles.

Emerson once observed that "the Americans take to this little contrivance, the railroad, as if it were the cradle in which they were born." They took to it (after first showing considerable hostility) in spite of such early inconveniences as irregular schedules, frequent breakdowns, and the likelihood of being showered with sparks from the wood-burning locomotives. A major annoyance was the lack of a standard-gauge track—as late as 1860 there were still a dozen gauges in use—which made it impossible for the rolling stock of one railroad to use the tracks of another. Worse than the inconveniences were the disastrous wrecks resulting from soft roadbeds, broken rails, and collapsed bridges.

Construction engineers gradually increased the safety and efficiency of the railroads. They built solid roadbeds using crushed rock for ballast, substituted cast-iron "T" rails for the old wooden rails covered with iron straps, learned how to make curves and negotiate grades, erected sturdier bridges, and improved the design of locomotives and cars. By the 1850's, though accidents still occurred with painful frequency, technological advances had reduced the risks of travel by railroad to a point where they were not much greater than by steamboat. The speed of the railroads (twenty to thirty miles an hour by 1860), their ability to get through the roughest terrain and to tap the remotest markets, their serviceability in winter when the canals froze over, made them the ideal solution to the country's transportation needs.

During the 1850's, in addition to an enormous expansion of railroad mileage, considerable progress was made toward the consolidation of small, independent lines to form trunk lines. In the South, although both Norfolk and Charleston had established rail connections with the Mississippi River at Memphis, most lines continued to be short and to serve merely as feeders for river transportation. The railroad network that had emerged by 1860 was largely a system that united the Northwest with the Northeast. The Baltimore and Ohio had now reached the Ohio River at Wheeling, the Pennsylvania Railroad had connected Philadelphia and Pittsburgh, and several lines had given Boston access to the Erie Canal and the Great Lakes. Meanwhile, the Hudson River Railroad from New York to Albany, together with the New York Central, formed by the consolidation of seven lines between Albany and Buffalo, had given New York a through route to the West. A second railroad, the Erie, had been built across southern New York State from Jersey City to Buffalo. Powerful corporations, controlled by railroad capitalists like Erastus Corning of Albany and John Murray Forbes of Boston, directed the construction and consolidation that produced the trunk lines. Most of the funds came from American and British investors, a little from state and local government subsidies.

In the West, where most of the railroad construction of the 1850's took place, various lines in Ohio, Indiana, and Illinois linked the Ohio and Mississippi rivers with the Great Lakes. The most important of these north-south lines was the Illinois Central, which by 1858 had given Chicago a connection with the rivers at Cairo. Other railroads ran eastward from Chicago, now the transportation hub of the West, to meet the Eastern trunk lines. By 1860 both the Erie and the New York Central either controlled or had agreements with a series of lines that gave them access to Chicago. Railroad bridges now spanned the Mississippi River, and new lines had penetrated as far west as Burlington, Iowa, and St. Joseph, Missouri.

Railroad-builders in the West depended on public support more than those in the East. State and local governments aided them with

The Growth of the Railroad Network 1850-60

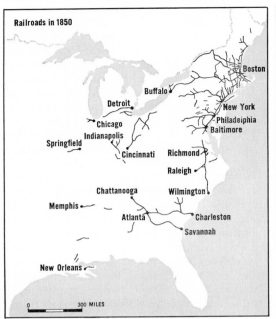

Railroads in 1850

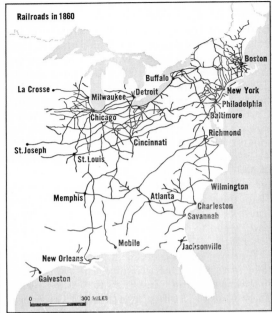

Railroads in 1860

loans, subsidies, and stock subscriptions, and in 1850 Congress passed a momentous bill providing the first of many railroad land grants. This act, whose chief sponsor was Senator Stephen A. Douglas, was for the benefit of the Illinois Central; it gave the state of Illinois three square miles of land in alternate sections on both sides of the proposed line (six square miles for each mile of track), with the understanding that the land would be turned over to the company as the railroad was built. Southern support was obtained by making a similar grant for a line from the Ohio River to Mobile. By 1860 approximately 28 million acres from the public domain had been granted to various states for railroad construction.

After 1850 there was much talk of a transcontinental railroad to be built with a federal subsidy, but sectional disagreement over the location of the route delayed action until after the start of the Civil War. Meanwhile, in 1855 the firm of Russell, Majors & Waddell, aided by a government subsidy, established regular overland freight service between Kansas and California. Three years later the Butterfield Overland Mail Company began to run subsidized semiweekly stagecoaches between St.

Louis and San Francisco. In the spring of 1860 Russell, Majors & Waddell introduced the pony express, which carried mail from St. Joseph, Missouri, to Sacramento in ten days. But in less than a year and a half the pony express was put out of business by a device that was revolutionizing communication: the electric telegraph. In 1844 Samuel F. B. Morse had demonstrated its practicality, and by 1860 the country had been tied together with fifty thousand miles of telegraph wire. In October 1861, when the Pacific Telegraph Company completed its line to San Francisco, communication between the Atlantic and Pacific coasts became a matter of minutes.

Agriculture   The revolution in transportation, the rapid growth of industry, and advances in agricultural technology profoundly affected the life of the American farmer. In New England the rural population declined as many families moved west in search of better land, or to the cities to find employment in the factories. Even so, in the 1850's a large proportion of the country's raw wool came from New England, while much wheat and corn were grown in New York and Pennsylvania. But farmers in the Northeast were rapidly turning from these crops to the production of fruits, vegetables, and milk for the growing cities nearby. Railroads enabled the owners of orchards, truck gardens, and dairy herds to make daily shipments to city markets from considerable distances. In this highly specialized and commercialized form, Eastern agriculture found new life and became a rewarding enterprise.

In the South the 1850's were prosperous years for the producers of the great staples (tobacco, rice, sugar, and cotton) with slave labor. By then the heart of the Cotton Kingdom had shifted from the Southeast to the Alabama-Mississippi Black Belt, the Mississippi delta, the valleys of the Arkansas and Red rivers, and the prairies of eastern Texas. With cotton selling for ten to twelve cents a pound, production rose from 2,469,000 bales in 1849 to 5,387,000 bales in 1859, and the South came near to monopolizing world markets. Able-bodied young slaves sold for $1,500 in the New Orleans market. In eastern Virginia, where a generation earlier soil exhaustion had produced agricultural stagnation, conditions had greatly improved. The slave-plantation system gained new vitality from the introduction of fertilizers, improved methods of cultivation, and systems of crop rotation. Throughout the South the plantations, though highly commercialized agricultural enterprises, were less affected by technological changes than the farms of the Northeast and Northwest. Planters continued to cultivate the staples with gangs of unskilled slaves using simple hoes and plows. As for the mass of nonslaveholding yeoman farmers, they often planted a few acres in cotton or tobacco, but in the main they raised corn and hogs for their own subsistence.

By 1860 the Old Northwest had become the center of wheat, corn, beef, and pork production. Responding to the needs of old markets in the plantation South and to the growing demands of the East and of Europe, native-born farmers and German and Scandinavian immigrants had opened up the virgin lands of northern Illinois and Indiana, southern Michigan and Wisconsin, and eastern Iowa and Minnesota. With their help the corn crop had increased from 592 million bushels in 1849 to 839 million bushels in 1859, the wheat crop from 100 million bushels to 173 million bushels.

Illinois and Indiana now led in hog production, Illinois in corn production, and Illinois, Indiana, and Wisconsin in wheat production.

Widening markets, the high cost of labor, and the abandonment of self-sufficient agriculture for specialized crops stimulated the improvement of farm implements and mechanization. To cut through the tough prairie sod, Western farmers needed plows that were more efficient than the old ones made of wood or cast iron and drawn by slow-moving oxen. In 1847 John Deere supplied this need when he opened a factory at Moline, Illinois, to manufacture light steel plows that cut deeper furrows and could be drawn by horses. The fifties also saw the substitution of grain drills for hand planting and the introduction of mowers to harvest the hay crop. Most important for the wheat farmers was the invention of mechanical reapers to replace hand sickles and cradles. In 1831 Cyrus Hall McCormick, a Virginian, built a successful reaper, and in 1847 he moved to Chicago to begin manufacturing them on a large scale. Mechanization advanced another step when threshing machines began to outmode the old method of flailing wheat by hand.

A growing number of Western farmers thought of agriculture as a business enterprise, rather than in Jefferson's terms as a way of life. Technological advances enabled them to cultivate more acres but also forced them to make heavier investments in implements and machinery. The railroads opened new markets to them but increased their dependence on the middlemen who financed, transported, stored, and marketed their crops. Specialization made them more efficient but increased their dependence on Eastern manufacturers for things they had once made for themselves. In short, the farmers were being caught up in the capitalist world of merchants, manufacturers, bankers, and railroad operators, and by 1860 some of them were showing signs of dissatisfaction with their place in this world. Out of their discontent would grow the farmers' movements of the post-Civil War years.

Industry   In 1851, at London's Crystal Palace Exhibition, the products of American industry and technology were shown to the world. More than a hundred of them won prize medals, including the McCormick reaper,

A New England mill, 1850.

which attracted by far the greatest admiration. The success of the American exhibits was an indication of the rapid progress the country had made in manufacturing since the founding of the first textile mills in the early nineteenth century.

The industrial growth of the 1850's far surpassed that of any previous decade. The capital investment of a half-billion dollars in 1849 had nearly doubled by 1859, the number of manufacturing establishments had increased from 123,000 to 140,000, and the annual value of their products had grown from $1,019 million to $1,886 million. Manufacturing was concentrated in the New England and Middle Atlantic states. The market was almost entirely a domestic one, with the Northeast exchanging its industrial surpluses for the foodstuffs and raw materials of the agricultural South and West.

Yet industry in the 1850's had certain characteristics indicating that the United States was still in the early stages of the Industrial Revolution. First, most of the manufacturing involved the processing of the products of American farms and forests. In 1860 the leading industry was the milling of flour and meal, whose value was about one-eighth of the total value of manufactures. Other important industries included lumber-milling, distilling, brewing, leather-tanning, and meat-packing. A second indication of industrial immaturity was the smallness of the typical manufacturing enterprises; on the average they employed fewer than ten workers and had a capital value of less than $7,500. Finally, as we have seen, the United States was still a large consumer of foreign manufactured goods and primarily an exporter of agricultural products.

Nevertheless, by 1860 the direction of Ameri-

The Lowell Operatives: A Reminiscence

Work began at five o'clock on summer mornings, and at daylight in the winter. Breakfast was eaten by lamplight, during the cold weather; in summer, an interval of half an hour was allowed for it, between seven and eight o'clock. The time given for the noon meal was from a half to three quarters of an hour. The only hours of leisure were from half past seven or eight to ten in the evening, the mills closing a little earlier on Saturdays. It was an imperative regulation that lights should be out at ten. During those two evening hours, when it was too cold for the girls to sit in their own rooms, the dining-room was used as a sitting-room, where they gathered around the tables, and sewed, and read, and wrote, and studied. It seems a wonder, to look back upon it, how they accomplished so much as they did, in their limited allowance of time. They made and mended their own clothing, often doing a good deal of unnecessary fancy-work besides. They subscribed for periodicals; took books from the libraries; went to singing-schools, conference meetings, concerts, and lectures; watched at night by a sick girl's bedside, and did double work for her in the mill, if necessary; and on Sundays they were at church, not differing in appearance from other well-dressed and decorous young women.

From Lucy Larcom, *Among Lowell Mill-Girls: A Reminiscence*, November 1881.

---

can economic development was clear. Textile manufacturing had already become the core of New England's economy: the investment in mills and machinery was more than a hundred million dollars, and the number of cotton spindles in operation had grown to 5,236,000—a 100 per cent increase since 1840. In 1844 Charles Goodyear had patented a method of "vulcanizing" raw rubber to make it resist heat and cold, and a new rubber-goods industry was soon manufacturing hundreds of products. In 1846 Elias Howe had patented a sewing machine, and five years later Isaac Singer had begun to manufacture and market an improved model. During the 1850's they were used in hundreds of factories making shoes and ready-made clothing. The iron industry had expanded to meet the demands of the railroads and the producers of farm machinery. Between 1840 and 1860 pig-iron production rose from 321,000 tons to 920,000 tons a year. Originally the rails and locomotives for American railroads had to be imported, but by the 1840's Pennsylvania iron manufacturers were able to meet domestic needs.

A few industries began to use the techniques of modern mass production. The manufacturers of guns, clocks, sewing machines, and farm implements introduced assembly lines in which unskilled workers, performing standardized tasks, made the finished product from interchangeable parts. In these and other industries the corporate form of business organization spread rapidly—during the 1850's the number of manufacturing corporations nearly doubled. Industry and the building and organizing of railroads were rivaling commerce as the road to wealth and economic power. Thus Amos and Abbott Lawrence of Boston, Phelps, Dodge & Company of New York, and many others, got their start in mercantile enterprises but transferred their capital to manufacturing, railroads, and mining. The industrial entrepreneur had already become an important figure in the country's economic life.

The Lowell Operatives: Contemporary Testimony

The first petitioner who testified was Eliza R. Hemmingway. She had worked 2 years and 9 months in the Lowell Factories; 2 years in the Middlesex, and 9 months in the Hamilton Corporations. Her employment is weaving—works by the piece.... She is now at work in the Middlesex Mills, and attends one loom. Her wages average from $16 to $23 a month exclusive of board. She complained of the hours for labor being too many, and the time for meals too limited. In the summer season, the work is commenced at 5 o'clock, A.M., and continued until 7 o'clock, P.M., with half an hour for breakfast and three quarters of an hour for dinner. During eight months of the year, but half an hour is allowed for dinner. The air in the room she considered not to be wholesome. There were 293 small lamps and 61 large lamps lighted in the room in which she worked, when evening work is required. These lamps are also lighted sometimes in the morning. About 130 females, 11 men, and 12 children (between the ages of 11 and 14) work in the room with her.... She thought there was a general desire among the females to work but ten hours, regardless of pay.

From *Massachusetts House Document No. 50*, 1945.

By 1860 American factories were employing 1,311,000 workers, the mines and transportation a half-million more. Although skilled labor was still in great demand, each craft felt severely threatened by the steady encroachments of the machines and of mass production. Already the factories had made nearly obsolete several old and honorable crafts, notably those of the cordwainers, coopers, and ironsmiths. As the factories grew in size and the ranks of the unskilled were filled with recent immigrants, the relations of labor and capital became increasingly impersonal. Employers began to think of their workers less as human beings than as commodities to be bought at the lowest price. They paid their employees six dollars a week or less for a working day of twelve to fifteen hours. They often ignored feeble state laws fixing maximum hours or regulating the labor of children. And they viewed with indifference the poor sanitary conditions and the high rate of industrial accidents in their factories. Conditions such as these touched the lives of only a small fraction of the population, but by the 1850's there had emerged in the factory slums of Eastern cities an unskilled, propertyless proletariat.

Middle-class reformers who took an interest in the plight of the laboring population usually urged low-paid workers to form their own cooperative workshops or to go west and become farmers. They seldom approved of direct economic action through trade unions. This, however, was the means by which factory workers eventually improved their condition. The promising labor movement of the 1830's (see p. 208) had been destroyed by the depression following the Panic of 1837, and it took many years for another movement to get started. A legal barrier was partially removed when the Massachusetts Supreme Court, in the case of *Commonwealth* v. *Hunt* (1842), ruled that trade unions were not in themselves conspiracies in restraint of trade, a rule that courts in other states soon accepted. But when workers resorted to strikes or boycotts they still ran into trouble with the old common-law doctrine of conspiracy. Trade unions were also handicapped by a hostile press, by a generally unfavorable public opinion, and by the ability of employers to recruit strikebreakers.

In the 1850's, though conditions showed little improvement, only a few American workingmen belonged to trade unions. In 1852 the International Typographical Union was formed, and by the end of the decade the stonecutters, hat-finishers, iron-molders, and machinists had also established national organizations. The other skilled crafts were organized only locally, while the mass of unskilled workers had no unions at all. Strikes for higher wages or shorter hours occurred in the shoe and textile industries and on the railroads, but they usually failed. Though trade unionism had made a new beginning, a formidable labor movement would not emerge until after the Civil War.

Economic Discontent in the South

The Colonial South   On the surface the economic conditions of the 1850's would seem to have given no cause for sectional conflict. The South was prospering, and its economy appeared to be neatly complementary to that of the North—each section needed the products of the other. And yet, throughout the decade, there was in the South an undercurrent of economic discontent.

Far more than that of the Northeast, even more than that of the Northwest, the economy of the South was based on agriculture. In 1860 the eleven states that were to form the Southern Confederacy produced less than one-tenth of the country's manufactured goods; they contained about half as many manufacturing establishments as the Western states. Moreover, there was little direct trade between Southern and European ports, most of the trade being carried on indirectly through Northern ports and in Northern ships. An Alabama editor complained,

With us every branch and pursuit of life, every trade, profession, and occupation, is dependent upon the North. . . . In Northern vessels [the Southerner's] products are carried to market, his cotton is ginned with Northern gins, his sugar is crushed and preserved by Northern machinery; his rivers are navigated by Northern steamboats, . . . his land is cleared with a Northern axe, and a Yankee clock sits upon his mantel-piece; his floor is swept by a Northern broom, and is covered with a Northern carpet; and his wife dresses herself in a Northern looking-glass.

Southerners resented this condition of dependency and searched for ways to strengthen their economy. As early as 1837 a group of Georgians had sponsored a convention at Augusta "to attempt a new organization of our commercial relations with Europe." During the 1840's and 1850's a series of commercial conventions urged the establishment of direct trade between Southern and European ports. While some Southerners planned steamship lines, others favored the building of railroads to divert Western trade to Southern cities. Neither goal was achieved.

For a time there seemed to be a better prospect of improving the South's industrial position. During the depression years of the 1840's, when the price of raw cotton was low, interest in manufacturing increased in the older states of the Southeast, and a number of factories were built. William Gregg of South Carolina, a vigorous propagandist for industrialization, demonstrated its profitability at his highly successful cotton factory in Graniteville. In the 1850's, however, the revival of agricultural prosperity made it difficult for industry to compete for capital. Moreover, the Northern manufacturer was usually able to undersell his Southern competitor and to provide a superior product. As a result, the South's economy remained agricultural.

Rumors of a Northern Conspiracy The failure of these various efforts toward economic diversification produced a state of mind in the South that contributed to sectionalism and ultimately to disunion. Agriculture, Jefferson had taught and Southerners believed, was the most productive pursuit of man, and the agrarian was the chief repository of human virtue. Yet the North had surpassed the South in wealth and population and had reduced her to a colonial status. This evil and unnatural condition, many Southerners believed, was the result of a sinister conspiracy planned by a close-knit body of Northern bankers, merchants, and manufacturers. The chief haunts of the conspirators were New York and Washington; their distinguishing characteristics were their essential unproductiveness and their skill in amassing wealth from the labor of others. Their special field of operation was the South, from which they extracted a major portion of their profits.

The Northern businessman, according to this conspiracy theory, took advantage of the plain, homespun Southerner, who was no match for the artful Yankee in the techniques of chicanery. By exacting exorbitant middlemen's charges, by rigging prices, by manipulating the money market, the Northern capitalists kept much of the wealth produced in the South flowing steadily into their coffers. The price of Southern property, wrote an indignant Virginian, "is dependent upon the speculative pleasure of the Merchants, Bankers, and Brokers of New York. And why? Because Wall Street can depress the money market when it pleases." The South, said a Mississippian, had permitted itself to fall into a condition of "serfdom" and to become "the sport and laughing stock of Wall Street." A Southern editor described New York as "a mighty queen of commerce . . . waving an undisputed commercial scepter over the South." With an "avidity rarely equalled," she "grasps our gains and transfers them to herself."

But Northern capitalists did not make their profits solely from their adroit maneuvers in a free economy. Rather, in advancing their conspiracy they had enlisted the support of the federal government. In November 1860 Senator Robert Toombs, in a speech before the Georgia legislature, described the political side of the Northern conspiracy to prostrate the South. No sooner was the government organized, he claimed, than "the Northern States evinced a general desire and purpose to use it for their own benefit, and to pervert its powers for sectional advantage, and they have steadily pursued that policy to this day." They demanded, and received, a monopoly of the shipbuilding business; they demanded, and received, a monopoly of the trade between American ports. The New England fishing industry obtained an annual bounty from the public treasury; manufacturers obtained a protective tariff. Through its policy of subsidizing "every interest and every pursuit in the North," the federal treasury had become "a perpetual fertilizing stream to them and their industry, and a suction-pump to drain away our substance and parch up our lands."

By the 1850's the notion that Northern profits were largely a form of expropriation of Southern wealth, that the South was "the very best colony to the North any people ever possessed," was having a powerful effect on Southern opinion. Southerners had convinced themselves, remarked a Northerner, "that in some way or other, either through the fiscal regulations of the Government, or through the legerdemain of trade, the North has been built up at the expense of the South." Not even agricultural prosperity could banish this thought from the Southern mind. When the sectional conflict was reopened in 1854, slavery transcended all other issues. However, as the historian Charles A. Beard has observed, it was not always easy to tell "where slavery as an ethical question left off and economics—the struggle over the distribution of wealth—began."

SUGGESTIONS FOR READING

Expansionism and Foreign Trade

American interests in Cuba, Central America, and the Far East are treated adequately in three general surveys of American foreign policy: S. F. Bemis, *A Diplomatic History of the United States* (rev. ed., 1955); T. A. Bailey, *A Diplomatic History of the American People* (6th ed., 1958); and J. W. Pratt, *A History of United States Foreign Policy* (1955). Allan Nevins, *Ordeal of the Union*, 2 vols. (1947), is informative on Cuba and Central America. Several excellent monographs may also be consulted: M. W. Williams, *Anglo-American Isthmian Diplomacy, 1815–1915* (1916); Dexter Perkins, *The Monroe Doctrine, 1826–1867* (1933); A. A. Ettinger, *The Mission to Spain of Pierre Soulé* (1932); and Basil Rauch, *American Interests in Cuba, 1848–1855* (1948). E. S. Wallace, *Destiny and Glory* (1957), is a vivid account of filibustering.

The most useful special studies of American–Far Eastern relations that deal with this period are: Tyler Dennett, *Americans in Eastern Asia* (1941); A. W. Griswold, *The Far Eastern Policy of the United States* (1938); P. J. Treat, *Diplomatic Relations Between the United States and Japan, 1853–1905*, 3 vols. (1932–38); and F. R. Dulles, *China and America: The Story of Their Relations Since 1784* (1946). Arthur Walworth, *Black Ships off Japan* (1946), is a readable account of the Perry mission to Japan. H. W. Bradley, *American Frontier in Hawaii* (1942), is the best study of early American interest in Hawaii.

The standard works on the growth of American foreign trade are E. R. Johnson and others, *History of Domestic and Foreign Commerce of the United States*, 2 vols. (1915), and J. H. Frederick, *The Development of American Commerce* (1932). The commerce of New England and New York City are the subjects of two distinguished books: S. E. Morison, *Maritime History of Massachusetts* (1921), and R. G. Albion, *The Rise of New York Port, 1815–1860* (1939). The best books on the clipper ships are A. H. Clark, *The Clipper Ship Era* (1910), and C. C. Cutler, *Greyhounds of the Sea* (1930).

Immigration and Nativism

Several excellent surveys of immigration to the United States are valuable for this period: G. M. Stephenson, *History of American Immigration* (1926); Carl Wittke, *We Who Built America* (1939); M. L. Hansen, *The Atlantic Migration, 1607–1860* (1940); and M. A. Jones, *American Immigration* (1960). Oscar Handlin, *The Uprooted* * (1951), is a sensitive study of the immigrant's problems. Four specific immigrant groups are the subjects of individual volumes: T. C. Blegen, *Norwegian Migration to America*, 2 vols. (1931–40); R. T. Berthoff, *British Immigrants in Industrial America, 1825–1950* (1953); Carl Wittke, *Refugees of Revolution: The German Forty-Eighters in America* (1952); and by the same author, *The Irish in America* (1956). The immigrant populations of two large eastern cities are studied in Oscar Handlin, *Boston's Immigrants* (1941), and Robert Ernst, *Immigrant Life in New York City, 1825–1863* (1949).

A perceptive account of mid-nineteenth–century nativism is in Nevins, *Ordeal of the Union*, cited above. R. A. Billington, *The Protestant Crusade, 1800–1860* (1938), emphasizes the anti-

* Available in a paperback edition.

Catholic aspect of the movement. John Higham, *Strangers in the Land* (1955), deals only briefly with Know-Nothingism in the 1850's, but it should be consulted for its distinctive interpretation. Two special studies are also useful: Sister M. E. Thomas, *Nativism in the Old Northwest, 1850–1860* (1936), and W. D. Overdyke, *The Know-Nothing Party in the South* (1950).

Economic Development

All of the books on agriculture, industry, transportation, and technology listed in the suggested readings for Chapter 8 are useful for this period. There are also several splendid chapters on the American economy at mid-century in Nevins, *Ordeal of the Union*, cited above, and in A. C. Cole, *The Irrepressible Conflict, 1850–1865* (1934).

A good introduction to the history of the railroads is Slason Thompson, *A Short History of American Railways* (1925). Problems of railroad promotion and finance can be studied in F. A. Cleveland and F. W. Powell, *Railroad Promotion and Capitalization in the United States* (1909); L. H. Haney, *A Congressional History of Railways in the United States to 1850* (1908); and by the same author, *A Congressional History of Railways in the United States, 1850–1877* (1910); and A. D. Chandler, Jr., *Henry Varnum Poor: Business Editor, Analyst and Reformer* (1956). An outstanding history of the New England railroads is E. C. Kirkland, *Men, Cities and Transportation, 1820–1900*, 2 vols. (1948). Railroad promotion in the Southeast is described in U. B. Phillips, *A History of Transportation in the Eastern Cotton Belt to 1860* (1908). T. C. Cochran, *Railroad Leaders, 1845–1890* (1953), contains important material on early railroad promoters and their social attitudes. The following histories of individual railroads are useful: F. W. Stevens, *The Beginnings of the New York Central Railroad* (1926); P. W. Gates, *The Illinois Central Railroad and Its Colonization Work* (1934); Edward Hungerford, *The Story of the Baltimore and Ohio Railroad, 1827–1927*, 2 vols. (1928); and by the same author, *Men of Erie* (1946); and R. C. Overton, *Burlington West* (1941).

In addition to the listings in the suggested readings for Chapter 8, the following books on industry and technology are worth consulting for this period: Waldemar Kaempffert, ed., *A Popular History of American Invention*, 2 vols. (1924); Allan Nevins, *Abram S. Hewitt: With Some Account of Peter Cooper* (1935); J. A. Kouwenhoven, *Made in America* (1948); D. J. Struik, *Yankee Science in the Making* (1948); and Mitchell Wilson, *American Science and Invention: A Pictorial History* (1954). The best book on labor in this period is N. J. Ware, *The Industrial Worker, 1840–1860* (1924). Hannah Josephson, *The Golden Threads* (1949), is excellent on the women textile workers of New England. Two good general treatments are J. G. Rayback, *History of American Labor* (1959), and H. M. Pelling, *American Labor* (1960).

The causes of economic discontent in the South can be studied in R. R. Russel, *Economic Aspects of Southern Sectionalism, 1840–1861* (1924); J. G. Van Deusen, *The Ante-Bellum Southern Commercial Conventions* (1926); Herbert Wender, *Southern Commercial Conventions, 1837–1859* (1930); and Clement Eaton, *The Growth of Southern Civilization* (1961).

13

The Gathering Storm

The hopeful mood of the early months of the Pierce Administration soon gave way to an atmosphere of increasing tension. Tempers hardened north and south, reducing the chances for finding a peaceful solution to the sectional crisis. Politics, as always the art of the possible, had to operate within a more and more constricted range. Slavery lay at the core of the problem. Sectional differences about national public policies were important and would have existed in the absence of the South's peculiar institution, but the debate could not have taken the turn it did had not the expectations of Americans crystallized around the question of slavery. For all the stubbornness of that issue, however, for all the political difficulties attending a time of tension, men had a choice about their destiny —a choice that they continually exercised. The choice was not simple and the men were not often wise. A harassed generation, they were struggling to control themselves and their destiny. They were testing the unity, the spirit, even the survival of the United States.

The Divisive Issue

The Kansas-Nebraska Act   Ironically, a miscalculated effort to dispose of the problem of slavery in the territories resulted instead in the polarizing of sectional attitudes about that issue. Stephen A. Douglas, a talented Illinois Democrat, senator from that state since 1847, was the chairman of the Committee on Terri-

tories in the upper chamber. No one had a larger experience with territorial politics; no one was more committed to the rapid settlement of the West; no one was more dedicated to the Union and its peaceful preservation. Douglas rejected alike the free soilers' demand that Congress should prohibit slavery in all territories and the Southern demand that Congress should protect it there. He stood instead for settling the question by local self-determination, by letting the majority of the people in each territory vote slavery up or down. This doctrine of popular sovereignty, already applied by the Compromise of 1850 to Utah and New Mexico, struck Douglas and like-minded men as twice blessed. They considered it democratic on its merits; they also believed it to be a practicable middle way between the controversial sectional extremes.

In January 1854 Douglas reported out a bill for the territorial organization of the Platte country, the area west of Missouri and Iowa. In keeping with his interpretation of the Compromise of 1850, his bill provided that the territorial legislature elected by the people should decide about slavery. Since the Platte, or Nebraska, country lay within the Louisiana Purchase, where the Missouri Compromise had governed the slavery question since 1820, Douglas' proposal tacitly abandoned that longtime sectional settlement. Consequently the bill triggered another sectional debate.

Douglas had hoped that his bill would still rather than inflame tempers. His contemporaries thought he also intended it to advance his ambitions for the presidency. A cocky, undersized, tireless scrapper, Douglas had a practiced ability for seizing a good political chance. He may have been concerned not only with "a final settlement of the controversy" over slavery in the territories but with capturing Southern support for his candidacy. Probably the Little Giant had still other motives. He said at the time that he had proposed the bill in order to remove the "barbarian wall" of Indians blocking settlement on the plains and to encourage thereby a "continuous line of settlement to the Pacific Ocean." To develop the West, he had to skirt the slavery question, for his influential colleague in the Senate, David R. Atchison of Missouri, had sworn to let the Nebraska area "sink in hell" before permitting it to be organized on a free-soil basis. Douglas, furthermore, was in a hurry. A survey of possible routes for a transcontinental railroad had favored a Southern line, but he was eager to win a Northern route that would enhance the growth of Illinois and especially of Chicago. Perhaps his holdings of real estate in that city enlarged his natural preference for his home state. In any case, local or self-interest dictated the necessity of organizing the Nebraska area quickly if it was to surround a vital railway line.

Douglas was no fool. Whatever his motives, he had surely estimated the chances for his bill. He apparently counted on its ambiguity about the moral question of slavery, on the tradition of sectional compromise, and on his own political influence to carry his measure past the objections of both free soilers and Southerners. Personally opposed to slavery, he was one of those who believed that it could not be adapted profitably to the climate and soil of the plains country, so manifestly inhospitable to cotton or tobacco culture. By temperament an adjuster rather than an agitator, he expected the logic of geography to preclude a theoretical debate on the dominant moral and political question of the day. It was in projecting his own feelings that he erred, for the men who stood on either side of him were not willing to let nature make policy.

The storm broke as soon as the bill reached the Senate in January 1854. Countering a free-soil amendment that reasserted the Missouri Compromise, Southern Democrats and their allies insisted on permitting slavery in the Nebraska country during its territorial phase—that is, until it became a state. Douglas yielded and rephrased his bill to read "that all questions pertaining to slavery in the Territories, and in the new states to be formed therefrom, are to be left to the people resident therein through their appropriate representatives." Still not content, the Southerners, who had the votes they needed, added an amendment that declared the Missouri Compromise "inoperative and void." Another amendment divided the area into the two separate territories of Kansas and Nebraska. As Douglas said, the revised bill, a considerable departure from his own original, equivocal draft, would "raise the hell of a storm." Yet he apparently expected Northern opposition to be less bitter and divisive than Southern resistance to the unamended bill had been. His efforts, and the persistent influence of the Pierce Administration, took the bill safely through an angry debate. The Senate passed it by a vote of 37 to 14; the House by the narrower margin of 113 to 100.

The National Response The debate over the Kansas-Nebraska Act marked the end of the uneasy truce of 1850, and set the tone of the rest of the decade. Douglas had sensed the strength of Northern sentiment against repeal of the Missouri Compromise, but he had failed to realize that the new legislation would intensify the slavery issue. He had supposed that once the first storm had blown itself out the issue would be more or less closed; the extension of slavery would be left to popular sovereignty, agitation would cease, and the whole problem would be out of the way. The storm did not blow itself out. A more accurate prophet was William H. Seward of New York, who had warned during the Senate debate that the bill would "end a cycle in the history of our country."

Southerners responded to the act with indifference, but in the North the response was indignant. Antislavery and free-soil men, their resentment increased by the failure of the Homestead bill (p. 277) to win enactment, began at once to try to reverse the policy of Congress. Their meetings and petitions denounced Douglas for his "criminal betrayal of precious

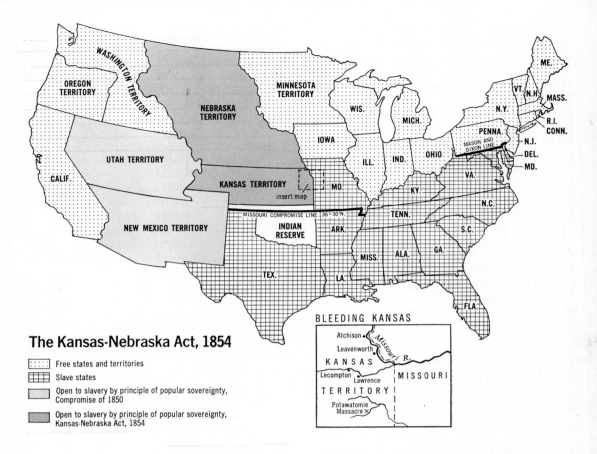

The Kansas-Nebraska Act, 1854

- :::: Free states and territories
- ⊞ Slave states
- ▨ Open to slavery by principle of popular sovereignty, Compromise of 1850
- ▨ Open to slavery by principle of popular sovereignty, Kansas-Nebraska Act, 1854

BLEEDING KANSAS

Atchison
Leavenworth
KANSAS
Lecompton
Lawrence
TERRITORY
Potawatomie Massacre ✕
MISSOURI
Missouri R.

rights." Never before, one Washington newspaper reported, had "a public man been so hounded and hunted." As Douglas said himself, he could have traveled from Boston to Chicago by the light of his burning effigies.

This temper speeded a significant political realignment that had already begun. The Whig party, moribund at best, was unable to adjust its heterogeneous factions and policies to the deep division over the issue of slavery in the territories. As the party died, most of its Northern adherents joined with more radical free soilers and abolitionists, and with some Northern Democrats disenchanted by Douglas' work. These coalitions formed local "anti-Nebraska" groups, some of which adopted the name "Republican." One, in Ripon, Wisconsin, called for a new party dedicated to "the sole issue of the non-extension of slavery." Before the end of the summer in 1854, the emergent party had its name and its basic principle.

Before then, the Democratic party in the North had begun to split, its free soilers disaffected, and the balance of its Northern membership caught between the intransigent demands of the South and the growing resentment they occasioned. In introducing his bill, in bending to Southern amendments to it, Douglas had inadvertently damaged the party he meant to strengthen, weakened the candidacy he wanted to serve, and revived the issue he proposed to bury.

The explosive potentialities of the Kansas-Nebraska Act were most immediate within the new territories. The act stipulated that the settlers could decide for themselves whether their territory might or might not contain slavery, but it did not say whether that initial decision would continue to operate once the territory had become a state. The future of slavery in the territories would depend, first, on the sentiment of the majority of original settlers; second, on their ability to mold the policies of the territorial government to their purpose; and, third, on the persisting dominance of their preference at the time of statehood. This situation invited, and the mood of the nation guaranteed, unceasing agitation of the slavery question during the entire territorial period.

Test in Kansas   The issue was joined on the plains of Kansas. Nebraska was surrounded by free soil; there geography and climate did decide against slavery. But Kansas adjoined Missouri, and Kansas became a symbol for Southerners determined to stamp out the infection of abolitionism, a symbol for free soilers resolved to conquer for their cause. Kansas in 1854 was virtually uninhabited, but that summer and fall a rush for new land quickly filled the territory. Most of the settlers were from the states adjacent to Kansas; most of them were relatively indifferent to the slavery question, though they brought no slaves to work their farms. They did bring with them, however, other characteristic frontier tensions—conflicts over Indian affairs, land titles, federal and local patronage, the location of county seats, the awarding of army and other contracts. To this powder keg the slavery issue applied a spark.

Since the people of Kansas were eventually to decide whether it should be a free state or a slave state, much depended on the attitude of the interested settlers. Both in the North and in the South determined efforts were made to see that the "right people" moved into the territory. In the East, the Massachusetts Emigrant Aid Company, later the New England Emigrant Aid Company, was set up to encourage and finance the emigration to Kansas of good antislavery men. This organization sponsored some 1,240 settlers, giving them advice and money in the free-soil cause. Similarly Southern promoters sponsored settlement, including one expedition of several hundred men from Alabama, Georgia, and South Carolina.

The first governor of the territory, Andrew H. Reeder, a Pennsylvania Democrat, found that several thousand settlers had preceded him to Kansas. In the fall of 1854 he called an election to choose a territorial delegate to Congress, and early in 1855 he called another election to name a territorial legislature. But Kansas elections developed unusual features. The Missouri counties which bordered Kansas on the east were strong proslavery areas, and the people in these counties, urged on by leaders like Senator Atchison, did not want a free-soil territory next door. Missourians by the hundreds swarmed across the border to Kansas to vote in the territorial elections. The antislavery settlers, though apparently in the majority, were heavily outvoted. On the face of the returns, the new territory had chosen a proslavery delegate to Congress and had elected a solidly proslavery legislature. The legislature, in turn, at once adopted a stringent slave code, providing the death sentence for anyone who helped a fugitive slave to escape and a prison term for anyone who held that slavery was not legal in Kansas.

Governor Reeder threw out some of the more obviously fraudulent returns, but the principal result of the elections stood. When the proslavery legislature requested Reeder's removal, President Pierce dismissed him and named Wilson Shannon of Ohio in his place. Antislavery settlers now called a convention of their own, drew up a constitution, conducted an extralegal "election" which the proslavery people boycotted, and announced that they had installed a new government in Kansas, with Charles Robinson as governor. The troubled territory now had two governors and two legislatures: one, the result of an election dominated by nonresidents; the other, an affair without legal basis.

Strong action in Washington might have kept the situation from getting so badly out of hand. Pierce might have asserted federal control, ordered a new election, and established a territorial government which could have won the respect of both parties. Instead, unwilling to use the authority of his office or to risk antagonizing his political friends, he let matters drift.

The antagonists in Kansas acted. The roving Missourians who kept crossing the line carried weapons to back up their arguments. New England abolitionists shipped boxes of rifles, "Beecher's Bibles," to the antislavery settlers. (An eminent antislavery clergyman, Henry Ward Beecher, had incautiously remarked that a rifle might be a more powerful moral agent on the Kansas plains than a Bible.) Sporadic shootings and barn-burnings culminated, in May 1856, in a raid by Missouri "border ruffians" on the free-soil town of Lawrence. They sacked the place, destroyed the type and press of an antislavery newspaper, and terrorized the inhabitants. A few days later John Brown, a grim abolitionist fanatic, retaliated. He and his sons and companions undertook a foray through the valley of Potawattomie Creek, where they stole horses, murdered five settlers, and mutilated their bodies. Brown claimed that he was an agent of the Lord, assigned to punish those who favored slavery. His inexcusable atrocities, lamentable by any reasonable standard, spurred a counterattack by proslavery men, who fell upon Brown's band, killed one of his sons, and burned the settlement at Osawatomie. Though federal troops prevented further private war, the slavery issue had brought blood and terror to Kansas.

His own larger passions aroused, Senator Charles Sumner of Massachusetts, an outspoken abolitionist, delivered, on May 19, 1856, a bitter speech, "The Crime Against Kansas," in which he poured invective on the proslavery men of the South. Sumner denounced South Carolina and, with unstinted personal meanness, one of her absent senators, Andrew Pickens Butler. Two days later Butler's nephew, Congressman Preston Brooks of South Carolina, stalked into the Senate chamber and beat Sumner unconscious with his cane. It was several years before Sumner again took part in Senate debates; meanwhile, Brooks's assault made Sumner a martyr in the eyes of the enemies of slavery, although to most Southerners he seemed a demagogue who had got what he deserved. The deplorable incident, coming on the heels of the bloodshed in Kansas, heightened the emotional strain of a nation stumbling to find some way to settle the slavery controversy.

The Election of 1856   The Administration of Franklin Pierce, begun in hope, died in futility. The nation, leaderless, was in ferment as the presidential campaign of 1856 approached. Convening at Philadelphia in June, the Republicans were confident. Their new party had already won control of most of the Northern state governments. Turning their back on the South and its votes, they adopted a strong free-soil platform that denounced the repeal of the Missouri Compromise, demanded that Congress prohibit slavery in the territories, urged that Kansas be admitted as a free state, and condemned the Ostend Manifesto (p. 288). The platform was not, however, an abolitionist pronunciamento. It did not say that the federal government should interfere with slavery in states where it existed. In effect, the Republicans advocated the containment of slavery, asserting only that it must not be allowed to expand any further. In addition, their platform called for internal improvements, a Pacific railroad, and general support for the country's growing (and largely Northern) industrialism. As their candidate for President, the Republicans nominated John C. Frémont, an antislavery man who lacked political experience but had won national recognition and some glory as an explorer and soldier in the West.

The Democrats, meeting in Cincinnati, drew their strength from both the North and the South and were eager for a compromise program that would hold the Union together and the party in office. Their platform explicitly denied the power of Congress to interfere with slavery in the states, upheld the Kansas-Nebraska Act—and so, at least by implication, the principle of popular sovereignty—urged the annexation of Cuba, and maintained a discreet silence on the question of whether or not a territorial legislature could outlaw slavery before the formation of a state government. In selecting a candidate, the Democrats passed over Douglas on the ground that he had become too controversial a figure, and nominated James Buchanan of Pennsylvania, who had been conveniently out of the country as American minister to England during the Kansas fracas. The choice of Buchanan was another sign of the Democrats' attempt to find a workable compromise; for the last time, the party was trying to win support in both sections by naming a Northern man with Southern principles. Buchanan, elderly and unaggressive, less principled than partisan, seemed certain not to rock the boat.

Buchanan won the election handily with 174 electoral votes against 114 for Frémont; Millard Fillmore, the Know Nothing candidate, got only the 8 votes of Maryland. In the popular vote, however, Buchanan had only 45 per

James Buchanan: Less principled than partisan.

cent of the total. Frémont carried all but five of the free states and could have won the election if he had taken Pennsylvania and either Illinois or Indiana. The Republicans had come close to victory without attracting a single Southern state.

The House Divided

Dred Scott   When Buchanan took office, the Kansas issue was still alive, bitterness over the slavery question still growing. Popular sovereignty, instead of settling the question of slaveholders' rights in the territories, had made that question more acute. Southerners were arguing that a territorial legislature was powerless to exclude slavery before the territory was ready to enter the Union as a state, for Congress, they contended, lacked that power, and the territories were the creatures of Congress. Some Southerners also maintained that Congress had a positive duty to protect slavery in the territories.

Buchanan, in his inaugural address in March 1857, remarked that the Supreme Court would soon rule on this question, expressed the hope that agitation on the matter might cease, and urged the nation to accept the Court's ruling, when issued, as a final settlement of the matter.

This was a disingenuous request, for the President already knew and approved of the Court's decision in the Dred Scott case.

Dred Scott—whose case reached the Supreme Court in 1856—was a slave whose owner had taken him from Missouri into Illinois and then into Wisconsin territory, which at the time had been free soil under the Missouri Compromise. Taken back to Missouri, Scott found himself the center of a test case when suit was filed in his behalf asking that he be declared a free man on the ground that his sojourn in free territory had automatically ended his servitude. The Missouri Supreme Court had ruled against this plea, holding that even in Wisconsin Scott had still been subject to Missouri law. A United States circuit judge, to whom the case next came, held that Scott, because he was a Negro, was not a citizen and therefore not entitled to bring suit under federal jurisdiction. Scott's lawyers then appealed to the United States Supreme Court. In conference in February 1857 the justices decided to dispose of the case by confirming the interpretation of the Missouri Court.

Several justices, however, soon changed their mind. John McLean of Ohio and Benjamin R. Curtis of Massachusetts prepared dissents which, in supporting Scott's plea, reviewed the question of the Missouri Compromise and, in finding that law constitutional, upheld the authority of Congress to regulate slavery in the territories. This antislavery opinion provoked the proslavery justices to spell out their views, which at least one of them—James M. Wayne of Georgia—had apparently resolved to do in any event. The proslavery majority now prepared to dispose of the Dred Scott case on the broadest grounds. Justice John Catron so informed Buchanan, and the President-elect urged Justice Robert C. Grier of Pennsylvania to stand with his five Southern brethren. Buchanan, then, had some responsibility for the six-to-three decision against Scott which the Court rendered just two days after the inauguration.

Though each of the justices issued a separate opinion, five of them concurred with the long, involved, and forceful opinion of Chief Justice Roger B. Taney. In essence, the majority announced that a Negro could not be entitled to the rights of federal citizenship. Negroes, Taney said, were inferior beings with "no rights which any white man was bound to respect." This doctrine shocked many Northerners, who were equally offended by Taney's second major point. The Missouri Compromise, he held, was unconstitutional because Congress had no power to prohibit slavery in the territories. Slaves, Taney said, were property; the Fifth Amendment guaranteed that no citizen should be deprived of his property without "due process of law"; thus Congress was restrained from forbidding slaveholding, and the law of 1820 was "therefore void." McLean and Curtis dissented. Curtis' powerful rebuttal argued that Negroes had been citizens in several states before the Constitution was adopted and that nothing in the Constitution deprived them of that status. The Constitution, Curtis continued, expressly granted Congress the power to "make all needful Rules and Regulations respecting the Territory . . . belonging to the United States," and the Missouri Compromise was therefore lawful.

Taney's opinion and Curtis' dissent heightened the controversy over slavery. The South rejoiced in the Court's ruling, which fully confirmed that region's attitude about race and about the Constitution. But the majority opinion cut the ground from under the Republican platform on slavery, and Northern Republicans recited Curtis' reasoning to support their own. As advocates of popular sovereignty realized, if Taney was right and Curtis wrong, then Douglas' position was of questionable constitutionality.

Fiasco in Kansas   Whatever its legal merits, popular sovereignty had still to meet the test of application in Kansas. Buchanan, eager to end the bewildering disorder there, named Robert J. Walker of Mississippi as territorial governor. In March 1857 Walker went to Kansas hoping to bring the territory under a legal government acceptable to all and to get a constitution adopted under which the territory could become a state. He summoned a constitutional convention, but he was obliged to turn over to the proslavery legislature all arrangements for the election of delegates. Most of the free-soil settlers, complaining that the election was rigged, boycotted it. Consequently, the convention that met in the fall of 1857 at the temporary capital of Lecompton

was controlled by the proslavery group. The delegates first adopted a constitution which made slavery legal in Kansas and then provided that when the constitution was submitted to the electorate no one could vote against it. Voters might accept the constitution as it was or else they might accept a slightly modified version which made slavery legal but did forbid the importation of additional slaves. The ratifying election was also boycotted by the free-soil people, and the Lecompton constitution was adopted by a one-sided vote.

To make matters even more bewildering, another election was held in the summer of 1858 to select members of a territorial legislature. Walker did his best to make this a fair election, and the free-state voters carried it; the new legislature then called a referendum on the Lecompton constitution, which the majority now rejected.

Walker came east to discuss his woes with the Administration. He wanted to cancel everything and start all over again, but Buchanan refused. Though the Lecompton constitution was patently a fraud, Southern leaders in the Democratic party were solidly in favor of it, and Buchanan, unwilling to lose their support, backed them up. Walker resigned, and the President presented the Lecompton constitution to Congress in a message that cited the Dred Scott decision to prove that Kansas was "as much a slave state as Georgia." The prompt admission of Kansas, he went on, would "restore peace and quiet to the whole country," whereas its rejection would be "keenly felt" by the fourteen slave states. This was too much for Douglas. Breaking with the South and the Administration, he spoke out vigorously against the Lecompton constitution. He was indignant at the highhanded way in which the slavery forces had taken over a territory in which most of the settlers were opposed to slavery, and he felt that his popular sovereignty doctrine had been distorted beyond recognition. The bill to admit Kansas passed the Senate by a vote of thirty-three to twenty-five, with Douglas joining the Republican minority, but it had no chance in the House.

Democrats in the lower chamber contrived a compromise which the Senate accepted. It provided for resubmitting the Lecompton constitution to the people of Kansas, and for a federal land grant if the constitution were adopted. The Republicans denounced the obvious bribe, but it had no discernible effect on the vote. In August 1858 in an honest election, the Kansans rejected the constitution, 11,300 to 1,788. By then, however, Buchanan's striking concessions to the Southern Democrats had alienated Douglas and his Northern Democratic supporters. The President who was expected to cement the party had helped to divide it in two.

The Panic of 1857 Meanwhile, in 1857, the country had experienced a brief but severe economic depression. The new railroad network had been built too far and too fast, with many lines reaching into thinly settled areas where there was no hope for immediate profits. In addition, the land boom that had spread across the Middle West and the Northwest had ended characteristically in a general collapse of land prices, widespread defaulting of mortgages, and a severe strain on the country's flimsy banking structure. On top of all this the end of the Crimean War in Europe deflated the overseas market for farm products, and American farmers found themselves unable to dispose of bumper crops of wheat and meat.

The depression hurt the North more than the South. The network of financial, manufacturing, and transportation interests in the North was much larger and more intricate than in the South, and hence felt the shock of the depression more keenly. Moreover, since the world market for cotton continued to expand, the cotton kingdom weathered the depression very well. All in all, Southerners had reason to conclude that their economy was more stable than that of the North. Their

Wall Street, the Panic of 1857.

leaders proclaimed that cotton was indeed king, and began to suggest that the South could manage handsomely by itself. They grew more confident that neither New England nor Europe could get along without Southern cotton, and that the prospect of losing it would compel the North, Great Britain, and France to accede to demands for "Southern rights."

Many Northern manufacturers, hard hit by the depression, decided that a higher tariff was one answer to their problems. Some moved into the Republican party, making it a big-business party as well as an antislavery party, and giving the South one more reason for hating it. Southerners, already convinced that Republican control of the federal government would bring about a ruinous policy toward slavery, now feared that it would also foster the exploitation of the agricultural South by the commercial North. As always, moreover, depression hurt the party in power, and Democrats, especially Southerners, faced the congressional campaign of 1858 anxiously.

The Election of 1858   The most memorable of the contests of 1858 occurred in Illinois, where Douglas, the Democratic senatorial nominee, opposed Abraham Lincoln, his Republican rival. Lincoln was by no means unknown. He had served a term in Congress, he had narrowly missed election to the Senate in the early 1850's, and he had received several votes for nomination as Vice-President in the Republican convention of 1856. Not yet a national figure, he had at least emerged from obscurity, and he was the logical candidate of the Illinois Republicans. His gaunt, ranging body; his homely, rugged features; his crisp, penetrating speech; his frontier background and straightforward ways made him a striking figure on the platform. His long service in the Whig party had given him a broad political acquaintanceship. His thoughtful conservatism tempered his Jeffersonian convictions with practicality. Even for "the Little Giant," Lincoln was a formidable opponent, and during the campaign he proved himself a shrewd and effective fighter.

Lincoln challenged Douglas to a series of debates which focused on the territorial problem, particularly the case of Kansas. By no means an abolitionist, Lincoln was a convinced free soiler and a telling critic of both popular

Stephen A. Douglas: "The Little Giant."

sovereignty and the Dred Scott decision. The Republicans, he pointed out, considered slavery "a moral, social and political wrong"; the Democrats did not. The Republicans intended to prevent the spread of the blight of slavery; the Democrats did not. At Freeport, Illinois, Lincoln put to Douglas a question much in men's minds: Was there any lawful way in which the inhabitants of a territory could keep slavery from their midst?

Douglas, eagerly rehearsing his own conviction, replied that the answer was simple. The inhabitants could not legally outlaw slavery—that much the Supreme Court had declared—but they could effectively keep it from their midst simply by refusing to adopt the strict slave code which would be needed to protect it. Unless such a code existed, no slave-

The Great Debate: Lincoln

I have stated upon former occasions ... what I understand to be the real issue in this controversy between Judge Douglas and myself. On the point of my wanting to make war between the Free and the Slave States, there has been no issue between us. So, too, when he assumes that I am in favor of introducing a perfect social and political equality between the white and black races. These are false issues.... The real issue in this controversy—the one pressing upon every mind—is the sentiment on the part of one class that looks upon the institution of slavery *as a wrong,* and of another class that *does not* look upon it as a wrong. The sentiment that contemplates the institution of slavery in this country as a wrong is the sentiment of the Republican party.... They look upon it as being a moral, social, and political wrong; and while they contemplate it as such, they nevertheless have due regard for ... the difficulties of getting rid of it in any satisfactory way and to all the constitutional obligations thrown about it. Yet ... they insist that it should, as far as may be, *be treated* as a wrong; and one of the methods of treating it as a wrong is to *make provision that it shall grow no larger.*

From Abraham Lincoln, Speech at Alton, Illinois, October 15, 1858.

owner would bring his valuable property into the territory, and the problem of slavery would never arise.

This reply satisfied most Northern Democrats as a logical, practical application of popular sovereignty, but to the proslavery Southern Democrats it seemed outrageous. Douglas had already broken with the Buchanan Administration; he was at war with the Southerners in his party; and he had killed the Lecompton constitution in Congress. Now he was saying, as he had before, that popular sovereignty really offered the South nothing. The "Freeport doctrine" was one part of the set of attitudes and purposes that cost Douglas his chance for his party's nomination in 1860, but that doctrine sufficed in Illinois in 1858.

Douglas won re-election, but not a popular majority. Through the country, the Democrats held tenuous control of the Senate. The Republicans gained the largest representation in the House, but Know Nothing congressmen kept them from a majority there. Lincoln,

though defeated, earned national Republican acclaim. His interrogation of Douglas had reminded Americans of the incompatibility of popular sovereignty and the Dred Scott decision. His tactic had thus advertised the split within the Democracy. And Lincoln's own program—his insistence on excluding slavery from the territories, his clear denunciation of the immorality of slavery, and yet his promise not to interfere with that institution where it already existed—gave to the Republican position the most compelling statement it had known. Lincoln also defined the long-range problem succinctly, and in so doing marked the gap between the purpose of his party and that of either of the Democratic factions. " 'A house divided against itself cannot stand,' " he had told the Republican state convention. "I believe that this government cannot endure permanently half *slave* and half *free.*"

The Great Debate: Douglas

We ought to extend to the negro race ... all the rights, all the privileges, and all the immunities which they can exercise consistently with the safety of society. Humanity requires that we should give them all these privileges; Christianity commands that we should extend those privileges to them. The question then arises, What are those privileges, and what is the nature and extent of them? My answer is, that that is a question which each State must answer for itself.... If the people of all the States will act on that great principle, and each State mind its own business, attend to its own affairs, take care of its own negroes, and not meddle with its neighbors, then there will be peace between the North and the South, the East and the West, throughout the whole Union.

Why can we not thus have peace?... The moment the North obtained the majority in the House and Senate by the admission of California, and could elect a President without the aid of Southern votes, that moment ambitious Northern men formed a scheme to excite the North against the South, and make the people be governed in their votes by geographical lines, thinking that the North, being the stronger section, would outvote the South, and consequently they, the leaders, would ride into office on a sectional hobby.

From Stephen A. Douglas, Speech at Alton, Illinois, October 15, 1858.

Denouement

Harper's Ferry   In the new Congress, the state of mind of the Southern Democrats, who were no longer able to shape public policy, had become alarming. In 1856 they had been content to abide with popular sovereignty and to assert that Congress lacked power to meddle with slavery in the states; now, reacting to the Freeport doctrine, they were close to insisting on a federal slave code for the territories. But the Northern Democrats would accept no such thing. The only national party left in the country was in imminent danger of splitting on a sectional basis. If the 1860 campaign offered only a choice between sectional loyalties, the federal Union would be tested as it had never been before.

In a time of quiet, such a test might have been avoided, or at least postponed. But there was no quiet. During 1859 continued by-elections kept politics at high heat. So did Buchanan's distribution of patronage to Douglas' enemies, and so did Republican proposals for the economic and land programs that both Democratic wings opposed. Most disturbing, in 1859 John Brown struck directly at slavery in the South itself.

Brown in his fifty-five years had engaged in more than twenty business ventures, most of them failures. Some terminated in bankruptcy, two in crime. He had regularly failed to pay his debts. Since 1855 he had depended for his livelihood on contributions from people whom he persuaded, remarkably, of his integrity and high purpose. Doubtless his fiery passion against slavery blinded his victims to his palpable record of dishonesty. The father of twenty children, Brown was the son of a mother who, like her own mother, had died insane. Three of his mother's sisters and two of her brothers were also intermittently insane. So were one of Brown's brothers, his sister, and her daughter. So, too, were Brown's first wife and one of his sons. If he was not himself mad, he was at least a monomaniac about religion and slavery, a psychopathic individual—not merely a madman—who revealed the symptoms of paranoia and, by his deeds, provoked those symptoms in others.

Brown's plan was to seize some stronghold in the Southern mountains where he could gather slaves together and arm them. This action, he felt, would touch off a general slave uprising; the slaveholders would be unable to suppress it; the peculiar institution would collapse. Brown had gained financial support from eminent New Englanders who hated slavery; most of them, by no means insane, however vengeful they may have been, were canny enough to keep themselves ignorant of exactly what he was planning, for they did not propose to be accessories before the fact in an insurrection which might fail and come to the gallows. At a hideout in the Maryland hills Brown recruited a handful of followers, collected weapons, and made ready for his stroke.

In October 1859 Brown led his strange company down across the Potomac to seize the government arsenal at Harper's Ferry, Virginia. In theory this bold stroke would give him the armaments he needed, the slaves of Virginia would flock in to join him, the nearby mountains would offer a safe retreat, and the great slave uprising would take place. Actually, the old man's planning was so fuzzy that his project never had a chance. He did manage to seize the fire-engine house at the arsenal,

John Brown: At the least, a monomaniac.

and a few bewildered slaves were induced or compelled to join him. In the incidental shooting a few men were killed. Brown himself stayed in the fire-engine house. State militia blocked all his escape routes, while a detachment of United States marines marched up the river from Washington under the command of a regular army officer, Lieutenant Colonel Robert E. Lee, who chanced to be in the capital at the time. The marines carried the fire-engine house by assault, took Brown and his followers prisoners, and transferred him to Charles Town, Virginia, to stand trial for treason. He was speedily convicted and on December 2, 1859, he was hanged.

The Virginia authorities would probably have been wiser simply to have had Brown adjudged insane and confined in an asylum. By hanging him, they made him a martyr. The one thing John Brown could do well was to die. From the moment of his arrest until the moment of his execution he behaved with dignity, courage, and restraint, and many Northerners who did not themselves believe in fomenting slave uprisings heaped praise upon him.

As a result, the Harper's Ferry raid took on an exaggerated importance. It had been the futile act of a madman and it had been denounced by most people in the North. But it had touched the South on a particularly sensitive nerve, for the dread of a slave uprising always lay just below the slave-owner's consciousness. John Brown had actually tried to stage one, apparently with the encouragement of antislavery people in the North, and on his death he was hailed there as a martyr, with public ceremonies of mourning. Many thoughtful Southerners were now convinced that the Northerners who wanted to abolish slavery meant also to inflict bloodshed and destruction on the people who held slaves.

The Election of 1860   The 1850's drew to a close with a presidential election which, instead of helping to harmonize the differences between the sections, put them almost beyond hope of settlement. At the Democratic convention in Charleston in April 1860 the differences within the party were quickly exposed as past healing.

Senator Douglas was the leading contender for the nomination, but even though a ma-

jority of the delegates probably would have accepted him, he could not muster the two-thirds vote the party rules required. The Buchanan Administration fought him as a matter of party politics; neither the President nor such influential party stalwarts as Howell Cobb of Georgia, John Slidell of Louisiana, or Jefferson Davis of Mississippi would accept a man who had broken with the party leadership on the Lecompton issue, and all the resources of federal patronage were arrayed against him. In addition, the extremists—William L. Yancey of Alabama, Robert B. Rhett of South Carolina, and Edmund Ruffin of Virginia—were determined to accept nothing less than a platform and a candidate explicitly committed to the proslavery position. Specifically, they wanted a federal slave code in the territories and a disavowal of anything resembling the Freeport doctrine. The fact that a campaign based on such a program could not hope to win in the North struck them as an advantage rather than a handicap. Above all, they were fighting against any implication that slavery could be contained, for they believed that containment would be the first step toward extinction. To avert containment they were ready to split both the party and the Union itself.

Men like Yancey represented only a minority in the South, but it was a determined, tightly organized, ably directed minority that knew exactly what it wanted. It wanted, ultimately, secession of the slaveholding states. Most Southerners in the spring of 1860 were not ready for secession; but if the Democratic convention and the election showed that an all-out "Southern-rights" candidate and platform could not win, then thousands of Southerners who still considered themselves Unionists might be willing to accept secession. This was the goal to which the Yancey group devoted itself at Charleston.

The convention fell into a prolonged row which left it unable to make any nomination at all. After days of wrangling the delegates refused to accept the demand for a slave code in the territories; at this point, most of the delegates from the cotton states walked out, agreeing to meet again with the other delegates in Baltimore in June. But at Baltimore the cotton-state delegates were excluded, pro-Douglas

Lincoln the candidate.

North could applaud the party's firm stand against any extension of slavery in the territories. For good measure the platform added a denunciation of Southern threats of secession, which were becoming more and more common. Then, looking for a candidate who could pull together the various elements in this still half-formed party, the delegates passed up the most prominent contender, William H. Seward, on the ground that he had been too outspoken, had made too many enemies, and was too closely indentified with the militant antislavery element. The nomination went instead, in part because of the skillful maneuvering of his floor managers, to Abraham Lincoln.

Now a fourth party entered the field, a party drawing its support from old-line Whigs, Know Nothings, and dissident Democrats, calling themselves the Constitutional Union party. They named John Bell of Tennessee as their candidate and prepared to campaign on a program which simply demanded support for the Union and the Constitution.

The campaign brought forth a great deal of marching, shouting, and spread-eagle oratory, but it contributed almost nothing to a discussion of the divisive issues themselves. Lincoln made no speeches, taking the position that he had already made his stand clear. Breckinridge preserved a similar silence. Bell argued that brothers ought not to quarrel, but to suggest a way in which the brothers might stop quarreling was beyond him and indeed beyond everybody else. Douglas did try to make a campaign of it, stumping the South, warning that secession would mean disaster, and valiantly and unsuccessfully calling on his countrymen not to let this row over slavery lead to a disruption of the Union. But most Northerners apparently believed that the Southerners did not really mean their defiant words about secession, and most Southerners seem to have believed that if secession did come the North would accept it once the shock had worn off. The country moved with increasing speed toward catastrophe.

The election results surprised no one. Lincoln received less than half of the votes cast, but he won a decisive majority in the electoral college—180 votes to 123 for all the rival candidates together. His victory was obviously sectional: he had received no popular votes in the

men were seated in their places, and then the representatives of Virginia, North Carolina, Tennessee, and Arkansas left the convention. The delegates who remained proceeded to nominate Douglas for the presidency; their antagonists, calling themselves the real Democratic party, held a convention of their own and nominated John C. Breckinridge of Kentucky. Douglas' platform endorsed popular sovereignty; Breckinridge's demanded a federal code to protect slavery in the territories. Now it was all but certain that the Republican candidate would be elected in the fall.

Fully aware of their opportunity and bent on seizing the proffered prize, the Republicans met in Chicago. They had little difficulty agreeing on a platform—calling for a higher tariff, free homesteads, internal improvements, and a Pacific railroad. These planks promised to attract votes in both the industrial East and the agricultural West. Idealists throughout the

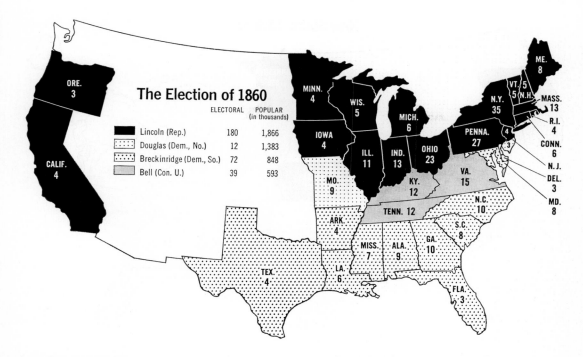

The Election of 1860

		ELECTORAL	POPULAR (in thousands)
■	Lincoln (Rep.)	180	1,866
⋯	Douglas (Dem., No.)	12	1,383
⋯	Breckinridge (Dem., So.)	72	848
▨	Bell (Con. U.)	39	593

deep South and very few in the border states. His 1,865,593 popular votes came to barely 40 per cent of the total. Douglas, who won a mere handful of electoral votes, ran second with 1,382,713, while Breckinridge and Bell between them polled 1,441,262. Nevertheless, Lincoln's election was wholly legal, and he was neither the first nor the last President to win the office with a minority of the popular vote.

Secession   The election of a Republican President profoundly disturbed the great majority of the people in all fifteen of the slave states. But the South was not, in November of 1860, in complete agreement about what to do next. Extremist leaders like Yancey and Rhett welcomed the Republican victory as justification for the secession they had dreamed of so long and so ardently, but secessionist sentiment in the South was by no means unanimous. Union sentiment remained strong. Lincoln had denied any intention of trying to free the slaves; a Southern majority still dominated the United States Supreme Court; and the Democrats still controlled the Senate. The South could perhaps be drawn into secession, but not en masse and not without careful leadership. It might not have gone at all if South Carolina had not dramatically exerted that leadership.

Anticipating Lincoln's victory, the South Carolina legislature had remained in session over election day, and immediately thereafter it summoned a state convention. On December 20, without a dissenting vote, the convention passed an ordinance of secession, proclaiming that the union previously existing between South Carolina and all the other states was dissolved. This action was the catalytic agent that led to action in other Southern states.

South Carolina obviously could not exist by itself as an independent nation. But if South Carolina could be compelled, by force, to return to the Union, the whole theory of the right and the feasibility of peaceful secession would be gone forever, and this was a theory which most Southerners held even though they may have doubted the advisability of exercising that right. Fundamental to political thinking in the South was the belief that any state could leave the Union if it wanted to, and to many Southerners this right was the ultimate defense against Northern interference with their cherished way of life. The Republican victory pointed to the possibility of such interference, perhaps not at once, but ultimately. Clearly the North had gained the balance of political power. Free population was

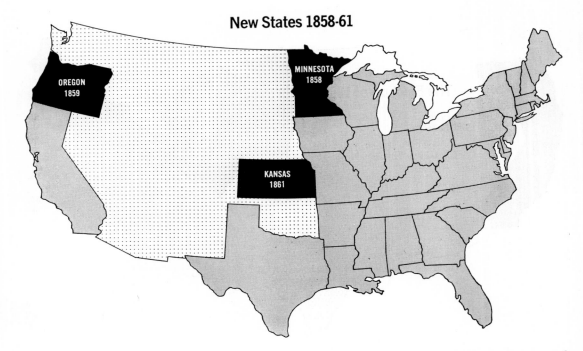

New States 1858-61

OREGON
1859

MINNESOTA
1858

KANSAS
1861

settling the open territories; California, Minnesota, and Oregon had come into the Union as free states; and urban and industrial development were swelling Northern population and strength. Northern demands for a high tariff, for internal improvements, for a national banking system would soon, given the trend of events, command congressional majorities. All this was portended by Lincoln's election, to which Southern extremists deliberately attached still more terrifying omens—the end of state rights, the freedom of the slaves, the violation of Southern white womanhood.

These expectations fed the sectional consciousness of the South and lent persuasion to South Carolina's quick, decisive act. Within six weeks, five other states adopted their own ordinances of secession—Georgia, Florida, Alabama, Mississippi, and Louisiana. A convention of delegates from these states met in Montgomery, Alabama, early in February 1861. They formed a new government to be known as the Confederate States of America, adopted a constitution similar to that of the United States, and named Jefferson Davis as President and Alexander H. Stephens of Georgia as Vice-President.

The Confederacy, to which Texas soon adhered, was made up of the states of the deep South, where cotton was king both on the small farms that produced most of the crop and on the large plantations of the *nouveau riche*. Here slavery was still a dynamic institution, and it was easy for men to believe that it had an enduring future. Though sentiment in these states was not unanimous for secession, though there was unquestionably more feeling for an undivided Union than was visible on the surface, the secessionist leaders had been well organized and forceful, and the new Confederacy came into existence on a wave of enthusiasm. Its adherents contemplated a rosy future—continuing profits from cotton, a commercial alliance with England, freedom from Northern lenders and sellers, expansion into the Caribbean or Mexico, the fulfillment of Southern reveries. Few men in the deep South, even among the Unionists, believed that the North would or could resist secession; fewer still thought the North would fight for union; almost none foresaw a terrible war and eventual defeat.

Yet secessionist arguments and expectations were not compelling outside of the cotton country. None of the border states at first joined the Confederacy. From Virginia to Missouri, eight slave states refused to secede. Their people disliked a Republican administration, but they did not believe that the election, in itself, required them to leave the Union. Many of them considered the secession of the cotton states as a political maneuver—a means of inducing the North to make concessions, after which the seceding states would return to the Union with guarantees of Southern rights.

No Compromise   While the states of the deep South were seceding and moving toward the Confederacy, most Americans in the months after the election hoped for a conciliatory solution. Especially in the border states men looked for a compromise that would restore the Union, preclude conflict, and erase the anxieties that had been growing for a decade.

Buchanan denied South Carolina's right to secede but also his right to use force to prevent her. The Union, he argued, was perpetual, but it rested upon consent. He hoped negotiations would bring back the seceded states; in contrast, they expected any agreement to legitimize their new status in Northern eyes.

In the Senate, a Committee of Thirteen searched vainly for a compromise. One was submitted to the Senate by John J. Crittenden of Kentucky. It prohibited slavery in territories "now held or hereafter acquired" north of the old Missouri Compromise line and protected it with a federal slave code in territories south of that line; further, it protected the domestic slave trade and endorsed a constitutional amendment prohibiting Congress for all time from interfering with slavery in the states. Lincoln and other leading Republicans opposed this proposal. They had no fear that slavery would ever take root in such territories as New Mexico, but they did fear that Southern expansionists would try to extend slavery and the American flag to Cuba and portions of Mexico and Central America. The Republicans, in short, would accept no program that encouraged the further spread of slavery.

Southerners were wholly dissatisfied with the concessions Lincoln approved. The President-elect was prepared to guarantee enforcement of the fugitive slave law and, if necessary by constitutional amendment, the right of the states to maintain slavery where it existed. When the

Southerners rejected these conditions, the impasse moved Crittenden to suggest a national referendum on his program, but the Republicans prevented that.

Efforts at compromise outside Congress also failed. At the request of the Virginia General Assembly, a convention of delegates from twenty-one states met in Washington early in February to seek some settlement. Ex-President Tyler presided over a company of distinguished men, but their differences quickly proved more marked than their agreements, and their proceedings were handicapped by the absence of delegations from the seceding states and six others. The Peace Convention, after three weeks of deliberation, sent Congress a plan for seven amendments to the Constitution which, taken together, rehearsed the ill-fated Crittenden proposal, and elicited only negligible support.

Now lingering hopes for compromise faded away. Even Buchanan had stiffened and reorganized his Cabinet, replacing state-righters with committed Union men. In his last message to Congress, on January 8, 1861, he appealed for patriotism, rejected the possibility of aggressive war against the seceded states, but also asserted his obligation as President to collect federal revenues and protect federal properties throughout the United States. "The Union," he concluded, "must and shall be preserved by all constitutional means. . . . The present is no time for palliations. Action, prompt action, is required."

In that spirit Buchanan decided to send a ship to reinforce the federal garrison at Fort Sumter, South Carolina. At first he considered dispatching a warship for this purpose, but his advisers persuaded him to send instead an unarmed, and therefore less threatening, merchantman. The *Star of the West*, carrying troops and ammunition, sailed from New York the first week in January. Before she entered Charleston harbor, the South Carolinians fired upon her, whereupon she came about and steamed away. Major Robert Anderson at Fort Sumter had been about to return the fire and protect the ship. But his guns stayed silent, and his small force was left without reinforcement or adequate supplies. But Fort Sumter remained under federal control, as did Fort Pickens in Florida and a few others. Elsewhere during January 1861 the Confederacy had seized federal forts and arsenals and other establishments. Buchanan failed to protect public property and collect public revenues; Southern independence asserted itself in deed as well as word; and the Confederates, it was clear, were ready to fight for the independence they had declared.

Lincoln Takes Over Lincoln's arrival in Washington was inauspicious. At the urging of friends who were afraid he might be assassinated, he reached the city after a secret ride through the night. He seemed preoccupied with patronage, indecisive about the national crisis, an awkward and inept man who would be the agent of powerful advisers like Seward, the designated Secretary of State.

But the new President's inaugural address revealed his true timber. There would be no invasion of the South, he said, no interference with the institution of slavery. Yet "we cannot separate," he maintained; the Union was not dissoluble; and he would use his power "to hold, occupy, and possess the property, and places belonging to the federal government." The "momentous issue of civil war" lay in the hands of the Confederates. Lincoln went on:

> The government will not assail *you*. . . . *You* have no oath . . . to destroy the government,

while I . . . have the most solemn one to "preserve, protect, and defend" it. . . . We must not be enemies. . . . The mystic chords of memory . . . will yet swell the chorus of the Union, when again touched, as surely they will be, by the better angels of our nature.

When Lincoln made this statement, he believed that Major Anderson had ample supplies to hold out for several weeks or months. There would be no fighting at Fort Sumter, as he saw it, unless South Carolina (or the Confederacy, which had by now asserted its own control over military matters in Charleston) opened fire and forced the issue. If there was to be a war, the Confederacy would have to start it.

Lincoln immediately learned that his calculations were wrong. Major Anderson's stock of foodstuffs was just about exhausted, and the day after delivering his inaugural address Lincoln was notified that the fort could hold out for only a few more weeks. Unless it could be supplied at once, Anderson would have to surrender. The overt act, as a result, would have to be taken by the federal government, for its efforts to supply Fort Sumter would almost certainly be taken by Jefferson Davis as a challenge, a warlike step against the new Confederacy.

Up to this point Lincoln had been firm but

conciliatory, eager to assert federal authority, reluctant actually to exercise it. To act against Sumter was to risk driving the upper South to secession. Not to act was to acknowledge disunion. Over Sumter, then, Lincoln and his countrymen faced their great crisis, and over Sumter and what it symbolized, opinion had hardened. The Confederates could not permit reinforcement without jeopardizing their claim to national independence. In the North, patriots believed that the destiny of America, of the whole democratic experiment launched in 1776, depended on preserving the Union. More selfish men had also begun to draw a hard line. Disunity would reduce the value of government securities and weaken the bonds of internal trade and commerce. Consequently the business community felt the need to save

the Union even at the cost of war. So also, most abolitionists were ready to risk war, which for them would be a crusade against slavery. And Republican politicians could permit secession only at the cost of destroying their young party.

Yet Lincoln hesitated. Only two of his Cabinet, Secretary of the Treasury Salmon P. Chase and Postmaster General Montgomery Blair, favored sending food to Sumter, and the commanding general of the army, Winfield Scott, advised against such a move. By April 1, most of the Cabinet had come to agree with Blair, but in a note to Lincoln on that day Secretary Seward talked wildly about cementing union sentiment, North and South, by drawing a European power into war. He had earlier gone as far as to negotiate indirectly

Stars and bars above Sumter.

on his own with Confederate commissioners in Washington, to whom he sent word that he wanted Sumter evacuated.

But Lincoln, steady as ever, reached a reasoned decision. Sumter, he concluded, had to be relieved, for anything less testified to Southern independence. But he would not dispatch an armed force. Rather, he would try to get supplies to Sumter peacefully; he would take a chance on war but leave the choice to the South. On April 4 the President completed arrangements for an expedition. He informed Governor Francis W. Pickens of South Carolina that "an attempt will be made to supply Fort Sumter with provisions only; . . . if such attempt be not resisted, no effort to throw in men, arms, or ammunition will be made, without further notice, or in case of an attack upon the Fort."

Pickens sent the message, received on April 8, to President Davis in Montgomery. Now the weight of decision lay there. The orders came back at once to demand evacuation, and, if Anderson refused, to "reduce" the place. On April 12 the harbor batteries opened fire, at the command of General Pierre G. T. Beauregard—acting, significantly, as an officer of the Confederacy; it was the Southern nation, not just South Carolina, that had taken the step. Major Anderson's men returned the fire, and the fort was badly battered; on the afternoon of April 13, with his food supplies depleted, Anderson agreed to surrender. The following morning—Sunday, April 14—he hauled down his flag, and his troops were allowed to embark for New York. Beauregard's forces moved into Fort Sumter. The Civil War had begun.

SUGGESTIONS FOR READING

General

Probably the best introduction to the period covered in this chapter is in the early part of J. G. Randall and David Donald, *The Civil War and Reconstruction* (2nd ed., 1961), a learned, judicious, and comprehensive work that is valuable not the least for its treatment of relevant bibliography. There is a longer account of the years 1854–61, distinguished for its clarity and scope and for the movement of its prose, in the latter part of Allan Nevins, *Ordeal of the Union*, 2 vols. (1947), and its sequel, *The Emergence of Lincoln*, 2 vols. (1950). Of equal stature, though its coverage begins in 1856, and of special significance for its interpretation of politics and the political process, is R. F. Nichols, *The Disruption of American Democracy* (1948). There are other important points of view in A. O. Craven, *The Coming of the Civil War* (1942); H. H. Simms, *A Decade of Sectional Controversy* (1942), and D. L. Dumond, *Antislavery Origins of the Civil War in the United States* * (1939); and there is a spirited narrative in Bruce Catton, *The Coming Fury* (1961).

The Kansas-Nebraska Act and Its Aftermath

A major concern of the general works cited above, the Kansas-Nebraska Act receives central and telling analysis in J. C. Malin, *The Nebraska Question, 1852–1854* (1953), and in a splendid essay, R. F. Nichols, "The Kansas-Nebraska Act: A Century of Historiography," *Mississippi Valley Historical Review*, XLIII, 2 (1956). On the aftermath of the Act, again apart from the general works already noted, P. W. Gates, *Fifty Million Acres: Conflicts Over Kansas Land Policy, 1854–1890* (1954), has major significance, as do two studies of John Brown: J. C. Malin, *John Brown and the Legend of Fifty-Six* (1942) and the essay on that disturbed figure in C. V. Woodward, *The Burden of Southern History* (1960). The birth and growth of the Republican party absorb A. W. Crandall, *The Early History of the Republican Party, 1854–1856* (1930), and J. A. Isely, *Horace Greeley and the Republican Party, 1853–1861* (1947), while the same subject, seen from the angle of two New England participants, is illuminated in M. B. Duberman, *Charles Francis Adams* (1961), and David Donald, *Charles Sumner and the Coming of the Civil War* (1960). The latter contains a brilliant analysis of Sumner the man and of his controversial caning.

* Available in a paperback edition.

The Court, the Economy, the Election

The classic studies of the Dred Scott case appear in two books of C. B. Swisher: *Roger B. Taney* (1935) and *American Constitutional Development* (1943), which can be supplemented in Vincent Hopkins, *Dred Scott's Case* (1951), and, with special profit, in the pertinent parts of the books of Nevins and Nichols cited above. Nevins also complements G. W. Van Vleck, *The Panic of 1857: An Analytical Study* (1943). Lincoln in the years 1858–60, as in the other years of his epochal life, has been the subject of a library of books, including the general studies already cited. For the beginning student, an outstanding further reading is the superb biography of B. P. Thomas, *Abraham Lincoln* (1952). A. J. Beveridge, *Abraham Lincoln, 1809–1858*, 2 vols. (1928), remains useful, and R. H. Luthin, *The First Lincoln Campaign* (1944), has instructive depth. For its sentiments and expressions of them, Carl Sandburg, *Abraham Lincoln: The Prairie Years*,* especially the one-volume 1929 edition, continues to win some admirers.

Secession and War

Among the many accounts of secession, one of the best is A. O. Craven, *The Growth of Southern Nationalism, 1848–1861* (1953), while two older works are still admirable for their scope and form: D. L. Dumond, *The Secession Movement, 1860–1861* (1931) and U. B. Phillips, *The Course of the South to Secession* (1939). There is significant additional material in Ollinger Crenshaw, *The Slave States in the Presidential Election of 1860* (1945). On the coming of war, P. S. Foner, *Business and Slavery: The New York Merchants and the Irrepressible Conflict* (1941), sets forth an interesting but, in the end, not entirely persuasive thesis. Much more important are the indispensable and somewhat conflicting analyses of David Potter, *Lincoln and His Party in the Secession Crisis, 1860–1861* (1950), and K. M. Stampp, *And the War Came: The North and the Secession Crisis, 1860–1861* (1950).

* Available in a paperback edition.

14

The Civil War

The Civil War tested the courage and stamina of men and women north and south. It tested the respective strengths of a society still essentially agricultural and of a society increasingly industrialized. It tested the qualities of leadership of dozens of soldiers and civilians who carried the greatest burdens Americans had known since the start of their national history. It tested Northern tolerance for the institution of slavery and Southern commitment to local self-determination. It tested the viability of two constitutions under conditions of crisis. Above all, it tested the meaning and determined the future of the federal Union. It was the great trial of the United States, the crucible from which the mature nation emerged.

The Stage for War

The Call to Arms   The bombardment of Fort Sumter released the explosive force of the sectional tensions that had accumulated during the preceding decade. Passion galvanized loyalties and dispelled irresolution. On April 15, 1861, President Lincoln called on the governors of the Northern states to furnish seventy-five thousand militia for ninety days to put down what he called the "combinations" of men who had seized control of the seceded South. Early in May he asked for forty-two thousand more volunteers to serve a three-year enlistment. He also enlarged the regular army and navy and declared a blockade of the Confeder-

ate coast. As recruitment began, the drums in every community beat the theme of dedication to the Union. Secession, in the view of the Administration, was illegal. The rebellion of Southerners had to be put down. That was the sole issue of the war as the President and later the Congress initially defined it. "The central idea pervading this struggle," Lincoln wrote, "is the necessity of proving that popular government is not an absurdity. We must settle this question now, whether, in a free government, the minority have the right to break up the government whenever they choose." Supporting the President, Horace Greeley of the New York *Tribune*, long preoccupied with the slavery question, for a time made the Union his first cause. And Stephen Douglas, who was soon to die, put the case fervently to a Chicago audience: "There can be no neutrals in this war; only patriots—or traitors."

With comparable fervor, the men of the Confederacy rallied to the flag of secession, to the theory of state rights, including the right to leave the Union, to the emotionally powerful appeal of local self-determination. Responding to Jefferson Davis' call for one hundred thousand troops, Southern volunteers marched forth with the verve and the certitude of their Northern counterparts. The very favor of the ministers of the Lord was thrown into the balance. Of the remaining national churches (some had split during the 1840's and 1850's), only the Roman Catholic failed to divide

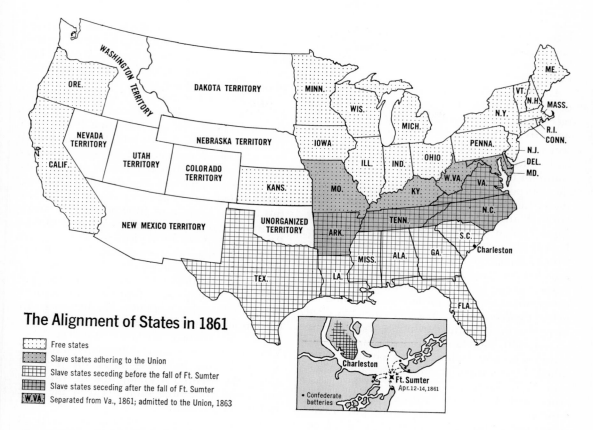

The Alignment of States in 1861

- Free states
- Slave states adhering to the Union
- Slave states seceding before the fall of Ft. Sumter
- Slave states seceding after the fall of Ft. Sumter
- W.VA. Separated from Va., 1861; admitted to the Union, 1863

Charleston

Ft. Sumter
Apr.12-14,1861

Confederate batteries

along sectional lines as the war began.

Confronted with a choice between two flags, between the attraction of Union and the pull of state rights, Virginia, North Carolina, and Arkansas refused to furnish federal troops and within a few weeks formally joined the Confederacy. Tennessee followed them in June. Kentucky and Missouri likewise refused troops, but remained in a state of indecision, their governors stoutly pro-Confederate, their people split between the two causes. The governor of Maryland was pro-Union, but his state also had divided loyalties, and he announced that Maryland would send men to help defend Washington but not to fight in the South. Of all the slave states, only Delaware remained loyal without qualification.

The Border States   The second wave of secession strengthened the Confederacy and made the control of the doubtful border states —Kentucky, Missouri, and Maryland—vital to the Union. Lincoln's vigorous policies held them in line. Until Congress met in July, the

President alone made the decisions of government. He decided boldly, improvising where no precedent existed, stretching the authority of his office beyond any previous practice. Besides his calls for troops and his proclamation of blockade, he ordered the disbursement of $2 million for "military and naval measures necessary for the defense and support of the government," and, when he had to, he used force without stint or let.

On April 19 the Sixth Massachusetts Infantry passed through Baltimore on its way to Washington. As it marched across town on its way from one railroad station to another, it fell afoul of a mob of disunionists. In the full-scale riot that developed, several soldiers and a larger number of civilians were killed, with many more wounded. Temporarily, Lincoln ordered additional contingents to bypass Baltimore, but in a short time he sent federal troops to occupy the city, authorized suspension of the writ of habeas corpus, ordered the arrest of suspects, and jailed a number of local officials. When the state legislature at length assembled, its secessionist leaders were kept from attending. Maryland was saved for the Union.

In Missouri Lincoln followed a similar course. Governor Claiborne Jackson was a secessionist; the legislature had a Unionist majority, and sentiment in the state as a whole seemed to be equally divided. The governor had called a contingent of state militia into camp on the edge of St. Louis, apparently for the purpose of seizing the federal arsenal there. Lincoln authorized Congressman Francis P. Blair of Missouri to organize a dimly legal "home guard" from among the pro-Union German residents of the city. These troops, armed and sworn into federal service, and led by Captain Nathaniel Lyon of the regular army, on May 10 captured the militia camp, disarmed the militiamen, and then released them on parole. As Lyon's men marched away from this singular triumph, they fell into a riot with St. Louis civilians, and, as in Baltimore, both soldiers and civilians were killed. Lyon's superior officer, Brigadier General W. S. Harney, then worked out an uneasy truce with Governor Jackson, but presently Lincoln removed Harney and put Lyon, promoted to brigadier general, in his place. Lyon promptly marched on Jefferson City, the state capital, driving the governor off in flight. Again the federal government had acted decisively, with scant regard for ordinary legal formalities. As a result Missouri was held in the Union, although Lyon's blow left a legacy of bitterness that expressed itself in continued guerilla warfare.

Kentucky for several months maintained her position of neutrality. As in Missouri, the governor was pro-Confederate while the legislature was predominantly Unionist. The state contained many Confederate sympathizers, but a majority of the inhabitants probably leaned toward the Union. During the summer, both Lincoln and Davis respected the state's neutrality, at least on the surface, although each executive exerted whatever political pressure he could. Troops for both armies were recruited in Kentucky, but were mustered into service outside the state. Confident that a policy of patience would prevail, Lincoln won his reward in September. Fol-

lowing the occupation of the town of Columbus by a Confederate force, the newly elected state legislature declared for the Union. This was a significant gain, for the region was to be a major highway of the war.

Lincoln used still another tactic in western Virginia. Few large plantations and few slaveholders lay beyond the Blue Ridge. For years many of the people who lived there had resented the domination of the state government by the plantation interests of the tidewater region, and now they displayed a strong anti-Confederate sentiment. Capitalizing on this feeling, Lincoln in June ordered an army of twenty thousand volunteers across the Ohio River and into western Virginia. The original aim was largely to secure the line of the Baltimore & Ohio Railroad, but after the outnumbered Confederates were crushed, the Administration gave definite encouragement to the separatist tendency of the area. In November 1861 the western counties split away and formed the new state of West Virginia, which Congress formally admitted to the Union in 1863. Thus the Federal authorities secured a major link in transportation and communication between the East and the Ohio Valley.

Lincoln's achievement in holding the crucial border states was vital to success in the war. In a revolutionary situation, he had resorted to revolutionary means. Anything less might have surrendered to the Confederacy the margin of ultimate victory.

The Confederacy Even without the border states, the South was optimistic. It had to wage only a defensive war, as the colonials had against the British. It had only to keep the North from conquest, and in that way to establish a separate Southern nation. Confederate leaders expected to protect their territory with relative ease. Though their railroad network was thin except in and near Virginia, they counted on the skill and valor of their troops to repel Northern thrusts anywhere along their front. Their men were conditioned to life outdoors, to shooting and riding; they knew the terrain; they would be fighting to protect their homes. Some Southern leaders also underestimated the bravery and tenacity of the Yankees. Few thought the war would last long, and fewer still realized what a variety of resources it would demand. The dominant belief in speedy triumph rested partly on the expectation of foreign intervention. The South's virtual monopoly of the world's cotton supply was presumed to make England with her textile mills, and France, too, a ready if not a willing potential ally.

The Confederacy also counted heavily on the brilliance of its commanders in the field. General Robert E. Lee and his able lieutenants represented the best in the American military tradition, the best, too, of the alumni of West Point, the cream of the prewar regular army. (In contrast to their officers, the enlisted men for the most part remained loyal to the Union.) Against growing odds—ultimately enormous odds—against opposing commanders of equal dedication and increasing experience and imagination, the most splendid Southern generals earned the admiration of their troops and of their enemy. So it was especially with Lee, whose dignity and daring, whose virtue as a man and virtuosity as a soldier, wrote a glorious chapter in the annals of all wars and in the history of mankind.

Yet set off against its assets, the South had telling liabilities. The population of the seceded states was only nine million, three and a half million of them Negroes, in contrast to the twenty-two million of the Union. Over the years of war the Confederacy could muster to arms only some nine hundred thousand men, less than half of the two million soldiers and sailors of the North, and with the attrition and exhaustion of battle, this difference told more and more. The Southern share of material resources was even smaller. Confederate troops lacked food, uniforms, supplies, and ammunition. Four-fifths of the nation's manufacturing lay in the North, most of the minerals, most of the total supply of grain and meat. The trans-Mississippi South had no rail route east, whereas the twenty-one thousand miles of track in the North—more than twice the Confederacy's mileage—linked East with West and let both regions carry the Union armies swiftly toward the borders of battle. So also, the North held most of the nation's shipping, and most of its banks and financial wealth. And the demands of war, the need for production, the opportunities for economic growth, spurred the industrialization of the Union,

Robert E. Lee: His achievement was dazzling.

while the South, without a pool of skilled labor or capital or business experience, harassed by blockade and attack, remained essentially agricultural—a country primarily of farms and plantations, of languishing commerce, few cities, and less industry—a fair country, to be sure, but ill equipped for waging war even in its own defense.

The Confederacy suffered not the least from the political theory that had produced it. Its constitution, besides protecting slavery, explicitly recognized state sovereignty and denied to the central government the authority to impose a protective tariff or to finance internal improvements. (Two other innovations set a single, six-year term for the President and gave him the right to veto specific items within a general appropriations act.) The constitution's emphasis on local rights and federal restraints ran counter to the needs of war. The Confederate Conscription Act of 1862, drafting men eighteen to thirty-five years old, as well as later draft acts, met immediate resistance. It exempted various professional men and all owners and overseers of more than twenty slaves, and it permitted a conscripted man to hire a substitute. These provisions, favoring the planters and their friends, alienated the farmers who had never fully trusted them. The draft also excited the opposition of die-hard state righters. The governors of Alabama, Georgia, and Mississippi opposed the law and its administration; there was constant evasion of the draft in the nonslaveholding areas; and there were increasing desertions from the army. Though the Union troops deserted more frequently, they were much more easily replaced. The Confederate government, reluctant to impose its authority, waited until 1863 to pass a useful tax law. Earlier and later it resorted largely to borrowing and to printing money to pay its bills. The states also printed currency, which fed the inflation that crippled the economy, made the various currencies nearly worthless, encouraged hoarding, and eventually hurt morale.

The theory and structure of Confederate government cost the South less than did the shortcomings of its civilian leaders. Alexander H. Stephens of Georgia, the Vice-President, a brilliant neurotic, made a fetish of state rights, opposed the draft and wartime restrictions on civil liberties, and detested President Jefferson Davis. The President's Cabinet, largely undistinguished, squabbled constantly, failed to win the confidence of its chief or the Congress, and suffered from Davis' continuing changes of mind and personnel. Davis was himself ill cast. A native of Kentucky who grew up in Mississippi, he graduated from West Point, served ably in the Mexican War and as Franklin Pierce's Secretary of War, and in the United States Senate spoke ardently and forcefully for Southern aims. He was honest, devoted, and energetic, but also rigid and petty. He had neither the executive experience, the political instincts, nor the flair with people which his trying office demanded. His ego was large, particularly about his military judgment, and that was at best erratic. And Davis was an inveterate meddler.

Indeed his interference and his errors can-

celed out much of the benefit the South might otherwise have garnered from her cotton and from the excellence of her field commanders. In the first year of the war Davis attempted to bring England and France to heel by boycotting shipments of cotton to them. This was an egregious mistake. The Northern navy then still lacked the strength to impose an effective blockade. Davis' decision therefore shut off the best source of Southern revenue and military supplies during the brief period in which they were available. The European textile mills, moreover, had an ample inventory of cotton. Consequently they felt no serious pinch until after the blockade was firm and the course of war had lessened the probability of making a cotton famine into a fulcrum for winning foreign aid. The course of war itself took errant paths because Davis played favorites, often switched commands out of pique or unreasoning impatience, and,

Winslow Homer: Sketch of Union troops.

jealous of Lee, paid too little heed to his informed and percipient counsel. The Confederacy, a nation struggling to be born, needed a Washington in charge; Jefferson Davis was not a Washington.

The Union   The ample resources of the Union allowed room for trial and error, of which the war produced an abundance. Obviously far stronger than the South in human and material resources, the North spent much of its advantage in folly, greed, dissension, and delay. The folly and the delay were frequently attributable to the military. Inadequate organization complicated the problems of the senior generals, who when the war began were by and large second-rate men. Before the war ended, the Union had found commanders in whom it could take large pride—Grant, Sherman, Thomas, and Sheridan, among others—but their predecessors, as we shall see, too often stumbled through sorry campaigns that should have been won.

Sorrier still was the greed of Northern war profiteers—contractors and suppliers who grew rich by overcharging the government and delivering shoddy goods. Never before in American history had the ethics of commerce been worse than during the Civil War, never had public graft more cynically encouraged private immorality. Washington, one newspaper commented, was "reeling in the whirl of dissipation." Though, as always, most public officials were honorable men, many at every level of government winked at profiteering or shared in fraud. One of them was Lincoln's first Secretary of War, Simon Cameron of Pennsylvania, whom the President had appointed against his better judgment in order to cement his party coalition. In January 1862, to his great relief, Lincoln was able to get rid of Cameron by naming him minister to Russia. His successor, Edwin M. Stanton,

Winslow Homer: Sketch of a Union soldier.

life and business profits to the hardships of service. Almost none of the industrial titans of the postwar period ever wore a uniform. Men of their means and temperament were favored by the provisions of the Union Conscription Act of 1863. It applied only to districts that had not supplied their quota of volunteers, a condition that helped to perpetuate the bounty system, and it permitted a drafted man to escape service by hiring a substitute or paying three hundred dollars. This discrimination, together with persisting antagonism to the principle of conscription, gave rise to opposition to the draft, to widespread draft evasion, and in places to violent protests. A draft riot in New York City, where local machine politics and immigrant hostility to the war inflamed the resentment of workingmen, lasted four days, during which mobs spent their ire partly in attacks on Negroes, whom they blamed for their predicament. Yet in spite of these difficulties, the Union, unlike the Confederacy, had a sufficient pool of able-bodied men from which to enlist the soldiers it needed.

So it was also with money to finance the war; the North had its troubles, but it got the necessary funds. The Republican commitment to positive government marked the Union's economic policies. By 1864 Congress had boosted tariff rates to 47 per cent, the highest figure in national history to that date. The duties yielded over $300 million during the war, and also erected a protective barrier between American industrialists and their European competitors. The absence of Southern representatives in Congress vastly eased the fulfillment of the Republican campaign promise on the tariff. Resulting industrial profits in turn permitted business to pay unprecedented excise taxes which Congress levied in 1862 and increased two years later. Breaking another precedent, the lawmakers in 1861 imposed a 3 per cent tax on annual personal incomes and later raised that rate to a peak of 5 per cent on incomes from $600 to $5,000, and 10 per cent on additional earnings. Over-all, these internal taxes produced some $250 million of wartime revenue. Seeking still more funds, Congress authorized the printing of paper currency, in all $431 million, which depreciated rapidly, though never so dramatically as did Confederate paper. At bottom, in

while often a difficult man, brought to the War Department the same efficiency that characterized the work of Gideon Welles, the able Secretary of the Navy.

The Union, like the Confederacy, had trouble raising troops. In 1861 the government offered $100 to each volunteer, a bonus later increased to $302 for recruits and $402 for veterans, and states, counties, and cities added bounties of their own. By 1864 a volunteer in New York City could get $375 in addition to the federal bonus, and the total bounty in parts of Illinois came to $1,056. Yet the system did not work well. Enlistments lagged, and "bounty-jumpers" drew their reward, deserted, and then volunteered again under assumed names. Bounties, moreover, did not attract the well-to-do, who preferred civilian mid-1864, Union greenbacks were worth only 39 cents on the gold dollar, but by the end of the war, as the credit of the government improved with the prospect of victory, their value had risen to about 67 cents. Finally, the Treasury relied on the sale of bonds and notes, which bore the heaviest load of wartime finance—some $2,600 million, almost three times the sum of all other sources of revenue combined.

The need to sell bonds hastened the passage of the National Banking Act of 1862 and amendments to it in the following year. This legislation also removed most of the confusion and irregularity in the chaotic system of state banks that had developed since Jackson's time. All national banks chartered under the new system had to invest one-third of their capital in federal bonds, and deposit these securities with the Treasury Department. They were allowed then to issue bank notes, legal tender, up to 90 per cent of the market value of their bonds. They were also subjected to regular federal inspection, an important protection for depositors. In 1865 Congress extended federal control over banking. A law of that year brought most of the banks under state charters within the national system by imposing a prohibitive 10 per cent tax on their bank notes.

During the war the Republicans also capitalized on their strength in Congress to pass the Homestead Act of 1862, which granted free farms of 160 acres to all citizens and applicants for citizenship who occupied and improved the land for five years. In the same year Congress established the Department of Agriculture and passed the Morrill Act, which offered states a land grant to endow colleges of agriculture and the mechanical arts. These laws, significant in themselves, attracted farmers to the party and to the Union cause. So, too, just as the tariff pleased industry, the railroad legislation of 1862 delighted other business interests. To the companies building the first transcontinental railroad, Congress made large land grants and a generous loan: $16,000 for each mile of level ground covered; $48,000 in the mountains, and $22,000 elsewhere. Again public policy followed Republican prescriptions.

In the North partisanship never flagged. A minority of Democrats opposed the war and called for a negotiated peace which would have endorsed secession. Strongest in the old Northwest, these Peace Democrats—"Copperheads," in Unionist vocabulary—found a militant leader in Ohio Congressman C. L. Vallandigham. Some of them joined subversive secret societies. All attacked Lincoln mercilessly. In the Indiana legislature the Copperheads were able temporarily to block important war legislation; for a time they controlled the lower house in Illinois; in 1863 they tried, but failed, to elect Vallandigham—then exiled in Canada—governor of Ohio. The great majority of Democrats, loyal to the Union, supported the war, but they objected to Republican economic policies and kept alive the party organization through which they expected ultimately to regain power. Horatio Seymour, their outstanding spokesman, won election as governor of New York in 1862 in a campaign addressed to the Democratic slogan: "The Constitution as it is and the Union as it was."

Lincoln, in the view of the Democrats, had assumed autocratic authority. They bitterly criticized his denial of habeas corpus in Maryland in 1861 and his further, broader denial, by a proclamation of 1862, wherever any person discouraged enlistment in the army or engaged in any other "disloyal practice." That proclamation also provided for military rather than civil trial. In the case of one Milligan, an Indiana Democrat accused of conspiracy to set free certain Confederate prisoners of war, a military tribunal decreed the death sentence. After the war, in 1866, the Supreme Court annulled that judgment and held that a civilian could not, under the Constitution, be tried by court-martial when regular civil courts were operating "in the proper and unobstructed exercise of their jurisdiction." But that ruling came too late to affect wartime practice, and Lincoln, resolved to restore the Union at any price, regretfully saw no alternative to making civil rights subordinate to victory while the battle raged.

The President's emphasis on union as his overarching objective won the allegiance of the Conservative Republicans, the wing of the party that followed his lead in subordinating all other considerations. Though they differed with him about particulars, they were as ready

Lincoln the President: A master of the office.

An Impression of Lincoln

Soon afterwards there entered, with a shambling, loose, irregular, almost unsteady gait, a tall, lank, lean man, considerably over six feet in height, with stooping shoulders, long pendulous arms, terminating in hands of extraordinary dimensions, which, however, were far exceeded in proportion by his feet. He was dressed in an ill-fitting, wrinkled suit of black, which put one in mind of an undertaker's uniform at a funeral; round his neck a rope of black silk was knotted in a large bulb, with flying ends projecting beyond the collar of his coat, and above that, nestling in a great black mass of hair, bristling and compact like a ruff of mourning pins, rose the strange quaint face and head, covered with its thatch of wild republican hair, of President Lincoln. The impression produced by the size of his extremities, and by his flapping and wide-projecting ears may be removed by the appearance of kindliness, sagacity, and the awkward bonhomie of his face; the mouth is absolutely prodigious;... the nose ... a prominent organ ... the eyes, dark, full, and deeply set, are penetrating, but full of an expression which almost amounts to tenderness.

From William Howard Russell, *My Diary, North and South*, 1863.

as he was to improvise, to court the support of Union Democrats, to temper partisanship and seek national unity. But the Radical Republicans were of another mind. By no means unanimous in their attitude toward the legislation of the war years, they were substantially unanimous in their impatience with Lincoln's military policies, their zeal to stamp out slavery, and their vindictiveness toward all Confederates and most Democrats. They were jealous also of the prerogatives of the Congress where their forceful and often intemperate leaders served, among them Senator Benjamin F. Wade of Ohio, Senator Zachariah Chandler of Michigan, and Thaddeus Stevens of Pennsylvania, a dominant voice in the House. These men and their fellows and their friends of the press (Horace Greeley was one) criticized the President unsparingly, often with small regard for the truth. Their special instrument was the Joint Committee on the Conduct of the War, which Congress created in 1861. Its hearings and its demands kept Radical pressure on the moderate Lincoln, who needed the Radicals' votes, and agitated the still divisive question of slavery among the people of the North, whose sentiments Lincoln wanted to direct uniformly to the issue of union.

A lesser President might have crumbled; Lincoln, a master of the office, did not. He was a superb conciliator, adept at bending to this force and diverting or isolating that. He was an accomplished tactician, adroit in the use of patronage, persuasive in conference, patient with the foibles of productive men. Neither praise nor abuse turned him, for he lived within himself, supported by his infinite faith in the righteousness of the Lord and of the Union cause. Like any man, he made mistakes and bowed to circumstances, but while he suffered continual doubts about the thousands of decisions that fell to him, he never doubted his mission or wavered in its pursuit. This conviction gave him the boldness that dressed the Constitution in battle armor, gave him the stamina to absorb not only the trials of his task but, much worse for him, the ache of compassion for every sufferer on both sides of the hideous war. The Union, a nation struggling to survive, needed a great leader; it was blessed by the presence of Lincoln.

The Course of Arms

The First Offensive: Bull Run   Lincoln, as the war began, had to make a difficult choice. To prevent a stalemate that would ensure the survival of the Confederacy, the North had to attack, to destroy the government of the Southern people and bring them back by force into the Union. The President had at hand a long-range plan developed by General Winfield Scott, the commanding general of the army, a veteran of the War of 1812 and the Mexican War, now seventy-four years old, no longer well, but not unwise. Scott's plan set a

framework within which the Northern war effort could reasonably evolve. Unfortunately, it did not satisfy either public opinion or the Radical Republicans.

The plan called for a close blockade of the Confederate coastline, a blockade which the navy began at once feverishly to implement, and for "containment" of the Confederacy all along the land frontier. An amphibious expedition was to open the Mississippi Valley, restoring the Middle West's traditional outlet to the sea and cutting off such Confederate states as Arkansas, Texas, and Louisiana. Then, separate armies were to strike inland,

Major Campaigns of the Civil War

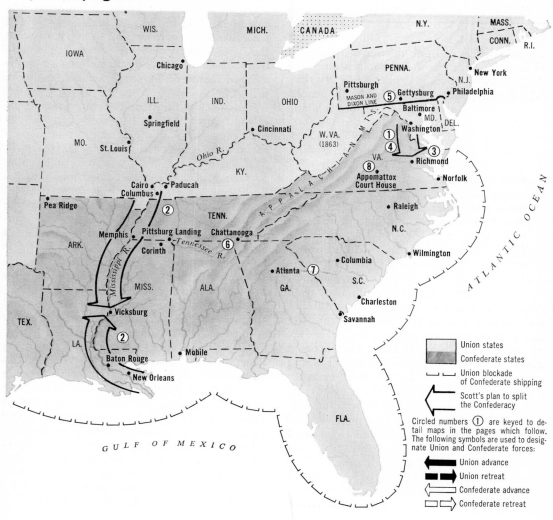

Union states

Confederate states

Union blockade of Confederate shipping

Scott's plan to split the Confederacy

Circled numbers ① are keyed to detail maps in the pages which follow. The following symbols are used to designate Union and Confederate forces:

Union advance

Union retreat

Confederate advance

Confederate retreat

progressively fragmenting the Southern nation and bringing it at last to full submission.

This strategy obviously would take a great deal of time, but many Northern people wanted decisive action quickly. Scott's plan, implying a slow and remorseless constriction, was dubbed the "Anaconda Plan" and was subjected to a good deal of derision. Horace Greeley's New York *Tribune* was already urging "Forward to Richmond"—the new capital of the Confederacy.

Swayed by this sentiment, the Administration early in June decided to attempt an overland advance across Virginia toward Richmond. It had some thirty-five thousand troops available for the operation, under the command of a competent regular army officer, Brigadier General Irvin McDowell. They were by no means ready for combat; their training had been sketchy, and the process of organizing them into an army was incomplete. But if they were to fight at all, it had to be soon, because most of them were ninety-day militia whose terms would expire by the middle of or latter part of July. In any case, the Confederate troops that would oppose them were equally green and undisciplined. The offensive got under way on July 16, but the raw column moved slowly. At last, on July 21, it met Confederate Brigadier General P. G. T. Beauregard and his army of twenty-five thousand men just beyond the sluggish stream of Bull Run, approximately thirty miles from Washington, and engaged in the first large-scale battle of the war.

McDowell's battle plan was good, but everything went wrong with it. A Union force failed to hold Confederate General Joseph E. Johnston and his twelve thousand men in the Shenandoah Valley. Slipping away, Johnston got most of his men to Bull Run, where they provided the reinforcements that Beauregard needed desperately. McDowell's flank attack on the Confederate force lagged, and although the untrained soldiers on both sides fought stoutly for several hours, the Union men were exhausted and confused by their marching. By mid-afternoon the Union attack had failed, and when McDowell tried to retreat his army fell apart and streamed back to Washington in a wild rout. Johnston and Beauregard found their own army so disorganized by victory that they could make no effective pursuit. They did not have to. The Union had suffered a humiliating defeat. For months to come, no more would be heard of "Forward to Richmond."

The shock of Bull Run convinced the people of the North that the war could not be won with ninety-day militia. The short-term regiments were sent home, and General George B. McClellan was called from western Virginia to take McDowell's place in command of a huge new force of three-year volunteers. An excellent organizer and administrator, the thirty-four-year-old McClellan devoted himself to the task of creating an army. In the fall Scott retired, and McClellan was made general-in-chief of all the Union armies. He was determined to undertake no new offensive until his soldiers were fully ready for combat. Lincoln supported him in this resolve, and throughout the summer and fall the war seemed to have an oddly static quality.

Lines for Battle   The appearance was deceptive, for away from the Washington-Richmond sector the lines for future battle were forming. While McClellan saw to his training program, the Union in the fall of 1861 launched amphibious expeditions to seal off as much as possible of the Confederacy's Atlantic coastline. On August 29 an army-navy force bombarded, captured, and occupied two Confederate forts at Hatteras Inlet, North Carolina, at one of the approaches to the intricate system of land-locked North Carolina sounds and rivers. During the winter months a second expedition followed, closing the entrances in the long, grass-grown sand dunes that lie between the sounds and the sea, capturing Confederate fortifications on historic Roanoke Island, and effectually shutting off North Carolina except for its most southerly port, Wilmington. Preceding the second expedition, a fleet of warships and transports dropped farther down the coast to seize Port Royal, South Carolina, establishing a secure base for the blockading squadrons and cutting all of South Carolina except Charleston itself off from ocean traffic. Still another expedition, during the winter, took Fort Pulaski at the mouth of the Savannah River in Georgia. By providing numerous Federal footholds along

the Confederate coast, these sallies compelled Richmond to disperse its troops to guard against sea-borne invasion.

Along the seacoast, the Federal government tried to seal in the Confederacy; in the West it wanted to open a path through the Confederacy as General Scott had advised. General John C. Frémont, in command in the West, was limited both as a soldier and as an organizer. But by early autumn 1861 he had begun to build up a powerful Union base at Cairo, Illinois, where the Ohio River joins the Mississippi. He left his country indebted to him for this move, and for putting an obscure brigadier general from Illinois, Ulysses S. Grant, in charge at Cairo. Then, unable to get along with the administration, Frémont de-

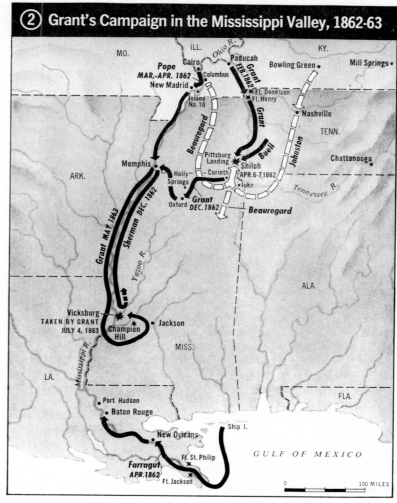

② **Grant's Campaign in the Mississippi Valley, 1862-63**

parted, giving way to sedate, paper-shuffling General Henry Wager Halleck. But before he left, Frémont had taken the steps that would bring the Anaconda Plan to vigorous life.

The Confederates realized that Federal troops at Cairo would soon march south. On September 4 the Confederate commander in the Mississippi area, Major General Leonidas Polk, decided to intervene by occupying Columbus, Kentucky, located on a high bluff overlooking the river, where batteries could deny passage to Federal steamboats. Grant countered by occupying Paducah, Kentucky, in order to control the mouths of the Tennessee and Cumberland rivers. In spite of itself, Kentucky now was in the war. Union troops moved into the northern part of the state and Confederates into the southern, and during November and December the lines faced each other, just out of contact, along an east-west line running from the Confederate strong point at Columbus through Bowling Green and off to the Cumberland plateau.

Here, as Washington presently saw, was the Confederacy's soft spot. Davis sent the man he considered his best soldier, General Albert Sidney Johnston, to take over-all command, but Davis was unable to give him as many soldiers as were needed. To hold his long line, Johnston had perhaps fifty thousand men; facing him were Grant, at Cairo, with twenty-five thousand, and Major General Don Carlos Buell, in front of Bowling Green, with something like eighty thousand. At St. Louis Halleck had a substantial force, with which he was methodically clearing Missouri of Confederate armies and preparing to reinforce Grant whenever an offensive should take place.

Attack in the West   Just after the end of the year the Federal drive began. The left wing of Buell's army, led by Virginia-born Major General George H. Thomas, crushed a small Confederate army under Major General George B. Crittenden in a sharp fight at Mill Springs, Kentucky, on January 19, 1862, destroying the eastern anchor of Johnston's long line. Early in February, Grant took fifteen thousand men up the Tennessee River, with a flotilla of Federal gunboats, and captured Confederate Fort Henry, just south of the Kentucky-Tennessee line. This move cut rail-

road communications between Johnston's center at Bowling Green and his left at Columbus —where General Beauregard of Bull Run fame was now in command—and Johnston was compelled to retire. He placed a substantial fraction of his command at Fort Donelson, Tennessee, on the Cumberland River, and led the rest back to Nashville; but Grant, strongly reinforced by Halleck, attacked Fort Donelson and on February 16 captured the place along with from twelve thousand to fifteen thousand Confederate soldiers.

The Union seizure of Forts Henry and Donelson added up to one of the decisive victories of the war. It destroyed Johnston's entire defensive line, compelling him to abandon the strong point at Columbus and to regroup his entire army in northern Mississippi. With virtually all of western Tennessee lost to the Confederacy, the way was opened for a Federal advance into the deep South. Simultaneously, a portion of Halleck's command under Major General S. R. Curtis drove the Confederates out of southwestern Missouri. Halleck sent another force down the Mississippi under Major General John Pope, who captured New Madrid, Missouri, and early in April took a strong Confederate fort at Island No. 10, in the Mississippi.

Aware that the Confederacy had been knocked off balance, Lincoln tried to get a Union army into eastern Tennessee, where the population showed strong Unionist sentiments. He urged Buell to occupy Knoxville and cut the vital railroad line that connected Virginia with the whole Tennessee area. McClellan supported this strategy, believing that it would help his own projected advance toward Richmond, but Buell refused to undertake it, arguing with some reason that the bad roads and the primitive character of the ground to be crossed would make it impossible for his army to be supplied. In addition, Halleck was hesitant in following up the Henry-Donelson triumph. Consequently Johnston and Beauregard gained time to regroup their forces at Corinth, Mississippi, and by the time Halleck at last sent Grant forward up the line of the Tennessee River, the Confederates were ready for him.

Grant established himself with forty thousand men at Pittsburg Landing, Tennessee, a

U.S.S. "Cairo" at Memphis.

short distance north of the Mississippi line, where he waited for Buell to join him with twenty-five thousand more. Johnston did not wait. With forty-five thousand men he advanced, and on April 6 and 7 his army and Grant's fought the most extensive battle yet seen on the North American continent, in a tangle of woodlands and pastures near a country meetinghouse known as Shiloh Church, not far from Pittsburg Landing. On the first day Grant's army, taken by surprise, was nearly driven into the river, but Johnston was killed in action, Buell's troops began to arrive in the evening, and on the following day the battered Confederates, now under Beauregard, had to retreat to Corinth. The battle had been extremely costly—some thirteen thousand Union casualties, more than ten thousand Confederate—but the victory was momentous. It left the Southern army in the Tennessee region cautiously on the defensive.

More Union victories followed. A powerful Union fleet under Flag Officer David Glasgow Farragut entered the Mississippi River from the gulf and ran past Forts Jackson and St. Phillip, near the mouth. On April 25 Farragut occupied New Orleans, the largest city in the Confederacy and its principal seaport. An army under General Butler followed, taking possession of New Orleans and moving on up the river to seize Baton Rouge; early in June a Federal fleet of river gunboats and rams annihilated a Confederate fleet at Memphis, throwing that city into Union possession and opening all of the upper Mississippi River. Halleck came down to Pittsburg Landing, where he assembled a powerful army of approximately 125,000 men, made up of the combined forces of Grant, Buell, and Pope. In a slow, methodical advance he drove Beauregard out of Corinth.

Thus by mid-spring of 1862 the Confederacy was on the verge of disaster. Of the Mississippi River it now controlled only the portion between Vicksburg, Mississippi, and Port Hudson, Louisiana. The area west of the river was fragmented. Halleck was in northern Mississippi with more than twice as many men as the Confederates could bring against him, apparently able to go anywhere he chose. Most of the South's Atlantic Coast had been closed, the navy's blockade at the ports which remained open was becoming increasingly effective, and in Virginia General McClellan was finally beginning his advance on Richmond, commanding an army of more than one hundred thousand men. Profound gloom prevailed in Richmond. In Washington, by contrast, Secretary of War Stanton was so confident that in June he temporarily suspended further recruiting.

Delay along the Peninsula But there was to be no end to the war that summer. The North suffered from the lack of a centralized military command. McClellan had served for approximately five months as general-in-chief, but in March the Administration, impatient with his reluctance to attack, removed him from the top position and reduced him to the command of the Army of the Potomac. Genuine coordination of the different military theaters did not exist, and as the big drive on Richmond commenced, the pressure in the West slacked off. Halleck, who had been given over-all command in the West, broke his huge army up into detachments and tried to occupy

territory rather than seek out and destroy the opposing Confederate armies. Grant found himself limited to holding western Tennessee. Buell was ordered to move on Chattanooga, but he was instructed to repair the railroad as he went, and his advance was painfully slow. No attempt was made to strike at the growing fortress of Vicksburg. Altogether, the Union offensive in the West became inactive just when it offered the greatest possibilities.

McClellan set out in mid-March, sending his army down the Potomac River and Chesapeake Bay by steamboat and taking up a position at the tip of the Virginia peninsula, between the York and James rivers, with his base at Fort Monroe. A scientific soldier with a deep streak of caution, he advanced slowly. General Joseph E. Johnston held a strong defensive position at Yorktown, and instead of trying to storm it—he had better than a two-to-one advantage in numbers—McClellan settled down for a methodical siege, moving up heavy mortars and artillery and preparing for a shattering bombardment. Johnston waited until McClellan had completed his preparations; then, on May 3, he evacuated the Yorktown line and drew off up the peninsula, pausing on May 5 to fight a savage but inconclusive rear-guard action at Williamsburg.

One of McClellan's problems arose from the Confederates' introduction of an iron-clad warship into naval warfare. In the spring of 1861 the Federals had abandoned the navy yard at Norfolk, Virginia. At that time they had burned and scuttled the powerful steam frigate *Merrimac*, which was in the yard for engine-room repairs. The Confederates raised and rebuilt this vessel, cutting it down to the berth deck and erecting an iron-plated citadel amidships, mounting powerful guns behind this protection, and equipping the ship with an iron ram at the bow. Rechristened *Virginia* (although usually referred to by its old name, *Merrimac*) this ship was slow, clumsy, and unseaworthy; but its four inches of armor made it almost invulnerable to ordinary gunfire, and when it came out into Hampton Roads early in March there was not a wooden warship in the navies of the world that could have stood up to it.

The *Merrimac* on its first appearance caused a near panic. It sank the Union frigate *Cumber-*

③ The Peninsular Campaign, 1862

PENNA.

MD.

Winchester MAY 25
Kernstown
Front Royal MAY 23
(W. VA.)
Potomac R.
Washington
McDowell MAY 8
Jackson
Shenandoah R.
Chesapeake Bay
Cross Keys JUNE 8
Port Republic JUNE 9
Jackson JUNE
Fredericksburg
McClellan MAR.-MAY
Pamunkey R.
Seven Days' Battles JUNE 25-JULY 1
Lee
Richmond
White House Landing
Chickahominy R.
Harrison's Landing
York R.
Williamsburg
Yorktown
James R.
VIRGINIA
Ft. Monroe
Monitor & Merrimac MAR. 9
Norfolk
0   75 MILES

land, forced the frigate *Congress* to surrender, drove the big steamer *Minnesota* aground, and threatened to destroy the whole Federal naval force around Fort Monroe. On March 9 this apparently irresistible warship suffered a check when the Federal navy brought on an ironclad of its own, the *Monitor*, a singular vessel with low freeboard and a revolving turret mounting two 11-inch guns. The *Monitor*'s keel had been laid in October 1861, and she was completed just in time to come down to Hampton Roads and meet the *Merrimac*. The two ships fought a wearing battle which demonstrated that warships without armor were now obsolete, and which ended the danger that the *Merrimac* might give the Confederacy control of all the lower Chesapeake Bay. But the *Monitor* gained no real advantage, and the *Merrimac* remained on the lower James River, barring that stream to Federal shipping and presenting a threat to McClellan's flank as he moved up the peninsula. The ship's existence did much to keep the cautious Union commander from making a bolder advance.

Eventually, however, the obstacle was removed. Johnston's withdrawal, coupled with Union possession of the North Carolina sounds —which opened the back door to Norfolk— compelled the Confederates to evacuate Norfolk on May 9. Since the *Merrimac* drew too much water to go up the James River to Richmond and was not seaworthy enough to go out into the open ocean, her crew had to destroy her once Norfolk was lost.

McClellan Repulsed McClellan continued to advance, moving his base presently to White House Landing on the Pamunkey River, some twenty-five miles east of Richmond. By the latter part of May he had established his army astride the Chickahominy River, with its advance elements less than ten miles from the Confederate capital. Here Johnston attacked him on May 31, at Seven Pines and Fair Oaks Station. The engagement was bloody and indecisive. Johnston himself was seriously wounded, and Jefferson Davis appointed Lee to command Johnston's army, the Army of Northern Virginia. McClellan held his position, waited for reinforcements, and prepared for another methodical advance to siege-gun range. And now the fortunes of war began to undergo an amazing reversal.

McClellan had nearly one hundred thousand men with him, and in northern Virginia —around Washington, in the lower Shenandoah Valley, and elsewhere—there were seventy thousand more Federal troops, most of which, McClellan believed, would shortly come down overland to join him. But in the Shenandoah Valley the Confederates had fifteen thousand soldiers led by a military genius, General Thomas J. Jackson, nicknamed "Stonewall" for his steadfast stand at Bull Run. Encouraged by Johnston and Lee, Jackson began a series of dazzling offensive maneuvers which convinced the Lincoln Administration that he had a larger army than was actually the case and that he intended nothing less than the capture of Washington.

In May, alarmed for the safety of Washington, the Administration hastily assembled troops to drive Jackson away, using a substantial number of the men whom McClellan was planning to include in his attack on Richmond. All in all, the Federals put nearly fifty thousand men in the Shenandoah, but Jackson, maneuvering skillfully and swiftly, now eluded them, now attacked and defeated them, leaving them wholly confused about his strength, his whereabouts, and his intentions.

The effect on McClellan's plans was disastrous. McClellan had posted approximately twenty-five thousand of his troops north of the Chickahominy River, believing that strong reinforcements would soon march down from Fredericksburg to join him there. Lee took advantage of the Union commander's awkward position by bringing Jackson and his men down from the Shenandoah. As the last week in June began, Lee found himself with a total force of about eighty thousand men. He was still outnumbered, but he boldly left a quarter of his army to confront McClellan's main body, took all the rest north of the Chickahominy, and on June 26 made a savage assault on McClellan's isolated right wing at Mechanicsville. The next day he made an even heavier attack at Gaines's Mill, driving the Union right wing south of the Chickahominy and compelling McClellan to shift his supply base from the Pamunkey River to the James. In order to make this change, McClellan was obliged to retreat. Lee followed him, trying to destroy the entire Union army, and fighting bitter engagements at Savage Station, Glendale, and Malvern Hill. At the end of a week's spirited combat McClellan had withdrawn to a defensive position at Harrison's Landing, on the James.

In the Seven Days' Battles—as this series of engagements became known—McClellan had lost upward of fifteen thousand men, Lee had lost close to twenty thousand. But McClellan's attempt to take Richmond had been repulsed. Outnumbered at all times, Lee had maneuvered in such a way that at the point of contact he had a decisive numerical superiority. With Jackson's aid he had induced the Federal government to retain thousands of troops in northern Virginia, a hundred miles and more from the scene of combat. He had grabbed the initiative.

Confederate Successes Lincoln now brought Halleck to Washington as general-in-chief, a logical step in itself, but a step that led the Federal high command to focus its attention entirely on the situation in Virginia, leaving affairs in the West to take care of themselves. General Pope was also brought east and given command of a new army, made up of the elements which had tried so unsuccessfully to destroy Jackson. Pope led them down the line of the Virginia Central Railway. The Union objective was to catch Lee at Richmond, in a pincers between Pope and McClellan. The plan might have succeeded, except that the Union commanders would not work in harmony, and Halleck lacked the force of personality to weld them into a proper team. When McClellan characteristically declined to advance on Richmond unless he were strongly reinforced, Halleck early in August ordered him to bring his army back by boat to the Washington area to join Pope.

Lee refused to allow the Federals time for regrouping. Leaving a contingent to watch McClellan's withdrawal, he marched north, maneuvered Pope into a retreat, forced him to make a stand along the upper Rappahannock River, and then boldly divided the Southern army and sent twenty-five thousand men under Jackson on a daring flanking movement aimed at Pope's rear. On August 28 and 29 Pope was brought to battle on the old field of Bull Run. Wholly unable to cope with Lee's generalship, he was driven back to the fortifications around Washington. McClellan's

troops had made such slow progress on their move up from the peninsula that only a part of them had been able to reinforce Pope. Discredited, Pope was relieved, and McClellan was told to take over and save the capital.

Lee's achievement had been dazzling. When he took command early in June, he had been pinned down in Richmond, doomed apparently to a hopeless defensive battle. He had beaten and driven away the attacking army, and by the end of August had transferred the scene of action from the environs of Richmond to the shores of the Potomac.

Lee's success in Virginia enabled the Confederacy to regain the initiative in the West. With Halleck's departure for Washington, and with the strong chance that troops from the West might have to be brought east, the whole Union campaign in the West had fallen into the doldrums. Grant was immobilized in western Tennessee, and Buell was making only glacial progress toward Chattanooga. Confederate General Braxton Bragg commanded an army of thirty thousand near Chattanooga, and General Edmund Kirby-Smith had twelve thousand more at Knoxville. While Pope was coming to grief in Virginia, these two suddenly moved north toward Kentucky, striking to cancel out all of the Union gains since Forts Henry and Donelson. Bragg side-stepped Buell, compelling that unhappy officer to follow in his footsteps. In the meantime, Lee, though his army had been badly mauled, boldly crossed the Potomac River and marched toward Pennsylvania.

In the spring the Confederacy had been visibly tottering, its leaders glumly contemplating the prospect of defeat. By autumn the Confederacy was on the offensive in the East and in the West. Union armies were hurrying to head them off, and the Confederate leadership had reason to hope that final independence might be won before winter.

The Crisis of the War

European Problems [Confederate resurgence brought to the point of crisis the deteriorating relations of the North with Great Britain.] British opinion about the war in America had been divided, partly along class lines. [Many of the nobility viewed the Southern planters as fellow aristocrats and rejoiced in the apparent collapse of popular government in the United States. Many supported the South's claim for self-determination. "The contest," wrote the London *Times*, "is really for empire on the side of the North and for independence on that of the South." But social reformers in Great Britain, engaged in a struggle to democratize their own society, befriended the North and attacked the "Slave Power." This was the position also of most of the laboring force, even those textile workers whose jobs were potentially imperiled by the possibility of a shortage of cotton. Self-interest attracted to the side of the Union British exporters of munitions and shippers who took over the carrying trade abandoned by the idled American merchant marine. But neither public opinion nor business considerations in themselves commanded British policy. It responded in the main to the impressions registered by the course of the war and to the negotiations over questions which the war raised.

The Union blockade created a first set of problems. In proclaiming it, Lincoln committed a tactical error, for a nation suppressing an "insurrection" does not "blockade" its own ports; it simply closes the ports held by the insurrectionists. The establishment of a blockade acknowledges the existence of a state of war—and, by implication, the existence of an enemy nation. Lincoln hoped to prevent the South from receiving status as a belligerent, but, logically enough, the British government met his proclamation of blockade with an announcement that it was extending full belligerent rights to the Confederacy. Now Jefferson Davis hoped to bring England to grant the Confederacy full recognition as a nation. Yet Davis' tactical error in boycotting cotton at the start of the war (p. 330) to a degree canceled out Lincoln's mistake, and the question of full recognition remained undecided.

The blockade itself was bound to create friction between the North and a maritime power as important as England. Yet the British kept in mind their own future needs, as a great sea power, for using the weapon of blockade against a continental enemy. They therefore did not deny the authority of the Union to impose a blockade, nor did they press interpreta-

tions of international law that might weaken the claims of a blockading country. But the situation nevertheless quickly gave rise to an incident that brought the Union to the verge of war with England. In the fall of 1861 Davis sent abroad two commissioners, James Mason of Virginia and John Slidell of Louisiana, to plead the Confederate cause in England and France. In November Captain Charles Wilkes in the Union warship *San Jacinto* stopped the British steamer *Trent*, removed Mason and Slidell, and carried them off directly to the United States, where they were imprisoned. His action, greeted enthusiastically at home, was denounced in London. British troops sailed for Canada, and Lord John Russell, the British foreign secretary, sent a sharp note demanding that the United States make apologies and release the prisoners forthwith. Lincoln could not afford war with England. The seizure of Mason and Slidell, moreover, violated long-standing American doctrine about freedom of the seas. Wisely, Lincoln ordered the release of the prisoners, who presently completed their journey.

Yet tension between the two nations did not much abate. With scant regard for the duties of a neutral, the British in 1862 permitted two cruisers, built for the Confederacy in Liverpool, to slip out to sea. Lincoln's minister to England, Charles Francis Adams, entered a vigorous protest, but the ships, the *Florida* and the *Alabama*, destroyed some $15 million of Northern commerce before the navy could capture them.

Even more disturbing in its long-run implications was England's association with Spain and France in a military expedition launched against Mexico by Napoleon III. The French emperor, taking advantage of the Civil War, hoped to re-establish his country's hold in the Western Hemisphere by setting up a puppet government in Mexico under Austrian Archduke Maximilian. This blatant violation of the Monroe Doctrine, possible only because of London's permissiveness and Washington's preoccupation, evoked an immediate denunciation from Secretary of State Seward, but French troops remained in Mexico (departing only after the Civil War in 1867, whereupon the Mexicans soon drove out the foreign government), and France, like England, blinked at the construction of Confederate commerce raiders in her ports. Worse still, Lee's victories in 1862 strengthened the arguments of pro-Southern Englishmen. Late in the summer Lord Palmerston, the Prime Minister, concluded that the time had come to grant full recognition to the Confederacy, if possible in conjunction with France and other powers, and to urge the Union to negotiate a peace. He decided, however, to await the outcome of Lee's invasion of the North. If it succeeded, the question of recognition would come before the Cabinet, probably to be resolved to the satisfaction of the South.

Again the Slavery Question Lincoln, brooding over the potentially ruinous course the war had taken, saw the need to touch men's minds and spirits. The North had not simply been losing battles; the spark and fire seemed to have gone out of the war effort. It was primarily the antislavery men who displayed a vigorous impulse to seek out and destroy the enemy in the field, and the President sought to engage and disseminate their ardor.

As Lincoln knew, the abolitionists wanted to strike at the Confederacy by attacking outright the institution of chattel slavery. In September 1861 General Frémont, then Union commander in Missouri, had announced that, as a war measure, the property of all Rebels in his district would be confiscated and their slaves set free. Lincoln immediately canceled that proclamation, which he feared might otherwise cost the Union the support of loyal slave-owners in the border states, but Frémont's action was portentous. It had a parallel in the policy of Major General Ben Butler of Massachusetts, an abolitionist who held command in the summer of 1861 at Fort Monroe. When fugitive slaves came into Butler's lines, he refused to send them back to their owners. Instead, he announced a novel interpretation of the rules of war. These slaves, he said, were the property of men in rebellion, and property used to support the rebellion was legitimate contraband of war that his army might seize. He would therefore treat slaves who had fled from Confederate masters as contraband; he would hold them, feeding and housing them and putting them to work for his own army. Both the War Department and the Congress supported him in this stand. Indeed, the Radical Republicans bit-terly criticized Lincoln's hesitation to declare all slaves free.

As the tide of battle turned against him, Lincoln, in order to enlist the drive and energy of the abolitionists, had to make the war a fight against slavery as well as a fight for the Union —a war for human freedom, grounded on a cause lofty enough to evoke a new wave of support. He maneuvered cautiously to that end. He had earlier supported, without much success, suggestions for compensated emancipation in the border states, and he had reluctantly signed an act of Congress providing for the confiscation of property of people in rebellion. In July 1862 he told the Cabinet that he proposed to use his war powers to issue a general proclamation of emancipation. This would be a purely military measure, offering freedom only to slaves in states that had seceded: it would be, in effect, a means of putting pressure on slaveholders to return to the Union. It might be illegal. But it would commit the Federal government to the policy of emancipation; it would portend complete emancipation for all slaves everywhere.

Secretary Seward, though he supported the idea, had urged delay. If such a proclamation were issued while the Union armies were staggering from a series of defeats, Seward warned, it would sound like a despairing cry for help rather than the bold announcement of a stirring new policy. The army had to win some decisive victory before the proclamation could be made. Lincoln agreed and put the draft of his projected proclamation in his desk, ready for use at an hour of triumph. It was not long in coming.

Antietam When Lee in September 1862 led his army into western Maryland, pointing toward an invasion of Pennsylvania, his purpose was to demonstrate that the South was going to win the war and that the North should therefore stop fighting. He crossed the Potomac, reached the town of Frederick, Maryland, and then paused. As Lee knew, McClellan and the hastily reorganized Army of the Potomac were coming up from Washington. Yet close at hand there was a garrison of ten thousand Federals at Harper's Ferry. Lying under the shadow of high mountains, Harper's Ferry was indefensible, its garrison a sitting duck. Lee, moreover, could not safely leave a

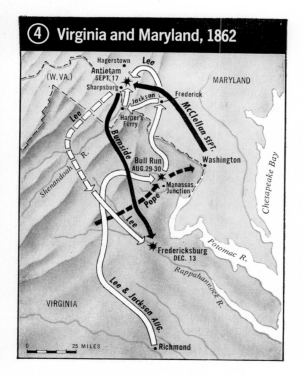

④ Virginia and Maryland, 1862

ably less than forty thousand, and lost at least ten thousand. Tactically the fight was a draw, but strategically it was a Confederate defeat. Lee withdrew into Virginia, his plan to invade the North shattered.

At last Lincoln had the victory he needed. On September 22, 1862, he issued a preliminary Emancipation Proclamation—an announcement that a final proclamation would be issued on January 1, 1863, unless the Confederacy meanwhile surrendered. The Emancipation Proclamation asserted freedom for slaves in those areas which were not under control of the Federal government, and left slavery untouched in the areas where Federal control was effective. It seemed a halting measure of dubious effect and shaky legality, and the Confederates denounced it as a call for a slave revolt. But they erred. Never again would the Federal government consider slavery a question for the states to settle; the Administration now was fighting not only to re-

force of this size astride his supply line while he moved north. With characteristic boldness, he once more divided his forces, occupying Hagerstown, Maryland, and the South Mountain passes with half of his men, and sending the other half under Stonewall Jackson to take Harper's Ferry.

The scheme might have worked, except that a copy of Lee's orders was lost, and got to McClellan, who had nearly reached the South Mountain barrier. Now McClellan found himself between the divided halves of Lee's army; if he moved fast he might destroy them separately and end the war in a week. Though he was not quick enough to win so conclusive a triumph, he did compel Lee to concentrate and give battle on the high ground above Antietam Creek, near Sharpsburg, Maryland, on September 17. (This action did not occur in time to save Harper's Ferry, which Jackson captured with its entire garrison.)

The battle of Antietam was the bloodiest single day's engagement of the entire war. Of eighty-seven thousand men, McClellan lost thirteen thousand. Lee's army, which had been subject to heavy straggling, numbered prob-

---

Antietam:
A Confederate View

The horse artillery did good service during the day but otherwise the cavalry was not engaged. Not so, however, General Stuart and his staff, for he was constantly riding over the field watching the progress of the action....

Standing on the hill in rear of our infantry lines toward the latter part of the day with General Stuart, a battery came past us at a trot from out of the action, whose ammunition had become exhausted, and I recognized one of its non-commissioned officers, my kinsman, Charles Trueheart, and we exchanged cordial greetings. Behind the battery came hobbling as best they could a string of fearfully mutilated horses which had been turned loose as they had received their wounds, and who had followed their comrades when they left the spot where they had been in action. After they had all passed, I saw a horse galloping after them and dragging something. Thinking it was his rider as he emerged from the clouds of smoke on the field of battle, I moved to intercept and stop the animal, but to my horror discovered that the horse was dragging his own entrails from the gaping wound of a cannonball, and after passing us a few yards the poor brute fell dead with a piercing scream.

From W. W. Blackford, *War Years with Jeb Stuart*, 1945.

store the Union but to make American freedom all-embracing and indivisible.

Since the time of national independence, the freedom of all Americans had been an essential objective of the nation's best ideals. The fact of slavery, the fact of the divisibility of freedom, had lain below the sectional controversies that rent the Union. The very course of war forced Federal troops in slave territory to come to grips with the South's anachronistic institution. Indeed, the waging of war against the Confederacy implied a contest also to abolish slavery, the pillar of the secessionist polity. Now, with the Emancipation Proclamation, the American Negro was to be "forever free."

After Antietam, the Confederate tide receded in the West as well as in the East. Bragg, invading Kentucky, found that the supposedly prosecessionist populace was not rising in his favor as he had expected it to. At Perryville on October 8 he fought an indecisive battle with Buell and then marched back to Tennessee. Kirby-Smith likewise withdrew, and the menacing counterstroke had come to nothing. Simultaneously, a Confederate army under General Earl Van Dorn, which tried to slip past Grant's army and join Bragg, was checked at Iuka, Mississippi, and soundly defeated in a battle at Corinth. Once more Union control in the West was firmly established.

The Confederacy had passed its high-water mark. Never again would it come so close to outright victory as it had at the beginning of the autumn of 1862. Lacking the sinews to make use of the initiative Lee had gained, it was once more back on the defensive.

This reversal cost the South its chance for British recognition. Following Lee's repulse at Antietam, the British government concluded that Southern prospects were dim. Furthermore, so long as the war was fought only for reconstruction of the Union, the British people might have consented to have their government take the Confederate side; but a war fought to end human slavery presented a very different case. The cotton famine—increasing, as the Federal blockade grew steadily more effective—brought economic distress to some British workers, who suffered extensive unemployment as the textile mills fell idle. Other workers profited from the boom in the arms trade and the merchant marine. And yet even those who suffered supported their liberal spokesmen, champions of the cause of freedom in America. The British government did not again come close to intervention in favor of the South.

Antietam and the Emancipation Proclamation had still another consequence. The change in Northern policy meant that the war must be fought to a finish. So long as reunion was the only issue at stake, there had been some possibility of a negotiated peace. But the South would not negotiate the slavery question. After Antietam, the divided nation was committed to an all-out, all-exhausting war.

The Attack Renewed   As a necessary first step toward the conquest of the South, Lincoln made a series of changes in Federal army command. He removed McClellan, appointing to his place Major General Ambrose E. Burnside, who had done well in the earlier operations along the North Carolina coast but who was to prove unfit for command of a large army. McClellan had met strong criticism from antislavery Republicans, including Secretary of War Stanton and Secretary of the Treasury Salmon P. Chase, for his slowness and his apparent reluctance to come to grips with his enemy. Opposed to the Emancipation Proclamation, the general was a hero to Northern Democrats who did not believe in making war to end slavery; and the Administration was now in a mood to equate softness on the slavery question with softness on the field of battle. McClellan went into retirement, his career as a soldier ended. Simultaneously, Lincoln removed one of his favorite lieutenants, Major General Fitz-John Porter, who had commanded the Fifth Army Corps and whom Pope had accused of disobeying orders at the second battle of Bull Run. The President also relieved Major General Buell, a friend of McClellan, who shared McClellan's position on slavery and his slowness to give battle. Buell's place in the West was taken by Major General William S. Rosecrans, who had fought with distinction at Iuka and Corinth.

Lincoln expected the new army commanders to take aggressive action without delay. To their credit, they tried, but with unfortunate results. Burnside, seeking to advance on Richmond by way of Fredericksburg, Virginia, crossed the Rappahannock on December 13,

1862, and made a clumsy assault on Lee's lines. Lee repulsed him with ease, inflicting twelve thousand casualties and suffering less than half that number himself. Burnside sullenly drew back across the river, the morale of his army temporarily shattered. (The soldiers of the Army of the Potomac, immensely fond of McClellan, felt that he would never have driven them into a disaster like that of Fredericksburg.)

In central Tennessee Rosecrans advanced against Bragg, and from December 30 to January 2 the two armies fought fiercely around Stones River near the town of Murfreesboro, Tennessee, thirty miles southeast of Nashville. Bragg's army had none the worst of it—at one point it almost won a shattering victory—but Bragg, unaccountably discouraged, retreated. Though the engagement seemed a Union victory, Rosecrans' army was so badly mangled that it could not resume the offensive for several months.

Grant, meanwhile, set out to capture Vicksburg. He marched south from the Corinth area, following the line of the Mississippi Central Railroad forty miles to the town of Oxford, Mississippi. Grant planned to attack Vicksburg from the east while a subsidiary army led by Major General William T. Sherman went down the Mississippi with a convoy of gunboats and hit the Confederate defenses south of the Yazoo River, just north of Vicksburg. This strategy would catch Confederate General John C. Pemberton between two fires; one or the other of the Union attacks ought to succeed.

The plan came to grief, however, when Confederate Van Dorn slipped behind Grant and on December 20, 1862, captured his base of supplies at Holly Springs. Simultaneously, Confederate cavalry under Major General Nathan Bedford Forrest—an untaught soldier who was rapidly becoming one of the most skilled cavalry leaders on either side—ranged across western Tennessee, disrupting Grant's line of communications. Grant was temporarily immobilized. Sherman, unaware of this development, reached the mouth of the Yazoo and made his attack, but Pemberton easily drove him off. The campaign against Vicksburg had bogged down.

The failure of the three Union offensives and the heavy casualties suffered in each produced a mood of gloom and discontent. War-weariness fed the doubts of the Peace Democrats and hurt the Republicans in the fall elections of 1862. The growing discontent in the North could, if it persisted, destroy the will to fight. In that case disunion and slavery would survive. Northern disillusionment would abate only if the war itself took a more favorable turn. Thus as 1863 began, the future of the nation, the future of democracy in the United States, depended on the recovery of the Federal soldiers in the field.

The Decision of War

Gettysburg   In January of 1863, while Rosecrans rested and refitted his battered army at Murfreesboro, Grant regrouped his entire force on the Mississippi River just above Vicksburg and prepared for a new campaign against that fortress. In the East, the Army of the Potomac, under new command, made ready for another offensive. The new leader was Major General Joseph Hooker, a dashing, hard-fighting soldier who restored the lost morale of his troops. Hooker planned to take most of his army off on a flanking maneuver, to cross the Rappahannock and Rapidan rivers some miles above Fredericksburg, and to come in on Lee from the rear. He had ample man power, some 120,000 men, whereas Lee, who had had to send part of his army on a temporary mission below the James River, had no more than half that number.

Hooker moved at the end of April. Holding the river bank opposite Fredericksburg with part of his army, he led the rest upstream to a position on Lee's left and rear at Chancellorsville and sent his cavalry on a long sweep to cut Lee's supply lines. This plan of battle, he believed, would compel Lee to retreat, and the retreating army could be assailed with overwhelming numbers. But Lee never did what his opponent expected. Instead of retreating, he attacked, sending Stonewall Jackson on a wide flanking march which struck and routed Hooker's right on May 1, 1863. After three days of desperate fighting in the wilderness area around Chancellorsville and on the high ground near Fredericksburg, Hooker was thoroughly defeated. Another Federal drive toward

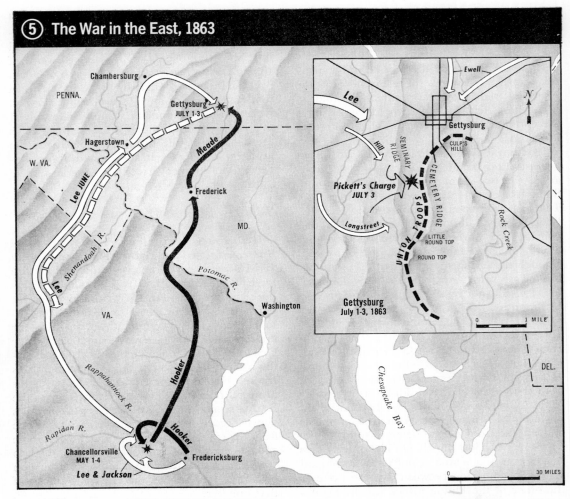

Chambersburg

PENNA.

Gettysburg
JULY 1-3

Hagerstown

Meade

W. VA.

Lee JUNE

Frederick

Shenandoah R.

Lee

MD.

Potomac R.

Washington

VA.

Rappahannock R.

Hooker

Rapidan R.

Hooker

Chancellorsville
MAY 1-4

Fredericksburg

Lee & Jackson

Chesapeake Bay

DEL.

30 MILES

Ewell

N

Lee

Gettysburg

Hill

SEMINARY RIDGE

CULP'S HILL

CEMETERY RIDGE

Pickett's Charge
JULY 3

UNION TROOPS

Longstreet

Rock Creek

LITTLE ROUND TOP

ROUND TOP

Gettysburg
July 1-3, 1863

0   1 MILE

Richmond had been thwarted. The Confederate victory, one of the most spectacular of the war, came at the cost of Stonewall Jackson's life. Wounded in battle, he died shortly after Hooker had retired north of the Rappahannock.

In the Mississippi Valley, however, the Union cause was beginning to prosper. Unable to attack the citadel at Vicksburg from the river, Grant boldly moved his army down the western bank and crossed over to Mississippi some thirty miles below Vicksburg. Cutting loose from his base, he marched to the Mississippi state capital at Jackson to drive off a Confederate force that was trying to come to Pemberton's rescue. After a sharp fight at Champion Hill, he drove Pemberton and his thirty

thousand men into the fortified lines at Vicksburg. With his right wing resting on the Mississippi River above Vicksburg, Grant was again in secure contact with his northern base. He was now reinforced, and he held entrenched lines that cut Pemberton off from the rest of the Confederacy. He had, moreover, enough men to keep General Joe Johnston (who had been given over-all command in the West) from breaking the constricting ring. By the end of May Grant's grip on Vicksburg was so firm that he was bound to capture both the fortress and its defending army unless the Confederacy could muster the strength to intervene.

Davis and Lee decided instead to make one more attempt to invade the North. A Confederate victory in Pennsylvania would imperil Washington and Philadelphia, would probably compel Lincoln to bring some of Grant's army east, and might even bring final Southern independence. Accordingly, early in June Lee crossed the Blue Ridge, heading for the Potomac. Hooker followed, maneuvering to keep between Lee and the Federal capital. On June 28, when Lee had his entire force in Pennsylvania and the Army of the Potomac was grouped in the vicinity of Frederick, Maryland, Lincoln abruptly removed Hooker from command and gave his army to Major General George Gordon Meade, a sharp-tempered, competent professional soldier. The showdown followed almost at once. On July 1, 1863, Lee's army collided with Meade's at Gettysburg, Pennsylvania, and the biggest battle of the war began.

For three days the Confederates desperately assaulted the Federals, who held a strong position on a chain of rocky hills just south of Gettysburg. Losses on both sides were prodigious. Several times the Union seemed on the very edge of defeat, but Lee lacked the strength to deliver the final blow. The climax came on the afternoon of July 3, when Lee assailed the Federal center with a column of fifteen thousand men led by Major General George Pickett. The Federals repelled the attack, shattering Lee's offensive power, and on the following day the Confederates began a slow, miserable retreat to Virginia. By mid-July the shattered Army of Northern Virginia was back in the lower Shenandoah Valley, decisively defeated. Losses on each side had run between twenty thousand and twenty-five thousand men—more than a fourth of the men engaged. The Confederate gamble on invading the North had failed.

Vicksburg and Chattanooga   More important even than the Union victory at Gettysburg was Grant's capture of Vicksburg on July 4, 1863. Pemberton had to surrender his thirty thousand men—a severe loss for the Confederacy, pinched as it was for man power —and the Mississippi River fell under Federal control all the way to the gulf. (The Confeder-

Union dead after Gettysburg.

ate strong point at Port Hudson surrendered as soon as the fall of Vicksburg became known.) The South west of the great river was irretrievably cut off. Taken together, the defeats at Gettysburg and Vicksburg reduced the Confederacy permanently to defensive warfare.

When Vicksburg fell, General Rosecrans moved his Army of the Cumberland against Braxton Bragg's Army of Tennessee. Maneuvering smartly, he compelled Bragg to retreat all the way to northern Georgia. Following incautiously, Rosecrans gave Bragg an opening for a counterstroke, which Bragg delivered at Chickamauga on September 19 and 20. Rosecrans' army was routed, saved from utter disaster only by the stand of the troops commanded by Major General George H. Thomas. Rosecrans retreated to Chattanooga, where he was replaced by Thomas, and Bragg followed

and entrenched on high ground overlooking the city.

If Bragg had attacked vigorously, he might have caused serious trouble, but he was content to wait in his entrenchments, believing that want of supplies would compel Thomas to surrender. Instead Grant, whom Lincoln now named to supreme command in the West, hastened to Chattanooga with substantial reinforcements. On November 24 and 25, in the twin battles of Lookout Mountain and Missionary Ridge, he drove Bragg's army back into Georgia and cemented Federal control over Tennessee.

With overwhelming strength the confident Federals awaited the opening of the 1864 campaign. The Union armies were now achieving the constriction and fragmentation of the Confederacy implied in the Anaconda Plan. At

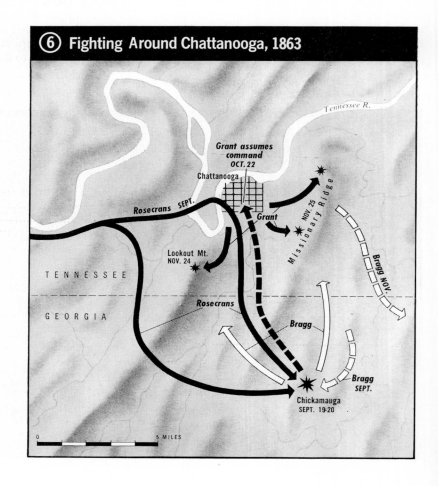

⑥ Fighting Around Chattanooga, 1863

Tennessee R.

Grant assumes command OCT. 22

Chattanooga

Rosecrans SEPT.

Grant

Missionary Ridge NOV. 25

Bragg NOV.

Lookout Mt. NOV. 24

TENNESSEE

GEORGIA

Rosecrans

Bragg

Bragg SEPT.

Chickamauga SEPT. 19-20

0   5 MILES

Vicksburg and at Chattanooga Grant had demonstrated that Northern resources, remorselessly applied, would bring victory. At Gettysburg, Meade had shown that the South lacked the resources to strike a decisive counterblow. The South was a doomed citadel, waiting to be taken. So persuaded, Lincoln in the spring of 1864 called Grant east and made him general-in-chief of all Union armies. Now the President had a commander who was prepared to pay whatever price victory might require.

The War and the Re-election of Lincoln

Grant set as his objective the defeat of the two major Confederate forces, the Army of Northern Virginia under Lee, and the Army of Tennessee, in northern Georgia, led now by General Joseph E. Johnston. Making his headquarters with Meade's Army of the Potomac, Grant on May 4 led it across the Rapidan

Ulysses S. Grant: Victory at any cost.

River to strike at Lee. Simultaneously, Major General William T. Sherman, now commanding the Federals in the West, led a powerful force against Johnston in the vicinity of Dalton, Georgia. These campaigns, proceeding slowly, brought ghastly casualties. The armies of Lee and Grant were in continuous contact for more than a month, fighting some of the most deadly battles in American history—the Wilderness, Spotsylvania Court House, Cold Harbor. In this month the Federals lost fully sixty thousand men, as compared with Confederate losses less than half as great. Grant, unable either to destroy Lee's army or to capture Richmond, settled down late in June to the slow, wearing siege of Petersburg, Virginia—a railroad center whose capture would lead to the fall of Richmond itself. Many people in the North felt that Grant had failed in his purpose and that the casualties his army had suffered were needlessly, intolerably, high. Sherman had had smaller losses, but he had been unable

---

Chickamauga:
A Union View

The march [to Rossville] was a melancholy one. All along the road, for miles, wounded men were lying. They had crawled or hobbled slowly away from the fury of the battle, become exhausted, and lain down by the roadside to die. Some were calling the names and numbers of their regiments, but many had become too weak to do this; by midnight the column had passed by. What must have been their agony, mental and physical, as they lay in the dreary woods, sensible that there was no one to comfort or to care for them and that in a few hours more their career on earth would be ended!...

Sammy Snyder lay on the field wounded; as I handed him my canteen he said: "General, I did my duty." "I know that, Sammy; I never doubted that you would do your duty." The most painful recollection to one who has gone through a battle is that of the friends lying wounded and dying and who needed so much when you were utterly powerless to aid them....

At this hour of the night (eleven to twelve o'clock) the army is simply a mob. There appears to be neither organization nor discipline. The various commands are mixed up in what seems to be inextricable confusion. Were a division of the enemy to pounce down upon us between this and morning, I fear the Army of the Cumberland would be blotted out.

From John Beatty, *Memoirs of a Volunteer*, 1879.

to destroy Johnston's army or to take the city of Atlanta, one of his important objectives. By midsummer a new wave of war-weariness swept the North, endangering Lincoln's re-election.

Even his renomination was contested. Many Radical Republicans wanted to supplant him in order to gain control of the party for themselves and their policies. Dissatisfied with Lincoln's conduct of the war, the Radicals were especially critical of his plans for reconstructing the South, and of his intended leniency toward the Confederate people and the seceded states (pp. 358–59). But, weakened by factionalism, the Radicals failed. The great majority of Republicans, joined by some War Democrats, adopted the name of the Union party for the campaign, renominated Lincoln, selected as his running mate Andrew Johnson, a Tennessee Democrat, and adopted a platform praising the Administration and promising a constitutional amendment to abolish slavery. The dissident Radicals bolted and selected General John C. Frémont as their candidate.

The Democrats, also divided, nominated General George McClellan. Their platform, drafted by C. L. Vallandigham, declared the war a failure and demanded an armistice and the negotiation of reunion. McClellan repudiated these planks, but his campaign could not entirely escape the taint of appeasement. His political strength mounted when Union losses rose and, with them, sentiment for a negotiated peace. His chances also depended on Frémont's making a strong race, and the Radicals, like the Democrats, profited when Lincoln's reputation suffered from Grant's setbacks. "This morning as for some days past," Lincoln reflected on August 23, "it seems probable that this Administration will not be re-elected."

But the war was grinding toward a different conclusion. In August 1864 a Federal fleet under Rear Admiral Farragut broke its way into Mobile Bay, closing one of the last ports which the Confederacy still possessed. In September and October a Union army, under energetic Major General Philip H. Sheridan, routed the troops of General Jubal A. Early and wrested the rich granary of the Shenandoah Valley from the Confederacy. In Georgia

President Davis, tired of General Johnston and his strategically sound delaying tactics, had put the fiery John B. Hood in his place. Hood gave battle to Sherman, was beaten, and had to give up Atlanta on September 1. With that victory Northern spirits soared. Frémont retired from the presidential contest, and in November Lincoln won re-election, polling 55 per cent of the popular vote and carrying the electoral vote 212 to 21.

The Bitter End   After the election Lincoln's generals moved swiftly. Sherman, copying the tactics Grant had used below Vicksburg, cut loose from his base at Atlanta and marched across Georgia to Savannah, devastating the country as he went. Hood took his army to northern Mississippi and moved north into Tennessee, hoping by this counterstroke to force Sherman's recall. He suffered a costly check at the battle of Franklin on November 30, and on December 15 and 16 Thomas struck him at Nashville, driving him away in complete disorder and almost destroying his army. Sherman, meanwhile, moved on, occupying Savannah just before Christmas. When 1865 began, the Confederacy consisted of little more than the Carolinas and the southern half of Virginia. Isolated Confederate armies still existed beyond the Mississippi and in southern Alabama, but they were unable to affect the outcome of the war.

The end, at last in sight, was not long de-

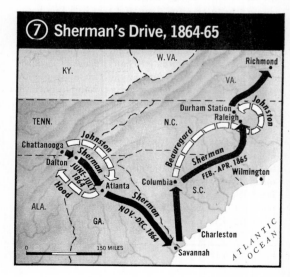

⑦ **Sherman's Drive, 1864-65**

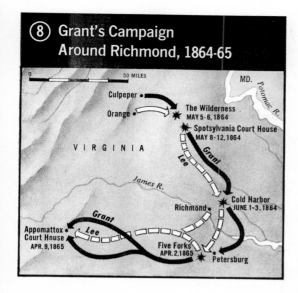

⑧ Grant's Campaign Around Richmond, 1864-65

VIRGINIA

MD.

Potomac R.

Culpeper •

Orange •

The Wilderness
MAY 5-6, 1864

Spotsylvania Court House
MAY 8-12, 1864

James R.

Cold Harbor
JUNE 1-3, 1864

Richmond •

Appomattox Court House
APR. 9, 1865

Five Forks
APR. 2, 1865

Petersburg

0   50 MILES

His occupying the chair of state was a triumph of the good sense of mankind, and of the public conscience. This middle-class country had got a middle-class president, at last. Yes, in manners and sympathies, but not in powers, for his powers were superior. This man grew according to the need. His mind mastered the problem of the day; and as the problem grew, so did his comprehension of it. Rarely was man so fitted to the event....

In four years—four years of battle-days—his endurance, his fertility of resources, his magnanimity, were sorely tried and never found wanting. There, by his courage, his justice, his even temper, his fertile counsel, his humanity, he stood a heroic figure in the centre of a heroic epoch. He is the true history of the American people in his time. Step by step he walked before them; slow with their slowness, quickening his march by theirs, the true representative of this continent; an entirely public man; father of his country, the pulse of twenty millions throbbing in his heart, the thought of their minds articulated by his tongue.

From Ralph Waldo Emerson, "Abraham Lincoln," 1865.

layed. During the winter of 1865 Sherman marched northward from Savannah, across the Carolinas. Confederate military resources had sunk so low that General Johnston, recalled to oppose him, confessed despairingly: "I can do no more than annoy him." From Tennessee a powerful Federal cavalry corps swung down through Alabama, capturing the original Confederate capital of Montgomery and destroying munitions works at Selma. Charleston fell, and a Federal army-navy expedition sealed off Wilmington, North Carolina, the South's last seaport. In desperation, Lee attacked Grant's lines before Petersburg, trying to disable his opponent so that he could then break away and join forces with Johnston, but his assault was unsuccessful. On April 2 Grant's troops shattered Lee's right flank in a battle at Five Forks, compelling Lee to evacuate Petersburg. Federal troops occupied Richmond, and the Confederate government fled south.

On April 9, at Appomattox Court House in southern Virginia, Lee had to surrender his army to Grant, and the war virtually came to an end. Johnston surrendered to Sherman a few days later. The surrender of the remaining Confederate contingents in the deep South and west of the Mississippi River followed in due course, and by early June the last vestige of Confederate resistance had disappeared. After

four years of struggle, after the loss of six hundred thousand lives, after the agony of fratricide, after the awful waste of hatreds, the ravages of destruction and grief, the Union had been restored.

The hour of triumph was marred by tragedy. On April 14, at Ford's Theatre in Washington, a fanatical actor, John Wilkes Booth, murdered Abraham Lincoln. His death dimmed the prospects for his cherished peace of reconciliation. Lincoln had instructed Grant and Sherman to arrange surrender on "the most liberal and honorable terms." Lincoln in his second inaugural address had called on the North to act "with malice toward none, with charity for all." Had he lived, he might not have been able to fashion national policy in the pattern of his magnanimity. But he would doubtless have tried, and, in the manner of his wartime efforts, tried skillfully. His assassination deprived the South of a great friend and the nation of a great leader, possibly the only American who had felt all of the grief and none of the hatred of the four terrible years.

SUGGESTIONS FOR READING

General

Here as in the preceding chapter the best introductory treatment, from the point of view alike of its text and its extensive, critical bibliography, is J. G. Randall and David Donald, *The Civil War and Reconstruction* (2nd ed., 1961). More extensive, but complete only to 1863, is Allan Nevins, *The War for the Union*, 2 vols. (1959–60). Valuable, too, are R. F. Nichols, *The Stakes of Power* (1961), and, especially on military matters, Bruce Catton, *This Hallowed Ground* (1956).

The Confederacy

The outstanding study of the Confederacy is the judicious, trenchant Clement Eaton, *A History of the Southern Confederacy* (1954). E. M. Coulter, *The Confederate States of America, 1861–1865* (1950), is important but less critical. There is a useful short account in C. P. Roland, *The Confederacy* (1960), and a good anthology in A. D. Kirwan, ed., *The Confederacy* * (1959). R. S. Henry, *The Story of the Confederacy* (1931), contains a clear narrative focused on military matters. The causes of the South's defeat are the subject of a series of incisive essays in David Donald, ed., *Why the North Won the Civil War* (1960). Among many special studies, one of the most engaging is B. J. Hendrick, *Statesmen of the Lost Cause* (1939), which examines Davis and his civilian associates. A more recent and more sophisticated treatment of the same subject is in R. W. Patrick, *Jefferson Davis and His Cabinet* (1944). Two works of F. L. Owsley are of the first importance: *King Cotton Diplomacy* (1931) and *State Rights in the Confederacy* (1925). Among the many biographies of significance are Hudson Strode, *Jefferson Davis*, 2 vols. (1955), and R. M. McElroy, *Jefferson Davis: The Unreal and the Real*, 2 vols. (1937), as well as R. R. Von Abele, *Alexander H. Stephens: A Biography* (1946). But the literature on the Confederacy, as on all matters related to the Civil War, is vast, and an interested student should consult the bibliography in Randall and Donald, cited above, for references beyond those that can be listed here.

Lincoln and the Union

The general studies cited above, and the Lincoln studies listed here, afford among them the appropriate points of departure for understanding the Union during the Civil War. Among additional important works, three bear upon significant diplomatic issues: E. D. Adams, *Great Britain and the American Civil War*, 2 vols. (1925); M. B. Duberman, *Charles Francis Adams* (1961); and the good biography of Seward in S. F. Bemis, ed., *The American Secretaries of State and Their Diplomacy*, 10 vols. (1927–29). F. L. Klement, *The Copperheads in the Middle West* (1960), explains the motivation of the group largely in economic terms, whereas disloyalty and danger are stressed by G. F. Milton, *Abraham Lincoln and the Fifth Column* (1942), and W. Gray, *The Hidden Civil War: The Story of the Copperheads* (1942). There are notable treatments of economic matters in Frederick Merk, *Economic History of Wisconsin During the Civil War Decade* (1916); Sidney Ratner, *American Taxation* (1942); W. C. Mitchell, *Gold, Prices and Wages under the Greenback Standard* (1908); and R. P. Sharkey, *Money, Class, and Party* (1959). Indispensable on its subject is J. G. Randall, *Constitutional Problems under Lincoln* (1926).

There is no end to Lincoln literature. The best short biography is Benjamin Thomas, *Abraham Lincoln* (1952). Among longer biographies, Carl Sandburg, *Abraham Lincoln: The War Years* [abridged version *], 4 vols. (1939), is distinguished for its passion, and J. G. Randall, *Lincoln the President*, 4 vols. (1945–55), completed by R. N. Current, for its depth and judgment. Among many anthologies, P. M. Angle, ed., *The Lincoln Reader* * (1947), stands out for its readability. Two especially incisive collections of essays are David Donald, *Lincoln Reconsidered* (1956), and R. N. Current, *The Lincoln Nobody Knows* (1958). Truly interested students will want to consult R. P. Basler and others, *The Collected Works of Abraham Lincoln*, 9 vols. (1953–55), and the thorough Jay Monaghan, ed., *Lincoln Bibliography, 1839–1939*, 2 vols. (1945). There is a more selective and critical bibliography in P. M. Angle, *A Shelf of Lincoln Books* (1946), and a good selection of Lincoln writings in P. M. Angle and E. S. Miers, eds., *The Living Lincoln* (1955), and R. P. Basler, ed., *Abraham*

* Available in a paperback edition.

Lincoln: His Speeches and Writings (1946). Especially significant on Lincoln as a politician are H. J. Carman and R. H. Luthin, *Lincoln and the Patronage* (1943); H. B. Hesseltine, *Lincoln and the War Governors* (1948); and T. H. Williams, *Lincoln and the Radicals* (1941). On Lincoln and military affairs, besides the books listed below, T. H. Williams, *Lincoln and His Generals* (1952), and R. V. Bruce, *Lincoln and the Tools of War* (1956), are particularly rewarding. Other useful Lincoln books, and biographies of Lincoln's associates, receive discerning assessment in Randall and Donald, cited above.

Military Events

Just about every significant general, Union or Confederate, and just about every significant engagement at arms, has been the subject of at least one, and ordinarily of several, books or essays. There are further shelves of volumes dealing more generally with the war, many of them memoirs, some of them stirring. The would-be specialist has no convenient terminus in his reading; the neophyte can begin profitably in any one of many places. For an exciting and informed start, an interested student might turn to the trilogy of Bruce Catton: *Mr. Lincoln's Army* (1951); *Glory Road* (1952); *A Stillness at Appomattox* * (1954). These volumes concentrate on Union forces in the East, but Catton's forthcoming volumes of the centennial history will give equal coverage to the Western theatre, which has already been ably described by E. S. Miers, *Web of Victory: Grant at Vicksburg* (1955), and F. D. Downey, *Storming the Gateway, Chattanooga, 1863* (1960), among other books. Jay Monaghan, *Civil War on the Western Border, 1854–1865* (1955), provides one of the good accounts available of the trans-Mississippi war, and the Northern navy absorbs several authors, among them R. S. West, Jr., *Mr. Lincoln's Navy* (1957), and C. E. Macartney, *Mr. Lincoln's Admirals* (1956)—both general accounts. There is also an intriguing but more technical study in J. P. Baxter III, *The Introduction of the Ironclad Warship* (1933). Of other accounts of a general nature, an excellent short one is Fletcher Pratt, *Ordeal by Fire: An Informal History of the Civil War* [*A Short History of the Civil War* *] (1955), and an excellent long one, K. P. Williams, *Lincoln Finds a General: A Military History of the Civil War*, 4 vols. (1949–56). David Donald has edited an informative picture history, *Divided We Fought: A Pictorial History of the War* (1952), as has R. M. Ketchum, *The American Heritage Picture History of the Civil War* (1960); and the common soldier has had admirable attention from B. I. Wiley, *The Life of Johnny Reb* (1943) and *The Life of Billy Yank* (1952). Also good on that subject is the anthology, H. S. Commager, ed., *The Blue and the Gray: The Story of the Civil War as Told by Participants*, 2 vols. (1950). *The Personal Memoirs of U. S. Grant*, 2 vols. (1885–86), are still an impressive testimony to the author's ability and humility, possibly the best of all Civil War memoirs, but W. T. Sherman, *Memoirs*, 2 vols. (1875), is also first-rate, and both men have had talented biographers, in particular Lloyd Lewis in his memorable *Sherman, Fighting Prophet* (1932) and *Captain Sam Grant* (1950)—the latter of which Bruce Catton is completing. On the Southern side, the literature, like the valor, balances that of the North, and D. S. Freeman stands out as one of the great historians of the conflict in his two classics, *R. E. Lee, A Biography*, 4 vols. (1934–35) and *Lee's Lieutenants*, 3 vols. (1942–44). Finally, not even a list as brief and selective as this should omit mention of the atlases of the Civil War: the most authoritative, H. S. Commager, 1958 edition of *Atlas to Accompany the Official Records of the Union and Confederate Armies* (1891–95); the more modern, in its design and use of symbols, V. J. Esposito, ed., *The West Point Atlas of American Wars*, 2 vols. (1959); and the motorists' handy J. B. Mitchell, *Decisive Battles of the Civil War* (1955).

* Available in a paperback edition.

15

Aftermath of War

In the decade after Appomattox, the vast social and industrial changes that had begun before the Civil War swept on. The American people continued their uninterrupted movement to the West and, at a quickened pace, to the cities. Immigration, light during the war years, resumed, bringing to the United States unprecedented numbers of Asians and non-English-speaking Europeans. North and south, on the farms and in the cities, native-born and immigrant alike felt the pressures of personal adjustment to new homes, new neighbors, new machines, new conditions of daily life.

In this time of transition, government, too, faced difficult problems, and for ten years those in authority used the power of government boldly and decisively to dispose of some of the nation's most pressing political issues. The war itself had settled three major questions: The triumph of Northern arms had established the Union as indivisible and indissoluble. So also, that victory had wiped out the institution of slavery. And it had assured, at least temporarily, Northern dominance in national politics. But no one was certain how the North would discharge it responsibilities, how the Union would in fact be restored, how the freed slaves would fare. These were thorny questions, especially for a generation that had just fought a fierce war, a struggle imbued with anxiety, death, and hatred. Emotions clouded the judgment of men confronted with the staggering political tasks of the postwar dec-

ade. The tensions of a time of transition, moreover, at once complicated political issues and diverted energies from them. Those who had expected victory to create a brave new world were disappointed.

The Problem of Reconstruction

Diversions   Union soldiers, eager to return to civilian pursuits, welcomed the rapid demobilization that released some eight hundred thousand men in six months. The government also dissolved the rest of its military apparatus. Conscription ceased, the standing army fell off within two years to traditional peacetime levels, the commanding staff scattered or retired, the navy relapsed to the desuetude of the prewar decade. With demobilization, the federal budget dropped about a billion dollars in one year, government contracts stopped, and over a million employees in wartime industries had to find other work. These adjustments produced a serious but brief economic slump. Recovery came in 1868 as a spurt in railway construction brought demands for iron, steel, lumber, and, consequently, for workers. With re-employment, the need quickened for the produce of farms and for the products of industries that finished foods and textiles. Until 1873, when depression returned, the opportunities of industrial growth and prosperity absorbed millions of Americans.

Prosperity fed a mood of confident materialism. Businessmen in particular exploited the opportunities for riches—new inventions, lucrative tactics for industrial and commercial competition and consolidation, exciting speculations (see Chapter 18). The accumulation of wealth caught the imagination and excited the expectations of many men in all ranks of society. There were each year more symbols to confirm their hopes—more factories, more residential palaces, more railroads and furnaces and bridges to signify the achievements of business and businessmen and the industrial conquest of the continent. Of these symbols perhaps the most stirring was the completion of the transcontinental railroad. The wartime loans and land grants (see p. 333) had sped the construction of the Central Pacific east from California and the Union Pacific west from Nebraska. Gangs of Chinese coolies pushed the tracks of the Central Pacific across the hazardous Sierra Nevada while Irish immigrants carried the line of the Union Pacific across the plains, often under danger of Indian attack. As the two roads raced for their share of federal subsidies, both subordinated quality to speed. Yet their accomplishment was none the less spectacular. The Union Pacific built 1,086 miles of track; the Central Pacific, 689. They met at Promontory Point, just northwest of Ogden, Utah. At ceremonies there on May 29, 1869, the telegraph recorded the blows of a silver sledge that drove in the golden spikes connecting the rails, and, with them, the two oceans, now separated by only a week's journey.

The lure of the golden spikes preoccupied most of the talented and ambitious in postwar America. Subsidies to railroads had had their wartime counterparts in the tariff that protected burgeoning industry from European competition, and in the Homestead Act that invited both settlement and speculation in the open West (see pp. 407–08). The itch to gamble, the urge to create, the desire to accumulate wealth and prestige, the drive for power—all these alone or together moved the majority of men who fashioned an age of enterprise out of the aftermath of war.

This seemed, to many men of noble hope and active conscience, a deplorable diversion from the mission of America. The pursuit of private profit or personal power, whatever its results, strayed wide of the mark of the idealists who had interpreted the war as a struggle for human freedom or a fight to preserve intact the United States, and thus the exemplary experiment in democracy. "The hot suns of modern progress" (the phrase belonged to Harriet Beecher Stowe) were distorting the meaning and compounding the problems of victory. "We hoped," Ralph Waldo Emerson wrote, "that in the peace . . . a great expansion would follow in the mind of the country; grand views in every direction. . . . But the energy of the nation seems to have expended itself." Emerson, of course, meant the nation's moral energy. It was by no means entirely expended, but the diversions of progress cost the nation much of the spirit and concentration needed for the politics of Reconstruction and reunion.

The Devastated South   The South especially needed the understanding and constructive intelligence of the whole nation. Emancipation had at one stroke wiped out billions of dollars of investment in slaves. It had lifted the Negroes to the status of freedom in a society that had no practice in and no plans for coping with the social and economic conditions of biracial living. Previously the South had counted on slavery to control relationships between white and black; now the South had no controls. But the two races remained, side by side, unaccustomed to their situation.

The South, moreover, was a devastated land. The war had taken the lives of a quarter of a million soldiers. Northern armies had destroyed most of the railways; Confederate bankruptcy had forced neglect of most of the roads; horses and mules were in short supply. The shortages of man power during the war and the havoc of Northern armies on the march had laid waste much of Southern agriculture. Fences, farmhouses, and outbuildings were burned or in the ruins of disrepair; crops were destroyed; livestock were either killed or left to stray. According to one contemporary report, "the country between Washington and Richmond was . . . like a desert." According to another, the path of General Sherman's march "looked for many miles like a broad, black streak of ruin and desolation." The cities had fared as badly. Industry was destroyed or abandoned; financial institutions were bankrupt; resources for business credit were wiped

Richmond: A devastated city in a devastated land.

out. Some fifteen thousand people in Atlanta and as many more in Richmond depended on federal relief for subsistence. Charleston, South Carolina, was "a city of ruins, of desolation, of vacant houses, of widowed women, of rotting wharves."

The South was also a conquered territory. Federal troops occupied the major towns, often with an understandable but lamentable disregard for the sensitivities of local citizens. The terms of surrender of course forbade the flying of Confederate flags and the wearing of Confederate uniforms, and the presence of Union blue provided daily reminders of defeat. The federal government imprisoned few Confederate leaders (Jefferson Davis was one), and in all respects the conquerors were, as victors go, not harsh. Indeed Northern relief for the destitute was as spontaneous as it was indispensable. But the evidences of defeat swelled the sorrows of devastation.

The South was on the whole reconciled to the failure of secession. Some die-hards—Confederate Secretary of the Treasury Judah P. Benjamin and General Jubal A. Early among them—expatriated themselves, others nursed a lifelong sulk, but most of the eminent and the plain alike accepted defeat. While proud of the spirit of the war years, they were ready to return to useful participation in the life of the nation. They immediately displayed remarkable energy in rebuilding the society and economy of their section (see Chapter 16). Over their political rehabilitation, however, they had no authority.

President Versus Congress   While the fighting still raged, Lincoln had taken initial steps toward re-establishing loyal governments in the seceded states. He always maintained that insurrectionists had temporarily grabbed power in the Southern states. They had never, in his view, seceded, for secession was impossible. On this theory he proceeded to use military force to set up loyal governments as quickly as he could, even when only a minority of the people of a state were loyal to the Union. He placed military governors over Tennessee, Louisiana, and Arkansas in 1862 and 1863, and in December of 1863 he proclaimed the general procedures by which the Southern people could remake their governments. With the exception of certain high public officials, he offered pardons to any Confederate who would take the oath to support "the Constitution of the United States, and the union of the States thereunder." When in any state one-tenth of the number who had voted in the presidential election of 1860 took this oath, they might establish a government without slavery which the President would recognize as the "true government." During 1864 Tennessee, Louisiana, and Arkansas, using the "10 per cent plan," set up new state governments.

The Radicals in Congress bitterly opposed Lincoln's plan. They argued that the seceded states had forfeited their rights, and that Congress had to determine the bases for Reconstruction. (Indisputably, Congress alone could pass upon the credentials of its members, a power sufficient to keep the representatives of states rebuilt on Lincoln's plan from taking their seats.) Lincoln, in the view of the Radicals, was much too lenient. In contrast, Benjamin F. Wade, Henry Winter Davis, and their fellow Radicals specified severe terms for Reconstruction in a bill that Congress passed in July 1864. By its terms, the provisional governor appointed in each seceded state was to enroll the white male citizens. If a majority of those enrolled took an oath to support the Constitution, they could elect a constitutional convention to form a new state government. No one who had held office in the Confederacy or in any of its states, no one who had voluntarily borne arms against the United States, could vote or serve as a delegate. The new government, moreover, was required to prohibit slavery, repudiate the Confederate debt, and prohibit voting and officeholding by former Confederate officials. Lincoln's pocket veto prevented this measure from becoming law, but the President endorsed its terms "as one very proper plan for the loyal people of any State choosing to adopt it." Southerners naturally preferred the presidential plan, which the Radicals would not accept. The problem called for statesmanship of the highest order, of which Lincoln was capable, but the assassin's bullet at Ford's Theatre put Andrew Johnson in the White House.

Johnson had been born to poverty and ignorance in North Carolina. A courageous, self-taught, energetic man, he had overcome the disadvantages of his background, represented

Andrew Johnson: Certain of his righteousness.

his adopted state, Tennessee, in the House and in the Senate, and served admirably as a loyal Democratic war governor. Though he had not opposed slavery, he detested the planter aristocracy and he was devoted to the Union. The Radicals, content with his nomination as Lincoln's running mate in 1864, expected to find him a malleable friend. They were wrong. Johnson was to be a pugnacious antagonist, a self-assured, intemperate, aggressive foe, certain of his duty, certain of his righteousness, and uncompromising—as well as frequently inept—in their pursuit.

Congress was in recess when Johnson took office in April 1865. At first vindictive toward the South, within a month he had adopted Lincoln's conciliatory tone. He retained all of Lincoln's Cabinet, preserved most of Lincoln's plan for Reconstruction (but not the 10 per cent plan), and embraced many of Lincoln's attitudes. Like Lincoln, Johnson considered Reconstruction primarily a presidential function. Like him, he hoped to restore the Southern states to the Union rapidly and on generous terms. Like him, he believed the war had been fought to preserve the Union and free the slaves. He opposed vindictiveness toward the South, opposed contrivances intended largely for partisan Republican advantage, and opposed both racial equality and federal policies designed to achieve it. On those issues—the last not the least—he clashed with the Radical program.

Following Lincoln's policy, Johnson in May 1865 issued a general amnesty proclamation that restored citizenship to former Confederates willing to swear the oath of allegiance and to endorse the abolition of slavery. The proclamation excepted Confederate officeholders and men with taxable property valued at over twenty thousand dollars, but those excepted could petition for special pardons, which Johnson granted liberally. The President also accepted the governments established according to Lincoln's plan in Arkansas, Louisiana, Tennessee, and Virginia, and encouraged the Reconstruction of the other seven

Thaddeus Stevens: Rancorous reformer.

Confederate states. Provisional governors in those states called conventions which Johnson asked to disavow ordinances of secession, repudiate war debts, and ratify the pending Thirteenth Amendment. Approved by Congress the previous January, that amendment forever ended slavery or involuntary servitude within the United States. By December 1865 the Thirteenth Amendment had been adopted. The Southern states, however, did not fully comply with Johnson's other requests. Some merely repealed their ordinances of secession without declaring them invalid in origin. Some tried to avoid repudiating their debts. None enfranchised any Negroes, though Johnson had suggested the advisability of providing for a limited Negro suffrage. Nevertheless the President considered the states reconstructed and also believed, as General Grant put it, that "the mass of thinking men of the South accept the present situation . . . in good faith." Had the decision been his to make, Johnson would unhesitatingly have seated the delegations of Southern congressmen arriving in Washington. Congress was of another mind.

The Shaping of Reconstruction

Seeds of Bitterness   Only the Democrats and a few Republicans were willing to receive the Southerners elected to Congress or to abide with Reconstruction as Johnson had planned it. The other Republicans, moderates and Radicals alike, demanded more than the South had yet yielded. Their attitude reflected the dominant public opinion of the Northern people, who could not believe that the "rebels," enemies in battle for four years, had reformed in nine months. The victors intended to impose stringent terms for Reconstruction, conditions that would set so high a price for disloyalty that it would never occur again. The Radicals proposed to go even further.

In the Congress that reconvened in December 1865, the Radicals were only a minority. But they were determined, personally powerful, politically adroit men, and they had in Thaddeus Stevens a leader distinguished for his parliamentary skill, his pith and sarcasm in debate, and his rancorous commitment to punishing the South. He wanted the South to pay the cost of the war. He wanted to "insure the ascendancy" of the Republican party, on which, he believed, the safety and glory of the nation depended. And if he was vindictive and partisan, he was also, as were his fellows, a daring champion of Negro rights. He advocated distributing all the public lands in the Southern states, and the private property of the "rebels," too, to the freed Negroes in order to establish each head of a former slave family on his own farm. "Forty acres . . . and a hut," Stevens said, "would be more valuable . . . than the . . . right to vote." But that right he and the other Radicals also eventually demanded for the Negro.

The Radicals were furious over Southern reluctance to accede even to Johnson's lenient recommendations, and over Southern suppression of the Negro. The moderates as well as the Radicals objected to the "black codes" which the former Confederate states adopted. Those codes represented the initial Southern effort to regulate the economic and social lives of the freed slaves. Many of the Negroes, without experience with freedom, drifted aimlessly about the country, expecting charity and avoiding work, sometimes stealing or carousing. The "black codes" were designed to discourage vagrancy and to minimize race friction. While they permitted the freedmen to make contracts and own property, they set special penalties for Negroes who broke labor contracts, and they forbade Negroes to carry arms, serve on juries, or marry whites. To most Northerners, the Radicals especially, these provisions seemed appallingly like the old slave codes. Indeed in many respects they were; the South had turned to the past for guidance in managing its problems.

But the past, in the mind of the Republicans, could not give guidance. The war was to have established at least the conditions of freedom and—as the Radicals saw it—the conditions of equality as well. But the "black codes" impaired the freedom of the Southern Negro, and white Southerners manifestly had not even begun to understand the desirability of Negro equality. Southern disdain for the freedmen pushed the moderates in Congress toward the Radical position and away from the President, who unwisely refused to consider any view but his own. Johnson's form of Reconstruction had permitted the Southerners precisely the license which Congress would not tolerate. Bitterly, doggedly, Congress struck back.

A Bitter Year Although the Republicans in Congress did not break with Johnson at once, they refused to recognize the Southern regimes he had called into being, and they asserted their authority over policy by creating an influential joint committee on Reconstruction. In February 1866 Congress passed a bill to undo the "black codes." This measure enlarged and extended the powers of the Freedmen's Bureau, an agency created by Congress in 1865 to provide humanitarian services for Southern Negroes. The bureau, a kind of guardian for its charges, had been effective in every Southern state, coordinating the work of voluntary benevolent societies, feeding migrants, finding them work and homes, rendering medical aid, establishing schools, defending freedmen from white terrorists. The new bill permitted the bureau to use military force to protect Negro rights. Though the moderates in Congress considered this step both necessary and equitable, many Southerners distrusted the bureau's agents, of whom a minority were ruthless or corrupt, and President Johnson condemned any resort to the military in time of peace. Vetoing the bill, he argued that the courts would adequately protect the freedmen, and that the continuation of the bureau "would inevitably result in fraud, corruption, and oppression."

Though the Senate did not override the veto, Radicals and moderates in April 1866 joined forces to pass a civil-rights bill. It declared all persons born in the United States, with the exception of untaxed Indians, to be citizens of the country and therefore entitled to the legal rights of white persons, regardless of the stipulations of any local statutes. The bill also authorized the use of troops to assure enforcement of its provisions and penalties. Again the President responded with a veto, but this time Congress overrode it. Indeed Congress went on to pass a second Freedmen's Bureau Act, which Johnson also vetoed. This time only three Republicans in the Senate voted to sustain him.

Congress next approved, with minor alterations, a constitutional amendment proposed by

Radical Doctrine
for Reconstruction

It is the opinion of your committee—

I. That the States lately in rebellion were, at the close of the war, disorganized communities, without civil government, and without constitutions or other forms, by virtue of which political relations could legally exist between them and the federal government.

II. That Congress cannot be expected to recognize as valid the election of representatives from disorganized communities, which, from the very nature of the case, were unable to present their claim to representation under those established and recognized rules, the observance of which has been hitherto required.

III. That Congress would not be justified in admitting such communities to a participation in the government of the country without first providing such constitutional or other guarantees as will tend to secure the civil rights of all citizens of the republic; a just equality of representation; protection against claims founded in rebellion and crime; a temporary restoration of the right of suffrage to those who had not actively participated in the efforts to destroy the Union and overthrow the government, and the exclusion from positions of public trust of, at least, a portion of those whose crimes have proved them to be enemies to the Union, and unworthy of public confidence.

From *Report of the Joint Committee on Reconstruction*, 1866.

its joint committee on Reconstruction. The first section of this sweeping amendment— ultimately the Fourteenth Amendment—embodied the provisions of the Civil Rights Act, thereby establishing their constitutionality. (These provisions, designed primarily to safeguard the rights of freedmen, were later to be interpreted by the federal courts as pertinent also to the rights of corporations, a development that some of the framers of the amendment welcomed.) The second section of the amendment tried to force the states to grant Negro suffrage by giving them a choice between enfranchising all male citizens or losing a number of seats in the House of Representatives proportionate to those excluded. The amendment also denied the right to hold office to former Confederates who had been federal or state officials before the war, until

Veto of the Radicals' Plan

The power ... given to the commanding officer over all the people of each district is that of an absolute monarch. His mere will is to take the place of all law. The law of the States is now the only rule applicable to the subjects placed under his control, and that is completely displaced by the clause which declares all interference of State authority to be null and void....

It is plain that the authority here given to the military officer amounts to absolute despotism. But to make it still more unendurable, the bill provides that it may be delegated to as many subordinates as he chooses to appoint, for it declares that he shall "punish or cause to be punished." Such a power has not been wielded by any monarch in England for more than five hundred years. In all that time no people who speak the English language have borne such servitude. It reduces the whole population of the ten States—all persons, of every color, sex, and condition, and every stranger within their limits— to the most abject and degrading slavery.

From Andrew Johnson, Veto of the Reconstruction Act, 1867.

Congress should by a two-thirds vote pardon them. This provision postponed indefinitely the return to national politics of the Southern leaders of the 1850's. Finally, the amendment stated that the Confederate war debt was never to be paid, the Union war debt was never to be repudiated, and owners of former slaves were never to be compensated for their loss.

Firm though it was, the Fourteenth Amendment was less harsh than some of the Radicals had hoped. It reflected something of a concession to the moderates, who tended to believe that, if ratified, it would put to rest the problems of Reconstruction. But the South would have none of it. Only Tennessee of the former Confederate states ratified the amendment, and Tennessee did so only after the establishment of voting qualifications favoring the Republicans and only after the use of outright force in the legislature. In return Congress readmitted Tennessee to the Union. Elsewhere Southern legislatures rejected the amendment out of hand. These rejections tended to reinforce Republican beliefs in Southern intransigence. So did an outbreak of race riots in the South, of which the worst were in Memphis and New Orleans. Although there were provocations on both sides, the spectacle of white mobs killing Negroes for whatever reason hardened the attitude of the North.

Johnson's behavior confirmed Radical hostility. In a fit of pique the President classified Stevens as a traitor, and he took the stump in opposition to Radical candidates in the congressional campaigns of 1866. Blustering his way through cities in the East and Middle West, Johnson flashed his temper at hissing audiences and surrendered the dignity of his office to vilification. This exhibition played into the Radicals' hands. When they swept the election, profiting in large part from their own wild charges against the President, they could claim that they had defeated him, that they had received a spanking mandate for their policies. They took it to be also a mandate for their passions.

Radicals in Control   Dominating the new Congress, the Radicals in March 1867 put through a drastic Reconstruction bill, quickly repassed it over another Johnson veto, and in 1868 added three supplementary measures to facilitate the administration of their program. These acts rested on the presumption that no lawful governments existed in the ten former Confederate states (the eleventh, Tennessee, had of course been readmitted). The legislation divided the states into five military districts, each of which was placed under a federal commander with authority over police, judicial, and civil functions—authority superior to that of the state governments and including the control of constitution-making. In order to regain representation in Congress, the people of a state had to meet various conditions: In elections for state constitutional conventions, Negroes were entitled to vote, but Confederate officeholders disqualified by the still-pending Fourteenth Amendment were not. The new state constitutions had to establish Negro suffrage and win approval by referendum from the electorate that had chosen the convention delegates, and from Congress as well. The state legislatures then elected had to ratify the Fourteenth Amendment. When enough states had done so to make that amendment a part of the Constitution of the United States, and only then, the states that had complied with Congress's demands would be readmitted.

Johnson condemned the Radical program as "without precedent . . . in palpable conflict with the plainest provisions of the Constitution . . . utterly destructive to . . . great principles of liberty." Unquestionably the Radicals were treating the South as a dangerous, conquered province. Whatever the merit of their motives, however precious the principles of equality, the Radicals were also violating cherished Anglo-American principles of freedom in order to impose their will. The tangle of ends and means did credit to no one; the harshness of the program occasioned indignation and defiance in the South, thus enlarging the tasks of the military commanders and fanning resentment toward both Yankees and Negroes.

The Radicals expanded their fiery authority over the federal government as well as over the Southern states. One of their laws declared that all military orders of the President and the Secretary of War had to be issued through the general-in-chief, who could not be removed or reassigned without the consent of the Senate. This diminution of the power of the presidency, an act of dubious constitutionality, made General Grant, who was drifting under Radical control, the effective commander in chief of the army. Another measure, designed to preclude a decision attacking the constitutionality of Reconstruction legislation, limited the appellate jurisdiction of the Supreme Court. The Radicals also managed to delay the seating of properly elected Democrats from Kentucky until after the Reconstruction laws were passed. Most boldly, Stevens and his fellows attempted to seize the presidency itself.

The Tenure-of-Office Act of March 1867, a direct assault on Johnson, declared that the President would be guilty of "high misdemeanor" if he removed without the Senate's consent any officeholder who had been appointed with the Senate's "advice and consent." Cabinet members, according to this law, were to hold office "during the term of the President by whom they may have been appointed and for one month thereafter." As Johnson's veto pointed out, the measure was doubtless unconstitutional, but his veto was overruled.

Johnson fought on. Secretary of War Stanton, an ally of the Radicals, had consistently undermined the President. When he refused to resign, Johnson, during a recess of Congress in August 1867, suspended him and made General Grant the interim Secretary of War. Johnson knew the Senate would challenge this move, but he wanted to test the Tenure-of-Office Act in the courts. He clearly believed that Grant, in accepting his new appointment, had agreed either to stay on until a court decision had settled the question, or else to resign before the Senate acted on the Stanton suspension; in the latter case, the President could appoint an alternative interim Secretary. But Grant did neither. Bewildered by the situation, yet sensing the growing power of Congress, he waited until, as expected, the Senate refused to endorse Stanton's suspension. Then Grant resigned. His resignation now kept the President from testing the constitutionality of his appointment and supported Stanton's refusal to vacate his office. The nonentity whom Johnson named to Grant's place was still puzzling over how to assume it when, in March 1868, the House of Representatives voted 126 to 47 to impeach the President.

The resolution of impeachment contained no bill of particulars against Johnson. An earlier attempt to pass such a resolution, based on accusations of corruption, had failed. In the debate over the successful resolution the old charges were rehearsed and the House indulged in an orgy of slander against the President. The set of eleven articles of impeachment which the House framed was a rambling, tautological, confused indictment emphasizing Stanton's dismissal. But in fact Johnson had not been guilty of "high misdemeanor" even under the Tenure-of-Office Act, for Stanton, a Lincoln appointee, had served much more than a month beyond the term of the President who named him. The articles of impeachment represented only the venomous effort of the Radicals to depose a President who hated and opposed them. If they succeeded in that effort, Johnson would be replaced by Ben Wade, the president pro tem of the Senate, and one of the most vengeful Radicals. Furthermore, their success would destroy the presidential system established by the Constitution; it would set a precedent for making the President the creature of a congressional majority, a precedent pointing toward parliamentary government in the British style.

The Radicals almost succeeded. Popular sentiment in the North supported their purpose. Chief Justice Chase of the Supreme Court, by virtue of his office the presiding judge at the Senate's trial of treason charges, was unable to establish all the rules for the conduct of the case which he recommended. But when in May the vote was taken, seven Republicans bravely sided with the Democrats, and the ballot stood 35 to 19 for conviction, one short of the necessary two-thirds majority. Johnson had barely survived the fatuous test. In the wake of his escape, Stanton resigned and the Senate adjourned.

No Republican seriously considered renominating Johnson in 1868. The tempers that surrounded the struggle over Reconstruction obscured even his achievements in foreign affairs. Johnson and Secretary of State Seward served the principles of the Monroe Doctrine well. In 1866 the President dispatched fifty thousand veteran troops under General Philip H. Sheridan to the Mexican border, and Secretary of State Seward demanded the withdrawal of French forces from Mexico. France complied, and a year later the Mexicans re-established their independence. Serving also the spirit of Manifest Destiny, Seward signed a treaty of friendship and commerce with China in 1868 and also negotiated a treaty to buy the Virgin Islands from Denmark for $7,500,000, but the Senate rejected the latter. In 1867 the Senate had almost unanimously approved a treaty for the purchase from Russia of Alaska for $7,200,000. Russia was eager to sell what seemed a barren tract of wasteland, and many Americans joked about Seward's "icebox." But time was to demonstrate the enormous strategic value of Alaska and the richness of her undeveloped resources. Seward had swung a magnificent bargain.

It was, however, Reconstruction, and not foreign policy, on which the Republican platform focused in 1868. Fashioned by the Radicals, the platform endorsed their policy and damned Johnson and the Democrats. (The party also acknowledged an emerging issue of potential importance by pledging payment of the national debt in gold.) The Radicals' high-handed methods had made them enough enemies to persuade the Republicans to seek a popular hero as their candidate. Unanimously they settled on Ulysses S. Grant and, as his running mate, Speaker of the House Schuyler Colfax. Grant had no political experience, but he had demonstrated a willingness to accede to the Radicals' advice. From their point of view, he was an ideal choice.

The Democrats had nearly insuperable obstacles to overcome. They had yet to rid their party of the taint of disloyalty. They had yet to find new leaders to replace their ablest prewar spokesmen. Their platform denounced Radical Reconstruction as unconstitutional. Hoping to raise a new and popular issue, the party endorsed an inflationary proposal—the "Ohio Idea"—popular among Midwestern farmers who had suffered during the slump of 1867. This proposal called for paying the principal of the government bonds sold during the war in gold, but the interest in greenbacks. The "Ohio Idea" appealed to debtors, who stood to benefit from inflation, and to critics of the "bloated bondholders"—the war profiteers. It appealed, too, to those Democrats who felt that the war debt had been contracted for an unworthy cause. But it distressed conservative eastern Democrats, who took solace in their successful effort to nominate Horatio Seymour of New York. A wealthy but scarcely a compelling man, a war governor with an unjust reputation for disloyalty, Seymour was badly handicapped in a race with Grant. No telling weight was added to the ticket by vice-presidential candidate Francis P. Blair of Missouri.

In a savage campaign, the Republicans concentrated on the alleged treason of the Democratic party and waved the "bloody shirt" of war. The Republicans could count on the support of Southern states dominated by carpetbag governments (see p. 366), a multitude of federal officeholders, and most Union veterans, to whom they promised generous pensions (a pledge the Democrats made, too, but less persuasively). Yet in spite of these advantages, and in spite of his appeal as a triumphant soldier, Grant ran just well enough to win. He carried the electoral college 214 to 80, but received only 52.7 per cent of the popular vote. Without the Negro vote, he would have had only a minority of the popular vote. Without the support of the six Southern states manipulated by the Radicals, he would have been in trouble. Radical Reconstruction, the "bloody

shirt," the memories of war—these had brought Republican victory. The lesson was plain. For continued control of the federal government, the Radicals had to retain their control of the South.

The Grant Era

The Reconstructed South   The Radical program of military Reconstruction resulted during 1868 in the readmission of most of the Southern states. Each of them met the statutory prescriptions, including approval of the Fourteenth Amendment, which accordingly received the ratifications necessary for adoption. In four states—Georgia, Mississippi, Virginia, and Texas—opposition to the Radical terms delayed Reconstruction and readmission, but military pressure had brought all of them into line by 1871. The Union was then completely restored, and the South was entirely under the rule of local administrations subservient to the Radicals and their doctrines.

Now the Radicals could advance their quest for Negro suffrage, a quest that had begun before 1868 but had played no significant part in the campaign that year. The Fifteenth Amendment, approved by Congress in 1869, in 1870 secured enough ratifications for adoption, including those of subservient Southern states. "The right of citizens of the United States to vote," the amendment provided, "shall not be denied or abridged by the United States or by any State on account of race, color, or previous condition of servitude." Congress, the second section said, had the power "to enforce this article by appropriate legislation." As it developed, however, Negro voting depended for the while on the practices of the Southern states.

In the South the period of "Black Reconstruction" cut raw wounds. Southerners tended to remember the era as one in which government fell to uneducated Negroes, to selfish Northern transients—"carpetbaggers"—and to a treacherous minority of Southern whites— "scalawags." It was a time, according to this memory, of unmitigated public corruption. But the recollection drew on evidence selected to confirm it.

Negroes never dominated the governments of the Southern states. They never held public

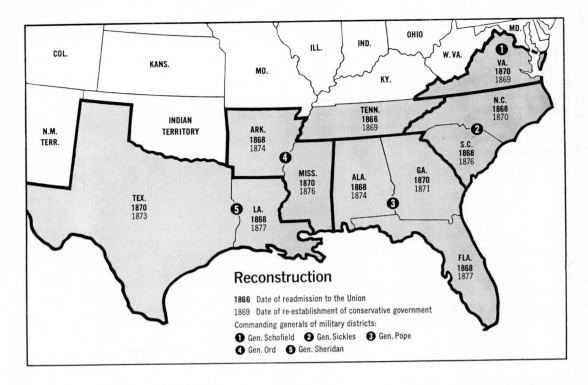

Reconstruction

1866 Date of readmission to the Union
1869 Date of re-establishment of conservative government
Commanding generals of military districts:
❶ Gen. Schofield ❷ Gen. Sickles ❸ Gen. Pope
❹ Gen. Ord ❺ Gen. Sheridan

offices in proportion to their numbers within the population; they had a legislative majority only in South Carolina; they won election to no governorship, to only two seats in the United States Senate, to only fifteen in the House of Representatives. Negroes elected to lower offices, to state legislatures, and to positions as justices of the peace, had on the whole qualifications equivalent to the average standard for incumbents in such undistinguished posts. And some Negroes elected to high office were enlightened, talented, forceful men.

In most of the Southern states, a majority of the voters were white, and most of them were not "scalawags." Among the whites who sought and held political power, some were simply renegades, others poor men in quest of social advancement and, possibly, revenge against the planter aristocracy. But most were planters and merchants recruited from the ranks of prewar Southern Whigs. This last group, anxious to develop the Southern economy and to promote interracial harmony, gradually lost out to carpetbaggers who employed less genteel tactics and made less moderate and practicable promises to the Negroes. Regrettably, the carpetbaggers drove the former Whigs away from the Republican party, which consequently lost its best chance to establish a broad basis in the South and to find a creative leadership there.

Yet the carpetbaggers and their associates in the Reconstruction governments also made positive contributions. Several of the state constitutions they adopted, copied from the best models in the North, endured for several decades. Their policies abetted the Negroes' transition to citizenship; extended social services, including compulsory education, previously unknown in many Southern states; and rebuilt the physical structure essential for economic growth—the cities and roads and railways.

That rebuilding involved letting contracts, granting charters and other privileges, and spending public money. And to each contract let, each charter granted, each dollar of public money spent, large temptations adhered: opportunities for graft and for handsome bribes from rival groups of promoters, especially from competing railroad interests. To those temptations officeholders throughout the South suc-

A Southern Historian Assesses Reconstruction

Radical Reconstruction had failed in every particular in which the Radical Congress had accused the Johnson governments.... The editor of *Scribner's Monthly* saw Southerners in despair and he blamed the Federal government: "They feel that they were wronged, that they have no future, that they cannot protect themselves, and that nothing but death or voluntary exile will give them relief." The editor of the *Nation* by 1870 had come to view the South with a light different from that of 1865. In the South the people had almost forgotten "that in free countries men live for more objects than the simple one of keeping robbers' hands off the earnings of the citizen." There people were worse off than they were in any South American republic; for in the latter place tyrants could be turned out through the right of revolution, but the South with the army on its back could no longer resort to this ancient remedy. Southerners must continue to suffer enormities "which the Czar would not venture toward Poland, or the British Empire toward the Sautals of the Indian jungle."

From E. Merton Coulter, *The South During Reconstruction*, 1947.

A Northern Historian Views Reconstruction

It was imperative in those first years after Appomattox that a way be found whereby the nation and the Negro might confidently look forward to the former slave's full and equal participation in American life. But the unique opportunity of those first years was squandered. Neither Southerners nor Northerners were capable of disenthralling themselves, as Lincoln had counseled; both continued to act within their historically determined attitudinal patterns. Lincoln himself, for that matter, failed to grasp the crucial nature of the postwar era, so far as the Negro was concerned. His plan for the rapid restoration of the southern states indicated that he was quite prepared to throw away the single opportunity for realizing the equalitarian precepts of the Declaration of Independence to which he so often referred. And though the Radicals succeeded in enshrining in the Constitution their vision of equality for all, thereby illuminating the path the nation was ultimately to follow, they were woefully unequal to the complicated and delicate task of implementing their vision. Having failed to meet the problem of the Negro at its inception, Americans have been compelled to grapple with it in each succeeding generation down to our own day.

From Carl N. Degler, *Out of Our Past*, 1958.

cumbed. There was graft in public printing, in the sale of public lands, in expenditures for official entertainment, in contracts for hiring prison labor and for marketing public bonds. Fraud and corruption infected all the Reconstruction governments, damaging morale, swelling state debts. But the increases in debt during the period arose mostly from the need to subsidize economic development, particularly the building of railroads, whose properties were often a lien against the obligations the states incurred. The graft and fraud, moreover, were not peculiar to the South and its carpetbag administrations. The Tweed Ring in New York City (see p. 375) and its counterparts in Chicago and Philadelphia were more corrupt than the statehouse gangs in Georgia or Florida or Texas. The carpetbaggers simply had no more moral stamina than other Democrats and Republicans the nation over during the era of Grant.

To most Southern whites at the time, however, the pattern of Reconstruction seemed a pattern of oppression, Africanization, and misrule. To relieve their situation they turned to violence. Among the secret terroristic agencies they founded, the most notorious was the Ku Klux Klan. Following its launching in 1866 in Tennessee, the Klan spread throughout the South, reaching its zenith between 1868 and 1871. It adopted weird rituals, a complex scheme of organization, and outlandish titles for its officers—Grand Dragons, Hydras, Titans, Cyclopes. Klansmen in white robes and hoods rode out at night on sheeted horses to intimidate Negroes and punish "scalawags." They often whipped or even killed their victims and sometimes engaged in outright pillage.

Northerners, particularly the Radicals, saw in the activities of the Klan and similar organizations fresh evidence of wickedness in the unrepentant South. Supported by public opinion, Congress passed three disciplinary measures. The Force Act of 1870 imposed severe penalties on anyone using force, bribery, or intimidation to prevent citizens from voting. It also placed congressional elections under federal supervision. A second Force bill in 1871

Southern freedmen: They needed a guardian.

strengthened the terms of the first. In the latter year Congress added a statute defining as high crimes the conspiracies and activities characteristic of organizations like the Klan. This measure authorized the President to suspend habeas corpus in suppressing such "armed combinations," which were deemed comparable to rebellion itself. In executing the act, Grant ordered federal troops to the most unruly areas, suspended habeas corpus in nine counties in South Carolina, and appointed commissioners who made hundreds of arrests on the charge of conspiracy. The Supreme Court later found the important provisions of the disciplinary legislation unconstitutional, but the acts applied long enough to permit the federal government to stamp out the Klan, which had virtually disappeared by 1872.

The force bills also helped the Radicals to preserve hegemony for their friends in the South. Though in several states before 1872 white political leaders found legal ways to unseat the carpetbaggers, elsewhere federal bayonets or the threat of bayonets perpetuated the authority of the Reconstruction administrations. This resort to military force in time of peace left a heritage of bitterness at least as deep and rankling as the memory of defeat in battle or fraud in Reconstruction government. The resulting mood contributed to the tension between the races and to the South's antagonism to the Republican party and its works. Radical Reconstruction, by no means empty of achievement, produced far more scars than monuments. The Radical program did not attain its finest purposes; in pursuing that program, moreover, the Radicals revealed their sorriest traits. The chapter they wrote was both ominous and unhappy, but not the darkest in the record of the black Grant years.

Government under Grant No president before 1869 had been so unqualified for office as was Ulysses S. Grant—a man who had no experience in politics, no capacity for absorbing such experience, no sensitivity for statescraft, and no judgment about men. Grant had impeccable personal integrity. He had as a soldier displayed the qualities of leadership and fortitude that won him deserved glory. He had, as his enemies in battle had learned, incomparable courage. But as a public servant Grant was a fool and a failure. He appointed an undistinguished Cabinet, of which several members were knaves who duped him shamelessly. He found most matters of public policy utterly bewildering. He did not himself generate the gross and greedy spirit of the time, but a stronger and wiser man would have yielded less readily than Grant to its rapacious temper. Truly pathetic in his inadequacies, he was also singularly obtuse about his choice of friends. He accepted expensive gifts from favor-hunters; he received personal loans from Jay Cooke, whose Northern Pacific Railroad was seeking federal subsidies; he welcomed the company of Jim Fisk, a conscienceless gambler in stocks.

Only one of Grant's official family performed in the manner of a statesman. Secretary of State Hamilton Fish, an able, honest, dignified gentleman, negotiated the Treaty of Washington of 1871, which resolved issues troubling Anglo-American relations. The treaty put to an end the strident demands of American chauvinists who had talked of acquiring Canada as compensation for the damage done by the *Alabama* and other Confederate commerce raiders built in England. It referred to arbitration the question of those ships and other matters as well. The German emperor judged one dispute over the international boundary in the channel between Vancouver Island and the state of Washington, deciding in favor of the United States. A special tribunal awarded $2 million to British subjects for damages suffered during the Civil War. The British, in the terms of the treaty itself, expressed "regret" about the *Alabama* and agreed to principles for arbitrating the American claims and for proper neutral behavior in the future. In accord with those principles, a special court awarded the United States $15,500,000. The treaty and the techniques it employed furthered international peace and Anglo-American understanding, achievements of which Secretary Fish could be proud.

The balance of the record of the Grant Administration afforded no occasions for pride. Spokesmen in Washington enjoyed an unparalleled orgy, an orgy that led, in the words of the *Nation*, a reform periodical, not only to "bad appointments but probably some of the worst ever made by a civilized Christian government." The President in 1870 dismissed two of the most culpable of his Cabinet, and in 1871 asked Congress for a civil-service law. But he administered that act reluctantly and ineffectively, and in 1873 Congress let expire its appropriation for a commission to supervise federal appointments.

Indeed Congress during Grant's term enjoyed free reign. The President shared the view of its leaders that it had responsibility for determining federal policy. In this view, it fell to the President to execute the laws but not to take the lead in formulating them. Grant happily rubber-stamped the legislation that came to his desk, legislation in which Congress revealed continuing solicitude for men of wealth. In 1872 it abolished what remained of the wartime income tax, a step that made regressive excise and import taxes the sole source of revenue for repaying the debt and for current account. Responding to the requests of lobbies for various business interests, some of them in conflict with others, Congress in 1869 raised the tariff rate on copper, in 1870 on steel rails, marble, and nickel. In deference to the pending election and to farmer sentiment, Congress lowered most duties by 10 per cent in 1872, but even then many rates, which in the time of Henry Clay had stood at about 25 per cent, had climbed to 500 per cent, and industrialists were not yet satisfied.

Indeed the greedy were insatiable. Grant's friend Jim Fisk tried to arrange for himself a magnificent bounty built on the ruin of others. With Jay Gould he engineered a fantastic attempt to corner the market in gold. Keeping their role secret, the two men set out to bid up the price of gold and to command the supply of it in New York. They almost succeeded, but on "Black Friday," September 24, 1869, the crash came, the price of gold fell, many speculators and some innocents were ruined, and the conspirators, their plot a failure, escaped only by repudiating their contracts. They managed that repudiation by hiring thugs to intimidate their creditors and bribing officials to refrain from prosecution. Nevertheless, Grant remained friendly with Fisk, who, with Gould, continued his bribing, his manipulating, his frenzied but remunerative finance.

The corruption associated with the Grant Administration in Washington, in New York, and in the South gave rise to a reform movement within the Republican party. In 1870 Carl Schurz, a German immigrant, a Civil War hero, and an emerging statesman, led the group in Missouri who, with Democratic support, carried the state's gubernatorial election. These and other Liberal Republicans, the name they chose, stood for civil-service reform, downward revision of the tariff, and gentler treatment of the South. At the Liberal Republican convention of 1872, however, some of the delegates were protectionists, others merely disappointed office-seekers. A series of squabbles and compromises produced a platform that was silent on the tariff—and it produced

Horace Greeley: An anomalous candidate.

as well a grotesque presidential candidate, Horace Greeley, a perfervid protectionist and lifelong castigator of Democrats. Yet the Democrats, still politically bankrupt, buried their reservations about policy and personality and named as their own candidates Greeley and his running mate, Governor B. G. Brown of Missouri.

The election was never in doubt. Grant, the unanimous choice of the Republican convention, had not yet lost his heroic mantle. Seven carpetbag governments in the South were working for him; the "bloody shirt" remained a persuasive symbol in the north; and business interests provided lavish funds to finance his campaign. The Republican platform, praising tariff protection and Radical Reconstruction, probably counted less than did the appeal of the candidate and the disorganization of the Liberal Republicans and their Democratic allies. Grant polled 55.8 per cent of the popular vote and swept the electoral college 286 to 63. A few weeks later Horace Greeley died, brokenhearted, aware that never before had poor government won so thunderous an endorsement.

The Collapse   In less than a year after Grant's second election, political scandals and economic distress had destroyed the brittle reputation of his Administration. A congressional investigating committee early in 1873 exposed the shocking history of the Crédit Mobilier, a construction company that had been formed allegedly to build the Union Pacific Railroad. Much of the money from contracts it received, however, went straight to its major shareholders. One of its officers, Congressman Oakes Ames, had sold shares in the company at bargain prices to other congressmen, who had in return prevented inquiries into the company's strange affairs. Among the cooperative beneficiaries were Vice-President Colfax and Congressman—later president—James A. Garfield. The disclosure of the chicanery did not seriously disturb the Republican Congress, which contented itself with a vote of censure against Ames. But the public was troubled, and, though the rascality dated back to 1868, it was associated with the Grant supporters who profited from and condoned it.

More staggering exposures followed apace. Five of them involved Cabinet officers: the

Secretary of the Treasury, the Secretary of the Navy, the Attorney General, the Postmaster General, and the Secretary of War. The last of these officials, William W. Belknap, had accepted annual bribes from traders at Indian posts. Though Belknap resigned in 1876, he was impeached by the House and barely saved from conviction by the Senate because several senators argued that their chamber lacked jurisdiction in the case. Grant's new Secretary of Treasury uncovered the notorious "Whiskey Ring," a conspiracy of hundreds of distillers who had bribed Treasury officials in order to evade federal taxes. Grant's private secretary, General Orville E. Babcock, participated in that and other corrupt adventures. "Let no guilty man escape," Grant had ordered, but he provided Babcock with a deposition that helped him to escape punishment. Surely the President had been taken in by his friends, but clearly he could not discriminate between an honest man and a rogue. He richly deserved the criticism he received.

Grant's administration also earned a share of the blame for the economic collapse that marked his second term. Although the splurge of speculation encouraged by the government contributed to the panic of 1873, its deeper causes lay in the rapidity of economic expansion in the United States. Entrepreneurs in rails and in industry, foreseeing no end to the soaring profits of the postwar years, had built productive facilities beyond the existing needs of the nation. To assist in those endeavors and to share in their returns, bankers had extended credit beyond the margin of safety. Europe had experienced similar developments. The signal of danger came in September 1873 with the failure of Jay Cooke and Company, a leading financial firm in the United States that had plunged heavily in rails. Panic followed. Within a year eighty-nine railroads had defaulted on their bonds, and business failures had aggregated some $228 million. During the ensuing four years of depression, one of the longest and worst in American history, three million laborers lost their jobs, wages fell, agricultural prices sank so low that farmers, unable to pay their mortgages, had to surrender their properties, their homes, their fondest dreams.

Depression and scandal bred protest as well as discontent. The Democrats in 1874 won control in twenty-three states, improved their position in the Senate, and elected a majority of the House of Representatives. Grangerism was flourishing among the harassed farmers of the West (see p. 482). The Republicans met these challenges and the problems of the time by espousing two economic policies that were to hold the dedication of the party for decades to come—high tariffs and hard money. Assisted by the votes of some Eastern Democrats, in 1875 the Republicans restored the duties they had reduced three years earlier. They also reaffirmed their faith in a currency based on, and fully convertible to, gold.

The money issue had received inconsistent treatment. From the time the war ended, most farmers and debtors, but not all of them, favored cheap money, the continued use of the greenbacks issued during the war without gold backing. The advocates of cheap money believed that it would lessen the burden of debt and that it could sustain or advance the prices of the products they sold. Most, but not all, businessmen favored a return to gold. It would stabilize the value of currency, thus reducing the uncertainty of commerce and exchange, and if it resulted in a deflation of domestic prices of manufactured goods, those lower prices would add some measure of protection against more expensive imports.

Immediately after the war the Treasury had retired some greenbacks, only to put them back into circulation after the slump of 1867. The legal status of the greenbacks, however, was uncertain. In 1870 the Supreme Court ruled that the issuance of greenbacks was unconstitutional. This decision jeopardized the validity of contracts calling for payments in money that had been legal tender since 1862, and it worried those who realized that retiring the greenbacks might overly contract the supply of money. To their satisfaction, the Court in 1871, its membership increased by two Grant appointments, reversed its earlier ruling and declared the greenbacks valid in all respects. This opinion settled the legal question but left open the question of policy.

In 1873, to relieve the deflation that accompanied the panic, the Treasury reissued $26 million of greenbacks retired earlier. The next year Congress, responding to sentiment for further inflation, authorized a further use of paper money up to a limit of $400 million. Now the business interests opposed to that policy persuaded Grant, who had been typically confused and indecisive, to veto the measure. After the congressional elections of 1874, but before the Democrats had assumed control of the House, the Republicans put through a bill drafted by Senator John Sherman and signed by Grant in January 1875. This measure provided for an increase in the number of national banks and in the amount of their bank notes, a change that met the demands of the South and the West for a more equitable share of both. The act also provided that after January 1, 1879, the Treasury would, on demand, redeem all legal-tender notes in coin. It permitted the Treasury to prepare for that step by selling bonds (which would, incidentally, furnish a basis for further bank notes). Overlooking the constructive clauses in the act, inflationists condemned it unsparingly and predicted disaster. As it developed, however, the date of resumption coincided roughly with the return of prosperity. That accident strengthened the conviction of Republicans in their "sound-money" policy. It occurred too late, however, to mitigate the unpopularity that the Grant regime had reaped from the depression and from the Administration's steady deference to business and industry.

The Twilight of Reconstruction   Scandal, depression, and the debates over the tariff and greenbacks during Grant's second term diverted congressional attention from the South. Concurrently, Northern business interests, preoccupied with their own worries and disenchanted by the corruption and disorder of carpetbag government, lost interest in Radical Reconstruction. The carpetbaggers in these years filched more and more from the public purse, made travesties of elections by parading Negroes to the polls, padding voting lists, stuffing ballot boxes. Their excesses completed the alienation of white Southerners. Openly now, without hoods or robes, Southern whites of all classes organized to intimidate the Negroes and the remaining scalawags. The carpetbag governments, receiving little support from Washington, gradually toppled. By 1876 Radical rule remained only in Louisiana, South Carolina, and Florida; the rest of the South had achieved "home rule."

The collapse of the carpetbaggers would doubtless have occurred even without the collapse of public morals and of the economy. The three debacles, related in time, derived from a common national mood. Avarice, corruption, and vindictiveness in the aftermath of war rotted the splendid fruits of wartime sacrifice and ideals. From victory, the federal government inherited a tripartite positive mission—to cement the Union that had been saved; to develop systematically and equitably the economy that had burgeoned; to provide for the Negro the social and political necessaries of freedom. Sometimes with the best intentions, more often with greed and venom, the men in charge of government failed. In restoring the South, they scarred it. In developing the economy, they delegated opportunity and power to a grasping, gambling, overprivileged few. They set high goals for the freedmen, helped them briefly to reach for those goals, and then left them to the mercy first of demagogues and then of embittered Southern whites. With too many people too intent on private comfort and convenience, with too many public men too susceptible to cupidity or wrath, government of the people and by their elected representatives too rarely and too intermittently directed its powerful energies to the nation's positive good.

SUGGESTIONS FOR READING   General

There is a concise and learned account of Reconstruction, and an incomparable analysis of the bibliography on that subject, in J. G. Randall and David Donald, *The Civil War and Reconstruction* (2nd ed., 1961). That excellent volume covers also the Grant years. A recent short and valuable study is J. H. Franklin, *Reconstruction: After the Civil War* (1962). Another general treatment of the period 1865–76, stressing social and economic conditions, is in Allan Nevins, *The Emergence of Modern America, 1865–1878* (1927). The politics of the period receive detailed but sometimes jaundiced treatment in Matthew Josephson, *The Politicos, 1865–1896* (1938). The national mood concerns P. H. Buck, *The Road to Reunion, 1865–1900* (1937).

Johnson, the Radicals and Reconstruction

H. K. Beale, *The Critical Year: A Study of Andrew Johnson and Reconstruction* (1958), provides a sympathetic analysis of the President and an interpretation of the Radicals emphasizing their economic motives. Johnson is severely criticized in E. L. McKitrick, *Andrew Johnson and Reconstruction* (1960), which takes direct issue with Beale's thesis. Of the more general studies of Reconstruction, two thorough accounts are marred by their pro-Southern, anti-Negro bias: W. A. Dunning, *Reconstruction: Political and Economic, 1865–1877* (1907), and E. M. Coulter, *The South During Reconstruction, 1865–1877* (1947). Even more biased, indeed often frenetic, is C. G. Bowers, *The Tragic Era* (1929), while R. S. Henry, *The Story of Reconstruction* (1938), is competent but bland and, on major questions of interpretation, evasive. W. E. B. DuBois, in *Black Reconstruction* (1935), overstates the achievements of the Negroes and views the aftermath of war through a Marxist prism. Also sympathetic to the Negro, but on other issues often curiously oblique, is J. S. Allen, *Reconstruction: The Battle for Democracy, 1865–1876* (1937). All in all, the general history of Reconstruction is notable for a lack of adequate attention, a condition historians are now rectifying. (General and special literature on the South and its postwar condition and problems through 1900 is listed in connection with Chapter 16, below. On American business, consult the listing following Chapter 18, below.)

The Grant Era

Here again there is a dearth of truly satisfactory books. There is a good general study of business in T. C. Cochran and William Miller, *The Age of Enterprise: A Social History of Industrial America* (1942), which also touches intelligently on public policy. Rendigs Fels, *American Business Cycles, 1865–1897* (1959), is authoritative on the Panic of 1873. For a balanced and significant analysis of the money question, see R. P. Sharkey, *Money, Class, and Party* (1959). Postwar diplomacy has had able attention, especially in Dexter Perkins, *The Monroe Doctrine, 1867–1907* (1937), and Allan Nevins, *Hamilton Fish: The Inner History of the Grant Administration* (1936), which also provides the best account of the topic described by its subtitle. On the scandals of Grant's time and on the responses to them, three worthy studies are D. G. Loth, *Public Plunder: A History of Graft in America* (1938); C. R. Fish, *The Civil Service and the Patronage* (1904); and E. D. Ross, *The Liberal Republican Movement* (1919). There is a first-rate analysis of Grant and the liberals in the beginning chapters of Eric Goldman, *Rendezvous with Destiny* * (1955). Also useful are C. M. Fuess, *Carl Schurz: Reformer* (1932), and G. G. Van Deusen, *Horace Greeley: Nineteenth Century Crusader* (1953).

* Available in a paperback edition.

16

The New South: Reunion and Readjustment

The central theme of American history during the quarter-century following Reconstruction was laissez faire—"let alone." In this period control over public policy was surrendered almost entirely to private interest. The six chapters that follow will reveal this philosophy at work in all sections of the country, in the city as in the countryside, in economics as in politics. Laissez faire profoundly affected the lot of Negro freedmen and Indians, the fate of buffaloes, natural resources, and public lands, the course of railroad operations, industrial management, and labor relations. After 1877 the center of historical forces and the focus of historical interest shift away from Washington. The federal government and the major political parties retreated from responsibility for public policy and fixed their attention narrowly on political maneuvers and trade in public offices.

White Southerners responded with fervor to the doctrine of laissez faire. Their enthusiasm sprang from a revolt against Reconstruction, the radical application of a philosophy that was the opposite of laissez faire. Disillusionment with Reconstruction, in fact, was spreading in the North as well as in the South, and Southerners were beginning to hope for support from their former enemies. The great experiment of the Radicals had failed to solve the two problems it was designed to solve: the status of the South in the nation, and the status of the Negro in the South. These two problems had torn and agitated the country for more than a generation, and Reconstruction proved no more successful than the Civil War had been in finding a solution. "We have tried for eight years," wrote Joseph Medill, the influential Republican editor of the Chicago *Tribune*, "to uphold Negro rule in the South officered by carpetbaggers, but without exception it has resulted in failure." Patience was running out in 1876, and the demand for some practical solution was growing more and more insistent.

The Return to Compromise

For sixteen years, ever since Fort Sumter, North and South had settled their differences by armed force—not only during the four years of war, but during the twelve years that followed as well. If the country was ever to give up force and return to peaceful ways of settling sectional disputes, it would have to revive the neglected art of compromise. The opportunity for a drastic change in relations between North and South and a return to the tradition of compromise on the classic model of 1850 came unexpectedly with the presidential election of 1876.

Tilden Versus Hayes   Economic depression, political scandal, and weariness with Grant's Southern policy clouded Republican prospects in 1876. The election of 1874 had returned the Democrats to control of the House of Representatives for the first time since the Civil War. During the next two years the depression that had started in 1873 deepened and discontent increased. Throughout 1876 reformers filled the air with exposures of new scandals in the corrupt Grant Administration. Growing disgust with corruption, more than anything else, led to the elimination of the two leading contestants for the Republican nomination. One was President Grant himself, for, incredible as it may seem, the general had permitted the Stalwarts (see p. 466) to persuade him for a time that he would make a logical candidate for a third term. He withdrew, however, before the Republican convention met. The second candidate to be knocked out of the race for the nomination was Congressman James G. Blaine of Maine, formerly Speaker and currently minority leader in the House.

Blaine was known best as the leader of the "Half-Breeds," rivals of the Stalwarts, and for his personal enmity with Roscoe Conkling, the Stalwarts' leader. A master of florid oratory and dramatic political maneuver, he commanded a large personal following and an army of political dependents. Blaine's opening maneuver in 1876 was the very opposite of compromise. Taking the floor on January 10, he artfully revived wartime bitterness over the suffering of Northern troops in the South's Andersonville prison camp. Gesturing dramatically, he declared that "the thumbscrews and engines of torture of the Spanish Inquisition did not begin to compare in atrocity with the hideous crime of Andersonville." And he charged that Jefferson Davis was "the man that organized that murder." Here was the classic example of "waving the bloody shirt"— of stirring up old war hatreds for partisan purposes. Southern congressmen responded heatedly in defense of Davis. Blaine thus succeeded in identifying the Democratic party anew with disloyalty and rebellion and in thereby diverting attention from the scandals of the Republican Administration. His strategy almost won him the Republican nomination and the presidency.

On the eve of the nominating convention, however, a congressional investigating committee suddenly produced a witness named James Mulligan, who said he had evidence that Blaine, while Speaker of the House, had improperly received $64,000 for granting favors to a railroad company. Boldly seizing the "Mulligan Letters," which contained the alleged evidence, Blaine quoted selectively from them and claimed that he had cleared his name of the charges. In the ensuing convention, however, the Mulligan affair and the disfavor of President Grant and the Stalwarts finally eliminated Blaine from the race.

The Republicans nominated Rutherford B. Hayes, a comparatively obscure figure from the strategically important state of Ohio. Three times governor of his state, Hayes had a creditable war record, an unblemished reputation, and an association with mild civil-service reform. In short, he was the ideal nominee for a party bedeviled by smirched reputations and beset by scandal. Of Whig antecedents and puritanical conscience, Hayes was conservative in his economic and financial views, conciliatory toward Southern whites, and philanthropic toward the freedmen. To balance the ticket, the Republicans chose Congressman William A. Wheeler of New York for Vice-President.

Stressing the issue of reform, the Democrats nominated Samuel J. Tilden, governor of New York. Before his election to the governorship in 1874, Tilden had won fame by smashing the notorious ring of Boss Tweed, head of Tammany Hall, and sending Tweed and others to jail; as governor, he had shattered a powerful organization of grafters known as the Canal Ring. Tilden had made a private fortune as a corporation lawyer serving railroads, and his conservative economic views and hard-money doctrines were more pleasing to the business community of the East than they were to the South and the West. Popular enthusiasm for Tilden's candidacy was further limited by his railroad associations, his secretive habits, and his poor health. In order to make up for these drawbacks, the Democrats named for Vice-President Thomas A. Hendricks of Indiana, who had served his state as senator and governor and held soft-money views.

The campaign of 1876 was a struggle of exceptional bitterness and trickery. For the first time in twenty years the Democrats had a reasonable hope of winning a presidential election, and they bore down hard on Republican corruption in high places and misrule in the

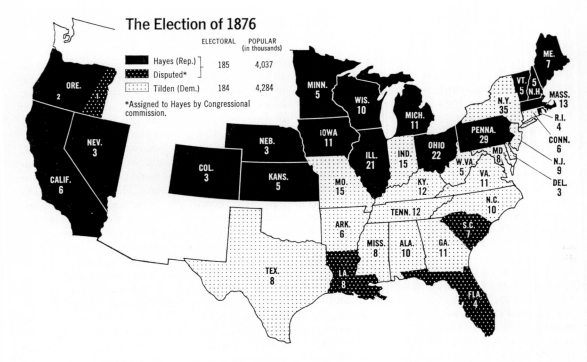

The Election of 1876

		ELECTORAL	POPULAR (in thousands)
■	Hayes (Rep.)	185	4,037
▨	Disputed*		
⋮	Tilden (Dem.)	184	4,284

*Assigned to Hayes by Congressional commission.

South. Their opponents countered with bloody-shirt oratory, charging that the Democrats were sympathetic to the rebels and attacking Tilden's personal integrity. When the returns came in, the Democrats seemed to have carried the day, for the majority of popular ballots were cast for Tilden with a quarter of a million to spare. And while Tilden was conceded 184 electoral votes, only one vote short of the 185 required for election, Hayes was conceded only 165. But nineteen of the twenty contested electoral votes lay in the three Southern states that were still under Republican government—South Carolina, Louisiana, and Florida. The twentieth vote, from the Republican state of Oregon, was claimed by the Democrats on a technicality. Tilden needed only one of the twenty votes to assure his election, while Hayes had to have them all to win a bare majority of one vote. Republican managers promptly claimed all the votes and announced a Hayes victory. Charging that the Democrats had used intimidation and fraud against Negro voters, Republican returning boards in the three Southern states threw out enough Democratic popular votes to give those states to Hayes. Both parties had resorted to

chicanery in the election, but modern scholars hold that Tilden deserved more than enough of the contested votes to win. On December 6 Republican electors met and cast the votes of the three states for Hayes, but on the same day a rival set of Democratic electors cast the votes of the same states solidly for Tilden.

Congress, with a Democratic House and a Republican Senate, now faced the problem of deciding which returns were authentic and which candidate had won. The Constitution was not explicit on who should count the electoral votes and the law was silent. As the weeks passed an ominous deadlock ensued and public anxiety mounted: only sixteen years before, a presidential election had precipitated a civil war, and already there was grave talk of Democratic war veterans organizing for resistance to the seating of Hayes. Probably more people expected a violent outcome in this crisis than in the crisis over Lincoln's election in 1860, but at the same time more people sensed the urgency of finding a peaceful solution.

The Compromise of 1877   Shocked by their predicament, the conservatives of North and South, particularly Northern Republicans and Southern Democrats, got together to devise a peaceful way out of the dilemma. They found they had much in common. Just as the Old Whigs had risen to the top in the new Republican party of the North, so they had gained prominence and power in the old Democratic party of the South. In both sections they were the people of conservatism, property, and compromise, and they had formerly marched together under the banner of the Whig party. Now they found themselves in opposing camps. Hayes's advisers urged him to attract Southern support by promising a new policy. They would have him abandon the carpetbaggers, scalawags, and Radicals and appeal instead to the ex-Whigs and Conservatives of the South for support in the disputed election as well as for recruits of the Republican party. An ex-Whig himself, Hayes fell in readily with their advice.

Hayes and his friends found other means of attracting Southern Conservatives. War had destroyed Southern capital, depression had dried up sources of Northern investment, and carpetbaggers had exhausted the credit of the states. The only source of capital left was the federal treasury, and Southern congressmen were knocking at its doors with hundreds of bills for internal improvements—for controlling floods along the Mississippi, for clearing harbors, river channels, and choked canals, for reconstructing depleted railroads, fallen bridges, broken levees, and public buildings. Southerners had already discovered that Republicans were consistently more sympathetic to such requests than were their fellow Democrats of the North, who lectured them sternly about "Grantism," public morals, and reform. Most powerful of the many lobbies promoting Southern measures was the one supporting the effort of Thomas A. Scott, president of the Pennsylvania Railroad, to get a subsidy of more than $200 million for the Texas and Pacific Railroad. General Grenville M. Dodge, the most astute railroad lobbyist of the Grant Era, organized the forces behind the Scott bill. Persuaded by intermediaries that Hayes as President would be friendly to the Texas and Pacific, Scott added his powerful influence to that of others seeking to win Southern support for Hayes in the electoral crisis.

In the meantime all the arts of compromise, neglected since 1861, were revived. Congress referred the disputed returns to an electoral commission created for the purpose, consisting of fifteen members drawn in equal numbers from the Senate, the House, and the Supreme Court. Seven were Republicans, seven were Democrats, and one, Justice David Davis, was an independent. At the last moment, however, Justice Davis was elected to the Senate from Illinois and his place on the commission was filled by a loyal Republican. The commission then decided by a strictly partisan vote of eight Republicans to seven Democrats to accept the Republican returns. Enraged at what they denounced as a "conspiracy" to defraud them of victory, many Democrats refused to abide by the vote of the commission and launched a filibuster that threatened to prevent any election whatever and bring on anarchy.

The deadlock was renewed. The Hayes forces intensified their efforts to win over Southern Democrats, thus enabling the latter to demand a higher price for their support. Not only did Hayes promise to withdraw federal troops from the South and leave the state governments in the control of Conservatives, but he agreed to appoint a Southern Democrat to his Cabinet and permit him to hand out patronage to his friends. The Republican candidate and his spokesmen emphasized that the new Administration would take a conciliatory attitude toward Southern needs and wishes generally, and particularly toward bills for internal improvements.

These Republican concessions and promises undoubtedly helped persuade Southern Democrats to accept the electoral commission's decision for Hayes, and the South's capitulation influenced many Northern Democrats to abandon the filibuster and accept the loss of a prize they were convinced they had rightfully won. Other influences worked toward the same end, including a patriotic urge to avoid anarchy and a yearning to return to traditional ways of peace and compromise. At last Hayes's dubious cause prevailed, and he was declared President only two days before he took office.

The Politics of Reconciliation The crisis of 1877 marked the end of one era and the beginning of another. The closing era had dawned with the martial zeal of troops singing,

Rutherford B. Hayes: President by compromise.

"Let us die to make men free." It had reached a crest of revolutionary fervor in 1868 with the determination, firmly and repeatedly announced, to make men equal as well as free— whatever the cost. By 1877 the revolutionary ardor had burned out, the high resolves and ideals had been forgotten, and many of the crusaders had fallen into disgrace. Men of this new era talked of peace at any price, of the need for order, conciliation, and getting on with business. They dismissed high ideals as impractical, used "politics" as a term of opprobrium, and insisted that "business" was the proper concern of the serious-minded.

President Hayes, perfectly sincere in his role as the man of conciliation and faithful to his promises to the South, appointed a Democrat, ex-Confederate General David M. Key, of Tennessee, to his Cabinet. After a few weeks of awkward hesitation Hayes withdrew the federal troops from South Carolina and Louisiana, and the last two carpetbagger governments promptly collapsed, never to be restored. All the Southern states and border states as well were now under Conservative control. In his courtship of the South's ex-Whig Democrats, Hayes appointed many of them to federal offices even though it meant turning down Republican applicants. The Texas and Pacific bill failed in spite of repeated endorsements by the President, but other bills for internal improvements in the South were enacted. Admirers cheered Hayes with the rebel yell during his three visits to the South—the first any President had paid since Lincoln viewed the ruins of Richmond.

Hayes's policy of conciliation pleased Southern Conservatives and eased somewhat the old tensions between North and South. But certain results of that policy disappointed the President. For one thing the ex-Whig Democrats of the South did not rally in numbers to the Republican standard as he had hoped they would. A ground swell of agrarian discontent and radicalism below the Potomac made it difficult for conservative Democratic leaders there to continue their cooperation with business-minded Republicans. Finally, congressmen of Hayes's own party resisted his policy of appeasing the South and appointing Democrats to office. And so the Republicans returned to the practice of bloody-shirt oratory and to charges of Southern disloyalty. Only a few Republicans seemed disturbed by their party's desertion of the carpetbaggers and the freedmen, its repudiation of the goals of Reconstruction policy, and its abandonment of the goal of equality.

Subordination of the Freedmen

The Abandonment of Equality The Radicals, so long as they had the power and so long as the country was in a responsive mood, had made equality for the freedman almost as much a war aim as freedom for the slave. By constitutional amendment and by detailed and explicit statutes, the United States was firmly committed to the principle of equal civil and political rights and to the use of federal power to guarantee them. Yet after Reconstruction the country quickly broke this commitment and virtually forgot about it for two generations. That the North was as remiss as the South was indicated by the conduct of federal troops in the South, the army's treatment of Negro soldiers, the policies of labor unions, and the discriminatory laws of Northern cities and states. Furthermore, the

Radical promise of equality was an embarrassment to Hayes's effort to reconcile the estranged South and to put aside bitter war memories.

In short, the white people of the North and South were reconciled at the expense of the Negroes. When Hayes visited Atlanta in the fall of 1877, he told the freedmen that their "rights and interests would be safer" if Southern whites were "let alone by the general government." This sentiment was greeted with "immense enthusiasm"—by the whites. "Let alone" became the watchword of government policy in race relations as well as in industrial and business affairs. Former champions of the freedmen in the North took up the new slogan and dropped their concern for the rights of the Negro. The *Nation* declared that the federal government should have "nothing more to do with him," and doubted that he could ever "be worked into a system of government for which you and I would have much respect."

The plea for reconciliation, the let-alone philosophy, and the prevailing disillusionment with high ideals and promises also had their effect on the Supreme Court. In a long series of decisions the Court underwrote white supremacy, state rights, and laissez faire and virtually nullified the Fourteenth and Fifteenth Amendments insofar as they applied to the rights of freedmen. In 1876 Chief Justice Morrison R. Waite, in *United States* v. *Cruikshank*, decided that the Fourteenth Amendment "adds nothing to the rights of one citizen as against another" and does not extend federal protection to other rights except when they are infringed by a state. Applying the same interpretation in the *Civil Rights Cases* of 1883, the Court pronounced the Civil Rights Act of 1875 unconstitutional. This act had provided that all persons, regardless of race, were entitled to "the full and equal enjoyment" of all public facilities such as inns and railroads, as well as theaters and other places of amusement. In holding that the Fourteenth Amendment was a prohibition against states only, the Court said in effect that the federal government could not lawfully protect Negroes against discrimination by private individuals. The Court joined the President in adhering to laissez faire.

Now, with the official approval of the federal courts, the acquiescence of many Northern liberals and Radicals, and the cooperation of the Republican party, the Negroes were subordinated to an inferior grade of citizenship. Their freedom was not seriously challenged, but their equality most certainly was. There was little they could do about it. Even Frederick Douglass, once the militant leader of the Negroes, accepted office under Hayes's administration, and so did Carl Schurz, one of their most outspoken white liberal friends. The high hopes and fine promises of earlier days were shattered.

The Road to Segregation   The freedmen were not yet wholly abandoned to their worst enemies nor entirely without friends of a kind. Harder times were to come, but meanwhile they fell under the paternalistic regime of the Southern Conservatives. These men were not insincere in their public pledge to protect the freedman in his rights—as they conceived those rights. They thought of the Negro as a subordinate and an inferior, but as having rights appropriate to his lower status. They were not fanatical racists bent on humiliating and ostracizing the Negro, as were the men who were to gain control of race relations in the future. The Conservatives considered themselves representatives of a superior race, but believed they had obligations as well as privileges. Among the obligations (not always honored, it is true) was a paternalistic responsibility for the underprivileged freedmen.

Deserted by their Northern friends and neglected by the federal government, the Negroes not unnaturally turned to the Southern Conservatives. They did this not out of love for their old masters, but out of a real need for protection against their enemies. They had nowhere else to turn. For their part, the Conservatives partially tamed the anti-Negro passions they had helped to arouse in overthrowing the carpetbaggers. In politics they sometimes used Negro votes against agrarian whites who were antagonized by the Whiggish, pro-business policies of the Conservative governments. Such prominent Conservative leaders as Wade Hampton of South Carolina, L. Q. C. Lamar of Mississippi, and Alexander H. Stephens of Georgia spoke out in favor of the freedmen's right to vote and invited their support. Although the Negroes were often coerced, intimidated, or defrauded, they nevertheless continued to vote in large numbers in many parts of the South for two decades after Reconstruction. What is more, they continued to hold minor offices and to keep at least one Negro congressman in Washington (in all but one term) until after the end of the century. To attract Negro support to the Democratic party, Governor Hampton of South Carolina appointed eighty-six Negroes to office during his Administration, and Governor Francis R. T. Nicholls of Louisiana also gave minor offices and political favors to Negroes. A common device was the "fusion principle," by which the Conservatives helped the Negro against the white wing of the Republican party in return for Negro assistance in the Conservatives' struggle against discontented whites of their own party. By this means the Conservatives strengthened their control over the Democratic party and kept the Republican party divided along racial lines within the South.

For a time the Conservatives restrained extremists who advocated systematic disfranchisement and rigid segregation of the Negroes. The idea of racial inferiority had struck roots long before the war, but segregation in its modern form was incompatible with slavery and unknown to the system. After the Civil War, the Negroes withdrew from the white-dominated churches to found their own. Except in a few brief experiments, the Radicals did not mix the races in the public schools of the South. In transportation and other public services, however, the races continued to mingle for two or more decades to an extent that would be unthinkable to a later era of Jim Crow.

The Conservatives themselves were partly to blame for opening the way to segregation and disfranchisement. In order to defeat the Populists, a radical movement of the early nineties that sought Negro support (see p. 482), they once again lifted the cry of white supremacy as they had in their struggle to overthrow the carpetbaggers. But this time they could not tame the passions they aroused, and the extremists took over. By 1900 all the Southern states had Jim Crow railroad cars; three required or authorized segregation in railway stations; and one had Jim Crow street cars. Eventually the harsh rule of segregation spread to public parks and buildings, sports and recreations, on through hospitals and prisons, and finally to cemeteries. Little protest came from the North, where the Negro also suffered increasing discrimination. And in 1896 the Supreme Court sanctioned segregation in "separate but equal" facilities as constitutional in the case of *Plessy* v. *Ferguson*.

Two years later, in 1898, the Supreme Court took another step toward laissez faire in the case of *Williams* v. *Mississippi* by approving a Mississippi scheme for depriving the Negro of the ballot. This plan, which had been adopted in 1890, combined the poll tax, the literacy test, and residence requirements to reduce the number of Negro voters to a handful. South Carolina followed suit in 1895, and the rest of the Southern states during the next twelve years.

Each state added minor variations to the Mississippi plan, but everywhere the result was the same. As the Negro disappeared from the polls, he also dropped out of the minor offices and public services on which he had managed to retain some hold. The last Negro congressman from the South left Washington in 1901.

By the end of the century, the great laissez-faire reaction had virtually undone the work of Reconstruction. The constitutional amendments guaranteeing equality before the law and at the ballot box had been practically nullified, and life itself was jeopardized by the spread of lynching. This crime reached its peak between 1889 and 1899, when an average of 187 lynchings a year occurred in the United States as a whole. Eighty-two per cent of the lynchings took place in the South, and the

Booker T. Washington: Spokesman of the Atlanta Compromise.

There is a New South, not through protest against the Old, but because of new conditions, new adjustments, and, if you please, new ideas and aspirations.... As ruin was never before so overwhelming, never was restoration swifter. The soldier stepped from the trenches into the furrow; horses that had charged Federal guns marched before the plow....

But what is the sum of our work? We have found out that in the summing up the free negro counts more than he did as a slave. We have planted the schoolhouse on the hilltop and made it free to white and black....

The South found her jewel in the toad's head of defeat.... The Old South rested everything on slavery and agriculture, unconscious that these could neither give nor maintain healthy growth. The New South presents a perfect democracy, the oligarchs leading in the popular movement: a social system compact and closely knitted, less splendid on the surface, but stronger at the core; a hundred farms for every plantation, fifty homes for every palace; and a diversified industry that meets the complex need of this complex age.

From Henry Grady, *The New South,* 1886.

---

great majority of the victims were Negroes.

The Atlanta Compromise   Freedom had not emancipated the Negroes from labor in the cotton field, for they continued to till the white man's land. At the end of the century a little more than 75 per cent of the Negro farmers in the South were croppers or tenants. Handicapped by prevailing agricultural depression and by their heritage of oppression, they contrived to live little better than they had under slavery. The exodus of the Negro to the North did not begin for more than a half-century after emancipation, but many freedmen did move into the towns of the South. There they went into the trades and crafts and shortly after the war were said to have outnumbered white artisans five to one. Employers increasingly discriminated against the colored workers, often at the insistence of all-white trade unions, which kept up a constant pressure to drive Negroes out of the better-paid, more attractive work and confine them to "Negro jobs." Gradually, Negroes disappeared from some skilled trades they had traditionally monopolized and were excluded almost entirely

from certain of the newer industries, such as textiles. Generally barred from labor unions, Negro workers were sometimes used as strikebreakers, thereby earning additional ill will from the unions.

By the 1880's the freedmen had become stratified into social and economic classes. The new Negro middle class, consisting largely of professional people and businessmen, was proportionately smaller and commanded far less wealth and power than the corresponding class of white people. Within the Negro society, however, its dominance was quite as strong. The Negro middle class, which reflected many of the attitudes, assumptions, and aspirations of the white middle class, found full expression in Booker T. Washington, the foremost leader of his race in the generation following Reconstruction.

Washington became head of an industrial school for Negroes at Tuskegee, Alabama, in 1881, but soon attained influence and power that far transcended this modest post and contrasted strikingly with his habitual attitude of humility. The foremost spokesman for his own

Our greatest danger is that, in the great leap from slavery to freedom, we may overlook the fact that the masses of us are to live by the productions of our hands; and fail to keep in mind that we shall prosper in proportion as we learn to dignify and glorify common labor, and put brains and skill into the common occupations of life.... It is at the bottom of life we must begin, and not at the top....

The wisest among my race understand that the agitation of questions of social equality is the extremest folly, and that progress in the enjoyment of all the privileges that will come to us must be the result of severe and constant struggle rather than of artificial forcing. No race that has anything to contribute to the markets of the world is long in any degree ostracized. It is important and right that all privileges of the law be ours, but it is vastly more important that we be prepared for the exercise of these privileges. The opportunity to earn a dollar in a factory just now is worth infinitely more than the opportunity to spend a dollar in an opera house.

From Booker T. Washington, *The Race Problem,* 1895.

---

race, he was also a leader of white opinion on racial policy and a powerful influence in shaping national philanthropic and educational policies. He believed that education for the Negro in that era should stress industrial training rather than intellectual development. In a famous speech delivered in Atlanta in 1895 Washington set forth a philosophy of race relations that came to be known as the Atlanta Compromise.

Washington's compromise in race relations received the support of Southern whites, Northern whites, and many Negroes. He conciliated the white South by abandoning the militant Reconstruction demand for equality, emphasizing economic opportunities instead of political rights, and identifying himself and his race with the industrial order established by the Conservatives. In the North, Washington sought friends for his race not among the agitators and idealists, but among the very wealthy industrialists, men able to establish rich philanthropic endowments and employ large numbers of unorganized and unskilled colored workers. To his own race he preached patience, Conservatism, and the primacy of material progress. Hard work, industrious habits, and the friendship of upper-class whites of the South and the North, he told them, offered more hope than protest and agitation. This submissive and compliant doctrine, widely accepted at the time, was rejected as "Uncle Tomism" by a later generation. It is only fair to Washington, however, to remember that he never spoke of his ultimate hopes for his race and to realize that in this period of reaction he could have accomplished little more than he did.

Politics in the New South

The Redeemers The new rulers of the South, claiming that they had "redeemed" their section from the carpetbaggers, spoke of themselves as the Redeemers. We have already seen that ex-Whigs played a prominent part in this redemption and in the reconstituted Democratic party. It was partly out of regard for their feelings, in fact, that the Democratic party was often called the Conservative party in the South. It deserved that name, for the

Old Whigs had brought their philosophy with them into their new party.

With some exceptions the Redeemers were businessmen or industrialists rather than planters. Only in Tennessee, Kentucky, and Georgia did the old planter element make a bid for power, but they were unsuccessful in each case. Mississippi, one-time principality of planter statesmen, was in the hands of five corporation lawyers, two of whom held the governorship for two decades and three of whom shared the state's Senate seats throughout the eighties. Redeemed Georgia was ruled by a triumvirate who speculated in railroads, coal and iron mining, and textiles. Virginia, still a countryman's state, was governed by city men for the benefit of bankers, bondholders, and railroad operators. In Tennessee the leader of the Redeemers was also general counsel of the Tennessee Coal and Iron Company; the first Redeemer governor of the state was president of the company, and his two successors were directors and officials. All were former Whigs and all were industrialists. Similarly, the Redeemers of Alabama were closely associated with the Louisville and Nashville Railroad, which helped put the new regime in power and won many favors in return. The Louisiana Lottery Company, originally chartered by the carpetbaggers and politically allied with them, turned against its former friends and helped the Redeemers seize power in 1877. The new rulers in return wrote a guarantee of the Lottery monopoly into the state constitution and protected its interests in other ways.

Although the Redeemers were often called "Bourbons," they did not really represent the restoration of the old order or cling to its values. They represented instead a new phase of the revolution that had been touched off in the South by the overthrow of the Confederacy, and in that revolution they played a more important and lasting role than the carpetbaggers and the scalawags, who have received far more attention. The Cotton Kingdom of slavery and the Radical regime of equalitarianism proved short and ephemeral compared with the new order of race relations, economic institutions, and politics established by the Redeemers.

The New Regime The new state constitutions framed by the Redeemers embodied a strong reaction against the government interference so characteristic of Reconstruction. They revealed suspicion and distrust of legislatures and placed such hampering restrictions upon government that positive action of any sort became difficult. The constitutions were, above all, laissez-faire documents. The new Southern governments also reacted against Reconstruction through their policy of "retrenchment," which meant cutting taxes and starving or eliminating tax-supported public services. The chief beneficiaries of the tax policy were the railroads, the utilities, and the factories whose burdens were lightened, and the chief victims were the public schools. The schools, which bore the stigma of carpetbagger support, were gravely crippled by the pinch of Redeemer retrenchment as well as by general poverty and depression. The Redeemers also cut appropriations for other public institutions, but none so drastically as those for prisons. The state governments actually turned prisoners into a source of revenue by leasing them as cheap labor to industrialists with the right political connections. The convict lease system, often marked by brutal exploitation, became one of the ugliest blots on the reputation of the new regime.

This was an era of corrupt government and lax public morals across the country, and it would be unfair to single out the Redeemers for special censure. They invited such censure, however, by the attack they made on graft and corruption in their campaigns to overthrow the carpetbaggers. Faced with no effective party of opposition, protected by long tenure of office, and consequently immune from criticism and exposure, the Redeemers fell into a laxity that eventually covered some of the state governments with disgrace. In the eighties one scandal after another came to light. Some were exposed only by the absconding of state treasurers, nine of whom were guilty of defalcation or embezzlement, and one of whom defrauded Louisiana of more than a million dollars. Such losses, as an Alabamian said, made a mockery of "niggardly economy in public expenditure."

In national affairs the Redeemers revealed their Whiggish heritage by lining up with conservative Northerners on questions of currency, banks, and internal improvements. In so doing they reversed the sectional diplomacy of Southern Democrats, who traditionally allied themselves with the West, and tied the South instead to the policies of the conservative wing of the party centered in the Northeast. To overcome the unpopularity of this shift in alignment, the Redeemers hushed the discussion of economic issues, stressed issues of race and tradition, and insisted on "white solidarity."

Stirrings of Revolt The "Solid South" won its name prematurely. Hardly had "home rule" been restored when revolt began to stir against the Redeemer regime. Once the pressure of occupation was removed, ancient class, party, and sectional antagonisms within the South began to reassert themselves, and local parties calling themselves Independents, or Greenbackers, or Readjusters organized for action. Poorly led, they were often cheated at elections and won only limited success, but they provide a clue to what was seething beneath the surface solidarity of Southern politics.

Many of the issues that prompted revolt against the Redeemer regime were profoundly felt. One source of unrest was resentment over the way the Conservatives used the Negro vote in the 1870's and 1880's to win political advantage over discontented whites. Upcountry whites in particular resented the huge political power of the white minority in the black belt, the power the carpetbaggers had derived from the same source and had used to the same end. Since the majority of Independents and other third-party men were small farmers, they found the Whiggish policies of the Redeemers little to their liking, particularly the pampering of railroads and corporations. Independents found further cause for resentment in the high-handed rule, the election chicanery, and the treasury scandals that became characteristic of Conservative rule. On national issues they usually sided with Western agrarians in support of soft money, greenbacks, and silver, and therefore rejected the Redeemers' alliance with the Northeast.

But the most disruptive issue of all was the "readjustment," or repudiation, of state debts. So disruptive was it, in fact, that it unseated the Redeemers in some states and threatened the security of the whole regime. By the end of Reconstruction, the Southern states had incurred a total debt of about $275 million, and in nine states there was talk of scaling the debts down or partially repudiating them. In one way or another these nine states contrived to reduce their total liabilities by $150 million. Naturally the states' creditors and bondholders protested bitterly, and in each state a faction of Redeemers fought the debt readjusters. In Tennessee the fight brought the Republicans back to power, and in Virginia it led to the triumph of a third party calling itself the Readjusters.

The advocates of repudiation argued that much of the debt was a heritage from carpetbagger looting, that the states themselves had derived little benefit from the sale of Reconstruction bonds, and that in any event the section was too impoverished and ravaged to carry the burden of Reconstruction debts. Those who argued that the debt must be repaid—the so-called funders—retorted that the honor of the states was worth any sacrifice. Virginia funders virtually closed the public schools by diverting school funds to bondholders. They starved out other public services and at last provoked their people to rebellion. The Readjusters took charge of the state in 1880, readjusted the debt, and passed a flood of liberal reform measures. The new party, however, quickly fell under the dictatorial control of William Mahone, who was a former Confederate general and subsequently a railroad executive. As soon as the Readjusters elected Mahone to the United States Senate he shifted his allegiance to the Republican party.

Encouraged by the revolt against the Conservative Democrats, the Republicans began to dream of returning to power in the South through an alliance with the local third parties. Even though the Republicans had little in common with these parties save their opposition to Democrats, they put aside President Hayes's commitment to the Southern Conservatives and threw their support to the reformers and debt repudiators. "Anything to beat the Bourbons," was the Republican policy. The Conservatives responded by reviving the tactics of fraud and intimidation once used against the carpetbaggers and employing them so effectively that by 1883 they had beaten all but the last spark out of the Independent revolt and shattered Republican hopes of exploiting it. Not for a decade was there to be further talk of insurgency in the South. This was the real period of the Solid South, of exclusively one-party politics, and of the most complete political torpor that ever settled over the region. It was not to be broken until the Populist revolt of 1892.

The Doctrine of the New South   There had long been advocates of industrialism in the South, but before the Civil War they had looked on factories as a means of buttressing the existing social order. Propagandists of the New South, by contrast, sought to replace the old order with an economy like that of the North, a business civilization of cities, factories, and trade, with new values and new aims. This was what the "New South" meant to its champions in the 1880's. "As for Charleston," declared an editor from that city in 1882, "the importation of about five hundred Yankees of the right stripe would put a new face on affairs, and make the whole place throb with life and vivid force."

Propaganda for the New South point of view found full voice during the 1880's and 1890's in such journals as the Baltimore *Manufacturers' Record*, the Louisville *Courier-Journal*, and the Charleston *News and Courier*. But more famous and effective was the Atlanta *Constitution*, edited by the orator Henry W. Grady. Full of the bustle and salesmanship of business enterprise, Grady exuded optimism and good will. In an address on "The New South" delivered in 1886 to the New England Society of New York he proclaimed:

> We have sowed towns and cities in the place of theories and put business above politics. We have challenged your spinners in Massachusetts and your iron-makers in Pennsylvania. . . . We have fallen in love with work. . . . We have let economy take root and spread among us as rank as the crab grass which sprung from Sherman's cavalry camps, until we are ready to lay odds on the Georgia Yankee, as he manufactures relics of the battlefield in a one-story shanty and squeezes pure olive oil out of his cotton seed, against any Down-easter that ever swapped wooden nutmegs for flannel sausages in the valleys of Vermont.

As models for young Southerners, Grady held up the hustler, the self-made man, the millionaire. What Grady and his friends were preaching was laissez-faire capitalism freed of restraints, a new industrial way of life, and a businessman's scale of values.

One sign of the popularity of the New South

doctrine was the Southerner's eagerness for Northern approval. "Beyond all question," declared a Richmond journal, "we have been on the wrong track and should take a new departure." And Henry Watterson, a Louisville editor and orator, thought that "the ambition of the South is to out-Yankee the Yankee." But the appeal of the New South doctrine would have been less compelling had it not been embellished by sentimental tribute to the past: a heritage "never to be equalled in its chivalric strength and grace," as Grady put it. The invention of a legendary Old South and the cult of the "lost cause" revealed the curiously divided mind and the conflicting impulses of the Southern people in the new era. They marched hopefully in one direction and looked back longingly in the other.

The inner tensions of the Southern mind were reflected in the career of the Georgia writer Joel Chandler Harris, author of *Uncle Remus* (1881). A gentle, rather wistful man of humble origins, Harris portrayed the old slave in quaint dialect with humor and affection, casting a spell of charm over memories of the ante-bellum plantation. But while he was writing his nostalgic stories about the Old South, Harris was also chief editorial writer for Grady's Atlanta *Constitution*, doing his daily best to encourage the growth of the New South of business and industry. Both the admirers of the old order and the propagandists of the new advocated sectional "reconciliation," urging that the North abandon its reformist aims and accept the new order in the South. In political terms reconciliation was simply an alliance between conservatives of both regions.

The Colonial Economy

The Agrarian Pattern   The dream and design of the new men of the South was to build an urbanized, industrialized society like that of the Yankees. But the habits and economic re-

Cotton-pickers in Virginia: Survival of the ante-bellum economy.

alities of the Old South were slow to change and hard to shake off. For all the factories that were constructed, 96.1 per cent of the North Carolinians and 94.1 per cent of the Alabamians were still not classified "urban" by the census of 1890. Only 8.5 per cent of the population of the South Atlantic states below Maryland was urban in 1890, as compared with 51.7 per cent of the population of the North Atlantic states from Pennsylvania up. By 1900 the urban population of those Northern states had further increased by nearly 7 per cent, that of the Southern states by only 1 per cent. The New South was still the most overwhelmingly rural and agrarian section of the country.

On the surface it would seem that deep changes had occurred in the distribution of land ownership in the South. The census of 1880 reported an amazing increase in the number of farms since 1860, and the average farm turned out to be less than half its former size. Optimists concluded that the Civil War had broken up the concentration of land in the hands of planters and had brought about "economic democracy." The truth was, however, that the old plantation lands had been parceled out in small plots among sharecroppers, each plot counting as a new "farm," and that large tracts of new land had been brought under cultivation. The sharecropper had replaced the slave, and his share of the crop depended largely on what the landlord furnished in the way of tools, work animals, and feed.

Ownership of the plantations had slipped from the old planters into the hands of merchants or other townsmen. Moreover, whatever efficiency and planning, whatever virtues of proprietorship, had resided in the old plantation system were largely missing from the sharecropper system. The old evils of land monopoly, absentee ownership, soil mining, and the one-crop system were not only retained but intensified. From a strictly economic point of view, cropping was probably as bad for the agriculture of the region as slavery had been.

The most desperate need of the Southern farmer after the war was credit. With no cash in hand, and no banks from which to borrow it, the farmer was at the mercy of merchants who were willing to advance supplies in return for a mortgage or "lien" on his future crop. The

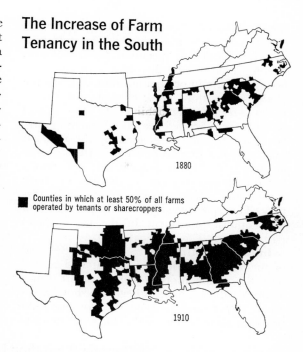

The Increase of Farm Tenancy in the South

1880

■ Counties in which at least 50% of all farms operated by tenants or sharecroppers

1910

farmer pledged an unplanted crop for a loan of unstipulated amount at an undesignated rate of interest. The amount of security fluctuated with the prospects of the harvest, the amount of credit with the hopes of the merchant, the amount of interest with the price of the goods. The lien system was a strange and deplorable makeshift. Once a lien was executed to a merchant, the farmer was bound to him until the debt had been repaid. Since the farmer was forced to part with his crop when prices were lowest, it is no wonder that many farmers failed to "pay out" at the end of the year. Trapped by the system, a man might continue year after oppressive year as a sort of peon, under lien to the same merchant and under the merchant's constant oversight. The lien system, in turn, fostered the stubborn persistence of the one-crop system; for the merchant would advance credit only against such cash crops as cotton or tobacco. The one-crop system was more characteristic of the new agricultural order than it had ever been of the old, and more and more the South had to turn to other sections for supplies it might have grown itself.

During the last quarter of the nineteenth century farmers were plagued by low prices and chronic depression the country over. The

Southern farmer shared these ills with farmers elsewhere, but he also suffered from a combination of burdens peculiar to the South. Among these was the heritage of military defeat, pillage, and occupation that had cost the section every third horse or mule and nearly half its agricultural machinery. On top of these burdens were heaped the ills of sharecropping peonage and the lien system. By the 1890's a spirit of grim desperation had settled on the farmers of the South, a spirit that long manifested itself in a suspicion of city folk and their ways and a resentment of wealth and its display. This spirit was to enter into the soul of the Populist movement in the years ahead (see p. 481).

Industrial Stirrings   Toward the end of the 1870's the depression that had settled over the nation in 1873 started to lift. Once again Northern investors began to show interest in opportunities below the Potomac and freed the springs of capital. The propagandists

of the New South boasted that the South, like the West, was an empire ripe for exploiting. "The way to clear and large profits is open," announced a Philadelphia editor in 1877. A book appeared in 1888 on *How to Get Rich in the South* and another in 1894 describing the South as *The Road to Wealth*. The Redeemers welcomed investors with open arms, tax exemptions, and promises of cheap and docile labor.

With the willing cooperation of Southern legislatures, speculators rounded up huge grants of public lands and mineral resources. Florida granted several million more acres than were in her public domain, and Texas surrendered an area larger than the state of Indiana. In 1877 the law reserving federal lands in five Southern states for homesteaders was scrapped and the rich Southern empire of timber, coal, and iron was thrown open to unrestricted exploitation. In the next decade nearly six million acres of federal lands were sold, most of them to Northern speculators,

A Georgia Plantation in 1860 and 1881

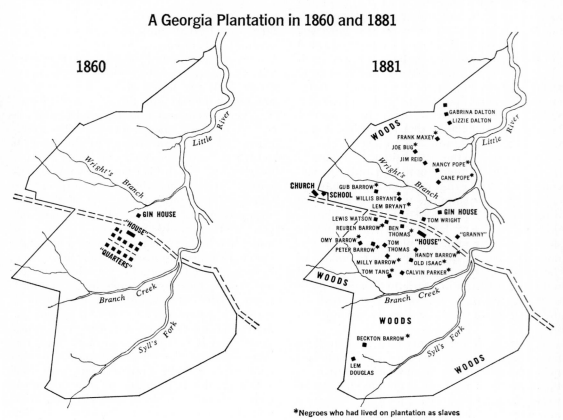

*Negroes who had lived on plantation as slaves

The Growth of the Railroad Network in the South

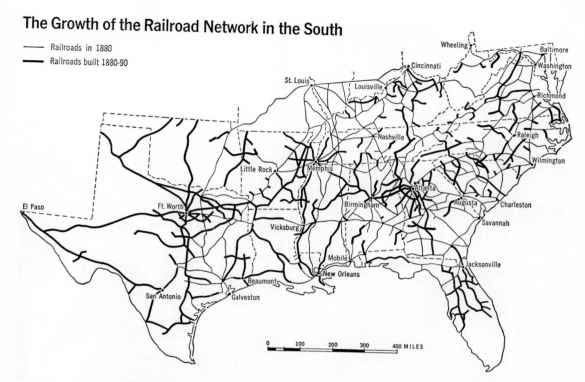

—— Railroads in 1880
—— Railroads built 1880-90

who indulged in a reckless destruction of forests and a rifling of other resources.

Exploitation of this sort, as well as more laudable schemes of industrial development, would have been impossible without dramatic improvements in transportation. Between 1880 and 1890 railroad mileage in the South as a whole increased from 16,605 miles to 39,108, a growth of 135.5 per cent, 50 per cent greater than the national rate of growth in mileage in the same period. Railroad development exposed to exploitation the landlocked mineral resources of the South, particularly the iron mines of Tennessee, Virginia, and Alabama. Between 1876 and 1901 pig-iron production increased seventeen times in the South, as compared with an eightfold increase in the country at large. Alabama, with its un-rivaled deposits of iron ore, coal, and limestone in unique proximity, quickly outstripped its Southern competitors, and by 1898 Birming-ham was the largest shipping point for pig iron in the country and the third largest in the world.

So long as the Southern economy stuck to its traditional role of supplying raw materials of mine, forest, and farm, it met with encourage-ment from Northern bankers and investors. Production of lumber and forestry products soared sensationally, as did the output of such fuels as coal and oil, and such ores as iron, sulphur, bauxite, phosphate rock, and manga-nese. Eastern capital entered each of these enterprises and Eastern control followed. The modern era of oil production, for example, opened with an unprecedented gusher at Spin-dletop, near Beaumont, Texas, in January 1901, and soon the newly opened fields of the Southwest became the province of three nomi-nally competing pipeline and refining com-panies presided over by Standard Oil. The story of the development and control of vast sulphur deposits in Louisiana and bauxite deposits in Arkansas was similar to that of oil in Texas.

The tobacco industry, the oldest in the region, discovered new markets and developed new techniques of manufacture during the new era. Until about 1885 tobacco was processed by the same methods and in the same areas as before the Civil War. But in the next fifteen years the industry was completely revolution-

Steamboats on the Mississippi: Vicksburg wharf in 1883.

ized by changes in consumer tastes, methods of manufacture, and areas of production. Leadership shifted from Virginia to the Carolinas, which grew the bright tobacco that pleased the new cigarette smokers. By 1900 the invention of new machinery and methods had thoroughly mechanized an industry that had once been largely handicraft. At the same time the size of factories increased dramatically and control of the industry became highly concentrated. The genius of concentrated control was a tall, rugged, redheaded North Carolinian named James Buchanan Duke, usually called "Buck," whose rise paralleled that of the industry. He started out in 1865 with two blind mules and a load of tobacco, all the war had left on his father's small farm. "Tobacco is the poor man's luxury," he observed, and on that insight he founded a fortune. By 1889 his firm was producing half the country's cigarettes, and the following year he absorbed his main competitors into the American Tobacco Company.

The true symbol of the New South, however, was the cotton mill, and the zeal of its promoters stirred up a veritable "cotton mill crusade." Actually, the industry was confined largely to the Carolinas, Georgia, and Alabama. Cotton manufacturing began in the Old South and continued to grow through war and Reconstruction, but between 1880 and 1900 the amount of capital invested in the Southern mills increased sevenfold. The mill-building fever infected whole communities. Much of the growth came at the expense of New England, which was unable to compete with the vast Southern supply of unorganized workers accustomed to long hours and low pay. The chief textile products of the South were unfinished goods that were sent north for final processing, and in this, as in the use of cheap labor, the cotton mills were typical of the South's new industries.

The Colonial Status   For all its boasts of industrial progress, the New South lagged far behind the rest of the country. So rapid

The Growth of the Southern Economy

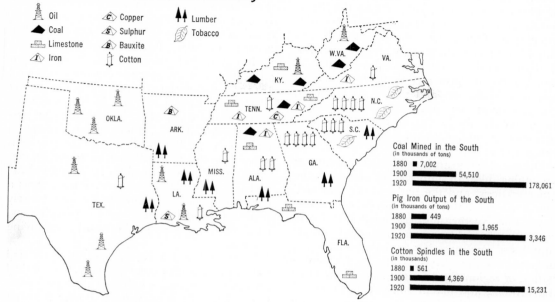

Legend:
- Oil
- Coal
- Limestone
- Iron
- *c* Copper
- *S* Sulphur
- *B* Bauxite
- Cotton
- Lumber
- Tobacco

Coal Mined in the South (in thousands of tons)
1880   7,002
1900   54,510
1920   178,061

Pig Iron Output of the South (in thousands of tons)
1880   449
1900   1,965
1920   3,346

Cotton Spindles in the South (in thousands)
1880   561
1900   4,369
1920   15,231

was the expansion of the North and West that by the end of the century the South had a smaller percentage of the nation's factories and a slightly smaller percentage of the nation's capital than it had in 1860. With few exceptions, the industries that did take root in the South were low-wage industries that gave the first rough processing to the agricultural, forestry, and mining products of the region. Transportation costs made it more economical to do this processing near the source of raw material, and large supplies of cheap, unskilled labor were an even stronger attraction to such industries. Cotton yarn, cottonseed oil, cane sugar, polished rice, fertilizers, liquors, and tobacco, and such forestry products as turpentine, resin, and lumber, constituted the bulk of the South's industrial output. The final processing of these products was usually done in the North, and from the final processing came the greatest profits.

There was no law relegating the South to a raw-material economy, no plot to exclude Southerners from the better-paying jobs and the more profitable industries. What, then, were the reasons for the persistent industrial backwardness of the section? A lost war, a late start, and a lack of capital were some of the reasons. These disadvantages might have been

overcome more readily, however, had it not been for certain artificial barriers: a host of practices and rules adopted to suit the convenience of private interests in the North while the South was out of the Union or later when the section was without significant influence in national decisions.

One of these barriers was the system of regional freight-rate differentials adopted in the seventies and eighties by private railway associations and later given legal sanction by the Interstate Commerce Commission. These differentials meant that shippers of manufactured goods in the South and West were charged far higher rates than shippers in the privileged "Official Territory," north of the Ohio and Potomac and east of the Mississippi. The system discouraged the Southern producer from competing in the richest market area, the Northeast, but enabled the Northeastern producer to penetrate the Southern market. At the same time, favorable "commodity rates" were provided for Southern raw materials. Taken together, these rate differentials discouraged the South from developing manufactures of its own and encouraged it to concentrate on raw materials. A price differential imposed on Birmingham steel by the Pittsburgh steel masters and their allied railroads had a similar effect. "Pittsburgh Plus" meant that buyers of Birmingham steel had to pay the Pittsburgh price *plus* the freight charge from Pittsburgh. Later, the "Birmingham Differential" replaced the freight charge with a straight additional charge of three dollars a ton. This scheme protected the Pittsburgh mills and their customers and prevented Southern manufacturers or potential manufacturers eager to enter the lists against Northern competitors from taking advantage of the decidedly cheaper steel of Birmingham.

During these years the Northeast assumed something like an imperial power over the other sections, and the national economy fell into a neomercantilism reminiscent of colonial days. The Northeast discouraged the rise of competing manufactures, promoted ample supplies of raw materials for its own factories, monopolized the carrying trade by the combination of regionalized freight rates, steel-price differentials, and patent control, and reduced foreign competition in its domestic markets by the protective tariff. In brief, the Northeast became for a long time the workshop of the nation, reserving for its own coffers the profits of processing, transporting, and distributing goods. The South was left to produce the raw materials for the new economic order, to serve as a tributary of industrial power.

Division of labor was, of course, inevitable in a national economy, and the South derived real benefits from its role in the form of increased job opportunities, payrolls, and taxable assets. On the other hand, this subordinate economic status imposed grave penalties on the South. As late as 1910 some 62 per cent of its workers were engaged in the extractive industries—agriculture, forestry, animal husbandry, fishing, mining. Throughout the country, these industries paid the lowest wages of all, and the wages of Southern workers were even lower than the national average. By 1900 the percentage of Southerners employed in manufactures was still about the same as it had been in all the states east of the Mississippi in 1850.

In wealth, living standards, and general welfare the Union was more a "house divided" now than when Lincoln first used the phrase. In 1880 the estimated per capita wealth in the South was $376 as compared with a national average of $870. No Southern state came within $300 of the national average nor within $550 of the average outside the South. In 1900 the national average in per capita wealth stood at $1,165 and in the South the average was $509. The earliest income estimates, those of 1919, indicate that per capita income in the South was about 40 per cent lower than the national average. Little wonder that the region was noted for its "poor whites" and its "poor blacks" as well. Poverty was a characteristic of the regional economy. Closely related to that poverty was a lag in literacy, education, libraries, public health, and living standard.

The South of the New Order was humbled politically as well as economically. Its political abasement, in fact, represents the most striking shift in the geography of power that has ever occurred in American history. In the seventy-two years between Washington and Lincoln, Southerners held the presidency for fifty years and the title of Chief Justice of the Supreme Court for sixty years. They furnished more than half the justices and diplomatic representatives to major powers, nearly half the men of Cabinet rank, and more than half the Speakers of the House of Representatives. During the next half century, by contrast, no Southerner save Johnson served as President or Vice-President, and the South furnished only 14 of the 133 Cabinet members, 7 of the 31 justices of the Supreme Court, 2 of the 12 Speakers of the House, and fewer than one-tenth of the diplomatic representatives to major powers. From the power and glory of the eighteenth and early nineteenth century the South had fallen to a lowly state. In the process of reunion it had lost much of its old distinctiveness, along with much of its power, and had become the frontier of a dynamic new order that was expanding southward as well as westward.

SUGGESTIONS FOR READING F. B. Simkins, *A History of the South* (1953), provides an informative survey of the period that emphasizes the sectional viewpoint, and W. B. Hesseltine and D. L. Smiley, *The South in American History* (1960), stresses national themes in regional history. C. V. Woodward, *Origins of the New South, 1877–1913* (1951), concentrates on the post-Reconstruction period.

An earlier and sketchier survey of the period that neglects agrarian movements is Holland Thompson, *The New South* (1921). W. J. Cash, *The Mind of the South* * (1960), contains original and provocative interpretations of uneven value.

The stresses and strains of sectional adjustment and reconciliation are the subject of P. H. Buck, *The Road to Reunion, 1865–1900* * (1960). C. V. Woodward, *Reunion and Reaction: The Compromise of 1877 and the End of Reconstruction* * (1956), investigates the complex national crisis of 1876–77. For the setting of industrial conflict see R. V. Bruce, *1877: Year of Violence* (1959). The development of President Hayes's policy toward the South is traced in Harry Barnard, *Rutherford B. Hayes and His America* (1954); Republican efforts to revive their party in the South are pictured in V. P. De Santis, *Republicans Face the Southern Question: The New Departure Years, 1877–1897* (1959).

The Negro's struggles after the abandonment of Reconstruction are illuminated in J. H. Franklin, *From Slavery to Freedom: A History of American Negroes* (1956), and in E. F. Frazier, *The Negro in the United States* (1949). Gunnar Myrdal, *An American Dilemma: The Negro Problem and Modern Democracy* (1944), has valuable historical essays on race relations in this period. Older views of the Negro are revised or discredited in V. L. Wharton, *The Negro in Mississippi, 1865–1890* (1947), and G. B. Tindall, *South Carolina Negroes, 1877–1900* (1952). C. V. Woodward, *The Strange Career of Jim Crow* * (1957), traces the origins and rise of segregation; and R. W. Logan, *The Negro in American Life and Thought: The Nadir, 1877–1901* (1954), depicts the deterioration of Reconstruction ideals of racial equality. Two works written in the period itself are especially recommended: Booker T. Washington's autobiography, *Up from Slavery* * (1901), and G. W. Cable, *The Negro Question: A Selection of Writings on Civil Rights in the South,* * ed. by Arlin Turner (1958).

Insight into the politics of the New South is furnished by biographies of popular leaders, such as F. B. Simkins, *Pitchfork Ben Tillman: South Carolinian* (1944); J. F. Wall, *Henry Watterson: Reconstructed Rebel* (1956); C. V. Woodward, *Tom Watson: Agrarian Rebel* (1955); W. A. Cate, *Lucius Q. C. Lamar* (1935); and N. M. Blake, *William Mahone of Virginia: Soldier and Political Insurgent* (1935). C. C. Pearson, *The Readjuster Movement in Virginia* (1917), is the best study of the first breach in the Solid South; and A. D. Kirwan, *Revolt of the Rednecks: Mississippi Politics, 1876–1925* (1951), is a colorful account of poor-white revolts. Paul Lewinson, *Race, Class and Party: A History of Negro Suffrage and White Politics in the South* (1932), shows how the race issue has been exploited. V. O. Key, Jr., *Southern Politics in State and Nation* (1949), treats of twentieth-century politics but sheds a bright light on earlier years.

Industrialization of the South is viewed critically and analytically by H. L. Herring, *Southern Industry and Regional Development* (1940), and from the New South viewpoint by Broadus Mitchell and G. S. Mitchell, *The Industrial Revolution in the South* (1930). N. M. Tilley, *The Bright Tobacco Industry, 1860–1929* (1948), recounts the revolutionary changes that overtook the South's oldest industry in this period. C. C. Rister, *Oil! Titan of the Southwest* (1949), tells of the boom period of a new industry. Broadus Mitchell, *The Rise of Cotton Mills in the South* (1921), stresses the "crusading" aspects of the movement for textile manufacturing. On the freight rate discriminations W. H. Joubert, *Southern Freight Rates in Transition* (1949), is useful. R. B. Nixon, *Henry W. Grady: Spokesman of the New South* (1943), is an able portrayal of the industrial propagandist. The plight of the Southern farmer is investigated in F. A. Shannon, *The Farmer's Last Frontier: Agriculture 1860–1897* (1945).

Southern men of letters have in recent years furnished some of the most profound insights into the life and history of the South. Willard Thorp, who calls the South "the most exotic and exciting region in America," has collected excellent examples in *A Southern Reader* (1955). Of special relevance to this period are some of the works of William Faulkner, foremost of the novelists, particularly *The Hamlet* (1940) and *Go Down, Moses* (1942).

* Available in a paperback edition.

17

The New West: Empire Within a Nation

After the Civil War the American people embarked on the conquest and exploitation of an area greater than all the territory that had been settled since the landing at Jamestown in 1607. Up to this time the settlers of the trans-Mississippi West had occupied only its eastern and western fringes, in one tier of states just beyond the Mississippi and in another tier half a continent beyond along the Pacific Coast. Between these two frontiers, separated by fifteen hundred miles, stretched a vast and fabulous expanse of ocean-like plains, spired and towering mountain ranges, grassy plateaus, painted deserts, and breath-taking canyons. Of all the American wests, this was the one that captured the imagination of the world; this was the image that would be perpetuated in song and story.

Americans had conquered many frontiers in the past, but the new West was different from all the others. Pioneer experience there was less like that of their forefathers in taming the forested "wests" of the East, and more like the imperialistic adventures of nineteenth-century Europeans in Africa and Asia. America was a nation with a built-in empire, an empire disguised as a nation. What Englishmen and western Europeans had to seek "somewhere east of Suez," the Yankee adventurer might find somewhere west of the wide Missouri. The impulse behind this late nineteenth-century quest was more than a desire for private gain. It partook of the strange drive

that was sending western man into all the remote corners of the world to impose his will upon people of color in exotic climates. If in Rudyard Kipling's Mandalay there were no Ten Commandments and the best was like the worst, so it was too in New Orleans in the time of the carpetbaggers, and so it was even more spectacularly in Deadwood Gulch and in a hundred mining towns, cow towns, and trading posts of the Wild West.

Subordination of the Indians

The Great Plains Environment   The steady westward advance of the American frontier ground to a halt in the 1840's and then (except for Utah, p. 268) skipped all the way to the Pacific Coast. What stopped the pioneer in his tracks was the forbidding new environment of the Great Plains. Abnormally dry, almost treeless, and mostly level, the plains had their own peculiar soil, weather, plant life, animal life, and human life. The woodcraft and Indiancraft that had enabled the frontiersman to master the humid, forested East were simply inadequate or useless on the treeless, arid plains, and so were his ax, his plow, his canoe, and his long rifle. And so, for that matter, were some of his laws and institutions. As Walter P. Webb writes: "East of the Mississippi civilization stood on three legs—land, water, and timber; west of the Mississippi not one but two of these legs were withdrawn—

water and timber—and civilization was left on one leg—land. It is small wonder that it toppled over in temporary failure." Major John Wesley Powell, explorer of the region, wrote in 1879: "The physical conditions which exist in that land and which inexorably control the operations of men, are such that the industries of the West are necessarily unlike those of the East and their institutions must be adapted to their industrial wants."

So harsh and uninhabitable did the plains appear that the Easterner wrote them off as wasteland; in American atlases and geographies from 1820 to 1860 this vast stretch of land was labeled simply "The Great American Desert." The dry winds parched the Easterner's throat, cracked his lips, and made his eyes smart. Everything was different. There were chinooks, or warm mountain winds, northers, blizzards, and hailstorms. All but the chinook could bring distress and disaster. Writing of the Texas plains, Colonel Richard I. Dodge warned: "Every bush had its thorn; every animal, reptile, or insect had its horn, tooth, or sting; every male human his revolver; and each was ready to use his weapon of defense on any unfortunate sojourner, on the smallest, or even without the smallest provocation."

The rivers dried up unexpectedly, and when they flowed, their unpalatable water concealed treacherous sands. The slight rainfall, usually under fifteen inches a year, made traditional methods of farming impracticable and demanded a new extensive agriculture to replace the old intensive type. Not for a generation after they reached the edge of the Great Plains did Americans begin to find satisfactory solutions to the problems posed by the new environment—the problems of water and wood, of fences and transportation, of agriculture and cattle-raising.

The animals native to the plains seemed to need little water—the jack rabbit and the prairie dog apparently none at all. The swift and elusive antelopes, coyotes, and wolves depended on speed for safety, and were difficult to bag. The one exception was the most famous, the most numerous, and, for human life, the most important plains animal of all, the buffalo, or American bison. This great, shaggy, lumbering beast, neither swift of gait nor alert to danger, could be overtaken by any good horse and was easy prey to a hunter armed with either bow and arrow or rifle. Though they existed in small numbers far east of the Mississippi in colonial days, the buffaloes found their true home on the Great Plains, from Canada to the Gulf of Mexico. So numerous were they that one authority believed it would be "as easy to count or to estimate the number of leaves in a forest as to calculate the number of buffaloes living at any given time during the history of the species previous to 1870." Estimates of the buffalo population around the end of the Civil War range from twelve million to fifteen million, and a single herd sighted in 1871 was said to contain at least four million.

Once the rebellious South had been put down, Americans turned anew to the conquest of the Great Plains. Here they encountered rebels of a different and even more difficult breed.

The Plains Indians   Of some three hundred thousand Indians left in the United States in 1865, more than two-thirds lived on the Great Plains. The frontiersman called them "wild Indians"—and so they were, in comparison with their sedentary and semi-civilized cousins of the eastern forests. The only mounted Indians the white man ever encountered, they were nomadic and nonagricultural. Above all, they were fierce, skillful, and implacable warriors—"the most effectual barrier," according to Webb, "ever set up by a native American population against European invaders in a temperate zone." Against all comers—Spanish, French, English, and American—they had held their own as masters of the plains for two and a half centuries.

The Spaniards had introduced horses into Mexico in the sixteenth century and the animals had multiplied and spread northward over the plains in wild herds. Before then, the plains Indian had been a miserable, earthbound creature, hard pressed to earn a living and defend himself. The horse revolutionized the life of the tribesmen and brought on the golden era of the plains Indians—an era that had about reached its peak when the Anglo-Americans first encountered them. The horse made the Indians more mobile and hence more nomadic than ever, less agricultural, more warlike, and above all far more effective buffalo hunters. The buffalo was even more in-

The plains Indians: Crow Camp, Montana, 1887.

dispensable to the plains Indians than the horse, for it provided them with food, clothing, shelter, and even fuel. Necessities, luxuries, ornaments, tools, bedding, their very tepees— all were fashioned from the flesh, bone, and hide of the buffalo. The nomadic tribes moved back and forth across the plains with the great herds and organized their life and religion around the hunt. Whatever threatened the buffalo threatened their very existence.

The plains Indians were generally superior in physique to the Indians of other regions. Although their culture varied from that of the peaceful tribes of the pueblos to that of fierce nomadic tribes, all the plains Indians shared the culture of neolithic man, using stone knives, stone scrapers, and bone awls as tools. The warriors carried bows and arrows and four-teen-foot, stone-tipped lances for hunting and warfare. Yet in combat the stone-age man asked no quarter of early industrial man. With his short three-foot bow and a quiver of two-score arrows or more, the Comanche would ride three hundred yards and get off twenty arrows with startling force and accuracy while the Texan was firing one shot and reloading his

long and cumbersome rifle. Even the Colt six-shooter, with which the white man began arming himself in the 1840's, did not entirely overcome the Indian's advantage. As armor he carried a loosely slung shield made of buffalo hide so tough that it could deflect a bullet. The arrows he used against an enemy, unlike those he used in the hunt, were fitted with heads that came off in the wound when the shaft was withdrawn.

The plains Indians lived on horseback, and in case of emergency even used their mounts as food. They could hang by a heel to one side of the horse and discharge arrows under its neck; they could execute intricate cavalry maneuvers controlled by a secret system of communications and signals that was the envy of white military experts.

Until the white man finally crushed the plains Indians, he was conscious of them mainly as warriors, as ruthless and dreaded enemies who held military supremacy in their own country. The Indian's conception of the conduct of war and the treatment of captives differed from that of the white man. "Cruelty is both an amusement and a study," wrote

Colonel Dodge of the plains Indians. "So much pleasure is derived from it, that an Indian is constantly thinking out new devices of torture, and how to prolong to the utmost those already known. His anatomical knowledge of the most sensitive portions of the human frame is wonderfully accurate. . . ." The Indian's reputation for cruelty was probably as much deserved as the white man's reputation for ruthlessness. The military struggle between the two races on the Great Plains was marked by a peculiar ferocity and savagery.

White Supremacy in the West So long as Americans thought of the plains as the "Great American Desert" and as "one big reservation" for the red man, conflict as well as contact between the races was rare. But in the 1850's the situation changed. Mass migrations got under way across the plains to Oregon; miners began to beg for protection; the Kansas and Nebraska Territories were organized; and politicians demanded that the Indians be pushed out to north and south to clear the way for transportation and settlement. In 1851 the federal government adopted a new Indian policy of "concentration," under which the chiefs of the plains tribes were persuaded to restrict their people to areas which the white man solemnly promised he would never violate. Caught between the mining frontier that, as we shall see, was closing in from the west, and an agricultural frontier advancing from the east, the plains Indian was soon to learn what the woods Indian had learned long before: that he could trust none of the white man's promises, however solemn. The red man was further embittered by the behavior of corrupt officials of the Indian Bureau of the Interior Department who defrauded him of his land, cheated him in trade, and sold him liquor, and by the treachery of a reckless breed of beaver trappers, gold prospectors, hunters, and outlaws. Then in 1858 and 1859 the Pike's Peak Gold Rush sent tens of thousands hell-bent for Colorado and trouble, soon to be joined by deserters and draft-dodgers from the Union and Confederate armies.

Indian war broke out in Colorado about the time the Civil War was starting in the East. The immediate provocation was the effort of government officials to force the Arapaho and Cheyenne to abandon all claim to the area

that had been granted them forever only ten years before. Many braves rejected the agreement made by their chiefs and took the war-path. After an intermittent warfare of pillaging, home-burning, and murdering that went on for more than three years, they sued for peace. Chief Black Kettle of the Cheyenne, after being assured of protection, was surprised and trapped by a force led by Colonel John M. Chivington on the night of November 28, 1864. Ignoring Black Kettle's attempts to surrender, the militia shot, knifed, scalped, clubbed, and mutilated the Indians indiscriminately until the ground was littered with men, women, and children. Chief Black Kettle and a few warriors escaped, but before a year had passed the Cheyenne and Arapaho, as well as the Kiowa and Comanche, were compelled to surrender their claims and move on to more restricted areas assigned by the white masters.

Hardly had peace been restored to the Southwest in the fall of 1865 when Indian war broke out in the Northwest. The bloody Sioux War of 1865–67 was brought on by many forces, but it was triggered by the demands of miners who had invaded the Sioux country. In response to their request, the federal government announced its intention to build a road through the foothills of the Big Horn Mountains to connect the mining towns of Bozeman and Virginia City with the East. Such a road would spoil one of the Sioux' favorite hunting grounds, and Chief Red Cloud warned that it would be resisted. Sioux warriors ambushed a party of soldiers under Captain W. J. Fetterman near Fort Phil Kearny in December 1866 and slaughtered all eighty-two members.

The Chivington and Fetterman massacres, together with scores of minor battles and endless shooting scrapes, prompted the federal government to review its Indian policy in 1867. Easterners clashed with Westerners, humanitarian impulses with fire-and-sword military policies, and at last authority over the Indians was split between the Department of the Interior, which would placate them with gifts, annuities, and reservations, and the War Department, which was accustomed to punish with violence. The Westerner's disgust was reflected in a letter signed "Texas" in the Chicago *Tribune:* "Give us Phil Sheridan, and send

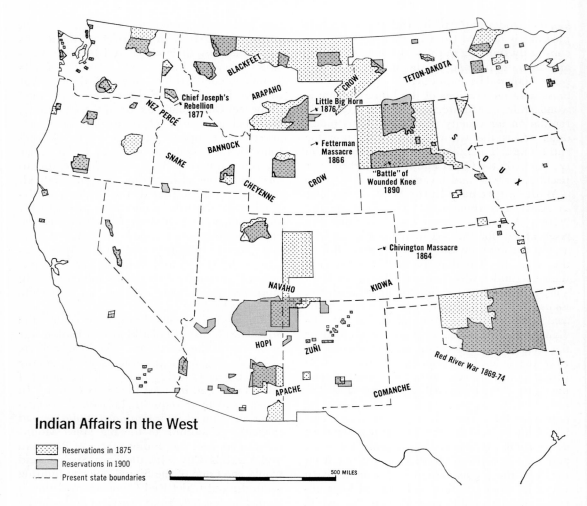

Indian Affairs in the West

Chief Joseph's
Rebellion
1877

NEZ PERCÉ

BLACKFEET

ARAPAHO

SNAKE

BANNOCK

CHEYENNE

CROW

Little Big Horn
1876

CROW

TETON-DAKOTA

S
I
O
U
X

Fetterman
Massacre
1866

"Battle" of
Wounded Knee
1890

Chivington Massacre
1864

NAVAHO

KIOWA

HOPI

ZUÑI

Red River War 1869-74

APACHE

COMANCHE

- Reservations in 1875
- Reservations in 1900
- - - Present state boundaries

0   500 MILES

Phil-anthropy to the devil." It is hard to say at times whether West or South was in fiercer revolt against the Eastern philanthropists. The East prevailed against the West as it had against the South, however, and sent out a Peace Commission of four civilians and three generals in the autumn of 1867 to end the Sioux War and to inaugurate a new policy of "small reservations" to replace the old one of "concentration." The new policy meant that the Indians were to abandon their way of life, submit to segregation in small out-of-the-way reservations on land spurned by the white man, and accept government tutelage in learning "to walk the white man's road." The Black Hills section of the Dakota Territory was to be set aside for the northern tribes. Poor lands in

the western part of what is now Oklahoma, of which the five civilized tribes of the Southeast had just been defrauded on false charges of treason because of their Confederate sympathies, were to be divided among the plains Indians of the Southwest.

The white man's treatment of the red man in these years contrasted strangely with his treatment of the black man. The same Congress that devised Radical Reconstruction to bring equality and integration to the Negro of the South approved strict segregation and inequality for the Indian of the West. General William T. Sherman, the deliverer of the Southern slaves, instructed General Winfield S. Hancock in 1867 that his principal mission to the Cheyenne and Kiowa was to "impress on them the imprudence of assuming an insolent manner and tone when they visit our posts."

But many Indians refused to renounce their way of life and enter meekly into the reservations. When they took the warpath in the summer of 1868, General Sherman unleashed his troopers and launched a decade of remorseless war against them. "I will urge General Sheridan to push his measures for the utter destruction and subjugation of all who are outside [the reservations] in a hostile attitude," Sherman wrote. "I propose that [he] shall prosecute the war with vindictive earnestness against all hostile Indians, till they are obliterated or beg for mercy. . . ." It took more than two hundred battles from 1869 through 1874 to restore peace, and in the Red River War alone fourteen pitched battles were required to beat the Indians of the Southwest into submission.

By the end of 1874 all seemed calm. Then in 1875, when government authorities permitted tens of thousands of gold prospectors to crowd into the Black Hills, the outraged Sioux and other northern Indians reacted violently. At the Battle of the Little Big Horn on June 25, 1876, the rash young General George A. Cus-

ter and 265 men were wiped out in the general's first, and last, stand in the new Sioux War. In spite of this victory, the Indians were compelled to surrender the following fall. Chief Sitting Bull and a few warriors fled to Canada but, facing starvation, they were forced to sue for peace in 1881. Chief Joseph of the Nez Percé Indians of Oregon led a rebellion that was repressed in 1877, and the survivors of this once-proud tribe were herded into a barren preserve in Indian Territory to be ravaged by disease and hunger. The last incident of the Indian wars was the sickening "Battle" of Wounded Knee in 1890, in which United States troops mowed down two hundred Dakota men, women, and children.

Long before the fighting ended, the near extermination of the buffalo herds had ensured the collapse of Indian resistance. At first the indiscriminate shooting of buffalo was motivated by little more than the desire for "sport," or for the diversion of railroad hands and passengers, who might incidentally help to clear the tracks and curb a nuisance. But in 1871, when it was discovered that buffalo pelts and leather could be marketed at a profit, the slaughter was organized on a commercial ba-

Extermination of the buffalo: Hides at Dodge City, 1874.

sis. Now professional hunters and skinners working in teams stepped up the butchery to three million buffalo a year. The advance of the railroads hastened the end of the herds. By 1878 the vast southern herd, the larger of the two main herds, had been wiped out. Five years later, when collectors tried to round up a few specimens of what had recently been the most numerous breed of large animals in the world, only remnants of the northern herd could be found in remote parts of Canada.

The virtual extinction of the buffalo is the classic example of the white man's heedless rapacity in the exploitation of nature; the United States Indian policy is the classic instance of his racial, cultural, and religious bigotry. Reformers and humanitarians won their fight against the policy of physical extermination of the Indian only to substitute their own policy of relentless destruction of Indian society, custom, religion, and tribal unity. This, they were convinced, was necessary if they were to "civilize" the red man, save his soul from "paganism," and integrate him into white civilization. In 1884 the Department of the Interior passed a criminal code forbidding and penalizing Indian religious practices, and in 1887 the Dawes Act struck at tribal authority and organization by breaking up reservation land into small family or individual holdings, with the best of the land usually sold to the whites. All Indians who received grants were to become citizens of the United States.

Thus the oldest residents of the land became the newest citizens. But their government simultaneously deprived them of the basic rights of citizens. Virtually imprisoned and pauperized on the reservations, they were constantly subjected to the withholding of rations—starvation—in an effort to compel them to abandon their tribal customs and loyalties. A government that guaranteed freedom of worship carried its religious persecution of the Indians to the point of espionage and armed violence. The sacred Sun Dance, the supreme expression of tribal unity, was ruthlessly destroyed as "pagan." The notorious corruption of the Indian Bureau and its agents was checked by civil-service reform in the 1880's, but this only meant that the misguided Indian policy was administered more efficiently and destructively than ever before. The real trou-

ble, according to the twentieth-century reformer John Collier, was not corrupt agents but "collective corruption; corruption which did not know it was corrupt, and which reached deep into the intelligence of a nation. It was such a collective corruption that dominated the plains Indian record and nearly the whole Indian record of the United States." Not until the "Indian New Deal" of 1934 was the old policy entirely abandoned for a new one designed to foster tribal culture and unity.

The Era of the Bonanzas

Webb in *The Great Frontier* distinguishes between the "primary windfalls" and the "secondary windfalls" that are gleaned from any frontier. The primary windfalls are the first easy pickings—gold, silver, furs—that are gained with little investment of energy or time. The secondary windfalls require more patience and expense. Usually the primary windfalls are grabbed up early in the game. The Spanish mined the precious metals in their quarter of the New World or seized them from the Indians in the sixteenth and seventeenth centuries, and the French gathered their bales of furs in Canada a little later. Entering the continent north of the gold and south of the furs, the Anglo-Americans were obliged to concentrate on secondary windfalls. Then late in the nineteenth century, after the frontier had become a prosaic matter of timber, corn, and cotton, they belatedly entered upon a fabulous phase of frontier history that for the rest of the world had faded into the mists of legend with the conquistadors and the Spanish treasure ships. The beaver pelts had been gathered, and we have seen what happened to the buffalo. But there remained the bonanzas of gold and silver and the lush grass left by the bison.

The Miner's Bonanza There had been gold rushes from time to time in the East, but from 1804 to 1866 the five-state Appalachian gold field had yielded only $19,375,890. An entirely new scale was set by the California yield of $555 million in a single decade, 1848–58. In the 1860's and 1870's the turbulent gold rush of the forty-niners (see p. 277) was to be repeated with variations time and again in the mountain areas of Nevada, Colorado, Arizona,

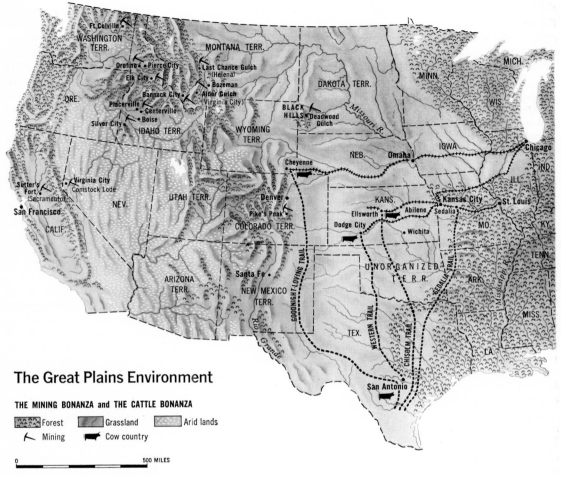

The Great Plains Environment

THE MINING BONANZA and THE CATTLE BONANZA

Forest ◦ Grassland ◦ Arid lands

Mining ◦ Cow country

0   500 MILES

Idaho, Montana, and Wyoming. Since the experienced Californians usually led the invasion of these areas, the mining frontier advanced eastward instead of westward. The Californians also developed the primitive technology of "placer" mining, by which "pay dirt" was washed in pans, "cradles," or sluice boxes. Armed with nothing more than a pick and shovel and a crude pan, the lucky prospector could gather up loose gold that had washed down through debris to bedrock. The richer deposits of gold, usually in deep-lying veins of quartz, could only be mined with machinery that was beyond the means of the prospector and had to await the corporation. It has been estimated that by 1868 placer miners, with their wasteful methods, had lost beyond recovery nearly $300 million in precious metals.

During the sixties placer mining was more and more superseded by quartz mining.

The lure of the bonanza—even the hope of modest pay dirt—was enough to keep thousands of prospectors feverishly exploring gulches and canyons for three decades. Working in groups—the lone prospector is largely mythical—they crisscrossed the vast mountain area in their obsessive quest. Few of them were qualified to interpret the evidence they uncovered, and some of the richest lodes were discovered by chance. Prospectors were entitled by law to one claim by pre-emption and one by discovery; latecomers were entitled to only one claim. The typical claim ran from side to side of a gulch and was one hundred feet wide. Only the exceptional claim really paid off, but the promise of fabulous riches and the wild thrill of discovery seemed reward enough. After the discovery came the inevitable leak of the secret and the headlong scramble by other prospectors to stake a claim. One such rush in 1861 was described by a witness:

> On Friday morning last, when the news of the new diggings had been promulgated, the store of Miner and Arnold was literally besieged. As the news radiated—and it was not long in spreading —picks and shovels were thrown down, claims deserted and turn your eye where you would, you could see droves of people coming in "hot haste" to town, some packing one thing on their backs and some another, all intent on scaling the mountains through frost and snow, and taking up a claim in the new El Dorado. In town there was a perfect jam—a mass of human infatuation, jostling, shoving and elbowing each other.

The prospectors' invasion of the interior was touched off by discoveries in Colorado and Nevada. A party of Southerners bound for California in 1849 had found signs of gold in Colorado, and two of them, John Beck and W. Green Russell, returned with a party of a hundred in 1858 to prospect more thoroughly. During the summer they made a number of small strikes in the vicinity of what was later to become Denver. Rumors of these finds, wildly and perhaps deliberately exaggerated, spread rapidly through the frontier region and started a rush for the Pike's Peak country that fall. During the winter news of the strike spread more widely, and by midsummer the Pike's-Peak-or-Bust rush had started some one hundred thousand people toward the new diggings. A new discovery in May 1859, followed by several smaller ones, had offered some justification for the excitement, but the great majority of fortune-hunters were doomed to disappointment. The dejected horde returning from Pike's Peak symbolized the disillusioned gold rusher of the period. Thousands of the unsuccessful miners, however, stayed on to become settlers and future citizens of Colorado.

In the meantime prospectors had struck it rich on the eastern slope of the Sierras in Nevada opposite the California fields on the western slope. Two Irishmen named Patrick McLaughlin and Peter O'Riley accidentally turned up a vein of bluish rock while digging a water reservoir for their modest placer operation. They were promptly bluffed out of a large share of their find by a loud-mouthed scamp named Henry Comstock, who sold out before he had more than an inkling of the treasure he had acquired: the incredibly rich Comstock Lode, the biggest bonanza of them all! At the first rumor, a thundering stampede of fifteen thousand claim-stakers blanketed the Washoe district. But most of the gold and silver was locked in veins of quartz, and little mining could be done until quartz mills and mining machinery were brought in. Not until 1873, after heroic tunneling operations and giant engineering feats under the direction of John W. Mackay and his partners, was the greatest lode of silver and gold struck. From 1859 to 1879 the total output of the Comstock mines was $350 million, of which 45 per cent was in gold and 55 per cent in silver. No deposits of equal richness have ever been recorded in ancient or modern mining history.

Perched on the roof of this subterranean treasure house on the steep side of Mount Davidson, 7,200 feet above sea level, was Virginia City, the most celebrated of the Western mining towns. Mark Twain, who arrived at the diggings in the early days, described the town in *Roughing It:*

> Virginia [City] had grown to be the "livest" town, for its age and population, that America had ever produced. The sidewalks swarmed with people—to such an extent, indeed, that it was generally no easy matter to stem the human tide. The streets themselves were just as crowded with quartz wagons, freight teams and other vehicles. The procession was endless. So great was the pack, that buggies frequently had to wait half an hour for an opportunity to cross the principal street. Joy sat on every countenance, and there was a glad, almost fierce, intensity in every eye, that told of the money-getting schemes that were seething in every brain and the high hope that held sway in every heart. Money was as plenty as dust; every individual considered himself wealthy, and a melancholy countenance was nowhere to be seen. There were military companies, fire companies, brass bands, banks, hotels, theatres, "hurdy-gurdy houses," wide-open gambling palaces, political pow-wows, civic processions, street fights, murders, inquests, riots, a whiskey mill every fifteen steps . . . a dozen breweries and half a dozen jails and station-houses in full operation, and some talk of building a church. The "flush times" were in magnificent flower!

New States 1864-90

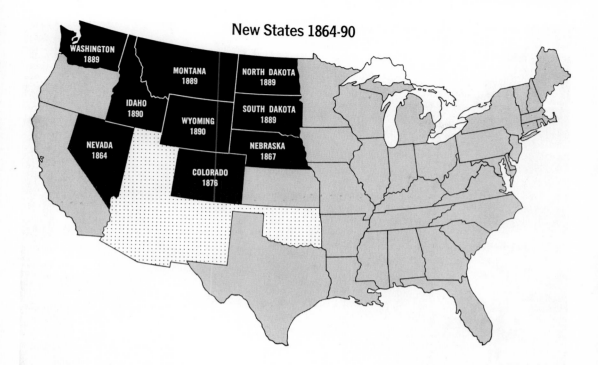

After Comstock one strike followed another in western Nevada. None was so rich as Comstock, but all served to attract an unstable population to the territory and increase the demand for statehood. Eight days before the election of 1864 Nevada became a state and promptly furnished three electoral votes for Lincoln.

In the meantime the future states of Washington, Idaho, and Montana were the scene of gold rushes and flush times. During the tragic years from Bull Run to Appomattox "yonder-siders" from California joined "pilgrims" from the East and seasoned prospectors from Nevada in stampedes to Orofino, Pierce City, Elk City, Boise, Placerville, Centerville, and Silver City. Some remained in Idaho as permanent settlers, but only fifteen thousand were living there in 1870. Many joined the great Montana gold rush around Bannack City, then jumped on to the spectacular diggings in Alder Gulch that produced $30 million of gold in three years, and ended up at Last Chance Gulch, where Helena was first laid out as a mining camp. A few more strikes after the war turned up the last surface gold in Idaho and Montana; then the placer miners passed on, leaving

scarred hills and ghost towns behind them. As in Nevada, the richest deposits lay in deep veins of quartz that could be reached only by expensive shafts and crushed only by heavy mills. Eastern capital moved in and opened up new mines in the seventies and eighties, one of which, the Bunker Hill and Sullivan Mine, discovered in 1885, yielded a quarter of a billion dollars in silver and lead.

During the early days of the gold rushes a motley and cosmopolitan assortment of humanity accumulated on the mining frontier. The population of one camp was somewhat unscientifically classified as "Saxon, Celt, Teuton, Gaul, Greaser, Celestial, and Indian." The 206 souls of another camp were more carefully tabulated as 73 American citizens, 37 Chinese, 35 British subjects, 29 Mexicans and Spaniards, 8 Negroes, and the rest assorted Europeans. Every camp of any size attracted its share of lawless outcasts—jailbirds, gamblers, prostitutes, deserters, desperadoes, stagecoach robbers. And every town had to decide whether or not to let the outcasts take over. As one observer described life in Last Chance Gulch in 1864: "Not a day or night passed which did not yield its full fruition of fights,

Gold rush town: Helena, Montana, June 1870.

quarrels, wounds, or murders. The crack of the revolver was often heard above the merry notes of the violin. . . . Pistols flashed, bowie knives flourished, and braggart oaths filled the air. . . ." The United States government was far off and preoccupied with other matters, and its arm was not always long enough to reach into Nevada and Idaho. As a result the miners developed their own informal codes of law and their own informal means of enforcement. Throughout the region there was a generous and sometimes loose resort to vigilantism, a more or less formalized lynch law intended to terrify the desperadoes.

The old mining frontier had its last mad fling in the Black Hills of what later became South Dakota. The army had finally given up as hopeless its effort to keep the insistent horde of prospectors out of the Sioux reservation, and in October 1875 it threw open the district to all who were willing to enter at their own risk.

Thousands of prospectors, still hopeful after two decades of disappointments, rushed in for one last chance. In a grand finale at Deadwood Gulch the miner's frontier outdid itself in a lurid caricature of its reputation. The curtain was rung down on the rowdiest brawls, the wildest desperadoes, and the most vigilant vigilantes of them all. After the Black Hills rush the prospectors and their supporting casts trooped off the scene, leaving mining to heavy investors and engineers. The frontier's "primary windfall" of precious metals had been stripped off, though the serious business of mining had only begun.

The Cattleman's Bonanza   The windfall of the early cattlemen was almost as rich and free as that of the early miners. The cows harvested the free crop of grass, turned it into beef and hides, transported these commodities to market on the hoof, and dropped calves along the way as replacements.

For a brief interlude between the passing of the Indian and the buffalo and the entry of the farmer and the barbed-wire fence, the Great Plains witnessed the most picturesque industrial drama ever staged—the drama of the open range and the cattle ranch. If the Southern planter could once claim that cotton was king, the Western cattleman could proclaim with equal fervor that grass was king. For the time being, at least, the plains were one limitless, fenceless, gateless pasture of rich, succulent, and ownerless grass that was his for the taking. Within an incredibly short period the red man's herds of bison had been replaced and outnumbered by the white man's herds of cattle.

The miner's invasion of the mountain and plains country came mainly from the Far West: the cattleman, his animals, and his ranch culture invaded from the South. Herdsmen had acquired some of the cowboy's arts and lingo on their long trek across the gulf states and the ante-bellum Southwest, but it was not until they had reached Texas and had begun to handle Spanish cattle from horseback that the craft took on its Mexican flavor and exotic style. A diamond-shaped area at the tip of Texas, with San Antonio at its apex, was the cradle of the future cowboy and his long-horned charges. The bulk of the cattle, a Spanish stock, grew up wild and were said to be "fifty times more dangerous to footmen than the fiercest buffalo." A tough, stringy, durable breed, wonderfully adapted to the plains, they multiplied so rapidly that they became a pest. Within just one decade the cattle population of Texas increased over 1,000 per cent, and by 1860 cattle were estimated at nearly five million in that state alone.

Even before the Civil War Texas cattlemen had made a few inconsequential drives to Northern markets, and after the war inducements multiplied. During the 1860's the population of the United States increased 22 per cent, while the number of cattle in the country decreased about 7 per cent. But the industrial revolution was piling up big meat markets in the cities and pushing the railroad out to the plains. At the end of the war cattle that brought three to five dollars a head in Texas could be sold for thirty to fifty dollars a head in northern markets. Fantastic profits had re-

The West: Cowboys

Those first trail outfits in the seventies were sure tough.... They had very little grub and they usually run out of that and lived on straight beef; they had only three or four horses to the man, mostly with sore backs, because old time saddle eat both ways, the horse's back and the cowboy's pistol pocket; they had no tents, no tarps, and damn few slickers. They never kicked, because those boys was raised under just the same conditions as there was on the trail—corn meal and bacon for grub, dirt floors in the houses, and no luxuries. In the early days in Texas, in the sixties, when they gathered their cattle, they used to pack what they needed on a horse and go out for weeks, on a cow-hunt, they called it then. That was before the name roundup was invented, and before they had anything so civilized as mess wagons....

In person the cowboys were mostly medium-sized men, as a heavy man was hard on horses, quick and wiry, and as a rule very good-natured; in fact it did not pay to be anything else. In character their like never was or will be again.

From E. C. Abbott and H. H. Smith, *We Pointed Them North*, 1955.

cently induced speculators to bring Confederate cotton through armed ranks of blue and gray to Yankee mills, and Texans were not to be daunted by the mere twelve or fifteen hundred miles that separated them from the fabulous meat markets in the North. In 1866 they set forth on the long drive north with more than a quarter of a million head. Taking the most direct route to the nearest railhead, Sedalia, Missouri, the cattlemen fell into the hands of thieves along the wooded parts of their route. Thereafter they kept to the open plains. The first town founded for the specific purpose of receiving cows for shipment was Abilene, Kansas, established by J. G. McCoy on the Hannibal and St. Joe Railroad in 1867. Of Abilene and its reputation, Webb writes:

Abilene was more than a point. It is a symbol. It stands for all that happened when two civilizations met for conflict, for disorder, for the clashing of great currents which carry on their crest the turbulent and disorderly elements of both civilizations—in this case the rough characters of the plain and of the forest. On the surface Abilene was corruption personified. Life was hectic, raw, lurid, awful. But . . . if Abilene excelled all later cow towns in wickedness, it also excelled them in service—the service of bartering the beef of the South for the money of the North.

Other cow towns followed—Wichita, Ellsworth, Dodge City—pushing farther and farther westward with the railroad, an indispensable adjunct to the cattle kingdom. The Texas trails themselves pushed in the same direction toward the Texas Panhandle and eastern New Mexico and Colorado. The trails shifted during the years of the long drive, to take advantage of the best grazing and water supplies. Some of them—the Goodnight-Loving Trail, the Western Trail, and the Chisholm Trail—left broad, brown, beaten tracks across hundreds of miles of grasslands. Riders of the long drive, beset by heartbreaking misfortunes, watched helplessly as the weight of their droves dwindled on the way to market. Nevertheless, the cowboys drove more than six million head of cattle northward over these trails between 1866 and 1888.

Not all the Texas cattle were sold directly for beef. Of the record drive of six hundred thousand in 1871 only half could find buyers and the rest spent the winter as "feeders" in the neighboring areas. It was mainly from this surplus of the Texas drives, many of them crossed with Hereford bulls to produce the white-faced hybrid, that the Great Plains area was stocked. Many herds were driven directly to the ranges of New Mexico, Arizona, Colorado, Wyoming, Montana, and the Dakotas to feed mining camps and railroad builders and to supply the ranchers' demand for fresh stock. Some Eastern cattle, called "pilgrims" (as were the miners from the East), contributed slightly to the stocking of the plains. In the amazing brief period of fifteen years, by 1880, the cattlemen and their ranches had spread over the whole vast grassland from the Rio Grande into Canada and up into the recesses of the Rockies.

With the boom of the 1880's, the monarchs of the cattle kingdom became intoxicated with the magnificence of their domain and its immediate prospects. The depression of the seventies had been rolled aside, the Indians had been driven into reservations, the railroads were coming on, and neither the homesteader nor barbed wire had yet arrived in menacing

quantity. Beef prices were soaring and the grass was growing higher by the hour. No wonder the cow king got a wonderful feeling that everything was going his way. His optimism spread abroad and investors from the four corners of the earth rushed to the plains to seek their fortunes, money hot in their pockets. Cheyenne, Wyoming, where a newly established cowman's club served caviar and rare wines, was described in 1882 by a local journalist:

> Sixteenth Street is a young Wall Street. Millions are talked of as lightly as nickels and all kinds of people are dabbling in steers. The chief justice of the Supreme Court has recently succumbed to the contagion and gone out to purchase a $40,000 herd. . . . A Cheyenne man who don't pretend to know a maverick from a mandamus has made a neat little margin of $15,000 this summer in small transactions and hasn't seen a cow yet that he has bought and sold.

As symbols of this spectacular adventure, the public took to its heart not the cow king but his hired hand, and there the cowboy has remained enshrined, his cult faithfully tended by votaries of screen and television. Known sometimes as "cowpoke" or "cowpuncher," names derived from an early method of prodding lagging critters with long poles, the cowboy is more popularly identified with the lariat and the branding iron. His picturesque accouterments—sombrero, spurs, long-heeled boots, chaps, gloves, and saddle, which he called his "workbench"—were strictly functional, not ornamental, and strictly adapted to life on horseback. There, indeed, much of his life was spent—eighteen hours or more a day during phases of the long drive or the roundup. Each cowboy had a "mount" of from eight to fourteen horses, depending on the work he was doing and the class of horses. Normally a hardworking man of Spartan and sober habits, the cowboy has come to share with the sailor a public image derived from his rare escapades of frantic recreation after long ordeals. The cowboy's two or three months in the saddle on the long drive built up as big a head of steam as a long voyage built up for the sailor. As for the cowboy's addiction to lethal six-guns, it was greatly exaggerated.

Violence of the shooting-iron sort, however, was unavoidable on the open-range cattle kingdom. With millions of dollars worth of property wandering at large on public lands, unfenced and poorly marked, the rustlers found the temptation overwhelming. Since government was remote and undependable, cattlemen resorted to private associations for protection and self-government in matters of roundup, branding, and breeding. These associations sometimes furnished all the government there was. The sort of justice they dispensed and the methods they used are suggested by a laconic item in the obituary of John S. Chisum of New Mexico, who died in 1884. Annoyed by Indians who had stolen some of his sixty thousand cattle in 1877, he armed a hundred men, moved against the presumed offenders, and "killed 175."

Even with free pasturage and virgin grassland, cattle-raising on the open range was extravagant and uneconomical. It exposed the herds to weather hazards, made adequate care of animals impossible and improvement of breeds difficult, encouraged rough and wasteful handling of cattle, and provoked costly and sometimes bloody range disputes. The approaching doom of the free range was further hastened by the expanding railroads and their loads of settlers, who staked claims and ran fences, and by the sheep-herders, who fouled the waterholes and stripped the grazing land. But the cattlemen contributed to their own downfall. They resorted to land fraud, monopoly, and ruthless violence to protect their interests. They even adopted for their own use that concrete denial of the open range, the barbed-wire fence: Charles Goodnight ran one all the way across the Texas Panhandle into New Mexico. Worse still, they overstocked and overgrazed the range.

The day of reckoning dawned in 1885, when beef prices started to tumble. During the severe winter of 1885–86 up to 85 per cent of the herds on the southern ranges either starved or froze to death. A bad drought the following summer scorched the grass and left the animals in poor condition. Then the legendary winter of 1886–87 fastened its cruel grip on the plains and brought panic to men as well as animals. When the thaw finally came, the emaciated corpses of enormous herds were left stacked up against fences or piled deep in coulees. A few grisly survivors staggered about on frozen legs.

The disaster spelled the end of the great beef bonanza. It ruined the larger corporations and many individual ranchers and took the heart out of the enterprise. There was little left of the reckless confidence with which cattlemen had greeted the great risks of the open range in its heyday. When nature smiled again and the public domain beckoned, some of the more hardy ranchers carried on in the old manner through the depressed nineties. But there was a steady and unmistakable retreat of investment to the security of privately owned pasturage, and a deliberate avoidance of the wild gambles and risks of the old days. Cattle had become a sober business instead of a high, wide, and handsome adventure.

The Farmer Moves West

Ever since 1607 American farmers had been moving west to break new ground. But in the last three decades of the nineteenth century they occupied and brought under cultivation more land than in all the years before 1870. It might seem natural to attribute this rapid expansion to the free-homestead policy adopted in 1862 (see p. 333). Before we jump to such a conclusion, however, it would be well to review that policy.

American Land Policy   The number of farms in the United States increased from some 2,000,000 in 1860 to 5,737,000 in 1900. And yet fewer than 600,000 homesteads were patented in those years, and they accounted for only 80,000,000 acres out of the more than 430,000,000 acres that were added to the total land in farms. Thus even if all the farmers who filed claims had been bona fide homesteaders, they would have accounted for fewer than one-sixth of the new farms and a little more than one-sixth of the added acreage. Actually, a great number of the so-called homesteads fell into the hands of large landholders and did not become farms until they were sold to settlers by speculators.

Nothing could have been further from the intention of the framers of the Homestead Act than the promotion of land monopoly. On the contrary, by distributing the bounty of free land among needy people they had hoped to defeat land monopoly. In practice, however, the great American promise of free land—a promise that was published around the world —turned out to be pretty much a delusion. One trouble was that few prospective homesteaders could afford to take advantage of the opportunity, because they lacked the capital to transport their families and possessions to the public domain, stock up with expensive machinery, and stick it out for years until the farm became self-supporting. Fewer still understood the new type of agriculture required on the arid plains. Two-thirds of all homestead claimants before 1890 failed at the venture. A realistic act would have provided the homesteader with credit and instruction in the new agriculture, and would also have set up safeguards against fraud. Uninhibited by such safeguards, the speculator hired men to stake out homesteads, falsely claim they had fulfilled the required conditions, and then turn over the land to their employer.

But the fundamental weakness of the Homestead Act was that it simply was not appropriate to the region where it applied. The law covered all public lands, of course, but by the time the act was passed the great bulk of public lands available for homesteading lay on the Great Plains and beyond. The Eastern congressmen who framed the law for the plains knew nothing about the needs of the people who were eventually going to live there. To the farmer back in the humid East a 160-acre tract seemed ideal for a family-sized farm—a good deal larger than the average, in fact. In the arid or semiarid West, however, land was useful only for intensive irrigated farming, extensive dry farming, or grazing. A 160-acre tract was too small for grazing or dry farming and too large for irrigated farming. Of the latter there was little anyway, so that the great Western complaint was against the smallness of holdings. If the East persisted in writing laws for the West that did not work, said the Westerners, then the West was justified in ignoring or violating them. Reflecting the ranchman's point of view, Webb writes: "The cattleman had to hold his own (and he did it pretty well) by evading the law and, as he would say, 'throwing in' with nature. He violated every land law made, in order that he might survive."

In land policy, as in Indian policy, it proved difficult to reconcile the views of East and West —particularly since the Eastern outcry was against land monopoly and the Western demand was for larger and larger units of land. One attempt to adjust land policy to Western needs was the Timber Culture Act of 1873, which permitted the homesteader to add another 160 acres of relatively treeless land to his holdings provided he would plant trees on one-quarter of it within four years. The law failed to increase rainfall, however, and homesteaders who tried to comply with its terms met with only moderate success. Nine out of ten claimants are said to have made no serious effort to forest their holdings.

A more absurd law was the Desert Land Act of 1877, which offered 640 acres to anyone who would pay twenty-five cents an acre down and promise to irrigate the land within three years. Upon presenting proof of irrigation and paying an additional dollar per acre the claimant could close the deal. The trouble here was that the law required irrigation where no water was to be had. Cattlemen seized on the Desert Land Act to enlarge their holdings, but at least 95 per cent of the "proofs" of irrigation were estimated to be fraudulent.

The Timber and Stone Act of 1878 permitted any citizen, or any alien with first papers, to buy at $2.50 an acre 160 acres of land "unfit for cultivation" and valuable chiefly for timber and stone. This act was as enticing an invitation to the timber barons as the Desert Land Act had been to the cattlemen. Using dummy entrymen to claim quarter-sections and deed them promptly to the corporation that paid them, lumber monopolists gobbled up vast empires of forest lands. As the Commissioner of the General Land Office reported in 1901, "immense tracts of the most valuable timber land, which every consideration of public interest demanded should be preserved for public use, have become the property of a few individuals and corporations." Timber and cattle interests grew bolder as time passed, and in 1903 alone they seized half as much land as they had secured from 1878 to 1900.

The laissez-faire philosophy of the period speeded the land speculator to the more desirable lands and locations well ahead of the homesteader. Taking advantage of cash sale and public auction of government lands, the speculator moved in early and cornered the choice lands, the probable town sites, and lands

Federal Grants to the Railroads

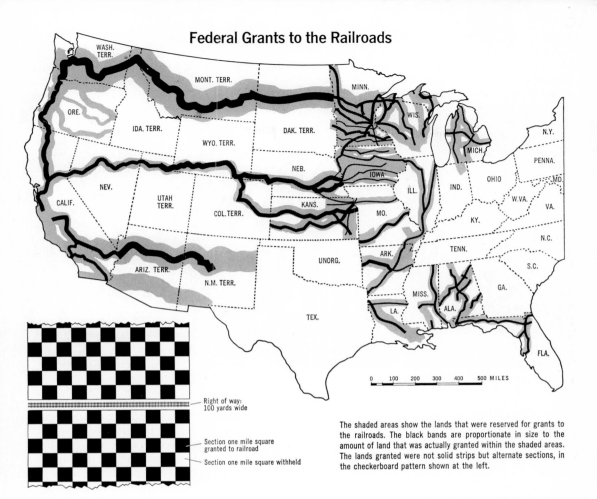

Right of way:
100 yards wide

Section one mile square
granted to railroad

Section one mile square withheld

The shaded areas show the lands that were reserved for grants to the railroads. The black bands are proportionate in size to the amount of land that was actually granted within the shaded areas. The lands granted were not solid strips but alternate sections, in the checkerboard pattern shown at the left.

along streams and roads to hold for high prices. When the bona fide homesteader finally arrived on the scene to stake out his claim, he usually had to choose from the least desirable and worst located tracts or else pay the speculator's price. In addition to about 100 million acres bought from the federal land office, the land jobbers bought up another 100 million acres from shrinking Indian reservations that became available under the government's policy of concentration, and 140 million acres from state land holdings. This accounted for some 340 million acres that were beyond the reach of homestead privileges.

Between 1850 and 1871 the federal government and the states had given railroad corporations 181 million acres of land to encourage construction (see p. 333), making the railroads the largest land jobbers of the West. But the form of the federal grants meant that many millions of acres in addition to the actual land granted were withheld from settlement. The railroad lands lay on both sides of the track, up to forty square miles for every mile of track laid in the territories and up to twenty for every mile laid in the states. This land was not arranged in solid strips, however, but in alternate sections, checkerboard fashion. But the whole solid strip was commonly withheld from settlement until the railroad chose its right-of-way and decided which alternate sections to keep. Great belts of land on either side of the tracks were placed beyond the homesteader's reach. At one time or another some three-tenths of the area of the country, and a much greater proportion of the West, was forbidden

Railroad and frontier: Scene at Omaha, 1868.

to use. Homesteaders were obliged either to accept areas remote from the rails or else pay the price the railroads asked. In 1887 this evil was alleviated by the Cleveland Administration (see p. 476), which threw open to settlement most of the land thus withheld.

The Advance of Settlement   The railroads became the principal colonizers as well as the biggest landowners of the New West. Rapid settlement along their lines meant larger revenues from passenger fares and freight charges and bigger profits from land sales. Railroads and states sold settlers nearly six times as much land as the farmers were able to obtain by homesteading. Each Western road had its land department and its bureau of immigration, and each Western state its agency to advertise and exaggerate opportunities for settlers. Steamship companies with an eye to emigrant passengers joined in the campaign abroad; working with railroad agents, they plastered Europe with posters and literature calculated to attract settlers to the "Garden of the West." The railroads provided what the Homestead Act had neglected: credit terms,

special passenger rates, and agricultural guidance and assistance for prospective purchasers and settlers. The success of the railroad colonizers was striking, and their campaigns in Europe infected whole countries with the "American fever." From Norway, Sweden, and Denmark, which were especially susceptible, peasants by the millions emigrated to the Northwest. By 1890 Minnesota had four hundred towns bearing Swedish names. Irish and German colonies were sprinkled across Minnesota, Nebraska, and Dakota Territory.

As in the past, however, the states immediately to the east of the advancing frontier furnished a large proportion of the new settlers. During the 1870's all but two of the states bordering on the Mississippi River lost population; their loss was the West's gain. In that single decade 190 million acres, an area equal to that of Great Britain and France combined, were added to the cultivated area of the country, mostly just to the west of the Minnesota-Louisiana tier of states. The line of settlement surged westward irregularly, first along the river valleys, rapidly along the growing rail-

The West: A Railroad Town

Here had sprung up in two weeks, as if by the touch of Aladdin's Lamp, a city of three thousand people; there were regular squares arranged into five wards, a city government of mayor and aldermen, a daily paper, and a volume of ordinances for the public health. It was the end of the freight and passenger, and beginning of the construction, division; twice every day immense trains arrived and departed, and stages left for Utah, Montana, and Idaho; all the goods formerly hauled across the plains came here by rail and were reshipped, and for ten hours daily the streets were thronged with motley crowds of railroad men, Mexicans and Indians, gamblers, "cappers," and saloon-keepers, merchants, miners, and mule-whackers. The streets were eight inches deep in white dust as I entered the city of canvas tents and pole-houses; the suburbs appeared as banks of dirty white lime, and a new arrival with black clothes looked like nothing so much as a cockroach struggling through a flour barrel.

It was sundown, and the lively notes of the violin and guitar were calling the citizens to evening diversions. Twenty-three saloons ... and five dance-houses amused our elegant leisure.

From J. H. Beadle, *The Undeveloped West*, 1873.

---

road lines, and out over the rolling plains. A frontier in Kansas that had not budged perceptibly in two decades forged rapidly ahead in the seventies, and both Kansas and Nebraska filled out to the edge of the semiarid plains by 1880. To the north the frontier advanced in a succession of three "Dakota Booms" roughly coinciding with three contemporaneous gold rushes. A demonstration of how to make a 100 per cent profit in wheat growing, put on by the Northern Pacific Railway after the Panic of 1873, started a rush that covered three hundred miles of the Red River Valley with "bonanza farms" ranging up to one hundred thousand acres in size, a remarkable commentary on the supposedly democratic land system. Further north in Dakota Territory was the special province of James J. Hill, inspired colonizer of the Northwest and head of the Great Northern Railway. Hill planned and directed the settlement of thousands of pioneers along the tracks of his road to the Pacific. By 1885 all of Dakota east of the Missouri River was settled and the population had increased 400 per cent in five years. The mountainous territories to the west, except for the Mormon settlements of Utah, were slower in attracting settlers, but by the mid-eighties homesteaders in western Nebraska and Wyoming were challenging the cattlemen there.

In the meantime settlers of the southwestern frontier were pushing ahead. The number of farms in Texas more than doubled during the seventies. As both the Texas and the Kansas frontiers approached the semiarid country to the west, avid land-seekers began to eye the tempting lands of the Indian Territory between the two states. Egged on by railroad companies with actual or projected lines in the territory, agitators defied the troops guarding the boundaries, repeatedly invaded the territory, and besieged Congress with demands to throw the cowed and defeated Indian tribes out of their last refuge. Congress yielded to their demands and on April 22, 1889, threw open some two million acres of the Oklahoma District in the heart of the territory. At the signal, a hundred thousand "Boomers" and "Sooners," riding on every conceivable vehicle, including fifteen trains with passengers jamming the roofs, swarmed into the District, staked it off in claims, and founded two cities—all within a few hours. Congress yielded to pressure again and created the Oklahoma Territory on May 2, 1890. In succeeding years one strip after another was opened—the largest, the six million acres of the Cherokee Outlet, in 1893—until the entire area of Oklahoma had been settled.

The superintendent of the census of 1890 discovered after the returns were in that something was missing: the long-familiar frontier. "Up to and including 1880," he reported, "the country had a frontier of settlement, but at present the unsettled area has been so broken into by isolated bodies of settlement that there can hardly be said to be a frontier line." Three years later Frederick Jackson Turner, a young historian from Wisconsin, undertook to interpret the meaning of this development in a paper entitled "The Significance of the Frontier in American History." A devoted son of the West, Turner declared that the influence of the East and Europe had been overemphasized: "The true point of view in the history of this nation is not the Atlantic coast, it is the

To the frontier the American intellect owes its striking characteristics. That coarseness and strength combined with acuteness and inquisitiveness; that practical, inventive turn of mind, quick to find expedients; that masterful grasp of material things, lacking in the artistic but powerful to effect great ends; that restless, nervous energy; that dominant individualism, working for good and for evil, and withal that buoyancy and exuberance which comes with freedom—these are traits of the frontier, or traits called out elsewhere because of the existence of the frontier. Since the days when the fleet of Columbus sailed into the waters of the New World, America has been another name for opportunity, and the people of the United States have taken their tone from the incessant expansion which has not only been open but has even been forced upon them. He would be a rash prophet who should assert that the expansive character of American life has now entirely ceased. Movement has been its dominant fact, and, unless this training has no effect upon a people, the American energy will continually demand a wider field for its exercise. But never again will such gifts of free land offer themselves.

From Frederick Jackson Turner, "The Significance of the Frontier in American History," 1893.

To Turner the westerner was a radical in both thought and actions, developing new ideas to meet new conditions. The modern trend of thinking, while far from uniform, tends to move in the opposite direction, with more and more people asserting that the West was essentially conservative. True enough the westerner made some unpleasant innovations such as the sod house, was forced to develop several new techniques as in the arid parts of the West, and supported certain drastic actions for his own advantage—as free land and the elimination of Indian power; and yet the great bulk of his customs, including the building of log cabins, was derivative. More basic, however, he accepted in general the virtues and ideals which he had been taught as a youth and which were common in the United States. He was a God-fearing man along traditional lines. He joined the rest of the United States in judging success as the attainment of wealth. He respected personal property and the sanctity of contracts just as did his eastern contemporary. In fact he had moved to the West not in protest at current ideals but to attain them more quickly. His objective was the same kind of life which he had envied in his eastern neighbors.

From Robert E. Riegel, *Current Ideas of the Significance of the United States Frontier*, 1952.

Great West." He believed, in fact, that "the existence of an area of free land, its continuous recession, and the advance of American settlement westward, explain American development." In other writings Turner maintained that contact with the frontier created the continuous rebirth and rejuvenation of democracy—a conclusion not easy to reconcile with the way land was distributed and the frontier advanced.

New Farms and New Methods The tribulations of the new pioneers of prairie and plain rivaled those of the Jamestown settlers in the early seventeenth century. Like the plagues that the God of Moses sent against the Egyptians, new calamities visited Western farmers with each season. Hardly had the winter blizzards ceased when melting snow brought flash floods to menace man and beast. Summer temperatures soared to 118°; drought and hot winds seared corn to crisp blades and whitened men's faces with the salt of sweat. Worst of all were the grasshoppers,

especially during the terrible plagues of the mid-seventics. The insects came in clouds that darkened the sun, cracked the limbs of trees with their weight, and covered the ground inches deep. After they had chewed the crops down to the roots, they stripped the few trees of leaves and tender bark, and even consumed the curtains at the farmers' windows. Prairie fires, dust storms, marauding Indians, claim-jumpers, and rattlesnakes further chastened the spirit of the pioneers and discouraged all but the sturdiest.

Gradually inventiveness and industry solved many of the problems of soil and climate and overcame the lack of wood and water. In his first few years the homesteader lived in a miserable sod house, half buried in the prairie and roofed with slabs of cut turf. But later, when the railroads brought down the cost of lumber, he built a frame house. The problem of how to fence his land in a woodless, rail-less, stoneless region was solved by the invention of barbed wire. Of the several types devised, the

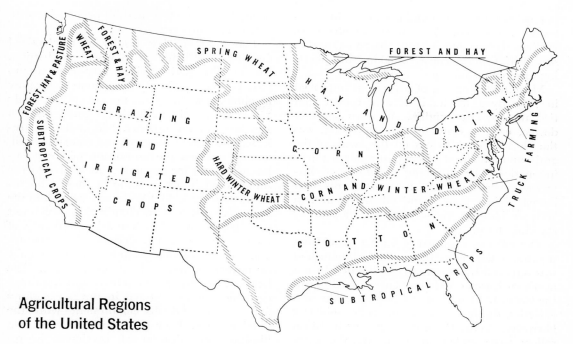

Agricultural Regions
of the United States

most successful was patented by Joseph F. Glidden, an Illinois farmer, in November 1874. Joining forces with a wire manufacturer, Glidden began mass production two years later, and by 1883 the Glidden factory was turning out six hundred miles of barbed wire a day. Farmers and cattlemen strung it up as fast as it was produced.

The problem of water supply was harder to solve. The only reliable sources of supply lay far below the surface, too deep to reach by open, hand-dug wells. And even when a well was drilled, pumping the water up two hundred to eight hundred feet by hand was impractical. The obvious solution was to harness the free power of the winds that steadily swept the plains, and by 1880 scores of small firms were producing windmills adapted to this purpose. The cost of digging a well ran up to two dollars per foot, and this expense, plus the cost of windmill, tower, tank, and reservoir, kept that solution beyond the means of the homesteader and the small farmer until near the end of the century. The big rancher, however, might have several windmills.

To meet the problem of cultivating soil in semiarid country without irrigation, West-erners developed the technique of "dry farming." They plowed deep into the earth to bring subsurface moisture up to the plant roots, and then harrowed the surface into fine particles to slow down evaporation. To break the tough soil of the plains and cultivate larger farms where labor was scarcer than ever, the farmer needed a new type of machinery. A revolution in farm machinery had started before 1860, and most of the basic patents had been granted by that year. But the mass production of machines came only after the Civil War.

The plow that most successfully broke the plains was devised by James Oliver of Indiana. After working on it for twenty-five years, by 1877 he had perfected the modern chilled-iron plow and smooth-surfaced moldboard. The old spike-tooth and disk harrows were replaced by a spring-tooth machine perfected in 1869. By the mid-seventies mechanical grain drills were in general use that automatically opened a furrow and dropped seed at proper intervals, and a little later a planting plow called a lister was developed for the deep planting needed in semiarid areas. Gigantic steam tractors the size of locomotives were used on the Pacific Coast for a brief period before the era of gasoline. On bonanza farms in California before 1900 these huge tractors were pulling sixteen plows, four harrows, and a seed drill, simultaneously breaking and planting as much as fifty acres a day.

Machine harvesting of wheat was improved in 1880 by a mechanical twine-binder that tied up the cut bundles. An even speedier device, used in drier parts of the West, was the "header," which cut off the heads of the grain and left the stalk for pasturage or plowing under. The threshing machine was improved over the years by refinements that increased its capacity and efficiency, and in 1884 a blowing device was developed for stacking straw.

The soft winter wheat of the East could not withstand the rigors of the new climate and was replaced by a new variety imported from northern Europe and by "Turkey Red" from the Crimea. To mill the hard grain of the new varieties, the basic idea of the roller mill was borrowed from Hungary, and chilled-iron rollers were added by 1879. By the early seventies the storage, loading, handling, and transporting of wheat had all been reduced to mechanical processes.

The most striking results of mechanized farming were achieved in wheat production. An acre that had required sixty-one hours to farm by hand took only three hours to farm by machine, and where one man could farm only 7½ acres by old methods he could take on 135 acres in the nineties. Mechanization released men from drudgery and stupefying toil, greatly reduced the proportion of the population needed for farming, and improved the standard of living of some of those who remained on the land. On the other hand, in the very states where mechanization was most prevalent there was a remarkable growth of tenancy in the last two decades of the century and a corresponding decline in the percentage of farmers working their own farms. The farmers, like the placer miners and the range cattlemen, were destined in the late eighties for trouble and disenchantment with the Golden West. They fell victims to their own illusions—the illusion of inexhaustible resources and the illusion of unlimited markets.

Sod house, Custer County, Nebraska, 1888.

The illusions of the farmer were part of a great national illusion dating from the early years of the Republic. This was what Henry Nash Smith in *Virgin Land* has called "The Myth of the Garden"—the myth that the West was a realizable utopia, an agrarian Eden where free land and honest toil would produce a virtuous yeomanry and the good life. According to the myth, the West was the true source of national regeneration, the means of realizing the ideals of democracy and equality, and it was celebrated by poets, novelists, and historians alike. "All of the associations called up by the spoken word, the West," wrote the Western novelist Hamlin Garland in 1891, "were fabulous, mythic, hopeful."

But the stark contrast between the hopes fostered by the myth and the harsh realities of experience could not escape even the dullest farmer. Far from utopian were the sod house, the dust storm, the grasshopper plague. "So this is the reality of the dream!" exclaims a character in a Garland novel. "A shanty on a barren plain, hot and lone as a desert. My God!" Far from equalitarian or democratic was a land system that fostered monopoly in the guise of distributing free land. It was a curious "safety valve" for the urban discontent of the East that sent homesteaders flocking to the city to escape the rural discontent of the West. The disillusionment with the Myth of the Garden that dates from these years helps explain the bitterness of the agrarian revolt that burst forth toward the end of the century.

Whether as myth or as reality, whether as the last stand of the first American or as the last frontier of miner, cattleman, and farmer, whether as man's last hope of equality or as a disillusioning experience with monopoly and inequality—this last of the nation's many wests left a profound imprint upon the American mind and the American legend.

SUGGESTIONS FOR READING

Two readable and comprehensive surveys of Western history have appeared in recent years: R. A. Billington, *Westward Expansion: A History of the American Frontier* (1960), which stresses the Turner thesis; and T. D. Clark, *Frontier America: The Story of the Westward Movement* (1959), which disclaims the thesis. The thesis itself appears in an essay by F. J. Turner, "The Significance of the Frontier in American History," in his *The Frontier in American History* (1920). W. P. Webb, *The Great Plains* * (1931), is the most provocative study of regional culture and environmental influences in our literature; his *The Great Frontier* (1952) examines the world significance of the New World frontiers since the Age of Discovery. J. A. Malin, *The Grassland of North America* (1947), brings agricultural and geographical science to the aid of historical understanding. Wayne Gard, *The Great Buffalo Hunt* (1959), is the best book on this dramatic subject. Allan Nevins, *The Emergence of Modern America, 1865–1878* (1927), has excellent chapters on the West. The West as symbol and myth in American thought is brilliantly analyzed in H. N. Smith, *Virgin Land* * (1957).

Two general histories of the Indians are recommended: Clark Wissler, *The American Indian* (1922), and Paul Radin, *The Story of the American Indian* (rev. ed., 1944). On the Plains Indians, F. G. Roe, *The Indian and the Horse* (1955), is excellent. Two champions of the red man's rights have left moving accounts: H. H. Jackson, *A Century of Dishonor* (1881), a stirring indictment; and J. J. Collier, *The Indians of the Americas* (1947), by a leader of policy reform. L. G. Priest, *Uncle Sam's Stepchildren: The Reformation of United States Indian Policy, 1865–1887* (1942), defends the reformers against their critics. Revealing books on military activities are R. G. Athearn, *William Tecumseh Sherman and the Settlement of the West* (1956); E. I. Stewart, *Custer's Luck* (1955); and C. C. Rister, *Border Command: General Phil Sheridan in the West* (1944).

On mining, T. A. Rickard, *A History of American Mining* (1932), is a fairly technical approach by an engineer. W. J. Trimble, *The Mining Advance into the Inland Empire* (1914), is a general treatment of activities in the Northwest, and G. C. Quiett, *Pay Dirt: A Panorama of American*

* Available in a paperback edition.

Gold-Rushes (1936), stresses the more colorful and violent parts of the story. C. H. Shinn, *The Story of the Mine* (1896), and *Mining Camps: A Study in American Frontier Government* (1885), are based on first-hand experience. For colorful reminiscences, see Mark Twain, *Roughing It* (1872), and Dan DeQuille, *History of the Big Bonanza* (1876, reprinted 1947).

The cattleman's bonanza is briefly surveyed in E. S. Osgood, *The Day of the Cattleman* (1929, reprinted 1957), and more fully in E. E. Dale, *The Range Cattle Industry* (1930). Maurice Frank, W. T. Jackson, and A. W. Spring, *When Grass Was King* (1957), is a roundup of recent scholarship. Lewis Atherton, *The Cattle Kings* (1961), is a thoughtful and sympathetic account. Of the vast cowboy literature, Andy Adams, *The Log of a Cowboy* (1931), and J. F. Dobie, ed., *A Texas Cowboy* (1950), contain firsthand experiences; J. B. Frantz and J. E. Choate, *The American Cowboy: The Myth and the Reality* (1955), is a realistic analysis.

The best history of agriculture in this period, especially in the West, is F. A. Shannon, *The Farmer's Last Frontier, 1860–1897* (1945). On the history of American land policy and its administration, two works of value are R. M. Robbins, *Our Landed Heritage: The Public Domain, 1776–1936* (1942), and B. J. Hibbard, *A History of the Public Land Policies* (1924). The history of the new farm machinery is found in Waldemar Kaempffert, *A Popular History of American Invention* (1924). The pioneer farm on the western frontier is pictured in Everett Dick, *The Sod-House Frontier, 1854–1890* (1937). Vivid fictional accounts are Willa Cather, *O Pioneers!* (1913) and *My Ántonia* (1918), O. E. Rølvaag, *Giants in the Earth* (1927), and Mari Sandoz, *Old Jules* (1935).

18

The Ordeal
of Industrialization

"The truth is," Senator John Sherman wrote his brother General William T. Sherman in November 1865, "the close of the war with our resources unimpaired gives an elevation, a scope to the ideas of leading capitalists, far higher than anything ever undertaken in this country before. They talk of millions as confidently as formerly of thousands." The high hopes and towering schemes of the industrial capitalists continued to mount over the decades, and before the end of the century they were talking of billions where they had once spoken of millions. There was reason for their optimism. Of all the nations that have industrialized their economies through capitalistic rather than socialistic methods, the United States offered its businessmen the greatest encouragement and the fewest obstacles.

The Civil War itself, as Senator Sherman suggested, had been a great smasher of barriers and opener of opportunities. "Such opportunities for making money," wrote Judge Thomas Mellon of Pittsburgh in 1863, "had never existed before in all my former experience." But the great war did more than give rein to fortune-builders. It created new attitudes and expectations on the part of the public, the government, and industry. It accustomed bankers, bookkeepers, and manufacturers to nationwide operations and large-scale organization. It pointed the way to mass markets and mass production, and it taught the government habits of openhanded and reckless generosity toward private enterprise that sought control of public funds and public resources.

Throughout the last third of the nineteenth century the federal government was controlled by men who were not only responsive to the wishes of the business community, but eager to further its interests. They used the prevailing philosophy of laissez faire to justify the lack of public policy and the virtual absence of restraints and regulation of business to protect public welfare and safeguard public health. When the government intervened at all, it was to extend loans, grant subsidies and franchises, hand over public resources, or protect home industries from foreign competitors. The Civil War eliminated the Southern planter as a rival of the industrialist for control in Washington, and no other class offered serious competition. Unlike European businessmen, the Americans had no heritage of canon law and feudal custom with which to contend. No royal prerogatives or aristocratic privileges barred them from certain fields of enterprise, and no pampered courtiers controlled vital trade routes. For the time being, the industrial entrepreneur was the lord of all he surveyed.

What he surveyed was a built-in empire, rich in coal, iron, oil, water power, lumber—most of the resources essential for great industrial power. Of bituminous coal, the unrivaled fuel of nineteenth-century industry, the United States had the greatest known deposits in the world. Petroleum fields in Pennsylvania had been tapped already and the vast oil fields of the Southwest were yet to be discovered. Employers had already learned to tap European resources for their labor supply, and after the Civil War immigrants came swarming to the New World in unprecedented numbers. Within the boundaries of the United States was the greatest free-trade market in the world, and around it Congress had erected a high protective tariff barrier.

It is no wonder that an economy that had already been expanding rapidly before the Civil War grew with explosive force in the decades that followed. In 1860 the United States was a second-rate industrial country, lagging far behind the United Kingdom, France, and Germany. But by 1890 the United States had stepped into first place, and the value of its manufactured goods almost equaled the combined production of all the three former leaders. Between the eve of the Civil War and the eve of the First World War American manufacturing productivity multiplied twelve times over.

The Railroad Empire

"The generation between 1865 and 1895 was already mortgaged to the railways," reflected Henry Adams, "and no one knew it better than the generation itself." This was the generation that planned, built, financed, and made the first attempts to control the most extensive railroad network in the world. The headlong haste and heedless ethics of its experience are caught in the national expression "railroaded through." No one, not even the enemies of the railroad, could be found in that age to deny its importance. Everyone knew it was the key to mass production and mass consumption, to the utilization of natural resources and the creation of a national market, and to the binding together and settlement of a two-ocean land mass. The railroad dominated the imagination, the politics, the economy, and the hopes of a generation, and the outsized cowcatcher and smokestack of the old-fashioned steam locomotive might well be taken as the symbol of the age. The poet William Ellery Leonard, who was born in 1876, entitled an autobiographical work *The Locomotive-God*, and the popular ballad-makers lavished on the iron horse a devotion they had formerly reserved for the flesh-and-blood steed and the sailing ship.

Building the Network   The laying of rails, which were mainly iron rather than steel until the eighties, went forward in fits and starts, impeded by panics and depression and spurred on by speculative booms and prosperity. Starting with only about 35,000 miles of railway at the end of the Civil War, during which less than 5,000 miles were laid, the country had doubled its mileage before the Panic of 1873. The next six years of depression added only some 16,000 miles. The 1880's, the great decade of railway expansion, opened with some 93,000 miles and ended with 166,000, an increase of more than 73,000 miles in ten years. By the end of the century the United States had a total of nearly 200,000 miles, or more than all Europe including Russia. In the meantime the ungainly little "bullgine" with the disproportionate funnel had evolved into a giant that could master mountain and plain, a giant that dwarfed any foreign make of locomotive. Greatly improved by the Westinghouse air brake and other inventions, the trains carried more passengers in 1900 than they did in any year of the 1930's.

To build this vast railway network was an undertaking comparable in magnitude with the construction of a navy, and for the United States it was even more costly and probably more essential to the national interest. European governments assumed responsibility for building and running their railroad establishments as readily as for their military establishments. In America, apart from a few state-owned roads of ante-bellum origin, initiative and management were left primarily in the hands of private enterprise. Even by 1880, before half the network was completed, an investment of more than $4,600 million had gone into the nation's railroads. By 1897 their stocks and bonds totaled $10,635 million as compared with a total national debt of less than $1,227 million. Edward Kirkland, the economic historian, concludes that the handling of railroad finances had "a greater effect upon the economy than the management of the national finances." Since such huge sums were far more than private American investors could supply, promoters turned to foreign investors and to local, state, and federal governments. By the

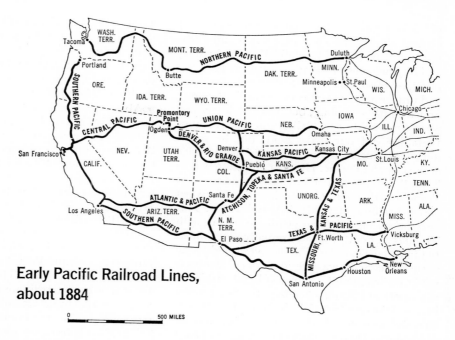

Early Pacific Railroad Lines, about 1884

0   500 MILES

end of 1898 Europeans, mainly British, owned $3,100 million worth of American railroad securities, about one-third of the whole.

While public enthusiasm for railroad building was at its height, government at all levels fairly thrust credit and resources upon the railroad promoters. Villages, towns, cities, and counties came forward with $300 million, and states with some $228 million more in the form of bonds and other commitments. The federal government lent approximately $65 million to six western railroads and extended even more important aid through grants of public land. In all, Congress committed 155,500,000 acres of the public domain, of which the railroads actually received more than 131,000,000 acres. In addition they received 49,000,000 acres from the states. There is no way of estimating realistically the dollar value of these lands and the resources upon them. Their main value to the railroads was not the cash they brought from sales, but the credit and security they supplied for stock issues. Although government subsidies were often obtained through bribery and were responsible for much corruption, the policy of subsidizing the railroads with grants of public land was probably justified in the long run. By attaching conditions to the land grants which obliged the railroads to furnish

cheap transportation for mail and military shipments, the government has enjoyed substantial savings over the years. Actually, less than 10 per cent of the railroad mileage of the country was built with federal land grants. And most of that mileage was on the roads built across the Great Plains, where investment was slow in yielding returns and where some form of public credit was essential.

The transcontinental lines called for the most heroic efforts and attracted some of the ablest—and some of the most unscrupulous—enterprisers. The completion of the Union Pacific–Central Pacific in 1869 (see p. 357) realized the ante-bellum dream of spanning the continent with rails, and within the next quarter of a century four more lines flanked the original one, two on either side: the Southern Pacific and the Santa Fe to the south and the Northern Pacific and the Great Northern to the north. Each line excited intense rivalries and ambitions in the cities they connected and the sections they served, as well as among the railroad builders and promoters.

Collis P. Huntington, one of the Californians behind the Central Pacific, took the leading role in pushing through the Southern Pacific, the second and southernmost of the transcontinentals. Like many railroad barons of his generation, Huntington was tough and cynical about business and politics and ruthless in his methods. He talked about bribing and buying congressmen as he would about the purchase of so many cattle. The son of a large and unprosperous Connecticut family, he grew up with little schooling, became a peddler, and went west with the California gold rush of 1849. He did not strike gold, but he made money as a merchant and a fortune as a builder of the Central Pacific. His next ambition was to build the Southern Pacific southward from San Francisco through California and westward across Arizona, New Mexico, and Texas. This enterprise brought a head-on clash with Thomas A. Scott, who was equally determined to build the Texas and Pacific over roughly the same route. Scott was president of the Pennsylvania Railroad and as powerful and ruthless a man as Huntington. The effect the Scott lobby had on the presidential election of 1876 has already been noted (see p. 377). But in spite of President Hayes's support of Scott's bill for a $200 million government subsidy for the Texas and Pacific, Congress failed to pass it. There were several reasons for the failure, but one important reason was Huntington, who once remarked, "It costs money to fix things so that I would know his bill would not pass." Huntington would stop at nothing, and nothing could stop him. In defiance of a War Department order he laid rails across an Indian reservation and then boasted to the President of his defiance. Scott continued to resist, but Huntington kept laying rails until at last he forced the Southern Pacific into El Paso, Texas, in 1881, and Scott gave up the struggle.

In the course of the contest with Scott, however, Huntington met his match in Jay Gould, the most notorious land pirate of all the railroad barons. Having looted the Erie and left it in ruins in 1873, Gould next seized control of the Union Pacific and forced its directors to buy up at exorbitant prices some lines that he had pieced together as a potential competition. Turning his attention to the Southwest, Gould won control of the Texas and Pacific and employed the same tactics to force his way into the Southern Pacific. Using a combination of the Texas and Pacific and the Missouri, Kansas, and Texas ("Katy") line, he threatened to block Huntington's way through the state of

Texas. He relented only after exacting a traffic-sharing agreement from Huntington and a large influence in the Southern Pacific. The Gould and Huntington lines joined near El Paso in 1882, and two years later the Southern Pacific reached New Orleans.

About the same time another major system, the Atchison, Topeka, and Santa Fe, usually known simply as the Santa Fe, entered the Southwest and threatened the Huntington-Gould monopoly. Financed by Boston capital, this road cut across Kansas and a corner of Colorado to reach Santa Fe, New Mexico. Huntington and Gould cleverly thwarted the Santa Fe's efforts to gain direct access to the coast by buying up its charter. Then in 1883 the Southern Pacific, on its own terms, permitted the Santa Fe to enter California on Southern Pacific lines. The competing Santa Fe was then subordinated to the monopoly, and by 1890 Gould was the virtual dictator of transportation in the Southwest.

The Northwest was somewhat more fortunate in its railroad pioneers and masters. The Northern Pacific had been chartered to build a line from Lake Superior to Puget Sound, but construction was halted in 1873 when Jay Cooke and Company as well as the railroad it was financing went bankrupt. Reorganized in 1875, the Northern Pacific was acquired in 1881 by Henry Villard, a German-born capitalist with large holdings in Oregon. Villard completed the line to Tacoma, Washington, in 1883, but he was never able to enjoy a monopoly of transportation in the Northwest. In 1878 a competing line under the management of James J. Hill had begun to push westward from St. Paul, parallel to the Northern Pacific. A Canadian by birth, Hill had a long-cherished dream of colonizing the Northwest. First he had acquired the two-hundred-mile track of the bankrupt little St. Paul and Pacific, and then had started building westward through Minnesota, North Dakota, Idaho, and across Washington for 2,775 miles to the Pacific. The Great Northern, as he renamed this line, had no land grant such as the Northern Pacific enjoyed. Consequently, in order to build up traffic and revenue, Hill had to rely on Canadian and American capital and his own efforts to settle the country. "We consider ourselves and the people along our line as co-partners in the prosperity of the country we both occupy," said Hill. He completed his line to Puget Sound in 1893. Built more carefully and solidly than its competitor, financed more soundly, and integrated more thoroughly in the economy of the region it served, Hill's Great Northern was the only transcontinental road to pull through the Panic of 1893 and the depression that followed.

East of the Mississippi railroads were built mainly to serve local needs and to promote the interests of particular cities. Hundreds of small lines using a variety of gauges were built after the Civil War, many without connections. The South alone had four hundred companies averaging not more than forty miles apiece. One task of the postwar generation was to fill in the gaps between lines and to weld them into an integrated national network. Through consolidation by lease, purchase, or merger, nearly two-thirds of the country's railroad companies were absorbed by the other one-third. In 1880 alone 115 companies lost their identity, and between 1880 and 1888 some 425 companies were brought under the control of other roads. The Pennsylvania Railroad by 1890 was an amalgamation of 73 smaller companies and some five thousand miles of rail.

One result of combination was the emergence of a few dominant systems in each section. In the Northeast, in addition to the Pennsylvania, were the New York Central, the Erie, and the Baltimore and Ohio. All competed to some degree, and all shared the same general aim of connecting the Eastern ports with the Western rivers and the Great Lakes. In the South the largest system was the Richmond and West Point Terminal (later the Southern Railway), which by 1890 had pieced together by financial jobbery some 8,500 miles of lines. Competing with it for north-south traffic were the Atlantic Coast Line and the Seaboard Air Line, smaller companies that were themselves the result of combinations of more than a hundred small lines. West of the Appalachians the powerful Louisville and Nashville served the mining and industrial areas of Kentucky, Tennessee, and Alabama; and the Illinois Central paralleled the Mississippi River down to New Orleans and connected with the Atlantic Coast at Savannah.

Consolidation sometimes, but not always,

James J. Hill: Railroad empire-builder of the Northwest.

brought improvements: steel rails to replace iron rails, safety precautions such as double-tracking and the block signal, and cheaper, more reliable, and more punctual service. In 1883 the American Railway Association divided the country into four time zones with an hour's difference between each, and in spite of outraged advocates of "God's time" regularized their timetables. The standard gauge of 4 feet 8½ inches for rails became virtually nationwide in May 1886, when the Southern roads moved one rail three inches closer to the other.

Competition and Disorder In spite of all these improvements, the American railroads were in serious difficulties. They were under heavy criticism and attack from the public, and they were suffering from grave and uncontrolled disorders within the industry itself. The troubles of the railroads were inherent in the very nature of American industry in the age of unrestricted competition. The mania for construction in the seventies and eighties provided all the major transportation areas with an overdeveloped network of railroads, much greater than was needed at the time. In the same period the looting by buccaneer operators saddled the railroads with heavy fixed costs due to wasteful construction and overcapitalization. In 1885 *Poor's Manual*, an authority on railroads, estimated that nearly one-third of the capitalization in that year represented "watered stock," that is, stock issued in excess of the value of assets. Railroad managers, faced with the demand to make profits on overcapitalized stock and the pressing need for traffic when there was not enough to go around, resorted to ruinous competitive wars of line against line. Competitors and interlopers paralleled each other's lines for purposes of blackmailing or ruining rivals. Railroads offered fantastic "rebates," secret rates below the published tariffs, to secure traffic of big shippers and overcharged outrageously to compensate where they had no competition. They often charged less for a long haul than a short haul, resorted to all kinds of rate jugglery and deception, and trusted neither client nor competitor. "No wonder that railroad managers accused each other of fraud and deception," testified one manager before a Senate committee in 1885. "Men who in all other relations of life were blameless winked at falsehoods, and dallied with deception, not because they were morally debased, but actually because they knew not the way out of the toils."

Competition under such circumstances, instead of being "the life of trade," and benefiting enterprise as well as the public, proved a curse to both. The railroads themselves suffered heavily from the rate wars, for they were often driven to cut rates below the cost of handling the business and thereby imperiled the dividends, if not the solvency, of the firm. Obviously the railroads had to find some way to stop piratical practices of rebate, rate-cutting, and blackmail. They sought solutions in treaties and solemn agreements—all of which proved unenforceable. A more formal device of railroad cooperation was the pool, an agreement to divide traffic on some proportional basis and charge uniform rates. But the pool agreements were also difficult to enforce

and were always breaking down. The temptation to gain advantage over competitors by violating agreements often proved irresistible. As Charles Francis Adams, Jr., a keen student as well as an executive of railroads, described the demoralization:

> Honesty and good faith are scarcely regarded. Certainly they are not tolerated at all if they interfere with a man's getting his "share of the business." Gradually, this demoralizing spirit of low cunning has pervaded the entire system. Its moral tone is deplorably low. . . . That healthy, mutual confidence which is the first essential to prosperity in all transactions between man and man, does not exist in the American railroad service taken as a whole.

If the railroad industry could not set its own house in order, then order would have to be imposed from outside. The problem was nationwide, but the federal government continued through the years of the worst railroad anarchy to practice laissez faire. The state governments took the initiative and made the first experiments in regulation and control. Their laws and commissions are often attributed to the "Granger Movement," the work of a farmers' organization (see p. 482), and associated with the Middle West. But the movement to regulate railroads was limited to no one class or section. Massachusetts and New York made important contributions, and states in the Southeast, the Southwest, and the Far West also participated. Merchants, wholesale dealers, and manufacturers were more prominent and effective than farmers in pressing for regulation in several areas. If pools were an unsatisfactory solution from the point of view of the railroads, they were even more offensive from the point of view of consumers who had to pay the exorbitant rates charged and submit to the abuses practiced. Shippers of all kinds suffered from the abuses and disorders of the railroads. In particular they resented rate and service discrimination between persons and places, favoritism that gave unfair advantages to powerful shippers and to cities where railroads had competition. A common grievance was the practice of charging more for a short haul than for a long haul. Small men resented bigness and the power it gave the railroads over legislatures, governors, and judges, and correctly charged some roads with using bribes

THE SCOURGE OF THE WEST.

The railroad as robber baron: 1885.

and free passes to corrupt or influence public officials. The low reputation railroads acquired by the underhanded means they had used to secure land grants, subsidies, and charters from federal and state governments continued to cling to them.

Popular resentment of abuses found expression in numerous state laws. In 1869 Massachusetts established a commission to supervise railroad activities and investigate grievances and made Adams a member. Within the next ten years a dozen more states established commissions modeled on that of Massachusetts. Several state legislatures in the Middle West adopted more thoroughgoing measures of regulation. Illinois, for example, laid down explicit and detailed provisions against discrimination and went further to give its commission power to bring suit "against any railroad corporation which may violate the provisions of this act." The Supreme Court upheld the constitutionality of the legislation in the case of *Munn* v. *Illinois* (1877) and declared that when private property is "affected with a public interest" it "must submit to be controlled by the public for the common good." Railroads nevertheless waged relentless war against such legislation, which in some states was

carelessly drawn, and limited its effectiveness from the start. Then in the Wabash case of 1886 (*Wabash, St. Louis, and Pacific Railway Co.* v. *Illinois*) a more laissez-faire Supreme Court reversed earlier decisions and held an Illinois statute invalid on the ground that it was the exclusive power of Congress to regulate interstate commerce. With the states thus excluded, any effective regulatory action would have to be taken by the federal government.

A second spur to federal action in 1886 was the report of a Senate committee headed by Senator Shelby M. Cullom of Illinois, which denounced railroads sharply for the "reckless strife" of their competition and for "unjust discrimination between persons, places, commodities, or particular descriptions of traffic." Railroad leaders themselves acknowledged the necessity for measures to end the anarchy in which they struggled, and the Republican platform of 1884 had declared that "the principle of the public regulation of railroad corporations is a wise and salutory one." The Interstate Commerce Act that eventually grew out of demands for regulation was a milestone in American history, but it was not a triumph of radicals over conservatives or of the people over the corporation.

The Interstate Commerce Act, passed by large majorities in both houses of Congress and signed by President Grover Cleveland on February 4, 1887, forbade railroads to engage in discriminatory practices, required them to publish their rate schedules, prohibited them from entering pooling agreements for the purpose of maintaining high rates, and declared that rates should be "reasonable and just." The act placed enforcement in the hands of an Interstate Commerce Commission of five members, who were to hear complaints and issue orders to the railroads to "cease and desist." For enforcement of its orders, however, the commission had to appeal to the courts, and there the advantage was consistently with the railroads. During the first eighteen years after the act was passed the Supreme Court heard sixteen cases brought before it by the Interstate Commerce Commission and decided fifteen for the railroads and against the commission. As an assertion of the federal government's right to regulate private enterprise and as a precedent for more effective measures in the future, the Interstate Commerce Act was important. But it did not provide any immediate solution to the problem of cutthroat competition. It was a conservative measure based on the old belief that competition was beneficial rather than harmful and adopted mainly to alleviate public anxieties.

Morgan and Banker Control   Within a year of the passage of the Interstate Commerce Act, the railroads began to return to the discriminatory practices that were now illegal. They were somewhat more secretive about rebates and blackmail competition, but it quickly became evident that the law had no teeth and that there was nothing to fear from the courts. With no effective government control, the industry appeared as anarchic as ever and management as quick to resort to speculative looting and stock-watering. Railroads generally continued to make profits and pay dividends through the 1880's and the early 1890's, but after decades of waste, mismanagement, and folly, many of them were in a shaky financial plight and in no condition to weather hard times. Railroad speculation and overexpansion had prepared the way for the panics of 1857 and 1873, and the first signal of the Panic of 1893 was the bankruptcy of the Philadelphia

and Reading Railroad on February 20. This panic was less closely connected with railroad overexpansion than the earlier panics, but it claimed more railroad victims. By the middle of 1894 there were 192 railroads in the hands of the receivers. "Never in the history of transportation in the United States," reported the Interstate Commerce Commission at that time, "has such a large percentage of railway mileage been under the control of receiverships." There were 40,818 miles of railway insolvent then, and 67,000 miles, or about one-third of the total mileage of the country, were foreclosed by the middle of 1898. Among the failures were some of the greatest systems in the country, including the Erie, the B. & O., the Union Pacific, and the Northern Pacific. To obtain the funds needed for reorganization, the distressed railroads turned to the bankers. They received not only reorganization but a measure of control that neither they themselves nor the state and federal governments had so far been able to contrive.

Numerous bankers took part in the railway reorganizations of the nineties, but none took so prominent and conspicuous a part as J. Pierpont Morgan, the dominant banker of his time. For a quarter of a century ending with his death in 1913, this tall, massive figure with piercing eyes and fiery nose was the very symbol of American financial power. Morgan began life near the top of the economic and social ladder, the son of a rich merchant from Hartford, Connecticut, who established a bank in London during the Civil War. He grew up with all the advantages of wealth, including a good education, travel and residence abroad, and study at the University of Goettingen, in Germany. He established his firm and his family in New York during the seventies in princely fashion, and began to collect treasures of art and rare books. His elegant steam yacht, *Corsair* (165 feet long at the water line), or its successors, *Corsair II* (204 feet) and *Corsair III* (302 feet), always awaited his pleasure in the harbor. Aboard his yacht or in the library of his home at 219 Madison Avenue the titans of industry and finance met at his call and submitted to agreements that made history in the world of business and sometimes in the world of politics as well. At such meetings he brought to bear his passion for order

J. Pierpont Morgan:
Private economic power.

and his distaste for competition. Morgan enhanced his reputation as a masterful peacemaker among railroads when in 1885 he intervened in a reckless war of blackmail competition between the New York Central and the Pennsylvania and persuaded them to abandon the destructive operation of parallel lines. It was natural that the managers of the sick railroads of the nineties should come to him, as to a famous surgeon, for the strong medicine and heroic surgery the bankrupt roads needed for recovery.

Other banking firms, such as Kuhn, Loeb & Company, employed the same methods as Morgan and charged huge fees for their services. First they ruthlessly pared down the fixed debt of the railroad, then assessed holders of the old stock for working funds, and next issued lavish amounts of new stock, heavily watered. To assure control along lines that suited them and to eliminate waste and ruinous competition, the bankers usually installed a president of their own selection and placed members of their own houses on the boards of railroad directors. Between 1894 and 1898 the House of Morgan reorganized the lion's share of big railroads, including the sprawling, demoralized Richmond Terminal, which became the Southern Railway, as well as the Erie, the Reading, the Norfolk and Western, the B. & O., the Cincinnati and Ohio, and, in alliance with James J. Hill, the Northern Pacific. Banker control was not the ideal solution or the final answer to the problems of competition and control, but it did curb prevailing anarchy, improve management and financial methods, and sometimes raise the standards and increase the efficiency of railroad service.

Industrial Empire

Carnegie and Steel The new industrial order of America was based on steel, and by 1870 the techniques of production, the supply of raw materials, and the home market were sufficiently developed to make the United States eventually the world's greatest steel producer. A cheap and practical process of making steel by forcing a blast of cold air through molten iron and cleansing it of impurities had been invented by Henry Bessemer, an Englishman, in 1857. A rival patent for the same process was held by William Kelly, a Kentucky ironmaster who claimed to have made the discovery before Bessemer. The two patents were merged in 1866, and the following year the first steel rails in the country were rolled for commercial use. In 1867 the United States made 1,643 tons of steel ingots; in 1897 it made 7,156,957. In the meantime new discoveries of ore deposits in the fabulous Lake Superior district opened exciting prospects for the ironmasters. Government surveyors in 1844 had discovered the Marquette Range in Michigan, including "a mountain of solid iron ore, 150 feet high." In 1868 the rich Vermilion Range in Minnesota was discovered, and in 1875 it was tapped by a railroad. Within the next decade the Menominee, the Gogebic, and the Mesabi mines—all within close proximity to Lake Superior and cheap water transportation—were opened up. Together they constituted the greatest iron-ore district in the world.

These opportunities brought a multitude of entrepreneurs into the field of iron and steel in quest of profits. By 1880 there were 1,005 iron companies in the nation, all of them subject to the competitive struggle under which the railroads labored, with all its uncertainties, anxieties, and ruthlessness. In fact the spread of the railroads intensified the competitive struggle in iron and steel by breaking down the protection against competition provided by distance, creating a national market. Like the railroad operators, the iron- and steelmasters resorted to cutthroat tactics, price-slashing, and blackmail. Faced with large fixed costs, they sometimes ran their plants at a loss rather than let them remain idle. They sought rebates and unfair advantages and rushed into pools, combinations, and mergers to hedge against competition. Out of the melee emerged one dominant figure, Andrew Carnegie, the most articulate industrialist America ever had.

Quite untypical of industrial leaders of his day in several respects, Carnegie was of immigrant and working-class origin, a voluble speaker, a facile writer, and a religious skeptic. He came to the United States from Scotland with his family when he was thirteen years old and went to work immediately to earn a living. At eighteen he became a telegraph clerk in the office of Thomas A. Scott, then a rising official of the Pennsylvania Railroad, and won his employer's favor and confidence. His service with Scott, which lasted through the Civil War, not only brought valuable acquaintance with the foremost railroad and industrial leaders of the country, but guided him in making shrewd and extremely profitable investments. With a salary of only $2,400 a year, he was receiving a millionaire's income from investments when he was twenty-eight years old. He was drawn into the iron business and then in 1872 into a venture for building a huge steel plant on the Monongahela River, twelve miles from Pittsburgh, a site with excellent river transportation and service from both the Pennsylvania and the B. & O. railroads. The new plant rolled its first rail in 1875.

Without pretense of engineering or technological skill, Carnegie was first of all a superb salesman with a genius for picking the right subordinates to supervise production. He was personally acquainted with all the railroad barons of the day and, as he said, simply "went out and persuaded them to give us orders." He did not have to remind them that steel rails lasted twenty times as long as iron. The supreme example of the industrial capitalist, Carnegie refused to permit his company to become a corporation, maintained it as a limited partnership, and retained a majority of the shares himself. Giving no hostages to the bankers, he used the firm's enormous profits to construct new plants, acquire raw materials, buy out competitors, and win fights with organized labor. His independent resources enabled him to go on building and spending even during depressions and thus to approach his goal of establishing an "integrated industry." He bought ore deposits in the Mesabi Range and ore ships on the Great Lakes, and he acquired docks, warehouses, and railroad lines to supply his great furnaces and mills with raw materials.

Carnegie had a remarkable gift for finding able lieutenants—men like Henry Clay Frick, Charles M. Schwab, Laurence C. Phipps, and Alexander R. Peacock. He pitted these men against one another in jealous competition, rewarding the successful with shares and partnerships. Like other capitalists of his day, he benefited from pools, rebates, and protective tariffs, but in time his power and resources became great enough to make him virtually independent of such devices. At the crest of his power he held the whole steel industry in his grasp. His trail to the top was strewn with ruined competitors, crushed partners, and broken labor movements. His bloody victory over labor at Homestead (see p. 439) had re-established the twelve-hour day. Carnegie increased his annual production from 322,000 tons in 1890 to 3,000,000 tons in 1900. Over the same decade he and his lieutenants increased the annual profits of the Carnegie Steel Company from $5,400,000 in 1890 to $40,000,000 in 1900. Carnegie's own share of the 1900 profits was approximately $25,000,000.

In the meantime Pierpont Morgan turned his attention from railroads to steel, and the bankers challenged the industrialists for the control of heavy industry. The American Steel and Wire Company, the first big combination in steel, was constructed without his help. Then in the summer of 1898 Morgan swung his support to Judge Elbert H. Gary of Chicago and other Midwesterners who merged several big concerns to form the Federal Steel Company, second only to Carnegie Steel in size. Quickly other mergers between hitherto competing steel firms sprang into being, "as if a giant magnet had moved over the surface of the industry," observed one historian. Morgan helped put together the National Tube Company and the American Bridge Company, and within two years the National Steel, the American Tin Plate, the American Sheet Steel, and the American Steel Hoop companies came into existence. The next obvious move in the drive for mergers was to combine the combinations —consolidate the whole industry into one vast

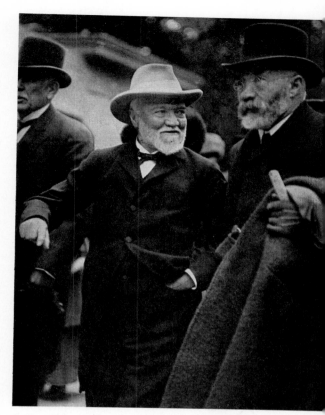

Andrew Carnegie (center): Steelmaster of Pittsburgh.

supercorporation, the greatest in the world. Blocking that dream was the mighty Carnegie Steel Company and the known prejudice of its head against banker control. Even Morgan threw up his hands when it was proposed that he buy up Carnegie Steel outright: "I don't believe I could raise the money," he said. The new combinations for making finished steel products then decided in the summer of 1900 to produce their own raw steel, free themselves from dependence on Carnegie, and cancel their contracts with him. Carnegie's response was a cable from Skibo Castle, his summer home in Scotland, declaring open war: "Have no fear as to result. Victory certain." He proposed to go into the production of finished steel products himself and drive all competitors to the wall.

Alarmed at the prospect of a war that would place the new steel combinations in deadly peril and demoralize the whole industry, Morgan determined to buy out Carnegie and consolidate the supercorporation. After a nightlong conference in the famous Morgan library, Charles M. Schwab agreed to take the matter up with Carnegie. The Scotsman scribbled a few figures on a scrap of paper and Schwab took it to Morgan. The banker glanced at it and said, "I accept." There was no bargaining. The figure was nearly a half billion dollars. In a few weeks he pushed and pulled the big steel companies into combination and on March 3, 1901, announced the organization of the United States Steel Corporation. The new concern brought under a single management three-fifths of the steel business of the country and was capitalized at nearly a billion and a half dollars.

The uneasy popular sentiment about the gigantic deal was reflected in the words the humorist Finley Peter Dunne put in the mouth of his Irish saloonkeeper, "Mr. Dooley":

> Pierpont Morgan calls in wan iv his office boys, th' prisidint iv a national bank, an' says he, "James," he says, "take some change out iv th' damper an' r-run out an' buy Europe f'r me," he says. "I intind to re-organize it an' put it on a paying basis," he says. "Call up the Czar an' th' Pope an' th' Sultan an' th' Impror Willum, an' tell thim we won't need their savices afther nex' week," he says. "Give thim a year's salary in advance."

Rockefeller and the Trusts An industrial giant of power and influence comparable to that wielded by Carnegie was John D. Rockefeller, who did for oil what the Scotsman did for steel. The two contemporaries were strikingly different in temperament and taste: Carnegie was exuberant and communicative, Rockefeller silent and taciturn; Carnegie was a skeptic and an agnostic, Rockefeller a Bible-class teacher and a devout Baptist. Both in their business methods and their achievements, however, there were many similarities. Both men showed the same astuteness in selecting lieutenants and putting them in the right jobs, the same abhorrence of waste and gambling, the same ability to transform depressions into opportunities for building, buying, and expanding. The Standard Oil Company, founded in 1872 with Rockefeller at its head, made ruthless use of railroad-rate discrimina-

tion, espionage, bogus companies, price-slashing, and other reprehensible practices. On the other hand, it had positive achievements to its credit, including improved and standardized products, the elimination of waste, and efficiency in distribution.

Rockefeller was the most oustanding American exponent of consolidation in industry. Of the trend toward consolidation he wrote:

> This movement was the origin of the whole system of modern economic administration. It has revolutionized the way of doing business all over the world. The time was ripe for it. It had to come, though all we saw at the moment was the need to save ourselves from wasteful conditions. . . . The day of combination is here to stay. Individualism has gone, never to return.

By "wasteful conditions" he meant the glutted markets in crude and refined oil, and the disorder, uncertainty, and wild fluctuation of prices and profits that attended free competition among thousands of small producers and hundreds of small refiners. Rockefeller hated free competition and believed that monopoly was the way of the future. His early method of dealing with competitors was to gain unfair advantage over them through special rates and secret rebates exacted from railroads.

The most notorious device of the sort was the short-lived South Improvement Company, by means of which Standard joined a few other oil companies in 1872 to demand special rates and secret advantages from the leading railroads in the Pennsylvania oil fields. They not only received large rebates on their own shipments, but also cash rebates on all shipments made by rivals outside the combination, as well as full and valuable reports on their competitors' business. The South Improvement scheme was soon exposed and had to be abandoned, but Standard continued to receive special advantages from the railroads and to use them to threaten or eliminate competitors. By such methods Standard Oil acquired some seventy-four refining companies and by 1878 was manufacturing a very large percentage of the national product of oil. When pipelines threatened the advantage gained through railroad favors, Standard quickly consolidated most of the pipelines in the Appalachian field into the United Pipe Lines Company, in which

Standard had controlling interest. Independent producers and refiners sought to escape the monopoly by building a pipeline across the Appalachian Mountains to the seaboard. Standard waged unrelenting war on the independent Tidewater Pipe Company, which succeeded in completing its line, but in 1883 it signed an agreement that gave Standard 88½ per cent of the business.

Rockefeller and his associates dealt competitors crushing blows with their nation-wide marketing organization, which could put irresistible pressure on competitors and force surrender. They strengthened their position further by manufacturing all commodities necessary to the trade, from barrels to bungs. Referring to his competitors, Rockefeller said: "They had not the means to build pipe lines, bulk ships, tank wagons; they couldn't have their agents all over the country; couldn't manufacture their own acid, bungs, wicks, lamps, do their own cooperage—so many things; it ramified indefinitely." He was convinced that small-unit enterprise and free competition were things of the past.

Standard Oil speeded up the progress of consolidation and the suppression of competition by forming a trust, first set up in 1879 and then revised in 1882. The trust was an old legal device, but Standard Oil lawyers put it to new use. They created a board of nine trustees, and persuaded all stockholders of twenty-seven competing oil companies to turn over their capital stock to the board and receive trust certificates in return. The trustees were now in position to harmonize and direct the affairs of a huge aggregation of capital, for according to the Standard Oil Trust agreement they were authorized "to hold, control, and manage the said stock and interests for the exclusive use and benefit" of the parties to the agreement. With competition thus brought under control, profits soared.

The Standard Oil Trust became the model for many imitators. Other American industries were plagued by much the same anarchy that had prompted the leaders in railroads, steel, and oil to force consolidation upon warring competitors. They had tried associations, agreements, and pools, but the trust had obvious advantages over the older devices. With the Standard Oil Trust as a pattern, some fif-teen new trusts appeared during the 1880's, including the American Cottonseed Oil Trust, the National Linseed Oil Trust, the National Lead Trust, the Whiskey Trust, and the Sugar Refineries Company.

The trust movement encountered active popular suspicion and hostility from the start. The American creed, bred of an agrarian heritage, held that business should be organized in small units, that competition should be unfettered, and that opportunity should be open to all. The trusts were an affront to this traditional faith: they were gigantic, all-powerful, even awe-inspiring. To the public, the trusts were the product of an evil plot born of greed, and that was the way the cartoonists pictured them in the newspapers and journals and the way popular political leaders described them in their speeches in the eighties. The popular attitude was not without foundation, for the trusts often did use their enormous power to the detriment of both consumers and small businessmen. A demand for government action against the trusts grew as rapidly as the trusts themselves.

As in railroad regulation, the state legislatures took the lead against the trusts. The laws they passed were never very effective, however, and the Wabash decision of 1886 limited the states here as it did in the regulation of railroads and left the problem up to the federal government. The growth of the trusts had stirred uneasiness in the East and the South as well as in the West, and by the campaign of 1888 all political parties of significance had inserted antitrust planks into their platforms. In that year John H. Reagan of Texas, the ex-Confederate postmaster general who had also fought for the Interstate Commerce Act, introduced an antitrust bill in the House (one of fourteen similar bills), and John Sherman of Ohio submitted one in the Senate. Debate in Congress revealed concern for the interests of both the consumer and the small business proprietor. It illustrated both the "folklore" of the old capitalism and apprehension about the new. The so-called Sherman Antitrust Act became law on July 2, 1890.

On the face of it the new act would seem to have spelled the end of every trust or trustlike combination. In effect it wrote common-law doctrine against monopoly into a federal statute. The opening sentence of the first section declares, "Every contract, combination in the form of trust or otherwise, or conspiracy, in restraint of trade or commerce among the several States, or with foreign nations, is hereby declared to be illegal." And the second section pronounces guilty of a misdemeanor "every person who shall monopolize, or attempt to monopolize, or combine or conspire with any other person or persons, to monopolize any part of the trade or commerce among the several States, or with foreign nations." The word "person" was specifically defined to include corporations, and the act fixed penalties, as the Interstate Commerce Act had not, for violations.

Efforts to enforce the act during the 1890's, however, proved most discouraging, for clever lawyers found loopholes and various ways of evading its provisions. Some trusts merely reorganized as huge corporations, while others pointed the way to the future by finding refuge in holding companies—that is, giant financial structures that held enough stock in member companies to control their policies. In the first five years after the act was passed, twenty-five new combinations came into being. Then in 1895 the first case under the Sherman Act was decided by the Supreme Court. A suit against the E. C. Knight Company of Philadelphia charged that in selling out to the American Sugar Refining Company it was guilty of furthering monopoly. Although the purchase rounded out one of the most complete monopolies in the country, the court decided that it did not violate the antitrust act. The court's reasoning was that manufacturing was not "commerce" within the meaning of the law, and that monopoly of manufacturing without "direct" effect on commerce was not subject to regulation by the federal government. *United States* v. *Knight* was an extreme instance of laissez-faire interpretation of the Constitution. After this signal that the law offered virtually no obstacle, consolidation went forward with a rush, and literally hundreds of new combinations sprang up in the next five years.

The course of Standard Oil from trust to holding company illustrates the trend. The company formally abandoned the trust agreement of 1882 under an Ohio court order in 1892, but in practice the same nine men who had served as trustees continued to conduct the business of the member companies for five years after the trust was formally dissolved. Charged with evading the court order, the trust reorganized in 1899 as a holding company under the laws of New Jersey, which permitted corporations of that state to own and control corporations of other states. The Standard Oil Company of New Jersey simply increased its stock some tenfold and exchanged it for stock of the member companies. These in turn elected directors of the New Jersey company, who carried on in the place of the old trustees. With concentration of control unimpaired and power enhanced instead of diminished, Standard made money as never before. In the eight years following its reorganization as a holding company, annual dividends on its stock varied between 30 and 48 per cent.

The Technology of Centralization
Concentration of ownership meant centralization of control. The management of a vast railroad network, a continentwide industry, or an international market from a central office in New York, Pittsburgh, or Chicago required a revolution in the technology of business administration and the technology of communication. American inventors outdid themselves to meet these demands. The number of patents issued to inventors jumped from fewer than two thousand a year in the 1850's to more than thirteen thousand a year in the 1870's and better than twenty-one thousand a year in the 1880's and 1890's. In those days the typical inventor was not a trained engineer in an industrial or university laboratory, but an individual tinkerer who frequently operated on a shoestring.

Such a man was Christopher L. Sholes, printer and journalist from Pennsylvania and Wisconsin, who invented a typewriter in 1867. He struggled vainly for six years to manufacture and market the machine before he sold his rights to the Remington Arms Company, which put the typewriter on the market in 1875. The year Sholes invented the typewriter, E. A. Callahan of Boston developed a superior stock ticker. In the summer of 1866 Cyrus W. Field employed new techniques to repair and improve his transatlantic cable, broken since 1858, and stock quotations spanned the ocean.

Numerous other inventions, including the adding machine (1888), quickened the pace of business transactions.

None of these inventions, however, could rival the importance of the telephone. This was the work of Alexander Graham Bell, a Scotsman who was educated in Edinburgh and London, emigrated to Canada in 1870, when he was twenty-three, and then to Boston two years later. As a teacher of speech to the deaf, he formed the ambition to "make iron talk"— to transmit speech electrically. His experiments over three years resulted in the magneto-electric telephone. He transmitted the first intelligible sentence on March 10, 1876, and a year later conducted a conversation between Boston and New York. The inventor and his supporters organized the Bell Telephone Company in 1877 and promptly plunged into law suits to defend their patent. The most formidable challenger was the Western Union Telegraph Company, which had originally spurned an opportunity to buy the patent for the "scientific toy" for a mere one hundred thousand dollars. Western Union settled out of court and left the field to Bell and his company, which continued to win hundreds of suits, improve the telephone, buy out competitors, and expand facilities. In 1885 the directors of Bell, led by Theodore N. Vail, organized the American Telephone and Telegraph Company. By 1900 it had become the holding company for the whole system, with some thirty-five subsidiaries and a capitalization of a quarter of a billion dollars.

The use of electricity for light is justly linked with the name of Thomas Alva Edison, who outdid his contemporary Bell as an inventor. The son of a Canadian who settled and prospered in Ohio, Edison grew up without formal schooling. He became a telegraph operator and while still quite young made some very profitable inventions to improve transmission. He then established himself as a businessman-inventor and built his own "invention factory," forerunner of the modern industrial research laboratory, at Menlo Park, New Jersey, in 1876. There in 1877 he invented the phonograph, and in later years his laboratories turned out hundreds of inventions or improvements, including the storage battery, the motion-picture projector, an electric dynamo, and

Andrew Carnegie: The Duties of Wealth

This, then, is held to be the duty of the man of wealth: To set an example of modest, unostentatious living, shunning display or extravagance; to provide moderately for the legitimate wants of those dependent upon him; and, after doing so, to consider all surplus revenues which come to him simply as trust funds, which he is called upon to administer, and strictly bound as a matter of duty to administer in the manner which, in his judgment, is best calculated to produce the most beneficial results for the community—the man of wealth thus becoming the mere trustee and agent for his poorer brethren, bringing to their service his superior wisdom, experience, and ability to administer, doing for them better than they would or could do for themselves.

From Andrew Carnegie, *The Gospel of Wealth and Other Essays*, 1901.

an electric locomotive. The electric light required a vacuum bulb with a durable filament. Edison made one that burned for forty hours in 1879 and improved it until it was commercially practicable. With the backing of J. Pierpont Morgan he organized the Edison Illuminating Company and moved to New York City to install an electric-light plant. On September 4, 1882, in the presence of Morgan, Edison threw a switch and the House of Morgan, the New York Stock Exchange, the New York *Times*, the New York *Herald*, and many smaller buildings in lower Manhattan began to glow with incandescent light.

Edison's plant used direct current, but in order to transmit electricity any distance its voltage had to be stepped up and then stepped down again. For this purpose alternating current and transformers were necessary. George Westinghouse of Pittsburgh, who had invented the railroad air brake in 1869, developed a power plant and a transformer in 1886 that could transmit high-voltage alternating current efficiently, safely, and cheaply over long distances. In spite of opposition from Edison and others with vested interests in direct-current plants, alternating current rapidly outstripped direct current for use in lighting.

For this type of current to be converted into mechanical power, an alternating-current mo-

Business Predators?

If our civilization is destroyed ... it will not be by ... barbarians from below. Our barbarians come from above. Our great money-makers have sprung in one generation into seats of power kings do not know. The forces and the wealth are new, and have been the opportunity of new men. Without restraints of culture, experience, the pride, or even the inherited caution of class or rank, these men, intoxicated, think they are the wave instead of the float, and that they have created the business which has created them. To them science is but a never-ending repertoire of investments stored up by nature for the syndicates, government but a fountain of franchises, the nations but customers in squads, and a million the unit of a new arithmetic of wealth written for them. They claim a power without control, exercised through forms which make it secret, anonymous, and perpetual. The possibilities of its gratification have been widening before them without interruption since they began, and even at a thousand millions they will feel no satiation and will see no place to stop. They are gluttons of luxury and power, rough, unsocialized, believing that mankind must be kept terrorized.

From Henry Demarest Lloyd, *Wealth Against Commonwealth*, 1894.

tor had to be developed. In 1888 Nikola Tesla, a Hungarian engineer who immigrated to the United States in 1884, invented such a motor. Westinghouse and his associates bought the patent, improved it with the aid of Tesla, and dramatically demonstrated the practicability of alternating current by illuminating the Columbian Exposition at Chicago in 1893, and by harnessing the might of Niagara Falls and transmitting the power over the countryside. While American industry continued to depend mainly upon steam and water for power until the end of the century, factories no longer had to hover around waterfalls and coal supplies. They were now ready for the electrical revolution that came in the twentieth century.

Laissez-Faire Conservatism

The Gospel of Wealth A survey of private fortunes conducted in 1892 revealed that there were 4,047 millionaires in the United States. These were new fortunes; very few of them dated from before the Civil War, when a millionaire was a rarity. Only 84 of the millionaires of 1892 were in agriculture, and most of those were cattle barons. The fortunes of the new plutocracy were based on industry, trade, railroads. The new plutocrats were the masters and directors of the economic revolution that was changing the face of American society.

To say that these men were "conservative" is to put a strain on customary usage of the word, for conservatives are usually opposed to change and devoted to tradition. Yet these men flouted tradition and preached "progress." To confuse customary usage further, they adopted the slogan "laissez faire," which was traditionally the doctrine of Jeffersonian and Jacksonian liberals and radicals. In one of the strangest reversals in the history of political thought, the new conservatives took over virtually the whole liberal vocabulary of concepts and slogans, including "democracy," "liberty," "equality," "opportunity," and "individualism," and turned it against the liberals. In short, they gave an economic and material turn to ethical and idealistic concepts. Man became economic man, democracy was identified with capitalism, liberty with property and the use of it, equality with opportunity for gain, and progress with economic change and the accumulation of capital. God and nature were thus in league with the Gospel of Wealth.

The new doctrine was conservative, however, in the sense that it was bent on defending the status quo, conserving the privileges by which vast accumulations of wealth were gained, and preventing government interference with those privileges. The laissez-faire conservatives naturally found comfort in classical economics, and those who had heard of them found special fascination in the biological theories of Charles Darwin and the sociological theory of Herbert Spencer. The ideas of the great English biologist, which were taken up by American scientists after the Civil War, found early acceptance in the older colleges, and were spread abroad by popular writers and lecturers. Herbert Spencer, an English philosopher, found zealous American apostles in John Fiske, a prolific writer and lecturer, and Edward L. Youmans, self-appointed salesman of Spencer's ideas. Spencer applied biological concepts, especially the concept of natural selection, to social principles and justified the unimpeded struggle for existence on the ground that "survival of the fittest" made for human progress. State interference in behalf of the weak would only impede progress. The tooth-and-claw competition of the postwar American economy prepared the perfect market for ideas that glorified laissez faire as the secret of progress. The people could readily see the industrial struggles around them in terms of the Darwinian jungle. It is not surprising that Darwin and Spencer were more readily acclaimed and more widely admired in America than they were in their native England. "The peculiar condition of American society," wrote the preacher Henry Ward Beecher to Spencer, "has made your writings far more fruitful and quickening here than in Europe." By 1903 more than 368,000 volumes of Spencer's works had been sold in the United States, and many Americans who had never opened one of them or even heard of the author spoke glibly of "the struggle for survival," "natural selection," and "the survival of the fittest." So thoroughly did these concepts become associated with laissez-faire conservatism that the new doctrine has appropriately been called "social Darwinism."

Professors, clergymen, and intellectuals as well as businessmen were captivated by the new philosophy. Professor William Graham Sumner of Yale, the most articulate and influential exponent, in an essay called "The Concentration of Wealth: Its Economic Justification," wrote, "What matters it then that some millionaires are idle, or silly, or vulgar. . . . The millionaires are a product of natural selection, acting on the whole body of men to pick out those who can meet the requirement of certain work to be done. . . . They get high wages and live in luxury, but the bargain is a good one for society." William Lawrence, the Episcopal Bishop of Massachusetts, announced, "Now we are in a position to affirm that neither history, experience, nor the Bible necessarily sustains the common distrust of the effect of material wealth on morality. . . . Godliness is in league with riches. . . . The race is to the strong." Rockefeller said, "The growth of a large business is merely a survival of the fittest . . . the working out of a law of nature and a law of God." Carnegie admitted that while this "may sometimes be hard for the

---

Industrial Giants?

The question of motive enters into any consideration either of economic vision or of business ethics; and it is important because some writers of the muckraking school have grievously misconstrued the motives ... of a whole generation of business leaders. They sum up these motives in the word "greed," as if it were greed which led Carnegie to build steel mills, Rockefeller to organize the oil industry, Westinghouse to develop the electrical industry, and Ford to manufacture motor cars. If we wish to misuse the word greed we can apply it in many contexts. We can say that Shakespeare was greedy for fame, Lincoln greedy for political power, and Duse greedy for applause. But such a word means nothing in the analysis of motive. What these figures were really interested in was competitive achievement, self-expression, and the imposition of their wills on a given environment. And these were precisely the motives which actuated Carnegie, Westinghouse, and Rockefeller.... The men who built the really towering economic structures were not thinking primarily of dollars, or they would have halted at the first story.

From Allan Nevins, *John D. Rockefeller*, 1940.

---

individual, it is best for the race, because it insures the survival of the fittest in every department."

By the time it had become fully elaborated, the Gospel of Wealth and its corollaries of social Darwinism included many propositions widely accepted. Among them were the following: (1) That the American economy was controlled for the benefit of all by a natural aristocracy, and that these leaders were brought to the top by a competitive struggle that weeded out the weak, the incompetent, and the unfit and selected the strong, the able, and the wise. (2) That politicians were not subject to rigorous natural selection, and therefore could not be trusted to the same degree as businessmen. (3) That the state should confine itself to police activities of protecting property and maintaining order, and that if it interfered with economic affairs it would upset the beneficent effect of natural selection. (4) That slums and poverty were the unfortunate but inevitable negative results of the competitive struggle, and that state intervention to eliminate them was misguided. (5) That the stewardship of wealth obliged the rich to try to ameliorate social injustice.

Though these ideas may be regarded as a rationalization of the rule of a privileged group, they were by no means confined to members of that group. They also became the common assumption of millions, a sort of folk faith. The popular demand for success stories like those in the novels of Horatio Alger, whose 119 books were filled with rags-to-riches heroes for boy readers, suggests that the mass of Americans were as firm in their faith in the Gospel of Work as they were in their faith in the Gospel of Wealth. The business creed absorbed and fostered both faiths for its own purposes.

In the Supreme Court the Gospel of Wealth found institutional support of great prestige and incomparable value. Under the persistent tutelage of Justice Stephen J. Field, the court had been converted by the mid-eighties to the view that Herbert Spencer's *Social Statics* coincided remarkably well with the will of the Founding Fathers and the soundest moral precepts of the ages. Interpreting the "due process" clause of the Fourteenth Amendment as a protection intended to cover corporate enterprise, the Court proceeded to declare state regulatory measures unconstitutional on the ground that they deprived corporations of property without due process of law. By the end of the century, the Court's laissez-faire interpretation of the Constitution had debarred the states in many fields from the exercise of ancient police powers for the protection of the public interest and the welfare of workers.

Social Critics and Dissenters   The Gospel of Wealth and the Darwinian apology for unrestrained capitalism did not meet with universal acceptance, however, for those doctrines were challenged by social critics, economists, and clergymen. The dissenters themselves were influenced by Darwin, but they interpreted the social implications of his theories in a different way. They rejected the survival-of-the-fittest concept of social progress and found a place for ethical values in economic theory, as well as a need for governmental intervention to restrain the strong and protect the weak. A strong religious impulse often motivated the nonclerical as well as the clerical critics of social Darwinism.

Lester Frank Ward, one of the founders of sociology in America, was an outspoken critic of Spencer's theories. Ward took a job in a Washington bureau in 1865, after service in the Union army, and remained in government work for some forty years. Largely self-educated, he compensated for his impoverished background by astonishing feats of learning. He mastered ten languages and several fields of science in addition to sociology, and, when he finally found acceptance in academic life, he entitled a course he gave at Brown University "A Survey of All Knowledge." His first book, *Dynamic Sociology* (1883), was a prodigious work of fourteen hundred pages that was not easily or widely read. He never achieved the acclaim or the influence his conservative rival, Professor Sumner, did. Ward pointed out that there was a difference between animal and human economics. Darwinian laws governed the former, but the human mind transformed the environment of human economics and substituted rational choice for natural selection. This was as it should be, for nature was terribly wasteful in her crude methods of evolution. Unrestrained competition actually prevented the fittest from surviving, and the doctrine of laissez faire killed off whatever benefits competition conferred by encouraging monopoly and by leaving no competitors to compete. For competition to survive, government regulation was necessary. Ward believed in social planning and had great faith in education. "Thus far," he wrote, "social progress has in a certain awkward manner taken care of itself, but in the near future it will have to be cared for." The caring, he said, should be done by social engineers, scientific planners, and managers of society.

A second self-taught social philosopher of the age, and the most original economist of them all, was Henry George, author of the famous book *Progress and Poverty* (1879). Born in Philadelphia, George traveled in the Orient and in 1868 settled in California, where he had ample opportunity to observe the land speculation, land monopoly, and social distress that played so important a part in his economics. Addressing himself to the problem of unequal distribution of wealth, he inveighed against the "shocking contrast between monstrous

Henry George:
The Nature of Property

What constitutes the rightful basis of property? What is it that enables a man justly to say of a thing, "It is mine"? From what springs the sentiment which acknowledges his exclusive right as against all the world? Is it not, primarily, the right of a man to himself, to the use of his own powers, to the enjoyment of the fruits of his own exertions? Is it not this individual right, which springs from and is testified to by the natural facts of individual organization—the fact that each particular pair of hands obey a particular brain and are related to a particular stomach; the fact that each man is a definite, coherent, independent whole—which alone justifies individual ownership? As a man belongs to himself, so his labor when put in concrete form belongs to him....

If production give to the producer the right to exclusive possession and enjoyment, there can rightfully be no exclusive possession and enjoyment of anything not the production of labor, and the recognition of private property in land is a wrong.

From Henry George, *Progress and Poverty*, 1879.

---

wealth and debasing want." Wealth is produced, he concluded, by applying labor to land, and capital is the surplus above the cost of labor. Labor therefore creates all capital. But capital, by withholding advantageous land sites until their value has been enhanced by labor in adjacent areas, reaps a profit out of all proportion to its contribution. This profit George called the "unearned increment." Since land should no more be monopolized than air and sunshine, George's solution was to tax land in such a fashion as to appropriate the unearned increment. This was to be done by a "single tax" which would make other taxes unnecessary and would result in common ownership of the land by the people. George's book and his lectures won him a political following at home and abroad and enabled him to make a strong showing as candidate for mayor of New York in 1886.

Another party born of a book was the Nationalist movement: this time the book was Edward Bellamy's *Looking Backward* (1888). The most successful of several utopian novels published during the eighties, Bellamy's book "looked backward" to the benighted 1880's from the collectivized society of the year 2000 A.D. By that time selfishness has been eliminated by the abolition of private property and the nationalization of industry. Competition is seen to have killed nineteenth-century society and its individualism. "Competition," says the protagonist, "which is the instinct of selfishness, is another word for dissipation of energy, while combination is the secret of efficient production." Bellamy's attack on the ethic of "survival of the fittest" appealed to a wide variety of people, who for a time sought to maintain a political organization. Nationalist clubs and periodicals fostered municipal ownership of utilities and public ownership of railroads. As agrarian reform mounted in the nineties, however, the Nationalists tended to join the farmers' parties and abandon their own organization.

From the viewpoint of a later day, the debate over laissez-faire doctrine and social Darwinism appears confused and paradoxical. If free competition was the goal of laissez faire, the industrialists who hated competition and sought to restrain it would seem to have embraced the wrong doctrine. If social Darwinism taught hands off by the government, the businessmen who sought subsidies, protection, and favors from the government again seemed inconsistent. But in so far as these doctrines were useful for the defense of the status quo and the discouragement of efforts to reform or change society by conscious purpose the conservatives were right in embracing them and the radicals in rejecting them.

The House of Labor

Man and the Machine In the long run industrialization raises the living standard and increases the opportunities of labor, but around the world labor has discovered that the revolution that establishes industrialization comes at heavy cost and that the worker's adjustment to the machine and the factory way of life is often painful and difficult. In America the labor shortage that had persisted since colonial times had kept the level of wages higher than the level that prevailed abroad; and yet the American worker had his full share of troubles in the grim iron age of industry.

Many of the adjustments the worker had to

make were hard to understand and painful to accept, for they meant loss of status and surrender of independence. The skilled craftsman who owned the tools he used was likely to be an individualist who took pride in the quality of his product and enjoyed a strong bargaining position. The new factory discipline offered a humbler role and a lower status. In the factory the worker surrendered his tools, nearly all the creative pride he took in his product, most of his independence, and much of his bargaining power. He became the tender of a machine that set the work pace and the employee of owners whom he probably never met and never saw. The craftsmanship that had been the skilled worker's source of pride and security was no longer of any significance, for his place at the machine could be taken by an unskilled worker. The growing impersonality of his relations to his work and his employer and the ever-increasing size of the industrial organization meant a sacrifice in security, identity, and the satisfactions that bestow meaning and value on work.

Adjustment would have been easier had the change been less swift and the worker better prepared. But the mechanization and expansion of the factory system hit a breath-taking pace during the 1880's. Between 1880 and 1890 the total capital invested in the production of machinery increased two and a half times, and the average investment in machinery increased 200 per cent for each establishment and 50 per cent for each employee. The manufacturer, with all his capital tied up in new machinery, was driven to seek a rapid return on his products, generally at low prices in a highly competitive market. The hard-pressed employer often made economies at the expense of the unskilled factory workers, who suffered low wages, long hours, and working conditions that impaired their safety, their comfort, and their health. The great body of legislation that now protects factory workers had not yet been written in the eighties and nineties. Employers thought nothing of using detectives and armed force to thwart the organization of labor unions, and in "company towns," where all houses, stores, and services were company-owned, employers subjected workers to endless harassments and petty tyranny. There was nothing but the urging of conscience and the weak protest of labor to restrain employers from cutting costs at the expense of their workers.

The average weekly wages of common laborers remained less than nine dollars throughout the nineties, and farm laborers got less than half that amount. After the depression of the seventies, however, there was a fairly steady increase in real wages—for those who had jobs. The rise in real wages helps explain labor's attachment to the system and its relative indifference to socialism. The millions who suffered unemployment during the depressions of the last three decades of the century were not even enumerated, much less assisted, by the government. The most insistent demand of organized labor was for the eight-hour day, but the main result was the adoption of a federal law passed in 1869, and amended in 1892, limiting the work day of federal employees to eight hours. In private industry, however, most workers continued to work a ten-hour day and a six-day week, and in steel and other industries they worked even longer. The accident toll taken by heedless negligence, and the damage done to workers' health by poor ventilation and lighting, dust and fumes, were all charged off as the cost of progress.

A special handicap of American labor was its lack of homogeneity. Workers divided by race, color, and national origin formed exclusive groups to protect their own privilege and to keep underprivileged groups at bay. Between 1882 and 1900 there were fifty strikes waged against the employment of Negro labor. Negroes sometimes served as strikebreakers, thereby increasing the resentment of white workers.

Immigrants formed the largest segment of the American labor force, except in the South, where few of them settled. There had been immigrant workers from the start in the United States, but now they were coming in greater numbers and from different parts of Europe, mainly the southern and eastern countries. Nineteenth-century immigration reached high tide in the 1880's, when nearly five and a quarter million immigrants arrived, two and a half million more than had come in the seventies and a million and a half more than were to come in the nineties. Set apart by language and culture, accustomed to lower wages and living standards, the newcomers often arrived single, without families to feed, and were willing to accept any work under almost any conditions. Native workers often looked down on them with contempt and spoke of work for which they were suited as "foreign jobs." The new immigrants crowded into the coal-mining and steel industries, with each wave pushing the earlier comers a step up the ladder. The bitterest and most implacable labor opposition to immigrants was directed at the Asiatics, particularly the Chinese of California. The Workingmen's party of California, led by Denis Kearney, an orator of Irish birth who blatantly exploited race prejudices of the West Coast, placed a provision in the state constitution in 1879 prohibiting corporations from hiring Chinese workers. Supported by labor organizations in the East, the Californians persuaded Congress in 1882 to suspend admission of Chinese immigrants for ten years.

Unions and Strikes   For a long time the attitude of American labor toward unions and collective bargaining was typically that of the skilled craftsman or the small shopkeeper. Native workers, and many immigrants as well, were reluctant to abandon the American dream of rising higher and higher in the social scale. Instead of accepting the new industrial order and its conditions, they looked back nostalgically to the past and longed for the good old days. Longings of this sort found expression in such slogans as "every man his own master," or "every man his own employer." Labor unions remained very weak throughout the nineteenth century, embracing not more than 1 or 2 per cent of the total labor force and less than 10 per cent of the industrial workers.

During and after the Civil War the typical national trade union was designed primarily to protect the status of skilled craftsmen. In 1866 William H. Sylvis, an iron-molder of Pennsylvania, attempted to unite the trade unions into a single organization called the National Labor Union. This organization, of which Sylvis became president in 1868, bore no resemblance to modern labor unions. It was led by visionaries and idealists who did not believe in strikes and who were unconcerned with the immediate needs of working people, apart from the eight-hour day. Sylvis stressed long-range reforms and humanitarian demands, and admitted farmers' societies and advocates of women's rights as members. The organization changed its name to the National Labor party in 1871, and after a feeble showing in the election of 1872 the new party went to pieces.

With many of the same generous impulses and naïve assumptions, the Noble and Holy Order of the Knights of Labor was founded in 1869. A secret fraternal order with high-flown titles and elaborate rituals, the Knights sought to unite all labor and welcomed all "toilers" of whatever color, race, nationality, or craft, whether skilled or unskilled. They excluded only gamblers, bankers, liquor dealers, and a few others—apparently on moralistic grounds. Utopian and nostalgic in many of their views, the Knights frowned on the use of the strike and promoted dreams of restoring the past. Their labor program, however, included demands for a federal bureau of statistics, equal pay for both sexes, the eight-hour day, and the abolition of child and prison labor. The two hundred or more consumer and producer cooperatives the Knights founded elicited great enthusiasm, but little profit. Many of their political demands resembled those of contemporary farmers' organizations, for they included paper money, an income tax, abolition of the national bank, and prohibition.

The Knights, like Sylvis, however, grasped one important fact of the new economy: that the consolidation of industry made necessary the consolidation of labor. They founded their General Assembly in 1878 with a view to centralizing control over labor in order to combat the monopolistic power of corporations. In 1879 they elected Terence V. Powderly as their Grand Master Workman. The dominant figure in the Order during the years of its power and influence, Powderly summed up many of its contradictions in his own person and views. A newspaperman described him at a labor convention in 1886 as elegantly dressed in "double-breasted, black, broadcloth coat, stand-up collar, plain tie, dark trousers and narrow small shoes," surrounded by "horny-fisted sons of toil" and acting "like Queen Victoria at a national Democratic convention." Powderly constantly preached against strikes, and yet it was as a result of strikes in 1885–86 that the Order made its most sensational gains.

These were spontaneous revolts rather than organized strikes, but under their stimulus membership soared from about one hundred thousand to over seven hundred thousand. The strength of the Order quickly ebbed after the upheavals of 1886, and two years later its membership had fallen to two hundred thousand. By 1893 it was virtually defunct.

In the meantime the American Federation of Labor, founded in 1881, was hammering out a labor philosophy more closely related to the realities of the industrial economy and more in harmony with the future. Rejecting the vague utopian radicalism of the Knights of Labor, the AFL foreswore political goals for economic objectives. Instead of embracing the brotherhood of all workers, it devoted its attention to gaining concrete benefits for skilled workers organized along craft lines. It was a loose alliance of national trade unions, each of which retained a large amount of autonomy, with jurisdiction over its own affairs and with the power to call its own strikes. Unlike the Knights, the AFL did not hesitate to acknowledge the strike and the boycott as legitimate means of collective bargaining. These principles were fully formulated by 1881 and reaffirmed when the AFL was reorganized in 1886.

As its first president the AFL elected Samuel Gompers, who retained the office for nearly forty years. An immigrant boy, born in London in 1850, Gompers grew up in the trade union movement. Under the impact of his experience in America he gradually put aside his earlier leanings to socialism and slowly shaped a pragmatic approach to the problems of labor. He felt that labor should accept the economic system and should try to win for itself a respectable place as a "legitimate" group within that system, as legitimate as business or the church. And to do so, he argued, labor would have to struggle day by day for higher wages and lower hours. "Unions, pure and simple," he said, "are the natural organization of wage workers to secure their present material and practical improvement and to achieve their final emancipation. . . . The way out of the wage system is through higher wages." The AFL grew rapidly as the Knights declined, and within fifteen years its membership had passed the million mark.

Labor's struggle to win acceptance and to improve its lot was marked by an extraordinary number of strikes and lockouts, conflicts that sometimes flared into bloodshed, particularly in time of depression. In July 1877 a series of wage cuts and abortive strikes provoked an upheaval of insurrectionary violence along the trunk lines of three big railroads. In the first show of violence, along the B. & O., federal troops were called in after a mob intimidated state militia. In Pittsburgh the community joined the strikers against the Pennsylvania Railroad and destroyed five million dollars' worth of property before being dispersed with heavy loss of life. Other disturbances broke out in Philadelphia, Harrisburg, Reading, Scranton, Buffalo, and Toledo, and farther west in St. Louis, Chicago, and San Francisco. Scores of people lost their lives, and property valued at millions of dollars went up in flames. The courts clamped down, the police became more ruthless, and the public began to withdraw its sympathy from the labor movement. Another upsurge of labor militancy occurred during the mid-eighties. With the Knights of Labor at the peak of their strength the loose rhetoric of labor solidarity ceased to be merely verbal and materialized in general strikes, sympathetic work-stoppage, and nationwide boycotts and political demonstrations. During 1886, a climactic year in labor history, 610,000 men were out on strike, more than three times the average of the five preceding years. Then on May 4, during an anarchist demonstration against police brutalities at Haymarket Square in Chicago, a bomb was thrown that killed a policeman and fatally wounded six other persons. A jury found eight anarchists guilty and four were hanged, though the identity of the bomb-thrower was never established. The incident smeared the whole labor movement, especially the Knights, with the charge of anarchism and subjected labor to public suspicion and hostility.

Resort to violence was common in the turbulent nineties, but often labor was merely replying to force with force. In the remote Coeur d'Alene district of Idaho company guards and miners fought it out in 1892 with rifles and dynamite until at last federal troops came in, crushed the strike, and turned the miners' jobs over to strikebreakers. At Carnegie's Homestead steel plant in Pennsylvania the same year

3,800 members of the Amalgamated Association of Iron and Steel Workers struck over wage cuts and working conditions. As a preparation for breaking the strike, Henry C. Frick, the manager, imported three hundred Pinkerton detectives. When they arrived at the plant on barges, the strikers resisted and a gun fight ensued that resulted in the death of three detectives and ten strikers, the wounding of a much larger number, and the surrender of the detectives. The sufferings of the workers stirred great public sympathy, a sympathy that was not entirely alienated by the attempt of an anarchist, who had no connection with the strike, to assassinate Frick. In the end, however, the strike failed miserably, and its failure destroyed unionism in the steel industry for nearly five decades to come.

The great depression that started in 1893 (see p. 485) brought on a new wave of wage cuts, layoffs, and strikes. More men were thrown out of work by strikes in 1894, a year of exceptional unemployment and labor violence, than in any previous year. The most important strike of that year, and of many years to come, was the big railroad strike centering in Chicago. It did not originate among railway workers but among factory workers in George M. Pullman's "model" company town just south of Chicago. The men were driven to desperation by five wage cuts in one year and no reduction in the high rents charged for company houses. The Pullman workers had recently joined the new American Railway Union, headed by Eugene V. Debs and frowned on by the older Railway Brotherhoods of the AFL. Although Debs urged caution, his union voted to refuse to handle Pullman cars if the management would not accept arbitration of the strike. Pullman rejected all arbitration, and the General Managers Association came to his aid by dismissing switchmen who boycotted his cars. The union then struck against the railroads and by the end of June 1894 nearly all railroad men on roads west of Chicago were on strike.

Acting for the railroads, the General Managers Association than appealed directly to the federal government to intervene with armed force and end the strike. There had been no violence so far, and the Constitution allowed federal intervention with troops only upon the request of the state government, a move that Governor John P. Altgeld strongly opposed. Railroad lawyers had no trouble persuading President Cleveland and Attorney General Richard Olney, himself a railroad attorney and director, that intervention could nevertheless be justified on the ground that the strike had obstructed the delivery of United States mail. Actually, the railroads themselves refused, against the union's wishes, to attach mail cars to trains boycotting Pullman cars. Nevertheless, Olney secured an injunction against the union, and on July 4 Cleveland sent some two thousand troops to Chicago to enforce the injunction and protect the mails. After the troops arrived, the union completely lost control of the situation, and mobs of looters destroyed cars and burned and stole property. Twelve people were killed and many arrested at the scene, but none were strikers. The effect of the troop action was to break the strike, a result that Olney, by his own confession, intended to accomplish.

The failure of the Pullman strike had important consequences for the future of American labor. Debs and other union officials were tried and sentenced to jail for contempt of court in disobeying the injunction against the union. The Supreme Court in upholding the sentence gave the use of the injunction in labor disputes a prestige it had never before enjoyed. And the government in suggesting that a strike might be construed as a conspiracy in restraint of trade under the Sherman Antitrust Act placed a powerful weapon in the hands of management for use against unions. Another unforeseen consequence of the Pullman strike and the Court's decision was to bring into national prominence for the first time the name of Eugene V. Debs. Within a few years he was to become the foremost leader of the socialist movement in the country, a position he was to hold during the years when that movement enjoyed its greatest strength.

Any realistic account of the ordeal of industrialization in America will tell of heedless waste and ruthless exploitation, of cutthroat competition and consolidation. Whatever economic progress came out of the grim struggle— and undoubtedly much was gained—was purchased at a high cost in brutalized labor, wasted resources, and deterioration in business and public ethics. Historians who emphasize the necessity for industrialization and the advantages ultimately derived from it remind us that the costs of industrialization have never been low, and that when reckoned in human suffering and social turmoil the price has been even more appalling in other countries than in the United States. And in all fairness, the American ordeal should be judged in comparison with that of England, which came before the American experience, and that of Russia, which came after it. In neither case does the American record, as bad as it was, suffer by comparison.

SUGGESTIONS FOR READING

Learning and wit combine to make E. C. Kirkland, *Industry Comes of Age: Business, Labor, and Public Policy, 1860–1897* (1961), a survey of most superior quality. A much briefer sketch of value is S. P. Hays, *The Response to Industrialism: 1885–1914* * (1957). I. M. Tarbell, *The Nationalizing of Business, 1878–1898* (1936), and T. C. Cochran and William Miller, *The Age of Enterprise* (1942), contain excellent chapters. Two older books still worth while are L. C. A. Knowles, *Economic Development in the Nineteenth Century* (1932), and D. A. Wells, *Recent Economic Change* (1890).

The railroad establishment of the period is described in G. R. Taylor and I. D. Neu, *The American Railroad Network, 1861–1890* (1956). Railroading in the West is treated in R. E. Riegel, *The Story of the Western Railroads* (1926), and in R. E. Overton, *Burlington West* (1941) and *Gulf to Rockies* (1953); in New England by E. C. Kirkland, *Men, Cities and Transportation*, 2 vols. (1948); and in the South by J. F. Stover, *The Railroads of the South, 1865–1900* (1955). On consolidation and management see E. G. Campbell, *The Reorganization of the American Railroad System, 1893–1900* (1938). Matthew Josephson, *The Robber Barons* (1934), stresses the misdeeds of the capitalists, and T. C. Cochran, *Railroad Leaders, 1845–1890* (1953), emphasizes their attitudes and problems. New light on government regulation comes from Lee Benson, *Merchants, Farmers, and Railroads* (1955).

On technological developments, Lewis Mumford, *Technics and Civilization* (1934), is suggestive. An authoritative work of reference is Vol. V of *A History of Technology*, ed. by Charles Singer *et al.*, entitled *The Late Nineteenth Century, c. 1850 to c. 1900* (1958). Roger Burlingame, *Engines of Democracy* (1940), is a narrative of inventions, and Waldemar Kaempffert, *A Popular History of American Invention*, 2 vols. (1924), is full of interesting detail. A good biography of a major inventor is Matthew Josephson, *Edison* (1959). Heavy industry and manufacturing generally are treated in V. S. Clark, *History of Manufactures in the United States from 1607–1928*, 3 vols., Vol. II (1929); a briefer account is Malcolm Keir, *Manufacturing Industries in America* (1920). H. C. Passer, *The Electrical Manufacturers, 1875–1900* (1953), reveals much about technical change and economic growth.

On the steel industry, Andrew Carnegie, *Autobiography* (1920), and his official biography, B. J. Hendrick, *The Life of Andrew Carnegie*, 2 vols. (1932), are highly informative, as is J. K. Winkler, *Incredible Carnegie* (1931). Oil and Rockefeller are the subject of more exhaustive studies, including Allan Nevins, *John D. Rockefeller*, 2 vols. (1940); R. W. Hidy and M. E. Hidy, *Pioneering in Big Business, 1882–1911* (1955); and P. H. Giddens, *Early Days of Oil* (1948). For contrasting points of view on Rockefeller, see Earl Latham, *John D. Rockefeller: Robber Baron or Industrial Statesman?* (1949). The trust and early regulatory legislation are most fully treated in H. B. Thorelli, *The Federal Antitrust Policy* (1954), but see also W. Z. Ripley, *Trusts, Pools and Corporations* (1905), John Moody, *The Truth About the Trusts* (1904), and H. D. Lloyd, *Wealth Against Commonwealth* (1894).

The business philosophy of laissez faire is perceptively treated in E. C. Kirkland, *Business in the Gilded Age* (1952) and *Dream and Thought in the Business Community, 1860–1900* (1956), and by R. G. McCloskey, *American Conservatism in the Age of Enterprise* (1951). Chapters in

* Available in a paperback edition.

R. H. Gabriel, *The Course of American Democratic Thought* (1940), are illuminating. Richard Hofstadter, *Social Darwinism in American Thought* * (1944), throws much light on both laissez faire and its critics; and so does Sidney Fine, *Laissez Faire and the General Welfare State: A Study of Conflict in American Thought, 1865–1901* (1956). The authority on Henry George is C. A. Barker, *Henry George* (1955). See Samuel Churgerman, *Lester F. Ward: The American Aristotle* (1939), and A. E. Morgan, *Edward Bellamy* (1944), for the best treatment of these men.

For detailed history, J. R. Commons and others, *History of Labour in the United States*, 4 vols. (1936), is indispensable; Vol. III is on this period. A useful brief survey is Henry Pelling, *American Labor* (1960). On the Knights of Labor, see N. J. Ware, *The Labor Movement in the United States, 1860–1893* (1929), and on its great rival see Philip Taft, *The A. F. of L. in the Time of Gompers* (1957). An important analytical study is Lloyd Ulman, *The Rise of the National Trade Union* (1955). Autobiographies of the two foremost leaders of labor are T. V. Powderly, *Thirty Years of Labor* (1889), and Samuel Gompers, *Seventy Years of Life and Labor*, 2 vols. (1925).

Industrial life and business struggles have been the subjects of such novels as Henry James, *The American* (1877); John Hay, *The Breadwinners* (1883), an antilabor work; W.D. Howells, *The Rise of Silas Lapham* (1885), the study of a businessman; and Theodore Dreiser, *The Financier* (1912) and *The Titan* (1914), portraits of industrial tycoons. Edward Bellamy, *Looking Backward, 2000–1887* (1888), is a utopian novel that started a reform party.

* Available in a paperback edition.

19

The Urban Society

"The United States was born in the country and has moved to the city." A great deal of American history is summed up in this observation by Richard Hofstadter. Old America was rural by birth, by breeding, and in outlook. The Founding Fathers, their children, and their grandchildren were typically country-men, and it was inevitable that their problems, their values, and their myths should have been shaped by the setting in which they lived. It was just as inevitable that the problems, values, and myths of modern America should be shaped by the urban environment that eventually replaced the old agrarian setting. The new environment created new problems and strained old institutions. It compelled new adjustments in politics, religion, education, and economic life, and it left a profound imprint upon the arts and literature.

America Moves to Town

The Pull of the City　In 1790, the year of the first census, only 3.35 per cent of the population lived in towns of eight thousand or more. By the end of the nineteenth century ten times that, a third of the population, was classified "urban" by this definition. The cities grew with the nation, of course, but after about 1820 they grew much faster than the nation. Between 1800 and 1890 the population of the entire country increased twelvefold, but over the same period the urban population multiplied eighty-sevenfold. In 1800 there

were only 6 cities with more than eight thousand people; by 1890 there were 448, and 26 of them had a population greater than one hundred thousand. More striking still was the rise of the American metropolis, the big city of more than half a million. The ancient world produced only two of that size, Rome and Alexandria, and Western Europe had only two by the end of the seventeenth century, London and Paris. By 1900 there were six cities that large in the United States and three of them had a population of over a million. Rapid urbanization was not limited to this country, but the pace was faster in the United States than in Europe. The New World metropolis grew at a pace unprecedented in history. Chicago more than tripled its size between 1880 and 1900, when it had more than a million and a half, and New York grew from not quite two million to nearly three and a half million in those two decades. Buffalo, Detroit, and Milwaukee more than doubled, and St. Paul, Minneapolis, and Denver more than quadrupled their size.

Urban growth was very unequally distributed, and some parts of the country did not really participate in the movement significantly until the twentieth century. In fact, half of the entire urban population in 1890 was in the North Atlantic states and only 7.7 per cent was in the South Atlantic states. More than half of the nation's city-dwellers lived in the five states of New York, Pennsylvania, Massachusetts, Illinois, and Ohio.

America Moves to Town

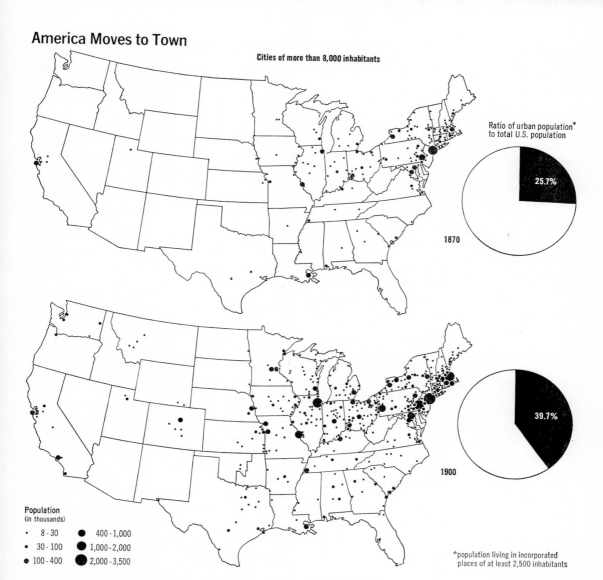

Cities of more than 8,000 inhabitants

Ratio of urban population*
to total U.S. population

25.7%

1870

39.7%

1900

Population
(in thousands)

- 8 - 30
- 30 - 100
- 100 - 400
- 400 - 1,000
- 1,000 - 2,000
- 2,000 - 3,500

*population living in incorporated
places of at least 2,500 inhabitants

Four-fifths of them lived north of the Ohio and Missouri Rivers. While by 1900 six out of ten people in the North Atlantic states and three out of ten in the Midwest lived in cities, scarcely one out of ten was an urbanite in the South. Urbanization affected all parts of the country, even the most remote, but in large areas toward the end of the century it was less an immediate experience than a distant and powerful lure.

The depopulation of the countryside was especially noticeable in the Midwest and the North Atlantic states. Some of it was due, as in

the past, to the lure of the West. But the pull of the city was growing stronger and stronger. Between 1880 and 1890 more than half the townships of Iowa and Illinois declined in population, and yet both states gained substantially in total number of inhabitants. Rural decline was even greater in the North Atlantic states, where the flight to the city had long been in progress. In New England 932 out of the total of 1,502 townships, including two-thirds of those in Maine and New Hampshire and three-fourths of those in Vermont, declined in population during the eighties. Thousands of farms were abandoned, houses were left to decay, and scores of deserted villages dotted the countryside. Yet in that decade New England, largely through the growth of her cities, actually gained 20 per cent in total population. As early as 1890 the number of industrial wage-earners in the whole country almost equaled the number of farm owners, tenants, and farm laborers combined.

Rural defenses against the ancient lure of the city reached a new low in the eighties and nineties. Those were the worst decades of agricultural depression (see Chapter 20), when everything seemed to go wrong with the farming economy. Crop prices were lower, debts greater, and mortgages heavier than ever before. At the same time the glamour and attraction of the city were enhanced by the glitter of the new electric lights, as well as by the telephones, the trolley cars, and a thousand other wonders. The city was the only place where one could enjoy such amenities, for they did not begin to penetrate the countryside to any extent and soften the contrast with urban comforts until well into the twentieth century. The contrast between rural ills and urban felicity made the farmer regard his harsh lot and isolation as even more intolerable than ever before, as indeed they were. Many farmers resorted to political rebellion for relief. A great many others simply moved to town.

City Lights and Cesspools   The new technology and the factories probably produced more discomforts and inconveniences than comforts and amenities for the city-dweller of the late nineteenth century. But to the outsider the advantages and attractions were more readily apparent. First among these were the bright lights that were replacing the dim gas lamps in the streets and the kerosene lamps and gas jets indoors. Cleveland and San Francisco led the way in 1879 by installing brilliant electric arc lamps in their streets, and their example was quickly followed in cities across the country. The noisy, sputtering arc lamp was impractical for indoor use, but for that purpose the incandescent light bulb patented by Edison in 1880 (see p. 431) became available in a few years and spread as swiftly as the growth of power plants permitted. In 1882 there were only thirty-eight central power stations in the whole country, but before the

end of the century there were three thousand. Improved lighting not only made cities safer at night, but it enabled factories to run night shifts, proved a boon to theaters and other amusement houses, and extended the hours of libraries, shops, and schools.

Electrical power provided the answer to a city problem that was even more pressing than that of lighting—the problem of moving vast numbers of people rapidly through the streets at rush hours. The old horse cars or mule-drawn coaches, the prevalent means of public transportation into the eighties, were much too slow as well as too small, smelly, and crowded. New York City, later imitated by Brooklyn, Chicago, and Boston, built an overhead railroad with four cars pulled by a tiny steam locomotive. But the heavy elevated roadway was expensive to build and shut out light from the streets, and the locomotives sprinkled pedestrians with soot and hot coals. To master her steep, hill-climbing streets, San Francisco developed cable roads, with the cars pulled by an endless cable sunk under the track level. Midwestern and Eastern cities also used them successfully in their level streets.

In the meantime, inventors had tinkered for years with the idea of an electric street railway, but Lieutenant Frank J. Sprague was the first to install and profitably operate one, a short line built at Richmond, Virginia, in 1887. The cars were powered by a current from an overhead trolley wire that tapped a central power-house. The success of the experiment started a revolution in urban transportation, for the electric trolley cars were faster, cheaper, and more comfortable than any of the older types. By 1895 some 850 lines, using ten thousand miles of tracks, were in operation. Boston in 1897 was the first city to put electric cars underground, and New York opened her subway to the public in 1904.

Cities took to the telephone eagerly and naturally, for without it the congestion and concentration of people that was to follow would have been insupportable. Within two years after Bell invented the instrument in 1876 (see p. 431), New Haven, Connecticut, had set up the first commercial switchboard, and in two more years eighty-five cities had telephone exchanges. The first telephone connection between cities was effected in 1877 between Boston and New York. Before the end of the century the whole country was laced with interconnecting lines and eight hundred thousand phones were in use—double the number in all of Europe.

Technology and invention were slower to yield solutions to city problems that were traditionally assigned to the public domain, such as street-paving, water supply, and sewage disposal, and in these matters progress was halting. In the seventies the streets even of the larger cities were poorly paved—usually with cobblestones or granite blocks along the eastern seaboard, with wooden blocks in the Midwest, and with gravel or macadam in the South. Brick became popular as pavement in the mid-eighties, especially in cities where it was manufactured. The national capital in 1878 set the pace in adapting asphalt to street-paving, the method that eventually proved the favorite, and by 1900 Washington was pronounced the best-paved city in the world.

Water supply and sewage disposal lagged far behind the demands and needs of mushrooming city populations. The typical urbanite of the seventies relied on the rural solution of individual well and privy or cesspool: Washington had fifty-six thousand cesspools in the mid-seventies, and Philadelphia even more. Improvement was slow, and large cities of the East and South depended mainly on drainage through open gutters to the end of the century. Pollution of water supplies by sewage as well as by the dumping of industrial waste accounted in large measure for the wretched public health records and staggering mortality rates of the period. The number of public waterworks multiplied more than fivefold in the eighties, but filtering and purification were slow to be adopted. Throughout the nineties the American city remained poorly prepared to accommodate the hordes that continued to pour in upon it.

The Immigrant and the City The cities grew at the expense of the European as well as the American countryside and village. For the pull of America was felt in Europe more powerfully than ever before, and the great majority of the immigrants crowded into the nation's cities. Like the new native city-dwellers, the immigrants were also countrymen, though in the old country they had been called peasants instead of farmers. In spite of the distance they had come, they were usually no more familiar with city ways and city life than Americans fresh from the farm, and for the immigrants the uprooting was even more of a shock and a bewilderment. Neither they nor native Americans were prepared to understand or cope with the urban crisis intensified by their sudden convergence upon the city from the ends of the earth.

Sources of Immigration 1871-1910

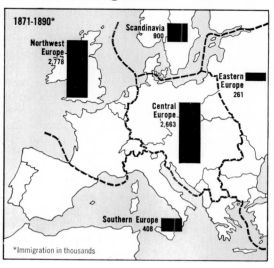

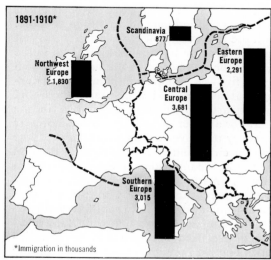

New immigrants.

Many observers have singled out the immigrants as the primary cause of the urban crisis. Actually, the percentage of foreign-born in the total population remained about the same; the immigrants came from much the same social class as they always had; and they came for the same old reason—to better their lot. But there were significant changes. For one thing they began to come in far greater numbers than ever before. From 1850 to 1880 about two and a half million had arrived per decade, with the rate falling off a bit in the sixties but picking up again in the seventies. Then in the eighties the number more than doubled, with nearly five and a quarter million arriving during that decade, and with nearly three and three-quarters million more landing in the next. For another thing they showed a greater tendency than ever to congregate in the large Eastern cities and less disposition to disperse over the countryside. This concentration naturally made them more conspicuous. And finally there came a shift to the so-called "new" immigration—from southern and eastern Europe—as contrasted with the "old" immigrants from northern and western Europe. The old immigrants had come typically from Britain, Ireland, Germany, or one of the Scandinavian countries, and were usually Protestant. The new immigrants were Italians, Austrians, Hungarians, Poles, Serbs, and Russians; they were Catholic or Jewish in religion, and had habits and ways that appeared outlandish to older Americans. Immigrants of the new type had made up only 1.4 per cent of the total immigration of the sixties, and less than 20 per cent in the eighties; but in the nineties their proportion suddenly climbed to more than 50 per cent, and in the next decade to more than 70 per cent. This increasing proportion of new immigrants happened to coincide with two tendencies: (1) an increasing concern over the ills of urban life, and (2) an increasing tendency to stress racial differences. Because of this coincidence, the new immigrants were blamed for many serious city problems that had little to do with racial or national origin.

There could be no doubt, however, that the foreigner and the immigrant had become conspicuous in American life. By 1890 one-fourth of the Philadelphians and one-third of the Bostonians and Chicagoans were of foreign birth, and in Greater New York four out of five

The New York East Side.

residents were of foreign birth or foreign parentage. Of the male population of the eighteen largest cities in the country there were two and a half times as many of foreign birth or foreign parentage as there were of the older American stock. New York City had half as many Italians as Naples and two and a half times as many Irish as Dublin. Understandably, the newcomers tended to huddle together clannishly by nationality. Jacob Riis, a New York journalist and reformer who had emigrated from Denmark in 1870, pictured a map of Manhattan in 1890 colored according to races and nationalities:

Between the dull gray of the Jew, his favorite color, and the Italian red, would be squeezed in on the map a sharp streak of yellow, marking the narrow boundaries of Chinatown. Dovetailed in with the German population, the poor but thrifty Bohemian might be picked out by the sombre hue of his life. . . . Dots and dashes of color here and there would show where the Finnish sailors worship their *djumala* (God), the Greek pedlars the ancient name of their race, and the Swiss the goddess of thrift.

Less colorfully, Jane Addams described the map of Chicago:

Between Halsted Street and the river live about ten thousand Italians—Neapolitans, Sicilians, and Calabrians, with an occasional Lombard or Venetian. To the south on Twelfth Street are many Germans, and side streets are given over almost entirely to Polish and Russian Jews. Still farther south, these Jewish colonies merge into a huge Bohemian colony, so vast that Chicago ranks as the third Bohemian city in the world.

Slums and Palaces   The city was the way of the future. But there was much about the city of the late nineteenth century to justify the old antiurban prejudice of agrarian America, the prejudice Jefferson voiced when he called the city "a sore on the body politic." To many the city did indeed seem a product of disease rather than a source of social health. The city of that period was the very embodiment of laissez-faire doctrine, for it grew without plan, with a minimum of control, guided mainly by the dictates of industrial enterprise

Splendor in New York: Mrs. Astor's art gallery.

and private greed. Even with an alert and informed citizenry and an honest and efficient municipal government a city would have faced staggering difficulties, and few cities could boast either asset.

The foulest product of the haphazard, laissez-faire growth was the city slum, an old evil that took on new life and descended to new depths in 1879 with the invention of the "dumbbell" tenement house, so named for the shape of its floor plan, in New York City. Designed to get the maximum return for the landlord, the new tenement was no better than a barracks honeycombed with rooms, many of them with no direct access to light or air. Lacking sanitary facilities, privacy, or health precautions, these tenements rapidly degenerated into human pigsties, vile-smelling and vermin-infested. According to Jacob Riis, in 1890 there were thirty-seven thousand tenement houses of this type in New York and more than 1.2 million people lived in them, half the city's population.

William Dean Howells, a realistic novelist, admitted in 1896 that from a distance the tenement might sometimes appear picturesque:

> But to be in it, and not have the distance, is to inhale the stenches of the neglected street, and to catch the yet fouler and dreadfuller poverty-smell which breathes from the open doorways. . . . It is to see the work-worn look of mothers, the squalor of the babes, the haggish ugliness of the old women, the slovenly frowziness of the young girls.

The worst of the tenement slums in New York, which had their counterpart in every urban community in the United States, were known by such names as "Bandit's Roost," "Misery Row," and "Murderer's Alley." Crime and prostitution flourished in these noisome horrors, and organized gangs operated securely within their protection. In years when the homicide rate in England and Germany was less than half that in the United States, and when the rate in Europe was declining, the ratio in the United States was increasing and lawlessness was growing at an alarming pace. Extremes of human misery and degradation had become common sights.

In the eighties and nineties the gulfs between social classes were dramatically emphasized rather than concealed. Unlike our day when Americans of every class tend to dress and look alike and all try to appear middle-class, the evidence and symbols of power and wealth were flaunted without apology. It was no accident that the economist Thorstein Veblen, in his *Theory of the Leisure Class* (1899), hit on the expression "conspicuous consumption." Displaying habits of consumption that were competitive as well as conspicuous, Chicagoans sported liveried servants and dwelt in lavish palaces built in plain view. The contrast with conspicuous poverty was glaring and unconcealed; squalor and splendor paraded the same streets. The palaces of the wealthy that lined New York's Fifth Avenue were paralleled a few blocks away by the desolation of Shantytown, inhabited by Irish paupers and goats and stretching along the East Side for sixty blocks or more. In the same year in which Jacob Riis published his shocking study of the slums, *How the Other Half Lives* (1890), Ward McAllister published his *Society As I Have Found It* (1890), lovingly recounting the extravagances of New York's Four Hundred, the self-elected social elite. One exploit of this set, a favorite example among protest groups, was the Bradley Martin costume ball staged in the Waldorf Hotel at a cost of $368,200. It took place on February 10, 1897, at the depths of the depression, when thousands of unemployed roamed the street, and was attended by guests decked in costumes costing as much as ten thousand dollars. Scenes of this sort help to explain the violence in the rhetoric of Populists and other protest movements of the nineties.

Howells, in a poem called "Society" (1895), compared the violent social contrasts of his day with "a splendid pageantry of beautiful women and lordly men" playing and dancing upon a magnificent floor that barely covered the crushed and bleeding bodies of the oppressed:

> And now and then from out the dreadful floor
> An arm or brow was lifted from the rest,
> As if to strike in madness, or implore
> For mercy; and anon some suffering breast
> Heaved from the mass and sank; and as before
> The revellers above them thronged and prest.

The Awakening of the Social Conscience

The city was a shock to the American conscience, not merely because of violent contrasts, abuses, and evils, but because the national conscience had taken shape in an agrarian culture and a rural past. So had national values, ideals, morals, folkways, and political institutions. American countrymen or European peasants who emigrated were repelled as well as fascinated by the city; they accepted it and rejected it at the same time. Their feelings were torn and their consciences were bruised by the experience.

The Challenge of the Bosses Probably the most flagrant offense against public morals in the last quarter of the nineteenth century was the corruption of city government. The politician bent on corruption could hardly have dreamed of a more promising combination of circumstances. The rapid growth of cities had made necessary the large-scale expansion of public utilities of all sorts—water, gas, transportation, electricity—as well as the construction of public buildings, sewage systems, docks, street and sidewalk pavement. For this work a multitude of valuable contracts, franchises, monopolies, subsidies, and privileges had to be granted. Such prizes were worth the ransom of kings, and there were plenty of predatory operators ready with the price. The corrupt politician was aided in his operations by an antiquated and complex form of municipal government modeled on that of the state. Clumsy city charters saddled the government with inappropriate legislative machinery, weak executive authority, and disorganized courts, making responsibility so difficult to fix that crime went unpunished. State legislatures, by interfering excessively with city affairs, added to the confusion and increased the opportunities for corruption.

Potter Palmer's mansion
in Chicago.

Not surprisingly, the cities were excessively burdened with debt. By 1880 city and town indebtedness ran to more than three-quarters of a billion dollars, more than three times the amount of state indebtedness. Yet for all their heavy expenditures the cities often received wretched service from the utilities they subsidized and were cynically and repeatedly defrauded by the public servants they elected. "With very few exceptions," wrote Andrew D. White, president of Cornell, "the city governments of the United States are the worst in Christendom—the most expensive, the most inefficient, and the most corrupt." And James Bryce, a generous but well-informed English critic, pronounced city government "the one conspicuous failure of the United States," far more serious in his opinion than the shortcomings of state and federal government.

The city machine dominated politics and the boss dominated the machine. Never has a more colorful set of politicians wielded such power as the great bosses of this period. With a disposition toward large girth, shiny hats, and heavy jewelry, the boss played the role of a freehanded spender, the Robin Hood of the masses. High in the annals of bossdom are the names of "Honest" John Kelley and Richard Croker of New York, Christopher L. Magee

and William Finn of Pittsburgh, Ed Butler of St. Louis, "King" James McManes of Philadelphia, and "Czar" Martin Lomasney of Boston. Revenue flowed into their coffers from office-seekers, contractors, public utilities, railroads, prostitutes, gamblers—anybody who happened to need protection or favors. Even pushcart peddlers and garbage collectors paid tribute to New York's Tammany. Boss McManes, as head of Philadelphia's gas trust, had 5,630 public jobs at his disposal; he died leaving an estate of more than two million dollars.

The city boss and his lieutenants in the wards and precincts found their most reliable supporters among the immigrants. These new voters certainly had no monopoly on ignorance and apathy, and many of them were intelligent and useful citizens. But they were usually unaccustomed to the ballot, unpracticed in the ways of democracy, and bewildered by city life in a strange land. Moreover, the great majority of them were unskilled laborers who lived close to the margin of existence, and were often in need of a job and a friend. The boss dealt primarily in jobs and votes. He had sprung from the immigrant community himself, shared its sense of solidarity, knew its members by name, and remained one of them.

He was in fact the natural leader of the immigrants, and they responded to him with group loyalty and devotion. They knew him as a man who "got things done," a man to whom they could always take their troubles. The boss made it his business to know their needs and give them tangible evidence of his interest in them. His favors took the form of getting them jobs, intervening with the law in their behalf, bailing them out of jail, paying burial money, distributing free coal, and handing out Christmas baskets. In short, he performed services for which there was as yet no public agency and which no one else was ready to perform.

Irish politicians were especially adept at these arts, and it was a prevailing conviction that, as one writer put it, "The function of the Irishman is to administer the affairs of the American city." A glance at the names heading the roster of bosses supports this conviction. One of them put his political theory in these words: "I think that there's got to be in every ward a guy that any bloke can go to when he's in trouble and get help—not justice and the law, but help, no matter what he's done."

The Immigrant and the Boss

What tells in holdin' your grip on your district is to go right down among the poor families and help them in the different ways they need help. I've got a regular system for this. If there's a fire ... any hour of the day or night, I'm usually there with some of my election district captains as soon as the fire-engines. If a family is burned out I don't ask whether they are Republicans or Democrats, and I don't refer them to the Charity Organization Society, which would investigate their case in a month or two and decide they were worthy of help about the time they are dead from starvation. I just get quarters for them ... and fix them up till they get things runnin' again....

Another thing, I can always get a job for a deservin' man. I make it a point to keep on the track of jobs, and it seldom happens that I don't have a few up my sleeve ready for use....

And the children—the little roses of the district! Do I forget them? Oh, no! They know me, every one of them, and they know that a sight of Uncle George and candy means the same thing. Some of them are the best kind of vote-getters.

From William L. Riordon, *Plunkitt of Tammany Hall*, 1905.

The Immigrant in the City

I am polish man. I want be american citizen.... But my friends are polish people—I must live with them —I work in the shoes-shop with polish people—I stay all the time with them—at home—in the shop —anywhere.

I want live with american people, but I do not know anybody of american. I go 4 times to teacher and must pay $2 weekly. I wanted take board in english house, but I could not, for I earn only $5 or 6 in a week.... Better job to get is very hard for me, because I do not speak well english and I cannot understand what they say to me. The teacher teach me—but when I come home—I must speak polish and in the shop also. In this way I can live in your country many years—like my friends—and never speak—write well english—and never be good american citizen. I know here many persons, they live here 10 or moore years, and they are not citizens, they don't speak well english, they don't know geography and history of this country, they don't know constitution of America.

From, "Letter of an Anonymous Polish Immigrant...," *Report of the Commission on the Problem of Immigration in Massachusetts*, 1914.

Theodore Roosevelt, who studied the matter, concluded that urban reformers would have to create social agencies to fulfill the role the boss played before they could replace him.

As the reformers found out for themselves, after a little experience, many "good" people supported the bosses and machines—educated, respectable, middle-class people who had been natives for at least three generations. Some of these "good" people were businessmen who were quite willing to cooperate with the machine to secure the favors, privileges, and exemptions they desired. Other respectable citizens voted regularly, if regretfully, for the machine because of their sincere devotion to the national party with which the machine was identified and their desire for a party victory. In short, city machine and city boss were buttressed by some of the strongest as well as by some of the weakest elements of the population. Anyone who undertook to change the system would need to be very powerful indeed.

Humanitarians and Reformers The conscience of the middle class was eventually stirred to indignation and action by the misery and degradation of the city. But first the middle class had to discover what poverty was. Early humanitarians and reformers did not understand the poor—the "depraved classes," as they called them. Attributing their plight to moral shortcomings, they sent agents of the Charity Organizations Society to discover which of the poor were "deserving." But it was the young social workers, patiently investigating and visiting the sweatshops and tenement firetraps, who began to establish contact between middle class and working class.

Inspired by English social reform literature and a visit to Toynbee Hall in the slums of London, Jane Addams took up the settlement-house idea and established Hull House on Halsted Street in Chicago in 1889. She wished, she said, "to share the lives of the poor" and to make social service "express the spirit of Christ." One such house had already been established in New York in 1886, and in the next ten years some fifty or more were founded in Northern and Eastern cities. They offered a variety of services, maintained playgrounds, nurseries, club rooms, libraries, and kindergartens, and conducted classes in various subjects. But perhaps of more significance was the education they provided for the young middle-class social workers who came to live in the slums to gain firsthand knowledge of the workers' problems. Within a few years the settlement houses had become the spawning ground of reformers and reforms.

Lillian Wald, founder of the Henry Street Settlement in New York, was the first to propose that a Children's Bureau be established in the federal government, and the first two heads of that bureau came from Hull House. Florence Kelley, also from Hull House, was the leading spirit in the National Consumers League, whose purpose was to eliminate child labor, night work, and long working hours for women, and to promote minimum-wage laws. Another organization that grew out of the same background was the Association for Labor Legislation, dedicated to the fight for decent labor standards. It was these middle-class reformers rather than the trade unions that launched the movement for social legislation in America. They led the agitation that put through the first child labor laws and they helped to focus the nation's attention on the evils of the slums. Work in the settlement houses was part of the training of such future reformers as Frances Perkins, Charles A. Beard, Henry Morgenthau, Jr., and Harry Hopkins.

On the political front the battle for municipal reform began under leaders recruited from the solid and substantial middle class. These included Seth Low and George William Curtis in New York, Edwin U. Curtis and Thomas W. Higginson in Boston, Lyman J. Gage in Chicago, and Joseph W. Folk in St. Louis. Good-government clubs, committees, commissions, and reform organizations for municipal improvement proliferated rapidly in the eighties. Every city of any size had one such organization, and the larger cities had several. One of the most prominent was the National Civil Service Reform League, founded in 1881, which published the magazine *Good Government* to promote its prime object, the merit system for city employees. In the early stages these organizations wasted a good deal of time in mass meetings that drafted wordy resolutions and accomplished nothing except to make the reformers look ineffectual if not ridiculous. Cynics called the good-government people the "goo-goos." Their efforts to expose corruption met with more success than their attempts to break the power of machine politics, but they kept up a running fight to lower the cost of city administration, to encourage law enforcement, and to improve public sanitation and education. They stirred up a good bit of excitement on occasion, but for a long time they seemed to be getting nowhere.

Not until after 1890 did the municipal reformers become an effective force for change and improvement. The cumulative experience of scattered reformers began to point the way to a concerted program, and the National Municipal League was launched on a wave of public interest in 1894. Within two years more than two hundred branch leagues were founded. The league put forward as its program a model city charter that embodied such advanced reforms as the short ballot, greater freedom from state interference, limited franchise for utilities, separate city and state elections, the merit system, government by experts, and, above all, more authority for the mayor. In 1880 only one of the nation's twenty-three principal cities was dominated by the mayor, but by 1900 there were twelve. By that year the battle for municipal reform was in full swing. The reformers still had much to learn, but they had aroused the electorate and they had gained experience and confidence through substantial victories. In 1894 the embattled hosts of reform in New York overthrew Boss Richard Croker and elected William L. Strong mayor, though Tammany returned to power after a brief period. Reformers in Chicago, Boston, and St. Louis also scored significant victories over their machines in the next few years.

The Conscience of the Church The church community was eventually to respond both in faith and in works to the human needs and social problems of city and industry. But in 1876, as Henry May has observed, "Protestantism presented a massive, almost unbroken front in its defense of the status quo." Slums, depressions, and unemployment were but necessary steps to progress, and suffering was the lot of man in good, orthodox theology. Religion was a spiritual and individual, not a social, concern, and salvation came through the striving of the individual with sin and conscience, not through social welfare and betterment. The church, middle class in outlook, was dedicated to the early social creed of individualism and laissez faire, and the mightiest preachers of that era expressed these attitudes forcefully and repeatedly. There was no better exponent of laissez faire and social Darwinism than Henry Ward Beecher in his Brooklyn pulpit.

Revivalism and professional revivalists were usually powerful propagators of the old-time religion—orthodox fundamentalism—and shared little or no social awareness. Throughout the eighties and nineties the annual revival was a regular feature of the program of Methodist, Baptist, Presbyterian, Congregational, and smaller churches. The most famous of the professional revivalists was Dwight L. Moody, an impressive figure of two hundred and eighty pounds who got his start with a successful campaign in Britain during the seventies. Returning to America in 1875, he set out with Ira D. Sankey, his equally weighty

singer, to "evangelize the world in this generation." Moody brought into play all his great executive and publicity talents to attract huge crowds, and with forceful and colloquial sermons converted sinners by the thousands in all parts of the United States. His popularity and his energy continued unflagging until his death in 1899. Moody and another famous revivalist, T. DeWitt Talmage, along with numerous imitators, marked the heyday of professional revivalism in America. Whether as a result of their work or for some other reason, Protestant churches grew rapidly in the last two decades of the century, increasing their membership from somewhat over ten million to almost eighteen million.

In spite of this growth, clergymen complained constantly that the working people were drifting away from the church. Moved either by the pulpit's lack of sympathy for their plight or by the elegance of the clothing they saw in the pews, workingmen found the churches of the older denominations less suited to their tastes than they once had been. Investigators reported that large working-class districts in the cities were without church facilities of any kind. Some of the poor and the lowly, as they had in the past, sought solace in new sects founded to restore the lost purity or the original doctrine of the old sects. Many of these "holiness" people were recruited from the Methodists, Baptists, and other Protestant denominations. Usually originating in the country and then moving to the city, a dozen or more pentecostal and millennial sects sprang up in the eighties and nineties.

A new sect of a different sort was the Church of Christ, Scientist, usually called Christian Scientist, which was chartered by a small group of the followers of Mary Baker Eddy in 1879. The prophet of the new faith was born in 1821 to a New England family of the pious, humble sort to which Joseph Smith, the Mormon prophet (see p. 267) had been born fifteen years earlier. Inspired by the help she received from a faith-healer in her own rather complex health problems, she developed the belief that "Disease is caused by mind alone." At the end of her long life in 1910, adherents of her church numbered a hundred thousand, her book *Science and Health* (1875) had sold four hundred thousand copies, and her estate was appraised at more than two and a half million dollars.

Addressing its appeal to the downtrodden, the Salvation Army invaded America in 1879 under the command of George Railton and seven women officers. Founded the year before in London by William Booth, it was born of his desire to reach the city poor. Using revivalist methods and brass bands to attract crowds, the uniformed army and its lassies preached repentance to "rumdom, slumdom and bumdom." Within a decade after the invasion they began to supplement repentance sermons with a social service program and sent "slum brigades" into the tenement districts to bring relief as well as the gospel to the poor.

It would have been impossible for the Catholic Church to ignore the working class and the social problems of the city. Since the "new" immigration was overwhelmingly Catholic, working-class, and urban, the American Catholic Church of the late nineteenth century became more than ever the church of the city, the worker, and the immigrant. The number of Catholics in the country increased from over six million to more than ten million in the last two decades of the century. Responsibility for training and adjusting the new Americans to their country compelled the church to adjust its social policy to urban needs and persuaded James Gibbons, then in Rome to be installed as cardinal, to defend the cause of American labor before the Holy See in 1887. American Catholics found support for their social policy in the loyalty of their communicants, which contrasted strongly with the defection and alienation of the masses of which European Catholics complained. The papal encyclical *Rerum novarum* of May 1891 enunciated social ideals and responsibilities for Catholics that gave additional sanction to the social views of the Americans.

In the meantime a small group of Protestant clergymen, at first responding as individuals to the social crises and labor struggles of the seventies, eighties, and nineties, had begun to shape a reinterpretation of their religion that in later years came to be known as the Social Gospel. Turning away from the traditional emphasis on spiritual and moral concerns, the new gospel stressed the social and pragmatic implications of Christian ethics and called for good works in social reform and betterment.

The Reverend Josiah Strong's book, *Our Country* (1885), which sold half a million copies in twenty years, has been called the *Uncle Tom's Cabin* of the movement. But Washington Gladden, a Congregational minister who wrote *Applied Christianity* (1886), was probably the most influential leader. Next in importance was R. Heber Newton, a liberal New York Episcopalian and an advocate of more sweeping reform. The Episcopal Church, the most aristocratic denomination and yet the one most influenced by the mildly socialistic doctrines then gaining attention in the parent Church of England, took most readily to the new gospel, while the Methodist Church, traditionally the church of the common man, tended to cling to rural individualism and resisted the Social Gospel at first. With a similar following and the additional restraint of such wealthy benefactors as John D. Rockefeller, the Baptists nevertheless moved earlier toward the social gospel under the inspiration of Walter Rauschenbusch. By 1895 the Social Gospel had reached maturity and its influence was being felt throughout American Protestantism and in secular thought as well. Its main impact, however, was not to come until the following century.

The Spread of Learning

Public Schools and Mass Media   The national determination to educate everybody was best reflected in the growth of public schools, which increased at an unprecedented speed after 1870. Free education for all became a foremost article in the American faith, and the schools were unfairly expected to solve all of democracy's problems, from poorly cooked meals to poorly adjusted races. Growing cities expected the schools to take over many functions that parents, police, and priests had once performed, and along the way to Americanize the children of the new immigrants. One measure of the hopes and aspirations thus aroused was the rapid expansion of the school system, especially in the cities. In 1870 only $69 million, or an average of about $15 per pupil, was spent on public education, and in the first school year of the new century $250 million, or nearly $23 per pupil, went into the school budget. By 1900 all but two of the states outside the South had compulsory school-attendance laws of some sort, and both the average school attendance and the length of the average school year had increased markedly. There were only 160 public high schools in the whole country in 1870 but by the end of the century there were more than six thousand. The cities, with a more concentrated school population and better transportation than rural communities, reaped the greatest benefits from the public school expansion. More and more of them extended public schools to include kindergartens, normal schools, night classes, and adult and vocational education.

Under the sway of the new theories of education the public schools gradually put aside the old authoritarian ways of the drillmaster and disciplinarian in the one-room country school. Like the preceding generation, which imported the progressive doctrines of Pestalozzi, the new generation brought from Germany the theories of Johann Friedrich Herbart, who believed that education could be made into a science. The Herbartians discouraged the teacher from assuming the role of policeman and urged her to teach the child in terms relevant to his natural interests by effective presentation. Cities and later states began to forbid the use of corporal punishment, and schools began to experiment with successive fads for new courses in sewing, cooking, and manual training. The traditional curriculum of classics gave way rapidly before the new emphasis on science and "practical" subjects.

Private schools still held on, particularly in the Eastern states, and certain ethnic and religious groups resisted being integrated into a uniform public school system. Unable to win public support for their own educational efforts, the Catholics in 1884 determined upon an elaborate expansion of their parochial schools and increased their number to nearly four thousand by 1900. The program was mainly designed to educate the immigrants of that faith in the cities, and most of the schools were located in New England and the Middle Atlantic states.

The federal government had made a gesture of assistance to public schools in 1867, when Congress laid the foundation of a bureau of education, but the Blair bill for federal aid distributed according to the proportion of illiterates in a state was defeated in the 1880's. Since support of the schools was left to local communities, improvement and growth varied widely with the distribution of wealth. In general, the rural districts lagged behind the urban areas and the West and South behind the East. But the South had a staggering burden of special disadvantages. In the first place it had about twice as many children per adult as the North, and it had considerably less than half the per capita taxable wealth with which to educate them. To complicate the matter, Southerners were not concentrated in cities and towns but scattered out thinly over the countryside. And on top of that, at the insistence of the whites, two separate school systems were maintained for the segregation of the races. At the century's end the schools of the South were still miserably supported, poorly taught, and wholly inadequate. Efforts to improve them accomplished little until the next decade.

In spite of the physical growth of the educational plant and the millions of dollars poured into public education, the average American adult by the turn of the century had only about five years of schooling. Illiteracy had been reduced, however, from around 17 per cent in 1880 to about 11 per cent twenty years later. For all the faddism and quackery, in spite of the low-paid teachers and the attempt to saddle them with all the problems of democracy, the public schools continued to increase in number and grow in popular esteem.

The popular faith in education and the craving for its benefits were reflected in other ways as well. One of these was the highly popular Chautauqua movement, which was started in 1874 at Lake Chautauqua, New York, by Methodist laymen as a camp meeting for training Sunday-school teachers. The idea spread over the country as a sort of informal adult education movement. It retained its pious, middle-class emphasis on temperance and morality and often made use of Methodist camp-meeting grounds. Small-town audiences sweated earnestly through long lectures on science and religion, thrilled to the illustrated travel lectures of John L. Stoddard, or relaxed with James Whitcomb Riley and Swiss bellringers. To supplement the summer meetings a home-study circle was formed in 1878, and ten years later a Chautauqua College began to offer correspondence courses and hand out degrees via the postman.

These years also brought a dramatic expansion of public libraries. Librarians laid claim to professional standing in 1876 when they organized the American Library Association. State and local tax money was tapped and private donors began to put large amounts into library building: Andrew Carnegie, the most munificent of them, launched his library benefactions at Pittsburgh in 1881. In the 1890's six library buildings costing more than a million dollars had been either started or completed. The most splendid were the Boston Public Library and the New York Public Library, both opened in 1895, and the Library of Congress, the largest and most costly in the world, opened in 1897. By 1900 there were more than nine thousand public libraries in the country, with a total of more than 45 million volumes.

The repetitive theme of "more and more and more" that drums through all phases of American life in the eighties and nineties (along with *more* unemployment and *more* depression) was nowhere so striking as in journalism, especially in periodicals. In the last fifteen years of the century the number of periodicals published increased by 2,200, most of them devoted to trades and special interests. More striking was the increase in the number and circulation of the periodicals for the general reader. There were only four such monthly magazines in the country in 1885 with circulations of a hundred thousand or more, and they were usually priced at thirty-five cents a copy. Twenty years later there were twenty such magazines with an aggregate circulation of more than five and a half million, and all but four of them sold at ten to fifteen cents a copy. The ten-cent monthlies had worked a revolution and had created a vast new reading public. More than price was involved in the revolution, however. The older journals, such as the *Century*, the *Atlantic*, or the *North American Review*, were sedate, leisurely, rather aloof, and upper-class in appeal and sympathy. Their new ten-cent competitors, such as *Munsey's*, *McClure's*, and the *Cosmopolitan*, were lighter in tone, with shorter articles and many illustrations. News-mindedness was an innovation of *Public Opinion* (1886), *Current Literature* (1888), and the *Literary Digest* (1890), and reform-mindedness was the theme of the *Forum* (1886) and *Arena* (1889) as well as the older *Nation* (1865) and *Independent* (1848).

Growing cities, increasing literacy, and expanding population combined to create greater and greater markets for newspapers and to heighten the temptation to vulgarize the product in order to exploit the potential market. The number of daily papers, largely confined to the cities, more than doubled, and the number of weekly and semiweekly papers increased more than 50 per cent between 1880 and 1900, while subscribers increased even more rapidly. By the end of the century the United States had more than half the newspapers in the world. Two potent influences were at work to change the character of American newspapers: one was advertising, which surpassed sales as a source of revenue in the nineties, and the other was the mass audience. To reach the masses the news columns became more sensational and vulgar. The father of the new school of journalists was Joseph Pulitzer, who bought the New York *World* in 1883 and ran its circulation up from fifteen thousand in 1883 to over a million by 1898. The assault on privacy and taste was continued and intensified by his imitator, William Randolph Hearst of the New York *Journal*.

The Higher Learning   For all the crassness and materialism that earned for it the name of "Gilded Age" the period could boast of substantial advances in higher education and scholarship. There was obviously much room for improvement. American colleges of 1870, even the better ones, were likely to be strongly sectarian, provincial, and undistinguished. The typical college professor of that year was harshly, but not very unfairly, described as "a nondescript, a jack of all trades, equally ready to teach surveying and Latin eloquence." The curriculum of Latin, mathematics, and theology, designed for the training of ministers, did not permit specialization or allow time for research. Library and laboratory facilities were inadequate, and the natural sciences were neglected. There were no graduate schools and no professional schools to speak of beyond theological seminaries. Collegiate pedagogy, like the Victorian family, was heavily authoritarian, with emphasis upon rules, discipline, rote learning, and recitations.

With Harvard in the vanguard and with Charles W. Eliot at its head, a small group of academicians undertook to reform the old collegiate order. The reforms they made were not universally acknowledged to be improvements in their day, nor are they yet, but they were widely if slowly imitated. One of them was the elective system, which resulted in a proliferation of courses and subjects from which the student chose according to his fancy. Additional reforms, such as an increase in the number of science courses and in the use of the laboratory method of instruction, were taken up rapidly, as were lectures and discussion periods as substitutes for rote recitation. Colleges were slower to follow Harvard's example of abolishing compulsory chapel attendance (1886) and relaxing student discipline. But there were numerous signs that the old collegiate system that had prevailed for centuries was passing. Among these signs were the decline of authoritarian norms and traditional curricula and a decrease in the proportion of clergymen on boards of trustees and in presidents' offices.

Accompanying these changes and reflecting the shift to a secular and scientific emphasis was an increase in German influence in academic circles. During the nineteenth century more than nine thousand Americans studied at German universities, all but about two hundred of them after 1850. In the 1880's some two thousand Americans were studying in Germany. The Johns Hopkins University, opened in Baltimore in 1876 with an inaugural address by Thomas Huxley, the Darwinian, was an expression of both English and German influence. Nearly all the faculty of the new university had studied in Germany, and the policies pursued by President Daniel Coit Gilman expressed many of the academic ideals of that country's universities. Among these were a stress on research and graduate study, and a shift from the attitude that professors and students were mere conservers of learning to the attitude that they were searchers and

advancers of knowledge. The new emphasis implied an increase in the scholar's stature, freedom, and prestige. Inspired more or less by the example of Johns Hopkins, fifteen major graduate schools or departments had been established by the end of the century.

Nearly three thousand students registered in American graduate schools in 1890, as compared with a mere handful two decades before. As quick as their fellow countrymen to organize themselves in national associations, the professional scholars founded scores of learned societies in the seventies and eighties: the Archaeological Institute of America (1879), the Modern Language Association (1883), and in the next ten years the American Historical Association, the American Economic Association, the American Mathematical Society, the American Physical Society, and the American Psychological Association, to mention only a few. Learned journals and books equal to Europe's best began to appear in America, and American-trained scholars began to acquire international reputations.

Medical and legal education was still primitive in the seventies and eighties. None of the schools of medicine or law required a college degree for admission, and the typical medical school turned its graduates loose on a helpless public after only a few months of haphazard lectures. Both medical and legal degrees could easily be bought. Between 1876 and 1900 eighty-six new medical schools were founded, but the Johns Hopkins Medical School, opened in 1894, was the first to require a college degree for admission and the first to have a full-time teaching staff. By the end of the century many states had established boards of medical examiners that tightened license requirements, and the schools themselves began to raise their standards in response. Comparable improvement in law schools was to come only later.

This was an era prolific in the birth of new institutions of higher learning, both public and private. In the last two decades of the nineteenth century the total number of colleges and universities in the country increased by nearly one hundred and fifty, though many of them had no valid claim to academic status and were often short-lived. Ten new state universities, all of them coeducational from the start, were founded between 1882 and

Modern Architecture:
The Principle

Amid the immense number and variety of living forms, he [Louis Sullivan] noted that invariably the form expressed the function, as, for instance, the oak tree expressed the function oak, the pine tree the function pine, and so on through the amazing series. And, inquiring more deeply, he discovered that in truth it was not simply a matter of form expressing function, but the vital idea was this: That the function *created* or organized its form. Discernment of this idea threw a vast light upon all things within the universe, and condensed with astounding impressiveness upon mankind, upon all civilizations, all institutions, every form and aspect of society, every mass-thought and mass-result, every individual thought and individual result.... The application of the idea to the Architectural art was manifest enough, namely, that the function of a building must predetermine and organize its form.

From Louis H. Sullivan, *The Autobiography of an Idea,* 1924.

1895. In the East, where coeducation was slower to win acceptance, Vassar was opened in 1861, Smith in 1871, and Bryn Mawr in 1885, while several of the older men's colleges opened affiliated women's colleges nearby. Numerous land-grant colleges, taking advantage of the Morrill Act of 1862 (see p. 333), sprang up to teach agricultural and mechanical arts. A fraction of the new industrial and commercial fortunes of the age went into the founding of universities bearing the names of Cornell (1868), Vanderbilt (1873), Hopkins (1876), Tulane (1884), Stanford (1885), and Clark (1887). The University of Chicago (1891) was one of the few that did not take the name of its benefactor, in this case John D. Rockefeller.

The history of higher learning of this period was not, however, purely a story of expansion and improvement. A mistaken conception of democracy led to the assumption of equality among all academic pursuits and justified the teaching of courses in almost any subject whatever, however trivial. Charlatans were often commissioned to teach such courses and almost anyone could take them. Institutions became overexpanded, overcrowded, and absurdly bureaucratized by a new species of academician known as the administrator. A misguided deference to the opinions of alumni, sports enthusiasts, and the unlettered public generally led to an anarchical confusion of values and grotesque distortions of academic purpose. For the first time in recorded history institutions of higher learning assumed the function of providing mass entertainment in spectator sports, and the comparative distinction of a university came to depend on its success in pursuing these commercial enterprises.

The businessmen who replaced the clergymen on the college boards of trustees were slow to acknowledge the status claimed by the new scholar and were sometimes quite unable to distinguish any difference between their relation to faculty members and their relation to "other employees." The trustees of seven well-known universities approved a statement published in the Chicago *Tribune* in 1899 to the effect that college professors "should promptly and gracefully submit to the determination of the trustees" in deciding what should be taught, and that "if the trustees err it is for the patrons and proprietors, not for the employees, to change either the policy or the personnel of the board." During the 1890's nine prominent faculty members were dismissed for presuming to express their opinions on such subjects as labor, railroads, and currency. Though there was no legitimate excuse for the gaucheries that for a time made American colleges a laughing stock of informed world opinion, we must remember that America was trying to spread the benefits of learning far more widely (and as a result more thinly) than had ever been attempted before.

Arts, Letters, and Critics

Artists and Their Work   In matters of taste the Gilded Age has acquired and for the most part deserved a deplorable reputation. Whether it was because the molders of fashion were insecure in their social position or new to their wealth or for some other reason, their taste ran to excesses in all things—in their clothing, their jewelry, and their houses, in interior décor and exterior ornament. They overloaded their rooms with bric-a-brac, their dresses with bustles, and their houses with gingerbread. They had no trouble finding architects, painters, and sculptors of the sort that would cater to their preferences, but the work these people left behind need not detain us.

Beneath the crass surface and behind the clutter of imitative art, however, there were genuinely original and creative spirits at work in the land. Artists, engineers, architects, sculptors, and painters honestly faced the realities of the new urban, industrial society and contrived original and powerful answers to its problems. It was the new city that gave them both their challenge and their opportunity. The bold spirit with which they met the challenge and seized the opportunity is caught in a statement by a Georgia-bred architect, John Wellborn Root, who did his work in Chicago:

> In America we are free of artistic traditions. Our freedom begets license, it is true. We do shocking things; we produce works of architecture irremediably bad; we try crude experiments that result in disaster. Yet somewhere in this mass of ungoverned energies lies the principle of life. A new spirit of beauty is being developed and perfected, and even now its first achievements are beginning to delight us. This is not the old thing made over; it is new. It springs out of the past, but it is not tied to it; it studies the traditions, but is not enslaved by them.

One achievement of the age that was daring and magnificent enough to meet Root's description was Brooklyn Bridge, a suspension such as had never before been built, with granite towers 276 feet high and with a central span of 1,600 feet. Sketched by John A. Roebling, who died before construction began, the great bridge was completed by his son Washington A. Roebling in 1883. A product of the new industrialism down to the last of the nineteen strands of steel cable and the last riveted girder, the bridge soared out of the soot and slums of Manhattan, monumental proof that the new society could produce a thing of beauty out of its materials. In the same city a landscape architect named Frederick L. Olmsted demonstrated that it was not necessary for a city to be the seat of an absolute monarch in order to create in its very center spacious, lovely, and exquisitely designed parks, such as Central Park, Olmsted's masterpiece. It was not his only great park, however,

Modern Architecture: The Application

It became evident that the very tall masonry office building was in its nature economically unfit as ground values steadily rose. Not only did its thick walls entail loss of space and therefore revenue, but its unavoidably small window openings could not furnish the proper and desirable ratio of glass area to rentable floor area.

Thus arose a crisis, a seeming *impasse*. What was to do?... The need was there, the capacity to satisfy was there, but contact was not there. Then came the flash of imagination which saw the single thing. The trick was turned; and there swiftly came into being something new under the sun. For the true steel-frame structure stands unique in the flowing of man and his works; a brilliant material example of man's capacity to satisfy his needs through the exercise of his natural powers....

The social significance of the tall building is in finality its most important phase. In and by itself, considered *solus* so to speak, the lofty steel frame makes a powerful appeal to the architectural imagination where there is any. Where imagination is absent and its place usurped by timid pedantry the case is hopeless. The appeal and the inspiration lie, of course, in the element of loftiness, in the suggestion of slenderness and aspiration, the soaring quality as of a thing rising from the earth as a unitary utterance.

From Louis H. Sullivan, *The Autobiography of an Idea*, 1924.

for he designed many more and left scarcely a major city in the country untouched by his influence.

The architect whom Root singled out to illustrate the new spirit in American art was Henry Hobson Richardson. Born in New Orleans but educated at Harvard and abroad, Richardson was a man of gargantuan ambitions and appetites, full of zest for any problem and equally ready to design churches, railroad stations, department stores, libraries, office buildings, anything. "The things I want most to design," he said, "are a grain elevator and the interior of a great river steamboat." Although he died in 1886 at the age of forty-eight, he left his buildings scattered across the country from Trinity Church in Boston to a monument on the Wyoming plains. Richardson came before the age of steel and glass and worked entirely in masonry, though he used the medium with spontaneous originality and with an eye to the coming era. His admirer John Root carried Richardson's example one step further in the Monadnock Building in Chicago, an office building of masonry, entirely without ornament and fifteen stories in height, as high as masonry construction would permit.

The problem of the skyscraper, called into being by the fantastic extravagance of unplanned city growth and overcrowding, could not be solved by masonry. What was required was a steel skeleton for support and walls reduced to mere fireproof curtains instead of supporting buttresses. With contributions from engineers and steelmasters as well as architects, Chicagoans achieved a solution in the Tacoma Building in 1888. With the arrival of the electric elevator and vertical transportation, the age of the skyscraper begins, and with that age the name of Louis Sullivan is intimately associated. Ranking with Richardson as one of the giants of the period, Sullivan was a capricious genius who commanded the respect of the ablest critics: Frank Lloyd Wright referred to him as *Der Meister*. Sullivan has been called the "father of the skyscraper," and yet he revealed the inner conflicts of his generation's adjustment to the city when he characterized the structure as "profoundly antisocial."

It is curious that Chicago, which contributed so many new and original architectural techniques, should also have been the host and creator of the "White City" at the Columbian Exposition of 1893, which represented a return to Renaissance classicism and eclecticism in the extreme. Although Daniel H. Burnham of Chicago supervised the building, the White City was mainly the work of Easterners, particularly the firm of Charles F. McKim, William R. Mead, and Stanford White. The architects were assisted by the most famous American sculptor of the period, Augustus Saint-Gaudens, and by Olmsted, whose landscaping included the lovely lagoon surrounded by gleaming white plaster buildings. The ephemeral dream city was undoubtedly an impressive spectacle, but Sullivan, who designed the only nonclassical structure in the Exposition, regarded it as "an appalling calamity"

whose influence would "last for half a century." What he feared was a reversion to the academic, classical models of architecture, and in the "Federal" style sponsored by McKim, Mead, and White in the national capital and elsewhere in the ensuing era Sullivan's fears were justified. On the other hand the example of a city intelligently planned for comfort and beauty stimulated the "city beautiful" movement, and under Burnham's guidance Washington, Cleveland, San Francisco, and Manila made impressive achievements in the art of city planning.

Some of the fine arts in what Lewis Mumford has called the "Brown Decades" were creditably served by American artists. John La Farge, a gifted interior decorator and art critic, executed thousands of stained glass windows and won the admiration of Richardson, for whom he did the windows of Trinity Church in Boston. Winslow Homer, a serious illustrator, occasionally struck the note of greatness in his paintings of the weather-beaten ruggedness of common life. But to find American painters who deserve to rank with the best of their European contemporaries one must turn to Thomas Eakins and Albert Pinkham Ryder. Eakins worked in relative obscurity outside fashionable currents and left a house full of unsold paintings at his death. A friend of Walt Whitman, whose portrait he painted, he had a salty contempt for pretense and loved to paint boxers, oarsmen, and surgeons at their work. Ryder was a painter of the sea and the night and has been compared with Melville in the symbolic and lyrical qualities of his art. Among his great symbolic paintings are *Death on a Pale Horse*, *The Flying Dutchman*, *Jonah*, and *Macbeth and the Witches*, all of them eerie, mystic, and tragic.

Beginnings of Realism   In letters as in arts the post-Civil War decades have had a poor reputation. Their writers have been tagged with the "genteel" label and condemned for complacency and blindness to the glaring faults of their society. Their reputation for shallowness, complacency, and prudery is not wholly unjustified, but the age was often as blind to its literary merits as to its social faults. It sometimes overlooked and sometimes misunderstood its best talent. Contemporaries of Emily Dickinson, the greatest American poet of the age, and one of the subtlest, never even heard of her, for she lived the life of a recluse and published only two poems before her death in 1886. They mistook Mark Twain, their greatest satirist, for a funny man and a writer for boys. They were misled by the surface mildness of William Dean Howells, their major critic and their leading realist, and they misunderstood when they did not neglect Henry James, their greatest artist. But any age that could produce Dickinson, Twain, Howells, and James should command respect and serious attention.

More completely and richly than any other writer, Mark Twain, who was christened Samuel Langhorne Clemens, embodied in his life and writings the sprawling diversity, the epic adventures, the inner tensions, and the cross-purposes of post-Civil War America. A Southerner by birth and heritage, he became a Westerner while the West was wildest, and settled in New England to live out his life. He was a child of the frontier and, like his America, a countryman who moved to the city, a provincial who was thrust into a strange new world. His literary record of the experience documents a whole epoch. "I am persuaded," the playwright George Bernard Shaw wrote Mark Twain, "that the future historian of America will find your works as indispensable to him as a French historian finds the political tracts of Voltaire."

Mark Twain's American odyssey started in Missouri on the banks of the Mississippi, where the East bordered on the West and the South overlapped the North. He joined the Confederate army when the war broke out, but, after a trivial accident that involved no fighting, he gave up the war and joined his brother in the Far West. He recorded his adventures in the Nevada mining camps in *Roughing It* (1872) and gave the period a name that has stuck in *The Gilded Age* (1873), a broad political and social satire. His boyhood and his later experience as a pilot on the great river found expression in two of his best works, *The Adventures of Tom Sawyer* (1876) and *Life on the Mississippi* (1883). But he surpassed all his other work in *The Adventures of Huckleberry Finn* (1884), the finest expression of the age in fiction and a masterpiece of American literature. A composite of satire and nostalgia, it dips deeper

Henry James, 1843–1916.

into irony than was characteristic of the age, for it aligns the sympathies of every decent reader with Huck, the river rat, against civilization itself and fixes the primitive, superstitious Nigger Jim as one of the noblest figures in American fiction. Mark Twain wrote a great deal more, but like the miners of his Nevada adventure and America itself, he was a spendthrift with his resources and he could not always tell the stuff that glittered from the real gold.

Howells, the friend of Twain and the generous friend of every creative spirit in letters of his time, was even more prolific. He wrote thirty full-length novels and five volumes of short stories, not to mention an endless stream of literary criticism. In his time he was rightfully called the dean of American letters and the foremost exponent of American realism.

Mark Twain, 1835–1910.

novel that exposes and attacks social injustice.

Henry James continued to develop as a writer after Howells and Twain began to decline. His wonderfully productive life carried over into the twentieth century, though the bulk of his work appeared before 1900. Unlike Howells and Twain, he was not interested in the common man. His typical subjects are Americans and Europeans of cultivated minds, usually in a cosmopolitan setting. *The American* (1877), *The Europeans* (1878), and *Daisy Miller* (1879) are treatments of national attitudes in transatlantic society. This was only the beginning of four decades of writing that included such masterpieces as *The Portrait of a Lady* (1881), *The Ambassadors* (1903), and *The Golden Bowl* (1904). Henry James was the most completely dedicated and probably the most wholly fulfilled American writer and artist of his time.

The age affords posterity one unflattering but fascinating portrait of itself drawn by a philosopher-historian who stands in a class by himself: Henry Adams, descendant of the two Presidents whose name he bore. Every serious student of the period must make his own acquaintance and his own peace with this querulous and opinionated critic. His main writing dealt with the history of another period, that of Jefferson and Madison. But his novels *Democracy* (1880) and *Esther* (1883) and more particularly his autobiographical *Education of Henry Adams* (1918) and *The Degradation of the Democratic Dogma* (1919) are the keys to his incisive critique. It was characteristic of him that he had the first two books published anonymously and the last two posthumously. Having mastered those, one is then better prepared to find Adams, in *Mont-Saint-Michel and Chartres* (1913), searching the monuments of the Middle Ages for their meaning to modern America, and projecting lines of change from the year 1200 to the year 1900.

After the end of the century and near the end of his life, Henry Adams looked back philosophically over the American experience since the Civil War. He was astonished at how much history had been telescoped into that brief span of years and how frightfully the pace of change had accelerated. At the outset of the period, in his youth, his fellow citizens were still grappling with stone-age men on the Great Plains and debating the issue of African slavery

Rejected by a later generation that unfairly associated him with complacency and materialism, Howells deserves better from the present perspective. In mid-life he reached a critical turning point marked by his reaction to the Haymarket executions in 1886, against which he conducted virtually a one-man protest among the intellectuals. The experience coincided with his reading of Tolstoy and Henry George, and he began calling himself a socialist and demanding a sterner realism that would confront the injustice and suffering of industrial society under plutocratic control. His fiction began at once to reflect his views. *Annie Kilburn* (1889) is an indictment of social injustice and the inadequacies of charity in a New England community, and *A Hazard of New Fortunes* (1890), the best expression of Howells' new phase and the climactic work of American realism, centers around a violent strike. *A Traveler from Altruria* (1894) is a utopian in their midst. America had been a land of villages and farms, a provincial outpost of Western civilization. But now, as he steamed into New York harbor in 1902, remembering his return from Europe in 1868, he searched in vain for landmarks of the earlier era. "The outline of the city became frantic in its effort to explain something that defied meaning," he observed. Titanic, uncontrollable forces "had exploded, and thrown great masses of stone and steam against the sky. . . . A Traveller in the highways of history looked out of the club window on the turmoil of Fifth Avenue, and felt himself in Rome, under Diocletian. . . . The two-thousand-years failure of Christianity roared upward from Broadway, and no Constantine the Great was in sight." Henry Adams' fellow Americans, less troubled by historical perspective and premonitions of things to come, called the spectacle "progress" and greeted the dawn of the twentieth century with a confidence that was apparently unbounded.

SUGGESTIONS FOR READING

A. M. Schlesinger, *The Rise of the City, 1878–1898* (1933), furnishes an introduction to the social history of urban America in this period. A. F. Weber, *The Growth of Cities in the Nineteenth Century* (1899), compares statistics of city growth in Europe and America. Lewis Mumford, *The Culture of Cities* (1938), *The City in History* (1961), and several other studies, transcends national history to study the phenomenon theoretically. Max Weber, *The City* (1958), is another theoretical study. Several cities are examined as types by C. McL. Green, *American Cities in the Building of the Nation* (1956).

Contemporary sources on urban slums and poverty include Jacob Riis, *How the Other Half Lives* (1890), *The Children of the Poor* (1892), and *The Battle with the Slum* (1902); see also Josiah Strong, *The Twentieth Century City* (1898), as well as Jane Adams, *Twenty Years at Hull House* * (1910). A recent history of American attitudes toward poverty is R. H. Bremner, *From the Depths: The Discovery of Poverty in the United States* (1956). A sensitive analysis of immigration is Oscar Handlin, *The Uprooted* * (1951). On the new immigrants see particularly I. A. Hourwich, *Immigration and Labor* (1923), and on their reception in the United States consult Barbara Solomon, *Ancestors and Immigrants* (1956), and John Higham, *Strangers in the Land* (1955).

On the boss, the machine, and the reformer a contemporary account, James Bryce, *The American Commonwealth*, 2 vols. (1888), is a classic. A muckraker who deals with this period informatively is Lincoln Steffens, *The Shame of the Cities* (1904). Later studies of value are F. J. Goodnow, *Municipal Problems* (1907), and Clifford W. Patton, *The Battle for Municipal Reform: Mobilization and Attack, 1875–1900* (1940).

The reaction of the Protestant churches to social problems is discussed in several books, notably H. F. May, *Protestant Churches and Industrial America* (1949); A. I. Abell, *The Urban Impact on American Protestantism, 1865–1900* (1943); and C. H. Hopkins, *The Rise of the Social Gospel in American Protestantism, 1865–1915* (1940). On the Catholics there is a fine brief account in J. T. Ellis, *American Catholicism* * (1956), and a longer study in Theodore Maynard, *The Story of American Catholicism* (1941). Allan Johnson's long sketch of Mary Baker Eddy in the *Dictionary of American Biography* is helpful on the origins of Christian Science. W. W. Sweet, *Revivalism in America: Its Origins, Growth and Decline* (1944), is a useful survey, and his *The Story of Religion in America* (1939) is also helpful.

The history of higher learning has been much illuminated by Richard Hofstadter and Walter Metzger, *The Development of Academic Freedom in the United States* (1955). For a stiff and amusing indictment see Thorstein Veblen, *Higher Learning in America* (1918). Merle Curti, *Social Ideas of American Educators* (1935), is instructive, and also is H. K. Beale, *Are*

* Available in a paperback edition.

American Teachers Free? (1936). R. H. Shryock, "The Academic Profession in the United States," *Bulletin of the American Association of University Professors*, Spring (1952), is most important.

The history of public education receives vigorous and needed reinterpretation in L. A. Cremin, *The Transformation of the School: Progressivism in American Education, 1876–1957* (1961). E. W. Knight, *Education in the United States* (1929), and E. P. Cubberly, *Public Education in the United States* (1934), are old-style surveys. A. E. Meyer, *An Educational History of the American People* (1957), is a useful reference work. On the South see C. W. Dabney, *Universal Education in the South*, 2 vols. (1936). R. O. and Victoria Case, *We Called It Culture: The Story of Chatauqua* (1958), is the best account of that movement. F. L. Mott, *A History of American Magazines, 1885–1905* (1957), is an exhaustive and excellent history. The newspapers are treated in W. G. Bleyer, *Main Currents in the History of American Journalism* (1927).

On the graphic arts there are several studies of value, notably Lewis Mumford, *The Brown Decades: A Study of the Arts in America, 1865–1895* * (1931); John Kouwenhoven, *Made in America: The Arts in Modern Civilization* (1948); and O. W. Larkin, *Art and Life in America* (1949). On architecture, see Wayne Andrews, *Architecture, Ambition and Americans* (1955), and on the growth of cities, Christopher Tunnard and H. H. Reed, *American Skyline* (1955).

Literary history in this era is penetratingly treated by Everett Carter, *Howells and the Age of Realism* (1954), who discusses Howells' contemporaries as well. E. H. Cady, *The Realist at War* (1958); G. N. Bennett, *William Dean Howells* (1959); and V. W. Brooks, *New England: Indian Summer, 1865–1915* (1940) and *The Confident Years, 1885–1915* (1952), are full of biographical incident. Alfred Kazin, *On Native Grounds* * (1942), starts his account at 1890 but has two illuminating chapters on that decade.

* Available in a paperback edition.

20

Political Stalemate and Agrarian Revolt, 1877-1896

National politics had normally been the vital center of American civilization, the arena in which the future was determined and important issues of the present were resolved. Under Presidents Hayes, Garfield, Arthur, Cleveland, and Harrison Americans still worked up a great deal of excitement over national politics, especially presidential politics, but it was the excitement of spectators rather than of participants. The audience was large and noisy, but the participants themselves were few in number and strictly professional. The outcome of the contests meant more to the contestants than to the spectators, for the elections determined which party would enjoy the spoils of victory—and often little else. Great issues were sometimes debated, but most of them were settled around the council tables of industrialists and financiers rather than in the halls of legislatures and in the meetings of cabinets. The doctrine of laissez faire that was so popular among businessmen was just as popular among politicians, for it spared them a great deal of trouble. Literally applied, it meant permitting men of power to have things their own way so long as they appeared to stay within the law. The political game played under these rules attracted men of great skill, but none of true greatness.

The Business of Politics

The Party Equilibrium Politics in the post-Reconstruction period was more of a business than a game, a highly competitive business, with the two major parties as the evenly matched competitors. The Democrats managed to elect only one of their candidates President (for two terms) in the fifty-two years between 1860 and 1912. And yet this gives a misleading impression of the relative strength of the Democratic and Republican parties. Actually, there was an extraordinarily narrow margin of difference in the popular vote the two parties polled in the two decades following 1876. In none of the presidential elections from 1876 to 1892 did the Republicans carry a majority of the popular votes, and in only one, that of 1880, did they receive a plurality—but even that plurality was less than one-tenth of 1 per cent. In three of the five elections, in fact, the difference between the popular votes for the two major party candidates was less than 1 per cent, and in that of 1876, even though the Democrats received a majority of nearly 3 per cent, they lost the election. In the electoral college votes, on the other hand, majorities ranged from one in 1876 to 132 in 1892. The narrow margin between victory and defeat encouraged the laissez-faire tendency of politicians, the tendency to avoid vital issues and take few chances.

The Republican party was a loose alliance of regional and interest groups with different and sometimes conflicting interests. The basic alliance was between the Northeast and the upper Midwest—an alliance that had been consolidated in 1860 and that had fought and won the Civil War. It hung together afterward partly because of wartime loyalties and memories of the heroic days of Lincoln, when the party had emancipated the slaves and saved the Union. Two other large groups traced their attachment to the party back to the Civil War: the Negroes and the Union army veterans. The Negroes remained loyal to the party of emancipation and continued to send one or two congressmen to Washington, but after the Republicans abandoned them in 1877 the freedmen diminished rapidly in political power. On the other hand the war veterans increased in political significance as the Grand Army of the Republic grew as a pressure group and as Congress responded with larger and larger pensions for veterans. Economic conflict and political rivalry opened breaches in party unity. Republican policies such as high tariff, sound money, and favors for railroads pleased Eastern industrialists, but Western grain-growers often resented these policies and threatened revolt. The noisiest quarrel within Republican ranks was the running war between the Half-Breeds, led by James G. Blaine of Maine, and the Stalwarts, led by Roscoe Conkling of New York. The long-winded battles between these factions fascinated the multitude, but there was no significant difference between them over any policy or issue that troubled the country—only over which of them should get the spoils of office. Each faction demanded all the offices.

The post-Reconstruction Democratic party was even more regional than the Republican. Its most reliable sources of support were the Solid South and the machine-dominated cities of the Northeast. And the disparity of outlook and interest between the provincial, Protestant, agrarian cotton farmers of the South and the underprivileged, Catholic, immigrant, industrial workers of the big cities was almost as great as that between the impoverished Negro and the affluent capitalist supporters of the Republican party. The Democrats also received support from Northeastern merchants and bankers who opposed protective tariff and favored contraction of the currency—"sound-money" men, they called themselves. The leaders of the party in the South, many of them of Whig background, preferred to be called Conservatives, and were often called Bourbons

by their opponents. They had much in common with the dominant Democratic leaders in the Midwest, who were also business-minded conservatives and were also known as Bourbons. Rank-and-file Democrats, farmers, industrial workers, and small businessmen in the West, the South, and the East, were often restive and sometimes rebellious under such leaders, but conservatives generally had things their way in the party until the mid-nineties.

On major issues no important differences existed between the two old parties, which were under equally conservative leaders. Politics became the art of blurring or avoiding issues. Not that there was any lack of important issues. To appreciate the emptiness, bankruptcy, and dullness of national politics in this period, one has only to recall the recurrent industrial crises and depressions of the period and the desperate plight of the victims. Their problems cried out for vigorous government action. But if they got a hearing in the political arena, it was through small third parties. The major parties preferred to avoid live issues and revive dead ones. In the North the Republicans "waved the bloody shirt," accusing the Democrats of rebellion and treason, and in the South the Democrats invoked the menace of "Negro rule" and called for white supremacy. It is true that a vast amount of lung power was devoted to the "platform" and its "planks" during campaigns, but the wind seems to have whistled over the heads of the voters.

"The American, like the Englishman," observed James Bryce in 1888, "usually votes with his party, right or wrong, and the fact that there is little distinction of view between the parties makes it easier to stick to your old friends." Party allegiance during these years was in fact remarkably rigid. In Indiana, for example, thirty-two counties remained unswervingly Republican from 1876 to 1892, and thirty-nine counties stuck as unswervingly with the Democrats, with neither group varying more than 3 per cent. Only twenty-one counties shifted at all, and with third parties in the picture neither of the major parties could muster a reliable majority in those counties until 1896. The same pattern had prevailed for years: two-thirds of the Democratic counties had been voting Democratic since 1844, and over four-fifths of the Republican counties had

The Consistency of the Vote, 1876-92

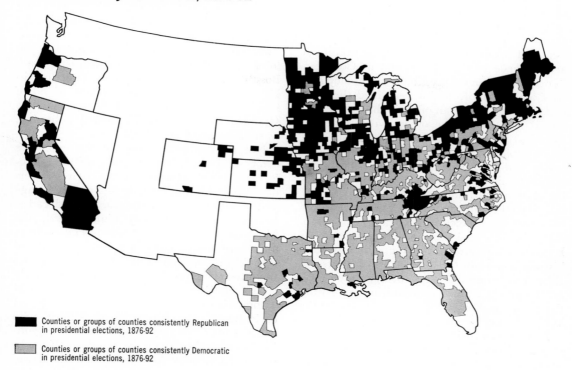

■ Counties or groups of counties consistently Republican in presidential elections, 1876-92

▨ Counties or groups of counties consistently Democratic in presidential elections, 1876-92

gone down the line for the old party since its founding in 1856. These rigid loyalties carried Hoosier voters right through war and peace, through a wide variety of candidates and policies, and through all the economic and social upheavals of the passing years.

Neither party was strong enough, however, to rely for victory on the allegiance of certain states or parts of states that could be counted "in the bag." There were always the "doubtful states"—that is, states with enough shifting voters to turn the tide either way. These states were thought to be Connecticut, New York, New Jersey, Ohio, Indiana, and Illinois, but the key states were New York and Indiana. In the 1880's the Republicans had to carry New York and all three of the Midwestern states to elect their candidate President. Since the whole contest hinged on a few states, it is no wonder that they commanded great bargaining power, absorbed most of the "slush funds" from the campaign treasuries, and gained desirable offices for their politicians. The strategic importance of the few doubtful Midwestern states

also helps to explain why five of the six Republican candidates for President from Grant to McKinley came from those states, including three from Ohio and one from Indiana. And as a running mate for their Midwestern candidate, the Republicans almost invariably chose a man from New York. The Democrats, on the other hand, usually reversed the regional order, though they picked their nominees from the same doubtful states. Their presidential nominees, with one exception, all came from New York—three of them had been governors of the state—and their vice-presidential nominees from Ohio, Illinois, or Indiana. In 1876, 1880, and 1884 the second place on the Democratic ticket went to the "strategic" state of Indiana.

The Spoilsmen and the Reformers From Grant to McKinley the power and influence of the presidential office was at low ebb. One reason was that no President between 1865 and 1897 enjoyed the advantage of having his own party in control of both houses of Congress throughout his tenure of office, so rapidly did control seesaw back and forth between the evenly matched parties. But more than that, the presidency was slow in recovering from the blows struck by Congress in its bitter fight with President Johnson and from President Grant's continual acquiescence in the domination of Congress. For a generation congressional supremacy and presidential subordination remained the rule. Senator John Sherman of Ohio, himself a perpetual aspirant to the office, wrote that the President "should be subordinate to the legislative department" and that he should merely "obey and enforce the laws." Ordinarily the President did not even have a voice in preparing the annual budget, and he was certainly not given the staff or the money to play the role of a real chief executive. To a large degree, Congress itself took care of administration. As Leonard D. White, a leading administrative historian, puts it, "The established course of the public business went on its appointed way, for the most part without requiring or inviting the collaboration of the man who sat in the White House."

Politics was really controlled by oligarchies of party bosses, many of them United States senators, who headed state machines and commanded armies of henchmen whom they paid off with public offices. In addition to Senators Blaine and Conkling were such potentates as Senator Zachariah Chandler, the fat, coarse, and cynical boss of Michigan, and Senator John A. "Black Jack" Logan of Illinois, a power in the Grand Army of the Republic. The patronage system placed at the disposal of the bosses the whole public service, an enormous booty in federal, state, and local offices, the "spoils" of political victory. The spoilsmen sometimes sold offices to the highest bidder, but more regularly they distributed them among faithful workers for service rendered and systematically taxed the holders for "contributions." The consequence of the system was a partisan, clumsy, ignorant, unstable, and often corrupt public service. After the Civil Service Reform Act of 1883 (see p. 473) began to curb the patronage as a source of revenue, politicians increasingly turned to big business for money and support. A new type of boss then began to replace the old flamboyant "stump politician," a quieter, more efficient "desk politician," who em-

ployed the methods of the corporation executive and worked hand in glove with the lobbyists and leaders of public utilities, railroads, heavy industries, and manufacturers. Matthew Quay, who kept a card index of the foibles of Pennsylvania politicians; "Easy Boss" Tom Platt, who replaced Conkling in New York; Arthur P. Gorman, the friend of business in Maryland; and Marcus Alonzo Hanna, Ohio industrialist turned politician, were bosses of the new type.

Not all the public men of the age were cynics and spoilsmen. A group of liberal reformers called Mugwumps by their deriders kept up a running crusade against patronage and corruption in office for two decades. Earnest, intelligent, and high-minded, the Mugwumps were men of high social position and conservative economic views, usually of Republican background. Foremost among them was George William Curtis, scholarly editor of *Harper's Weekly*, whose cartoonist Thomas Nast made a career of ridiculing and caricaturing the corrupt. Carl Schurz, who called Curtis "the intellectual head, the guiding force" of the movement, was himself a hero of the Mugwumps. Another of their luminaries was E. L. Godkin, editor of the *Nation*. Devoted to laissez-faire principles and unconcerned over the deeper ills of the economy, the reformers of this school confined their economic program to tariff reform and sound money and fixed their hopes on achieving honest and efficient government through civil-service reform. Spoilsmen sneered at "snivel service," and Senator Conkling described the reformers as "the man milliners, the dilettanti and *carpet knights* of politics" and accused them of "canting self-righteousness."

The influence of the Mugwumps was largely confined to the literate upper class, for they were isolated from the mass of voters by their attitudes and their social position. The Mugwump had an aristocratic disdain for the masses, a fear of the "radicalism" of the farmer and labor movements, and a contempt for the "demagogues" who led them. He regarded the urban immigrant as the tool of "unscrupulous bosses" and rural unrest in the South and West as a seedbed of economic heresies. The various reform movements of the period were not on speaking terms with each other, or they spoke different languages. Grangers, Green-backers, and Alliancemen of the West and the South (see pp. 482–84) demanded reforms in the currency, banking, and credit systems that chilled the blood of Eastern reformers. Agrarian reformers were at the same time divided among themselves: Northerner against Southerner, Republican against Democrat. Both the urban Mugwumps and the rural agrarians had trouble understanding the impulses and strivings of labor reformers. The cause of reform, its forces divided and mutually suspicious, languished and faltered through the eighties.

The Conservative Ascendancy

Hayes in the White House We have already seen how the means used to elect Rutherford B. Hayes cast widespread doubt on his title to the presidency. Even prominent leaders of his own party referred to him publicly as "His Fraudulency," and powerful Republicans of both the Stalwart and the Half-Breed factions resented his withdrawal of troops from the South, his desertion of the carpetbaggers, and his appeasement of the Southern conservatives. He antagonized many reformers, on the other hand, by rewarding the notorious politicians of the Louisiana returning board who had aided him in 1876. To add to his handicaps, the Democrats controlled the House during the first two years of his Administration and both Senate and House during the last two years. He did not strengthen his position when he announced that he would not run for re-election. Hayes was never an astute politician, but he did not lack courage and determination. From the start of his Administration he set out resolutely to redress the balance between the executive and legislative branches and regain for the presidency some of the powers that Congress had pre-empted, particularly the powers of appointment and removal of office-holders.

The nominations for the Cabinet that he sent to the Senate were his first challenge to congressional dominance, for they included names unwelcome to the bosses—notably the name of Carl Schurz for Secretary of the Interior. "Hayes has passed the Republican party to its worst enemies," said Senator Zach Chandler. The Senate balked and refused confirmation on the whole list at first, but under pressure of public opinion later yielded to the President. An old device that the House used to coerce the President was the "rider," a piece of legislation the President had to approve in order to secure the needed appropriation to which it was tied. The Democratic majority of the House used the rider repeatedly in an attempt to force Hayes to accept the repeal of Reconstruction laws providing federal protection of elections. Determined to resist the pressure and make the executive "an equal and independent branch of the Government," Hayes vetoed seven such bills, compelled acceptance of his independence, and gained a clear-cut victory over congressional encroachment.

A more daring and direct blow for reform was the one Hayes struck at the spoils system in its most powerful entrenchment, the New York Custom House Ring, the center of Senator Conkling's machine. A commission appointed by the President in 1877 and headed by John Jay of New York investigated the Custom House patronage system and reported that it was "unsound in principle, dangerous in practice, demoralizing in its influence on all connected with the customs service," and that it was ridden with "ignorance, inefficiency, and corruption." Conkling's lieutenants, Collector of the Port Chester A. Arthur and naval officer Alonzo B. Cornell, refused to clean up the corruption and declined to resign. At Conkling's demand the Senate refused to confirm appointment of the successors whom Hayes nominated, but the President stubbornly persisted, dismissed Arthur and Cornell while the Senate was in recess, and eventually filled their places with men of his own choice. Hayes had won a battle with the spoilsmen, but not a war. His orders that office-holders not be assessed for political contributions or required to do political campaigning were ignored. His promise of "thorough, radical and complete" civil-service reform remained unfulfilled, and the spoilsmen continued to rule the roost.

Economic crises and social protest in the worst years of the depression caught the Hayes Administration without a policy and without real comprehension of what was happening.

The first great industrial conflict in our history started with a strike on the B. & O. Railroad in July 1877 (see p. 438). The strike spread spontaneously and rapidly throughout all sections save New England and the South, affecting two-thirds of the railroad mileage in the country. At the request of four state governors, Hayes set the fateful precedent of using federal troops to intervene in a strike and restore order. The President incurred additional ill will from labor, especially on the west coast, by vetoing a bill passed in 1879 to restrict Chinese immigration. As a matter of fact, Hayes agreed with labor opinion that the importation of cheap "coolie labor" by mining and railroad corporations of the West was undesirable and wished to restrict it. He vetoed the bill because it violated the Burlingame Treaty of 1868, but after the veto he began negotiations for a new treaty with China. The treaty of 1880 acknowledged the right of restriction and in 1882 Congress passed a bill stopping Chinese immigration for the next decade. For all this, however, Hayes received little gratitude from labor.

Monetary Policy in Politics The President also took the unpopular side in a series of debates over national currency policies that divided both parties during his Administration. Hayes held the conservative, laissez-faire doctrine that the sole duty of the government was to maintain the value of currency and that the only way to do this was by the demonstrated ability of the Treasury to redeem currency at face value in gold. His opponents held, on the other hand, that it was the duty of the government to manage the currency so as to prevent or correct injustice and to relieve distress and suffering. People in debt—and this included a growing majority of the farmers—held that the contraction of the amount of currency in circulation, making it scarcer and more valuable, increased the burden of their debts and compelled them to pay off their creditors in dollars more valuable than the ones they borrowed. Farmers maintained that the same monetary policy also depressed the price of their crops and compelled them to raise more and more bushels of wheat and pounds of cotton to earn a dollar. As we shall see, this was not the only explanation for the growing agricultural distress of the time, but the farmer was perfectly right that crop prices were falling and that monetary policy was related to the decline in prices.

The first clash between Hayes and the discontented agrarians occurred over a movement to repeal the Specie Resumption Act of 1875, which obliged the Treasury to resume the redemption of legal-tender notes in specie at full face value by January 1, 1879, and to reduce the number of greenbacks in circulation. The measure thus contracted the currency and at the same time appreciated its value, the two things most complained of by farmers and debtors. Advocates of repeal, called Greenbackers, argued that fulfillment of the act would further depress prices and increase the burden of private and public debt. They denounced as outrageous the proposal to redeem war bonds that had been bought with greenbacks worth less than forty cents to the dollar with currency worth one hundred cents to the dollar. A National Greenback party had polled an insignificant vote in the election of 1876, but in the following year the movement gained recruits from labor and additional support from farmers and in February 1878 reorganized as the Greenback Labor party. In the fall elections the new party polled a remarkable total of 1,060,000 votes and elected fourteen representatives to Congress. Resisting all pressure, much of it from his own party, Hayes clung to the policy of resumption and supported Secretary of the Treasury John Sherman in building up a gold reserve to redeem the currency. Two weeks before the deadline of January 1, 1879, however, greenbacks became worth their face value in gold and no run on the gold reserve developed. Resumption was an accomplished fact. The Greenbackers nominated James B. Weaver of Iowa for President in 1880, but their issue was dead and they attracted little attention.

Inflationist sentiment, by no means dead, found a new outlet in the movement for the free coinage of silver just as the greenback cause was becoming hopeless. Once again Hayes took the unpopular side. The silver question was to become one of the most hotly debated issues in the history of American politics during the next two decades, but before 1875 it attracted no popular interest. The official government ratio of sixteen to one—

sixteen times as much silver in a silver dollar as there was gold in a gold dollar—had undervalued silver ever since the gold rush of 1849 had lowered the price of gold. As a consequence, silver miners sold their product commercially rather than offer it to the Treasury at a loss, and silver dollars virtually disappeared from circulation. In recognition of this, Congress abolished the coinage of silver dollars and put the country on the gold standard in 1873. In the meantime, new silver mines in Nevada, Arizona, and Colorado flooded the market and the price of silver began to drop. Miners then discovered that the Treasury rejected their product and that their European market had been reduced by widespread adoption of the gold standard abroad. Denouncing demonetization of silver as the "Crime of 1873," they demanded that free coinage at the old ratio be restored. Inflationists took up their cry because they saw in silver a means of halting currency contraction, getting cheaper money, raising crop prices, and securing debtor relief.

So rapidly did the silver movement spread in the West and the South that by the fall of 1877 an overwhelming majority of the lower house of Congress voted for a bill for the "free and unlimited coinage of silver" introduced by Representative Richard "Silver Dick" Bland of Missouri. The Bland bill would have stopped the sale of government bonds for gold and driven that metal out of circulation, since it would have produced silver dollars worth less than ninety cents (and still falling in value) and made them legal tender. Yet the bill commanded so much support in both houses that Hayes knew it would be passed over his veto. Before the Senate acted, however, Senator William B. Allison of Iowa amended and weakened the bill, and in that form it was passed over Hayes's veto in February 1878. The Bland-Allison Act deprived the inflationists of their objective of "unlimited coinage," and substituted the requirement that the Treasury buy not less than $2 million and not more than $4 million worth of silver per month and coin it into dollars. The act did not have the effects that the conservatives feared and the inflationists desired. For one thing the government consistently purchased the minimum amount of silver required by the act and stood ready to redeem the silver coin and notes in gold. And for another, the depression lifted in 1879, gold flowed in from abroad, and crop prices improved temporarily for reasons other than monetary policy. Silverites were to return to the battle in stronger force, but for more than a decade they made no change in the law.

In spite of the unpopularity of his stand on silver and quarrels with Congress, Hayes ended his administration on an upswing of confidence and respect. The lifting of the long depression, the decline in unemployment, and the rise in farm prices during his last year in office undoubtedly helped. But his stubborn fight for his convictions, even unpopular ones, and the new reputability he had brought his party won grudging respect for the President. "I am now experiencing one of the 'ups' of political life," he wrote near the end of his term. Ordinarily such an upturn would have started a "draft" for a second term to overcome his announced intention to retire, but no such movement developed. His party virtually ignored him and he became scarcely more than a spectator during the struggle to nominate his successor.

The Garfield Tragedy   The Republicans brought their bitter feuds to the Chicago nominating convention under the banners of rival candidates. The Stalwarts were united under Conkling's leadership to name Grant for a third term. The Half-Breeds were determined to have the prize for their own leader, Blaine; and Secretary of the Treasury John Sherman maneuvered to make himself available as a compromise candidate. For more than two years Grant's friends had kept him out of domestic quarrels and in the public eye by sending him on a round of foreign travels. The ex-President took the lead on the first ballot of the convention and maintained it for thirty-five consecutive ballots, with Blaine a close second and Sherman a poor third. When it became clear that none of the three could marshal a majority, the Blaine and Sherman forces joined on the thirty-sixth ballot and nominated Congressman James A. Garfield of Ohio as a dark horse. Garfield had managed Sherman's campaign and led the anti-Grant forces at the convention. To conciliate the defeated faction, the convention then nominated Conkling's lieutenant, Ches-

James A. Garfield: Victim of spoilsman politics.

votes by claiming credit for the current economic recovery. Garfield made what he could of his log-cabin birthplace (the last President to claim that distinction) and sought frantically to win the support of mutually hostile factions of his party. His managers did the most decisive work of the campaign in the doubtful states of Ohio, New York, and Indiana, using large amounts of money to carry Indiana by a bare seven thousand votes and New York by twenty thousand. Garfield won by a scant margin of less than forty thousand popular votes in the country at large, though his electoral vote was 214 to 155 for Hancock.

President Garfield's brief tenure in the White House began with embarrassments, continued with unhappiness, and ended in tragedy. A handsome, massive figure of a man, with a reputation for courage under fire in the war and for resourcefulness as party leader in the House, Garfield was not without a degree of integrity. Under the extraordinary pressures of his new office, however, he wavered in purpose. His first impulse was to conciliate all the warring Republican factions and please as many people as possible. He knew that his major obligation for his office was to Blaine, however, and he acknowledged it by making the senator Secretary of State. Blaine promptly used his influence over the President to undermine and destroy the power of his sworn enemy Conkling. Garfield's most aggressive move against the Stalwarts was to replace the man whom Hayes had made collector of the port of New York (in the name of civil-service reform) with William H. Robinson, the leading opponent of the Conkling faction in New York. This precipitated a violent war between the factions of spoilsmen and a torrent of abuse and charges of bad faith against the President. Conkling blocked the confirmation of Robinson and other appointments in the Senate until May. The President's will was hardened when he suddenly learned that a plunder ring of Stalwarts had stolen more than $4 million of public funds over the past five years by means of fraudulent "Star Route" mail delivery contracts in the Post Office Department. Conkling and the junior senator from New York, Thomas C. Platt, then resigned their seats in the Senate to make what later proved to be a futile effort to seek re-election and vindica-

ter A. Arthur, the deposed spoilsman of the New York Custom House, for Vice-President. The platform contained ambiguous planks for tariff and civil-service reform and called for generous treatment of Union veterans and restriction of Chinese immigration.

Prospects for revenging Governor Tilden by nominating him in 1880 looked promising to the Democrats, but Tilden, like Hayes, declined to run for the presidency again. The party nominated instead General Winfield Scott Hancock, a Pennsylvanian and a Union hero in the Battle of Gettysburg. Hancock had no political experience, but his nomination was an effective answer to the charge of disloyalty that was so often thrown at his party. His running mate was William H. English, from the "doubtful" state of Indiana. The platforms of the two parties were nearly indistinguishable, their nominees almost equally undistinguished, and the campaigns they waged demagogic and sometimes unprincipled. The Republicans enjoyed somewhat less success with the bloody-shirt issue than they had in former years, but they probably won

tion at the hands of the New York legislature.

At the very height of the furor over spoils and corruption, on July 2, 1881, Charles J. Guiteau, a crazed and disappointed office-seeker, shot the President in the back and shouted: "I am a Stalwart and Arthur is President now." Garfield died of the wound on September 19 and the next day Stalwart Chester A. Arthur took the oath and was, indeed, President.

The Arthur Interlude The new President was a wealthy, easygoing man with expensive tastes, elegant clothes and carriages, and twenty years of experience as a spoilsman in the Conkling camp of New York politics. His first year as President did little to dispel the fear that Garfield's martyrdom had been in vain and that the spoils system was there to stay. He did not turn over patronage to Conkling, as many expected, but after Blaine resigned the President filled the Cabinet with friends of Grant and Conkling. Arthur did prosecute with vigor the criminals charged with the Star Route post-office frauds, one of whom claimed to have provided the money for carrying Indiana for Garfield and Arthur. But the guilty men escaped punishment, and the President's efforts not only failed to win over the reformers, but alienated his former followers. The fall elections of 1882 were a stinging rebuke to the President, for they drove his party from control of the House of Representatives and gave the Democrats a majority of nearly a hundred seats.

One cause of the Democratic landslide was the nation's shock over Garfield's assassination and revulsion against the system of patronage and spoils associated with the tragedy. Popular indignation put new power behind the demands of the small band of reformers who, having fought the spoilsmen since the 1860's, had in 1881 organized the National Civil Service Reform League, with George William Curtis as president. It was ironic that "Chet" Arthur, long the very symbol of spoils politics, should be cast in the role of civil-service reformer, but he firmly told Congress that "action should no longer be postponed" and promised his full cooperation. In January 1883 large bipartisan majorities in both houses of Congress passed a Democratic bill sponsored by Senator George H. Pendleton of Ohio. The

Civil Service Act (often called the Pendleton Act) established a bipartisan Civil Service Commission of three members, appointed by the President with Senate confirmation, who were to administer competitive examinations and select appointees on the basis of merit and an apportionment among the states according to population. Arthur demonstrated his good faith by naming as head of the commission Dorman B. Eaton, an outstanding reformer who drafted the act, and appointing two prominent friends of reform as the other commissioners. At first the act affected only some fourteen thousand officials, about one-tenth of the total number of federal employees, but it empowered the President to expand the proportion of "classified" posts—jobs subject to the merit system. By the end of the century 40 per cent were classified and the federal civil service was securely established.

While the Civil Service Commission was the most important achievement of the Arthur administration, it was not the President's only assertion of independence and conscience, nor his only praiseworthy effort. Two such efforts, both of them futile, as it turned out, were in response to the problem of a surplus of over $100 million accumulated in the United States Treasury by excessive tax revenues. The solution favored by Congress was to spend the surplus in lavish appropriations for river and harbor improvements and pork-barrel handouts. Arthur vetoed one such bill, only to have Congress pass it over his veto. The President's solution to the Treasury surplus included the reduction of taxes, particularly the high protective tariff duties. To this end he appointed a Tariff Commission that made an elaborate study and recommended a moderate reduction of about 20 per cent in the revenues, but a lobby of industrialists frustrated the President's plans for reform. As an incidental means of reducing the Treasury surplus, Arthur's naval construction program was more successful. The navy had deteriorated since the Civil War to a collection of wooden antiques with cast-iron guns and rotten hulls. It did not boast a steel vessel or a rifled gun afloat. Arthur awakened Congress out of its indifference and started the construction of new fighting ships. The three cruisers begun in his administration had numerous defects, but he is properly credited with sweeping away barriers of ignorance and clearing the way for a modern navy. In this as in other ways Arthur proved worthier of the office he held than anyone had reason to believe when he took it.

Changing the Conservative Guard
The chances of Arthur's succeeding himself as President in 1884, never very strong in any case, were greatly weakened by the Democratic tidal wave of 1882, in which he lost control of his own state. He later won approval from the reform, especially the Mugwump, element, but not their support, and he proved unable to unite his own faction of the party behind his candidacy. Blaine remained the dominant figure in the Republican party, and his nomination seemed more and more likely as the convention approached. Curtis, Schurz, and other Mugwumps spurned Blaine and supported their own candidate, Senator George Edmunds of Vermont, to the end. Ignoring the reformers and overriding the Arthur supporters, the Blaine men nominated their candidate without difficulty and named John A. Logan, favorite son of Illinois, for Vice-President. The Yankee Mugwumps promptly decided to bolt the party provided the Democrats nominated the rising hope of the reformers, Grover Cleveland, governor of New York.

Cleveland's rise in New York politics had been recent but rapid. Elected mayor of Buffalo in 1881, he accepted the Democratic nomination for governor in 1882 and won an easy victory because of the split in the Republican party of the state. A burly figure of 240 pounds, determined jaw, and hard eyes, he was known for his rugged honesty and his habits of hard work and thrift—the common man turned reformer. But Cleveland was a thoroughgoing conservative as well, a believer in sound money and a defender of the right of property. As governor he enhanced his reputation for scorn of popularity by vetoing a popular bill reducing the fare on Jay Gould's elevated railroads in New York City to five cents. Similarly, he risked the wrath of labor by vetoing a bill limiting the working day of New York streetcar conductors to twelve hours, and with even greater recklessness he defied "Honest" John Kelley, boss of Tammany Hall. Businessmen, middle-class taxpayers, and re-

formers of the Mugwump school admired the independence and integrity of Cleveland. The nomination of Blaine and the promise of Mugwump support made Governor Cleveland the logical standard-bearer for the Democrats in 1884. He was nominated with the aid of state bosses and financed in his campaign by corporate wealth. His running mate was Thomas A. Hendricks, yet another available candidate from the shifting counties of Indiana.

The presidential campaign of 1884 was one of the most sensational, abusive, and frenzied in our history, and yet it managed to avoid all vital issues. "The public is angry and abusive," wrote Henry Adams. "Every one takes part. We are all doing our best, and swearing like demons. But the amusing thing is that no one talks about real interests." Cleveland said little at all, and Blaine talked a great deal without saying very much. There was no significant difference between the party platforms. In the absence of public issues, popular attention focused on the private life and personal morals of the candidates. Democrats and Mugwumps took the initiative by reviving the Mulligan Letter charges (see p. 375) that had deprived Blaine of the nomination in 1876 and by publishing additional Mulligan letters to prove that Blaine had been guilty of underhanded deals with railroad promoters. George William Curtis declared that the issue was "moral rather than political." Thereupon the Republicans retaliated with charges that Cleveland was the father of an illegitimate son born to the widow Maria Halpin of Buffalo. Cleveland did not deny the story but urged his friends to "tell the truth"—that he had assumed responsibility for the child, whether he was actually the father or not. Republican paraders chanted, "Ma! Ma! Where's my Pa?" and Democrats responded with a jingle on Blaine, "The monumental liar from the State of Maine." The campaign deteriorated into scandalmongering that became more and more irresponsible.

Cleveland had to carry New York to win the election, and the extreme closeness of the contest in that state concentrated attention on a number of intangible factors, any one of which might conceivably be decisive. These intangibles included the unknown strength of the Mugwump support, the strength of the Greenback third-party ticket, the effect of Conkling's disaffection on Blaine's strength and of Tammany Hall's hostility on Cleveland's chances, as well as a number of factors touching labor sentiment, particularly the Catholic issue, anti-British bias, and prohibition. As the election approached, Blaine appeared to have a slight advantage in New York, but on October 29, just a week before election day, two events put powerful propaganda in the hands of Democratic strategists. Before a meeting of New York clergymen the Reverend Samual D. Burchard told Blaine that the antecedents of the Democratic party were "Rum, Romanism, and Rebellion." Blaine failed to rebuke the indiscretion, and his opponents swiftly plastered cities having a significant Catholic vote with the Republican slander of their religion. That evening Blaine spoke at a dinner in his honor attended by two hundred of the country's wealthiest men, including Jay Gould and other well-hated millionaires. Newspapermen were excluded, but the Democratic press followed the lead of the New York *World*, which filled half its front page with a cartoon of "The Royal Feast of Belshazzar Blaine and the Money Kings," picturing the senator glorifying the plutocrats and wallowing in luxury while unemployed labor shivered outside in the hunger and want of a depression. Such incidents as these have been pronounced decisive factors in the election.

Whatever the explanation, the tide turned narrowly in Cleveland's favor. In addition to all the Southern states, he carried the doubtful states of Indiana, New Jersey, Connecticut, and New York—the last by a plurality of a mere 1,149 votes. His share of the votes in the country as a whole was only about twenty-nine thousand greater than Blaine's. Mugwumps and reformers rejoiced at the victory, but it is a mistake to conclude that a moral crusade had defeated Blaine. Actually, he polled only .09 per cent less of the total vote than Garfield had in 1880 and a larger percentage than the Republican candidates were to poll in 1888 and 1892. At any rate, the long Republican rule was at an end, and the Democrats were back in power for the first time in twenty-four years.

Grover Cleveland: Defender of the right of property.

Cleveland in Command   No one could be sure of the new President's views on any of several leading issues, but everyone could be sure he was a conservative. His inaugural address promising adherence to "business principles" bore this out, and so did his Cabinet appointments, which included representatives of the most conservative and business-minded wing of the party in the East and South. The new Administration signified the return of the party of the "outs" and the political rehabilitation of the South, but no break with the past on fundamental issues.

If there was any policy to which Cleveland had a clear commitment, it was civil-service reform, and it was over this issue that he came near to wrecking his Administration. He came to office with two masters to please: the Mugwump reformer and the hungry spoilsman of his own party with an appetite for office whetted by twenty-four years of anticipation. The President's first moves delighted the reformers. Defying the Democratic bosses and spoilsmen, he retained in office some able Republicans and personally examined applications for office far into the night. Party leaders besieged the President with patronage demands and insisted that he accept their definition of civil-service reform which, according to one senator, "meant turning out of office of Republicans and putting honest Democrats in their places"—*all* their places. The party press thundered against his "ingratitude." Within a few months he yielded to pressure and Republican heads began to roll. Carl Schurz wrote, "Your attempt to please both reformers and spoilsmen has failed," and Cleveland broke with the Mugwumps. By the end of four years he had removed about two-thirds of the 120,000 federal officers. He did increase the list of classified jobs to 27,380, nearly double the number when he took office, but he filled the Civil Service Commission with weak and incompetent men.

In the role of Treasury watchdog and thrifty steward of public funds, Cleveland showed more independence and consistency than he did as civil-service reformer. For one thing, he sternly rebuked a scandalous pensions racket run by a powerful lobby for Union veterans of the Civil War. Agents of this lobby used private bills to push through Congress thousands of dubious claims, hundreds of them obviously fraudulent. Previous Presidents, who feared the Grand Army of the Republic, had always signed these bills, but Cleveland called a halt and took to investigating individual claims himself, vetoing many of them, often with sarcastic comment. In January 1887 Congress passed a Dependent Pension Bill that provided a pension for all honorably discharged disabled veterans who had seen as much as ninety days of service if they were unable to work, regardless of the cause of their disability. The President defied the wrath of the GAR and its half-million members and vetoed the bill.

Cleveland believed that, except in rare circumstances, the President should confine himself to the execution of the laws and was not obliged to furnish leadership to Congress.

In spite of the storms of social protest in the mid-eighties, Congress enacted little legislation of lasting significance, and the President's influence upon that was largely negative. His Secretary of the Interior, L. Q. C. Lamar, showed initiative in compelling railroads and cattle barons of the West to give up 81 million acres of public lands which they illegally withheld from settlement. But Cleveland himself deserves no credit for what was probably the most important act passed during his Administration, the Interstate Commerce Act of 1887 (see p. 424). He regarded the whole idea with suspicion and signed the bill reluctantly and "with reservations."

In his fight for tariff reform, however, Cleveland rose to the full heights of leadership that earned him the distinction of being the outstanding President between Lincoln and Theodore Roosevelt. The forthright stand he eventually took on this issue contributed to his defeat for re-election, but it fulfilled his promise of rugged integrity and dedication to duty. Typical of the man was his reply to an adviser who counseled compromise and caution: "What is the use of being elected or re-elected, unless you stand for something?" To appreciate the risks he ran and the foes he encountered, one needs to glance back over the history of the tariff issue.

The Tariff in Politics   The issue was as old as the Republic, but since the Civil War it had taken on a new importance and complexity and was treated with caution and evasiveness by politicians of both parties. The tariff acts of the Civil War had been justified on the grounds that high internal war taxes on American industries put them at a competitive disadvantage that had to be offset with protective tariff duties to enable Americans to compete with foreign manufacturers on equal terms. Beginning with modest rates of 18.8 per cent on dutiable goods in 1861, a succession of acts raised the average to 40.3 per cent in 1866. No politician at the end of the war would admit publicly that these rates were anything but a temporary expedient. But while the American producers were soon relieved of the burden of internal war taxes, the protective tariff remained unrepealed. American industry quickly adjusted to the prices, dividends, and profits made possible by freedom from competition from abroad. Producers who enjoyed or desired these advantages organized to press their needs on Congress. Politicians learned the great power of the tariff lobby, and both major parties, the Republicans explicitly and the Democrats tacitly, accepted the principle of protection—though with dissent in each party.

From time to time a President would make a gesture of reform, but Congress would regularly respond with jugglery that left the situation unchanged or made a mockery of reform. The Tariff Act of 1870 reduced the duties on coffee, tea, spices, and other articles not produced in this country, but left the protective duties virtually unaltered. Reformers tried again in 1872 and actually effected a reduction of 10 per cent in the protective duties, but the cut was quietly restored three years later on the ground that the panic of 1873 had reduced federal revenues. Two Democratic bills for reform in 1876 and 1878 never got out of committee. We have already seen (p. 473) how President Arthur's efforts on tariff reform came to naught in 1883.

In the meantime, tariff reformers were stirring up public demand for action. The reformers included most of the Mugwumps and many intellectuals, but they included in addition many practical politicians, such as S. S. "Sunset" Cox of New York, with a mass appeal of a kind that the Mugwumps rarely enjoyed. It was not difficult for editors like Henry Watterson of the Louisville *Courier-Journal* and congressmen like William S. Holman of Indiana to bring home to the farmers of the South and the West the injustices of the tariff. They hammered away at the point that high tariff meant high prices, that the outrageous profits of protected industries were taken out of the pockets of consumers, and that the tariff was "the mother of monopoly." The reformers also pointed out that surplus revenues, bringing in $100 million or more a year in excess of expenditures, kept needed currency out of circulation when money was tight. The just solution, according to the reformers, was not to give away the surplus by pork-barrel appropriations, or to reduce it by cutting taxes on luxuries, but to lower the tariff on necessities that was mainly responsible for excess revenues.

Cleveland hesitated for three years to take an aggressive stand. He knew that a minority of some forty Democratic congressmen had combined with Republicans to defeat tariff-reform bills in 1884 and 1886, and Democratic leaders assured him that an all-out fight on the issue would split the party and lose the next election. Finally deciding that a bold stand was his duty, however, the President went the whole way and devoted his entire annual message of December 1887 to the tariff question. He made a slashing attack on the injustice, inequity, and absurdity of existing rates, ridiculed the need to protect century-old "infant industries," and denounced high rates as "the vicious, inequitable and illogical source of unnecessary taxation." The House of Representatives, with a Democratic majority, responded to the President's demand by adopting a bill sponsored by Roger Q. Mills of Texas. Far from radical, it did place such raw materials as lumber, wool, and flax on the free list and made moderate reductions of about 7 per cent in rates for finished goods. The Republican-controlled Senate then rejected the Mills bill, as expected, and adopted a highly protective bill that was buried in the House committee by the Democrats. The deadlock of tariff reform produced the first clear-cut economic issue between parties since Reconstruction and provided the leading issue of the 1888 election.

For their presidential candidate the Republicans chose Benjamin Harrison of Indiana, whose chief attractions were that he came from a doubtful state and that he was the grandson of former President William Henry Harrison, "Old Tippecanoe," of log-cabin and hard-cider fame. During a single term in the United States Senate the candidate had proved himself a champion of generous pensions for Union veterans and a defender of the protective tariff, and on these matters he was in complete harmony with the Republican platform of 1888. His running mate was Levi P. Morton, a wealthy New York banker. The Democrats naturally renominated President Cleveland, and for their vice-presidential candidate they chose the elderly and ailing ex-senator Allen G. Thurman of Illinois.

Although the Democratic platform endorsed Cleveland's demand for tariff reform, the party made a protectionist the chairman of its national committee. The campaign for Cleveland's re-election was handicapped, therefore, by halfhearted and ineffective leadership. It was also afflicted by the performance of Governor David B. Hill, a shifty politician who carried New York handily for himself but lost it for Cleveland by a handful of votes. By contrast, the Republican campaign had a vigorous leader in Senator Matt Quay, boss of a ruthless machine in Pennsylvania. With the support of industrialists who were aroused by Cleveland's challenge to the tariff, Quay collected and spent a huge campaign fund. Republican strategists made telling use of this fund to purchase votes and rig elections in Indiana and New York. Inventing new tricks as well as reviving old ones, they publicized a letter that the unwary British minister to the United States had written a Californian who represented himself as a naturalized Englishman seeking advice on how to vote. The minister's intimation that a vote for Cleveland would do the mother country the most good caused indignation among Americans and cost the Democrats many Irish-American votes.

In spite of much talk about tariff reform, the election did not turn on that issue. Cleveland actually carried the manufacturing states of New Jersey and Connecticut, and the Democrats gained ground in Michigan, Ohio, and California, normally protariff states. Cleveland polled a plurality of almost one hundred thousand popular votes, but Harrison won the electoral vote 233 to 168. It was an extremely narrow victory for the Republicans. As usual, the outcome had hung on a few evenly divided states—Indiana, New York, Rhode Island, and Ohio—and Harrison had carried them all, each by a few thousand votes. The decisive factors in what was probably the most corrupt presidential election in national history appear to have been trickery and bribery in Indiana and New York.

Harrison and Reaction   President Harrison complained that he could not name his own Cabinet because party managers "had sold out every place to pay the election expenses." Heavy obligations to Blaine dictated his appointment as Secretary of State, and other appointments paid off regional bosses,

high-tariff groups, and donors to the campaign fund. John Wanamaker, the wealthy Philadelphia merchant, became Postmaster General and promptly turned over the post-office patronage to hungry spoilsmen. In spite of his commitment to civil-service reform, Harrison watched the process in silence. To appease the reformers he made young Theodore Roosevelt a member of the Civil Service Commission. But the President pleased neither the reformers nor the spoilsmen and lost strength in both camps.

For the first time since 1875 the Republicans in 1889–91 held the presidency and a majority in both houses of Congress. Each majority was extremely slight, however, and under existing House rules the Democratic minority could frustrate the majority by simply not answering roll call and thereby depriving the House of a quorum. Speaker Thomas B. Reed of Maine earned the title of "Czar" by sweeping aside the rules over the indignant protest of the minority and running House proceedings with an iron will. Under Reed in the House and the protectionist Senator Nelson W. Aldrich of Rhode Island in the Senate, the Republican majority won the name of the "Billion Dollar Congress." Their solution for the growing Treasury surplus was not to lower the tariff revenues that produced it, but to give away the surplus to their friends. With this policy they greeted the protectionist lobby, the veterans' pension lobby, and the pork-barrel lobby with open arms.

The American Iron and Steel Association, the Industrial League, and other protectionists were the first to benefit. Reed appointed William McKinley, a high-tariff representative from Ohio whom he had just defeated in a contest for the speakership, as chairman of the House Ways and Means Committee, and the new chairman assumed the task of fulfilling Republican pledges of higher tariff rates. The McKinley Tariff Bill, which became law on June 10, 1890, raised an already scandalously high tariff scale even higher, an ad valorem increase of about 4 per cent. Its purpose was not merely to be protective, but to be prohibitive; not merely to discourage foreign competition, but to eliminate it; not merely to protect infant industries, but to call new industries into being. To aid the Sugar Trust, the bill put raw sugar on the free list, but granted American sugar growers a compensatory subsidy of two cents a pound. As a rather hypocritical gesture of help to farmers, duties were raised on farm products that generally needed no protection anyway. Finally, there was a "reciprocity" clause intended not as a means of lowering tariffs but as a threat to raise them in this country if other countries did not lower theirs.

Faced with an indignant reaction in the agricultural sections against the favoritism of the McKinley Tariff, Republican congressmen now hastened to take steps of appeasement. Representatives from the silver-mining states and the Western states in favor of currency expansion had been promised that the party would "do something for silver" in return for their reluctant support of the tariff bill. The measure finally contrived to fulfill this commitment was the Sherman Silver Purchase bill, named for the senator from Ohio. It was designed to replace the Bland-Allison Act of 1878 (see p. 471), which had fixed a minimum amount of silver that the federal Treasury was required to purchase each month in dollars. Under this law the Treasury had put about $378 million in silver into circulation without relieving the scarcity of currency. The Sherman Act fixed the amount of silver to be purchased in ounces rather than dollars: four and a half million ounces a month, approximately the amount of current production of the metal. The silver was to be paid for in treasury notes of full legal-tender value which could be redeemed in either gold or silver at the discretion of the government. The bill was passed by a straight party vote, with Democrats opposing on the grounds that it provided no adequate relief. As it turned out, the government subsequently chose to redeem the notes only in gold, and as the price of silver dropped the Treasury was required to spend fewer and fewer dollars to purchase the stated number of ounces. The act produced no more currency expansion than its predecessor had. The product of weak and shifty statesmanship, it pleased neither side and contributed nothing of importance toward solving the currency problems of the nation.

Another reform act passed about the same time, the Sherman Antitrust Act, bearing the name of the same Ohio senator, became law in July 1890 (see discussion on p. 429). Although many congressmen were absent when the vote was taken, the Sherman Antitrust Act was adopted with only one vote against it in the Senate and none in the House. It had little effect during the following decade, for no Administration during those years showed any interest in enforcing it.

In order to please Union veterans of the GAR, Harrison appointed Corporal James Tanner, a cynical pensions lobbyist, as commissioner of pensions. The new commissioner publicly declared that he favored "an appropriation for every old comrade who needs it," and as quickly as he could in a brief term of office he added millions to the pension budget. Congress assisted him with the Dependent Pension Act of 1890, similar to the one Cleveland had vetoed in 1887, which declared all Union veterans with at least ninety days' service in the Civil War eligible for a pension if they were unable to provide for themselves for any reason at all. Their widows and children were also made eligible for pensions. The number of pensioners increased by one-third in three years and reached nearly a million, more than twice the number of Union veterans surviving at the time.

The legislative program of the Billion Dollar Congress did wonders in taking care of the Treasury surplus. The prohibitive tariff rates set by the McKinley Act reduced income, and the combination of excessive pensions and silver purchases increased expenditures. Still in a mood of generosity and still finding some of the surplus left, Congress hastily devised more handouts in the form of subsidies to steamship lines, lavish pork-barrel bills for river-and-harbor improvements, enormous premiums for government bondholders, and the return of federal taxes paid during the Civil War by Northern states. These handouts wiped out the surplus in the Treasury by 1894—a year when a surplus was badly needed—and the problem has never troubled the United States since.

The first Congress of the Harrison Administration promoted the interests of politicians and businessmen—that is, if they belonged to the right party or were engaged in the right business. To other interests, particularly farmers and small businessmen, Congress appeared a wasteful dispenser of favors to the privileged. The congressional elections of 1890 came as a severe rebuke. The Republicans were overwhelmed by a revolt that penetrated traditional strongholds in Ohio, Michigan, Illinois, Wisconsin, and Kansas, even Massachusetts. They were reduced to 88 seats in the House of Representatives, the smallest number in thirty years, while the Democrats took 235 seats. Republicans hung on to a small majority in the Senate. But the election of 1890 ran up danger signals for conservative leaders of both the old parties, a depression was on the way, a third-party revolt was shaping up, and a new era of reform was in the making.

The Agrarian Revolt

The Decline of Agriculture   The spirit of revolt flamed up most fiercely in the agricultural sections of the South and the West, and it was fed by acute economic distress and a deep sense of grievance. American farmers reached the lowest point in their history in the 1890's. The past was not the golden age they sometimes dreamed of, but they had certainly been better off before and were to be much better off in the future. But ever since the 1860's agriculture had been slipping backward while the cities and factories had been surging forward. Farmers knew they were being left behind, and they suspected the government of indifference, if not hostility, to their interests. They searched everywhere for the causes of their plight and the cure for their troubles. Some of their guesses were shrewd and accurate, but they never grasped the larger causes of their troubles.

What the American farmers did not see was that they were caught up in an international crisis that afflicted agriculture in many parts of the world and provoked rebellion abroad as well as at home. The agrarian crisis resulted from a revolution in communication and transportation that created a worldwide market for agricultural products. Ships first steamed through the Suez Canal in 1869, the year locomotives first steamed across the North American continent. The network of railroad and steamship lines was swiftly paralleled by a network of telegraph and telephone lines that linked continents and tied the world together. In the meantime vast new tracts of land were brought under cultivation in South America, Australia, and Canada, as well as in the trans-Mississippi West, and simultaneously a new technology of mechanized cultivation increased productivity enormously.

Forced to compete in a world market without protection against their competitors or control over output, American farmers watched the prices of their product decline as productivity mounted. It did not seem fair: the more they grew, the less they earned. And as their income diminished, their expenses increased. They had to buy expensive farm machinery in a protected market and sell their crops in an unprotected market. As the gap between income and expenses widened, farmers were increasingly forced to mortgage their land or borrow money to cover the gap. Farmers were therefore chronically in debt, and debtors always suffered most keenly from deflationary monetary policies such as those the government had pursued ever since the resumption of specie payments in 1879 (see p. 470). Contracting the amount of currency in circulation resulted in lowering the price that crops brought and increasing the difficulty of paying off debts. Farmers in debt had reason for opposing contraction and demanding expansion of currency.

It was no wonder that agrarian discontent was most bitter in the South and the West, for the growers of the staple crops of those sections were most dependent on exports. The price of their cotton and wheat had been falling steadily for two decades. From 1870 to 1873 cotton had averaged about 15.1 cents a pound; from 1894 to 1898 it dropped to an average of 5.8 cents. Over the same period wheat prices dropped from 106.7 to 63.3 cents a bushel, and corn from 43.0 to 29.7. These were market prices, after transportation and warehouse charges had been paid, not the lower prices the farmer received. In 1889 corn was actually selling for ten cents in Kansas, and farmers were burning it for fuel. Georgia farmers were getting five cents a pound for their cotton at a time when economists were estimating that it cost about seven cents a pound to produce. During several of these years the nation's farmers were running a losing business. Western farmers were kept going mainly by the appreciation of land values, and Southern farmers mainly by sheer habit and the momentum of generations, for in the South land values were declining as well as crop prices.

The ills of agriculture were reflected in the growing number of mortgages and tenant farmers. Nearly a third of the country's farms were mortgaged by the end of the nineties— 45 per cent of those in Wisconsin, 48 per cent in Michigan, and 53 per cent in Iowa. In Kansas, Nebraska, North Dakota, South Dakota, and Minnesota there were by 1890 more mortgages than families. In the Southern states mortgages were far fewer, but only because land was such a drug on the market that it could not be mortgaged. The South's substitute was the lien system, the worst credit system of all (see p. 387). Fewer and fewer farmers owned the land they worked, and more and more labored for a landlord, often an absentee landlord. The number of tenant farms increased from 25.8 per cent of all the farms in 1880 to 35.3 per cent at the end of the century.

Understandably, the farmer blamed others for his woes. He singled out the railroads as the archenemy, and the offences he attributed to them were by no means wholly imaginary, though sometimes exaggerated. The complaint that it took one bushel of wheat or corn to pay the freight on another bushel was no exaggeration. The main victims of rate discrimination were in the South and the West, where rates were frequently two or three times what they were between Chicago and New York. Railroads favored large over small shippers and one locality over another and flagrantly dominated politics and bought up legislatures. The national banks were also a natural target for agrarian abuse, for they were located and run for the convenience of city people, not for countryfolk. They were concentrated in nonagricultural areas, and their rules forbade them to lend money on real estate and farm property. Farmers believed that they manipulated bank-note currency against agricultural interests and were indifferent to seasonal needs for money for the movement of crops.

Few could deny the validity of the complaint that the farmer bore the brunt of the tax burden. Stocks and bonds could easily be concealed from the view of the tax collector, but not livestock and land. Railroads and corporations could pass the taxes on to the consumer, but the farmer could not pass on his taxes. The tax laws, like the bank laws, worked to the farmer's disadvantage. And so did the tariff laws. Southerners, with their long antitariff tradition, felt this more keenly than did the Westerners, and they lost no opportunity to press their views that farmers were doubly victimized by the tariff—as sellers in a free-trade market and as buyers in a protected market. Sharing none of the benefits of protection, they were compelled as consumers to foot the bill and pay the additional cost of protected goods. The injustice was all the harder to bear for those who believed that the tariff was "the mother of trusts." By fixing prices and defeating competition at home, trusts levied tribute on the consumers of all types of goods. Antitrust and antimonopoly feeling ran high in all farmer organizations. While agrarian theorists were wrong in attributing their plight to a conspiracy, they were right in contending that they had a legitimate grievance against a system that worked so consistently to their disadvantage.

In their more desperate moods the farmers sometimes felt that nature herself was conspiring with their oppressors. In the late eighties and early nineties natural calamities came one on top of another with stunning impact—droughts on the plains that not merely damaged the crops but destroyed them; floods in the lower Mississippi Valley that not merely destroyed the crops but left the land unusable; grim, blizzard-bound winters on the high plains that destroyed not merely domestic animals but wild ones as well and threatened the survival of man himself. Less spectacular, but contrasting sharply with the new urban way of life, was the loneliness, the drudgery, and the isolation of rural life in America in those years. This was the ancient lot of farmers, but the growing glitter of the city made it less tolerable than ever, especially when coupled with the grinding, ceaseless pressure of economic ills and grievances. To Thomas E. Watson of Georgia, who was to whip agrarian wrath into a frenzied crusade, the farmers of his region seemed to move about "like victims of some horrid nightmare . . . powerless—

oppressed—shackled." It is not surprising that their protests sometimes sounded a bit irrational.

Agrarian Protest   There was nothing irrational, however, about the farmers' impulse to organize and protest against their lot. The Patrons of Husbandry, organized in local "granges" and better known as the Grangers, served as a model for later and more powerful movements. Founded in 1867 by Oliver Hudson Kelley, a government employee in Washington who was moved by the plight of Southern farmers, the Grange grew slowly until the pinch of depression quickened interest in the early seventies. By 1874 the estimated membership was about one and a half million, and growth continued into the next year. In 1875 the Grange was strongest in the Midwest, the South, the Southwest, and the border states of Missouri and Kentucky. It was officially described as a secret social order for "working together, buying together, selling together, and generally acting together for . . . mutual protection and advancement."

Seeking to eliminate the profits of the middleman, Grangers founded cooperatives for buying and selling, for milling and storing grain, even for banking and manufacturing. These enterprises often suffered from inexperience and lack of capital, but some of them flourished and saved their members money. Membership fell off rapidly after 1875, but the Grangers left their imprint upon law and politics. While their order officially declared itself "nonpolitical," individual members joined agrarian third parties and swelled the farmer's influence in state legislatures. They actually received more credit than they were due for the so-called Granger laws that were adopted in the early seventies by Midwestern states to regulate grain elevators and railroads. Eight "Granger" cases came before the Supreme Court in 1877, and in *Munn* v. *Illinois*, the most significant of them, the Court upheld the "police power" of state regulation (see p. 434). Curtailed and hampered by subsequent decisions, the right of the public to control great corporations nevertheless held securely in the future.

The Grange dropped out of political prominence in the late seventies after inspiring a number of similar and smaller agricultural societies. Easily the most important was the Farmers' Alliance, really two organizations of independent origins, a huge one in the South and a much smaller one in the Midwest. Each of them underwent changes of names with reorganizations but were commonly known as the Southern Farmers' Alliance and the Northwestern Farmers' Alliance. The Southern Alliance had originated in 1875 in a frontier county of Texas, but it amounted to little until it launched a program of rapid expansion in 1886 under the energetic leadership of Dr. C. W. Macune. The Alliance took in several rival agricultural societies, including the Agricultural Wheel, with its home base in Arkansas, and the Farmers' Union of Louisiana. Agents spread out through all the cotton-growing states and found farmers everywhere eager to join. And they joined by the hundreds of thousands—at one time the national organization claimed as many as three million members, though it never made a really accurate count. Affiliated with them was a separate Colored Farmers' National Alliance and Cooperative Union that claimed one and a quarter million Negro members.

The Southern Alliance took in tenants and landowners, as well as rural mechanics and other classes of country people. With a highly centralized national organization, it established its own press, which was supported by hundreds of local weekly papers, and a lecture bureau that kept reform ideas circulating among its members. The Alliance went in for cooperatives even more extensively than the old Grange. Hundreds of Alliance stores and warehouses, marketing agencies, gins, tanneries, and mills sprinkled the South, though most of them were short-lived.

The Northwestern Alliance, organized by Milton George of Chicago in 1880, did not agree with the Southern Alliance in its policies of secrecy, centralized control, and separate organization for the Negro, and resisted pressure to join it for fear of being overwhelmed by the larger society. But in 1889 the Southern Alliance changed its name to the National Farmers' Alliance and Industrial Union and persuaded the three strongest state alliances of the Northwestern Alliance, those of Kansas and North and South Dakota, to join them. In the same year the Alliance gained the endorsement of the Knights of Labor and formed a political combination with the organization.

The character of the Alliance is reflected in the "demands" drawn up at its annual conventions. The Ocala Demands, for example, voted at the convention in Ocala, Florida, in 1890, called for the government to establish a "Subtreasury System." This would permit farmers to store nonperishable crops in government warehouses or elevators and receive treasury notes lending them up to 80 per cent of the local market value of the grain or cotton deposited. The government loan was secured by the crops and repaid when they were sold, thus enabling the farmer to hold his produce for the best price. * Other demands were the abolition of national banks, a substantial increase in the amount of money in circulation, the free coinage of silver, a federal income tax, the reduction of tariff rates, the direct election of senators, "rigid" control of railroad and telegraph companies—and, if that did not work, "government ownership" of both.

Though the Alliance, like the Grange, professed to be strictly "nonpolitical," it was clear that its demands could be realized only by political means. Using their demands (similar to the ones adopted later that year at Ocala) as a yardstick, Southern Alliance men required all Democratic candidates in the 1890 elections to "stand up and be measured." As a result, the Alliance seemed at the time to have come near taking over the Democratic party in the South, for it elected four governors, secured control of eight legislatures, and elected forty-four congressmen and three senators who were pledged to support Alliance demands. Instead of working within one of the old parties, Alliance men in the West hastily set up independent third parties, the names of which varied from state to state, and nominated their own candidates. Their most striking successes were in Kansas, where they elected five congressmen and a senator; in Nebraska, where they took control of both houses of the legislature and elected two congressmen; and in South Dakota, where they elected a senator. In other Western states their vote came largely at the expense of the Republicans and ac-

* The idea was embodied in the New Deal measure of 1936 creating the Commodity Credit Corporation.

counted in part for the large number of Democratic congressmen elected in 1890. The election served notice on both old parties that the farmers were on the march.

The Populist Crusade   Their successes in 1890 inspired Westerners with the ambition to form a national third party to promote Alliance ideas. Southerners hung back, however, in order to try out their plan of working within the Democratic party. They were quickly disillusioned, for all the Southern Democratic congressmen elected on an Alliance platform, with the exception of Tom Watson, entered the Democratic caucus and voted for a conservative anti-Alliance Georgian for Speaker. Whereupon Watson, red-headed and a rebel by temperament, left his party and became the "People's party" candidate for Speaker with the support of eight congressmen from the West. Thus the new party, often called the Populist party, had a congressional delegation before it had a national organization. The National Alliance, however, under the leadership of President Leonidas L. Polk of North Carolina, was moving rapidly in the Populist direction. On February 22, 1892, a huge Confederation of Industrial Organizations met at St. Louis, attended by delegates from the Knights of Labor, the Nationalists, the Single-Taxers, Greenbackers, Prohibitionists, and other curiously assorted reform groups, but dominated by delegates from the National Alliance. The delegates officially founded the People's party and called for a convention to nominate a ticket for the presidential election of 1892.

Shortly before the convention met in Omaha on July 4, the Populists were deprived of their strongest candidate by the death of Polk. The party nominated the old Greenback campaigner of 1880, General James B. Weaver of Iowa, for President, and, to balance the Union general with a Confederate one, chose General James G. Field of Virginia as his running mate. The platform emphatically reiterated Alliance principles on money, credit, transportation, and land, and evoked the wildest enthusiasm for its planks on government ownership of railroads and monetary reform. Populist principles, embodying the agrarian reform ideas of two decades, had become a sacred creed. The fervor and violence of Populist

The Populist Protest

A vast conspiracy against mankind has been organized on two continents, and it is rapidly taking possession of the world. If not met and overthrown at once, it forebodes terrible social convulsions, the destruction of civilization, or the establishment of an absolute despotism.

We have witnessed for more than a quarter of a century the struggles of the two great political parties for power and plunder, while grievous wrongs have been inflicted upon the suffering people. We charge that the controlling influences dominating both these parties have permitted the existing dreadful conditions to develop without serious effort to prevent or restrain them. Neither do they now promise us any substantial reform. They have agreed together to ignore in the coming campaign every issue but one. They propose to drown the outcries of a plundered people with the uproar of a sham battle over the tariff, so that capitalists, corporations, national banks, rings, trusts, watered stock, the demonetization of silver, and the oppressions of the usurers may all be lost sight of. They propose to sacrifice our homes, lives and children on the altar of mammon; to destroy the multitude in order to secure corruption funds from the millionaires.

From *The Omaha Platform of the People's Party*, 1892.

rhetoric is illustrated by the following excerpt from the Preamble to the platform, written and delivered by Ignatius Donnelly of Minnesota, foremost Populist writer and orator:

> We meet in the midst of a nation brought to the verge of moral, political, and material ruin. corruption dominates the ballot-box, the legislatures, the Congress, and touches even the ermine of the bench. The people are demoralized. . . . The newspapers are largely subsidized or muzzled, public opinion silenced, business prostrated, homes covered with mortgages, labor impoverished, and the land concentrated in the hands of capitalists. . . . The fruits of the toil of millions are boldly stolen to build up colossal fortunes for a few. . . .

Eastern conservatives were frightened by the Populist tone and built up a distorted image of the movement as an insurrection of hayseed anarchists or hick communists. The very nicknames of Populist leaders lent themselves to such propaganda—names such as Lemuel H. "Calamity" Weller of Iowa, Congressman "Sockless" Jerry Simpson of Kansas, Governor Davis H. "Bloody Bridles" Waite of Colorado, and orator James H. "Cyclone" Davis of Texas—not to mention the endlessly quoted advice of Mary E. Lease of Kansas to "raise less corn and more hell." It is quite true that some of the Populist leaders were fanatical and narrow-minded, and that the majority of Populist voters were provincial and ill-informed folk with a poor understanding of the troubles that beset them. Populists tended to oversimplify issues, to embrace panaceas, to talk loosely of "conspiracy" against them, and to use violent and desperate language.

It is only fair to the Populists, however, to recall that the plight of the people for whom they spoke was desperate. We must also recall that their conservative opponents, much better educated as a rule, entertained absurd monetary and economic theories of their own and talked wildly of conspiracies and subversives themselves (see p. 492). To their credit it should be remembered that the Populists were the first important movement in this country to insist that laissez-faire economics was not the final solution to industrial problems and that the federal government had some responsibility for social well-being. Most of the Populist demands that seemed so wild at the time accepted as respectable within a surprisingly short time and were eventually written into law. The Populists' main service was to usher in a long-needed and long-delayed era of reform and to reveal the empty pretense of the political game as played by the old parties.

The first task of the Populists was to bridge the cleavages between parties, sections, races, and classes that kept apart the forces of reform that they wished to unite. First they sought to revive the old agrarian alliance between South and West that had been effectively broken by the Civil War. Second, they felt that both the Republicans and the Democrats were bent on keeping natural allies divided, and sought to replace the old parties with a third party. Third, they tried to unite farmers of the South who were divided by racial barriers, and both whites and Negroes worked hard at the effort. Finally, the Populists sought to create an alliance between farmers and labor. The Populists enjoyed some success with all four of these alliances, but sectional animosities were kept alive by the bloody-shirt issue, old party loyalties were hard to break, racial antagonism was inflamed by white-supremacy propaganda, and labor did not always see eye to eye with the farmer. In view of all these handicaps the Populists made a surprisingly good showing in their first appearance at the polls. They cast a little more than a million votes for their presidential candidate and broke into the electoral college with twenty-two votes. They also elected ten representatives, five senators, three governors, and some fifteen hundred members of state legislatures.

The Depression and the Silver Issue

Cleveland and the Silverites Somewhat sobered by the Populist threat, the Democrats and the Republicans conducted their 1892 campaigns with more dignity than usual. Cleveland, the choice of conservative Democrats, was nominated by the first ballot of his party's convention, and Harrison was the equally inevitable nominee of the Republicans. Adlai E. Stevenson* of Illinois became Cleveland's running mate, and Whitelaw Reid, editor of the New York *Tribune*, was the Republican nominee for Vice-President. Both platforms were evasive on the monetary issues that stirred the greatest interest among voters. Harrison was handicapped by the necessity of defending the unpopular McKinley Tariff and by his inability to stir enthusiasm among his supporters. Cleveland improved his poll of 1888, and 1884 as well, winning 5,555,426 votes to 5,182,690 for Harrison, and 277 electoral votes to Harrison's 145. Not only did the Democrats carry the doubtful states of New York, New Jersey, Connecticut, and Indiana, but also the normally Republican states of Illinois, Wisconsin, and California. It was not quite a landslide, but it was the most decisive victory either party had won in twenty years.

President Cleveland moved back into the White House and surrounded himself with a thoroughly conservative Cabinet of Easterners and Southerners who were as completely out of touch with the radical discontent of the

* Grandfather of the Democratic candidate for president in 1952 and 1956.

An Antipopulist Rejoinder

What's the matter with Kansas?

We all know; yet here we are at it again. We have an old mossback Jacksonian who snorts and howls because there is a bathtub in the State House; we are running that old jay for Governor. We have another shabby, wild-eyed, rattle-brained fanatic who has said openly in a dozen speeches that "the rights of the user are paramount to the rights of the owner"; we are running him for Chief Justice, so that capital will come tumbling over itself to get into the state....

Oh, this is a state to be proud of! We are a people who can hold up our heads! What we need is not more money, but less capital, fewer white shirts and brains, fewer men with business judgment, and more of those fellows who boast that they are "just ordinary clodhoppers, but they know more in a minute about finance than John Sherman"; we need more men who are "posted," who can bellow about the crime of '73, who hate prosperity, and who think, because a man believes in national honor, he is a tool of Wall Street. We have had a few of them—some hundred fifty thousand—but we need more.

From William Allen White, "What's the Matter with Kansas?" 1896.

---

country as he was himself. Almost immediately the financial panic of 1893 shattered his peace and ushered in the worst depression the nation had experienced up to that time. The panic had actually started ten days before Harrison left office, when the Philadelphia and Reading Railroad went bankrupt and the New York Stock Exchange was shaken by the greatest selling spree in its history. Two months after Cleveland's inauguration the market collapsed. Banks called in their loans and credit dried up. Unstable financial conditions abroad, especially the failure of Baring Brothers of London in 1890, had started a drain on the gold reserve that became increasingly severe after 1893. One great railroad after another—the Erie, the Northern Pacific, the Union Pacific, the Santa Fe—went down in failure. "Mills, factories, furnaces, mines nearly everywhere," reported the New York *Commercial and Financial Chronicle* in August, "shut down in large numbers, and commerce and enterprise were arrested in an extraordinary degree." By the end of the year five hundred banks and more than fifteen thousand business firms had fallen into bankruptcy. Populist Donnelly's apocalyptic picture of "a nation brought to the verge of ruin" seemed about to be translated into reality.

Learned economists still argue about the causes and remedies of depressions, and there can be no doubt that the causes of the depression that settled over the country in 1893 were highly complex. But President Cleveland had a simple explanation and a simple remedy, and never did a dogmatist cling more tenaciously to his theory. His explanation was that the Sherman Silver Purchase Act (see p. 479) had caused the depression and his remedy was to repeal the act and maintain the gold standard at all costs—that is, continue to redeem all United States Treasury notes in gold. The economic consequences of Cleveland's remedy do not appear to have been decisive one way or the other, but the political consequences were disastrous. No issue since slavery had divided the people more deeply than silver. It split both old parties, disrupted Populism, and caused a revolution in the Democratic party that overthrew conservative control.

The trouble was that Cleveland's theory clashed head on with a more popular theory held with equal dogmatism by the silverites. According to them, the cause of the economic disaster lay in the "Crime of '73" that demonetized silver, and the remedy lay in the free and unlimited coinage of silver at a ratio of sixteen to one of gold. The arguments and the sources of support for the silver movement had not changed since the Bland-Allison Act of 1878 (p. 471), but the movement had acquired new strength and additional recruits. The admission of six new Western states—Montana, North Dakota, South Dakota, and Washington in 1889, and Idaho and Wyoming in 1890—brought reinforcements to the silverites in Congress, especially in the Senate. In the meantime American silver producers suffered additional reductions in their market from the demonetization of silver in Europe and India and became more desperate for relief through free coinage in the United States. At the same time debtor agrarians saw free coinage of silver as one hope of relief from deflation and currency contraction and increased their cry for "free silver." In place of the inadequate relief provided by the Sherman Silver Purchase Act, they demanded unlimited and free coinage.

Cleveland stubbornly insisted, on the other hand, that the Sherman Act was the whole cause of the trouble and demanded its repeal. He was convinced that the silver certificates issued under this act and redeemed in gold were responsible for the constant drain on the gold reserve and for the menace to the gold standard. The only way to restore confidence and prosperity, he held, was to maintain the gold standard, and that required the maintenance of a gold reserve of $100 million in the Treasury. There was a case to be made in favor of the gold standard in the 1890's, but there were many causes for the drain on the gold reserve, and there were many causes of the depression other than the threat to the gold standard. But under relentless pressure by the President, Congress finally repealed the Sherman Act. Cleveland got his way by relying on Republican support and splitting his own party.

Repeal of the Sherman Act seemed to have no effect, for the drain on the gold reserve continued unabated, and so did the depression. Business confidence was not restored, and the hoarding of gold increased. The Treasury surplus that the Billion Dollar Congress had been so eager to spend was no more, and the McKinley Tariff had sharply reduced tariff revenues. Holders of gold and silver certificates, doubting the ability of the government to maintain the gold standard, started a run on the Treasury; and panic in Europe caused continual withdrawals. In January 1894 the gold reserve sank below $62 million, and to save the situation the President desperately resorted to a $50 million bond sale. The gold came in from the sale of bonds, but since much of it was withdrawn from the Treasury by the bankers in order to pay for the bonds, the net gain was not great. A second government bond sale was necessary in November; it too brought only temporary relief; and more bond sales were required. Each of these loans was additional proof to the silverites that Cleveland was interested in nothing but maintaining the gold standard and pleasing Wall Street bankers. The third bond sale, in February 1895, caused the greatest indignation of all. This

Coxey's Army on the march.

time the President yielded to the demand of J. Pierpont Morgan that the sale be kept private, and the syndicate of bankers that handled the loan drove a hard bargain for their services and were accused of making large profits, though Morgan refused to reveal how much. The bond issue yielded over $65 million to the government, half of it from Europe, and the bankers scotched some of the drain on the gold reserve. Nevertheless, another issue was necessary in January 1896. The four bond sales did save the gold standard, but they did not stop the decline of the gold reserve, nor restore prosperity. Each one further intensified the silverites' hatred of the President. These bond sales enhanced Cleveland's reputation for courage but not for wisdom: they failed to cure the depression and they led to political disaster.

The Politics of Depression The blight that had been familiar to farmers for years now began to fall on the factory and the city. Railroad construction fell off drastically, dividends halted, and investment in all businesses declined sharply. Bankers, businessmen, and employers seemed stricken with a failure of nerve. They laid off men, cut wages, closed factory doors, and swelled the army of jobless men. A hundred thousand of them shuffled through the streets of Chicago, and visitors to the "dream city" at the Exposition in 1893 wondered at the miles of sleeping men who lined the tracks of the elevated railway. "What a spectacle!" exclaimed Ray Stannard Baker, a cub reporter, "What a human downfall after the magnificence and prodigality of the World's Fair."

The year 1894 was the most brutal of the depression. Between two and a half and three million, perhaps as many as one out of five workers, were thought to be unemployed, but no one really knew, and the unemployed felt

The Supreme Court
and the Income Tax:
The Government's Argument

RICHARD OLNEY:

The constitutional objection [is] nothing but a call upon the judicial department of the government to supplant the political in the exercise of the taxing power; to substitute its discretion for that of Congress.... It is inevitably predestined to failure unless this court shall, for the first time in its history, overlook and overstep the bounds which separate the judicial from the legislative power—bounds, the scrupulous observance of which it has so often declared to be absolutely essential to the integrity of our constitutional system of government.

JAMES C. CARTER:

Nothing could be more unwise and dangerous—nothing more foreign to the spirit of the Constitution—than an attempt to baffle and defeat a popular determination by a judgment in a lawsuit. When the opposing forces of sixty millions of people have become arrayed in hostile political ranks upon a question which all men feel is not a question of law, but of legislation, the only path of safety is to accept the voice of the majority as final.

From *Pollock* v. *Farmers' Loan and Trust Co.*, 157 U.S. 429, 1895.

---

that no one in the government really cared. Some cities provided a little work relief, but this was wholly inadequate, and when hungry men turned to the federal government, they were met with cold indifference or angry rejection. Jacob S. Coxey of Massillon, Ohio, a well-to-do businessman who was a Populist and was quite untypical of his class in other ways, proposed a plan of federal work relief on public roads to be financed by an issue of $500 million in legal-tender treasury notes. The "Good Roads" bill was designed to end the depression by providing monetary inflation and internal improvements as well as work relief for the unemployed. When Congress refused to pass it, Coxey declared, "We will send a petition to Washington with boots on." "Coxey's Army" marched peacefully from Massillon to the Capitol, picking up sympathizers on the way, including one hundred students from Lehigh University and a few visionaries and eccentrics, and paraded into Washington on May Day, about five hundred

strong. They were cheered by crowds, but Coxey and his lieutenants were arrested by the police and some fifty people were beaten or trampled. No less than seventeen "industrial armies" started for Washington in 1894, and some twelve hundred men arrived. They were peaceful and sober as a rule, but it was the obvious sympathy they stirred over the country that frightened the government, even President Cleveland, into the mistaken idea that a spirit of rebellion threatened to bring on mob rule.

Not only the government but private employers resorted to violence in countering labor protest. An extraordinary number of strikes, some fourteen hundred in all, occurred during 1894, many of them provoked by wage cuts. More than 660,000 men were thrown out of work by strikes or lockouts. Management countered by using ruthless violence, employing secret police, or securing injunctions from friendly courts. In the Pullman strike of July, as we have seen (p. 439), the federal government used troops of the regular army to crush the workers. Cleveland earned as much hostility from labor by his use of troops as he had from agrarians by his sale of bonds.

In the meantime, the only serious piece of reform the second Cleveland Administration undertook, the reform of the tariff, met with complete failure. To fulfill their campaign pledges, the Democrats did put through the House a bill containing modest reductions in tariff that had been framed by William L. Wilson of West Virginia. But in the Senate the protectionists of both parties fell upon it with six hundred amendments that restored the old rates and actually raised some of them. The Wilson-Gorman Act, which Cleveland denounced as "party perfidy and party dishonor" and allowed to become law without his signature, made a mockery of the Administration's pretenses of tariff reform. The only sop to reformers was an amendment slipped in by the agrarians and deplored by the President which provided for a small income tax of 2 per cent on incomes over four thousand dollars. The Supreme Court, which shared Cleveland's unpopularity as an agency of reaction, promptly declared the income tax unconstitutional by a vote of five to four. For relief of suffering among the unemployed, on the farms, and in the cities, for restoring credit, and for assisting industry afflicted by depression, Cleveland's Administration refused to take any responsibility beyond maintaining the gold standard.

The spirit of despair and resentment abroad in the land was perfectly suited to the appeal of the Populists. In the fall elections of 1894 the third party increased the vote it polled in 1892 by 42 per cent. In the West the Populists lost Nevada, which went over to the Silverites, a new party, and Colorado and Idaho went Republican, so that the over-all strength of the party declined. But in the South Populists exploited hatred of Cleveland, and with evangelistic campaigns and camp-meeting techniques they piled up gains that frightened the Democrats. In spite of violence and fraud and racist propaganda more blatant than the Democrats had used since the overthrow of Reconstruction, the Populists captured North Carolina, with Republican aid, and mustered more strength in the supposedly conservative states of Georgia and Alabama than they commanded in any Western state save Nebraska. The Democrats barely retained control of the Senate and suffered heavy losses in the House. Many prominent Democratic congressmen went down to defeat as the Republicans recouped their losses in the previous election and took control of the House with a majority of 140 seats.

The Democratic party was, in fact, in the midst of revolution almost as profound as that of 1860. Again it was a sectional split, but this time it was the Northeast that was isolated instead of the South. West and South joined hands in the name of the free coinage of silver, but silver merely served as a symbol for dozens of other sectional issues. And Grover Cleveland became the personification of the Northeastern conservatism against which the two agrarian regions were in revolt. Never since Johnson had a President been so detested and abused by members of his own party as was Cleveland. Southern and Western Democrats deserted him in droves and outdid the Republicans and Populists in denouncing him. "He is an old bag of beef," Democratic Congressman "Pitchfork" Ben Tillman told his South Carolina constituents, "and I am going to Washington with a pitchfork and prod him in his old fat ribs."

The Supreme Court and the Income Tax: The Argument That Prevailed

JOSEPH H. CHOATE:

You cannot hereafter exercise any check if you now say that Congress is untrammelled and uncontrollable. My friend says you cannot enforce any limit. He says no matter what Congress does ... this Court will have nothing to say about it. I agree that it will have nothing to say about it if it now lets go its hold upon this law....

I have thought that one of the fundamental objects of all civilized government was the preservation of the rights of private property. I have thought that it was the very keystone of the arch upon which all civilized government rests, and that this once abandoned, everything was in danger.... According to the doctrines that have been propounded here this morning, even that great fundamental principle has been scattered to the winds....

If it be true, as my friend said in closing, that the passions of the people are aroused on this subject, if it be true that a mighty army of sixty million citizens is likely to be incensed by this decision, it is the more vital to the future welfare of this country that this court again resolutely and courageously declare, as Marshall did, that it *has* the power to set aside an act of Congress violative of the Constitution ... no matter what the threatened consequences of popular or populistic wrath may be.

From *Pollock* v. *Farmers' Loan and Trust Co.*, 157 U.S. 429, 1895.

Early in 1895 prominent Democrats in the South and West set to work systematically to use the silver issue as a means of taking over control of their party and unseating Cleveland and the conservatives. With financial support from the silver miners, they held silver conventions all over the South and West to which they invited Populists and urged them to give up their more radical demands and "come down to silver." They distributed great quantities of silver propaganda such as Ignatius Donnelly's *The American People's Money* (1895) and the famous booklet by William H. "Coin" Harvey, *Coin's Financial School* (1894). In the latter, "Professor Coin" laid bare the "conspiracy of Goldbugs," proponents of the gold standard, and "proved" that the free and unlimited coinage of silver was the panacea for all economic ills. The work of the silver Democrats against Cleveland was so effective that after the state conventions in the summer of 1896 no state Democratic organization south of the Potomac and only three west of the Alleghenies remained in the hands of the President's friends. There was no longer any doubt that the Silverites would be able to wrest control of the national Democratic convention from Cleveland.

McKinley and Gold Versus Bryan and Silver   Nor was there any doubt that the Republican convention would nominate William McKinley of Ohio when it met at St. Louis in June. McKinley's nomination had been assured by the systematic and patient work of his devoted friend Marcus Alonzo Hanna, who not only rounded up the necessary votes before the convention, but financed and managed his friend's preconvention campaign. A blunt and forthright businessman from Cleveland, Hanna had made a fortune in coal, iron, banking, shipping, and street railways before he retired from business in 1895 to devote full time to fulfilling his ambition of putting McKinley in the White House. McKinley's nomination rolled forward as planned on the first ballot, and Garret A. Hobart, a relatively unknown corporation lawyer from New Jersey, was the vice-presidential nominee. A protectionist platform was obviously called for, since McKinley's name had become synonymous with high tariff. The only doubt was how explicit the plank on the gold standard should be. Hanna had already decided upon a forthright endorsement, but he cleverly hung back at the convention and permitted himself to be "persuaded" by Eastern delegates to accept the statement that "the existing gold standard should be preserved." Upon the adoption of the gold plank, Senator Henry M. Teller of Colorado led a small group of Western silver Republicans from the hall and they withdrew from the party.

Eastern Republicans had reason to doubt McKinley's firmness on gold. In the political lingo of the battle of standards, politicians were classified as "Goldbugs," "Silverbugs," or "Straddlebugs," and the Ohioan was often classed with the third group. He had voted for both the Bland-Allison Act and the Sherman Silver Purchase Act and continued to speak kindly of silver as an American product that deserved "protection" and to favor compromise when compromise had become untenable. In 1896, however, he accepted his party's decision for gold. He was an experienced and skillful politician who had served in Congress from 1876 to 1892, with the exception of one term, and had been governor of Ohio for two terms, completing the second in 1895. A kindly, impressive-looking, rather solemn man, McKinley sincerely shared Hanna's devotion to the interests of American business. The campaign caricature of McKinley as the spineless puppet of the millionaire boss had no foundation in fact, for the evidence is that Hanna constantly deferred to his friend and respected his wishes.

The Democratic convention at Chicago exhibited all the disorder and spontaneity that the Republicans had been spared under Hanna's direction. Cleveland supporters, still full of fight, arrived from the East to clash with red-hot silver orators from the South and the West amid a din of hisses and catcalls and rebel yells in which only the leather-lunged could make themselves heard. But the Easterners had neither the strength to control the convention nor a suitable candidate to put before it, and the agrarian rebels rode over them roughshod. They adopted a platform strongly influenced by Governor John P. Altgeld of Illinois, the friend of the Pullman strikers (see p. 439) and the pardoner of the Haymarket Riot anarchists. The platform, which denounced virtually everything Cleveland stood for, also struck out fiercely at protective tariff, the national banks, trusts, and the Supreme Court; it demanded an income tax and, most important of all, free coinage of silver at the ratio of sixteen ounces of silver to one of gold.

Altgeld was disqualified as a candidate by foreign birth, and the convention passed over Congressman Richard P. "Silver Dick" Bland, the most prominent contender. At the strategic moment a handsome young ex-congressman, William Jennings Bryan of Nebraska, captured the attention and the imagination of the silver forces with a speech that mounted to a thrilling peroration: "You shall not press down upon the brow of labor this crown of thorns, you shall not crucify mankind upon a cross of gold." Bryan was nominated on the fifth ballot, and, to balance the ticket,

Arthur Sewall of Maine, a banker and businessman who opposed the gold standard, was nominated for Vice-President.

While he was only thirty-six and little known in the East, Bryan was already widely known as a peerless orator in the West and the South, where he had been campaigning for three years to prepare the revolt of the silver forces. Bryan had some naïve ideas about money and harbored suspicions of the East, "the enemy's country," as he once called it. He was no radical, and his ties were with the simple agrarian past rather than with the complex future. But conservatives were wrong to dismiss him as a one-idea fanatic. He had an intuitive grasp of the deep mood of protest that stirred the mass of voters, and he expressed that mood in a moral appeal to the conscience of the country. His real service was to awaken an old faith in social justice and to protest against a generation of plutocratic rule.

In their next maneuver, the silver leaders of the "revolutionized" Democrats persuaded the Populist party, which held its convention in St. Louis after the Democratic convention had met, to make Bryan its candidate as well. The proposal deeply divided the Populists, who neither wanted to split the reform forces with a separate ticket nor give up their own party identity. Western Populists were eager to nominate Bryan, but Southern members, always more radical and less devoted to silver, wanted a separate Populist ticket and no compromise. Bryan's nomination was at last secured through trickery. Senator William V. Allen of Nebraska, chairman of the convention, told the Southerners that the Democrats had agreed to withdraw Sewall and accept Thomas E. Watson as their vice-presidential nominee if the Populists would nominate Bryan. Southern radicals bitterly resisted fusion with the Democrats, whom they had been fighting for four years. But when their hero Watson agreed to compromise, they reluctantly consented and nominated Bryan and Watson. Only later did they learn that the Democrats refused to withdraw the banker Sewall.

Two more parties were created out of bolters from the old parties. The National Silver Republicans endorsed the Democratic candidates. Later on, the gold Democrats, with encouragement and financial support from

Faith in social justice: Bryan in 1896.

Hanna, organized the National Democratic party and nominated a separate ticket that was intended to contribute to Bryan's defeat.

The contest between McKinley and Bryan in 1896 has taken on the legendary character of the combat between Goliath and David— except that it turned out quite differently. Bryan played the David role admirably—the lone youth armed with nothing but shafts of oratory pitted against the armored Gold Giant and all his hosts. Actually, reformers of many schools rallied to Bryan's cause, including Henry George of the Single Taxers, Edward Bellamy of the Nationalists, W. D. P. Bliss of the Christian Socialists, Eugene V. Debs of the Railway Union, and Samuel Gompers of the American Federation of Labor, all of whom campaigned for him. Bryan's chief reliance, however, was upon his own voice. In a campaign without precedent at that time, he traveled eighteen thousand miles by train,

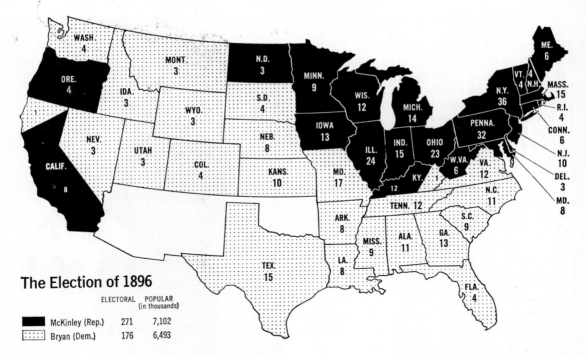

The Election of 1896

	ELECTORAL	POPULAR (in thousands)
■ McKinley (Rep.)	271	7,102
⁙ Bryan (Dem.)	176	6,493

made more than six hundred speeches, and talked to some five million people. He spoke not only of silver, but of the price of crops, the cost of mortgages, the need for credit, and the regulation of railroads. The powerful popular response to his campaign aroused great hopes for victory.

It also aroused a hysterical wave of fear among conservatives and facilitated Hanna's collection of campaign funds. He exacted tribute from every great trust, railroad, bank, and tycoon with any stake in the outcome and built up a treasure chest undreamed of before that time. The fund has been estimated everywhere between $3.5 million and $15 million— as against a mere $300,000 at Bryan's disposal. Hanna spent the money lavishly but shrewdly, sending out propaganda by the ton and the carload, and speakers by the battalion. He also transported trainloads of people from representative groups, all expenses paid, to hear McKinley read well-prepared speeches from his front porch in Canton, Ohio, from which the candidate never stirred. The press assisted Hanna with blasts of ridicule and charges of socialism and anarchism against Bryan. The Philadelphia *Press* described the

"Jacobins" of the Chicago convention as "hideous and repulsive vipers." President Cleveland called them "madmen" and "criminals," and the New York *Tribune* referred to Bryan as a "wretched, rattle-pated boy." Employers of labor joined in with threats to close up shop or cut wages if Bryan were elected.

The combination of powers was too much for the resources of Bryan. He polled 6,492,559 votes, more votes than any victorious candidate had ever polled before, nearly a million more than Cleveland polled in 1892, but it was still not enough. McKinley won with 7,102,246 votes, a plurality of 609,687, and an electoral vote margin of 271 to 176. Bryan did not carry a single state north of the Potomac or east of the Mississippi. He did not even carry the farming states of Iowa, Minnesota, or North Dakota. What is more significant, he carried no industrialized, no urbanized state. This may well be the main reason for Bryan's defeat. In spite of widespread unrest among labor, Bryan did not win labor's support, which might have given him victory. He really had little to offer either labor or the cities. Like many other American reformers of his day, he had something of significance for the present, but his true ties were with the past. McKinley and Hanna may not have been looking very far into the future, but they had a firmer grip on the present. They were also able in one way or another to influence labor, and they evidently won the confidence of the urban middle class. Their victory meant a return to conservatism and another businessman's regime.

The Aftermath of '96 The election was followed swiftly by a revival of the economy and the end of the long depression. The upturn had little if anything to do with the saving of the gold standard or the victory of McKinley. The price of wheat had started to climb before the election, though hardly enough to have influenced the outcome. But in 1897 the European wheat crop fell off 30 per cent, and American farmers doubled their exports of the previous year. Prices continued to rise and the whole economy began to revive. Discoveries of gold in Australia and Alaska revived the flow of gold into the country, and gold production was further increased by discoveries of pay dirt in South Africa and the development of the cyanide process for extracting the metal from ore. The inflation that the agrarians and silverites had demanded came, ironically enough, not through silver but through gold. The influx of gold and capital stimulated industrial expansion, and that in turn touched off a boom in iron and steel.

With a Republican majority in both houses, McKinley called a special session of Congress in the summer of 1897 to further his favorite type of legislation, additional protective tariff. The Wilson-Gorman Tariff of 1894 was already high enough for most protectionists, but not for the President. Congress complied by passing a bill framed by Nelson Dingley of Maine which raised duties to an average of 52 per cent. McKinley avoided action on the gold standard until gold was flowing in and silver sentiment was waning. But in his annual message of 1899 he called for legislation, and Congress adopted by a party vote the Gold Standard Act, which he signed on March 14, 1900. The act declared that the gold dollar was henceforth the sole standard of currency, thus writing an end to a generation of controversy, but without producing any significant economic effect, either good or bad.

One significant but often overlooked result of the election of 1896 and the return to prosperity was the demoralization of the Populist movement. Fusion with the enemy party and abandonment of principle for the sake of silver had demoralized the Populists and all but destroyed their party. "The sentiment is still there, the votes are still there, but confidence is gone," thought Tom Watson. The following decade was to see a new upsurge of reform and the realization of many of the old Populist demands, but they were achieved under urban, not rural, leadership. Nineteenth-century agrarian radicalism made its last significant bid for leadership of a national reform movement in 1896.

SUGGESTIONS FOR READING The political history of this period is treated most readably, though not with the greatest detachment, in Matthew Josephson, *The Politicos, 1865–1896* (1938); less readably and with a bias in the opposite direction in E. P. Oberholtzer, *A History of the United States Since the Civil War*, 5 vols. (1917–37). On the nineties, a helpful recent synthesis is H. U. Faulkner, *Politics, Reform and Expansion, 1890–1900* (1959). W. E. Binkley, *American Political Parties: Their Natural History* (1943), is interpretive; E. H. Roseboom, *A History of Presidential Elections* (1957), is factual; and C. A. M. Ewing, *Presidential Elections from Abraham Lincoln to Franklin D. Roosevelt* (1940), is analytical. Richard Hofstadter, *The Age of Reform: From Bryan to F. D. R.* (1955), is revisionary and challenging. Two sectional studies of politics are C. V. Woodward, *Origins of the New South, 1877–1913* (1951), and H. S. Merrill, *Bourbon Democracy of the Middle West, 1865–1896* (1953).

Key biographies are Harry Barnard, *Rutherford B. Hayes and His America* (1954); R. G. Caldwell, *James A. Garfield: Party Chieftain* (1931); G. F. Howe, *Chester A. Arthur* (1934); D. S. Muzzey, *James G. Blaine: A Political Idol of Other Days* (1934); Allan Nevins, *Grover Cleveland: A Study in Courage* (1932); and H. J. Sievers, *Benjamin Harrison: Hoosier Statesman* (1959). (On Bryan and McKinley, see below.)

On the politics and issues of reform the literature is rich. On reformist mentality, see Eric Goldman, *Rendezvous with Destiny: A History of Modern American Reform* * (1952), and the book by Hofstadter cited above. Civil service reform is the subject of three excellent recent studies: L. D. White, *The Republican Era: 1896–1901* (1958); P. P. Van Riper, *History of the United States Civil Service* (1958); and Ari Hogenboom, *Fighting the Spoilsmen* (1961). Still valuable on tariff reform are F. W. Taussig, *The Tariff History of the United States* (1894), and I. M. Tarbell, *The Tariff in Our Times* (1911). Pensions for veterans are treated by J. W. Oliver, *History of the Civil War Military Pensions* (1917), and W. H. Glasson, *Federal Military Pensions in the United States* (1918). Monetary controversies of the period are examined in D. R. Dewey, *Financial History of the United States* (6th ed., 1918); D. C. Barrett, *The Greenbacks and the Resumption of Specie Payments, 1862–1879* (1931); and J. A. Barnes, *John G. Carlisle* (1931), a biography of Cleveland's Secretary of the Treasury.

Agricultural conditions and movements are authoritatively examined in F. A. Shannon, *The Farmer's Last Frontier: Agriculture, 1860–1897* (1945). For light on farmers' organizations, see chapters in Allan Nevins, *The Emergence of Modern America, 1865–1878* (1927); and for greater detail, S. J. Buck, *The Granger Movement* (1913); J. D. Hicks, *The Populist Revolt* (1931); R. B. Nye, *Midwestern Progressive Politics: A Historical Study of Its Origins and Development, 1870–1958* (1951; rev. ed., 1958), and Theodore Saloutos, *Farmer Movements in the South, 1865–1933* (1960). A suggestive survey is C. C. Taylor, *The Farmers' Movement, 1620–1920* (1953); and a special study is F. D. Haynes, *Third Party Movements Since the Civil War, with Special Reference to Iowa* (1916).

The depression of the nineties and its political repercussions are intelligently discussed in G. H. Knowles, *The Presidential Campaign and Election of 1892* (1942); and economic causes of the trouble in F. B. Webeg, *The Background of the Panic of 1893* (1929). The serious student will be fascinated by source materials in Hamlin Garland, *Main-travelled Roads* * (1891), for agrarian ills; W. H. Harvey, *Coin's Financial School* (1894), and Ignatius Donnelly, *The American People's Money* (1895), for silver propaganda; and H. D. Lloyd, *Wealth Against Commonwealth* (1894), for an exposure of monopoly. Scholarly studies of labor protest are D. L. McMurry, *Coxey's Army* (1929), and Almont Lindsey, *The Pullman Strike* (1942). On the latter event, see also Harry Barnard, *"Eagle Forgotten": The Life of John Peter Altgeld* (1938), and Ray Ginger, *Altgeld's America—Lincoln Ideal Versus Changing Realities* (1958).

On Populism and Bryanism and the crisis of 1896, many biographies and studies already mentioned are relevant. Two recent biographical works are of special interest: Margaret Leech, *In the Days of McKinley* (1959), and P. W. Glad, *The Trumpet Soundeth: William Jennings Bryan and His Democracy* (1960). The latter book does not attempt to fill the need for a full study of Bryan, which is not entirely met by Paxton Hibben, *The Peerless Leader* (1929), or M. R. Werner, *Bryan* (1929). Bryan's own account of *The First Battle* (1897) is worth consulting. Still the best account of McKinley's good friend is Herbert Croly, *Marcus Alonzo Hanna* (1912), though Thomas Beer, *Hanna* (1929), is entertaining. Agrarian leaders prominent in 1896 are pictured in C. V. Woodward, *Tom Watson: Rebel* (1938), and F. B. Simkins, *Pitchfork Ben Tillman* (1944).

* Available in a paperback edition.

21

Empire
Beyond the Seas

The United States was not born in isolation, nor with any bias against expansionism. On the contrary, the long colonial experience was lived out in the midst of international rivalries. Independence itself was painfully won and precariously defended by taking shrewd advantage of those rivalries. Expansionism was a fundamental policy in the new nation's negotiations with foreign powers. Louisiana, Florida, Texas, New Mexico, California, Oregon, the Gadsden Purchase, and the Alaska Purchase—in fact the acquisition of all the continental area of the country beyond the original colonies—are dramatic evidence of expansionism, vigorously and steadily pursued.

After about a century, ending in 1867 with the purchase of Alaska, the nation lapsed into what might almost be called isolationism, though a better term would probably be withdrawal, or preoccupation. At any rate, the United States called a halt to expansion and showed only indifference or apathy toward foreign affairs for a quarter of a century or more. Toward the end of the 1880's, however, expansionism reawakened in a new form— overseas expansion—and concern over foreign affairs revived. A war with Spain, though not itself prompted by expansionism, actually brought overseas possessions, colonies, millions of colonial subjects, protectorates—a whole empire. A republic became an empire, a country long preoccupied with internal affairs turned into a world power. One phase of isolationism ended, and with it one phase of American innocence.

Withdrawal and Return

The Period of Withdrawal   The United States' withdrawal from world affairs was not due to any lack of advocates of aggressiveness. William H. Seward, Secretary of State under Lincoln and Johnson, proposed, among other things, intervention in Korea, acquisition of the Hawaiian Islands, and adventures in the Caribbean. He could muster no support for these undertakings, however, and only with difficulty persuaded Congress to accept the Alaska bargain offered by Russia. Moved by scheming friends, President Grant devised a treaty for the annexation of Santo Domingo, though the Senate rejected it in 1870. Other expansionists agitated in vain for the annexation of Canada, for intervention in the Cuban rebellion in 1868–78, for securing a naval station in Samoa in the seventies, and for grabbing naval harbors in Haiti during the eighties. The standard arguments against such schemes were that it was against American principles to govern without the consent of the governed, that we should abstain from foreign entanglements, avoid large naval commitments and expenditures, and refrain from absorbing peoples of alien race and tradition. One name for this policy was "continentalism"—the idea that the nation should acquire no territory outside its continental limits.

The fact is that Americans in the seventies and eighties were preoccupied with their built-in empire of the West and their economic colonialism in the South, absorbed in political and economic problems of a domestic character, largely content to stay at home, and more or less indifferent to the rest of the world. When Cleveland became President in 1885 the State Department had only sixty employees, including clerks. Secretaries of State were usually political appointees with little knowledge of foreign affairs. Until the 1880's the United States navy was an obsolete and antiquated collection of wooden ships that provoked foreign ridicule. The American merchant marine had virtually disappeared from the seas, and the army was reduced to a handful of Indian-fighters. America still enjoyed—complacently took for granted—nature's marvelous boon of security—military security that was not only effective but relatively free. Wide oceans, weak neighbors, and rivalries that kept her potential enemies divided accounted for this blessing of free security. No other great nation enjoyed it, and only the habit of relying upon it can account for the tendency of the United States to engage in heated disputes with foreign powers in which her threats and boasts were out of all proportion to her military strength.

Some of these disputes were with Great Britain, then the mightiest power in the world, and any such dispute was likely to become a game between the major political parties. The game was to see who could "twist the lion's tail" the hardest and who could curry the most favor with the Irish and other anti-British elements. One of the disputes during Cleveland's first Administration was merely a renewal of the perennial bickering over fishing rights along the coasts of British North America—a dispute that dated back to the dawn of independence. The termination of a fisheries agreement in 1885 exposed American fishermen to harassments from Canadians who were jealous of foreign competition in their own waters. Yankee vessels were required to pay new fees, were refused the privilege of buying bait and tackle, and were seized by Canadian patrol craft for trifling violations. The approach of the presidential election of 1888 brought on a new outburst of John Bull-baiting from both parties and prevented the ratification of a compromise treaty. At last the negotiators worked out a *modus vivendi* that met most of the American complaints.

Off the western shores of the continent the United States and Canada were simultaneously embroiled in another dispute—this one over the fur-seal industry in and out of the Bering Sea. The destructive hunting of seals in the open seas beyond the territorial waters of the United States was threatening to exterminate the herds, and in 1886 American revenue cutters began to seize Canadian sealing vessels. In reply to British protests, the United States advanced an arrogant claim to exclusive jurisdiction over the Bering Sea with the contention that the seals were domestic animals that had wandered out of bounds. The American position was in obvious conflict with the traditional policy of "freedom of the seas." A court of arbitration rejected the American claims and prescribed regulations for the industry that were put into effect by both governments.

The only other embroilment to ruffle the relatively calm waters of foreign affairs during Cleveland's first Administration occurred in the Samoan Islands of the remote South Pacific. The landlocked harbor of Pago Pago on Tutuila Island had stirred the interest of naval officers of the United States and other countries. In 1878, after rejecting the proposal of annexation or guardianship made by a Samoan chieftain, the Hayes Administration negotiated a treaty granting the United States the right to establish a naval station at Pago Pago. Germany and Great Britain secured similar treaties the following year, granting them naval station rights in the same harbor and elsewhere. Competition among the traders of these three nations, and the intrigues of their consuls with rival native chieftains, precipitated a tropical squall of international temper in the mid-eighties. Alarmed by the threat of bloodshed, Cleveland called a conference among the three powers which met in Washington in the summer of 1887 but accomplished nothing. Conditions grew worse when Germany set up a new regime in the islands, and seven warships anchored at Samoa prepared for hostilities. A sudden storm of hurricane force in Apia Harbor brought peace unexpectedly by sinking all but one of the warships on March 15, 1889, less than two weeks after Cleveland's term ended. Harrison's Administration worked out a tripartite protectorate of the islands with

Germany and Great Britain.

In spite of all these flurries and alarms, little had happened down to 1889 to divert Cleveland from his determination, announced in his first annual message to Congress in 1885, to adhere to "the tenets of a line of precedents from Washington's day, which proscribe entangling alliances," and to oppose "acquisition of new and distant territory or the incorporation of remote interests with our own." Yet the old tradition of isolation, abstention, and withdrawal was near its end, for America was now about to plunge into imperialism and world affairs.

Manifest Destiny Revived The old doctrine of "manifest destiny" (see p. 260) that sped the conquest of California and Oregon in the 1840's had been based on a rather simple faith in the superior vitality of the American people and the beneficence of their political institutions. The new-model manifest destiny that flourished in the late nineteenth century was ornamented by fashionable ideas and scientific notions. In particular the new imperialists found in Darwinism a source of support and rationalization. If industrialists could justify the rise of monopoly in terms of "natural selection," the imperialists could use the same defense for their conquest of "natives" and "backward peoples" in tropical climes. The domination of the "fittest" was thus given the sanction of reputable science. Impulses of aggression and mastery were part of nature's plan for the evolution of man, and to resist them was to go against the law of the universe. Ordinary rules of right and wrong did not apply in this sphere, for responsibility was shifted from conscience to nature. Moreover, the ethics of war and international relations were even more primitive than those of business, for there one was dealing with "the lesser breeds without the law," rather than with civilized adversaries.

Nor did the question of who was the "fittest" present the imperialists with any problem: those who were the fittest to rule were those who had the power and craft to do so. The concept of a superior breed of rulers was perfectly attuned to prevailing ideas about race and racial superiority, particularly to the cult of Anglo-Saxon superiority that prevailed among the upper classes of the East and, with

The Anglo-Saxon Mission

It is not necessary to argue ... that the two great needs of mankind, that all men may be lifted into the light of the highest Christian civilization, are, first, a pure, spiritual Christianity, and, second, civil liberty. Without controversy, these are the forces, which in the past, have contributed most to the elevation of the human race, and they must continue to be, in the future, the most efficient ministers to its progress. It follows, then, that the Anglo-Saxon, as the great representative of these two ideas, the depositary of these two great blessings, sustains peculiar relations to the world's future, is divinely commissioned to be, in a peculiar sense, his brother's keeper. Add to this the fact of his rapidly increasing strength in modern times, and we have well nigh a demonstration of his destiny.... It seems to me that God, with infinite wisdom and skill, is training the Anglo-Saxon race for an hour sure to come in the world's future.

From Josiah Strong, *Our Country*, 1885.

a different emphasis, among the whites of the South. Some preferred the term "Teutonic" and others "Aryan" to describe the superior race, but the terms were often used interchangeably and were sufficiently vague to cover almost all white people with whom one shared friendly feelings.

Religiously inclined exponents of racial superiority believed it had divine sanction. Josiah Strong, an evangelical leader and social reformer, wrote in his popular book *Our Country* (1885) that the Anglo-Saxon was "divinely commissioned to be, in a peculiar sense, his brother's keeper," and pictured the American branch of the family moving "down upon Mexico, down upon Central and South America, out upon the islands of the sea, over upon Africa and beyond." Professor John W. Burgess of Columbia University assigned the Teutonic nations "the mission of conducting the political civilization of the modern world." A Darwinian lecturer and writer, John Fiske, shared with many historians and philosophers of his time the conviction that it was the manifest destiny of the English-speaking people to establish sovereignty of the seas and to bestow the blessings of benevolent rule and superior institutions on less fortunate people around the globe.

American Interests

Indications are not wanting of an approaching change in the thoughts and policy of Americans as to their relations with the world outside their own borders.... The interesting and significant feature of this changing attitude is the turning of the eyes outward, instead of inward only, to seek the welfare of the country. To affirm the importance of distant markets, and the relation to them of our own immense powers of production, implies logically the recognition of the link that joins the products and the markets—that is, the carrying trade; the three together constituting that chain of maritime power to which Great Britain owes her wealth and greatness. Further, is it too much to say that, as two of these links, the shipping and the markets, are exterior to our own borders, the acknowledgment of them carries with it a view of the relations of the United States to the world radically distinct from the simple idea of self-sufficingness? We shall not follow far this line of thought before there will dawn the realization of America's unique position, facing the older worlds of the East and West, her shores washed by the oceans which touch the one or the other, but which are common to her alone.

From Alfred T. Mahan, *The Interest of America in Sea Power*, 1897.

But such a grand mission could hardly be accomplished with an antiquated navy. No one was more aware of this fact than Captain Alfred T. Mahan, the foremost exponent of navalism in his time. Mahan was the author of such books as *The Influence of Sea Power upon History* (published in 1890 but delivered as a series of lectures at the new Naval War College in 1886) and *The Interest of America in Sea Power* (1897). "Whether they will or no," wrote Mahan in 1890, "Americans must now begin to look outward." He advanced a program of mercantile imperialism that included the building up of foreign markets, the expansion of the merchant marine, the construction of a navy to protect it, and the acquisition of overseas bases that would enable the fleet to operate in distant seas. Only by these means, he argued, could America keep pace with rival nations. Mahan was the prophet of world power for the United States, and he spoke a language of hard realism that was new to his fellow countrymen. "When he speaks," wrote an admirer, "the millennium fades, and this

stern, severe, actual world appears." His books were translated into many languages, he was honored in England, and he was studied assiduously in Japan. He was a prophet with honor at home as well as abroad, for his influence was strong in shaping naval policy in Washington and in molding opinion and inspiring ambitions among such rising statesmen as Henry Cabot Lodge and Theodore Roosevelt.

Big-navy agitators worked hard and effectively through the eighties. In 1881 Congress established a Naval Advisory Board that began at once to press for larger naval appropriations, and in 1883 Congress authorized the Secretary of the Navy to construct three cruisers and in 1886 two battleships, the *Maine* and the *Texas*. This construction was still guided by the concept of the navy as a defensive force, but the Naval Act of 1890, which authorized the building of three more battleships, the *Indiana*, the *Massachusetts*, and the *Oregon*, all heavier and more powerful ships, announced the intention of the government to have a navy that could meet a potential enemy anywhere on the high seas. Before the end of the century the United States had moved up from twelfth to third place among naval powers. Thereafter the big-navy advocates began to reap the cumulative benefits of an expanding fleet: new bases and coaling stations, a stronger argument for a canal to connect the Atlantic and the Pacific, an even larger navy to protect the additional bases, and even more bases to accommodate the larger navy.

Another stimulus that quickened America's response to imperialist propaganda was the example set by the European nations that were carving up Africa and Asia, snatching island kingdoms in the Pacific, and casting eyes on South America. Driven by lust for power and greed for trade, they made protectorates of Morocco, Algeria, Tunis, and Libya in North Africa. The British worked southward from the Sudan and northward from the Cape to realize Cecil Rhodes's dream of an African empire. French, Germans, Belgians, and Italians took all the rest, save Ethiopia. The predatory powers moved in on the crumbling dynasty of China from bases already established in Asia: the French from Indochina, the British along the Yangtze Valley, and the Russians from Siberian possessions. Japan felt cheated after her victory over China in 1894 when she received only Formosa as booty. Americans began to wonder if they were not falling behind the times, whether they would ever be able to protect their interests if they did not enter even belatedly into the imperialist adventure, and "take up the white man's burden" along with the rewards and plunder that went with it.

Domestic affairs furnished further arguments for foreign adventure. The Indians had been subdued and the built-in empire of the West had been "settled" by 1890—at least according to formal census reports. The South had resumed control of the domestic "white man's burden." Some theorists, including young Theodore Roosevelt, believed that foreign adventures might divert farmers and laborers and the nation from preoccupation with economic ills.

All these impulses—the doctrine of racial superiority, the sense of national mission, and the excitement of the Darwinian struggle, along with an expanding navy, an interest in foreign markets, and the example set by old and admired European nations—combined to prepare America for a new era of involvement in foreign affairs.

The New Diplomacy

Imperialistic Stirrings   The break with the old tradition was finally made by James G. Blaine, Secretary of State under Harrison. Blaine had served briefly in the same office eight years earlier under Garfield, and revived the tradition of earlier Republican expansionism under Seward and Grant. Like them he also sought naval bases in Santo Domingo and Haiti, though with no more success. His followers expected him to pursue a "spirited policy" in keeping with his nickname of "Jingo* Jim." Actually Blaine exerted a moderating influence in the settlement of the Samoan incident with Germany and Great

* The word was popularized by a jingle printed in the Detroit *News* during the fisheries dispute with Great Britain and Canada:

> We do not want to fight
> But, by jingo, if we do
> We'll scoop in all the fishing grounds
> And the whole Dominion, too.

Britain held over from the previous administration. The three-power protectorate over the islands to which he agreed was, however, without precedent and constituted one of the first steps toward overseas imperialism.

Closer to Blaine's interests was Latin America, especially the promotion of United States trade with her sister republics, the obtaining of naval bases in the Caribbean, and the construction of an isthmian canal. Eight years earlier he had urged calling an international conference of the American republics, and the idea materialized when he became Secretary of State for the second time. Delegates arrived in the fall of 1889 and were treated to a six-thousand-mile barnstorming tour of the country, but when they settled down to consider Blaine's proposals on trade and arbitration treaties they could not agree. All they would accept was the setting up of an information center, which later became the Pan-American Union. More than a half century was to pass before Pan-American conferences would finally accept the sort of agreements Blaine tried to effect in 1889.

In the early nineties a new martial spirit in America found expression in a succession of chauvinistic outbursts, "jingoism" it was called. One such outburst almost brought the United States to the point of war with Chile, a republic with not one-twentieth its population. In October 1891, when a party from the cruiser *Baltimore* went on shore leave in Valparaiso, a mob of Chileans killed two of the American sailors and injured seventeen others. The State Department sent a stern protest to the Chilean government demanding an apology. Jingoistic papers demanded that the upstarts be taught a lesson, and warmongers made the American eagle scream. President Harrison inserted a sword-rattling passage in his annual message to Congress and dictated a stiff note to Chile that was in effect an ultimatum threatening to break off diplomatic relations. He followed this with another message to Congress virtually inviting it to declare war at a time when the apologies he had demanded from Chile were hourly expected. Preparations for hostilities were actually initiated by army and navy. Chile fortunately capitulated with apologies and indemnities and the war scare passed over.

The bellicose mood of the jingo editors and politicians did not pass over, however. Rather it continued to mount during the nineties. "The number of men and officials in this country who are now mad to fight somebody is appalling," said the anti-imperialist editor of the *Nation*, E. L. Godkin, in 1894. "Navy officers dream of war and talk and lecture about it incessantly. The Senate debates are filled with predictions of impending war and with talk of preparing for it at once." The irresponsible warmongering of the period was indeed appalling, though it should be remembered that nineteenth-century Americans knew nothing of the total wars to come. They regarded the Civil War as an exception and still thought of war as an heroic affair limited to professionals and filled with splendor and glory. It was an illusion slow to die.

Even the antiexpansionist Cleveland was not immune to the new spirit, as he showed in his handling of relations with Britain in the dispute over the boundary between British Guiana and Venezuela. It was an old dispute that went back into the colonial history of Venezuela, but the discovery of gold in the disputed territory, combined with a bit of Venezuelan propaganda suggesting that British aggression was a challenge to the Monroe Doctrine, stirred up the Anglophobia and pugnacity of the jingo editors of the United States. In 1895 Cleveland's Secretary of State, Richard Olney, demanded that Great Britain conform to the Monroe Doctrine, as he very broadly interpreted it, by submitting the boundary dispute to arbitration. He accompanied this demand with the truculent assertion that the United States today "is practically sovereign on this continent, and its fiat is law upon the subjects to which it confines its interposition." The tone of the note, coupled with his request for a quick reply, gave it the flavor of an ultimatum.

The British foreign minister, Lord Salisbury, took his time in replying, and when he did reply four months later he repudiated Secretary Olney's interpretation of the Monroe Doctrine and flatly refused to submit the dispute to arbitration. After receiving this rebuff, Cleveland sent a special message to Congress deploring "a supine submission to wrong and injustice and the consequent loss of national self-respect" and asking that he be authorized to appoint a commission to determine the boundary and that the commission's decision be enforced at whatever cost. Congress promptly complied and war sentiment mounted. "Let the fight come if it must," wrote Theodore Roosevelt, who hoped to participate personally. "I rather hope that the fight will come soon. The clamor of the peace faction has convinced me that this country needs a war." The risk was altogether disproportionate to the American interest at stake, but it was not at all disproportionate to the chauvinistic mood of the day. Fortunately Britain saw fit to back down. Suddenly finding herself in trouble in South Africa with no ally in Europe on which she could count for support, Great Britain decided to court a friend instead of make an enemy in the New World. She switched to a conciliatory tone and signed a treaty with Venezuela providing for arbitration, which turned out to be mainly in her favor. The upshot of the incident was to enhance American nationalist feeling, but paradoxically it also ushered in an era of Anglo-American understanding.

The Hawaiian Question   When it came to expansion overseas, however, Cleveland clung consistently to traditional views and stood firm against the annexation of Hawaii. American interest in these islands dated back to the China trade in the late eighteenth century. Traders were followed by American missionaries, who converted the native Polynesians to Christianity in the second quarter of the nineteenth century, and the missionaries were followed by American sugar-growers. Efforts to annex the islands under President Pierce and again under Secretary Seward failed, but in 1875 a reciprocity treaty was signed opening a free market in the United States to Hawaiian sugar-planters. Sugar production in the islands multiplied tenfold in the next twenty years in response to the free American market. So dependent did the industry become on this market, however, that when the McKinley Tariff of 1890 admitted other foreign sugar on the same terms and subsidized domestic producers, the blow precipitated an economic crisis in the island kingdom and contributed to a political crisis.

King Kalakaua, the last but one of the

reigning family, had been forced by the white business community in 1887 to accept a new constitution that curbed his power, made his ministers responsible to the legislature, and brought the legislature under control of the propertied classes. The dissolute old king was succeeded in 1891 by his sister Liliuokalani, who made it apparent that she was determined to overthrow the constitution her brother had accepted, shake off white control, and restore royal prerogatives. Alarmed at this political threat and distressed over the economic slump caused by the new tariff policy, white business leaders in the islands decided that annexation by the United States was the only solution to their problems. In their plans to overthrow "Queen Lil" they received definite encouragement from members of Congress as well as members of President Harrison's administration, which had all along been more favorable to annexation than had Cleveland.

In January 1893 a committee of businessmen-revolutionaries took the queen's announcement that she was going to proclaim a new constitution as the signal for revolt and demanded that she abdicate. Thereupon United States minister John L. Stevens, an annexationist whom Blaine had picked for the office, ordered marines ashore from the cruiser *Boston*, and raised the American flag. The queen then capitulated, as she said, "to the superior force of the United States of America." A month later, on February 15, Harrison sent to the Senate a treaty annexing the islands. It might have gone through then and there had it not been for the declared preference of Cleveland, who was to begin his second Administration in a few days, that the matter be held over until his inauguration. As soon as he became President again he dispatched a special commissioner to investigate the situation in the islands. The commissioner's report convinced Cleveland that the great majority of the natives supported the queen and that the coup of the white clique could not have been carried off without the aid of Minister Stevens and the marines. Cleveland therefore not only withheld the annexation treaty but insisted that it was his duty to restore Queen Lil. The revolutionary provisional government refused to step down, however, and continued to rule, biding their time until

William McKinley: "Duty determines destiny."

a more imperialist-minded Administration came to power.

Cleveland's firm resistance to annexation, as compared with Harrison's receptive attitude, helped to make the question something of a party issue. The Republican platform of 1896 contained a plank favoring Hawaiian annexation, and though McKinley had previously shown no interest in the matter, he was quickly won over after he became President in March 1897. Comparing him with Cleveland, commissioners from Hawaii reported that there was "the difference between daylight and darkness." On June 16, 1897, Secretary of State John Sherman signed a treaty of annexation and McKinley sent it to the Senate. Congress was strongly interested in Hawaii and alarmed by the interest Japan was manifesting in the islands, but the sentiment against overseas expansion was still too strong to be overcome, and the treaty languished for more than a year without action. Only in July 1898, after the war with Spain had opened the floodgates of expansionism, did the annexation of Hawaii take place.

War with Spain

The Cuban Crisis   The expansionists and imperialists did not cause the war with Spain. They merely exploited it for their own purposes. The war itself grew out of deplorable conditions in Cuba that seemed intolerable to an aroused popular sentiment in the United States. Spanish misgovernment of the island had given rise to numerous revolts and a Ten Years' War, 1868–78, that brought little relief for Cuban ills. A new civil war broke out in February 1895. As in the case of the Hawaiian revolution, American tariff policy contributed to the uprising, for the tariff law of 1894, by imposing a duty on raw sugar, had added economic suffering to political discontent. Both the Cubans and the Spaniards used savage methods. The Cubans systematically destroyed sugar mills, cane fields, and other property, and early in 1896 the Spanish commander, General Valeriano Weyler, resorted to the brutal policy of "reconcentration." This meant driving the entire population of large areas of Cuba—including women, children, and old people—into cities and towns fortified with barbed wire and under armed guard. Left without food or sanitation, the prisioners fell victim to famine and disease, which swept thousands of them to their death. Within two years two hundred thousand, or approximately one-eighth of the total population, were estimated to have been wiped out.

The American press exaggerated the Spanish atrocities, but the sufferings of the rebels were horrible enough in any case to arouse deep sympathies among Americans. The sufferings, moreover, were those of a neighbor, and they were incurred in a fight for independence from a manifestly unjust imperial ruler. Little more was required to whip up popular sympathy for the Cuban patriots and animus against Spain, especially in years when the public mind was as susceptible to jingoism as it had recently proved to be in far less serious disputes with Chile and Great Britain. Indications were abundant that influential Americans were "spoiling for a fight," and the Cuban *junta* that established itself in New York to dispense propaganda, solicit aid, and arouse sympathy was not without support.

One strong ally of the interventionists was the "yellow press" of New York City. Led by William Randolph Hearst's New York *Journal* and Joseph Pulitzer's New York *World*, which were currently engaged in a war for circulation, the press sent a corps of reporters and artists to cover the Cuban conflict and supply the papers with vivid human-interest stories and pictures. The barbarities of the Spaniards were played up and the atrocities of the Cubans glossed over, with the result that the newspaper coverage constituted powerful propaganda for the rebel cause. Waves of sympathy for the insurgents swept the country, and when the struggle continued to drag on with no prospect of Spain's relenting, much of the sympathy began to turn into a demand for American intervention and war with Spain.

American businessmen did not share the interventionist sentiment. Even those who had investments in Cuba or carried on trade with the island, though they desired an end to the revolt, feared that more harm would come from war with Spain than from continuation of the civil war in Cuba. Financial journals and industrial leaders warned that war would endanger the domestic business revival that was beginning in 1897 and menace the gold standard. On the other hand, Protestant religious journals and both Republican and Democratic newspapers clamored loudly for intervention and war, though they insisted that they did so on purely humanitarian grounds and disclaimed any desire to annex Cuba or gain territory. Theirs was a moralistic aggression, with imperialism disavowed. Avowed imperialists, including Roosevelt, Lodge, and Mahan, were also for war, but for the express purpose of conquest, expansion, and military glory. Two contrasting sets of aggressive impulses, both frustrated in the nineties, sought outlet in an idealistic crusade for Cuban freedom. One set embraced the impulses of protest and humanitarian reform; the other embraced the impulses of national self-expression, aggressiveness, and expansion. The first was embodied in Populism, Utopianism, the Social Gospel, and radical labor movements—all of which had suffered frustrations in the nineties, most recently in the downfall of Populism and Bryan and the triumph of conservatism and McKinley. The second group included the big-navy advocates, the patriotic societies, and the statesmen and propagandists of imperialism, whose programs had been blocked by cautious business interests and the antiexpansionist foreign policy that had prevailed since Grant's administration. The convergence of these two groups in support of intervention in Cuba goes far toward explaining why Americans worked themselves up into a mood for war with Spain.

American Intervention   When Grover Cleveland was President, he had opposed intervention in Cuba on every front. He had resisted pressure from Congress to accord the insurgents belligerent rights, had sought to suppress gun-running into Cuba from the States, and had tendered his good offices to Spain to settle the colonial war. McKinley tried hard to curb the jingoes and halt the drift to war. He adhered to the Cleveland policy when he took office, and six months later a satisfactory settlement seemed to be in the making. A change of government in Spain brought in a Prime Minister who recalled General Weyler and offered Cuba a considerable measure of self-government in local affairs. The offer proved unacceptable, however, since the Spaniards in Cuba opposed rule by native Cubans and the insurgents refused to settle for anything short of complete independence. Further hopes for a peaceful solution were disrupted by a series of fateful incidents, or accidents, that brought relations between the United States and Spain to the breaking point.

The first incident was the publication on February 9, 1898, of a stolen private letter from the Spanish minister in Washington, Dupuy de Lôme, who indiscreetly described President McKinley as "weak and a bidder for the admiration of the crowd" and said that the Cuban rebels should be suppressed by force. Dupuy de Lôme resigned before his government had time to respond to Washington's inevitable request for his recall. Then, six days later, the battleship *Maine* blew up in Havana Harbor with a loss of 260 officers and enlisted men. The Spanish government has-

tened to offer condolence and propose a joint investigation. An investigation by American naval officers reported that the *Maine's* bottom plates had been thrust inward, indicating an external explosion, but the cause of the tragedy was never discovered. It is highly improbable that the Spanish government would have plotted such an act, but the jingo press held Spain guilty and raised the cry "Remember the Maine!" Before the report of the *Maine* explosion was completed, Congress unanimously voted a defense appropriation of $50 million, and on March 19 Senator Redfield Proctor of Vermont delivered a speech painting the shocking conditions he had found in Cuba during a recent unofficial visit. His calm tone and matter-of-fact manner convinced many who had heretofore been skeptical of the lurid stories in the yellow press that action was indeed necessary.

On March 27 McKinley proposed to Spain a peaceful settlement in which she would abandon her reconcentration policy at once, grant an armistice until October 1, and enter into peace negotiations with the insurgents through his offices. This was not an ultimatum, though he followed it the next day with a telegram saying that independence would be the only satisfactory outcome of the peace negotiations. Spain was confronted with a cruel dilemma: if she rejected McKinley's demands she faced a disastrous war, and if she complied with them she faced a revolt that might overturn the government and possibly the throne. Her appeals for support from European powers won sympathy, but the only tangible response was a visit to President McKinley by the ambassadors of six powers who begged him not to intervene with armed force. Despairing of European aid, Spain replied on March 31 to McKinley's proposals by agreeing to abandon reconcentration and to grant an armistice upon the application of the insurgents. She hedged on the point of independence, but volunteered to submit to arbitration the question of who was responsible for sinking the *Maine*. She followed up on April 9 by declaring an armistice on her own without waiting for the insurgents to take the initiative. The following day the American minister in Madrid cabled that he believed Cuban independence and a solution satisfactory to all

could be worked out during the armistice.

Spain had gone far toward meeting the President's demands, far enough according to his minister in Madrid to assure a peaceful solution. But ignoring these assurances, caught up in the popular cry for war, McKinley on the day after receiving his minister's cable, April 11, sent a warlike message to Congress. He alluded to Spain's concessions to American demands in passing, but did not stress them. There was, it is true, ground for doubt that the Spanish government could make good its promises. Congress paused only to debate whether it should recognize the insurgent government as well as the independence of Cuba, decided on the latter only, and adopted

the resolution on April 19 by a vote of 42 to 35 in the Senate and 311 to 6 in the House. An amendment to the resolution, which was prepared by Senator Henry M. Teller of Colorado and adopted at the same time without dissent, renounced any intention of annexing or governing Cuba and promised to "leave the government and control of the Island to its people." The Teller Amendment proclaimed American righteousness and abstention with respect to Cuba, but as the author of the resolution carefully pointed out, left the country a free hand "as to some other islands," which also belonged to Spain. Spain responded by declaring war on April 24 and Congress followed suit the next day. The American declaration of war was made retroactive to April 21, since the President had established a blockade of the Cuban coast on April 22.

The Little War   Within ten weeks of the declaration of war the fighting was over and the victory assured. For the country at large—and the readers of headlines in particular—it could not have been a more "splendid little war," as John Hay described it, or one conforming more completely with the romantic imagination of the budding imperialists. The whole war seemed to have been fought to the stirring music of "The Stars and Stripes Forever," the battle song of the war, played by a marine band in dress uniform. Even the participants chose to remember it in the manly prose of Richard Harding Davis or in the heroic sketches of Frederic Remington, two of the numerous writers and artists who "covered" the story of one of the best-publicized wars in history. The Spanish-American War was, in short, the most popular of all American wars. Disillusionment takes a bit of time, especially among noncombatants, and this war was over even before weariness could set in—save among combat troops.

The most hardened skeptics were thrown off balance less than a week after the war started by Commodore George Dewey's dazzling naval victory in Manila Bay on the opposite side of the globe. Assistant Secretary of the Navy Theodore Roosevelt, who had secured the Commodore's assignment to the command, had taken advantage of his superior's temporary absence to direct Dewey two months earlier to be thoroughly prepared for action. On receiving news of the war and his final instructions, Dewey had immediately steamed out of Hong Kong, slipped through the straits of Boca Grande during the night of April 30, and at dawn opened fire on the weak and inferior Spanish squadron at Manila. Before breakfast, and without losing a man, he had sunk the whole fleet to the last of its ten ships. Dewey had crushed Spanish power in the Pacific.

Unfortunately the army was not as well prepared as the navy, but the public did not learn about that until later. The account of the expeditionary force to Cuba that the public read and gloried in was the sort supplied by the debonair reporter Richard Harding Davis:

Dewey's Campaign in the Pacific, 1898

It was a most happy-go-lucky expedition, run with real American optimism and readiness to take big chances, and with the spirit of a people who recklessly trust that it will come out all right in the end, and that the barely possible may not happen. . . . As one of the generals on board said, "This is God Almighty's war, and we are only His agents."

That was one way of putting it. At least Davis was accurate about the expedition's optimism and recklessness. The army, with only some 26,000 men at the start of the war, had no adequate plans, equipment, or supplies. The War Department was crippled by antiquated methods, utterly incompetent administration, and inefficient and negligent officers. General William R. Shafter, a three-hundred-pound Civil War hero, presided over the chaos at Tampa preceding the embarcation of the expeditionary force. Transportation broke down and confusion reigned. The thousands of volunteers who rushed to the colors eager for glory could not be supplied with guns, tents, or blankets. With hopeless inefficiency they were clad in heavy woolen winter uniforms for a summer campaign in the sweltering tropics. Food was inadequate, repulsive, and some-

The Cuban Campaign, 1898

times poisonous, sanitation was conspicuously wanting, and medical supplies were almost nonexistent. Over the expeditionary force there spread the stench of dysentery and illness and eventually the horror of plague, the yellow jack. The fact was that blundering inefficiency brought the army to the brink of disaster.

The Spaniards blundered badly too, but with an unstable government, a tradition-bound leadership, and a backward economy, they had more excuse for inefficiency than the Americans, who had none of these handicaps. Yet for all their pride in industrial progress and their reputation for bustling efficiency and technological know-how, the Americans made a mess of their war effort. The government seemed unable to adopt the vigorous administrative methods that would have made effective use of the country's vaunted industrial superiority. The scandal reflected a quarter-century of federal lassitude and laissez-faire philosophy. As it turned out, the real explanation of the quick American military success lay in the even more incredible inefficiency and blundering of the Spaniards.

The enemy obliged by immobilizing its naval power in Cuban waters, a small force of four cruisers and three destroyers under the command of Admiral Pascual Cervera, in Santiago Harbor, where it was immediately block-

aded by a vastly superior fleet commanded by Admiral William T. Sampson. The blockade ended the threat to the landing of an expeditionary force, and after much backing and filling and countermanding of orders a force of some 18,000 regulars and volunteers got under way from Tampa, partly equipped, partially trained, and poorly led. The most publicized unit of volunteers was the Rough Riders, commanded by Colonel Leonard Wood, who was loudly supported by Lieutenant Colonel Theodore Roosevelt, second in command. The landing force blundered slowly ashore on June 20 and somehow established a beachhead at Daiquiri, a few miles east of Santiago.

With some two hundred thousand troops in Cuba, the Spaniards could have destroyed the Americans utterly. But they had only about thirteen thousand men at Santiago and were so handicapped in transportation that they could not bring their superior forces to bear, and so unfortunate in military leadership that they could not employ what power they had at hand to their best advantage. Even so they came near inflicting a disaster upon the invaders. The American objective was to capture the ridges known as San Juan Hill that surrounded Santiago and then to take the town in whose harbor Admiral Cervera was blockaded. So poorly was the command organized, however, that the American units were largely without coordinated control in their attack. It was in the capture of Kettle Hill, a flanking outpost of San Juan Hill, that Theodore Roosevelt established his reputation for martial zeal and heroism. Later he was to describe the attack volubly and frequently as a "bully fight" that was "great fun," something of a rollicking skylark. Actually the fight, in which his was by no means the only part, was a pretty desperate and bloody affair marked by a reckless display of courage and a great many needless casualties. The capture of the heights proved decisive in the land fighting, for Santiago was now closely invested. But, under counterattack and without supplies, the American troops were soon in a dangerous plight. On July 3 Roosevelt wrote Lodge, "We are within measurable distance of a terrible military disaster," in desperate need of reinforcements, food, and ammunition.

Flag-raising at Guantanamo Bay, Cuba, 1898.

On that very morning, however, Admiral Cervera hoisted anchor and steamed out of Santiago Harbor to face his doom for the honor of Castile. He knew perfectly well that he was far outclassed and outgunned by the four United States battleships awaiting him just outside the harbor, but he gave battle rather than surrender without a fight. The American battle line opened up with its thirteen-inch guns, and one after another the Spanish ships went down gallantly, guns ablaze. It was all over in a few hours, with four hundred enemy killed or wounded and with only one American killed. The next day was the Fourth of July, and orators had not had such an opportunity since the day after Gettysburg and Vicksburg.

The enemy ashore was now powerless, and the Spanish forces surrendered Cuba on July 16. Puerto Rico was taken within the next two weeks virtually without resistance, and on August 12 a peace protocol was signed. The next day Manila fell to the troops that were sent over after Dewey's victory in May, and the war was over. In actual battle casualties the price of victory was comparatively small. But only after the close of the war did the major losses begin to mount: losses due to disease, mainly typhoid, malaria, and yellow fever. By the end of the year the total deaths in the American army in all theaters of war had risen to 5,462, only 379 of which were the direct result of combat or wounds.

The White Man's Burden

Mr. McKinley and His Duty   The armistice deliberately left open the question of the disposition of the Philippine Islands. They had scarcely figured at all in the war motives of most Americans, who, in Reinhold Niebuhr's phrase, were bent on fighting a "pure-minded war." To seize those possessions and to rule them by force without consent of their inhabitants would be to violate both the humanitarian motives that prompted the war and the oldest and profoundest American political traditions. Knowing these things in their hearts, whether they admitted them or not, the imperialist-minded minority scarcely dared hope at the onset of the war that their dreams would materialize. As it turned out they were on the eve of sensational success.

Hawaii was the first sign. In the spring before the war the cause of annexation had looked fairly hopeless. But in the excitement of the Dewey and Sampson victories the traditional arguments were swept aside and the "large policy" of Hay, Lodge, Mahan, and Roosevelt prevailed. The New York *Tribune* maintained that Hawaii was "imperative" as a halfway station to the Philippines, and another expansionist argued later that the Philippines were imperative as an outpost for Hawaii. On June 15 the House of Representatives, and on July 6 the Senate, adopted a joint resolution annexing Hawaii. The large policy was now on the way to further enlargement.

The enlargement was facilitated by the flexible conscience of President McKinley, who once regarded forcible annexation as "criminal aggression" but now saw in it "the hand of Almighty God." He advanced his insights in the form of such epigrams as "Duty determines destiny," but he did not answer the New York *Evening Post*'s query, "Who determines duty?" At any rate the destiny of the Philippines was becoming pretty manifest as McKinley's epigrams and actions multiplied. Even before Dewey's victory was confirmed he sent a force to capture and hold Manila, and before the end of May Lodge was writing Roosevelt, "The Administration is now fully committed to the large policy that we both desire."

The President was swimming with the tide, as he usually did. And the commercial and industrial interests now helped swing the tide toward expansionism. Though they had opposed the war for fear of its effect on recovery and the gold standard, once the war started and news of the victories poured in and the potentialities of expansion for the advancement of trade became manifest, the business community swung about in support of the policies it had so recently opposed. Big business saw the Philippines as a key to the China trade and listened appreciatively to Senator Albert Beveridge's declaration that "the trade of the world must and shall be ours."

At the same time the religious press, with the support of the missionary movement, stepped up support for the "imperialism of righteousness." Annexation would further the cause of world evangelization, extend the blessings of civilization and sanitation, and "civilize" more of the heathens. It was this sentiment that McKinley reflected later in recounting how he had reached his decision through prayer "to educate the Filipinos, and uplift and civilize and Christianize them, and, by God's grace, do the very best we could by them, as our fellow men for whom Christ also died."

A more cynical approach to imperialism was that of editor Henry Watterson, who proposed to "escape the menace and peril of socialism and agrarianism" by means of "a policy of colonization and conquest." The most popular reasoning, however, was to attribute imperialism to a determinism of some sort: the hand of God, the instinct of race, the laws of Darwin, the forces of economics and trade—anything but rational and responsible decision. Though many Americans seemed willing to surrender to imperialist policies, few would admit they did so because they wanted to.

McKinley revealed his intentions pretty clearly by the choice of commissioners he sent to negotiate with Spain at the peace conference held in Paris. Three of the five peace commissioners were open and avowed expansionists. Another indication was his seizure of Spain's island of Guam—whose inhabitants mistook the American bombardment for a salute and apologized for having no ammunition with which to return it. In his instructions to the peace commissioners the President took the moral position that "without any desire or design on our part" the United States had assumed duties and responsibilities that it must discharge as became a nation of noble destiny. Impressed by the popular response to speeches he made along this line of "responsibility," he instructed the commissioners in October with regard to the Philippines that "duty requires we should take the archipelago."

John Hay, who had recently become Secretary of State, cabled the delegation in Paris to hold out for the whole of the Philippine Islands. The Spanish commissioners resisted the demand to the point of risking a renewal of hostilities. McKinley stuck to his position that we should "not shirk the moral obligation of our victory," but made one concession, an offer to pay $20 million for the Philippines. The Spaniards capitulated and the treaty was signed December 10, 1898. By its terms Spain was to give up control over Cuba and surrender Guam, Puerto Rico, and the Philippine Islands to the United States.

In thus abandoning American tradition and his own earlier convictions, President McKinley showed little evidence of grasping the implications of his decision for American foreign policy and future involvement in power rivalries and wars in the Far East. There is little reason, however, to doubt the sincerity of the reasons he offered a year later, though some critics question that they came to him in a flood of prayerful illumination. The reasons he offered were: that it would be cowardly and dishonorable to give the Philippines back to Spain, "bad business and discreditable" to let France or Germany seize them, impossible to leave them to their own devices since they were unfit for self-rule, and absolutely necessary to follow the humanitarian impulses to "civilize and Christianize" the Filipinos by taking possession of their land. He did not see fit to propose the establishment of a protectorate over the islands with the promise of self-government and later of independence.

The Debate on the Philippines The treaty with Spain committed the country to imperialism in the Far East and the Caribbean. But first it had to be ratified by the Senate, and the question of ratification precipitated a debate that spread far beyond the Senate chamber and cast more light on the issues of annexation than had the President's speeches and the expansionists' slogans. After the drums of war were silenced and the people began to think more soberly, it became apparent that there was formidable opposition to the President's policy, perhaps enough to defeat it. Far more opposition came from

Democrats than from Republicans, and the sentiment was strong enough to unite even such Democratic extremes as Bryan and Cleveland. But prominent members of McKinley's own party, including Speaker Reed of the House and Senator George F. Hoar of Massachusetts, broke with the Administration over the question, as did Senator Eugene Hale of Maine. To the very last it was doubtful whether the President could muster the two-thirds of the Senate required to ratify his treaty.

Even before the treaty was signed an Anti-Imperialist League was organized that attracted the support of many distinguished men. As president, the League elected George S. Boutwell, formerly Grant's Secretary of the Treasury and later Republican senator from Massachusetts. Among the vice-presidents were such contrasting figures as Grover Cleveland and Samuel Gompers, Andrew Carnegie and Carl Schurz, John Sherman and Charles Francis Adams. Intellectuals, novelists, and poets rallied to anti-imperialism in great numbers, among them President Eliot of Harvard and President David Starr Jordan of Stanford, along with William James, William Dean Howells, William Graham Sumner, Hamlin Garland, William Vaughn Moody, and Mark Twain. In a bitter satire Mark Twain assured his countrymen that the "Blessings-of-Civilization Trust" had the purest of motives. "This world-girdling accumulation of trained morals, high principles, and justice cannot do an unright thing, an unfair thing, an ungenerous thing, an unclean thing," he wrote. "It knows what it is about. Give yourself no uneasiness; it is all right."

Some of the anti-imperialist arguments showed remarkable prescience. George Boutwell foresaw a war with Japan as a consequence of American expansion in the western Pacific, and following that the rise of a warlike China in alliance with Russia that would turn against American holdings. A favorite argument was based on the doctrine of the Declaration of Independence: no government without the consent of the governed. We had fought the Revolution for that principle and had intervened in Cuba on the same ground; how could we now shamelessly adopt the doctrines we fought to overthrow? Or, as Senator Hoar put

God has ... made us the master organizers of the world to establish system where chaos reigns. He has given us the spirit of progress to overwhelm the forces of reaction throughout the earth. He has made us adepts in government that we may administer government among savage and senile peoples. Were it not for such a force as this the world would relapse into barbarism and night. And of all our race He has marked the American people as His chosen nation to finally lead in the regeneration of the world. This is the divine mission of America, and it holds for us all the profit, all the glory, all the happiness possible to man....

What shall history say of us? Shall it say that we renounced that holy trust, left the savage to his base condition, the wilderness to the reign of waste, deserted duty, abandoned glory?... Our fathers would not have had it so. No! They founded no paralytic government, incapable of the simplest acts of administration.... They unfurled no retreating flag.

That flag has never paused in its onward march. Who dares halt it now—now, when history's largest events are carrying it forward?

From Albert J. Beveridge, Speech in the U.S. Senate, January 9, 1900.

it, how could we "strut about in the cast-off clothing of pinchbeck emperors and pewter kings?" Other objections were that the Asiatic people could not be assimilated into our tradition, that imperialism would lead to militarism and racist dogma at home, that overseas expansion was unconstitutional and inconsistent with the Monroe Doctrine. Southerners viewed the new imperialism as a revival of carpetbaggery and warned of the difficulties of reconciling races of contrasting color and heritage.

The imperialist-minded defenders of the treaty revived with new assurance their old arguments of naval strategy, world power, and commercial interests, and incorporated the moralistic line of McKinley on duty, destiny, humanitarianism, and religious mission. In the latter vein Senator Beveridge declared, "It is God's great purpose made manifest in the instincts of our race, whose present phase is our personal profit, but whose far-off end is the redemption of the world and the Christianization of mankind." Senator Lodge dismissed

the consent-of-the-governed argument as of no account because that principle had been ignored or violated before, notably in the Louisiana Purchase, in order to advance the national interest. He emphasized and exaggerated the supposed economic advantages of the Philippines, their resources, their trade, and the opportunities for investment there. He stressed the political expediency of keeping the islands: they were not ready for self-government, would lapse into anarchy, or would be seized by more ruthless powers.

In the meantime the Senate continued its deliberations, the outcome still in doubt. Before the end of the debate the anti-imperialists were confused by a strange maneuver and strategic blunder of William Jennings Bryan. Although he was a strong opponent of the acquisition of the Philippines, he decided that the Senate should approve the treaty to assure peace and should leave the future disposition of the islands to be decided at the polls. He undoubtedly believed that this move would provide him with a winning issue in the presi-

Acquisition of the Philippines:
Retrospective Criticism

The Russian writer, Anton Chekhov, who was also a doctor, once observed that when a large variety of remedies was recommended for the same disease, it was a pretty sure sign that none of them was any good and that the disease was incurable. Similarly, when one notes the variety of arguments put up by the expansionists for the territorial acquisitions of 1898, one has the impression that none of them was the real one—that at the bottom of it all lay something deeper, something less easy to express, probably the fact that the American people of that day, or at least many of their more influential spokesmen, simply liked the smell of empire.... But by the same right of retrospect one is impressed with the force and sincerity of the warnings of the anti-expansionists and the logic, as yet never really refuted, of their contention that a country which traces its political philosophy to the concept of the social compact has no business taking responsibility for people who have no place in that concept and who are supposed to appear on the scene in the role of subjects and not of citizens.

From George F. Kennan, *American Diplomacy, 1900–1950*, 1951.

Filipino insurrectionists: A desire for freedom.

dential election of 1900, but he miscalculated. Approval of the treaty confronted the voters with a *fait accompli*. Bryan's advice won some Senate votes over to the side of the Administration, though not enough to assure victory. On February 5, 1899, the very day before the final ballot was set, the drama of the decision was complicated and intensified by the arrival of news that the Filipinos had taken up arms in open revolt against the United States. There could be no more doubt of their desire for freedom, nor that the United States was now in the same position formerly occupied by discredited Spain. The effect of this news is impossible to estimate. The issue remained in doubt until the roll call the next day recorded fifty-seven in favor of the treaty and twenty-seven against, or more than the necessary two-thirds majority.

The motives that prompted America to "take up the white man's burden," as Rud-

yard Kipling urged her to do, were even more complex than the motives of the war that prepared the way for the decision. Part of the motivation was fear, the fear of appearing silly and playing the fool in the eyes of the world. Part of it was an uglier impulse of aggression. "The taste of empire is in the mouth of the people even as the taste of blood in the jungle," said the Washington *Post*. A more attractive variant, described in the twentieth century by George F. Kennan, was "an urge to range themselves among the colonial powers of the time, to see our flag flying on distant tropical isles, to feel the thrill of foreign adventure and authority, to bask in the sunshine of recognition as one of the great imperial powers of the world."

McKinley's Vindication of 1900 It was Bryan's mistake, in planning to make the election of 1900 a popular referendum on imperialism, to believe that the anti-imperialist sentiment of the great debate of 1898–99 could be sustained, revived, or even strengthened. Nearly two years were to pass between the ratification of the treaty and the presidential election, and by that time much water had passed under the bridge. Empire was no longer a dangerous menace to tradition and a decision that had to be worried out; it was an accomplished fact to which the people were growing accustomed. They did not like the war that was being waged to suppress Emilio Aguinaldo and his Filipino patriots, even though censorship kept some of its worst aspects from them. That war was to drag on for three years, during which the United States was to use more men to suppress freedom in the Philippines than it had used to bring freedom to Cuba. And the new American rulers were to repeat in grotesque imitation the tortures and brutalities of their Spanish predecessors. But all that was taking place on the other side of the widest of oceans. When pressed, people admitted, "Peace has to be restored."

At home there were plenty of distractions to divert a burdensome conscience. The most important was the gradual return to prosperity. The war itself served as an additional stimulus. Business regained its nerve, trade quickened, and the economy bustled into activity.

As the farmers and laborers sloughed off the burden of depression, their radicalism declined. "The Spanish War finished us," wrote Tom Watson of the Populist party. "The blare of the bugle drowned the voice of the reformer." The war, coupled with returning prosperity, mounting racism, and the legacy of the Populists' demoralizing fusion with Bryanism in 1896 (see p. 491), did just about finish the party. In the 1900 campaign it split into two feuding factions, neither of which could make a substantial showing. Many of the Populists of the Southwest and Midwest were attracted to the new Social Democratic

party, which was founded in 1900 and nominated Eugene V. Debs of Pullman strike fame as its presidential candidate.

Although McKinley's policies had little to do with the revival of the economy, he was billed as "the advance agent of prosperity," and he prospered politically with the return of good times. With a Cabinet that was if possible even more conservative than he was himself, McKinley's first Administration had proved as willing and cooperative as Hanna and the business community could have hoped. The Dingley Tariff of 1897 lifted the rates to a new high, and the gold standard was now safe.

The presidential nominees of the two major parties in 1900 were pretty much a foregone conclusion. The Republicans had no hesitation about McKinley, but only with some difficulty did they settle upon the military hero and New York governor, Theodore Roosevelt, whom neither McKinley nor Hanna wanted, for Vice-President. The Democrats returned to Bryan and picked the Silverite Adlai E. Stevenson, who had been Cleveland's running mate in 1892, for second place. The Democratic platform stressed imperialism as the "paramount issue" and on Bryan's insistence revived the demand for free silver. Bryan soon discovered that he had two fairly moribund issues on his hands, however, and shifted his emphasis to monopoly and special privilege.

Bryan, in a poorer showing than he had made in 1896, lost his own state of Nebraska, as well as Kansas, South Dakota, Utah, and Wyoming—all silver states he carried before. The election neither revived the silver issue nor provided a mandate on imperialism. Even if the voters opposed imperialism, they could express their disapproval only by voting against prosperity. To the majority of voters in 1900 McKinley meant prosperity rather than imperialism or gold, and with him conservatism was triumphant once more.

SUGGESTIONS FOR READING   The general histories of American diplomatic relations by Bemis, Pratt, and Bailey see this period from somewhat different points of view. F. R. Dulles, *The Imperial Years* (1956), is an informed and perceptive general study beginning with Cleveland's first Administration. E. R. May, *Imperial Democracy* (1961), reveals how America emerged as a great power. The world context of imperialism is best seen in P. T. Moon, *Imperialism and World Politics* (1926), and the American variant and its rationalization are described and richly illustrated and exposed in A. K. Weinberg, *Manifest Destiny* (1935). On Latin-American affairs the most informative studies are S. F. Bemis, *The Latin American Policy of the United States* (1943), and Dexter Perkins, *The Monroe Doctrine, 1867–1907* (1937); and on the Far East a helpful work is A. W. Griswold, *The Far Eastern Policy of the United States* (1938).

Secretaries of State and their policies are examined in C. C. Tansill, *The Foreign Policy of Thomas F. Bayard, 1885–1897* (1940), and A. F. Tyler, *The Foreign Policy of James G. Blaine* (1927); see also the sketches in Vol. IX of Bemis, *American Secretaries of State*.

The revival of the expansionist impulse is traced in Harold and Margaret Sprout, *The Rise of American Naval Power, 1776–1918* (1939), and reflected in many works of the period, particularly Josiah Strong, *Our Country* (1885), and A. T. Mahan, *The Influence of Sea Power upon History, 1660–1783* (1890). Leading expansionists of the 1880's and 1890's are portrayed in W. D. Puleston, *Mahan* (1939); H. K. Beale, *Theodore Roosevelt and the Rise of America to World Power* (1956); and H. F. Pringle, *Theodore Roosevelt: A Biography* * (rev. ed., 1956). C. A. Beard, *The Idea of National Interest* (1934), takes a skeptical view of expansionism. The instance of Hawaii is examined in S. K. Stevens, *American Expansion in Hawaii, 1842–1898* (1945).

The crisis in Cuba and the war with Spain are treated by Julius W. Pratt, *The Expansionists of 1898* (1936), with emphasis on motives; by Walter Millis, *The Martial Spirit* (1931), with coverage of diplomatic and military aspects; and by Frank Freidel, *The Splendid Little War* (1958), with many wonderful photographs and contemporary sketches. R. S. West, Jr., *Admirals of the American Empire* (1948), is useful on naval aspects of the war. The influence of newspapers is examined in M. W. Wilkerson, *Public Opinion and the Spanish-American War* (1932), and J. E. Wisan, *The Cuban Crisis As Reflected in the New York Press, 1895–1898* (1934). Orestes Ferara, *The Last Spanish War* (1937), uses Spanish sources. Penetrating analyses of the theories and motives of American imperialists are found in Richard Hofstadter, *Social Darwinism in American Thought* * (rev. ed., 1955), and by the same author, "Manifest Destiny and the Philippines," in Daniel Aaron, *America in Crisis* (1952), pp. 173–200. G. F. Kennan, *American Diplomacy* * (1951), has sober reflections on this and subsequent American crusades. R. H. Davis, *The Cuban and Porto Rican Campaigns* (1898), and Theodore Roosevelt, *The Rough Riders* (1899), are full of the euphoria and illusions of the war period.

Valuable discussions of the peace negotiations and the aftermath of the war are Tyler Dennett, *John Hay* (1933); F. E. Chadwick, *The Relations of the United States and Spain*, 2 vols. (1909–11); and J. W. Pratt, *America's Colonial Experiment* (1950). England's example and approval are pictured in C. S. Campbell, *Anglo-American Understanding, 1898–1903* (1957), and in L. M. Gelber, *The Rise of Anglo-American Friendship: A Study in World Politics, 1898–1906* (1938). Matthew Josephson, *The President Makers, 1896–1919* (1940), throws light on the election of 1900, and Margaret Leech, *In the Days of McKinley* (1959), illuminates not only the same subject but also many aspects of the war with Spain.

* Available in a paperback edition.

22

Theodore Roosevelt and the Progressive Movement

That which strikes the visitor to America today," a friendly English observer wrote soon after the turn of the century, "is its prodigious material development." Industry was growing more swiftly than ever before. Cities spread, wealth increased, and so did "the stress and rush of life." Yet the United States, as another Englishman had noted, was still a "land of stark, staring, and stimulating inconsistency." While technology advanced, rural ways of life and habits of mind persisted. Americans had yet to accommodate to the social and cultural changes stimulated by industrial and urban growth. They had yet to adjust their laws and their techniques of government to an age of large and complex private organizations. They had yet to recognize the international responsibilities of their national power. They had yet to fulfill their national promise of individual dignity, liberty, and decency for all men.

The unprecedented productivity of the economy made comfort potentially available to all Americans. This possibility in turn highlighted the striking contrasts between the few and the many, the white-skinned and the dark, the urban and the rural—the striking contrast between national aspiration and national achievement. Out of an awareness of that contrast, out of the tensions of material development, out of a consciousness of national mission, there emerged the efforts at adjustment and reform that constituted the progressive movement, a striving by men of good will to understand and improve their prosperous society.

A Land of Growth and Contrasts

National Wealth and the Business Elite During the first decade of the twentieth century the number of people in the United States, their average age, and their average per capita wealth and income all increased. This growth gave confidence to most members of a generation that tended to measure progress in terms of plenty.

There were almost seventy-six million Americans in 1900, almost ninety-two million in 1910. Advances in medicine and public health, resulting in a declining death rate, accounted for most of this increase, which was accompanied by a continuing movement of people within the United States. In the West the rate of growth was highest—along the Pacific slope, more than 73 per cent. But growth occurred everywhere, especially in the cities, where it proceeded three times as fast as in rural areas. The cities, in the pattern of the past (see p. 445), absorbed almost all of the three million immigrants who came largely from eastern and southern Europe. Usually swarthy and unlettered, ordinarily Catholics or Jews, these newcomers differentiated the cities further and further from the patterns of life which rural America remembered and

Population 1900

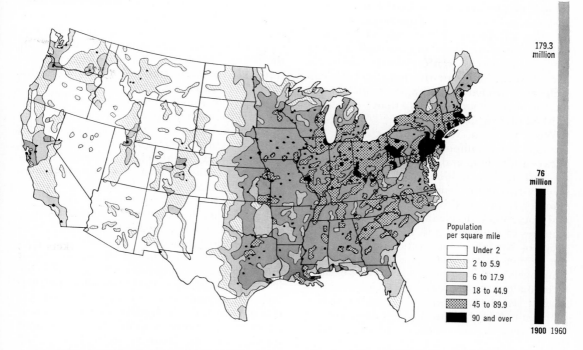

Population per square mile

☐	Under 2
▨	2 to 5.9
▨	6 to 17.9
▨	18 to 44.9
▨	45 to 89.9
■	90 and over

179.3 million

76 million

1900 1960

revered. As the cities increased in number and size, they and their new suburbs transformed the neighboring countrysides.

Moreover, the nation, spurred by the pace of private investment, was recovering from the depression of the nineties. During the first decade of the century, capital investment more than doubled and the total value of the products of industry rose over 76 per cent. By a larger margin than ever before the average per capita income of Americans led that of all other nations. But all groups did not share equally in national wealth. Though unemployment became negligible, the average real income of wage-earners was falling, partly because prices rose faster than wages, partly because an increasing percentage of business profits was going to investors.

Those who were already rich were at once the agents and the beneficiaries of the process of industrial expansion and consolidation which followed the patterns of the 1880's and 1890's. Corporate mergers and reorganizations gave a dominant influence to a few huge combinations in each of many industries—among others, railroading, iron and steel and

copper, meat-packing, milling, tobacco, and petroleum. By 1909, 1 per cent of all the business firms in the nation produced 44 per cent of all its manufactured goods. The consolidators had become the richest and in some ways the most powerful men in the United States. They guided the process of investment. They controlled the boards of directors of the great American banks and industries, and thus through their agents guided the policies of big business, which dominated the country. Its startling growth and burgeoning product seemed to them to confirm their own wisdom and their optimism about the economic future of the United States. They were proud of their accomplishment, and not without cause, for it was impressive to behold.

The "Leaden-Eyed" The magnificence of American wealth and its products contrasted sharply with the sorry lot of the American poor whom society, as the poet Vachel Lindsay put it, had made "oxlike, limp, and leaden-eyed." In 1910 the nonagricultural laboring force consisted of more than thirty million men and eight million women, most of whom worked too long, earned too little, and lived meanly. While the richest 1 per cent owned 47 per cent of the national property and received 15 per cent of the annual national product, a large part of the industrial population, between one-third and one-half, lived in poverty. Their children ordinarily left school to find work—only one-third of the American children enrolled in primary schools completed their courses; less than one-tenth finished high school.

Work for men, women, and children was arduous. Four million laborers were on the job between fifty-four and sixty hours each week; at least half a million, between sixty and seventy-two hours. Industrial accidents were common and conditions of work unhealthy and sometimes despicable, as in the textile factories of the South and the garment sweatshops of New York and other cities. Usually the worker had to suffer his disasters alone. Employers' liability laws, where they existed, were inadequate; there was no social insurance against accident, illness, old age, or unemployment. And the slums, where most workers lived, were as bad as they had been in the 1890's.

Skilled laborers fared better. The crafts-union movement, well launched in the nineties, made significant gains during the early years of the twentieth century. Membership in the affiliates of the American Federation of Labor rose from 548,000 in 1900 to 1,676,000 in 1904 and, in the face of strong resistance from employers, to about 2,000,000 by 1914. These unions and the railroad brotherhoods continued to strive for the objectives which Samuel Gompers and their other leaders had defined earlier. Especially in the building and metals trades, they were able to win from management agreements providing for collective bargaining, higher wages, shorter hours, and safer conditions of work.

The crafts unions were effective, intelligent, but in some respects selfish, agencies of change. Though they excited opposition from business managers not yet prepared to grant labor any voice in industrial decisions, they had no quarrel with the concentration of industrial power. Indeed their leaders recognized that labor had benefited from the stability produced by the restriction of competition. The American Federation of Labor did, however,

demand the right to organize workers into national trades unions, consolidations that would parallel the consolidations of capital. In order to organize, labor needed to be unshackled from state and federal prohibitions on the strike and the boycott, and needed, too, state and federal protection from antiunion devices. The unions welcomed legislation setting standards of safety and employers' liability, but otherwise they preferred to rely on their own power, rather than on the authority of the state, to reach their goals. So it was that Gompers and his associates persisted in opposing legislation on wages and hours, matters that they intended to settle through collective bargaining.

Bargaining, however, even when possible, assisted only union members, and the crafts unions were generally unconcerned with organizing the unskilled bulk of the labor force. Indeed Gompers, along with other labor leaders, looked down on the unskilled, particularly the immigrants (though he himself was one of them). Crafts leaders feared that management would hire unskilled and unorganized immigrants and Negroes to replace skilled workers (though in fact skilled workers were competing not with the unskilled, but with an advancing technology and mechanization). This fear doubtless intensified prejudices against Asians, Negroes, and southern and eastern Europeans—prejudices that fed growing sentiments for the restriction of immigration and for racial segregation. Organized labor condoned Jim Crow and sparked the agitation that led in 1902 to the permanent exclusion from the United States of Chinese immigrants, and in 1907 to the effective exclusion of Japanese.

In short, the unions did no more than management or landlords to help the majority of workers. Within that majority were numbered the American Negroes, of whom almost 90 per cent still lived in the South, but more and more in the cities there. In 1910 almost a third of all Negroes were still illiterate; all were victimized by the inferior facilities for schooling, housing, traveling, and working which segregation had imposed upon them. Worse still, the incidence of lynchings and race riots remained high—a shameful condition dramatized by mass killings in Atlanta in 1906 and by riots in Abraham Lincoln's own Springfield, Illinois, in 1908. As racist concepts spread in the North as well as the South, the American Negro experienced his darkest hours since the Civil War. A few Negro intellectuals, led by W. E. B. DuBois, a Harvard Ph.D., in 1905 organized the Niagara Movement for political and economic equality. With some support from informed whites, it was expanded in 1909 by the formation of the National Association for the Advancement of Colored People. But the NAACP, though a hopeful portent, was some years from becoming an influential instrument of reform.

In both North and South, conscientious middle-class men and women, long engaged in sporadic battles for political reform, tended to blame the immigrants and the Negroes for the shameful conditions that still characterized urban government (see p. 450). Yet the candidate for a reform administration needed the votes of the poor, as did the farmer or small businessman who wanted to limit the privileges of the rich and powerful. The continuing struggle for political reform and for restrictions on wealth forced the polite to learn more about the unfortunate. With that learning there came a larger understanding, a growing interest, whetted by compassion, in improving the lives of those whom machine politics, in its own way, exploited.

Politics had not created the glaring inequities in American life, but politics did reflect and sustain them. Politics might also erase them, and during the first decade of the twentieth century there occurred a flowering of remedial political ideas, and of remedial social ideas which politics could implement. The thoughtless and extravagant behavior of the very people who profited most from American wealth and productivity was generating a pervasive, corrective discontent.

Protest and Reform

Agrarian Demands   The new century brought unparalleled prosperity to American farmers. As domestic and world markets revived, the prices of farm products and the value of farm land just about doubled within a decade. And yet the farmer was still suspicious of finance and bankers, of industry and middlemen, of cities and foreigners. But prosperity tempered farmers' hostilities, softened their rhetoric, turned their energies from outright attack to flanking maneuvers by which they sought to procure for themselves a larger share of urban culture and comforts and of the business profits of agriculture.

Farm organizations and farm leaders continued to press for political reforms designed to give voters a stronger and more direct voice in government. These reforms, they hoped, would help them obtain public policies that would aid agriculture—better roads and marketing facilities, cheaper credit, technical advice on planting and cultivation, more and cheaper electric power, assistance to cooperatives, lower taxes on land, larger appropriations for rural schools, tariff adjustments that would facilitate sales abroad. These practicable goals, some of which entailed special privileges for farmers, challenged the special privileges and the superior power which big business had long enjoyed. Though far from altruistic, the farmers were lending their voice to the cause of reform.

In Washington their spokesmen continued to urge the creation of agencies to monitor the growth and the practices of the great consolidations. Perpetuating the agrarian bias against monopoly, representatives of farming states and communities also argued that industrial power should be splintered by enforcing the languishing antitrust laws. Many farm leaders believed that control should extend not only to the prices farmers paid for transportation or received for their crops, but also to the treatment accorded to labor. Thus the objectives of farm politics sometimes merged with the objectives of urban reformers.

Art and Literature of Protest   Those objectives took shape as artists, journalists, and social workers exposed the conditions of filth and misery which violated the ideals of middle-class Americans. Realistic literature and art, candid and conscientious journalism, reached the hearts of ladies and gentlemen of good will and helped enlist them in the causes of reform.

Theodore Dreiser, an immigrant's son schooled in poverty, used his powerful novels to describe the barren life of the poor "as simply and effectively as the English language will permit." His *Sister Carrie* (1901), *Jennie*

Theodore Dreiser: Protest and despair.

as he had, in "the unending limbo of toil." His fellow Socialist and novelist, Upton Sinclair, writing *The Jungle* (1906) in a similar vein, showed how those who labored in the crooked and poisonous world of the Chicago packing houses "hated their work . . . the bosses . . . the owners . . . the whole place, the whole neighborhood." The poet Carl Sandburg, remarking the waste that appalled so many writers less able than he, railed at the stockyards and at "Pittsburgh, Youngstown, Gary—they made their steel with men."

Realistic painters, representatives of the "ash-can school," produced canvases which one of their number, John Sloan, called "unconsciously social conscious." Sloan, Robert Henri, William Glackens, George Luke, and others, experimenting with new brush techniques and new relationships of form, found compelling subject matter and communicative feeling in dirty alleys, dank saloons, and squalid tenements—"chapters out of life" which they interpreted with beauty that expressed the sorrow and injustice of an experience previously unrecorded in fashionable galleries.

The art of men like Sloan, Sandburg, and Dreiser, for whom social criticism was often a secondary purpose, supplemented and sharpened the message of outraged authors of a deliberate literature of exposure. Social workers, sociologists, and economists recited the facts of poverty in the magazine *Charities and the Commons*, in reports like *The Tenement House Problem* (1903), in books like Robert Hunter's *Poverty* (1904), Father John A. Ryan's *A Living Wage* (1906), John Spargo's *The Bitter Cry of the Children* (1906), Walter Rauschenbusch's *Christianity and the Social Crisis* (1907), and Frances Kellor's *Out of Work* (1915). These documents demonstrated that between half and two-thirds of all working-class families had incomes too small to buy food, shelter, and clothing—incomes that left nothing for recreation or education, little even for union dues or church contributions. No thoughtful student of the facts could any longer believe that poverty was a function of sloth or moral turpitude; clearly there was something wrong with a society that permitted so much misery while it pretended to a Christian ethic and a generous standard of living.

Gerhardt (1911), *The Financier* (1912), and *The Titan* (1914) revealed the human tragedy of inadequate wages, of insecure, hopeless, mechanical existence. Most of Dreiser's characters, driven by greed or sex to bestial violence, tried to fight their way into more splendid circumstances, but he made it poignantly clear how great were the odds against them, how cruel the cost of success, how sorry the lot of those success left behind. Frank Norris, a lesser talent than Dreiser, made his *The Octopus* (1901) a vehicle for condemning the inhumane policies of the Southern Pacific Railroad. In spite of the evils he recounted, he professed a faith that "all things . . . work together for good," but he continued his indictment of wealth in *The Pit* (1903). Jack London, a Socialist, was optimistic only about the ultimate triumph of those who had lived,

Tragedy confirmed this lesson. In 1911 a fire at the Triangle Waist Company in New York resulted in the death of 146 employees, mostly girls, who could not escape from the building where management had been as stingy about safety as about wages (four or five dollars for a seventy-hour week). This episode shook public opinion and precipitated official investigations. These led ultimately to new factory laws and immediately to broader support of organizations already advocating legislation to regulate wages, hours, and conditions of work, especially for women and children.

But humanitarian striving, effective though it was, influenced fewer Americans than did the hortatory, often sensational, journalism of exposure. *McClure's* set the pace for the inexpensive, middle-class magazines. It published Ida M. Tarbell's devastating account of the business methods of the Standard Oil Company, Lincoln Steffens' exposés of the role of respectable citizens as well as ward politicians in the corrupt government of a dozen cities and states, Burton J. Hendrick's disclosures of the fraudulent practices of various insurance companies, and Ray Stannard Baker's indictments of railroad mismanagement, labor-baiting in Colorado, and race discrimination in the South. Though other "muckrakers" (the phrase was Theodore Roosevelt's) sometimes enlivened their work with willful exaggerations, they had no need to distort. The bare facts stirred the awakening conscience of middle-class Americans into indignation over the high-handed conduct and ruthless ethic of the powerful. Disenchantment with the mighty, like compassion for the poor, swelled the ranks of reform.

Protests of the Intellectuals Meanwhile American intellectuals were formulating the attitudes and techniques on which reform was to rely. These new attitudes, taken together, suggested the need for skepticism about rigid, formal systems of thought. They suggested also the importance of rigorous, dispassionate inquiry as a foundation for knowledge, and of constant testing of hypotheses and modification of them on the basis of experience. These principles, derived from the methods of science, were expected to yield ideas for social action. Indeed for the innovative proponents of the developing philosophy of pragmatism, the value of any idea depended on its utility for the thinker and his society.

Among the influential intellectuals of the early century, none better stated the case for enlightened skepticism than did Justice Oliver Wendell Holmes, Jr., who recognized that the prejudices of judges often determined their interpretations of the law. Explaining the divergences between law and ethics, Holmes questioned the propensity of courts to upset the decisions of popularly elected legislatures. Though he understood the fallibility of the majority, he preached judicial restraint, for he understood also the judiciary's fallibility and its tendency to artificiality and arrogance.

The artificiality and formalism of prevalent theories of social Darwinism invited the attack of William James and John Dewey, the fathers of American pragmatism. A psychologist as well as a philosopher, James emphasized the vagaries and the resilience of the mind, and warned against imprisoning intellectual creativity within arbitrary or mechanistic systems. For him the truth of an idea or an action lay in its consequences, as it did also for Dewey, who conceived of philosophy as an instrument for guiding action, an instrument he himself used in advocating experimentation in education and government. Tolerance and freedom of belief and of expression, Dewey noted, were essential if ideas were to enjoy a competitive chance to prove their merit.

In a similar spirit Charles Beard doubted the ability of scholars to find final truths in history, and mercilessly attacked the partial truths that clothed with rectitude the motives of the Founding Fathers. Though Beard himself misread their purpose, his *An Economic Interpretation of the Constitution* (1913) weakened forever the traditional approach to American history.

Thorstein Veblen continued to strip away the façade of contemporary institutions as he had in the nineties. His *The Theory of Business Enterprise* (1904) explained the cultural and economic importance of the machine process, and his *The Instinct of Workmanship* (1914) showed that wasteful and destructive monopolistic practices frustrated man's basic drive to create. Veblen's uncompromising analyses "fluttered the dovecotes of the East," but they contained insights from which reformers, economists, and sociologists were then and later to borrow freely and with reward.

Other less angry and less probing students of contemporary economic institutions directed attention to reform. The writings of John R. Commons on labor, Jeremiah W. Jenks on industry, and William Z. Ripley on railroads were characteristic of moderate, but perceptively critical, scholarship. These experts, often counselors to state and federal regulatory or investigatory commissions, understood that business managers were not ordinarily bad men, but that they were too often timid or limited men, lacking in power and imagination. With Ripley, the economists Henry C. Adams, Richard T. Ely, and Simon Patten viewed man not as the creature of deterministic forces but as the maker of beneficent change. They urged that the principles of management be applied to government, and that the state be empowered to solve public problems which business could not.

All in all, American intellectuals were growing more and more skeptical about their culture and society, and more and more confident in the ability of free, informed, alert minds to conceive and to achieve a better world. Their doubts, their faith, and their impatience for change accorded with the restlessness of a self-critical era and animated the diverse social thrusts which constituted the progressive movement.

Progressivism in the Cities and the States
Democratic government had failed most blatantly in American cities. Now municipal reform organizations, many of them founded in the nineties, succeeded gradually in winning home-rule charters and permission to regulate franchises or to provide for public ownership of vital services. The experiments of Galveston, Texas, with a commission form of government, and of Staunton, Virginia, with a city-manager, demonstrated how efficient these substitutes for an aldermanic system could be. Over a hundred cities had copied them by 1910. The form of government, however, was less important than its spirit, which in city after city drew inspiration from the examples set by mayors like Hazen Pingree of Detroit and Samuel "Golden Rule" Jones of Toledo.

The work of these men and others like them impinged continually on state government,

partly because urban reform could not proceed without improvements in state laws. A wave of reform in the agricultural Middle West began in Wisconsin with the election of Robert M. La Follette as governor in 1900. "Battle Bob," who set precedents for the entire region, had tried for years to overcome the regular Republican machine. A loyal party man, he built his own faction of those who shared his rural democracy. Before he became United States senator in 1906, La Follette made his administration a model of honesty and efficiency, established a fruitful liaison between the government and the state university whose distinguished faculty included many valuable advisers on public policy, and overcame the opposition of the Old Guard in the legislature. At the governor's urging, Wisconsin passed laws providing for a direct primary, civil service, restrictions on lobbying, conservation, effective control of railroads and banks, higher taxes on all corporations (previously under-taxed), and the first state income tax. Wisconsin had become, as Theodore Roosevelt later said, "the laboratory of democracy."

As in Wisconsin, progressive government also drew heavily on rural support in Iowa, Minnesota, the Dakotas, Oregon, Arkansas, Mississippi, Georgia, and South Carolina. Progressive administrations limited the privileges of corporations, especially railroads, and put into effect sundry devices of popular democracy—the direct primary, the initiative and referendum, penalties for corrupt political practices, frequently women's suffrage, sometimes machinery to instruct legislators on whom to elect as United States senator.

Progressivism won similar victories in industrial states, though here the impetus for reform came from the middle class of cities and suburbs. In New Jersey the "New Idea" arose among prosperous suburbanites who were fighting to prevent valuable new rapid-transit and other franchises from falling into exploitative hands, to empower a state commission to regulate commutation fares, to extract taxes from corporations (instead of from real estate alone) to defray the costs of public schooling. Objectives like these, along with the characteristic middle-class hostility toward machine politics, brought the "New Idea" into alliance with the reform mayor of Jersey City. In 1904

"The System": Wisconsin

But there was the good State of Wisconsin ruled by a handful of men who had destroyed every vestige of democracy in the commonwealth. They settled in private conference practically all nominations for important offices, controlled conventions, dictated legislation, and had even sought to lay corrupt hands on the courts of justice....

The pass abuse had grown to extraordinary proportions in Wisconsin, and the power to give passes, franks on telegraph and telephone lines, free passage on Pullman cars, and free transportation by express companies had become a great asset of the machine politicians....

Clubs were formed in Madison where members of the legislature could be drawn together in a social way and cleverly led into intimate associations with the corporation men who swarmed the capital. In one of the principal hotels a regular poker game was maintained where members who could not be reached in any other way, could win, very easily, quite large sums of money. In that way bribes were disguised.... It was notorious that lewd women were an accessory to the lobby organization. Members who could not be reached in any other way were advised that they could receive good positions with railroad corporations after the legislative session was over.

From Robert M. La Follette, *La Follette's Autobiography*, 1913.

the resulting coalition of independent Republicans began to convert New Jersey into the progressive community that in 1910 elected the Democrat Woodrow Wilson as governor, and that during his administration completed, under bipartisan auspices, the program of the "New Idea."

New York, New Hampshire, Massachusetts, Michigan, California, and to a lesser degree Ohio, all states with important industrial centers, had political experiences not unlike New Jersey's, though none elected a governor who was so quickly and dramatically successful as Wilson. Reform in these and other industrial and semi-industrial states led to major improvements for the working force, though labor itself was rarely of a progressive temperament. Before 1915, twenty-five states passed employers' liability laws; five limited the use of injunctions preventing strikes or boycotts; nine passed minimum-wage laws for women; twenty

granted pensions to indigent widows with children; other restricted hours and conditions of work.

The Progressive Attitudes and Motives

The strivings of the progressives revealed a great deal about the progressives themselves—their faith in pure democracy, their hostility to large aggregations of private power, their confidence in public regulatory agencies, their humanitarian temper. And yet they were a diverse group, and their movement was a concatenation of similar but independent movements. In rural areas, it emerged from social responses like those that had motivated Populism; it borrowed much from Populism, and it retained an agrarian flavor modified by time, experience, and prosperity. In the cities, however, progressivism was a political expression of the anxieties and attitudes of the liberal intellectuals and social critics of the nineties and the early century. The middle-class men who absorbed those attitudes and formed the ranks of reform were both good-hearted and worried. They partook of the long national heritage of humanitarian democracy, but where they had long been inactive in

"The System": Pittsburgh

Boss Magee's idea was not to corrupt the city government, but to be it; not to hire votes in councils, but to own councilmen; and so, having seized control of his organization, he nominated cheap or dependent men for the select and common councils. Relatives and friends were his first recourse, then came bartenders, saloon-keepers, liquor dealers, and others ... who were ... dependent ... upon the maladministration of law....

Business men came almost as cheap as politicians, and they came also at the city's expense.... The manufacturers and the merchants were kept well in hand by many little municipal grants and privileges, such as switches, wharf rights, and street and alley vacations.... A foundry occupies a block, spreads to the next block, and wants the street between....

As for the railroads, they did not have to be bought or driven in; they came, and promptly, too. The Pennsylvania appeared early, just behind Magee, who handled their passes and looked out for their interest in councils and afterwards at the State Legislature.

From Lincoln Steffens, *The Shame of the Cities*, 1904.

public matters, they now mobilized, partly because they had gained a better understanding of the urgency of social reform, partly because they saw that change was needed if they were to preserve the things they valued. The unrest of the nineties had been a searing experience. Violence had trembled below the surface of society, threatening the comfortable middle-class world. And with prosperity returned and violence abating, middle-class men hastened to remove the inequities that had bred disquiet.

Professional men, white-collar men, and small businessmen, moreover, felt their prestige and their well-being threatened by the advancing power of big business, big city machines, and—more rarely—big labor. They had to organize to protect themselves and their standing, and to monitor their giant rivals. Mostly native Americans, they resented the immigrant or second-generation political boss. Mostly men of modest means and often men of old family, they resented the purchased prestige and paraded vulgarity of the newly rich. Though some of them were bureaucrats, successful servants of big business and finance who realized that they had to discipline the behavior of their corporations if they were to survive criticism, more of them were the victims of bigness and consequently anxious to fragment as well as to regulate it. Where labor unions were strong economically and politically, as in California, they too became targets for the attack on power. But more often the attack was pointed toward corporations that dealt directly with many customers—monopolies or near-monopolies selling transportation, utilities, and food—or that were saddled (sometimes unjustly) with especially bad reputations.

The urban progressives were middle-class men, but not all—or even most—middle-class men were progressives. Those who were, were the most socially conscious, perhaps the most anxious, but also, by and large, the younger men, educated, ambitious, and adventurous. They drew much of their inspiration from the most dynamic national exponent of their spirit and purpose, President Theodore Roosevelt. Without Roosevelt, progressivism would doubtless have happened, but it could not have been quite what it became. Nor would it have been nearly so much fun.

The Republican Roosevelt

In September 1901 McKinley died, the third President to be assassinated in less than forty years. His successor, Theodore Roosevelt, whom Mark Hanna had called "that damned cowboy," had set his political course for the White House long before McKinley's death gave him the prize ahead of schedule. "It is," wrote Roosevelt, "a dreadful thing to come into the Presidency this way; but it would be a far worse thing to be morbid about it." The gift of the gods to Roosevelt—at forty-two the youngest chief executive in history—was joy in life, and for eight exciting years he brought that joy to his office.

The son of patrician parents, a graduate of Harvard, an accomplished ornithologist and an enthusiastic historian, Roosevelt chose early in life to make politics his career, for he wanted to rule—and he chose to work not as an independent but as a loyal Republican, for he wanted to win. He served successfully, with occasional time out as a rancher in the Dakotas, as an assemblyman in New York, a United States Civil Service commissioner, a New York City police commissioner, Assistant Secretary of the Navy, colonel of the celebrated Rough Riders, and governor of New York. Senator Thomas C. Platt, the long-time boss of the state Republicans, developed serious apprehensions about Roosevelt's successful ventures in reform and managed in 1900 to get him out of New York by arranging his nomination for Vice-President, a position Roosevelt accepted with somewhat resigned grace but with characteristic vigor.

Roosevelt and the Presidency As a campaigner Roosevelt displayed the qualities which were to give him during his presidency an enormous influence with the people. As had no President since Jackson, he captured their imagination, indeed their adulation. To the Americans who acclaimed him he was many wonderful things—policeman, cowboy, hero in arms, battler for the everlasting right. He was that familiar squeaky voice, that toothy grin, that animal energy, that Harvard accent exhorting the worthy to reform. Roosevelt was also a learned man, at home with ideas, receptive to the advice of the men of ideas whom he

T. R. on the Rights of Labor

The gravely significant attitude toward the law and its administration recently adopted by certain heads of great corporations renders it desirable that there should be additional legislation as regards certain of the relations between labor and capital....

It is to be observed that an employers' liability law does not really mean mulcting employers in damages. It merely throws upon the employer the burden of accident insurance against injuries which are sure to occur. It requires him either to bear or to distribute through insurance the loss which can readily be borne when distributed, but which, if undistributed, bears with frightful hardship upon the unfortunate victim of accident....

It is all wrong to use the injunction to prevent the entirely proper and legitimate actions of labor organizations in their struggle for industrial betterment.... It is futile to concede, as we all do, the right and the necessity of organized effort on the part of wage-earners and yet by injunctive process to forbid peaceable action to accomplish the lawful objects for which they are organized.

From Theodore Roosevelt, Special Message to Congress, 1908.

---

brought to Washington. As one Englishman put it, he was more remarkable than anything in the United States, except perhaps Niagara Falls.

Roosevelt was also a skilled politician and an imaginative statesman who made the presidency a great office and used it boldly. He conceived of the President as "a steward of the people bound actively and affirmatively to do all he could for the people"; he set out therefore as President to define the great national problems of his time, to propose for each a practicable solution, to win people and Congress to his proposals, and to infuse the executive department with his own dedication to efficient enforcement of the laws.

Roosevelt summoned to federal service a remarkable group of advisers and subordinates, one of the ablest sets of public servants that had ever been seen in any country. The President's example and support inspired them; his reorganizations of federal agencies gave scope to their talents. They included, among others, Elihu Root, McKinley's Secretary of War whom Roosevelt continued in that office and later made Secretary of State; William Howard

Taft, Root's successor in the War Department; Chief Forester Gifford Pinchot and Secretary of the Interior James R. Garfield, eminent conservationists; United States District Attorney Henry L. Stimson, who was to serve in various capacities under five other Presidents; Interstate Commerce Commissioners Charles Prouty and Franklin K. Lane; and Attorney General William H. Moody, whom Roosevelt later appointed Associate Justice of the Supreme Court, an office he conferred also on Oliver Wendell Holmes, Jr.

In filling dozens of lesser federal offices, Roosevelt assured his own control of his party. Winning over some of the adherents of Mark Hanna, replacing others, he manipulated patronage so deftly that the old senator had lost his control of Republican affairs months before he died in February 1904. By that time Roosevelt could count on the support of every important state delegation to the forthcoming national convention. He could rely, too, on

---

T. R. on Preparedness

It is idle to assume, and from the standpoint of national interest and honor it is mischievous folly for any statesman to assume, that this world has yet reached the stage, or has come within measurable distance of the stage, when a proud nation, jealous of its honor and conscious of its great mission in the world can be content to rely for peace upon the forbearance of other powers.... Events still fresh in the mind of every thinking man show that neither arbitration nor any other device can as yet be invoked to prevent the gravest and most terrible wrongdoing to peoples who are either few in numbers, or who, if numerous, have lost the first and most important of national virtues—the capacity for self-defense....

I can not recommend to your notice measures for the fulfillment of our duties to the rest of the world without pressing upon you the necessity of placing ourselves in a condition of complete defense.... There is a rank due to the United States among nations which will be withheld, if not absolutely lost, by the reputation of weakness. If we desire to avoid insult, we must be able to repel it; if we desire to secure peace, one of the most powerful instruments of our rising prosperity, it must be known that we are at all times ready for war.

From Theodore Roosevelt, Special Message to Congress, 1908.

T. R. campaigning:
Steward of the people.

the influential party leaders, for he had satisfied the most urgent demands of the liberal wing without offending or frightening the stand-patters.

Roosevelt and the Trusts Roosevelt, always a gradualist, fashioned a circumspect domestic program which he dressed in a pungent rhetoric. At the outset of his administration he indicated that he would accept the advice of the Old Guard in the Senate on tariff and monetary policies, matters about which they were most sensitive. He was himself much more worried about the problems of industrial consolidation. The "absolutely vital question," Roosevelt believed, "was whether the government had power to control" the trusts. The Supreme Court's decision in the E. C. Knight case (1895) suggested that it did not (see p. 430). Seeking a modification of that interpretation, Roosevelt in 1902 ordered his

Attorney General, Philander C. Knox, to bring suit for violation of the Sherman Act against the Northern Securities Company.

The President had chosen his target carefully. The Northern Securities Company was a mammoth holding company for the Northern Pacific, the Great Northern, and the Chicago, Burlington, and Quincy railroads. A battle for the stock of the Northern Pacific, key to control of transportation in the Northwest, had led in 1901 to panic on Wall Street. The antagonists made peace by creating the Northern Securities Company for the immediate purpose of quieting the market and for the ultimate purpose of monopolizing the railroads of a rapidly growing region. Those who had fought and then made their profitable peace were titans of finance: J. P. Morgan and Company, the Rockefeller interests, James J. Hill, and E. H. Harriman. Rightly or wrongly, their names had become symbols of unbridled power. The panic they had brought on, a calamity for many brokers, drew attention to their ruthless speculation; the holding company they formed, in which 30 per cent of the stock was water, cast a long shadow of fear over the Northwest, where farmers, suspicious as ever of monopolies, expected freight rates to soar.

While several states initiated legal action against the holding company, Roosevelt had Knox begin his preparations in secret. Announcement of the federal government's suit stunned Wall Street. Morgan, with the arrogance of an independent sovereign, tried in vain to have his lawyer settle things with the Attorney General. His failure, like Roosevelt's attack, symbolized a transfer of power from lower New York to Washington, where it belonged. In 1903 a federal court ordered the dissolution of the Northern Securities Company, a decision the Supreme Court sustained the next year. Heartened by the outcome, most Americans agreed with Roosevelt that it was "impossible to overestimate the importance" of the case.

The government proceeded against forty-four more corporations during Roosevelt's term in office. In 1902 action began against the "beef trust," so unpopular with sellers of livestock and buyers of meat; equally unpopular were four defendants in cases started in 1906 and 1907, the American Tobacco Company, the Du Pont Corporation, the New Haven Railroad, and the Standard Oil Company.

Roosevelt's revival of the Sherman Act won him a reputation as a "trust-buster," but he never believed that the fragmentation of industry could solve the nation's problems. He had, he felt, to establish the authority of the federal executive to use the antitrust law in cases of monopoly or flagrant misbehavior. Trust-busting, however, was in his view an ultimate weapon, inappropriate in the case of most enterprises which had legitimately reduced the cost of production and won for the nation the industrial leadership of the world. The growth of industry was, he argued, natural, unavoidable, and beneficial. Breaking up corporations whose only offense was size would be impossible unless the government also abolished steam, electricity, large cities, indeed all modern conditions. The need was for continuous, informed, and expert regulation, which only the federal government could properly undertake.

The Square Deal   In December 1901 Roosevelt made his first, modest recommendations to Congress for creating the efficient system of control on which, he believed, the orderly development of industrial life depended. He asked for an act to expedite antitrust prosecutions, which Congress passed in 1903. Without opposition it then also enacted his proposal for forbidding the granting or receiving of rebates, a practice that powerful shippers had forced upon unwilling railroads. There was, however, serious congressional resistance to Roosevelt's major objective, the creation of a new Department of Commerce and Labor with a Bureau of Corporations empowered to gather and release information about industry. Such a bureau was essential if the government was to learn what businesses to regulate, and how. Precisely on that account, conservative Republican senators blocked Roosevelt's bill. The President saved it by announcing that John D. Rockefeller was secretly organizing the opposition to it. The culprit was actually one of Rockefeller's subordinates, but the purport of Roosevelt's charge was accurate, and the consequent public clamor persuaded both houses of Congress quickly to pass the controversial law.

The act gave Cabinet status to the Bureau of Labor, primarily a fact-finding agency that had demonstrated its usefulness to Roosevelt and to workingmen by its fair and accurate reporting during the strike of anthracite coal miners that began in May 1902 and lasted until October. The managers of the Eastern coal-carrying railroads that owned most of the mines would not negotiate with the union, the United Mine Workers, which was demanding recognition, an eight-hour day, and a 10 to 20 per cent increase in pay. Labor's orderly conduct and willingness to arbitrate won growing public approval, particularly after the intransigent owners, speaking through George F. Baer, the president of the Reading Railroad, insisted that "God in his Infinite Wisdom has given control of the property interests" to the directors of large corporations. This attitude invited public antagonism at a time when fuel was short and the days were growing chilly.

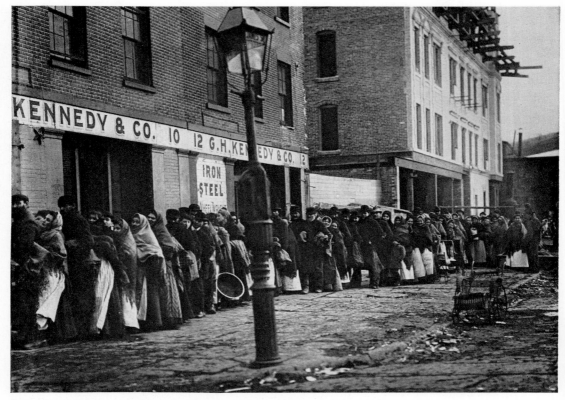

Queue for coal, autumn 1902.

Reflecting a growing sentiment, most of the press called for federal intervention.

Roosevelt, sympathetic with the workers and worried about the coal shortage, had hesitated to enter the dispute only because his advisers felt that he lacked the legal authority. Early in October he summoned the mine operators and John Mitchell, the union chief, to the White House. Mitchell again offered to submit to arbitration but the owners remained obdurate. Indeed, they demanded that the President issue an injunction and, if necessary, use the army to end the strike. Their "arrogant stupidity" provoked Roosevelt instead to let them know indirectly that he was prepared to use troops to dispossess them and produce coal. With this kind of intervention in the offing, Mark Hanna, Elihu Root, and other conservative men who were already working for peace quickened their efforts, enlisted the help of J. P. Morgan himself, and on October 13

persuaded the mine-owners to accept a compromise settlement. By its terms the miners resumed work and a commission appointed by the President arbitrated the questions at issue. In March the commission awarded labor a 10 per cent raise, a reduction in working hours to nine and in some cases eight per day, but not recognition of the union. The owners in return received a welcome invitation to raise coal prices 10 per cent.

Roosevelt's actions stamped him as a friend of labor. He was the first President to bring both labor and capital to the White House to settle a dispute, the first to get them both to accept the judgment of a commission appointed by the executive, the first to coerce the owners of a crucial industry by threatening to take it over. All this contrasted vividly with the course of the federal government during the Pullman strike (see p. 439).

Roosevelt, however, in other labor episodes

insisted on the open shop for government workers and resisted not only all radical unionism but also the principle of the union shop in industry. He believed, as he put it, in "the right of laboring men to join a union . . . without illegal interference." This was less than Gompers advocated, but it was much more than most businessmen or conservative politicians were yet willing to concede. It was a position characteristic of Roosevelt—advanced but not radical, cautious but not timorous.

His purpose during the coal strike, Roosevelt explained during the campaign of 1904, had been to give both sides a "square deal." The phrase caught on and became a familiar label for his first Administration. He liked the connotation of the phrase, which suggested his "appeal for common sense, courage and common honesty." His intention was to abolish privilege and enlarge individual opportunity. His "natural allies," he said, were "the farmers, small businessmen and upper-class mechanics," middle-class Americans "fundamentally sound, morally, mentally and physically." Like him, they abhorred extremes; like him, they judged in moral terms. They were not radicals or even Populists, but they were fed up with the behavior of the Rockefellers and the Baers. They warmed, therefore, to Roosevelt's fusillades against those he later called the "malefactors of great wealth." They accepted and cheered his image of himself as a champion of fairness.

The Election of 1904 That was the basis of his campaign for re-election. It was the basis, too, for his appointment to office of qualified men from minority groups, Negroes, Catholics, Jews, Americans of Hungarian and German and Irish extraction. His appreciation of the inherent dignity in every man encouraged him to invite to lunch Booker T. Washington, the Negro educator who doubled as an adviser on patronage. There was, to be sure, a happy compatibility between Roosevelt's conscience and the needs of politics, but that did not detract from his conscience, though it manifestly strengthened his campaign. He took no chances. A new pension order, making age alone a sufficient qualification for eligibility, held the GAR to the GOP. The official platform contained standard Republican platitudes about the tariff and prosperity, sops to the Old Guard, as was the lackluster nominee for Vice-President, Senator Charles W. Fairbanks of Indiana. But the real platform was Roosevelt's record, and the real issue was the man.

That made things difficult for the Democrats. As Bryan complained, Roosevelt had captured his banner, perhaps not by intention but nevertheless with effect. The Republicans now marched as the party of reform. Conservative Democrats were delighted to return to the formulas of Grover Cleveland's days, to a platform emphasizing strict construction of the Constitution and a candidate—Judge Alton B. Parker—chosen for his safe views and close ties to New York wealth.

Parker conducted a dull campaign until the vision of impending defeat persuaded him to charge that Roosevelt's campaign manager, George B. Cortelyou, was blackmailing corporations for contributions. Cortelyou, who had been Secretary of Commerce, had indeed had access to the findings of the Bureau of Corporations, but he neither resorted to blackmail nor needed to. Wealthy Republicans, loyal party men in spite of their reservations about Roosevelt, had responded without stint to the usual appeals for funds. Parker's charges reminded the electorate that Roosevelt's campaign was well-endowed, but served otherwise only to provoke from the President an indignant denial. Indeed Roosevelt went further and directed his party treasurer to return any contributions that had come from predatory wealth. The treasurer ignored the order, just as the voters by and large ignored Parker's accusations. Roosevelt could have won without much financial support. In a landslide victory, he received 57.4 per cent of the popular votes (7,628,461) to Parker's 37.6 per cent (5,084,223), and 336 electoral votes to the Democrat's 140. The people had endorsed their steward. And their steward rejoiced in their confidence and in the prospect of a term of his own.

Roosevelt and Reform

The Regulation of Business When Congress convened in December 1904, the progress of reform in Washington and in the states was gathering momentum. Success bred daring, and Roosevelt, President now in his own right, at once took advantage of the mandate he had helped to create. His prime objective was railroad regulation. Decisions of the Supreme Court had stripped the Interstate Commerce Commission of authority over railway rates or rebates, which the roads continued to grant in spite of the government's efforts to enforce the antirebate act of 1903. The only feasible remedy was to give the Commission power to set reasonable and nondiscriminatory rates, and to prevent inequitable practices. Farmers and small businessmen and their representatives were increasingly demanding that remedy. But the railroads, their privileged customers, and the devotees of conservative economic theory opposed federal rate-making, which would for the first time in American history give the national government authority to determine prices, the sacrosanct prerogative of private enterprise.

For Roosevelt, laissez-faire theory was not sacred, but moral corporate behavior was. In 1904 and 1905 he urged Congress to endow the ICC with the power to adjust rates against which shippers had complained. During the long debate that ensued, Roosevelt advanced his purpose skillfully. Concentrating on the railroad issue, he gave up a tentative plan to press for a downward revision of the tariff, which agrarian Republicans as well as Democrats favored. The President had never considered the tariff a vital matter, for in his opinion it was not a moral question. It was, however, an issue that divided his party. So, rather than risk division, he conceded to the Old Guard on tariff reform. At least partly on that account, Joseph G. Cannon, the influential Speaker of the House, supported the President's railroad bill and the House passed it by an overwhelming margin.

Handling the Senate was more difficult. There Nelson Aldrich of Rhode Island, a masterful Republican strategist, delayed a vote while the railroads underwrote a national publicity campaign which Roosevelt answered in a series of vigorous speeches. In 1906 Aldrich outmaneuvered the senators managing the railroad bill, but the President, a dogged and inventive antagonist, ultimately forced Aldrich to endorse the Hepburn Act. It gave the ICC the authority upon complaint from a shipper to set aside existing rates and to prescribe substitutes, subject to court review. This was less than the most vocal critics of the roads had wanted, for they suspected the courts of pro-business bias, but it was just what Roosevelt was after. The act, a major victory for him, was a keystone in his intended system of continuous, expert federal regulation of American industry.

Congress in 1906 passed several notable laws. One was an Employers' Liability Act for the District of Columbia and all common carriers. Another was a pure food and drug bill of which the chief exponent was Dr. Harvey W. Wiley of the Department of Agriculture. For several years this measure, twice approved by the House, had faltered. Now a series of articles by Samuel Hopkins Adams exposed the dangers of patent medicine, aroused public opinion, and speeded the enactment of the legislation. In a similar way, the publication of Upton Sinclair's *The Jungle*, with its description of the scandalous conditions in meat-packing houses, led Roosevelt to order a special investigation. This confirmed Sinclair's findings and precipitated the passage of a federal meat-inspection law.

In 1906 Roosevelt also sent Congress a series of recommendations on which it did not act, including proposals for a law to provide for the physical valuation of railway properties as a basis for establishing rates, for federal control of railway securities, and for the abolition of child labor. Labor problems were much on his mind. The National Association of Manufacturers had won a number of victories in its drive to cripple unions by obtaining injunctions against strikes and boycotts, the unions' most effective weapons. The NAM was also exhorting legislators to oppose all labor legislation. Fighting back, Gompers and his associates submitted to Roosevelt and the Congress a Bill of Grievances voicing their traditional demands, especially for relief from injunctions granted under the Sherman Act. The American Federation of Labor struck politically as well, campaigning in 1906 against congressmen unfriendly to labor, most of whom were Republicans. Caught between his growing sympathy for labor's goals and his partisan loyalties, Roosevelt endorsed all Republican candidates but exhorted them to mend their ways.

New Ideas and the Old Guard   The gulf between the President and the Old Guard widened in 1907 and 1908. They especially differed about conservation. In 1902 Roosevelt, an ardent conservationist, had spurred the passage of the Newlands Act, which set aside a portion of receipts from the sale of public lands for expenditures on dams and reclamation. Pushing on, largely on the advice of Gifford Pinchot, he had withdrawn from private entry valuable coal and mineral lands, oil reserves, and water-power sites. He had proceeded vigorously against cattlemen and lumbermen who were poaching on public preserves. These policies offended the Western barons who had become rich by exploiting the nation's natural resources (see p. 408). In 1907 their representatives attached a rider to an appropriation bill for the Department of Agriculture which prevented the creation of new forest reserves in six Western states without the consent of Congress. Roosevelt had to sign the bill, for the department had to have funds, but before signing he added seventeen million acres to the national reserves. He later vetoed bills that granted water-power sites to private interests but did not provide for federal supervision of water-power development.

In 1908 Roosevelt called a National Conservation Congress, which forty-four governors and hundreds of experts attended. It led to annual meetings of governors and to the creation of state conservation commissions. Congress, more and more hostile, ignored recommendations for river and flood control made by the Inland Waterways Commission, which Roosevelt appointed, and refused to provide funds to publish the report of another of his boards, the Country Life Commission, which advocated federal assistance for rural schools and roads, and for farmers' cooperatives. Yet Roosevelt had succeeded in making the conservation of human and natural resources an issue of the first importance to thousands of Americans. Like him, they were dedicated to preserving the public domain and to mobilizing the intelligence of man to temper the course of nature.

Roosevelt's policies jarred many businessmen who blamed him for the financial panic that occurred in the autumn of 1907 and for the brief depression that preceded and followed it. The basic causes of the slump were beyond his control. Productive facilities had expanded beyond the country's immediate capacity to consume, but the differential was small and would probably have led to no serious trouble if the nation's banking and monetary systems had been stronger and if financiers had not been guilty of speculative excesses. Panic began only after depositors learned that several New York trust companies had failed in an expensive attempt to corner the copper market. As runs began on these and other, sound, banks, some had to close and all had to call in loans from creditors in New York and throughout the country. J. P. Morgan, at his most magnificent in this crisis, supervised a pooling of the funds of the leading Manhattan banks with which to support the threatened institutions. Undoubtedly this action prevented general disaster.

Morgan and his fellows could not have succeeded without assistance from Washington. Their complex maneuvers depended in part on the purchase by the United States Steel Corporation of controlling shares of stock in the Tennessee Coal and Iron Company. That transaction, however, was unthinkable if there was any danger that it might lead immediately to an antitrust suit. So informed, Roosevelt, without making "any binding promise," urged Morgan's associates to proceed. The government had earlier given the banks more important but less dramatic help through the United States Treasury.

Though the panic quickly subsided, it had demonstrated the urgency of financial reform. It was ridiculous for a great nation in a time of crisis to have to fall back on Morgan or any other private banker. And it was vital to relax the general monetary stringency that intensified the crisis. Both the President and his detractors endorsed the action of Congress authorizing a commission, with Nelson Aldrich as chairman, to study and report on monetary and banking policy.

Roosevelt meanwhile had condemned the "speculation, corruption and fraud" that contributed to the panic. His messages to Congress of December 1907 and January 1908 disclosed his zeal for further reform. After repeating many of his earlier recommendations, the President called for federal incorporation and regulation of all interstate business, federal regulation of the stock market, limitation of injunctions against labor, compulsory investigation of labor disputes, extension of the eight-hour law for federal employees, and personal income and inheritance taxes. He went on to castigate the courts for declaring unconstitutional a workmen's compensation law, and to condemn "predatory wealth" for its follies and its unscrupulous opposition to "every measure for honesty in business." An avid foe of socialism, which was then gaining adherents, Roosevelt in private warned that a revolution would break out if rich men and blind judges made the lot of the worker intolerable. Without reform, capitalism could not survive.

The goals Roosevelt defined and the principles he enunciated were the chart and compass of progressives in 1908 and for many years thereafter. He did not invent them, but he recognized their importance, gave them effective expression, put the dignity of his high office at their service, and converted to them the thousands who felt the integrity and the vitality of his person. Before he left the White House, he drew the lines of battle and recruited the legions for reform. All this he did with a faith in the progress that conserves; a belief that power properly inheres in the federal government rather than in any private group; a conviction that the holder of power has an obligation to promote justice and enforce orderly and moral behavior; and a confidence in his own ability to handle power to those ends. Those beliefs and that confidence also guided his foreign policy.

Roosevelt and World Power

National Power and Responsibility
During the first decade of the twentieth century, more and more Americans, including those who considered themselves progressives, subscribed to a new doctrine of manifest destiny (see p. 497). Along with these concepts there grew up other, sounder ideas about the international role of the United States. The writings of Alfred T. Mahan, the experience of the Spanish War, and awareness of the

swelling ambitions and power of Germany and Japan persuaded an influential minority of Americans of the importance of naval preparedness and national defense. Some, like Roosevelt, Root, and Senator Henry Cabot Lodge, also realized that every powerful nation had a stake in world order and an obligation to preserve it, that—in other words—a great country like the United States could not escape international involvement.

Roosevelt as President continually reminded his countrymen of the oneness of the world. Nineteenth-century progress in transportation, communication, and production, he warned, had created situations of potential chaos in which only the availability of power and, when necessary, the application of force could establish a tolerable equilibrium. He therefore preached preparedness to his frequently reluctant countrymen. For Roosevelt, preparedness was not simply militarism. It entailed, too, the preservation and development of natural and human resources. Sharing the Anglo-Saxon bias of his time, Roosevelt urged Americans of old stock to increase their birth rate. But all Americans, regardless of national origin, could, he maintained, contribute to national well-being if they saw to their physical fitness and cultivated clear minds, clean souls, and brave hearts.

High character and the strenuous life were not in themselves enough, for preparedness ultimately involved the size, equipment, and leadership of the military services. The President heartily supported the reform of the outmoded army organization that Secretary of War Root had begun to plan under McKinley. Root set up an Army War College, demanded rigorous tests for the promotion of officers, and in 1902 asked Congress to authorize the creation of a general staff and the incorporation of the state militia into the regular army. Congress hesitated, partly because the national guard and its aggressive lobby, as well as some senior but inflexible regular officers, opposed incorporation of the guard, partly because of the belief, especially among rural Americans, that the militia was a democratic institution and a general staff a "Prussian" and militaristic agency. Roosevelt and Root had to give up their plan for the militia, but Congress approved a modification of the general-staff plan which permitted the modernization of the army to get under way.

Roosevelt also demanded the construction of a modern navy strong enough to protect American interests and to further his "large view" of national obligations. The United States, he realized, could no longer depend on the British fleet for protection. It had to keep pace with the building program of Japan and Germany and with rapid changes in naval technology. His constant prodding caught the public imagination and wore down the opposition of congressmen who favored thrift even at the cost of national strength. Before he left office, the navy's effectiveness had been doubled. Anything less would seriously have impeded the nation's performance in the next war. The navy and the army profited, too, from the enthusiastic recognition the President gave to military service and to dedicated and imaginative commanders. His zeal for discipline and morale led him to discharge without honor the Negro troops who refused to reveal the names of the few soldiers who had shot up the anti-Negro town of Brownsville, Texas, in 1906. This was a hasty decision, which American Negroes resented, but the motives that guided the President were those that on happier occasions brought him to rid the services of incompetent officers and to advance the careers of outstanding men like General Leonard Wood and Commander William S. Sims. The country as well as the services benefited from his actions, as they did from his penetrating discourses on the indispensability of might in the affairs of nations.

A strong nation, in the view of Roosevelt and others who subscribed to the new manifest destiny, had the duty of imposing civilization and justice in the backward territories it ruled. In the Insular cases of 1900 and 1901, the Supreme Court held that inhabitants of the recently acquired American empire were not American citizens and did not have a right to the liberties guaranteed by the Constitution unless Congress expressly conferred them. Except for Hawaii and Alaska, which were destined for statehood, the Court's rulings left the determination of colonial policy to the Roosevelt Administration. It adopted a variety of experiments. The navy administered Guam and Tutuila, where it had coaling stations. Puerto Rico elected its own house of delegates, though its decisions had to be confirmed by a council and executed by a governor appointed in Washington. The American protectorate in Cuba ended in May 1902 with the inauguration of the first government under Cuba's new constitution. The next year, however, a formal treaty between Cuba and the United States provided for American intervention in the event of a foreign threat or domestic disturbance. Insurrection in Cuba in 1906 forced Roosevelt most reluctantly to exercise the right of intervention. As soon as possible, after three years of gentle rule, the Americans withdrew. Earlier, the President had insisted that in return for the rights accorded by the Cuban treaty, the United States had a moral duty to aid the Cuban economy by granting special tariff rates to Cuban sugar, a concession he wrung from protectionist congressmen after a stiff legislative struggle in 1903.

He was unable, in spite of repeated attempts, to obtain tariff concessions for the Philippines. Those islands presented a number of difficult problems. Occasional episodes of cruelty by American army officers during the suppression of the independence movement (see p. 511) had whetted native resentment. It began to abate in 1902 when Congress passed an organic act for the Philippines, Roosevelt abolished the office of military governor, and William Howard Taft, the first civilian governor, proclaimed a general amnesty. A wise and patient proconsul, Taft got along well with the elected assembly and furthered municipal home rule, improvements in public health, civil affairs, education, and transportation. He was successful, too, in delicate negotiations with the Vatican and Catholic friars in the islands for the purchase of lands which the Church claimed but the Filipinos held and deserved to keep. Like Roosevelt and Root, Taft did not believe the Philippines would be ready for independence for many years. Though native patriots and American anti-imperialists remained impatiently committed to that goal, Taft's able and benign administration gradually won the confidence of the islanders, assisted the development of their economy, and helped them prepare for ultimate self-government.

International Interests in the Caribbean

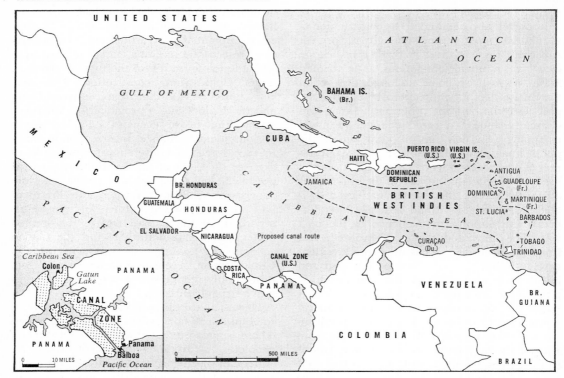

Policing the Hemisphere Roosevelt's foreign policies, like his colonial policies, were derived from his assumption that it was "incumbent on all civilized and orderly powers to insist on the proper policing of the world." This was, of course, a high-handed assumption, which Roosevelt defended when he had to by arguing that only with stability could there be justice. An imperious manner characterized his methods as well as his objectives. As President, he believed, he had to conduct foreign policy himself, for in that field the Congress and "the average American" did not "take the trouble to think carefully or deeply."

Stretching his constitutional authority to its limits, Roosevelt intervened to preserve stability and American hegemony in the Caribbean, where, with Mahan, he felt the United States could not afford a rival. Like the other small states in that area, Venezuela had borrowed money in Europe, which Cipriano Castro, her prodigal dictator—Roosevelt considered him a "villainous little monkey"—lacked either the means or the will to repay. In December 1902 England, Germany, and Italy, demanding payment for their citizens, blockaded Venezuela, and fired on one of her ports. Venezuela asked the United States to arrange arbitration, to which England and Germany agreed. But a German ship again bombarded a port, infuriating the President and many other Americans, and later Germany briefly opposed referring the dispute to arbitration. During the controversy Roosevelt implied to the German ambassador that the United States would insist on that solution. He recalled years later that he threatened if necessary to dispatch a naval squadron under Admiral George Dewey. His memory probably exaggerated his role, but whatever he actually did he certainly was indignant over Germany's conduct.

The best way to keep Europe at home, the President believed, was to keep order in the Caribbean. Yet a selfish conception of order gave Roosevelt a flimsy basis for incontinent behavior in Panama. In December 1901 the Senate ratified the second Hay-Pauncefote Treaty by which England acknowledged the right of the United States alone to build and fortify an isthmian canal, so long an American dream. Such a canal would facilitate inter-coastal shipping and, more important, would make it easier for the navy to move from ocean to ocean. The preferred route had at one time been through Nicaragua, where a sea-level canal could be built, but the commission of experts which Congress had authorized had come to prefer a lock canal through Panama, which would provide the cheapest and shortest route between the coasts of the United States. Accordingly, in June 1902 Congress directed the President to negotiate with Colombia for the acquisition of a strip of land in Panama, provided that the old French canal company, which had begun work decades earlier, agreed within a reasonable time and on reasonable terms to sell the United States its titles and equities in the area. Members of the American commission had valued the French holdings at not more than $40 million. This was only half of the company's own estimate, but the company accepted the revised figure.

With that matter settled, Roosevelt pressed Colombia to surrender control of the land in return for $10 million and an annual rental of $250,000. A treaty to that effect was rejected by the Colombian government, which wanted more money and greater rights of sovereignty in the zone. Roosevelt, outraged at what he considered "blackmail," though the Colombian request was scarcely that, let it be known privately that he would smile upon insurrection in Panama. Predictably, in November 1903 insurrection occurred (if it had not, the President was prepared to ask Congress for authority to take the zone from Colombia). The United States aided the revolutionists, used a warship to prevent Colombian forces from landing, and immediately recognized the new, independent Republic of Panama, which promptly accepted Roosevelt's terms for a canal zone.

Roosevelt boasted that he "took Panama," and most Americans at the time condoned his behavior. But the episode was a national disgrace. There was even suspicion of scandal. Agents of the French company, eager to unload their otherwise worthless assets, had influenced the State Department and members of Congress to favor the Panama route and had helped to foment the insurrection. Roosevelt had no personal stake in their game, but his ruthless pursuit of his own interpretation of national advantage was no more ethical than was their pursuit of profit. Yet he persuaded himself that his conduct was impeccable, for, he argued, he had stamped out lawlessness in Colombia and disorder in Panama. Thus he perverted his insistence on stability in the Caribbean into a rationalization for imperialism.

That perversion took much of the gloss off his message to Congress of December 1904, in which he announced that the United States would not interfere with Latin-American nations that conducted their affairs with decency, but that "brutal wrongdoing" might require intervention by some civilized power, and that the United States could not "ignore this duty." The Monroe Doctrine told Europe to stay out of the Americas; the Roosevelt Corollary asserted that the United States had a right to move in. In 1905 Roosevelt interceded in Santo Domingo to end the cycle there of debt, revolution, and default. He imposed American supervision of customs collections and finance, establishing a trust fund to repay the European-held debt. The convention containing those terms was blocked in the United States Senate, which was growing restive under the President's single-handed conduct of foreign affairs, but Roosevelt substituted an executive agreement which protected his policy until the Senate accepted a modified treaty in 1907.

The Balance of Power The international police power which Roosevelt arrogated for the United States he expected other civilized nations to exercise elsewhere—Japan in Korea, England in Egypt and India. Stable and prosperous nations, however, had in his view no right to proceed against each other. World order depended on their restraint and on the shifting balances of their power. British restraint preserved the growing Anglo-American entente during a dispute about the Alaskan boundary. Canada in 1902 claimed

The Alaskan Boundary Settlement, 1903

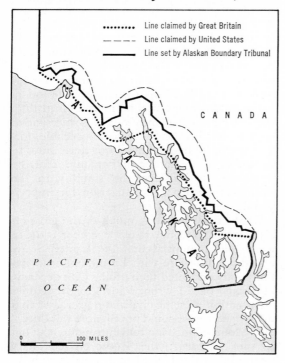

- ········· Line claimed by Great Britain
- – – – – Line claimed by United States
- ——— Line set by Alaskan Boundary Tribunal

CANADA

PACIFIC

OCEAN

0   100 MILES

Alaskan lands which cut off newly discovered Canadian gold fields from the sea. Roosevelt rightly judged the claim weak, but he wounded Canadian sensibilities by his blustering refusal to arbitrate (for, he said, arbitration usually resulted "in splitting the difference"). To help Canadian officials save face, in 1903 he submitted the issue to negotiation but instructed the commissioners he appointed to concede nothing. He also took pains to inform London of his order. The single English commissioner voted with the three Americans against the two Canadians, thereby straining temporarily the bonds of empire but serving both the merits of the issue and the cause of transatlantic friendship.

As he contemplated the balance of power in Europe, Roosevelt was grateful for England's friendship, dubious about Russia's immediate strength (though he recognized her great potentials), and more and more anxious about Germany. Had the Kaiser had the "instinct for the jugular," Roosevelt thought, he would have kept a sharp eye on Russia. As it was,

Germany was more jealous of France and England, and the Kaiser entertained "red dreams of glory" that might disrupt Europe and thus the whole world.

Aware of the network of European alliances that would engage every continental power in a contest between any two, the President worried about the tensions that flared in 1905 over French and German rivalry in Morocco. The Kaiser secretly asked Roosevelt to persuade England not to support France. Roosevelt at first hesitated to intervene, for, as he put it, the United States had "no real interest in Morocco." It did have a major stake in preserving peace, however, and Roosevelt overcame his disinclination to appear "a Meddlesome Mattie" and carried on the difficult negotiations that brought all parties, including the United States, to a conference at Algeciras, Spain, in January 1906.

Roosevelt's instructions to the American delegates revealed his anti-German bias, his conviction that the entente cordiale between France and England preserved the essential balance of power in Europe. Though American participation had little effect on the outcome of the conference, at which France won a diplomatic victory, Roosevelt's role was nevertheless significant. He had served peace. Furthermore, he had demonstrated to Europe and to the American people, many of whom criticized his departure from the course of isolation, that the President of the United States recognized the nation's inexorable and legitimate concern in any European crisis. In the twentieth century, the bounds of national security could not stop at the water line.

They extended across the Pacific as well as the Atlantic. In Asia, Roosevelt judged, slumbering China was of no account, but to prevent dislocations of power he accepted the prevailing fiction of her territorial integrity, and he gave lip service to the principle of the Open Door. To stabilize the Orient he counted primarily on a balance between Russia and Japan. He welcomed an Anglo-Japanese defensive alliance of 1902, which committed both signatories to preserve the status quo in Asia, but in 1904, when the Russo-Japanese War began, he brooded about its "immense possibilities . . . for the future." A Russian triumph, he concluded, would be "a blow to

Portsmouth Conference:
"Immense possibilities
. . . for the future."

civilization"; on the other hand, the elimination of Russia's "moderative influence" on
Japan would be equally unfortunate. That
possibility seemed imminent after Japan's
initial naval and land victories and the outbreak of revolution in Russia. Though Roosevelt was partial to the Japanese, he intensified
his effort through mediation to arrange a peace
that would preserve a safe equilibrium. He
proceeded without the knowledge of Congress,
working secretly and deftly through personal
friends in the diplomatic corps of Japan, Germany, and Great Britain. By the summer of
1905 Russian distress and Japanese financial
infirmity brought both belligerents to accept
a peace conference at Portsmouth, New Hampshire.

The President's brilliant diplomacy continued at the conference, which produced a
settlement that exactly suited his purpose and
incidentally earned him a Nobel Prize for
Peace. Japan took over the southern half of
the island of Sakhalin, Port Arthur, and the
South Manchuria Railroad, but Manchuria
remained a part of China where the Open
Door still presumably permitted all nations to
trade and invest, and Russia retained all of
Siberia, the source of her basic weight in
Asian politics. The Japanese failed to get the
huge idemnity they had wanted, which made
the treaty and Roosevelt the object of considerable public criticism in Japan. But her
government was satisfied, particularly because
the United States, like Russia, had recognized
Japan's primacy in Korea.

Also in 1905 Taft and Japanese Foreign
Minister Taro Katsura reached an agreement
by which the United States permitted Japan

The Far East after the Portsmouth Treaty, 1905

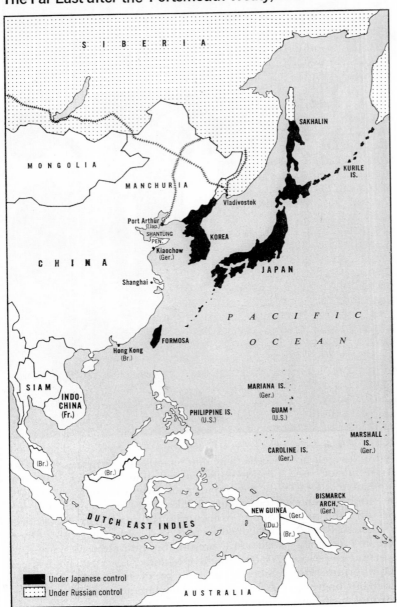

to occupy Korea. This, too, was a victory for the President's realistic diplomacy. The United States, he knew, lacked the means to interfere in Korea, and Japan had to be kept friendly and content or she could easily conquer the Philippines which Congress would not arm.

Japanese-American relations might have re-mained excellent had it not been for the problem of immigration. In 1900 Tokyo agreed to deny passports to emigrant laborers bound for the United States. But Japanese workers continued to make their way to the West Coast through Hawaii, Mexico, and Canada. Especially in California, where deep-rooted prejudice against all Asians had resulted in the national exclusion of Chinese immigrants, anti-Japanese feeling rose, revealing itself in the press, in the debates of the legislature, and in race riots. In 1906 San Francisco segregated Asian school children. The proud Japanese protested officially to Washington. Roosevelt assured them that he had no sympathy with the "outrageous agitation" of the Californians. He could not, however, silence the yellow press or control the "idiots" in the California legislature, nor could he prevent racial discrimination by barring the immigration of all laborers, for Congress opposed so stringent a law. Yet he was wholly unwilling to ask the Japanese to concede any racial inferiority. The State Department resolved the crisis by negotiating the "Gentlemen's Agreement" of 1907, an official but informal understanding that bound both countries to stop unwanted immigration between them.

This crisis focused attention on the whole immigration question. Roosevelt understood why organized labor objected to unrestricted immigration, Asian or European, and to a degree he shared the middle-class prejudice against the unrestricted entry of southern and eastern Europeans. Still, he feared that a general debate about immigration in 1906 would complicate relations with Japan and possibly divide the Republicans, some of whom were urging enactment of a literacy test for immigrants. He recommended the appointment of a fact-finding commission, a solution that would delay debate, appease the restrictionists, and, he believed, throw light on a complex subject. Modifying his proposal, Congress in 1907 authorized a commission of nine members, of whom three were to be selected by the President, three by the Speaker of the House, and three by the President of the Senate. Those who were appointed to the commission, of which Senator Dillingham became chairman, approached the task with a considerable bias for the restriction of immigration.

Besides provoking a debate on immigration policy, the Japanese-American crisis stirred up loose talk of war. There was probably less in Japan than in the United States, where racists spoke of irreconcilable conflict and where the President was apparently worried in 1907 that Japan intended to provoke war. His anxiety may have been contrived to stir Congress into pushing ahead with the naval building program. In any case, there was no need for alarm, although years later Roosevelt said that he had detected "a very, very slight undertone of veiled truculence" in Japan's communications. "It was essential," he then decided, "that we should have it clearly understood by our own people especially, but also by other peoples, that the Pacific was as much our home waters as the Atlantic." And he sailed the battle fleet around the world to make his point clear.

Had Japan been belligerent, she could have demolished the American ships that entered Tokyo Bay. Instead she welcomed them heartily. Yet Roosevelt believed their presence curbed any Japanese urge toward aggression and was therefore "the most important service" he ever rendered to peace. It was certainly a fine example of one of his favorite adages: "Speak softly but carry a big stick." Good will rather than fear led the Japanese ambassador to propose a declaration of friendship. In the Root-Takahira Agreement of 1908, both nations promised to uphold the status quo in the Pacific and to respect the Open Door and China's territorial integrity.

"A council of war never fights," Roosevelt wrote in his *Autobiography*, "and in a crisis the duty of a leader is to lead." As President he personally conducted the nation's foreign policies, acting sometimes with skill, sometimes with daring, sometimes with scant regard for the opinion of public or Congress or for the rights or sensitivities of other nations. Yet on the whole his record was impressive. As he knew, and as he instructed, the United States had become part of an interdependent world; the use of force could keep isolated troublespots from erupting into general war; power was an essential element in world affairs; and the United States, a powerful nation, had an obligation to keep its power in a state of readiness and, when necessary, to use it well.

The Election of 1908   No harm came from the concentration of power in one man's hands, Roosevelt observed, "provided the holder does not keep it for more than a certain, definite time, and then returns it to the people from whom he sprang." An American President, he believed, should serve only two terms.

So he announced in 1904 that he would not run again, and though he gloried in his office, he resisted the strong sentiment for his renomination in 1908 and used his power in the party to ensure the nomination of William Howard Taft, whom he had selected as the man most able to perpetuate his policies.

Some progressive Republicans would have preferred New York's governor, Charles Evans Hughes, but the President's endorsement and Taft's own excellent reputation kept the party united. With the tide of progressivism rising, the Democrats turned again to Bryan, who ran with more prudence than before, but not fast enough. He had the support of the leaders of organized labor, who applauded the Democratic plank urging the restriction of injunctions, and he made what he could of an attack on the Republican tariff. But Taft polled 52.0 per cent of the popular vote and carried the electoral college 321 to 162. Taft's identification with Roosevelt elected him. In 1901 Roosevelt had inherited a conservative administration. Increasingly he had enlisted with reform. When he bowed out in 1909, off to hunt in the African jungles, a majority of Americans had come to adulate him and to expect progressive government as a matter of course. It remained to be seen what Taft would do with his inheritance.

SUGGESTIONS FOR READING

General

G. E. Mowry, *The Era of Theodore Roosevelt* (1958), provides the best comprehensive account of the developments during the first twelve years of this century. There is an indispensable, stimulating, and original interpretation of progressivism and its adherents in Richard Hofstadter, *The Age of Reform* * (1955). Another important and spirited account appears in the relevant chapters of Eric Goldman, *Rendezvous with Destiny* * (1952). S. P. Hays, *The Response to Industrialism* * (1957), offers an interpretation suggested by the book's title. Among various older studies that remain useful, J. R. Chamberlain, *Farewell to Reform* (1932), stands out, not the least because of its statement of a point of view characteristic of its time.

Progressivism

The various aspects of progressivism have received wide contemporary and historical treatment. One of the best places to begin reading is in a lucid and moving study of the underprivileged and their champions, R. H. Bremner, *From the Depths* (1956). Two of those champions revealed their concerns in J. A. Riis, *How the Other Half Lives* * (1890), and Jane Addams, *Forty Years at Hull House* * (1935). The contributions of the churches receive a thorough and compelling analysis in H. F. May, *Protestant Churches and Industrial America* (1949). Philip Taft, *The A.F. of L. in the Time of Gompers* (1957), provides a systematic, friendly account of the trade unions. Among the important interpretations of progressive intellectuals, besides the volumes listed in the preceding paragraph, are Daniel Aaron, *Men of Good Hope* * (1951); Morton White, *Social Thought in America: The Revolt Against Formalism* * (1949); D. W. Noble, *The Paradox of Progressive Thought* (1958); Sidney Fine, *Laissez Faire and the General Welfare State* (1956); and H. F. May, *The End of American Innocence* (1959). These should be read in conjunction with the contemporary works mentioned in the text and with such revealing autobiographies as those of Lincoln Steffens and William Allen White. Progressive ferment and achievement in various regions, states, and cities have had excellent treatment in C. V. Woodward, *Origins of the New South (1951)*; R. B. Nye, *Midwestern Progressive Politics* (1951); G. E. Mowry, *The California Progressives* (1951); R. E. Noble, *New Jersey Progressivism Before Wilson* (1947); and Arthur Mann, *Yankee Reformers in the Urban Age* (1954).

Roosevelt and His Administration

The best introduction to Theodore Roosevelt remains his autobiography, which can be profitably supplemented by reading in his voluminous collected works (the National Edition

* Available in a paperback edition.

[1926] is handiest) and published letters, E. E. Morison, ed., *Letters of Theodore Roosevelt*, 8 vols. (1951–54). Carleton Putnam provides a glowing account of Roosevelt in *Theodore Roosevelt: The Formative Years* (1958). Henry Pringle, *Theodore Roosevelt* * (1931), for all its discernment, tends to see its subject from the point of view of the depression years in which it was written. A more judicious and learned biography is W. H. Harbough, *Power and Responsibility* (1961). J. M. Blum, *The Republican Roosevelt* * (1954), focuses on Roosevelt as politician and President, and H. K. Beale, *Theodore Roosevelt and the Rise of America to World Power* (1956), offers an informed and rigorous analysis of Roosevelt's foreign policy. Among other special studies of important public policies in Roosevelt's time, some of the most rewarding are E. L. Peffer, *The Closing of the Public Domain* (1951), which should be supplemented by Gifford Pinchot's autobiography; O. E. Anderson, Jr., *The Health of a Nation* (1958); B. H. Meyer, *History of the Northern Securities Case* (1906); and relevant chapters from W. Z. Ripley, *Railroads: Rates and Regulations* (1915). There is a wealth of good autobiography by and biography of the men around Roosevelt. Besides those autobiographies noted earlier, Robert La Follette's is important, and among the most readable and instructive biographies those that most successfully introduce the period are: C. G. Bowers, *Beveridge and the Progressive Era* (1932); N. W. Stephenson, *Nelson W. Aldrich* (1920), a sympathetic treatment of a great conservative; P. C. Jessup, *Elihu Root*, 2 vols. (1938), a distinguished and detailed work; Henry Pringle, *The Life and Times of William Howard Taft*, 2 vols. (1939), which is both learned and laudatory; and E. E. Morison, *Admiral Sims and the Modern American Navy* (1942).

* Available in a paperback edition.

23

Progressivism
in Crisis and Triumph

Republicans celebrating the inauguration of William Howard Taft in March 1909 had cause for joy but not for complacency. Their party had won four successive presidential elections, and its national leaders had preserved the alliances on which its majority rested. But the partners in these alliances—the Old Guard, urban progressives, and Western agrarians—were growing uneasy with one another. The Democrats, secure in the South and in many Northern cities, were gaining strength among labor unions and farmers. In 1906 and 1908 the Republicans had lost seats in the House of Representatives, and in 1908 they had also lost several governorships. If they hoped to remain in power, they would have to satisfy their restive factions and close ranks against their opposition.

Insurgency

President Taft   Taft, the new President and head of the party, had excellent intentions. A kindly, learned man, he saw the need for social welfare legislation, understood the purposes of the Roosevelt reforms, for which he had worked with skill, and meant to keep his promise to preserve and further his predecessor's program. He was also a loyal Republican who hoped to strengthen his party, which in his opinion was the only fit instrument of government. In a placid time he might have done well.

He was, however, seriously handicapped for the job he had to do. Taft was almost a caricature of the fat man—genial, usually easygoing, often lazy. He was also untrained in politics, for his career had been on the bench and in appointive, administrative offices. He had no instinct for manipulation, no nerve for controversy. His reluctance to use the full powers of the presidency grew out of his interpretation of the Constitution, which led him to believe that he should not interfere in the course of legislation, something that in any case he found uncomfortable. He was uncomfortable, too, in the company of men who did not share his background of old family, personal means, and Eastern education. He preferred talking with Nelson Aldrich rather than with La Follette, whom in any event he considered one of the party's troublemakers.

The President was by nature and conviction a conservative whose highest confidence was in the law as he and other judges had studied and shaped it. The bench, he believed, was the appropriate arbiter of social issues. He was suspicious of direct democracy because he did not trust the majority to make laws. He was also cautious about enlarging the power of the executive for fear that it might encroach upon the traditional authorities of the other branches of government.

Taft was not unresilient. He accepted the need for change. But he did not particularly like it and he did not at all like to be rushed. Yet he came to his office when the progressives were in a hurry. And they expected him, on the basis of his commitment to Roosevelt's program, to keep pace with them. He held his own view of that program, expecting an easy pace, an advance in which each forward step was measured carefully against the footprints trailing through the past.

The Tariff   Taft began boldly by calling a special session of Congress to revise the tariff. He and Roosevelt had insisted upon a plank in the Republican platform promising modification of the tariff, and his speeches had suggested that he preferred a moderate downward revision. Republican representatives of manufacturing interests were still wedded to high protectionism, but the Midwestern farmers and their party spokesmen were convinced that the Dingley duties (see p. 493), by protecting the trusts from foreign competition, were sustaining artificial prices for manufactured goods. Furthermore, as proponents of the "Iowa Idea" argued, Europeans had to sell in the American market in order to earn dollars to buy American agricultural surpluses.

The Western progressives counted on the President's support in getting the tariff lowered, but even before the special session got under way they experienced their first disappointment. Taft appointed a Cabinet of conservatives, five of them corporation lawyers. He also turned down young George Norris of Nebraska and other insurgents in the House of Representatives who appealed for his support in their effort to restrict the power of the Speaker, "Uncle Joe" Cannon of Illinois, an arch-Tory and protectionist. And when debate on the tariff began, Taft made no gesture in behalf of the revision he had advocated.

The Ways and Means Committee of the House, of which Sereno Payne of New York was chairman, reported out a tariff bill that made modest concessions to reform. It reduced some duties and imposed an inheritance tax graduated from 1 to 5 per cent. The House quickly accepted the bill, though the Democrats fought for larger reductions and for a graduated income tax.

In the Senate, however, the Old Guard carried the day. The Finance Committee, of which Nelson Aldrich was chairman, struck out the inheritance tax, made over eight hundred amendments to the House bill, and even slightly increased the average rates of the

William Howard Taft: Kindly conservative.

Dingley Tariff. On the floor of the Senate, Albert Beveridge of Indiana and Jonathan Dolliver of Iowa (both former lieutenants of Roosevelt), La Follette, and several other progressives attacked the swollen tariff schedules one by one and joined the Democrats in urging an income tax. Aldrich, retreating guardedly, accepted a compromise that set a 2 per cent tax on corporate income and assured passage of a constitutional amendment authorizing a personal income tax. But the compromise did not affect the tariff itself, which went to a conference committee of the two houses in July 1909. Taft now interceded to obtain reductions in a number of schedules, but most of these revisions benefited manufacturers rather than farmers or consumers.

The bill as it finally passed was a triumph for the protectionists. During the struggle Taft had lost his chance for reform and had alienated the insurgent Midwesterners and their constituents. Stubbornly, the President in September widened the breach. In a series of implausible speeches he extolled Aldrich and scolded the progressives who had voted against

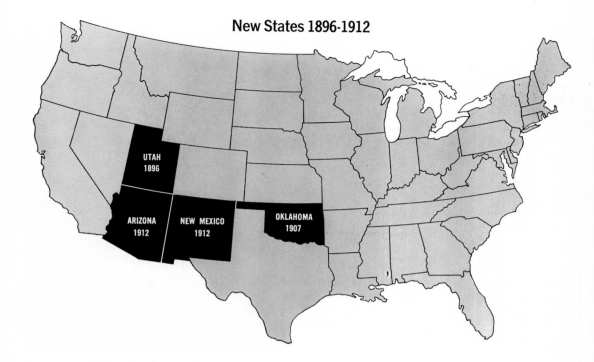

New States 1896-1912

UTAH
1896

ARIZONA
1912

NEW MEXICO
1912

OKLAHOMA
1907

the tariff, which he declared the best the party had ever enacted.

A Divided Party When Congress met again in 1910, the insurgents no longer expected help from the White House. Attacking at once, Norris and his associates made common cause with the Democrats and passed a resolution transferring much of Speaker Cannon's authority to the House Rules Committee. The insurgents then joined the Democrats to amend Taft's railway bill, though the President made support of that bill a test of party loyalty. The measure empowered the Interstate Commerce Commission to fix rates on its own initiative. But it also established a Court of Commerce with broad powers of review over the Commission's decisions, thereby giving the traditionally conservative judiciary a determining veto. The bill also permitted railroads to acquire competing lines. The Democratic-progressive coalition supported the first of those three provisions, attacked the others, and succeeded in eliminating the third. Moreover, it amended the bill to bring telephone and telegraph companies under the Commission's jurisdiction, to prescribe equal rates per mile for long and

short hauls, and to provide for the physical valuation of railway properties as a basis for determining fair rates.

In the Senate Aldrich eliminated the provision calling for physical valuation and preserved the Commerce Court by making a trade with the Democrats. In return for their help on the railway bill, he agreed to the admission of Arizona and New Mexico, which were sure to elect four Democratic senators in 1912. This was a Pyrrhic victory: It saved the Administration's face, but it also saved many of the progressive features of the railroad measure, the Mann-Elkins Act. It did not long prevent a physical-valuation law (which Congress passed early in 1913), and it precipitated open warfare within the Republican party. The insurgents had defied the President, who had unwisely raised the question of party regularity. Now he retaliated by denying them patronage and starting a campaign to defeat them in the fall elections.

Meanwhile Taft had got caught up in a damaging controversy. His Secretary of the Interior, Richard A. Ballinger, with Taft's approval, had returned to the public domain millions of acres of land and many valuable water-power sites that Gifford Pinchot, Roosevelt's trusted friend, had previously had withdrawn. Pinchot, the "Sir Galahad of the woodlands," was still chief forester. Frankly hostile to Ballinger, he became suspicious of his motives when he learned from Louis R. Glavis, an investigator in the General Land Office, that Ballinger had been instrumental in selling certain government coal lands in Alaska to a wealthy syndicate controlled by J. P. Morgan and David Guggenheim. Pinchot took the case to Taft, who ruled for Ballinger on every count and discharged Glavis. Though he considered Pinchot a "crank," Taft politely urged him to drop the issue and stay in office.

The indignant Pinchot had other plans. He supplied material for two magazine articles attacking Ballinger. He also wrote a letter praising Glavis for Dolliver to read to the Senate. Taft had no choice but to dismiss Pinchot, though he knew that in so doing he would seem to oppose Roosevelt's conservation policies and possibly antagonize the Colonel. His worst fears materialized. A joint congressional committee in 1910 exonerated Ballinger, but Louis D. Brandeis, counsel for the opposition, made a brilliant case against both the secretary and the President. Though Taft was an effective conservationist, Brandeis' argument cost him his laurels and identified him once again with reaction. The political damage was compounded when Pinchot greeted Roosevelt after the Colonel emerged from the African jungles. In the future Roosevelt always saw the matter Pinchot's way.

The Election of 1910   Taft felt that Roosevelt's friends had plotted to cause a rupture between him and the Colonel. Maybe they had; Pinchot and Dolliver were zealous men. But even if they had not, the Colonel would have heard disturbing tales from the progressives whom the President had tried to purge in the struggle over his railway bill. Immediately after Roosevelt's triumphant return to New York, the insurgents set out for his home at Oyster Bay to enlist his help. Roosevelt, who was temperamentally incapable of remaining out of politics and who was sensitive to a coolness on Taft's part, now decided that his principles needed defending. He embarked on a speaking tour during which he endorsed the Administration, party harmony, and various

Eastern conservatives, but gave even stronger praise to Beveridge and other insurgents. By implication, in supporting them he was criticizing the President. He also re-emphasized the points he had made in his last messages to Congress. At Osawatomie, Kansas, invoking the spirit of John Brown, Roosevelt announced his New Nationalism, a program of social welfare, federal regulation of business and industry, and direct democracy. In that address he frightened conservatives by attacking the courts for having invalidated progressive labor legislation.

The friction within the Republican party contributed to Democratic gains in the elections of 1910. In states where Old Guard candidates were running, progressive Republicans tended either to stay at home or to split their tickets. Where progressives were candidates, some of the Old Guard avoided the polls on election day, often with the thought that in this way they were casting a vote against Roosevelt and reform. The Democrats in many states managed to identify themselves with progressivism and to identify the Republican tariff with the rising cost of living, a particularly sensitive issue among city-dwellers. The Democratic campaign went over the top. The party won several governorships, including those of New York and New Jersey, which had been safely Republican for many years. For the first time since 1892, the Democrats elected a majority to the House of Representatives. The Republicans' loss of New York and the defeat of Senator Beveridge in Indiana saddened Roosevelt. The Democratic victories over Old Guard candidates in the East and the victories of progressive Republicans in the West repudiated Taft. Over-all, the returns suggested that only an insurgent could save the Republicans in the presidential election of 1912, but the Old Guard, tense and defensive, prepared to resist the temper of the time.

Taft's closest political associates began in 1911, by the adroit use of patronage, to strengthen their factions in the North and to wrap up the Republican organizations in the South, which were significant only for the votes they cast at national conventions. At the same time, La Follette began to recruit support for his own candidacy, which was endorsed by many progressives. Some of them, however, privately hoped to draft Roosevelt, whose personal appeal remained strong even after his announcement that he had retired from politics.

A Divisive Foreign Policy   During the year Taft succeeded in intensifying party discord and stirring the Colonel to action. In January 1911 the President submitted to Congress a reciprocity agreement with Canada. It put on the free list many agricultural products, including important raw materials for industrial use, and some manufactured goods. Western progressives, fearing the competition of Canadian farmers, opposed the measure. So did most high-tariff advocates, who objected to any breach in the wall of protection. Together they rejected the agreement. But Taft called a special session in April during which the Democrats, delighting in the discomfort of the Republicans, helped Administration forces to put the measure through. The Canadians, however, disturbed by the prospect of economic competition and Americanization, in September repudiated the agreement. Another tariff debate had produced only more scars. The Democrats kept them open, with help from Republican insurgents, by passing a series of bills reducing specific schedules— "pop-gun" tariffs that the President systematically vetoed.

Taft's foreign policy also aroused opposition. His Secretary of State, Philander C. Knox, negotiated treaties with Nicaragua and Honduras providing for the assumption of their European-held debt by American investors and for the appointment of Americans to direct their finances and thus assure the collection of those debts. Though the Senate rejected the treaties, Knox pursued his policy throughout the Caribbean with considerable success.

Taft and Knox also emphasized the possibilities for American investments in China. At the instigation of the State Department, American bankers agreed to join in various commercial projects there, including an international railway consortium. Roosevelt was aghast at these developments. Aware of Japan's growing power, he had urged Taft to abandon commercial competition with the Japanese in China. It was more important, the Colonel argued, to cultivate Japanese friendship and to arrange a clearer understanding about Japanese immigration.

Roosevelt also opposed arbitration treaties that Taft negotiated with France and England. Taft was dedicated to world peace and was confident that international problems could be solved by courts of law. In the summer of 1911 he submitted to the Senate treaties with France and Great Britain that bound the signatories to arbitrate all differences "susceptible of decision by the application of the principles of law or equity." These treaties excited the hopes of the thousands of Americans who considered them an important step toward avoiding wars. But Roosevelt wrote angry articles denouncing the arbitration of questions involving "territory" or "national honor," and he cooperated with like-minded senators who succeeded in amending the treaties so drastically that the President would not ratify them. Taft was dismayed by the outcome and offended by Roosevelt's scathing language.

Roosevelt Revolts   Roosevelt in turn was offended ideologically and personally by Taft's antitrust policies. These rested upon decisions of the Supreme Court in 1911 in the Standard Oil and American Tobacco cases, both of which had been initiated during Roosevelt's Administration. The Court found that the corporations were monopolies guilty of violating the Sherman Act, which the decisions now clearly applied against industrial holding companies (in contrast to the ruling in the Knight case [see p. 430]). Yet the decisions also pronounced the "rule of reason," which held that only unreasonable restraints of trade were unlawful. This was a necessary corollary to antitrust law, for an undiscriminating application of the Sherman Act would destroy the structure and impede the functioning of American business. But whereas Taft was content to have the Court take upon itself the authority to define reasonableness, Roosevelt believed that an administrative agency should make that judgment and should base it on considerations of economic efficiency and business behavior.

This difference of opinion was exemplified in the case of the United States Steel Corporation, that largest of all holding companies, which Taft chose to prosecute. Roosevelt, who considered the company guiltless, concluded

A Case for Bigness

If the anti-trust people really grasped the full meaning of what they said, and if they really had the power or the courage to do what they propose, they would be engaged in one of the most destructive agitations that America has known. They would be breaking up the beginning of a collective organization, thwarting the possibility of cooperation, and insisting upon submitting industry to the wasteful, the planless scramble of little profiteers. They would make impossible any deliberate and constructive use of our natural resources, they would thwart any effort to form the great industries into coordinated services, they would preserve commercialism as the undisputed master of our lives....

It is said that the economy of trusts is unreal. Yet no one has ever tried the economies of the trust in any open, deliberate fashion. The amount of energy that has had to go into repelling stupid attack, the adjustments that had to be made underground—it is a wonder the trusts achieved what they did to bring order out of chaos, and forge an instrument for a nation's business.

From Walter Lippmann, *Drift and Mastery*, 1914.

---

dance of industrialism while controlling and preserving the institutions which had made that abundance possible. Roosevelt stood an excellent chance of winning the election. Taft had no such chance, but his dander was up, and the Old Guard cared more about nominating him, defeating Roosevelt, and dominating the party than about beating the Democrats.

The Taft forces, moreover, had in their hands the party apparatus through which they could control the convention. In some states Roosevelt's supporters managed to pass legislation establishing preferential primaries for the nomination, but in the end only thirteen states held such elections. They gave 36 delegates to La Follette, 48 to Taft, and 278 to Roosevelt—an overwhelming mandate for the Colonel. Taft, however, controlled the South, New York, and the crucial national committee, which with its affiliates disposed of 254 contested seats at the convention. With a cynical disregard for the merits of the contestants, it allotted 235 of the contested seats to

that Taft had acted largely to persecute and embarrass him, for the prosecution, which resulted ultimately in an acquittal, and the congressional hearings which it provoked, publicized Roosevelt's negotiations of 1907 with J. P. Morgan (see p. 529).

Taft's antitrust and foreign policies widened the breach between himself and Roosevelt and gave Roosevelt a chance to rationalize what he would undoubtedly have done anyway. In February 1912 Roosevelt announced that his hat was in the ring. A furious battle for the Republican presidential nomination was under way.

The struggle was really between Roosevelt and Taft, who denounced each other with unrestrained personal vehemence. Though La Follette remained in the race, most of his supporters of 1911 deserted him for Roosevelt. La Follette was a dedicated reformer but a captive of agrarian ideas ill suited to the needs of an urban and industrial society. Roosevelt, now just as progressive and vastly more sophisticated and popular than La Follette, had in his New Nationalism formulated a program that promised to distribute the abun-

---

A Case Against Bigness

I think we are in a position, after the experience of the last 20 years, to state two things: In the first place, that a corporation may well be too large to be the most efficient instrument of production and of distribution, and, in the second place, whether it has exceeded the point of greatest economic efficiency or not, it may be too large to be tolerated among the people who desire to be free. I think, therefore, that the recognition of those propositions should underlie any administration of the law....

It seems to me that there is a distinct peril in the community in having one organization control a very large percentage of the market.... Where there is found to be a combination in restraint of trade, if the combination controls 40 per cent or more of the market, that creates a presumption of unreasonableness. I am inclined to think that an inquiry into our experience of the last 20 years would justify making of that presumption irrefutable, and that no corporation ought to control so large a percentage if we desire to maintain competition at all.

From Louis D. Brandeis, Testimony Before the Committee on Interstate Commerce, U.S. Senate, 62 Cong., 1st Sess., 1911.

La Follette in Wisconsin, his laboratory of democracy.

Taft delegates. The rigged convention then renominated the President on the first ballot.

The Bull Moose   Before the balloting took place, however, most of the Roosevelt men bolted, crying fraud. In August they reconvened as delegates of the new Progressive party. To that convention there came social workers, intellectuals, and industrialists attracted by Roosevelt's personality and program, and Republican politicians disenchanted with their factional rivals—all imbued with a revivalist spirit that led them to choose "Onward, Christian Soldiers" as their marching song. Roosevelt, "strong as a Bull Moose," told them they were standing at Armageddon battling for the Lord, and accepted the nomination they tendered with thundering unanimity.

The Progressive party was a politician's Gothic horror, hastily and inadequately organized, but with a powerful leader. Roosevelt probably knew in his heart that by splitting the Republican party he was assuring the election of a Democrat. He and Taft, however, had by June gone too far to turn back toward compromise, which the events of four years had in any case made difficult. The split was much more than just a personal falling-out. Taft's adherents by and large stood for the status quo. Some, to be sure, were of a progressive mind but were unwilling to break with their party. Many were genuinely frightened by Roosevelt's advocacy of the recall of state judicial decisions by referendum, a proposal that in their view would substitute the fickle and untutored will of the majority for the presumed majesty of the courts. Mostly they stayed with Taft because they considered him and his sponsors safe, whereas they considered Roosevelt, his friends, and his platform downright alarming.

The Bull Moose platform was incontestably adventurous, a charter of progressive reform for its own time and for years to come. It advocated the familiar devices of popular democracy—presidential primaries, women's suffrage, the initiative and referendum, and popular election of United States senators. It advocated, too, a comprehensive social welfare program—conservation of natural and human resources, minimum wages for women, the restriction of child labor, workmen's compensation, social insurance, a federal income tax,* and the limitation of injunctions in labor disputes. Finally, in keeping with Roosevelt's ideas about the proper role of government, it called for expert federal commissions to adjust the tariff and to regulate interstate business and industry. Party and candidate alike stood for social justice and popular rule. As it developed, however, they faced formidable competition as champions of reform from a united and inspired Democratic party.

Progressivism at Zenith

Woodrow Wilson   The Democratic candidate in 1912 had found his way into politics by an unusual route. Woodrow Wilson, the son of a Southern Presbyterian minister, had abandoned a brief and unrewarding career in law for one in education. After earning his doctorate at The Johns Hopkins University, Wilson taught history and political science at Bryn Mawr, Wesleyan of Connecticut, and Princeton, his own alma mater, of which he became president in 1902. He first won national attention for his writings, especially his earliest book, *Congressional Government* (1885), which criticized the weakness of the executive and the inefficiencies of Congress and praised the British parliamentary system. As president of Princeton Wilson initiated a number of celebrated educational reforms. In order to minimize the distractions of undergraduate life and to develop an atmosphere conducive to learning, he proposed to assimilate the undergraduate clubs into larger residential units modeled after the colleges at Oxford and Cambridge. The alumni blocked this apparent challenge to the clubs, but the suggestion drew further attention to Wilson, as did his losing battle with faculty members and wealthy alumni over plans for a graduate

* The Sixteenth Amendment, which provided for an income tax, was already before the states, as was the Seventeenth, providing for popular election of senators. Both were ratified in 1913.

school. Though these struggles brought on his resignation, they also gave him a reputation as a champion of democracy in education.

Wilson resigned in 1910 to accept the Democratic nomination for governor of New Jersey. He had always had political ambitions. As a young man he had cultivated his forensic talents and dreamed of serving in the United States Senate. He owed his gubernatorial nomination to Democratic machine leaders who were impressed, as were his wealthy New York friends, by his stature and his presumably conservative economic views. But during the campaign Wilson adopted the program of New Jersey progressives. As governor he made a brilliant record that put New Jersey in the van of progressive states (see p. 521) and put Wilson in the lead for the Democratic Presidential nomination.

But in 1912 the Democrats, like the Republicans, were caught in a momentous struggle over selecting a candidate. Wilson had offended his conservative sponsors, who now helped organize a movement to defeat him. Though he was a Southerner, they were particularly successful in the South where Congressman Oscar Underwood of Alabama captured most of the state delegations. In the East, the city machines, alarmed by Wilson's treatment of their counterparts in New Jersey, embarrassed him by publicizing sections of his *History of the American People* (1902), which disparaged the new immigrants. In the farming West, moreover, the favorite candidate was Speaker of the House Champ Clark, the folksy "Ol' Hound Dawg" of Missouri. Bryan Democrats there rightly judged that Wilson was not one of them. And they resented a letter he had written in 1907, now published by his opponents, in which he had expressed the wish that something be done to knock Bryan "into a cocked hat."

Bryan recognized that Wilson had had a change of heart and during the national convention at Baltimore took the floor to castigate any candidate supported by Tammany. Tammany had moved New York into the Clark column, thus contributing to his majority. But it took a two-thirds vote to nominate, and while the Wilson and Underwood men stood fast, Wilson's floor leaders gradually made the deals that turned the convention their way.

One of those deals assured the vice-presidential nomination to Thomas R. Marshall of Indiana, a politician best remembered for his fetching assertion that what the country needed was "a good five-cent cigar." On the forty-third ballot Wilson won a majority of the votes; on the forty-sixth, Underwood withdrew and Wilson received two-thirds and the nomination.

The Election of 1912   The basic contest in 1912 was between the Democrats and the Progressives. Certain of the South, assisted elsewhere by the Republican schism, the Democratic leadership took pains to preserve party unity by placating the factions that had opposed Wilson and by appealing to the urban ethnic groups which had long sustained the party's political machines. But Wilson, though

Woodrow Wilson: "Free men need no guardians."

the odds were with him, could not take Roosevelt for granted. He had to meet the challenge for progressive votes.

In many respects the Bull Moose and Democratic platforms were similar, but there were several significant differences between them. Where the Progressives endorsed a protective tariff, the Democrats called for sharp downward revision. Where the Progressives demanded powerful federal regulatory agencies, the Democrats emphasized state rights. The Democrats did not spell out a broad social welfare program, but they did advocate limiting the use of injunctions against labor unions. The party's continuing insistence on that issue held the allegiance of Gompers and most of his associates in the American Federation of Labor. Moreover, farmers responded enthusiastically to Democratic promises to make loans for agriculture cheaper and more readily available.

More than the platforms, the attitudes of the candidates marked the differences between the parties. Roosevelt's New Nationalism assumed that the consolidation of the economy was inevitable and healthful. He welcomed big business but demanded big government to supervise it and to promote the welfare of nonbusiness groups. The political theorist Herbert Croly expressed these ideas forcefully in *The Promise of American Life* (1909), an influential book that helped Roosevelt and like-minded men articulate their principles. It demanded positive, comprehensive federal planning for the national interest and for social reform.

Wilson had reached dissimilar conclusions. There lingered in his mind a complex of ideas he had cherished since youth. He was a devout Presbyterian who held men individually responsible to God for their actions. Guilt in business affairs, he believed, was also personal guilt. Where a corporation misbehaved, his instinct was to punish its officers as the Lord punished sinners. He was more the stern prophet than the stern promoter. He was also convinced that laissez-faire principles of economics would work if only the state would protect and encourage competition. It should, he felt, act as a handicapper resolved to make the race equitable at the start and as a policeman determined to keep the runners in their

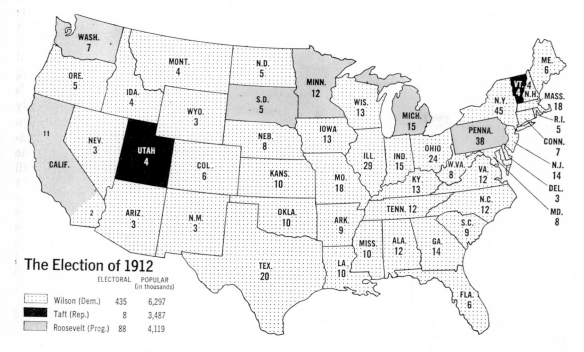

The Election of 1912

		ELECTORAL	POPULAR (in thousands)
⬚	Wilson (Dem.)	435	6,297
■	Taft (Rep.)	8	3,487
▨	Roosevelt (Prog.)	88	4,119

Map labels: WASH. 7, ORE. 5, MONT. 4, N.D. 5, MINN. 12, IDA. 4, WYO. 3, S.D. 5, WIS. 13, MICH. 15, ME. 6, VT. 4, N.H. 4, N.Y. 45, MASS. 18, R.I. 5, 11, NEV. 3, UTAH 4, COL. 6, NEB. 8, IOWA 13, ILL. 29, IND. 15, OHIO 24, W.VA. 8, VA. 12, PENNA. 38, CONN. 7, N.J. 14, DEL. 3, MD. 8, CALIF., 2, ARIZ. 3, N.M. 3, KANS. 10, MO. 18, KY. 13, TENN. 12, N.C. 12, S.C. 9, OKLA. 10, ARK. 9, MISS. 10, ALA. 12, GA. 14, TEX. 20, LA. 10, FLA. 6

lanes. An enemy of political and business corruption, a believer in popular democracy, a
proponent of regulation to prevent industrial
abuses, Wilson was a progressive, but of a type
uncomfortable with Croly's formulations.

Another able intellectual, Louis D. Brandeis
of Massachusetts, one of the splendid legal
thinkers of his time, helped Wilson organize
his developing ideas. The great corporations,
Brandeis argued, controlled credit, raw materials, and markets. They prevented competition and guarded their own inefficient methods, excessive profits, and overcapitalized
values. They had corrupted government,
Brandeis went on, and had to be prosecuted
and broken up. He also urged that the rules of
competition be defined by law, and that federal
programs be launched to provide credit for
small and new businesses. His ideas and the
data with which he supported them confirmed
Wilson's own theories, which the candidate
set forth in the program he called the New
Freedom.

Roosevelt's plans, Wilson said, would result
in "partnership between the government and
the trusts." The Democratic alternative would
ensure a free economy and preserve free government. "Free men," he asserted, "need no

guardians." Indeed they could not submit to
guardians and remain free, for submission
would produce "a corruption of the will."

Wilson called for "regulated competition"
in preference to "regulated monopoly." He
feared that individuals were being "swallowed
up" by great organizations, and he condemned
what he considered "an extraordinary and
very sinister concentration in . . . business."
He demanded "a body of laws which will look
after the men . . . who are sweating blood to
get their foothold in the world of endeavor."
Roosevelt called Wilson's program "rural
Toryism." In a sense it was. But Wilson affirmed the hopes of the farm, of the small
town, of middle-class America. His theme won
many hearts.

Wilson won a telling victory, though he
got only 41.9 per cent of the popular vote and
a smaller total vote than Bryan had in 1908.
Roosevelt received only 27.4 per cent and Taft
only 23.2. In the electoral count Wilson led his
rivals 435 to 88 and 8, and the Democrats
carried both houses of Congress. The Democrats, who ran best in the areas of their traditional strength, had needed the Republican
division to win. The returns were just as clearly
a triumph for reform. Taft's miserable show-

ing revealed the voters' disdain for standpat government, while the dissatisfaction with existing conditions was evidenced by the nearly one million votes for Socialist candidate Eugene V. Debs and by the remarkable support won by the Bull Moose party in its initial test.

Wilson and the Tariff   Wilson realized that he could work most efficiently through his own party. Indeed he regarded the presidency as somewhat like the office of Prime Minister in England. He considered himself a party leader with the right to hold party members in Congress to his programs and, if necessary, to appeal over their heads to the electorate. From the first he set out to unite the Democratic factions—the Southerners, the Northern city machines, the progressives; to use his united party to legislate; and to endow it with a record and reputation that would make a majority of Americans prefer it to any rival.

Wilson, however, had neither the temperament nor the experience to get along with professional politicians. A tense and angular man, he was incapable of displaying good fellowship he did not feel. But he knew his limitations and compensated for them by selecting a group of skilled advisers. Among others they included Bryan, the new Secretary of State, influential as always with the agrarian liberals; Albert S. Burleson, Postmaster General, a veteran Southern congressman popular among the party regulars on the Hill; Secretary of the Treasury William G. McAdoo, a progressive businessman who had the confidence of those who had made Wilson's nomination possible; Joseph P. Tumulty, the President's private secretary, a young Irishman wise in the ways of machine politicians and professional journalists; and Colonel Edward M. House, an urbane Texan who attached himself to Wilson and became his "second personality." Though House had neither title nor office, he quickly acquired important responsibilities as a liaison man between the President and leaders of the party and the Congress, as well as between the President and foreign heads of state. Describing House's facility in his role, one observer said enviously that he could "walk on dead leaves and make no more noise than a tiger."

Informed and assisted by his subordinates,

Wilson made his own major decisions and gave a personal stamp to his executive leadership. Right after his inauguration he called a special session of Congress to fulfill the Democratic pledge of tariff revision. He dramatized the session and his intended role by appearing personally, as had no President since Jefferson's time, to address the Congress. He had already begun a fruitful cooperation with the committees responsible for tariff recommendations. In May 1913, only a month after the President's address, the House passed a bill reducing average ad valorem rates about 11 per cent, adding a number of consumer goods to the free list, and eliminating the protection of iron, steel, and various other products of the trusts. To make up for the attending loss in revenue, the bill levied a modest graduated income tax, which ratification of the Sixteenth Amendment had legalized two months earlier.

The test of Wilson's leadership came in the Senate, where the Democrats had a majority of only three votes. Democratic senators from sugar- and wool-producing states were reluctant to leave those products on the free list where the House had placed them. Wilson urged them to vote with their party, but they wavered and lobbyists for protection tried to exploit the chance for logrolling. The President then called on public opinion to "check and destroy" the "intolerable burden" of "insidious" lobbyists. His statement helped to initiate an investigation of the private interests of all senators, some of whom, it developed, stood to profit personally from the protection of wool and sugar. With a refreshed sensitivity to public opinion, all but two Democrats voted for the party's bill. It kept sugar and wool on the free list and reduced the general level of rates another 4 per cent. It also, thanks to the efforts of progressives in all the parties, doubled the maximum surtax on personal incomes.

The tariff of 1913, the Underwood-Simmons Tariff, removed an accumulation of privileges and, without abandoning protection, reduced previously swollen schedules to dimensions that permitted a healthy international trade. It also made a significant modification in the federal tax structure by shifting some of the burden to those best able to bear it. It was a convincing demonstration that the Democrats could achieve the goals of the New Freedom,

Federal Reserve Districts and Banks

9 Minneapolis
7 Chicago
12 San Francisco
10 Kansas City
8 St.Louis
1 Boston
2 New York
3 Philadelphia
4 Cleveland
Richmond **5**
Atlanta **6**
Dallas **11**

4 Federal Reserve districts
• District banks

and it was an acknowledged triumph for Wilson's leadership.

Banking Reform Pressing his gains, the President had urged the special session of Congress to correct the nation's anachronistic money and banking system. The panic of 1907 (see p. 529) had underscored the inflexibility of currency and the inelasticity of credit. The events of the panic also suggested that financial power was concentrated in the hands of a small group of Eastern private bankers. That situation had been the subject of investigation by a House committee chaired by Congressman Arsène P. Pujo. Its findings, later popularized in Louis Brandeis' *Other People's Money* (1914), persuaded many progressives that there existed a "money trust."

Southern and Western agrarians had long assumed that there was a bankers' conspiracy against their interests and had long agitated for monetary reform. By 1913 the bankers themselves were in favor of reform, but of their own kind. The experience of the panic and the report of Aldrich's Monetary Commission (see p. 529) led most of them to advocate central control of the banking system and the creation of a currency responsive to, and partly based on, the expansion and contraction of commercial paper—that is, loans that banks made to business.

The bankers, taking as their models the Bank of England and the controversial Second United States Bank, wanted a central bank to be authorized by the government but privately controlled. They also wanted it to issue currency on its own liability. The conservative Democrats modified those proposals by replacing a single central bank with a number of regional banks supervised by a federal board. This modification, the plan Wilson at first favored, failed to satisfy the party's progressive and agrarian factions. To meet their minimum demands, the President agreed that the government should appoint the supervising board and that the bank notes issued by the new system should be obligations of the United States.

These concessions fell short of the program advanced by Southern agrarians. They called for a prohibition of interlocking directorates, for public control of the regional banks, for permitting reserve banks to discount agricultural paper, and for preventing the use of commercial paper as a basis for currency. Bryan mediated their differences with Wilson, who saw that he had to meet them part way. Accordingly he conceded the discounting of agricultural notes and promised later to take care of interlocking directorates. In return, the militants supported the rest of the bill, which the House passed in September 1913.

There was resistance again from conservatives in the Senate. Wilson overcame some of it by another appeal for party responsibility and by a timely use of patronage. Again he took his case to the people, asserting that bankers were trying to defeat the measure by creating artificial fears of impending panic. Although Senate conservatives managed to increase the percentage of gold reserves required for the issue of bank notes and to reduce the authority of the Federal Reserve Board, the Democrats were sufficiently united to pass the bill without further changes in December 1913.

The Federal Reserve Act was the most significant statute of Wilson's administration. The Federal Reserve Board and the regional reserve banks gave the United States its first efficient banking system since the time of Andrew Jackson. Their power over currency and credit put into responsible hands the means to provide the flexibility of short-term credit which was so badly needed. The regulatory authority of the board assured a greater degree of public control over banking than had ever existed before. Indeed the act remedied almost all the deficiencies in American banking and currency which informed men then recognized. Without the new system the country could not have adjusted to the financial strains of the First World War. There was still need to ease long-term agricultural credit and (though it was not yet understood) to endow public authorities with effective instruments to modulate the business cycle. But the new law was nonetheless impressive. Americans of all points of view and parties applauded it and the President's "great exhibition of leadership" in guiding it through Congress.

The New Freedom Completed   When Congress met in regular session in 1914, Wilson presented his program for regulating industry. The tariff had furthered the New Freedom by reducing protection for the products of the trusts. The Federal Reserve Act had made credit more readily available to small and new enterprises. The obvious drift of public opinion and public policy had helped to persuade the Morgan partners to resign from many of their directorates. Now the President asked Congress to make it impossible for interrelated groups to control holding companies, to create a commission to help dissolve corporations found in restraint of trade, and to define unfair business practices.

These recommendations, too strong for conservatives, did not satisfy either labor leaders,

---

Program for the New Freedom

We have itemized with some degree of particularity the things that ought to be altered and here are some of the chief items: A tariff which cuts us off from our proper part in the commerce of the world, violates the just principles of taxation, and makes the Government a facile instrument in the hands of private interests; a banking and currency system based upon the necessity of the government to sell its bonds fifty years ago and perfectly adapted to concentrating cash and restricting credits; an industrial system which, take it on all its sides, financial as well as administrative, holds capital in leading strings, restricts the liberties and limits the opportunities of labor, and exploits without renewing or conserving the natural resources of the country; a body of agricultural activities never yet given the efficiency of great business undertakings or served as it should be through the instrumentality of science taken directly to the farm, or afforded the facilities of credit best suited to its practical needs; water courses undeveloped, waste places unreclaimed, forests untended, fast disappearing without plan or prospect of renewal, unregarded waste heaps at every mine.

From Woodrow Wilson, First Inaugural Address, 1913.

---

who urged that unions be exempted from the Sherman Antitrust Act, or Bull Moosers, who advocated a strong regulatory agency. Louis Brandeis had moved closer to the Bull Moose point of view, and he now drafted a bill which Wilson supported. It created a Federal Trade Commission to prevent the unlawful suppression of competition. The measure passed, but only after Southern Conservatives had helped the Republicans amend it to provide for broad court review of the commission's orders.

A companion measure, the Clayton bill, was also amended before enactment. As the House passed it, it followed the prescriptions of Wilson's message, defined unfair practices, and forbade interlocking directorates. Senate conservatives modified that prohibition by exempting instances that did not tend to decrease competition. That standard gave the courts great latitude in deciding antitrust cases. It was also in the Senate, however, that friends of labor added to the bill a statement declaring that labor was not to be considered a commodity, a mere article of commerce. The

House had earlier included a clause exempting labor unions and farm organizations from antitrust prosecutions, but only when those groups were lawfully pursuing legitimate aims. As the courts were to interpret the Clayton Act, the reservation about legitimate aims just about canceled the exemption.

The antitrust laws of 1914 failed to prescribe business conduct to the extent Wilson had sought, and they failed to give unions the freedom of activity Gompers had urged. The Federal Trade Commission, moreover, had less power than many progressives had recommended. But the weaknesses of the legislation were not immediately apparent, and in any event the laws did improve federal arrangements for dealing with private industry. They constituted another, though a limited, victory for the Administration. In less than two years Wilson had reached the major statutory goals of his New Freedom.

The voters responded favorably in the elections of 1914. Superficially, the Democrats suffered that year, for the Republicans made sizable gains. But the Democrats retained control of both houses of Congress. The collapse of the Progressive party helped the Republicans in the Northeast, where they made their best showing. Elsewhere the Democrats picked up progressive support, and in the new Congress that sat in 1915 and 1916 Southern and Western agrarians had a larger voice than they had had before. The returns convinced perceptive Democratic strategists that they could carry the nation in 1916 only by winning the progressives of the West. Once more, reform had won a mandate.

In Behalf of Social Justice   This mandate made an impression on Wilson, who had given signs of turning toward the right. Before the election he had blocked bills that outlawed child labor and that established federal banks to make long-term loans to farmers. His appointments to the Federal Reserve Board and the Federal Trade Commission had on the whole been conservative. After the election he adjusted to the demands of congressional and national politics. He encouraged the progressive Democrats who in 1916 succeeded in passing the Federal Farm Loan Act and the Child Labor Act. Though he also endorsed legislation permitting firms engaged in export trade to combine to meet foreign competition, he did so primarily in order to strengthen American competition against foreign cartels. On matters of international trade the President had learned to respect the arguments of the Progressive party, and he supported an act in 1916 creating a nonpartisan, expert tariff commission designed, among other things, to prevent the dumping of unprotected goods in the American market.

In 1916 Wilson also practically ordered Congress to establish the eight-hour day at ten-hour pay for railway labor. Congress responded with the Adamson Act. In this case the President acted largely to prevent a threatening strike which would have tied up shipments of war materials for France and England, but his intercession won the plaudits it deserved from organized labor. Labor leaders and reformers had earlier found convincing evidence of Wilson's progressive intentions in his nomination of Louis D. Brandeis as Associate Justice of the Supreme Court.

Wilson's effective use of influence to overcome the opposition to the Brandeis appointment symbolized the President's commitment to progressivism. He had moved a long way from his position of 1912 toward that of Roosevelt and the Bull Moose. Indeed he had a right to boast that the Democrats had opened their hearts to "the demands of social justice" and "come very near to carrying out the platform of the Progressive Party" as well as their own.

Wilson and Moral Diplomacy

The Force of Moral Principle   In making foreign policy Wilson and Secretary of State Bryan were guided by attitudes they shared with most progressive Americans, particularly rural folk, social workers, and Protestant social gospelers. "The force of America," the President said during one crisis, "is the force of moral principle." As he and Bryan interpreted moral principle, it ruled out imperialism, colonialism, and war, which were all presumed to be avoidable as well as undesirable. Moral principle involved a duty to work for peace both by example and through diplomacy. It also involved obedience to the law. Wilson and Bryan felt that they had a mission to teach semideveloped countries to live according to the kind of legal and con-stitutional system which existed in the United States. They believed that that system was not only especially efficient but also especially ethical. They believed, too, that there was a definable body of international law that moral nations should obey in their relations with one another. And they placed their hope for peace in that law rather than in systems of alliances or in defensive or deterrent military build-ups.

Their quest for peace and international decency led Wilson and Bryan to distrust the career men in the navy, the army, and the State Department, whom they considered conventional and even cynical. The President and the Secretary of State were willing to risk offending the experts and losing the benefits of their informed advice in order to strike out along new diplomatic paths. Bryan launched his idealistic program in 1913 and 1914 by negotiating treaties with Great Britain, France, Italy, and twenty-seven lesser powers. These treaties provided for submitting all disputes among the signatories to permanent com-missions of investigation. For one year, while investigation proceeded, the parties to the treaties promised that they would neither go to war nor increase their armaments. At the end of that year they could either accept or reject the findings of the investigation, but Bryan expected the "cooling-off" period to remove the chance of war. Though Roosevelt ridiculed the plan, humanitarians throughout the west-ern world applauded the treaties and the spirit that produced them.

That spirit impelled Wilson in 1913 to with-draw American support from the Chinese railway consortium which Taft had helped to arrange (see p. 544). The United States, Wil-son said, could not be a partner to foreign in-terference in Chinese affairs. He also recog-nized the new Republic of China, the first major recognition that government received.

The most imminent threat to China's na-tional integrity was Japan, whose relations with the United States had deteriorated be-cause of the troublesome race issue. Wilson had characteristic Southern prejudices about race. During his Administration there was in-creasing segregation of Negroes within the federal service. Never an enemy of "Jim Crow," Wilson made no effort to dissuade

California politicians who were in any case determined in 1913 to prohibit Japanese from owning land in their state. On the President's advice, they passed a statute which achieved that end indirectly, and without violating American treaty obligations. But the Japanese were nonetheless humiliated. Their ambassa-dor protested to the State Department; there were anti-American disturbances in Japan; and the Joint Board of the Army and Navy, deeming war probable, advised Wilson to move warships into Chinese and Philippine waters. The President resorted instead to conciliatory diplomacy. The ensuing exchange of notes eased the crisis and ended talk of war, but the issue remained unresolved, and the Japanese remained understandably resentful.

That resentment contributed to a new con-troversy in 1915. The preoccupation of Eu-ropean powers with the war then raging on their own continent gave Japan a chance to make twenty-one extraordinary demands of China. Had China agreed to the treaty con-taining the demands, she would have become a political and economic dependency. Ameri-can protests, supplemented by pressure from England, persuaded the Japanese temporarily to moderate their terms. The episode revealed how tenuous the balance of power in Asia had become. It also disclosed Bryan's commitment to long-standing national policies. The United States, he warned Japan in a portentous note, could not recognize any agreement impairing the Open Door Policy, the treaty rights of Americans, or the political or territorial in-tegrity of China.

Confusion in Latin America   As in Asia, so in Latin America, Wilson intended to abandon "dollar diplomacy" with its attend-ant intrusions on the sovereignty of weak nations. He hoped also, while preserving the strategic lifeline to the Panama Canal, to cultivate the friendship of Latin-American peoples and to help them to achieve a higher standard of living and a more democratic gov-ernment. He began convincingly by nego-tiating a treaty with Colombia providing both apology and indemnity for Roosevelt's Pana-manian adventure. But Roosevelt's friends in the Senate prevented ratification of that treaty, and the Administration's benign purposes soon produced policies that seemed imperialistic to those they were designed to assist.

A combination of circumstances made moral diplomacy difficult. The small nations in and around the Caribbean were, as they had long been, impoverished and turbulent. Unwilling to have the United States government assume and service their debts, Wilson relied on private bankers whose motives he suspected. He could not permit turmoil in the area to breed revolutions or European intercessions that might endanger the approaches to the isthmus. Consequently he turned to American troops and American dollars to keep order. Since the local forces of order were often also the forces of reaction, Wilson at times resisted reform. Experienced diplomats might have been able to promote stability, but Wilson let Bryan turn out career men and send to the Caribbean area "deserving Democrats" lacking any qualifications except faithful party service.

Yet the President tended to attribute qualities of justice and legality to the reactionary government Bryan supported in Nicaragua and to the protectorates the Administration established in Santo Domingo and Haiti. Wilson never fully appreciated the intensity of the anti-American feeling his policies provoked. That feeling impeded his efforts to establish a Pan-American pact, to which Chile and Argentina were in any event unready to subscribe.

The President's unselfish intentions pulled him deep into Mexican affairs. During the late nineteenth century, large landholders, the army, the hierarchy of the Church, and foreign investors had sustained a dictatorial government in Mexico which had suppressed the landless, uneducated, impoverished peasants and workers. In 1911 a revolution overthrew the government, but in 1913 General Victoriano Huerta engineered a *coup d'état* that restored a reactionary regime under his domination. The revolutionists, who called themselves Constitutionalists, continued to resist under Venustiano Carranza, their able and implacable leader. Though his forces controlled much of the country, the major European powers recognized the Huerta government. President Taft had delayed recognizing the Huerta regime only because he hoped first to settle various outstanding American claims.

Americans with financial interests in Mexico urged Wilson to recognize Huerta, but the President would have no formal dealings with a government of assassins. He therefore refused to appoint an ambassador to Mexico. He did, however, send a series of special agents whose reports intensified his dislike for the regime but also led him erroneously to believe that the United States could decree a solution to her neighbor's problems.

Wilson followed a policy of "watchful waiting" until October 1913, when Huerta, supported by British oil interests, proclaimed himself military dictator. The President then demanded that Huerta retire. The United States, he assured the Mexicans, sought no land but only the advancement of "constitutional liberty."

To cut off the dictator's support, Wilson promised to protect British property if a Constitutionalist victory endangered it. He also, in 1914, drove through Congress a law repealing the exemption from tolls for American coastal shipping using the Panama Canal. That exemption, as the British had argued, violated an Anglo-American treaty that pledged the United States not to discriminate against British shipping using the canal. In full agreement, Wilson timed his action to serve his Mexican policy as well as international good faith. The danger of war in Europe made the British particularly solicitous of American friendship, and in March 1914 they withdrew their recognition of Huerta.

Meanwhile Wilson had told Carranza that the United States would join him in war against Huerta if he would keep the revolution orderly. Opposed to any American interference, Carranza rejected the indiscreet offer. But since he needed the arms which an American embargo denied all Mexicans, his representatives assured Wilson that he would respect property rights. Somewhat skeptically, the President in February 1914 lifted the embargo.

Armed Conflict in Mexico Soon thereafter Wilson seized an excuse for intervention. On April 10, 1914, an Huertista colonel arrested some American sailors who had gone ashore at Tampico. Though the Mexicans immediately apologized, American Admiral Henry T. Mayo insisted that they make a formal salute to the American flag. After the Mexicans declined, Wilson prepared to occupy

The United States and Mexico, 1914-17

Vera Cruz, Mexico's most important port. On April 20 he asked Congress for authority to use military force "to obtain from General Huerta . . . the fullest recognition of the rights and dignity of the United States."

The next day, before Congress could act, Wilson ordered the navy to seize Vera Cruz in order to prevent a German merchant ship from landing arms for Huerta. Several Americans were killed in the action that followed. While American newspapers predicted war and Wilson ordered war plans drawn up, the Constitutionalists as well as the Huertistas denounced the violation of their national sovereignty.

Fortunately both countries accepted an offer of mediation from Argentina, Brazil, and Chile. Though Wilson told American negotiators to insist on Huerta's removal and on the "necessary agrarian and political reforms," the final agreement said nothing about those matters. Indeed it was never even signed by the Constitutionalists, who had become the dominant faction in Mexico. Huerta abdicated in July and Carranza marched into Mexico City in August 1914, angry with the United States and disdainful of Wilson's aid and advice.

During 1915 the revolution in Mexico reached high pitch. Violence sometimes accompanied reform. The destruction of private property and attacks on priests and nuns excited American demands for intervention,

especially among Catholics, Republicans eager to embarrass Wilson, and jingoes spoiling for a war. The President, however, refused to let the unfortunate episodes of the revolution obscure his understanding of its laudable objectives. He had no affection for Carranza, but he resisted the pressure of the jingoes; partly because he dared not let embroilments in Mexico tie his hands in the crisis then developing with Germany. In October 1915 he recognized the *de facto* existence of the Constitutional government.

Within a few months the bandit leader Pancho Villa, in command of a band of guerillas in northern Mexico, created a new crisis. An opponent of Carranza, Villa had earlier posed as an advocate of restraint and thus had persuaded Wilson to give him support. In January 1916 Villa revealed his true self. He murdered a group of Americans whom he had removed from a train in Mexico. In March he killed nineteen more during a raid on Columbus, New Mexico. Again there were demands in the United States for war, but Wilson tried to contain the situation. He ordered an expedition to cross the border and punish Villa but to avoid engaging the Constitutionalists.

The futile pursuit of Villa aroused Mexican tempers. In April Carranza insisted the Americans leave his country. Wilson refused and negotiations faltered. When Villa brazenly raided Texas, the President called up the national guard for service on the border and commissioned plans for a full-scale invasion. Twice there were serious skirmishes between American and Constitutionalist soldiers. Carranza, however, needed to devote his full energies to his domestic affairs, and Wilson had growing problems in Europe. Both men, moreover, genuinely desired peace. In July 1916 they agreed to appoint a joint commission to resolve their differences. Although Carranza later rejected its decision, the danger of war had passed. In January 1917 Wilson called the troops home, and two months later he granted the Constitutionalists *de jure* recognition.

In the balance Wilson's restraint outweighed his impulsiveness. In attempting to impose American standards upon the Mexicans, the President dangerously offended those he wanted to help. But he also succeeded in withstanding the demands for war which he had

Pancho Villa: Brazen bandit.

inadvertently fanned. He succeeded most of all in grasping the need for reform in Mexico. No other head of state of a major power was as perceptive or as friendly. For all his miscalculations, the President in the end protected the cause of agrarian and political reform. The American people in varying degree shared his confusions and his distaste for the excesses of revolution. Most of them, however, also shared his sympathy for Mexico's troubles and his reluctance to permit disagreement and discord to grow into war.

Problems of Neutrality

War in Europe   In August 1914 a crisis within the empire of Austria-Hungary brought on the war in Europe that had been brewing for more than a decade. Ambitious Germany dominated the alliance of the Central Powers, including Austria-Hungary and Turkey. On the other side were the western powers, France and England, their ally, Russia, and soon also Italy, a partner bought by promises of more lands.

Though most Americans had known that war was threatening, they were shocked by the outbreak of hostilities and unprepared to face the problems war imposed on them. Relieved that war seemed so far away, they had yet to learn that distance alone could not insulate the United States. Most progressives tended to believe that selfish commercial rivalries had moved the European nations toward disaster. They believed, too, that the United States could serve the world best by concentrating on further reform at home, by setting a noble example of peace and democracy. Even those who were not progressives were slow to assess the actual causes of war, slow to recognize the intensity of nationalistic emotions that war bred, slower still in seeing how those emotions

The European Powers at War

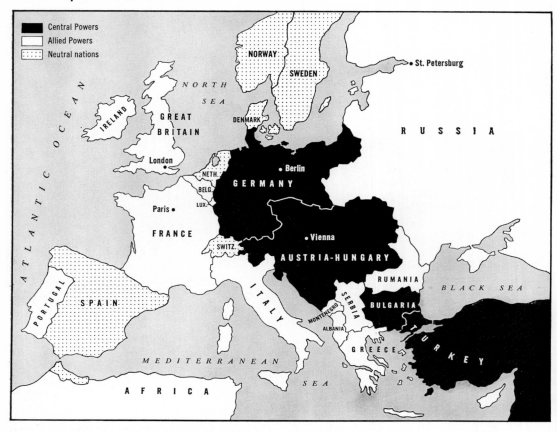

blocked a return to peace. Americans, like other western men, had no experience with the shocks of total war, calculated brutality, and mass hatred.

The Administration's initial statements of policy gave official sanction to attitudes that prevailed throughout the nation. Wilson expressed his faith that the United States could play "a part of impartial mediation," and he urged his countrymen to be "neutral in fact as well as in name." But impartiality of sentiment was impossible. Many Americans of various national origins identified themselves with the loyalties of their forebears. The German-Americans and Irish-Americans particularly supported the Central Powers. British-Americans favored the western Allies. The similarities between British and American speech and institutions, furthermore, fostered widespread sympathy for England. Wilson himself had

long been an admirer of England's culture.

Belligerents in both camps tried to enlist American emotions. The Germans circulated stories alleging that the British blockade was causing mass starvation; the British published accounts of atrocities allegedly committed by German soldiers. Both sides exaggerated, but propaganda won few converts. The course of the war itself, however, made a deeper impression. Germany's invasion of Belgium in August 1914, which violated a treaty pledging Germany to respect Belgian neutrality, was an early act of aggression that offended many Americans. Propaganda could not erase that evidence of German ruthlessness, and evidence was to come of German intrigue within the United States. The Allied cause gradually gained adherents, though very few even among them favored American participation in a war across the Atlantic.

Captured U-boat: Effectiveness
depended upon surprise.

Neutral Rights   While Wilson remained
firm in his purpose to be neutral in fact, he
upheld neutral rights to trade and use of the
ocean. Those traditional objectives of American diplomacy had, the President believed, a
clear basis in law and morality. His standards
for defining neutral rights were "the existing
rules of international law and the treaties of
the United States." But these rules were uncertain, especially under the unprecedented
conditions created by the tactics of the submarine, the novel weapon on which Germany
counted heavily. Particularly with Germany,
but also with England, troubles arose over
Wilson's interpretations of American neutral
rights.

The British, who controlled the seas, were
determined that the Allies alone should receive munitions and other essential war materials from the United States. They therefore
established a tight blockade of Germany and
narrowly limited the kinds of goods that
American ships could carry to neutral ports
from which they could be sent on to Germany.
The British also diverted suspect shipping to
their own ports, confiscated many cargoes,
interfered with American mail in order to
intercept military and economic information,
and ultimately forbade British subjects to do
any business with American firms "black-
listed" for violating British rules.

Wilson protested often and vigorously
against these and other British practices that
infringed upon traditional neutral rights. The
British, engaged in total war, considered him
peevishly legalistic. But, since they had to

The War at Sea

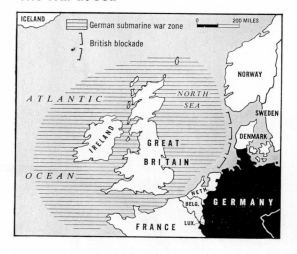

have American supplies, they made the basic objective of their diplomacy "the maximum blockade that could be enforced without a rupture with the United States."

The success of that policy owed much to the increasing good will Americans felt for England. It owed something, too, to the growing importance of war production for the American economy. Allied demands for war materials stimulated American heavy industry and provided a market for American agriculture. Indeed, with a wise solicitude the British even provided funds to help stabilize the price of cotton at a level satisfactory to the Democratic South.

There were no international rules against selling war materials to the Allies. And if Wilson had refused to permit such sales, he would have indirectly aided the Central Powers. Nor were there any rules to prevent American bankers from making loans to finance Allied purchases. Bryan at first maintained that such loans violated "the true spirit of neutrality," but early in 1915, when the Allies were desperate for funds, he partially reversed himself. Before the end of that year the State Department had approved enormous loans, arranged by American financiers, without which England and France could not have continued to buy the materials they had to have. Thereafter almost every segment of the national economy would have suffered from a

diplomatic rupture with the Allies or from a German triumph.

The Germans, who were unable to transport supplies through the British blockade, protested against American sales of war materials to the Allies and against British interpretations of maritime law. They also sent out submarines to destroy Allied shipping. These U-boats created the issue on which German-American relations ultimately foundered.

The Submarine Problem   Submarines could not operate according to the traditional rules governing the conduct of ships bent on destroying commerce. Their effectiveness depended upon surprise. They could not warn their prospective targets before attacking them, or remove crews or passengers from stricken ships. They were too small to rescue survivors of their sinkings. Yet Wilson insisted, as most Americans thought he should, that the Germans observe traditional international law.

The submarine issue arose in February 1915, when Germany proclaimed a war zone around the British Isles. Enemy ships, she warned, would be sunk on sight, and neutral ships would be in danger of misidentification. In a sharp reply Wilson called the sinking of merchant ships without visit and search "a wanton act." The destruction of an American ship, he declared, or the loss of American lives on belligerent ships, would be regarded as "a flagrant violation of neutral rights." It would be an offensive act for which he would hold Germany to "strict accountability." His note expressed the horror most Americans felt toward the barbarity of modern weapons. It left the Germans with a choice between abandoning their strategic plan or risking American antagonism.

They chose to take the risk. In April 1915 an American went down aboard a British ship. On May 1 an American ship was torpedoed. Six days later the Germans sank the British passenger liner *Lusitania* and with her died hundreds of men, women, and children, many of them Americans whom the Germans had warned not to embark. That sinking shocked the nation. A minority wanted to break off relations with Germany, which in their view was guilty of "murder" and "piracy," as Theodore Roosevelt put it. Most men of that mind hoped soon to see the United

States at war. At the other extreme, those who sympathized with Germany and those who considered war the worst possible calamity were eager to arbitrate the issue, if necessary to prohibit travel on the ships of belligerents. The majority of Americans were angry, determined to win some redress, but anxious to avoid hostility. Like Wilson, they hoped the problem could be negotiated away.

"There is such a thing," the President told one audience, "as a man being too proud to fight. There is such a thing as a nation being so right that it does not need to convince others by force." In that spirit he began his negotiations. It did not matter, he told Berlin, that the *Lusitania* carried munitions as well as passengers. That was a secondary consideration. The United States was concerned with the "sacred . . . rights of humanity," particularly "the right to life itself." The sinking was an "illegal and inhuman" act, and Wilson demanded an apology and reparations. Since submarines could not be used without violating "principles of justice and humanity," he also by implication demanded that they should not be used at all.

The extremists were dissatisfied. Roosevelt called the President "yellow." Bryan, who had urged Wilson to adopt the principles of the "cooling-off" treaties, considered the notes to Germany too harsh. Sadly he resigned from the Cabinet, to be replaced by Robert Lansing, a New York lawyer with a talent for diplomatic phraseology. As he and the President continued to negotiate, the Germans met them halfway. They would not admit the illegality of the sinking, but in February 1916 they offered an apology and an indemnity. By and large the American people were relieved. As Lansing put it, they desired only honorable friendship.

Peace with Honor   So long as the war continued, however, the submarine issue might involve the United States. The national interest as well as the interests of the besieged people of Europe impelled Wilson to attempt to arrange a peace. He had sent Colonel House to Europe in January 1915 to investigate the possibility of mediation, but House had found the Germans adamant in their decision to hold Belgium and destroy England's naval power. In October, however, the colonel concocted a plan for peace which Wilson approved. They intended to force Germany to negotiate by warning that otherwise the United States might enter the war on the Allied side. If the Germans were agreeable to negotiations, House hoped to bring them to reasonable terms at the conference table. Again, failure, according to the plan, would invite American participation in the war. In London in January and February 1916 House made progress toward his goal. Indeed it looked as if the British would accept an offer from Wilson for a peace conference in the autumn. But the enterprise collapsed when Lansing tried to revise American policy toward the submarines.

Wilson and Lansing had decided to ease the submarine issue by attempting to persuade the Allies not to arm their merchantmen. In that event the U-boats could issue warnings before attacking. The Germans naturally welcomed the idea, for their purpose was not to kill sailors but to destroy cargoes and bottoms. To their delight, just as House was completing his negotiations in England, Lansing suggested that Allied merchantmen be disarmed. The British of course refused. Lansing had earlier suggested to the Germans that if the Allies declined, Germany might declare unrestricted submarine warfare against all armed ships. In February 1916 the Germans made precisely that declaration. But Lansing then doubled back, reasserted Wilson's original submarine policy, and announced that the United States would not warn Americans against travel on armed ships. "Strict accountability" still applied.

The conflicting strands of American diplomacy had increased the chances of national involvement in the war. The Roosevelt Republicans prepared to make a major campaign issue during 1916 of the embarrassment the President had caused the Allies. At the opposite pole of opinion, Bryan, La Follette, and other agrarian progressives saw a "sort of moral treason" in letting American citizens create crises by sailing on endangered ships. Resolutions forbidding such travel failed in Congress only because Wilson exerted all his influence to defeat them.

One month later, in March 1916, a German submarine without warning torpedoed an unarmed French steamer, the *Sussex*. The President's policy seemed to have failed completely. But he did not retreat from his principles. After much reflection, in April he sent Germany an ultimatum. Unless it immediately abandoned "its present method of submarine warfare," the United States would "sever diplomatic relations." The Kaiser's advisers decided that, since they lacked the submarines to conduct a useful blockade of England, it was more important to keep the United States neutral. In May Germany acceded to Wilson's demand. Submarines would observe the rules of visit and search, the Germans said, but they might remove that limitation unless the United States compelled England to obey international law.

In spite of the threat that Germany might revert to its earlier tactics, most Americans were again relieved. Unaware of the reasons for the German decision, they felt that the President had avoided war, maintained justice, and conquered the submarines with his pen. The *Sussex* pledge seemed to promise peace with honor, a happy formula—especially in a campaign year.

Americanism and Preparedness   As the war went on, it revealed to Americans as well as to Europeans the terrors of organized brutality and the dangers of organized passions. Intelligence and decency and orderliness gave way before the strains of continual fear. Though the United States was far from the fields of battle, even here timid men sought some symbol which would seem to protect them from the disturbances around them. Other men seized the chance to create symbols they could use for their own selfish ends. So it was that the most avid foes of labor unions underwrote a campaign to equate the open shop with "Americanism." So it was that those who distrusted Negroes or Catholics or Jews now did so in the name of Americanism. It was a word that the opponents of women's suffrage used, a word used also by the advocates of a literacy test for immigrants. The Senate blocked an amendment to enfranchise women, and Congress in 1915 passed a bill establishing a literacy test. Wilson vetoed it, pointing out that it abridged the traditional right of asylum and tested education rather than talent.

The President resisted the spirit of frightened conformity which Roosevelt exalted in the name of Americanism. The name, however, had a political magic which no politician could safely ignore, and Wilson himself used it to describe his foreign policy. In 1915, condemning the sabotage of munitions production for the Allies, he attributed it to extremists among the German- and Irish-Americans. Calling on all others to dedicate themselves to the national honor, the President planned to make his version of Americanism the keynote of his campaign for re-election.

The position that Wilson and his party took on preparedness also accorded with the middle-of-the-road attitudes of most Americans. Even after the war began, they tended, like the President, to consider arms and munitions the unnecessary tools of evil men. Again like the President, they had an instinctive dislike for widespread military training and a large standing army, neither of which had any place in the American tradition. That tradition persisted, in spite of the nature of modern war, in viewing the militia and a citizen-soldiery as adequate safeguards for national security. Four months after the sinking of the *Lusitania*, Wilson expressed a popular sentiment when he said he saw no need "to stir the nation up in favor of national defense."

Moved by the possibility of war in Europe and Mexico, a vocal minority began to teach their countrymen the need to prepare, pointing out that it took time to produce weapons and to train armies and navies for twentieth-century warfare. Theodore Roosevelt led these advocates of preparedness. He was sometimes too strident to be convincing, but more moderate men gradually put their ideas across. During 1915 Secretary of War Lindley M. Garrison and his three Republican predecessors all urged preparedness. It had become a political issue, and Wilson's Democratic advisers warned him that he had better do something about it.

In July 1915 the President instructed the armed services to make plans for expansion. In November, asking for much less than they had recommended, he proposed a volunteer army of four hundred thousand men who were to serve only a few months in each of several successive years. Even this modest proposal met opposition from agrarian liberals in Congress, most of them Democrats, some of them with great influence. To win support for his program, Wilson went on a speaking trip that took him halfway across the continent. During that tour he came out for a "navy second to none."

Yet in 1916 the President had to make concessions to his opponents. Still close to the middle of the road, he first rejected the War Department's plan for creating a large reserve force under the regular army, and he also appointed a new Secretary of War,* Newton D. Baker, a progressive with a reputation for antimilitarism. Wilson and Baker then accepted a plan for the army which had been formulated by the national guard lobby and was sponsored by Southern agrarians. In adopting this plan, the House of Representatives "federalized" the guard by giving the War Department larger but still incomplete authority over state units. The Senate, however, rewrote the bill, modeling it closely on the earlier suggestions of the War Department.

Wilson again demonstrated his leadership by working out a successful compromise. The law which he supported and Congress enacted in May 1916 doubled the regular army and gave the War Department more authority than had the House bill. The President's influence helped, too, to carry a measure accelerating the building of a strong navy. The agrarians scored one success: In the face of Administration opposition, they fashioned the revenue legislation to pay for the defense program. It increased surtaxes on personal income and put new taxes on inheritances. Those best able to pay would have to foot the bill for preparedness.

Taken together, the army, navy, and tax laws of 1916 satisfied the majority of Americans. The Democrats had given the preparedness issue a progressive stamp and had identified their party with national defense. The measures fell short of the demands of the armed services, but they met the most urgent requirements of a nation that still hoped and expected to remain at peace.

The Election of 1916   For the Republicans one major problem in 1916 was how to

* Garrison had resigned partly because of his view on national defense, partly because he opposed Wilson's policy for increasing home rule in the Philippines.

reassimilate the Progressive party. Roosevelt had kept it alive largely to further his own ambitions, but the Old Guard would not countenance his nomination on the Republican ticket, and the Colonel cared more about defeating Wilson than about nursing old grudges. In order to regain Bull Moose votes, the Republicans selected a candidate with a progressive record, Charles Evans Hughes. He had been a successful reform governor of New York and in 1912, as an Associate Justice of the Supreme Court, had stayed neutral in the party split. He was an able man and a strong candidate whose cause may have been hurt rather than helped by Roosevelt's obsessive attacks on Democratic foreign policy.

Although Wilson had planned to run on the issues of Americanism and progressivism, foreign policy became a central factor in the campaign. At the Democratic convention, as the keynote speaker described the recurrent crises in foreign policy, he explained how Wilson had resolved each one and concluded each time with the phrase "We did not go to war." Each time the delegates responded jubilantly. The party managers sensed that their most effective slogan would be, "He kept us out of war." Its effectiveness probably grew as Roosevelt sounded more and more bellicose and as Hughes explained that he would have been tougher on Mexico and Germany than Wilson had been. The President himself told the voters that he was "not expecting this country to get into war," and Democratic propagandists advertised: "Wilson and Peace with Honor? or Hughes with Roosevelt and War?"

There were, of course, other issues. The Irish-American and German-American extremists embarrassed Hughes by supporting him openly, but he failed to repudiate them publicly while Wilson deliberately attacked them. The Democrats had made a progressive record that was especially persuasive with those from the defunct Bull Moose who could not yet tolerate the thought of voting Republican again.

By and large, rural America voted for Wilson, as did labor, the liberals, and most intellectuals. The contest was so close that it hinged on the ballots in California and Minnesota, which were counted only after early

Eastern returns had put Hughes ahead. Hughes went to bed election night thinking that he had won. But the South and the West reversed the verdict. Wilson received 49.4 per cent of the popular vote to Hughes's 46.2 per cent and carried the electoral college 277 to 254. The mandate was narrow, but the appeal of peace and progressivism had prevailed.

The Road to War

Wilson knew very well how tenuous was the nation's hold on peace. Before election day the British had tightened their regulations on neutral trade and the Germans had intensified their submarine campaign against the Allies. The war could not be contained much longer. Either Wilson had to find ways to end it or else he would have to sacrifice peace or honor —or both.

The President planned to send a dramatic note to the belligerents. He was ready, his draft said, to pledge the "whole force" of the United States to end the "war of exhaustion and attrition" and to keep the future peace. The draft asked each side for "a concrete definition" of the objectives for which it was fighting. It also demanded that a peace conference be called immediately. Furthermore, Wilson intended to employ every pressure short of war to assist the more reasonable side. While he was still reworking his draft, in December 1916, the German chancellor announced his government's readiness to negotiate. Briefly Wilson was encouraged.

The offer, however, hid a corrupted spirit. The Germans made the gesture out of confidence of impending victory. Masters of the eastern front where the Russians were collapsing, the Germans expected to smash France and England if their terms were rejected. They had also secretly decided that, if negotiations failed, they would resume unrestricted submarine warfare. And their secret terms were harsh—they would insist on territory along the Baltic, in the Congo, and in Belgium, France, and Luxembourg.

Slowly Wilson discovered the truth. He dispatched the note he had been drafting, but the Germans replied that they wanted no neutral at the peace table. The Allies publicly rejected the President's proposal but privately let him know they would negotiate if the German conditions were reasonable. Then in January 1917 the Germans at last revealed their grasping terms and announced that their submarines would sink at sight all ships, belligerent or neutral.

For several weeks Wilson would not admit that he had either to surrender his principles or go to war. He broke off relations with Germany, but he told Congress he wanted no conflict. He remained outwardly temperate even after learning on February 25 that Germany was plotting against the United States. That day the British communicated to Washington secret orders of the German foreign minister, Arthur Zimmermann, which they had intercepted. Those orders told the German minister to Mexico that, in the event of war with the United States, he should invite Mexico and Japan to join the Central Powers.

Wilson, while still hoping to avoid war, had meanwhile pressed his interpretation of neutral rights. He had asked Congress for authority to arm American merchant vessels and to employ any other means that might be necessary to protect American ships and citizens at sea. To win votes for his proposal, he made the Zimmermann note public on March 1, 1917. A wave of anti-German sentiment swept the country, but the Democratic House of Representatives withheld the broad authority the President wanted, and in the Senate a dozen antiwar progressives talked a stronger bill to death.

That "little group of willful men," as Wilson called them, struggled in vain. The Zimmermann note had dissolved the myth that the war was strictly European. The President on his own ordered the merchantmen armed, and on March 18, two weeks after his second inauguration, U-boats sank three American ships. Moreover, the first Russian revolution established a limited monarchy and a responsible parliament, temporarily destroying the despotism that had made Americans reluctant to associate with the Allied cause. And the Allies could no longer fight without American men, money, and material. The combination of events converted even the most ardent peace advocates in the Cabinet to the necessity for war.

Wilson was agonized by a conclusion he could not escape. War, he told one confidant, "would overturn the world we had known," lead to "a dictated peace," require "illiberalism at home." Sadly he predicted that "the spirit of ruthless brutality" would enter the very "fibre of our national life." His pain was shared by every progressive, for progressivism had based its faith on the peaceful, reasonable improvement of the lot of man in a world of quiet and intelligence. It was also, however, a moral faith, and in the view of Wilson and other progressive intellectuals, Germany had violated moral principles. She had forced war on France and Belgium. She was bent on conquest. Whatever the definitions of neutral rights, no one was immune from German aggression, and there could be no real peace while it went unpunished.

With those thoughts in mind, Wilson on April 2 addressed the special session of Congress he had summoned. On April 4 the Senate by a vote of 82 to 6, and on April 6 the House of Representatives by a vote of 273 to 50, passed a resolution recognizing the existence of a state of war with Germany.

Program for a Just War

The world must be made safe for democracy. Its peace must be planted upon the tested foundations of political liberty. We have no selfish ends to serve. We desire no conquest, no dominion. We seek no indemnities for ourselves, no material compensation for the sacrifices we shall freely make. We are but one of the champions of the rights of mankind. We shall be satisfied when those rights have been made as secure as the faith and the freedom of nations can make them....

It is a fearful thing to lead this great peaceful people into war, into the most terrible and disastrous of all wars, civilization itself seeming to be in the balance. But the right is more precious than peace, and we shall fight for the things which we have always carried nearest our hearts,—for democracy, for the right of those who submit to authority to have a voice in their own governments, for the rights and liberties of small nations, for a universal dominion of right by such a concert of free peoples as shall bring peace and safety to all nations and make the world itself at last free.

From Woodrow Wilson, War Message to Congress, 1917.

SUGGESTIONS FOR READING

General

The best general account of the Taft years and of the breakup of the Republican party is in G. E. Mowry, *The Era of Theodore Roosevelt* (1958). A. S. Link, *Woodrow Wilson and the Progressive Era* (1954), covers the succeeding years to the American entry into the war with equivalent vigor and insight. Also useful are relevant parts of Eric Goldman, *Rendezvous With Destiny* * (1952), and Richard Hofstadter, *The Age of Reform* * (1955). An older book of G. E. Mowry, *Theodore Roosevelt and the Progressive Movement* * (1946), contains a more detailed account—and less friendly to T.R.—than that in the same author's later work.

Progressives and Regulars

The case for Taft is set forth cogently in Henry Pringle, *Life and Times of William Howard Taft*, 2 vols. (1939), but this study should be compared with the Roosevelt biographies listed in connection with the preceding chapter, and with A. T. Mason, *Bureaucracy Convicts Itself* (1941), which takes Pinchot's part in his controversy with Ballinger. For an understanding of progressive social ideas, it is essential to read Herbert Croly, *The Promise of American Life* (1909), Walter Weyl, *The New Democracy* (1912), and Walter Lippmann, *Drift and Mastery* * (1914), as well as the autobiographies of La Follette and William Allen White. Two significant studies of progressive thought, besides those referred to in the previous chapter, are Walter Johnson, *William Allen White's America* (1947), and C. B. Forcey, *The Crossroads of Liberalism* (1961). There are no comparable studies of conservative thought, but that subject gets useful treatment in Richard Leopold, *Elihu Root and the Conservative Tradition* (1954), and in the introduction by E. E. Morison to Vol. V of *The Letters of Theodore Roosevelt* (1952).

* Available in a paperback edition.

The outstanding work on Wilson is A. S. Link's continuing biography, of which three strong volumes have been published: *Wilson: The Road to the White House* (1947), covering the period through the election of 1912; *Wilson: The New Freedom* (1956), concentrating on domestic policies through 1914; and *Wilson: The Struggle for Neutrality* (1960), analyzing foreign policy through 1915. Two recent, brief studies of Wilson are J. M. Blum, *Woodrow Wilson and the Politics of Morality* * (1956), and J. A. Garraty, *Woodrow Wilson* (1956). These are less sympathetic than two older works: H. C. F. Bell, *Woodrow Wilson and the People* (1945); and R. S. Baker, *Woodrow Wilson: Life and Letters*, 6 vols. (1927–37). Of the special studies of Wilson's diplomacy, the best are A. S. Link, *Wilson the Diplomatist* (1957), and Harley Notter, *The Origins of the Foreign Policy of Woodrow Wilson* (1937). There is an especially keen analysis of the issues of American foreign policy in R. E. Osgood, *Ideals and Self-interest in America's Foreign Relations* (1953). The European scene gets thorough treatment in S. B. Fay, *Origins of the World War*, 2 vols. (1930), and B. E. Schmitt, *The Coming of War*, 2 vols. (1930). The case for isolation imbues both C. C. Tansill, *America Goes to War* (1928), and Walter Millis, *The Road to War* (1935). Of the various studies of the Wilsonians, one is indispensable: Charles Seymour, ed., *The Intimate Papers of Colonel House*, 4 vols. (1921–28). Also useful, particularly on domestic issues, is A. T. Mason, *Brandeis: A Free Man's Life* (1946). J. A. Garraty, *Henry Cabot Lodge* (1953), presents an understanding account of one of Wilson's foremost antagonists. The literature on Wilson and his time will be richly expanded with the publication, not yet begun, of his letters and papers under the editorship of A. S. Link.

* Available in a paperback edition.

24

The First World War

The American nation was unprepared for the First World War. To begin with, the nation did not have a clear sense of purpose. Many German- and Irish-Americans were unreconciled to fighting on the side of the Allies. Smaller groups of pacifists saw no excuse for any fighting, and some progressives believed that the United States had no business involving itself in what they considered to be a struggle between European imperialists. The majority of Americans were in full accord with the decision to go to war, but they were confused about its origins and objectives. Like the President, they had hoped to remain neutral. Like the President, they regarded the submarine issue as a matter of morality. They had little if any understanding of the threat to the nation's interest that aggression in Europe had created.

Indeed the moral temper of the times led men to seek utopian rather than realistic reasons for the actions to which they were committed. To accommodate that temper, and to convert the dissenters, Wilson defined American war aims in idealistic terms. The spirit of his war message and later addresses was noble as well as persuasive. It helped transmute the fervor of progressivism into the selfless bravery of the "great crusade." But it also turned some fervor into frenzy, and it led men to expect a paradise that no war could give them.

The United States was also unprepared for the total mobilization demanded by modern war, and for the special strengths required to

fight a war overseas. The increases in the army in 1916 had been adequate at best for defending the nation's borders from attack. Even in April 1917 the Administration hoped that the Allies would need only money and war materials. But the war missions which England and France sent to Washington quickly dispelled Wilson's hopes by making it clear that the Allies had to have reinforcements as fast as the United States could supply them.

Yet the nation lacked the necessary army, the plans and facilities to raise it, the guns and tanks and airplanes to equip it, the ships to transport it, and even the tools and the organization to produce the materials of war. In every respect—emotional, economic, military—mobilization was urgent. But mobilization was bound to be painful for a people who could scarcely imagine the hardships it would entail.

The Armed Forces on Land and Sea

Selective Service   The President and his military advisers agreed that conscription was the only efficient and democratic way to recruit a large army. In the House of Representatives, however, the Speaker and the chairman of the Military Affairs Committee, both Democrats, led the opposition to the Administration's selective service bill. Many of the bill's opponents considered conscription a threat to democracy. Others had a romantic attachment to the tradition of voluntary mili-

Embarkation: The Yanks are coming.

tary service. But if war had ever been romantic, it was no longer so, and selective service, as Wilson argued, spread the obligation to serve among all qualified men without regard to their social position. The House passed the bill in May, but only after mollifying American mothers by raising the minimum draft age from nineteen, which the army recommended, to twenty-one.*

In the Senate the Republicans wasted three weeks in a futile effort to force the Administration to accept the volunteer division which Theodore Roosevelt was organizing. Roosevelt and his admirers believed that even though his troops were half-trained they would make up the deficiency in dash. But the officers he wanted were needed to staff newly drafted divisions, and the Colonel, brave as ever, was also stout, elderly, partially blind, and without

experience in trench warfare. The Selective Service Act finally passed by the Senate left Wilson free to dispose of volunteer units as he saw fit, and he saw fit to reject Roosevelt's. Though Roosevelt might have dramatized the war effort if he had been given the chance, the President and the army chiefs believed it more important to preserve the principles of selective service and to avoid the embarrassments caused by political generals.

Early in June 1917 over nine million men registered quietly with the local officials whom the War Department authorized to supervise the draft. Before the war ended, over twenty-four million had registered and almost three million had been inducted into the army. At no time was there any significant opposition to conscription, and the drafted troops fought as heroically as the two million volunteers who enlisted in the various armed services.

The army's top command was strictly professional. Bypassing General Leonard Wood,

* It was necessary in 1918 to lower the minimum age to eighteen.

American Operations on the Western Front, 1918

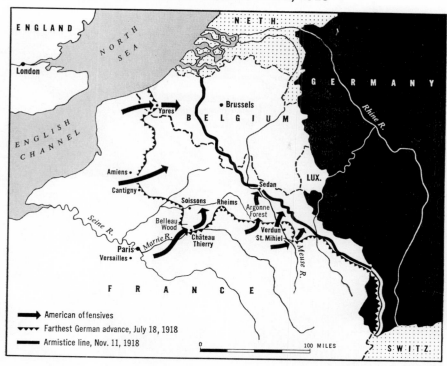

an intimate of Roosevelt, Wilson made General John J. Pershing head of the American Expeditionary Force and gave his decisions consistent support. "Black Jack" Pershing, a laconic, stern West Pointer, pursued two controversial policies. He refused to send troops into battle until they had completed their training, and he insisted on preserving a separate identity for the AEF, though the French and British were impatient for reinforcements and anxious to merge American units with their own.

The War in the West   In the fall of 1917 German offensives routed the Italians and destroyed the Russian army. The Bolshevik Revolution of November removed Russia from the war and left the western front, manned by war-weary French and British troops, exposed to the full attack Germany was certain to mount the following spring. The alarmed Allies created the Supreme War Council to direct their resistance and urged Pershing to supply men, trained or untrained. But Pershing still declined. In the spring, however, as

the Allied lines crumbled before a furious German offensive, Wilson agreed to the appointment of French Marshal Ferdinand Foch as supreme commander, and Pershing put his four available divisions at Foch's disposal.

During May 1918 the Germans pushed the French back to the Marne River, only fifty miles from Paris. Foch then called up one American division and a few regiments of marines who met the Germans at Château Thierry, carried the intensive battle there, and in June drove the enemy out of Belleau Wood.

Gambling for a quick victory before more American forces could reach France, the Germans in July struck at the sector of the Marne between Rheims and Soissons. Here some eighty-five thousand Americans helped to turn the attack, and eight divisions of Yanks participated in the French counteroffensive which cleaned out the sector early in August. The American First Army under Pershing then took over the southern front near St. Mihiel and routed the Germans there in an independent offensive in September. Late that

France: Fear, drudgery, exhaustion.

month Pershing attacked the German lines between Verdun and Sedan. This Meuse-Argonne engagement, which lasted more than a month, produced a costly but crucial American victory. Along with the success of French and British forces on the northern and central fronts, it crushed the German army and set the stage for an armistice (see p. 577).

The triumph exacted extraordinary expenditures of nerve and flesh, for in some respects the First World War was the most ghastly in history. By 1917 the opposing armies in the west were facing each other from lines of trenches which were in places only hundreds of yards, or less, apart. Continually within range of enemy artillery, soldiers in the trenches were exposed also to the poison gases which both sides used extensively. Hand grenades, machine guns, rifles with a high muzzle velocity, as well as bayonets and some-

times tanks, served as the basic tools for soldiers attacking "over the top" toward the enemy lines, where the defense was similarly equipped. Casualties ran high, particularly during offensives, and American troops, along with their allies and foes, suffered a high incidence of shell shock, a form of battle fatigue, and of tuberculosis, a companion of the poison gas and the mud, cold, wet, and filth of the trenches. For most soldiers the war was an awful combination of fear, drudgery, and exhaustion.

The signal exceptions were the aviators. In the infancy of the air age, the airplane was used primarily for observation and light bombing, but opposing squadrons of fighter pilots struggled for control of the air. Their craft were simple and slow, their tactics rudimentary. Yet the new knights of the air wrote a special chapter of military history in their man-to-man combat in the skies, and American aces dramatized for their countrymen the potentialities and the importance of aerial warfare.

The Yanks had reached France just in time. The Allies needed the new man power to stop the Germans' gamble for victory—a gamble that would probably have succeeded had reinforcements failed to appear. Yet the Americans, indispensable during the last months of war, and gallant and effective then, arrived only after the Allies had held the Germans for almost four terrible years. Over fifty thousand Americans died in France, but the war took the lives of three million English, French, and Russian soldiers. The role of the American army was both relatively small and absolutely vital.

The War at Sea   So too was the role of the American navy. In all but one respect the war at sea had been won by the success of the British navy in bottling up the German fleet. As the British admiralty admitted, however, the German submarines also had to be brought under control. During 1917 U-boats sank more than twice the tonnage of shipping that the Allies and Americans built that year. Hard pressed to supply themselves, the British could not guard the American lines of supply to Europe, and the Americans could not afford to risk transporting an army aboard ships unprotected from enemy submarines.

The United States Navy had the ships and the men to take over the patrol of the Western Hemisphere and to assist the English in patrolling the waters around the British Isles. Thirty-five American destroyers reached England in July 1917; during 1918 more than three hundred other ships of various classifications joined them.

Even with the American destroyers, both those afloat and those being built,* the Allies lacked the antisubmarine vessels to root the U-boats out of the ocean. Two American plans proved to be at least as important as the ships themselves. One was a favorite idea of the President, who overruled the experts and insisted in 1918 on laying mines between Scot-

* The warship building program was reorganized to concentrate on destroyers.

land and Norway in an effort to contain the U-boats at their bases. This costly operation was incomplete when the war ended, and only partially effective, but by that time the convoy system had minimized the submarine danger.

Admiral William S. Sims, the ranking American naval officer in Europe and one of the great naval intelligences of the century, was the primary exponent of the plan for using destroyers and other men-of-war to escort convoys of merchantmen across the Atlantic. Though British skippers preferred to sail alone rather than to proceed in formation under naval command, Sims in the summer of 1917 overcame their objections and the resistance of the British admiralty. By the end of 1917 the use of convoys had cut shipping losses in half.

The escorted convoys and the patrolling American destroyers were so effective that not one American soldier was lost in transit to Europe. The bridge of ships to France carried the troops and supplies that the Germans had expected to destroy. The miracle of transportation turned the tide of war. This was a great American achievement, but it was possible only because the British also provided bottoms for men and equipment, and only because the Yanks at the front could use Allied cannon, tanks, and airplanes.

The Home Front

Problems of Production   By themselves the eventual prodigies of American war production would have been too little and too late for victory. Since there were no precedents for economic mobilization, the Administration had to feel its way along in creating agencies to supervise production and distribution and to allocate vital goods and services. When war came, the army did not even have information about the uniforms and shoes it would need. There was no inventory of national resources, no adequate plan for priorities or for stockpiling critical materials. Most of the first nine months of the war were spent in experimentation, in learning about mobilization, and in tooling up for production.

The lost time was especially serious for the aviation program. American planners were so slow in designing an aircraft engine, and the lumber industry was so slow in manufacturing the parts for aircraft bodies, that American aviators had to fly in British and French machines all through the war. The situation was almost as desperate in the production of artillery and tanks, which, like airplanes, were a new weapon. The building program for transports and cargo vessels collapsed completely, and the government had to rely on ships seized from neutrals or purchased from private industry.

These and other difficulties spurred the Senate Military Affairs Committee to investigate the conduct of the war. As 1918 began, the Democratic chairman of that committee asserted publicly that the military effort had been impeded by waste and inefficiency in every bureau of government. Republican senators, joined by several Democrats, urged that a war cabinet of three distinguished citizens be set up to exercise the powers that Congress had conferred upon the President. If that measure had passed, Wilson would have become a figurehead. Even as it was, the Senate committee was close to assuming the role of its predecessor which had harassed Lincoln during the Civil War.

The President, however, had already begun to solve the problems of mobilization. Neither during 1917 nor later, moreover, did any scandal taint the administration of the war. Aware of the threat from the Senate, Wilson admitted the delays and disappointments, but he also praised the "extraordinary promptness and efficiency" with which his associates were dispatching their unfamiliar tasks. To strengthen his position, he prepared a bill giving him sweeping authority to reorganize and manage all executive agencies. This measure, which Senator Lee S. Overman sponsored, passed Congress in April 1918 and enabled the President to complete his own plans.

Economic Mobilization   Those plans had taken shape slowly, but as they matured the Administration put the nation's economy on an effective war footing. In the spring of 1917 England, France, and Italy urgently needed food. Stretching the mandate of the Council of National Defense, which Congress had authorized the year before, the President in May established a food control program under Herbert C. Hoover, who had acquired an international reputation as director of the Belgian Relief Commission. Wilson also asked Congress for emergency authority over agriculture. The Lever Act of August 1917 granted him that authority, together with limited power to control the prices of certain scarce commodities. Wilson at once created the Food Administration. With Hoover at its head, that agency set high minimum prices to stimulate the production of wheat and pork, managed the distribution of those and other foodstuffs, and persuaded the public to observe meatless and breadless days. The success of Hoover's policies made possible the victualing of the nations fighting Germany.

To put American industry on a wartime footing proved more difficult. The General Munitions Board, another offshoot of the Council of National Defense, showed itself incapable of coordinating the conflicting demands of the American armed services and the Allied purchasing commissions. Consequently, in July 1917 Wilson appointed a War Industries Board with authority to pass on all American and Allied purchasing, to allocate raw materials, to control production, and to supervise labor relations. The WIB, however, failed to elicit the cooperation of the armed services, and the resulting confusion became a special target of the investigations of the Senate Military Affairs Committee.

In March 1918 the President rewrote the charter of the War Industries Board and named a new chairman, Bernard M. Baruch, who enlisted the help of some hundred outstanding business leaders. Now concerned largely with establishing industrial priorities, the WIB eliminated bottlenecks, developed processes to reduce waste, and speeded the conversion of plants to war production. The agency was helped in its task by a reorganization of the general staff of the army. Secretary of War Newton D. Baker created functional divisions within the staff and put each division under an experienced officer selected without regard to seniority. With the army and the WIB cooperating, Baruch became virtually the industrial dictator of the United States. Under his direction the incomparable abundance of the country could now be funneled into the war effort.

As in agriculture and industry, so in fuel, transportation, and labor, peacetime practices faltered under the stress of war. To relieve the critical coal shortage, the Lever Act empowered the President to fix the price of coal high enough to encourage operators to work marginal mines. In August 1917 he established the Fuel Administration under President Harry A. Garfield of Williams College. This agency set an attractive price for coal, and the resulting production was ample for the nation's needs. Snarls in railway transportation, however, impeded coal deliveries, and for four days in January 1918 Garfield closed all east-coast plants that used coal for any but vital purposes.

This emergency order underlined the crisis in railroading. The roads had tried to handle the extraordinary wartime traffic on the basis of voluntary cooperation, but in the absence of unified authority delays and tie-ups became worse and worse, and the snow and freezing weather of December 1917 precipitated a total collapse of internal transportation. With congressional approval, Wilson therefore established the United States Railway Administration under William G. McAdoo. Exercising an even greater authority than Baruch had over industry, McAdoo improved the railways' equipment, strengthened their finances, and successfully adjusted their operations to the demands of war.

Labor in Wartime   In April 1918 the President created the National War Labor Board, which unified the various agencies that had been established to prevent labor disturbances and the attending losses in production. Under the joint chairmanship of ex-President Taft and Frank P. Walsh, a labor lawyer, the WLB heard more than twelve hundred cases and forestalled many strikes, but it lacked the information it needed to set labor policies for the entire country. To remedy that deficiency, Wilson in May 1918 appointed the War Labor Policies Board under Felix Frankfurter, a young law professor who had been the War Department's labor adviser. The WLPB surveyed national labor needs and practices and standardized wages and hours. At its recommendation, the President created the United States Employment Service, an agency which placed almost four million workers in essential war jobs.

REMEMBER
·BELGIUM·

Buy Bonds
Fourth
Liberty
Loan

While keeping the country free from serious strikes, the government's labor agencies and policies also advanced the peacetime objectives of social reformers and union leaders. Membership in the American Federation of Labor grew more than 50 per cent, reaching over 3,200,000 by 1920. The government demanded an eight-hour day for war industry wherever it could and insisted on decent working conditions and living wages. Even though the cost of living rose 50 per cent, booming wages and full employment permitted a gratifying increase of 20 per cent in average *real* income. Though management groups hostile to labor were impatient with wartime controls, their profits were high. The over-all experience demonstrated dramatically that enlightened federal labor policies could bring to the laboring force unprecedented comfort and personal dignity without damping business enterprise.

Indeed the wartime experience confirmed the insights of men like Herbert Croly (see p. 548). Working together in the emergency agencies, businessmen and public servants learned a new respect for each other. They refined the techniques of organization and administration and applied them vigorously and unselfishly in the national interest. The organization of agriculture and labor proved to be as rewarding as the organization of industry, which had proceeded so much further during the days of peace. The wartime experience provided a precedent and a pattern for organizing a government beset by emergency. It was a compelling proof of the coming of age of an industrial society, a compelling rejoinder to advocates of the receding agrarian myth.

Propaganda, Public Opinion, and Civil Liberties   This very increase in efficiency, however, gave some of the wartime agencies a dangerous authority over the minds of men. A week after war was declared, Wilson created the Committee on Public Information to mobilize public opinion. George Creel, chairman of the CPI, was a progressive journalist of uncompromising self-assurance who worked out with newspapermen a voluntary censorship that kept the public reasonably well informed while safeguarding sensitive information. He also hired hundreds of artists and writers to mount a propaganda campaign without precedent in American history.

The CPI stressed two major points. One argued, as Wilson did, that the United States was fighting only for freedom and democracy. The other maintained that the Germans were all Huns, diabolic creatures perpetrating atrocities in an effort to conquer the world for their lust and greed. The releases of the Creel committee intensified the unreasoning attitudes of a nation at war. They hinted that German spies had an ear to every wall. Often they carried antiunion overtones, labeling as treason all work stoppages, whatever their real cause. More often they implied that all dissent was unpatriotic, and that pacifists and socialists had hidden sympathies for the enemy.

This propaganda helped to sell war bonds, combat absenteeism in the factories, and reconcile some doubters to the war. But the price was high. The attitudes the CPI encouraged were the same as those fostered by private vigilante groups like the National Protective Association, which cultivated a kind of war-madness. There were continual spy scares, witch hunts, even kangaroo courts that imposed rash sentences of tar and feathers. The innocent victims were usually German-Americans or antiwar radicals. The orgy of hatred had its ridiculous as well as its outrageous side. Americans stopped playing German music and stopped teaching or speaking the German language; they called sauerkraut "liberty cabbage"; and in Cincinnati they even removed pretzels from the free-lunch counters of saloons.

It was essential, of course, to protect the country from espionage and sabotage, but wartime legislation and its administration exceeded reasonable bounds. The Espionage Act of 1917, which Wilson requested, provided penalties of up to twenty years in prison and a ten thousand dollar fine for those who helped the enemy, obstructed recruiting, or incited rebellion within the armed services. One section gave the Postmaster General authority to deny the use of the mails to any publication which in his opinion advocated treason or forcible resistance to the laws. The Trading-with-the-Enemy Act, which Congress passed in October 1917, added sweeping authority to censor the foreign-language press.

In 1918 Congress went still further. The rising hysteria was stimulated by the demands of the Attorney General and by the violence of the syndicalists in the Industrial Workers of the World, who had tried to tie up copper production. Copying state statutes, Congress passed the Sabotage Act and the Sedition Act, which empowered the federal government to punish any expression of opinion that, regardless of whether or not it led to action, was "disloyal, profane, scurrilous or abusive" of the American form of government, flag, or uniform.

The recklessness of Congress in stocking such an arsenal had its source in the frenzy of the people. Timid in the face of public opinion, state and federal officials and judges made a mockery of the right of freedom of speech and belief. Just as those administering the draft subjected conscientious objectors to needless humiliations, often imprisonment, so those administering the Espionage, Sedition, and other wartime laws made conformity a measure of loyalty. The mails were closed to publications whose only offense was a statement of socialism or anti-British bias. Men were haled into court who had done no more than criticize the Red Cross or the financing of the war, or who had merely declared that war was contrary to the teachings of Jesus Christ. Of over fifteen hundred arrests for sedition, only ten were alleged to be for actual sabotage. The government's own immoderation and its failure to control private vigilantes shocked men of good will and good sense, blemished the Administration's war record, and exaggerated passions that long outlived the crisis itself.

Politics in Wartime Those exaggerated passions sometimes found expression in partisan, sectional, and factional politics. Though Wilson expressed the wish that politics might be adjourned for the duration, wartime problems raised conflicts of interest and irresistible opportunities to pursue partisan advantages. The Republicans, determined to prevent the Democrats from getting all the credit for American successes, criticized the conduct of the war. But that criticism, much of it valid, hurt the Democrats less than did the behavior of a few Southerners in key congressional posts who consistently voted against war legislation.

Southern agrarians and Western progressives demanded heavy income, inheritance, and excess-profits taxes to prevent war profiteering. Conservatives, in contrast, preferred federal borrowing and excise or sales taxes of various kinds, arguing that future generations should share the cost of a war fought in the national interest, and that taxes on consumption would help check wartime inflation. The Administration took a sensible middle position. In all, the war cost about $33.5 billion dollars, of which $10.5 billion was raised by taxes, the balance by Treasury borrowing in four Liberty Loan campaigns and one Victory Loan campaign. Secretary of the Treasury McAdoo had intended taxes to carry a larger share, but the soaring cost of the war upset his calculations. As it was, wartime taxes were heavier than they had ever been in the United States. The Revenue Act of October 1917 imposed new and larger excise and luxury taxes, a graduated excess-profits tax on business, and increased estate and personal income taxes. It raised the maximum surtax on income to 63 per cent, and the Revenue Act of 1918 lifted it and the excess-profits tax still higher.

The revenue measures passed during the war established a truly progressive tax structure which placed a heavy but equitable burden on those best able to carry it. They paid, but they also complained. And, especially in the Northeast, Republican politicians won middle-class support by contending that the agrarian Democrats were deliberately punishing the nation's industrial regions. By 1918 the tax issue was being hotly debated by moneyed men who had once supported less expensive progressive policies.

The Republicans also made gains among Midwestern farmers who had defected to the Democrats in 1916. The Lever Act empowered the Administration to control the price of wheat but not the price of cotton, and the Western farmers resented the larger profits of their Southern brethren and the Democratic votes in Congress which made those profits possible.

The Democratic coalition of 1916 was hurt by other issues as well. Southern votes were crucial in overriding Wilson's veto of an act of 1917 establishing a literacy test for immigrants. The urban laboring force found the Southerners' support of Prohibition even more exasperating. Advocates of the prohibition of the manufacture and consumption of alcoholic beverages had been gaining strength since 1900, and during the war they achieved their goal. First, a section of the Lever Act limited the production of whiskey, and a section of the Selective Service Act limited its sale near army camps. Later, in December 1917, Congress adopted the Eighteenth Amendment—the Prohibition Amendment—and submitted it to the states for ratification.*

Northern liberals, disturbed by the Administration's threats to civil liberties, were also irritated by Southern resistance to the women's suffrage amendment, which senators from Dixie blocked until January 1919. Only then did Congress acknowledge the contribution of women to war work and remove the injustice of limiting suffrage on the basis of sex.†

* It was ratified in January 1919.
† The Nineteenth Amendment was ratified in August 1920.

As the coalition of interests that had elected Wilson in 1916 fell apart, the Republicans effected a powerful reorganization of their party under the astute direction of their able and aggressive national chairman, Will Hays. They approached the elections of 1918 (see p. 578) with more confidence than they had had in a decade, and their campaign threatened not only Democratic control of Congress but also the program for a liberal peace on which Wilson pinned his most fervent hopes.

Constructing the Peace

A Liberal Program   During the war, sentiment for a liberal peace developed on both sides of the Atlantic, especially in England and the United States. The plans of various humanitarian groups differed in detail, but they usually advocated four common principles: the substitution of an international comity for the alliance system; the substitution of arbitration for armaments; the institution of self-government among all peoples; and the avoidance of seizures of territories and demands for reparations.

Wilson embraced these objectives. In 1916 he publicly advocated the idea of a league of nations. In 1917 he began to meditate seriously on the components of a generous peace— a peace without victory. Soon after the United States declared war, he assigned the task of preparing detailed peace plans to Colonel House and a staff of experts. While they were at work, the President in a series of addresses spelled out his own goals, which reflected the kind of idealism that had earlier characterized his New Freedom and his neutrality policies.

It was necessary, Wilson believed, to remove the military party, including the Kaiser, from authority in Germany, to divest Germany of power over other peoples, to establish democratic self-government in Germany and among each of the national groups rescued from her domination or the domination of her allies. It was necessary then to bring all nations into a world parliament whose collective, democratic judgment would guard the peace. "Peace," he said, "should rest upon the rights of peoples, not the rights of governments— the rights of peoples great or small . . . to freedom and security and self-government and to . . . economic opportunities."

This grand vision underestimated the role of power in world affairs and the selfishness of nations torn by war. Even so, Wilson might have won commitments from the Allies to a liberal peace if he had tried. He did not. By his own choice the United States had fought not as one of the Allies but as an "associated" belligerent, with the others but not of them. This was the Administration's way of paying tribute to the questionable tradition of avoiding "entangling alliances." Wilson chose, too, to avoid facing squarely the punitive intentions of the Allies, intentions that they had recorded in secret treaties. He simply ignored the existence of those treaties, with their clauses providing for the division of German, Austrian, and Turkish territories and for the exaction of huge indemnities. Apparently he felt no need to insist that America would help the Allies only if they gave up their punitive intentions.

The course of revolution in Russia focused the attention of the world on the problems of peace. After taking over the government in November 1917, the Bolsheviks began to arrange a separate and humiliating surrender to Germany. They also set out, in a reign of terror, to solidify their hold at home and to advance the communist revolution elsewhere. In order to embarrass the Allies, they disclosed the terms of the secret treaties they found in the czar's archives. Both David Lloyd George, the British Prime Minister, and Wilson countered by reasserting their dedication to a just peace.

In January 1918, while the war was still raging, Wilson announced his celebrated Fourteen Points. Five were broad: open diplomacy, by which he meant an end to secret agreements; free use of the seas in peace and war; the reduction of armaments; the removal of barriers to free trade; and an impartial adjustment of colonial claims. Eight points pertained to the principle of national self-determination: German evacuation of Russian territory; the restoration of Belgian independence; the return to France of Alsace-Lorraine (which Germany had conquered in 1870); the establishment of an independent Poland; and the autonomous development of each of the peoples of Austria-Hungary and

European Turkey. The fourteenth and crowning point called for forming "a general assembly of nations" to afford "mutual guarantees of political independence and territorial integrity."

These objectives conflicted not only with the ambitions of the Allies but also with the attitudes of many Americans. Though there was much enthusiasm for the President's ideals, there was also opposition from those who wanted protective tariffs, from those who resisted internationalism of any kind, and particularly from those whose war-born hatreds demanded revenge, a march on Berlin, and gallows for the Kaiser.

The Armistice and the Election of 1918
The President was by no means soft. In October 1918, as the Allies drove through the German lines, the German high command urged the chancellor to propose an armistice to Wilson on the basis of the Fourteen Points. During the ensuing exchange of notes, Wilson took a position charitable enough to lead the Germans on, but firm enough to make them admit defeat. This satisfied all the Allied chiefs of state and military commanders except Pershing, who urged unconditional surrender. The British and French, exhausted by four years of war and frightened by the westward surge of Bolshevism, were eager for an armistice so long as it gave them security. And Wilson, aware of their views, realized that an armistice would save thousands of soldiers from death in battle.

He demanded withdrawal of German forces from all invaded territory and immediate cessation of aerial and submarine warfare. When the Germans acceded to these conditions, which were designed to make renewed hostilities impossible, Wilson on October 23 opened negotiations with the Allies and suggested to the Germans that reasonable terms would depend on their establishing a democratic government. This suggestion precipitated the overthrow of the Kaiser, who abdicated on November 9.

The Allied leaders chafed at the Fourteen Points; the British explicitly rejected the point on the freedom of the seas, and the French demanded reparations for civilian damages. They would have insisted on further changes had Colonel House not threatened to make a separate peace if they did not assent to the rest of the Fourteen Points, which were to be the basis for an armistice. The Americans on their part ultimately agreed to add terms forcing the Germans to withdraw well beyond the east bank of the Rhine and to surrender vast quantities of war materials, including their submarines.

These were tough conditions. But even so the Republicans attacked the President's foreign policy, insisting, as Roosevelt put it, on dictating peace to the hammer of guns instead of to the clicking of typewriters. This demagoguery frightened many Democratic leaders who, with a congressional election coming on, were tempted to seek votes by flag-waving. But Wilson refused to let politics interfere with his carefully devised program. He yielded, however, to his advisers' demand for a blanket endorsement of all Democratic candidates. Angry himself at the onslaughts of men like Roosevelt, Wilson on October 25 urged the people to vote Democratic if they approved of his policies at home and abroad. The Republicans, he said, had been prowar but anti-Administration. The return of a Republican majority would be a repudiation of his leadership.

This appeal made Wilson's foreign policy more than ever a partisan issue. It infuriated the Republicans, and though it helped some Democratic candidates it did not prevent the Republicans from gaining control of both houses of Congress. The Republicans profited from many issues, but their leaders later claimed that it was foreign policy that had determined the outcome. On November 11, 1918, only a few days after the election, men of all parties rejoiced at the news that an armistice had been arranged. Now, as Wilson turned to negotiating the terms for peace, he had to reckon with a Republican majority in the Senate, where partisanship could complicate the ratification of any treaty he submitted.

Negotiating Peace

The Background of the Paris Conference Wilson failed to appoint any influential Republican to the American delegation preparing to leave for the peace conference at Paris. To advance his liberal program he chose to head the delegation himself, thus becoming the first President to go overseas on a diplomatic mission. Though his critics complained that he would slight his duties at home, his able performance at Paris justified his decision. Wilson named to the delegation Secretary of State Lansing and Colonel House, in his view obvious choices, and two others: General Tasker H. Bliss, a military expert, and Henry White, a career diplomat, ostensibly a Republican but in no sense a politician or a representative of the Senate. The President would not consider Henry Cabot Lodge, the powerful chairman-designate of the Senate Foreign Relations Committee, whom he despised. He passed over Elihu Root and ex-President Taft, an ardent internationalist. The delegation was to be Wilson's instrument, under his domination, but any advantage this control gave him during negotiations was overshadowed by the disadvantages inherent in slighting the Republicans.

Wilson also slighted public opinion. He had little talent for dealing with journalists, many of whom distrusted his official press representative, George Creel. Moreover, at the peace conference he had to yield to the other negotiators' insistence on secret sessions. The American press interpreted this decision as a violation of the principle of open diplomacy, even though there was no secret about the decisions reached at the conference. If Wilson's press relations had been better, American newspapers could have helped explain the President's difficulties to a public which did not fully understand the necessity for give-and-take.

Wilson had to bargain endlessly with the Allies, for their objectives often conflicted with his. He felt strongly that the Fourteen Points should be accepted as guides for the peace settlement. He did not expect a perfect peace, but he thought that a league of nations could continually improve the terms of a peace treaty, and he counted on enlisting the moral force of the world behind the league and the principle of justice. His optimism grew during his tour of Europe before the conference opened. Crowds greeted him as a savior, and he mistook their gratitude for victory as an endorsement of his goals.

Actually, the peoples of Europe and Asia,

Dover, England: Crowds greeted Wilson as a savior.

with unimportant exceptions, supported the demands of their own spokesmen. Four of these men were, with Wilson, the major architects of the peace. There was the inscrutable and resourceful Count Nobuaki Makino of Japan, ambitious for territory, as was the cultured and adroit Vittorio Orlando of Italy; there was the perspicacious but shifty British Prime Minister, David Lloyd George, who had promised his electorate vast reparations; there was the French Premier, Georges Clemenceau, cynical, tenacious, weary, aloof, determined to crush Germany forever. These men were bound by treaties to support one another's claims. Their armies, moreover, actually held most of the lands they planned to annex or assign.

Over large parts of the world neither they nor Wilson could exercise much influence. The Bolshevik Revolution had made Russia unwelcome at the conference, and she stood apart brooding, dissatisfied, a mighty and ominous force. There was, furthermore, con-

tinuing war within her borders while the peace conference sat. British troops in the northern part of European Russia were trying to assist anti-Bolsheviks there, and in Siberia a Japanese army was pushing west. The Japanese had begun operations allegedly to protect Czech prisoners of war from the Bolsheviks and to keep munitions from the Germans. They stayed on, however, with an eye to conquest, and in order to keep watch on them the United States sent troops to Siberia. The Bolsheviks, resenting the presence of foreigners, believed the Japanese and the Americans were agents of counterrevolution, as some authorities in Washington and Tokyo would have liked them to be.

Revolution and counterrevolution infected all Russia's European neighbors. The empire of Austria-Hungary had simply ceased to exist. In the territories it once had ruled, the quarrels of self-conscious ethnic groups, complicated by the conniving of communists, were forging the new states which were to speckle the map of central and eastern Europe whether the men at Paris willed it or not. Within Germany the new republican government faced revolution at the borders, Red plots within, and a populace exasperated by a food shortage imposed by the continuing Allied blockade. With the world in turmoil and Europe exhausted by war, the Paris conference had an unpropitious setting. With the Allies opposed to a liberal peace, moreover, the odds against Wilson's program were enormous.

The League of Nations Wilson's plans for a charter for a league of nations included the disposition of former German colonies. In order to bring about an impartial and equitable settlement of colonial claims, as the Fourteen Points promised, Wilson hoped to put the German colonies under the guardianship of small neutrals like Switzerland and Sweden. These neutrals were to be trustees for the league and were to help the backward colonial peoples to move along the road toward independence.

The British and Japanese, however, would not surrender the territory in Africa and the Pacific that they had seized during hostilities. According to a secret treaty between them, German islands in the Pacific north of the Equator were to go to Japan and islands south of the Equator were to go to Australia and New Zealand. Yet Wilson prevented the outright transfer of colonies by persuading the Allies to accept instead a system of "mandates," which obliged their holders to render annual accountings and to help subject peoples to stand alone. The compromise gave the Allies a pocketful of territory but it also subjected them to surveillance in their administration of that territory. Though the mandate system was imperfect, Wilson felt that the league would gradually better it.

Yet the concepts of a league met opposition from the French, who wanted a military alliance of the victors against Germany. Japan further complicated Wilson's negotiations by demanding a statement of racial equality pledging member nations of a league not to discriminate against the nationals of other members. But the President had help from the Italians, who were pleased by his endorsement of the northern boundary they wanted, and from the British, who shared his hopes for the

league. The racial pride of the Japanese was assuaged by their new mandates, and the French accepted the idea of a league after they realized that they could obtain their objectives elsewhere in the treaty. Wilson in return let the French and British dodge the question of self-disarmament. In the end his draft served as the basis for the Covenant of the League of Nations which the responsible committee approved and reported to the peace conference in February 1919.

It was a simple document. Each signer of the treaty was to have one vote in a Body of Delegates of the League. Larger authority rested with the Executive Council, which was to consist of representatives from the United States, the British Empire, France, Italy, Japan, and four states selected by the Body of Delegates. Decisions of the Council required a unanimous vote except when a Council member was itself a party to a dispute. The Covenant also established a permanent secretariat, an international Bureau of Labor, and the mandate system. It provided for the admission of new members by a two-thirds vote of the delegates, and for amendment by a three-fourths vote.

The main purpose of the League was to keep the peace. To that end, the Covenant obliged signatories, before they resorted to war, to submit disputes either to inquiry by the Council or to arbitration by the Permanent Court of International Justice which the Council was to create. Member nations were to punish any breach of this article by severing economic relations with the offending state. The Council, moreover, might recommend that members of the League contribute military and naval units to protect its principles. And the Council was to advise on means of ensuring that member nations lived up to Article 10, which Wilson considered the heart of the Covenant. This article bound signatories "to respect and preserve against external aggression the territorial integrity and . . . political independence of all members of the League."

The League was not a superstate. It could only recommend but could not compel the recruitment and use of military force. Its deliberations would not bind Germany or Russia until the victorious powers invited them to join. But the Covenant did create the first meaningful international organization in modern history. It also fulfilled Wilson's purpose of recognizing war and the threat of war as everybody's business and of providing a forum for the nations of the world to discuss problems that might lead to conflict. In his view, the Covenant organized the moral force of the world.

Consequently the President was distressed by the opposition to the League which he confronted during a brief trip home. The essence of that opposition was Republican partisanship, but it fed on other attitudes as well. Many German-Americans still resented the war and its outcome. Many Irish-Americans believed Wilson should have insisted on Irish independence. The President pointed out that that was a question for England to resolve, but he was pointedly cool toward his Irish critics. He was even less patient with those Americans who hesitated to depart from what to them was a national tradition of isolation from Europe. They thought of the past as having been sterilized from the Old World. They thought of the Monroe Doctrine as a kind of shield from European wars and woes. And they viewed the Covenant as an "entangling alliance." These and other confusions

---

Fear of the League

This treaty ... imperils what I conceive to be the underlying, the very first principles of this Republic. It is in conflict with the right of our people to govern themselves free from all restraint, legal or moral, of foreign powers.... Next to the tie which binds a man to his God is the tie which binds a man to his country, and all schemes, all plans, however ambitious and fascinating they seem in their proposal, but which would embarrass or entangle and impede or shackle her sovereign will, which would compromise her freedom of action I unhesitatingly put behind me.

Since the debate opened months ago those of us who have stood against this proposition have been taunted many times with being little Americans. Leave us the word American, keep that in your presumptuous impeachment, and no taunt can disturb us, no gibe discompose our purposes.

From William E. Borah, Speech in the U.S. Senate, November 1919.

Need for the League

America is going to grow more and more powerful; and the more powerful she is the more inevitable it is that she should be trustee for the peace of the world.... All Europe knew that we were doing an American thing when we put the Covenant of the League of Nations at the beginning of the treaty.... The most cynical men I had to deal with ... before our conferences were over ... all admitted that the League of Nations, which they had deemed an ideal dream, was a demonstrable, practical necessity. This treaty cannot be carried out without the League of Nations....

The rest of the world is necessary to us, if you want to put it on that basis. I do not like to put it on that basis. That is not the American basis. America does not want to feed upon the rest of the world. She wants to feed it and serve it. America ... is the only national idealistic force in the world, and idealism is going to save the world.... That is the program of civilization.

From Woodrow Wilson, Speech at Helena, Montana, November 1919.

---

bred susceptibility to the propaganda of Wilson's opponents.

On March 4, 1919, the day before the President returned to Paris, Senator Henry Cabot Lodge produced a round robin signed by thirty-seven Republican senators, four more than were needed to defeat the treaty. It stated that the Covenant was unacceptable and insisted that consideration of the League be deferred until after a treaty had been completed. In a speech that night, Wilson condemned the "careful selfishness" of his critics and their "ignorance of the state of the world." The Covenant would be intimately tied to the treaty itself, he said. That interrelationship was essential for working out the problems of the conference, and the President was understandably annoyed. But his strong language intensified the partisanship that provoked it.

The Treaty of Versailles Though Wilson would not separate the League from the treaty, he realized that the Covenant would have to be modified to meet the suggestions of ex-President Taft and other moderates. The revisions which the President sponsored on his return to Paris would certainly have been demanded by the Senate in any event. They defined procedures for withdrawal from the

Europe in 1920

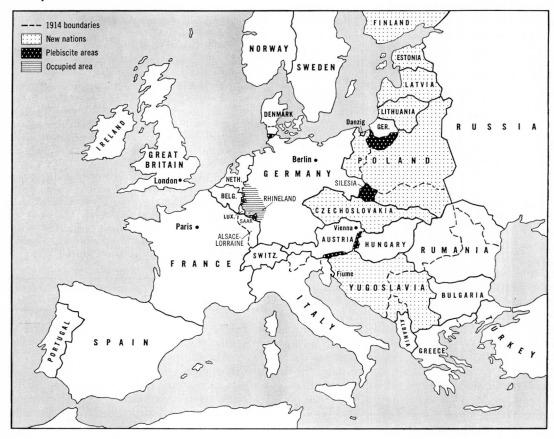

League, stated that the acceptance of mandates was optional, and excluded from the purview of the League domestic issues such as immigration and regional agreements such as the Monroe Doctrine. By reopening the question of the Covenant, however, Wilson exposed himself to the bargaining of his associates, who once more pressed their demands for Europe and Asia. The President secured his revisions, but only at an inflated price.

Clemenceau, still determined to assure French security, insisted that Germany be dismembered. He urged that two new states, Poland and Czechoslovakia, be set up on Germany's eastern border. Both states would absorb some German land and population. He also asked for the creation of a Rhenish buffer state, to be splintered off from Germany's west, and for the cession to France of the Saar

Basin, a bountiful source of coal and iron, as well as of Alsace-Lorraine. Wilson balked at these extreme demands and argued that the League itself would protect France from German aggression. Clemenceau scoffed and called the President pro-German. For ten days the conference stalled. Early in April Wilson cabled for the *George Washington* to stand by to take him home. This threat to depart, though perhaps petulant, was effective, for Clemenceau bowed to the proponents of compromise.

The treaty drew generous boundaries for Poland and Czechoslovakia, but it also arranged for the League to conduct a plebiscite to determine the disposition of a part of Silesia coveted by both Germans and Poles. To give Poland access to the sea, the treaty drew a narrow corridor through Germany that put some Germans under Polish rule. But Poland's need for a major port outweighed ethnic considerations, and Danzig, the port in question, was made a free city under League supervision. France received Alsace-Lorraine and temporary economic concessions in the Saar, but the League was to administer the Saar and after fifteen years was to conduct a plebiscite there. France could also occupy the Rhineland for fifteen years; after that time the area was to be demilitarized but left a part of Germany. The German army was limited to a token force of one hundred thousand.

Furthermore, Wilson and Lloyd George agreed to a special security treaty pledging their nations to assist France if she were attacked. Clemenceau realized, even if Wilson did not, that the United States Senate would reject the special treaty, but in that case the Rhineland could be occupied indefinitely. All in all, Clemenceau obtained as much safety for France as any treaty could reasonably provide.

The French and the English also pushed Wilson into accepting their demands for reparations far in excess of what Germany could pay, and in violation of the prearmistice agreement to limit payments to the cost of civilian damages. The President let the Allies include the cost of pensions, which later permitted the reparations commission to calculate that the Germans owed some $120 billion, the fantastic figure that had been the British objective. The reparations clause of the treaty, moreover, specifically attributed the cause of war to "the aggression of Germany," a phrase that rankled in German minds for years to come, however accurate it may have been. Along with the economic dislocations that were bound to grow out of the exorbitant reparations imposed on Germany, the war-guilt clause proved to be a threat to future peace.

At the time, however, the President's troubles with Italy seemed more ominous. Before the conference, Wilson had agreed to a northern frontier for Italy at the line of the Brenner Pass, which put two hundred thousand Austrians under Italian rule. This meant that he had nothing left to trade when the Italians also insisted on taking Fiume, an Adriatic port surrounded by Yugoslav land. When the Italians discovered that all the powers were antagonistic to their claim to Fiume, they baldly marched into the city. Wilson appealed to the Italian people in the name of justice, but they, with their leaders, resented the President's idealistic but miscalculated intrusion. The Italians left Paris in a rage, and though they returned to sign a treaty that did not give them Fiume, the incident confirmed the Italians in their pursuit of deceitful diplomacy, alienated Italian-Americans from Wilson's treaty, and almost disrupted the conference.

The Japanese seized on the confusion to advance their own claims. They were seeking endorsement for their economic ambitions in China and for their assumption of the German leasehold at Kiaochow and of German economic privilege in the Shantung Peninsula. The Chinese, of course, opposed the whole program, which Japan's secret treaties with France and England condoned. Furthermore, late in 1917 Secretary of State Lansing had reached an understanding with Viscount Kikujiro Ishii by which Japan affirmed her support of the Open Door and of China's territorial integrity; but in return the United States recognized Japan's special interest in Chinese provinces adjoining Japanese possessions. Since Shantung was just such a province, Wilson found it hard to oppose the Japanese demands, especially after the whole conference seemed about to disintegrate. He accepted a compromise that by and large restricted the Japanese to former German holdings, less Kiaochow, which Japan promised to surrender. Though many Americans, including two of the delegates, thought the President conceded too much, he had obtained, as he said, a solution "as satisfactory as could be got out of the tangle."

The same could be said of the whole treaty that the victors and the vanquished signed at Versailles in 1919. It was severe, but Germany had lost the war she had expected to win, and the Allies were much less severe than she would have been. The treaty followed the Fourteen Points as closely as world conditions permitted. Wilson had conceded little, if anything, more than he had to, and the Allies had moved a long way toward his program. Europe had a new map that approximated ethnic groupings as closely as possible. This, to be sure, involved some compromises of the principle of self-determination and created some boundaries that conflicted with the military defense and the economic needs of the new states. But these difficulties and others could be negotiated later in the forum of the League. As Wilson had predicted, the League was inextricably part of the treaty, a "convenient, indeed indispensable" instrument, "the hope of the world." He had yet, however, to bring two-thirds of the Senate over to his way of thinking.

The Struggle over Ratification

The Senate and the Treaty Wilson brought the treaty home to a people predisposed in its favor. Though few Americans were familiar with the whole long document, most had learned something about the League, millions were enthusiastic about it, and the majority had no serious objection to it. But the people could not vote on the treaty. The question of its ratification, and thus the portentous question of what direction American foreign policy would take, were for the Senate to debate and decide.

Of the ninety-six senators forty-nine were Republican, but only fourteen were irreconcilably against the League and the treaty. The other thirty-five were resolved to Republicanize Wilson's work. They intended not to reject the treaty but to make its adoption contingent on a number of reservations, of which the most significant had to do with Wilson's League of Nations. Twenty-three Republicans favored a list of strong reservations drafted and sponsored by Senator Lodge; twelve were willing to settle for milder reservations. Since only four of the forty-seven Democrats opposed the treaty, a coalition of Democrats and moderate Republicans would have commanded a majority vote. And a majority was all that was needed to settle the kind of reservations that would be demanded. Such a coalition, moreover, could probably have attracted the necessary two-thirds vote for ratification. But the crucial coalition was never formed.

The Democratic leaders knew they had to make concessions to their opponents, but they felt that they also had to wait for instructions from the President. They never received those instructions, for Wilson refused to compromise

an issue he considered both personal and moral.

It was Lodge who had made the issue personal. Lodge had endorsed the round robin and the strategy of insisting on reservations; Lodge had packed the important Foreign Relations Committee with irreconcilables and strong reservationists. Lodge, the majority leader of the Senate, was a dogmatic partisan determined to hold his party together and to win in 1920. If necessary, he was willing to sacrifice anything to those objectives. He honestly believed that the League as Wilson had planned it was a threat to national sovereignty. Furthermore, he put his faith in armies and navies and the balance of power, the "large view" of his old friend Theodore Roosevelt, who had just died. A narrow, bitter, ruthless, often exasperating man, Lodge was also moved by mean considerations, including the prejudices of his many Italian- and Irish-American constituents. He was a formidable antagonist who hated Wilson as Wilson hated him.

Lodge's reservations struck the President as unnecessary and immoral. Wilson objected to the very idea of making the ratification of the treaty subject to reservations. He also held that reservations would mean that the treaty would have to be renegotiated, though the British, the French, and the State Department did not think so. Two of the reservations would have made Congress the sole judge of whether the United States should accept a mandate and whether it should withdraw from the League. Two others reserved to the United States exclusive authority over tariff policy, immigration, and the Monroe Doctrine. Wilson argued that the revised Covenant already covered those issues. Another reservation exempted the United States from any decision of the League on which any member and its self-governing dominions had cast in the aggregate more than one vote. The American veto in the Council, Wilson noted, made superfluous such an ungracious protest against the seats of the British Dominions in the Body of Delegates. The President especially opposed the reservation on Article 10, which stated that the United States would assume no obligation to preserve the territorial integrity or political independence of any other country without the approval of Congress. To Wilson this would be a violation of the essential spirit of the League—the moral obligation to protect the peace of the world.

In the abstract Wilson was probably right, but the politics of the Senate made compromise necessary. Even if Lodge's reservations did make the United States seem timid and selfish, they would have damaged the League far less than would outright rejection of treaty and League alike. Senator Gilbert Hitchcock, the Democratic minority leader, advised Wilson to work out some sort of compromise with Lodge, as did Colonel House, Robert Lansing, Bernard Baruch, and many other friends of the President.

But Wilson would not listen, and his personal efforts to persuade individual Republicans to adopt his point of view were futile. Moreover, as the days passed, Lodge used public hearings on the treaty to vent the objections of Irish nationalists, Republican partisans, and other opponents. Gradually the public tended to become bored with the whole question, dubious about the Covenant, and amenable to Lodge's purpose. Wilson had advocated a degree of national involvement in foreign affairs greater, in all probability, than most Americans, after reflection, were willing to accept. And their willingness gradually shrank. The idealism of wartime was fading into the problems of the postwar period. Inflation, unemployment, and fears of Bolshevism deprived Wilson of the public enthusiasm for a generous peace and for a genuine internationalism on which he had relied.

The President's Collapse   In order to arouse new enthusiasm for the League, Wilson set out in September 1919 on a speaking tour across the country. He hoped to stir up a passion for his program that the Republican Senators would not be able to withstand. His train moved through the strongholds of isolationism, over eight thousand miles, stopping thirty-seven times for him to address the voters. As he proceeded through the Middle West to the Pacific Coast, then south, and then east, he was greeted by larger and larger crowds. But their applause did not change one vote in the Senate. Indeed Wilson's attacks on his opponents stiffened their resolution to resist, and his absence from Washington impeded

Democratic efforts to find a basis for compromise. The President was superbly eloquent, particularly in explaining the moral imperatives of Article 10, but his strenuous efforts taxed his limited strength without achieving his political purpose.

On September 25 Wilson spoke at Pueblo, Colorado. That night he could not sleep. His head hurt mercilessly. Frightened by the President's exhaustion, his physician canceled the remainder of the trip. Back in Washington Wilson was too tired to work, too tense to rest. On October 2 he fell to the floor unconscious, the victim of a cerebral thrombosis, a blood clot in his brain.

The stroke did not kill the President, but it paralyzed his left side, thickened his speech, totally disabled him for almost two months, and prevented him thereafter from working more than an hour or two at a time. For six months he did not meet with the Cabinet. For six weeks he could not execute the minimum duties of his office. Though his mind was not injured, his emotional balance was upset and he became petulant, suspicious, and easily moved to tears. He was unable to think of compromise with a clear mind, unable to assess men or situations with accuracy. His collapse was a tragedy not only for himself but also for a nation facing a momentous crisis in foreign policy.

On November 6, while Wilson was still bedridden, Lodge presented his reservations to the Senate. It was obvious that the Republicans had the votes to adopt them but not the two-thirds needed to ratify the treaty after the reservations had been attached. The Democratic leaders hesitated to move without the President's consent, and he gave stringent orders on November 18 that they were to reject the treaty so long as it was shackled by the Lodge reservations. They were then to move that the treaty be accepted on Wilson's terms, either as it stood or with mild interpretive reservations of which he approved. This order conceded nothing to the Republican moderates, who stood behind Lodge. Though nonpartisan friends of the League preferred accepting Lodge's reservations to rejecting the whole treaty, the Democrats on November 19 voted to reject the treaty with those reservations. Consequently the resolution to adopt the treaty as Lodge had modified it failed by thirty-nine to fifty-five. Lodge blocked debate of the interpretive reservations that the Democrats then proposed, and minutes later a resolution to approve the unamended treaty also failed, thirty-eight to fifty-three.

The Final Rejection But the treaty was still not dead. The moderate Republicans and the Democrats were stunned by what they had done and felt they had to try again. Furthermore, organizations representing some twenty million Americans petitioned for compromise and ratification. The same hope was voiced by the British and French press and by the British government. Influential Democrats without exception tried to persuade the President to relieve his party of the hopeless battle to defeat the Lodge reservations.

But Wilson, the victim of fantasies produced by ill health, would still not hear of concessions. Instead, on January 8, 1920, he wrote a blistering letter to his fellow Democrats. The majority of the people wanted ratification, he said. Let the Senate accept the treaty without tampering with it or else reject it. If there was any doubt about public opinion, Wilson warned, the issue could be resolved at the next election, which would be "a great and solemn referendum."

This was the counsel of a deluded man, for presidential elections turn on many issues, not just one. The Democratic party had been losing strength for three years, and the treaty, if the Senate rejected it again, would be impossible to resuscitate. Recognizing the folly of Wilson's position, Senator Hitchcock and other Democrats tried to work out a satisfactory compromise on the reservations. They failed, partly because the Republican irreconcilables warned Lodge against compromise, partly because Lodge himself probably did not want to rescue the treaty now that he realized Wilson would yield nothing on Article 10.

The President, increasingly peevish, forced Secretary of State Lansing to resign, allegedly for arranging unauthorized Cabinet meetings, but actually because Lansing had criticized some of the transactions at Paris. Though Wilson's action alienated many of his friends, he remained the head of his party and on March 8 he again instructed the Democrats to hold the line.

His adherents prevailed. The Lodge reservations, only slightly modified, were adopted once more, this time with some Democratic help. On March 19, the day of the final test, half the Democrats voted to ratify the treaty with the reservations. But twenty-three Democrats, twenty of them Southerners, did the President's bidding. Together with twelve irreconcilables, they voted against ratification and thus prevented by a margin of seven the two-thirds majority needed for adoption.

There was to be no "solemn referendum." The Democratic presidential nominee in 1920, James M. Cox, supported the League, but sometimes with hesitation. The Republican plank on the treaty was deliberately vague, as was the Republican candidate, Warren G. Harding. Though Harding enjoyed the full support of both Republican isolationists and Republican internationalists, he chose to consider his smashing victory a repudiation of the treaty.

The Senate had made the telling decision. In rejecting both treaty and League, the Senate had turned America's back to Europe. The rejection destroyed the best available chance for developing world peace, the best potential force of liberal internationalism. Perhaps the irreconcilables, the forceful spokesmen of isolation, could have defeated the treaty in any event, but it was not they who did so, though they helped. Wilson's stubbornness also helped, and Lodge's partisanship even more. Indeed partisanship was the real culprit, and the outcome of the fight revealed how severely domestic politics could damage foreign policy.

The damage, in the end, affected the whole world, for without the United States the League never had a chance to fulfill Wilson's vision. That vision, which rested on the moral intent and the idealistic promise of the President's peace program, was the most compelling image democracy could offer to the world. Men could believe in both the intent and the promise because they knew that the United States had fought a totally unselfish war, and they knew too that under Wilson the United States at home had experienced the New Freedom, with its heartening reforms, inspiring to all peoples.

With the defeat of the treaty, a great democracy seemed to have renounced its persuasive claims to the imagination of men everywhere. And its renunciation came just at the time when Bolshevism was advancing its false claims more effectively than ever before. The American retreat opened the way for both the protagonists of reaction and the protagonists of communist revolution. It cost the United States and her allies the true fruits of a gallant victory. It made a travesty of the noble effort to create a world safe for the democracy Americans cherished.

SUGGESTIONS FOR READING

The War

Historians have given the experience of the United States during the First World War less attention than it merits. The biographies of Wilson and the Wilsonians, noted in connection with the preceding chapter, provide some useful data and insights. More complete is F. L. Paxson, *American Democracy and the World War*, 3 vols. (1936–48). There are adequate discussions of economic mobilization in B. M. Baruch, *American Industry in War* (1941) and *The Public Years* (1960). The relevant chapter of Sidney Ratner, *American Taxation* (1942), is important on its subject. On the administration of the War Department, Frederick Palmer, *Newton D. Baker*, 2 vols. (1931), offers considerable information; the Navy Department receives perceptive treatment in Frank Freidel, *Franklin D. Roosevelt: The Apprenticeship* (1952). The most rewarding of the war memoirs is J. J. Pershing, *My Experiences in the World War*, 2 vols. (1931), but there are more useful accounts of military developments in J. G. Harbord, *The American Army in France* (1936), and E. E. Morison, *Admiral Sims and the Modern American Navy* (1942). There are a number of admirable studies of propaganda, censorship, and civil liberties in wartime, including J. R. Mock and Cedric Larson, *Words That Won the War* (1939); H. C. Peterson, *Propaganda for War* (1939); H. C. Peterson and G. C. Fite, *Opponents of War, 1917–1918* (1957); and the classic Zechariah Chafee, *Free Speech in the United States* (rev. ed., 1941).

The Peace

The student of peace-making and of the American rejection of the peace treaty has at his disposal a voluminous literature which is continually growing. One excellent place to begin reading is in the penetrating analysis of H. H. Rudin, *Armistice, 1919* (1944). Two detailed accounts of the negotiations at Paris, which applaud Wilson's efforts, are D. F. Fleming, *The United States and the League of Nations, 1918–1920* (1932), and Paul Birdsall, *Versailles Twenty Years After* (1941). Also laudatory, and essential on its topic, is R. J. Bartlett, *League to Enforce Peace* (1944). There is a critical but persuasive analysis in T. A. Bailey, *Woodrow Wilson and the Lost Peace* (1944). The same author, in *Woodrow Wilson and the Great Betrayal* (1945), provides a trenchant study of the rejection of the treaty. Also significant on that subject are: J. A. Garraty, *Henry Cabot Lodge* (1953); R. W. Leopold, *Elihu Root and the Conservative Tradition* (1954); and M. C. McKenna, *Borah* (1961). There are conflicting views about the conduct of government during Wilson's illness in E. B. Wilson, *My Memoirs* (1938), and J. M. Blum, *Joe Tumulty and the Wilson Era* (1951). Among the accounts of contemporaries friendly to Wilson, two of the most valuable are D. F. Houston, *Eight Years with Wilson's Cabinet*, 2 vols. (1926), and Herbert Hoover, *The Ordeal of Woodrow Wilson* * (1958). Two important unfriendly statements appear in H. C. Lodge, *The Senate and the League of Nations* (1928), and J. M. Keynes, *Economic Consequences of the Peace* (1919). Several of the books here listed cover the question of the League in the election of 1920, a subject further explored in J. M. Cox, *Journey Through My Years* (1946), and Frank Freidel, *Franklin D. Roosevelt: The Ordeal* (1954).

* Available in a paperback edition.

25

Retreat
from Responsibility

No date marked the start of the progressive movement in the United States and no date marked its end. The inauguration of Theodore Roosevelt in 1901, however, had marked the beginning of a period in which the federal government gave intense attention to making the nation and the world a better place in which to live. The new sense of responsibility in Washington reflected the temper of the American people at large, who believed that man had both the duty and the capacity to shape his environment. This progressive faith later yielded to a complex of anxieties, many of them irrational, that turned a majority of Americans away from reform. For a time they found it more comfortable to subordinate mind to emotions. They succumbed to fatigue, fear, selfishness, and thoughtlessness. This retreat from responsibility began to grip the nation soon after the armistice of 1918. It played a part in America's rejection of the Treaty of Versailles, and it helped set the course of domestic affairs as well.

Transition from War

Demobilization   When the war ended, the government had no plans for demobilization. It simply lifted the controls it had imposed on the economy during the war. In accord with public sentiment, it hastened the discharge of the soldiers, many of whom were unable to find a job when they returned to civilian life. Though unemployment declined

after February 1919, it persisted in troubled areas for another half-year, and it soured thousands of veterans who had expected a hero's welcome to include a job.

Immediately after the armistice the War Industries Board began to close up shop, confident that private industry would be able to switch back to a peacetime economy with no help or direction from the federal government. That was a miscalculation. While industry bid for new plants and machinery, consumers dug out their wartime savings to make the purchases they had long postponed. Their demands for housing and automobiles were particularly strong. Inflation struck the country. During 1919 the cost of living climbed 77 per cent above prewar levels; during 1920, another 28 per cent.

The government developed only piecemeal and inadequate remedies for unemployment and inflation. There was as yet no body of economic ideas to explain the need for over-all federal policies to ease the process of reconversion. Wilson, moreover, was preoccupied with peacemaking and hampered by an opposition Congress. And yet the record was not completely bare. The Revenue Act of 1919, which raised tax rates even higher than they had been during the war, carried on the policy of progressive taxation, ensured the government the income it needed, and helped check inflation. The Merchant Marine Act of 1920 enabled the government to sell to private industry the ships it had ordered during the war.

Although this act produced unimpressive results, its purpose was to get the government out of the shipping business and to stimulate the lagging merchant marine, which was so important to national defense. In 1920 the Water Power Act set up a Federal Power Commission, consisting of the Secretaries of War, Agriculture, and the Interior, to license the building and operation of dams and hydroelectric plants. This was a clumsy arrangement, and it failed to regulate the hydroelectric industry. But its very failure drew attention to the need for genuine public control.

Both Congress and the public were anxious to settle the question of what should be done with the railroads, which the government was still running. Private management wanted them back, but labor had found that public administration was more generous and more efficient. An attorney for the railway brotherhoods, Glenn E. Plumb, proposed a plan for nationalizing the roads. The AFL supported the Plumb plan, but elsewhere it evoked little enthusiasm. Wilson announced that he would return the railways to their owners unless Congress came up with some other scheme, and Congress in the Transportation Act of 1920 extended the tradition of mixed capitalism by turning the railroads back to their private owners while subjecting them to increased supervision.

The Transportation Act gave the Interstate Commerce Commission control over the issue of railroad securities, authorized it to oversee the uses to which the railroads put the proceeds of those issues, and strengthened its power over the setting of railroad rates. The act also made special provisions to strengthen the finances of weak roads, to permit pooling of traffic, and to regroup railroads into a limited number of systems. The roads, shippers, and investors applauded the act, but labor was disappointed, particularly because arbitration of labor disputes by the new Railway Labor Board was not to be compulsory.

The new law took the government out of the railroad business and did a good deal to complete the program of regulation that progressives had put forth twenty years before. Yet it was far from being a genuine "transportation" act, for it did nothing to regulate the trucks and airplanes which would soon cut into the railroads' monopoly of transportation. Neither the commission nor the railroads could cope with the new kinds of competition and the financial and public problems they created. At best the Transportation Act was a fulfillment of past strivings rather than a plan for the future.

Labor Strife   In the years right after the war, the nation's policy-makers seemed to be turning more and more to the past. The Administration, which had sympathized with the goals of organized labor for so long, now began to favor management. This policy-reversal was prompted by several forces: Wilson's advisers were growing impatient with the strikes that continued to cripple the nation's industries; management had launched a successful campaign to associate all unions with radicalism; and the country at large was infected by an almost hysterical fear of radicalism in any form.

The enforced wartime truce between labor and management ended in 1919. The unions then set out to consolidate their gains and to bring wages in line with the rising cost of living. And the National Association of Manufacturers, the National Civic Federation, and other management groups set out to reestablish the open shop, which they liked to call "the American way." Management propaganda extolled the beneficence of business and warned that unions and union demands were inspired by foreign and radical influences. Nevertheless, many of the first strikes after the war were successful, notably those of clothing, textile, telegraph, and telephone workers.

The AFL faced its crucial test in the steel industry. Unfortunately, it selected as secretary of its organizing committee William Z. Foster, whose record seemed to confirm management's charges of labor radicalism. Though Foster was unreliable, the steelworkers had grave grievances. Most of them put in a twelve-hour work day in return for subsistence wages. After attracting a substantial minority of workers, the union called a strike in September 1919, for management had rejected its demands for recognition, an eight-hour day, and decent pay. Episodes of violence punctuated the strike. Public opinion, misled by the steel companies' propaganda, condoned the widespread use of state and federal troops to prevent picketing. The United States Steel

Company alone used thousands of strike-breakers. In January 1920 the union gave up, thoroughly beaten.

Meanwhile, in November 1919 the bituminous coal miners had walked out under the leadership of their new and colorful president, John L. Lewis, who was radical only in his pugnacious manner. A wartime agreement had governed wages in the mines, but the union claimed that the armistice had made that agreement inapplicable. As Lewis observed, there was no ceiling on the rising price of coal. The miners demanded a 60 per cent wage increase, a six-hour day, and a five-day week. When the operators refused to negotiate, the miners prepared to strike. With Wilson's approval, Attorney General A. Mitchell Palmer ruled that the wage agreement was still in effect and obtained an injunction against the union. Lewis then called off the strike because, as he put it, "we cannot fight the government." Still the miners refused to go back to work until the government ordered an immediate 14 per cent increase in pay and set up an arbitral commission which ultimately awarded another 27 per cent. The miners' other demands were denied.

The most celebrated postwar strike had run its course two months earlier. The Boston police found that they could not stretch their prewar wages to cover postwar living costs. Denied a raise and restive because of other grievances, they secured a charter from the AFL and threatened a strike in August 1919. The mayor appointed a citizens' committee which suggested that most of the policemen's demands, except recognition of their union, be granted. The police commissioner, however, a declared enemy of organized labor, rejected the suggestion and fired nineteen of the union's leaders. On September 9 the policemen went out on strike. Volunteer vigilantes were unable to control the gangs of looters who brought Boston to the point of anarchy. The American middle class was shocked and scared. But just then the governor of Massachusetts, Calvin Coolidge, called out the national guard to restore order. The strike failed and many of the police were dismissed.

The whole episode was as unnecessary as it was lamentable. Coolidge could have supported the mayor and overruled the police commissioner before the strike began. The police should never have left their stations, for whatever their grievances they had a professional obligation to maintain law and order. Certainly there was nothing in the episode for anyone to be proud of. Coolidge, however, won a national reputation by putting down the strike. The American people knew little about the facts of the case, but they long remembered the governor's somewhat irrelevant response to Gompers' request that the policemen be reinstated: "There is no right to strike against the public safety by anybody, anywhere, any time." Coolidge was correct, of course, but only a people unwilling to examine the context of his policy would have deemed him heroic.

The Red Scare   A scrupulous examination of the state of the nation would have prevented the hysteria that swept much of the country in 1919. Vastly exaggerating the strength of communism in the United States, Americans let old prejudices and new fears lead them into shameful persecutions.

There was genuine cause for concern about the march of Bolshevism in Europe. In March 1919 Soviet leaders organized the Third International as an agency for world revolution, and during the rest of that year the communists made striking gains in Germany, Hungary, and along Russia's frontiers. The International fed on the postwar disintegration of eastern Europe—a disintegration the United States did little to check.

Within the United States, however, communism was feeble. In 1919 the Socialist party, its ranks depleted and its morale low, broke into three factions. Some forty thousand moderates retained the old name. One left-wing faction of about twenty thousand, almost all of them immigrants, formed the Communist Labor party. Another militant group of between thirty thousand and sixty thousand, also largely immigrant, joined the Communist party of America under native-born leaders. Some of these leaders—John Reed, a successful journalist and former Harvard cheerleader, for one—made a good deal of noise, but the three groups together constituted less than half of 1 per cent of the population.

During the war public and private propaganda had generated hatred and fear of the Germans, and Americans had already begun to fight the shadows of their anxieties. In the postwar months they transferred much of this hate to the nation's immigrants, whom the suspicious middle class had long stereotyped as radical. Hysteria reached pathological proportions under the influence of business propaganda that branded all labor as radical, under the spur of politicians who exploited the mood of the nation for their own advantage, and under the stimulus of sporadic episodes of violence.

There were early outbreaks of hysteria in February 1919, when the Seattle Central Labor Council called a general strike to support shipyard workers who had walked out in quest of higher pay and shorter hours. Some of the Seattle labor leaders were unquestionably radical, and a general strike was itself a radical technique. But Mayor Ole Hanson grossly exaggerated the Red menace and used troops to stamp out the strike.

Scare headlines and legislative investigations of alleged Red activity kept the public edgy. In April the handiwork of a few lunatic radicals created near-panic when bombs were mailed to Mayor Hanson, Senator Thomas W. Hardwick of Georgia, and thirty-six other eminent citizens, including John D. Rockefeller, Justice Holmes, the Postmaster General, and the Attorney General. The post office intercepted all the bombs except one, which wounded Hardwick's maid. In June there were several direct bombings. One weapon exploded in front of the Washington home of Attorney General A. Mitchell Palmer, damaging the building and dismembering his would-be assassin, an Italian anarchist.

The bombings of April and June had been plotted by dangerous, probably insane criminals. They were not, however, a part of communist strategy, for the leaders of international communism recognized that simple terror would be an ineffective weapon for overturning a strong, capitalist state. But most Americans did not differentiate among radicalisms. They grew more frightened every day, and they saw Red in everything they feared or disliked. Opponents of the League of Nations condemned all internationalism as Red internationalism. Congressman James F. Byrnes of South Carolina warned that the Reds were inciting a Negro uprising in the South. One

Columbia professor even suggested that Albert Einstein's theories, with which he disagreed, were the product of a "deep mental disturbance" that was bringing Bolshevism to both politics and physics.

The mood of the nation endorsed the witch hunts conducted by Attorney General Palmer. A Quaker, a progressive Democrat who had worked effectively for women's suffrage and labor reforms, an enthusiast for the League of Nations, Palmer had enjoyed a deserved reputation as a liberal until he took office in March 1919. Then he threw his department, especially the Federal Bureau of Investigation, into a strenuous campaign against aliens and radicals. He may have been hoping to advance his candidacy for the Democratic presidential nomination in 1920. If so, he overreached himself. But he did succeed in violating the Anglo-American heritage of civil liberties.

Congress refused to pass a sedition bill that Palmer had drafted, but the Attorney General on his own authority ordered a series of raids beginning in November 1919. During the first raid his agents arrested 250 members of the Union of Russian Workers and beat many of them up, but the Justice Department could find cause to recommend that only 39 of them be deported. In December Palmer cooperated with the Labor Department in deporting 249 aliens to Russia, most of whom had committed no offense and were not communists. A nationwide raid on January 1, 1920, led to the arrest of some 6,000 people, many of whom were American citizens and noncommunists. They were handcuffed, marched through the streets, and herded into prisons and bull pens; some were seized on suspicion only, taken without warrants from their homes, and held incommunicado. The raids revealed no evidence of a grand plot. (Fewer than 600 of the aliens arrested were deported, though more would have been sent packing had Secretary of Labor William B. Wilson not seen to it that all received a fair trial.) Nevertheless, few Americans spoke out against the high-handed tactics of the Attorney General, the chief legal officer of the United States.

His ambitions soaring, Palmer continued to warn the nation about Red plots. But the outbreak he predicted for May 1, 1920, failed to materialize, and gradually the public began to

Vanzetti's Last Statement in Court

I am not only innocent of these two crimes, but ... in all my life I have never stole, never killed, never spilled blood, but I have struggled all my life, since I began to reason, to eliminate crime from the earth....

You already know that we were radicals, that we were underdogs.... We were tried during a time that has now passed into history. I mean by that, a time when there was hysteria of resentment and hate against the people of our principles, against the foreigner....

I am suffering because I am a radical and indeed I am a radical; I have suffered because I was an Italian, and indeed I am an Italian; I have suffered more for my family and for my beloved than for myself; but I am so convinced to be right that if you could execute me two times, and if I could be reborn two other times, I would live again to do what I have done already.

From Bartolomeo Vanzetti, Last Statement in Court, April 9, 1927.

tire of his unfounded alarms. The tide of Bolshevism had started to recede in Europe, and Palmer and his imitators had made themselves ridiculous. They could, of course, also be ruthless, as was the New York legislature which expelled five innocuous Socialists, all properly elected members of the Assembly. This travesty on the American elective system evoked sharp denunciations, the most influential from Charles Evans Hughes. By the summer of 1920 the Red scare was over, the hysteria spent. In September Americans were horrified by a bomb explosion at the corner of Broad and Wall Streets in New York; but they accepted the episode for what it was, the work of a crazed individual, not the product of a Bolshevik conspiracy as Palmer maintained.

The Red scare left ugly scars. The constitutional rights of thousands of Americans had been violated. Hundreds of innocent people had been deported. Many states had enacted sedition laws even more extreme than those passed during the war. And there lingered a less strident but still pervasive nativism that in the years ahead was to condone the new Ku Klux Klan, an organization dedicated to the hatred of Negroes, Catholics, Jews, and foreigners. Nativism set the stage for a major

reversal of immigration policy, which had for so many decades kept the gates of America open to newcomers. In February 1921, over Wilson's veto, Congress passed a law limiting the number of immigrants in any year to 3 per cent of the foreign-born of each national group who had been living in the United States in 1910. Even this restrictive quota, which just about choked off immigration from Asia and central and southern Europe, was later to be reduced (see p. 611).

Hatred of aliens and radicals made a travesty of justice in the celebrated case of two Italians, confessed anarchists, Nicola Sacco and Bartolomeo Vanzetti. They were arrested, tried, and convicted for murdering two employees of a shoe company in South Braintree, Massachusetts, during a payroll robbery in 1920. Yet there was no compelling evidence against them, and they were condemned essentially for their language and their beliefs. The judge who conducted the trial referred to them privately as "those anarchist bastards." Many of the best people of Boston felt the same way, and most of them, including the presi-

Eulogy to Sacco and Vanzetti

——know this where you lie,
this is the glory of earth-born men and women,
not to cringe, never to yield, but standing,
take defeat implacable and defiant,
die unsubmitting. I wish that I'd died so,
long ago; before you're old you'll wish
that you had died as they have. On this star,
in this hard star-adventure, knowing not
what the fires mean to right and left, nor whether
a meaning was intended or presumed,
man can stand up, and look out blind, and say:
in all these turning lights I find no clue,
only a masterless night, and in my blood
no certain answer, yet is my mind my own,
yet is my heart a cry toward something dim
in distance, which is higher than I am
and makes me emperor of the endless dark
even in seeking! What odds and ends of life
men may live otherwise, let them live, and then
go out, as I shall go, and you. Our part
is only to bury them....

From Maxwell Anderson, *Winterset*, copyright 1935 by Anderson House. Permission to reprint granted by Anderson House.

Sacco and Vanzetti: "You will kill the brave men."

dents of Harvard and M.I.T., approved the decision to deny a retrial. Felix Frankfurter, the novelist John Dos Passos, the poet Edna St. Vincent Millay, and other defenders of justice tried for six years to save Sacco and Vanzetti, but they failed. The cause attracted attention throughout the world and engaged the hearts of men who were to provide liberal leadership in the years to come. But in 1927, when Sacco and Vanzetti were electrocuted, the wounds of the Red scare festered again and liberalism seemed beaten. The forces of respectability and conformity and regression seemed to be united against justice and decency and democracy. "All right," Dos Passos wrote a decade later, ". . . you will kill the brave men. . . . all right we are two nations."

The Election of 1920 The American public had small appetite for defiance in 1920. The Red scare seemed to have drained away the last vestiges of crusading zeal. Americans, weary of public matters great and small, withdrew to a private world of pleasure, entertainment, and sensationalism. Theodore Roosevelt's lament of 1916 was pertinent in 1920: the country was not in a heroic mood.

Neither were the political parties. The confident Republicans met in Chicago to select their presidential nominee from a large group of aspirants, among whom probably the best

known was General Leonard Wood, who claimed the mantle of Roosevelt and stood for nationalism, militarism, and hell-fire for radicals. Wood's closest rival was Governor Frank O. Lowden of Illinois, an experienced executive popular among farmers and businessmen in the Midwest. Senators Hiram Johnson of California and Robert La Follette of Wisconsin appealed to the outnumbered progressives, as did Herbert Hoover, who had announced that he would accept nomination.

The professionals who controlled the party machinery had plans of their own. National Chairman Will Hays, Senator Henry Cabot Lodge, Senator Boies Penrose of Pennsylvania, and businessmen Harry Sinclair and Edward L. Doheny intended to name a candidate they could manage. For six ballots Wood and Lowden stood each other off. Then, during an adjournment, the bosses met in the Blackstone Hotel suite of George Harvey, a New York editor once a friend but now a bitter foe of Wilson. In this, the most celebrated of smoke-filled rooms, they arranged for the nomination to go to Senator Warren G. Harding of Ohio. The convention selected Harding on the tenth ballot, and then the delegates, ignoring the orders of the bosses, named Calvin Coolidge for Vice-President.

Harding was a handsome, semi-educated

Harding in Florida: A complaisant disposition.

political hack with a modest talent for golf; a larger taste for women, liquor, and poker; a complaisant disposition; an utterly empty mind; and an enduring loyalty to the Republican creed of 1890. He was probably the least-qualified candidate ever nominated by a major party. His platform fitted his creed exactly. It promised lower taxes, higher tariff, restriction of immigration, and—with opportunistic generosity—aid to farmers. It damned the League of Nations but called vaguely for an "agreement among nations to preserve the peace"—a phrase that made the isolationists happy and that Harding's wordy speeches did nothing to clarify. Yet a number of Republican internationalists, among them Taft, Root, and Hughes, endorsed Harding. If they lacked faith in their candidate, as well they might have, they were too close to 1912 to risk another schism, some of them were skeptical about the League as a vehicle for internationalism, and all of them were tired of eight long years of Democratic dominance.

The Democrats were at odds with themselves. The failure of President Wilson, in spite of his illness, to disclaim ambition for the nomination impeded the candidacy of his son-in-law, William G. McAdoo, probably the ablest of the hopefuls. Attorney General Palmer had begun to run out of gas before the convention met. And in any event the Democratic bosses, almost as powerful as their Republican counterparts, wanted no candidate who was identified with the Wilson Administration. They preferred Governor James M. Cox of Ohio, a man with a progressive record, a good vote-getter, and an opponent of Prohibition.

After thirty-seven ballots Palmer released his delegates, but McAdoo still could not muster the necessary two-thirds vote; on the forty-fourth ballot the convention selected Cox. As his running mate, the delegates chose a young Wilsonian with a magic political name, Assistant Secretary of the Navy Franklin D. Roosevelt. The platform was pro-League (though it allowed for amendments to the Covenant), in favor of tax reduction and Philippine independence, noncommittal about Prohibition, and otherwise undistinguished. So, except in contrast to Harding, was the Democratic candidate. Cox had about him a pleasant way, a certain prim yet persuasive manner, and a satisfactory record; but he also had a quality of littleness, at least in comparison with the national candidates of the preceding decade.

Cox and Roosevelt waged a hard campaign, in which they stressed the League issue as Wilson had hoped they would. But the Democrats had no real chance of winning, for the movement toward the Republicans, still the normal majority party, had begun in 1918 (see p. 576), and it accelerated in 1920. Midwestern farmers, alienated by wartime controls, were now troubled by falling prices. Much of the once-progressive middle class had come to resent high taxes and labor strife. Urban Democrats of the North were suspicious of Southern "drys," and Irish-Americans were hostile toward Wilson's foreign policy. Many independents could not forgive Palmer his behavior, or Wilson his sometimes open endorsement of it.

All these factors combined to produce a Republican "earthquake," as one Democrat put it. Harding received 61 per cent of the popular vote, carried every state outside the South and also Tennessee, and led Cox by 404 to 127 in the electoral college. The Republicans also swept the congressional elections, obtaining a majority of 22 in the Senate and 167 in the House of Representatives. Not only had the voters repudiated Wilson and internationalism; they had also repudiated progressivism. They restored to power the Republicans who had stuck with the party when Roosevelt bolted in 1912. Harding, for all his limitations, had caught the purpose of his constituency when he called for a return to "not nostrums, but normalcy." He invented the last word, which in 1920 seemed to connote escape from responsibility, even from reality. His Administration soon gave the term a venal overtone.

"I sympathize deeply with you, madame, but I cannot associate with you."

Normalcy

All the Advantages   Harding, his Secretary of State, Charles Evans Hughes, and the Republican majority in the Senate quickly buried the issue of the Treaty of Versailles. In his first message to Congress the President stated that the United States would have nothing to do with the League of Nations, not even with its health program. Since the rejection of the treaty left the United States still technically at war with the Central Powers, the Senate passed again a resolution establishing a separate peace with Germany—a resolution that Wilson had vetoed. Harding signed it in July 1921, and Hughes then negotiated peace treaties with Germany, Austria, and Hungary. Like the resolution, these treaties claimed for the United States all the rights and advantages, but none of the responsibilities, of the Paris settlement.

The pursuit of advantages without responsibility—in Wilson's words "an ineffaceable stain upon . . . the honor of the United States"—also engaged the Harding Administration as a diplomatic partner to American oil companies. Their pressure persuaded the President to champion a treaty with Colombia, ostensibly designed only to indemnify that republic with $25 million for her loss of land and honor when Roosevelt assisted the Panama-

nian revolt. The treaty had been under consideration for several years, but Roosevelt's friends had blocked it while he still lived. In 1921, two years after his death, Colombia was preparing to withdraw all private rights to subsurface oil deposits. This possibility helped to move even Lodge to seek the good will which would permit Standard Oil to obtain concessions from the Colombian government. In April 1921 the Senate ratified the treaty; Colombia ratified it in 1922; and American investments there, largely in oil, grew from about $2 million to $124 million by 1929. The State Department opened even richer prospects for profit by persuading the British to share with American companies the enormous oil fields of the Middle East.

The outstanding diplomatic venture of Harding's term was a 1921 conference on naval disarmament, which the President was rather reluctant to summon. At the time of his inauguration, the Navy Department was urging the completion of the vast building program that had been launched five years earlier (see p. 563). But businessmen were impatient to cut federal expenses so that taxes could be reduced, and they grumbled about the cost of the program. Continued naval expansion, moreover, was provoking an armament race with two recent associates, Great Britain and Japan, sea powers who were unwilling to stand idly by while the American navy grew. Fearful that this competition might lead to war, Senator William E. Borah of Idaho suggested a three-power meeting on naval limitation. In his view, for which there was growing popular support, the Republicans could make disarmament the fulcrum for world peace. Though Harding disagreed, large majorities in both houses of Congress endorsed Borah's scheme in a resolution attached to the naval appropriations bill of 1921.

This move was welcomed by the British government, which foresaw trouble in the naval rivalry between Japan and the United States. Britain was also eager to terminate the defensive alliance she had made with Japan in 1902, an alliance that the Dominions, especially Canada, disliked. The agreement bound both powers to respect each other's interests in the Orient and to assist each other should the interests of either be attacked by two other countries. The British felt that the arms race was intimately associated with stability in the Far East, particularly because the United States and Japan had been at odds over such questions as China's future, the Siberian intervention, and the disposition of former German islands in the western Pacific. Harding proposed a conference on naval limitations on the same day the British called for a conference on the Far East. They agreed to discuss both matters at a single meeting in Washington.

The double agenda made it necessary to invite all the major naval powers—the United States, Great Britain, Japan, France, and Italy—as well as smaller powers with interests in the Far East—China, Portugal, Belgium, and the Netherlands. Everyone agreed that Bolshevik Russia should be excluded, and her protests were ignored. Of the powers that were invited, only Japan was hesitant, worried lest she lose either her alliance with England or her newly acquired Pacific islands. She accepted, however, on the condition that the conference would not consider matters that constituted accomplished facts.

The delegates assembled on November 11, 1921, to commemorate the third anniversary of the armistice. The next day Harding greeted them with an emotional speech. Next the delegates heard an address by Secretary of State Charles Evans Hughes, who had been named presiding officer. Instead of dealing in the usual platitudes of such occasions, Hughes presented the conference with a detailed plan for naval disarmament. The United States was to scrap thirty capital ships, half old and half being built; the British were to give up twenty-three; Japan, seventeen. This destruction of more than 1,878,000 aggregate tons afloat, on the ways, or planned, would establish a capital-ship tonnage ratio among the three nations of 5:5:3. The ratio was to persist for ten years, during which the powers would observe a moratorium on the construction of capital ships. France and Italy were each to have one-third the tonnage allotted the United States and Great Britain.

Hughes's speech, one of the most dramatic in diplomatic annals, stirred the amazed delegates to cheers. The Japanese, however, disliked being on the short end of the ratio, which wounded their pride and might threaten their national security. Starting with a demand for a 10:10:7 ratio, they bargained successfully to keep their newest battleship, which Hughes had destined for the junk heap. They accepted the Five Power Naval Treaty only after the United States and England had agreed not to fortify their possessions in the western Pacific.

Another agreement, the Four Power Treaty, bound the United States, Great Britain, Japan, and France to respect each other's rights affecting insular possessions in the Pacific, to refer disputes in that area to a joint conference, and to consult each other in the event of a threat from another power. Moreover, the treaty specifically supplanted the Anglo-Japanese alliance.

Now Hughes pressed on to conclude a Nine Power Treaty that committed all the nations at the conference to observe traditional American policies in the Far East. They agreed to respect the territorial and administrative integrity and the independence of China, and to uphold the Open Door.

The Washington treaties were a considerable achievement. As the British had intended, and as the United States later maintained, they were integrally related to each other, and together they reduced tension in the Far East.

Indeed, in the wake of the treaties, Japan restored Shantung to China's sovereignty, withdrew from Siberia, and granted the United States cable rights on the former German island of Yap. The naval treaty, moreover, marked the first time in history that major powers had consented to disarm. Hughes had made a virtue of necessity, for he had really given up nothing he had any reasonable chance of getting. The economy-minded Congress, as Lodge reported, would not have continued to expand the navy and would have looked askance at the cost of fortifying Guam or the Philippines.

Yet the Washington settlement also had shortcomings. It left the powers free to construct auxiliary naval vessels, such as destroyers, cruisers, and submarines, which were to prove vital weapons in the future. It provided no mechanism for policing the islands of the western Pacific or for protecting China. Thus it largely perpetuated the postwar status quo, for the western Pacific was still a Japanese lake. Japan when she chose could build up her fleet, fortify her mandate islands, and encroach upon China, unless the United States was prepared to defend her stated policies. The test of the settlement lay not in its terms but in whether or not the powers chose to honor them. As Wilson had asserted, peace was a matter of continuous negotiation and accommodation. And as Roosevelt had preached, power was ever a factor in the affairs of nations.

Hughes had done remarkably well, but the spirit with which Americans greeted his accomplishment was ominous. In ratifying the Four Power Treaty, the Senate added a reservation asserting that the United States recognized "no commitment to armed force, no alliance, no obligation to join in any defense." Despite Hughes's admonitions, Congress and the public in 1922 and for years thereafter were unwilling to keep the navy even up to treaty strength. In short, the American people accepted words as realities, and the Washington settlement proved to be another case of seeking all the advantages and none of the responsibilities.

The Best Minds Advantages rather than responsibilities were also the goal of the representatives of business and finance who shaped the domestic policies of the Harding

Andrew Mellon: "Government is just a business."

Administration. The President had promised to recruit for government the "best minds" of the country. Hughes met that standard, as did Secretary of Agriculture Henry C. Wallace, who had long devoted himself and his Iowa newspaper to the cause of agricultural reform. But Wallace's influence was outweighed by that of Herbert Hoover, the new Secretary of Commerce, who used his department to promote the interests and enlarge the markets of American business. Hoover, in Harding's view, had proved his worth by acquiring a magnificent fortune. That was the President's surest criterion for finding the "best minds."

Foremost among Harding's advisers was Secretary of the Treasury Andrew Mellon, a reticent multimillionaire from Pittsburgh whose intricate banking and investment holdings gave him, his family, and his associates

Equality of Opportunity?

To the average man, it seems not unfair that the taxpayer with an income of over $200,000 a year should pay over half of it to the Government.... Taxation, however, is not a means of confiscating wealth but of raising necessary revenues for the Government.

One of the foundations of our American civilization is equality of opportunity, which presupposes the right of each man to enjoy the fruits of his labor after contributing his fair share to the support of the Government, which protects him and his property. But that is a very different matter from confiscating a part of his wealth, not because the country requires it for the prosecution of a war or some other purpose, but because he seems to have more money than he needs. Our civilization, after all, is based on accumulated capital, and that capital is no less vital to our prosperity than is the extraordinary energy which has built up in this country the greatest material civilization the world has ever seen. Any policy that deliberately destroys that accumulated capital under the spur of no necessity is striking directly at the soundness of our financial structure and is full of menace for the future.

From Andrew W. Mellon, *Taxation: The People's Business*, 1924.

control, among many other things, of the aluminum monopoly. A man of slight build, with a cold and weary face, Mellon exuded sober luxury and contemptuous worldliness. "The Government is just a business," he believed, "and can and should be run on business principles."

Great businesses, as Mellon knew, thrive on innovation and expansion. Yet the only business principle he considered relevant to government was economy. With small regard for the services that only government could furnish the nation, Mellon worked unceasingly to cut federal expenditures. Expenses had to be cut if he was to achieve his corollary purpose: the reduction of taxes, especially taxes on men of means. It was better, he argued, to place the burden of taxes on lower-income groups, for taxing the rich inhibited their investments and thus retarded economic growth. A share of the tax-free profits of the rich, Mellon reassured the country, would ultimately trickle down to the middle- and lower-income groups in the form of salaries and wages. Robert La Follette

paraphrased this regressive theory succinctly: "Wealth will not and cannot be made to bear its full share of taxation."

The quest for economy in government had some beneficial results. In 1921 Harding signed the Budget and Accounting Act, which improved the budgeting procedures of the federal government. Previously each executive department had made its own requests for appropriations. Now a new official, the Director of the Budget, was to advise the President on the preparation of an over-all, annual budget, and another officer, the Comptroller General, was to audit all executive accounts. Though rudimentary, the new system was essential for efficient government, whatever its expenditures. It also served Mellon's purpose, for Harding's first Director of the Budget, Charles G. Dawes, a Chicago banker, made economy the touchstone of the budget that was presented to Congress in 1922.

Primarily in order to hold expenditures down, Harding opposed a veterans' bonus bill which Congress debated in 1921, and he vetoed it when it passed the next year. The American Legion, an organization of World War veterans, led the lobby that demanded "adjusted compensation" for all servicemen. The Legion argued that soldiers had fought for a pittance while civilians were drawing high wartime wages. The bonus was to set matters right by granting veterans either an extra dollar for each day of service (a dollar and a quarter for overseas service) or a paid-up twenty-year insurance policy of about the same value. It might be argued that veterans do indeed deserve something more than gratitude from their country, but this bonus was little more than a raid on public funds supported by an energetic and increasingly influential pressure group. The newly created Veterans Administration was already taking care of the disabled. Veterans were not necessarily the neediest candidates for public assistance. And military service was in any case an obligation, not a job. Yet the veterans were simply acting in the spirit of the time when they continued to seek special advantages. Congress overrode a second veto in 1924 and granted a bonus in the form of paid-up twenty-year insurance policies, against which the veterans could immediately borrow limited funds.

Meanwhile, Mellon had advanced the tax program of the business community. In 1921 he urged Congress to repeal the excess-profits tax and to reduce the surtax on personal income from a maximum of 65 per cent to 32 per cent for 1921, and 25 per cent thereafter. These proposals would have prevailed had it not been for the opposition of a group of Western Republican senators who joined with the Democrats to preserve the progressive principles of wartime revenue legislation. Together they were able to force Harding to accept a bill that incorporated many of their changes. The Revenue Act of 1921 did eliminate the excess-profits tax, but it fell short of Mellon's other goals. It held the maximum surtax on personal income at 50 per cent, and it granted some tax relief to lower- and middle-income groups by raising exemptions for heads of families and their dependents. Expressing the disappointment of the Administration and its supporters, the New York *Herald* called the act "a thoroughly bad job."

The Administration had better luck with its tariff policy. Following the tradition of their party, Republican leaders set out at once to restore the protective rates that had prevailed before 1913. Though they experienced some delay, two developments eased their way. The spread of industry in the South had dispelled much of the traditional Democratic resistance to tariff protection. More important, farm representatives had concluded that they would profit from protective rates on farm products. This was a delusion, for the farmer really needed larger markets abroad and help at home in marketing his produce and obtaining credit. But the members of the informal farm bloc, the same men who had joined forces against Mellon's tax bill, pushed through prohibitive duties for twenty-eight agricultural commodities in the Emergency Tariff Act of 1921. During the discussion of the tariff that continued the following year, the leaders of the farm bloc, except for Senators William E. Borah, George Norris, and Robert La Follette, rivaled the spokesmen of industry in their zeal for protection. Consequently there was no spirited debate on the tariff, as there had been in 1909.

With no significant dissent, Congress in 1922 passed the Fordney-McCumber Act, which re-established prohibitive tariff rates. The act did instruct the Tariff Commission to help the President determine differences in production costs between the United States and other nations. And it did empower the President to raise or lower any rate by 50 per cent, on the commission's recommendation. In practice, however, the commission was strongly protectionist, and of the thirty-seven rates that were altered during the life of the act, thirty-two were actually increased.

The tariff of 1922 enriched American monopolists, but it damaged foreign trade. By preventing Europeans from selling their goods in the United States, it made it impossible for them to buy American products, including agricultural surpluses, except by borrowing dollars and thus increasing the large debts they had incurred during the war. This was an unhealthy situation both for the United States and for Europe.

Nullification by Administration The restoration of tariff protection was only one part of a concerted effort by the Administration to restore the conditions of the nineteenth century. Wherever they could, Harding and his associates rolled back the accomplishments of the progressive movement.

The President could not tear down the apparatus that had been constructed for regulating business and industry, but he succeeded in rendering that apparatus useless by turning it over to the very interests it had been designed to regulate. Harding and his successor named to the Federal Trade Commission three men who were, in the phrase of George Norris, fearless advocates of big business. The Federal Reserve Board supported the views of Andrew Mellon, an ex officio member, and D. R. Crissinger, a lawyer and banker from Marion, Ohio, Harding's home town, whom the President made comptroller of the currency and later governor of the board.

Crissinger's small mind and pliant judgment characterized the temper of the new administrators throughout the federal government. Their appointment, as Senator Norris said, "set the country back more than twenty-five years." And, he added, they achieved "the nullification of federal law by a process of boring from within."

The Administration also stood aside while

management continued its attack on labor unions and labor legislation. In April 1922 bituminous coal operators, determined to cut costs, announced major reductions in wages, some of them almost 50 per cent. The miners themselves realized that the industry was in trouble, largely because of overproduction, and they were reconciled to lower pay. But they also suspected the operators of trying to destroy their union. They struck, as did the anthracite miners, in order to establish the principle of industry-wide collective bargaining. In June there were outbreaks of violence, of which the worst was in Herrin, Illinois, where strikebreakers and miners waged a small war. Harding then interceded. Sure of their man, the mine operators announced that they were quite willing to arbitrate if only the miners would return to work pending a settlement. But the union, with a good idea of what that settlement would be, declined to arbitrate. Harding ordered the mines reopened, requested the states to use troops to protect those miners who wanted to work, and promised to send federal support if it was needed. The union then called off the strike on the condition that there would be a federal investigation of the issues in dispute.

In September 1922 Congress authorized the President to appoint a commission of inquiry. After making a careful survey, the commission revealed the pitiful, even desperate, state of life in the coal towns. The commission supported neither compulsory arbitration, which the operators wanted, nor complete unionization, which the miners had advocated. Instead, it recommended various federal controls over the mining industry, but Congress and the Administration ignored the report. Deprived of the public guidance that might have saved it, the coal industry also failed to discipline itself during the decade that followed. The operators continued to lose markets to other fuels, and they transferred much of their distress to the miners by way of layoffs and wage cuts. The defeat of the union provoked timidity and bickering among its leaders and a decline in its rank-and-file membership.

The railroads were also having labor troubles, and again the Administration aligned itself with management. In 1922 the national Railway Labor Board approved a 12 per cent reduction in the wages of shopmen, thereby precipitating a strike that lasted two months. It ended only when the Attorney General got an injunction that forbade the union to picket or in any way to encourage workers to leave their jobs.

In this and other rulings the federal courts, acting in the spirit of the executive establishment and its sponsors, took advantage of the permissiveness of the Clayton Act (see p. 553). Contrary to Gompers' hopes, the injunction was still a handy instrument for breaking strikes. In the same spirit, the courts sustained "yellow-dog" contracts that bound employees not to join unions. The courts' hostility toward labor not only helped management's campaign for the open shop but also destroyed social legislation designed to protect the poorest and weakest workers. The Supreme Court in 1922, in the case of *Bailey* v. *Drexel Furniture Company*, declared unconstitutional a federal statute levying a prohibitive tax on products manufactured by children. The Court had ruled earlier, in *Hammer* v. *Dagenhart* (1918), that federal laws to control child labor were an unconstitutional invasion of the police powers of the states. In the Bailey case, it said that Congress could not use its tax power to accomplish this unconstitutional purpose. The decision perpetuated child labor, especially in the Southern textile mills. It also circumscribed the sovereign power of the federal government to tax.

The Supreme Court was just as opposed to regulation of wages, hours, and working conditions by the states as it was to regulation by the federal government. In 1923, in *Adkins* v. *Children's Hospital*, it held unconstitutional a District of Columbia statute establishing minimum wages for women. Ignoring the social and economic arguments for the act, the majority of the Court found it a violation of the freedom of women to contract to sell their labor as they pleased. The Adkins decision contravened the spirit of the Clayton Act, which asserted that labor was not a mere commodity. The decision also left labor defenseless, for neither federal nor state governments could insist on minimum standards of health and decency while the attitudes of the courts denied the unions much of their opportunity to recruit membership or to strike for fair treatment.

The farmers fared better politically, but not economically, under the Harding Administration. In 1922 agricultural prices began to recover from their postwar slump, but the farmers were harassed by high interest charges on mortgages and by heavy taxes on land. Advancing technology raised production and expanded surpluses even though the number of farms and of agricultural workers was steadily declining. And advancing industrialism continuously reduced the farmers' share of the national income. Agriculture during the early 1920's was not generally impoverished, though segments of it were. But even the more privileged farmers were anxious about their future and resentful of their diminishing influence on American life. They were jealous, too, of the conveniences, especially electricity, automobiles, and entertainment, which were becoming more and more common in the cities.

In 1921 and 1922 the discontent of farmers generated considerable political force in the South and the Midwest, and the farm bloc in Congress won a series of victories. With few exceptions, however, the leaders of the farm bloc failed to understand the basic difficulties. They gave little attention to enriching social life on the farm. And as their infatuation with tariff protection indicated, they were confused about the problem of agricultural surpluses.

They made their mark instead where the objectives of the fading progressive movement helped them to define their goals. The Packers and Stockyards Act of 1921 authorized the Secretary of Agriculture to issue cease and desist orders for the purpose of preserving competition among packers, and to compel commission merchants and stockyards to charge reasonable rates. The Grain Futures Act provided the same control over grain exchanges. In 1922 the Capper-Volstead Act exempted farm cooperatives from the antitrust laws, and Congress added a representative of agriculture to the Federal Reserve Board. In 1923 the Agricultural Credits Act established twelve Intermediate Credit Banks to make loans to cooperatives and other farm groups for six months to three years. The loans were to help cooperatives to withhold crops from the market when prices were temporarily low. These statutes strengthened the farmer's ability to conduct his business, and they created instruments

---

A Virtuous Poor?

The standard furnished by the statute ... is so vague as to be impossible of practical application with any reasonable degree of accuracy. What is sufficient to supply the necessary cost of living for a woman worker and maintain her in good health and protect her morals is obviously not a precise or unvarying sum—not even approximately so.... Morality rests upon other considerations than wages; and there is, certainly, no such prevalent connection between the two as to justify a broad attempt to adjust the latter with reference to the former.... Nor is there ground for distinction between women and men, for, certainly, if women require a minimum wage to preserve their morals, men require it to preserve their honesty. For these reasons, and others which might be stated, the inquiry in respect of the necessary cost of living and of the income necessary to preserve health and morals, presents an individual and not a composite question, and must be answered for each individual considered by herself and not by a general formula prescribed by a statutory bureau.

From *Adkins* v. *Children's Hospital*, 261 U.S. 525, 1923.

---

for controlling the middlemen to whom he sold his produce. But they did not provide him with new markets, nor did they ease his mortgage burden.

In the off-year elections of 1922, agrarian dissent carried anti-Administration candidates to victory in Republican primaries in most of the West. In November the resurgent Democrats reduced Republican majorities to eight in the Senate and eighteen in the House. And of the Republicans who were elected, so many were disenchanted that the Administration no longer controlled Congress. The returns heartened intellectuals and farm and labor leaders who were hoping to restore liberal government in 1924. More immediately the elections assured key committee assignments to strong men in both parties who were dubious about the Administration's program and methods. Those men, using Congress' power of investigation, soon exposed the Harding regime to publicity it could not afford.

The Harding Scandals The President of the United States sets the tone of his Administration. The first two decades of the twentieth century had been marked by McKinley's kindness, Theodore Roosevelt's strenuosity, Taft's decent ineffectuality, and Wilson's soaring idealism. Warren Harding brought to government the qualities of his own weak person. He was an ignorant, naïve, confused man whose loose standards made him particularly vulnerable to his intellectual deficiencies and to the corrupt character of the hail fellows with whom he instinctively surrounded himself.

Harding was ruefully aware of some of his limitations. On one occasion, after listening to a long discussion about taxes, he confessed to a secretary:

> John, I can't make a damn thing out of this tax problem. I listen to one side and they seem right, and then—God!—I talk to the other side and they seem just as right. . . . I know somewhere there is a book that will give me the truth, but, hell, I couldn't read the book. I know somewhere there is an economist who knows the truth, but I don't know where to find him and haven't the sense to know him and trust him when I find him. God! what a job.

As he suspected, the President did not know whom to trust. Though a few members of his Cabinet—Hughes, Hoover, and Mellon in particular—were men of large talent, more of his advisers were distinguished by their lack of qualifications. Uncomfortable with the "best minds," Harding preferred the kind of tawdry companionship he had known in his native Marion, Ohio. He made one former crony, "Ed" Scobey, the director of the mint. Another home-town friend, Old Doc Sawyer, a homeopath, became White House physician with the rank of brigadier general. Harding appointed his own brother-in-law, a missionary of the Adventist church, superintendent of federal prisons. As head of the Veterans Bureau he selected Charles R. Forbes, whom he had met by chance during a jovial holiday in Hawaii. For the office of Secretary of the Interior the President chose Senator Albert B. Fall of New Mexico, a bitter partisan with a reputation for shiftiness. The new Attorney General was Harry M. Daugherty of Ohio, who had advanced his own career largely by promoting Harding's. Daugherty's intimate, Jesse Smith of Ohio, came along as an unofficial influence. These, and a few others, constituted the "Ohio gang" who met continually with Harding at a house on K Street. There

councils of state had an incidental but insinuating part in the rounds of poker, whiskey, and women that made the President feel at home.

For two years the Ohio gang flourished. Early in 1923, however, Daugherty decided he had to tell Harding of the rumors he had heard about Charles Forbes. The cheerful head of the Veterans Bureau had pocketed an impressive fraction of the $250 million which his agency spent lavishly for hospitals and hospital supplies. Harding permitted Forbes to go abroad and resign, but in March a Senate committee began to investigate the Veterans Bureau, whose legal adviser, lacking the courage of his rascality, committed suicide. Yet ultimately Forbes was exposed, tried, convicted, and sentenced to prison.

There was a second suicide in May. Jesse Smith had been selling his influence at the Justice Department to lawbreakers who paid handsomely for forgiveness or immunity. When stories of his dealings finally reached the obtuse President, he told Daugherty that Smith had to leave. Briefly Smith returned to Ohio, but on May 23, back in Daugherty's familiar apartment, he killed himself.

It was later revealed that one of Smith's ventures involved Thomas W. Miller, Harding's alien property custodian, who had agreed to a dubious disposition of the control of the American Metal Company. The attorney in that transaction was John T. King, the Republican National Committeeman from Connecticut. King's fee was $441,000 in bonds, of which $50,000 went to Miller and $200,000 to Smith, who gave a block of bonds to Daugherty's brother. The proceeds from the sale of that block of bonds, about $50,000, were deposited in an account which the Attorney General managed. Eventually Miller went to jail for accepting a bribe, but two divided juries in 1926 saved Daugherty, who refused to testify on his own behalf for fear of self-incrimination.

Albert Fall was less fortunate. In 1921 he persuaded Harding to transfer to the Interior Department control over naval oil reserves at Elk Hill, California, and Teapot Dome, Wyoming. The next year Fall secretly leased Elk Hill to the oil company of Edward L. Doheny, and Teapot Dome to the company of Harry F.

Sinclair. But the leases could not be kept secret very long. In October 1923 a Senate committee under the chairmanship of Thomas J. Walsh, a Montana Democrat, began an investigation which a special commission completed in 1924. The inquiries disclosed that Doheny had "lent" Fall $100,000 and that Sinclair had given the Secretary of the Interior a herd of cattle for his ranch, $85,000 in cash, and $223,-000 in bonds. In 1927 the government won a suit for cancellation of the leases. Though another remarkable verdict acquitted Doheny, Sinclair, and Fall of conspiracy to defraud the government, Sinclair was convicted of tampering with a jury, and in 1929 Fall was convicted of bribery, fined $100,000 and sentenced to a year in jail. He was the first Cabinet officer ever to go to prison.

Harding knew of the exploits of only Forbes and Smith. In June 1923, before setting out on a speaking tour through the West, the President unburdened himself to William Allen White: "My God, this is a hell of a job. I have no trouble with my enemies. . . . But my damned friends, my God-damned friends, . . . they're the ones that keep me walking the floor nights!" Depressed and tired, Harding grew "nervous and distraught" as he traveled; his speeches disappointed his audiences; his seemingly endless bridge game involved even the reluctant Herbert Hoover, who never played again. Late in July, while in Seattle on the way home from Alaska, the President suffered acute pain. Dr. Sawyer diagnosed it as indigestion, perhaps from tainted crab meat. But other physicians in the party believed that Harding had had a heart attack, a diagnosis that was confirmed by a San Francisco specialist. On August 2, in a room at the Palace Hotel, Harding died, the victim of a coronary or cerebral thrombosis.

Sawyer's incompetent and unconvincing diagnosis bred doubts on which melodrama thrived. One Nan Britton, who claimed to have been Harding's mistress and to have borne him an illegitimate daughter, suggested that he had been poisoned by his jealous wife. The cheapness of Harding's life made the story plausible, but the truth was less exciting. A middle-aged man, overweight, with a tendency toward high blood pressure and an immodest taste for booze, tired, disappointed by his friends, despondent, had died of a bad heart and poor circulation. Only death saved him from sharing the disgrace of his companions.

Vulgarity and scandal were the sordid fruits of normalcy, of a government that sought all the advantages of power but none of the responsibilities, of organized self-interest that sought special favors in bonuses, bounties, lower taxes, and higher tariffs. The scandals passed, but the spirit that nurtured them lived on. They left the "best minds" and the nicest people strangely unabashed. So it was that the Democratic candidate who in 1924 condemned the scandals was said to be campaigning in bad taste. So it was that New York newspapers called the senators who investigated Teapot Dome "scandalmongers," "mudgunners," and "assassins of character." In the United States of the 1920's not even scandal could stay the pursuit of profits and the retreat from responsibility.

SUGGESTIONS FOR READING

General

W. E. Leuchtenburg, *The Perils of Prosperity, 1914–32* * (1958), provides a crisp and thoughtful account of the period and the issues covered by this chapter. Also lively, but less judicious, is F. L. Allen, *Only Yesterday* * (1931).

The Red Scare

R. K. Murray, *The Red Scare* (1955), contains the most comprehensive narrative about the subject. It has to be supplemented, however, by the lucid treatment of civil liberties in Zechariah Chafee, *Free Speech in the United States* (rev. ed., 1941), the masterful analysis of G. L. Joughin and E. M. Morgan, *The Legacy of Sacco and Vanzetti* (1948), the excellent study of labor in Irving Bernstein, *The Lean Years* (1960), and the penetrating treatments

* Available in a paperback edition.

of nativism in John Higham, *Strangers in the Land* (1955), and Oscar Handlin, *Race and Nationality in American Life* * (1957), and *The American People in the Twentieth Century* (1954).

Harding and Normalcy

There is a short but incisive evaluation of the Harding years in A. M. Schlesinger, Jr., *The Crisis of the Old Order* (1957), and a fuller narrative in J. D. Hicks, *Republican Ascendancy* (1960). The economy and its problems receive able handling in George Soule, *Prosperity Decade: From War to Depression, 1917–1929* (1947), but for a richer discussion of taxation and of agriculture, respectively, the relevant chapters of R. E. Paul, *Taxation in the United States* (1954), and Theodore Saloutos and J. D. Hicks, *Agricultural Discontent in the Middle West, 1900–1939* (1951), are particularly valuable. The Harding scandals get the treatment they merit in S. H. Adams, *Incredible Era* (1939), and Karl Schriftgiesser, *This Was Normalcy* (1948). Two stimulating studies of the Washington Conference are H. H. and M. T. Sprout, *Toward a New Order of Sea Power* (1940), and J. C. Vinson, *The Parchment Peace* (1950). Also important are the pertinent parts of A. W. Griswold, *The Far Eastern Policy of the United States* (1938), and F. R. Dulles, *Forty Years of American-Japanese Relations* (1937). Two biographers have given first-rate attention to the diplomacy of Harding's Secretary of State: M. J. Pusey, *Charles Evans Hughes*, 2 vols. (1951), and Dexter Perkins, *Charles Evans Hughes and American Democratic Statesmanship* (1953).

* Available in a paperback edition.

26

A New Age of Business

Calvin Coolidge believed in the kind of luck that Horatio Alger had immortalized. If a man worked hard, saved his pennies, respected the authorities, and kept his mouth shut, an invisible hand would contrive an occasion to make his reputation. Coolidge took no chances while he waited for his breaks. The son of a Vermont storekeeper, he worked his way through Amherst College, studied law in Northampton, Massachusetts, and entered politics there, winning successively those minor state offices on which undistinguished politicians build their ordinary careers. His patient course endeared him to the Massachusetts Republicans, who valued his unquestioning acceptance of things as they were, his unwavering preference for inaction, and his obvious personal honesty.

In 1919, twenty years after he first won public office, Coolidge achieved national prominence for his role in stopping the Boston police strike. His delay in dealing with that episode invited anarchy, but his terse defense of his ultimate policy suited the temper of the time (see p. 590), and his friends used his new reputation to generate the boom that made him the Republican choice for Vice-President. In that post Coolidge dispatched his ceremonial duties with quiet pleasure, warned Americans against the "Reds in Our Women's Colleges," and awaited his next break. When Harding died, Coolidge luck had him at home, where his father, a notary public, administered the oath of office. The event was a blessing for the

most privileged Republicans, for the accession of Calvin Coolidge gave them a new President who cloaked normalcy with respectability.

A New Cult of Enterprise

Coolidge and the Business Creed Personally neat, even prim, deliberately laconic and undemonstrative in public (though given in private to temper and garrulity), Coolidge scrubbed the White House clean of the filth that Harding had left. Grace Coolidge, the new first lady, erased scandal with her natural dignity, charm, and warmth. The President chose two lawyers of impeccable integrity, Owen J. Roberts and Atlee Pomerene, to prosecute the rascals in government. That choice bypassed Attorney General Daugherty, who could not be trusted, and yet permitted Coolidge, always sensitive to party feelings, to keep Daugherty in office until March 1924, when the mounting evidence of the Attorney General's rascality forced his retirement. To his place Coolidge named an eminent former dean of the Columbia Law School, Harlan Fiske Stone, whose appointment completed the shift from obscenity to virtue.

In other respects Coolidge left the national government unaltered. As much as Harding, Coolidge subscribed to the creed of American business. "The business of America is business," Coolidge believed. "The man who builds a factory," he once said, "builds a temple. . . . The man who works there wor-

An Adman?

Let us begin by asking why he was so successful in mastering public attention and why, in contrast, his churches are less so?... In the first place he recognized the basic principle that all good advertising is news. He was never trite or commonplace; he had no routine. If there had been newspapers in those days, no city editor could have said, "No need to visit him to-day; he will be doing just what he did last Sunday." Reporters would have followed him every single hour, for it was impossible to predict what he would say or do; every action and word were news....

Can you imagine the next day's issue of the *Capernaum News,* if there had been one?...

PROMINENT TAX COLLECTOR JOINS NAZARETH FORCES

MATTHEW ABANDONS BUSINESS TO PROMOTE NEW CULT

GIVES LARGE LUNCHEON

❊ ❊ ❊

Every advertising man ought to study the parables of Jesus ... schooling himself in their language. ... They are marvelously condensed, as all good advertising should be.... Jesus had no introductions. A single sentence grips your attention; three or four more tell the story; one or two more and the application is driven home.

From Bruce Barton, *The Man Nobody Knows,* 1925.

---

ships there." The President himself worshiped wealth and those who had it. Worldly possessions were for him evidence of divine election. He stood in awe of Andrew Mellon. He took a smug delight in his own eminence, but he was absolutely euphoric when his office commanded for him the deference of the rich. Coolidge, as William Allen White put it, was "sincerely, genuinely, terribly crazy" about wealth.

This passion coincided exactly with the theories of business spokesmen. There were, they preached, a superior few and an inferior many. And they were easy to distinguish, for "a man is worth the wages he can earn." Material success marked the elite, and to them the others should leave the important decisions about society. The 1920's witnessed a renaissance of the conservative dogmas of the 1880's now clothed in new metaphors. Bruce Barton, a magnificently successful advertising man, gave the gospel its most popular phrasing in his best-seller of 1925, *The Man Nobody Knows.* To his infinite satisfaction, Barton, the son of a minister, discovered that Christ was a businessman. "Jesus," he wrote, ". . . picked up twelve men from the bottom ranks of business and forged them into an organization that conquered the world." The parables made incomparable advertisements; the Gospel, an incomparable business school. "Great progress," Barton concluded, "will be made in this world when we rid ourselves of the idea that there is a difference between *work* and *religious work.*"

Coolidge was devoted to the dominant values of his time, to business, materialism, elitism, and their corollaries. If only the rich were worthy, it followed that the poor would upset or corrupt the management of all affairs, including the affairs of state. Government should therefore beware the counsels of the majority. Since poverty was the wage of sin, government should not tax the virtuous rich in order to assist the unworthy and thriftless poor. And since the virtuous rich best understood their own interests, government should not interfere with the businesses they ran, though it should help promote them.

No devotee of laissez faire ever abhorred government more than Coolidge did. "If the Federal Government should go out of existence," he said, "the common run of people would not detect the difference . . . for a considerable length of time." The federal establishment justified itself, he added, "only as it served business." Its grandest service was to minimize itself, its activities, and its expenditures. So persuaded, Coolidge slept more than any other President in this century. He also did less when he was awake. His favorite rule consisted "in never doing anything that someone else can do for you." And he said less. "Four-fifths of all our troubles in this life," he told one agitated senator, "would disappear if we would only sit down and keep still."

Silence, inactivity, gentility, complacency—these were the sum and the substance of the Coolidge calculus. He was shrewd and self-righteous and marvelously representative of the mood of an acquisitive society. He was also

Coolidge cloaked normalcy with respectability.

a personality, a man about whom other men told stories, some adulatory, others bitter. But for a season adulation reigned.

Productivity and Plenty   The extraordinary prosperity of the 1920's cast a mantle of credibility over the doctrines of business and its representative President. It was easy for him and others of like mind to interpret prosperity as majestic proof of their beliefs. As the country came out of the short slump of 1921, unemployment became negligible except in sick industries like textiles and coal. By 1923 the average money wages of industrial workers were twice what they had been in 1914, and they continued to advance through 1928. Real wages rose, too, steadily though less dramatically. By 1928 they were about one-third higher than they had been fourteen years earlier. Several factors accounted for those increases. Many employers had begun to realize that higher wages removed one of the incentives that prompted workers to join unions, and that they also provided purchasing power that swelled the market for industrial products. Wages stretched further as prices fell, especially the price of food and of goods manufactured in industries where mechanization pushed productivity to new peaks.

The profits that came with mechanization invited investment in new plants and new tools. Investment was encouraged also by the growing national market, by the permissive climate of inactive government, and by Mellon's gradual success in persuading Congress to reduce taxes on large incomes. While investment provided the means for building more and more productivity into American industry, management was mastering new ways to use machinery and to organize production more effectively.

The American system of manufacturing that flowered during the 1920's had deep roots. It depended on the concept of continuous fabrication by which raw materials entered a plant to emerge after multiple operations as finished products. That concept was at least as old as the first Lowell textile mills. It depended also on machine tools capable of producing standard, complex artifacts with interchangeable parts—the kinds of tool and the kind of standardization that Eli Whitney had developed for guns a century before Coolidge's inauguration. More immediately, the American system of manufacturing depended on two recent and interrelated developments. One was the emerging profession of industrial engineering, with its concern for continuous process, improved machinery, specialization of jobs, and time-motion studies of performance. The other was an emerging cult of productivity, a rationalization of the glories of making and distributing and consuming ever more bountifully. Americans had long honored that objective, but never more avidly than in the 1920's.

The founding father of "scientific management" was Frederick W. Taylor. Born in a comfortable family in Germantown, Pennsylvania, in 1856, Taylor had to interrupt his gentleman's education at Harvard because of poor eyesight. Moving into an entirely different kind of environment, he learned the trades of pattern-maker and machinist in a Philadelphia pump works and in 1878 went as a common laborer to the Midvale Steel Company. By 1885 he had earned his Master of Engineering degree at Stevens Institute; a year later he became chief engineer at Midvale. His preoccupation in those years was with machinery, which he mastered, invented, and loved. His driving concern was with efficiency, with making machines and the men who attended them produce more and faster. Those interests led him to establish his own consulting practice on production, on "systematizing shop management."

Taylor's system started with a close study of every step in manufacturing. He sought data to determine the fair capacity of both machines and men. By applying those data, by breaking the process of manufacturing into separate parts, and by specializing the function of the man and machine involved in each part, he could substantially increase the rate of production. His classifications of jobs and of capacity, he believed, would lead also to higher wages as workers first met and then exceeded their calculated goals. In *Shop Management* (1911), Taylor called for the abolition of unevenness in the process of production. The aim of every establishment, he wrote, should be to give each workman the highest grade of work of which he was capable, to call on each to turn out his maximum, and to pay each in accordance with his product. "This means," he argued, "*high wages* and *low labor cost*." It also meant time-motion studies, discipline, pressure, and incentives for speed-up. For

Taylor efficiency was a fetish, but he got results. Before he died in 1915 (with a watch in his hand, John Dos Passos surmised), he had caught the attention of management and had aroused the fears of labor leaders, who suspected that piecework and the speed-up would grind profits out of workers' fatigue. In spite of those fears, Taylorism spread. It was praised by Louis Brandeis and institutionalized by a Taylor Society.

Taylor was the philosopher of the machine process. Henry Ford was its commanding general. In 1911, Ford opened his plant at Highland Park, Michigan. There he and his fellow executives arrived at Taylor's principles along their own routes and began to turn out automobiles at prodigious rates. The Ford Motor Company outsped all industry in specializing the tasks of men and machines. After 1913 it also applied the idea of continuous motion, using conveyor belts, gravity slides, and overhead monorails to feed the machinery by which workers stood. The modern assembly line turned out the Model T's that put America on wheels. As his production and market grew, Ford cut prices and increased wages. To be sure, the wages he claimed to pay did not reach all his workers, the speed-up at the Ford company was notorious, and the company tolerated no unions. But the five-dollar day that Ford announced in 1914 seemed to mark the dawn of a new era, and so did Ford's staggering profits. In the mid-1920's Ford had become, in the phrase of Upton Sinclair, the Flivver King.

By that time Ford's production techniques had become standard in the automobile and other industries; Taylor's dream was coming true. The Model T was a very stark car, but America's machines were also producing more comfortable, more sumptuous, and more complex mechanisms. During Coolidge's tenure in office, for the first time in the history of any nation, a mass market developed for cars, for radios, for refrigerators and vacuum cleaners. There was, in a sense, no longer any problem of production. The available stocks of American raw materials, workers, machines, and techniques could saturate the nation, and much of the world, with the necessities and conveniences of modern civilization.

Businessmen, however, were interested in

more than just the science of production. Their restrictive labor policies during the 1920's kept the rise in real wages well below the rise in profits. And they guarded their market jealously, trying to produce only as much as the market could absorb without a break in prices. Large industries characterized by firms with heavy fixed costs had long since learned the importance of administered, noncompetitive pricing, and had long since contrived the consolidations that made for industrial stability. During the 1920's the tendency toward consolidation proceeded at an accelerating tempo, in old industries as well as new. And as consolidation advanced, managers became more and more skillful in governing costs, price, and output.

These developments disturbed Americans for whom the production and distribution of wealth were more precious objectives than amassing profits. The Nobel prize-winning novelist Sinclair Lewis, in *Dodsworth* (1929), told of an automobile manufacturer who was forced to sell out to a giant holding company, a fictional General Motors. Dodsworth, deprived of the satisfaction of producing cars himself, and unwilling to serve as a subordinate in a great corporation, sought vainly to find new satisfactions in the culture of Europe. But in the end he came back to the United States to embark on the manufacture of trailers. He was the kind of business engineer who adhered to a commitment to production that Lewis felt ordinary business managers were destroying.

Thorstein Veblen made the most devastating comparisons between those who made goods and those who made money. In *The Engineers and the Price System* (1921) and *Business Enterprise* (1923) he condemned businessmen for artificially curtailing output for the sake of profit—a practice he labeled "sabotage." He called for a revolution of technicians, of men committed to production, who would free industry of pecuniary restraints and use the machine process to provide plenty for all mankind. There was a legacy of Populism in Veblen's ideas, a naïveté in his attitude toward competition, and a strong dose of Marxism. But his simplifications had both merit and influence. Whereas business managers often planned only for profit, Veblen urged public

Sabotage?

It should not be difficult to show that the common welfare in any community which is organized on the price system cannot be maintained without a salutary use of sabotage—that is to say, such habitual recourse to delay and obstruction of industry and such restriction of output as will maintain prices at a reasonably profitable level and so guard against business depression.... In any community that is organised on the price system, with investment and business enterprise, habitual unemployment of the available industrial plant and workmen, in whole or in part, appears to be the indispensable condition without which tolerable conditions of life cannot be maintained. That is to say, in no such community can the industrial system be allowed to work at full capacity for any appreciable interval of time, on pain of business stagnation and consequent privation for all classes and conditions of men. The requirements of profitable business will not tolerate it. So the rate and volume of output must be adjusted to the needs of the market, not to the working capacity of the available resources, equipment and man-power, nor to the community's need of consumable goods.

From Thorstein Veblen, *The Engineers and the Price System*, 1921.

planning for the general welfare. His message helped to bridge the space between the progressive era and the next era of reform.

Republican Symbols: 1924 In the Coolidge era, however, the impulse for reform flagged. The spirit of that time saw no conflict between profits and productivity. It found a symbol in the person of Herbert Hoover, who seemed to have walked right out of American mythology. Son of an Iowa farmer, descended of pioneer stock, orphaned at ten, Hoover went west, worked his way through Stanford University, married a banker's daughter, and as an engineer in Asia earned his first million before he was forty. He was the hero of Belgian relief, the successful Food Administrator of Wilson's war Cabinet, and, in the opinion of one London newspaper, "the biggest man . . . on the Allied side" at Paris. By 1920 Hoover's name stood for personal success, for food for the hungry, and for rigor in administration. His reputation reached its height while he was serving under Harding and Coolidge as Secretary of Commerce.

To that office Hoover applied, as it were, the principles of scientific shop management. His department studied business trends, fought economic waste through its Office of Simplified Practice, and prompted American commerce and investment abroad. Concurrently it encouraged trade associations to sustain prices and profits by adjusting production to demand. Hoover personally organized the relief of victims of the Mississippi flood of 1927, avoided associating with politicians, and harbored an ambition as broad and inconspicuous as his conservative blue suits. He stood at once for laissez-faire doctrines, humanitarian endeavor, and quiet and humorless efficiency. Coolidge, increasingly jealous of Hoover's reputation, could barely tolerate "the wonder boy."

The President did not suffer any rival kindly. A shrewd political manipulator, he rapidly brought the machinery of the Republican party under his control. As the nominating convention of 1924 approached, he had only one serious, though unlikely, opponent—not Hoover, who was biding his time, but Henry Ford. The Flivver King had run as a Democrat, and lost, in the race for senator from Michigan in 1918. His publicity men, who wrote much of what he signed, had begun in 1922 to suggest that he might be available as a Republican candidate for the White House. The prospect was both preposterous and alarming. Away from his machines, Ford was a ludicrous, semiliterate figure, the captive of folk prejudices. He was opposed to tobacco, liquor, and ballroom dancing. He had published and circulated anti-Semitic propaganda. He detested labor unions and Wall Street, both of which he felt were the tools of an international Jewish conspiracy. But this nonsense had an unfortunate appeal to the uneducated, and a third of those who were polled by *Collier's* in a straw ballot of 1923 named Ford as their first choice for President.

Ford's candidacy may not have been serious, though many people thought it was. He was, however, deadly serious in his proposal to take over the government dam, nitrate plant, and other facilities constructed during the war at Muscle Shoals on the Tennessee River. He proposed to purchase the nitrate works for less than 5 per cent of what they had cost the gov-

ernment, to lease the water-power facilities for a hundred years for less than 10 per cent of what it would cost the government to complete them, and to have the government pay him simply by issuing new paper money. In return, he hinted that he would be able to produce fertilizer for American farms at half its current price. As Senator Norris said, this was the "most wonderful real estate speculation since Adam and Eve lost title to the Garden of Eden."

Norris exposed and defeated the scheme, which would have destroyed his cherished plans for the public development of the Tennessee. Yet before the chimera vanished, Coolidge, after talking with Ford, recommended that Congress sell Muscle Shoals to private interests. Ford himself soon put an end to his presidential boomlet by announcing that the nation was "perfectly safe with Coolidge." There may have been no bargain, but the coincidence of events suggested that both men were trading in character.

It was a striking commentary on the times that Ford's nitrate project was even proposed. It was no less striking that Ford's candidacy seemed to be the only barrier to Coolidge's renomination. Robert La Follette and Hiram Johnson, dedicated, doughty old progressives, could muster between them only forty-four votes at the Republican convention that gave Coolidge over a thousand votes on its first and decisive ballot. Only a dozen years earlier almost half the Republicans had cast their lot with Theodore Roosevelt.

One Nation Divisible

For White Protestants Only   The temper of the twenties was marked by narrowness and provincialism as well as by prosperity and complacency. The attitudes on which the Red scare had fed survived the passing of the scare itself. Among many Americans there lingered an intolerance of all -isms, a distrust of foreign nations, and a dislike, often bordering on hatred, of people of foreign origins. Much of the farm community had long been susceptible to those feelings, and organized labor had endorsed the racial as well as the economic arguments of those who advocated that immigration be restricted.

In 1924 Congress adopted the recommendations of the Dillingham commission (p. 537) and passed the National Origins Act. This based annual immigration quotas temporarily on the proportion of descendants of each nationality resident in the United States in 1890, and after 1927 limited immigration to 150,000 a year, selected on the proportion established by the census of 1920. Those quotas ended all but a trickle of immigration from southern and eastern Europe. The act, furthermore, included a provision that west coast racists had been urging for years. It forbade the immigration of Asians, thus terminating the Gentlemen's Agreement (see p. 537) and insulting the race-sensitive Japanese. "It has undone the work of the Washington Conference," Charles Evans Hughes wrote, "and implanted seeds of . . . antagonism."

Asians, Negroes, Catholics, and Jews were all victims of the prejudice based on the ethnic self-consciousness of white, Protestant Americans of older stock. Even many educated and comfortable people, who should have known better, attributed to race, religion, or national origin varying qualities of character and intelligence, always with the assumption that Americans of old stock were a superior breed. That kind of bigotry thrived among Southern whites, but it also appealed to the poorer and semi-educated who lived or had grown up in rural or small-town America. They tended, as they had for at least half a century, to blame their personal disappointments on the growth of cities and industry, and to express their anxieties in hostility toward those who peopled the cities.

These prejudices were the stock in trade of the Ku Klux Klan, an organization founded in Georgia in 1915 on the model of its Reconstruction predecessor. It recruited only "native born, white, gentile Americans," and it gave them a sense of importance by admitting them to membership in a group dedicated to persecuting an alleged enemy within the country. It also gave them a uniform—white-hooded sheets; a hierarchy, with such titles as Exalted Cyclops, Klaliff, and Klabee; and a ritual—"klodes" to sing, and a secret grip or "klasp."

In 1920 two professional fund-raisers realized that there was money to be made out of the Klan, which was then still small. They

Mencken on the Klan

The remoter and more forlorn yokels have risen against their betters—and ... their uprising is as hopeless as it is idiotic.... The truth is that the strength of the Klan, like the strength of the Anti-Saloon League ... has always been greatly overestimated. Even in the most barbarous reaches of the South ... it met with vigorous challenge from the start, and there are not three Confederate States to-day in which, on a fair plebiscite, it could hope to prevail. The fact that huge hordes of Southern politicians jumped into night-shirts when it began is not proof that it was actually mighty; it is only proof that politicians are cowards and idiots. Of late all of them have been seeking to rid themselves of the tell-tale tar and feathers; they try to ride the very genuine wave of aversion and disgust as they tried to ride the illusory wave of popularity. As the Klan falls everywhere, the Anti-Saloon League tends to fall with it.

From H. L. Mencken, *Prejudices: Sixth Series*, 1927.

organized a membership drive and arranged to share with local officers the profits from increased initiation fees and from the sale of uniforms and insignia. By 1925 membership approached five million. The Klan used floggings, kidnapings, cross-burnings, arson, even murder to terrorize whole communities. It was especially vicious in its treatment of Catholics. An Alabama jury acquitted a Klansman who had murdered a priest; a Klan mob burned a Roman Catholic church in Illinois; the Klan and its sympathizers attempted to crush parochial schools in Oregon; and in Oklahoma they inspired the impeachment of a governor who had declared martial law in a brave effort to rout the organization. Increasingly powerful in politics, the Klan held the balance of power in several states.

At its zenith in 1923 and 1924, the Klan by its very excesses attracted increasing opposition. In 1924 William Allen White, its implacable enemy, lost the Kansas governorship to one of the Klan's friends, but White's campaign set a sensible example. In some states the Klan began to fade, especially after "Dragon" David Stephenson of Indiana kidnaped and assaulted his secretary and connived to keep her from medical attention after she took poison. Convicted in 1925 of second-degree murder and sentenced to life imprisonment, Stephenson demanded a pardon from his fellow Klansman, Governor Ed Jackson. When Jackson refused, the vindictive "Dragon" opened a "little black box" whose contents provided evidence that sent one congressman, the mayor of Indianapolis, and various lesser officers to jail. Most important, the Klan, which had pretended to guard civic purity and feminine virtue, now stood exposed for what it was—corrupt, sordid, and licentious.

Prohibition The Prohibitionists, who were always strongest in rural areas and particularly among fundamentalist sects, considered liquor an instrument of the devil. Unaware of the complex personal and social problems that provoke excessive drinking, they insisted that alcoholism was created by alcohol itself and by the saloonkeepers who sold it.

Whiskey and beer seemed to them, moreover, the potions of immigrants and political bosses, the poison of the corrupt city.

The Prohibition Amendment of 1919 also drew strength from the delusion of many progressives that legislation could somehow control personal behavior of all kinds. Yet before long only the most rabid or stubborn "drys" failed to recognize the difficulties of enforcement. The Prohibition Commissioner, in his quest to prevent the manufacture, transportation, and sale of alcoholic beverages (defined by the Volstead Act of 1919 as one-half of 1 per cent by volume), had to depend on a small force of agents who were often third-rate political appointees with neither the background nor the intelligence to resist bribes or needless violence. They simply could not police the millions of Americans who wanted to drink

The Klan: Floggings, kidnapings, cross-burnings, arson, murder.

and who either made their brews at home or, more often, bought their beer or whiskey from the hundreds of "bootleggers" who earned an illegal, sometimes dangerous, but remunerative living supplying it.

Smugglers brought whiskey in across the Canadian border, or on fast boats from the Caribbean, or from vessels hovering off the miles and miles of the nation's coasts. To supplement the supplies of these "rum-runners," there were countless domestic distillers of illicit whiskey, much of it bad and some of it poisonous. It was easy to buy whiskey by the case, the bottle, or the drink. Indeed "speakeasies," illegal saloons, did business in every major city, and obliging policemen and cabdrivers were glad to tell strangers where they were.

The traffic in bootlegging provided a new and rich source of income and influence for organized crime. In 1920 the most notorious gangland chief, "Scarface" Al Capone, moved to Chicago, where within seven years he had established a sixty-million-dollar enterprise in whiskey, drugs, gambling, and prostitution. His private army of about a thousand gangsters, who were charged with protecting his domain, accounted for most of the one hundred and thirty murders in the Chicago area in 1926–27. Such was Capone's influence that not a single murderer was convicted. In New York, Philadelphia, Kansas City, and elsewhere, gangsters put high public officers on their payroll and transformed machine politics into agencies for crime.

Prohibition, manifestly unenforceable, had not created organized crime, but it had given gangland a vast privilege to exploit—a privilege that repeal of Prohibition would at least remove. Urban "wets," who had opposed Prohibition from the first, led the movement for repeal, supported by more and more former "drys." The most adamant foes of repeal were the moralists of the countryside who had failed to distinguish between liquor and crime, and who identified both with immigration and the city.

Last-Ditch Fundamentalism Rural hostility to urban culture also showed itself in matters of the mind. The unsophisticated have always fallen prey to antiscientism, partly because they do not understand the methods of science, partly because they resent many of the changes that science and technology bring about. Though most Americans admired the technological advances of the 1920's and recognized them as the products of earlier scientific strivings, some were distressed by the complexities and uncertainties of a machine civilization, by its speed, its capacity for destructive as well as constructive power, its overwhelming challenge to the ways of the "good old days." To these Americans science seemed threatening and mysterious. In the rural areas that modern culture had just begun to reach, men clung to the convictions that stood as a bulwark between them and the city, its life, and its ideas. There Protestant fundamentalism seized on science as an archenemy.

The fundamentalists insisted that the Bible must be accepted as literal truth. More than sixty years after the publication of Darwin's *Origin of Species*, more than a generation after educated men had reconciled Darwinism with Christianity, American fundamentalists still rejected the concept of biological evolution and attacked those who taught it. In the postwar years William Jennings Bryan, a "dry," a fundamentalist, a folk hero of a kind, and now an old and frustrated man, enlisted in the anti-evolutionist crusade. Strengthened by his leadership, the anti-evolutionists scored partial victories in several Southern states. Bryan himself in 1925 assisted the lobby that pressured the Tennessee legislature into passing a statute making it illegal to teach any theory that denied the account of creation recorded in Genesis.

The American Civil Liberties Union, responding to this challenge to the freedom of inquiry, offered counsel to any Tennessee teacher who would test the law. More in amusement than in anger, John T. Scopes of the mountain town of Dayton lectured from a Darwinian text, was arrested, and was bound over for trial. Among the lawyers who defended him were Clarence Darrow, the most famous pleader of the time, and Arthur Garfield Hays, a celebrated advocate of civil liberties. Assisting the prosecution was Bryan, who had been retained by the World's Christian Fundamental Association. The all-star cast in the Dayton "monkey trial" engaged the interest of the entire nation.

Darrow and Bryan at Dayton:
Creation took centuries.

The prosecution contended that the only issue was Scopes's violation of the law, but the defense raised the question of the validity of the law itself. The case reached its climax when Bryan took the stand as an expert on the Bible. Joshua had made the sun stand still, the Commoner said; the whale had swallowed Jonah; if it was in the Bible, it was so. As Darrow pressed the cross-examination, Bryan revealed an invincible ignorance of modern learning. Exhausted by the strain of testifying and by the laughter of the spectators, he died, heartbroken, soon after the trial.

Scopes was convicted for violating the law, but the state supreme court reversed the decision on a technicality, and the constitutionality of the statute could not be tested. There was no longer any reason to test it. Bryan had admitted in his testimony that creation took centuries; a "day" in Genesis might be an eon. That admission cost the fundamentalists their argument, and the ridicule of Bryan's performance had lost them their cause.

But by 1925 the blind innocence of fundamentalism, together with the pernicious zeal of the Klan, had estranged the ordinary citizen from the intellectual and had divided the underprivileged of the farms from the underprivileged of the cities. Protestant laborers had been set against Jewish and Catholic laborers. Americans whom prosperity either did not reach or did not beguile had been sealed off into separate and often hostile groups.

The Election of 1924   This estrangement made it difficult for the Democratic party to select a national candidate in 1924. One of the two leading contenders was William G. McAdoo, Wilson's son-in-law and Secretary of the Treasury. McAdoo had won the acclaim of liberals for his administration of the railroads during the war (p. 573), but he had lost their favor by taking a job as counsel to Edward L. Doheny, one of the scoundrels of Teapot Dome. Yet McAdoo, ardently "dry" and equivocal about the Klan, held the support of the South and the West. His major rival, Alfred E. Smith, the governor of New York, was a "wet," a Catholic, and a Tammany man. The darling of the Eastern cities, Smith was anathema to the rural delegates, in spite of his progressive record.

The convention met in New York's Madison Square Garden during a July heat wave. To the party's shame a motion not to include a plank in the platform condemning the Klan by name passed by $543\frac{3}{20}$ to $542\frac{3}{20}$. There followed a nine-day deadlock over the nomination. Through ninety-five ballots the hoarse voice of the aged Bryan vied with the raucous noise of the Tammany gallery, and the contest was relayed by radio to millions of American homes. The split in the party had become irremediable, the sweltering delegates had become exhausted. At last Smith and McAdoo withdrew by mutual agreement. On the 103rd ballot the convention nominated John W.

Davis for President and Charles Bryan as his running mate. They were an unlikely brace. Davis, who had served as solicitor general and briefly as ambassador to Great Britain during the Wilson Administration, was a cultivated gentleman and an eminent corporation lawyer identified with the House of Morgan. The progressives who disdained him could find small solace in Bryan's younger brother Charley, at best a cockboat in the wake of the Commoner's leaky man-of-war. Wall Street and Nebraska could not be squeezed onto a single ticket, but the prolonged bitterness of the convention had made a saner choice impossible.

A third nomination stirred wider interest. The resurgence of progressive candidates in the congressional election of 1922 had owed much to the Conference for Progressive Political Action, an organization of farm leaders, social workers, former Bull Moosers, and Socialists. Now the leaders of the Conference began to talk about running a separate ticket in 1924. The communists forced their hand by taking over the Farmer-Labor party and offering its nomination to Battle Bob La Follette. Then almost seventy, iron-gray, still the indomitable Daniel in the lion's den of "the interests," La Follette scorned the offer. The communists, he wrote, sought only to divide and confuse the progressive movement: "I protest their being admitted." La Follette's response prompted his supporters to form a new Progressive party, which named La Follette and the liberal Montana Democrat, Burton K. Wheeler, as its national candidates.

La Follette's candidacy attracted a host of tireless battlers for reform, among them Felix Frankfurter, John R. Commons, and Jane Addams. It was endorsed by the American Federation of Labor and, curiously, by the Socialists. La Follette stood for conservation, public ownership of water power, increased taxes on wealth, curbing the authority of the Supreme Court, limiting the use of injunctions in labor disputes, the popular election of judges, the direct election of Presidents, the end of child labor, and a national referendum on declarations of war. But he emphasized the evil of monopoly, ringing again the changes of his early campaigns in Wisconsin. The *Wall Street Journal* called his platform "Wisconsin

Bolshevism"; the head of the Communist party in the United States called it "the most reactionary document of the year." Both statements were nonsense. The platform and the campaign were simply refurbished Grangerism, rather seedy and out of place in 1924, yet still appealing to many farmers, and the only haven for progressives who could stomach neither Coolidge nor Davis.

The Republicans ignored Davis and harped on La Follette's radicalism. They need not have worked as hard as they did nor have spent the millions they poured into the campaign, for the nation voted overwhelmingly to "keep cool with Coolidge." The President carried thirty-five states to Davis' twelve and La Follette's one, Wisconsin. Coolidge won 382 electoral votes to his opponents' 149. And his popular vote, over 15,000,000, exceeded the combined total of Davis, who polled less than 8,500,000, and La Follette, who had slightly more than 4,800,000. Prosperity and "Silent Cal" had enjoyed a major triumph.

Yet the Progressives had made a point, though their party died in 1925 with La Follette. The point was simply that there was room in politics for dissent from the business creed. The lesson was not lost on the Democrats, who realized that they had to close ranks and reconstruct a coalition that welcomed men of all colors, all parentages, all sections. If the Democrats were to win in the future they would have to be "unequivocally the party of progress and liberal thought." That phrase was Franklin Roosevelt's, who saw small chance for a victory before 1932.

Grandiose Illusions

The Good Life   Americans were optimistic during Coolidge's second term. The middle class in particular, more comfortable than ever before, experienced a sense of well-being. They admitted no limit to a personal success symbolized by material possessions. They were, they thought, a virtuous people, except for an unavoidable minority of knaves and fools, and they neither liked nor trusted the "knockers." They preferred the "boosters," the men with their eyes and hearts set on the rosy future.

Some of the boosters channeled their optimism into the expanding advertising profession. National advertising flourished in the twenties. It offered an attractive substitute for more painful forms of competition, like price-cutting, which, in any event, were being curtailed by trade agreements and informal arrangements among manufacturers. Advertising also helped identify brands for consumers who were buying more and more of their goods in stores and producing fewer and fewer at home. Advertising men believed they were "inspiring citizens to live a more abundant life." They were creating new wants and encouraging discontent with possessions outmoded, but not necessarily outworn. Advertisers sold the ingredients of the good life—health in orange juice, cleanliness in soap, popularity in deodorants, romantic love in voguish clothes.

As one General Motors executive put it, advertising had to make people "healthily dissatisfied with what they have. . . . The old factors of wear and tear . . . are too slow." Built-in obsolescence paved the road to business success. Manufacturing prettier, more comfortable cars than Ford did, changing models annually (while also meeting competitive standards in engineering), General Motors won primacy in the automobile industry largely by catering to luxury and fashion.

Advertising also created and sold reputations, both corporate and personal. Public-relations experts, taking over the new game of ballyhoo as their own, fabricated heroes on demand. Some of the celebrated athletes of the 1920's, for example, owed part of their fame to sheer ballyhoo. To be sure, Bobby Jones in golf, Bill Tilden in tennis, Jack Dempsey in boxing, and Babe Ruth in baseball were athletes of genuinely heroic proportions. But their proportions were overdrawn, and cynical public-relations men learned to conceal the boorish behavior of Ruth, among others, by planting stories of fictitious noble deeds.

The prospering tabloid newspapers catered to a mass audience that delighted in sensationalism and hero worship. The art of sham was especially effective when it could concentrate on sex. It publicized the new heroes and heroines of the booming motion-picture industry—Rudolph Valentino, the Casanova of the silent films, whose untimely death broke thousands of adolescent hearts; Clara Bow, the "It" girl, whose curves and curls entranced a male multitude; Mary Pickford, the sweet charmer whom a plucky lad could more properly admire; and Charlie Chaplin, the incomparable clown.

Outside of Hollywood, standard success stories followed classic forms—farm boys conquered the city while remaining pure, poor boys struggled and saved their way to wealth, nice boys met and married beautiful rich girls. The protagonist's gleaming teeth, curly hair, lithe muscles, humility, and hard work assured a happy ending. And ordinary Americans could do just as well through diligent use of the right toothpaste, hair lotion, and correspondence course. But the plot was used too often to boost sales and circulation, and it was beginning to run thin. Just then a real hero revived the faith.

In the spring of 1927 there was startling news of a young man flying solo, east across the Atlantic, in a small monoplane. No one before had made that flight alone. The prayers of the nation followed Charles A. Lindbergh, Jr., to France. His safe landing set off a jubilee; Coolidge sent a cruiser to bring him home; New York extended ecstatic greetings. Briefly, sham and commercialism hid from authentic daring and clean-cut youth. Lindbergh took it calmly. After writing another stanza to his saga by marrying Anne Morrow, the daughter of a Morgan partner, he tried to escape the tabloids and the confetti. Myths need a foundation in truth, and the Lindbergh story had been as genuine as it was refreshing. When it faded from the headlines, myth fed once again on the exploits of hired muscle men who drew crowds to mammoth stadiums and testified about the proteins packaged in breakfast cereals.

Advertising and public relations and ballyhoo, like the newspapers and magazines and radio that carried them, exported urban ways to rural people. They disseminated a common set of symbols to diverse groups. They told farmers and laborers and suburbanites to admire the same success stories and buy the same cars and cosmetics. They told them all to spend their money to increase their comfort, to prove their mettle, to live "the good life." They encouraged installment buying to ensure the

Lindbergh at take-off: Authentic daring.

sale of an expanding national product. They helped Americans with rising wages to forget about the frustrations of their dull and routine jobs. The spurious self-esteem that sprang from possession and fashion would endure only so long as Americans could count on steady income and easy credit; but so long as prosperity lasted, advertisers gilded the promises of a commercial culture, the only brand of Americanism they really understood. This crass and transient boom was rooted in illusion, in calling things by the wrong names and then accepting the names as true. That illusion fostered waste in the name of progress. Meanwhile, the slogans of public life, based on other illusions, bred danger in the name of safety.

The Image of America Abroad   The Coolidge Administration was continually involved in Latin-American affairs. But often it

succeeded only in obscuring national purpose and generating ill will among Latin Americans. Secretary of State Hughes, moved by a concern for peace and order, had helped to bring about the peaceful settlement of several Latin-American boundary disputes. During his tenure, the United States also sponsored a conference of Central American powers which agreed to withhold recognition from any government established by a *coup d'état*. But this genuflection to stability ignored the realities of Central American politics, for where the government in power had complete control over elections, a *coup d'état* or revolution was the only means of ousting it.

When anarchy visited Nicaragua, Coolidge had no choice but to act unilaterally. First, in 1925, he withdrew a token force of marines from that nation, which then seemed capable of servicing its foreign debt and preserving its internal stability. But the appearance was deceptive. Almost at once revolution broke out, and Coolidge again landed the marines, in time some five thousand. Regrettably, in its quest for order, the United States chose to support the reactionary faction, whose identification with large landowners and foreign investors had helped provoke the revolution in the first place.

The marines contained the fighting but they could not bring it to an end. American bankers were lending money to the conservative faction for the purchase of munitions in the United States, and the rebels were receiving some arms from sympathetic Mexico. Increasingly uncomfortable, Coolidge in 1927 named Henry L. Stimson as his personal emissary to negotiate a peace. Stimson succeeded in arranging an effective truce and an honest election, in which the rebel general triumphed. The marines, however, remained until 1933.*

Though the United States clearly had no territorial ambitions, Latin Americans resented its habit of intervening in local affairs whenever it saw fit. At the Pan-American Conference of 1928 the Argentine delegation sponsored a proposal that "no American country have the right to intervene in any other American country." The United States succeeded in defeating the proposal, but in so doing it heightened the resentment. Late in 1928 the State Department concluded that intervention was not justified by the Monroe Doctrine or by the interests of American investors. But it was still not ready to announce this attitude or to surrender its claim to unilateral intervention in the interests of national self-defense. This offense to the sensitivies of Latin-American nationalists continued to cloud hemispheric friendship. Beyond the borders of the United States at least, words were not as convincing as deeds.

Latin-American liberals, moreover, identified the United States with the forces of reaction. Even more than the Nicaraguan episode, developments in Mexico contributed to that view. In 1925 Plutarco Elias Calles, the new president of Mexico, revived the spirit of the

* They also remained in Haiti but in 1924 left the Dominican Republic, where President Wilson had sent them.

revolution of 1910, which had for several years been in eclipse. He sponsored laws that permitted foreigners to acquire land only if they renounced the protection of their own government, and laws that defined all subsoil deposits as the inalienable property of the Mexican nation. Oil companies, American and other, were required to apply for a renewal of their concessions before 1927. Four large American companies refused. Their spokesmen in the United States, asserting that Mexico was on the road to Bolshevism, demanded military intervention. They were supported by some American Catholics incensed by Calles' anticlericalism. The clumsy diplomacy of Coolidge's ambassador to Mexico complicated the situation, but in January 1927 the United States Senate by unanimous vote passed a resolution demanding the peaceful settlement of all contested issues—by arbitration, if necessary.

Several months later Coolidge appointed a new ambassador, Dwight W. Morrow, with the overriding commission "to keep us out of war with Mexico." Morrow's patient negotiations led to a temporary relaxation of the Mexican land laws and to an uneasy accord between the Mexican government and the Catholic Church. These holding operations restored friendly relations. Yet Morrow's admirable performance could not erase the hostility earlier created by American diplomacy. To reformers south of the border American amity was colored by oil.

Europeans resented a different kind of diplomacy of the dollar. During the First World War the United States had lent the Allies $7 billion and after the war another $3.3 billion. The recipients had spent their loans almost entirely on American military products and relief supplies. With the return of peace, they regarded the loans merely as one part of the total Allied resistance to Germany, an American contribution toward a victory to which Europeans had given a larger share of flesh and blood. So they were reluctant to repay either the loans or the interest on them. And even those who wanted to square accounts found it difficult to pay. The European nations had depleted their own reserves before borrowing from the United States, and now they found it impossible to replenish those reserves in an American market sealed off by the tariff.

The only way they could meet their obligations to the United States was to draw on the huge reparations that had been imposed on Germany at Versailles. But Germany lacked both the means to pay and the will to scrimp in order to exonerate a war guilt she did not really accept. In 1923 she defaulted, and French and Belgian troops occupied the Ruhr Valley. The Germans there cut down coal production, while the German government inflated its currency recklessly, and the resulting economic distress in both France and Germany seemed to forebode economic collapse and possibly even armed conflict.

The crisis commanded American attention as well as European. Earlier, Charles Evans Hughes had suggested that an international commission of experts, including Americans, be appointed to examine the whole reparations problem. The deadlock in the Ruhr now persuaded the French to agree. The committees that then met recommended what was called the Dawes Plan, in recognition of the participation of Charles Gates Dawes, who was soon to become Coolidge's running mate. That plan, which went into effect in 1924, arranged for an international loan to stabilize German currency and for a flexible, graduated scale of reparations payments. Five years later another American, Owen D. Young, headed a second committee which substantially reduced the payments. The Allies, satisfied by these terms and concurrent European political agreements, withdrew their forces from the Ruhr and the Rhineland.

American money, however, played a more significant role in the European crisis than did either Dawes or Young. Between 1924 and 1931 Germany managed to meet her payments only because her government, her municipalities, and her businessmen were able to borrow $2.6 billion in the United States. In turn, only the reparations collected by the Allies enabled them to keep up their payments on their American war debts. The interdependence of debts and reparations payments was obvious, but the United States refused to acknowledge it. Most Americans, moreover, most of their congressmen, and certainly their President rejected the notion that the debts had in any sense been offset by the Allied losses in battle. For Coolidge, as for most of his constituents, the debts were business obligations pure and simple. When the French proposed that the burden of debt be eased, the President unhesitatingly turned them down. "They hired the money," he said. The spirit behind that phrase overshadowed all the efforts of Dawes and Young. So long as it prevailed, Europe regarded Uncle Sam as Uncle Shylock.

Deluded Diplomacy　The Administration resisted the facts of international politics as strongly as it resisted the facts of international economics. Like most Americans, Coolidge believed in disarmament, not only because he knew that it would reduce federal expense, but also because he presumed that it would assure peace. But he did not understand, or at least would not admit, the importance of power in international affairs and the indispensability of armed services adequate to national defense, whatever the cost.

The niggardly military budgets requested by the Administration and voted by Congress would in themselves have inhibited the development and testing of modern weapons. But the conventional men in control of the army and the navy husbanded their meager appropriations and resisted spending anything on airplanes and submarines, even though those weapons had clearly made traditional military tactics and strategy obsolete. The refusal of the services to develop aircraft infuriated General William ("Billy") Mitchell of the Army Air Service, whose bombers had sunk a battleship in 1921. In an oracular report two years later, he warned the authorities of the vulnerability of battleships. In 1925, after the navy's sheer incompetence had resulted in the destruction of a dirigible, Mitchell attacked his superiors in public and urged the creation of a separate air command. A court-martial suspended him from duty for five years. The flurry over the episode persuaded Coolidge to appoint a civilian board of inquiry under Dwight Morrow, but it shrugged off Mitchell's arguments. The Administration denied public funds to promote commercial aviation as well. By 1929 the productive capacity of the American aircraft industry had fallen to 7,500 planes a year, little more than a third of the capacity available at the war's end. In the absence of responsible public policy, the United States alone of the major powers slept smugly through the morning of the air age.

Coolidge was less complacent about international naval competition. The Five Power Treaty had applied only to battleships and aircraft carriers, and the signatories had continued to build auxiliaries. Late in 1924 Congress authorized the construction of eight cruisers. Hoping to avoid the expense of further construction and to end the naval rivalry, the President invited the powers to a conference in 1927. Italy, already infected by Mussolini's fantasies of military glory, refused to attend. So did France, who was unhappy with the small ratio she had already received at Washington and was reluctant, in the face of Italian resurgence, to commit herself to further self-restraint. Coolidge, dedicated to a policy of isolation from European affairs, had failed to assess these obstacles to disarmament. He failed also to negotiate a preliminary understanding essential to any agreement with the British. As a consequence, the English-speaking delegates at the 1927 conference wrangled to no purpose while the Japanese stood contentedly aside.

Coolidge had already retreated from an earlier, cautious gesture toward internationalism. The Permanent Court of International Justice called for by the League of Nations Covenant had been established in 1921. The purpose of this World Court was to adjudicate certain types of cases, to render advice whenever the League requested it, and to arbitrate cases brought before it. Americans had long hoped for the development of a body of law that could be applied to international affairs, and in 1923 Harding, influenced by Hughes, recommended conditional American adherence to the Court. Coolidge made the same recommendation in his first annual message. But, even though Hughes had drafted four reservations to the Court's protocol to protect the United States from contact with the League itself, the isolationists in the Senate balked. After a long delay the Senate adopted a fifth reservation that would limit the Court's right even to render advisory opinions to the League. This reservation specified that the Court could give no opinion, without American consent, on any question in which the

United States claimed an interest. In 1926 the Senate finally voted adherence to the Court if the reservations were accepted. When the members of the Court then tried to clarify the meaning of the reservations, Coolidge declared that clarification constituted rejection, and that there was no prospect of American adherence to the Court.* This denouement, followed by the failure of the naval armaments conference, left the Administration's diplomatic record singularly barren.

During his last months in office, however, Coolidge's diplomacy won wide acclaim. Salmon O. Levinson, a Chicago lawyer, had been recommending that the great powers sign an agreement condemning war. Professor James T. Shotwell, who had been advancing the same suggestion independently, also proposed sanctions to enforce such an agreement. The idea of outlawing war caught the attention of many Americans, including William E. Borah, chairman of the Senate Committee on Foreign Relations. Shotwell urged it upon Aristide Briand, the French foreign minister, who promptly used it for his own purposes. In April 1927, in a gesture of good will to compensate for Franco-American friction over disarmament and war debts, Briand wrote an address to the American people in which he proposed a pact outlawing war. Coolidge was irritated by Briand's resorting to irregular channels to announce his scheme, but the popular enthusiasm for the proposal forced the President's hand. The State Department asked Briand to submit his plan formally.

Secretary of State Frank B. Kellogg now outflanked Briand. Intent on avoiding a bilateral agreement which would imply some sort of alliance between the United States and France, Kellogg recommended instead "an effort to obtain the adherence of all the principal powers of the world to a declaration renouncing war as an instrument of national policy." While Briand stalled, the Secretary of State circulated the draft of a declaration he had drawn up on his own. He also let it be known that the United States would consent to sign the pact in Paris. Briand then accepted the American scheme, and in August 1928

* Both Hoover and Franklin Roosevelt later recommended adherence to the Court on terms like those contemplated by Hughes. But the Senate declined.

fifteen nations meeting in Paris endorsed a treaty by which they renounced war and promised to settle all disputes, whatever their nature, by "pacific means."

Americans were jubilant over the banishment of war—so jubilant that they tended to ignore qualifications made in diplomatic notes exchanged by the signatories. These set down reservations safeguarding France's interpretations of her own self-defense and Great Britain's obligations to her empire. In recommending ratification of the pact, the Senate Foreign Relations Committee reported that ratification would not, in its view, curtail the right of the United States to self-defense and to its own interpretations of the Monroe Doctrine, nor would ratification oblige the United States to take any action against a violator of the Kellogg-Briand pact. So interpreted, the pact won approval by a vote of eighty-five to one. But so interpreted, it was, in the words of Senator Carter Glass of Virginia, "worthless, but perfectly harmless." Though sixty-four nations ultimately signed it, it was merely an expression of an eternal hope.

For most Americans that expression was enough; the Paris pact, a triumph. To declare perpetual peace without assuming the responsibility for preserving it suited the nation's mood of isolation. Now the nation could cut its expenditures, disarm, collect its debts, and trust to reassuring words for sunny safety. Yet the hocus-pocus that sold peace in multilingual print was not unlike the hocus-pocus that sold beauty in a bottle.

Get Rich Quick   Of all the grandiose illusions of the 1920's none was more beguiling than the prospect of easy riches. It rested on the simple faith that the value of property would constantly increase, and that the man who bought today could sell tomorrow at a handsome profit. Those who had property to sell nourished this faith, and they were helped by the ready credit that enabled speculators to borrow what they needed. The hucksters and the boomers, moreover, made the allure of speculation a favorite fantasy of the time.

For a while in the mid-twenties the quest for a bonanza drew thousands of Americans to ventures in Florida real estate. The population of Miami more than doubled between 1920 and 1925, and other Florida cities and resorts along the Atlantic and Gulf coasts also mushroomed. Florida's boomers pointed to the warm winter climate, the ready accessibility of their region to vacationers from the north, the prospect of an American Riviera replete with pastel cottages, golf courses, power boats, cabanas by the sea, and grand hotels in golden cities where the business of recreation would thrive in a perpetual Mardi gras. Imagination covered swamps and barren sands with towns and building lots burgeoning with joy and dollars. As the greedy rushed to buy the dream, a few who invested early and sold at the peak of the boom made fortunes. Their success lured others. Most of the transactions took the form of binders—agreements to buy property which could be had for a fraction of the value of the property itself. These binders could be sold and sold again, each time for more money.

For every sale, of course, there had to be a buyer. The trade in binders was profitable only so long as someone came along to bid them up, and once people began to compare the dream with the reality the buyers were bound to disappear. The balloon began to deflate in the spring and summer of 1926. That fall it burst when a hurricane swept through the Miami area, wiping out towns, destroying developments that had emerged from the dream stage, and wrecking the railroad to Key West. The grand plans of the boomers were laid away; the millions of dollars in speculative profits were wiped out; and the Florida craze was over.

But a much larger boom was already under way. During the prosperous twenties most of the gains from increased productivity and from the growing market for manufactured goods were funneled into corporate profits. And as profits rose, enhanced by Mellon's tax favors to business, so did the value of corporate shares. Initially that rise reflected a genuine increase in the worth of corporate properties and in the earning potential of the corporations themselves. In the mid-twenties, however, the price of stocks began to soar at a dizzying pace. Investors who were looking for securities that would give them a reasonably safe return now had to compete with speculators who were after overnight fortunes. The flood of speculation lifted the price of stocks just as it had lifted the price of Florida real estate. To meet the demand and to keep it active, promoters organized investment trusts and multitiered holding companies whose only assets were hope and good will. They offered their new issues to eager buyers deluded by greed and by a naïve confidence in the surging market. In 1923 new capital issues totaled $3.2 billion; in 1927, $10 billion, much of it purely speculative. The volume of sales on the New York Stock Exchange leaped from 236 million shares in 1923 to 577 million in 1927 and to 1,125 million a year later.

Corporations themselves speculated. As the market rose, corporations found that they earned less by investing their reserves in new facilities than by putting them into brokers' loans—that is, loans that brokers made to their customers to enable them to gamble far beyond their cash resources. In "buying on margin," as this practice was called, customers relied on brokers' loans to cover most of the cost of their stock purchases. Brokers and customers alike expected that the growing value of the stocks would make it easy enough to repay the loans. Meeting the pressing demand for brokers' loans, or "call money," corporations emptied their surpluses into the money market, where they received staggering returns.

Instead of tempering the boom, public officials encouraged it. The Federal Reserve System had two means of tightening credit—that is, of making loans more expensive. It could contract the supply of money by selling government securities or by raising the rate of interest at which banks borrowed from the Federal Reserve. But the Federal Reserve chose to use its power to keep interest rates low. It did so for good reason—in order to discourage the import of gold from Europe and to facilitate American loans to Europe, then still in need of investment funds for economic rehabilitation and development. (If interest rates had gone way up, Europeans and Americans would both have tended to invest more of their money within the United States.) Even if the Federal Reserve had tightened credit, however, it could not have controlled the call-money market which the corporations were feeding, for speculators were willing to borrow at usurious rates to finance their march to riches.

In the absence of federal authority over either credit or the chicanery of promoters, the best weapon available to the government was simple candor. There was, however, none of that. Secretary of the Treasury Mellon knew exactly what was going on; indeed he was himself deep in speculation. Yet whenever sober businessmen questioned the state of the market, he or his colleagues in the Administration invariably responded with soothing reassurances. And Coolidge went along. Early in 1927 William Z. Ripley, a Harvard economist, visited the White House. Disturbed by the excesses of speculators and by the secrecy and deceit of corporations, Ripley lectured the President on the prevalent "double-shuffling, honey-fuggling, hornswoggling and skulduggery." Coolidge, feet on desk and cigar in teeth, asked gloomily: "Is there anything we can do down here?" Ripley answered that the regulation of securities was the responsibility of the states, not of the federal government. Relieved, the President relaxed and put the incident out of his mind.

By the end of the year brokers' loans had reached nearly $4 billion. In January 1928 Coolidge reassured the dubious few by announcing that this volume of loans was perfectly natural. Shortly thereafter Roy Young of the Federal Reserve Board, a close friend of Herbert Hoover, told a congressional committee that the loans were "safely and conservatively made." These sanctions hastened the tempo of the boom and gave a Midas touch to 1928, an election year.

To Coolidge the ascending figures on the ticker tape were evidence of the nation's prosperity and of his own sagacity. He was as much honey-fuggled as hornswoggling. Like the brokers and speculators, he was at once the prisoner and the propagator of the grandiose myths that bemused the nation.

Nonconformity and Dissent

The Jazz Age Some Americans, however, were repelled by materialism and its delusions. Disappointed by a progressive faith that seemed to have failed, they were alienated by the emptiness of business civilization. They were equally cynical about serving mankind and about striving for worldly success. Finding only futility in the past and the future, they chose to seek out the pleasures of the present, to live for their private selves and for immediate self-expression. If this search was ultimately unsatisfying, it was at least fleetingly fun.

These men and women, many of them young, were no more immoral or promiscuous than men and women had been before. But they dropped pretense. They revealed their impatience with traditional standards of conduct openly and often. One symbol of their protest was jazz, with its sensuality, its spontaneity, its atavistic rhythms, and with the sinuous and intimate dancing it inspired. Jazz was ungenteel, even un-Caucasian, above all uninhibited. It expressed not only protest and art of a kind but also a controversial change in sexual mores.

That change sprang largely from the ways in which city living altered family life. The nuclear family of the city and suburb (man, wife, children) existed in a private world quite different from that of the kinship family of the country, where grandparents, aunts, uncles, and cousins provided support and discipline, and where community was more common than aloneness. The very impersonality of the city obliged its inhabitants to meet and resolve the problems of their lives with neither help nor impediment. Not every marriage was equal to the challenge.

Having won the vote, women now demanded equal rights to jobs, to income, to their own apartments, to cigarettes, to whiskey, and to sexual satisfaction in matrimony or sometimes outside it. Unhappy men and women, at one time without escape from oppressive marriages, each year sought more and more divorces under laws that were growing increasingly lenient. Probably the incidence of premarital and extramarital sexual experience also rose. To some extent, especially for young people, adventures in sex released part of a rebellion against the reigning culture and its neopuritanical code.

During the twenties, moreover, even the unrebellious were learning to understand the significance of sex in human nature. The most important contributions to that understanding were made by Sigmund Freud, whose doctrines had first reached America in the years before the war. After the war Freudian psychology rapidly became a national fad, ordinarily in vastly simplified and distorted forms. Freud himself, while demonstrating that neurotic symptoms and behavior could usually be attributed to sexual tensions, did not advocate promiscuity. His first concern was with creating a system of analysis that would enable a doctor to help a patient find the emotional sources of his disorders, behavioral or somatic. On the basis of that discovery sick people could then reconstruct their lives.

His popularizers, however, often concentrated on the libido, the antisocial, the powerful and personal and sexual instinct in man, rather than on the social experiences that contained it or permitted it constructive release. The average American met Freudian ideas only in the tabloids, where they were made to endorse almost any escape from sexual starvation.

In their undistorted form, Freudian doctrines did not excuse adultery or condone lechery, but they did explain the importance of sex, which prudery was reluctant to admit. They also called attention to the need for latitude and compassion in judging behavior, sexual or otherwise. And, incidentally, they demonstrated the harrowing inadequacy of the values of a pecuniary culture.

A Literature of Alienation   "Society was something alien," Malcolm Cowley wrote about himself and his literary contemporaries of the 1920's. ". . . It was a sort of parlor car in which we rode, over smooth tracks, toward a destination we should never have chosen for ourselves." Gertrude Stein called the young writers of the time "a lost generation," and Cowley agreed. It was lost, he later concluded,

> because its training had prepared it for another world than existed after the war . . . because it accepted no older guides to conduct and because it had formed a false picture of society. . . . The generation belonged to a period of transition from values already fixed to values that had to be erected. . . . They were seceding from the old and yet could adhere to nothing new.

This generation of artists turned its back on progress, on economics, on Main Street and on Wall Street. "It was characteristic of the Jazz Age," said novelist F. Scott Fitzgerald, one of its high priests, "that it had no interest in

Fitzgerald: "They were seceding from the old, and yet could adhere to nothing new."

had succeeded in the career of the spirit. For him and for his admirers, not progress or business, but art, was the distillation of experience.

That same conviction motivated the young masters whose experiments with literary form gave a new beauty and vitality to American letters. Encouraged particularly by Ezra Pound and Gertrude Stein, and inspired by their prewar poetry, the novelists Ernest Hemingway and William Faulkner and the poet T. S. Eliot raised the national literary reputation to its all-time zenith. Hemingway's *The Sun Also Rises* (1926) and *A Farewell to Arms* (1929) expressed a deep revulsion against nineteenth-century standards of conduct and idealizations of war. In *The Sound and the Fury* (1929) Faulkner used Freudian insights and adventurous prose to expose the awful tensions between self and society, and the exacerbation of those tensions in the culture of the Deep South. Eliot's "The Love Song of J. Alfred Prufrock" (written in 1911, published six years later) made impotence the weary symbol of modern man. His *The Waste Land* (1922), probably the most emulated poem of the decade, provided a text in fragmentation and despair.

politics at all." George Jean Nathan, the drama critic, announced: "I decline to pollute my mind with such obscenities." And the editor of *The Smart Set*, H. L. Mencken, wrote: "If I am convinced of anything, it is that Doing Good is in bad taste."

These men and their fellows detested the business culture. Many of them fled, some to Paris, others to Greenwich Village, still others to an impenetrable privacy of creativity. And they attacked the civilization they hated. Sinclair Lewis peopled the Midwest with confused men and women, trapped by their own futile materialism and unthinking gentility, narrow, unhappy, stifled. Lewis' *Main Street* (1920) and *Babbitt* (1922) created satirical symbols of American life that persisted for a quarter of a century, not in the United States alone, but in Europe as well.

Sherwood Anderson exercised a larger influence on his literary compatriots. A compassionate critic of small-town America, Anderson abandoned a business career, after a nervous breakdown in 1912, to devote himself to writing. His *Winesburg, Ohio* (1919) was a moving, autobiographical novel of alienation. Perhaps more important, he exemplified the religion of art, for he had escaped Babylon and

All these works were vastly more significant for their form than for their content. They revealed alienation and spoke of protest, but their authors were first, and most self-consciously, artists. So, too, were the other Americans who shared in the extraordinary literary renaissance of the period. It had begun before 1920; it continued beyond 1929; but it came to crescendo during the Coolidge era. The experimental forms of literature and of the fine arts were themselves a break with tradition. They were based on the deliberate artistic manipulation of concepts of time, of man, of sound, of meaning. Art, if it was not a distillation of all experience as its devotees believed, was at least a distillation of aesthetic expression without equal in the American past. And the artist's alienation from society freed his creative mind, which enriched the perceptions and satisfactions of generations yet unborn.

But the religion of art could also be as futile as materialism itself. Dada, for example, a Paris vogue in which some American expatriates shared, was the ultimate in obscurity, the end of the line in the search for pure art, where "Order = disorder; ego = nonego; affirmation = negation." What did Dada mean? "DADA HAS NO MEANING."

Alienation ordinarily denied social responsibility. The artists who rejected their national culture also accepted most of its claims. They turned away from the Coolidge era not because of its inequities but because of its superficial accomplishments. In contrast to the progressive intellectuals who had preceded them, they sought private escapes and private satisfactions, and they surrendered society to its shortsighted masters. This escapism, even desertion, deprived the nation of the assistance of many of its most imaginative minds.

Worse still, some Americans cast off democracy along with materialism. They took at their word the Mellons and the Fords and the Coolidges who believed that the business cult was the democratic ideal. They concluded that democracy generated a vulgar, selfish, pecuniary civilization. The critic Van Wyck Brooks, in his *The Ordeal of Mark Twain* (1920), wrote about the Gilded Age, with the twenties much in mind, as "a horde-life, a herd-life, an epoch without sun and stars," which condemned the artist, and the soul, to frustration. Eliot also scorned democracy and remained rootless until he found salvation in the church, as Brooks did in sentimentality. H. L. Mencken was more acid. He ridiculed not only Prohibition, the Ku Klux Klan, and censorship, but also the whole American people, whom he considered a sodden, brutish, ignorant mob. Democracy, for him, was government by orgy. As for democracy as a theory, "all the known facts lie flatly against it." Irving Babbitt, who formulated an aristocratic doctrine of the "inner check," had no patience with the "sickly sentimentalizing of the lot of the underdog," no confidence in social reform, no hope except in pseudo-Platonic comforts, and thus no real hope. The price of complacent materialism was alienation; and the bill of despair that went with alienation was ominously high.

Progressive Still Yet disenchantment did not lead all critics to alienation. Some drew on their undaunted progressive spirit to point out anew the paths toward a good society. John Dewey (see p. 519) continued to examine the practical consequences of social policies in *Human Nature and Conduct* (1922) and *Individualism Old and New* (1929). These books urged experimentation in education for selfless citizenship, and public rather than private planning for social rather than pecuniary goals. Charles Beard (see p. 519) in his *Rise of American Civilization* (1927) stressed the historical significance of economic change. A year later he called for social engineering, national planning, to organize advancing science and technology for the general good. John R. Commons (see p. 520) worked out theories and techniques for social insurance, and among his fellow economists Irving Fisher showed that the government had to manage the nation's money supply if it was to achieve desirable social and economic ends. William T. Foster and Waddill Catchings put forth even more novel ideas. They attacked the belief that savings flowed automatically into investment, and that business cycles righted themselves. If the nation was to avoid depressions, they insisted, government would have to resort to public spending when private investment faltered.

In public life, too, the progressives persevered, though they suffered major setbacks. In 1926, when Mellon again advocated tax relief for the rich, his dwindling opponents could find no telling argument against cutting taxes. Federal revenues were then more than ample for the costs of government, and no one had yet developed a cogent program for spending to improve the nation's housing, roads, and natural resources. Without difficulty, the Administration put through Congress a revenue act that cut in half the estate tax and the maximum surtax on individual incomes. It also made minor reductions in the normal tax on small incomes. Two years later Congress eased the tax on corporations. Mellon had carried the field.

Private utility companies were almost as successful. Sales of electric power doubled during the twenties, and ingenious promoters with very little cash managed to monopolize the industry by setting up complex holding companies. By the end of the decade ten utility systems controlled approximately three-fourths of the nation's light and power business. The promoters kept the cost of electricity unreasonably high and through financial sleight of hand manipulated securities at the expense of bewildered stockholders. They also carried on a massive propaganda campaign and financed a powerful lobby to beat back demands for public supervision and for public distribution of electrical power.

The reformers were led by George Norris. He preached:

> The power trust is the greatest monopolistic corporation that has been organized for private greed. . . . It has bought and sold legislatures. . . . It reaches into every community and levies its tribute. . . . It has undertaken to bribe the minister in the pulpit. . . . It has even entered our public schools and tried to poison the minds of our children.

Among those who agreed with Norris, Governor Smith of New York and his successor, Franklin Roosevelt, advocated state ownership and operation of public power. Gifford Pinchot, governor of Pennsylvania, organized a survey in 1923 that paved the way to public rural electrification. Many municipalities built or acquired their own power plants and Nebraska, Norris' home state, established a public power system.

Farm politics particularly exercised Washington during Coolidge's second term. With real income falling, farmers began to step up their demands for a government marketing plan. Such a plan had first been suggested in the lean years right after the war. Now it became the basis for legislation sponsored by Senator Charles L. McNary of Oregon and Representative Gilbert N. Haugen of Iowa. At the heart of the proposal was a two-price scheme—a high domestic price and a low foreign price for staple crops. By purchasing farm surpluses, the government was to sustain a balance of supply and demand that would keep commodity prices at "parity" (see p. 653). This meant that the government would be underwriting the prosperity of the American farmer. The government would sell farm surpluses abroad for whatever price it could get, and any loss would be offset by an equalization tax levied on farmers or on those who processed and transported farm products.

Congress rejected the McNary-Haugen bill in 1924. But it passed a revised measure in 1927 and another one in 1928. Coolidge vetoed both versions. The bill, he said, would create a vast and clumsy bureaucracy, would improperly delegate taxing power from Congress to the administrators of the program, and would involve the government in trying to fix prices. Such prices, he argued, would be artificial and would encourage farmers to overproduce. Moreover, if the American government began to dump farm surpluses abroad, foreign governments would be bound to retaliate. The last two objections were undoubtedly sound, but Coolidge's concern for minimized government and a laissez-faire economy was unconvincing. After all, the government used the tariff, which was simply one kind of taxation, to aid industry. And the tariff, combined with the marketing practices of big business, led to artificial prices for manufactured goods. In fact, it was those very prices that kept farmers' costs high while their incomes were falling. Coolidge's vetoes, as the economist Rexford G. Tugwell put it, revealed "a stubborn determination to do nothing." Yet the farmers' spokesmen continued to insist that government had to do something to lift commodity prices if farmers were to earn a decent living. They had been repulsed for the time being, but their commitment to the idea of parity remained as strong as ever.

The debate over farm policy, like the debate over public power and taxation, highlighted the policy issue that dominated the late twenties: Was the federal government to be the handmaiden of business, the servant of the wealthy? Or was the government to treat all men equitably, and to build a society in which all could obtain a fair share of the nation's wealth? Intellectuals like Dewey and Commons, and politicians like Norris and Smith, insisted on the second alternative. They were insisting that Americans, both in their private lives and in their conduct of public affairs, accept a responsibility that the spirit of the times rejected.

The Election of 1928 Calvin Coolidge announced that he "did not choose to run" in 1928. He might have been persuaded to accept a draft, but the Republican convention nominated Herbert Hoover on its first ballot. Professional politicians had little liking for Hoover, who was never one of them, and Midwestern farmers had little enthusiasm for a man who had opposed the McNary-Haugen bill as vehemently as had Coolidge. But businessmen trusted Hoover; his reputation for efficiency

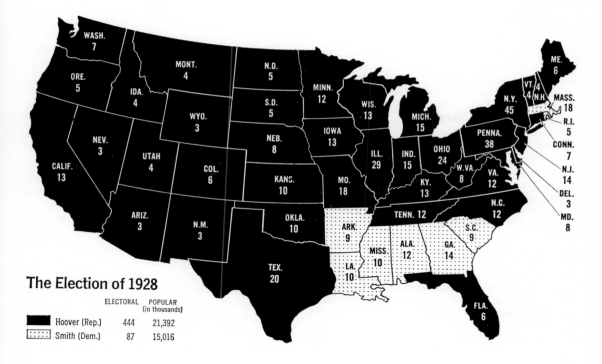

The Election of 1928

	ELECTORAL	POPULAR (in thousands)
■ Hoover (Rep.)	444	21,392
⬚ Smith (Dem.)	87	15,016

and humaneness was at its peak; and his personal success more than compensated for his lack of public glamour.

Hoover stood stolidly on a platform that attributed good times to Republican rule, praised the protective tariff, endorsed Prohibition, offered only platitudes to labor, and warned farmers of the evil of "putting the government into business." In his campaign speeches Hoover emphasized the virtues of individualism and "the American system" of free enterprise. There lay the source of prosperity. "We in America," Hoover said, "are nearer to the final triumph over poverty than ever before in the history of any land. . . . Given a chance to go forward with the policies of the last eight years, we shall soon with the help of God be in the sight of the day when poverty will be banished from this nation."

The Democrats nominated Al Smith. Those who had kept the nomination from him in 1924 could no longer deny his claims. As governor of New York he had made a record for efficiency as compelling as Hoover's. He had reordered the state's finances. He had reorganized its administration. He had promoted public health and public recreation, workmen's com-

pensation, and civil liberties. As a national candidate, Smith stood for public ownership of the principal power sites and generating plants, and he endorsed the McNary-Haugen Plan.

"Socialism," Hoover retorted. But Smith was no radical. Indeed, he blurred his own liberalism by deferring to the temper of the time. He accepted the need for protective tariffs. He chose as his campaign manager John J. Raskob, a Republican industrialist identified with Du Pont and General Motors who had unstinted enthusiasm for Coolidge. The Democratic campaign may have reassured the conservatives, but it converted almost none of them, and it disappointed the liberals.

Raskob's appointment, furthermore, reopened the party wounds of 1924, for, like Smith, Raskob was a Catholic and a "wet." Rural America dug out its old suspicions of the city, booze, Tammany, and the pope. Particularly in the South, fundamentalist preachers associated Smith with all the old fears and hates. Smith explained that his religion had not and would not affect his policies, and his record confirmed his words. But the suspicious

A Catholic for President

I am unable to understand how anything I was taught to believe as a Catholic could possibly be in conflict with what is good citizenship. The essence of my faith is built upon the Commandments of God. The law of the land is built upon the Commandments of God. There can be no conflict between them....

What is this conflict about which you talk? It may exist in some lands which do not guarantee religious freedom. But in the wildest dreams of your imagination you cannot conjure up a possible conflict between religious principle and political duty in the United States except on the unthinkable hypothesis that some law were to be passed which violated the common morality of all God-fearing men. And if you can conjure up such a conflict, how would a Protestant resolve it? Obviously by the dictates of his conscience. That is exactly what a Catholic would do. There is no ecclesiastical tribunal which would have the slightest claim upon the obedience of Catholic communicants in the resolution of such a conflict.

From Alfred E. Smith, Article in the *Atlantic Monthly*, May 1927.

took their cue instead from his East Side accent, his brown derby, his chewed cigar, his open advocacy of repeal, his unabashed cityness. Hoover, on his part, made no convincing effort to dispel the religious issue. And with the ethnic issue he had no real quarrel: Smith accepted men for what they were; Hoover was a dedicated "lily white."

More than bigotry, prosperity defeated Smith, for probably no Democrat could have outraced Santa Claus. Smith received only 87 electoral votes to Hoover's 444; some 41 per cent of the popular vote to Hoover's 58. Five Southern states and all the border states went Republican. The Grand Old Party had won another landslide.

The returns, however, were not that unambiguous. Smith polled twice as many votes as Davis had in 1924. He carried the dozen largest cities, which the Republicans had won handily four years before. The Democrats also cut into the traditionally Republican agricultural vote in the West. The farmers had doubts about Santa Claus, and in the cities the ethnic issue cut both ways, helping the Democrats in the urban North as much as it hurt them in the rural South. In 1928, as in 1924, the vote dramatized the need for Democratic unity and for a positive commitment to social reconstruction. But their prospects seemed poor, for the Coolidge era ended much as it had begun. Prejudice had divided the underprivileged, and prosperity had obscured public irresponsibility. Most Americans, as they had shown at the polls, were remarkably content. And confident, too. The stock market boomed as it awaited Hoover's inauguration and the nation's final triumph over poverty.

SUGGESTIONS FOR READING

General

The outstanding general accounts of the Coolidge years and their implications are in A. M. Schlesinger, Jr., *The Crisis of the Old Order* (1957), which focuses on the culture and the politics of the time, and W. E. Leuchtenburg, *The Perils of Prosperity, 1914–32* * (1958), which is shorter but more inclusive. F. L. Allen, *Only Yesterday* * (1931), while often rather casual, has charm and flair, and J. D. Hicks, *Republican Ascendancy* (1960), is sober and usually solid. The most entertaining and perceptive biography of Coolidge is W. A. White, *A Puritan in Babylon* (1938); the President emerges as a hero in C. M. Fuess, *Calvin Coolidge* (1940).

Business Enterprise

The economics of prosperity are described in George Soule, *Prosperity Decade: From War to Depression, 1917–1929* (1947); the institutions of business, in T. C. Cochran, *The American Business System: A Historical Perspective, 1900–1955* (1957); the business creed, in J. W. Prothro, *The Dollar Decade: Business Ideas in the 1920's* (1954). On the Ford Motor Company, its master, and the automobile industry in general, the pre-eminent works are Allan Nevins and F. E. Hill, *Ford: The Times, the Man and the Company* (1954), and *Ford: Expansion and*

* Available in a paperback edition.

Challenge (1957). There is also an acid and scintillating analysis in Keith Sward, *The Legend of Henry Ford* (1948). The best introduction to F. W. Taylor is his own *The Principles of Scientific Management* (1907). Siegfried Giedion, *Mechanization Takes Command: A Contribution to Anonymous History* (1948), offers brilliant observations about technology, which is handled on a more elementary level in Stuart Chase, *Men and Machines* (1929). By far the fullest and best account of labor during the 1920's is in Irving Bernstein, *The Lean Years* (1960). Two studies of the first rank on corporate concentration and on the stock market, respectively, are A. A. Berle, Jr., and S. F. Means, *The Modern Corporation and Private Property* (1932), and Thomas Wilson, *Fluctuations in Income and Employment* (1948). E. A. Goldenweiser, *American Monetary Policy* (1951), deals expertly with its subject.

Ideals and Ideologies

The works mentioned in the text, and other works of the authors noted there, provide a good point of departure for studying the artists and intellectuals of the 1920's. For that purpose, Malcolm Cowley, *Exile's Return* * (1934), is very rewarding, and so are Alfred Kazin, *On Native Grounds* * (1942), and Edmund Wilson, *The Shores of Light* * (1952) and *The American Earthquake* (1958). Among the outstanding literary biographies are Mark Schorer, *Sinclair Lewis* (1961); F. O. Matthiessen, *The Achievement of T. S. Eliot* * (1927); Arthur Mizener, *The Far Side of Paradise* * (1951), on Scott Fitzgerald; C. A. Fenton, *The Apprenticeship of Ernest Hemingway* (1954); and C. H. Baker, *Hemingway: the Writer as Artist* (1956). Carvel Collins' forthcoming study of William Faulkner will be of great value. American anti-intellectuals and bigots receive their just rewards in N. F. Furniss, *The Fundamentalist Controversy, 1918–1931* (1954); Ray Ginger, *Six Days or Forever?* (1958), on the Scopes trial; and J. M. Mecklin, *The Ku Klux Klan* (1924). Among the engaging works on the ideology and politics of Prohibition, and on the crime it helped to spawn, are Andrew Sinclair, *Prohibition: The Era of Excess* (1962); Herbert Asbury, *The Great Illusion* (1950); Charles Merz, *Dry Decade* (1931); Virginius Dabney, *Dry Messiah: The Life of Bishop Cannon* (1949); F. D. Pasley, *Al Capone* (1930); and Raymond Moley, *Tribunes of People* (1932).

Public Issues and Public Men

Two important accounts of major federal public policies in the period 1923–29 are in the pertinent parts of R. E. Paul, *Taxation in the United States* (1954), and Theodore Saloutos and J. D. Hicks, *Agricultural Discontent in the Middle West, 1900–1939* (1951). Agricultural matters also receive useful treatment in J. D. Black, *Agricultural Reform in the United States* (1930), and M. R. Benedict, *Farm Policies of the United States, 1790–1950* (1953). On the campaign of 1924, there is a brief review in R. B. Nye, *Midwestern Progressive Politics* (1951), and a longer analysis in K. C. MacKay, *The Progressive Movement of 1924* (1947). The fullest study of the election of 1928 is E. A. Moore, *A Catholic Runs for President* (1956). Oscar Handlin, *Al Smith and His America* (1958), is short and thoughtful; an earlier biography, still useful, is Henry Pringle, *Alfred E. Smith: A Critical Study* (1927). Among the autobiographies and biographies of other public men of the time, some of the more rewarding are B. C. and Fola La Follette, *Robert M. La Follette*, 2 vols. (1953); Frank Freidel, *Franklin Roosevelt: The Ordeal* (1954); G. W. Norris, *Fighting Liberal* (1945); Herbert Hoover, *Memoirs*, 2 vols. (1951); E. E. Morison, *Tradition and Turmoil: A Study of the Life and Times of Henry L. Stimson* (1960); and H. L. Stimson and McGeorge Bundy, *On Active Service in Peace and War* (1948). The last two shed significant light on the foreign policy of the Coolidge years, on which R. H. Ferrell, *Peace in Their Time* (1952), is also valuable.

* Available in a paperback edition.

27

The End of an Era

The United States met the new year of 1929 with a smile and a swagger. The national habit of confidence had grown during three decades in which both the reformers of the early century and the merchants of the new age of business believed they were fashioning a national Eden. A college graduate of the class of 1901, fifty years old in 1929, could believe with them that they had succeeded. As evidence of success, he might point to the statutes left over from progressivism, the great war won, the apparent unlikelihood of future war, and the largess of good times. Not since the mid-nineties, not for a generation, had the nation suffered a serious depression.

President Hoover

Business Plans   "I have no fears for the future of our country," the new President announced at his inauguration. "It is bright with hope." Hoover had what seemed to be just the right experience for national leadership—technical training, business success, and public service. He had, too, a grasp of the economics of industry, and a faith in the future of enterprise. There was no nonsense about Hoover, none of T. R.'s boyishness or Wilson's dreaminess, none of Harding's incontinence or Coolidge's folksiness. The new President was a serious man who kept in shape by playing medicine ball in the early morning. He would, most people thought, keep the nation in shape,

and lead it to ever higher plateaus of prosperity.

Hoover approached his office like a businessman with a business plan. He reorganized the inefficient presidential staff by creating a secretariat in which each member was assigned a specific place and duty. Government was to be neat. It was also to be respectable. Hoover appointed a Cabinet of solid citizens, men who stood for what the business community admired. With one exception, they were distinguished only for that stance. The exception was Secretary of State Henry L. Stimson, a conservative, to be sure, but also a man whose superior perceptions soon made him as uncomfortable as he was valuable. Andrew Mellon continued as Secretary of the Treasury. Among the others were Secretary of Agriculture Arthur M. Hyde, whom few farmers considered a friend, and Secretary of War James W. Good, a former utilities lawyer who preserved his private loyalties while serving, by virtue of his office, as head of the Federal Power Commission.

The utilities had other reasons for rejoicing. Hoover himself, according to the solicitor of the Federal Power Commission, interceded to prevent private companies from being regulated rigorously. The President also proposed that the federal government withdraw its control from all public lands and from all new reclamation and irrigation projects. The states, he said, were "more competent to manage

Herbert Hoover, 1928: "I have no fears for the future of our country."

. . . these affairs." This was a debatable assertion, but it suited Hoover's purpose. In conservation, as in most other matters, he was determined to keep federal government small in size and small in power.

Hoover's farm program reflected that determination. Like Coolidge, he rejected the McNary-Haugen scheme. But he recognized the need for some aid to agriculture and he summoned a special session of Congress to provide it. The President suggested that the best way to help the American farmer would be to raise the tariff and to give him federal assistance in marketing his produce—policies that would not, he said, undermine the farmer's initiative. In the Agricultural Marketing Act of 1929 Congress acted on Hoover's suggestions. It created a Federal Farm Board of nine members who were to be advised by committees representing the cooperative associations that marketed each of the major commodities. It also provided a revolving fund of $500 million from which the board could make loans to cooperatives to help them market their crops more effectively. Another provision, inserted by the farm bloc, permitted loans to be made to stabilization corporations "for the purpose of controlling any surplus." In other words, these corporations could influence prices so long as the Farm Board lent them enough money. But the Farm Board had no control over production. Consequently, not even generous loans for stabilization could long sustain prices if they should begin a major decline. From the first, farmers were dissatisfied with the legislation of 1929.

They gained nothing at all from Hoover's proposal to give them more tariff protection. The President lacked the political skill to guide a tariff bill through Congress. In 1929 Congress put the matter aside. In 1930 industrial lobbyists and their friends in the Republican majority carried protection to its all-time high. The Hawley-Smoot Tariff of that year raised average ad valorem rates from about 32 per cent to about 40 per cent. It increased rates on some seventy farm products and over nine hundred manufactured goods. More than a thousand economists urged Hoover to veto the bill. It would, they pointed out, raise the cost of living, encourage inefficient production, hamper American export trade, including trade in agricultural surpluses, and provoke foreign bitterness and retaliation. Though these arguments were entirely correct, Hoover signed the measure. Like the Agricultural Act of 1929, it reflected the continuing influence of business interests in Washington, and their continuing shortsightedness.

The Crash   Dramatic evidence of that shortsightedness had already appeared in the stock market, the barometer of prosperity. It soared during the early months of 1929, but the unbridled speculation of investors and promoters began to worry conservative financiers and the President too. He privately urged the New York Stock Exchange to curb the manipulation of securities, but with no success. Hoover would not ask Congress to interfere, for he "had no desire to stretch the powers of the Federal Government" that far. Instead he supported the Federal Reserve Board when it warned banks against making loans for speculative purpose, and he approved the Board's increase in the rediscount rate to 5 per cent in June and 6 per cent in August 1929. But the higher cost of funds for speculation did not check the speculative fever.

Gamblers in stocks paid no heed to other warnings. The first signs of danger began to appear during the summer of 1929. Residential construction fell off more than a billion dollars; business inventories trebled; the rate of advance in consumer spending dropped some 400 per cent. From June onward, industrial production, employment, and commodity prices declined steadily. Indeed the August increase in the rediscount rate came at a time when legitimate enterprise could ill afford it.

Yet the stock market boomed on. Ignoring the evidence of industrial decline, undeterred by the advancing cost of brokers' loans, speculators bid shares to new peaks. The morning after Labor Day the New York *Times* average of selected industrial stocks stood at 452, up more than 200 points since early 1928. American Tel. and Tel. had reached 304; General Electric, 396; Radio Corporation of America, 505. The market seemed strong, but it was sustained only by deluded confidence. In one week brokers' loans had risen $137 million and New York banks had borrowed $64 million to carry the weight of speculation.

During September and most of October the market wavered, moving gently downward. Some days were worrisome, but none of the captains of finance in New York or their lieutenants in Washington voiced alarm. Then on October 23 security prices crumbled in a wave of frenzied selling. Panic was temporarily averted when a group of New York bankers met next morning at J. P. Morgan and Company and agreed to pool their resources to hold the market up. The senior Morgan part-

ner assured reporters that the heavy selling had been "due to a technical condition," not to any basic cause. The following day President Hoover gave the nation further reassurance. "The fundamental business of the country," he said, ". . . is on a sound and prosperous basis."

They were wrong. During the next fortnight the market shuddered to collapse. As values fell, all the bets made on a rising market paid off in panic. An uncontrollable decline swept past the support the bankers had organized. By mid-November the New York *Times* average had fallen to a shattering 224. In less than a month the securities listed on the New York Stock Exchange lost $26 billion—more than 40 per cent—of their face value. Nor was the descent over. In July 1932 the *Times* average hit bottom at a mere 58.

Contrary to Hoover's assertion, the fundamental business of the country was on an unsound basis. Excessive industrial profits, along with skimpy industrial wages, were distributing one-third of all personal income to 5 per cent of the population. The shortage of purchasing power among consumers had a particularly bad effect on the vital construction and automobile industries. The surfeit of disposable income among the rich, together with the swollen profits of corporations, had encouraged speculation. When trouble came, the jerry-built corporate structures of many businesses, especially the utilities, toppled. Nor could the American banking system meet the strain, for bankers, though they had been aware of the loose practices of their profession, had long refused to discipline themselves.

Business had failed to keep its house in order. Even worse, it had persuaded the government to follow unwise policies. The government's tax policies had served to make the rich richer and the poor poorer. The government's enmity toward labor unions had made it impossible for labor and management to develop the habit of collective bargaining, which might have done a good deal toward correcting the maldistribution of income. High protective tariffs and the absence of any positive agricultural program had cut into the farmers' foreign market and had impaired their purchasing power. The federal government had made no effort to regulate the practices that created overcapitalized and monopolistic holding companies and that kept the prices of industrial products artificially high. For almost a decade the government had followed a monetary policy that had fanned speculation instead of tempering it, and then, even at the brink of disaster, Hoover had opposed regulation of the stock exchanges.

The market in the fall of 1929 suddenly revealed the unsoundness that had been developing for years, and the crash itself brought the sagging economy down. It wiped out savings and confidence alike. The mood of despair that settled over the nation stifled any renewal of private investment which might have encouraged recovery. It also dispelled the confidence of Americans in the business elite. The dominance of businessmen and industrialists, in government and out, had brought, not a new Eden, but a panic that marked the onset of the most baleful depression in all history.

The Onset of Depression

The Hoover Policies: First Phase Few of the leaders of American business and politics, either Republican or Democrat, had expected the crash. And when it came, very few of them understood what had caused it or foresaw the severity of the depression it was to bring. Most of them agreed with the head of Bethlehem Steel, who announced in December 1929 that "never before has American business been as firmly entrenched for prosperity as it is today." Most of them agreed also with Andrew Mellon, who recommended letting the economy run down to the depths, from which it would presumably recover automatically, as it had in the 1870's and 1890's. This policy would entail great suffering, but those who believed that the economy operated according to mechanical laws believed too in the inexorability of business cycles, and in the wisdom of leaving them alone, suffering or no. "Liquidate labor," Mellon advised, "liquidate stock, liquidate the farmers."

Hoover knew better. Though he remained convinced that the economy was basically sound and that government should not interfere with business, he took steps to prevent the spread of depression. In a series of conferences he tried to persuade business leaders to keep wages and prices up voluntarily. He called on the Federal Reserve to make it easy for business to borrow. He encouraged the Farm Board to provide funds to help the stabilization corporations in their efforts to sustain commodity prices. Above all, he hoped, by offering private advice and by making public pronouncements, to restore the nation's confidence in business.

Hoover welcomed the tariff act of 1930 (see p. 631), for he was convinced that business would be encouraged by a continuation of protection. To hearten businessmen further, he recommended and Congress in 1930 provided cuts in personal and corporate income taxes. The reductions gave the wealthy more disposable income to use for investment, though few chose to use it that way, but they gave lower-income groups little additional money to spend on consumption. Yet the reductions, inadequate and unbalanced as they were, wisely risked a deficit in government revenues in the hope of stimulating the private sector of the economy. Congress, moreover, followed Hoover's advice by making modest appropriations for public works. These gave some boost to the sick construction industry and to the heavy industries that supplied it, and indirectly to the men who were employed in those industries.

But these efforts were too meager to check the contraction in private spending, investment, and employment that followed the crash. Hoover would not countenance any more spending because he was determined to keep the federal budget balanced, or as close to balanced as possible. This, he believed, was sound finance, and it was also an unshakable article of business faith. Large federal deficits would have frightened the business community, which the President wanted to soothe. To that purpose, during 1930 the President continually applied the balm of official optimism. True, official gloom would have caused further alarm; but Hoover acted as if his conferences with business leaders had succeeded, whereas wages and prices actually continued to decline.

The Blight of Depression "We have now passed the worst," Hoover announced wishfully in May 1930, "and . . . shall rapidly recover." The statistics told a different

New York bread line:
The despair of sullen men.

story. In 1929 new capital issues in the United States, a rough yardstick of investment, had totaled $10 billion; in 1930 they dropped to $7 billion. As the depression deepened, the figure reached $3 billion in 1931 and $1 billion in 1932. Investment was discouraged by the decline in corporate profits, which fell off steadily from $8.4 billion in 1929 to $3.4 billion in 1932. At the same time, the rate of business failures rose—over 100,000 businesses went under in the period 1929–32. And banks were failing too. In 1929, 659 banks with total deposits of about $200 million closed their doors; in 1930, 1,352 banks with deposits of $853 million; in 1931, 2,294 banks with deposits of almost $1,700 million, at the rate of

almost 200 a month. Each collapse buried the cash and savings of depositors, most of whom had no other resources.

By the last quarter of 1930 industrial production had fallen 26 per cent below the 1929 level. By mid-1932 it was off 51 per cent from that level. Unemployment mounted: four million in October 1930; nearly seven million a year later; almost eleven million by the fall of 1932. Even those who kept their jobs were earning less and less. Between 1929 and 1933 the total annual income of labor dropped from $53 to $31.5 billion. Average manufacturing wages came down 60 per cent, average salaries 40 per cent. Farmers fared even worse: their income declined from $11.9 to $5.3 billion.

In 1929 national income touched $81 billion; by 1932 it had shrunk to $49 billion.

Liquidation carried a frightful burden of human suffering. Thousands of middle-class families, their incomes dwindling, sometimes entirely gone, lost next their savings, then their insurance, then, unable to pay their mortgages, their very homes. The optimism of the twenties gave way to gloom and fear. The times were even harder on laboring men and their families. The lost job, the fruitless search for work, the shoes worn through and the clothes worn thin, the furniture and trinkets pawned, the menu stripped of meat and then of adequate nutrition, no rent, no joy, no hope; and finally the despair of bread lines—these visited every city, leaving in their path sullen men, weeping women, and hungry children. So, too, on the farm—vanished incomes, foreclosures, tenancy, migrancy, and with them, as in the cities, the death of self-respect.

Hoover had predicted the abolition of poverty in America. Instead, within two years there mushroomed around America's cities settlements of shacks built of empty packing boxes, where homeless men squatted, reduced to desultory begging. A new Eden? "Brother, can you spare a dime?"

The Hoover Policies: Second Phase   In the congressional elections of 1930 the Democrats conducted a confident and rousing campaign. The intensification of depression hurt the Republicans, as depression had always hurt the party in power. Democratic publicists exploited the situation by launching a fierce attack on Hoover. Though he had been by no means unenlightened, he was, by virtue of his office, the most exposed target for abuse. The Democrats made his name a synonym for hardship. A "Hoover blanket" was yesterday's newspaper; a "Hoover flag" was an empty pocket turned inside out. Rough tactics and national discontent produced a slim Democratic victory, the first since 1916. The Republican majority in the Senate was reduced to a single vote, leaving that body dominated by a coalition of Democrats and Western agrarians. The Democrats won a bare majority in the House.

The new Congress was not to meet for a year, but in December 1930 the Democratic minority of the old Congress (which had been elected in 1928) used the rump session to develop a program for unemployment relief. Hoover, irritated by the Democratic campaign and appalled by its success, met the challenge with a reassertion of his own policies.

The President felt that relief was strictly a local problem. The cities, he insisted, with help from private charity, should and could take care of the needy. This was a fallacious assumption, for nowhere in the nation was there an adequate system of relief. Local public funds in 1929 paid three-fourths of the cost of relief (by 1932, four-fifths), but the localities had neither the means to raise revenue nor the capacity to borrow to defray their mounting obligations. Their relief agencies and programs, moreover, had concentrated on helping unemployables, people unable to work. Local administrators had neither the experience nor the facilities to cope with mass unemployment, and private charity was clearly incapable of meeting the nation's massive need for immediate relief.

As the winter of 1930–31 came on, cold and hunger moved into the homes of the unemployed. Relief payments in New York were only $2.39 a week for a family, and even less in most other cities. Two Texas cities barred relief for Negroes. Detroit, unable to tax or borrow, dropped a third of the needy families from its relief rolls; St. Louis cut off half, and children there combed the dumps for rotting food.

In October 1930 the President appointed an Emergency Committee for Employment under Colonel Arthur Woods. Though Hoover told the committee that relief was a local responsibility, Woods recommended a federal public works program. The President rejected it, and in April 1931 Woods resigned.

Meanwhile Senator Robert Wagner, a New York Democrat, had introduced bills providing for federal public works and a federal employment service. Along with Wagner, Senator Robert M. La Follette, Jr., "Battle Bob's" son and successor, and Republican Senator Bronson Cutting of New Mexico urged federal spending for public works and relief. All this Hoover opposed on the ground that federal action was unnecessary.

The President was prepared to act quickly when drought destroyed cattle and crops in the

Southwest during the summer of 1930. Unhesitatingly he advised appropriations to enable farmers to borrow money for seed and feed and fertilizer. But he opposed a scheme for distributing surplus wheat to the unemployed. He was willing, the Democrats suggested, to feed starving cattle but not starving women and children.

Understandably hurt by that criticism, Hoover defended himself in February 1931 by expressing his dedication to individualism, local responsibility, and mutual self-help. But in the face of depression, the virtues of economic individualism and private charity were drowned out by the demands of the helpless. Hoover's dedication to keeping the federal government small in size and small in power was breaking the lives of four million unemployed and their families. The President was a compassionate man whose honest convictions had glued him to inaction.

Hoover's interpretation of the economic ups and downs of 1931 strengthened his convictions. Between February and June of that year the economic indexes rallied slightly, partly because of a normal seasonal upturn. The gains, while tiny, persuaded the President, and others bent on optimism, that recovery was under way. Then in the spring and summer of 1931 financial panic swept over Europe. The American crash had precipitated the collapse abroad by drying up the loan funds on which the European economy and the interrelated reparations and war-debt payments had come to depend. And the European collapse in turn drove foreigners to dump American securities in their scramble for dollars, thereby driving American stock prices down even further. Moreover, shortages in exchange forced one European nation after another to devalue its currency. This action disrupted international trade, and the prices of American agricultural commodities plummeted. Before the end of the summer, the indexes had resumed their decline. Again the depression deepened.

The fault, Hoover concluded, lay in Europe. All the calamities since 1929, he came to believe, had originated in the Old World. The war had taxed the world economy beyond repair; the United States had regrettably become involved not only in war but in a morass of bad loans as well. European bankers had collaborated with their New York associates to create the easy-money conditions on which speculation had fed (see p. 622), and from that collusion was born the panic of 1929. Then, just as recovery beckoned, European disaster in 1931 had reversed the gains so arduously won. This view of the causes of the depression reasserted the persistent myth of American innocence—even wounded innocence, for as Hoover saw the situation American business shared little of the blame; he himself shared none. Hoover's theory, moreover, excused him from embracing the domestic policies he had rejected, for if the basic cause of depression lay outside the United States the most appropriate action would clearly be to ease the strains abroad and to protect the American economy from them.

Diplomacy in Depression

A Set of Good Intentions   The foreign policies on which the Hoover Administration embarked in 1929 were marked by good will and moral purpose. The President and his able Secretary of State, Stimson, believed, as had their immediate predecessors, that the world had fought its last major war a decade earlier. Europe, they expected, could take care of itself, as could Asia and Latin America, with occasional advice from the United States. The aroused morality embodied in the Kellogg-Briand pact would prevent aggression and discourage militarism. Indeed Hoover expected the powers to put an end to their arms race in the very near future.

Initially Hoover and Stimson made some progress toward their benign goals. While still President-elect, Hoover had carried friendship to Latin America during a ten-week tour that publicized the "good neighbor" policy.* In Argentina he promised to abstain from intervention in the internal affairs of the nations south of the border. He kept his word. In 1930 Stimson announced that the United States henceforth would grant diplomatic recognition to *de facto* governments. Moreover, Hoover set about withdrawing the marines from Nicaragua, a task that was completed in 1933, and he arranged to remove them from Haiti.

* A phrase later used by and ordinarily associated with Franklin Roosevelt.

In 1930 the President formally repudiated the Roosevelt corollary to the Monroe Doctrine (see p. 533). A memorandum written by former Assistant Secretary of State J. Reuben Clark, which Hoover ordered published, denied that the Doctrine justified intervention in Latin America. "The Monroe Doctrine," Stimson later added, "was a declaration of the United States versus Europe—not . . . versus Latin America." Nor did Hoover regard the Doctrine as a mandate for collecting the private debts of Americans. Some fifty revolutions or attempts at revolution shook the "good neighbors" of the hemisphere during his administration. But he kept hands off, even though these disturbances often resulted in the repudiation of debts owed to American citizens and in the nationalization of their properties. Although the State Department fell into argumentative negotiations that ran on for many years, the United States did not resort to force. By abandoning dollar diplomacy and protective imperialism, Hoover initiated a new era of hemispheric friendship and solidarity.

This success contrasted with the Administration's diplomatic disappointments in Europe and its agonies in Asia. Intent on naval disarmament, Hoover welcomed the cooperation of Ramsay MacDonald, the head of the new Labor Cabinet in England. Their preliminary negotiations prepared the way for the multipower conference that met in London in 1930. There the Americans, the British, and the Japanese extended the "holiday" on the construction of capital ships, and American and British representatives evolved a formula for limiting the construction of cruisers, destroyers, and submarines. Naval experts of the English-speaking nations, however, deplored a compromise that increased Japan's ratio for cruisers and destroyers and gave her equality in submarines. In effect, this arrangement recognized her primacy in the western Pacific. She would have accepted nothing less, and neither the Hoover nor the MacDonald government wanted to engage in an expensive naval race. Neither, moreover, considered Japan unfriendly. They confirmed, therefore, only what they had already conceded.

Even so, they failed to close the door on a naval race. The French, frightened by the militarism of fascist Italy, refused to limit their naval program unless the United States promised to help France in the event of aggression. Such a pledge was unthinkable to Hoover, the Senate, or the American people. When France and Italy would not subscribe to significant parts of the London treaty, England insisted on adding a clause permitting her, the United States, or Japan to expand their fleets if their national security was threatened by the building program of some other power. This "escalator" clause meant that naval limitation was conditional upon the self-restraint of a resurgent Italy and an alarmed France. If they began to build, England could follow suit, which would open the way for Japan. Yet the Hoover Administration and the American people accepted disarmament as a fact and let the navy languish. Again the nation saved money at the expense of security.

Monetary Diplomacy   When the panic struck European banks and security markets in 1931 (see p. 636), the focus of Hoover's diplomacy shifted to money. American investors, hard hit by the depression, cut off the loans to Germany that had so far enabled her to pay reparations for her part in the First World War. Without this source of income, the former Allies were unable to keep up payments on their debts to the United States. Even before the distressed German president appealed for help in the spring of 1930, Hoover had begun to think about a one-year moratorium on all intergovernmental debts and reparations payments. The idea was admirable, but Hoover said nothing about it until he had made sure of congressional support, and he failed to consult the French. When he announced his proposal late in June, England and Germany endorsed it, but France held back, still hopeful of collecting reparations. The French also suspected that the American proposal was partly designed to enable Germany to pay back private debts she owed in the United States. During the two weeks before France endorsed the moratorium, the accelerated flight of funds from Germany forced widespread bank failures.

To his shock, the President discovered that Europe's distress directly embarrassed American banks. They had lent some $1.7 billion, on a short-term basis, without collateral, to Central European banks, especially in Germany. Bank runs in Europe meant that these loans could not be collected, and the solvency of the American banks that had made them was threatened. The loans were part of a complex network of obligations among banks in many countries. In order to stop demands for payments back and forth among them, Secretary Stimson and other American representatives in July 1930 negotiated an emergency "standstill" agreement. It was later extended to September 1931, and again to March 1933. The standstill agreements froze private debts just as the moratorium had frozen public debts. This gave financiers time to try to protect the banks of the western world from bankruptcy, and time to delay putting pressure on borrowers for loans due.

But the freezing came too late to stop panic. Depositors, their confidence in banks shaken, demanded their money, which they intended to hoard. A run on the Bank of England, for decades the world's foremost symbol of financial stability, drained its gold and forced Great Britain off the gold standard in September 1931. That nation made gold the property of the government, refused to convert paper currency into gold except under conditions the government set, and devalued the pound— that is, increased the cost of gold in terms of British currency. England also established a special government fund to manage the value of the pound in terms of other currencies. By the end of 1931 every major power except Italy, France, and the United States was also forced off the gold standard, and each depreciated its currency and attempted to control its value in international exchange. These efforts at control were often designed to produce selfish advantages in trade, as were the prohibitive tariffs which invariably accompanied devaluation. Exchange controls and high tariffs actually impeded world trade and, worse still, gave rise to international suspicion and distrust.

Hoover had shown commendable initiative in arranging the moratorium and the standstills, but he never saw to the bottom of the problem. He failed to recognize that America's high protective tariffs were among the first and worst impediments to world commerce. And he would not support the cancellation of war debts. At the Lausanne Conference of 1932,

England and France finally admitted Germany's bankruptcy and agreed to scale reparations down to an insignificant sum provided that the United States would scale war debts down equivalently. Most American bankers favored that plan, as did Stimson, who urged cancellation of "these damn debts." But Congress, reflecting public opinion, would not even consider a new debt commission, and Hoover, equivocal himself, demanded that the European nations resume payments on their debts after the moratorium expired. The debtor nations—except for Finland, whose obligation was tiny—had no choice but to default.

The defaults, like the demand that forced them and the long stalemate over debts and reparations that preceded them, engendered ill feeling on both sides of the Atlantic. The resulting distrust weakened the will of the democracies to resist the black forces gathering in Germany and Japan.

Fire Bells in the Orient   Japan broke the peace of the world. Since her victory over Russia in 1905, she had dominated the economy of southern Manchuria, the northeastern section of China. Tokyo was willing to acknowledge China's political claim to the area so long as it did not collide with Japanese military interests and economic privileges. During the late twenties such a collision grew increasingly likely. In China Chiang Kai-shek took over the central government and broke with the communists who had been his allies. Chinese nationalists hoped soon to have the whole country under their control. But the Russians still managed the Chinese Eastern Railway, and were developing its Pacific terminus, the Siberian city of Vladivostok. Alarmed by the construction there, Japan resolved to reinforce southern Manchuria. Here she confronted Chiang Kai-shek, who was determined to yield nothing further to any foreign power.

In the fall of 1931 the Japanese army in effect took over the Tokyo government. In September Japanese troops occupied Mukden and other Manchurian cities, and moved rapidly to establish political control over the province. This violation of the Nine Power Treaty and the Kellogg-Briand pact was perfectly timed. China turned to the League of

Japanese troops in Shanghai:
Fire bells in the Orient.

Nations for help, but the West was paralyzed by depression.

Even in good times Japan would probably have had little to fear. The British were opposed to any strong action in Manchuria. American public opinion, though it condemned Japan's behavior, was vehemently against any measures that might precipitate war. Hoover, anxious to avoid war at any cost, rejected Stimson's suggestion that the United States might have to cooperate with the League in imposing economic sanctions on Japan.

With almost no room to maneuver, Stimson proceeded cautiously. He hoped at first to strengthen the civilian moderates in the Japa-

nese cabinet and to persuade them to end the occupation of Manchuria. But in January 1932 the Japanese army drove on. Now Stimson resorted to moral condemnation, the only weapon Hoover would countenance. In identical warnings to China and Japan, he revived the doctrine Bryan had enunciated in 1915. The United States, Stimson warned, would not recognize any change brought about by force that impaired American treaty rights or Chinese territorial integrity. Japan scoffed politely.

Before the end of January the Japanese invaded Shanghai, bombarded the city, and killed thousands of civilians—all on the pretext that they were retaliating against a Chinese boycott. America's warning had proved no deterrent. Yet once again Hoover refused to consider economic sanctions. Stimson could turn only to sterner words.

In February he published a long letter to Senator Borah, "in many ways," he later said, "the most significant state paper" he ever wrote. In it he reiterated the nonrecognition doctrine and lamented the failure of other nations to endorse it. He also recalled the interdependence of the various Washington treaties of 1922. Stimson wrote:

> No one of these treaties can be disregarded without disturbing the general understanding and equilibrium. . . . The willingness of the American government to surrender its commanding lead in battleship construction and to leave its positions at Guam and in the Philippines without further fortification, was predicated upon, among other things, the self-denying covenants contained in the Nine Power Treaty.

Stimson had hoped that his letter would encourage China, inform the American public, exhort the League and Great Britain, and warn Japan. But sentiment did China no good. Americans were to learn little about aggression for another decade, the League and its members shared Hoover's addiction to confining deterrence to words, and Japan was confident that neither the President nor his constituents were prepared to heed Stimson's counsel.

In 1932 the Assembly of the League, with Japan abstaining, unanimously adopted a resolution incorporating the nonrecognition doctrine. A year later a League commission of inquiry named Japan the aggressor in Manchuria and called on her to return the province to China. Japan simply withdrew from the League and, though she also left Shanghai temporarily, prepared to continue her aggressions. In the absence of sanctions against her, she was unimpressed by the concepts of international law and order which Stimson had invoked and the League had endorsed.

Stimson, a disciple of Theodore Roosevelt, did not need to be reminded that power and the will to use it were essential to world peace. But the lesson was lost on the vast majority of his countrymen, including Congress. In the early weeks of 1933 Congress passed a bill granting independence to the Philippine Is-

lands, largely in response to pressure from American interests eager to raise the tariff barrier between themselves and their Filipino competitors. The measure, enacted over Hoover's veto, demonstrated that Congress was willing to throw the islands to the mercy of Japan, and it canceled the veiled but vigorous warning in Stimson's letter to Borah.

The story was very much the same in Europe, where the German Nazis were marching to power. At a World Disarmament Conference in Geneva in 1932, the French proposed that an international army be established and that all powers submit to the compulsory arbitration of disputes. Hoover countered with a plan for the immediate abolition of all offensive weapons and the reduction by one-third of existing armies and navies. But with the United States still unwilling to guarantee their security, the French were unimpressed by the arithmetic of arms reduction, and the conference adjourned in July with nothing accomplished. In 1933 Germany was Hitler's.

Good will and high moral purpose had no meaning in the Germany of the Nazis or the Japan of the Imperial Army. The world, Stimson realized, no longer resembled the one into which he had been born, or even the one he thought he had understood in 1929. For men who hoped for disarmament and peace and the rule of law, the hour of peril had arrived. Neither the American people nor their leaders had brought mankind to the edge of disaster, nor could they alone have prevented the collapse of world order. But the foreign policies of the United States lacked the force and the courage to check depression or aggression.

The Depths of Depression

The Hoover Policies: Third Phase
Hoover, William Allen White once said, was "constitutionally gloomy, a congenital pessimist who always saw the doleful side of any situation." The President took no joy in his office or in its potentialities for leadership. As he put it himself, "I can't be a Theodore Roosevelt." Grim and aloof, Hoover was nonetheless resolute. Just as he tried to halt the panic in Europe in 1931, so did he try to buttress the United States against the effects

of that panic. By the fall of that year he had reached certain conclusions that were to shape his policies during the coming months. He intended to do everything he could to keep the nation on the gold standard, in his view an indispensable condition of economic health. The business and financial community shared that belief passionately, as it had for almost a century. The President also intended, again with ardor and with the blessing of men of means, to strive for economy and a balanced budget. He was prepared, however, to use federal funds and federal authority on an unprecedented scale to rescue the banks and industry from their troubles. The effects of their recovery, he thought, would then trickle down to the farmers and laborers, who were to receive little direct aid from the federal government.

The new Congress convened in December 1931. At Hoover's suggestion it appropriated $125 million to expand the lending powers of the Federal Land Banks. Also at his urging, but not until July 1932, it established a system of home loan banks with a capital of $125 million for discounting home mortgages. The purpose of this scheme was to enable savings banks, insurance companies, and building and loan associations to obtain cash for the mortgages they held instead of having to foreclose them. The act not only helped to keep the assets of the lending institutions liquid, but also, as Hoover said, it spared hundreds of Americans the "heartbreaking . . . loss of their homes." And it set a significant precedent for more extensive legislation later on.

In February 1932 Congress amended the Federal Reserve Act of 1914 as requested by the President and Secretary of the Treasury Ogden Mills. (Hoover had rid himself of the increasingly unpopular Mellon by appointing him ambassador to Great Britain.) The act of 1914 had required that Federal Reserve currency be backed by gold or certain safe kinds of commercial paper—bank loans to business. By 1932 there was so little commercial activity that gold had come to form almost 70 per cent of the reserve stock. Yet foreigners were withdrawing gold at an increasing rate, and domestic hoarding had reached alarming proportions. Hoover and Mills therefore recommended making government bonds and larger classes of safe commercial paper acceptable as collateral for Federal Reserve notes.

The new law, the Glass-Steagall Act, freed about a billion dollars' worth of gold to meet the demands of Europeans who were converting their dollars to gold. This enabled the United States for the time being to retain enough gold to remain on the gold standard without putting controls on gold movements or on transactions in foreign exchange. Yet the continuing outflow of gold even further reduced bank reserves and thus the availability of bank loans to business. This situation further depressed prices and added to the burden of debts contracted when prices were high. To hold to the gold standard was in keeping with the theories of classical economics, with its emphasis on the automatic workings of domestic and international trade and of the business cycle. Yet now that mechanism spun the business cycle downward and helped depression feed upon itself.

In spite of the Glass-Steagall Act, moreover, many banks remained weak. To supplement their resources, Hoover in the fall of 1931 persuaded New York bankers to create a National Credit Association with a $500 million pool. But the halfhearted use of this fund doomed the effort to failure. The President then gave in to the urgings of Eugene Meyer, governor of the Federal Reserve Board and formerly head of the War Finance Corporation established in 1918. Meyer proposed revising that agency in the form of a Reconstruction Finance Company to make loans to banks, railways, and insurance companies. Hoover, hoping that the psychological lift provided by this scheme would justify the cost of financing it, made it the keystone of his recovery policy in 1932.

In January Congress created the Reconstruction Finance Corporation with a capital stock of $500 million and the power to borrow three times that sum in guaranteed, tax-free bonds. It was authorized to lend money to banks and insurance companies and, with the approval of the Interstate Commerce Commission, to railroads. Most of the $1.5 billion the RFC disbursed before March 1933 went to banks and trust companies. The RFC, however, could lend funds only against adequate collateral, and it could not buy bank stock. Its loans increased bank indebtedness, but it could not satisfy the banks' basic need for new capital.

The RFC kept its transactions secret for five months, largely because Hoover feared that publicity would incite runs on the weak banks that were receiving the loans. More than half of the $126 million that the RFC dispersed during those months went to three large banks. One of them was the bank of Charles G. Dawes, who resigned as president of the RFC only a month before the loan went through. In July 1932 the Democrats in Congress, to Hoover's dismay, put through an amendment compelling the RFC to report its transactions. Thereafter the number of loans made to large institutions fell off.

The Muddle of Relief   Late in 1931 Hoover appointed a new committee on unemployment with Walter S. Gifford as its head. Gifford, the president of the American Telephone and Telegraph Company, agreed with Hoover that relief was the responsibility of local government and private charity. Yet Gifford could not convincingly defend this view. In January 1932 he confessed to a Senate committee that he did not know how many people were out of work; he did not know how many needed help, how much help they needed, or how much money localities were raising or could raise. But of one thing he seemed certain: the "grave danger" of taking "the determination of these things into the Federal Government."

The gravest danger, in the view of the President and most congressmen of both parties, was that the budget might be thrown further out of balance. Yet throughout 1932 the need for federal spending increased. In the words of Senator Edward P. Costigan, Colorado's progressive Republican, "nothing short of federal assistance . . . can possibly satisfy the conscience and heart and safeguard the good name of America." With La Follette, Costigan introduced a bill granting a modest $375 million for relief, but the Administration blocked it. Sensing the political importance of the issue, the Democratic leadership now began to press for direct federal aid to the unemployed and for deficit spending for public works.

Hoover, however, insisted on limiting any relief program to RFC loans to localities and on limiting public works to self-liquidating projects, like bridges and housing, which could return enough income from tolls or rentals to pay back the initial cost of construction. But many states had nearly exhausted their legal authority to borrow from any source, and few projects had emerged from the drawing board. Consequently the President's restrictions put a lower ceiling on spending than the Democrats had contemplated.

Even so, Hoover endorsed a federal program without precedent in American history. After a partisan wrangle, in January 1932 he signed a bill that authorized the RFC to lend $1.5 billion for local self-liquidating public works and $300 million at 3 per cent interest to supplement local relief funds.

The relief loans, the President said, were to be based on "absolute need and evidence of financial exhaustion." This limitation kept them small. The governor of Pennsylvania asked for a loan of $45 million (three-fourths of the sum, he noted, that would allow the jobless in the state a mere thirteen cents apiece a day for food for a year). The RFC let him have only $11 million (enough for little more than three cents a person a day). By the end of 1932 the RFC had allotted only $30 million for relief loans and even less for public works.

The outlook of the nation's farmers seemed as hopeless as that of the unemployed workers in the cities. Even before the depression destroyed the European market for farm commodities, the Federal Farm Board had recognized that it could never stabilize farm prices without some control over farm production. When in 1932 American prices followed world prices down to bewildering lows, the stabilization corporations made a brief but futile effort to brake the decline. They lost $354 million in market operations, accumulated huge stocks of unsalable commodities, and finally in the summer simply gave up. Wheat, which had brought $2.16 a bushel in 1919 and $1.03 in 1929, sank to 38 cents. Cotton, corn, and other prices suffered comparably. Farmers found themselves without enough income to meet their mortgage payments or even to buy food for their families. And certainly they lacked the money to buy manufactured goods, which still sold at prices sustained by industry.

In December the members of the Federal Farm Board urged Congress to do something about regulating acreage and production as a first step in setting up some sort of program for boosting farm prices. The only alternative was agricultural bankruptcy. Yet Hoover and Secretary of Agriculture Hyde rejected the idea of imposing federal controls on agriculture. Before the year ended, farmers in Nebraska were burning corn to keep warm, forming angry posses in Minnesota to prevent foreclosures, and joining Milo Reno's militant Farmers' Holiday Association in Iowa to block the shipment of produce until prices rose.

Moods of Despair   Father John Ryan, the Catholic social reformer, despaired for the state of the nation. "I wish," he said, "we might double the number of Communists in this country, to put the fear, if not of God, then . . . of something else, into the hearts of our leaders." Communism had a particular appeal to the intellectuals who had been alienated by the culture of the Coolidge era, men like Malcolm Cowley and Sherwood Anderson. But the theories of Karl Marx had little appeal for the general public. The communists organized "hunger marches" in Washington and Detroit and preached revolution elsewhere, but Communist party membership was little more than one hundred thousand.

Rural Violence

There was an air of immense earnestness about the farmers. They had been swung completely out of their usual orbit, but they are absolutely sure of the righteousness of their cause. An old man with white mustache said:

"They say blockading the highway's illegal. I says, 'Seems to me there was a Tea-party in Boston that was illegal too. What about destroying property in Boston Harbor when our country was started?'" He sets the note of the evening.

"If we farmers go down bankrupt," says one of the younger men, "everything in this country goes down. If we get enough to live on, everybody's going to go to work again."... There is a cry:

"Truck!"

They hurry out in the roadway. All of them carry heavy stakes, some made from axe handles.... Beside the road, handy to use, are heavy spiked logs and planks bristling with spikes to throw in front of trucks. This truck is empty. There is a short conference. The truck passes on its way.

"Good-night, boys," calls the driver. "Good luck!" He is one of them, part of the movement that is just beginning to realize its power.

From Mary Heaton Vorse, "Rebellion in the Cornbelt: American Farmers Beat Their Plowshares into Swords," *Harper's Magazine*, December 1932.

Though desperate Americans spurned communism, they gave way to hatred and violence. Farmers brandished shotguns to prevent foreclosures, defying the law to defend their homes. The president of the Farmers' Union damned the rich as "cannibals . . . who live on the labor of the workers." Some of the prosperous took out "riot and civil commotion insurance" and began to suggest that the United States needed a fascist dictator like Mussolini.

In the spring of 1932 some fifteen thousand unemployed veterans converged on Washington from every region of the country. They announced that they planned to stay in the capital until Congress voted full and immediate payment of the bonus. The year before, over Hoover's veto, Congress had authorized loans up to 50 per cent of the value of each adjusted service certificate (see p. 598). But those funds had been spent, and the unemployed veterans, like all other unemployed Americans, were in dire need of help. When the Senate voted down the bonus bill, half the

Bonus army: The burning of Anacostia Flats.

veterans went home. But the rest had no place to go and no way of getting there, so they camped in a muddy shanty town on Anacostia Flats and in vacant government buildings.

Their plight evoked the sympathy of the chief of the District of Columbia police, who treated them generously and intelligently. But their presence worried the Administration. Hoover, anxious to get rid of them, had Congress pass a bill that permitted them to borrow against their bonus certificates in order to get funds for transportation home. Still the veterans waited around after Congress adjourned, hoping at least for a conference with the President.

Late in July the Administration ordered the eviction of all squatters from government buildings. In the ensuing melee, brought about largely by the small corps of communists among the veterans, two men were killed and several policemen wounded. Secretary of War Patrick Hurley had been looking for just such an incident. At his request, the White House now called in the army—four troops of cavalry and four infantry companies, with six tanks, tear gas, and machine guns. Under the personal command of General Douglas Mac-Arthur (whose junior officers included Dwight D. Eisenhower and George Patton), the troops rode into Anacostia Flats, drove out the veterans and their families, and burned their shacks. Crowing over his triumph, Mac-Arthur called the veterans "a mob . . . animated by the essence of revolution." The Administration published reports claiming that most of them had been communists and criminals.

Neither a grand jury nor the Veterans Administration could find evidence to support those charges. The bonus marchers were destitute men. Whether or not they merited special treatment, they deserved, as did unemployed Americans everywhere, compassion and assistance. They received first indifference and veiled hostility, then vicious armed attack. That treatment and the attitude that prompted it appalled the nation.

With government callous and blundering,

Roosevelt's arrival at Chicago, 1932: "Let it . . . be symbolic that . . . I broke traditions."

with the business elite defensive about the disrepute it had brought on itself, with depression still spreading, Americans began to fear that the whole political and economic system might collapse. Yet they waited patiently, as they had so often before in times of trouble, to see whether the presidential campaign would give them a vote for a brighter future.

The Changing of the Guard   In the summer of 1932 the Republicans renominated Hoover and his Vice-President, Charles Curtis. A minority of the delegates to the convention were dissatisfied with the Administration's policies but were unwilling to repudiate the President. The convention was listless, for the delegates realized that the electorate, rightly or wrongly, blamed the party for the depression and regarded Hoover as the symbol of the party.

The Democrats, in contrast, sniffed victory ahead. A majority of the delegates came to Chicago pledged to Franklin D. Roosevelt, who had been the front runner for the nomination since his spanking re-election as governor of New York in 1930. He had the nerve for politics, the sense of fun, and the zest with people that had once made his distant cousin, Theodore Roosevelt, the most popular man in America. Franklin Roosevelt, moreover, had worked effectively with Tammany Hall, had

made friends with the masters of other Northern machines, and yet had always preserved close relations with the Southern wing of the party. Basically a conservative in his economic thinking, Roosevelt was a progressive in his attitude toward government, an activist, and a humanitarian.

Roosevelt, though by no means a radical, stood to the left of his serious opponents. Their one hope was to organize a coalition to keep him from getting the two-thirds vote necessary for nomination. Al Smith, still a favorite of the machines and jealous of any rival, hoped to be nominated once again. Ambition had soured Smith's best instincts. When Roosevelt before the convention called for help for "the forgotten man at the bottom of the economic pyramid," Smith remarked testily, "This is no time for demagogues." But Smith lacked allies. The McAdoo faction still opposed him, and now backed Speaker of the House John N. Garner. After Roosevelt had failed to win the necessary vote in three ballots, McAdoo, evening up the old scores of 1924 (see p. 614), switched California's critical delegation to the New York governor. This put Roosevelt across and in return his lieutenants arranged second place on the ticket for Garner.

In a characteristically dramatic gesture, Roosevelt broke precedent by flying to Chicago

Hoover on Federal Relief

The proposals of our opponents will endanger or destroy our system.... I especially emphasize that promise to promote "employment for all surplus labor at all times." At first I could not believe that anyone would be so cruel as to hold out a hope so absolutely impossible of realization to these 10,000,-000 who are unemployed. And I protest against such frivolous promises being held out to a suffering people. It is easily demonstrable that no such employment can be found. But the point I wish to make here and now is the mental attitude and spirit of the Democratic Party to attempt it. It is another mark of the character of the new deal and the destructive changes which mean the total abandonment of every principle upon which this government and the American system is founded. If it were possible to give this employment to 10,000,000 people by the Government, it would cost upwards of $9,-000,000,000 a year.... It would pull down the employment of those who are still at work by the high taxes and the demoralization of credit upon which their employment is dependent.... It would mean the growth of a fearful bureaucracy which, once established, could never be dislodged.

From Herbert Hoover, Campaign Address in New York, October 1932.

to accept the nomination before the convention adjourned. "Let it . . . be symbolic that . . . I broke traditions . . . ," he told the cheering delegates. "Republican leaders not only have failed in material things, they have failed in national vision, because in disaster they have held out no hope. . . . I pledge you, I pledge myself to a new deal for the American people."

Roosevelt began to define that New Deal during his campaign. He was often deliberately vague and took pains to avoid offending any large bloc of voters. He hedged on the tariff. He made much of his party's demand for the repeal of the Eighteenth Amendment: Prohibition was still an important political issue in 1932, but it had no immediate bearing on the depression, which was the overriding concern of Americans. But he also set forth vigorous lines of attack on the nation's economic ills. At the Commonwealth Club in San Francisco, Roosevelt said that "government . . . owes to everyone an avenue to possess himself of a portion of that plenty sufficient for his needs,

through his own work." In its dealings with business, government was to "assist the development of . . . an economic constitutional order." And such an order, he pointed out, demanded national planning.

Roosevelt's plans drew on the ideas which progressives had nurtured throughout the twenties, and promised assistance to the victims of depression. He called for strict public regulation of the utilities and federal development of public power. He advocated federal controls on agricultural production as a part of a program to support commodity prices, and federal loans to refinance farm mortgages. He expressed interest in the schemes for currency inflation that agriculture leaders were urging as a means to raise prices and reduce the weight of debt. He appealed to the business community by demanding cuts in government spending in order to balance the budget, but in the same speech he also promised to incur a deficit whenever human suffering made it necessary.

Roosevelt's oratorical flair and personal ebullience contrasted with Hoover's heavy

F. D. R. on Federal Relief

We have two problems: first, to meet the immediate distress; second, to build up on a basis of permanent employment.

As to "immediate relief," the first principle is that this nation, this national Government, if you like, owes a positive duty that no citizen shall be permitted to starve....

In addition to providing emergency relief, the Federal Government should and must provide temporary work wherever that is possible. You and I know that in the national forests, on flood prevention, and on the development of waterway projects that have already been authorized and planned but not yet executed, tens of thousands, and even hundreds of thousands of our unemployed citizens can be given at least temporary employment....

Third, the Federal Government should expedite the actual construction of public works already authorized....

Finally, in that larger field that looks ahead, we call for a coordinated system of employment exchanges, the advance planning of public works, and unemployment reserves.

From Franklin D. Roosevelt, Campaign Address in Boston, October 1932.

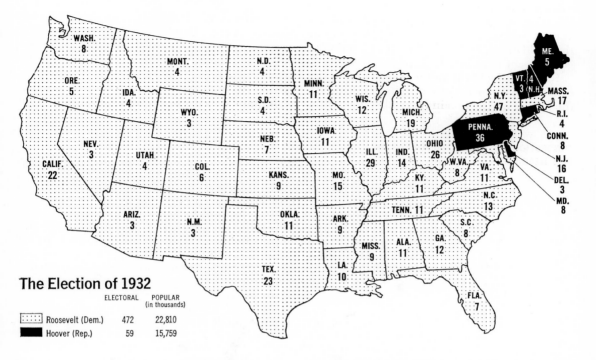

The Election of 1932

	ELECTORAL	POPULAR (in thousands)
Roosevelt (Dem.)	472	22,810
Hoover (Rep.)	59	15,759

speech and grim manner. The President emphasized his dedication to budget-balancing and the gold standard, defended his record, and charged his opponent with recklessness. The policies Roosevelt advocated, Hoover said, "would destroy the very foundations of our American system." If they were adopted, "grass will grow in the streets of a hundred cities, a thousand towns."

That rhetoric reflected Hoover's gloom. It obscured his own expansion of federal control, and it exaggerated Roosevelt's intentions. Actually the Democrat's campaign disappointed many intellectuals who felt, as Walter Lippmann earlier had, that Franklin Roosevelt was "a highly impressionable person, . . . without strong convictions. . . . a pleasant man, who, without any important qualifications for the office, would very much like to be President."

But there were significant differences between the two candidates and their ideas, between Hoover's pessimism and Roosevelt's effervescence, between Hoover's belief that the origins of the depression lay outside the United States and Roosevelt's belief that they were internal, between Hoover's impulse to-

ward caution and Roosevelt's impulse toward experiment, between Hoover's identification with industry and finance and Roosevelt's identification with the forgotten men and with the intellectuals and social workers who championed them. Hoover in his last campaign speech was right in associating Roosevelt with Norris and La Follette, right in asserting that the contest was between two philosophies of government. Both philosophies were fundamentally American, but Hoover's looked backward while Roosevelt's looked eagerly ahead.

The people had a real choice when they went to the polls in November. Dismissing radicalism (the Socialists polled only 881,951 votes, the Communists 102,785), they swept the Democrats into office. Roosevelt won over 57 per cent of the popular vote and carried the electoral college 472 to 59. The Democrats also gained a large majority in both houses of Congress. The vote, a protest against the Administration, gave Roosevelt a clear mandate for change. He carried most of the agricultural West as well as the South; he carried the great cities by majorities larger than Smith's in 1928. After twelve years the farmers and the workers once again had the determining voice in

Washington. They had repudiated business and its policies and servants, had thrown out the Old Guard, and had taken the direction of government back into their own hands.

Roosevelt had faith in the people and in the capacity of democracy to solve its problems. At the time of his election in November 1932 little

else remained of the national confidence of March 1929. Depression had stripped the American people of most of their illusions. Now they had given the new Administration a chance to prove the viability of Roosevelt's faith. At bottom it was also still their own faith, and still the best hope of mankind.

SUGGESTIONS FOR READING

Hoover and His Policies

Arthur M. Schlesinger, Jr., *The Crisis of the Old Order* (1957), provides a critical and detailed analysis of the Hoover Administration and its problems. Also critical, though the author intends to be sympathetic, is H. G. Warren, *Herbert Hoover and the Great Depression* (1959), while the relevant chapters in J. D. Hicks, *Republican Ascendancy* (1960), are unsympathetic and those in W. E. Leuchtenberg, *The Perils of Prosperity* * (1958), lucid but brief. The most ardent defense of the Administration appears in Herbert Hoover, *Memoirs: The Great Depression, 1929–1941* (1952), which may be supplemented by another book of similar spirit, R. L. Wilbur and A. M. Hyde, *The Hoover Policies* (1937). On Hoover's foreign policies, there is significant material in the biographies of Stimson mentioned in connection with the preceding chapter, and in R. H. Ferrell, *American Diplomacy in the Great Depression* (1957).

Depression

All the volumes noted above of course deal with the depression. Its impact is also poignantly revealed in the pertinent parts of I. Bernstein, *The Lean Years* (1960), and D. A. Shannon, ed., *The Great Depression* * (1960). There are excellent descriptions of the stock market crash in F. L. Allen, *Only Yesterday* * (1931), and J. K. Galbraith, *The Great Crash* * (1955). The skillful analysis of the latter should be compared with the also able view in Thomas Wilson, *Fluctuations in Income and Employment* (1948). Within his excellent general study of American radical intellectuals, *Writers on the Left* (1961), Daniel Aaron discusses the influence of the depression on the spread of radicalism.

F.D.R. and 1932

Franklin D. Roosevelt's governorship and first presidential campaign receive important treatment in A. M. Schlesinger, Jr., *Crisis of the Old Order* (1957), which is brilliant and panoramic on those subjects, and in Frank Freidel, *Franklin D. Roosevelt: The Triumph* (1956), a work of outstanding scholarship and compelling judgments. Less comprehensive but still useful are parts of J. M. Burns, *Roosevelt: The Lion and the Fox* (1956), and R. G. Tugwell, *The Democratic Roosevelt* (1957).

* Available in paperback edition.

28

The New Deal

The winter of 1932–33 was a season of despair unique in American history. The ever-deepening depression, the lengthening bread lines in the cities, the angry mobs of farmers in the countryside, the apparent immobility of the national government, the spreading misery and resentment—all combined to stamp society with an unprecedented sense of bewilderment and defeat. Some Americans were even beginning to feel that the traditional system of democratic capitalism had reached the end of its tether. Talk of alternative systems was in the air—of communism, of fascism, and of strange new local panaceas, like Technocracy, which sought to substitute for the price system an economy based on the measurement of electric energy. Never had Americans been so baffled and so desperate.

The Interregnum

The Failure of Cooperation   The four-month interval between the election in November 1932 and the inauguration of the new President the following March compounded the feeling of national impotence.* Herbert Hoover had striven valiantly according to his

---

* The Twentieth Amendment, providing for inauguration on the January 20 after the election and eliminating future lame-duck Congresses, was ratified by the required thirty-nine states by February 6, 1933, but, according to its own provisions, was not to take effect until October 15, 1933.

lights to arrest the downward plunge of the economy, but his policies had not been effective. Now, as a lame-duck President, he exerted little influence, and he frustrated any chance of constructive collaboration with his successor during the interregnum by his continued insistence on policies that Roosevelt had already condemned and that the electorate had rejected. Thus in February Hoover called on Roosevelt to make a series of conservative declarations which he thought might calm the country; at the same time, he wrote privately to a Republican senator, "I realize that if these declarations be made by the President-elect, he will have ratified the whole major program of the Republican Administration; that is it means the abandonment of 90 per cent of the so-called new deal." This was an invitation, not to cooperation, but to capitulation.

Through these weeks the country remained in a mood of gloomy suspense. The session of Congress beginning in January 1933 produced little in the way of positive action. In February the Senate Finance Committee called leading businessmen to Washington to give their ideas on how the country could get out of the depression. John W. Davis, who had been the Democratic candidate for President in 1924 and was now the leader of the American bar, summed up the general testimony when he said, "I have nothing to offer, either of fact or theory." The sense of desperation became every day more acute. The head of the Farm

Bureau Federation told a Senate Committee, "Unless something is done for the American farmer we will have a revolution in the countryside within less than twelve months." Alfred E. Smith observed that this was a crisis worse than war. "And what does a democracy do in a war? It becomes a tyrant, a despot, a real monarch. In the World War we took our Constitution, wrapped it up and laid it on the shelf and left it there until it was over." An attempt on the President-elect's life by a madman in Miami, Florida, in February heightened the sense of national anxiety.

The Banking Crisis   In February 1933 the spreading panic began to concentrate on one of the weakest links in the economy—the banking system. Over five thousand banks had failed in three years; as the economy continued its downward spiral, more and more people determined to play it safe by converting their savings to cash. The mounting pressure on financial institutions, the lines of depositors waiting to draw out their savings, the threat of further runs on the banks, led the governor of Michigan in mid-February to proclaim a bank holiday—that is, to order the temporary closing of the banks in his state. This act set off a chain reaction in other states. As the clock struck midnight on the last day of Hoover's administration, with banks shutting their doors across the land, the retiring President said, "We are at the end of our rope. There is nothing more we can do."

Franklin D. Roosevelt

His Personal Background   The new President was fifty-one years old. The Roosevelt name was, of course, well known in American politics. Like his distant cousin Theodore, Franklin Roosevelt had come from a patrician background which equipped him with both a high sense of civic responsibility and a certain disdain for those whose chief claim to attention was their capacity to make money. Like Theodore, Franklin was a man of boundless charm, vivacity, and energy. As a young man he had been much influenced by Theodore, and their careers offered curious parallels. Both had made their political debuts in the New York assembly; both had served as Assistant Secretary of the Navy in Wash-

ington; both had been governor of New York; both had been candidates for the vice-presidency.

Unlike Theodore, Franklin was a member of the Democratic branch of the Roosevelt family. He was less of an intellectual than Theodore, less interested in books and ideas; he was also less of a lay preacher, less moralistic and evangelical. His urbane and conciliatory manner, indeed, led some observers to suppose him too compliant for hard responsibilities and decisions. None the less, his record suggested a man of parts. As second in command in the Navy Department during the First World War, he had been an aggressive and resourceful executive. As candidate for Vice-President in 1920, he had been a vigorous and articulate campaigner. In 1921 he had been stricken by an acute attack of poliomyelitis. This illness deprived him of the use of his legs; many thought it would end his public career. The iron determination of his comeback revealed an inner spirit that was not only gallant but tough. He had been an able and imaginative governor of New York; no state had taken so many positive measures to contain the effects of depression. His capture of the Democratic nomination in 1932 was the work of a resolute and crafty politician.

The superficial affability of Roosevelt's manner actually concealed an enormously complex and contradictory personality—at once lighthearted and somber, candid and disingenuous, open and impenetrable, bold and cautious, decisive and evasive. Throughout his life he pursued certain public ends—especially the improvement of welfare and opportunity for the great masses of people—with profound steadiness of purpose; but the means he employed to achieve these ends were often inconsistent and occasionally unworthy. Yet his capacity to understand and project the grand moral issues of his day—and his readiness to use all the resources of presidential leadership to prepare the country for necessary action—enabled him to command the confidence of a great majority of Americans during his terms in office, despite the bitter and persistent opposition of a powerful minority.

His Ideas   Roosevelt was a child of the progressive era. Theodore Roosevelt and Woodrow Wilson had been his early inspirations. Government seemed to him a necessary and proper instrument of the general welfare, and he had no inhibitions about calling on it to redress matters when "rugged individualism" left parts of the population or sections of the country without adequate protection. The problems of 1933 were novel. Progressivism had been a philosophy of social welfare rather than of economic growth, and progressives were no less baffled than conservatives by economic collapse. But, where faith in the sovereign virtue of laissez faire constrained conservatives from taking positive government action, progressives like Roosevelt, with activist temperaments and a pragmatic attitude toward social policy, were quite ready to invoke positive government to bring about economic recovery.

So far as economics were concerned, Roosevelt had attitudes rather than theories. In his campaign for the presidency, he had identified himself with two main ideas—action and planning. "The country needs," he had said in 1932, "and, unless I mistake its temper, the country demands bold, persistent experimentation. . . . Above all, try something." As to what should be tried, his views were less definite. His campaign speeches made it evident that he favored action in a number of specific fields—agricultural and industrial planning; federal relief and public works; social insurance; conservation; securities regulation; government retrenchment and a balanced budget. But it was not easy to see how these elements fitted together into a consistent and comprehensive program.

Certain of his advisers had more clear-cut ideas. A group of college professors, mostly recruited from Columbia University, had served as his campaign brain trust. A book of 1932, *The Modern Corporation and Private Property*, by Adolf A. Berle, Jr., and Gardiner C. Means, provided the foundation for their analysis. The trend toward economic concentration, they contended, was irreversible. Already it had transformed great parts of the old free market of classical economics into "administered" markets, in which basic economic decisions were made, not by equations of supply and demand, but by the policies of those who ran the great corporations. In their opinion this change in the structure of the market ren-

dered classical laissez-faire theory obsolescent.

What did this mean for public policy? Another Columbia economist, Rexford G. Tugwell, urged the President-elect to bold conclusions. If concentration was inevitable, Tugwell argued, then control over the nation's economic life could not be safely left in private hands. It was precisely such private control, according to Tugwell, that had brought about the depression; in the twenties the gains of economic productivity had gone into profits, savings, and speculation when they should have gone into a build-up of purchasing power through the payment of higher wages to workers and higher prices to farmers. The only way to operate the modern integrated economy at capacity, in Tugwell's view, was organized public planning.

Men like Berle, Tugwell, Means, and Raymond Moley, who acted as nominal head of the brain trust, were in a sense heirs of Theodore Roosevelt's New Nationalism, carrying the philosophy of "concentration and control" several steps further. Their predisposition toward new institutions for central planning was reinforced by the views of those who, recalling America's last national emergency, the First World War, reverted to wartime economic mechanisms in the battle against depression. Indeed, the Reconstruction Finance Corporation of the Hoover Administration was itself simply a revival of Wilson's War Finance Corporation; the same man—Eugene Meyer—ran both agencies (see p. 641). Now men once associated with the War Industries Board, like Bernard Baruch, Hugh S. Johnson, and George N. Peek, began to sponsor schemes of industrial and agricultural planning.

Not all those around Roosevelt accepted the virtues of national planning. Others close to him—especially Associate Justice Louis D. Brandeis of the Supreme Court and Professor Felix Frankfurter of Harvard—were heirs of Wilson's New Freedom. They rejected the thesis of inevitable economic concentration, distrusted the idea of central planning, and advocated policies designed to plan, not for control, but for competition. Still others, though these were more powerful in the Democratic party in Congress than in the President's immediate circle, were inflationists in the tradition of William Jennings Bryan, hoping to

Inauguration Day, 1933: A New Deal for the American people.

bring about economic recovery through the expansion of the means of payment. And others, like Lewis W. Douglas, whom Roosevelt was about to appoint Director of the Budget, were sound-money, laissez-faire Democrats in the school of Grover Cleveland, deeply committed to the gold standard and the annually balanced budget.

Roosevelt presided benignly over the clash of debate around him. Disagreement stimulated him, enabled him to compare the merits of competing arguments and personalities, and reassured him that the crucial questions of policy would come to him for decision. His choice of Cabinet members reflected his desire for a variety of views and his confidence that he could control men of divergent opinion. To the State Department he named Cordell Hull of Tennessee, a respected Southern politician who had sponsored the income-tax amendment during the Wilson Administration but who was now somewhat conservative in his domestic views and a passionate foe of international trade barriers. Two vigorous progressive Republicans—Henry A. Wallace of Iowa and Harold L. Ickes of Illinois—were appointed to Agriculture and Interior; the first woman in history to go into the Cabinet, Frances Perkins

of New York, became Secretary of Labor; and the other posts were filled by Democratic politicians from widely scattered parts of the country or, in the case of the Treasury, by William Woodin of New York, a flexible-minded businessman.

The Hundred Days

The Inauguration   On March 4, 1933, millions of Americans clustered around their radios to hear the new President deliver his inaugural address. "Let me assert my firm belief," Roosevelt began, "that the only thing we have to fear is fear itself." Then he assailed the business leaders whose incompetence and misconduct, he said, had been largely responsible for the economic disaster. "This Nation asks for action, and action now," he concluded, adding that he would seek from Congress "broad Executive powers to wage a war against the emergency, as great as the power that would be given to me if we were in fact invaded by a foreign foe."

The words of the inaugural address, with their confidence and their promise of action, thrilled the nation. And action itself was quick to follow. Immediately after the inauguration,

Roosevelt declared a national bank holiday and called Congress into special session. When Congress convened on March 8, it received at once a special message on the banking crisis and a draft of emergency banking legislation. In less than eight hours the House and Senate shouted through the bill and returned it to the President for signature. The unprecedented combination of decision and speed in the passage of the act electrified the country and called forth a spectacular outpouring of hope.

Quick to seize advantage of the national mood, the President set forth the next item on his program—a bill calling for the reduction of government expenses, including veterans' pensions. "Too often in recent history," he told Congress, "liberal governments have been wrecked on rocks of loose fiscal policy." He quickly followed his economy message with a call for the amendment of the Volstead Act to legalize light wines and beers. The prompt enactment of both the economy and beer bills meant, among other things, the defeat of the two most powerful lobbies in the nation's capitol—the veterans and the prohibitionists. All this activity increased the sense of exhilaration with which the nation watched developments in Washington. "At the beginning of March," wrote Walter Lippmann, "the country was in such a state of confused desperation that it would have followed almost any leader anywhere he chose to go. . . . In one week, the nation, which had lost confidence in everything and everybody, has regained confidence in the government and in itself."

The First New Deal: Agricultural Planning So far the Roosevelt program had been dashing in style but exceedingly orthodox in content. On March 16, however, Roosevelt's leadership entered a new phase. On that day he sent to Capitol Hill a message calling for a bold national policy in agriculture. "I tell you frankly that it's a new and untrod path," he warned Congress, "but I tell you with equal frankness that an unprecedented condition calls for the trial of new means."

The condition was indeed unprecedented. The per capita cash net income of the American farmer had declined from $162 to $48 between 1929 and 1932; farm prices had fallen 55 per cent; and, since industrial prices had not fallen correspondingly, the farmer's purchasing power was only about 60 per cent of what it had been in 1929. The farmer's fixed charges—especially the burden of mortgage debt assumed at higher price levels—weighed more heavily than ever on him. In some areas, the farmer was not even able to clear the cost of production. And since the individual farmer saw no way to fight falling prices except to increase his production, all he did was to put more produce on the market and drive prices down faster and further.

The central idea in the administration proposal was "agricultural adjustment." This plan aimed to increase farm income by controlling production; and it aimed to control production by offering benefit payments to farmers who agreed to regulate their plantings according to a national plan. The adjustment programs were to be financed by processing taxes collected at the flour mill or textile mill or packing house. No program would go into effect until a majority of farmers indicated they wanted it by voting in a referendum; and the local administration of the plan was to be as much as possible in the hands of the farmers themselves. The ultimate object was to restore to the farmer substantially the terms of trade he had had in 1909–14—that is, to give his produce the same exchange value it commanded in the years directly before the First World War. This concept was known as "parity."

The agricultural adjustment bill that emerged from conferences between the Department of Agriculture and leading farm organizations incorporated, in addition to benefit payments, a number of other approaches to the farm problem. It gave the government authority, for example, to maintain prices through loans on or purchase of nonperishable crops, which would then go into government storage; it also conferred authority to withdraw land from cultivation through leasing and to regulate the release of commodities for sale through marketing agreements and quotas. The inflationists in Congress added an important amendment giving the President power to issue greenbacks, to remonetize silver, and to alter the gold content of the dollar.

In the meantime, trouble was mounting in

the countryside. In late April a mob marched on a judge in Le Mars, Iowa, who had refused to suspend foreclosure proceedings, took him from his bench, put a rope around his neck, and nearly lynched him. The Farmers' Holiday Association, the most radical of the farmers' groups, renewed its threat of a farm strike. Alarmed by the rising agrarian wrath, the governor of Iowa called out the National Guard and placed half a dozen counties under martial law. "For all of the loose talk in America about red revolution and menaces of the kind that exist only in the hysterical imagination of patrioteers," said the New York *World Telegram*, "Americans are slow to understand that actual revolution already exists in the farm belt."

The passage of the Agricultural Adjustment Act on May 12 established the Agricultural Adjustment Administration and opened the New Deal's campaign to raise farm income. The first task was to cut down production in areas already overwhelmed by surpluses. Thus a carry-over from previous years of eight million bales of cotton had driven cotton prices down to five cents a pound. Yet, by the time the act had passed, some forty million acres had already been planted in new cotton. The only way to save the cotton-grower was to persuade him to plow under the planted crop in return for benefit payments. This the AAA proceeded to do in a whirlwind plow-up campaign of some ten million acres in the spring and summer. In corn and hogs, acting on the recommendation of the Farm Bureau and the Grange, the AAA dealt with the market glut by buying and slaughtering some five million little pigs.

No one perceived more sharply the irony of destroying plenty in the midst of want than the men who ordered the job to be done. "To destroy a standing crop goes against the soundest instincts of human nature," said Henry Wallace. Yet industry, the Secretary of Agriculture pointed out, had in effect plowed under much of its potential output after 1929 by cutting down on production; how in all logic could agriculture be denied the same right of self-protection? "We must play with the cards that are dealt," the Secretary said. "Agriculture cannot survive in a capitalistic society as a philanthropic enterprise."

And indeed the terrible logic of scarcity worked. As production declined—aided, in the cases of wheat and corn, by the searing droughts of 1933–34—prices rose. Between 1932 and 1936 gross farm income increased by 50 per cent, and cash receipts from marketing (including government benefit payments) nearly doubled. The parity ratio rose from 55 in 1932 to 90 in 1936. Though the AAA was occasionally disturbed by top-level policy conflicts, it won extraordinary acceptance among farmers and conducted its complex administrative operations with smoothness and effect. In agriculture, planning seemed a surprising success.

The First New Deal: Industrial Planning
Yet agricultural planning covered only the lesser part of the American economy. By 1933 American industry was employing some five million fewer workers than in 1929 and producing less than half the value of goods. Businessmen, striving to maintain a margin of profits, saw no choice but to cut costs—i.e., to lower wages and lay off employees. But the more wages and employment were reduced, the more mass purchasing power declined, until the resultant spiral threatened to carry everything down in what Hugh S. Johnson called a saturnalia of destruction.

There was increasing agreement that the only way to stop the industrial decline was through joint planning by government and business. This view was backed not just by Tugwell, with his belief in public management of the economy, and by Johnson, with his memory of the War Industries Board. Powerful voices in business, especially the United States Chamber of Commerce, now urged that the private trade association be given authority to fix prices, divide markets, and "stabilize" industrial production. The only hope for recovery, it seemed, was to limit the play of what Johnson called "the murderous doctrine of savage and wolfish individualism, looking to dog-eat-dog and devil take the hindmost."

In the spring the Administration worked out a so-called national industrial recovery bill, divided into two parts. The first part was designed "to promote the organization of industry for the purpose of cooperative action among trade groups" through codes of fair competition carrying with them exemption from the antitrust laws; an important provision—the famous Section 7a—sought to win labor support by offering federal guarantees of the right of trade unions to organize and bargain collectively. The second part of the bill provided for the establishment of a Public Works Administration with an appropriation of $3.3 billion. Roosevelt signed the bill on June 16, calling it "a challenge to industry, which has long insisted that, given the right to act in unison, it could do much for the general good which has hitherto been unlawful. From today it has that right."

Two agencies were set up under the National Industrial Recovery Act—the National Recovery Administration, with General Johnson as head, and the Public Works Administration under Harold L. Ickes. Johnson combined considerable pragmatic knowledge of the workings of the economy with the talent of a showman and the evangelism of a missionary. He saw the NRA as a great national crusade designed to restore employment and regenerate industry in an excitement of torchlight processions, giant rallies, and airplane dashes around the country. Finding the negotiation of codes with specific industries disappointingly slow, Johnson came up in July with the idea of a "blanket code" in which cooperating employers would pledge themselves to observe NRA standards on minimum wages and maximum hours; the Blue Eagle, modeled on the Indian thunderbird, became the symbol of compliance. For a moment, in the revivalist atmosphere conjured up by Johnson, the Blue Eagle carried all before it. Two million employers accepted the blanket code, and the great industries of the country, one by one, began to accept special codes.

As a result, the NRA was soon able to end the price-cutting, wage-cutting spiral. To this emergency purpose, however, it added long-term objectives. In the economic field, it hoped to bring about permanent re-employment by raising wages and shortening working hours. In the social field, it sought to bring about long overdue reforms: the abolition of child labor, an improvement of working conditions, an encouragement of labor organization, an extension of fair-trade practices.

Soon the NRA began to overextend its efforts. Instead of concentrating on codification in the major industries, it allowed itself to be tempted into setting up codes for local and service trades. There was good humanitarian reason for this effort, for these were precisely the trades where the sweatshop was most deeply entrenched. But it involved the NRA in a host of petty enforcement problems, which at once distracted its energies and dissipated its credit. Johnson was reluctant to use the NRA's coercive powers, since he wanted to avoid a court test of the NRA's constitutionality. Consequently his chief reliance against those whom he denounced as "chiselers" was the compulsion of public opinion. So long as the nation felt itself in acute crisis, this compulsion worked. But as soon as economic conditions began to grow better, more and more employers tried to beat the codes.

Within the NRA, moreover, there was constant pressure from trade associations to use the code mechanism as a means of raising prices. Many businessmen felt that price-fixing would be an appropriate *quid pro quo* for their concessions on wages, hours, and collective bargaining. On the other hand, many within the NRA and out argued that excessive price increases would defeat the whole policy of expanding purchasing power; they feared, moreover, that price-fixing would turn the codes into a vehicle for precisely the sort of monopoly Congress had tried to outlaw in the Sherman Act. An investigation by a special committee in 1934 under the chairmanship of Clarence Darrow, the criminal lawyer, purported to substantiate the charge that the NRA had become the instrument of monopoly.

In the meantime, the labor provisions in Section 7a had given a great stimulus to trade union organization, and this embittered many employers. Hugh Johnson, in addition, was an unstable person, and his increasingly erratic course further complicated the NRA's existence. Roosevelt eventually forced him out in the fall of 1934 and replaced him by a five-man board. By now the NRA was passing the political point of no return. In 1933 nearly everyone had been for it. By 1935 most people—except for the trade associations and the trade unions—were against it. When the Supreme Court finally declared the National Industrial Recovery Act unconstitutional in 1935, the Administration accepted the verdict with relief and sought new roads to recovery and reform.

The End of the Hundred Days The AAA and the NRA set the pattern of national planning and were, in this sense, the crucial measures of the First New Deal. But they by no means exhausted the achievement of the special session of 1933. During the Hundred Days after March 4, 1933, Roosevelt sent fifteen messages to Congress and saw fifteen major bills through to enactment.

One sequence of actions sought to lessen the dead weight on the economy of a burden of debt contracted when the price level was much higher. Since the closing of the banks and the Economy Act had a deflationary impact, the Administration from an early point looked for means to induce a general price increase. Conservative officials, especially Budget Director Douglas, were profoundly opposed to anything that savored of inflation. On the other hand, many Southern and Western members of Congress could hardly wait to set the printing presses to work turning out greenbacks. Roosevelt himself had no desire for currency inflation, but he was determined to bring about a rise of prices—not so fast as to

Harry L. Hopkins: Servant to the New Deal.

absorb the increases in wages and farm income, but fast enough to reduce the drag of debt on the economy. It seemed increasingly evident to him that the United States had to choose between the old gold standard and the price-raising policy, and he had no hesitation about the choice. The gold standard had not been in operation, in any case, since March 4, 1933, and on April 18 Roosevelt determined to abandon it altogether. In a few weeks Congress confirmed the departure from gold by passing a resolution providing for the abrogation of the gold clause in public and private contracts.

In the meantime, the inflationist amendment to the Agricultural Adjustment Act (see p. 653) had bestowed a variety of monetary powers on the President. He protected the independence of American monetary policy by refusing at the London Economic Conference in July to peg the dollar at a fixed value in international exchange, and, when farm prices sagged in November, Roosevelt, always eager for action, embarked on a gold-purchase program designed to raise the price level by Treasury purchases of gold. The economics of this program was of doubtful validity. But the program did little harm, and it permitted Roosevelt to retain control of monetary policy at a time when both inflationists and bankers were demanding that he take action that he deemed positively harmful. By January 1934 the pressure had died down sufficiently for the Administration to end the gold-purchase experiment and to stabilize the value of the dollar at 59.06 per cent of its last official gold value. The gold policy, along with the banking and securities legislation of 1933–34, shifted the financial capital of the nation from Wall Street to Washington.

Other actions of the Hundred Days were designed to reduce the human cost of depression. The Home Owners' Loan Act, one of the most popular of New Deal measures, saved countless homes by providing means for the refinancing of mortgages. More precedent-breaking was the Federal Emergency Relief Act, which established for the first time a system of federal relief. Under the resourceful direction of Harry L. Hopkins, a New York social worker, a succession of agencies (the best known, launched in 1935, was the Works

The Extent of Erosion, 1935

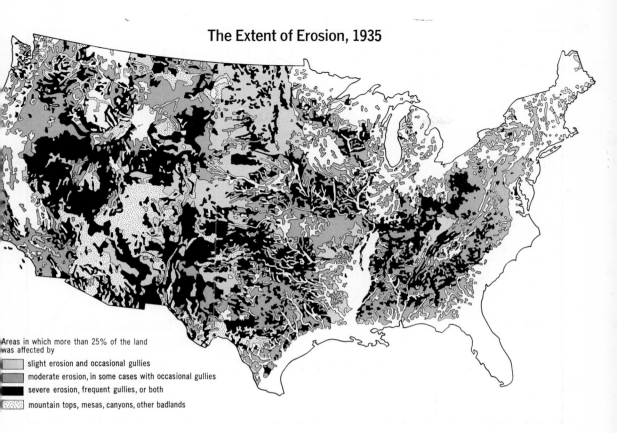

Areas in which more than 25% of the land was affected by

- slight erosion and occasional gullies
- moderate erosion, in some cases with occasional gullies
- severe erosion, frequent gullies, or both
- mountain tops, mesas, canyons, other badlands

Progress Administration) tackled the problem of aid for the unemployed. In Hopkins' view the solution lay in "work relief" rather than in "doles"—that is, in jobs rather than in cash handouts. Though the work-relief program led to a certain amount of made work, known invidiously as "boondoggling," it also built roads, airports, and schools, improved parks and waterways, produced plays and concerts, maps and guidebooks, and sustained the morale and preserved the skills of millions of Americans unable through no fault of their own to find private employment. Where Hopkins' WPA specialized in light public works, Ickes' Public Works Administration concentrated on heavy and durable projects, ranging from dams and bridges to irrigation projects and aircraft carriers. The activities of PWA not only stimulated the national economy but permanently improved the national estate in a great variety of ways.

Another measure of the Hundred Days linked work relief to the conservation of natural resources. This was the Civilian Conservation Corps, an organization that recruited young men between the ages of eighteen and twenty-five to work in the countryside. CCC camps were set up in all parts of the country, and CCC boys played a useful role in protecting and developing reservoirs, watersheds, forests, and parks. Roosevelt himself had been deeply interested in conservation since the days of Theodore Roosevelt and Gifford Pinchot; and the dust storms of the early thirties, whirling up from the parched and eroded land of the Great Plains, emphasized the urgent need for a revitalized national conservation policy. A "shelterbelt" of trees was planted along the one hundredth meridian from Canada to Texas; other measures were undertaken to promote reforestation, to control overgrazing and to encourage farmers to plant soil-improving crops and adopt other soil conservation practices.

In some respects the most striking innovation of the Hundred Days was an effort to rescue

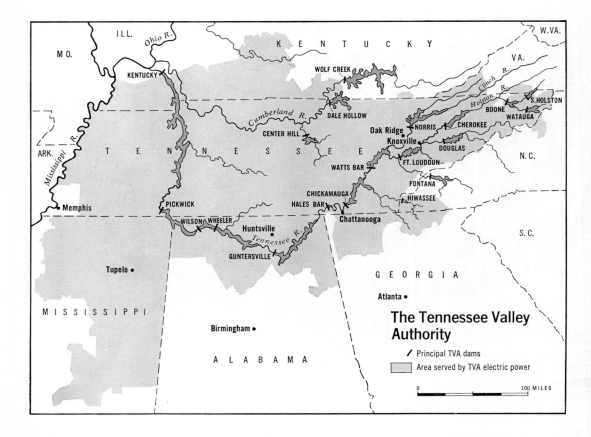

The Tennessee Valley Authority

/ Principal TVA dams

▨ Area served by TVA electric power

0   100 MILES

nothing less than an entire region. The Tennessee Valley was a conspicuous example of what later generations would know as an "underdeveloped" territory. Recurrent floods washed away the topsoil; the forests were thin and overcut; income was less than half the national average; in the highland counties, over half the families were on relief. Only two out of every hundred farms had electricity. Yet the Valley also contained one of the most valuable power sites in the country, at Muscle Shoals, Alabama; and some people, especially Senator George W. Norris of Nebraska, saw in cheap electric power the means of transforming life in the Valley. The disposition of Muscle Shoals had been a bitter issue in congressional politics since the First World War. Norris' bills providing for government operation of hydroelectric plants had fallen under the vetoes of Republican Presidents; Hoover in 1931 had angrily denounced the public power idea as "the negation of the ideals upon which

our civilization has been based."

Many factors converged in the Valley: not only electric power and conservation but fertilizer production, flood control, inland waterways and, above all, the hopeless cycle of human poverty. In a bold change of perspective, Roosevelt now saw all these elements as parts of a single problem. The answer, he believed, was not a collection of separate and unrelated reforms but multipurpose development under the direction of a single authority. In April 1933 he called on Congress to establish "a corporation clothed with the power of Government but possessed of the flexibility and initiative of a private enterprise" charged with "national planning for a complete river watershed."

Despite the opposition of the power companies of the area, whose executives claimed that the Valley already had all the power capacity it could absorb for years to come, Congress passed the bill establishing the

Tennessee Valley Authority in May 1933. The TVA proved to be one of the most dramatically successful of all New Deal undertakings. Seeking at every opportunity to win local collaboration under TVA director David E. Lilienthal's slogan of "grass-roots democracy," the TVA built dams and powerhouses, cleared the rivers, replenished the soil, rebuilt the forests, and brought the magic of electricity into the farthest corners of the Valley. The region vibrated with a new life and a new hope. Soon visitors came from all over the world to inspect the result. No other New Deal agency had such international impact.

The Struggle for Recovery

The Conquest of Fear The Hundred Days, wrote Arthur Krock of the New York *Times*, gave Washington the sensations of a man with a life-and-death appointment thousands of miles away who suddenly found himself switched from an ox-cart to an airplane. And throughout the nation the special session of 1933 induced a tremendous revival of confidence. In this revival, the personality of the President himself played a basic role. As late as the 1932 campaign, Franklin Roosevelt had still been a hazy figure. Now his speeches, his radio "fireside chats," his twice-a-week press conferences made him seem almost a constant presence in the homes of Americans who had suffered too long under presidential indifference. He radiated energy, decision, and good cheer; and his superb personal faith, along with the explosion of administrative inventiveness and political audacity in Washington, convinced the people that they had a chance to recover control of their economic destiny.

During 1933 Roosevelt enjoyed almost universal support. As the crisis receded, however, opposition began to emerge—first from the business community on Roosevelt's right, then in a clamor of discordant voices on his left. At the start his critics made little dent in his popularity. The congressional election of 1934 provided an almost unprecedented national endorsement of the President's program. The Administration actually increased its strength in both the House and the Senate, and, when the smoke cleared, the Republicans held the governorship in only seven states.

Roosevelt thus confronted the congressional session of 1935 with top-heavy majorities in both houses. But the policy momentum of 1933 had begun to slacken; full economic recovery still seemed distant; and the voices of criticism were now speaking out with new confidence. The American Liberty League, an organization formed in 1934 by a group of conservative businessmen and politicians, offered the most active opposition on the right. On the left the most powerful of the new leaders was Huey Long of Louisiana.

As governor of Louisiana, Long had brought new roads and schools and textbooks to the state; but the price for his impressive program of social improvement was spreading corruption and repression. By 1935 he ruled his native state almost as a dictator. In national politics, Long's role was more purely that of a demagogue. His "Share Our Wealth" movement had no serious theory or program. It was rather a means of stirring existing resentments over the maldistribution of wealth in the hope that the Kingfish, as Long fondly called himself, could be propelled into the presidency.

Another rising leader was a California physician, Dr. Francis E. Townsend, who proposed a two-hundred-dollar monthly pension for all over sixty-five. No group in the population save the Negroes had suffered more from the depression than the aged, and the Townsend Plan seemed for a while in 1935 to be developing genuine mass support. Both Long and Townsend were openly hostile to the New Deal. A third leader, Father Charles E. Coughlin, the famous "radio priest" of Royal Oak, Michigan, had originally endorsed Roosevelt and the New Deal but by 1935 was drifting into opposition. He established in that year the National Union for Social Justice, an organization that appealed especially to the Populist traditions of the Middle West and to the Irish Catholic masses of the great cities. Coughlin's particular nostrum was the nationalization of the banks.

Long, Townsend, and Coughlin were hawking competing patent medicines for the nation's economic ills. But they drew their following from much the same audience—baffled and disoriented members of the old-American lower middle class who were seeking attention

The Act establishes a compulsory retirement and pension system for all carriers subject to the Interstate Commerce Act.... The Act is invalid because several of its inseparable provisions contravene the due process of law clause of the Fifth Amendment.... The Act is not in purpose or effect a regulation of interstate commerce within the meaning of the Constitution....

The petitioners' sole reliance is the thesis that efficiency depends upon morale, and morale in turn upon assurance of security for the worker's old age. ... The question at once presents itself whether the fostering of a contented mind on the part of an employee by legislation of this type, is in any just sense a regulation of interstate transportation. If that question be answered in the affirmative, obviously there is no limit to the field of so-called regulation....

We feel bound to hold that a pension plan thus imposed is in no proper sense a regulation of the activity of interstate transportation. It is an attempt for social ends to impose by sheer fiat ... a means of assuring a particular class of employees against old age dependency.

From the Majority Opinion of the U.S. Supreme Court by Mr. Justice Owen J. Roberts, *Railroad Retirement Board* v. *Alton Railroad Co.*, 295 U.S. 300, 1935.

and protection. The emergence of these new movements signified a discontent which the President could hardly ignore.

The Second New Deal

Stalemate in 1935 Yet how was this discontent to be met? The bag of tricks of 1933 was now empty, and, though the policies of the Hundred Days had ended despair, they had not produced recovery. The gross national product, though nearly $20 billion larger than in 1933, was still $30 billion less than in 1929. Four million more workers were employed in 1935 than in 1933, but nine million were still unemployed. The New Deal had done remarkable things, especially in social reform, but the formula for full recovery evidently still eluded it. Roosevelt, in short, was still in economic trouble and, as the clamor of the demagogues and the fractiousness of the new Congress in the first months of 1935 made clear, might

well be in increasing political trouble. It grew more and more apparent that he needed a new forward thrust of policy if he was to maintain his control.

The Supreme Court further increased the pressure against the policies of 1933. For two years the Administration had delayed tests of the constitutionality of New Deal legislation; but at last the dam was breaking. Early in 1935 the Court invalidated a provision of the National Industrial Recovery Act prohibiting interstate shipment of "hot" oil—that is, oil produced in violation of production quotas fixed by state laws. A few weeks later, the gold resolution of 1933, one of the foundations of the nation's monetary policy, barely escaped judicial veto in a bitter and somewhat ambiguous five-to-four decision. Then the Court, in another five-to-four decision, declared against the whole idea of a federal pension act for railroad employees. And, on May 27, 1935, the celebrated "Black Monday" of New Deal annals, the Court in three sweeping decisions killed a farm mortgage relief act, rebuked the President for what it declared to be an illegal exercise of his removal power, and condemned the entire National Industrial Recovery Act as unconstitutional.

The NRA case, irreverently known as the "sick chicken" case, involved some Brooklyn poultry dealers, the Schechter brothers, who had been charged with violations of the Live Poultry Code. The Court pronounced unanimously against the Recovery Act on two grounds: that it delegated excessive powers to the executive, and that it ascribed to Congress powers of economic regulation which could not be justified under the commerce clause. This second objection was particularly devastating. The language used in the decision seemed to say that the Court regarded mining, manufacturing, agriculture, and construction as "essentially local" activities. In a press conference a few days later, Roosevelt called the action of the Court "more important than any decision probably since the Dred Scott case." He concluded, "We have been relegated to the horse-and-buggy definition of interstate commerce."

New Directions in Policy In invalidating the NRA, the Supreme Court knocked out the keystone of the early New Deal experiment in national planning. Moreover, the Court's action came at a time when Roosevelt himself was perhaps losing faith in the efficacy of national planning, and when the New Dealers most identified with the planning idea were beginning to lose their political usefulness. Roosevelt had little choice now but to seek new ideas and new men. Always the activist, he turned to those best prepared to offer him a convincing program of action. He found this program in the Brandeis-Frankfurter group (see p. 651).

During the Hundred Days, the neo-Brandeisians, with their desire to "plan for competition," had played a subordinate though hardly negligible role. They contributed to the enactment of two important laws: the Securities Act of 1933, requiring full disclosure of relevant information in the issuance of new securities; and the Glass-Steagall Banking Act, providing for the separation of commercial and investment banking. But they disapproved of the main direction of 1933 as embodied in the NRA, rejecting both the philosophy of irreversible economic concentration on which it was based and the program of national planning to which it led. During 1934 the neo-Brandeisians moved a little more to the forefront. Two members of the group in particular, Thomas G. Corcoran and Benjamin V. Cohen, revealed exceptional skill as legislative draftsmen and congressional persuaders. They wrote the Securities Exchange Act of 1934 which carried the fight against deceit and scandal in the securities market a further step by establishing new standards of behavior and a new agency—the Securities and Exchange Commission—to enforce them. In 1935, when Roosevelt was groping for a new program, he found the Brandeis-Frankfurter group overflowing with ideas.

The President's support in February of a bill to deconcentrate public utility holding companies demonstrated a growing interest in the idea of breaking up big business instead of accepting it as an economic necessity. Roosevelt was still unwilling for some months to move unequivocally along the new lines, but the mounting hostility of business and the Court's condemnation of the NRA cut his remaining ties with the Hundred Days. Thereafter Roosevelt shook off his indecision and

The Scope of Congressional Power: A Permissive View

I am unable to concur in the decision of this case. The gravest aspect of the decision is that it does not rest simply upon a condemnation of particular features of the Railroad Retirement Act, but denies to Congress the power to pass any compulsory pension act for railroad employees....

The fundamental consideration which supports this type of legislation is that industry should take care of its human wastage, whether that is due to accident or age. That view cannot be dismissed as arbitrary or capricious. It is a reasoned conviction based upon abundant experience. The expression of that conviction in law is regulation. When expressed in the government of interstate carriers, with respect to their employees likewise engaged in interstate commerce, it is a regulation of that commerce....

The power committed to Congress to govern interstate commerce does not require that its government should be wise, much less that it should be perfect. The power implies a broad discretion and thus permits a wide range even of mistakes.

From the Minority Opinion of the U.S. Supreme Court by Chief Justice Charles E. Hughes, *Railroad Retirement Board* v. *Alton Railroad Co.*, 295 U.S. 300, 1935.

moved boldly ahead on neo-Brandeisian principles. In a message to Congress on June 19, 1935, calling for a new tax law, the President committed himself to the view that "without . . . small enterprises our competitive economic society would cease. Size begets monopoly." The New Deal had abandoned the faith in "concentration and control" and was moving into a new phase.

With the revival of Roosevelt's leadership, the 1935 session broke the log-jam that had blocked action for months. The result was a program of legislative achievement surpassed only by the Hundred Days itself. A new $4.8 billion relief bill, establishing the Works Progress Administration, had already passed in April. But the elimination of the NRA had created an urgent need for new laws continuing elements of the NRA program. Thus the Wagner Labor Relations Act replaced Section 7a of the National Industrial Recovery Act; by giving new authority to the National Labor Relations Board, the Wagner Act provided more reliable guarantees for collective bargaining. The Public Contracts Act applied NRA wage and hour standards to firms doing business with the federal government. The Guffey Coal Act tried to put the NRA Coal Code into constitutional form. No one could be sure whether these laws would survive the Supreme Court, though they had been drawn up to avoid the more obvious defects of the National Industrial Recovery Act.

Most important of all, the Congress passed in August the Social Security Act, setting up the Social Security Board to operate both a national plan of contributory old-age and survivors insurance and a federal-state plan of unemployment compensation. Both programs were of inestimable importance in providing men and women a measure of protection against hazards and vicissitudes beyond their control. They laid the basis for what later was to be termed the "welfare state." In addition, the Social Security Act, along with other measures of the session, helped further to consolidate the political alliance between the New Deal and organized labor.

Other acts of the 1935 session were designed to restore competition to the economy. The Public Utilities Holding Company Act, passed in late August after weeks of violent altercation and high-pressure lobbying, struck at financial concentration in public utilities, especially at the exaggerated development of holding companies, which had so often arisen in response, not to the needs of efficient operation, but to the desire for financial gain. The much disputed "death sentence" provision limited each holding company after 1938 to a single integrated public utility system unless it could make a convincing economic case for holding more than one system. The tax law of 1935, with its substitution of a graduated for a uniform corporation income tax, sought to discriminate in favor of small business. And the Banking Act of 1935, by giving the Federal Reserve Board control over "open-market operations"—that is, the purchase or sale of government securities in order to enlarge or contract the base of the money supply— greatly reduced the power of private bankers over the money market.

The Philosophy of the Second New Deal
The First and Second New Deals shared the same broad objectives. Both aimed at economic recovery and social reform. They diverged somewhat in their ideas and methods, partly as a consequence of the change in national mood between 1933 and 1935. The desperation of 1933 seemed to demand sweeping economic measures; at the same time, it produced a large measure of political unity. The partial recovery of 1935 increased political disunity and decreased the desire for radical economic change.

Consequently the Second New Deal was economically more conservative but politically more radical than the First. It was economically more conservative in the sense that, while the First New Deal had accepted the logic of the administered market and tried to invent new institutions to do what competition had once done to keep the economy in balance, the Second New Deal revived the classical model of a freely competitive market as the objective or policy. It was politically more radical in the sense that, while the First New Deal had sought government-business cooperation to achieve national objectives, the Second New Deal, persuaded that free competition could be restored only through rigorous government enforcement of the rules of the competitive game, was zestfully antibusiness in rhetoric. If "a concentration of private power without equal in history" was the great menace to the American economy, as Roosevelt told Congress in 1938, if "private enterprise is ceasing to be free enterprise and is becoming a cluster of private collectivisms," then the way out was a program "to stop the progress of collectivism in business and turn business back to the democratic competitive order." His basic thesis, Roosevelt said, was "not that the system of free enterprise for profit has failed in this generation, but that it has not yet been tried." In 1938 the antimonopoly drive picked up new speed with the appointment of Thurman Arnold as head of the Antitrust Division of the Department of Justice and with the establishment of the Temporary National Economic Committee to survey the concentration of economic power.

The fight against economic concentration, however, constituted only part of the Second New Deal. The First New Deal had offered programs for both reform and recovery; the

Second New Deal was, at the start, just a program of reform. But a new philosophy of recovery through the use of the federal budget was beginning to emerge within the Administration. The chief spokesman for this new view was Marriner Eccles of the Federal Reserve Board, who contended that, when the decline of private spending brought about a depression, it was the obligation of government to offset the decline by increasing public spending. Eccles felt that the deliberate creation of compensatory government deficits would stimulate capital formation and purchasing power until the consequent rise in national income produced enough revenue to bring the budget once again into balance. In 1935 these ideas were still tentative and unorthodox, even among New Dealers. The New Deal was spending large sums, true enough, and it was running budgetary deficits (the largest in the prewar years was $4.5 billion, in 1936); but it was doing these things in response to conditions, not to theories. In 1936 the English economist John Maynard (later Lord) Keynes gave this approach its first extended theoretical justification in his influential book, *General Theory of Employment.* The Second New Dealers found Keynesian ideas increasingly congenial, and the alliance with the compensatory spenders was decisive in the final evolution of New Deal policies.

The 1936 Election

The Estrangement of Business The emergence of big government and big labor in the early thirties meant that the business community no longer enjoyed unchallenged primacy in American society. Resentment over loss of status, resentment over government regulation, resentment over uncertainty and strain—all these emotions, joined in many cases to a sincere conviction that the New Deal was a first step toward a totalitarian state, gradually produced among businessmen a state of open and bitter opposition to the Roosevelt Administration. The attitude of the Supreme Court seemed to validate the notion that the New Deal was using unconstitutional means to achieve unconstitutional objectives. When the Court returned in 1936 to its assault on the New Deal—vetoing the Agricultural

Adjustment Act in January, the Guffey Coal Act and the Municipal Bankruptcy Act in May, and a New York minimum wage law in June—its actions deepened convictions on both sides that an impassable gulf existed between the America of individualism and the America of reform. Hoover denounced the New Deal as an attack on "the whole philosophy of individual liberty." His Secretary of the Treasury, Ogden Mills, said, "We have to turn back many centuries to the days of absolute autocrats to find so great a power over the lives of millions of men lodged in the hands of a single fallible being." The family of J. P. Morgan told visitors not to mention Roosevelt's name in his presence lest it excite his blood pressure. Some conservatives began to trace the New Deal to subversive foreign ideas—to fascism or, more generally and fashionably, to communism. At the height of the holding company fight, and on occasion thereafter, rumors were even put into circulation that Roosevelt was a madman given to wild bursts of maniacal laughter.

The 1936 Campaign The "hate-Roosevelt" feeling, the conviction that the New Deal represented the end of the American way of life, permeated the conservative wing of the Republican party. Other Republicans, however, recognizing the hard fact of Roosevelt's popularity and, in many cases, agreeing with his policies, opposed Hoover's notion of making the 1936 campaign an all-out fight against the New Deal. This view prevailed in the Republican convention of 1936. The Republicans nominated Governor Alfred M. Landon of Kansas, a former Bull Moose Progressive, who, while conservative on matters of public finance, had shown himself tolerant of many aspects of the New Deal and distinctly liberal on questions of social reform. Frank Knox, a newspaper publisher from Chicago, was chosen as Landon's running mate. The Democrats meanwhile renominated Roosevelt and Garner. The forces of Coughlin, Townsend, and Long (Long himself had been assassinated in September 1935) coalesced in the Union party and nominated Congressman William Lemke of North Dakota for the presidency.

At the start Landon took a moderate line, accepting New Deal objectives but arguing that only the Republican party could achieve them economically and constitutionally. In the later stages of the campaign, however, he found himself making more and more extreme accusations against the Roosevelt Administration until in the end his line was almost indistinguishable from Hoover's. In a moment of last-minute desperation the Republican high command even decided to make an issue of the social security program, which was due to go into effect on January 1, 1937. The Social Security Act, declared Frank Knox, "puts half the working people of America under federal control." The Republican National Chairman said that every worker would have to wear metal dog-tags carrying his social security number.

Such efforts were unavailing. Roosevelt conducted his campaign in a mood of buoyant confidence. He was aware, however, of the bitterness of feeling against him; and, in indignation over the social security panic, he gave vent to bitterness of his own before the campaign was over. "Never before in all our history have these forces [of selfishness and greed] been so united against one candidate as they stand today," he said. "They are unanimous in their hate for me—and I welcome their hatred." The election revealed that the attacks on Roosevelt and the New Deal had made little impression on the voters. In a victory without precedent in American politics, Roosevelt carried every state except Maine and Vermont. The Republicans were routed, and the Union party sank without a trace. William Allen White, the great country editor from Emporia, Kansas, wrote, "The water of liberalism has been dammed up for forty years by the two major parties. The dam is out. Landon went down the creek in the torrent."

The Supreme Court Fight

The Court Versus the New Deal   Roosevelt opened his second administration by issuing a vigorous call for an extension of the New Deal. "I see one-third of a nation illhoused, ill-clad, ill-nourished," he said in his inaugural address. But he faced a formidable roadblock in his determination to push ahead his reform program. That roadblock was the Supreme Court. By the end of its 1936 term the Court had heard nine cases involving New

Deal legislation. In seven of these cases a majority of the Court had found the legislation unconstitutional, though three verdicts of unconstitutionality were by the narrow margin of five to four and two more by six to three. In addition, the Court, having in 1923 (*Adkins* v. *Children's Hospital*) denied the federal government power to set minimum wages, had now denied that power to the state of New York, thereby apparently saying that no power existed in the United States to outlaw the sweatshop.

So sustained and devastating a use of the judicial veto to kill social and economic legislation was without precedent. Moreover, the minority, which in several cases had affirmed its belief in the constitutionality of the disputed laws, comprised by far the more distinguished members of the Court—Louis D. Brandeis, Benjamin N. Cardozo, Harlan F. Stone, and, on occasion, Chief Justice Charles Evans Hughes. "Courts are not the only agency of government that must be assumed to have a capacity to govern," Stone had warned his conservative brethren in the AAA case. He added: "While unconstitutional exercise of power by the executive and legislative branches of the government is subject to judicial restraint, the only check upon our own exercise of power is our own sense of self-restraint." The record of 1935–36 gave Roosevelt no hope that this check would be effective.

The whole future of the New Deal appeared to hang in balance. Such laws as the Social Security Act, the Wagner Act, and the Holding Company Act seemed the next candidates for execution by the Court. And, so long as the majority's narrow reading of the Constitution prevailed, there was little chance that the New Deal could take further steps to meet the problems of the forgotten third of a nation. During 1936 Roosevelt and his Attorney General, Homer Cummings of Connecticut, came to feel that, before anything else could be done, something had to be done about the Court. They considered and then dismissed the idea of a constitutional amendment, partly because of the difficulties of the ratification process, partly because the amendment itself would be at the mercy of judicial interpretation. In any case, the trouble seemed to lie, not with the Constitution, which they regarded as a spacious charter of government, but with the Court majority. They concluded that the best solution would be to do something directly about the personnel of the Court.

"Packing" the Supreme Court In February 1937 Roosevelt sent a message to Congress calling for the reorganization of the federal judiciary. He contended that the Supreme Court could not keep up with its work burden, and that the interests of efficient administration required the appointment of an additional justice for each justice aged seventy or over. The argument about overcrowded dockets was disingenuous and gave the Court plan an air of overslickness from which it never recovered. Chief Justice Hughes was soon able to demonstrate that the Court had, in fact, been keeping abreast of its responsibilities. In two speeches in March, Roosevelt tried to wrench the debate back to the real issue. The Court, he said, had "cast doubts on the ability of the elected Congress to protect us against catastrophe by meeting squarely our modern social and economic conditions." His object was "to save the Constitution from the Court and the Court from itself." But it was too late. The protest against the measure was now too great to be easily diverted.

Those who had disliked the New Deal from the start found in the Court plan verification of their claim that Roosevelt was trying to destroy the American system. And many who had supported the New Deal were genuinely shocked both by the idea of "packing" the Court and by Roosevelt's circuitous approach to his objective. The proposal set in motion a bitter national debate. In Congress the Republicans held back and allowed dissident Democrats to lead the fight against the President. The measure might have carried in some form, however, had not the Court itself suddenly changed its attitude toward New Deal legislation. On March 29, 1937, the Court in effect reversed its decision of 1936 and affirmed the constitutionality of a Washington minimum wage law. Two weeks later it sustained the Wagner Act. Plainly the Court majority had abandoned the narrow ground of 1935-36; in Robert H. Jackson's phrase, it had retreated to the Constitution. The way had apparently been cleared for the New Deal without the appointment of a single new justice. And the resignation of one of the conservative justices in June, giving the President his first Supreme Court appointment, made his plan of enlarging the Court seem less necessary than ever. The bill was defeated, though Roosevelt could later claim with some justice that, if he had lost the battle, he had won the war.

Social and Economic Crises

The Rise of the CIO The Court battle had struck a blow at Roosevelt's prestige and at the unity of the Democratic party. And the surging militance of organized labor was creating new problems. The NRA had given the trade union movement its first impetus to mass organization since the First World War. Under the leadership of John L. Lewis and the United Mine Workers, a great campaign had begun in 1933 to organize the unorganized in the mass-production industries. This campaign soon led to a major conflict within the labor movement itself. The American Federation of Labor was dominated by craft unions; under the craft theory, the automobile industry, for example, was to be organized, not by a single union, but by as many different unions

John L. Lewis: United Mine Worker.

Auto Workers' sit-down, Flint, Michigan, 1937.

as there were different crafts involved in making a car. But Lewis, as head of one of the few industrial unions in the AFL, thought instinctively in terms of organization, not by craft, but by industry. Moreover, craft unionism had signally failed to organize the basic industries, to which industrial unionism seemed peculiarly adapted. The consequence was a fight within the AFL between craft unionism and industrial unionism, culminating in the expulsion of Lewis and his associates in 1936 and their formation of a rival labor federation, the Congress of Industrial Organizations.

The CIO came into existence at a time when workers throughout the country, especially in the mass-production industries, were hungering for organization in unions of their own choosing. The spontaneous character of the labor uprising was shown in 1936 and 1937 by the development of a new strike technique, frowned upon by national labor leadership—the "sit-down strike," in which workers sat down by their machines in factories and refused to work until employers would concede them the right of collective bargaining. To many employers, the sit-down strike threatened property rights and smacked of revolution; its vogue led them to fight all the more

savagely against any recognition of national unions as bargaining agents.

But the CIO pushed its organizing campaigns ahead vigorously, especially in automobiles and steel. There were shocking moments of violence. In May police shot and killed ten pickets outside the Republic Steel plant in Chicago in what became known as the Memorial Day massacre. In Detroit Walter Reuther and other leaders of the United Automobile Workers were brutally beaten by company guards at Henry Ford's River Rouge plant. But the decision of General Motors to negotiate with the UAW in February 1937 and of United States Steel to negotiate with the Steel Workers Organizing Committee in March meant the beginning of the end. The battle for collective bargaining was substantially won. Union membership, which had been less than 3 million in 1933 and barely over 4 million at the start of 1937, grew to 7.2 million by the end of the year and to 9 million by 1939.

The Recession of 1937–38 The years 1935 and 1936 had been ones of steady economic improvement. So marked was the trend toward recovery that leading bankers began to raise the panic cry of inflation, though resources and labor were still widely underemployed. Under pressure from the bankers,

A Case
for a Balanced Budget

Let me say at the outset that I never objected to spending money when the alternative would have been human suffering.... But I did feel that, in a capitalist economy, recovery had to depend basically on private business. I wanted to see a free enterprise economy as flourishing as the twenties but operating more soundly and more equitably. It seemed vital to me that the government try sincerely to build a feeling of confidence in its financial operations so that businessmen would be encouraged to take over their proper role of invigorating the economy. I did not believe in the notion that a large, permanent deficit was necessary to "compensate" for inadequacies of private investment or for deficiencies of private purchasing power....

Business conditions had continued to improve in 1935 and 1936 and I had decided that the time had come to make an all-out attempt to get the budget balanced—to give business and agriculture a chance to create jobs on their own.... This was the moment, it seemed to me, to strip off the bandages, throw away the crutches and see if American private enterprise could stand on its own feet.

From Henry Morgenthau, Jr., "The Fight to Balance the Budget," *Collier's*, 1947.

the Federal Reserve Board tried to put on the brakes by raising reserve requirements in 1936 and 1937. This action had some effect. But it was less significant in arresting the upward swing than the decline between 1936 and 1937 in the federal government's net contribution to the economy. In 1936 the payment of the veterans' bonus of $1.7 billion on top of relief and public works expenditures and the normal costs of government resulted in a net government contribution of $4.1 billion. In 1937 several factors—the collection of taxes under the Social Security Act as well as the attempt to reduce public spending and to move toward a balanced budget—resulted in a decrease of the net government contribution to $800 million, a drop of $3.3 billion in a single year. Private business spending was unable to fill the gap created by the contraction of public spending.

The collapse in the months after September 1937 was actually more severe than it had been in the first nine months of the depression (or, indeed, than in any other period in American history for which statistics are available). National income fell 13 per cent, payrolls 35 per cent, durable goods production 50 per cent, profits 78 per cent. The increase in unemployment reproduced scenes of the early depression and imposed new burdens on the relief agencies.

The recession brought to a head a policy debate within the Administration. One group, led by Henry Morgenthau, Jr., the Secretary of the Treasury, had supported the policy of government retrenchment and favored balancing the budget as soon as practicable. Another group, led by Hopkins of the WPA and Eccles of the Federal Reserve Board, urged the immediate resumption of public spending. Roosevelt himself inclined for a while to the first group; but, as the downward slide speeded up, he reluctantly accepted the necessity for spending. In March 1938 a new spending program was announced. In a short time, this program began to reverse the decline, and by 1939 the

A Case
for Countercyclical Spending

An unbalanced budget, I began to argue, was not an independent condition created by a government decision. It reflected a deep-seated unbalance in the economy, and it was the economy that first had to be balanced, and its governmental bookkeeping effects secondarily. A policy of adequate governmental outlays at a time when private enterprise is curtailing its expenditures does not reflect a preference for an unbalanced budget. It merely reflects a desire and the need to put idle men, money, and material to work....

It was misleading to talk about the federal government as though it were an individual, a family, a corporation, a city, or a state.... Unless their outgo balances their income, they ultimately go broke. But the federal government is in a different category. To begin with, it can make and change the rules of the game according to the needs of the nation. It alone has the power to issue money and credit and thus influence the price structure. Through its power of taxation it has the means to control the accumulation and distribution of wealth-production. And, finally, it has the power to mobilize the resources of the whole nation for the benefit of all the people in it.

From Marriner S. Eccles, *Beckoning Frontiers: Public and Personal Recollections*, 1951.

gross national product was larger than in 1937. The recession, however, killed Roosevelt's hope of attaining full economic recovery before the end of his second term.

1938 and the Purge The Court fight, the new aggressiveness of organized labor, and the resumption of the spending policy all tended to widen the gap between the liberal and the conservative wings of the Democratic party. The liberals were mostly Northerners, the conservatives mostly Southerners, and other events of 1938 hastened the alienation of the Bourbon Democrats from the New Deal. Southern employers were bitterly opposed to the Administration's Fair Labor Standards (or Wages and Hours) Act, which was finally passed in June 1938; they objected that its policy of setting minimum wages and maximum hours and outlawing child labor would increase labor costs. Southern planters were equally bitter against the Farm Security Administration and its activities on behalf of tenant farmers and sharecroppers. The release in August 1938 of a government report on economic conditions in the South and Roosevelt's description of the South as "the nation's No. 1 economic problem," seemed to express a determination to extend the New Deal into the South. Conservative Democrats in Congress prepared to resist; and the alliance between Southern Democrats and Northern Republicans, tentatively initiated in 1937 during the Supreme Court fight, began to harden in 1938 into a major obstacle to further New Deal legislation. The House Committee on Un-American Activities, dedicated under the chairmanship of Martin Dies of Texas to the harrying of radicals in and out of government, became an instrument of conservative retaliation against the New Deal.

The defection of the Southern conservatives raised difficult problems for the Administration. Roosevelt felt that many conservative Democrats had taken a free ride on the popularity of the New Deal; their refusal to support liberal policies, in his judgment, served to blur essential distinctions in American politics. "An election cannot give a country a firm sense of direction," he said in June 1938, "if it has two or more national parties which merely have different names but are as alike in their principles and aims as peas in the same pod."

Accordingly he decided to make the New Deal itself an issue in the Democratic primary elections. In August he began to intervene personally in state primaries in the hope of replacing anti-New Deal Democratic senators and congressmen with liberals. Such intervention was a striking departure from precedent, and his opponents were quick to denounce it as a "purge." The almost complete failure of Roosevelt's efforts was a prelude to Administration setbacks in the general election: the Republicans gained seven seats in the Senate and eighty in the House.

The year 1938 marked the end of the forward thrust of the New Deal. The public demand for reform seemed to be slackening, and the drift toward war in Europe was leading both the President and the people to shift their attention to foreign policy. In his state-of-the-union message in January 1939 Roosevelt spoke significantly of the need "to invigorate the processes of recovery in order to *preserve* our reforms."

The American People in the Depression

The Trauma of Depression The depression had been a severe shock to the American people—to their expectations, their values, and their confidence in themselves and their future. Mute evidence of a declining faith in their prospects was the sudden slowdown of the marriage and birth rates. Population grew at a rate of less than a million a year; the total population increase (to 131.7 million in 1940) was hardly more than half that of the preceding decade. In 1938 there were 1.6 million fewer children under ten than there had been five years before. With the increase in life expectancy (from fifty-six in 1920 to sixty-four in 1940), the proportion of people over sixty-five increased from 5.4 per cent in 1930 to 6.9 per cent in 1940. In the perspective of depression, America began to look like an aging country, its population growth slowing to a stop, its future limited. The demographic trend led economic theorists to argue that the nation had reached "economic maturity" and that it could not hope to resume growth without aggressive government intervention.

Americans brought up in the tradition of the

bright future and the happy ending found it hard to adjust to bread lines, government relief, and mass unemployment. Some fell into listlessness and apathy. Others, unwilling to concede that the old story had come to an end, flocked behind one or another of the social demagogues with their promises of miraculous deliverance. A few believed that depression was an inherent and ineradicable evil of the capitalist system and concluded that the only way out was to abolish capitalism.

Some of these, excited by the success of fascism in Italy and Germany, formed fascist groups, bearing such names as the Silver Shirts. In a vivid novel, *It Can't Happen Here*, Sinclair Lewis showed how a 100 per cent American fascist movement could take over the United States. But, though the American fascists diligently imitated many of the Nazi techniques and appeals (including anti-Semitism), they had little impact on American life.

More of those who despaired of capitalism turned toward Marxism. In 1932 just under a million Americans voted against the capitalist system. Most of the votes went to the Socialist party, a reformist group under the appealing leadership of Norman Thomas; but over one hundred thousand voted for the Communist ticket. The communist movement, the more serious and menacing of the two, was controlled by a hard core of disciplined conspirators, faithfully conforming to the turns and twists of the party line laid down in Moscow. Not all those who joined the party, however, were aware of its conspiratorial nature. At one time or another during the decade, a large number of people passed rather quickly through the movement, attracted at first by the apparent idealism of communist promises but soon bored by the sectarian dogmatism of communist analysis or repelled by the ruthless dishonesty of communist performance. Secret communists had some success in penetrating certain labor unions and even a few government offices.

The Shake-up of the People   If depression induced despair, it also compelled change. In particular, it discredited and disrupted the structure of status and prestige which had ruled the United States in the twenties. The businessman had been the culture hero of the prosperity decade. In 1929 his New Era had

exploded in his face. In the thirties his pretensions to wisdom were derided, his leadership rejected, and he himself often dismissed as a fool if not a crook. A midget perched impudently on the knee of the mighty J. P. Morgan at a congressional investigation became the symbol of the new skepticism about men of wealth.

People from outside the business community—especially politicians and intellectuals—were now in power. Still smarting from their own sense of inferior status in the twenties, they often took undue pleasure in rubbing the nose of the once-arrogant businessman in the mess he had helped to create. And in their wake came a rush of the "forgotten men" of America for status—men who had been denied opportunities in the past because of their class or ethnic origin. The New Deal, by revising the structure of status, brought about both a social and an ethnic revolution.

The Social Revolution   Organized labor's rise to respectability typified the tendencies of the decade. In 1933 the presidents of the six great steel companies blanched and fled when Secretary of Labor Frances Perkins proposed to introduce them to William Green of the American Federation of Labor for a discussion of the NRA steel code. Four years later, when United States Steel signed up with the CIO, labor had achieved substantial recognition. The business community had gradually accepted the right of other groups to participate in national economic decisions. Even though the depression continued to restrict economic opportunity, members of once marginal groups—not only wage-earners but tenant farmers, sharecroppers, old folks, and even intellectuals and women—now had unprecedented chances for fulfilled lives.

The social revolution also enhanced the quality of life, particularly in the countryside. Though the Supreme Court knocked out the original AAA in 1936, the principle of national responsibility for the agricultural economy had been established, and the government continued its programs of agricultural assistance and control in other forms. No other federal agency had such an impact on the quality of country life as did the Rural Electrification Administration. When it was founded in 1935, only about one farm in ten had power-line

Migratory workers: The grapes of wrath.

electric service, and these were mostly in the neighborhood of towns or cities. Through low-interest loans to rural cooperatives, the REA enabled farmers to build their own power lines and generate their own electricity. The spread of electricity transformed the countryside.

While the price support and rural electrification programs made life far more tolerable for commercial farmers, they left untouched wide areas of rural poverty, especially among subsistence farmers. Toward the end of the decade, poor farmers and agricultural workers displaced by changes in agricultural technology began to head west in a pathetic search for new employment. John Steinbeck's *The Grapes of Wrath* (1939) offered a memorable picture of the exodus of the "Okies" (from Oklahoma) and the "Arkies" (from Arkansas). This migration was part of a general westward shift of people which resulted, for example, in the near doubling of the population of California between 1920 and 1940. In time and with economic recovery, most of the migrants were absorbed in the new communities.

The Ethnic Revolution   Immigration substantially stopped in the thirties (except for refugees from fascism toward the end of the

decade). The last wave of immigrants, mostly from southern and eastern Europe, in the earlier part of the century had not yet achieved full acceptance in American society; the upheaval of depression gave many Italians, Poles, South Slavs, and Jews unprecedented opportunities. Where craft unions, for example, had often discriminated against the "wops" and the "hunkies," as against the Negroes, the industrial unions of the CIO opened their doors to them. Similarly the New Deal gave them their first chance in politics and public service.

Roosevelt himself had no patience with the old-American attitude of superiority toward more recent immigrants. "Remember, remember always," he once told the Daughters of the American Revolution, "that all of us, and you and I especially, are descended from immigrants and revolutionists." Of the 214 federal judges appointed by Harding, Coolidge, and Hoover, only 8 were Catholics; of the 196 appointed by Roosevelt, 51 were Catholics. Political figures in the great cities, like Mayor Fiorello La Guardia of New York, acted as brokers in gaining recognition for ethnic minorities previously shut out from political preferment. Concurrently, there was a notable decline in the foreign-language press and a more effective assimilation of ethnic minorities into American life.

Most striking of all, perhaps, was the rise of the Negro, who for many years had been the victim of economic and political neglect. During the depression he was, in the phrase of the day, "the first man fired and the last man hired." And though he had voted Republican since the Civil War, the Republican administrations had shown little concern for his welfare; Negro leaders had denounced Hoover as "the man in the lily-White House." Roosevelt brought to Washington an unprecedented sympathy for Negro problems. New Deal agencies generally conformed to local folkways, but they made special efforts to help Negroes; Roosevelt himself repeatedly denounced lynching; and the Northern Democrats in the Senate took the initiative in sponsoring bills to make lynching a federal crime. By 1936 Negro voters had begun to shift to the Democratic party.

The Recovery of American Faith   The release of energy brought about by the New Deal, the invigorating sense that the "forgotten man" was not forgotten and could still make a place for himself in American life—all this gradually began to heal the trauma of depression. The million votes cast against the capitalist system in 1932 dwindled to 275,000 in 1936 and to 145,000 in 1940. The image of America as an exhausted nation, impotent before the challenge of mass unemployment, gave way to the image of a purposeful and idealistic society, capable of meeting its problems with energy and conviction.

In the twenties, the intellectuals who scorned the American present had turned to "debunking" the American past. In the thirties, when the American present was acquiring purpose and dignity, they saw purpose and dignity throughout American history. The title of John Dos Passos' book *The Ground We Stand On* (1941) summed up the new attitude toward the past. "In times of change and danger," Dos Passos wrote, "when there is a quicksand of fear under men's reasoning, a sense of continuity with generations gone before can stretch like a lifeline across the scary present." Other skeptics of the twenties joined Dos

Passos in taking a more affirmative view of American traditions. In *The Prodigal Parents* (1938) Sinclair Lewis transformed George F. Babbitt from a butt into a hero. Van Wyck Brooks, who had once seen American culture as pinched and sterile, now portrayed it in *The Flowering of New England* (1936) and succeeding volumes as rich and abundant. Even H. L. Mencken, though he took small comfort in the America of the thirties, dedicated his main energies to bringing up to date his loving study of *The American Language* and to writing his own nostalgic recollections of an earlier America. The publication of a number of important biographies—Carl Van Doren on Franklin, Marquis James on Jackson, Carl Sandburg on Lincoln, D. S. Freeman on Lee, Allan Nevins on Cleveland, Henry Pringle on Taft, Bernard De Voto on Mark Twain, Ralph Barton Perry on William James—helped meet the new national desire to repossess the past in all its solidity. This impulse came into happy conjunction with the New Deal in the valuable series of state guidebooks produced by the WPA.

The New Pattern of American Society   The recovery of American faith in the thirties both derived from and contributed to the capacity of the American people to reassert a measure of control over their social and economic destiny. In so doing, American society was striking out on its own in defiance of the prevailing ideologies of the day. Both laissez faire and Marxism were philosophies of economic determinism with exceedingly narrow views of social possibility. The New Deal, with all its improvisations, contradictions, sentimentalisms, and errors, did have the signal and decisive advantage of rejecting economic fatalism. By affirming a faith in intelligent experiment, it enormously expanded the range of social possibility and helped lead America toward a new society beyond classical capitalism and beyond classical socialism.

By Roosevelt's second term the essential pattern of the new society was complete. The American nation had renounced laissez faire without embracing socialism. Government had acquired the obligation to underwrite the economic and social health of the nation. The budget provided the means by which the government through the use of fiscal policy could compensate for a decline in private economic activity. The state had abandoned efforts at the direct control of industrial production, but industry had to accept ground rules covering minimum standards of life and labor, and the state continued to intervene to maintain, in some form or other, the free play of competition. Special areas of economic activity required more comprehensive government control—banking, transportation, public utilities, agriculture, oil. Human welfare was to be protected through various forms of public insurance. A collection of "built-in stabilizers" —minimum wages, unemployment compensation, farm price supports, social security payments—were to help secure the economy against future crashes like that of 1929.

Was a Middle Way Possible?   All these measures involved more government intervention in the economy than some had previously thought either government or the economy could stand. This was the critical question raised by the New Deal—whether a policy of limited and piecemeal government intervention in economic life was feasible; whether a mixed system was possible which gave the state power enough to assure economic and social security but still not so much as to create an all-powerful dictatorship.

To this question, doctrinaires on both right and left had returned a categorical *no* through the decade. Ogden Mills stated the issue with precision: "We can have a free country or a socialistic one. We cannot have both. Our economic system cannot be half free and half socialistic. . . . There is no middle ground between governing and being governed, between absolute sovereignty and liberty, between tyranny and freedom." Hoover himself was equally clear on the point: "Even partial regimentation cannot be made to work and still maintain live democratic institutions."

In such sentiments, at least, the critics of capitalism agreed enthusiastically with the conservatives. "Either the nation must put up with the confusions and miseries of an essentially unregulated capitalism," said a radical weekly in 1935, "or it must prepare to supersede capitalism with socialism. There is no longer a feasible middle course." The proponents of individualism and the proponents of collectivism agreed on this if on nothing else; no modified capitalism was possible, no mixed economy, no middle way between laissez faire and socialism. If that conclusion had turned out to be true, it would have had fateful consequences for the future of the world.

But the New Dealers cheerfully rejected the conclusion. They detested the mystique of either/or and believed that there was more on heaven and earth than could be found in any ideology. Roosevelt himself was the humane pragmatist par excellence. His aim was to steer between the extremes of individualism and statism by moving always, in a favorite phrase, "slightly to the left of center," avoiding alike "the revolution of radicalism and the revolution of conservatism." The profound New Deal faith in intelligence, compassion, and experiment demonstrated in the end that a managed capitalist order could combine personal freedom and economic growth. The decade of the New Deal, with all its confusion and recrimination, rekindled confidence in free society, not in America alone, but throughout the western world.

SUGGESTIONS
FOR READING

General

The most comprehensive account of the years from 1933 to 1937 is to be found in A. M. Schlesinger, Jr., *The Coming of the New Deal* (1959) and *The Politics of Upheaval* (1960). J. M. Burns, *Roosevelt: The Lion and the Fox* (1956), carries the story through 1940 and contains invaluable insights. Among the useful shorter accounts are Dixon Wecter, *The Age of the Great Depression* (1948), which emphasizes social history; D. W. Brogan, *The Era of Franklin D. Roosevelt* (1951), lively with a political focus; Dexter Perkins, *The New Age of Franklin Roosevelt* * (1957), a briefer account; and Basil Rauch, *History of the New Deal* (1944), which is detailed and fluent. John Gunther, *Roosevelt in Retrospect* * (1950), is vivid and sympathetic.

* Available in a paperback edition.

Memoirs and Biographies

Memoirs of the New Dealers and biographies based on their papers throw important light on Roosevelt and his problems. R. E. Sherwood, *Roosevelt and Hopkins* * (1948; rev. ed., 1950), provides an intimate view of an important friendship and a favorable account of relief policies. Frances Perkins, *The Roosevelt I Knew* (1946), is significant for its compassion; R. G. Tugwell, *The Democratic Roosevelt* (1957), for its retrospective reflections; *The Secret Diary of Harold L. Ickes*, 3 vols. (1953–54), for its gossip and atmosphere. On politics, two illuminating memoirs are J. A. Farley, *Behind the Ballots* (1938), and Edward Flynn, *You're the Boss* (1947). J. M. Blum, *From the Morgenthau Diaries* (1959), recounts in detail the activities of the Secretary of the Treasury, one of the President's influential advisers. H. S. Johnson, *The Blue Eagle* (1935), presents a contemporary view of the National Recovery Administration. There is a valuable contemporary critique of the early New Deal in Raymond Moley, *After Seven Years* (1939), and a sometimes critical retrospective narrative of significant economic policies in M. S. Eccles, *Beckoning Frontiers* (1951). Samuel Rosenman writes as a close counselor to the President in his *Working with Roosevelt* (1952). There is indispensable personal material in Eleanor Roosevelt, *This I Remember* * (1949). Though there is no useful edition of Roosevelt's private papers, one vital source for study of the man and his times is Samuel Rosenman, ed., *The Public Papers of Franklin D. Roosevelt*, 9 vols. (1938–50).

New Deal Political Thought

Students wishing to study New Deal political thought in the important works of the time should consult, as the text suggests, at least the following influential sources: A. A. Berle, Jr., and G. C. Means, *The Modern Corporation and Private Property* (1932), significant on economic concentration; M. S. Eccles, *Economic Balance and a Balanced Budget* (1940), significant on countercyclical spending; R. G. Tugwell, *The Battle for Democracy* (1935), and H. L. Ickes, *The New Democracy* (1934), both important on social goals and public planning, as is H. A. Wallace, *New Frontiers* (1934); and D. E. Lilienthal, *TVA* (rev. ed., 1953), on regional development.

Special Studies

The outstanding studies of the economic history of the 1930's include the analytical Thomas Wilson, *Fluctuations in Income and Employment* (1948); K. D. Roose, *Economics of Recession and Revival* (1954); and the more dated and rigid Broadus Mitchell, *Depression Decade* (1947). Also useful are the following more specialized works: R. E. Paul, *Taxation in the United States* (1954); J. E. Reeve, *Monetary Reform Movements* (1943); G. G. Johnson, Jr., *The Treasury and Monetary Policy* (1939); J. K. Galbraith and G. G. Johnson, Jr., *Economic Effects of Federal Works Expenditures, 1933–38* (1940); A. H. Hansen, *Full Recovery or Stagnation* (1938); and H. A. Millis and E. C. Brown, *From the Wagner Act to Taft-Hartley* (1950).

There is a lively contemporary account of social and intellectual currents in F. L. Allen, *Since Yesterday* * (1940), and there are stimulating retrospective essays in Isabel Leighton, ed., *The Aspirin Age* (1949). Two thoughtful studies of the appeal of communism, particularly to artists and intellectuals, are in Murray Kempton, *Part of Our Time* (1955), and Daniel Aaron, *Writers on the Left* (1961). For an alarmed and informed, as well as entertaining, contemporary assessment of the lunatic right, see R. G. Swing, *Forerunners of American Fascism* (1935).

Samuel Lubell, *The Future of American Politics* * (1952), identifies important political changes in the period. A. M. Bingham, *Insurgent America* (1935), describes the radical politics of the mid-thirties, and George Wolfskill, *The Revolt of the Conservatives* (1962), displays the reaction on the right. On the Supreme Court fight, four especially rewarding studies are R. H. Jackson, *The Struggle for Judicial Supremacy* (1941); A. T. Mason, *Harlan Fiske Stone* (1956); Joseph Alsop and Turner Catledge, *168 Days* (1938); and M. J. Pusey, *Charles Evans Hughes*, 2 vols. (1951). The same subject is treated by one of the masters of constitutional history, E. S. Corwin, in his *Twilight of the Supreme Court* (1934), *Court over Constitution* (1938), and *Constitutional Revolution, Ltd.* (rev. ed., 1946).

* Available in a paperback edition.

29

The Shadow of War

When Franklin D. Roosevelt became President in 1933, the American democracy was profoundly absorbed in its internal problems. After the crusade of 1917, the nation had quickly reverted to its traditional isolationism. The rejection of the League of Nations in 1919 marked the return to the prewar policy of eschewing foreign entanglements. The resurgence of economic nationalism in the twenties reinforced the determination of the Republican administrations to extirpate Wilsonian error and steer an independent American course. Though such gestures as the Kellogg-Briand Pact and the Stimson Doctrine (see pp. 621, 639) showed that the United States had not totally turned its back on the outside world, both were characterized by a naïve faith in moral suasion and a studied avoidance of political commitment. The coming of the depression completed the process of turning inward. In 1933 Colonel House, the old Wilsonian, could write, "We seem determined not to have a friendly power in the entire world, and in this I think we have succeeded."

Suggestions were multiplying, moreover, that the uneasy peace established after the First World War was in jeopardy. The evident intention of the Japanese Empire to expand onto the mainland of Asia filled others than Stimson with apprehension. Equally alarming was the growing militancy of Germany and the consequent renewal of tension in Europe. On January 30, 1933, thirty-three days before Roosevelt told Americans that they had nothing to fear but fear itself, Adolf Hitler became the new Chancellor of Germany. Nineteen days after Roosevelt's inauguration the *Reichstag* conferred dictatorial powers on the Nazi leader. The German *Führer*'s fanatical determination to revise the system established at Versailles in 1919 implied an ominous challenge to the whole postwar structure of international order.

Roosevelt and World Affairs

Preparation for Statesmanship Few American politicians could rival Roosevelt in the breadth of his world experience. Between 1885 and 1931 he had made thirteen trips to Europe, and, though he had never visited the Far East, family tradition—his maternal grandfather had been active in the China trade—gave him a vivid interest in Asia and especially in China. He had come of age, moreover, when the United States, under Theodore Roosevelt, was first beginning to recognize the responsibilities of world power. As a young man, he was greatly influenced, not only by the aggressive diplomacy of his presidential cousin, but by the strategic philosophy of Admiral Alfred T. Mahan.

His service under Woodrow Wilson as Assistant Secretary of the Navy gave him direct and varied experience in international affairs. Almost alone among the members of the Wilson Administration, he instantly perceived the

Reichstag, 1933: Roosevelt was convinced that Hitler meant war.

catastrophic implications of the events of the summer of 1914. While Wilson strove to maintain American neutrality, young Roosevelt made no secret of his desire to build up American naval power or of his passionate belief in the Allied cause. When America entered the war, he dealt effectively both with problems of economic mobilization at home and with problems of coalition strategy and diplomacy abroad.

But the war did more than give him a chance to apply the principles of strategy he had learned from Mahan. It placed those principles in a new setting. To Mahan, Roosevelt now added Wilson: the combination defined the framework of his own future philosophy of foreign policy. He became an ardent supporter of Wilson in his fight for the League, and he made the League a key issue in his campaign for the vice-presidency in 1920. He retained his sharp concern with the actualities of national power but now saw power in the context, not of nationalist self-assertion, but of international order. His approach to foreign policy thereafter represented a union of Mahan's realism and Wilson's idealism.

During the twenties Roosevelt opposed the drift toward isolationism and moralism in foreign affairs. He condemned the Republican tariff policy, derided the pretensions of the Kellogg Pact, and constantly pleaded the case for international collaboration. "If the World War showed anything more than another," he said, "it showed the American people the futility of imagining that they could live in smug content their own lives in their own way while the rest of the world burned in the conflagration of war." But, as depression accentuated the isolationist mood after 1929, Roosevelt moved somewhat with the prevailing winds. As candidate for the Democratic nomination in 1932, he announced that in existing circumstances he no longer favored American participation in the League.

The Roosevelt Style in Foreign Policy At bottom, however, Roosevelt retained faith in internationalism. He signalized this by naming as Secretary of State Cordell Hull, an unregenerate Wilsonian and low-tariff man. "In pure theory," he once wrote Hull, "you and I think alike but every once in a while we have to modify principle to meet a hard and disagreeable fact!" Roosevelt was far more ready than Hull to temper the internationalist creed, but he respected his Secretary of State's capacity to recall him to the true faith.

Toward the State Department itself, Roosevelt's attitude was one of disdain mingled with a certain mistrust. He instinctively understood the problems of military as of political leaders, but he was often impatient with the professional diplomat and his rules and prejudices. Foreign-service officers, he tended to believe, represented a narrow social group and knew little of American life.

This attitude molded his own style in foreign affairs. His conduct of foreign policy was marked by imagination, insight, and also a certain dilettantism and insouciance. He remained the brilliant amateur, better in the main than the professionals, bolder, more creative, more compelling, but often deficient in steadiness and follow-through. Given this attitude, he tended toward personal diplomacy. He used personal agents and emissaries to bypass the professionals, and his basic faith, not always realizable in practice in these early years, was in direct negotiation among heads of state.

Uniting the Western Hemisphere

The Good Neighbor "In the field of world policy," Roosevelt said in one of the scant references to foreign affairs in his inaugural address, "I would dedicate this Nation to the policy of the good neighbor—the neighbor who resolutely respects himself and, because he does so, respects the rights of others—the neighbor who respects his obligations and respects the sanctity of his agreements in and with a world of neighbors." Though this thought was evidently intended to be general in its import, its immediate sphere of application was Latin America, and in time the Good Neighbor policy came to refer specifically to United States policy in the Western Hemisphere.

Latin Americans had not recently considered the United States a good neighbor. From the time of Theodore Roosevelt's corollary to the Monroe Doctrine (1904), Washington had insisted on its "right" to intervene in the internal affairs of Latin-American republics. This intervention covered a variety of practices, from economic pressure to military occupation. Roosevelt himself had participated in such intervention when the United States marines occupied Haiti during the Wilson Administration. In the twenties, however, Roosevelt and other North Americans—among them Sumner Welles, a former chief of the Latin-American Division of the State Department and an old friend of Roosevelt's—had become critical of the policy of intervention. In the meantime, accumulating resentment throughout the hemisphere resulted in a sharp rebuff to the United States at the Havana Conference of 1928. The Hoover Administration, recognizing the gravity of the situation, began to recede from the Theodore Roosevelt corollary and to withdraw American troops from Nicaragua and Haiti.

Roosevelt's Latin-American policy got off to an ambiguous start. Welles, recalled to public service, went to Cuba as ambassador to arrange the transition from the brutal Machado dictatorship to a new constitutional regime. The dislodgment of Machado, however, eventually brought into power a revolutionary government which the United States declined to recognize. In response to the American attitude, a conservative government came into power and duly received recognition. Though Roosevelt at the same time speeded up plans for withdrawing the marines from Haiti, Latin Americans in the fall of 1933 were convinced that policy in Washington was as bad as ever.

From Montevideo to Buenos Aires The Seventh International Conference of

American States met at Montevideo in December 1933 in an atmosphere of extreme hostility toward the United States. The American delegation, however, led by Cordell Hull with Welles's able assistance, soon induced a change in Latin-American attitudes. The United States, reversing its policy of five years before in Havana, now accepted (with minor qualifications) a proposal declaring that "no state has the right to intervene in the internal or external affairs of another." The Montevideo Conference, by establishing inter-American relations on the principle of nonintervention, brought into being a new epoch in hemispheric relations.

The United States proceeded to show that it meant to live up to its Montevideo pledge. In May 1934 it abrogated the unpopular Platt Amendment, thereby abandoning its treaty right to intervene in the affairs of Cuba. In recognizing the revolutionary Martínez government in El Salvador in 1934, it abandoned the policy of nonrecognition of revolutionary governments in Central America. The Panama Treaties of 1936 renounced the right to intervene in Panama and recognized Panama's responsibility in the operation and protection of the Canal. A treaty of 1940 terminated United States financial controls in the Dominican Republic. The establishment of the Export-Import Bank in 1934 provided a means of extending credit to Latin-American states and thereby encouraging trade within the hemisphere.

Relations with Mexico provided a test of the new policy. The hostility of the radical Mexican government toward the Roman Catholic Church in the early thirties had produced demands in the United States that Washington intervene in Mexico. The expropriation of foreign-owned petroleum companies renewed this pressure in 1938. Washington declined to intervene, however, confining its activities to urging the Mexican government to provide American owners their due compensation.

The ability of the United States to live at peace with a left-wing Mexican regime on its southern borders helped inspire confidence throughout the hemisphere in the reality of the Good Neighbor policy. By December 1936, when Roosevelt himself attended the Inter-American Conference at Buenos Aires, the ex-ceptional warmth of his reception attested to the transformation in Latin-American attitudes toward the colossus of the north.

Early Relations with Europe

The London Economic Conference American relations with European nations had been bedeviled since 1919 by the question of war debts. Pressure for the cancellation of these debts mounted as the depression deepened. A good deal of this sentiment emanated from the international banking community, and Roosevelt suspected that the bankers wanted to wipe out intergovernmental debts in order to make it easier to collect debts owed to themselves. In any case, the European nations, feeling that America had contributed dollars to a cause to which they had contributed blood, increasingly resented "Uncle Shylock's" insistence on getting his money back. Beginning in 1933, most European nations, except for Finland, began to suspend payment. War debts thereafter became a dead issue—except to the United States Congress, which retaliated in 1934 by passing the Johnson Act prohibiting loans to defaulting governments.

From the European viewpoint, war debts were only a part of the larger problem of world economic relations. By the early thirties, in the panic of depression, governments everywhere were building walls of protection in the hope of defending their national economies against the worldwide decline. Economic nationalism took more than one form, however. The Hoover version was nationalist in trade, internationalist in finance: Hoover thus advocated raising the protective tariff to new levels and at the same time argued that recovery depended on the restoration of a world gold standard. In this belief, he agreed to United States participation in an international economic conference favored by the gold-bloc nations and scheduled for London in the spring of 1933.

Roosevelt and the early New Dealers, on the other hand, believed that recovery was to be achieved primarily through domestic planning. "I shall spare no effort to restore world trade by international economic readjustments," the new President said in his inaugural address, "but the emergency at home cannot wait on that accomplishment." The New Dealers consequently mistrusted the international gold standard as a threat to national programs for recovery. Yet, unlike Hoover, they rejected the steeply protective tariff, favoring instead the system of reciprocal trade agreements which Hoover assailed in 1932 as "a violation of American principles." The Roosevelt version of economic nationalism was thus internationalist in trade, nationalist in finance.

When the London Economic Conference opened in June 1933, it became evident that the gold bloc, led by France and Italy, was determined to force through an agreement stabilizing foreign exchanges. By now the American government was fully committed to its program of raising commodity prices through reducing the value of the dollar—a policy obviously incompatible with immediate stabilization of the dollar in terms of an international standard. Roosevelt therefore declined to subordinate his domestic policy to international stabilization. This view emerged only gradually in the course of the conference; and meanwhile the antics of the American delegation had dissipated American influence in London. As the gold bloc continued to press for stabilization, Roosevelt, in what he conceived as an effort to recall the conference to more fruitful topics, sent a testy message scolding the conference for succumbing to the "old fetishes of the so-called international bankers." This "bombshell" message threw the conference into consternation. Though some Englishmen, among them J. M. Keynes and Winston Churchill, defended Roosevelt, the predominant reaction was to criticize him for "wrecking" the conference. Actually the conference was doomed anyway, since the gold bloc insisted on stabilization on its own terms, and these terms would have required the American President to renounce monetary policy as a weapon in his fight for domestic recovery.

Liberalizing American Trade   Roosevelt soon made it clear that his opposition to the international gold standard did not mean a belief in economic self-containment. In March 1934 he asked Congress for authority to enter into commercial agreements with foreign nations and to revise tariff rates in accordance with such agreements up to 50 per cent either way. This proposal for the executive negotia-

tion of reciprocal trade agreements raised a storm of opposition, partly because some congressmen—and the protectionist lobbies—objected to the weakening of the congressional role in tariff-making, partly because manufacturers feared the new system would result in lower rates. Senator Arthur H. Vandenberg of Michigan condemned the proposal as "Fascist in its philosophy, Fascist in its objective." Only two Republicans supported the bill in the House, only three in the Senate. But, with Hull's devoted backing, the bill became law in June 1934.

Actually the preamble of the act stated that its purpose was to increase American exports, an objective fully acceptable to protectionists and one which, by itself, would do little to help the United States adjust to its postwar position as a creditor nation. As administered by the State Department, however, the Reciprocal Trade Agreements program sought to increase imports and thereby to revive world trade. By the end of 1935, agreements were in effect with fourteen countries; by 1945, with twenty-nine countries. While the program did little in the thirties to relieve the balance-of-payments problem between the United States and foreign countries (indeed, debts owed to the United States grew steadily during the thirties), it did display America's hope of bringing about a larger measure of economic internationalism.

Disarmament   In an effort to compose matters after the breakup of the London Economic Conference, Roosevelt wrote to Ramsay MacDonald, the British Prime Minister, "I am concerned by events in Germany, for I feel that an insane rush to further armaments in Continental Europe is infinitely more dangerous than any number of squabbles over gold or stabilization or tariffs." From an early point—earlier, indeed, than any European statesman of comparable rank—Roosevelt was convinced that Hitler meant war. Yet, while he saw the approaching horror with unusual clarity, he also saw it with a certain aloofness. This was partly the result of geography, which conferred on the United States the luxury of detachment; partly the result of politics, for Roosevelt had little choice but to defer to the isolationist preferences of the vast majority of the people; partly the result of the depression, which gave the American domestic scene first claim on his attention.

The combination of concern and aloofness produced a basic contradiction in the heart of his foreign policy. From the moment of his inauguration, Roosevelt addressed himself to two problems: first, how to stop the world drift toward war; and, second, if that drift proved irresistible, how to make sure that the United States would not be involved. Plainly the goals of international peace and national isolation— of world disarmament and American neutrality—were in latent conflict. World disarmament implied American cooperation in a world system. Rigid neutrality implied a systematic reduction of America's international commitments. In 1933 and 1934 the tension between these two ideas complicated the conduct of America's foreign policy.

Disarmament had been a major theme of foreign affairs in the twenties, when a succession of conferences established a system of tonnage quotas governing the naval strength of the great powers. Efforts to work out formulas for land armaments had proved less successful. A new disarmament conference, beginning in Geneva in 1932, had bogged down because of Germany's demand for equality in armed strength—a demand the Germans based on Article 8 of the League Covenant with its call for general arms reduction. It had proved impossible to reconcile the German position with the insistence of other nations, especially France, on having reliable protection against a possible recurrence of German aggression.

The replacement of the Weimar Republic by the Nazi regime now gave the German demand for equality a new and ominous cast. In May 1933 Roosevelt authorized the American representative at Geneva to say that, if a substantial reduction of armaments were effected by international agreement, the United States was prepared to consult with the other states in case of a threat to peace. If the other states identified an aggressor and took measures against aggression, the United States, if it concurred in their judgment, would "refrain from any action tending to defeat such collective effort which these states may thus make to restore peace." In other words, the United States would forego its traditional insistence on neutral rights, including the freedom of the

seas, in the interest of supporting measures of collective security.

This was a striking development. For the first time since Wilson, the American government was making proposals which seemed to involve, not just edifying rhetoric, but concrete commitments to world peace. Or at least the President of the United States was prepared for such commitments. To make these proposals meaningful, the Administration now asked Congress to pass a resolution authorizing the executive at his discretion to embargo arms shipments to aggressor nations.

The congressional isolationists had not paid much attention to the Geneva statement. But the arms embargo resolution confronted them with the actuality of an internationalist policy. The Senate Foreign Relations Committee rose to the occasion and amended the resolution to compel the President to embargo arms shipments to *all* nations involved in a war. This amendment obviously destroyed the original purpose of the resolution, which was to discriminate against aggressors. Its effect would now be to strengthen those who had arms already and to abandon those who had none. The Administration tried in vain to defeat the amendment. Failing, it dropped the resolution itself, thereby canceling the effect of the American initiative at Geneva. What the President had proposed the Congress had now disowned. This failure of the Roosevelt Administration's first effort to throw American power in the balance against world aggression confirmed the deep-seated skepticism in European chancelleries over the seriousness of American diplomacy.

It seems unlikely, however, that even congressional approval of the arms embargo could have saved the Geneva conference. Hitler, now hell-bent on rearmament and committed to a revolt against the entire Versailles system, would probably not have accepted international disarmament on any terms. When Germany walked out of the League in October 1933, the hope of controlled land disarmament was dead. And the withdrawal of Japan from the League in 1933 and the Japanese decision in 1934 to terminate the Washington Naval Treaty signaled the end of international efforts at naval disarmament. By 1934 the hope of averting war through disarmament had gone.

The American government had been prepared to cooperate in the supervision of a disarmed world. It was not prepared to cooperate in keeping the peace at the risk of war in a world intent on rearmament. If disarmament had failed, the alternative, in the American view, was neutrality.

Relations with Great Britain and the Soviet Union   The collapse of disarmament was accompanied by a deterioration in American relations with the leading anti-Hitler powers. Roosevelt's bombshell message had exasperated London; and the policies of the British government now succeeded in exasperating Washington. Thus in 1933 Sir John Simon, the British Foreign Secretary, made an official protest to Washington over the American decision to build four 10,000-ton cruisers —a protest which made sense only if Britain had something to fear from the American navy. And an important faction in the British Cabinet, led by Neville Chamberlain, the Chancellor of the Exchequer, so deeply distrusted the United States that in 1934 it seriously considered whether Britain should base its strategy on cooperation with Japan instead of with the United States. At this point Roosevelt instructed his roving emissary, Norman Davis, to impress Simon "and a few other Tories" with the fact that

> if Great Britain is even suspected of preferring to play with Japan to playing with us, I shall be compelled, in the interest of American security, to approach public sentiment in Canada, Australia, New Zealand and South Africa in a definite effort to make these Dominions clearly understand that their future security is linked with us in the United States.

Happily, the Japanese themselves soon took care of the problem by presenting the British with rearmament demands so extreme that even the pro-Tokyo Cabinet members had to abandon their policy.

Roosevelt's efforts to establish friendly relations with the Soviet Union were hardly more successful. For some time before 1933, people had been growing restive in the United States over the absence of diplomatic relations with the Soviet Union. Businessmen saw in Russia a potential market for American surplus production; depression consequently whetted their demand for a new policy toward Moscow. At the same time, the renewal of Japanese aggression argued for a normalization of Soviet-American relations as a means of restraining the Japanese. "The world," Cordell Hull told Roosevelt, "is moving into a dangerous period both in Europe and in Asia. Russia could be a great help in stabilizing this situation."

Roosevelt decided to see what he could do. In October 1933 Maxim Litvinov, the Soviet Commissar for Foreign Affairs, came to Washington. After a series of talks Roosevelt and Litvinov worked out agreements designed to cover the main points at issue between the two countries. In one document Litvinov gave a remarkably detailed pledge to refrain from any intervention in American internal affairs —a pledge which covered not only the Soviet government itself but any organizations "under its direct or indirect control." Another memorandum provided what seemed to be a formula for the settlement of the Russian debts to the United States. The discussions concluded in the establishing of formal relations between the two governments.

Despite this beginning, relations soon returned to the prerecognition state of mistrust. The attempt to make the Soviet government live up to its promises on propaganda and debts led to interminable negotiation, argument, recrimination, and frustration. American diplomatic representatives in Moscow encountered harassment and hostility. Finally, when American communists came to Moscow in July 1935 for the seventh congress of the Comintern, their presence seemed, in the view of the American ambassador, to constitute "a flagrant violation of Litvinov's pledge to the President" and to place "beyond question of fact that the Government of the United States would be juridically and morally justified in severing diplomatic relations with the Soviet Union." Though the government did not go this far, relations with Soviet Russia had reached a low ebb less than two years after recognition.

Isolationism at Flood Tide

The Rout of the Internationalists   The breakdown of attempts to strengthen relations with Britain and the Soviet Union coincided with a crystallization of isolationist sentiment in the United States. By the early 1930's, few Americans were prepared to make an all-out defense of Wilson's decision of 1917. A school of "revisionist" historians had launched a reconsideration of such problems as German "war guilt" and American entry into the war. Their scholarship seemed to reveal the war as the product, not of a struggle of good against evil or even of democracy against autocracy, but of rivalries among virtually indistinguishable imperialist powers. If this were so, then Wilson's crusade for democracy was phony, and the United States had been drawn into the war under false pretenses.

The logical next question was: Who had drawn the United States in and why? The new disillusion was clinched in 1934 and 1935 by the work of a Senate committee set up under the chairmanship of Gerald P. Nye of North Dakota to investigate the munitions industry. The Nye Committee unearthed a wealth of documentation purporting to show that the United States had been shoved into war when international bankers, especially the House of Morgan, saw no other way to guarantee repayment of the vast credits they had granted to the western Allies. To demonstrate that no President could be trusted with discretionary power in matters of war and peace, Nye charged Wilson with duplicity in pretending to be ignorant of the secret treaties.

The Nye Committee completed the work of consolidating the isolationist philosophy. The isolationists could conceive of no world war that would present a moral issue between the antagonists or a strategic threat to American security; in fact, they were convinced that American freedom could not survive another holocaust. America's best contribution to peace and democracy, in their judgment, lay in absolute rejection of the power struggles of Europe and Asia. These views summed up the prevailing opinion of the American people.

Roosevelt was quickly to learn the new power of organized isolationism. In January 1935, a short time after the stunning Democratic victory in the 1934 elections, he sent the Senate a recommendation that the United States join the World Court. "At this period in international relationships," he said, "when

every act is of moment to the future of world peace, the United States has an opportunity once more to throw its weight into the scale in favor of peace." Joining the World Court could hardly have been a more innocuous act, and the Administration confidently supposed that it could command the necessary two-thirds vote without trouble. But the isolationist bloc staged an extraordinary appeal to public opinion which prompted an outpouring of protest and the defeat of the resolution. Isolationism and internationalism were joined in clearcut battles and the outcome was ominous. Roosevelt wrote to Elihu Root, who had proposed a world court at The Hague a generation before, "Today, quite frankly, the wind everywhere blows against us."

The Design of Neutrality   The next problem, as Nye, Arthur Vandenberg, and their Nye Committee colleagues saw it, was to make sure that the forces which had brought about American participation in the First World War would never have their way again.

If America had been drawn into that war to ensure the repayment of debts owed to American bankers and munitions-makers, then to keep out of war it would be necessary to forbid loans and the export of arms to belligerents. If America had been drawn into that war because American ships carried supplies to belligerent nations or because American citizens insisted on traveling on belligerent ships, then to keep out of war such actions should be prohibited. If America had been drawn into war by the unneutral decisions of a President with too much discretion in the conduct of foreign policy, then the President should be denied the opportunity to tamper with neutrality. The Nye group demanded a new American neutrality policy—one that might even involve the surrender of certain classical neutral rights, such as the freedom of the seas, in the interests of absolute immunity.

Given the mood of 1935, even the State Department seemed prepared to go a considerable distance toward this objective. Still, a decisive difference remained between the Administration and the Nye Committee. Both agreed that the President should have authority to prohibit American ships from carrying arms and munitions, to withdraw the protection of the government from Americans traveling on belligerent vessels and to impose an embargo on arms and loans. But the Administration wanted the President to be able to use these powers at his discretion; the senators, with the image of the perfidious Wilson in their mind, wanted to make it mandatory that he use them against *all* belligerents—which would, of course, nullify American influence in the case of conflict. In the end the Senate passed a mandatory bill, the House a discretionary bill. The resulting compromise of August 31, 1935, contained a mandatory arms embargo but made it good only until March 1, 1936; in other respects—such as American travel on belligerent vessels—it gave the President discretion. The Administration decided to accept the measure rather than risk further exacerbation of isolationist sentiment through a veto. On signing the bill, Roosevelt warned that "the inflexible provisions . . . might have exactly the opposite effect from that which was intended."

Neutrality on Test

Italy Invades Ethiopia   Early in October 1935 Italian troops crossed the frontier into Ethiopia. Roosevelt promptly reiterated the national determination to keep free of foreign entanglements, but he added significantly that he did not expect Americans to be indifferent to assaults on freedom abroad—a marked contrast to Wilson's appeal of 1914 that his countrymen be "neutral in fact as well as in name." In his message to Congress in January 1936, Roosevelt outspokenly indicted nations that were committed to the "fantastic conception that they, and they alone, are chosen to fulfill a mission and that all the others among the billion and a half of human beings in the world must and shall learn from them and be subject to them."

At the same time, he issued a proclamation of neutrality and invoked the mandatory arms embargo. The supposition in Washington was that the embargo would hurt Italy more than Ethiopia, since Ethiopia lacked dollars to buy arms in the United States and ships to carry them away. Actually the arms embargo did Italy little initial harm, since it had its own munitions industry. Where the restriction of American exports really could hurt the Italian

war-making capacity was in raw materials, especially in oil. But the Neutrality Act covered only implements of war. Roosevelt accordingly followed up the arms embargo with a call for a voluntary restriction of other exports. This action initiated the experiment in what became known as the "moral embargo."

The moral embargo aroused the protests of the Italian government as well as of American oil companies, and moral suasion did not turn out to be effective. Oil shipments to Italy, for example, were 600 per cent larger in August and September 1935 than they had been for the same two months in 1934. Nevertheless, Washington's attitude remained important. The American policy preceded by many weeks any comparable action by the League, and it strengthened the hands of those in Geneva who were contending for economic sanctions against Italy. The League decision was finally taken in a limited way (not including oil, for example) on November 18, 1935.

When Congress convened in 1936, one of its first tasks was to replace the neutrality resolution of 1935. The Administration tried to increase the presidential role in the management of neutrality; but the parliamentary situation grew hopelessly confused, and in the end it seemed simpler to extend the existing act until May 1, 1937, with an amendment banning credits to belligerents. One apparently minor change did, however, increase executive discretion: it was now up to the President to decide that a state of war existed before the act could be invoked.

"One cannot help feeling," Roosevelt wrote his ambassador to France in the midst of the neutrality debate of 1936, "that the whole European panorama is fundamentally blacker than at any time in your lifetime or mine." The outbreak of civil war in Spain on July 17, 1936, deepened Roosevelt's sense of a general European disintegration. In a speech at Chautauqua, New York, four weeks later, he set forth with earnestness his hatred of war, his commitment to neutrality, and his determination to resist the forces which might draw the United States into another world conflict. His private correspondence reflected a belief that somehow a conference among heads of state might avert the drift to Armageddon; but he could find no formula which offered any prom-

The twin spirits of autocracy and aggression: Italy conquers Ethiopia.

ise of success and, in consequence, he took no action.

The attempt of Spanish fascists under General Francisco Franco to overthrow the democratic government of Spain created new problems in 1936. The mandatory embargo applied to wars between nations, not to revolutions within a single nation: so, early in January 1937, Congress, with Roosevelt's full support and with but one negative vote in both houses, enacted a resolution aligning the United States with Britain and France in a program of nonintervention and in banning shipments of implements of war to either side in Spain.

Then Congress faced once again the question of renewing or rewriting the existing neutrality legislation. The main innovation in the 1937 debate was the so-called "cash-and-carry" proposal, which provided that, once the President had proclaimed the existence of a state of war, no nonmilitary goods could be shipped to a belligerent until the purchaser acquired full title and took them away himself. The Administration supported this idea in order to head off a drive for an automatic embargo on all goods. Ironically, the amendment would clearly have the unneutral effect of favoring the maritime powers, notably Britain and Japan, and of closing American markets to interior nations, notably Germany and China. Nevertheless, Congress adopted the provision by sweeping majorities.

Aggression in the Far East

The Problem of China For many Americans the problems of Europe had come to seem more remote, or at least less America's business, than the problems of the Far East. As far back as the announcement of the Open Door Doctrine, the acquisition of the Philippines, and Theodore Roosevelt's mediation of the Russo-Japanese War, America had conceived of itself as playing a direct role in the affairs of East Asia. By the First World War Washington had concluded that the great threat to American interests in the Far East would come from Japanese expansion. Both the Washington Naval Conference and the Stimson Doctrine were parts of a general policy designed to restrain Tokyo's imperial aspirations.

Roosevelt, who regarded the plight of China with sympathy, endorsed the Stimson Doctrine even before he took office. In the first months of his presidency he asked what the United States could do short of war to prevent Japan from overrunning China. It was easier to raise such questions than to answer them. Far Eastern experts in the State Department counseled a policy of inaction. China, they believed, was too weak and disunited to qualify for American help. Only by giving the Japanese their head, they suggested, could the world be made to understand the sinister nature of Japanese purposes.

Then the Tangku truce of May 1933 brought hostilities between China and Japan to a temporary end. But in April 1934 the spokesman for the Japanese foreign office, Eiji Amau, arrogantly warned western countries against any financial or military assistance to China and demanded a free hand in China for Japan. Soon thereafter Japan denounced the Five-Power Treaty.

What could America now do to contain Japanese ambitions? To the State Department, the cornerstone in an effective containment policy was the rapid build-up of the United States navy. It is true that diplomacy by itself could do little in the Far East. Yet the State Department's commitment to the naval thesis led it to oppose taking interim anti-Japanese or pro-Chinese measures until the navy had been sufficiently strengthened. So long as America remained weak in Asian waters, Cordell Hull reasoned, any attempt to oppose the Japanese or to help the Chinese would be pinpricks that would serve only to provoke Tokyo unnecessarily. Naval superiority became, in short, not only the indispensable condition for a future American policy in East Asia but also a powerful argument against present action. Thus the State Department generally opposed proposals to condemn Japan or to render financial assistance to China.

The Renewal of Japanese Aggression In the meantime, the Chinese, under the able leadership of Chiang Kai-shek, were making impressive progress toward the unification of their nation. Perhaps wishing to halt the process before it went too far, the Japanese used troop clashes at the Marco Polo Bridge in July 1937 as an excuse for a new invasion of China. By the end of the month, Japanese soldiers had seized Peking and Tientsin. The subsequent bombing of Shanghai by Japanese planes and the appalling sack of Nanking in December deeply horrified Americans. The Chinese retreated to the interior, established their capital at Chungking, and prepared to keep up their resistance.

Popular sympathy in the United States was wholly with the Chinese, but the official reaction in Washington was cautious. Britain and America warded off Chinese pressure for invocation of the Nine-Power Treaty (see p. 596) and instead allowed the matter to go to the League for perfunctory condemnation. The President, however, displayed his solicitude for the Chinese cause by refusing to proclaim the existence of a state of war between China and Japan. Without such a proclamation, the arms embargo and the cash-and-carry provision for nonmilitary commodities would not go into effect. Most observers felt that these provisions would hurt China, which had to import implements of war, more than they would Japan, which had ample stockpiles and a productive capacity of its own. Thus between July and November 1937 the value of licensed munitions shipments to China was $86 million; to Japan, $1.5 million. Moreover, an arms embargo would not cut off what Japan needed most—oil and scrap metal. And the application of cash-and-carry would favor Japan as a naval power. Since neither China nor Japan had formally declared war on the other, it was not difficult for Roosevelt to refuse to find that they were at war.

Awakening the Nation

The Quarantine Speech   As it became evident that virtuous generalities were not enough to stem the drift toward war, Roosevelt began to consider other possibilities. Early in 1937 he permitted Secretary of the Treasury Morgenthau to begin confidential exchanges with Neville Chamberlain, the British Chancellor of the Exchequer, over the possibility of Anglo-American cooperation to keep the peace. Apart from amending the Neutrality Act, however, Chamberlain could not think of much that the United States could do. When Roosevelt proposed a personal meeting, Chamberlain, now Prime Minister, replied, "I cannot suggest any way in which the meeting between us could be expedited. . . . We must wait a little longer." Chamberlain had little use for the United States—"it is always best and safest," he said in 1937, "to count on nothing from the Americans but words." And he dedicated himself to the hope that Hitler could be made reasonable by a program of political appeasement.

The renewal of warfare in China now heightened the sense of international urgency. It apparently also turned Roosevelt's attention to an idea which had been in the back of his mind for many years—the deterrence of aggression by holding over potential aggressors the threat (as he had put it in a "Plan to Preserve World Peace" written for a prize competition in 1923) of "the severance of all trade or financial relations, and the prohibition of all intercourse." Carrying his campaign to alert the nation to the heart of American isolationism, Roosevelt, in a speech at Chicago in October 1937, declared that "the present reign of terror and international lawlessness" had reached a stage "where the very foundations of civilization are seriously threatened." If

---

F. D. R.: The Contagion of War

It seems to be unfortunately true that the epidemic of world lawlessness is spreading.

When an epidemic of physical disease starts to spread, the community approves and joins in a quarantine of the patients in order to protect the health of the community against the spread of the disease....

War is a contagion, whether it be declared or undeclared. It can engulf states and peoples remote from the original scene of hostilities. We are determined to keep out of war, yet we cannot insure ourselves against the disastrous effects of war and the dangers of involvement. We are adopting such measures as will minimize our risk of involvement, but we cannot have complete protection in a world of disorder in which confidence and security have broken down....

Most important of all, the will for peace on the part of peace-loving nations must express itself to the end that nations that may be tempted to violate their agreements and the rights of others will desist from such a course. There must be positive endeavors to preserve peace.

From Franklin D. Roosevelt, Speech at Chicago, October 1937.

Gerald P. Nye: The Contagion of Isolationism

There can be no objection to any hand our Government may take which strives to bring peace to the world so long as that hand does not tie 130,000,000 people into another world death march.

I very much fear that we are once again being caused to feel that the call is upon America to police a world that chooses to follow insane leaders. Once again we are baited to thrill to a call to save the world.

We reach now a condition on all fours with that prevailing just before our plunge into the European war in 1917. Will we blindly repeat that futile venture? Can we easily forget that we won nothing we fought for then—that we lost every cause declared to be responsible for our entry then?

From Senator Gerald P. Nye, Statement in the New York *Times*, October 1937.

---

aggression continued, he said, "let no one imagine America will escape." In a cryptic passage, he compared "the epidemic of world lawlessness" to an epidemic of physical disease and advocated a "quarantine" to protect the community against the contagion.

Aftermath of the Quarantine Speech Roosevelt's main purpose was undoubtedly educational: he wanted to awaken the nation to the dangers of world war. A secondary purpose was very likely to explore the readiness of the American people to support some form of boycott of aggressors—moral, diplomatic, perhaps economic.

In the international sphere, the quarantine speech encouraged the British to call the signatories of the Nine-Power Treaty to a conference at Brussels to deal with the new Sino-Japanese conflict. But first the British sent word to Washington that they could do nothing about imposing sanctions against Japan unless they received "assurance of military support" in the event of Japanese retaliation. Roosevelt declined to give such guarantees; the British declined to act without them; and the Brussels Conference came to nothing.

In the meantime, Under-Secretary of State Sumner Welles suggested that Roosevelt follow up his quarantine speech by convening a conference of neutral nations to set forth a peace program based on certain standards of international behavior. In January 1938 the plan was submitted to Chamberlain. But the British Prime Minister, now wholly absorbed in the appeasement policy, briskly rejected the American initiative on the ground that it ran the danger of "cutting across our efforts here." Winston Churchill later wrote that Chamberlain's decision was "the loss of the last frail chance to save the world from tyranny otherwise than by war." Though Churchill exaggerated the probable effectiveness of the plan, Chamberlain's behavior did discourage Roosevelt from further efforts at Anglo-American collaboration. He left Chamberlain free to pursue his experiment in appeasement without distraction.

Within the United States the first reaction to the quarantine speech was not unfavorable. But it soon became evident that most Americans, while sharing their President's detestation of dictators, had an even greater desire to avoid anything that might invite the risk of war. When Japanese planes sank the American gunboat *Panay* in the Yangtze River in December 1937, the nation accepted Japanese apologies and indemnification with relief. And interest was rising throughout the nation in an amendment to the Constitution offered by Congressman Louis Ludlow of Indiana proposing to make the declaration of war a matter of popular plebiscite except in case of invasion. On top of all this, the country was evidently sinking into an economic recession, and the Administration needed united congressional support for its new recovery program. Given all these circumstances, Roosevelt doubtless felt that he could not risk dividing his party and the nation on issues of foreign policy. Accordingly, after the British rejection of the Welles plan, he did nothing more with the quarantine idea.

The idea, vague enough at best, thus perished between American reluctance and British indifference. It left an indelible mark, however, on the popular consciousness as the nation struggled to define the issues of totalitarianism and aggression.

The Road to War

The End of Appeasement In 1936 Germany had moved into the Rhineland. In March 1938 Germany continued its course of expansion by invading and annexing Austria. In the following months Adolf Hitler began to use the plight of the German minority in the Sudetenland as a pretext for demands on the government of Czechoslovakia. In August Roosevelt, speaking at Kingston, Ontario, expressed deep concern over the growing

Munich: An abject capitulation.

European crisis. Chamberlain asked that he make no more such speeches lest they provoke the Germans.

As the Czech crisis deepened in September, Chamberlain requested a personal conference with Hitler. There followed a series of meetings attended by Hitler, Chamberlain, Prime Minister Daladier of France, and eventually Mussolini. No representatives of Czechoslovakia were present. In the interval between the talks at Godesberg (September 23) and those at Munich (September 29), when it seemed as if Chamberlain were standing firm against Hitler, Roosevelt sent him an encouraging cable ("GOOD MAN") and brought pressure on Hitler to resume negotiations. But the Munich meeting produced an abject capitulation of the democratic powers. Czechoslovakia had no choice but to acquiesce bitterly in the result.

The first reaction in the United States was one of heartfelt relief: the appeasement policy seemed to have averted war. But in a short while people began to compute the price of appeasement: not just the establishment of German hegemony in central Europe, but the incentive offered everywhere to intimidation and aggression. "There can be no peace," Roosevelt said in a speech on October 26, 1938, "if national policy adopts as a deliberate instrument the threat of war."

Rearmament   During the 1920's neither the executive nor Congress had been much interested in national defense. As a result, the regular army had fallen well below the size authorized by the National Defense Act of 1920 and the navy below the levels permitted by the various international agreements. When Roosevelt came into office in 1933, the army ranked seventeenth in the world in active strength. From the start of his Administration, he had tried to rebuild American military and naval power. Thus the Public Works Administration constructed cruisers and aircraft carriers; and in 1935 Congress authorized the army to increase its enlisted strength to 165,000. In a message to Congress in January 1938 Roosevelt called for larger appropriations, declaring the existing defense establishment "inadequate for purposes of national security" in the light of the multiplying armaments of other nations. In May Congress responded to his request by passing the Naval Expansion

Act. In the months after Munich, he requested vast increases in the defense budget. In order to expand the productive capacity of the American aircraft industry, he encouraged British and French purchasing missions to place defense orders in the United States.

In other respects Roosevelt began to tighten his ship in preparation for storms ahead. Following the failure of his "purge" in 1938 (see p. 668), he moved toward a tacit political truce, moderating his liberal objectives in the hope of gaining support for his foreign and defense policies. He also worked for unity in the American hemisphere. In December 1938 a new Inter-American Conference produced the Declaration of Lima, whereby the American republics announced their collective determination to resist fascist threats to peace and security.

The Neutrality Act remained the greatest obstacle to a positive policy; and in 1939, as the Munich settlement seemed to be growing increasingly unstable, Roosevelt considered how best he might modify the neutrality system in order to make American aid available to democratic nations. Hitler's invasion of Czechoslovakia on March 15, 1939, persuaded even Neville Chamberlain of the bankruptcy of appeasement. The State Department denounced Germany's "wanton lawlessness," and the Administration stepped up its campaign for the repeal or at least the modification of the arms embargo. As Cordell Hull put it, the law "plays into the hands of those nations which have taken the lead in building up their fighting power. It works directly against the interests of the peace-loving nations." But neither argument nor pressure was of any avail. The isolationist senators, confident that there would be no war in 1939, insisted that the matter be laid over to the next session of Congress.

In Europe events rushed toward climax. The invasion of Czechoslovakia was followed by the German occupation of Memel (March 23), the collapse of the Spanish Republic (March 28), and the Italian invasion of Albania (April 7). Through the summer Hitler carried on a war of nerves against Poland, using a German minority in Danzig as his tool. In the meantime his emissaries were secretly negotiating a nonaggression pact with the Soviet

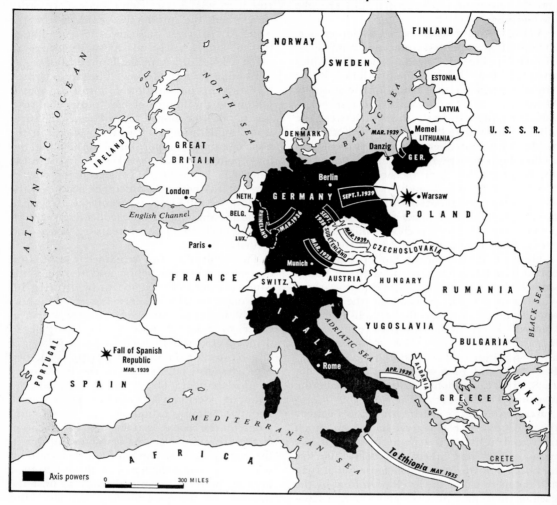

Union. On August 23 the German-Russian pact was signed in Moscow. The next day Britain and Poland signed a pact of mutual assistance. On September 1 Germany attacked Poland. Two days later Britain and France declared war on Germany. The Second World War was now under way.

America and the War

First Reactions "When peace has been broken anywhere," Roosevelt said in a fireside chat on the evening of September 3, 1939, "the peace of all countries everywhere is in danger." He reaffirmed his determination "to use every effort" to keep war out of America. But he added, "I cannot ask that every American remain neutral in thought. . . . Even a neutral cannot be asked to close his mind or his conscience." On September 5 he issued the proclamation of neutrality. At the same time he indicated that he would call Congress into special session in order to repeal the arms embargo.

The isolationists now threw all their efforts into a defense of the embargo. The isolationist leaders in the Senate, backed by former President Hoover and by such national figures as

Colonel Charles A. Lindbergh, as well as by the American Communist party, declared that Roosevelt's course was leading straight to war. The opposition was strong enough to compel the Administration to accept restrictive compromises in exchange for the elimination of the embargo. Thus hedged around, the neutrality revision bill passed Congress, and the President signed it on November 4, 1939. The new law placed the arms trade on a cash-and-carry basis. Where the previous legislation had favored Germany, with its well-established war industries, the new law enabled Britain and France to buy war materials in the United States so long as they paid cash and carried their purchases away in their own ships.

Meanwhile the Nazi Air Force and Panzer divisions had subdued Poland in a three-week campaign. The French and British had been able to do little to create a diversion on the western front, and after the reduction of Poland the war settled into an aspect of apparent quiescence which won it the derisive name of "the phony war." Britain and France seemed relatively slow to seize the advantages now open to them to make war purchases in the United States. While public-opinion polls showed an overwhelming public preference in America for the Western Allies against Germany (in October 1939 62 per cent of the population favored all possible aid to the Allies short of war), less than 30 per cent favored American entry into the war even if Britain and France were in danger of defeat.

American emotions were perhaps more deeply engaged when the Soviet Union, having advanced into eastern Poland in September, moved into the small Baltic republics of Latvia, Estonia, and Lithuania in October and invaded Finland in late November. The American people, remembering Finnish punctiliousness in the payment of war debts, grew particularly indignant over the onslaught on the "gallant little Finns." Roosevelt sharply condemned "this dreadful rape." Isolationists, however, were more alert than ever not to let emotion over Finland drag the nation closer toward war. The Administration's cautious program of aid to Finland encountered strong opposition in Congress and had hardly gone into effect when the "Winter War" came to an end in March 1940.

Blitzkrieg Hitler was already preparing the blow which, he hoped, would destroy the will of his Western antagonists. On April 9, 1940, Germany attacked Denmark and Norway. An Anglo-French attempt to land forces in Norway miscarried, and by the end of the month Norwegian resistance was broken. Popular discontent in Britain over the Chamberlain government now reached new heights. Chamberlain was forced to resign, and Winston Churchill, who had long criticized the appeasement policy and, after the outbreak of war, had served as First Lord of the Admiralty, became Prime Minister.

Chamberlain was in the course of resigning on May 10 when the Nazi forces struck again. Without warning, German mechanized divisions invaded the Netherlands, Belgium, and Luxembourg. In a week they were thrusting deep into northern France. The British and French tried to resist, but they were unable to cope with the speed of the German attack. The main part of the British forces retreated to Dunkirk, where they were evacuated across the British Channel by a heroic flotilla of small boats conjured up from British ports. In a few days Italy joined the war, invading France from the south. "The hand that held the dagger," Roosevelt said grimly, "has struck it into the back of its neighbor." Soon Paris fell, Marshal Pétain became head of the French government, and on June 22 France and Germany signed an armistice at Compiègne. The next day, from London, General de Gaulle pledged continued French resistance.

The success of the Nazi blitzkrieg had a stunning effect on American opinion. Citing "the almost incredible events of the past two weeks," Roosevelt asked Congress for more than a billion dollars in additional defense appropriations, calling in particular for the annual production of fifty thousand warplanes. He also set up a National Defense Advisory Commission to plan defense production. And he began to consider how he could aid Britain, now standing alone against the Berlin-Rome Axis. Churchill's rise to power meant the end of the glumness that had marked Anglo-American relations during the Chamberlain period. Roosevelt, who had for some months exchanged letters with the new Prime Minister, recognized him as a man of congenial temperament and stature. When Churchill offered his own people nothing but "blood, toil, tears and sweat," when he promised to "wage war by sea, land and air, with all our might and with all the strength that God can give us," he made a profound appeal to the American imagination.

But Britain needed more than sympathy. On May 15 Churchill sent Roosevelt a long list of specific requirements, including old destroyers, new aircraft, and materials of war. For the moment Washington could do little, partly because of America's own defense needs, partly (as in the case of the destroyers) be-

cause it was feared that congressional assent would not be forthcoming. After Dunkirk the American government did scrape together small arms and ammunition for the British to use in the desperate eventuality of a German invasion. But the problems of American policy were now further complicated by the approach of the 1940 presidential campaign.

The Election of 1940

The Third Term   The struggle between isolationists and interventionists cut across

Churchill: Nothing but "blood, toil, tears and sweat."

Evacuation at Dunkirk, 1940.

party lines. Thus Roosevelt found some of the most effective supporters of his foreign policy in the ranks of internationalist Republicans—a fact which he acknowledged in June 1940, when he appointed Henry L. Stimson of New York as Secretary of War and Frank Knox of Illinois as Secretary of the Navy. However, the main drive of the Republican party was isolationist. When the Republicans gathered in Philadelphia to select a presidential candidate, they read Stimson and Knox out of the party and prepared to choose between two candidates, Senator Robert A. Taft of Ohio and Thomas E. Dewey of New York, both identified with isolationism.

They did not allow, however, for the enthusiasm with which a group of internationalist Republicans rallied support for a dark-horse candidate, Wendell L. Willkie of Indiana. Willkie, an affable and articulate businessman, had magnetic qualities of person-

ality which justified the title of "the rich man's Roosevelt." As president of Commonwealth & Southern, a leading public utilities holding company, Willkie had won attention as an antagonist of the New Deal during the fight over the Tennessee Valley Authority. Actually he had been a Democrat himself most of his life; his personal views and values were on the liberal side; and, most critically of all in 1940, he sympathized with the Roosevelt policy of aid to Great Britain. To general astonishment, the Willkie forces staged a blitzkrieg of their own at Philadelphia, and the former Democrat emerged as the Republican candidate.

As for the Democrats, Roosevelt had failed, whether through design or negligence, to develop an heir apparent. For many months the more ardent New Dealers had demanded that he stand himself for a third term. A group of conservative Democrats, led by Vice-President Garner and Postmaster General Farley, sought to organize opposition on the ground that a third term would violate a sacred American tradition. But the international urgencies made Roosevelt seem to most Democrats the indispensable candidate. The Democratic convention accordingly renominated him at Chicago in July, though it swallowed rather hard at his insistence on Henry A. Wallace, the Secretary of Agriculture, for Vice-President.

Foreign Policy and the Campaign
While Americans concerned themselves with presidential politics, the German *Luftwaffe* launched a series of savage air assaults against England. The Royal Air Force put up a magnificent defense in what became known as the Battle of Britain. But if Britain hoped to repulse an anticipated German invasion—as well as maintain its own lines of supply—it needed immediate reinforcement of its battered destroyer fleet. Churchill, renewing his request for American destroyers, cabled Roosevelt on July 31, "I must tell you that in the long history of the world this is a thing to do *now.*"

Though the United States had over-age de-

The U.S.-British Destroyer-Bases Agreement, 1940

CANADA

NEWFOUNDLAND

■ Argentia

UNITED STATES

ATLANTIC

■ Bermuda

OCEAN

BAHAMA IS.

CUBA ■ Great Exuma I.

■ Antigua

■ Jamaica ■ St. Lucia

Caribbean Sea Trinidad ■

Georgetown

BR. GUIANA

■ Bases acquired by U.S. from British

SOUTH AMERICA

stroyers to spare, the Naval Appropriations Act seemed to require prior approval of the Chief of Naval Operations before they could be released. Moreover, Roosevelt feared the political repercussions in a campaign in which he was already under attack for unneutral acts. But he was persuaded that he could legally release the destroyers without amending the law, and he received assurances that Willkie, the Republican candidate, would not attack the transaction. Accordingly, on September 2 the United States agreed to transfer fifty destroyers to Britain in exchange for ninety-nine-year leases and grants of naval and air bases in Newfoundland and the Caribbean.

Willkie's support of conscription also enabled the Administration to obtain a Selective Service Act in August. Still, though Willkie's internationalism minimized the role of foreign policy in the campaign, it did not altogether eliminate peace and war as an issue. Indeed, as the campaign wore on, the Republican candidate, rattled both by his own inexperience and by discordant counsel among his advisers, assailed Roosevelt's foreign policy more and more extravagantly in terms which he himself would later dismiss as "campaign oratory." Thus in October he began to ask audiences whether anyone "really thinks that the President is sincerely trying to keep us out of war." Soon he predicted that Roosevelt, if elected, would have the nation in war by April 1941. Democratic politicians told Roosevelt that Willkie's charges were politically damaging and had to be met. By the end of the campaign Roosevelt was himself assuring American parents: "I have said this before, but I shall say it again and again and again: Your boys are not going to be sent into any foreign wars."

The election showed that Roosevelt still retained the national confidence. He received 27 million popular votes against 22 million for Willkie; the electoral college margin was 449 to 82. But he received only 54.8 per cent of the vote as against 60.8 per cent in 1936. Because of the equivocal way in which both candidates had presented the foreign issues—had, indeed, somewhat misrepresented their own convictions—the election did not serve either to clarify public thinking or to produce a setting for future action.

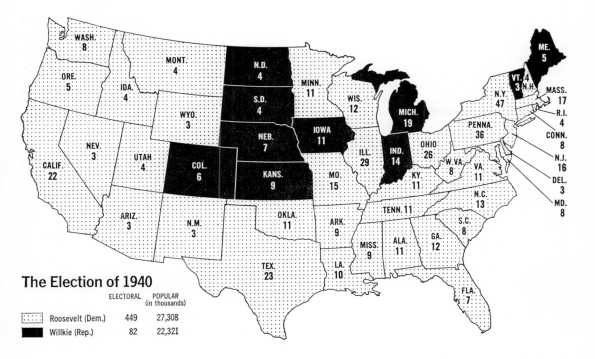

The Election of 1940

	ELECTORAL	POPULAR (in thousands)
Roosevelt (Dem.)	449	27,308
Willkie (Rep.)	82	22,321

Aid Short of War

The Lend-Lease Act   Through 1940 Britain had been able to get the goods it needed under the system of cash-and-carry. As the war moved into 1941, however, both bases of the system seemed in peril—"cash" because Britain's supply of American dollars was nearing the point of exhaustion, "carry" because of the growing effectiveness of the German submarine campaign against British shipping. In an eloquent letter to Roosevelt early in December, Churchill emphasized the urgency of these two problems.

Churchill's letter precipitated in Roosevelt's mind a decision to end the phase of assistance by quibble and ingenuity and to inaugurate a more explicit policy of aid to Britain. "The thing to do," he told Secretary of the Treasury Morgenthau, "is to get away from a dollar sign. I don't want to put the thing in terms of dollars or loans." As he explained to his press conference, if a neighbor's house was on fire, you would not waste time arguing about the cost of the hose; you would put the fire out and get the hose back afterward. Why not say to England, "We will give you the guns and the ships you need, provided that when the war is over you will return to us in kind the guns and ships we have loaned to you"?

In January 1941 the Administration introduced the so-called lend-lease bill to carry out Roosevelt's intention. The measure authorized the President to sell, transfer, exchange, lend, lease, or otherwise dispose of war equipment and other commodities to the "government of any country whose defense the President deems vital to the defense of the United States." So sweeping a proposal aroused bitter isolationist opposition. "The lend-lease-give program," said Senator Burton K. Wheeler, "is the New Deal's triple A foreign policy; it will plow under every fourth American boy." (Roosevelt called this "the rottenest thing that has been said in public life in my generation.") Among those who testified against the bill were Charles A. Lindbergh, Charles A. Beard, the historian, and Joseph P. Kennedy, the former ambassador to England; Wendell Willkie led a parade of witnesses in its favor. But public sentiment strongly supported the proposal, and it became law on March 11, 1941. "Through this legislation," Roosevelt said, "our country has determined to do its full part in creating an adequate arsenal of democracy."

The Battle of the Atlantic The Lend-Lease Act decisively committed the economic power of the United States to the support of Britain. More than this, it implied at least a partial commitment of American naval power; for, if America deemed aid to Britain vital to American security, then clearly America had better make sure that goods intended for Britain actually arrived there. Shortly after the passage of lend-lease, the Germans joined the challenge by extending the North Atlantic war zone westward to the coast of Greenland. Through the spring of 1941 the Germans were destroying half a million tons of merchant shipping a month; ships were sinking twice as fast as they could be replaced. It is, Churchill told Roosevelt, "in shipping and in the power to transport across the oceans, particularly the Atlantic Ocean, that in 1941 the crunch of the whole war will be found."

An obvious answer was for Roosevelt to order the American navy to escort and protect transatlantic convoys, and some advisers urged this course on him. Such a policy would have constituted, however, an invitation to undeclared hostilities; the President evidently regarded it as too radical a step. Instead he proposed an eastward extension of the area in which American naval and air patrol was clearly legitimate. While this move lessened, it by no means resolved, Britain's problem of the Atlantic lifeline.

Unlimited National Emergency Roosevelt's policy of aid to Great Britain was not limited only by the fear of an adverse public reaction. It seems likely that the President himself cherished the hope, which many around him had abandoned by the spring of 1941, that Hitler might be defeated without direct American military involvement in the war. Accordingly he shied away from actions that might make American entry into the war unavoidable.

Yet he confronted the hard fact that Britain's situation seemed to be growing steadily worse. And in the United States itself the attitude of business-as-usual impeded full mobilization of the economy for defense production. The Office of Production Management had succeeded the National Defense Advisory Commission in January 1941, but the new agency lacked adequate authority over allocations and priorities. Many businessmen were disinclined to convert their facilities to defense needs. Strikes in defense industries, some of them instigated by communists, further kept the country from living up to its full responsibility as the "arsenal of democracy." Some positive step seemed necessary to galvanize America and to reassure Britain. On May 27, 1941, the President addressed a forceful speech to the nation, concluding with a proclamation "that an unlimited national emergency exists and requires the strengthening of our defense to the extreme limit of our national power."

Isolationism's Last Stand

The Great Debate   The slow unfolding of American policy had been accompanied by an intensification of public debate over the relative merits of isolationism and intervention. In 1940 the Committee to Defend America by Aiding the Allies was established under the chairmanship of the Kansas editor William Allen White to argue the moderate interventionist position; some who felt that this committee did not go far enough set up the Fight for Freedom Committee in 1941 to contend for American entry into the war. On the other side, the America First Committee condemned the policies which it believed were taking the country down the road to disaster. Each side took its case to the public through newspaper advertisements, radio broadcasts, and mass meetings.

The resulting debate became more bitter even than the arguments of the thirties over the New Deal. It was, in addition, unpredictable, cutting across political, economic, and geographical lines. Isolationists were to be found in all parts of the country, in all social classes and in all political parties. Still, to a considerable degree, isolationism as a political force represented the conservative Republican wing of the business community, especially in the Middle West. Progressives like Burton K. Wheeler, Socialists like Norman Thomas and (until the Nazi attack on Russia) the commu-

nists also criticized Roosevelt's policies. Most isolationists were patriotic Americans, sincerely persuaded that Hitler's victory in Europe, though admittedly distasteful, carried no important threat to American security. The German-American Bund and the fringe of pro-Nazi groups in America also, of course, endorsed the isolationist position.

The Isolationist Dilemma   Most Americans remained uncertainly in the middle of the violent debate. "I am 100 per cent plus against our participation in this criminal war," wrote Josephus Daniels, the old Wilsonian, once Roosevelt's chief as Secretary of the Navy in the First World War, now ambassador to Mexico, "but, of course, I trust that Europe will be delivered from totalitarian governments and the scourge of force." This was the isolationist dilemma: at some point, the two sentiments were bound to collide. George W. Norris, the patriarch of American liberalism, told an interviewer that he was the only one left of the six senators who had voted against war in 1917:

> . . . viewing the aftermath of the war, I feel justified in what I did. Yet now . . . I do not like to think how a future generation called upon to combat this terror will feel about us who did not nip it in the bud. . . . If the policies of Hitler or Mussolini or Japan are carried out to their logical conclusion, the civilized world will ultimately have to contend against the barbarous conduct they have inaugurated.

An analysis of votes in Congress during these years shows, not a rigid isolationist-interventionist division, but a large middle bloc trying to steer a course between the two extremes. Most members of Congress, like most Americans, wished that all-out support of Britain short of war would somehow bring British victory without American participation. In providing Britain such support, they edged steadily toward involvement. Yet involvement was not their purpose; it was rather the last resort which they earnestly hoped to avoid. Men like Henry L. Stimson, Harold L. Ickes, and the members of the Fight for Freedom Committee felt that Roosevelt himself, by refusing to call for an American declaration of war, was engaged in self-delusion. Still the President's policy of hoping for the best while preparing for the worst expressed the predominant sense of the American people in 1941.

Hitler Widens the War   After the Soviet Union attacked Finland, Roosevelt had condemned Stalin's regime as "a dictatorship as absolute as any other dictatorship in the world." None the less, American diplomats noted growing evidence of tension between Germany and Russia and in the winter of 1940–41 even told a skeptical Kremlin that a German attack might be in the making. Stalin remained impervious to warnings, however; and, when Hitler, despairing of an early defeat of Britain, decided to eliminate the potential threat of Russia by a sudden blow, the Soviet regime was taken completely by surprise. The Nazi invasion of the U.S.S.R. on June 22, 1941, brought the European war into a new phase.

Winston Churchill had long since decided that, in such an eventuality, he would offer Russia full British support. "I have only one purpose," he said, "the destruction of Hitler. . . . If Hitler invaded Hell, I would make at least a favorable reference to the Devil in the House of Commons." Roosevelt was ready to accept this policy. Despite warnings that Russia could not be expected to hold out for very long against the Nazi onslaughts, he sent Harry Hopkins to Moscow in July. Hopkins' relatively optimistic report confirmed Churchill and Roosevelt in their decision to do what they could to stiffen Soviet resistance.

Most Americans supported this decision. The American communists, of course, rapidly reversed their position, called off their antiwar agitation, and became passionate proponents of national defense. From an isolationist viewpoint, however, Hitler's new embroilment strengthened the case against American participation.

The Atlantic Charter   A long-sought meeting between Roosevelt and Churchill took place in early August off Argentia on the coast of Newfoundland. The conversations between the two leaders ranged widely over the problems of both Europe and the Far East. While Roosevelt avoided military commitments, he did agree with Churchill on "certain common principles in the national policies of their respective countries on which they base their hopes for a better future for the world." In the document they drew up, known as the Atlantic Charter, Britain and the United States disclaimed territorial aggrandizement, affirmed the right of all peoples to choose their own form of government and to express freely their wishes concerning territorial changes, assured all states equal access to trade and raw materials ("with due respect to their existing obligations"), proposed collaboration among all nations in the economic field, and promised "after the final destruction of the Nazi tyranny" the disarmament of all aggressor nations "pending the establishment of a wider and permanent system of general security."

In the meantime, American troops had relieved the British garrison in Iceland in July, an act technically justified on the ground that Iceland was really part of the Western Hemisphere. This occupation now enabled American destroyers to escort convoys as far as Iceland, leaving the British navy to conduct them the rest of the way. The question of what American ships should do if they encountered a German raider was left unanswered until a U-boat fired on the destroyer *Greer* early in September. "From now on," said Roosevelt, "if German or Italian vessels of war enter the waters the protection of which is necessary for American defense, they do so at their own risk." In October the Germans badly damaged one American destroyer and sank another, the *Reuben James*, with considerable loss of life. In November Congress revised the Neutrality Act to allow merchantmen to carry arms and to proceed to British ports.

Both the Argentia meeting and the new developments in the Atlantic goaded the isolationists into ever more impassioned attacks on the Administration. In an extraordinary speech at Des Moines in September, Charles A. Lindbergh declared that "the three most important groups who have been pressing this country toward war are the British, the Jewish and the Roosevelt administration." He went on to say of the Jews, "Their greatest danger to this country lies in their large ownership and influence in our motion pictures, our press, our radio, and our government." Though most isolationists disowned the Lindbergh line, a disturbing strain of anti-Semitism began to appear in isolationist discourse. Some observers felt that the dynamics of isolationism was propelling its supporters ever more steadily in a pro-Nazi direction.

The Japanese Dilemma Despite the loss of coastal China in 1937 and the failure of the Brussels Conference (see p. 685), the Chiang Kai-shek government had kept up a stalwart resistance against the Japanese invasion. The Chinese plight increasingly enlisted the sympathy of the United States and Britain, and, though both governments were reluctant to provoke Japanese retaliation, they began in 1938 to seek ways to get financial assistance to China.

Though the Japanese grumbled a good deal, their response to these Anglo-American gestures was less explosive than the State Department had predicted. One reason for this restraint was the extent to which the Japanese war effort had itself become dependent on the United States. In 1938, for example, the United States supplied Japan with 90 per cent of its metal scrap, 91 per cent of its copper, and 66 per cent of its oil. This trade confronted Washington with embarrassing problems. It was sanctioned by the Japanese-American commercial treaty of 1911, and the commodities involved were beyond the reach of existing neutrality legislation. To call for a "moral" embargo of the sort used in the Italo-Ethiopian conflict would penalize China as well as Japan. Its hands thus tied, the United States was left in the position of fueling a war machine of which it profoundly disapproved. In an effort to regain freedom of action, Washington informed Tokyo in July 1939 of its intention to terminate the commercial treaty.

Chastened by this bulletin, the Japanese government was even more staggered by the announcement of the Soviet-Nazi pact in August 1939. The consequence was a temporary setback to the fire-eaters in Tokyo and an improvement of relations with the United States. In January 1940 Washington informed Tokyo that, while it would not renew the commercial treaty, it would not for the time being disturb the existing trade. For a few months relations between the two countries jogged along. Then the Nazi successes in Europe transformed the situation. The expansionists in Tokyo felt their long-awaited opportunity had come to seize the colonial empires of France and the Netherlands, even perhaps of Britain. The relatively moderate government was overthrown. In its place came a tough government, dominated by the military and dedicated to the achievement of a "new order in Greater East Asia."

The Problem of Japan The immediate American response to the change in Japanese policy was the imposition of an embargo on essential materials, especially aviation gasoline and scrap metal. Since this action could be justified in terms of America's own defense needs, it did not have the flavor of an open affront to Japan. It was the first of a series of measures by which Washington sought quietly to restrict exports to Japan. Behind the scenes, American representatives took part in staff discussions with British and Dutch officials to consider plans for the defense of the western Pacific in case a Japanese attack forced the United States into war.

Within Japan an argument continued between a moderate group, hoping for an accommodation with the United States, and a radical group, demanding American acceptance of Japanese hegemony in East Asia. The sticking-point was American insistence on Japanese withdrawal from China. It has been subsequently argued that, if the United States had only been willing to compromise on China, the moderates would have regained control in Tokyo, and Japan would never have embarked on its course of southward expansion. Roosevelt and Hull, however, had good reason for not wishing to abandon China; and, in any case, such abandonment might simply have encouraged the extremists.

Washington felt that by prolonging negotiations it could stave off a Japanese drive southward. Accordingly 1941 was marked by long, intricate, and repetitious discussions between the two countries. For a time, the policy of delay worked, and Japan refrained from acts of aggression. Then the Nazi attack on the Soviet Union freed Japan for adventures to the south. In mid-July 1941 Japanese troops invaded southern Indochina. At this point Roosevelt told the Japanese ambassador that, if Japan withdrew from Indochina, he would secure its neutralization and gain Japan access to its raw materials. If, on the other hand, Japan persisted in its course, and especially if it moved into the Dutch East Indies, the

Pearl Harbor, December 7, 1941: "A terrible lesson."

United States would help the Dutch and probably cut off oil exports to Japan. When Japan did not reply, Roosevelt on July 26 froze Japanese assets in the United States, and a few days later he placed an embargo on oil shipments to Japan.

These actions brought about a moment of reappraisal in Tokyo. Prime Minister Konoye, a moderate, favored one more attempt to reach an agreement with the United States. But the army and navy proposed a war plan to eliminate Allied power in the Far East and to conquer the Dutch East Indies. At an Imperial Conference in early September, the Japanese leaders reached their decision: "If by the early part of October, there is no reasonable hope of having our demands agreed to in the diplomatic negotiations . . . we will immediately make up our minds to get ready for war." The minimum demands to which America and Britain were expected to accede included the termination of aid to China, the

recognition of the Japanese position in Indochina, the resumption of trade with Japan, and the agreement not to reinforce their Far Eastern bases.

The Rising Sun over the Pacific   The military planners pressed their preparations for war. Under the pressure of Admiral Yamamoto, they added a plan for a carrier-based surprise strike against the American fleet at Pearl Harbor. In mid-October Konoye resigned, to be replaced by General Tojo, the Minister of War. On November 5 the new government set as its final deadline November 25 (later November 29). It also prepared a final offer to Washington along the line of the minimum demands of September. Tojo told Admiral Nomura, the Japanese ambassador, that other matters would be negotiable but that Japan could never yield on the question of China.

By intercepting and decoding secret Japanese messages, the Americans had been able to follow some of the Japanese moves. Officials in Washington thus realized that the end was drawing near. Late in November American forces in the Pacific, including those in Hawaii, were sent the first of a number of alerts ordering them onto a war footing. Everyone expected attack; but the conviction was absolute that the Japanese would strike toward the south. In Washington, Cordell Hull continued to meet with Japanese representatives. On December 6 Roosevelt sent a final appeal to the emperor.

In the meantime, a striking force of Japanese carriers had left the Kuriles on November 26 and was making its way toward Pearl Harbor. On December 7, 1941, the Japanese launched a devastating attack on the American fleet and air force in Hawaii. An epoch in American history had come to an end.

"In the past few years—and, most violently, in the past few days—we have learned a terrible lesson," said Franklin Roosevelt two days later. ". . . We must begin the great task that is before us by abandoning once and for all the illusion that we can ever again isolate ourselves from the rest of humanity." He added, "We are going to win the war, and we are going to win the peace that follows."

SUGGESTIONS FOR READING

General

There are brief, general accounts of United States foreign policy in Allan Nevins, *The New Deal and World Affairs* (1951), and Dexter Perkins, *The New Age of Franklin Roosevelt* * (1957), as well as in the standard textbooks on diplomatic history by T. A. Bailey, S. F. Bemis, R. W. Leopold, and J. W. Pratt. Neither those volumes nor any others provide adequate coverage of the early foreign policy of the New Deal. For the period from 1937 on, however, there is the superbly balanced, comprehensive, two-volume study of W. L. Langer and S. E. Gleason, *The Challenge to Isolation* (1952) and *The Undeclared War* (1953). The developments covered in those volumes are treated from the isolationist view in C. A. Beard, *American Foreign Policy in the Making, 1932–1940* (1946), and C. C. Tansill, *Back Door to War* (1952). Point after point, Beard is corrected and refuted in Basil Rauch, *Roosevelt: From Munich to Pearl Harbor* (1950).

Memoirs and Biographies

The memoirs of four American policy-makers are indispensable. Cordell Hull, *Memoirs*, 2 vols. (1948), is copious and detailed. H. L. Stimson and McGeorge Bundy, *On Active Service in Peace and War* (1948), is powerful and lucid. Important also are Sumner Welles, *A Time for Decision* (1944), and Herbert Feis, *Seen from E. A.: Three International Episodes* (1947). Stimson's policies receive understanding analysis in E. E. Morison, *Turmoil and Tradition* (1960), and sometimes unfair attack in R. N. Current, *Secretary Stimson* (1954). Harry Hopkins has a learned and sympathetic biographer in R. E. Sherwood, *Roosevelt and Hopkins* * (1948; rev. ed., 1950). For conflicts between the Treasury and State Departments over foreign monetary policy through 1938, see J. M. Blum, *From the Morgenthau Diaries* (1959).

Special Topics

There are some useful special studies of New Deal foreign policies. On the Good Neighbor policy there are accounts in E. O. Guerrant, *Roosevelt's Good Neighbor Policy* (1950), and Bryce Wood, *The Making of the Good Neighbor Policy* (1961). More specialized are H. F. Cline, *The United States and Mexico* (1953), and E. D. Cronon, *Josephus Daniels in Mexico* (1960). R. P. Browder, *The Origins of Soviet-American Diplomacy* (1953), concentrates on the recognition of Russia. A perceptive analysis of the interests of the United States in the Orient is A. W. Griswold, *The Far Eastern Policy of the United States* (1938). The best treatment of the developing tensions in Japanese-American relations is in Herbert Feis, *The Road to Pearl*

* Available in a paperback edition.

Harbor (1950), which is well supplemented by P. W. Schroeder, *The Axis Alliance and Japanese-American Relations, 1941* (1958). Also instructive is the memoir of Ambassador Joseph C. Grew, *Turbulent Era* (1952).

On the threat of Nazism there are A. L. C. Bullock's excellent biography, *Hitler: A Study in Tyranny* * (1952); W. L. Shirer's long and sometimes superficial *Rise and Fall of the Third Reich* * (1960); the classic volumes of Winston Churchill, *The Gathering Storm* * (1948) and *Their Finest Hour* * (1949); the scholarly H. L. Trefousse, *Germany and American Neutrality* (1951); and relevant chapters in Gordon Craig and Felix Gilbert, eds., *The Diplomats, 1919–1939* (1953). The later Churchill volume discusses American aid to England, but in less complete and documented form than does the authoritative study by H. D. Hall, *North American Supply* (1955). American defense planning is described in M. S. Watson, *Chief of Staff: Prewar Plans and Preparations* (1950). For the great debate about foreign policy, see Walter Johnson, *Battle Against Isolationism* (1944), which describes the work of the Committee to Defend America by Aiding the Allies, and, for an account of the opponents of that purpose, W. S. Cole, *America First* (1953).

* Available in a paperback edition.

30

The World in Flames

The bitter wreckage of ships and planes at Pearl Harbor ended the illusion that the United States could be a world power and still be safe from world conflict. In the shocking strike from the placid Hawaiian skies, the Japanese did more than cripple the Pacific Fleet, destroy hundreds of airplanes, and kill nearly twenty-five hundred men (the navy lost three times as many men in this single attack as it had lost in the Spanish-American War and the First World War put together). The date which, as Roosevelt put it in his address to Congress, would "live in infamy" also brought to an abrupt end the national debate between isolationism and internationalism. On December 11, 1941, Germany and Italy declared war on the United States. The age of innocence was over.

America Organizes for War

Mobilization of Production The outbreak of war found the American economy in a condition of semimobilization. During 1941 the Office of Production Management had presided over a gradual shift from civilian to defense production: by Pearl Harbor about 15 per cent of industrial output was going for military purposes. Still, much of the economy continued to operate on principles of "business as usual." Through 1941 businessmen resisted pressure to convert industrial facilities to war production; labor leaders conducted strikes for higher pay and better working conditions;

the OPM itself lacked the authority to allocate materials and to enforce priorities. In August, Roosevelt established the Supplies, Priorities, and Allocations Board, but this new coordinating agency lacked effective power.

Nevertheless, for all the apparent confusion, the defense output was steadily rising. Between January and December 1941, munitions production increased 225 per cent. By the time of Pearl Harbor, military spending was reaching a monthly rate of nearly $2 billion, aircraft production an annual rate of nearly twenty-five thousand. By this time the American economy was turning out everything the American services required, in notable contrast to the First World War, when the American government depended throughout on European factories for many types of arms and munitions.

Yet this progress, though impressive, was not nearly enough for the harsh requirements of total war. After the Japanese attack, Roosevelt laid down unprecedented production objectives for 1942: sixty thousand planes, forty-five thousand tanks, twenty thousand antiaircraft guns, eight million tons of shipping. To achieve such formidable goals demanded a further centralization of the defense effort. In January 1942 the President accordingly gave basic responsibility over production to a new agency, the War Production Board.

Though its charter conferred on the WPB broad powers over the whole economy, the new chairman, Donald Nelson, construed his mandate modestly. He had an intelligent grasp of the issues involved in economic mobilization, but he lacked force as an administrator. Thus he relinquished to the military control over the setting of industrial specifications, the letting of contracts, and the entire process of procurement. Since the services lacked an over-all production program, the immediate result was a chaos of requisitions in all directions. In the first six months of 1942, government procurement officers placed over $100 billion of war contracts—more goods on order than the American economy had ever produced in a single year in its history. The structure of central control quickly buckled under the strain. The priority system broke down; sometimes more priorities were issued than goods existed. Production programs competed with each other for labor, for machine tools, and especially for scarce materials. Too often production lines had to suspend because of stoppages in the flow of materials. All this led to demands by the military that they be given full control over war production. Nelson, backed by the President and Congress, succeeded in fending off these recurrent proposals. In 1943 the WPB's Controlled Materials Plan finally introduced order into the allocation of critical materials.

As he had relinquished authority over procurement, Nelson similarly relinquished areas of authority over vital commodities. In December 1942 the War Food Administration assumed direction of the nation's food program. Shortages in oil and rubber brought about the appointment, also outside the WPB, of "czars" with exceptional powers to expedite production and distribution. The War Manpower Commission, granted operating authority at the end of 1942, supervised the mobilization of men and women for both civilian and military purposes. And the Office of Scientific Research and Development, under the direction of Dr. Vannevar Bush, conducted scientific and technical mobilization; its scientists and engineers were responsible for radar, short-range rockets (especially the "bazooka"), the proximity fuse, and other remarkable gains in military technology.

Though Nelson thus parceled out authority which his critics thought should have been hoarded in the WPB, the war output nevertheless kept increasing. In 1942 alone the pro-portion of the economy committed to war production grew from 15 to 33 per cent. By the end of 1943 federal expenditures for goods and services constituted a sum larger than the total product of the economy when Roosevelt took office a decade earlier. The gross national product grew from $100.6 billion in 1940 to $213.6 billion in 1945 (in 1957 dollars, from $218.8 billion to $333.9 billion). The WPB continued to be shaken by feuds, both internal and external; Nelson himself was forced out in 1944. Still, in one way or another, the WPB succeeded in releasing and guiding the productive energies of the economy to enable America in a surprisingly short time to outproduce all other nations in the world.

The Fight for Stabilization   This extraordinary feat of economic expansion was a result of the stimulus provided by government spending to the productive talents of American managers and workers. Federal purchases of goods and services rose from $6 billion in 1940 to $89 billion in 1944 (from $15 billion to $155 billion in terms of 1957 dollars). Total federal spending during the war years came to over $320 billion—an amount twice as great as the total of all previous federal spending in the history of the republic.

How was this prodigious expenditure to be paid for? The first resort was to a broadening and deepening of the tax structure. In October 1942, for example, Roosevelt by executive order limited salaries to $25,000 net after taxes. By the end of the war surtaxes were taking away 94 per cent of net income in the highest brackets; and people at every level were paying taxes which would have seemed inconceivable a short time before. Total tax revenues in the war years came to about $130 billion. As a result of this mighty effort, the government was able to meet about 41 per cent of the cost of the war on a pay-as-you-go basis—a much larger proportion than during the First World War.

The rest of the defense bill was made up by borrowing. In 1944 alone the excess of expenditures over receipts amounted to more than $50 billion—a figure over twice the total size of the accumulated debt in 1941. By the end of the war the national debt had grown to about $280 billion, nearly six times as large as it had been when bombs fell on Pearl Harbor. The budgetary deficits so loudly bewailed in New Deal days now seemed negligible compared to the deficit spending of war. An incidental effect was to prove the Keynesian argument that public deficits would end the depression: unemployment rapidly vanished in 1941 and 1942, and old New Deal agencies like the Works Progress Administration gave up the ghost. The problem became, not to find jobs for people, but to find people for jobs.

The tremendous increase in public spending raised up the specter of inflation. The shift from civilian to war production meant that the quantity of goods available for purchase was shrinking just as the quantity of money jingling in people's pockets was increasing. By 1944, for example, the production of civilian automobiles, of washing machines and other consumer durables, of nondefense housing and the like had virtually come to an end. Unless prices were to soar out of sight, means had to be found to hold the volume of spendable money down to the volume of available goods.

One resort was to fiscal and monetary policies. Taxation was an obvious means of reducing the supply of spendable money in people's hands. The war-bond drive was another way by which the government sought to persuade people to put their money away instead of using it to bid up prices; nearly $100 billion worth of the various series of war bonds was sold in these years. But it was evident from an early point that such indirect measures would not be enough to eliminate the "inflationary gap"—the gap, that is, between too few goods and too much money. As early as August 1941 Roosevelt had accordingly established the Office of Price Administration under the direction of Leon Henderson, a hard-driving New Deal economist. The OPA did not at first have the statutory authority to control prices directly; but this defect was partly remedied by the passage of the Emergency Price Control Act a few weeks after Pearl Harbor, though Henderson still lacked effective control over wages and farm prices.

Price control presented one of the toughest problems of war administration. Every economic interest wanted rigid policing of the other fellow's prices but tended to believe that anyone who policed its own prices was subverting the free-enterprise system. The OPA, operating at first on the theory of piecemeal price-fixing, tried to impose ceilings whenever prices in any commodity showed signs of rising. In April 1942 it added a general price freeze, aimed at holding most prices and rents at the level of March 1942. It joined to this a system by which necessities of life in short supply—meat, gasoline, tires—were rationed to the consumer through an allotment of coupons. Local rationing boards assumed responsibility for administering this program.

But the lack of control over wages and farm prices handicapped the stabilization effort. The farm bloc had succeeded in writing into the Emergency Price Control Act a provision permitting price ceilings only on agricultural commodities which had reached 110 per cent of parity—a stipulation which invited a steady increase in food prices. This increase in food prices inevitably brought about demands by workers for increased wages. The War Labor Board, established in January 1942, sought to meet this issue by the Little Steel formula of July, which allowed wage increases to keep pace with a 15 per cent increase in the cost of living since January 1941. None the less, the inflationary spiral continued. Finally, in September 1942, Roosevelt requested new authority to stabilize the cost of living, including farm prices and wages. The result was the Stabilization Act of 1942 and the creation of the Office of Economic Stabilization under the direction of Supreme Court Justice James F. Byrnes.

Byrnes made a manful attempt to coordinate the various elements in the stabilization program; but special interests continued unabashed guerrilla warfare against price control in their own sectors. The farm bloc was unrelenting in its demand that exceptions be made for itself. John L. Lewis led the United Mine Workers in a fight against the Little Steel formula; for a time in 1943 the government was forced to seize and operate the coal mines. Henderson, who had affronted Congress by the unquenchable zeal of his war against inflation, had been forced to resign in December 1942. But a "hold-the-line" order in April 1943, followed by a campaign in May to "roll back" food prices, helped bring the price level to a plateau by mid-1943. For the rest of the war the OPA, under the able direction of Chester Bowles, was able to maintain substantial price stability. Indeed, in the whole period between the outbreak of the European war and the final defeat of Japan, the cost of living rose only about 29 per cent. For all its unpopularity, especially among businessmen, politicians, and farm leaders, the OPA was one of the war's brilliant successes.

The problem remained of concerting the efforts of various agencies dealing with production and stabilization. During 1942 Roosevelt had tried to do the coordination job himself in the spare moments left over from the military and diplomatic business of the war. This did not work, however, and in May 1943 he set up the Office of War Mobilization and put Byrnes in charge. Employing his judicial and political skill to intervene when operating agencies disagreed, Byrnes did an effective job in pulling together the infinitely ramified strands of America's domestic war effort.

The People Behind the Lines   The attack on Pearl Harbor caused a tremendous surge of national unity behind the government. Throughout the war, the morale of the nation remained high. None the less, like any period of war, this was a period of upheaval. People were uprooted from familiar settings and thrust into new places and new responsibilities. The new social fluidity created both anxiety and opportunity.

Anxiety derived from worries about the war itself. The spate of rumors following the Pearl Harbor attack dramatized the public hunger for military information. To deal with the Pearl Harbor situation Roosevelt appointed Justice Owen Roberts of the Supreme Court as a head of a Special Board of Inquiry, and to coordinate the general release of information to the public he established in June 1942 the Office of War Information under Elmer Davis, a greatly respected news commentator. Congressional mistrust of the OWI's domestic information activities eventually caused a reduction of its role at home, and in the end it made its major contribution as an agency of psychological warfare overseas.

Anxiety also derived from alarm over enemy activity within the United States. But fear of the enemy within was much less than it had been during the First World War, and the years 1941–45 were not marred by the widespread assaults on civil freedom which had

characterized the years 1917–20 (see pp. 590–93). Perhaps because the issues now seemed ideological rather than national, German-Americans and Italian-Americans were not subjected to jingoistic harassments. The tragic exception to this general tolerance was the fate of the over one hundred thousand Japanese-Americans—the Nisei—who were brutally removed from their homes along the Pacific Coast and relocated in internment camps in the interior—an act wholly unjustified and subsequently profoundly regretted.

Of native Americans suspected of sympathy for fascism, some had their publications—for example, Father Coughlin's *Social Justice*—denied the mails. Toward the end of the war, an effort to convict a number of American fascists in a mass sedition trial miscarried. In the meantime, the Department of Justice had taken effective steps against Nazi agents and organizations. So far as is known, no acts of enemy sabotage were committed in the United States during the war. In the main, Attorney General Francis Biddle strove with success to maintain an atmosphere of moderation. Both government and people generally respected the distinction between heresy and conspiracy.

If war meant anxiety, it also meant opportunity. In the acceleration of events during the Second World War, no group gained more than the Negroes. The national folkway of discrimination constituted a spectacular contradiction to the official rhetoric of freedom; from an early point, Negro leaders were determined to make the libertarian pledges of the war apply to their own people as well as to the victims of Nazism in Europe. Their first demand was for equality of opportunity in employment. When Philip Randolph, president of the Brotherhood of Sleeping Car Porters, threatened a mass Negro march on Washington in 1941, Roosevelt issued his historic Executive Order 8802 forbidding discrimination in hiring practices in defense industries and establishing a Fair Employment Practices Commission. During the war years the FEPC, aided by the shortages in the labor market, did an effective job in expanding economic opportunities for Negroes. Progress was also made in reducing segregation in the armed services. The assertion of Negro rights sometimes increased racial tensions; a shameful series of riots in Detroit in June 1943 resulted in the death of over thirty persons, white and Negro. But, on balance, the Negroes were more than able to maintain the momentum of the thirties in the fight for equality.

Early Politics of the War Political developments after Pearl Harbor quickly refuted the isolationist prediction that war must doom democracy and free discussion. The processes of economic mobilization, in particular, created strains; and groups anxious to protect favored positions or to ventilate grievances generally found ample representation in the ranks of Congress. Thus the resentments of businessmen and farmers against the OPA, and also against organized labor, took up a great deal of congressional time. The dominating conservative coalition of Republicans and Southern Democrats also seized the opportunity to liquidate New Deal agencies which appeared to have lost their function. On the other hand, Congress also provided disinterested and responsible counsel on many aspects of the war effort. The most notable expression of this was the Senate War Investigating Committee, which, under the able chairmanship of Harry S. Truman of Missouri, exposed waste and confusion in the defense effort and made valuable recommendations.

Relations with Congress presented Roosevelt with difficult problems. The chairmen of the Senate Military and Naval Affairs Committees were both isolationists; the chairman of the House Military Affairs Committee was later convicted of attempting bribes in connection with war contracts; and most of the congressional leaders were conservatives. The 1942 congressional election took place in an atmosphere suffused with wartime irritations, especially over the OPA's efforts to hold prices and rents down. It resulted in striking Republican gains—ten seats in the Senate, forty-seven in the House. This outcome confirmed the conservative complexion of the Congress and filled the Republicans with high hopes for the presidential election of 1944.

The War in Europe

Beat Hitler First The manifold activities at home, however, only provided the backdrop for the essential problem of war—victory over the enemy. For the United States there were, in essence, two enemies—the Japanese, advancing rapidly into Southeast Asia in the weeks after Pearl Harbor; and the European Axis, now engaged in savage warfare on the Russian front and presumably preparing an eventual invasion of England. The immediate problem for the United States was to decide where first to throw its military might—against Germany or against Japan.

American military planners had already given this problem careful consideration and had concluded by March 1941 that, if the United States entered the war, American strategy must be to beat Hitler first. There were several reasons for this decision. For one thing, Germany, with its command of most of the western coast of Europe and its access to the Atlantic, presented a direct threat to the Western Hemisphere; there was particular concern over Axis penetration of Latin America. For another, Germany seemed far more likely than Japan to achieve some revolutionary breakthrough in military technology. In addition, Great Britain was fully engaged in fighting the Axis, while in the Far East China was both less active in its resistance to Japan and less accessible to outside support.

The Nazi attack on the Soviet Union in June 1941, far from reversing the Europe-first argument, was considered to reinforce it; for the Russo-German war increased both the chance of defeating Germany and the urgency of doing so before Germany absorbed Russia. Nor did the Japanese attack on Pearl Harbor shake the American decision. When Winston Churchill came to Washington in December 1941, he found complete agreement on his proposition that "the defeat of Germany, entailing a collapse, will leave Japan exposed to overwhelming force, whereas the defeat of Japan would not by any means bring the World War to an end." For a moment in July 1942, General George C. Marshall and Admiral Ernest J. King, the Chiefs of Staff of the army and navy, succumbed to irritation over the delays in planning for a second front in Europe and advocated a major American offensive in the Southwest Pacific. But the "Hitler-first" strategy survived this crisis and determined the subsequent course of the war.

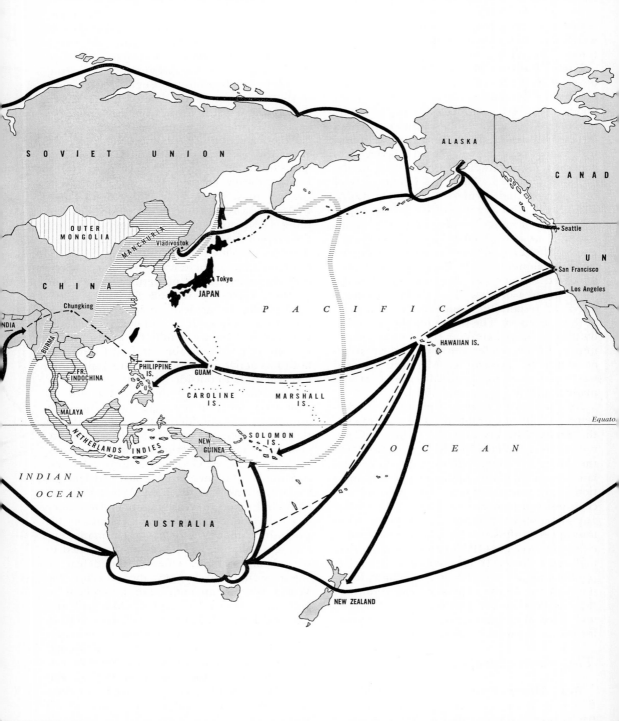

GREENLAND

ICELAND

Quebec

Argentia

New York

gton

Signing of the
Atlantic Charter
Aug. 1941

Casablanca Conference
Jan. 1943

Casablanca

MOROCCO

ALGERIA

TUNISIA

LIBYA

Cairo Conferences
Nov., Dec. 1943

EGYPT

NORWAY

SWEDEN

FINLAND

• Leningrad

• Moscow

GREAT
BRITAIN

London

FRANCE

GERMANY

ITALY

SPAIN

SOVIET UNION

Yalta Conference
Feb. 1945

• Stalingrad

Yalta

TURKEY

SYRIA

IRAQ

Teheran Conference
Nov. 1943

Teheran

IRAN

CHINA

INDIA

Suez
Canal

SAUDI
ARABIA

ATLANTIC

VENEZUELA

COLOMBIA

DOR

PERU

BRAZIL

OCEAN

BOLIVIA

PARAGUAY

FRENCH WEST AFRICA

NIGERIA

FR. EQ.
AFRICA

SUDAN

ETHIOPIA

KENYA

BELGIAN
CONGO

TANG.

ANGOLA

NO. RHO.

SO.
RHO.

MOZAMBIQUE

MADAGASCAR

INDIAN

OCEAN

S.W.
AFR.

BECH.

UNION
OF SOUTH
AFRICA

URUGUAY

CHILE

ARGENTINA

The Second World War

Allied nations	Axis powers
Neutral nations	Area of maximum Axis control
Allied supply lines	Area of German submarine operations
U.S. air supply lines	

Diverging Strategies in Europe   The agreement between the United States and Britain on beating Germany first was not matched, however, by agreement on the best way of doing it. British strategy was clearly formulated: it was to postpone any direct assault on Germany until a combination of naval blockade, aerial bombing, psychological warfare, and military attack on the Axis periphery had sufficiently weakened Germany's capacity to resist. In Churchill this strategy had an exceptionally eloquent and resourceful champion. The British Prime Minister had long been identified with the circuitous approach to the German foe. The Dardanelles campaign during the First World War had resulted from his dislike of the policy of direct assault. "No plan could be more unpromising than the plan of frontal attack," he had written in his history of the First World War. ". . . It is a tale of the torture, mutilation, or extinction of millions of men, and of the sacrifice of all that was best and noblest in an entire generation."

Where the British strategy was to attack the enemy where he was weakest; the American was to attack the enemy where he was strongest. From the American viewpoint, the Churchill plan of "pecking at the periphery" would waste resources without winning victory. As Roosevelt used to observe when Churchill advocated a landing at one or another European point remote from Germany, "All right, but where do we go from there?" The Joint Chiefs of Staff felt that only a massive thrust across the English Channel and France into the heart of Gemany would achieve victory. In their view—a view generally shared by Roosevelt—all Anglo-American efforts should be concentrated on establishing a second front in France.

Detour to North Africa   The American strategy was strongly supported by the Soviet Union, in desperate need of relief from the hammer blows of the German army and air force. But, though the British accepted the necessity of a cross-channel invasion in principle, they continued to object in practice. They felt that the Americans underestimated the difficulties of amphibious landings on fortified coasts; they regarded American troops as untried; and they doubted whether the American economy could quickly achieve the production levels necessary to sustain a great invasion. There were particularly ominous shortages in landing craft and in modern tanks. Accordingly, when the American Joint Chiefs submitted in the spring of 1942 a plan for the invasion of France later that year, the British, after some hesitation, turned it down.

Still, something had to be done in 1942, if only to maintain the morale of the Russians. Churchill consequently proposed, as a substitute for a cross-channel attack, an invasion of North Africa. The American Joint Chiefs opposed this idea; they felt that a North African diversion, by committing Anglo-American forces to a Mediterranean campaign as well as by pre-empting necessary men and materiel, would delay the invasion of France, perhaps until 1944. But Roosevelt accepted Churchill's argument that an invasion of North Africa in 1942 could be a preliminary to a cross-channel attack in 1943. In July the decision was made to invade North Africa in the autumn. The operation was placed under the command of General Dwight D. Eisenhower.

On November 8, 1942, Anglo-American forces disembarked at Casablanca in Morocco and at Oran and Algiers in Algeria. The landings achieved tactical surprise. Within short order, local resistance came to an end. But the military success raised complex political problems. The collaborationist regime of Marshal Pétain, established at Vichy and in control of the unoccupied portions of southern France, exercised nominal authority in North Africa. The United States, which had maintained diplomatic relations with the Vichy government, had some hope of winning the support of pro-Vichy officials and military leaders in Algeria and Morocco. Roosevelt and Churchill supposed that General Charles de Gaulle, commander of the Free French in London, would be unacceptable to the North African French, who had sworn oaths of loyalty to Pétain. But the Americans believed that General Henri Giraud, who had recently escaped from a German prison camp, would be exempt from De Gaulle's unpopularity. The situation was further complicated when, by pure accident, the invasion happened to catch in Algiers Admiral Jean François Darlan, a prominent French collaborationist and Pétain's successor-designate.

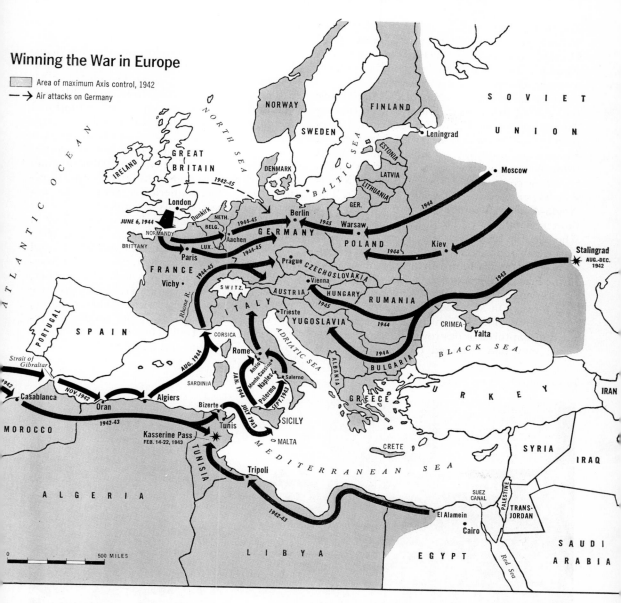

Winning the War in Europe

▫ Area of maximum Axis control, 1942
━➤ Air attacks on Germany

Giraud's prestige in North Africa turned out to be much overrated. Darlan, on the other hand, proved as ready to collaborate with the Americans in 1942 as he had been with the Germans in 1940. Ignoring Pétain's appeal for resistance, Darlan on November 11 signed an armistice agreement with Eisenhower and ordered a ceasefire. As part of the arrangement, Eisenhower recognized Darlan as *de facto* political chief in North Africa—an action which provoked a storm of criticism in England and the United States from those who feared that it inaugurated a policy of making deals with fascists. Roosevelt defended Eisenhower's action as "a temporary expedient, justified solely by the stress of battle." To his press conference, he quoted a Balkan proverb: "My children, you are permitted in time of great danger to walk with the Devil until you have crossed the bridge." The Darlan deal undoubtedly accelerated the Anglo-American military success in Algeria and Morocco, and Darlan's assassination on December 24 spared Roosevelt and Churchill what would have been a vexing political embarrassment.

In the meantime, the North African fighting had shifted to the east. Hitler, after ordering the occupation of Vichy France, rushed German troops by sea and air to Tunisia. General Eisenhower promptly advanced into Tunisia from the west, while the British Eighth Army, under the command of General Bernard Montgomery, entered from Tripoli to the east. The Anglo-American forces encountered the brilliant generalship of Field Marshal Rommel, who came to be known as the Desert Fox; and American troops received a disconcerting baptism of fire at his hands in the Battle of Kasserine Pass in February 1943. None the less, the Anglo-American vise closed inexorably on the Axis forces. On May 12, 1943, the Axis troops surrendered. The British and Americans had not only captured or destroyed fifteen Axis divisions; they had regained the Mediterranean

for their shipping and had thereby laid open to attack what Churchill called the "soft underbelly" of the Axis. In addition, the Americans had gained indispensable combat experience.

The Mediterranean or France? "All right, but where do we go from there?" Roosevelt had asked. As the Joint Chiefs of Staff had feared, the British, while still agreeing in principle that the decisive attack on Germany must come from the west rather than from the south, now advocated moving on into Sicily and Italy in order to maintain the initiative in the Mediterranean. The Americans reluctantly accepted the logic of this argument. The result was the Anglo-American invasion of Sicily in July and of Italy in September. At first, when Mussolini toppled from his dictatorial seat and the new Italian government, under Field Marshal Pietro Badoglio, made haste to surrender, it seemed as if this campaign would produce quick results. But, despite the Italian collapse, the German forces in Italy put up dogged resistance; and the Italian front soon was marked by the most bitter and bloody fighting of the

GI's in Sicily.

European war. When Allied progress up the spine of Italy was stopped at Monte Cassino early in 1944, an attempt was made to circumvent the enemy by amphibious landings at Anzio near Rome late in January. But for many weeks Allied troops could not break out of the Anzio beachhead, and Rome itself did not fall for another four months. In the end, the Italian campaign—especially beyond Rome—cost more and achieved less than its proponents had expected.

In the meantime, argument continued over the long-postponed invasion of France. The British service chiefs, however, still wanted to delay Overlord (the code name for the cross-channel operation) for the sake of new adventures in the Mediterranean. "It is certainly an odd way of helping the Russians," Churchill argued as late as November 1943, "to slow down the fight in the only theatre where anything can be done for some months." But the American Joint Chiefs, with Soviet backing, insisted on a firm commitment to a second front in France. At the end of November 1943, Churchill finally consented to May 1944 as a target date.

The actual invasion, shaped, as Churchill said, "mainly by the moon and the weather," did not take place until June 6. The Germans, deluded by elaborate stratagems, did not expect an attack in Normandy and refused to believe it when it took place. The Allied forces were thus able to consolidate their position on the French coast and fan out for movement along a larger front. On July 25 General Patton's Third Army broke through into Brittany. The war in France now developed extraordinary speed and mobility. American and British divisions raced toward Paris, which was liberated on August 25; and by September 13 Allied forces had penetrated deep into Belgium and crossed the German frontier at Aachen.

These developments, on top of the long-sustained Anglo-American air offensive against Germany, made Hitler's situation more desperate every day. From 1942, when the British and American air forces took substantial command of the air, Germany had been subjected to a series of devastating air raids. By the autumn of 1944, Allied air attacks—which by the end of the war amounted to 1.5 million bomber sorties and 2.7 million tons of bombs dropped

—were exerting a heavy toll on German production (most essentially, of fighter aircraft), rail and road transportation, and civilian morale. In addition, a Soviet offensive, timed to coincide with the Anglo-American landings in France, was driving the Germans back on the eastern front. An attempt on Hitler's life on July 20, 1944, provided evidence of the resistance within Germany to further prosecution of the war.

General Montgomery, the top British commander in the west, now urged Eisenhower to concentrate all Allied resources on ending the war by a single decisive thrust into Germany. The Supreme Commander, looking at Allied port and trucking facilities, concluded that logistic support was lacking for the Montgomery plan. Accordingly, in a highly controversial decision, he settled instead for a "broad-front" strategy of building up strength along the entire western front in preparation for a general advance into Germany. Critics have subsequently insisted that this decision prolonged the European war for an additional six months.

Southern France or the Ljublana Gap? A final argument over strategy remained. The Americans had long wished to follow up the invasion of Normandy with troop landings in southern France; Eisenhower regarded this as essential to the invasion of Germany. The British opposed the plan. Churchill wanted to switch the whole operation to the east and mount instead an invasion through Trieste and the Ljublana Gap of Yugoslavia toward Vienna.

It was this debate that gave rise to the subsequent myth that Churchill, wishing to forestall the Soviet advance into eastern Europe, favored a Balkan invasion rather than a second front in France. Actually Churchill's Mediterranean strategy of 1942–43 was based entirely on military considerations; Churchill himself has never claimed—nor has historical research ever revealed—that this strategy was designed to thwart Soviet expansion. Moreover, Churchill never advocated an invasion of the Balkans, as an alternative to the second front or otherwise. As he wrote Roosevelt in October 1943, "I have never wished to send an army into the Balkans, but only by agents, supplies, and Commandos to stimulate the intense guerrilla

My advice is: As soon as your Chiefs of Staff have completed the plans for the northern offensive to your satisfaction, you should send them by a most trusted messenger and advocate to Churchill and his War Council as the American plan which you propose and intend to go ahead with if accepted by Britain....

And then having done that, you should lean with all your strength on the ruthless rearrangement of shipping allotments and the preparation of landing gear for the ultimate invasion.... It should be pushed with the fever of war action, aimed at a definite date of completion not later than September. The rate of construction of a number of landing barges should not be allowed to lose the crisis of the World War. And yet that is the only objection to the offensive that, after talks with British critics here, I have heard made.

If such decisive action is once taken by you, further successful dispersion of our strength will automatically be terminated. We shall have an affirmative answer against which to measure all such demands; while, on the other hand, so long as we remain without our own plan of offensive, our forces will inevitably be dispersed and wasted.

From Henry L. Stimson, Letter to President Roosevelt, March 1942.

---

prevailing there"—and the guerrillas he wished to stimulate were the Yugoslav Partisans under the leadership of the communist Josip Broz, Tito. Indeed, the only recorded champion of a second front in the Balkans was Stalin himself, who urged this course on Churchill in 1940. The proposed attack through the Ljublana Gap in 1944—the "stab in the Adriatic armpit," as Churchill called it —would have left most of the Balkans untouched.

By 1944, it is true, Churchill was becoming increasingly concerned over the spread of Soviet power, and a definite object of the Ljublana plan was to beat the Russians to Vienna. The Americans rejected the proposal, partly because of the logistic difficulties presented by an Istrian campaign, partly because of their indifference to postwar political considerations. And so the invasion of southern France took place according to schedule on August 15, 1944. Eisenhower later wrote,

"There was no development of that period which added more decisively to our advantages or aided us more in accomplishing the final and complete defeat of the German forces." With the fresh Allied advance up the Rhone Valley, the iron ring around Germany was drawing tight.

The War in the Pacific

Holding the Line   Though the European theater of war had acknowledged priority, the United States and Great Britain could hardly afford to neglect the war in the Far East. Pearl Harbor had only marked the beginning of a period of exultant Japanese aggression. "For three months after the Pearl Harbor attack," Admiral Samuel Eliot Morison has written, "the Pacific was practically a Japanese lake." One after another the bastions of western empire fell to the Japanese: Guam, Wake Island, and Hong Kong in December 1941; Singapore in February 1942; Java in

---

The storm of Cherbourg by a sea-landed army in the face of German opposition, probably in superior numbers and with strong fortifications, was a hazardous operation. If it succeeded, the Allies would be penned up in Cherbourg and the tip of the Cotentin peninsula, and would have to maintain themselves in this confined bomb and shell trap for nearly a year under ceaseless bombardment and assault. They could be supplied only by the port of Cherbourg, which would have to be defended all the winter and spring against potentially continuous and occasionally overwhelming air attack. The drain which such a task would impose must be a first charge upon all our resources of shipping and air-power. It would bleed all other operations.... Moreover, it was not apparent how this unpromising enterprise would help Russia. The Germans had left twenty-five mobile divisions in France. We could not have more than nine ready by August for "Sledgehammer," and of these, seven must be British. There would therefore be no need for the recall of German divisions from the Russian front.

As these facts and many more presented themselves ... I did not have to argue against "Sledgehammer" myself. It fell of its own weakness.

From Winston S. Churchill, *The Hinge of Fate*, 1950.

March; the Philippines in May. Japanese forces were moving into Burma and threatening advances as far to the east as India and to the south as Australia. Japanese politicians were looking forward to the formation of the Greater East Asia Co-Prosperity Sphere, where Japan would mobilize the power of East Asia behind a wall of air and naval defense. It seemed indeed the epoch of the Rising Sun in the Pacific.

This fantastic sequence of events left America and Britain no choice but to conduct an active—even desperate—defense. The Allied forces in the Pacific, knowing that the European war had priority, often felt themselves the step-children of the war. Still, even when they believed themselves starved for supplies, their situation was by no means hopeless. The Japanese had failed to destroy a single aircraft carrier at Pearl Harbor; and the American carrier striking force was not only able to secure the South Pacific supply line between Hawaii and Australia but could conduct sporadic harassments of the enemy (including a raid on Tokyo in April 1942).

Moreover, the Japanese themselves, instead of pausing for prudent consolidation, succumbed to the temptations of success and struck out on ambitious new programs of conquest in the spring of 1942. The Japanese political leaders hoped to extend the sway of the emperor by isolating and perhaps invading Australia; and Admiral Yamamoto, the chief Japanese sea lord, wished to force the American Pacific Fleet into a final engagement before it had a chance to recoup the losses of Pearl Harbor. In May 1942, therefore, the Japanese occupied Tulagi in the Solomon Islands and launched a naval expedition across the Coral Sea toward Port Moresby in Papua, New Guinea. But an American carrier task force intercepted the Japanese ships, and, in an extraordinary battle of carrier-based aircraft, the Americans turned back the enemy. This was the first sea battle in history in which the ships involved exchanged no shots—indeed, did not even come within sight of one another.

The Battle of the Coral Sea marked the high point of Japanese initiative in the south. Yamomoto now shifted his operations to the north central Pacific. A month later, the bulk of the Japanese navy—some two hundred ships—

headed toward Midway Island and the western Aleutians. But the Americans, having broken the Japanese code, were able to anticipate the Japanese intentions and to deploy their forces accordingly. There followed the decisive naval battle of the war, in which the American fleets, brilliantly led by Admiral Spruance and Admiral Fletcher, defeated the Japanese, destroyed four aircraft carriers and many other ships, and forced the enemy into disorderly retreat. The Japanese never again had sufficient naval air strength to take the long-range offensive. The balance of striking power was shifting to the United States.

The Road to Tokyo   The threat to communications from Hawaii to Australia remained, however, so long as the Japanese held their bases in the Solomons and the Bismarcks. Moreover, the Bismarcks Barrier, a chain of small islands, gave the Japanese a powerful defense block athwart the road to Tokyo. It seemed essential to deal with this situation before doing anything else, and intelligence that the Japanese were building an airstrip on the island of Guadalcanal in the Solomons precipitated American action against both Guadalcanal and Tulagi in August 1942. There followed six months of exceptionally savage fighting in the steaming, fetid jungles of Guadalcanal and in the serene waters around the island. By February 1943 the marines and the army had finally forced the Japanese to abandon Guadalcanal.

The Pacific war was still officially considered a holding action. But in January 1943 the American Joint Chiefs, noting that only 15 per cent of Allied resources was being used in the Pacific, argued for the allocation of enough additional strength to permit the launching of an offensive. The British acquiesced, stipulating only that Pacific operations should be kept within such limits as would not handicap the war against Germany. The American planners —for, by agreement, the Pacific war was accepted as essentially an American responsibility—were now free to consider the question of the best route to Tokyo.

The strategy of the European war represented a compromise between diverging American and British views; the strategy of the Pacific war represented a compromise between the diverging views of the American army and

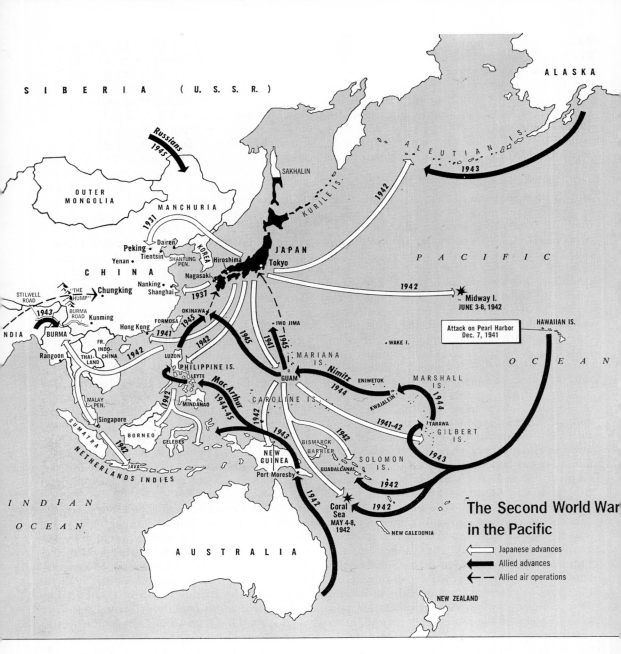

The Second World War
in the Pacific

⇨ Japanese advances
➡ Allied advances
⇢ Allied air operations

the American navy. Both services, furthermore, had unusually articulate representatives in the debate. General Douglas MacArthur, who had been American commander in the Philippines and had been evacuated to Australia early in 1942 to take command of the army in the South Pacific, argued forcefully for an advance on Japan along what he called the "New Guinea-Mindanao Axis"—that is, from the South Pacific through New Guinea to the Philippines, and thence to Japan. Admiral Chester Nimitz, on behalf of the navy, contended for an advance through the central Pacific—the Gilbert, Marshall, Caroline, and Mariana Islands—to Formosa and the Chinese coast, and thence to Japan. MacArthur protested that this would be

Marines at Tarawa.

a gravely mistaken diversion of limited resources. But the navy responded persuasively that a single axis of advance would allow the Japanese to concentrate their defensive action. In the end the Joint Chiefs decided on parallel offensives along both routes.

The invention of a new tactical technique facilitated the American offensive. Up to this point, the aggressive use of forward bases by the Japanese had enabled them to reinforce points under siege. But in March 1943, in the Battle of the Bismarck Sea, General George Kenney's bombers destroyed a Japanese troop convoy headed for New Guinea—an action which dissuaded the Japanese thereafter from attempting to move large bodies of troops within range of Allied air power. As a consequence, American forces could simply bypass the stronger Japanese bases, knowing that the Japanese would not risk large-scale reinforcement, and leave them to wither on the vine. This "leapfrogging" technique became the basic pattern of the American counteroffensive.

The two-pronged offensive got under way in June 1943. In the next nine months it produced solid results. By March 1944 Nimitz' forces had leapfrogged at Tarawa and Kwajalein, and MacArthur's forces had broken the Bismarcks Barrier. Nimitz was now moving into the Marianas; in June the Pacific Fleet under Admiral Spruance smashed the Japanese navy again in the Battle of the Philippine Sea; MacArthur continued to press along the northwest coast of New Guinea toward the Philippines. The time was approaching for a final strategic decision about the road to Tokyo.

Luzon or Formosa? The culmination of the disagreement between MacArthur and Nimitz came over the question of the jumping-off place for Japan. MacArthur insisted on the recapture of the Philippines, and especially of Luzon, as the indispensable preliminary. He invoked not only strategic arguments—that Luzon would be a safer staging area for invasion than Formosa—but also political and emotional arguments; as he put it to Roosevelt, was the President willing "to accept responsibility for breaking a solemn promise to eighteen million Christian Filipinos that the Americans would return?" Admirals King and Nimitz, on the other hand, advocated leapfrogging part or all of the Philippines in the interest of an immediate attack on Formosa. It was not entirely an army-navy difference; many senior naval officers in the Pacific supported MacArthur, and some army planners in Washington supported King. In a conference at Pearl Harbor in July 1944, Roosevelt leaned toward the MacArthur view, but did not settle the question in MacArthur's favor until early October.

Once given the signal, MacArthur lost no time in moving ahead. On October 20 he disembarked on the beach at Leyte, saying, "People of the Philippines: I have returned." A few days later, in the Battle for Leyte Gulf, the American navy in the Philippines completed the destruction of Japanese naval striking power; in terms of the number of ships engaged, this was the greatest naval battle of all history. MacArthur's troops meanwhile pressed on toward Manila while Nimitz' forces were making their way toward Japan from the central Pacific. This steady advance of American arms, reinforced by a stern naval blockade and ever more devastating air attacks, meant that the iron ring was gradually tightening around Japan.

The Riddle of China   At the time of Pearl Harbor, Washington had hoped that China, which had been resisting Japanese aggression since 1937, could play a leading role in bringing about Japan's ultimate downfall. Indeed, through the war, Roosevelt, in face of Churchill's skepticism, persisted in treating China as if it were a major power. However, the Nationalist regime of Chiang Kai-shek, driven into the interior, cut off from sources of supply, exhausted by four years of war and demoralized by inflation, intrigue, and graft, was increasingly incapable of serious action against the enemy.

Keeping China in the war nevertheless remained a major American objective. In 1941 and 1942 the Chungking government received only a thin trickle of supplies flown over the "hump" of the Himalayas from India. Then in 1943 an assortment of Chinese, Indian, and American troops, under the command of General Joseph W. Stilwell, began to construct a road and pipeline across northern Burma to Kunming. Soon Stilwell was sent to Chungking as commander of the American forces in China with orders to maximize the Chinese contribution to the war against Japan. But, where Stilwell saw only one enemy, he rapidly discovered that Chiang Kai-shek saw two: not only the Japanese, but the increasingly powerful Chinese communists, now spreading out from their base in Yenan.

The rise of Chinese communism had come about in the thirties as the Kuomintang lost its revolutionary dynamism under the stress of power, war, and corruption. Seeking particularly to mobilize the poverty-stricken and land-hungry peasants, the communists began to win respect, even among some westerners, as an embodiment of reform, austerity, and discipline. War sharpened the contrast between the self-indulgence of Chungking and the dedication of Yenan and thereby enhanced the communist appeal. Chiang himself seemed to be paying less and less attention to Japan in his preoccupation with the threat of Mao Tse-tung and his Eighth Route Army. By 1944, four hundred thousand Nationalist troops had been diverted to check the spread of communist influence. Stilwell, instructed to get as many Chinese divisions as possible—whatever their politics—into action against the Japanese, soon came to consider Chiang a main obstacle to the fulfillment of his mission.

In June 1944 the Fourteenth Air Force began to attack Japan from Chinese airstrips. This action provoked the Japanese into counterattacking the bomber bases and renewing their offensive against Chungking. Now the difficulties between Stilwell and Chiang came to a head. A brave, narrow, intense man, Stilwell was devoid of diplomatic skill and baffled by the unfathomable depths of Chinese politics. When the Joint Chiefs recommended that the Chinese army be placed under Stilwell's command, Chiang instead demanded his dismissal. Roosevelt complied. The military potential of China was disappearing in the swirl of Chinese civil discord.

The Fourth Term

Politics as Usual   The congressional elections of 1942 brought into office the most conservative Congress Washington had known for a decade. During the next year Congress took every occasion to repudiate the reform mood of the thirties. Its refusal in the spring to continue the National Resources Planning Board was a symbolic rejection of the whole idea of New Deal planning. Its passage in June of the Smith-Connally Act over Roosevelt's veto bestowed on a reluctant government new powers to crack down on trade unions in labor disputes. Congress repealed the $25,000 net salary limitation, liquidated the National Youth Administration, harassed the Farm Security Administration, and sought in a variety of ways to curtail nonwar public functions and expenditures.

Roosevelt himself gave ground before the conservative attack. In a press conference in December 1943 he explained that the New Deal had come into existence because the United States was suffering from a grave internal disorder. But in December 1941 the patient had been in a bad external smashup. "Old Dr. New Deal didn't know 'nothing' about legs and arms. He knew a great deal about internal medicine, but nothing about surgery. So he got his partner, who was an orthopedic surgeon, Dr. Win-the-War to take care of this fellow who had been in this bad accident." Roosevelt went on to praise the ministrations of Dr. New Deal but added, "At the present time, obviously, the principal emphasis, the overwhelming first emphasis should be on winning the war." Such New Dealers who had survived in wartime Washington, like Harry Hopkins, shared the President's belief that domestic reform had to take second place.

The occupation of the White House by Dr. Win-the-War meant a certain disenchantment in the American liberal community. Though Roosevelt retained the essential confidence of liberals, he was no longer articulating their day-to-day hopes. In their frustration, they listened to other voices. They found consolation in particular in Vice-President Henry Wallace, with his celebration of "the century of the common man," and, more surprisingly, in Wendell Willkie, the Republican presidential candidate of 1940 (see p. 691). In the years after his defeat, Willkie had shown himself a political leader generous in disposition and

courageous in utterance. His book *One World*, published in 1943 after his trip as a presidential emissary to Britain, the Soviet Union, the Middle East, and China seemed to sum up the best aspirations of America in its sturdy assertion of liberal internationalism.

The Campaign of 1944 As the titular leader of the Republican party, Willkie retained hopes of a second presidential nomination in 1944. But his liberal ideological tendencies, on top of a chronic political maladroitness, had estranged most of the leaders of his party. After suffering a bad defeat in the Wisconsin presidential primary in April, he withdrew from the race. Thomas E. Dewey, who had been elected governor of New York in 1942, was now emerging as the favored Republican contender. A young man—he had just passed his forty-second birthday—he had already gained a notable reputation for executive efficiency and vigor. The Republican convention, meeting in Chicago at the end of June, promptly nominated Dewey on the first ballot. To balance Dewey's mild inclinations toward liberalism and internationalism, Governor John W. Bricker of Ohio, a conservative isolationist, was named for second place.

The Democrats renominated Roosevelt without suffering the trauma of 1940. "For myself, I do not want to run," he wrote the chairman of the Democratic National Committee in July. ". . . All that is within me cries to go back to my home on the Hudson. . . . But as a good soldier . . . I will accept and serve." The real struggle in the Democratic party was over the vice-presidential nomination. Wallace, with the ardent support of the labor-liberal wing of the party, sought renomination. But the Democratic bosses opposed him, and, though Roosevelt said he "personally" would vote for Wallace if a delegate, it was evident that he was not insisting on Wallace's renomination. Roosevelt's personal preference seems to have been James F. Byrnes. When Ed Flynn of New York and Sidney Hillman of the Amalgamated Clothing Workers vetoed Byrnes, Roosevelt said he would be "very glad to run" with either Senator Harry S. Truman of Missouri or Justice William O. Douglas of the Supreme Court. The contest narrowed down to Truman and Wallace, and Truman won on the third ballot.

The campaign was overshadowed by the war. The initial restraint of Dewey's speeches failed to stir the electorate. He stepped up the harshness of his attack, but his main achievement was to force Roosevelt himself into the arena. An uproariously successful speech before the Teamsters Union in Washington on September 23 showed that the old campaigner had lost none of his magic. In October he sought to meet doubts about his health by riding around New York City all day in an open car through pouring rain. In the meantime, he spoke with eloquence about the need for liberalism and internationalism in the postwar world. The Political Action Committee of the Congress of Industrial Organizations took an aggressive role in bringing out the vote. On November 7 Roosevelt received 25.6 million popular and 432 electoral votes as against 22 million and 99 for Dewey. The Democrats lost one seat in the Senate, gained twenty in the House, and captured five governorships. The election was a categorical confirmation of Roosevelt as America's chosen leader for the peace.

The Diplomacy of Coalition

The Question of War Aims   Though American participation in the war was the consequence of Japanese attack, the United States even before Pearl Harbor had indicated the broad outlines of its ideas on the postwar settlement. In his message to Congress on January 6, 1941, Roosevelt had declared that the United States looked forward to a world founded upon "four essential human freedoms —freedom of speech and expression, freedom of worship, freedom from want, freedom from fear." In August of the same year, the Atlantic Charter (see p. 696) further particularized the American conception of the postwar world, laying stress on national self-determination, equal access to trade and raw materials, and a lasting peace to be achieved through a permanent system of general security. On January 1, 1942, twenty-six nations, led by America, Britain, the Soviet Union, and China, signed a joint declaration subscribing to the Atlantic Charter, pledging their full resources to victory, promising not to make a separate peace, and dedicating themselves to "defend life,

liberty, independence, and religious freedom, and to preserve human rights and justice in their own lands as well as in other lands." Roosevelt called this a "declaration by United Nations," and his phrase was employed thereafter to describe the grand alliance.

In practice, three of the United Nations— the United States, Britain, and the Soviet Union—were more important than the rest; and the main issues of coalition diplomacy proceeded from the relations among these Big Three. The United States and Britain, with their common traditions and interests, had little difficulty in establishing an effective partnership. Roosevelt and Churchill regarded each other with mutual respect and delight and were almost immediately on terms of intimate understanding. The formation of the Anglo-American Combined Chiefs of Staff in December 1941 guaranteed close military coordination between the two countries; a series of combined boards were subsequently set up in other fields. Friction, of course, was not entirely eliminated. Not only were there persistent differences over European strategy, but it soon became evident that Churchill might resist too rigorous an application of the Atlantic Charter to the British Empire. "We mean to hold our own," he said in November 1942. "I have not become the King's First Minister in order to preside over the liquidation of the British Empire." None the less, disagreements were held within a framework of reciprocal confidence.

The Soviet Union, on the other hand, had its distinctive and impassioned ethos and ideology, as well as a separate set of strategic interests. Though Stalin had adhered to the Atlantic Charter, he had no intention of permitting its application, say, to the Baltic republics which he had so recently annexed. Roosevelt and Churchill, aware of the importance to the war effort of ending the legacy of mistrust between the democratic and communist states, were eager to do everything honorable to win Soviet friendship. At the same time, they were determined not to surrender vital interests or principles in the process. When in December 1941 Stalin asked the British to recognize the Soviet conquest of the Baltic republics, Churchill was at first inclined to do so in exchange for an Anglo-Soviet treaty; but, under

The return from Casablanca, 1943: The decision was for unconditional surrender.

pressure from Roosevelt and Cordell Hull, the British changed their minds and held firm. The Soviet Union surprisingly acquiesced in this decision and signed a twenty-year treaty of alliance in the spring of 1942 with no reference to frontiers. "This was a great relief to me," Churchill later wrote, "and a far better solution than I had dared to hope."

The Early Wartime Conferences   It soon became evident that the diplomacy of coalition required not only constant communication among the nations but periodic face-to-face meetings among their leaders. Thus Churchill followed his Washington visit in December 1941–January 1942 with a second Washington visit in June, in which he was primarily concerned with military and scientific matters, and with a visit to Moscow in August, where he explained to a glum Stalin the reasons for the postponement of the second front ("Now they know the worst," he wrote Roosevelt, "and having made their protest are entirely friendly; this in spite of the fact that this is their most anxious and agonizing time").

The successes in North Africa at the end of 1942 opened a new phase of the war and emphasized the need for a conference among all three leaders. Stalin, however, felt that he could not leave the Soviet Union; so Roosevelt

and Churchill met with their staffs at Casablanca on the Atlantic coast of Morocco in January 1943. The Casablanca Conference laid plans for future military action in the Mediterranean. Roosevelt and Churchill also sought, with little success, to unite the anti-Vichy French by bringing about a reconciliation between General de Gaulle and General Giraud. The main contribution of Casablanca, however, was the doctrine of "unconditional surrender."

By unconditional surrender Roosevelt meant no more than the surrender by Axis governments without conditions—that is, without assurance of the survival of the political leadership that had brought on the war. "It does not mean," he explained at Casablanca, "the destruction of the population of Germany, Italy, or Japan, but it does mean the destruction of the philosophies in those countries which are based on conquest and the subjugation of other people." Contrary to popular myths, unconditional surrender was not a last-minute improvisation by the President. It had been discussed in the State Department since the preceding spring and had been raised with Churchill (who, in turn, raised it with the British War Cabinet) before the press conference at which it was announced. The reasons behind the doctrine were partly to overcome the misgivings generated by Anglo-American willingness to deal with Darlan but even more to prevent Hitler from breaking up the Allied coalition by playing off one side against the other. The fear that the Soviet Union might seek a separate peace with Germany haunted British and American policy-makers in 1942–43, and unconditional surrender seemed the best insurance against such an eventuality.

Critics have subsequently claimed that unconditional surrender stiffened Axis resistance and prolonged the war. While this argument has an initial plausibility, it is not easy to substantiate with regard to the European war. Thus unconditional surrender had no effect at all in delaying the Italian surrender. In the case of Germany, no one seems to have been deterred from surrendering who would have surrendered otherwise, and up to the last moment such Nazi leaders as Goering and Himmler were sure they could work out their own deals with the Allies. An associated argument that unconditional surrender played into the hands of the communists seems odd in view of the fact that Stalin tried hard in 1944 to persuade Roosevelt and Churchill to modify the doctrine.

From Big Two to Big Three   Roosevelt and Churchill met again in Washington in May 1943, and in Quebec in August. Both meetings dealt mainly with Anglo-American military questions. The Soviet Union still remained outside the conference circuit until October, when Cordell Hull and Anthony Eden, the British Foreign Secretary, journeyed to Moscow to pave the way for a meeting of the Big Three.

Relations between the Soviet Union and its western allies were now in a somewhat ambivalent posture. On the one hand, there were indications that the nationalist emotions released by what the Russians called the Great Patriotic War had forced ideological preoccupations into a subordinate place in the Soviet Union. In May 1943, for example, the Comintern, the instrumentality of communist revolution, was dissolved. Stalin himself seemed more a traditional national leader than a world revolutionist. On the other hand, the shadows of future problems were casting themselves ahead, especially in the liberated

nations. The Soviet Union had protested Anglo-American policy in North Africa and Italy. It had made clear its disinclination to relinquish the part of Poland it had seized in 1939, and in April 1943 it broke off relations with the Polish government-in-exile in London because the Poles asked the International Red Cross to investigate German charges that the Russians had massacred several thousand Polish officers at Katyn. In Yugoslavia, the communist Partisans, led by Marshal Tito, were already in conflict with a monarchist resistance movement of Chetniks led by General Mihailovich. A similar feud between communist and noncommunist guerrillas divided the resistance movement in Greece.

But such events remained in the background when the Foreign Secretaries met in October. Molotov, the Soviet Foreign Secretary, went agreeably along with a statement of pieties advocated by Hull and soon issued as the Declaration of Moscow; this included affirmation of "the necessity of establishing at the earliest practicable date a general international organization . . . for the maintenance of international peace." The Moscow Conference also resolved differences over Italy and established the European Advisory Commission to plan for German collapse. There were, Churchill later wrote, many signs during the conference that the Soviet government sincerely desired permanent friendship. "They had met us on a number of points, both large and small, about which we foresaw difficulties."

The next step was the long delayed personal meeting of the three leaders. This was arranged for Teheran in late November, but it was preceded by a separate conference in Cairo where Roosevelt and Churchill met with Chiang Kaishek. The resulting Cairo Declaration promised to strip Japan of its conquests, to free Korea, and to return Manchuria and Formosa to China—a series of decisions founded on the optimistic assumption that Nationalist China could become the guarantor of postwar stability in the Far East. Because the Soviet Union was not at war with Japan, Stalin did not wish to participate in the Cairo meeting.

Although the conference in Teheran concentrated on military problems, the three participants did consider such other questions as

Germany, the territorial problems of eastern Europe and the Far East, and the shape of future international organization. Roosevelt and Stalin came away from this first encounter reasonably impressed with each other, though Roosevelt was doubtless deceived on the extent to which his persuasiveness could beguile Stalin into genuine partnership with the West. "We came here with hope and determination," the three men wrote in the Declaration of Teheran. "We leave here, friends in fact, in spirit and in purpose."

Postwar Planning   By 1944 the suspense was substantially over. Barring unforeseen developments, it was only a matter of time before the Allied rings would finally close around Germany and Japan. The approach of victory lent new urgency to postwar planning—not only planning for long-range international organization, but even more urgently for the immediate problems of feeding and succoring the war-ravaged world. In November 1943 the United Nations Relief and Rehabilitation Administration had been set up. In July 1944 an international monetary conference at Bretton Woods, New Hampshire, recommended the establishment of an International Bank for Reconstruction and Development and of an International Monetary Fund. In August–September a conference at Dumbarton Oaks in Washington laid the foundation for the permanent political structure of the United Nations, envisaging a Security Council, on which the United States, Britain, Russia, China, and, in due course, France would have permanent seats, and a General Assembly of all member nations.

But the creation of broad frameworks for postwar political and economic collaboration did not solve immediate problems either of the enemy countries or of conflicts among the Allies themselves. For these problems the more specific means of personal diplomacy still seemed essential. The fate of Germany posed especially perplexing questions. All members of the Big Three had played around at one time or another with notions of German dismemberment; this approach seemed to prevail as late as the Teheran Conference. But when the European Advisory Commission took over, dismemberment receded into the background. The EAC concentrated instead on determin-

ing the zones of Allied occupation. In the end, after a protracted dispute between Britain and the United States, Britain took the northwestern zone, America the southwestern, and Russia the eastern. Berlin, though situated in the Soviet zone, was to be jointly held; the question of access to Berlin was left, on military advice, to the commanders in the field.

As for the German economy, the most drastic proposals came from the United States Treasury Department in August 1944. Secretary Morgenthau urged both territorial transfers and partition; in addition, he recommended the dismantling of German heavy industry and the transformation of Germany into an agricultural state. For a moment Roosevelt fell in with the Morgenthau plan. Even Churchill accepted it briefly during the second Quebec Conference in September. But in a few weeks this scheme dropped by the wayside.

Growing doubts about Soviet policy compounded the uncertainty over the future. The Polish question was more acute than ever. Churchill, in an effort to restore the position of the Polish government-in-exile in London, had been urging that government to accept Soviet territorial demands, including the Curzon line to the east and (in compensation) the Oder-Neisse line to the west; in November 1944 the British government pledged support for the Oder-Neisse line even if the United States refused to go along. But Stalin continued to reject the London regime. In August the Polish Home Army, whose affiliations were with London, set off a revolt against the Germans in Warsaw. The Red army, a few miles outside the city, declined to aid the uprising; moreover, the Soviet Union refused to permit planes carrying supplies to Warsaw from the west to land on Russian soil. This could only seem a calculated attempt to destroy noncommunist Poles. In addition, the Soviet Union was setting up a group of procommunists in Lublin as the nucleus of a postwar Polish government.

In October Churchill paid another visit to Moscow in an effort to clarify the dilemmas of liberation. His effort to bring about a reconciliation between the London and Lublin Poles failed; but he and Stalin agreed on a scheme for southeastern Europe, according to which Britain would recognize Russia's predominant interest in Rumania and Bulgaria and Russia would recognize Britain's predominant interest in Greece, with Yugoslavia and Hungary split fifty-fifty. Roosevelt felt that this arrangement foreshadowed a revival of prewar "spheres of influence" but was prepared to go along with it as a rule of thumb for the period immediately after military liberation. On his return, Churchill told the House of Commons, "Our relations with Soviet Russia were never more close, intimate and cordial than they are at the present time."

Triumph and Tragedy

The Big Three at Yalta Roosevelt's re-election in November 1944 found the Allied forces pressing hard down the last mile to victory. But bloodshed was far from over. With Eisenhower's forces deployed along the length of the Siegfried line, the Germans saw an opportunity in December 1944 to launch an attack through weak points in the American line at the Ardennes Forest. The desperate German offensive resulted in some early breakthroughs, but the Americans held at Bastogne, and, after weeks of severe fighting, the Battle of the Bulge came to an end in January. On the other side of the world, the Japanese continued their resistance. It took months of hard fighting before Manila was liberated in February 1945, and Luzon was not finally cleared till July. The forces of Admiral Nimitz coming in from the central Pacific had to fight every step of the way before they could gain such islands to the south of Japan as Iwo Jima (in February) and Okinawa (in April).

The approach of victory did not simplify the political problems of the triumphant coalition. In December communist resistance groups revolted against the British-backed provisional government of newly liberated Greece. Though the Soviet Union made no objection to Churchill's prompt military intervention in Greece, the fact that local communists had taken such initiative seemed a poor omen for the future. The Polish tangle showed no signs of unraveling. The fate of Germany remained undecided. The future of eastern Europe and the Far East was still swathed in obscurity. The persistence of these

problems argued for another meeting of the Big Three. They met in a conference at Yalta in the Crimea in February 1945.

Some of the decisions taken at Yalta pertained to Europe. The most critical of these had to do with the liberated nations of eastern Europe. Roosevelt and Churchill rejected Stalin's proposal that they accept the Lublin government in Poland. Instead, after long discussions, the three leaders agreed on a reorganization of the Polish government to include leaders from abroad. They added, "This Polish Provisional Government of National Unity shall be pledged to the holding of free and unfettered elections as soon as possible." For liberated Europe in general, the conference promised "interim governmental authorities broadly representative of all democratic elements in the population and pledged to the earliest possible establishment through free elections of governments responsive to the will of the people." With regard to Germany, the conference postponed decisions on dismemberment and on future frontiers, evaded a Russian demand for heavy reparations, and endorsed the EAC provisions for zonal occupation (adding a zone for France) and for an Allied Control Council.

The Yalta discussions also dealt with the Far East, where the American Joint Chiefs were most anxious to secure from Stalin a precise commitment about entering the war. While Stalin had said vaguely in 1943 that the Soviet Union would declare war on Japan after the defeat of Germany, there was a danger that Russia would let the United States undertake a lengthy and bitter invasion of Japan and then move into Manchuria and China at the last minute to reap the benefits of victory. Moreover, the military estimated that the invasion of Japan, scheduled for the spring of 1946, might cost over a million casualties to American forces alone—another reason for desiring early and full Soviet participation. In discussions with Roosevelt, Stalin agreed to declare war on Japan within two or three months after the surrender of Germany on condition that the Kurile Islands and southern Sakhalin be restored to Russia and that the commercial interests of the Soviet Union in Dairen and its rail communications be recognized. When Roosevelt ob-

Churchill, Roosevelt, and Stalin at Yalta, 1945: "Hopeful assumptions were soon to be falsified."

tained the assent of Chiang Kai-shek to these measures, the Soviet Union would agree "that China shall retain full sovereignty in Manchuria" and would conclude a treaty of friendship and alliance with the Chiang Kai-shek government.

A third topic at Yalta was the organization of the United Nations. Here the Soviet Union accepted American proposals on voting procedure which it had opposed at Dumbarton Oaks and agreed that a United Nations conference should be called at San Francisco in April to prepare the charter for a permanent organization. Roosevelt attached great importance to the apparent Soviet willingness to collaborate in a structure of international order and doubtless supposed that the United Nations would provide the means of remedying the omissions or errors of the various summit conferences.

Roosevelt and Churchill returned from Yalta well satisfied. Churchill told the House of Commons:

The impression I brought back . . . is that Marshal Stalin and the Soviet leaders wish to live in honourable friendship and equality with the Western democracies. I feel also that their word is their bond. I know of no Government which stands to its obligations, even in its own despite, more solidly than the Russian Soviet Government.

It is true that during the war the Soviet government had discharged its military commitments with commendable promptitude. The Yalta agreements were something different, however; they represented the first experiment in postwar political collaboration with the Soviet Union. Here, as Churchill himself later wrote, "Our hopeful assumptions were soon to be falsified. Still, they were the only ones possible at the time." If the United States and Britain had proceeded at Yalta on the opposite assumption—that is, of Soviet postwar hostility—before sufficient evidence was in to convince the world of the correctness of that assumption, then the onus for starting the cold war would have rested on the West.

In subsequent years some critics have written as if Roosevelt and Churchill had perpetrated a "betrayal" at Yalta. They have contended that Poland, Rumania, and China were "sold down the river." A glance at the text of the Yalta agreements makes it hard to sustain such charges. Far from things having been made easy for Stalin at Yalta, he was obliged thereafter to *break* the pledges he made there in order to achieve his aggressive purposes. If the Yalta agreements had been kept, for example, eastern Europe would have had freely elected democratic governments, and Chiang Kai-shek would have been confirmed in control of China and Manchuria. Communism gained no territory as a result of Yalta

Allied Victory in Europe

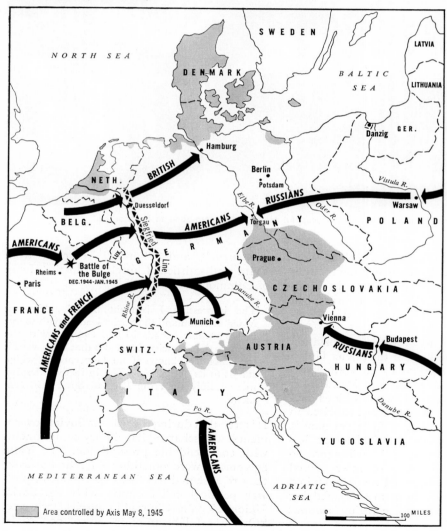

Area controlled by Axis May 8, 1945

0   100 MILES

(except the Kurile Islands) which was not already, or about to be, in communist hands anyway as a result of the military operations of communist armies—and such operations could have been checked only by the application of countervailing force from the West.

Victory in Europe For the Soviet Union cooperation with the West had been a wartime policy, to be continued so long as Nazism remained a threat. The Yalta Conference, taking place in the shadow of the Ardennes counteroffensive, still partook of the wartime mood of cooperation. But in the weeks after Yalta the military picture began to alter rapidly. The Crimean talks had barely started before the American Third Army breached the Siegfried line. A fortnight after Roosevelt left Yalta, the Ninth Army had reached the Rhine at Düsseldorf. With the end of the war in sight, the Soviet need for wartime cooperation was disappearing: it was now time to begin the postwar battle for Europe. Within a few weeks after Yalta the Soviet Union took swift action in Rumania and Poland to frustrate the Yalta pledges of political freedom. Stalin himself opened up a savage political offensive against the west, charging that the United States and Britain were engaged in separate peace negotiations with Germany. Roosevelt replied with indignation that he deeply resented these "vile misrepresentations." At the same time, the Soviet Union signaled to the communist parties of the west (and, through a public condemnation of the collaborationist policies identified with the American Communist Earl Browder, especially to the American Communist party) that the period of antifascist collaboration was over.

At the end of March 1945 Roosevelt cabled Churchill that he was "watching with anxiety and concern the development of the Soviet attitude"; this attitude, he said, portended danger, not only for immediate issues, but for "future world cooperation." The American President sent stern warnings to the Soviet leader and on April 12 told Churchill, "We must be firm. . . . Our course thus far is correct." But Roosevelt, worn out by his immense exertions and by his long years of terrible responsibility, was reaching the end. Later the same day he died of a massive cerebral hemorrhage, as truly a casualty of war as any man who died in battle. The world mourned his loss.

These ominous political developments put military problems in a new context. As the Anglo-American armies plunged ahead into Germany, Churchill argued in March and April that they should race the Russians to Berlin. "From a political standpoint," he said, "we should march as far east into Germany as possible." But General Eisenhower replied, "I

Joe and Ivan: Torgau, 1945.

The Atomic Bomb:
A Plea for Restraint

The development of nuclear power not only constitutes an important addition to the technological and military power of the United States, but creates grave political and economic problems for the future of this country.

Nuclear bombs cannot possibly remain a "secret weapon" at the exclusive disposal of this country for more than a few years. The scientific facts on which their construction is based are well known to scientists of other countries. Unless an effective international control of nuclear explosives is instituted, a race for nuclear armaments is certain to ensue following the first revelation of our possession of nuclear weapons to the world. Within ten years other countries may have nuclear bombs.... In the war to which such an armaments race is likely to lead, the United States, with its agglomeration of population and industry in comparatively few metropolitan districts, will be at a disadvantage compared to nations whose population and industry are scattered over large areas.

We believe that these considerations make the use of nuclear bombs for an early unannounced attack against Japan inadvisable. If the United States were to be the first to release this new means of indiscriminate destruction upon mankind, we would sacrifice public support throughout the world, precipitate the race for armaments, and prejudice the possibility of reaching international agreement on the future control of such weapons.

From Report to the Secretary of War from the Committee on Social and Political Implications, June 1945.

---

regard it as militarily unsound . . . to make Berlin a major objective." The imperative consideration, in the view of the American Joint Chiefs, was the destruction of the German armed forces; and this, Eisenhower believed (incorrectly, as it turned out), required the pursuit of the remaining German troops to a supposed last stand in the so-called National Redoubt to the south.

A month later, Churchill renewed his pleading, this time in connection with Prague. The Allied liberation of Prague, he said, might "make the whole difference to the postwar situation in Czechoslovakia." He went on to propose that Allied forces remain as far east as they could until Soviet Russia clarified its intentions with regard to Poland and Ger-

many. Harry S. Truman, who had succeeded to the American Presidency, hesitated at suggestions for deeper American involvement in central Europe, partly because of a fear of prejudicing future Soviet cooperation with the United Nations, partly because of the need for redeploying American troops to the Pacific. He accordingly treated the problem as a tactical one to be decided by the commander in the field. Eisenhower, for his part, declined to abandon strictly military criteria in the absence of orders from above. Though he could have put American troops into Prague far in advance of the Red army, he refused to do so. It is by no means clear that Churchill's plan would have basically changed the postwar balance in Europe. But it seems evident that the American generals, as General Omar Bradley later wrote, "looked naïvely on this British inclination to complicate the war with political foresight and non-military objectives."

By now events in Europe were rushing to climax. Hitler's thousand-year *Reich*, racked by months of Allied bombing and now overrun by Allied armies from both west and east, was falling to pieces. The German dictator himself took refuge in his bunker in Berlin and on April 30 committed suicide. On May 3 the process of piecemeal German surrender began, culminating in a final ceremony of unconditional surrender at Eisenhower's headquarters in Rheims on May 7. As Churchill later wrote, the end of hostilities was "the signal for the greatest outburst of joy in the history of mankind." He added somberly that he himself moved amid cheering crowds "with an aching heart and a mind oppressed by forebodings."

Victory in the Far East   While the European war was coming to its troubled end, American forces continued to make steady progress in the Pacific. But Japanese resistance grew every day more fanatical. The use of kamikaze suicide planes and the last-ditch fighting in Iwo Jima and Okinawa seemed to confirm the horrendous American estimates of casualties to be expected in an invasion of the homeland. Within civilian Japan, though, opinion was not so united or so fanatical. Sensible people recognized that the war was irretrievably lost. After the invasion of Okinawa in April, the emperor appointed a new Prime

Minister and instructed him to explore the possibilities of peace.

In the meantime, an extraordinary new factor entered into American calculations. In 1939 the scientist Albert Einstein had called Roosevelt's attention to the possibility of using atomic energy for military purposes. In the next years the government sponsored a secret $2 billion operation known as the Manhattan Project to attempt the building of an atomic bomb. A brilliant collection of physicists, working under the direction of J. Robert Oppenheimer in Los Alamos, New Mexico, steadily broke down the incredibly complex scientific and technological problems involved in the production of the weapon. On April 25, 1945, Secretary of War Stimson could tell President Truman, "Within four months we shall in all probability have completed the most terrible weapon ever known in human history, one bomb of which could destroy a whole city."

The next question was how and when this frightful weapon should be employed. On June 1 a special committee recommended to the President that the bomb be used against Japan as soon as possible. Many Manhattan Project scientists, intimately aware of the ghastly character of the weapon, opposed this recommendation, favoring a preliminary demonstration to the world in a desert or on a barren island. But this course was rejected, partly because of the fear that the bomb might not go off, partly because only two bombs would be available by August and it seemed essential to reserve them for direct military use.

Within Japan, the new government was still looking for a way out. In July it requested Soviet mediation to bring the war to an end, though it added, "So long as the enemy demands unconditional surrender, we will fight as one man." Moscow delayed its reply to this request while Stalin departed for a new Big Three meeting at Potsdam, near Berlin. At the same time, the American government, following the Japanese peace explorations through decoded cable intercepts, came to the conclusion that the best way to hasten the end of the war would be to issue a solemn plea to the Japanese to surrender before it was too late. This warning was embodied somewhat cryptically in a declaration issued at Potsdam by

The Atomic Bomb: The President's View

I realize the tragic significance of the atomic bomb.

Its production and its use were not lightly undertaken by this Government. But we knew that our enemies were on the search for it. We know now how close they were to finding it. And we know the disaster which would come to this nation, and to all peaceful nations, to all civilizations, if they had found it first.

That is why we felt compelled to undertake the long and uncertain and costly labor of discovery and production.

We won the race of discovery against the Germans.

Having found the bomb we have used it. We have used it against those who attacked us without warning at Pearl Harbor, against those who have starved and beaten and executed American prisoners of war, against those who have abandoned the pretense of obeying international laws of warfare. We have used it in order to shorten the agony of war, in order to save the lives of thousands and thousands of young Americans.

We shall continue to use it until we completely destroy Japan's power to make war. Only a Japanese surrender will stop us.

From Harry S. Truman, Radio Address, August 1945.

Truman and Clement Attlee, who had succeeded Churchill as British Prime Minister, urging the Japanese to give up or face "the utter devastation of the Japanese homeland." The Japanese government was inclined to accept this ultimatum, but the military leaders disagreed. On July 28 the Japanese Prime Minister, in a statement designed for domestic consumption, pronounced the Potsdam Declaration "unworthy of public notice."

Truman had already been informed while at Potsdam that the first bomb test in New Mexico on July 17 had been a triumphant success. The rejection of the Potsdam Declaration now convinced him that the militarists were in control of Tokyo and that there was no point in delaying the use of the bomb. Actually the Japanese were still awaiting Stalin's return from Potsdam in the hope of obtaining Soviet mediation. But it would have required a positive statement from Tokyo to change President Truman's mind, and none was forthcoming. On August 6, in a blinding flash of heat and horror, the first atomic bomb fell on Hiroshima, killing nearly eighty thousand people and reducing the city to rubble. With Tokyo still silent about surrender, the remaining bomb was dropped three days later on Nagasaki with results almost as appalling. On the day before, Soviet Russia had declared war on Japan. The Japanese now at last agreed to accept the Potsdam Declaration on condition that the emperor be permitted to preserve his status. The act of surrender took place on September 2, 1945.

The decision to drop the atomic bomb was the most tragic taken in the long course of American history. It may well be that only so drastic a step could have ended the war and thereby averted the losses which an invasion would have brought to both sides. On the other hand, thoughtful observers have wondered whether the American government, with Japan essentially beaten and on the verge of capitulation, had exhausted all the possible alternatives before at last having recourse to the bomb—whether there were not resources of negotiation or demonstration that should have been first attempted, with the bomb held in reserve as a weapon of last resort. Here perhaps the doctrine of unconditional surrender had terrible consequences. Certainly, though the bomb terminated the war, it also placed America for many years in an ambiguous position before the world as the only nation to have employed so horrible a weapon.

Victory thus came—but in a way which converted triumph into tragedy. The Second World War was at an end. Perhaps twenty million persons, soldiers and civilians, had died during the five years. In the United States sixteen million men had been under arms; total casualties amounted to over a million, with nearly three hundred thousand deaths in battle. Now, in the autumn of 1945, the world stood on the threshold of a new epoch in human history—an epoch incalculably rich in hazards and potentialities. With faltering steps, mankind was entering the atomic age.

SUGGESTIONS FOR READING

The Second World War: The Home Front

There is no adequate short history of the United States during the Second World War, nor is there a good general treatment of the domestic economy and society in that time. The best survey of defense mobilization is in the Bureau of the Budget, *The United States at War* (1946). Eliot Janeway, *The Struggle for Survival* (1951), describes the conflicts within the federal government over mobilization policy and administration; Bruce Catton, *War Lords of Washington* (1948), focuses on the influence of big business in the resolution of those conflicts; both books are somewhat polemical. A rewarding memoir is D. M. Nelson, *Arsenal of Democracy* (1946), which reviews some of the work of the War Production Board. See, too, H. M. Somers, *Presidential Agency: OWMR* (1950), and R. H. Connery, *Navy and Industrial Mobilization in World War II* (1951). There are two useful studies of the problem of price stabilization: J. K. Galbraith, *Theory of Price Control* (1952), and L. V. Chandler, *Inflation in the United States, 1940–1948* (1951). Also relevant to that question, and indispensable on questions of wartime finance, are two books of R. E. Paul: *Taxation for Prosperity* (1947) and *Taxation in the United States* (1954). On the mobilization of science and technology, there is the incisive study of J. P. Baxter III, *Scientists Against Time* (1946). R. G. Hewlett and O. E. Anderson, Jr., *The New World* (1962), provides the most authoritative account of the development of the atomic bomb.

Jack Goodman, ed., *While You Were Gone: A Report on Wartime Life in the United States* (1946), accomplishes the purpose suggested in its title. Helpful on the same subject are Reuben Hill, *Families Under Stress* (1949), and W. F. Ogburn, ed., *American Society in Wartime* (1943). For the Japanese-American issue, Morton Grodzins, *Americans Betrayed* (1949), is revealing. On politics during the war years, see Jonathan Daniels, *Frontier on the Potomac* (1946), and Roland Young, *Congressional Politics in the Second World War* (1956).

The Second World War: Military Operations

On this topic there is general narrative, too brief to be satisfactory, in Fletcher Pratt, *War for the World* (1951). S. E. Morison reviews American strategy in *Strategy and Compromise*

(1958); aspects of that subject concern K. R. Greenfield, ed., *Command Decisions* (1959), and —more journalistically—H. W. Baldwin, *Great Mistakes of the War* (1950). J. F. C. Fuller, *The Second World War, 1939–45* (1948), provides a crisp and dogmatic account. The role of the American services is intensively portrayed in three multi-volume series: Department of the Army, Office of the Chief of Military History, *The United States Army in World War II;* S. E. Morison, *History of United States Naval Operations in World War II;* and W. F. Craven and J. L. Cate, *The Army Air Force in World War II.* There is indispensable background and comment in the six volumes of W. L. S. Churchill, *The Second World War* * (1948–53), and in H. L. Stimson and McGeorge Bundy, *On Active Service in Peace and War* (1948), and E. E. Morison, *Turmoil and Tradition* (1960).

From the specialized literature about the war, still growing, any selection must omit some titles of merit; many are noted in a check list of 150 paperbacks by H. O. Werner in the *United States Naval Institute Proceedings* (August 1959). Among the formidable number of war memoirs, the most useful on the European theater are those of Dwight D. Eisenhower, Omar Bradley, Bernard Montgomery, Frederick Morgan, H. H. Arnold, and W. Bedell Smith; on the Pacific theater, those of Joseph Stilwell, Claire Chennault, Robert Eichelberger, George C. Kenney, Walter Kreuger, and, as recounted by Walter Whitehill, Ernest J. King. Chester Wilmot, *The Struggle for Europe* (1952), provides a stimulating but vulnerable interpretation; for another interpretation, see Trumbull Higgins, *Winston Churchill and the Second Front* (1960). Policy in the Pacific receives able treatment in Herbert Feis, *The China Tangle* (1953) and *Japan Subdued* (1961), which should be supplemented by C. F. Romanus and Riley Sunderland, *Stilwell's Mission to China* (1953); J. K. Eyre, *The Roosevelt-MacArthur Conflict* (1950); and T. H. White and Annalee Jacoby, *Thunder Out of China* * (1946).

The soldier's view of the war can be found in three books by Ernie Pyle: *Here Is Your War* (1943), *The Story of G. I. Joe* * (1945), and *Brave Men* * (1944), and also in Bill Mauldin, *Up Front* (1945). See, too, the *New Yorker Book of War Pieces* (1947), and such novels as J. G. Cozzens, *Guard of Honor* (1948); Norman Mailer, *The Naked and the Dead* * (1948); James Jones, *From Here to Eternity* * (1951); and Joseph Heller, *Catch-22* * (1961). There is an important sociological study in S. A. Stouffer, *et al.*, *The American Soldier*, 2 vols. (1949).

The Second World War: Diplomacy

Herbert Feis has written most fully and intelligently about the diplomacy of the war, the subject of his two books cited above and also of his monumental *Churchill, Roosevelt, Stalin* (1957), and his *Between War and Peace* (1960). On Soviet-American relations, J. R. Deane, *The Strange Alliance* (1947), is also useful. W. L. Langer, *Our Vichy Gamble* (1947), is valuable though defensive on Franco-American problems. For postwar planning there is important material in E. F. Penrose, *Economic Planning for the Peace* (1953), and R. N. Gardner, *Sterling-Dollar Diplomacy* (1956). Also significant are two books of J. L. Snell, ed.: *The Meaning of Yalta* (1956) and *Wartime Origins of the East-West Dilemma over Germany* (1959). There are also a number of useful memoirs and biographies, particularly Cordell Hull, *Memoirs*, 2 vols. (1948); R. E. Sherwood, *Roosevelt and Hopkins* * (1948); W. D. Leahy, *I Was There* (1950); J. F. Byrnes, *Speaking Frankly* (1947); E. R. Stettinius, Jr., *Roosevelt and the Russians* (1949); and Sumner Welles, *Seven Decisions That Shaped History* (1951).

* Available in a paperback edition.

31

The Cold War

The greatest war in history had come to an end. But victory brought relief rather than exhilaration. In 1918 many Americans had supposed that success on the battlefield would by itself guarantee peace and freedom and that the United States, once war was won, could safely retire from international responsibility. By 1945 most Americans knew better. Their country was now inextricably mixed up in world affairs and could no longer escape a world destiny. This fact confronted the United States with a series of unaccustomed burdens: It had to make peace with the defeated states. It had to help meet the desperate needs of war-ravaged nations for relief and reconstruction. It had to come to terms with the unleashed power of the atom. It had to hold together an uneasy wartime coalition lest quarrels among the victors produce a third world war. It had to lay the foundations for an enduring structure of world order. And at home it had to prevent a repetition of the economic depression, the political hysteria, and the intellectual stagnation which had followed World War I.

Truman Takes Over

The New President   Moreover, the nation faced these problems under a new and relatively inexperienced leader. "I feel as though the moon and all the stars and all the planets have fallen on me," Harry S. Truman told newspapermen on the April day in 1945

when he heard the report of Roosevelt's death. "Please, boys, give me your prayers. I need them very much." The new President could hardly have taken over in less auspicious circumstances. An inconspicuous back-bencher from Missouri who had barely retained his own seat in the Senate four and a half years before, he had to fill the awesome place of the man who had dominated the affairs of the United States and the world for a dozen years. And he had to do all this as a comparative unknown, without a Cabinet of his own choosing, without a personal following in Congress or in the country, without even adequate instruction on his government's policies and objectives. He could depend only on the popular sympathy which rushed to him in his plight, on the power of the office of the President, and on his own abilities and resources.

His past did not throw great light on his potentialities. On the record he seemed a Missouri courthouse politician of a familiar sort, a beneficiary of the notorious Pendergast machine in Kansas City, a Democratic wheel horse in the Senate, an old-time political pro whose chief attribute was loyalty to his organization and his President. On the other hand, those who knew him valued the spontaneous sense of decency which had led him to fight the Ku Klux Klan at the height of its power in Missouri, the courage in adversity which had enabled him to hold his Senate seat in 1940, and the deep dedication to the popular welfare he had displayed throughout his public career.

Churchill and Truman at Potsdam: "New perils loomed and glared."

Even back in Kansas City, for all his machine associations, his personal record was spotless. In the Senate he had shown an unwavering allegiance to the New Deal. As chairman of the Senate Committee to Investigate the National Defense Program, he had discharged a delicate job with intelligence and responsibility. He kept on his desk a motto from Mark Twain: "Always do right. This will gratify some people, & astonish the rest." No one could tell what the chemistry of the presidency would do with this strangely assorted mixture of human elements.

The First Truman Months Initial impressions were not encouraging. In his fourth week as President, Truman casually signed, without even reading, an order which abruptly stopped the delivery of goods under the lend-lease program. During the war, the United States had sent abroad over $50 billion worth of goods under that program, of which

60 per cent went to Great Britain and 22 per cent to the Soviet Union. The sudden termination of these deliveries caused resentment abroad and some real hardship. "This experience brought home to me," Truman subsequently wrote, "not only that I had to know exactly where I was going but also that I had to know that my basic policies were being carried out. If I had read that order, as I should have, the incident would not have occurred. But the best time to learn that lesson was right at the beginning of my duties as President."

The candor, the humility, and the cockiness were all characteristic. Though he never totally divested himself of a tendency to shoot from the hip, Truman gradually developed authority in his new role. His wide knowledge of history gave him a vigorous sense of the dignity and power of the presidency. He worked hard. He accepted responsibility: he used to say of the presidential desk, "The buck stops here."

He sifted his advisers until he found those he could trust. Slowly he transformed a Roosevelt Administration into a Truman Administration. By July 1945 at Potsdam, Winston Churchill, calling on Truman the morning after his arrival, was impressed with "his gay, precise, sparkling manner and obvious power of decision."

Making the Peace

The Postwar Atmosphere   This power of decision was almost immediately put to the test. Relations between the Soviet Union and the West had begun to deteriorate before Roosevelt's death, and the evident Soviet determination after Yalta to fasten a pro-communist regime on Poland sped up the process. In April, Truman conveyed in sharp language his disapproval of the Soviet course to V. M. Molotov, the Soviet Foreign Minister. "I have never been talked to like that in my life," Molotov said. "Carry out your agreements," Truman replied, "and you won't get talked to like that."

But stern words were not enough. In late May 1945 Truman sent Harry Hopkins to

The Partition of Germany and Austria

::::: Occupied by U.S.	+++ Occupied by U.S.S.R.
Occupied by France	Transferred to Poland
||||| Occupied by Gr. Britain	

Moscow. Hopkins pointed out to Stalin that recent Soviet actions had caused great concern in America and that "if present trends continued unchecked the entire structure of world cooperation . . . would be destroyed." Hopkins emphasized that Poland had become the "symbol" of the ability of the West to work out problems with the Soviet Union. The talks produced minor Soviet concessions on Poland and the United Nations, but no basic relaxation; Stalin was evidently determined to push a "hard" line. As Churchill later described the situation in the summer of 1945, "The agreements and understandings at Yalta, such as they were, had already been broken or brushed aside by the triumphant Kremlin. New perils, perhaps as terrible as those we had surmounted, loomed and glared upon the torn and harassed world."

It was in this atmosphere that Truman, Stalin, and Churchill (accompanied by Clement Attlee, who succeeded Churchill as Prime Minister of Great Britain in the midst of the conference) met at Potsdam outside Berlin at the end of July. The main items on the Big Three agenda were Japan, Poland, peace treaties with the Nazi satellites, and the German settlement. The talks on Japan led to the Potsdam Declaration (see p. 727). The western powers acquiesced in a temporary Polish occupation of Germany up to the Oder-Neisse line, with the final territorial decision to be reserved for the peace conference. The task of drawing up peace treaties with the minor Axis powers was assigned to a newly established Council of Foreign Ministers.

Occupation of Germany   As for Germany, the three powers proposed a joint occupation by the United States, Britain, Russia, and France. Each nation was to supervise its own zone of occupation, but each was also to participate in an Allied Control Council responsible for matters affecting Germany as a whole. The objectives of the occupation included disarmament, demilitarization, denazification, the trial of war criminals, the breaking up of cartels, the democratization of politics, and the encouragement of libertarian ideals.

Though the Potsdam Conference marked a retreat from the punitive proposals which had been considered a year earlier at Quebec, the

Hermann Goering at the Nürnberg trials.

American occupation authorities at first imposed severe political and economic measures on Germany. American troops were forbidden to "fraternize" with Germans. An International Military Tribunal established at American instigation tried twenty-two top Nazis in Nürnberg from November 1945 to October 1946; nineteen were convicted, of whom twelve were sentenced to death. Restrictions on the German economy kept the German living standard low.

In time, however, the burden of supporting the German economy (a burden aggravated by the reparations exacted from German production by the Soviet Union), on top of the evident Soviet determination to establish East Germany as a separate economic unit, led to a change in American policy. In a speech at Stuttgart on September 6, 1946, Secretary of State James F. Byrnes asked that Germany be "enabled to use her skills and her energies to increase her industrial production and . . . make her economy self-sustaining." After 1946 the western powers encouraged German economic recovery. In 1949 the German Federal Republic was established with Konrad Adenauer as Chancellor. The Allied occupation came to its formal end in October 1954.

Occupation of Japan   Truman, after his exposure to Soviet methods at Potsdam, concluded on his way home that he would allow the Russians no part in the control of a defeated Japan. Consequently, the Japanese occupation, unlike that of Germany, was an essentially American enterprise. Like the German occupation, however, it began in a mood of severity which, as circumstances changed, became progressively more benign.

At first General Douglas MacArthur, as Supreme Allied Commander, instituted a series of political and economic purges, culminating in the establishment of an International War Crimes Tribunal and the trial and punishment of leading officials in previous Japanese governments. At the same time he imposed on Japan a number of reforms designed to transform the defeated country into a model western democracy. A new constitution, adopted under American direction in 1946, renounced war as a sovereign right, adding that "land, sea and air forces, as well as other war potential, will never be maintained." The *zaibatsu*, the great family trusts, were threatened with dissolution; trade unions were encouraged, women were given the vote, land was redistributed among the peasants, the educational system was reorganized, and Shinto was abolished as the state religion.

After 1947 the emphasis of American policy began to change. As in the case of Germany, the United States began to look with favor on the idea of permitting an increase in Japanese production in order to reduce the burden on American taxpayers. At the same time, the growing aggressiveness of the Soviet Union raised the question of whether a disarmed Japan would not leave a dangerous power vacuum in the Far East. A peace treaty with Japan, finally negotiated in 1951, registered the altered American attitude. The treaty terminated the occupation, conceded to Japan as a sovereign nation "the inherent right of individual or collective self-defense," and opened the way for American troops to remain in Japan through bilateral agreement.

Treaties with Lesser Axis Powers In the meantime, the Council of Foreign Ministers sought to clear up the unfinished business of the war by negotiating peace treaties with Germany's European allies. Through 1946 Secretary of State Byrnes, despite obstacles and discouragements, persevered in his effort to find a meeting-ground with the Russians. In December 1946 treaties were finally concluded with Italy, Bulgaria, Hungary, Finland, and Rumania. Though the eastern European treaties all contained solemn pledges to preserve political and intellectual freedom, in effect they turned the countries (except for Finland) over to Soviet-dominated governments. No agreement was reached on Austria until 1955.

Despite the manifest defects of the eastern European treaties, Truman accepted them and the Senate ratified them. This was partly in the hope that the treaties might introduce an element of stability into Europe and partly in order to gain Soviet assent to the treaty with Italy. Inequities in the peace settlement, it was supposed, would be eventually resolved in the new world organization.

Experiment in World Order

Launching the United Nations While the leaders of the victorious coalition worked in their sometimes clashing ways to bring the war to its formal conclusion, they were also trying to establish a system of international order to preserve the peace they had fought so hard to win. The United Nations had begun as a wartime coalition. Then the Dumbarton Oaks conference of 1944 had laid down the main lines for a postwar structure; and on April 29, 1945, representatives had met at San Francisco to adopt a United Nations Charter and create a permanent UN organization.

The Charter, essentially an American product, was in the direct line of descent from the Covenant of the League of Nations. It was dominated by the belief that the best way to keep peace was through conciliation, backed up when necessary by collective military strength. The principal UN organs were the General Assembly, the Security Council, the Economic and Social Council, the Trusteeship Council, and the Secretariat. Of these, the Assembly and the Security Council had the widest authority. The Assembly was the general legislative body of the organization, though its powers were limited to discussion and recommendation. The Security Council was the agency of action; it was to this body that the architects of the UN assigned, in the language of the Charter, "the primary responsibility for the maintenance of international peace and security." The Security Council consisted of five permanent members—the United States, Britain, Russia, France, and China—with six further members to be elected each year by the General Assembly. The Charter gave the Council authority to settle international disputes by peaceful means—through investigation or mediation or whatever method seemed suitable. If such methods failed, Chapter 7 of the Charter authorized the Council to determine whether there existed a threat to the peace and to take appropriate measures against any state that broke the peace. If necessary, it might use armed force supplied by the member states.

However, the Charter also limited the Council's authority to invoke these powers. The most notable limitation was the provision giving each permanent member a veto. While neither the United States nor the Soviet Union would have joined the UN without this means of protecting its interests, the effect of the provision was to render the Council impotent to deal with infractions by the great powers. By

1961 the Soviet Union had used its veto ninety-five times, the United States never. Hobbled by the veto, the Security Council began to decline in importance. By the end of the 1950's, as the total membership in the UN rose to over one hundred nations, the General Assembly began to be the main focus of decision and attention.

Collective Economic Effort Surrounding the UN was a constellation of subsidiary and related agencies, among which the United Nations Relief and Rehabilitation Administration (UNRRA) assumed an immediate importance. Between 1945 and 1947, UNRRA carried food, clothing, and other supplies to the people in the war-ravaged areas of eastern Europe and China. American citizens played a leading administrative role in UNRRA, and the United States government contributed most of its financial support—some $2.7 billion.

While UNRRA tackled the immediate crisis, the economic agencies devised at the Bretton Woods Conference of 1944 sought to build a long-term world economic framework. The International Bank for Reconstruction and Development supplied capital for investment in economically underdeveloped areas. The International Monetary Fund was to stabilize currency and promote world trade. Other UN agencies—the Food and Agricultural Organization, the International Trade Organization, the World Health Organization, the International Labor Organization (taken over from the League)—had more specialized roles. In addition, the newly organized United Nations Educational, Scientific, and Cultural Organization (UNESCO) fostered international efforts to raise cultural standards and promote intellectual exchange.

Except for UNRRA, however, these international agencies could do little to meet immediate economic problems. Countries whose economies had been disrupted by war desperately needed imports from the United States but lacked the dollars to pay for them. The cessation of lend-lease forced them to buy goods on international account, and the result was an extraordinary imbalance in international payments. In 1946 the rest of the world owed the United States $7.7 billion; in 1947, $11.5 billion. To meet this yawning "dollar gap," the United States resorted to a number of expedients—a $3.75 billion loan to Great Britain in 1946, loans by the Export-Import Bank, sales of surplus property on credit, and so on.

The Challenge of the Atom The most fateful responsibility confronting the United Nations was to bring the incalculable new force of atomic energy under control. The United States still enjoyed a monopoly of nuclear power, and in the winter of 1945–46 a sharp debate had gone on in Washington over whether the atomic program should be under military or civilian control. Truman himself believed that, while the government had to have an absolute monopoly of the ownership and production of all fissionable materials, the government program should be run by civilians. This view was embodied in the McMahon Act, which, among other things, set up a civilian Atomic Energy Commission. Truman designated as its first chairman David E. Lilienthal of the Tennessee Valley Authority.

In the meantime, the government was developing a plan for the international control of atomic energy through the United Nations. This proposal, presented in June to the United Nations Atomic Energy Commission by Bernard Baruch, the American delegate, called for an International Atomic Development Authority empowered to own and operate the materials and facilities involved in the production of atomic energy. The proposed agency was to have power to punish violations of its rules, and it was to be exempt from the great-power veto.

The imaginative sweep of the plan, especially its elimination of the veto, forecast a tremendous stride forward toward international cooperation. But the Russians feared that the Baruch plan would give the United States permanent control over atomic developments. Their counterproposal called for the cessation of production and the destruction of stockpiles *before* the imposition of controls. It also retained the veto. These provisions were unacceptable to the United States. Though the United Nations Commission adopted the American plan, the threat of Soviet veto prevented further action in the Security Council. Atomic negotiations entered a stalemate from which they were not to emerge for years.

Test at Bikini: The new world.

The Cold War Begins

The Breakup of the Coalition The impasse on atomic control was but one expression of a deeper conflict. As the Yalta Conference had shown, the United States was eager to make a try for postwar collaboration. Even as relations deteriorated in the months after Yalta, the United States had proceeded to demobilize its armed forces—striking evidence of the nation's peaceful intent. "In 1945–46," Truman later said, "the American people had chosen to scuttle their military might." By the summer of 1946, the army and navy were down to 1.5 million and seven hundred thousand men, respectively. Nor was Congress willing to compensate by acting on Truman's recommendation for universal military training, though it agreed to continue selective service.

The American government continued through 1945 and 1946 to seek agreement with the Soviet Union on peace treaties, on atomic energy, and on other issues. But American confidence in Soviet purposes was now subjected to a series of shocks. During the war, the Soviet had sent troops into Iran, promising to withdraw them six months after the termination of hostilities. Then in December 1945 pro-Soviet forces established a revolutionary regime in the province of Azerbaijan. In January 1946 Iran charged before the Security Council that the Soviet Union was interfering in her internal affairs. The Soviet Union rejected these charges and then declined to meet the March deadline for the withdrawal of its troops. A sharp protest from Truman, however, brought about a change in Soviet policy. The troops were withdrawn in May 1946, and crisis was temporarily averted.

But the Soviet action seemed only a tactical

retreat before American pressure. In an important speech on February 9, 1946, Stalin made clear his belief that the capitalist system rendered war inevitable. On March 5, Winston Churchill, speaking at Fulton, Missouri, with Truman beside him on the platform, responded by warning against the "expansive tendencies" of the Soviet Union. "From Stettin in the Baltic to Trieste in the Adriatic," he said, "an iron curtain has descended across the Continent." What should the West do to meet the Russian challenge? "I am convinced that there is nothing they admire so much as strength, and there is nothing for which they have less respect than weakness, especially military weakness."

Revolution in China The most conspicuous communist gains, however, seem not to have been the result of premeditated Soviet design. Moscow had long regarded the Chinese Communist party with disdain. Stalin seems to have believed nearly as firmly as the United States in the capacity of the Nationalist regime of Chiang Kai-shek to organize China. If he had not, he would hardly have stripped Manchuria of nearly a billion dollars' worth of industrial equipment in 1945. But Stalin plainly underestimated the revolutionary possibilities in China—the ancient resentments against foreign domination, the pent-up demand for agrarian reform, the growing revulsion against the corruption and terrorism of the Kuomintang, and the skill and tenacity with which the Chinese Communists were to exploit these discontents.

When the Japanese surrendered, China was battered and exhausted. In the north the Communist armies, fanning out from Yenan, were in control; in the center were the Japanese armies; in the southwest corner were the armies of Chiang Kai-shek. American policy still looked to Kuomintang-Communist cooperation under Chiang's leadership; but, to bring this about, it was considered first necessary to establish the primacy of the Nationalist regime. Accordingly, an American airlift operation dropped Nationalist armies from the skies to occupy such key northern and western cities as Peking and Shanghai. Then at Yalta Stalin was induced to recognize Chiang as the ruler of China—a recognition confirmed by the Sino-Soviet pact of August 1945 (in which the Nationalist government made concessions to the Soviet Union opposed by the State Department and beyond anything required by Yalta).

The next step was to be a coalition government. Though this proposal was later said to have been made by Communist agents, many people in 1945 considered it the best way to neutralize the Communist army and the Communist party. As so resolute an anti-Communist as General Claire Chennault put it, "There is only one way out. . . . That is for us to sponsor thorough political reconstruction at Chungking, followed by true unification between Chungking and Yenan." Generals Wedemeyer and MacArthur joined in a similar recommendation in December 1945. The new American ambassador to China, General Patrick J. Hurley, took enthusiastic personal charge of this effort. When a disenchanted Hurley resigned in November 1945, Truman appointed General George C. Marshall to continue his work.

For a time Marshall appeared to be making progress. But neither the Nationalists nor the Communists really subscribed to the unification policy. The Nationalists, beguiled by their apparently overwhelming military strength, believed that they could win a civil war; the Communists were committed by their ideology to total domination. By the end of 1946 full-scale war seemed inevitable. In January 1947 Marshall abandoned his mission, blaming its failure on the reactionaries in the Kuomintang as well as on the Communists.

Though the Nationalists scored early military successes, they disregarded the counsel of their American military advisers and soon began to overextend themselves. The Communists, welded together by quasi-religious conviction and helped by the increasing popular hatred of the Nationalist government, now started to win victories. With each victory they captured more arms and attracted more deserters. In 1947 Truman sent Wedemeyer to China on a fact-finding tour. "The only basis on which national Chinese resistance to Soviet aims can be revitalized," Wedemeyer reported, "is through the presently corrupt, reactionary and inefficient Chinese National government." Therefore the United States should aid that government. But "until drastic political and economic reforms are undertaken United States aid cannot accomplish its purpose."

The United States continued its economic and military assistance, but Chiang made no serious attempt at reform. Nor did anyone in the United States call for the all-out military intervention which alone might have averted a Communist victory. In 1947 and 1948 the Nationalist armies began a retreat from Manchuria. By January 1949 they had abandoned Peking and Tientsin. Shanghai fell in May, Canton in October. By the end of the year, the Nationalist regime, driven from the mainland, had withdrawn to the island of Formosa.

The collapse of the Nationalist regime later provoked a bitter political debate in the United States. It is hard to accept the view that anti-Nationalist prejudice in the State Department caused the Nationalist downfall, or that more American money and arms would have saved Chiang. As Wedemeyer explained the Nationalist defeat, it was "lack of spirit, primarily lack of spirit. It was not lack of equipment. In my judgment they could have defended the Yangtze with broomsticks if they had the will to do it." It was Chiang's failure to retain the support of his own people that brought about his defeat—this plus the efficiency, incorruptibility, and ruthless fanaticism of Mao Tse-tung and the Chinese Communist party.

Confusion on the Home Front

The Process of Reconversion While foreign affairs thus presented Truman with a series of frustrations, things at home were very little better. As soon as the war ended, he decided to dissipate all doubts about where he stood on domestic issues. His message to Congress of September 6, 1945, was his answer to the question (as he later wrote) of whether "the progress of the New Deal [was] to be halted in the aftermath of war as decisively as the progress of Woodrow Wilson's New Freedom had been halted after the first World War." In this document and in six additional messages in the next three months, Truman laid out the main elements of what was to be called after 1948 the Fair Deal—full employment legislation, public housing, farm price supports, the nationalization of atomic energy, health insurance, a permanent Fair Employment Practices Commission, and an updating of New Deal legislation on conservation, social security, and minimum wages. Truman evidently saw himself as both the continuer and the consolidator of Roosevelt's brilliant improvisations. A man of orderly administrative habits, he tried to systematize the presidency and to rationalize the recently expanded government.

At the same time, he was faced with the problem that had so long worried economists and businessmen—the problem of reconverting the nation's economy from war to peace without creating depression. Predictions of eight or ten million unemployed had been common in 1945. But the American economy showed far more resilience than anyone expected. Between 1945 and 1946 government purchases of goods and services declined from $83 billion to $31 billion—a decline which, according to theorists, should have brought in its wake a disastrous fall in the national output and a rise in unemployment. But the gross national product declined by only $4 billion in the same period, and employment actually increased by three million.

This extraordinary achievement was due in great part to the pent-up demand for consumer goods after the deprivations of the war years. It was also due to sensible government policy. The Servicemen's Readjustment Act of 1944, known popularly as the G.I. Bill of Rights, assisted veterans in a variety of ways to find employment, education, and medical care; between 1945 and 1952 the government provided veterans with $13.5 billion for education and training alone. In addition, Congress considered in the winter of 1945–46 a so-called full employment bill, committing the government to use federal investment and expenditure to assure "a full employment volume of production." Though conservative opposition succeeded in diluting the Murray-Wagner bill, the Employment Act of 1946, enacted in February, established the Council of Economic Advisers and charged the federal government with responsibility for maintaining a high level of economic activity.

The Ordeal of Inflation Inflation rather than depression was the greater threat to the economy. After the Japanese surrender, the Office of Price Administration planned to end price controls and rationing as rapidly as goods came into the market to take up excess spending power. But the OPA had never been popular with many businessmen and farmers, and the effort to continue wartime controls even for a limited period encountered mounting public resistance.

The rise of "black markets" testified to the determination of buyers and sellers alike to evade controls. Organized labor, seeking wage increases after years of wartime denial, increased the pressure on the stabilization program. In October 1945 Truman had conceded that a general 24 per cent wage rise might be possible without inducing a corresponding rise in prices. But this did not satisfy the unions. In early 1946 a series of strikes, especially in steel, coal, and the railroads, threatened further wage increases. In the spring Truman ordered the government to seize both the coal mines and the railroads. The coal strike was soon settled; but, when the Brotherhood of Engineers and Trainmen refused to accept the President's compromise offer, he asked Congress for power to draft the strikers into the army—a request which even conservatives deemed intemperate and which the Senate rejected.

Against this background Truman in the spring of 1946 called for the extension of the OPA with full powers. Instead, Congress, dominated by a coalition of Republicans and Southern Democrats, passed a bill which so weakened the OPA that the President, on the advice of OPA director Chester Bowles, vetoed it. There followed an interval in July 1946 with no controls at all. During this period prices shot up almost 25 per cent. By the time Congress passed another bill a few weeks later, it was too late to put back the lid. An attempt to roll back meat prices under the new act led to new waves of bitterness against the Administration. Producers withheld meat from the market, and consumers denounced Truman for their meatless tables. After the election in November, Truman abandoned all controls. The conservative assault on the OPA was, in the end, responsible for the largest price rise in a single year in all American history. Wholesale prices increased more from 1946 to 1947 than they had during the Second World War.

The Election of 1946   By the fall of 1946 the country was convinced that the Adminis-

tration was inept and floundering. Labor disliked Truman because of his violent reaction to the railroad strike, farmers because of his meat policy. Conservatives opposed him because of his professions of liberalism; liberals questioned the sincerity of these professions. The old New Dealers were disturbed by the steady elimination of New Deal personalities from the government. Harold Ickes departed in February in a lurid eruption of flames and sulphur, charging that Truman was turning the nation's resources over to the oilmen. In September, Truman discharged Henry A. Wallace, his Secretary of Commerce, when Wallace condemned the increasing firmness of United States policy toward the Soviet Union.

As the fall campaign drew near, the Republicans asked with penetrating effect, "Had enough?" "To err is Truman" became a popular joke. To no one's surprise, the Republicans carried both houses of Congress for the first time since 1930 and won governorships in twenty-five states. In the eyes of the nation, Truman had been repudiated. Some observers —even a thoughtful Democratic senator, J. William Fulbright of Arkansas—proposed that the President resign.

Truman Assumes the Initiative

The Truman Doctrine   But Truman had no intention of resigning. And, with Soviet pressures against the West assuming more definite shape, the need for executive energy was growing urgent. Truman had already shown his determination to maintain personal control over foreign policy when he reprimanded his Secretary of State, James F. Byrnes, for not keeping him adequately informed during the Council of Foreign Ministers meeting in Moscow in December 1945. At the end of 1946, Byrnes resigned because of ill health, and Truman appointed General George C. Marshall to take his place. Marshall's unique national eminence helped remove the discussion of foreign policy from a partisan context. So too did the constructive collaboration of Arthur H. Vandenberg, a Republican senator from Michigan, whose long record as an isolationist gave his views special weight among conservatives.

The Soviet Union in the meantime was

stepping up a war of nerves against Greece and Turkey. The Greek situation was particularly critical. That unhappy country, after years of German occupation, was now torn by a bitter civil war between the monarchy, supported by Great Britain, and a communist-dominated resistance movement, supported by Yugoslavia and other Soviet satellites. Probably only the presence of British forces had prevented Greece from falling to the communists in 1944–45. But the drain on Britain's depleted treasury was severe. On February 21, 1947, London notified Washington that Britain would have to withdraw all support to Greece by April 1.

The loss of Greece and Turkey would mean the extension of the Iron Curtain across the eastern Mediterranean. Moreover, Truman felt, if the United States stood by and permitted independent states to be seized by the communists, resistance to communism would decline everywhere. On March 12, 1947, he appeared before Congress to urge what later became known as the Truman Doctrine. "I believe," Truman said, "that it must be the policy of the United States to support free peoples who are resisting attempted subjugation by armed minorities or outside pressures." He added that American help "should be primarily through economic and financial aid. . . . The seeds of totalitarian regimes are nurtured by misery and want." He accordingly asked Congress to pass a bill granting $400 million in aid to Greece and Turkey over the next fifteen months. Truman's request opened up a brief but intense national debate, with conservatives joining communists and fellow travelers in opposing the proposal. But Congress passed the Greece-Turkey aid bill in May. In the next years, an American mission helped restore the Greek economy and reorganize the Greek army. After Tito's break with Stalin cut off support for Greek guerrillas from the north, the civil war in Greece came to an end.

The Containment Policy   The Truman Doctrine was the first application of a philosophy that had been evolving for some time in the minds of American policy-makers. The most extended statement was made by George F. Kennan, a member of the foreign service with long experience of the Soviet Union. Writing anonymously in *Foreign Affairs* in July 1947, Kennan argued that Soviet communism

was like "a fluid stream which moves constantly, wherever it is permitted to move, toward a given goal. Its main concern is to make sure that it has filled every nook and cranny available to it in the basin of world power."

If Soviet policy was committed to "pressure, increasing constant pressure," then "the main element of any United States policy toward the Soviet Union must be that of a long-term, patient but firm and vigilant containment of Russian expansive tendencies." Kennan made it clear that he was not advocating "threats or blustering or superfluous gestures of outward 'toughness.' " He sought rather "the adroit and vigilant application of counter-force at a series of constantly shifting geographical and political points, corresponding to the shifts and maneuvers of Soviet policy." Through such means, said Kennan, and especially if the United States meanwhile convinced the world of its own continuing vitality as a free nation, it could force a measure of moderation and circumspection on the Kremlin and "promote tendencies which must eventually find their outlet in either the break-up or the gradual mellowing of Soviet power." The answer to Soviet expansion, in short, was a policy of containment; and the logic of containment meant a systematic program to build the collective strength of the West.

The Marshall Plan   The Truman Doctrine was an emergency effort to shore up crumbling positions in Greece and Turkey. It had been made necessary by a larger economic problem—the hard-pressed condition of Britain, confronted by a staggering deficit in its international balance of payments, as well as by acute shortages in food and power. And Britain's plight was symptomatic of the plight of all western Europe. With UNRRA coming to an end in March 1947, with 1947 crops damaged or destroyed over millions of acres by severe winter weather, with little evidence of industrial recovery, with communist parties and the Soviet Union threatening political and economic action, western Europe faced a frightening crisis. "The patient is sinking," said Secretary Marshall, "while the doctors deliberate."

In a speech at Cleveland, Mississippi, in May, Undersecretary of State Dean Acheson raised the question of how foreign countries could acquire the dollars they needed to meet their American debts. "The facts of international life," said Acheson, ". . . mean that the United States is going to have to undertake further emergency financing of foreign purchases if foreign countries are to continue to buy in 1948 and 1949 the commodities which they need to sustain life and at the same time rebuild their economies." But Congress was likely to balk at more foreign credits along the line of the British loan of 1946. In an address at the Harvard Commencement on June 5, 1947, Marshall accordingly set forth a revolutionary new proposal. After describing the European crisis, he called on the European countries themselves to draw up a plan for European recovery. "This is the business of the Europeans. . . . The role of this country should consist of friendly aid in the drafting of a European program and of later support. . . . The program should be a joint one, agreed to by a number, if not all, of European nations." Marshall added, significantly, "Our policy is directed not against any country or doctrine but against hunger, poverty, desperation, and chaos."

This was the proposal which, as the British Foreign Secretary, Ernest Bevin, later told Parliament, he "grabbed . . . with both hands." Within three weeks, representatives of Britain, France, and the Soviet Union met in Paris to discuss the Marshall offer. Though Molotov arrived with a retinue of eighty-nine economic experts, he soon made it clear that the Soviet Union rejected any general program of European recovery. His departure left Britain and France to join with fourteen other European nations (including Turkey) in a collective response to the Marshall offer. The Soviet attitude also eased the way for support of the Marshall Plan by the United States Congress.

By mid-September the sixteen Marshall Plan nations had outlined a four-year European recovery program to cost an estimated $22.4 billion. The program had four main goals—increased production, internal financial stability, European economic cooperation, and a resolution of the dollar gap. The cost of the program was reduced to $17 billion when the Administration submitted a bill to Congress in December. The communist take-over in Czechoslovakia in February 1948 helped

The Marshall Plan

The truth of the matter is that Europe's requirements for the next 3 or 4 years of foreign food and other essential products—principally from America —are so much greater than her present ability to pay that she must have substantial additional help, or face economic, social, and political deterioration of a very grave character.

The remedy lies in breaking the vicious circle and restoring the confidence of the European people in the economic future of their own countries and of Europe as a whole. The manufacturer and the farmer throughout wide areas must be able and willing to exchange their products for currencies the continuing value of which is not open to question.

Aside from the demoralizing effect on the world at large and the possibilities of disturbances arising as a result of the desperation of the people concerned, the consequences to the economy of the United States should be apparent to all. It is logical that the United States should do whatever it is able to do to assist in the return of normal economic health in the world, without which there can be no political stability and no assured peace.

From George C. Marshall, Commencement Speech at Harvard University, 1947.

strengthen sentiment for action. Congress finally enacted the first appropriation at the end of March.

For the next four years the Economic Cooperation Administration, working with the Organization for European Economic Cooperation, made possible the economic recovery of Europe. ECA missions in each of the cooperating countries helped work out national programs of economic reconstruction. It was an extraordinary exercise in economic planning, and the results were equally extraordinary. By July 1951 the Marshall Plan countries had raised their industrial output about 40 per cent above the 1938 level. The total cost of the program was about $12.5 billion—considerably less than the original estimates. And the effect of economic recovery was to reduce the communist parties of western Europe to virtual impotence and to give free institutions in Europe a new lease on life.

The First Berlin Crisis   The Marshall Plan checked the Soviet hope that economic disintegration might bring communism to

Autumn 1948: Nearly five thousand tons of supplies a day for Berlin.

western Europe. In response Moscow began to organize its own economic bloc in eastern Europe. And, as the communist political and economic offensive faltered, the Soviet Union presented the West with a new challenge in the spring of 1948 when it cut off West Berlin by blockading all highway, river, and rail traffic into the former German capital. The evident purpose was to force the western powers out of Berlin.

The West now had several alternatives, all unattractive. If it retreated, it would lose a bastion of western defense and encourage the Soviet Union to believe that it could win its objectives through a show of force. If it tried to break the blockade by sending armed convoys to Berlin, it ran the risk of a third world war. General Lucius Clay, the American commander in Germany, proposed a third course —that the West circumvent the blockade by

supplying West Berlin through an airlift. Truman adopted Clay's suggestion. On June 26, 1948, the airlift went into operation. The minimum daily supply required to keep the 2.1 million inhabitants of West Berlin alive was calculated to be about forty-five hundred tons of goods. By October American and British planes were flying in nearly five thousand tons a day. When it became apparent that even winter weather could not halt the airlift, Moscow began to entertain second thoughts. After negotiations in the early months of 1949, the Russians finally, on May 12—321 days after the start of the airlift—ended the blockade.

The Berlin crisis, following so closely on the communist coup in Czechoslovakia, convinced many western Europeans of the need for some sort of regional defense agreement against possible Soviet aggression. Led by Bevin of Britain and Spaak of Belgium, Britain, France,

Belgium, the Netherlands, and Luxembourg joined in March 1948 to sign the Brussels Pact providing for military and economic collaboration. The Senate responded to this initiative by passing the Vandenberg Resolution in June expressing American approval of such arrangements. Bevin argued, however, for more explicit American commitments; and Truman agreed that only "an inclusive security system" could dispel the fear that the Soviet army might overrun western Europe before effective help could arrive. Accordingly, negotiations on such a system began in Washington in July. By October the countries involved had agreed in principle on a North Atlantic Alliance in which (in the language of Article 5 of the final pact) "an armed attack against one or more of them in Europe or North America shall be considered an attack against them all." The treaty was signed in Washington on April 4, 1949, by the United States, Britain, France, Italy, Belgium, the Netherlands, Denmark, Norway, Portugal, Luxembourg, Iceland, and Canada. The creation of the North Atlantic Treaty Organization (NATO) completed the work of the Marshall Plan in immunizing western Europe against Soviet aggression.

In the meantime, the United States had taken steps to restore her military strength. The Second World War had convinced many Americans that the armed services should be brought under unified command. The professional navy fought bitterly against unification, but in July 1947, with the approval of Secretary of the Navy James Forrestal, Congress passed the National Security Act. While this act did not achieve the thoroughgoing unification for which some had hoped, it created the framework for unified action—a single Secretary of Defense, a permanent Joint Chiefs of Staff, a National Security Council, a Central Intelligence Agency, and a National Security Resources Board. Forrestal himself became the first Secretary of Defense.

The Eightieth Congress at Home

The Resurgence of Conservatism Despite his failure in the 1946 election, Truman as President, ably seconded by Marshall in the State Department and Vandenberg in Congress, had thus made impressive accomplish-

ments in foreign affairs. In domestic policy, however, his accomplishments were less impressive. In his annual message of 1947 his references to domestic matters were subdued and sketchy— in marked contrast to the sweeping program of September 1945.

The dominant figure of the Eightieth Congress was Robert A. Taft of Ohio, son of the former President and a senator of inexhaustible force, knowledge, and self-confidence. His admirers regarded him as the epitome of old-fashioned American wisdom; others said that he had the best mind in Washington until he made it up. Taft was particularly concerned with ending what he regarded as the privileged position created for organized labor by the Wagner Act of 1935. The atmosphere for change was propitious. The pent-up exasperation of American businessmen against the "labor bosses" burst out in full force after the 1946 elections. Some members of Congress demanded such extreme measures as the abolition of industrywide bargaining; and the Hartley bill, passed by the House in the spring of 1947, included this and other punitive proposals. In the Senate, Taft accepted certain modifications in the Hartley bill; but the resulting measure—the Taft-Hartley Act, enacted in June 1947—was still drastic enough to outrage labor leaders, some of whom extravagantly denounced it as a "slave labor" act. Truman vetoed the bill, but Congress promptly passed it over his veto.

The unions objected most of all to the outlawing of the closed shop and to the revival of the government injunction as a means of dealing with labor disputes. The bill also called for the registration of unions, prohibited union contributions to political parties, demanded that union officials file noncommunist affidavits, gave new powers to employers to canvass workers in National Labor Relations Board elections, and forbade certain "unfair" labor practices, such as secondary boycotts and jurisdictional strikes. And, though the act itself permitted a measure of union security through the "union shop" (i.e., a contract requiring workers to join the union after being hired, as distinct from the closed shop which demands that they join before being hired), its Section 14b declared that state laws affecting union security had priority over federal laws.

This provision invited the states to pass so-called "right-to-work" acts forbidding that union membership be required as a condition of employment. Such laws were passed in eighteen states between 1944 and 1956. Although the act checked union attempts to organize unorganized workers, especially in the South, it had much less effect on strong unions than had been anticipated.

The passage of the Taft-Hartley Act was powerful evidence that the conservatives had gained the upper hand in domestic policy. So too was the passage in 1947 of a proposed Twenty-second Amendment forbidding presidential third terms—a belated act of vengeance against Franklin D. Roosevelt; the amendment was eventually ratified by the required thirty-six states in February 1951. The Eightieth Congress ignored Truman's legislative recommendations and passed bills, including a major tax reduction in 1948, over his veto.

Truman Fights Back   But Truman's success in foreign affairs had given him new confidence. In 1948 he began to reassert in vigorous language his objectives of 1945. He followed a militant state-of-the-union message with "a message a week" through the winter and spring of 1948. Most of the special messages reaffirmed earlier positions; but in his civil-rights message of February 2, 1948, Truman broke new ground.

In December 1946 Truman had set up a President's Committee on Civil Rights to recommend more effective means of protecting individual freedoms. A year later the Committee, under the chairmanship of Charles E. Wilson of General Electric, released a report entitled "To Secure These Rights." After a memorable analysis of the state of personal freedom in America, the committee concentrated on "civil rights" in the narrow sense—issues of racial and religious discrimination—rather than on "civil liberties"—freedoms of conscience and expression. It recommended a permanent commission on civil rights, a mandatory FEPC, anti-lynching and -poll-tax laws, and a strengthening of civil-rights statutes and enforcement machinery. In his message of February 1948, Truman made these proposals part of his executive program. This attempt to realize the promises of the Declaration of Independence for all Americans, regardless of race or color, represented Truman's boldest initiative in the domestic field. Nothing he did aroused more controversy.

In the meantime, the approach of the 1948 election sharpened interest in party politics. Truman's situation seemed far from promising. The Democratic party had been in disarray since the 1946 election. The civil-rights proposals had outraged the conservative Democrats of the South. The Truman Doctrine and the Marshall Plan had outraged communist sympathizers in the North, as well as innocent liberals like Henry A. Wallace, whose concern for world peace led them to overlook the disruptive Soviet role in foreign affairs. A new anticommunist liberal group, Americans for Democratic Action, while deeply opposed to Wallace, was skeptical of Truman. Old-line Democratic bosses shared this skepticism. As the Democratic convention drew near, a "dump-Truman" movement acquired momentum within the party.

The anti-Truman forces were unable to agree on an alternative, however, and in the end Truman won renomination with little difficulty. The choice of Senator Alben Barkley of Kentucky for the vice-presidency was exceptionally popular. The adoption of a strong civil-rights plank after a floor fight brought the Truman-Barkley ticket the enthusiastic support of Northern liberals. Then Truman himself concluded a fighting acceptance speech with an electrifying promise to call a special session of Congress on July 26 ("which out in Missouri we call 'Turnip Day'") to test the readiness of the Republicans to live up to their platform pledges. "They can do this job in fifteen days," he said, "if they want to do it."

The 1948 Campaign   The Republicans had once again nominated Governor Thomas E. Dewey of New York. Governor Earl Warren of California received the vice-presidential nomination. Dewey campaigned with the quiet confidence of a man who could not lose. Republican optimism swelled even further when a communist-dominated Progressive party nominated Wallace for the presidency and when the diehard Southern Democrats formed the States Rights Democratic party (better known as the Dixiecrats) and nominated Strom Thurmond of South Carolina.

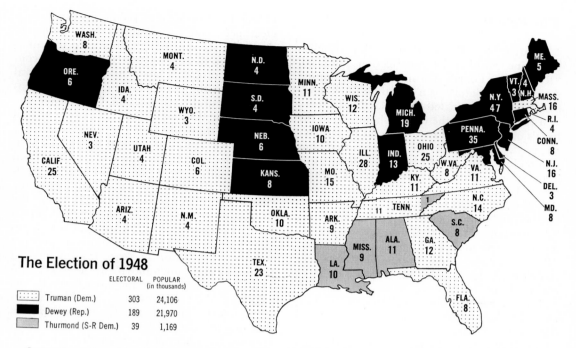

The Election of 1948

	ELECTORAL	POPULAR (in thousands)
Truman (Dem.)	303	24,106
Dewey (Rep.)	189	21,970
Thurmond (S-R Dem.)	39	1,169

WASH. 8 · ORE. 6 · MONT. 4 · N.D. 4 · MINN. 11 · ME. 5 · VT. 4 · N.H. · N.Y. 47 · MASS. 16 · IDA. 4 · S.D. 4 · WIS. 12 · MICH. 19 · R.I. 4 · NEV. 3 · WYO. 3 · NEB. 6 · IOWA 10 · OHIO 25 · PENNA. 35 · CONN. 8 · UTAH 4 · COL. 6 · ILL. 28 · IND. 13 · W.VA. 8 · N.J. 16 · CALIF. 25 · KANS. 8 · MO. 15 · KY. 11 · VA. 11 · DEL. 3 · ARIZ. 4 · N.M. 4 · OKLA. 10 · ARK. 9 · TENN. 11 · 1 · N.C. 14 · MD. 8 · MISS. 9 · ALA. 11 · GA. 12 · S.C. 8 · LA. 10 · TEX. 23 · FLA. 8

Only Truman thought he could win. The special session of Congress adjourned without doing anything, thus providing him with the issue he needed. He began a lively "give 'em hell" campaign across the country, telling audiences at every whistlestop that the record of the "do-nothing, good-for-nothing" Republican Eightieth Congress proved the worthlessness of Republican campaign promises. By election day, Truman had traveled 31,700 miles and delivered 356 speeches. A fall in the price of corn and hogs alarmed the farmers; this, reinforced by the fear that the Eightieth Congress, in cutting funds for the Commodity Credit Corporation, had left inadequate storage space for grain, turned the Corn Belt toward the Democrats. The Dixiecrat revolt confirmed the Negroes in their Democratic allegiance, while the Wallace movement eliminated communism as an issue between the major parties and kept the Catholics in the Democratic camp. The Democratic coalition put together by Roosevelt in the preceding decade remained intact. Neither Dewey's personality nor his campaign roused much enthusiasm, even among his supporters. Truman, on the other hand, emerged as a tireless campaigner, a pungent orator, an indomitable fighter, and—in contrast to his opponent—an intensely *human* being. By late October, shouting crowds greeted Truman's appearances with the joyful cry, "Pour it on, Harry."

"My one-man crusade," Truman later said, "took effect. . . . I never doubted that they would vote for me." Everyone else doubted, however. Public-opinion polls forecast a sure Republican victory. The Chicago *Tribune* put out an election extra announcing Dewey as the next President in eight-column banner headlines. But the Truman-Barkley ticket clung to an early lead through a long night; and, when the results became clear the next morning, the Democratic party was the surprise victor. Truman received 24.1 million popular votes against 22 million for Dewey, and 303 electoral votes against 189. Thurmond carried four states (South Carolina, Mississippi, Alabama, and Louisiana) and polled 1.2 million votes. Wallace polled 1.2 million votes. In addition, the Democrats captured both houses of Congress. Truman had at last established himself as a President in his own right. As for the pollsters, one wit observed, "Public opinion polls reach everyone in America, from the farmer in his field right up to the President of the United States, Thomas E. Dewey."

The Fair Deal

Return to Frustration An English magazine entitled its postelection editorial, "Roosevelt's Fourth Term." Truman himself regarded his victory as a mandate for liberalism. "We have rejected the discredited theory that the fortunes of the nation should be in the hands of a privileged few," he said in January 1949. ". . . Instead, we believe that our economic system should rest on a democratic foundation and that wealth should be created for the benefit of all. The recent election shows that the American people are in favor of this kind of society and want to go on improving it." His state-of-the-union message was a ringing summons to a new era of social reform. "Every segment of our population and every individual," he concluded, "has a right to expect from his government a fair deal."

Truman lost no time in pressing for his Fair Deal. The agricultural proposals of Secretary of Agriculture Charles F. Brannan envisaged a new approach to the farm problem through the support of income rather than prices; under the Brannan Plan, farm income from perishable commodities would be maintained by "production payments" made directly to the farmers, while prices would be allowed to find their own level in the market. In medical care, Truman, on the recommendation of Federal Security Administrator Oscar Ewing, offered a nationwide scheme of compulsory health insurance. In civil rights, he called for a permanent FEPC.

But the bolder Fair Deal ideas roused fierce opposition. The Brannan plan was condemned as "socialistic," and the American Medical Association led a successful campaign against the Ewing health plan, which it stigmatized as "socialized medicine." A Senate filibuster killed the FEPC. In addition, Congress refused to repeal the Taft-Hartley Act and rejected Truman's requests for federal aid to education and for middle-income housing. On the other hand, though thwarted in his legislative program for civil rights, Truman was able through executive action to abolish segregation within the government and the armed services. And, though Congress turned down the more spectacular Fair Deal proposals, it did pass a housing act in 1949 providing for low-income public housing, slum clearance, and urban renewal; it improved the social security system, increased the minimum wage to 75 cents, extended the soil conservation program, and enlarged the federal effort in public power, flood control, reclamation, and rural electrification. On balance, the Eighty-first Congress enacted more liberal legislation than any Congress since 1938.

The year 1949 was marked by the first serious economic troubles since the war. Several factors—particularly the cash surpluses collected by the government on all levels, the sharp decline in inventory purchases, and the drop in the export trade—combined to turn a near-inflationary situation in 1948 into a recession in 1949. The gross national product fell about $9 billion in 1949, from a peak of $266 billion; unemployment reached 4.6 million, or 7 per cent of the labor force. By the middle of the year, however, the tide had begun to turn. Though the Eightieth Congress had not reduced taxes in 1948 for Keynesian reasons, the effect of tax reduction was to release funds for consumer spending. With this fiscal stimulus, reinforced by increased government expenditures, the economy began to right itself before the downturn could develop momentum. By the end of 1949 recovery was well under way.

The Fair Deal Abroad Though Truman's primary concern in 1949 was with domestic affairs, he did not see the Fair Deal as merely a domestic policy. In a listing of points in his inaugural address, he placed particular emphasis on Point Four—"a bold new program for making the benefits of our scientific advances and industrial progress available for the improvement and growth of underdeveloped areas." With western Europe presumably secure against communism, the next priority was to prevent the uncommitted third of the world from falling into communist hands. "There will be no quick solution for any of the difficulties of the new nations of Asia and Africa," he said, "—but there may be no solution at all if we do not press forward with full energy to help these countries grow and flourish in freedom." The war against poverty "is the only war we seek."

The object of Point Four was to furnish the new nations with technical assistance for developing their own resources. Congress declined to take action on Point Four in 1949; but Truman renewed his request in 1950 and finally obtained a minimal $35 million with which to establish the Technical Cooperation Administration. In subsequent years Congress made more funds available to Point Four. By 1952 America's "technical missionaries" were at work in thirty-three countries, improving agricultural productivity, fighting typhus and malaria, launching irrigation and hydroelectric projects, and teaching people to read and write.

As for the contest with the Soviet Union, the Administration viewed its situation in 1949 with complacency. The American atomic monopoly seemed an effective deterrent to major war. The forward drive of communism in Europe had been stopped, in Berlin as well as in western Europe. If China was "lost," nothing could be done about it, except, in the phrase of the day, to "let the dust settle." All these circumstances encouraged the President to call for reductions in the defense budget.

As early as 1946, Truman had laid down as a general principle that defense spending should not amount to more than one-third of the national budget (less interest charges on the debt). This "ceiling" had kept major national security expenditures at an average of about $13 billion a year in 1947–49. Air-atomic power had first claim on these funds, and both Congress and the public tended to feel that, if the Strategic Air Command were kept strong enough, there was no need to worry about other kinds of military force.

In 1948, however, the Joint Chiefs of Staff declined to accept responsibility for the $15 billion ceiling proposed by the President for 1949–50, and Secretary Forrestal argued in vain for larger expenditures. But, after Forrestal's resignation and death early in 1949, his successor, Louis A. Johnson, supported by the former Chief of Staff General Dwight D. Eisenhower, cheerfully collaborated with Truman and the Bureau of the Budget in holding down defense spending. Johnson expressed the prevailing philosophy when he observed, "You would conclude, if you read Stalin's books, and what Stalin said, that he doesn't look to a clash of arms, that he expects America to spend itself into bankruptcy." The fear that spending

---

The Soviet Challenge

The possibilities for American policy are by no means limited to holding the line and hoping for the best.... It is rather a question of the degree to which the United States can create among the peoples of the world generally the impression of a country which knows what it wants, which is coping successfully with the problems of its internal life and with the responsibilities of a World Power, and which has a spiritual vitality capable of holding its own among the major ideological currents of the time. To the extent that such an impression can be created and maintained, the aims of Russian Communism must appear sterile and quixotic, the hopes and enthusiasms of Moscow's supporters must wane....

Thus the decision will really fall in large measure in this country itself. The issue of Soviet-American relations is in essence a test of the over-all worth of the United States as a nation among nations. To avoid destruction the United States need only measure up to its own best traditions and prove itself worthy of preservation as a great nation.

From George F. Kennan, "The Sources of Soviet Conduct," *Foreign Affairs*, July 1947.

---

would overstrain the economy spurred on the program of military cutbacks. In 1949 the armed forces lost about 10 per cent of their personnel. The army was reduced to about ten active divisions. The capability to fight a limited war dwindled; military calculations rested on the idea of a full-scale retaliatory air strike against the Soviet Union.

The Truman retrenchment left the United States in an all-or-nothing military posture. If war broke out, it seemed that Washington would either have to do nothing or else blow up the world. Some observers feared that this defense posture would invite the communists to launch an aggression in some marginal area where the United States would not wish to respond by atomic war and would find it hard to respond in any other way.

Experiment with Limited War

The End of the Atomic Monopoly The Truman defense program was based on the assumption that the United States monopoly of atomic weapons would last indefinitely. But on September 22, 1949, Truman issued a laconic statement: "We have evidence that within recent weeks an atomic explosion occurred in the U.S.S.R." With one stroke the Soviet Union had not only broken the atomic monopoly but had shown the world that its economy was capable of the most advanced achievements in science, technology, and production. The short-lived era of American invincibility had come to an end.

The American response to this prospective change in the world balance of power was slow and uncertain. On January 30, 1950, Truman concluded a bitter argument among his scientific advisers by directing the Atomic Energy Commission to proceed with the construction of a hydrogen bomb, a weapon that promised to be even more fearful than the atomic bomb. At the same time, he instructed the National Security Council to undertake a basic reappraisal of America's strategic position. The result was a document known as NSC 68, which called for an increase in military expenditures and a more ample provision for

The Shifting Front in Korea

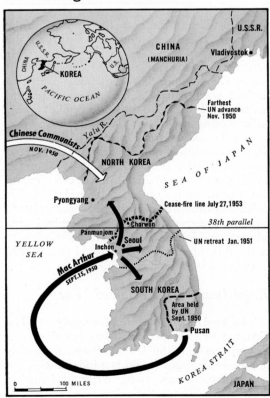

limited war. But, before NSC 68 could be translated into concrete policy, a new development challenged the thesis that air-atomic power by itself would assure American security.

War in Korea   When American and Soviet troops entered Korea after the collapse of Japan in 1945, they had accepted the thirty-eighth parallel as a military dividing line. The Americans expected that the occupying forces would withdraw and that Korea would become a free and united nation, as provided for by the Cairo Declaration of 1943. But time and the cold war converted the military demarcation into a political frontier. In 1948 the Russians set up a People's Democratic Republic in North Korea, while the Americans recognized the Republic of South Korea. In June 1949 the bulk of the American army of occupation withdrew from South Korea. The position of the new republic in the American security system was not altogether clear. Both General Douglas MacArthur and Secretary of State Acheson declared that South Korea lay outside the American defense perimeter in the Pacific; should an attack occur, Acheson said, "The initial reliance must be on the people attacked to resist it and then upon the commitments of the entire civilized world under the Charter of the United Nations."

On June 25, 1950, North Korean troops crossed the thirty-eighth parallel in a surprise invasion of South Korea. Now Truman was confronted with what he later recalled as the toughest decision he ever had to make. Without hesitation, he committed American forces under General MacArthur to the defense of South Korea. At the same time he instructed Acheson to bring the matter up before the United Nations Security Council. The fortunate absence of the Soviet delegate, who was boycotting the Security Council in pique over its refusal to seat a delegate from Communist China, made it possible for the UN to condemn the North Korean aggression without incurring a Soviet veto.

The original UN intention in South Korea was simply to repel the North Korean invasion. At first the Communists drove the UN troops—made up of ROK (Republic of Korea) forces and American troops, soon to be reinforced by a smattering of units from other nations, especially Great Britain and Turkey—back to the southeastern corner of the peninsula. But on September 15, in a daring move, MacArthur landed an amphibious force at Inchon behind the enemy lines. By September 27 the UN forces were in Seoul, and by October 1 they had recovered almost all of Korea below the thirty-eighth parallel.

Crossing the Thirty-Eighth Parallel The Inchon victory raised new issues. The question was whether the UN forces, having repelled the invader, should pause at the frontier, or whether they should pursue the enemy into North Korea. On October 3 the Chinese Communist Foreign Minister told the Indian ambassador in Peking that the Red Chinese would intervene if UN forces crossed the thirty-eighth parallel. But the Chinese warning was discounted. The Truman Administration and the British Labor government agreed with MacArthur that the war should be carried to the enemy. On October 7 the UN General Assembly, "recalling that the essential objective was the establishment of a unified, inde-

pendent, and democratic Korea," authorized UN forces to move ahead into North Korea.

On October 15 Truman and MacArthur met at Wake Island. When the President asked the General about the chances of Chinese or Soviet intervention in Korea, MacArthur replied, "Very little. . . . We are no longer fearful of their intervention. . . . If the Chinese tried to get down to Pyongyang there would be the greatest slaughter." He added that he believed all enemy resistance would end by Thanksgiving. Superbly confident, MacArthur ignored the cautions from Washington and deployed his forces in a thin line across North Korea. On November 24 he declared that his final drive to end the war was "now approaching its decisive effort." Two days later, a Chinese Communist army drove a flying wedge through the central sector. The UN forces retreated in disarray two-thirds of the way down the peninsula. MacArthur gloomily announced, "We face an entirely new war."

Korea: The objective was democracy.

Relations between MacArthur and Washington, not easy in victory, now became prickly in defeat. Years of proconsulship had charged a naturally proud and flamboyant personality with a conviction of independent authority. In particular, MacArthur showed a disposition to issue public statements at variance with official policy and often in implied criticism of it. A barrage of messages after his November defeat suggested that the blame lay, not in faulty intelligence or faulty tactics, but in the Washington decision to limit the war to Korea and to forbid attack on Chinese bases in Manchuria. This "privileged sanctuary," said MacArthur in one public *démarche*, was "an enormous handicap, without precedent in military history." On December 6 Truman ordered MacArthur to clear all subsequent statements with Washington.

No Substitute for Victory?   The tension between MacArthur and Truman reflected a fundamental disagreement over the purpose of the war. MacArthur believed that the United States had no choice but to pursue the war to a victorious conclusion. If this required an enlargement of the war—the bombing of Manchurian bases, the blockade and bombing of China, the entry of the Chinese Nationalists— then so be it. Even if such action alienated the United Nations and America's European allies, that risk had to be run. "In war there is no substitute for victory. . . . War's very object is victory, not prolonged indecision."

The Administration, on the other hand, saw the conflict as a limited war for limited objectives. If Manchuria was a privileged sanctuary, so were Okinawa and Japan. To use all the national power and transform a limited war into a general war against Communist China would be, in General Omar Bradley's phrase, to fight "the wrong war, at the wrong place, at the wrong time, and with the wrong enemy." To commit American military strength to the mainland of Asia might mean abandoning Europe to Soviet aggression— or provoking Soviet intervention in Asia. As Dean Acheson stated the case, "We are being asked to undertake a large risk of general war with China, risk of war with the Soviet Union, and a demonstrable weakening of our collective security system—all of this in return for what? In return for measures whose effectiveness in

bringing the conflict to an early conclusion are judged doubtful by our responsible military authorities."

The Administration was content to achieve the original objective of its intervention—the integrity of South Korea. And a reversal of military fortunes now gave hope that this limited goal could be won. General Matthew B. Ridgway, who had taken command of the 8th Army in December, had rallied the UN forces and begun to recover the initiative. By March most of South Korea was once again free of Communists, and Ridgway's troops were pressing on the thirty-eighth parallel. The time seemed right for negotiation.

On March 20 Washington informed MacArthur that the United States and the United Nations felt that "further diplomatic efforts toward settlement should be made before any advance with major forces north of the thirty-eighth parallel." MacArthur's reply, a defiant public statement calling for enemy surrender,

Retreat in Korea, January 1951: "An entirely new war."

killed the President's move toward negotiation. "By this act," Truman later said, "MacArthur left me no choice—I could no longer tolerate his insubordination." For the moment, however, the President contented himself with a reaffirmation of his earlier directive requiring clearance of all public statements. Then on April 5, Congressman Joseph Martin of Massachusetts, the Republican leader in the House, read a new letter from MacArthur challenging Administration policy. On April 11, Truman relieved MacArthur of his command.

Truman's decision caused an outburst of public indignation in the United States. Senator Joseph McCarthy of Wisconsin characterized the President as a "son of a bitch" and ascribed MacArthur's recall to the machinations of a White House clique besotted by "bourbon and benzedrine." Senator William Jenner of Indiana declared, "This country today is in the hands of a secret inner coterie which is directed by agents of the Soviet Union." The fever reached its pitch on April 19 when MacArthur, returning to the United States for the first time in fourteen years, addressed a joint session of Congress. He concluded with a reference to a barracks-room ballad popular in his youth "which proclaimed most proudly that 'old soldiers never die; they just fade away.' And like the old soldier of that ballad," he went on, "I now close my military career and just fade away, an old soldier who tried to do his duty as God gave him the light to see that duty."

There followed an extraordinary inquiry into the circumstances of MacArthur's dismissal by the Senate Foreign Relations and Armed Services committees. Beginning on May 3, MacArthur, Acheson, Bradley, and a number of other military and civilian leaders underwent a congressional interrogation which, in time, canvassed the most basic problems of global strategy. When the hearings ended on June 25, over two million words had been transcribed. This ventilation of the issues dispelled much of the turbulence generated by MacArthur's return. When Administration senators asked MacArthur to relate his Korean strategy to the world situation, the General replied, "I have asked you several times not to involve me in anything except my own area. My concepts of global defense are not what I am here to testify on. I don't pretend to be the authority now on those things." By taking this position, MacArthur permitted the Administration to persuade the country that the President and the Joint Chiefs, having the global interests of the country in view, might have been justified in overruling MacArthur's local recommendations. In a short time, Truman rode out the storm; and MacArthur in due course began to fade away.

The Korean War: Repercussions

The West Rearms The first consequence of the Korean War was a reversal of the United States policy of military retrenchment. Major national security expenditures increased from $13 billion in 1949–50 to $22.5 billion in 1950–51 and to $44 billion in 1951–52; only 33 per cent of the budget in 1950, they reached 67 per cent in 1952. Two years after the attack on South Korea, the nation had 3.6 million men under arms—an increase of nearly 2.2 million. The army had doubled its number of divisions, the air force had grown from forty-eight groups to ninety-five wings, and the navy had doubled its number of big carriers.

Nor was rearmament confined to the United States. The Korean War, on top of the Soviet achievement of atomic weapons, had compelled a widespread reconsideration of communist intentions. Under American inspiration, Britain and France launched rearmament programs, and in September 1950 Acheson persuaded his European allies to go along with a measure of rearmament in Germany. In 1951, NATO forces were united under the command of General Eisenhower, and the United States agreed to station four American divisions in Europe. By 1952 SHAPE (Supreme Headquarters, Allied Powers in Europe)

at Versailles had substantial military strength at its disposal.

The renewed military effort had its impact on the American economy. The gross national product rose from $264 billion in 1950 to $339 billion in 1952. At the same time there was a violent increase in prices during the first months after the start of the Korean War. This was not caused by stepped-up defense spending, then still largely in prospect, but rather by a burst of panic buying on the part of businessmen and consumers afraid of shortages and price increases. Between the invasion of South Korea and the beginning of general price and wage controls in January 1951, the cost of living rose, on the average, nearly 1 per cent per month, and wholesale prices more than 2 per cent per month. Thereafter, prices leveled off, partly because of the controls and partly because tax increases produced a cash budgetary surplus which offset inflationary tendencies. At the same time, in March 1951, a continuing struggle between the Treasury and the Federal Reserve Board was resolved by a so-called "accord." Until this time, the Federal Reserve had been forced to support government bond prices and keep down interest rates. The accord secured what came to be known as the "independence" of the Federal Reserve Board in pursuing monetary policies (meaning, in practice, tight-money, high-interest-rate policies) which might or might not be compatible with the general economic programs of the government.

The Politics of Fear The rearmament effort of 1950–52 caused surprisingly little economic dislocation. The Korean War had a sharper impact on the morale and self-confidence of the American people. For some years concern had been rising over the dangers of subversive activities within the United States. The disclosure by a Canadian Royal Commission in 1946 of a communist spy ring in Canada prompted the American government to step up its own counterespionage activities. In October 1947 Truman instituted a federal loyalty program to deal with communist penetration. Under this program, loyalty boards set up in federal agencies checked the loyalty of all federal employees. In November Truman established a Loyalty Review Board to guard against injustice. "Disloyal and subversive elements must be removed from the employ of government," he said. "We must not, however, permit employees of the Federal government to be labelled as disloyal . . . when no valid basis exists for arriving at such a conclusion."

Despite these precautionary efforts, the loyalty program—as a consequence of over-zealous investigators, ignorant or malicious informers, and apprehensive loyalty boards—began to assume a drastic and promiscuous character. By December 1952, 6.6 million people had been checked for security. Of the 25,750 who received full FBI field investigations, 5,900 withdrew before or during adjudication and 490 were dismissed as ineligible on loyalty grounds. No cases of espionage were uncovered by the investigations. The outcome was an impressive testimonial to the public service, but it was purchased in many cases at a pitiful human cost. "It was not realized at first," Dean Acheson later wrote, "how dangerous was the practice of secret evidence and secret informers, how alien to all our conceptions of justice and the rights of the citizen. . . . Experience proved again how soon good men become callous in the use of bad practices."

The government also initiated prosecutions against the eleven top communist leaders under the Smith Act of 1940, which prohibited groups from conspiring to advocate the violent overthrow of the government. Throughout the country, citizens anxious to protect their communities against the dread infection sometimes, in ardor or panic, failed to distinguish between communism and traditional American radicalism or mere dissent.

In 1948 and 1949 concern about communist infiltration crystallized around the case of Alger Hiss, a former State Department official who had been denounced as a communist spy by an admitted former spy, Whittaker Chambers, before the House Un-American Activities Committee. At first, public sympathy had favored the gracious Hiss over the unprepossessing Chambers. Then Chambers produced microfilms of classified State Department documents allegedly delivered to him by Hiss in 1937 and 1938. Since the statute of limitations barred indictment for espionage, Hiss was brought to trial early in 1949 for perjury.

The nation watched with fascinated atten-
tion as the two principals dueled in the courtroom. Each man's version of the events contained discrepancies, and the jury was unable to agree on a verdict. A second trial, however, resulted in Hiss's conviction on January 21, 1950. Four days later, when asked to comment on the case, Dean Acheson said, "I do not intend to turn my back on Alger Hiss."

On February 10, in London, Dr. Klaus Fuchs, a respected British scientist of German origin, was arrested on the grounds of atomic espionage. The pace of disclosure was quickening: if men like Hiss and Fuchs were communist agents, who might not be?

The day before the news about Fuchs, a little-known senator from Wisconsin, Joseph R. McCarthy, gave a speech in Wheeling, West Virginia. "I have here in my hand a list," he said—a list of communists in the State Department; whether he said there were 205 or 81 or 57 or "a lot" of communists (and this was a question around which much controversy would revolve) was in the end less important than his insistence that these communists were "known to the Secretary of State" and were "still working and making policy." With this speech, a remarkable new figure began a brief but lurid career on the national stage.

The Rise of McCarthyism McCarthy's charges prompted an astonished Senate to appoint a subcommittee under Senator Millard Tydings of Maryland to look into his allegations. In July 1950, after weeks of hearings, the Tydings Committee declared that McCarthy had worked a "fraud and a hoax." Yet, for all the apparent failure of his charges, the hearings also revealed the facility, agility, and lack of scruple with which McCarthy operated. His most characteristic weapon was what Richard Rovere called the "multiple untruth"—a statement so complicated and flexible and grandiose in its mendacity as almost to defy rational refutation. To this McCarthy added unlimited impudence, an instinct for demagoguery, and an unmatched skill in alley-fighting. If the Tydings Committee thought it had disciplined McCarthy, it was wrong. In the election of 1950, McCarthy's intervention in Maryland, marked by a broad hint that Tydings, a conservative Democrat whom Roosevelt had tried in vain to purge in 1938, was procommunist, brought about

From the beginning we will bring into government men and women to whom low public morals are unthinkable. Thus, we will not only drive wrong-doers and their cronies out of government. We will make sure that they do not get into government in the first place....

Then we will begin to move forward. With that accomplished, we will make these our objectives, our immediate aims for the government of the United States:

First, to save: That means an administration which knows how to practice the wiser spending of less of the people's money;

Second, to streamline: That means an administration which knows how to make government the more efficient servant of the people;

Third, to decentralize: That means an administration which is determined effectively to bring government close to the people. It means, also, faith in the people to act more wisely in their own behalf than can a bureaucrat removed a thousand miles from the scene of action.

Fourth, to unify: That means an administration able to make the whole government a joint, cooperative enterprise for the whole people's benefit.

From Dwight D. Eisenhower, Campaign Address at St. Louis, September 1952.

Tydings' defeat. From that moment, the Wisconsin senator became a formidable figure in the Senate, with whom no one thereafter tangled lightly.

The Korean War had wrought a significant change in the public atmosphere. It had created a climate which transformed McCarthy's crusade from an eccentric sideshow, like that of Martin Dies, into a popular movement. If communists were killing American boys in Korea, why should communists be given the benefit of the doubt in the United States? In some quarters a storm of near-hysteria blew up, and for a moment membership in any liberal or internationalist organization seemed to provide some senator or congressman with grounds for indicting a man's loyalty to his country. Politicians who knew better quailed, especially when they noted the fate of Tydings in 1950 and of William Benton of Connecticut, McCarthy's next major senatorial opponent, in 1952.

Though Truman's loyalty program had in

some respects overridden traditional safeguards of civil freedom, it did not go nearly far enough for McCarthy and his followers. In September 1950, Congress passed the McCarran Internal Security Act, establishing a Subversive Activities Control Board to follow communist activities in the United States, and setting up bars against the admission to the country of anyone who had once been a member of a totalitarian organization.* Truman vetoed the bill: "We need not fear the expression of ideas—we do need to fear their suppression. . . . Let us not, in cowering and foolish fear, throw away the ideals which are the fundamental basis of our free society." But Congress passed the bill over his veto.

The spectacle of McCarthyism infuriated the President. "All this howl about organizations a fellow belongs to gives me a pain in the neck," he wrote when someone attacked Secretary of the Air Force Thomas K. Finletter for the crime of belonging to the United World Federalists. "Liberty can be endangered by the 'Right' as well as by the 'Left,'" he warned. He told the American Legion, "Slander, lies, character assassination—these things are a threat to every single citizen everywhere in this country. When even one American—who has done nothing wrong—is forced by fear to shut his mind and close his mouth, then all Americans are in peril. It is the job of all of us—of every American who loves his country and his freedom—to rise up and put a stop to this terrible business."

The 1952 Election

Truman in Retreat   But, in the backwash of the Korean War, the movement of opinion favored McCarthy. The Administration and its leading officials—especially Secretary of State Acheson—fell under unsparing

---

* A second McCarran Act, also passed over Truman's veto, was the Immigration and Nationality Act of 1952. While this bill finally abolished the Asian exclusion provisions of 1924, it retained the national origins quota system which discriminated in favor of immigrants from northern and western Europe and which critics condemned as a form of racism built into federal law. It also required that foreigners visiting the United States go through so complicated a system of loyalty checks that many came to feel that the United States regarded them as potential criminals.

attack as communist sympathizers. It was charged that China had been "lost" because of procommunists in the State Department. "One might say," James Wechsler has written, "that Mr. Truman spent his last two years in office leading the democratic resistance to a Communist assault abroad while seeking to prove to his countrymen that he was neither a captive nor an agent of Communism at home." The Republicans scored impressive gains in the congressional elections of 1950 and looked forward with increasing confidence to 1952.

Their confidence grew with revelations of spreading corruption within the Administration. A congressional investigation of the Reconstruction Finance Corporation in 1951 exposed collusion and payoffs—mink coats and deep freezes—in RFC loans. Soon the phrase "five percenter" became the colloquialism for the fixer who would arrange profitable transactions with the government for a 5 per cent fee. In a few months, further exposures revealed extensive corruption in the Bureau of Internal Revenue and in the tax division of the Department of Justice. In addition, the Senate Crime Investigation Committee, under the chairmanship of Estes Kefauver of Tennessee, set forth before rapt television audiences the connections between politics and organized crime in big cities.

"There are two Trumans," Elmer Davis once said, "—the White House Truman and the courthouse Truman. He does the big things right, and the little things wrong." The disclosures of 1951–52 called attention to the decline which had taken place in the governmental service from the relatively incorruptible thirties—a decline brought about in part because Truman's ill-concealed scorn for the "professional liberal" had driven many of the old New Dealers from government to be replaced by party hacks. When the facts got out, moreover, Truman, constrained by loyalty to old political associates, seemed grudging in his response; and, though the necessary housecleaning finally took place, it took place too late for him to recapture public confidence.

A rebuff by the Supreme Court increased the Administration's confusion. Fearing that a steel strike would handicap the prosecution of the Korean War, Truman, on August 8, 1952, ordered government seizure of the steel

Stevenson: A New Day

Government has three duties.

First, government is an umpire, denying special privilege, ensuring equal rights, restraining monopoly and greed and bigotry....

Second, government has the duty of creating an economic climate in which creative men can take risks and reap rewards, so that our economic life will have a continuous flow of fresh ideas and fresh leadership; and, of course, it means the building of solid defenses against the greatest threat to that flow—depression....

Third, government has the duty of helping the people develop their country.

The Federal Government made the Louisiana Purchase, and on that land a nation grew to greatness. No private corporation would have built Grand Coulee Dam, yet in the Grand Coulee country people are building their homes and establishing their private business, and farmers are converting desert into garden....

We take our stand upon the fundamental principle that the role of government is, to sum up, just this: To remove the roadblocks put in the way of the people by nature and by greedy men; to release the energies of the people, so that free men may work the miracles of the future as they have worked the miracles of the past.

From Adlai E. Stevenson, Campaign Address at St. Louis, October 1952.

plants after all efforts to avert a strike had failed. The steel companies argued that the seizure was illegal, and they were upheld by the Supreme Court on June 2. A seven-week shutdown followed, and at last the companies accepted a settlement which gave them more latitude on price increases than Truman had wished. All this strengthened the idea of a "mess in Washington" and helped substantiate a growing national conviction that the Democratic party had been in power too long.

The Campaign of 1952 Robert A. Taft's triumphant re-election to the Senate in 1950 over determined liberal and labor opposition made him the leading contender for the Republican nomination in 1952. But the powerful Eastern wing of the party, fearing that the Ohio senator was too strong, too isolationist, and too conservative, turned to General Dwight D. Eisenhower. Though

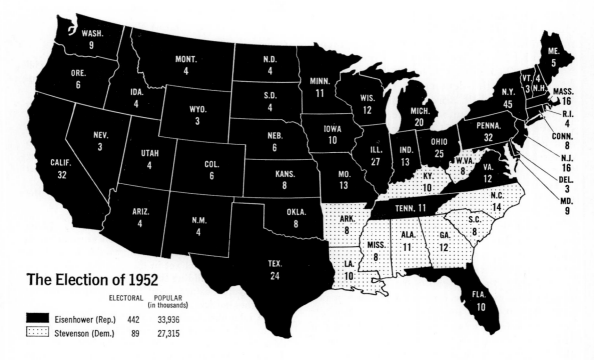

The Election of 1952

	ELECTORAL	POPULAR (in thousands)
■ Eisenhower (Rep.)	442	33,936
⬚ Stevenson (Dem.)	89	27,315

Eisenhower had expressed doubt in 1948 that a military career was suitable qualification for the presidency, he finally succumbed to the pressure. The contest between the Taft and Eisenhower forces reached its angry climax at the Chicago convention in July. There the Eisenhower supporters outmaneuvered their opposition in a battle over contested delegates. Eisenhower was nominated on the first ballot. Senator Richard M. Nixon of California became his running mate.

Truman had meanwhile withdrawn from the Democratic picture. Though his choice for the Democratic nomination—Governor Adlai E. Stevenson of Illinois—at first demurred, the Democratic convention in Chicago drafted Stevenson for the top place on the ticket. Little known to voters outside Illinois, Stevenson in the next three months established himself with extraordinary success as a brilliant, literate, and eloquent candidate. His campaign pledge was to "talk sense to the American people." He explained in a series of remarkable speeches that the problems of the age had no easy solution and called for restraint and sacrifice. Labor backed him, and he won particular support among intellectuals.

The Republican campaign was based on the themes of "Korea, communism, and corruption." Eisenhower appealed to the national desire to end the war in Korea, to drive communists out of government, to clean up the mess in Washington, and to free the economy from taxation and regulation. Nixon, a more experienced campaigner, reinforced these themes with particular emphasis, referring to the Democratic candidate, for example, as "Adlai the appeaser . . . who got a Ph.D. from Dean Acheson's College of Cowardly Communist Containment." "I further charge," Nixon added, "that Mr. Truman, Dean Acheson and other administration officials for political reasons covered up this Communist conspiracy and attempted to halt its exposure." Intellectual supporters of Stevenson were dismissed as "eggheads."

The campaign was interrupted by a revelation that Nixon had been a beneficiary of a fund collected on his behalf by California businessmen. For a moment, Eisenhower considered asking Nixon to resign from the ticket. But an effective television speech in an autobiographical vein enabled the vice-presidential candidate to win back the ground he had lost and to recover his partner's confidence. When Eisenhower, late in the campaign, declared his intention to go to Korea if elected, he clinched his victory. The popular vote showed 33.9 million for Eisenhower, 27.3 million for Stevenson; the margin in the electoral college was 442 to 89. Twenty years of Democratic rule had come to an end.

In the meantime, the cold war persisted. United Nations forces were combating the Chinese and North Koreans in Korea. The Soviet Union was seeking to consolidate its position in eastern Europe and to renew its pressures against western Europe. The emerging nations of Asia, Africa, and Latin America, striving for political independence and economic development, were themselves becoming a battlefield in the cold war. The new American President confronted difficult problems on every side.

SUGGESTIONS FOR READING

General

Truman's *Memoirs*, 2 vols. (1955–56), are pithy and revealing though sometimes controversial. E. F. Goldman, *The Crucial Decade* * (1956), is a fluent survey of the Truman years. Useful, too, are Jonathan Daniels, *The Man from Independence* (1950), and L. W. Koenig, ed., *The Truman Administration* (1956).

Foreign Policy

There is a brief analysis of postwar foreign policy in Herbert Agar, *The Price of Power: America Since 1945* * (1957), and another brief interpretation of the basic issues involved in G. F. Kennan, *American Diplomacy: 1900–1950* * (1951). H. B. Westerfield, *Foreign Policy and Party Politics: Pearl Harbor to Korea* (1955), is thoughtful, and R. E. Neustadt, *Presidential Power* (1960), contains valuable sidelights. Among the significant books by or about the policy-makers themselves, besides Truman's cited above, are J. F. Byrnes, *Speaking Frankly* (1947); McGeorge Bundy, ed., *The Pattern of Responsibility* (1952), compiled from the speeches of Dean Acheson; W. B. Smith, *My Three Years in Moscow* (1950); Walter Millis, ed., *The Forrestal Diaries* (1951); and A. H. Vandenberg, Jr., and J. A. Morris, eds., *The Private Papers of Senator Vandenberg* (1952). For a characteristic criticism of Truman, see R. A. Taft, *A Foreign Policy for Americans* (1951), and, on Taft's views, Norman Graebner, *The New Isolationism* (1956).

Material of special importance for Germany may be found in L. D. Clay, *Decision in Germany* (1950), and the indispensable Hajo Holborn, *American Military Government* (1947), as well as Drew Middleton, *The Struggle for Germany* (1949), and E. H. Litchfield, ed., *Governing Postwar Germany* (1953). On postwar policy in Japan the following are all useful: E. M. Martin, *Allied Occupation of Japan* (1948); Russell Brines, *MacArthur's Japan* (1948); and especially R. A. Fearey, *Occupation of Japan* (1950), and E. O. Reischauer, *The United States and Japan* * (1957 ed.). By far the best work on problems of atomic energy in the immediate postwar period is the authorized but judicious study by R. G. Hewlett and O. E. Anderson, Jr., *The New World* (1962). Two good studies of the early years of the United Nations, already the subject of many publications, are L. M. Goodrich and E. I. Hambro, *Charter of the United Nations* (1949), and E. P. Chase, *The United Nations in Action* (1950). An important memoir on that subject is Trygve Lie, *In the Cause of Peace* (1954). S. E. Harris, ed., *Foreign Economic Policy for the United States* (1948), covers the subject of its title, as does R. F. Mikesell, *United States Economic Policy and International Relations* (1952).

There is a short, general account of the diplomatic and military aspects of the Korean War in Carl Berger, *The Korea Knot, a Military-Political History* (1957), and a longer, essential military narrative in Department of the Army, *Korea—1950* (1952); see also M. W. Cagle and F. A. Manson, *The Sea War in Korea* (1957). J. W. Spanier takes the view of a neutral in his *The Truman-MacArthur Controversy and the Korean War* (1959), and Trumbull Higgins

* Available in a paperback edition.

that of a skeptic in *Korea and the Fall of MacArthur* (1960). The general is adored in Courtney Whitney, *MacArthur: His Rendezvous with History* (1956), and evaluated in R. H. Rovere and A. M. Schlesinger, Jr., *The General and the President* (1951).

Domestic Affairs

There are discussions of specific domestic issues in H. A. Millis and E. C. Brown, *From the Wagner Act to Taft-Hartley* (1950); Estes Kefauver, *Crime in America* (1951); P. H. Douglas, *Ethics in Government* (1952); and G. A. Graham, *Morality in American Politics* (1952). Indispensable on the Employment Act of 1946 is S. K. Bailey, *Congress Makes a Law* (1950). On Negro civil rights, two important works are A. M. Rose, *The Negro in Postwar America* * (1950), and C. V. Woodward, *The Strange Career of Jim Crow* * (1957). On politics, Samuel Lubell has written two vital books, *The Future of American Politics* * (rev. ed., 1956) and *Revolt of the Moderates* (1956). "Mr. Republican" has an uncritical biographer in W. S. White, *The Taft Story* (1954), and uncritical, too, is K. M. Schmidt, *Henry Wallace: Quixotic Crusader* (1960). For the 1952 campaign, Adlai E. Stevenson, *Speeches* (1952), is both eloquent and essential. No one better distinguishes between political rhetoric and political reality than does J. K. Galbraith in *Economics and the Art of Controversy* (1959).

There are thoughtful treatments of questions of civil liberties and loyalty in Alan Barth, *The Loyalty of Free Men* (1951), and Sidney Hook, *Heresy, Yes—Conspiracy, No* (1953); see, too, Walter Gellhorn, *Security, Loyalty, and Science* (1950) and *The States and Subversion* (1952), and H. D. Lasswell, *National Security and Individual Freedom* (1950). The most incisive study of the junior senator from Wisconsin is R. H. Rovere, *Senator Joe McCarthy* * (1959). E. A. Shils, *The Torment of Secrecy* (1956), offers a stimulating analysis of the background of McCarthyism. Alistair Cooke, *A Generation on Trial* (1950), reviews the Hiss case with much sympathy for the accused. Hiss's argument in his own behalf, *In the Court of Public Opinion* (1957), is less persuasive and less gripping than the autobiographical Whittaker Chambers, *Witness* (1952).

* Available in a paperback edition.

32

The Eisenhower Years

By 1952, the American People had endured nearly a generation of unrelenting crisis. In the years since 1929, they had experienced the worst depression in their history, the worst hot war, the worst cold war, the worst limited war. During these years, moreover, they had been led by two aggressive Presidents who believed strongly in positive government and in vigorous national action. But a people's capacity for high-tension political life is limited. Just as the first two decades of the twentieth century—the activist decades dominated by Theodore Roosevelt and Woodrow Wilson —produced by 1920 a condition of near national exhaustion, so the thirties and the forties left the American people—or a good many of them—weary of public commitment and ardently desirous of respite. By 1952 they were frustrated and spent; they wanted to be let off public affairs and to resume the private course of life. The pursuit of "normalcy," however, was far more difficult in the stormy fifties than it had been thirty years before. In 1920 Americans could turn their back on public issues; in the fifties this was no longer easy or safe. Communist competition abroad and the unprecedented rate of population growth at home confronted the nation with problems it could not reject. The people manfully accepted the existence of these problems but tackled them without enthusiasm or urgency or strong sense of purpose.

The Eisenhower Style

The New President   President Dwight D. Eisenhower embodied the popular mood. He was sixty-two years old on his inauguration, and was already a national hero, long admired and beloved by his countrymen. After quiet years in the peacetime army, Eisenhower had been one of that group of remarkable military men who burst on the public attention during the Second World War. His notable service as Supreme Commander of the Allied forces in Europe was followed by a postwar tour of duty as Chief of Staff in the United States. In 1948 he became president of Columbia University, but in 1950 he yielded to Truman's request that he return to Europe as Supreme Commander of the NATO forces. He resigned this post to seek the Republican nomination in 1952.

Eisenhower's professional career had kept him aloof from party politics, and the appearance of being "above" politics was an important source of his popular strength. People weary of the "mess in Washington" and yearning for an end to the controversies of the New Deal era saw in Eisenhower a leader who might heal the nation's wounds. His own affable personality and accommodating temperament qualified him all the more for the role of national conciliator. Moreover, as the candidate of the modern-minded Republicans, he could

Under the Constitution the President of the United States is alone responsible for the "faithful execution of the laws." Our government is fixed on the basis that the President is the only person in the executive branch who has the final authority. Everyone else in the executive branch is an agent of the President. There are some people, and sometimes members of Congress and the press, who get mixed up in their thinking about the powers of the President. The important fact to remember is that the President is the only person in the executive branch who has final authority, and if he does not exercise it, we may be in trouble. If he exercises his authority wisely, that is good for the country. If he does not exercise it wisely, that is too bad, but it is better than not exercising it at all.

Yet our government is so vast that branches of the administrative machinery do not always tie in smoothly with the White House. The Cabinet presents the principal medium through which the President controls his administration. I made it a point always to listen to Cabinet officers at length and with care, especially when their points of view differed from mine.

I never allowed myself to forget that the final authority was mine. I would ask the Cabinet to share their counsel with me, even encouraging disagreement and argument to sharpen up the different points of view. On major issues I would frequently ask them to vote, and I expected the Cabinet officers to be frank and candid in expressing their opinions to me. At the same time, I insisted that they keep me informed of the major activities of their departments in order to make certain that they supported the policy once I had made a decision.

From Harry S. Truman, *Memoirs*, Vol. I, *Year of Decisions*, 1955.

---

be expected to lead his long-embattled party to accept both the internationalist policies and the social and economic changes of the Roosevelt-Truman epoch.

Eisenhower's Conception of the Presidency   Eisenhower began as an exponent of the Whig theory of the presidency. He was convinced that Roosevelt and Truman had aggrandized the executive branch at the expense of the other branches of government and that it was his duty to "restore" the constitutional balance. In his dealings with Congress, he believed that his job was simply to propose policies; thereafter the legislators were free to

"vote their own consciences." He disliked the idea of exerting pressure on Capitol Hill: "I don't think it is the function of the President of the United States to punish anybody for voting what he believes." Even within his own official family he did not insist on his own views. He once said of his Cabinet, "I have given way on a number of personal opinions to this gang." He was not, he remarked many times, the desk-pounding sort of President.

In running the presidential establishment, Eisenhower rejected the haphazard methods of his civilian predecessors in favor of the military staff system, with the principal acting on recommendations from his subordinates. Former Governor Sherman Adams of New Hampshire, as the chief of the executive staff, controlled the flow of information and recommendations to the President (except in foreign affairs, where Secretary of State John Foster Dulles had a similar role). Adams once said, "I count the day lost when I have not found some new way of lightening the President's load." A Cabinet secretariat was set up, along with other devices designed to institutionalize the White House, until at last observers could write of "mechanizing the President."

Eisenhower's conception of the presidency was fundamentally nonpolitical. "In the general derogatory sense," he observed in 1955, "you can say that, of course, that I do not like politics." But, while the Eisenhower reorganization gave the White House a superficial orderliness which it had heretofore lacked, his commitment to the staff system tended to confine his knowledge of public matters to problems

I think any President who tries to follow what he believes to be public opinion will in the long run come a cropper.... The President, I think, always has a job, day in and day out—not merely in times of crisis—but trying to get an informed public opinion.... I went to the people in every way I could....

I have not much patience with the desk-pounding type of leadership.... Leadership is a matter of influencing people. And you sometimes have to influence people who are hostile as well as friends.

From Dwight D. Eisenhower, Interview on CBS–TV, February 1962.

submitted to him through channels by his staff. He rarely even read the daily newspapers. As a consequence, he drew on fewer sources of information and ideas than some of his predecessors and had less personal impact through the government. Some observers welcomed this application of military staff methods to the presidency; others wondered whether the presidency could be run on this basis. Sam Rayburn, the veteran Democratic leader in the House, once said of Eisenhower, "No, won't do. Good man, but wrong business."

Eisenhower's Political Purposes Eisenhower's political philosophy combined moderation with a desire to correct past error. "The middle of the road," he once said, "is derided by all of the right and the left. They deliberately misrepresent the central position as a neutral, wishy-washy one. Yet here is the truly creative area within which we may obtain agreement for constructive social action compatible with basic American principles, and with the just aspirations of every sincere American." If such statements struck waspish critics as sonorous platitudes, many Americans found in them appealing notes of sincerity.

To achieve the middle of the road, Eisenhower felt it necessary to redress what he regarded as the excesses of the New Deal–Fair Deal years. While he accepted the basic New Deal revision of the economic and social structure, he hoped now to roll back the power of the federal government and, where possible, to transfer governmental functions from Washington to the states or to the private economy. Before the election, he had come to terms with Robert A. Taft on domestic policy. On their joint behalf, the conservative leader had issued a statement pledging Eisenhower to "the reduction of federal spending and taxes," the whittling down of the federal budget to $60 billion by 1955–56, the repudiation of the "left-wing theory that the Executive has unlimited powers," and resistance to "statutory extension of power by the creation and extension of federal bureaus." This pledge reflected Eisenhower's general fear of "statism" and his belief "that without free enterprise there can be no democracy." The President himself cited such federal activities as the Tennessee Valley Authority as examples of "creeping socialism." He promised what he called a

---

The Presidency: J. F. K.

The job of the next President will be the hardest since Roosevelt, and I think Roosevelt had the hardest of all except Lincoln and perhaps Washington. The job will be tremendous, and a great responsibility will center on the President. The real dilemma we face is whether a free society in which each of us follows our own self-interest can compete over a long period of time with a totalitarian society....

There are many short-term advantages which a totalitarian possesses in that kind of competition.... The responsibility of the President, therefore, is especially great. He must serve as a catalyst, an energizer, the defender of the public good and the public interest against all the narrow private interests which operate in our society. Only the President can do this, and only a President who recognizes the true nature of this hard challenge can fulfill this historic function....

Congress is quite obviously not equipped to make basic policy, to conduct foreign relations, to speak for the national interest in the way that a President can and must.... I ... believe that in the next two or three decades there will be greater demands upon the President than ever before—and the powers are there, if the man will use them.

Quoted in James M. Burns, *John Kennedy: A Political Profile*, 1959.

"revolution" in the federal government, "trying to make it smaller rather than bigger and finding things it can stop doing instead of seeking new things to do."

His Cabinet agreed that business was more trustworthy than government. In domestic affairs the Cabinet was dominated by Secretary of the Treasury George M. Humphrey, an Ohio businessman who reinforced deeply conservative views with a strong and attractive personality. When the new Secretary of Defense, Charles E. Wilson of General Motors, was asked whether he foresaw a conflict between his business and official commitments, he replied, "I cannot conceive of one because for years I thought what was good for our country was good for General Motors, and *vice versa*." The Secretary of the Interior, Douglas McKay of Oregon, summed up the general attitude when he said, "We're here in the saddle as an Administration representing business and industry." The conspicuous exception in this business-oriented Cabinet was

Eisenhower: The modern Republican.

the Secretary of Labor, Martin Durkin of the Plumbers Union, whose appointment prompted the remark that the Cabinet consisted of "eight millionaires and a plumber." His presence displeased prominent Republicans like Taft (who termed the appointment "incredible"); and after eight months of vain effort to persuade the Administration to go along on Taft-Hartley revision, Durkin resigned.

Dulles and Foreign Policy

John Foster Dulles   The urgent problems confronting the Administration, however, were in foreign affairs. Here the central figure was the Secretary of State, John Foster Dulles. Few Americans seemed so well pre-

pared by inheritance and experience for international responsibility. The grandson of one Secretary of State (John Foster) and the nephew of another (Robert Lansing), Dulles had begun his own diplomatic career as his grandfather's secretary at the age of nineteen in the Hague Conference of 1907. He had been at Versailles in 1919; and, though he was an isolationist in the late thirties, he had emerged by 1944 as the leading Republican spokesman on foreign affairs. The Truman Administration had several times called on Dulles' unquestioned talents as a negotiator, particularly in connection with the Japanese Peace Treaty.

By profession a lawyer and by avocation an eminent Protestant layman, Dulles united a talent for close legal argument with a penchant for high moral principle. This combination won him the total confidence of President Eisenhower, who, in line with his theory of the presidency, gave Dulles greater control over foreign policy than had ever been enjoyed by a Secretary of State. Others who dealt with Dulles were less ecstatic. One British Foreign Secretary, Herbert Morrison, spoke of his "duplicity" and "his remarkable and regrettable custom of saying the right thing in the morning and doing the wrong thing in the afternoon." Another, Sir Anthony Eden, wrote, "My difficulty in working with Mr. Dulles was to determine what he really meant and in consequence the significance to be attached to his words and actions."

Though Dulles himself was identified with many aspects of the Truman-Acheson foreign policy, he had grown violently critical of that policy as the 1952 election drew near. Now he felt that containment would commit the United States to a policy of indefinite coexistence with communism, whereas the proper American purpose, in his view, was not to coexist with the communist threat but to end it. Containment was, as he put it in the Republican foreign policy plank, "negative, futile and immoral." "We will abandon the policy of containment," Dulles said, "and will actively develop hope and resistance spirit within the captive peoples." While the program of "liberation" would be "a peaceful process," those who did not acknowledge what could be accomplished by propaganda and moral pressure "just do not know what they are talking about." The mere statement by the United States "that it wants and expects liberation to occur would change, in an electrifying way, the mood of the captive peoples." By such means the cold war could be brought to an end; moreover, the cost would be far less than the cost of containment. In short, the infusion of "dynamism" into American foreign policy would push back communism and balance the budget, both at the same time.

How was dynamism to be infused? The "liberation" policy was one means. Another was to encourage the forces of anticommunism to take the offensive. Thus Eisenhower, in his first state-of-the-union message, canceled Truman's order of 1950 to neutralize the Straits of Formosa, thereby "unleashing" Chiang Kai-shek and his Nationalist forces, presumably for a reconquest of the mainland. The Republican platform had also pledged the repudiation of "all commitments contained in secret understandings such as those of Yalta which aid Communist enslavement," and Eisenhower reaffirmed this pledge in his state-of-the-union message.

In making these declarations, Eisenhower and Dulles were in part moving to satisfy the right wing of the Republican party. Aware that Acheson's difficulties with Congress had impaired his effectiveness in the State Department, Dulles was determined to retain the confidence even of those who were most radically opposed to internationalist policies.

Ending the Korean War   The first order of business, however, was to end the Korean War. Eisenhower fulfilled a campaign pledge by visiting Korea in the interval between the election and his inauguration. Ceasefire negotiations, which had begun in July 1951, continued to drag on, however, as did hostilities; indeed, some of the heaviest fighting of the war took place around Porkchop Hill in the Chorwon area in July 1953.

The sticking-point in the truce negotiations was whether, and how, prisoners of war should be repatriated. Many of the 173,000 North Koreans in United Nations hands had made clear that they did not want to return to North Korea. United Nations negotiators accordingly rejected Communist insistence on compulsory repatriation. By the spring of 1953, however, the display of American military resolution, underwritten by western rearmament, apparently convinced the Communists that they had pushed military aggression about as far as they could. They consequently modified their position on forcible repatriation. President Syngman Rhee of South Korea, seeing the collapse of his hopes for a united Korea, opposed the end of hostilities and even ordered the unilateral release of some twenty thousand North Korean prisoners. But an armistice was finally concluded at Panmunjom on July 27, 1953.

The armistice provided for a demilitarized zone between the opposing armies, established a Neutral Nations Supervisory Commission to carry out the armistice terms, and called for a political conference to settle remaining questions, including the future of Korea and the fate of prisoners of war who refused to return to their homelands. Now the conflict shifted from the battlefield to the negotiations tent. The political conference was never held, and relations between North and South Korea remained hostile. During the next few years each side charged the other with repeated violations of the armistice agreement. The United States signed a mutual defense treaty with South Korea in 1954 and kept an un-

certain hand in South Korean affairs for the rest of the decade. In the end, the increasingly arbitrary actions of the aging Syngman Rhee caused widespread protest both in South Korea and in Washington, culminating in the overthrow of the Rhee regime in April 1960 and the establishment of a new government with American support.

The Korean War had lasted three years and one month. During that time 33,629 Americans had lost their lives in battle, along with about 3000 from other UN countries and about

The Far East

Member nations of SEATO

Nations which have bilateral treaties with the U.S.

Communist bloc

50,000 South Koreans. The total Communist battle casualties were estimated at 1.5 million. For all the bitterness and frustration the war produced at home, it had stopped Communist aggression in Korea, strengthened the authority of the United Nations, and convinced the communist world that the democratic nations were determined to meet and overcome military challenges.

Releasing Chiang Kai-shek Eisenhower's decision to deneutralize the Straits of Formosa led Chiang Kai-shek to garrison or reinforce a number of small islands near the mainland, notably Quemoy, Matsu, and the Tachens, and to use these islands as bases for guerrilla and intelligence raids against the mainland. Walter Robertson, Assistant Secretary of State for Far Eastern Affairs, felt that Formosa should keep alive "a constant threat of military action" in the hope that Communist China would one day collapse. This policy meant, however, that the United States might be drawn into a full-scale war on behalf of Chiang Kai-shek; and the misgivings this prospect aroused both in the United States and in the United Nations were heightened in September 1954 when Nationalist planes raided Amoy in response to a Communist bombardment of the offshore islands.

A mutual security pact, designed to guarantee Formosa and the neighboring Pescadores Islands, was already under negotiation with Chiang Kai-shek. In order to "releash" Chiang, provisions were inserted restricting the use of Nationalist force to defense operations except in agreement with the United States. By the time the treaty came before the Senate in January 1955, the situation in the Formosa Straits had grown even more explosive. Some of Eisenhower's military advisers were urging him to commit United States forces to the defense of Quemoy and Matsu; they evidently believed that a showdown with Red China could not be avoided, and that the time to have it was now. General Matthew B. Ridgway, the Chief of Staff, disagreed. He had no doubt that the United States should go to war, if necessary, for Formosa and the Pescadores; "but the juridical, historical and geographical background of Quemoy and Matsu is radically different. To go to war for Quemoy or Matsu to me would

seem an unwarranted and tragic course." Such proposals, he contended, reflected thinking "which trends dangerously toward acceptance of the doctrine of 'preventive war.'" Moreover, they would isolate America from her allies, most of whom accepted the British view that Quemoy and Matsu were legally part of the mainland.

Eisenhower agreed with Ridgway and declined to commit himself to the defense of the offshore islands per se. But, since the mutual security pact with Chiang Kai-shek did not cover the offshore islands, Eisenhower asked Congress for a resolution authorizing military action if necessary to repel Chinese Communist aggression in the area of the Formosa Straits. The Administration made it clear that it would defend Quemoy and Matsu only if an attack on these islands was part of an attack on Formosa. As Dulles put it, "The United States has no commitment and no purpose to defend the coastal islands as such." Though the Formosa resolution gave the President no powers he did not already possess, it was conceived (and resented by the opposition) as a means of implicating Congress in military action.

The situation remained risky. In February 1955 Washington induced Chiang to evacuate the Tachen Islands, but failed in later efforts to persuade him to reduce his troop commitments in Quemoy and Matsu. In August 1958, after a long period of quiescence, the Chinese Communists resumed their heavy bombardment of the offshore islands. Eisenhower stated again that the United States would not become involved "merely in defense of Quemoy and Matsu" but made clear American determination to resist any action which seemed part of an assault on Formosa. He added that it was "not a good thing" to station so many troops on islands which "as of themselves, as two pieces of territory, are not greatly vital to Formosa." The strong American stand evidently deterred the Chinese from an attack on Quemoy and Matsu.

The matter flared up briefly in the 1960 presidential campaign when Vice-President Nixon advocated an unconditional commitment to the defense of the islands and the Democratic candidate, Senator John F. Kennedy, appeared to favor disengagement.

New Directions in Soviet Policy

The Death of Stalin   During the first years of the Eisenhower Administration, the Soviet Union seemed to be modifying its foreign policy. These modifications were forecast in a statement presented by Stalin to the Nineteenth Party Congress in October 1952, and they gathered momentum after his death on March 5, 1953. Though the next years were marked by bloody and obscure feuds among the Soviet leaders, resulting in the victory of N. S. Khrushchev by 1957–58, the policy shift proceeded with surprising consistency. Now the main communist target became the underdeveloped world rather than Europe, and the main communist tactic became economic and political penetration rather than military or conspiratorial action.

Stalin in 1952 had called on the communists to pick up "the banner of nationalism where it had been dropped by the bourgeoisie." During the decade the Soviet Union launched a major campaign to win over the new nations of, first, Asia and the Middle East, then Africa, and, by the end of the decade, Latin America. This campaign employed a variety of tactics and appeals: the support of nationalist and anticolonial movements; economic and technical assistance to underdeveloped countries; and, above all, the contention, enormously appealing to nations struggling to emerge from centuries of oppression and stagnation, that communism provided the formula for swift economic and social modernization. Nothing was more critical to this campaign than the projection of the Soviet Union itself as the nation whose prodigious economic, scientific, and technological achievements verified its claim to be the master of the future. This image of the U.S.S.R. was reinforced by the fact that the Soviet rate of industrial growth in the fifties averaged about three times as high as that of the United States, and by the astonishing and unexpected major Soviet technical breakthroughs—the hydrogen bomb in August 1953, the first intercontinental ballistic missile and the first earth satellite (Sputnik) in 1957, the first moon satellite (Lunik) in 1959, and the first man in space in 1961.

The new Soviet strategy was accompanied by incessant propaganda to the effect that the communists alone were interested in peace— claims expressed, for example, in repeated proposals of grandiose but vague plans for general disarmament. This program was designed partly (as in the covert instigation of "peace" movements in western countries) to weaken the western will to invoke military sanctions. But there is also evidence to suggest that, as Soviet leaders assessed the frightening implications of nuclear weapons, they began to reconsider the Lenin-Stalin doctrine of the inevitability of war. Khrushchev first announced the modified doctrine—that the conflict between capitalism and communism was to be decided, not by war, but by peaceful competition between social systems—at the Twentieth Party Congress in February 1956 (a party conclave rendered the more notable by his famous "secret speech" in which he denounced the crimes of Stalin).

The American Response   The shock of the Korean War continued to dominate American policy. Though Churchill in England sensed the beginnings of a shift in Soviet policy and urged a summit meeting in 1953, Secretary of State Dulles still saw the communist threat as essentially one of military aggression. His main objective in Europe in 1953 was thus to carry forward the policy of German rearmament, to which the West had already acceded in principle in 1950. Dulles hoped that the German contribution would be part of a unified West European military effort through a European Defense Community. When the French balked at the idea of the EDC, Dulles, speaking in Paris in December 1953, warned that continued delay in establishing "political, economic and military unity" in West Europe would compel an "agonizing reappraisal" of United States policy. This warning seemed to mean that, if the EDC were not ratified, the United States might withdraw from Europe; but, since the United States was presumably in Europe not to defend the European nations but to protect its own national interests, the threat was ineffective. Eventually German rearmament took place through NATO, to which West Germany was admitted in October 1954.

Dulles' more considered response to the new Soviet policies came in a speech of January 12, 1954, in which he announced policy decisions recently taken by Eisenhower and the National Security Council. "The basic decision," Dulles said, "was to depend primarily upon a great capacity to retaliate, instantly, by means and at places of our choosing." He explained that this meant abandoning the "traditional" policy of "meeting aggression by direct and local opposition" and "more reliance on deterrent power and less dependence on local defensive power." In other words, local communist aggression was presumably to be countered in the future, not by limited war, but by a threat to retaliate directly against the Soviet Union or Communist China. The threat by itself, Dulles apparently thought, would be sufficient to stop aggression. As he put it on another occasion, the "necessary art" was "the ability to get to the verge without getting into the war. . . . If you are scared to go to the brink, you are lost."

The doctrine of "massive retaliation" was presented as a "new look" in American strategy. The older policy "could not be continued for long without grave budgetary, economic, and social consequences"; the new look would permit "a selection of military means instead of a multiplication of means." By reducing the need for local defensive power, it would lower the cost of national defense, bringing "more bang for the buck." According to General Maxwell D. Taylor, later Army Chief of Staff, Admiral Arthur Radford as chairman of the Joint Chiefs of Staff was "determined to eliminate from military planning any consideration of the possibility of conventional war with the Soviet Union." "The budget makers," said General Taylor, "have become the real strategy makers." Defense expenditures were cut from about 12 per cent of the gross national product in 1953 to 8.5 per cent by 1959. Critics, however, contended that reliance on the nuclear deterrent had not worked even when the United States had an atomic monopoly, and that it was bound to be ineffective now that the Soviet nuclear arsenal made retaliation a two-way street. If one nuclear deterrent now canceled out the other, did this not reduce the chance of nuclear war, and was there not therefore a need for more, rather than less, local defensive power? Dulles' pride in getting to the verge of war without getting into the war was promptly denounced as "brinksmanship."

Crisis in Indochina The new doctrines were put almost immediately to the test. Since December 1946 a war had been going on in Indochina between the French army and the so-called Vietminh, a nationalist group under communist leadership. By 1954 the French position was desperate. The *sale guerre*, as it was known, had become bitterly unpopular in France, while the long French refusal to make concessions to Indochinese nationalism and the attempt to set up a puppet state under the former Emperor Bao Dai had destroyed backing for the French among the Indochinese. In the meantime, the Vietminh, assisted by the Chinese Communists, had moved from one military success to another. In March 1954 they placed substantial French forces under siege in the fortress of Dien Bien Phu.

President Eisenhower promptly declared that Indochina was of "transcendent" concern to the United States and suggested that its fall to the communists would be like knocking down the first in a row of dominoes; "you have a beginning of a disintegration that would have the most profound influences." If the disintegration was to be stopped, the logic of massive retaliation presumably called for a direct blow at Communist China. But there is no evidence that such a policy was ever seriously considered. Instead, when the French commander at Dien Bien Phu pleaded for American support, Dulles proposed to Sir Anthony Eden, the British Foreign Minister, the possibility of local intervention. "I am fairly hardened to crises," Eden later wrote, "but I went to bed that night a troubled man. I did not believe that anything less than intervention on a Korean scale, if that, would have any effect in Indochina." In Washington Vice-President Nixon had already suggested the possibility of "putting American boys in." But the opposition of General Ridgway, Congress, and the British led Eisenhower to reject the plan for intervention.

Dien Bien Phu fell on May 7. In France Pierre Mendès-France came to power with a mandate to end the war. In the next weeks, negotiations at Geneva, in which the United States ostentatiously declined to take part, resulted in an agreement to divide Vietnam

Dien Bien Phu, 1954:
The "sale guerre" divided
Vietnam.

at the seventeenth parallel, with eventual unification to come through free elections. As in
the case of Korea, unification was never
achieved, and Vietnam remained a divided
country. For a time Premier Ngo Dinh Diem,
with strong American backing, succeeded in
bringing order to the Republic of South
Vietnam; but by late 1961 opposition to his
authoritarian regime, even by anticommunists,
was on the increase. Communist guerrillas,
supported from North Vietnam, were murdering local government officials in the countryside. In the meantime, communist pressure
continued to mount against the states of Laos
and Cambodia, which had also been established as independent states by the Geneva
Conference.

The readiness of the communists to accept
an armistice in Indochina seemed a further
indication of their confidence that they could
win in Asia by nonmilitary methods. Yet
Washington persisted in its view that the essential communist threat was military. On
September 8, 1954, Dulles brought together
three Asian states (the Philippines, Thailand,
and Pakistan) with the United States, Britain,
France, Australia, and New Zealand in a
new Southeast Asia Treaty Organization
(SEATO). A special protocol extended the
organization's protection to South Vietnam,
Laos, and Cambodia. The refusal of such nations as India, Burma, and Indonesia to participate prevented SEATO, however, from
providing the region with a genuine mutual

defense system; and, in any case, the critical problems in Southeast Asia in the rest of the decade were political and economic rather than military—a development emphasized when Asian and African nations, meeting at Bandung in Indonesia in April 1955, affirmed their neutralism, their hatred of colonialism, and their desire for economic development.

In the Middle East Dulles pursued a similar strategy, inducing the British to create a regional defense organization under the Baghdad Pact of 1955 (later known as CENTO—the Central Treaty Organization). Though the United States continued its aid program to underdeveloped countries, that program became subordinate to the mutual security system. The aid itself was predominantly military —the Point Four idea receded, the very name being dropped—and it went in the main to such embattled states as South Korea, Formosa, and South Vietnam. Denouncing neutralism as "immoral," Dulles hoped to force all nations to choose sides in the cold war. Some observers felt that he had undue faith in the capacity of military pacts to stabilize underdeveloped areas. Critics referred acidly to his "pactomania."

Parley at the Summit　　The Soviet Union persisted in its post-Stalin line, and pressure for top-level negotiations continued to mount. The termination of the Indochinese War suggested for a moment that the communists wanted to reduce international tension. So too did successful negotiation in May 1955 of a treaty between the U.S.S.R. and the West terminating the four-power occupation of Austria. Accordingly, Eisenhower finally consented to take part in a face-to-face meeting with Russian, British, and French representatives at Geneva in July 1955.

For a moment the conference seemed a powerful demonstration of the will to peace on the part of the world leaders. "The United States will never take part in an aggressive war," Eisenhower declared. Prime Minister Bulganin of the Soviet Union obligingly replied, "Mr. President, we believe that statement." But the conference was singularly barren of concrete results. An agreement on Germany perished immediately because of conflicting interpretations; the American proposal of an "open skies" plan of reciprocal air

inspection came to nothing. The meagerness of the "spirit of Geneva" was underlined by the failure of a meeting of foreign ministers the following October.

Even before Geneva a new threat to the already precarious situation in the Middle East had arisen in communist Czechoslovakia's offer to supply Egypt with arms. This offer—which for some reason was not challenged by the West at Geneva—evidently signaled a renewal of the Soviet attempt to penetrate what had long been regarded as an Anglo-French sphere of influence. It also called attention to the rising tide of Arab nationalism in the Middle East, a development that threatened to upset all calculations, whether of the West or of the communists.

The Road to Suez　　The center of this nationalist upsurge was the new regime in Egypt, installed by a *coup d'état* in 1952 and, since 1954, under the bold and purposeful leadership of Colonel Gamal Abdel Nasser. The Egyptian nationalists were concerned not only with modernizing their poverty-stricken country but with asserting Egyptian interests throughout the Middle East. Nasser had two main grievances: the existence of the state of Israel and the continued British control over the Suez Canal and Sudan.

The Republic of Israel had come into existence with the enthusiastic backing of the Truman Administration in May 1948. Armies from neighboring Arab states had promptly tried to destroy the new nation but Israeli forces had repelled them, and an uneasy armistice resulted. Israeli security was further strengthened by a declaration of 1950 in which Britain, France, and the United States guaranteed the armistice lines. None the less, though checked for the moment, the Arab states were still sworn to the eventual annihilation of Israel.

The Eisenhower Administration, feeling that its predecessor had overcommitted itself to Israel, proclaimed in 1953 a new policy of "impartiality." In May 1953 Dulles visited Egypt, presented the head of the revolutionary regime with a silver pistol as a gift from the President, and made clear his desire to help improve relations between the new government and Britain. In 1954 he induced the

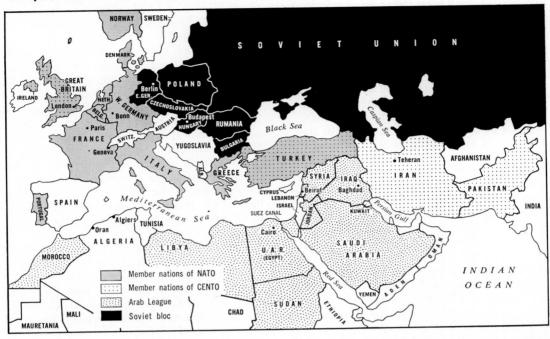

British to withdraw their troops from the Suez Canal Zone. But the Baghdad Pact policy conflicted with the Administration's Egyptian policy, for the pact exalted Egypt's chief Arab rival, Iraq, and portended Egypt's diplomatic isolation. Moscow accordingly "leaped over" the northern-tier countries of the Middle East and established direct relations with Cairo. At the same time Nasser stepped up Egyptian raids across the Israeli border—raids that provoked Israeli reprisals.

The first American response to the Soviet-Egyptian *rapprochement* was to redouble its courtship of Nasser. When Washington heard that the Soviet Union might subsidize the construction of a great dam at Aswan on the Nile, it offered to arrange western financing of the dam. But such gestures had little effect on Nasser's expansionism or on his friendship with Moscow. Egypt already dominated Syria; in March 1956 Nasser incited a revolution in Jordan; and in May he recognized Communist China. On the understanding that the Soviet Union could not after all finance the dam, Dulles withdrew the American offer on July 19, 1956, just as Egypt was about to ac-

cept it. He did so in a manner that was calculated to humiliate Egypt. Nasser immediately retaliated by nationalizing the Suez Canal.

The Suez Fiasco   Britain and France regarded Nasser's seizure of the canal as a threat to western Europe's vital supplies of oil from the Middle East. Moreover, Sir Anthony Eden, now the British Prime Minister, saw Nasser on the model of Hitler and believed that appeasement would only inflame his ambitions and invite the spread of Soviet influence. France felt that Nasser's support was helping to prolong a nationalist revolt in Algeria. Together, Britain and France were determined to nip the Nasser movement in the bud, and the nationalization of the canal provided a suitable pretext for action.

For a time Eden expected the sympathetic understanding of the United States. Thus he understood Dulles to agree with him that Nasser must be made to "disgorge what he has swallowed." But despite shows of private indignation, Dulles really felt that the use of force against Nasser would only alienate the new nations of Asia and Africa by demonstrating that western imperialism was not dead. Accordingly, he tried to divert the Anglo-French reaction by proposing schemes for international management of the canal. But his delaying actions only convinced London and Paris that he was stringing them along and had no intention of pressing the case against Nasser. By October communication between London and Washington had pretty well broken down.

In the meantime, another element in this complicated drama was approaching its climax—namely, Israeli resentment over the Egyptian border raids and Israeli fear that Egyptian rearmament would permanently alter the balance of power in the Middle East. On October 16 Eden conferred in Paris with Guy Mollet, the French Premier. Whether their intention was to concert Anglo-French action with a projected Israeli attack on Egypt is not clear. In any case, Israel attacked Egypt on October 29. Two days later Britain and France entered the war against Egypt on the patently spurious excuse of trying to localize the conflict. Ironically, one of the effects of the Anglo-French intervention was to save the Egyptian forces from probable defeat by the Israelis.

The situation was further complicated by an uprising against communist domination in Hungary beginning on October 24. Though deeply involved in the brutal suppression of this revolution, the Soviet Union threatened to use force—including the hint of long-range missiles against western Europe—to "crush the aggressors" in Egypt. This threat, along with the fear of estranging the ex-colonial world, led President Eisenhower to bring intense personal pressure on Eden to call off the Suez expedition. At the same time, a run on Britain's gold reserves threatened the stability of the pound, and Secretary of the Treasury Humphrey informed London that Britain could expect no financial aid from the United States until a definite statement on withdrawal had been made. On November 6 Eden gave in and ordered a ceasefire.

The American government now initiated immediate action in the United Nations—backed by the Soviet Union and opposed by Britain and France—to condemn Israel as the aggressor. The swift movement of events produced a certain euphoria in Washington. "For the first time in history," said Vice-President Nixon, "we have shown independence of Anglo-French policies toward Asia and Africa. . . . This declaration of independence has had an electrifying effect throughout the world." The effect was probably less electrifying than the Vice-President supposed; much of the world ascribed the American sense of urgency to fear of Soviet missiles rather than to a passion for international morality. Moreover, the rigid American line in the UN resulted in the rescue and reinstatement of Nasser without rebuke for past Egyptian harassment of Israel. None the less, the Anglo-French adventure was ill-conceived and ill-prepared, and Dulles was right in supposing that gunboat imperialism was obsolescent.

For a moment Suez had a shattering effect on Anglo-American relations. But the resignation of the sick and distracted Eden, followed by the determination of his successor, Harold Macmillan, to restore good relations, dispelled the memories of Suez in a surprisingly short time.

The Return to Containment   The Dulles period had begun with vigorous predictions of dynamic new departures in American foreign policy. By 1956, however, that policy had shown itself less distinctive than had been predicted. "Liberation" had vanished as a result of American inaction in the face of upheavals in East Germany in 1953 and in Hungary and Poland in 1956. "Massive retaliation" had faded in the aftermath of Dien Bien Phu. "Agonizing reappraisal" had been dropped from the diplomatic lexicon. Chiang Kai-shek had been released. Even the pledge to denounce the secret wartime agreements had dwindled into a denunciation of the Soviet "violation of the clear intent of these agreements."

The Administration continued to insist that it was reversing Truman-Acheson policies. "Isn't it wonderful," said Nixon in 1954, "finally to have a Secretary of State who isn't taken in by the Communists, who stands up to them?" But observers were more impressed by continuities than by reversals. Though the Dulles-Eisenhower tone was measurably more moralistic than that of Acheson and Truman, the policies themselves seemed much the same.

Modern Republicanism at Home

McCarthy: Zenith   As Eisenhower inherited the Korean War from Truman, so too he inherited the domestic problems created by the frustrations of that war, and especially the problem of McCarthyism. Some voters, indeed, had supported Eisenhower in the belief that a Republican President would be better able to discipline McCarthy than a Democrat. But the campaign was not reassuring on Eisenhower's readiness to take on the McCarthy problem. In 1951 McCarthy had denounced General George C. Marshall as part of "a conspiracy so immense and an infamy so black as to dwarf any previous venture in the history of man." During the campaign, Eisenhower, to avoid offending McCarthy, deleted a paragraph of praise for Marshall from a speech in Wisconsin. This action foreshadowed the President's reluctance to engage himself personally in the McCarthy issue. As he later put it, "I will not get in the gutter with *that* guy."

For over a year, the Eisenhower Administration tried to get along with McCarthy. There followed a singular and, in retrospect, almost incredible chapter in American history. The Wisconsin senator, agile and unscrupulous as ever, took full advantage of the Administration's tolerance to promote his own influence and power. Before 1953 only the bully of the Senate, he now began, as chairman of the Senate Committee on Government Operations, to swagger without challenge through the executive branch in his pursuit of communists and fellow travelers.

One of his main targets was the State Department. He began with an investigation of the Voice of America, the government agency for foreign broadcasts. On the basis of rumors provided by disgruntled employees, McCarthy and his chief counsel, Roy Cohn, proceeded to disrupt the Voice's operations and demoralize its personnel. Next McCarthy moved in on the International Information Administration and for a few months exerted direct control over its appointments and policies. Cohn, accompanied by his committee colleague, G. David Schine, made a whirlwind tour of United States information offices in Europe, plucking offending books from the shelves and terror-izing employees—an adventure which would have been richly comic had it not humiliated the United States government before the world.

What was even more humiliating was the government's refusal to put up any resistance. In anticipation of the Cohn-Schine tour, Dulles ordered State Department libraries to remove books by "authors who obviously follow the Communist line or participate in Communist front organizations." Such books as the thrillers of Dashiell Hammett, *The Selected Works of Tom Paine*, and even Whittaker Chambers' *Witness* were banned; a number of the proscribed books were actually burned. By June 1953 the panic had spread so widely that the President himself intervened to arrest it. "Don't join the book burners," he said. "Don't think you are going to conceal faults by concealing evidence that they ever existed."

But Dulles' acquiescence was part of a premeditated strategy. More determined than ever to avoid what he deemed the errors of Acheson, he was ready to collaborate with McCarthy and even to anticipate his needs. Veteran foreign-service officers whose political reporting had aroused McCarthy's ire were drummed from the service. A McCarthy disciple, W. Scott McLeod, was appointed chief of State Department personnel. When Harold Stassen, the director of the foreign aid program, objected to McCarthy's negotiations with Greek shipowners over trade with Communist China, Dulles, with the encouragement of Vice-President Nixon, called in McCarthy and conveyed a tacit apology. In January 1954, five senior American diplomats warned from retirement of the "sinister results" of such policies. "The conclusion has become inescapable," they said, ". . . that a Foreign Service officer who reports on persons and events to the very best of his ability and who makes recommendations which at the time he conscientiously believes to be in the interest of the United States may subsequently find his loyalty and integrity challenged and may even be forced out of the service and discredited forever as a private citizen."

McCarthy: Decline   Encouraged by the Administration's attitude, road-company McCarthys sprang up across the land. What was conceived as an effort to guard the national security became a heresy hunt employing the techniques traditionally used to ferret out non-conformists—guilt by association, loyalty oaths, testimony of secret informers, black-lists, suppressions of speech and assembly, interrogation and intimidation by legislative committees. In the 1954 campaign Vice-President Nixon spoke with pride of the number of "security risks" who had been driven from government. One notable victim was the great physicist, Dr. J. Robert Oppenheimer, the father of the atomic bomb, whose security clearance was withdrawn in 1953 on the basis of information well known to security officers a decade before when Oppenheimer was working in the Manhattan Project. A review board under the chairmanship of Gordon Gray declared that the Oppenheimer case "demonstrated that the Government can search . . . the soul of an individual whose relationship to his Government is in question." It added that national security "in times of peril must be absolute."

Thoughtful people began to wonder whether such ideas as these might not be the most subversive of all. A dissenter on the Gray board observed, "All people are somewhat of a security risk." George Kennan said that "absolute security" was an unattainable and self-devouring end—that its frenzied pursuit would lead only to absolute tyranny. "Our internal security system has run wild," said Dr. Vannevar Bush, the eminent scientist. "It is imperative to our real security that the trend be reversed." Judge Learned Hand summed up the feelings of many Americans when he wrote,

> I believe that that community is already in process of dissolution where each man begins to eye his neighbor as a possible enemy, where non-conformity with the accepted creed, political as well as religious, is a mark of disaffection; where denunciation, without specification or backing, takes the place of evidence; where orthodoxy chokes freedom of dissent; where faith in the eventual supremacy of reason has become so timid that we dare not enter our convictions in the open lists to win or lose.

Judge Hand concluded, "The mutual confidence on which all else depends can be maintained only by an open mind and a brave reliance upon free discussion."

If the Korean War had given McCarthy his opportunity for influence, the end of that war in July 1953 brought about his decline. As the war frustrations receded, McCarthyism began to lose its emotional base. By now, in his increasingly erratic course, McCarthy had become embroiled with the army. He had uncovered a dentist who, after invoking the Fifth Amendment to avoid answering questions about communist affiliations, had been promoted and given an honorable discharge, and he now sought to terrify the whole military establishment with the question, "Who promoted Major Peress?" He also launched a sensational, if unproductive, search for communists and spies in the army signal corps installation at Fort Monmouth, New Jersey. The matter was further complicated by the efforts of Roy Cohn to obtain favored treatment for his sidekick, Schine, who had recently been drafted. For a time Vice-President Nixon tried to reconcile McCarthy and Secretary of the Army Robert Stevens. But, goaded beyond endurance, the army finally fought back. The denouement took place in a series of televised hearings from April 22 to June 17, 1954.

The Army-McCarthy hearings were a compelling spectacle, marked by vivid and sharply etched personalities and passages of passion and conflict. They commanded a fascinated audience, amounting at times to twenty million people. Viewers trained through long exposure to TV westerns to distinguish between good and bad guys had little trouble deciding to which category McCarthy belonged. After thirty-five days of the grating voice, the sarcastic condescension, the irrelevant interruption ("Point of order, Mr. Chairman, point of order"), and the unsupported accusation, McCarthy effectively achieved his own destruction. The spell was at last broken. On July 30 Senator Ralph Flanders of Vermont introduced a resolution of censure. A select committee under Senator Arthur Watkins of Utah recommended censure. On December 2 the Senate censured McCarthy by a sixty-seven to twenty-two vote. The Wisconsin senator was finished. His subsequent appearances were dispirited and ineffective. His death in 1957 merely ratified his political demise.

In the meantime the Supreme Court, under the leadership of its new Chief Justice, Earl Warren of California, sought in the 1956–57 term to repair the holes that had been torn in the fabric of American freedom. The Watkins and Sweezy cases, with their condemnation of exposure "for the sake of exposure," restricted somewhat the scope of public investigation into private beliefs and associations. The Yates case, which set aside one count in the conviction of a group of California communists, narrowed the judicial interpretation of the Smith Act of 1940 and emphasized the distinction between "the statement of an idea which may prompt its hearers to take unlawful action, and advocacy that such action be taken." The Jencks case required that Federal Bureau of Investigation reports, if used by the prosecution in a criminal trial, be made available to the defense. These decisions stirred up a passing furor and led to congressional attacks on the Court. In the longer run, their impact was less drastic than civil libertarians hoped or than the heirs of McCarthy feared. Indeed, the Court itself sharply qualified the implications of Watkins and Sweezy by the Barenblatt and Uphaus decisions in the 1958–59 term, removing most limits on federal and state legislative investigations in the area of communism.

By the end of the decade the atmosphere of the McCarthy era seemed dim, remote, and improbable. Though traces survived in occasional committees, laws, oaths, and interdictions, as well as in wrecked lives, the robust tradition of American civil freedom had begun at long last to reassert itself. But the ability of this talented demagogue to intimidate a government and almost a nation remained a disturbing memory.

Eisenhower Economics: Inflation   With the decline of McCarthyism, the power of the radical right receded. Now liberated from serious harassment on the far right, and strengthened by the collaboration of the moderate conservative leader, Robert A. Taft (until his death in July 1953), the Eisenhower Administration prepared to reorder American society according to the values of "modern Republicanism." Modern Republicanism meant in practice an acceptance of the social and economic framework created by the New Deal, but an acceptance qualified by two abiding resolves—to preserve the value of the dollar, and to contract the activity of the federal government. It meant, as Eisenhower liked to put it, being "conservative when it comes to money and liberal when it comes to human beings."

The commitment to a stable dollar dominated domestic economic policy. The Administration adhered to the orthodox, or "demand-pull," theory of inflation—i.e., that inflation was caused by too much money chasing after too few goods. Accordingly, it proposed to combat inflation by reducing purchasing power through raising the interest rate (bank rates on short-term business loans rose from 2.7 per cent in 1950 to 5 per cent by 1959) and trying to balance the federal budget. The Administration was prepared to push deflationary measures even at the risk of slowing down the nation's rate of economic growth.

Despite such attempts to restrict demand, prices mounted through the decade. Though the inflation caused by the Korean War was followed by comparative price stability in 1952–55, prices rose in 1955–58 by 8 per cent. The climb persisted—contrary to the expectations of orthodox economic theory—even through the recession of 1957–58. Moreover, the true extent of inflation was disguised by a drop in farm prices. If farm prices had risen along with other prices, the general price index would have been about eight points higher by 1960.

What caused prices to rise even in depression? Some economists contended that the emerging form of inflation was not a buyers' ("demand-pull") but a sellers' ("cost-push") inflation, brought about by the ability of concentrated industries to raise prices or wages through decisions independent of the market. One such industry was steel, where through the decade the unions demanded a series of wage increases, and management responded, after a ritual of strike and settlement, with price increases even greater than required to absorb the new wages. One study, measuring the impact on the general price level of the increase in steel prices, concluded that, if steel prices had behaved like other industrial prices, the total wholesale price index would have risen 52 per cent *less* in the period between 1953 and 1960. Obviously inflation of this sort could not be stopped by policies that were aimed solely at repressing demand.

The Administration thus failed to preserve the value of the dollar. The consumer price index rose from 113.5 in 1952 to 125.7 in 1960, and the purchasing power of the dollar declined from 88.1 to 80.3.

Stable Prices or Growth? The Administration's concern to preserve the value of the dollar meant that if recession set in the government would be inclined to let things work themselves out, even at the cost of temporary unemployment, rather than risk inflation through undue lowering of the interest rate or undue increases in public spending. Indeed, powerful members of the Administration, notably Secretary of the Treasury Humphrey, believed that budgetary deficits would aggravate depressions, and that the reduction of government spending was the best way to offset economic decline.

As a consequence, the Administration declined to pursue a positive policy of stimulating economic growth. Though the gross national product increased from $347 billion ($399 billion in 1959 prices) in 1952 to over $500 billion by 1960, the rate of economic growth declined from 4.3 per cent in the years 1947–52 to 2.5 per cent in the years 1953–60. A good deal of this slowdown was caused by recessions in 1953–54, 1957–58, and 1960–61.

The 1953–54 recession was occasioned by an $11 billion drop in government spending at the end of the Korean War. At its lowest point, there were about 3.8 million unemployed—6 per cent of the labor force. This recession was brought to an end in the winter of 1954–55 by the Revenue Act of 1954, which reduced federal taxes by $7.4 billion, and by an easing in Federal Reserve monetary policy.

The 1957–58 recession was both sharper and shorter. It was caused by a cutback in inventories and by a marked decline, following the boom of 1955–57, in gross private domestic investment; and it was aggravated by a drop in exports. Unemployment rose to 5.4 million, or 7 per cent of the labor force. The federal deficit for the fiscal year 1958–59, which pumped $12.4 billion into the economy, was probably responsible for bringing this setback to a quick end.

Eisenhower Economics: Big Government
The Administration's effort to reduce the size of the federal government was almost as disappointing. The intention was to cut down federal activity in every direction—spending, taxation, regulation, public power—and at the same time to stimulate local and private activity. As the President put it in 1954, "We will reduce the share of the national income which is spent by the [national] government."

At first this shifting of the burden met with some success. While the per capita size of the national debt declined from $1,697 in 1950 to $1,595 in 1958, the per capita size of the total state and local government debt rose from $159 to $336. The tax relief in the Revenue Act of 1954 was directed largely to upper-income groups, in an effort to encourage private investment.

In power development, the Administration favored corporate over public activity. The great power site at Hell's Canyon on the Snake River went to the Idaho Power Company, a Maine corporation, for the construction of three low dams in place of the high multipurpose federal dam urged by public power advocates. In an evident effort to check the expansion of TVA, the Administration arranged with the newly formed Dixon-Yates syndicate to erect a steam power plant in Arkansas to provide electricity for TVA customers. The circumstances under which the Dixon-Yates contract was negotiated were so disreputable, however, that the Administration was finally forced to repudiate it and eventually sued for its cancellation as "contrary to public policy." In the development of atomic energy, and, later, space communications, the Administration again tried to encourage private corporations. Offshore oil lands were turned over to the adjacent states. In 1955 the Department of Health, Education and Welfare even refused during the polio season to distribute free shots of scarce Salk vaccine to school children.

In keeping with the same principle, regulatory commissions were now staffed more largely by men sympathetic to the industries they were supposed to regulate; this practice provoked widespread public criticism, especially of the Federal Communications Commission and the Federal Power Commission.

Particularly close to the President's heart was the vision of transferring countless functions from the federal government to the states.

When his Commission on Intergovernmental Relations failed to come up with a comprehensive program for such transfers, Eisenhower in 1957 appealed personally to the Governors' Conference for action. After working for a year, the resulting committee of governors and federal officials could find only two minor programs, costing $80 million, to recommend for transfer from federal to state hands.

The notion of a sweeping shift of federal functions either to state and local governments or to private business seemed doomed to frustration. In 1960 the size and structure of the federal government were much what they had been in 1952. Indeed, for all the concern with budget-balancing, the Eisenhower Administration achieved a budgetary surplus less than half the time and piled up an over-all deficit of $18.2 billion. This record disturbed the more conservative members of the Administration. When Eisenhower sent Congress a $72 billion budget in 1957, Secretary of the Treasury Humphrey said that, if the "terrific" tax burden were not reduced, "I will predict that you will have a depression that will curl your hair." Clearly, however, a modern industrial society in a world threatened by war could not revert to the simpler practices of the early republic.

The Farm Problem   No domestic economic problem seemed more intractable than agriculture. The basic cause of this problem was the technological revolution taking place on the countryside. During the nineteen fifties output per man-hour on the farms went up 84 per cent (as against an increase of 28 per cent in industry). As a consequence, though farm population decreased by 4.8 million in the decade and the number of farms by 1.1 million, farm output increased far beyond demand and piled up huge surpluses.

To prevent a total collapse of farm prices, the government, under the price support system devised in the thirties and revised in the Second World War, took most surpluses off the market. This program proved increasingly costly. By 1958 the government investment in farm surpluses was about five times as high as it had been in 1952, and federal agricultural spending was about six times as high. Indeed, Secretary of Agriculture Ezra T. Benson, for all his laissez-faire predilections, spent more

money on agriculture than all previous Secretaries of Agriculture together. Yet despite the billions of dollars transferred to farmers through the price support, soil bank, and surplus removal programs, the economic plight of the farmers grew steadily worse. In a period of general growth, income received by farmers from agricultural sources dropped from $17.3 billion in 1952 to $13.6 billion in 1959. The parity ratio—the ratio between the prices received and prices paid by farmers—fell from 100 in 1952 to 80 in 1960. And the predicament of noncommercial farmers, who lived outside the support and market system, and that of migratory workers, with per capita incomes in many cases averaging $200 a year or less, was a reproach to American affluence. By the end of the decade, the farm problem seemed as far from solution as ever.

The Battle of Desegregation   The gravest domestic issue, however, lay in social rather than economic policy. The struggle to assure Negroes their full rights as American citizens had resumed, after a long quiescence, during the New Deal and had gathered momentum during and after the Second World War. Though most of President Truman's civil-rights program of 1948 was rejected by Congress, his fight for that program established civil rights as a national issue.

Thwarted in the Congress, the champions of civil rights now turned to the courts. The Supreme Court, once chary of taking on cases involving Negro rights, was more willing in the years after the war. One important decision (*Shelly* v. *Kraemer*, 1948) removed the government's sanction from restrictive covenants—that is, private efforts to exclude ethnic minorities from buying houses in specified neighborhoods. Others required state educational institutions in the South to admit Negroes when the training available to them in Negro institutions was not demonstrably equal (*Sipuel* v. *University of Oklahoma*, 1948; *Sweatt* v. *Painter*, 1950). All these decisions reflected the essentially Fabian tactics of the Court under Chief Justice Fred M. Vinson of Kentucky (1946–53). The Vinson Court sought to work toward equal rights within the inherited legal framework—that is, by accepting the *Plessy* v. *Ferguson* doctrine (see p. 381) of "separate but equal," construing it literally, and rejecting separate facilities when they were not in full and exact fact equal.

After 1953 the Eisenhower Administration completed the process of ending segregation in the government and the armed services. But President Eisenhower was skeptical about what the government could do to promote equal rights. "It is difficult through law and through force to change a man's heart." Since the Administration did not advance civil-rights legislation with vigor, Negro organizations turned even more to the courts for remedy. Beginning in 1952 attorneys for the National Association for the Advancement of Colored People (NAACP) argued before the Supreme Court against state laws requiring the segregation of children in public education. On May 17, 1954, in the case of *Brown* v. *Board of Education of Topeka*, the Court, speaking through Earl Warren, the new Chief Justice, responded with a unanimous decision reversing *Plessy* v. *Ferguson* and outlawing racial discrimination in public schools. "We conclude," the Court said, "that in the field of public education, the doctrine of 'separate but equal' has no place. Separate educational facilities are inherently unequal." A subsequent decision on May 31, 1955, called on school authorities to submit plans for desegregation and gave to local federal courts the responsibility of deciding whether the plans constituted "good faith compliance." The Court concluded by ordering action "with all deliberate speed."

The border states moved toward compliance. But in South Carolina, Georgia, Alabama, and Mississippi, resistance began to harden, especially after the spread in 1955–56 of the militantly segregationist White Citizens' Councils and a manifesto by Southern congressmen, on March 11, 1956, condemning the decision. Some Southern states passed laws to frustrate the Supreme Court ruling. A favorite device was to divert state funds to what might be passed off technically as a private school system. Extreme segregationists revived the pre-Civil War doctrine of nullification under the more mellifluous name of "interposition," which Senator Harry Byrd of Virginia described in 1956 as "a perfectly legal means of appeal from the Supreme Court's order." And fanatics incited violence, as in Clinton, Tennessee, in 1956.

The Crisis of Little Rock   The strategy of resistance came to a climax in 1957 in Little Rock, Arkansas. Governor Orval Faubus, contending that integration would threaten public order, mobilized the Arkansas national guard in an effort to deny nine Negro students enrollment in the Central High School. Up to this time, President Eisenhower had been reluctant to take action in support of the desegregation decision. The year before, he had said, "We must all . . . bring about a change in spirit so that extremists on both sides"—meaning apparently those who wanted extremely to carry out the decision and those who wanted extremely to block it—"do not defeat what we know is a reasonable, logical conclusion." But Faubus' open challenge compelled the President to defend the Constitution. After a face-to-face discussion with Eisenhower, Faubus withdrew the national guard. When the Negro boys and girls then entered Central High School, they were mobbed by crowds of angry whites. On September 24, 1957, Eisenhower sent federal troops into Little Rock. Order was restored, and Negro children entered the school.

Another outburst of mob violence took place in New Orleans, Louisiana, in November–December 1960. Despite such episodes, however, slow gains were made toward putting the 1954 decision into effect. By September 1960, 765 out of the 6,676 school districts in the South had been desegregated. In the meantime, Congress had taken further action on behalf of civil rights. The Civil Rights Act of 1957 established a Civil Rights Commission to investigate denial of voting rights or equal protection of the law because of race, color, national origin, or religion. A subsequent act in 1960 authorized the courts to appoint federal referees to safeguard Negro voting rights against proved abuses and made it a federal offense to obstruct court orders by threat of violence. The Civil Rights Commission, ably backed by the Department of Justice under Attorney General William P. Rogers, made an earnest attempt to use these powers to increase Negro voting.

Negroes themselves were taking an increasingly prominent part in the struggle. Negro lawyers like Thurgood Marshall of the NAACP argued the constitutional cases. And

Little Rock, 1957: Separate but equal had no place.

in the South new Negro leaders emerged to urge the assertion of Negro rights through non-violent resistance. Beginning in December 1955, the Negroes of Montgomery, Alabama, under the inspiration of a young minister, Dr. Martin Luther King, Jr., boycotted the city's segregated bus system. King, who was strongly influenced by Thoreau and Gandhi, counseled his followers to avoid provocation and to confront "physical force with an even stronger force, namely, soul force." The boycott, reinforced by suits in the federal courts, achieved the desegregation of the bus system in a year. Passive resistance was widely used in the winter of 1959–60 to challenge the refusal to serve Negroes at Southern lunch counters. The rapid spread of "sit-in" demonstrations through the South, and the remarkable support they evoked in the North, testified to the rising moral force of the protest against segregation. Governor LeRoy Collins of Florida spoke for many moderate Southern whites when he said, "If a man has a department store

and he invites the public generally to come into his department store and trade, I think then it is unfair and morally wrong to single out one department and say he does not want or will not allow Negroes to patronize that one department."

By 1960 Negroes were still far from the goal of integration. But considerable progress had been made in assuring the right to vote, some progress had been made in school desegregation, and vast progress had been made in gaining acceptance for the moral case against discrimination. The rather pallid Southern filibuster against a civil-rights bill in 1960 was marked by the fact that, with one or two exceptions, no one tried to argue the philosophy of white supremacy. This fact, combined with the restraint and nobility of Negro leadership on the King model, held out the best prospect for an eventual resolution of a profound and tragic problem.

Eisenhower and Politics President Eisenhower's popularity continued unabated.

He was applauded by the people, not as a party leader, but as a national hero above party; consequently, his own popularity far exceeded that of the Republican party. As early as the Congressional elections of 1954, the Democrats recaptured control of both the House and the Senate. Democratic optimism about presidential prospects in 1956 increased when Eisenhower suffered a coronary thrombosis on September 24, 1955, followed by an attack of ileitis on June 8, 1956. Eisenhower decided none the less to run for re-election. "Some of my medical advisers," he said, "believe that adverse effects on my health will be less in the Presidency than in any other position I might hold." Most voters accepted with sympathy his need for a more carefully regulated life, made affectionate jokes about his long hours on the golf course, and accorded him undiminished confidence.

The Democrats in 1956 renominated Adlai Stevenson, whose penetrating comments on national issues had kept him easily in the forefront among the leaders of the party; Estes Kefauver, who had been Stevenson's chief rival till shortly before the convention, received the vice-presidential nomination. The campaign was less lively than the 1952 campaign, and Eisenhower won by a larger margin, partly because of the rush of support to him after the Suez crisis. He carried the popular vote by 35.6 million to 26 million, which gave him a decisive electoral college vote of 457 to 73.

On November 25, 1957, Eisenhower was again stricken, this time by an occlusion of a branch of the middle cerebral artery. Again he recovered, and again the illness had no perceptible effect on his popularity. But other factors, especially the Administration's reluctance to move swiftly against the recession of 1957–58, had damaged confidence in his government. At the same time, the Administration's claim to rectitude had been tarnished by a series of scandals. These scandals had forced the resignation of the Secretary of the Air Force, the chairman of the Republican National Committee, the chairman of the Interstate Commerce Commission, the General Services Administrator, the Public Buildings Administrator, a number of lesser officials, and, finally, in September 1958, Sherman Adams, the Assistant to the President. Adams, it was disclosed, had accepted expensive gifts and hospitality from Bernard Goldfine, a businessman with cases pending before the government. Eisenhower resisted pressure for Adams' resignation, saying simply, "I need him." But he was finally forced to yield.

The 1958 elections brought a Democratic landslide. The Democratic majority in the House—282 to 153—was the largest since 1936. In addition, the Democrats gained a 62 to 34 majority in the Senate. The most conspicuous Republican victory was that of the

Eleanor Roosevelt, Harry Truman, and Adlai Stevenson.

liberal Nelson Rockefeller as governor of New York. But the Democratic sweep had little effect on the President's conservative policies. The departure of Adams, ironically, led Eisenhower to play a more active personal role himself. In his last two years in office he succeeded, through the use or threat of the veto, in blocking most of the Democratic welfare and public investment proposals. His intervention in 1959 transformed a moderate labor reform bill, sponsored by Senator John F. Kennedy of Massachusetts, into a much stiffer antiunion measure, the Landrum-Griffin Act. His posture in domestic affairs remained to the end one of dogged defense of the budget.

Peace in the Nuclear Age

The Cold War Thaws   Suez and Hungary dealt strong blows to the precarious equilibrium of peace in October–November 1956. But the two episodes offset each other: since both West and East were preoccupied with internal troubles, each refrained from overt intervention in the other's difficulties. In the meantime, other currents seemed for a moment to be carrying the world toward a relaxation of tension. Within the Soviet Union the process of de-Stalinization appeared to have reduced the role of terror in Soviet society and to have opened up contacts with the outside world. Moreover, Soviet as well as western leaders were increasingly impressed by the incalculable perils presented by the new weapons—by the fact, for example, that a single plane could deliver more destructive power than all the planes in all the air forces delivered during the Second World War. Also the problem of radioactive fallout had come sharply to the world's attention in 1954 when both the United States and the Soviet Union tested large-yield nuclear weapons in the atmosphere. As scientists analyzed the long-term effects of radioactive contamination on the bones, blood, and germ plasm of man, concern mounted over the continuation of nuclear testing. In March 1958 the Soviet Union suspended testing, and the United States and Britain followed suit in October (while Russia briefly resumed). A permanent test ban, as well as the prevention of surprise attack, were

for some years under inconclusive negotiation between Russia, Britain, and the United States at Geneva.

The trend toward negotiation was not without its setbacks. In the months after Suez, Colonel Nasser had set up the United Arab Republic and extended his program of subversion and infiltration throughout the Middle East, thereby provoking a new wave of unrest which threatened the pro-western governments of Lebanon and Jordan. In an effort to stabilize the situation, and at the request of the two governments, Washington and London ordered troops into the area in July 1958. The Anglo-American forces were withdrawn in the fall after anxieties had subsided. Khrushchev at first demanded a summit meeting over Lebanon but did not press the issue.

More serious was Khrushchev's demand of October–November 1958 that West Berlin be made a demilitarized free city under international control with access to the West guaranteed by East Germany, and that West Berlin agree not to tolerate "subversive activity" against East Germany. If the West failed to negotiate a new status for West Berlin within six months, Khrushchev threatened, Russia would sign a separate treaty with East Germany. The western powers replied by stating their firm determination "to maintain their position and rights in Berlin, including the right of free access."

Khrushchev grew more conciliatory early in 1959; and, on the strong recommendation of Prime Minister Macmillan after a visit to Moscow in February, the West in March accepted a summit meeting in principle. Even Secretary of State Dulles, now ravaged by cancer, acquiesced in the drift toward negotiation. In April Dulles resigned, to be replaced by Christian A. Herter; five weeks later Dulles was dead. Though a foreign ministers' meeting in Geneva in May resulted in a deadlock over Berlin, the movement toward the summit continued. In the summer of 1959 Vice-President Nixon paid a visit to Russia and Poland, and Anastas Mikoyan, a veteran Soviet leader, toured the United States. This exchange paved the way for an extraordinary visit to the United States by Prime Minister Khrushchev. The Khrushchev tour, marked by a series of comic incidents, reached its climax in private talks between Khrushchev and Eisenhower at Camp David in Maryland. Following these talks, the United States agreed to a summit meeting and Khrushchev agreed to drop his time limit on Berlin. For a moment the "spirit of Camp David" seemed to renew and extend what had been known briefly four years before as the "spirit of Geneva."

Growth of Soviet Power   Though there was evidence of a slight "thaw" in the cold war, the Soviet Union was continuing to increase its military and technical power. Sputnik in October 1957 was followed by Lunik—the first earth rocket to reach the moon—in 1959. The Soviet Union was thus moving toward a military and technical lead in those areas that were most vividly identified with the future. The fact that a nation so recently dismissed as semiprimitive had attained such scientific and industrial distinction made a strong impression in parts of the world seeking their own modernization—and by 1961 forty-seven out of the more than one hundred member states of the United Nations were Asian or African. The Soviet gains inevitably led observers to comment on the apparent decline in the power and influence of the United States.

But the rising power of the Soviet Union was being challenged in the East. The Chinese Communists, still in the first ardor of revolutionary fanaticism, were rigid and doctrinaire in their Marxist commitment. Moreover, they may have supposed that the vast population of their nation rendered it uniquely invulnerable to an atomic holocaust. In any case, they opposed Khrushchev's talk of "peaceful coexistence" and disliked the whole move toward the summit. Presumably they found support among diehard Stalinists in the Soviet Union.

Explosion at the Summit   Yet the powers continued their uneasy climb toward the summit. After protracted preliminaries, the meeting was finally scheduled for Paris on May 16, 1960. Then on May 5 Khrushchev announced the shooting down of an American plane over the Soviet Union on May 1. He gave no details, and Washington promptly announced that the plane had been on a meteorological flight and had somehow strayed from its course. On May 7 Khrushchev glee-fully sprung his trap. The pilot was alive, he said, and had confessed to Soviet authorities that he was engaged in an espionage flight. Khrushchev added, "I am quite willing to grant that the President knew nothing about the plane."

The pilot's story was indeed true. At irregular intervals for about four years, the American government had been sending the U-2, an aircraft capable of flying at exceptional heights, on intelligence missions over the Soviet Union. At this point the Administration decided to take an unusual step, unprecedented in modern history: it owned up to the act of espionage. Secretary Herter went on to argue that the United States was morally entitled to conduct such flights in order to protect the free world from surprise attack. Herter and, soon, Vice-President Nixon implied that the flights would continue; Eisenhower, rejecting Khrushchev's proffered escape clause, accepted full responsibility for the flights.

No one knows whether Khrushchev had long since decided to wreck the summit and seized upon the U-2 incident as a pretext; or whether he still hoped, even after the U-2 incident, to have a useful meeting but found his position undercut by the American decision to defend and even perhaps to continue the flights—a decision which appeared to substantiate Peking's contention that "peaceful coexistence" was impossible. In any case, Khrushchev came to Paris demanding that Eisenhower apologize for the flights and punish those responsible. Eisenhower rejected these demands, the western allies loyally rallied behind him, and the summit collapsed.

Khrushchev made it clear that he would have no serious dealings thereafter with the Eisenhower Administration. But, within the communist world, he continued his debate with those who would repudiate "peaceful coexistence." A meeting of eighty-one Communist parties in Moscow in October–November 1960 patched up a compromise between the Soviet and Chinese viewpoints with a statement that the strength of the communist camp meant that war was not "fatally inevitable," but that if the "imperialist maniacs" should ever start a war "the peoples will sweep capitalism out of existence and bury it."

The Black Year   The U-2 fiasco and the ensuing confusion of lies, contradictions, and self-righteous avowals which cascaded out of Washington accelerated the decline of American influence in the world. This decline was dramatically underlined in June 1960 when, following a series of anti-American riots in Tokyo, the Japanese government requested that President Eisenhower cancel a scheduled visit to Japan. The fact that angry mobs prevented the visit of the American President to a country into which the United States had poured billions of dollars since the war was an alarming symptom of the decay of American prestige.

At the same time a startling reversal in America's world financial position became evident. Since the war the great international monetary problem had been the shortage of dollars abroad and the consequent flow of gold to the United States. Then, beginning in 1958, the United States balance of payments resulted in deficits which had to be made up by an outflow of American gold. While the balance of payments on normal account (i.e., exclusive of aid programs) remained favorable, America's capacity to maintain the large international programs deemed necessary to free-world security was threatened. The basic reason for the annual deficits of nearly $4 billion was the net reduction in foreign purchases of American goods. The basic remedy would therefore be to increase American productivity, to eliminate barriers to American exports, and in other ways to restore the competitive position of American production in the world market.

Even more alarming were developments within the American hemisphere. Ever since the Second World War, the Good Neighbor policy of the thirties had suffered neglect. With her attention fixed first on Europe and then on Asia, the United States had paid little heed to events south of the border. Meanwhile, in the 1940's, Latin America itself was swept by social and political ferment. Everywhere the historic oligarchies were being challenged by rising popular groups often allied with young army officers. The wave of unrest affected most of the Central American states and all the South American republics except Paraguay. The resulting revolutions sometimes (as

in Argentina) took authoritarian, sometimes (as in Venezuela) democratic, forms. Then toward the end of the forties a counterrevolutionary reaction set in, beginning in Ecuador in 1947. By 1954 thirteen Latin-American presidents were military men. Now a new surge of protest arose against dictatorships, bringing the overthrow of, among others, Perón of Argentina in 1955, Pérez Jiménez of Venezuela in 1958, Batista of Cuba in 1959, and Trujillo of the Dominican Republic in 1961.

All through this ebb and flow, Washington, insofar as it thought about the hemisphere at all, tried to fit it into the framework of the cold war. The Truman Administration concentrated on a program of inter-American military cooperation—a program that was expanded under the Eisenhower Administration. By the end of fiscal year 1958, the twelve participating countries had received $317 million in grants for military aid. In the same period Latin America as a whole received about $225 million in Point Four aid and loans of $2 billion through the Export-Import Bank. Washington made no response to the problems of economic development in Latin America comparable to the Marshall Plan. In political matters, though Truman began by pledging the United States "to do everything possible, in accordance with its international obligations, to fortify democratic forces in this hemisphere," he ended by signing mutual defense assistance pacts with dictatorial regimes.

The Eisenhower Administration stepped off the path of nonintervention—but only to help bring about the overthrow of a semicommunist regime in Guatemala in May–June 1954. Eisenhower also pressed the policy of friendship to dictators. The Administration granted a loan to the Perón regime in Argentina. Vice-President Nixon, visiting Cuba in 1955, praised the "competence and stability" of the Batista dictatorship. In November 1954 Eisenhower himself presented the Legion of Merit to two Latin-American dictators—Pérez Jiménez of Venezuela (for his "spirit of friendship and cooperation" and for his "sound foreign-investment policies") and Manuel Odría of Peru. When Nixon visited these two countries in May 1958, after the dictators had been thrown out, the people's resentment against

Central and South America, 1954-62

UNITED STATES

Batista overthrown 1959
Attempted anti-Castro invasion 1961
Soviet military aid, U.S.quarantine1962

Magloire overthrown 1956

U.S. broke diplomatic ties 1960
Trujillo assassinated 1961
Diplomatic ties restored 1962

Pérez Jiménez overthrown 1958
Anti-Nixon riots 1958

MEXICO

Miami

Havana

Mexico City

BAHAMAS
(Br.)

CUBA

HAITI
DOMINICAN REP.

JAMAICA

PUERTO RICO

BR. HONDURAS

GUATEMALA HONDURAS

EL SALVADOR

NICARAGUA

CARIBBEAN SEA

Arbenz overthrown 1954
Castillo Armas assassinated 1957

CANAL ZONE

COSTA RICA

PANAMA

Diaz overthrown 1956

Anti-U.S. riots 1959

Rojas Pinilla forced out 1957

TRINIDAD

Caracas

VENEZUELA

GUIANAS

BR.
SURINAM
FR.

Bogotá

COLOMBIA

ECUADOR Quito

PERU

Lima

PACIFIC OCEAN

Odria overthrown 1956
Anti-Nixon riots 1958
Military coup 1962

BRAZIL

Quadros resigned 1961

La Paz

Brasília

BOLIVIA

Vargas overthrown 1954

PARAGUAY

Asunción

Chavez overthrown 1954

Rio de Janeiro

Average annual per capita income 1955-57

■ under $100	░ $200-299	
▒ $100-199	▤ $300-699	

VENEZUELA
COLOMBIA GUIANAS
ECUADOR
PERU BRAZIL
BOLIVIA
PARAGUAY
CHILE ARGENTINA URUGUAY

CHILE

Santiago

URUGUAY

ARGENTINA Montevideo

Buenos Aires

Punta del Este Conferences 1961, 1962

Perón overthrown 1955
Frondizi overthrown 1962

ATLANTIC OCEAN

Fidel Castro, 1960:
Communism moved west.

United States identification with the hated regimes led to mob violence. The fact that the Vice-President of the United States should be stoned and spat upon in Latin America revealed how far relations had deteriorated since the high noon of the Good Neighbor policy.

The course of the Cuban revolution of 1958–59 was even more ominous. The hemisphere hailed the overthrow of the Batista regime and welcomed the advent of a revolutionary government led by Dr. Fidel Castro. In 1959 Dr. Castro's visit to the United States was something of a triumphal tour. In Cuba he initiated a long-needed program of social and agrarian reform. But he combined this program with a terrorism which, if less than that of his predecessor, still showed a brutal disregard for the processes of justice. In time, surrounded increasingly by communists and lashed on by the intensities of his own turbulent personality, Castro converted Cuba into the nearest equivalent of a Soviet satellite state in the Western Hemisphere. When he climaxed a series of provocations by ordering that the United States cut its embassy staff in Havana to eleven persons, the Eisenhower Administration broke relations in January 1961.

For all his excesses, Castro became for a time a hero throughout much of Latin America. The rapid spread of the *fidelista* enthusiasm, especially among poverty-stricken workers and underemployed intellectuals, suggested the magnitude of the problem the United States faced in restoring the unity of the hemisphere.

End of the Republican Era

The Election of 1960 As the election of 1960 approached, Vice-President Nixon soon outdistanced Governor Rockefeller for the Republican nomination. Henry Cabot Lodge, the ambassador to the United Nations, became Nixon's running mate. The Democrats turned to Senator John F. Kennedy of Massachusetts, who had established himself as the most popular candidate in the primaries. The Democratic Senate leader, Lyndon B. Johnson, who had run second to Kennedy in the convention balloting, accepted the vice-presidential nomination. A movement to draft Adlai Stevenson

evoked fervent support but failed to attract enough delegates.

The 1960 campaign was marked by an innovation in American politics—a series of television "debates" in which the two candidates responded to questions put to them by newspapermen. Observers believed that Kennedy's poise and command in these confrontations damaged the Republican argument that he was too young and inexperienced for the presidency. The campaign itself revolved around the question of America's condition as a nation. "Militarily, economically and diplomatically," Nixon declared, "we maintain and have a position of strength unparalleled in the history of this country." In foreign affairs, "Communist prestige in the world is at an all-time low and American prestige is at an all-time high." Kennedy, in contrast, found the national situation troubling, even perilous. The United States, he contended, was falling behind both in the world competition with communism and in meeting its own goals of economic growth and social progress. The process

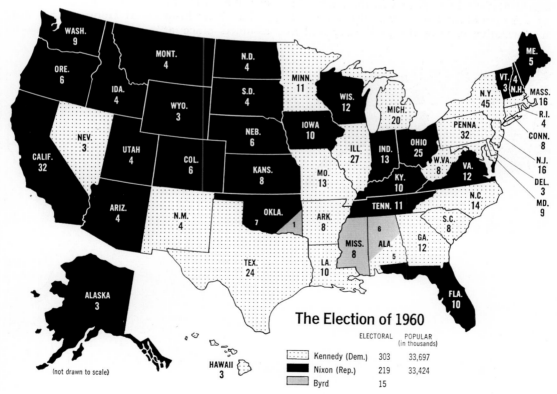

The Election of 1960

	ELECTORAL	POPULAR (in thousands)
Kennedy (Dem.)	303	33,697
Nixon (Rep.)	219	33,424
Byrd	15	

of decline could be reversed only by a "supreme national effort" under strong presidential leadership to "get the country moving again"—a "New Frontier."

The popular vote was the closest since 1888. With the admission of Alaska (January 3, 1959) and Hawaii (August 21, 1959), there were now fifty states in the Union. Kennedy's popular margin was only 119,057 out of 68.3 million votes; taking into account the votes for splinter-party candidates, he was a minority victor. The margin in the electoral college was more decisive—303 for Kennedy to 219 for Nixon (with 15 Southern votes for Senator Harry F. Byrd of Virginia).

The New Frontier   Kennedy, 43 years old, was the youngest man as well as the first Roman Catholic elected to the American presidency. The son of Joseph P. Kennedy, chairman of the Securities and Exchange Commission and later ambassador to London under Roosevelt, Kennedy had graduated from Harvard with honors, served heroically in the war, and won a seat in the House of Representatives in 1946 and in the Senate in 1952. A man of intelligence and drive, he had an affirmative view of the presidency and a

high sense of America's global responsibilities.

With Kennedy's election, the first of the established states of the world was turning to a new generation for political leadership. The newly emerging nations had long since accepted the generation born in the twentieth century—the generation of Nasser and Castro, Sukarno and Nkrumah. That was natural enough; national liberation was classically a task for the young and daring. But the older world had thus far resisted the claims of this generation. This was true for the new-old states of Asia, such as China, India, and Japan, as well as for nearly all the nations of Europe, and it was true for communist nations as well as for democratic and fascist ones. At the time of Kennedy's election Mao Tse-tung was 67, Nehru 71, Ikeda of Japan 61, Khrushchev 66, Tito 68, Macmillan 66, Adenauer 84, De Gaulle 70, and Franco 68.

The generation which was born during the First World War, grew up during the depression, fought in the Second World War, and began its public career in the atomic age had at last arrived at the seats of power.

The New Frontier at Home   Kennedy assumed office at a time of relative social

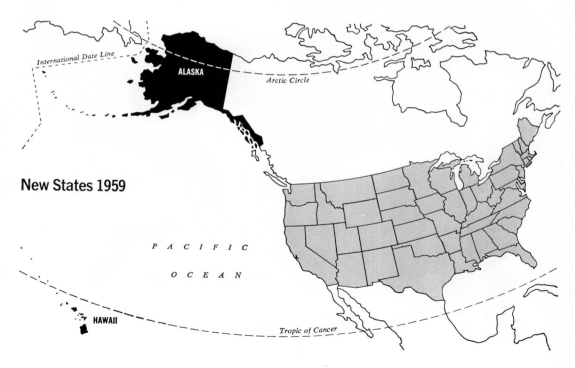

New States 1959

tranquility though of mild economic stringency. In January 1961 the gross national product was around $500 billion—nearly $9 billion less at uniform prices than a year earlier. Almost 8 per cent of the labor force, about 5.4 million people, were unemployed. Though conditions improved by the end of 1961, largely because of a rise in spending stimulated by an increase in government cash contributions to the economy, the first months of 1962 saw business investment fall off and unemployment grow. Worried by this relapse, by the possibility of more price inflation, and by the continuing problem of the nation's balance of payments, the Administration urged business and labor to hold down prices and wages and to increase productivity. Accordingly, the steel workers accepted a new contract calling for only nominal gains, but the major steel companies, led by United States Steel, announced a major price rise. Angry, Kennedy reprimanded the head of Big Steel and initiated antitrust action. The companies then retreated, but the episode provoked a wave of business criticism of the Administration reminiscent of the Roosevelt years. The stock market, already declining, reflected this mood and the slackening in corporate profits during a plunge in May 1962 that wiped out the speculative advances of the preceding several years.

Yet Kennedy did not panic. Again asking the cooperation of business as well as labor in an economic program rooted in Keynesian principles, the President also persuaded Congress to enact some of his earlier recommendations for tax changes designed to stimulate corporate investment in improved facilities. While resisting, as did congressional leaders, demands for quick, general tax relief, he also promised, in so far as necessary, to press later for both reductions and reform. By autumn the economic indices were again rising, though still too slowly to satisfy the Administration's objectives for national growth.

Neither the gains of 1961 nor the temporary losses of 1962 significantly affected the reluctance of Congress to accept the President's domestic policies. Elected by an exceptionally narrow popular margin and confronted by the powerful coalition of Republicans and Southern Democrats that had controlled domestic

policy since 1938, the new President felt that he had in any case to proceed with caution. None the less, the Eighty-Seventh Congress completed a substantial legislative program in 1961–62, including the establishment of a program to deal with economically distressed areas, a liberalization of social security, an increase in the minimum wage, a reform in the federal regulation of drugs, and an omnibus housing bill. Perhaps most important, Congress in September 1962 passed the President's trade bill, which gave him extensive authority to adjust tariff schedules for the purpose of cooperating with the western European nations in their developing Common Market. However, the Administration failed to win approval for its agricultural program; for its proposals to restrict tax deductions for business expense accounts and to withhold taxes on interest and dividends; for medical assistance for the old through the Social Security system; for establishing a new Department of Urban Affairs; and—most depressing—for its bill for federal aid to education. That measure failed in part because the first Catholic President, determined to confine the aid to public institutions, encountered the opposition of some of the Catholic hierarchy.

In the field of civil rights, the Administration concentrated on executive rather than legislative action. The President's brother, Attorney General Robert F. Kennedy, took new steps to end segregation in interstate transportation and to secure the right of Negroes to vote. In October 1962 the President ordered federal troops into Oxford, Mississippi, to protect a Negro student in the right, assured him by the courts, to attend the University of Mississippi. In addition, an unprecedented number of Negroes received responsible federal appointments. Such Southern cities as Atlanta, Memphis, and Dallas began the peaceable desegregation of schools or restaurants, and the popular movement for equality of opportunity continued to grow.

With the President's record one issue in the campaigns of 1962, the Democrats held their commanding control of Congress. Kennedy prepared to advance his "New Frontier."

Kennedy and Foreign Affairs Urgent international problems assailed the new President and his secretary of state, Dean Rusk. A festering crisis in the small but strategic Indochinese kingdom of Laos was reaching a new point of danger. This nation of two million persons had gained independence from France in 1953. Fearing that a neutral Laos might fall to the communists and provide a gateway into Southeast Asia, the United States in the next years poured nearly $400 million into Laos in the hope of establishing a reliable pro-western regime; this amounted to more than $150 for every Laotian—more aid per capita than had been received by any other country. The aid produced neither military nor political strength, and by 1960 the country was divided between pro-western, neutralist, and pro-communist forces.

The intensification of civil war in the winter of 1960–61 raised for a moment the prospect of open intervention by both the Soviet Union and the West. Kennedy, however, abandoned the policy of trying to build a pro-western state in the swamps and jungles of Laos and decided to explore instead the possibilities of genuine neutralization. Though the situation in Laos remained confused, protracted negotiations resulted by the end of 1961 in agreements which tested this neutrality policy. In 1962, after further trouble and new threats of Soviet and western intervention, a new settlement established a tripartite regime in Laos whose three ruling princes represented the western, neutralist, and communist factions.

The new Administration had also to confront recurrent crises in the Republic of the Congo, which had received its independence from Belgium in June 1960. The infant republic, dangerously short of trained leadership, soon became a swirl of political confusion, marked by conflicts between tribalism and nationalism as well as between pro-western and pro-communist tendencies. In July 1960 the Congo government asked the United Nations to intervene, and for many months thereafter a UN security force sought to stabilize the situation. The assassination of the left-wing leader Patrice Lumumba in February 1961 and the death in an airplane accident of Dag Hammarskjöld, the UN General Secretary, in September further complicated matters. A new central government, formed in August 1961, was soon threatened by secessionist tendencies in the wealthy state of Katanga under the leadership of Moise Tshombe, as well as by potential disaffection in the Lumumbist regime at Stanleyville. The United States continued to back United Nations efforts to make the central government strong enough to deal with both extremes.

The crises in Laos and the Congo were expressions of continuing unrest in the ex-colonial world. The Kennedy Administration took a number of steps to indicate American sympathy with the nations struggling to achieve their political and economic identity. Adlai Stevenson, named United States ambassador to the United Nations, voted in favor of a resolution calling for a UN inquiry in Angola and urging Portugal to introduce reforms preparing the way for the granting of independence. So also, the foreign assistance program underwent a revision in concept so that an increasing share of aid would go to develop economies rather than to build armies. The establishment of the Peace Corps was intended to channel the idealism of individual Americans into face-to-face cooperation in underdeveloped countries. An expanded Food for Peace program sought to utilize American agricultural abundance to foster development in the emergent nations.

Latin America: Crisis and Hope
Among other inheritances from the preceding Administration was a force of anti-Castro Cubans which had been trained and equipped in Central America since the spring of 1960. Confronted with the choice of disbanding this group or permitting it to try an invasion of their homeland, the Administration decided to let the exiles go ahead. A Cuban Revolutionary Council, organized in March 1961, assumed responsibility for the action. Its membership consisted of the liberal (as against the communist) wing of the original revolutionary movement; its chairman, Dr. Miro Cardona, had been Castro's first prime minister.

On April 17, 1961, about twelve hundred Cubans landed on the Bahia de Cochinas (Bay of Pigs) on the southern coast of Cuba. After three days of fighting, the invasion collapsed. The result was a serious blow to American prestige. For a moment the bright promise of the New Frontier seemed blighted. But Kennedy took full responsibility, remarking wryly that victory had a hundred fathers but defeat was an orphan. He also cut off all commerce between Cuba and the United States. During the balance of 1961 and 1962 Castro avowed with increasing boldness his commitment to Marxism-Leninism, but his rhetoric, his tirades against the United States not the least, failed to obscure Cuba's deepening agricultural crisis, the continuing delays in his promised economic development, and the ruthlessness of his dictatorship.

Whatever Cuba's fate, the President placed his hopes for Latin America in the Alliance for Progress, which he first outlined in March 1961. This program sought to add a social and economic dimension to the Good Neighbor policy of Franklin Roosevelt. It called for a concerted, hemisphere-wide effort to raise living standards and emphasized the need for social reform to make economic aid effective. An inter-American conference at Punta del Este, Uruguay, in August 1961 resulted in the acceptance by the Latin-American states (except for Cuba) of the goals of the Alliance.

The Alliance was accompanied by a determined effort to support progressive democratic forces in Latin America and to oppose military dictatorship. This resulted in a notable change in Latin-American attitudes toward the United States. In November 1961, when American naval units appeared off the coast of the Dominican Republic to strengthen a transition regime against an attempt by brothers of the late dictator Trujillo to seize power, the American flag was cheered by prodemocratic crowds. Kennedy's dramatically successful visits to Venezuela, Colombia, and Mexico in the next months showed that the United States was recovering its popularity of Good Neighbor days in the southern half of the hemisphere.

Despite Washington's new economic and diplomatic policies, however, Latin-American affairs continued to be characterized by confusion and instability. The Alliance for Progress was slow in producing tangible results. Such great countries as Brazil and Argentina fell into internal turmoil. When a military coup nullified the results of a democratic election in Peru in July 1962, Washington received only nominal support from most Latin-American countries in its policy of suspending relations with the military *junta*.

In the meantime, Cuba remained an irritant in hemispheric relations. A second Punta del Este conference in January 1962 resulted in a united declaration that the Castro regime was incompatible with the principles of the Organization of American States, but a resolution excluding Cuba from the OAS only just gained the two-thirds vote necessary for OAS decisions, and efforts to enlist hemispheric support behind sanctions against Castro failed. In the late spring and summer of 1962, when the Soviet Union stepped up its delivery of arms and military technicians to Cuba, the problem entered a new phase. Supported by Congress, the President informed Cuba and the Soviet Union that the United States was prepared at any cost to protect the security of the Western Hemisphere. Yet the Soviet Union, unheeding, supplied Cuba with offensive missile emplacements and jet aircraft capable of delivering atomic weapons throughout the Caribbean, the eastern half of the United States, and much of South America. On October 22, 1962, Kennedy therefore ordered the navy to quarantine further arms shipments to Cuba from any nation, demanded the dismantling of the missile sites and warned that the United States would interpret any atomic attack from Cuba as the responsibility of the Soviet Union, and would retaliate accordingly. The OAS voted to support the United States, and several Latin-American countries offered military assistance. By November 20 Khrushchev had stripped Cuba of the missiles and agreed to take back the jets. Kennedy then lifted the quarantine. But the United States still faced the tensions inherent in the defense of freedom close to its shores.

Relations with the Soviet Union Most critical of all was the new Administration's relationship with the Soviet Union. In the hope of making a visible step toward disarmament, Kennedy had ordered a review of the American position on a nuclear test ban as soon as he assumed office. When American negotiators returned to Geneva in March 1961, they brought with them concessions designed to meet Soviet objections to previous proposals. But the Soviet negotiators now repudiated earlier agreements, and the discussions got nowhere. The reasons for Soviet obduracy became evident in August when the Soviet

Union resumed nuclear testing in the atmosphere and in late October 1961, when it exploded a nuclear device nearly three thousand times larger than the bomb dropped on Hiroshima.

Confronted with the possibility that a second round of testing might enable the Soviet Union to gain a decisive lead in nuclear weaponry, Kennedy reluctantly ordered the resumption of American testing in March 1962. The Administration persisted, however, in its attempts to bring all testing to an end. In August 1962 American negotiators at the disarmament conference in Geneva again asked the Soviet Union to sign a treaty outlawing all nuclear tests under international inspection, or, if this was unacceptable, a treaty outlawing all tests in environments where violations could be detected by national monitoring systems—i.e., in the atmosphere, the oceans, and outer space. The Soviet Union rejected both proposals. By September 1962

"Go, baby, go": Colonel John H. Glenn, Jr., launched into orbit, February 20, 1962.

the Soviet Union had since 1949 exploded nuclear devices with a total yield of 250 megatons as against 140 megatons for the United States since 1945.

In an address to the United Nations in September 1961, Kennedy presented an American plan for general and complete disarmament. The establishment of the Arms Control and Disarmament Administration also expressed the Administration's concern with arms reduction. But the somber international atmosphere also made it equally important in the Administration's view to build the strength and unity of the free nations. This objective was furthered in part by increasing the United States defense budget and accelerating the program for the exploration of space. During 1962 that program resulted in several successful manned space flights and in a momentous probe of the planet Venus by a space capsule loaded with miniature instruments. Though the Soviet Union could still provide more thrust for manned capsules than could the United States, in other, more portentous ways the American effort was keeping pace with or exceeding its rival's. The strength of the free world gained, too, from American support for such unifying undertakings as the Organization for Economic Cooperation and Development and the European Common Market.

The decade-old crisis over the future of Berlin remained particularly ominous. When Kennedy and Khrushchev met at Vienna in June 1961, the Soviet leader threatened to make a peace treaty with East Germany before the end of the year, declared that this treaty would extinguish western rights of access to West Berlin, and called for the conversion of West Berlin into a neutralized free city. Kennedy responded by making clear that the United States felt it had vital interests in the freedom of the people of West Berlin and the freedom of access to West Berlin. On returning to the United States, he ordered an increase in American armed strength. "We cannot permit the Communists to drive us out of Berlin," he said, adding, "While we are ready to defend our interests, we shall also be ready to search for peace." In expressing a willingness to continue negotiation, Kennedy had the support of Prime Minister Harold Macmillan and the British government but encountered objections

from President de Gaulle of France and, to a lesser degree, from Chancellor Adenauer of Germany. Eventually Khrushchev abandoned his end-of-the-year deadline for the end of 1961, only to renew it some months later for the end of 1962. In the meantime, the erection by the communists of a wall cutting off East Berlin from West Berlin increased tensions in Berlin itself.

The Future of Peace   The persistence of the cold war as a fact of international life was intolerable for some Americans, yearning for a less complicated epoch of history. They demanded a policy aimed at "total victory"; and they apparently believed that such victory could be achieved by unmasking what they considered to be an all-pervasive communist conspiracy within the United States, by cutting government spending, and by initiating war against Cuba, if not against the Soviet Union. Under the leadership of Robert Welch, a candy manufacturer who professed his "firm belief that Dwight Eisenhower is a dedicated, conscious agent of the Communist conspiracy," such people joined local chapters of Welch's John Birch Society.

This represented, however, the view of an extremist minority. The John Birch Society seemed one more expression of the politics of frustration; and its leadership was far less formidable than that of Huey Long in the thirties or of Joe McCarthy in the early fifties. Most Americans appeared to respond to President Kennedy's warning against the temptation of simple and drastic solutions. "We must face the fact," Kennedy declared in November 1961, "that the United States is neither omnipotent nor omniscient—that we are only six per cent of the world's population —that we cannot impose our will upon the other ninety-four per cent of mankind—that we cannot right every wrong or reverse each adversity—and that therefore there cannot be an American solution to every world problem."

In these terms—"determined to defend the frontiers of freedom, by an honorable peace if peace is possible, but by arms if arms are used against us"—Kennedy led the United States into the next phase of the thermonuclear epoch. Prime Minister Harold Macmillan of Great Britain had well stated humanity's problem. He said,

The East-West conflict cannot be resolved by weakness or moral or physical exhaustion of one side or the other. It cannot, in this nuclear age, be resolved by the triumph of one side over the other without the extinction of both. I say, therefore, we can only reach our goal by the gradual acceptance of the view that we can all gain more by agreement than by aggression.

Prognosis Yet agreement remained a difficult objective with an adversary passionately committed to the infallibility of its own party, policy, leadership, and dogma. None the less, in the long run there seemed reason for the open society to view the future with confidence, for if the world could avoid thermonuclear suicide—whether through the maintenance of a "balance of terror" between the nuclear powers or through the establish-

ment of a system of world disarmament—the processes of modernization, contrary to Marxist prophecy, would vindicate the mixed society and render communism obsolete.

Marx had contended that capitalism would be the inevitable casualty of the modernization process, and that communism would be its inevitable fulfillment. In these terms communism claimed the certification of history. But history seemed to have refuted that case. It showed rather that the mixed society, as it modernized itself, could overcome the internal contradictions which in Marx's view doomed it to destruction, and that communism was historically relevant to the preliminary rather than to the concluding stages of modernization.

Marx rested his case for the inevitable communist triumph on the theory that capitalism contained the seeds of its own destruction. He argued that the capitalist economy generated inexorable inner tendencies—"contradictions" —which would infallibly produce its downfall. One inexorable tendency was the increasing wealth of the rich and the increasing poverty of the poor. Another was the increasing frequency and magnitude of economic crisis. Together such tendencies would carry society to a point of revolutionary "ripeness" when the proletariat would rise in its wrath, overthrow the possessing classes, and establish a classless society. Marx saw no way of arresting this process, because the capitalist state could never be anything but the "executive committee" of the capitalist class.

This was Marx's fatal error. The capitalist state in developed societies, far from being the instrument of the possessing class, became the means by which other classes of society could redress the balance of social power. This was true in the United States from the age of Jackson. The liberal democratic state accomplished two things in particular: It brought about a redistribution of wealth which defeated Marx's prediction that the rich would grow richer and the poor poorer; and it brought about an economic stabilization which defeated Marx's prediction of ever intensifying economic crisis. The democratic parties of the developed nations, in short, used the state to force capitalism to do what both the laissez-faire capitalists and the Marxists had said was impossible: to control the business cycle and to reapportion income in favor of the lower classes.

At the same time, history threw new light on the role of communism. Marx, regarding communism as the climax of the modernization process, expected that it would come about first in the most developed nations. On the contrary, it came about in nations in the early phases of development, like Russia and China; and it appealed to such nations precisely because they saw it as a means of rapid modernization. Instead of being the culmination of industrialization, as Marx held, communism would seem to be a form of social organization to which states have sometimes resorted in the hope that it would shorten the process of economic development. We do not know what would happen to communism in a fully developed society; but, if it should survive in anything like its present form, it would be because of the efficiency of its apparatus of terror, not because it is the natural expression of the institutions of modernity.

History thus shows plainly that communism is *not* the wave of the future, *not* the form of social organization toward which all societies are irresistibly evolving. Rather, communism appears to be a phenomenon of the transition from stagnation to development. The open society, founded on a diversification of ownership within a framework of law, freedom, and social justice, would seem far more likely to contain the resilience, the *élan*, and the creativity necessary to meet the long-term challenge of modernization.

SUGGESTIONS FOR READING

General

It is still too soon for satisfactory studies of the Eisenhower years to have appeared. Of the general works available, the most informative is R. J. Donovan, *Eisenhower: The Inside Story* (1956), which covers only the first of Eisenhower's two administrations. That limitation also characterizes the laudatory M. J. Pusey, *Eisenhower, the President* (1956), and the sharply critical Marquis Childs, *Eisenhower: Captive Hero* (1958). For illuminating sidelights, see R. H. Rovere, *Affairs of State: The Eisenhower Years* (1956). Of the few available memoirs, the most valuable and revealing is R. M. Nixon, *Six Crises* (1962); see also Sherman Adams, *Firsthand Report* (1961). President Eisenhower's own memoirs are scheduled for publication.

Foreign and Military Policy

On American defense strategy during the Eisenhower years, there is significant material and a variety of points of view in the following books: W. W. Rostow, *The United States in the World Arena* (1960); H. A. Kissinger, *Nuclear Weapons and Foreign Policy* * (1957); S. P. Hunt-

* Available in a paperback edition.

ington, *The Common Defense: Strategic Programs in National Politics* (1961); M. B. Ridgway and H. H. Martin, *Soldier: Memoirs of Matthew B. Ridgway* (1956); M. D. Taylor, *Uncertain Trumpet* (1959); Herman Kahn, *On Thermonuclear War* (1960). These all relate also to foreign policy, as do E. J. Hughes, *America the Vincible* (1959); R. E. Osgood, *NATO: The Entangling Alliance* (1962); and, especially on the Suez crisis, Anthony Eden, *Full Circle* (1960). For Dulles' views before he took office, see J. F. Dulles, *War or Peace* (1950). Also of interest is A. E. Stevenson, *Putting First Things First* (1960).

Domestic Issues

On the peak and decline of "McCarthyism," besides the studies listed in connection with the previous chapter, the important works include Michael Straight, *Trial by Television* (1954); C. P. Curtis, *The Oppenheimer Case* (1955); and J. A. Wechsler, *The Age of Suspicion* (1953). J. L. O'Brian, *National Security and Individual Freedom* (1955), explores the Eisenhower security policies. On Eisenhower's economic policies, three useful studies are E. L. Dale, *Conservatives in Power: A Study in Frustration* (1960); S. E. Harris, *The Economics of the Political Parties* (1962); and A. H. Hansen, *Economic Issues of the 1960's* (1960). For Kennedy's policies in his prenomination campaign, see J. F. Kennedy, *The Strategy of Peace* * (1960); his important speeches during his first year in office are collected in J. F. Kennedy, *To Turn the Tide* * (1962). J. M. Burns, *John Kennedy: A Political Profile* * (1959), is a discerning biography, and there is a vivid account of the 1960 election in T. H. White, *The Making of the President* * (1960).

* Available in a paperback edition.

33

Mid-Century Perspectives

The American people entered the sixties—the eighteenth decade of their national existence—in a mood of anxious self-appraisal. At the end of the Second World War their nation had seemed economically, militarily, and ideologically the strongest in the world. Some Americans even spoke with flamboyance of the twentieth as the "American Century." But the moment of euphoria passed. By the sixties, Americans had a sense, new to their experience, of being on the defensive—of being shoved and harried by peremptory and hostile historical forces. As they looked ahead, the changing configurations of world power—not only the advance of communism but the awakening of vast continents new to the world's power balance—threatened to isolate and beleaguer the West. And anxiety was compounded by the realization that the arms race was equipping mankind with the ultimate power—the power to abolish itself. Some responded to this situation with impatience, anger, and an insensate desire to strike out against the symbols of frustration. Others girded themselves for an indefinite time of competition in which they believed that, with sufficient *élan*, purpose, and fortitude, the proponents of the open society could demonstrate the superior vitality of free institutions.

The challenge of the future had never been more exacting. The United States could hold its own in the shadowed decades ahead only through a mighty national exertion. Still, the nation retained incalculable resources of energy, talent, and wealth with which to meet that challenge. Poised between the triumphs of the past and the inscrutable ordeal ahead, the American nation lingered in apprehension and hope.

The American People after the War

The Population Boom   An unexpected spurt in population increased the burden on existing institutions. The fall in the birth rate during the depression had led demographers to predict that the nation's population would soon level off. Instead, the return to prosperity in the war years produced a swing to earlier marriages and larger families. At the same time, medical advances—the introduction of penicillin and other antibiotics, of antipolio vaccines, and of new surgical techniques—brought about a steady drop in the death rate. Between 1935 and 1957 the birth rate rose from 16.9 to 25 per thousand, the death rate fell from 10.9 to 9.6, and the life expectancy rose toward 70. Furthermore, about 2.25 million immigrants entered the country in the fifties—more than in any decade since the twenties. The nation's population had grown only about 9 million in the thirties; it grew 19 million in the forties and 28 million in the fifties. The increase in the fifties alone was almost equal to the total population of the country a century earlier and took place at about the same rate in the United States as

Population 1950

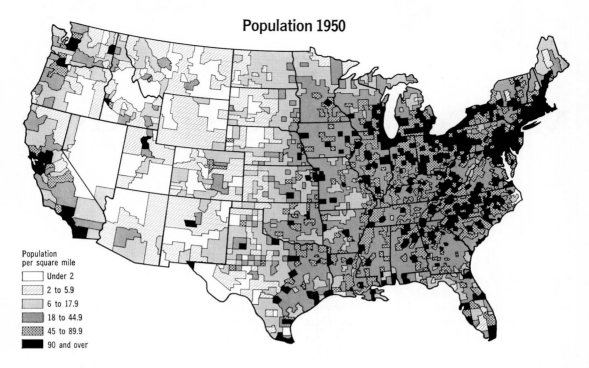

Population
per square mile
- ☐ Under 2
- ▨ 2 to 5.9
- ▦ 6 to 17.9
- ▩ 18 to 44.9
- ▦ 45 to 89.9
- ■ 90 and over

in India. Though the birth rate declined a little at the end of the decade, there was every expectation that at least 4 million babies would be born each year for some time to come.

The census of 1960 enumerated a total of 179,323,175 Americans. The West continued to show the greatest regional increase; its rate of 38.9 per cent was more than double the national rate of 18.5 per cent. California alone grew 5.1 million, accounting for nearly one-fifth of the total growth. About 85 per cent of the increase took place in cities of over fifty thousand and the suburban areas around them, and two-thirds of this—about 17.6 million—was in the suburbs themselves. The number of suburbanites increased from 36.8 to 54.4 million, a gain of 48 per cent. And mobility continued to mark American life: 19.9 per cent of Americans, about 31.5 million people, moved from one place to another in the year ending April 1960.

Economic Changes Despite the slow-down in the rate of economic growth in the fifties, America remained the richest nation known to history. The gross national product increased (in 1960 prices) from $362 billion in 1950 to over $510 billion in 1961. The New

Deal and the war had meanwhile wrought important changes in the distribution of wealth. In 1928 the 1 per cent of Americans with the highest income commanded nearly one-fifth of all income after taxes. By 1946 the top 1 per cent commanded less than 8 per cent. In 1928 the top 5 per cent received over a third of all income; by 1946 their share had declined to 18 per cent. Between 1941 and 1950 both the lowest fifth and the second-lowest fifth enjoyed a 42 per cent increase in income. The growing importance of insurance and welfare benefits played an important part in this re-apportionment of income.

These improvements produced what the economist J. K. Galbraith called "the affluent society." But, comforting as they were, they eliminated neither the nation's extreme wealth nor its extreme poverty. For example, between 1949 and 1956, according to the National Bureau of Economic Research, the share of total wealth held by the top 1 per cent increased from 20.8 to 26 per cent. The 1.6 per cent of the adult population who possessed more than $60,000 of estate tax wealth owned at least 80 per cent of privately held corporate stock, practically all state and local government bonds, and nearly 90 per cent of corporate bonds.

At the bottom of the income ladder, the Joint Committee on the Economic Report told the Congress in 1956, "Of every 10 families in the United States, one family still receives a real money income of less than $1000, and slightly more than two families have a real income of less than $2000," adding that there had been little change in these figures since 1948. About 25 million American families were living on less than $4,000 a year in 1960, and probably 40 million individuals on less than $3,000. Nor was this poverty, as many Americans supposed, limited to subsistence farm areas or to nonwhites. A good deal of it was in the slums of American cities. The terribly poor included men and women over 65 (of whom more than a third in 1957 had incomes of less than $36 a week); unskilled workers and especially migratory laborers; and, to some degree, certain minority groups— Negroes, Puerto Ricans, Mexicans, Indians. In addition, industrial obsolescence had created regional pockets of poverty, such as the coal fields of West Virginia and the textile towns of New England. It was evident by the early sixties that continued increases in general economic well-being would not necessarily wipe out these pockets of poverty. An irreducible element of "structural" poverty remained, requiring specific and local treatment.

Despite the persistence of poverty, the redistribution of income had reduced the differences between the classes in American society. Wage-earners began to make as much money as white-collar workers or professional people. In many communities, for example, the plumber had a higher income than the schoolteacher. And white-collar workers as a proportion of the total labor force had more than doubled since 1900, while the percentage of unskilled workers had dropped by half. During the fifties the number of white-collar workers finally passed the number of blue-collar workers. The increase in the productivity of machines contributed, of course, to the decline in the size of the wage-earning group. During the fifties the total manufacturing output increased 40 per cent, with only a 9 per cent increase in the number of persons employed, and only a small part of that among production workers.

By 1960 almost half the labor force, omitting farmers, were in managerial, professional, clerical, or sales jobs.

The New Technology   These changes resulted from the extraordinary advances in the techniques of production summed up in the word "automation." The distinctive element in automation was the introduction of self-regulating devices into the industrial sequence based on the "feedback" principle. Feedback devices transmitted information to the machine leading to the continuation or correction of its operations and thereby far extending the possibility of automatic control. Such devices were commonly electronic, and electronics became the most dramatic of the postwar industries. Sales in electronics soared from $2.5 billion in 1950 to well over $10 billion by the end of the decade. The electric computer in particular revolutionized every aspect of industry from production to marketing. It also intensified problems of technological unemployment. No one could foretell how many workers might lose their jobs to Univac. At the same time, automation held out new hopes of raising the general level of abundance.

These technological miracles stemmed in part from heavy investments in research by both business and government. The weapons race, for all its attendant horror, stimulated research and development in pure as well as applied sciences. In the middle fifties total research and development spending, both public and private, came to about $5.6 billion. By 1960 the figure had risen to $12.4 billion. Of the 1960 figure about one-fifth went into research; of this perhaps one-third went to basic research; and about one-fourth of the federal support for basic research was dispensed by the military establishment. Many scientists considered the outlay for pure research inadequate. They also expressed concern over the failure of the educational system to turn out enough trained scientists and engineers.

The Culture of Affluence

A Middle-Class Society   These economic and technological changes made the middle class more than ever the center of American society. Not only were the characteristic middle-class occupations—professional,

technical, managerial, sales, clerical—expanding faster than any other, but many wage-
earners were now able to emulate middle-class
standards of consumption and behavior. More
people than ever before had white-collar jobs,
white-collar incomes, white-collar educations,
and white-collar values.

Everyone welcomed the democratization of
comfort—the fact that so many Americans
could aspire to amenities once reserved for
wealthy elites. Some wondered, however,
whether the price of affluence had to be a
homogenized society in which everyone grew
more and more like everyone else. Two features
of the affluent society aroused special apprehension: the role of salesmanship, and the role
of large organizations.

Advertising had long been an essential lub-
ricant for the economic system. But the new
importance of consumption and of services
gave salesmanship a position of unprecedented
dominance. Where once advertising had been
primarily a means by which rival producers
could compete for larger shares of the market,
it now acquired a new function—the manufacture of wants to be satisfied by the voracious
economic machine. "As a society becomes increasingly affluent," wrote J. K. Galbraith,
"wants are increasingly created by the process
by which they are satisfied." Between 1947–49
and 1957 the amount of money spent on advertising more than doubled. The $10.3 bil-
lion spent for advertising in 1957 nearly
equaled the total net income of American
farmers and was about three times the amount
spent that year on higher education. Advertisers, who spent $57 per family in 1940, were
spending almost four times as much by 1960.
Advertising became a pseudo-science for the
manipulation of taste and the "engineering"
of consent. People began to fear the secret
machinations of those whom one best-selling
book dubbed the "hidden persuaders." In the
demonology of liberals, Madison Avenue displaced Wall Street as the headquarters of
social wickedness.

As the unceasing barrage of advertising
tended to reduce the individual to a unit in a
mass market, the rise of the great organization
appeared to divest him even further of a sense
of identity. More and more people were spending their whole life in organizations—their

The Contemporary Economy: A Liberal View

The Soviet Union has revealed a breath-taking series
of scientific and technical advances. No one or at
least not many have suggested that she was handicapped in doing so by too small a Gross National
Product. Those who once talked so resonantly of
production have been silent, at least on this subject.
It has become evident that our failure to match this
achievement was the result of the failure to concentrate the requisite resources on the desired
ends.... Too much was attributed to fortuitous factors—unwise budget cuts, the perverse personality
of the Secretary of Defense, interservice conflict,
and generally poor administration. We have not yet
seen that the causes were far deeper—that our
economy, and the economic theory that explains and
rationalizes its behavior, immobilizes all but a minor
fraction of the product in private and, from the
standpoint of national security, irrelevant production. We have not seen that the problem is far more
than one of a bigger budget—that it is one of our
attitude toward the goals of society itself. A society
which sets as its highest goal the production of private consumer goods will continue to reflect such
attitudes in all its public decisions. It will entrust
public decisions to men who regard any other goal
as incredible—or radical. We have yet to see that
not the total of resources but their studied and rational use is the key to achievement.

From John Kenneth Galbraith, *The Affluent Society*,
1958.

days in great corporations, their nights in
great suburban developments. "Togetherness"
was proposed as a national aspiration. The
homogenized society seemed to offer preference
to those who had no rough edges, eschewed
peculiarities, excited no suspicion, and played
the game according to the rules. In a training
film circulated by a leading chemical company, the sound track said, as the camera
panned over men in white coats in a company
laboratory, "No geniuses here; just a bunch of
average Americans working together." Both
corporation and suburb appeared to foster a
pervasive, benign, and invincible conformity.
It had become, it was said, a case of the bland
leading the bland. The tranquilizer seemed the
decade's symptomatic drug.

An older generation, remembering its
springtime of revolt—cultural in the twenties,

political in the thirties—regarded the young people of the fifties as a "silent generation" composed of "careful young men" who wanted only a steady job, a home in the suburbs, and a company retirement plan. Private security had reputedly become an obsessive goal. The titles of popular books in the fifties expressed the fashionable apprehensions: *The Man in the Gray Flannel Suit*, *The Status Seekers*, *The Lonely Crowd*, and, above all, *The Organization Man*. In this last work, W. H. Whyte, Jr., argued that the old Protestant-individualist code was giving way before a new collective ethic. This new ethic, arising from the bureaucratization of society, sanctioned as "morally legitimate" the pressures which society might genially exert against the free-wheeler. Whyte saw three major assumptions in the collective ethic: the group, rather than the individual, as the source of creativity; "belongingness," rather than personal fulfillment, as the ultimate need of the individual; and the attainment of "belongingness" through the application of "science" to human relations. Popular novels, like Herman Wouk's *The Caine Mutiny*, embodied the new ethic by suggesting that the worst sinner was the man who challenged the organization. No matter how cowardly or mad Captain Queeg was, his executive officer, Lieutenant Maryk, should not have relieved him of his post. In so doing, Maryk threatened the whole philosophy of command. The true villain, Wouk argued, was not Queeg but the rootless intellectual, Lieutenant Keefer, who had filled Maryk's mind with subversive doubts about the sacredness of authority.

Instruments of Adjustment: Education
Around the turn of the century, in a necessary revolt against the sterile formalism of the Victorian school, John Dewey had started the movement for "progressive education." His desire had been to bridge the gap between education and experience, to devise better ways of teaching classical subjects to larger numbers of students, and to use the schools as a means of preparing boys and girls for the concrete problems of their society. Only in this way, he contended, could the school system meet the requirements of mass education.

A later generation of progressive educators carried this program further than Dewey himself would have wished to go. A conference of educators declared in 1945, "In the United States the people have adopted the ideal of secondary education for all youth. As this ideal is approached, the high school is called upon to serve an increasing number of youth for whom college preparation or training for skilled occupations is neither feasible nor appropriate." To meet this need, professional educators went all out on so-called life adjustment programs. Courses in cooking, driving, and dating began to appear in curricula and were even required for graduation. Enrollments in algebra, geometry, physics, and Latin decreased. It seemed almost as if social adjustment were replacing intellectual training as the main function of the educational system.

Some of the teachers' colleges themselves, with their emphasis on method rather than content, contributed to the dilution of the curriculum. Professional educators, through powerful lobbies, controlled certification requirements in many states and insisted that candidates for public-school jobs take a specified number of course hours, not in the subject itself, but in how to teach it. Under these standards, many of the nation's leading scholars could not have qualified for positions in local public schools.

By the fifties the educational system was coming under increasing criticism. Part of this criticism was ignorant, reactionary, and tinctured with McCarthyism. Local groups attacked school superintendents for such offenses as mentioning the United Nations or requiring students to read the short stories of Ernest Hemingway. John Dewey was denounced as a sinister influence on American education. On the other hand, thoughtful observers, who sympathized with Dewey's original effort, felt that the time had come to arrest the softening of the curriculum and to restore intellectual discipline as the center of the educational enterprise.

Competition with the Soviet Union increased the pressure for a return to "basic" education. President Eisenhower reported in 1957 that, when a Russian graduated from high school, he had had five years of physics, four years of chemistry, one year of astronomy, five years of biology, ten years of mathematics through trigonometry, and five years of a foreign language. At the same time, according to the Department of Health, Education and Welfare, only one out of three American high-school graduates had had a year of chemistry, only one out of four a year of physics, and only one out of three more than a year of algebra. Comparisons of this sort roused fears that educational reform might put undue emphasis on mathematics and science at the expense of the humanities; but such proponents of reform as Dr. James B. Conant offered a balanced program, with adequate attention to classical as well as to technical studies, and with provision for both intellectual and vocational training. The reformers, impressed by evidence that less than half the boys and girls in the top 10 per cent of intellectual ability ever entered college, sought particularly to rescue the gifted child and to stop this national wastage of brain power.

Instruments of Adjustment: Mass Culture
The mass media too seemed to be accelerating the tendency toward uniformity. The postwar years saw a steady drop in the number and variety of newspapers and magazines. In 1916 the United States had 2,461 daily newspapers, with competing papers in more than half the cities; New York and Boston had ten or more dailies in active competition. By 1960 the total number had fallen to about 1,750 daily papers. Only seventy-six communities had papers that genuinely competed with one another. In 95 per cent of American communities, newspaper ownership was a monopoly. In twenty states there were no cities at all with competing dailies; in eleven more there was only one such city. More than half the newspaper circulation was controlled by 110 chains. An increasing number of papers bought not only columns and features and comic strips but even editorials from national syndicates. The story was much the same in magazines.

The new and compelling medium of television carried the process of homogenization a step further. Originally developed in the nineteen-thirties, television went on the popular market in the late forties. By 1960 nearly 90 per cent of American households had television sets—more than had running water or indoor toilets. It was estimated that these families spent five hours a day watching the tiny screen. From the age of three, according to one survey, the average child dedicated between one-sixth and one-seventh of his waking hours to television. "The strongest sustained attention of Americans," said Dr. Frank Stanton, president of the Columbia Broadcasting System, "is now, daily and nightly, bestowed on television as it is bestowed on nothing else." Programing was dominated by three large networks and a collection of advertising agencies. The result dismayed thoughtful viewers. Edward R. Murrow, who himself had done much to elevate the medium, wrote, "Television in the main is being used to distract, delude, amuse and insulate."

Advertisers seeking the widest possible market naturally favored programs that would alienate as few people as possible. The "great audience," as Gilbert Seldes called it, dominated mass culture, putting a premium on the lowest common denominator. The theater and the films, though sometimes displaying flashes of originality and talent, were often diluted or deformed to meet the supposed requirements of the great audience. And, on a far lower level, comic books offered children (and retarded adults) prefabricated installments of eroticism and sadism. Such consequences of mass culture filled some sensitive observers with alarm and gloom. The ultimate effect of the mass production of cultural products, they contended, would be to degrade taste, corrupt sensibility, smother spontaneity, and, instead of preparing the participant for a serious aesthetic experience, enslave him to substitute gratifications. The triumph of mass culture, it was argued, would mean the doom of high culture and the debasement of society.

The Cultural Explosion   Others, however, were less pessimistic about the cultural consequences of affluence. The optimists were willing to concede that the mass media promoted uniformity, but they argued that, in most cases, it was uniformity upward. The level of popular taste, they said, had been steadily rising, and the mass media, by enlarging the range of cultural possibilities, had enriched the experience of the individual. They saw America, not as declining into an air-conditioned, neon-lighted nightmare of vulgarity, but as committed to a distribution of high culture on a scale never before known to history. For the first time in human affairs, aesthetic experience was available, not just to the elite, but to the masses.

Thus in the fifties Americans spent more money on concerts than on baseball games. Over half the world's two thousand symphony orchestras were in the United States. The invention of the long-playing record made every dwelling its own concert hall. Nearly ten million Americans were taking instruction in musical instruments. The number of museums had quadrupled in the last quarter-century. Architecture had never been more daring and imaginative; the modern house spread across the country, and new office buildings, like Mies van der Rohe's Seagram building in New York, soared and gleamed in bronze and glass. Television had given a single performance of Shakespeare's *Richard III* a larger audience than all the theater audiences that had seen it since its opening in 1597. And the extraordinary rise of the paperback book—selling a million copies a day by 1960 and bringing the book industry one-fifth of its annual income—meant that every family could easily stock its shelves, not just with thrillers and westerns, but with great works of scholarship and with the classics of the ages. Books of all sorts became a billion-dollar industry in 1960.

To such statistics the pessimists replied that optimism rested on the fallacy that high culture could be acquired without pain. Popularization—especially as expressed in a *Reader's Digest* simplification of a complex philosophical or scientific theory—made things spuriously easy and deprived the mind of the hard discipline necessary for genuine cultivation. Mass culture consumed—and thereby vulgarized—everything. Even the rebel found a market and was thereby thwarted in his rebellion. Society in the past had tried to destroy the avant-garde by excluding it; now it destroyed the avant-garde far more effectively by welcoming it. Nothing was more characteristic than for critics to be absorbed by the shoddy culture they had been condemning—for "sick" comedians to be a success in nightclubs, and for highbrow artists to shine on the Ed Sullivan show. The satirical cartoonist Jules Feiffer portrayed a medieval scribe who used to petition the barons and merchants and clergy for reform, only to be tossed into the dungeons and beaten for his pains. Then his

country prospered, with rich harvests and fruitful commerce. He again sent out his exhortations, and now the barons invited him to lecture at each foreclosure, the merchants asked him to form a fact-finding committee, and the clergy discussed his work at every subsequent sacrifice; "if suppression cannot disarm criticism," he mournfully concluded, "amiable acceptance can."

The mass-culture debate left one clear impression: that the future was by no means foreclosed. Mass culture certainly contained the tendencies its critics found so ominous; but the very prevalence of the criticism itself helped provide the antidote. If the optimists turned out to be right, it would ironically be because the pessimists' unflinching insistence on the highest intellectual and aesthetic standards prevented mass culture from realizing its own worst potentialities.

The Quest for Identity

The "Beat Generation" Clearly, the mass culture of the affluent fifties did not answer man's deepest longings. The popularity of the tranquilizer demonstrated the pervasiveness of anxiety. Nothing revealed the inner unrest more vividly than the evident disaffection of a portion at least of the youth of the country. Even the silence of the "silent generation" suggested withdrawal from a society whose purpose was repugnant or unintelligible. Just as the rise of the "lost generation" in the twenties had expressed a rejection of the official values of that prosperous decade, so the rise of the "beat generation" in the fifties implied a repudiation of the contemporary American ethos.

The rebels of the fifties were far more desperate, chaotic, and pitiful than their light-hearted and talented predecessors. The "beat generation" included both "hipsters," proletarian in origin, sometimes criminal in inclination, apostles of inarticulate, violent revolt, and the middle-class "beatniks," lineal descendants of the bohemians of an earlier day, vindicating their withdrawal by experiments in verse, sometimes intoned to the accompaniment of a jazz band, and by an addiction to Zen Buddhism. Hipsters and beatniks congregated in San Francisco and New Orleans, shared a special vocabulary, admired "cool cats" like James Dean and Marlon Brando, and lost no opportunity to exhibit their biting contempt for the "squares" of the world. Sympathetic observers saw in these "anti-heroes" a brave attempt to heighten the integrity of individual experience and reject the suffocating embrace of a sick society. Others saw in them a tiresome conformity of their own and dismissed them as "rebels without a cause," dedicated to an aimless and pathetic flight from responsibility. As the beat novelist, Jack Kerouac, put it in an exchange between two characters in *On The Road*, "We gotta go and never stop going till we get there." "Where we going, man?" "I don't know, but we gotta go."

The Boom in Religion   Another expression of spiritual disquietude was the apparent surge of interest in religion in the years after the war. Though statistics on religion are notoriously unreliable, it appears that in the second quarter of the century church membership grew twice as fast as population. In 1940 total church membership was estimated at 64.5 million; in 1950 at 86.8 million; and in 1958 at 109.6 million. Never before in American history had so many persons claimed affiliation with organized religious bodies, though church membership in the twentieth century was far less exacting and definite than it had been a century earlier. When public opinion polls inquired into religious affiliation, 95 per cent of the respondents declared themselves Protestants, Catholics, or Jews, and 97 per cent of the population asserted a belief in God. The old-fashioned, militant, free-thinking tradition, from Ethan Allen through Robert G. Ingersoll to Clarence Darrow, seemed to have disappeared.

The religious boom had diverse manifestations. During the fifties, for example, the President opened his Cabinet meetings with prayer. Special rooms were set aside for religious meditation in the Capitol and the United Nations, in airports and even in factories. Religious books led the best-seller lists. Revivalists, headed by the popular Dr. Billy Graham, staged extraordinary mass meetings. The words "under God" were added to the pledge of allegiance to the flag. Religious songs even appeared on the Hit Parade.

This religious awakening was conspicuously nontheological, however, and indifferent to fine points of doctrine. Faith became good in general, and the old issues which had divided Christians for centuries receded into insignificance. President Eisenhower once said, "Our government makes no sense unless it is founded in a deeply felt religious faith—and I don't care what it is." Another observer remarked that faith was becoming a "detachable commodity." The point seemed to be, not *what* people believed, but *whether* they believed. William Lee Miller wrote, "It is almost as though the only thing we have to believe in is Belief itself."

Public opinion polls revealed the oddly nonspecific character of the new religiosity. According to one survey, 80 per cent of the respondents said they regarded the Bible as the revealed word of God, but only 35 per cent could name the four Gospels, and over half could not name even one. Seventy-five per cent said they believed in an afterlife with God as judge, but only 5 per cent admitted any concern about going to hell. Eighty per cent believed that Christ was the son of God, but, when a number of eminent Americans were asked to rate the hundred most significant events in history, they listed the birth of Christ fourteenth, along with the invention of the airplane and the discovery of the X-ray.

In place of the austere intellectual structure of historical Christianity, the best-selling religious books of the period purveyed a "cult of reassurance"—Rabbi Joshua Loth Liebman's *Peace of Mind* (1946), Bishop Fulton J. Sheen's *Peace of Soul* (1949), the Reverend Norman Vincent Peale's *The Power of Positive Thinking* (1952). "Don't doubt," wrote Peale. "Doubt closes the power flow." These and other books portrayed God as the man upstairs, someone up there watching over me, the everlasting source of protection and comfort. The new, nondoctrinal faith seemed designed to dispel anxiety, to induce self-confidence and even self-righteousness, to guarantee success for the individual in his professional career and victory for the nation in its struggle against atheistic, materialistic communism. Religious affiliation seemed to provide a means by which Americans could define themselves in their community and their society. Religion became part of "belonging," a quick way to establish social identity.

Many traditional Christians looked askance at the popular religious boom. "Much of this apparent revival of religious interest," said Bishop Henry Knox Sherrill, "seems to place the emphasis on using God for our own purposes of success, of health, of freedom from burdens and strain. [But] the heart of true religion has to do with offering ourselves to God." A more authentic revival of religious concern concentrated on intellectual and moral issues. Here the leading figure was Dr. Reinhold Niebuhr of Union Theological Seminary; and Niebuhr's great work, *The Nature and Destiny of Man* (1939), provided a massive and searching restatement of traditional Christian faith in terms of the urgencies of the mid-twentieth century. The "neo-orthodoxy" of Niebuhr and his followers could hardly have differed more from the cult of reassurance. Where the Niebuhrians sought the independence of Christian faith from contemporary culture, the Pealians identified faith with the values of contemporary society. Where one urged the church to re-establish transcendent norms and reaffirm its distinctive message, the other wanted faith to sanction the official society. Niebuhr himself sharply criticized the notion that public avowals of religious concern constituted genuine religious belief. "The greatest corruption of all," he wrote, "is a corrupt religion." He agreed that religion could produce peace of soul, but not the peace of positive thoughts or of self-congratulation; true religion aimed rather at the "peace of God which passeth all understanding." "That peace passes understanding," added Niebuhr, "precisely because it is a peace with pain in it." The object of faith was to induce not contentment but contrition, not complacency but repentance.

This religious revival criticized the attempt to make religious affiliation the emblem of social or political respectability. Both the neo-orthodox and the agnostics could unite in supporting the statement of Supreme Court Justice Robert H. Jackson:

The day that this country ceases to be free for irreligion, it will cease to be free for religion—except for the sect that can win political power.

. . . It is possible to hold a faith with enough confidence to believe that what should be rendered to God does not need to be decided and collected by Caesar. . . . We start down a rough road when we begin to mix compulsory public education with compulsory godliness.

For the neo-orthodox, the quest for identity through religion was not to be achieved by becoming a vestryman or attending interfaith banquets. If religion could save men's souls, it would only be in the traditional manner of an internal tumult leading to regeneration and salvation.

Literature and Identity   The quest for identity also dominated much of the writing in the postwar years. Literature once again provided a symbolic means by which man could come to terms with the intractable dilemmas of his experience and his age.

On balance, the writing produced in the years after the Second World War was, except for poetry and perhaps drama, markedly inferior to American writing after the First World War. No new novelists arose with the impact of Hemingway, Fitzgerald, Faulkner, Dreiser, Dos Passos, or Lewis. Though Faulkner wrote some of his greatest books after the Second World War, the work of Hemingway and especially of Lewis and Dos Passos fell off; the other great writers of the twenties were dead by 1945. Of the novelists who had emerged in the thirties, James Gould Cozzens showed solid growth after the war. *Guard of Honor* (1948) was a deeply observed novel of wartime, and *By Love Possessed* (1957), though baroque in manner, struck critics as an impressive exploration into moral ambiguities. J. P. Marquand continued to record business, society, and politics with a deft and sure satiric touch; the cumulative effect of his work was to provide an unsurpassed panorama of upper-middle-class life. Neither James T. Farrell nor John Steinbeck equaled their work of the thirties.

Of the postwar writers, none had established himself as of the first rank. In many respects, J. D. Salinger appeared to speak most directly to the preoccupations of the new generation. His novel *The Catcher in the Rye* (1951) was a poignant and searching account of an adolescent crisis of identity, and a series of brilliant short stories, especially *Franny and Zooey* (1961), explored the possibilities of sainthood in modern life. Saul Bellow's *The Adventures of Augie March* (1953) placed the search for identity in a picaresque context; his *Seize the Day* (1954) dealt effectively with the ordeal of self-recognition. James Jones's *From Here to Eternity* (1951) and Norman Mailer's *The Naked and the Dead* (1948) were richly promising war novels by writers who subsequently found trouble defining their own identity in the postwar years. Mailer's *Advertisements for Myself* (1959) offered a sensitive, distraught, and compulsively articulate account of one writer's attempt to orient himself in the America of the fifties. Mary McCarthy in *The Company She Keeps* (1942), *A Charmed Life* (1955), and *Memories of a Catholic Girlhood* (1957) supplied variations on the problem of identity as seen by an exceptionally intelligent and astringent American woman.

The level of poetry was higher than that of fiction. Robert Frost, Wallace Stevens, Marianne Moore, Archibald MacLeish, and others continued to write distinguished verse in the years after the war. Among the younger poets Robert Lowell was pre-eminent. *Lord Weary's Castle* (1946) and *Life Studies* (1959) represented perhaps the most successful effort to penetrate and resolve the obsessive literary concern with identity. In the theater, Arthur Miller revived the social drama in strong and somber plays such as *Death of a Salesman* (1949) and *The Crucible* (1953), and Tennessee Williams specialized with brilliant if cold effect in the pathology of modern life in such plays as *A Streetcar Named Desire* (1947) and *Cat on a Hot Tin Roof* (1955).

The "Self-Conscious Society" If on the surface the fifties, like the twenties, seemed a decade of acquiescence and content, underneath the surface these years, again like the twenties, were a decade of questioning, ferment, and self-criticism. Discontent produced self-appraisal. The result was a series of studies examining the tone and structure of American life and seeking to identify the distinctive problems of the affluent society.

The writings of J. K. Galbraith explored the implications of affluence. Whyte's *Organization Man* concentrated on the plight of the individual in the new collective world. The journalist, Vance Packard, highlighted aspects of

---

Contemporary America: An Angry View

Today, the enemy is vague, the work seems done, the audience more sophisticated than the writer. Society has been rationalized, and the expert encroaches on the artist. Belief in the efficacy of attacking his society has been lost, but nothing has replaced the need for attack. If, then, a number of important intellectuals and writers now see it as their function to interpret American society from within (the curious space relations of politics which equate right to within and left to without), must one necessarily assume that the motives are more serious than exhaustion?...

Really, the history of the twentieth century seems made to be ignored. No one of the intellectuals who find themselves now in the American grain ever discuss—at least in print—the needs of modern war. One does not ever say that total war and the total war economy predicate a total regimentation of thought. Rather, it is suggested that society is too difficult to understand and history impossible to predict....

Everything is viewed in a static way. We are democratic, we support the West, and the American artistic caravan is no longer isolated. The important work is to search out the healthy aspects of American life, and decide whether we can work with the movies.... It is worth something to remind ourselves that the great artists ... are almost always in opposition to their society, and that integration, acceptance, non-alienation, etc. etc., have been more conducive to propaganda than art.

From Norman Mailer, "Our Country and Our Culture," *Advertisements for Myself*, 1959.

---

manipulation and waste in the American economy in a series of popular, if splashy, books. Other aspects of society attracted scrupulous scholarly attention. Gunnar Myrdal, the Swedish economist, supervised a magistral study of the race question in *An American Dilemma: The Negro Problem and Modern Democracy* (1944). The zoologist, Dr. Alfred C. Kinsey, subjected the sex habits of Americans to detailed and disillusioning scrutiny in *Sexual Behavior in the Human Male* (1948) and *Sexual Behavior in the Human Female* (1953). F. X. Sutton, Seymour Harris, and others dissected *The American Business Creed* (1956). Paul Goodman's *Growing Up Absurd* (1960) offered a provocative account of the background of juvenile disaffection in American society. Walter Lippmann, Gilbert Seldes, Jacques Barzun, Louis Kronenberger, Thomas Griffith, Dwight Macdonald, and others assessed the quality of American culture. Eric Larrabee's *The Self-Conscious Society* (1960) appraised the process of appraisal.

Much of this enterprise of self-criticism was influenced by the works of the lawyer-sociologist David Riesman, especially *The Lonely Crowd: A Study of the Changing American Character* (1950). Riesman saw the American evolution in terms of a striking metaphor—the change from what he called the "inner-directed" man to the "other-directed" man. The inner-directed man was one whose fulfillment came from the effort to realize goals implanted within. Such character types, in Riesman's view, were typical of a society dedicated to production. But the shift from production to consumption had wrought changes in the American character structure. The other-directed man was one who took his standards from the group in which he aspired to live, and who realized himself only as he became identified with what he deemed respectable and enviable in the world outside himself. The inner-directed man felt guilty when he violated his inner ideals. The other-directed man had no inner ideals to violate. His moral life came, not from interior direction, but from the compulsion to be in harmony with the crowd. He felt guilty when he deviated from the group consensus. These were the terms in which Riesman invited Americans to review their own standards and purposes.

Out of his analysis Riesman emerged with the ideal of "autonomy"—that is, the individual's capacity to conform to the behavioral norms of society joined with a *freedom to choose* whether to conform or not. "Autonomy," wrote Riesman, "is never an 'all or nothing' affair; it does not come about suddenly, but sometimes imperceptibly, and always as the result of a continual struggle with the forces of the culture which oppose it. I like to interpret the conception that 'Man is born free; and everywhere he is in chains,' to mean that man is born a slave—a slave to his biological and cultural inheritance—but that he can become, through experience and experiment, increasingly free."

The Struggle for National Purpose

The New Conservatism   The search for identity began with the private individual who found that economic affluence did not necessarily allay psychological discontent. But the search soon led on to a reappraisal of mid-century America, and a consideration of how in public terms the promise of American life could be realized. In the late fifties and early sixties, Americans began to debate whether the effort to satisfy private, individual motives would provide sufficient direction to guide the Republic, or whether the pull of private purposes would disrupt society unless it was subordinated to some overriding public purpose. The debate raised issues of political philosophy and led men to formulate the principles of both a New Conservatism and a New Liberalism.

The return of conservatism to political power in 1953 (see pp. 759–62) created a favorable climate for a conservative political philosophy. The historical and philosophical basis for this effort was laid by Russell Kirk in *The Conservative Mind* (1953). The excessive optimism and rationalism of liberalism, Kirk argued, gave rise to illusions about man and society. In place of liberalism he called for a philosophy that would give full weight to the requirements of tradition, order, prescription, hierarchy, and authority. In these terms he conducted a searching and sometimes powerful critique of conventional liberalism.

Kirk's moral premises were in the tradition of Edmund Burke, who greatly admired the reciprocal social obligations of feudal society. But his political conclusions were in the tradition of Adam Smith, who sought to dissolve feudal obligations in order to release the energy of individuals. Thus Kirk condemned the federal school-lunch program as a "vehicle for totalitarianism" and proposed that the TVA and other public power projects be turned over to private corporations. The conflict between Burke and Smith remained an unresolved tension in Kirk's argument. Other conservatives, influenced by the Austrian economists Friedrich von Hayek and Ludwig von Mises, became wholehearted champions of the laissez-faire liberalism of the nineteenth century. The most prominent members of this group—Henry Hazlitt, William F. Buckley, Jr., Senator Barry Goldwater—were persevering in their insistence that the danger to freedom came from the activity of government. Goldwater, for example, in his book *The Conscience of a Conservative* (1960), proposed that the graduated income tax be abolished and that the federal government withdraw from the bulk of its public programs at a rate of 10 per cent a year.

Others of the New Conservatives reached different conclusions. Writers like Peter Viereck (*Conservatism Revisited*, 1949) and Clinton Rossiter (*Conservatism in America*, 1955) construed conservatism in the spirit not of Herbert Spencer but of Hamilton, Disraeli, and Winston Churchill. They were by no means averse to government intervention on behalf of the poor and defenseless. As Rossiter put it, "The negative theory of government proclaimed by most men on the Right ignores the complexities of modern American society and thwarts the effective discharge of the conservative mission." He added, "The new conservatism should look anew at the power of government to aid men in their pursuit of happiness." The Rossiter-Viereck rejection of "doctrinaire individualism" resulted in a "conservative" philosophy which endorsed the purposes, if not always the methods, of the New and Fair Deals. Conservatives of this school preferred Adlai Stevenson and John F. Kennedy to Robert A. Taft and Barry Goldwater.

The New Conservatism flowered for a season in the fifties. But it seemed to many a hot-house growth. The practical conservatives of the Eisenhower era paid little attention to the academic meditations of the conservative intellectuals. And some of the New Conservatives themselves began to wonder whether a rigid laissez-faire philosophy was, in fact—as conservatism ought to be—an expression of the nation's historical experience. If the essence of conservatism was the conservation of a society's essential heritage, then, as Louis Hartz brilliantly demonstrated in *The Liberal Tradition in America* (1955), what was to be conserved in America was after all the heritage of liberalism springing from John Locke. Eventually Peter Viereck, the most perceptive of the New Conservatives, recoiled from the movement he had helped to inspire. He wrote, "Theirs becomes

---

Contemporary Democracy: A Conservative View

In the effort to understand the malady of democratic government I have dwelt upon the underlying duality of functions: *governing*, that is, the administration of the laws and the initiative in legislating, and *representing* the living persons who are governed, who must pay, who must work, who must fight and, it may be, die for the acts of the government. I attribute the democratic disaster of the twentieth century to a derangement of these primary functions....

In this century, the balance of the two powers has been seriously upset. Two great streams of evolution have converged upon the modern democracies to devitalize, to enfeeble, and to eviscerate the executive powers. One is the enormous expansion of public expenditure, chiefly for war and reconstruction; this has augmented the power of the assemblies which vote the appropriations on which the executive depends. The other development which has acted to enfeeble the executive power is the growing incapacity of the large majority of the democratic peoples to believe in intangible realities. This has stripped the government of that imponderable authority which is derived from tradition, immemorial usage, consecration, veneration, prescription, prestige, heredity, hierarchy.

From Walter Lippmann, *The Public Philosophy*, 1954.

---

an unhistorical appeal to history, a traditionless worship of tradition, a rootless appeal for roots."

The New Liberalism   None the less the New Conservatism had scored effective points against the old liberalism. In particular, it had challenged the belief in human perfectibility so long associated with the liberal tradition—a challenge effectively reinforced by man's capacity for cruelty as revealed in the totalitarian movements of the twentieth century. But the question remained whether liberalism was dependent on optimism about man and society, or whether it could not rest equally well on more somber and ambiguous views of human nature.

During and after the Second World War some thinkers tried to re-establish liberalism on the basis, not of man's perfectibility, but of his frailty. "The excessively optimistic estimates of human nature and of human history with which the democratic credo has been historically associated," Reinhold Niebuhr wrote in *The Children of Light and the Children of Darkness* (1944), "are a source of peril to democratic society; for contemporary experience is refuting this optimism and there is danger that it will seem to refute this democratic ideal as well." In this and other works, Niebuhr attempted to show that democracy had a more realistic defense than that provided by the conventional liberal culture. An acceptance of original sin, in Niebuhr's view, constituted no serious argument against democracy. Rather the contrary; for, if all men were sinful, then a particular group of men, possessed of special authority, would be all the more subject to the corruptions of pride and power. As Niebuhr summed up his argument, "Man's capacity for justice makes democracy possible; but man's inclination to injustice makes democracy necessary." The doctrine of human fallibility thus appeared on reflection to strengthen rather than weaken the political philosophy of liberalism.

The New Liberalism, acknowledging the imperfection of man, resisted the panic conclusion that, because man was imperfect, the only solution was rule by an elite. "The children of light," said Niebuhr, "must be armed with the wisdom of the children of darkness but remain free from their malice. They must know the power of self-interest in human society without giving it moral justification. They must have this wisdom in order that they may beguile, deflect, harness and restrain self-interest, individual and collective, for the sake of the community."

The Renaissance of Public Purpose
The New Liberalism thus retained the conviction that democratic wisdom could control individual selfishness in the interests of the general welfare. To do this, however, democratic wisdom had to embody a conception of overriding purpose to which individual self-interest might be plausibly subordinated. The trouble with the America of the fifties, in the New Liberal view, was the assumption that what was good for one or another private interest was good for the country. Secretary of Defense Charles E. Wilson had given this idea its classic formulation (see p. 761); but many of his critics objected less to the principle of Wilson's Law than to his choice of benefici-

aries. They often seemed to assume that, if government would only cater to labor or to the farmers rather than to General Motors, then all would be well with the Republic. But unless government was dominated by a conception of the *public* interest, the welfare state would degenerate into what the educator Robert M. Hutchins called "the pressure group state, which cares [only] for the welfare of those who are well enough organized to put on the pressure."

What did the public interest require? In the economic field it led people to consider the question of the "allocation of resources"—the uses to which the nation put its annual income. Because so large a proportion of the national income went to satisfy private needs, it was argued, public needs had received inadequate attention. As a result, the United States, with twice as large an annual output as the Soviet Union, was spending half as large a proportion of that output for education or for defense. Equally important, the United States seemed to be failing to expand its own public services—schools, hospitals, and so on—to keep pace with its own rapid population growth. In 1957 only 10.3 per cent of total nondefense output was devoted to public purposes—substantially below the corresponding figure in 1939 (13.4 per cent) and only a little higher than that in 1929 (7.5 per cent). As F. M. Bator, the leading student of this problem, has written, "Of the resources left over for private and public 'civilian' consumption and capital formation— left over, that is, after military provision for survival—we have been committing in the postwar period only a slightly larger fraction to such communal uses as schools, roads, sanitation, urban renewal, etc., than we did in 1929 and a smaller share than in 1939."

"The line which divides our area of wealth from our area of poverty," wrote J. K. Galbraith, "is roughly that which divides privately produced and marketed goods and services from publicly rendered services." Galbraith envisaged the typical American family driving its two-toned, air-conditioned, power-steered automobile through rotting cities along badly paved streets made hideous by litter into a countryside rendered largely invisible by billboards. "They picnic on exquisitely packaged food from a portable icebox by a polluted stream and go on to spend the night at a park which is a menace to public health and morals. Just before dozing off on an air mattress, beneath a nylon tent, amid the stench of decaying refuse, they may reflect vaguely on the curious unevenness of their blessings. Is this, indeed, the American genius?"

By the early sixties many people felt an increasing need to restore the "social balance" between personal and national investment. And, though few argued that steering more resources into the public sector would cure the spiritual ailments of the affluent society, it seemed probable that the resulting improvements in education, medical care, housing, and community planning would improve the chances for the individual to win his own spiritual fulfillment. The final lesson of the affluent society was that affluence was not enough—that solving the quantitative problems of living only increased the importance of the quality of the life lived. These qualitative problems seemed next on the American agenda.

The impending threat of leisure, assuming an international stabilization, increased the importance of the quality of national experience. When people began to go to work at eighteen, work a twenty-hour week, and retire at fifty, the affluent society would be faced by a situation never before experienced, except by small minorities, in the whole course of history—that is, a lifetime spent more at leisure than at labor. Whether the American approach to leisure would be narcotic or creative might determine the whole national future. In this connection thoughtful citizens noted the warning in the Report of the President's Commission on National Goals (1960): "In the eyes of posterity, the success of the United States as a civilized society will be largely judged by the creative activities of its citizens in art, architecture, literature, music, and the sciences."

New Frontiers

As so often in the American past, self-appraisal appeared a prelude to action. By the early sixties observers perceived a stirring in the nation that might signify a new gathering of its

The Contemporary Challenge: A Courageous View

Whether we like it or not, this is a time *of* change. As a people that set out to change the world, I think we should like it, however difficult the challenges. For no nation is at its best except under great challenge. The question for us now is whether in a changing world we will respond in a way befitting "the land of the free and the home of the brave"— whether we will be at our best in these crucial years of our world leadership—whether we will measure up to the task awaiting us.

That task is to do all in our power to see that the changes taking place all around us—in our cities, our countryside, our economy, within the Western world, in the uncommitted world, in the Soviet empire, on all continents—lead to more freedom for more men and to world peace. It is only when the iron is hot that it can be molded. The iron of the new world being forged today is now ready to be molded. Our job is to shape it, so far as we can, into the world we want for ourselves and our children and for all men.

This will require that we recapture our national purpose and redouble our energy. For we seem to have lost both the sense of the promise of America and the will to fulfill it.

From John F. Kennedy, *The Strategy of Peace*, 1960.

forces. A young President summoned the people to a supreme national effort. The "silent generation" appeared to be finding its voice. The discussion of national purpose reminded Americans that their ancient ideals were not automatically self-fulfilling and that to realize the promise of American life required intelligence, stamina, and will.

The future remained darkly impenetrable. Eight generations of Americans had prepared the nation for this ultimate testing. Traditions of freedom, justice, and individual dignity, stretching back to the Greece and Judea of old, had woven the fabric of the American faith. To the ninth generation now lay the task of revindicating the American ideal in a revolutionary age—the duty of showing oppressed peoples in all countries that the revolution which had begun so valiantly in 1776 would not rest until the rights of man had been established everywhere in the world.

The Culture and the Society

Students seeking to broaden their own perspectives about mid-century America might begin with two recent books that have already become classics of a kind, David Riesman, et al., *The Lonely Crowd* * (1950), a study of American character, and Reinhold Niebuhr, *The Irony of American History* * (1952), an interpretation of American aspirations and achievements. F. L. Allen, *The Big Change: America Transforms Itself* * (1952), contrasts the United States of the early century with the nation after the Second World War. In his *American Capitalism* * (1962 ed.), J. K. Galbraith examines the counterbalances among large interest groups and big government, while in his *The Affluent Society* (1958) he discusses uses and misuses of American plenty. W. H. Whyte, Jr., looks at the impact of large business organizations on their personnel in *The Organization Man* * (1956). American advertising and its implications receive stimulating treatment in Martin Mayer, *Madison Avenue, U.S.A.* * (1958); Vance Packard, *The Hidden Persuaders* * (1957); and D. J. Boorstin, *The Image* (1962). The relationship between American advertising and American character, along with other questions about American character, concern D. M. Potter in his pithy *People of Plenty: Economic Abundance and the American Character* * (1954). Aspects of American values and of the uses of leisure are analyzed from two points of view in Gilbert Seldes, *The Great Audience* (1950), and Winston White, *Beyond Conformity* (1961). C. W. Mills takes a negative view of the new middle class in *White Collar: American Middle Classes* * (1951). The particular values of businessmen are discussed in F. X. Sutton, et al., *The American Business Creed* * (1956). Eric Larrabee, *The Self-conscious Society* (1960), reviews and explicates the American thrust for self-evaluation. Among recent, valuable studies of education are Arthur Bestor, *The Restoration of American Learning* (1955) and *Educational Wastelands* (1953), both critical of current practices; J. B Conant, *American High School Today* * (1959), which presents a constructive program for improvement of public secondary education; Robert Ulich, *Crisis and Hope in American Education* (1951); and Benjamin Fine, *Our Children Are Cheated* (1947). Also important is Richard Hofstadter and C. D. Hardy, *The Development and Scope of Higher Education in the United States* (1952). All the foregoing issues and many others receive comment rooted in a broad understanding of American history in Max Lerner, *America as a Civilization* * (1957). *The Library of Congress Series in American Civilization* emphasizes recent conditions and developments; see especially R. E. Spiller and Eric Larrabee, eds., *American Perspectives* (1961).

Political Thought

Contradictory interpretations of American conservatism appear in Clinton Rossiter, *Conservatism in America* (1962 ed.), and Russell Kirk, *The Conservative Mind: From Burke to Santayana* (1953). Two influential but antagonistic commentators speak for a conservative viewpoint in Walter Lippmann, *The Public Philosophy* * (1955), and Barry Goldwater, *The Conscience of a Conservative* * (1960). Of the liberal point of view, four useful expressions are Reinhold Niebuhr, *The Children of Light and the Children of Darkness* * (1944); J. K. Galbraith, *The Liberal Hour* (1960); and A. M. Schlesinger, Jr., *The Vital Center* * (1962 ed.) and *The Politics of Hope* (1963). Daniel Bell, *The End of Ideology: On the Exhaustion of Political Ideas in the Fifties* * (1959), is incisive and critically sympathetic toward current liberal doctrines. There is an excellent explanation of liberal fiscal policy in F. M. Bator, *The Question of Government Spending* (1960), and of liberal foreign policy in W. W. Rostow, *The United States in the World Arena* (1960). C. W. Mills, *The Power Elite* * (1956), and R. H. Rovere, *The American Establishment* (1962), discuss aspects of the locus and use of political and social power. On national goals and purposes, with emphasis on what they should be, see J. W. Gardner, *Excellence: Can We Be Equal and Excellent Too?* (1961); the President's Commission on National Goals, *Goals for Americans* * (1960); *The National Purpose* * (1960), compiled from articles in *Life;* and *Prospect for America* * (1961), consisting of Rockefeller Panel Reports on issues of foreign and domestic policy.

* Available in a paperback edition.

Appendix

The Declaration of Independence *

The unanimous Declaration of the thirteen United States of America.

When, in the Course of human events, it becomes necessary for one people to dissolve the political bands which have connected them with another, and to assume, among the Powers of the earth, the separate and equal station to which the Laws of Nature and of Nature's God entitle them, a decent respect to the opinions of mankind requires that they should declare the causes which impel them to the separation.

We hold these truths to be self-evident, that all men are created equal, that they are endowed by their Creator with certain unalienable Rights, that among these, are Life, Liberty, and the pursuit of Happiness. That, to secure these rights, Governments are instituted among Men, deriving their just Powers from the consent of the governed. That, whenever any form of Government becomes destructive of these ends, it is the Right of the People to alter or to abolish it, and to institute new Government, laying its foundation on such Principles, and organizing its Powers in such form, as to them shall seem most likely to effect their Safety and Happiness. Prudence, indeed, will dictate that Governments long established should not be changed for light and transient causes; and, accordingly, all experience hath shewn, that mankind are more disposed to suffer, while evils are sufferable, than to right themselves by abolishing the forms to which they are accustomed. But, when a long train of abuses and usurpations, pursuing invariably the same Object, evinces a design to reduce them under absolute Despotism, it is their right, it is their duty, to throw off such Government, and to provide new

* Reprinted from Worthington C. Ford, ed., *Journals of the Continental Congress*, 1774–1789 (Washington, D.C., 1904–37), Vol. 5, pp. 510–15. The original spelling, capitalization, and punctuation have been retained.

Guards for their future Security. Such has been the patient sufferance of these Colonies; and such is now the necessity which constrains them to alter their former Systems of Government. The history of the present King of Great Britain is a history of repeated injuries and usurpations, all having in direct object the establishment of an absolute Tyranny over these States. To prove this, let Facts be submitted to a candid world.

He has refused his Assent to Laws the most wholesome and necessary for the public good.

He has forbidden his Governors to pass Laws of immediate and pressing importance, unless suspended in their operation till his Assent should be obtained; and when so suspended, he has utterly neglected to attend to them.

He has refused to pass other Laws for the accommodation of large districts of People, unless those People would relinquish the right of Representation in the legislature; a right inestimable to them and formidable to tyrants only.

He has called together legislative bodies at places unusual, uncomfortable, and distant from the depository of their Public Records, for the sole Purpose of fatiguing them into compliance with his measures.

He has dissolved Representative Houses repeatedly, for opposing, with manly firmness, his invasions on the rights of the People.

He has refused for a long time, after such dissolutions, to cause others to be elected; whereby the Legislative Powers, incapable of Annihilation, have returned to the People at large for their exercise; the State remaining in the mean time exposed to all the dangers of invasion from without, and convulsions within.

He has endeavoured to prevent the Population of

these States; for that purpose obstructing the Laws for Naturalization of Foreigners; refusing to pass others to encourage their migrations hither, and raising the conditions of new Appropriations of Lands.

He has obstructed the Administration of Justice, by refusing his Assent to Laws for establishing Judiciary Powers.

He has made Judges dependent on his Will alone, for the tenure of their offices, and the amount and payment of their salaries.

He has erected a multitude of New Offices, and sent hither swarms of Officers to harrass our People, and eat out their substance.

He has kept among us, in times of Peace, Standing Armies, without the Consent of our legislatures.

He has affected to render the Military independent of and superior to the Civil Power.

He has combined with others to subject us to a jurisdiction foreign to our constitution, and unacknowledged by our laws; giving his Assent to their Acts of pretended Legislation:

For quartering large bodies of armed troops among us:

For protecting them, by a mock Trial, from Punishment for any Murders which they should commit on the Inhabitants of these States:

For cutting off our Trade with all parts of the world:

For imposing Taxes on us without our Consent:

For depriving us, in many cases, of the benefits of Trial by Jury:

For transporting us beyond Seas to be tried for pretended offences:

For abolishing the free System of English Laws in a neighbouring province, establishing therein an Arbitrary government, and enlarging its Boundaries, so as to render it at once an example and fit instrument for introducing the same absolute rule into these Colonies:

For taking away our Charters, abolishing our most valuable Laws, and altering fundamentally the Forms of our Governments:

For suspending our own Legislatures, and declaring themselves invested with Power to legislate for us in all cases whatsoever.

He has abdicated Government here, by declaring us out of his protection, and waging War against us.

He has plundered our seas, ravaged our Coasts, burnt our towns, and destroyed the Lives of our People.

He is at this time transporting large Armies of foreign Mercenaries to compleat the works of death,

desolation and tyranny, already begun with circumstances of Cruelty and perfidy scarcely paralleled in the most barbarous ages, and totally unworthy the Head of a civilized nation.

He has constrained our fellow Citizens, taken Captive on the high Seas, to bear Arms against their Country, to become the executioners of their friends and Brethren, or to fall themselves by their Hands.

He has excited domestic insurrections amongst us, and has endeavoured to bring on the inhabitants of our frontiers, the merciless Indian Savages, whose known rule of warfare, is an undistinguished destruction of all ages, sexes and conditions.

In every stage of these Oppressions, We have Petitioned for Redress, in the most humble terms: Our repeated Petitions, have been answered only by repeated injury. A Prince, whose character is thus marked by every act which may define a Tryant, is unfit to be the ruler of a free People.

Nor have We been wanting in attentions to our British brethren. We have warned them from time to time of attempts by their legislature to extend an unwarrantable jurisdiction over us. We have reminded them of the circumstances of our emigration and settlement here. We have appealed to their native justice and magnanimity, and we have conjured them by the ties of our common kindred, to disavow these usurpations, which, would inevitably interrupt our connexions and correspondence. They too have been deaf to the voice of justice and consanguinity. We must, therefore, acquiesce in the necessity, which denounces our Separation, and hold them, as we hold the rest of mankind, Enemies in war, in Peace Friends.

WE, THEREFORE, the Representatives of the UNITED STATES OF AMERICA, in GENERAL CONGRESS assembled, appealing to the Supreme Judge of the World for the rectitude of our intentions, DO, in the Name, and by Authority of the good People of these Colonies, solemnly PUBLISH and DECLARE, That these United Colonies are, and of Right, ought to be FREE AND INDEPENDENT STATES; that they are Absolved from all Allegiance to the British Crown, and that all political connexion between them and the State of Great Britain, is and ought to be totally dissolved; and that, as FREE and INDEPENDENT STATES, they have full Power to levy War, conclude Peace, contract Alliances, establish Commerce, and to do all other Acts and Things which INDEPENDENT STATES may of right do. AND for the support of this Declaration, with a firm reliance on the protection of divine Providence, we mutually pledge to each other our Lives, our Fortunes, and our sacred Honour.

The Constitution of the United States of America *

We the people of the United States, in Order to form a more perfect Union, establish Justice, insure domestic Tranquility, provide for the common defence, promote the general Welfare, and secure the Blessings of Liberty to ourselves and our Posterity, do ordain and establish this CONSTITUTION for the United States of America.

ARTICLE I

SECTION 1. All legislative Powers herein granted shall be vested in a Congress of the United States, which shall consist of a Senate and House of Representatives.

SECTION 2. The House of Representatives shall be composed of Members chosen every second Year by the People of the several States, and the Electors in each State shall have the Qualifications requisite for Electors of the most numerous Branch of the State Legislature.

No Person shall be a Representative who shall not have attained to the Age of twenty-five Years, and been seven Years a Citizen of the United States, and who shall not, when elected, be an Inhabitant of that State in which he shall be chosen.

Representatives and direct Taxes † shall be apportioned among the several States which may be included within this Union, according to their respective Numbers, which shall be determined by adding to the whole Number of free Persons, including those bound to Service for a Term of Years, and excluding Indians not taxed, three fifths of all other Persons.‡ The actual Enumeration shall be made within three Years after the first Meeting of the Congress of the United States, and within every subsequent Term of ten Years, in such Manner as they shall by Law direct. The Number of Representatives shall not exceed one for every thirty Thousand, but each State shall have at Least one Representative; and until such enumeration shall be made, the State of New Hampshire shall be entitled to chuse three, Massachusetts eight, Rhode-Island and Providence Plantations one, Connecticut five, New-York six, New Jersey four, Pennsylvania eight, Delaware one, Maryland six, Virginia ten, North Carolina five, South Carolina five, and Georgia three.

When vacancies happen in the Representation from any State, the Executive Authority thereof shall issue Writs of Election to fill such Vacancies.

The House of Representatives shall chuse their Speaker and other Officers; and shall have the sole Power of Impeachment.

SECTION 3. The Senate of the United States shall be composed of two Senators from each State, chosen by the Legislature thereof, for six Years; and each Senator shall have one Vote. *

Immediately after they shall be assembled in Consequence of the first Election, they shall be divided as equally as may be into three Classes. The Seats of the Senators of the first Class shall be vacated at the Expiration of the second Year, of the second Class at the Expiration of the fourth Year, and of the third Class at the Expiration of the sixth Year, so that one-third may be chosen every second Year; and if Vacancies happen by Resignation, or otherwise, during the Recess of the Legislature of any State, the Executive thereof may make temporary Appointments until the next Meeting of the Legislature, which shall then fill such Vacancies. †

No Person shall be a Senator who shall not have attained to the Age of thirty Years, and been nine Years a Citizen of the United States, and who shall not, when elected, be an Inhabitant of that State in which he shall be chosen.

The Vice President of the United States shall be President of the Senate, but shall have no vote, unless they be equally divided.

The Senate shall chuse their other Officers, and also a President pro tempore, in the absence of the Vice President, or when he shall exercise the Office of the President of the United States.

The Senate shall have the sole Power to try all Impeachments. When sitting for that purpose, they shall be on Oath or Affirmation. When the President of the United States is tried, the Chief Justice shall preside: And no person shall be convicted without the Concurrence of two thirds of the Members present.

Judgment in Cases of Impeachment shall not extend further than to removal from Office, and disqualification to hold and enjoy any Office of honor, Trust, or Profit under the United States: but the Party convicted shall nevertheless be liable and subject to Indictment, Trial, Judgment, and Punishment, according to Law.

SECTION 4. The Times, Places and Manner of holding Elections for Senators and Representatives, shall be prescribed in each state by the Legislature thereof; but the Congress may at any time by Law make or alter such Regulations, except as to the Places of Chusing Senators.

The Congress shall assemble at least once in every

---

* Original spelling, capitalization, and punctuation have been retained.

† Modified by the Sixteenth Amendment.

‡ Replaced by the Fourteenth Amendment.

* Superseded by the Seventeenth Amendment.

† Modified by the Seventeenth Amendment.

Year, and such Meeting shall be on the first Monday in December, unless they shall by Law appoint a different Day.*

SECTION 5. Each House shall be the Judge of the Elections, Returns and Qualifications of its own Members, and a Majority of each shall constitute a Quorum to do Business; but a smaller number may adjourn from day to day, and may be authorized to compel the Attendance of absent Members, in such Manner, and under such Penalties, as each House may provide.

Each House may determine the Rules of its Proceedings, punish its Members for disorderly Behavior, and, with the Concurrence of two thirds, expel a Member.

Each House shall keep a Journal of its Proceedings, and from time to time publish the same, excepting such Parts as may in their Judgment require Secrecy; and the Yeas and Nays of the Members of either House on any question shall, at the Desire of one fifth of those Present, be entered on the Journal.

Neither House, during the Session of Congress, shall, without the Consent of the other, adjourn for more than three days, nor to any other Place than that in which the two Houses shall be sitting.

SECTION 6. The Senators and Representatives shall receive a Compensation for their Services, to be ascertained by Law, and paid out of the Treasury of the United States. They shall in all Cases, except Treason, Felony, and Breach of the Peace, be privileged from Arrest during their Attendance at the Session of their respective Houses, and in going to and returning from the same; and for any Speech or Debate in either House, they shall not be questioned in any other Place.

No Senator or Representative shall, during the Time for which he was elected, be appointed to any civil Office under the Authority of the United States, which shall have been created, or the Emoluments whereof shall have been increased, during such time; and no Person holding any Office under the United States shall be a Member of either House during his continuance in Office.

SECTION 7. All Bills for raising Revenue shall originate in the House of Representatives; but the Senate may propose or concur with Amendments as on other bills.

Every Bill which shall have passed the House of Representatives and the Senate, shall, before it become a Law, be presented to the President of the United States; If he approve he shall sign it, but if not he shall return it, with his Objections, to that House in which it shall have originated, who shall enter the Objections at large on their Journal, and proceed to reconsider it. If after such Reconsidera-

* Superseded by the Twentieth Amendment.

tion two thirds of that House shall agree to pass the bill, it shall be sent, together with the objections, to the other House, by which it shall likewise be reconsidered, and if approved by two thirds of that House, it shall become a Law. But in all such Cases the Votes of both Houses shall be determined by Yeas and Nays, and the Names of the Persons voting for and against the Bill shall be entered on the Journal of each House respectively. If any Bill shall not be returned by the President within ten Days (Sundays excepted) after it shall have been presented to him, the Same shall be a Law, in like Manner as if he had signed it, unless the Congress by their Adjournment prevent its Return, in which Case it shall not be a Law.

Every Order, Resolution, or Vote to which the Concurrence of the Senate and House of Representatives may be necessary (except on a question of Adjournment) shall be presented to the President of the United States; and before the Same shall take Effect, shall be approved by him, or being disapproved by him, shall be repassed by two thirds of the Senate and House of Representatives, according to the Rules and Limitations prescribed in the Case of a Bill.

SECTION 8. The Congress shall have Power To lay and collect Taxes, Duties, Imposts and Excises, to pay the Debts and provide for the common Defence and general Welfare of the United States; but all Duties, Imposts and Excises shall be uniform throughout the United States;

To borrow money on the credit of the United States;

To regulate Commerce with foreign Nations, and among the several States, and with the Indian Tribes;

To establish an uniform Rule of Naturalization, and uniform Laws on the subject of Bankruptcies throughout the United States;

To coin Money, regulate the Value thereof, and of foreign Coin, and fix the Standard of Weights and Measures;

To provide for the Punishment of counterfeiting the Securities and current Coin of the United States;

To establish Post Offices and post Roads;

To promote the Progress of Science and useful Arts, by securing for limited Times to Authors and Inventors the exclusive Right to their respective Writings and Discoveries;

To constitute Tribunals inferior to the Supreme Court;

To define and punish Piracies and Felonies committed on the high Seas, and Offenses against the Law of Nations;

To declare War, grant Letters of Marque and Reprisal, and make Rules concerning Captures on Land and Water;

To raise and support Armies, but no Appropriation of Money to that Use shall be for a longer Term than two Years;

To provide and maintain a Navy;

To make Rules for the Government and Regulation of the land and naval forces;

To provide for calling forth the Militia to execute the Laws of the Union, suppress Insurrections and repel Invasions;

To provide for organizing, arming, and disciplining the Militia, and for governing such Part of them as may be employed in the Service of the United States, reserving to the States respectively, the Appointment of the Officers, and the Authority of training the Militia according to the discipline prescribed by Congress;

To exercise exclusive Legislation in all Cases whatsoever, over such District (not exceeding ten Miles square) as may, by Cession of particular States, and the acceptance of Congress, become the Seat of the Government of the United States, and to exercise like Authority over all Places purchased by the Consent of the Legislature of the State in which the Same shall be, for the Erection of Forts, Magazines, Arsenals, dock-Yards, and other needful Buildings;—And

To make all Laws which shall be necessary and proper for carrying into Execution the foregoing Powers, and all other Powers vested by this Constitution in the Government of the United States, or in any Department or Officer thereof.

SECTION 9. The Migration or Importation of such Persons as any of the States now existing shall think proper to admit, shall not be prohibited by the Congress prior to the Year one thousand eight hundred and eight, but a tax or duty may be imposed on such Importation, not exceeding ten dollars for each Person.

The privilege of the Writ of Habeas Corpus shall not be suspended, unless when in Cases of Rebellion or Invasion the public Safety may require it.

No Bill of Attainder or ex post facto Law shall be passed.

No capitation, or other direct, Tax shall be laid unless in Proportion to the Census or Enumeration herein before directed to be taken.

No Tax or Duty shall be laid on Articles exported from any State.

No Preference shall be given by any Regulation of Revenue to the Ports of one State over those of another: nor shall Vessels bound to, or from, one State, be obliged to enter, clear, or pay Duties in another.

No Money shall be drawn from the Treasury, but in Consequence of Appropriations made by Law; and a regular Statement and Account of the Receipts and Expenditures of all public Money shall be published from time to time.

No Title of Nobility shall be granted by the United States: And no Person holding any Office of Profit or Trust under them, shall, without the Consent of the Congress, accept of any present, Emolument, Office, or Title, of any kind whatever, from any King, Prince, or foreign State.

SECTION 10. No State shall enter into any Treaty, Alliance, or Confederation; grant Letters of Marque and Reprisal; coin Money; emit Bills of Credit; make any Thing but gold and silver Coin a Tender in Payment of Debts; pass any Bill of Attainder, ex post facto Law, or Law impairing the Obligation of Contracts, or grant any Title of Nobility.

No State shall, without the Consent of the Congress, lay any Imposts or Duties on Imports or Exports, except what may be absolutely necessary for executing its inspection Laws: and the net Produce of all Duties and Imposts, laid by any State on Imports or Exports, shall be for the Use of the Treasury of the United States; and all such Laws shall be subject to the Revision and Control of the Congress.

No State shall, without the Consent of Congress, lay any duty of Tonnage, keep Troops, or Ships of War in time of Peace, enter into any Agreement or Compact with another State, or with a foreign Power, or engage in War, unless actually invaded, or in such imminent Danger as will not admit of delay.

ARTICLE II

SECTION 1. The executive Power shall be vested in a President of the United States of America. He shall hold his Office during the Term of four years, and, together with the Vice-President, chosen for the same Term, be elected, as follows:

Each State shall appoint, in such Manner as the Legislature thereof may direct, a Number of Electors, equal to the whole Number of Senators and Representatives to which the State may be entitled in the Congress: but no Senator or Representative, or Person holding an Office of Trust or Profit under the United States, shall be appointed an Elector.

The Electors shall meet in their respective States, and vote by Ballot for two persons, of whom one at least shall not be an Inhabitant of the same State with themselves. And they shall make a List of all the Persons voted for, and of the Number of Votes for each; which List they shall sign and certify, and transmit sealed to the Seat of the Government of the United States, directed to the President of the Senate. The President of the Senate shall, in the Presence of the Senate and House of Representatives, open all the Certificates, and the Votes shall then be counted. The Person having the greatest Number of Votes shall be the President, if such Number be a Majority of the whole Number of Electors appointed; and if there be more than one who have such Majority, and have an equal Number of Votes, then the House of Representatives shall immediately chuse by Ballot one of them for President; and if no Person have a Majority, then from the five highest on the List the said House shall in like Manner chuse the President. But in chusing the President, the Votes shall be taken by States, the Representation from each State having one Vote; a quorum for this Purpose shall consist of a Member or Members from two-thirds of the States, and a Majority of all the States shall be necessary to a Choice. In every Case, after the Choice of the President, the Person having the greatest Number of Votes of the Electors shall be the Vice President. But if there should remain two or more who have equal votes, the Senate shall chuse from them by Ballot the Vice-President.*

The Congress may determine the Time of chusing the Electors, and the Day on which they shall give their Votes; which Day shall be the same throughout the United States.

No person except a natural-born Citizen, or a Citizen of the United States, at the time of the Adoption of this Constitution, shall be eligible to the Office of President; neither shall any Person be eligible to that Office who shall not have attained to the Age of thirty-five years, and been fourteen Years a Resident within the United States.

In Case of the Removal of the President from Office, or of his Death, Resignation, or Inability to discharge the Powers and Duties of the said Office, the same shall devolve on the Vice President, and the Congress may by Law provide for the Case of Removal, Death, Resignation, or Inability, both of the President and Vice President, declaring what Officer shall then act as President, and such Officer shall act accordingly, until the disability be removed, or a President shall be elected.

The President shall, at stated Times, receive for his Services a Compensation, which shall neither be increased nor diminished during the Period for which he shall have been elected, and he shall not receive within that Period any other Emolument from the United States, or any of them.

Before he enter on the execution of his Office, he shall take the following Oath or Affirmation:—"I do solemnly swear (or affirm) that I will faithfully execute the Office of President of the United States, and will, to the best of my Ability, preserve, protect, and defend the Constitution of the United States."

SECTION 2. The President shall be Commander in Chief of the Army and Navy of the United States, and of the Militia of the several States, when called into the actual Service of the United States; he may

require the Opinion, in writing, of the principal Officer in each of the executive Departments, upon any subject relating to the Duties of their respective Offices, and he shall have Power to Grant Reprieves and Pardons for Offenses against the United States, except in Cases of Impeachment.

He shall have Power, by and with the Advice and Consent of the Senate, to make Treaties, provided two thirds of the Senators present concur; and he shall nominate, and by and with the Advice and Consent of the Senate, shall appoint Ambassadors, other public Ministers and Consuls, Judges of the supreme Court, and all other Officers of the United States, whose Appointments are not herein otherwise provided for, and which shall be established by Law: but the Congress may by Law vest the Appointment of such inferior Officers, as they think proper, in the President alone, in the Courts of Law, or in the Heads of Departments.

The President shall have Power to fill up all Vacancies that may happen during the Recess of the Senate, by granting Commissions which shall expire at the End of their next Session.

SECTION 3. He shall from time to time give to the Congress Information of the State of the Union, and recommend to their Consideration such Measures as he shall judge necessary and expedient; he may, on extraordinary occasions, convene both Houses, or either of them, and in Case of Disagreement between them, with respect to the Time of Adjournment, he may adjourn them to such Time as he shall think proper; he shall receive Ambassadors and other public Ministers; he shall take Care that the Laws be faithfully executed, and shall Commission all the Officers of the United States.

SECTION 4. The President, Vice President and all civil Officers of the United States, shall be removed from Office on Impeachment for, and Conviction of, Treason, Bribery, or other high Crimes and Misdemeanors.

ARTICLE III

SECTION 1. The judicial Power of the United States, shall be vested in one supreme Court, and in such inferior Courts as the Congress may from time to time ordain and establish. The Judges, both of the supreme and inferior Courts, shall hold their Offices during good Behaviour, and shall, at stated Times, receive for their Services, a Compensation, which shall not be diminished during their Continuance in Office.

SECTION 2. The judicial Power shall extend to all Cases, in Law and Equity, arising under this Constitution, the Laws of the United States, and treaties made, or which shall be made, under their Authority;—to all Cases affecting ambassadors, other public ministers and consuls;—to all cases of admiralty

* Superseded by the Twelfth Amendment.

and maritime Jurisdiction;—to Controversies to which the United States shall be a Party;—to Controversies between two or more States;—between a State and Citizens of another State; *—between Citizens of different States,—between Citizens of the same State claiming Lands under Grants of different States, and between a State, or the Citizens thereof, and foreign States, Citizens or Subjects.

In all Cases affecting Ambassadors, other public Ministers and Consuls, and those in which a State shall be Party, the supreme Court shall have original Jurisdiction. In all the other Cases before mentioned, the supreme Court shall have appellate Jurisdiction, both as to Law and Fact, with such Exceptions, and under such Regulations as the Congress shall make.

The trial of all Crimes, except in Cases of Impeachment, shall be by Jury; and such Trial shall be held in the State where the said Crimes shall have been committed; but when not committed within any State, the Trial shall be at such Place or Places as the Congress may by Law have directed.

SECTION 3. Treason against the United States, shall consist only in levying War against them, or in adhering to their Enemies, giving them Aid and Comfort. No Person shall be convicted of Treason unless on the Testimony of two Witnesses to the same overt Act, or on Confession in open Court.

The Congress shall have power to declare the Punishment of Treason, but no Attainder of Treason shall work Corruption of Blood, or Forfeiture except during the Life of the Person attainted.

ARTICLE IV

SECTION 1. Full Faith and Credit shall be given in each State to the public Acts, Records, and judicial Proceedings of every other State. And the Congress may by general Laws prescribe the Manner in which such Acts, Records and Proceedings shall be proved, and the Effect thereof.

SECTION 2. The Citizens of each State shall be entitled to all Privileges and Immunities of Citizens in the several States.

A Person charged in any State with Treason, Felony, or other Crime, who shall flee from Justice, and be found in another State, shall on demand of the executive Authority of the State from which he fled, be delivered up, to be removed to the State having Jurisdiction of the crime.

No Person held to Service or Labour in one State, under the Laws thereof, escaping into another, shall, in Consequence of any Law or Regulation therein, be discharged from such Service or Labour, but shall be delivered up on Claim of the

* Modified by the Eleventh Amendment.

Party to whom such Service or Labour may be due.

SECTION 3. New States may be admitted by the Congress into this Union; but no new State shall be formed or erected within the Jurisdiction of any other State; nor any State be formed by the Junction of two or more States, or parts of States, without the Consent of the Legislatures of the States concerned as well as of the Congress.

The Congress shall have Power to dispose of and make all needful Rules and Regulations respecting the Territory or other Property belonging to the United States; and nothing in this Constitution shall be so construed as to Prejudice any Claims of the United States, or of any particular State.

SECTION 4. The United States shall guarantee to every State in this Union a Republican Form of Government, and shall protect each of them against Invasion; and on Application of the Legislature, or of the Executive (when the Legislature cannot be convened) against domestic Violence.

ARTICLE V

The Congress, whenever two-thirds of both Houses shall deem it necessary, shall propose Amendments to this Constitution, or, on the Application of the Legislatures of two-thirds of the several States, shall call a Convention for proposing Amendments, which, in either Case, shall be valid to all Intents and Purposes, as part of this Constitution, when ratified by the Legislatures of three-fourths of the several States, or by Conventions in three-fourths thereof, as the one or the other Mode of Ratification may be proposed by the Congress; Provided that no Amendment which may be made prior to the Year One thousand eight hundred and eight shall in any Manner affect the first and fourth Clauses in the Ninth Section of the first Article; and that no State, without its Consent, shall be deprived of its equal Suffrage in the Senate.

ARTICLE VI

All Debts contracted and Engagements entered into, before the Adoption of this Constitution, shall be as valid against the United States under this Constitution, as under the Confederation.

This Constitution, and the Laws of the United States which shall be made in Pursuance thereof; and all Treaties made, or which shall be made, under the Authority of the United States, shall be the supreme Law of the Land; and the Judges in every State shall be bound thereby, any Thing in the Constitution or Laws of any State to the Contrary notwithstanding.

The Senators and Representatives before mentioned, and the Members of the several State Legislatures, and all executive and judicial Officers, both of the United States and of the several States, shall be bound by Oath or Affirmation to support this Constitution; but no religious Test shall ever be required as a qualification to any Office or public Trust under the United States.

ARTICLE VII

The Ratification of the Conventions of nine States shall be sufficient for the Establishment of this Constitution between the States so ratifying the same.

Done in Convention by the Unanimous Consent of the States present the Seventeenth Day of September in the Year of our Lord one thousand seven hundred and Eighty seven, and of the Independence of the United States of America the Twelfth. In Witness whereof We have hereunto subscribed our Names.

Articles in Addition to, and Amendment of, the Constitution of the United States of America, Proposed by Congress, and Ratified by the Legislatures of the Several States, Pursuant to the Fifth Article of the Original Constitution.

AMENDMENT I *

Congress shall make no law respecting an establishment of religion, or prohibiting the free exercise thereof; or abridging the freedom of speech, or of the press; or the right of the people peaceably to assemble, and to petition the Government for a redress of grievances.

AMENDMENT II

A well regulated Militia, being necessary to the security of a free State, the right of the people to keep and bear Arms shall not be infringed.

AMENDMENT III

No Soldier shall, in time of peace, be quartered in any house, without the consent of the Owner, nor in time of war, but in a manner to be prescribed by law.

AMENDMENT IV

The right of the people to be secure in their persons, houses, papers, and effects, against unreasonable searches and seizures, shall not be violated, and no Warrants shall issue, but upon probable cause, supported by Oath or affirmation, and particularly describing the place to be searched, and the persons or things to be seized.

* The first ten amendments were passed by Congress September 25, 1789. They were ratified by three-fourths of the states December 15, 1791.

AMENDMENT V

No person shall be held to answer for a capital or otherwise infamous crime, unless on a presentment or indictment of a Grand Jury, except in cases arising in the land or naval forces, or in the Militia, when in actual service in time of War or public danger; nor shall any person be subject for the same offence to be twice put in jeopardy of life or limb; nor shall be compelled in any criminal case to be a witness against himself, nor be deprived of life, liberty, or property, without due process of law; nor shall private property be taken for public use, without just compensation.

AMENDMENT VI

In all criminal prosecutions, the accused shall enjoy the right to a speedy and public trial, by an impartial jury of the State and district wherein the crime shall have been committed, which district shall have been previously ascertained by law, and to be informed of the nature and cause of the accusation; to be confronted with the witnesses against him; to have compulsory process for obtaining witnesses in his favor, and to have the Assistance of Counsel for his defence.

AMENDMENT VII

In suits at common law, where the value in controversy shall exceed twenty dollars, the right of trial by jury shall be preserved, and no fact tried by a jury, shall be otherwise reexamined in any Court of the United States, than according to the rules of the common law.

AMENDMENT VIII

Excessive bail shall not be required, nor excessive fines imposed, nor cruel and unusual punishments inflicted.

AMENDMENT IX

The enumeration in the Constitution, of certain rights, shall not be construed to deny or disparage others retained by the people.

AMENDMENT X

The powers not delegated to the United States by the Constitution, nor prohibited by it to the States, are reserved to the States respectively, or to the people.

AMENDMENT XI *

The Judicial power of the United States shall not be construed to extend to any suit in law or equity, commenced or prosecuted against one of the United States by Citizens of another State, or by Citizens or Subjects of any Foreign State.

* Passed March 5, 1794. Ratified January 8, 1798.

AMENDMENT XII *

The Electors shall meet in their respective States and vote by ballot for President and Vice-President, one of whom, at least, shall not be an inhabitant of the same State with themselves; they shall name in their ballots the person voted for as President, and in distinct ballots the person voted for as Vice-President, and they shall make distinct lists of all persons voted for as President, and of all persons voted for as Vice-President, and of the number of votes for each, which lists they shall sign and certify, and transmit sealed to the seat of the government of the United States, directed to the President of the Senate;—The President of the Senate shall, in the presence of the Senate and House of Representatives, open all the certificates and the votes shall then be counted;—The person having the greatest number of votes for President, shall be the President, if such number be a majority of the whole number of Electors appointed; and if no person have such majority, then from the persons having the highest numbers not exceeding three on the list of those voted for as President, the House of Representatives shall choose immediately, by ballot, the President. But in choosing the President, the votes shall be taken by states, the representation from each state having one vote; a quorum for this purpose shall consist of a member or members from two-thirds of the states, and a majority of all the states shall be necessary to a choice. And if the House of Representatives shall not choose a President whenever the right of choice shall devolve upon them, before the fourth day of March next following, then the Vice-President shall act as President, as in the case of the death or other constitutional disability of the President.—The person having the greatest number of votes as Vice-President, shall be the Vice-President, if such number be a majority of the whole number of Electors appointed, and if no person have a majority, then from the two highest numbers on the list, the Senate shall choose the Vice-President; a quorum for the purpose shall consist of two-thirds of the whole number of Senators, and a majority of the whole number shall be necessary to a choice. But no person constitutionally ineligible to the office of President shall be eligible to that of Vice-President of the United States.

AMENDMENT XIII †

SECTION 1.   Neither slavery nor involuntary servitude, except as a punishment for crime whereof the party shall have been duly convicted, shall exist

* Passed December 9, 1803. Ratified September 25, 1804.

† Passed February 1, 1865. Ratified December 18, 1865.

within the United States, or any place subject to their jurisdiction.

SECTION 2.   Congress shall have power to enforce this article by appropriate legislation.

AMENDMENT XIV *

SECTION 1.   All persons born or naturalized in the United States, and subject to the jurisdiction thereof, are citizens of the United States and of the State wherein they reside. No State shall make or enforce any law which shall abridge the privileges or immunities of citizens of the United States; nor shall any State deprive any person of life, liberty, or property, without due process of law; nor deny to any person within its jurisdiction the equal protection of the laws.

SECTION 2.   Representatives shall be apportioned among the several States according to their respective numbers, counting the whole number of persons in each State, excluding Indians not taxed. But when the right to vote at any election for the choice of electors for President and Vice-President of the United States, Representatives in Congress, the Executive and Judicial officers of a State, or the members of the Legislature thereof, is denied to any of the male inhabitants of such State, being twenty-one years of age, and citizens of the United States, or in any way abridged, except for participation in rebellion, or other crime, the basis of representation therein shall be reduced in the proportion which the number of such male citizens shall bear to the whole number of male citizens twenty-one years of age in such State.

SECTION 3.   No person shall be a Senator or Representative in Congress, or elector of President and Vice-President, or hold any office, civil or military, under the United States, or under any State, who, having previously taken an oath, as a member of Congress, or as an officer of the United States, or as a member of any State legislature, or as an executive or judicial officer of any State, to support the Constitution of the United States, shall have engaged in insurrection or rebellion against the same, or given aid or comfort to the enemies thereof. But Congress may by a vote of two-thirds of each House, remove such disability.

SECTION 4.   The validity of the public debt of the United States, authorized by law, including debts incurred for payment of pensions and bounties for services in suppressing insurrection or rebellion, shall not be questioned. But neither the United States nor any State shall assume or pay any debt or obligation incurred in aid of insurrection or rebellion against the United States, or any claim for the loss or emancipation of any slave; but all such debts,

* Passed June 16, 1866. Ratified July 28, 1868.

obligations, and claims shall be held illegal and void.

SECTION 5. The Congress shall have the power to enforce, by appropriate legislation, the provisions of this article.

AMENDMENT XV *

SECTION 1. The right of citizens of the United States to vote shall not be denied or abridged by the United States or by any State on account of race, color, or previous condition of servitude—

SECTION 2. The Congress shall have power to enforce this article by appropriate legislation.

AMENDMENT XVI †

The Congress shall have power to lay and collect taxes on incomes, from whatever source derived, without apportionment among the several States, and without regard to any census or enumeration.

AMENDMENT XVII ‡

The Senate of the United States shall be composed of two Senators from each State, elected by the people thereof, for six years; and each Senator shall have one vote. The electors in each State shall have the qualifications requisite for electors of the most numerous branch of the State legislatures.

When vacancies happen in the representation of any State in the Senate, the executive authority of such State shall issue writs of election to fill such vacancies: *Provided*, That the legislature of any State may empower the executive thereof to make temporary appointments until the people fill the vacancies by election as the legislature may direct.

This amendment shall not be so construed as to affect the election or term of any Senator chosen before it becomes valid as part of the Constitution.

AMENDMENT XVIII §

SECTION 1. After one year from the ratification of this article the manufacture, sale, or transportation of intoxicating liquors within, the importation thereof into, or the exportation thereof from the United States and all territory subject to the jurisdiction thereof for beverage purposes is hereby prohibited.

SECTION 2. The Congress and the several States shall have concurrent power to enforce this article by appropriate legislation.

SECTION 3. This article shall be inoperative unless it shall have been ratified as an amendment to

the Constitution by the legislatures of the several States, as provided in the Constitution, within seven years from the date of the submission hereof to the States by the Congress.

AMENDMENT XIX *

The right of citizens of the United States to vote shall not be denied or abridged by the United States or by any State on account of sex.

Congress shall have power to enforce this article by appropriate legislation.

AMENDMENT XX †

SECTION 1. The terms of the President and Vice-President shall end at noon on the 20th day of January, and the terms of Senators and Representatives at noon on the 3d day of January, of the years in which such terms would have ended if this article had not been ratified; and the terms of their successsors shall then begin.

SECTION 2. The Congress shall assemble at least once in every year, and such meeting shall begin at noon on the 3d day of January, unless they shall by law appoint a different day.

SECTION 3. If, at the time fixed for the beginning of the term of the President, the President elect shall have died, the Vice-President elect shall become President. If a President shall not have been chosen before the time fixed for the beginning of his term, or if the President elect shall have failed to qualify, then the Vice-President elect shall act as President until a President shall have qualified; and the Congress may by law provide for the case wherein neither a President elect nor a Vice-President elect shall have qualified, declaring who shall then act as President, or the manner in which one who is to act shall be selected, and such person shall act accordingly until a President or Vice-President shall have qualified.

SECTION 4. The Congress may by law provide for the case of the death of any of the persons from whom the House of Representatives may choose a President whenever the right of choice shall have devolved upon them, and for the case of the death of any of the persons from whom the Senate may choose a Vice-President whenever the right of choice shall have devolved upon them.

SECTION 5. Sections 1 and 2 shall take effect on the 15th day of October following the ratification of this article.

SECTION 6. This article shall be inoperative unless it shall have been ratified as an amendment to the Constitution by the legislatures of three-fourths of the several States within seven years from the date of its submission.

* Passed February 27, 1869. Ratified March 30, 1870.

† Passed July 12, 1909. Ratified February 25, 1913.

‡ Passed May 16, 1912. Ratified May 31, 1913.

§ Passed December 17, 1917. Ratified January 29, 1919.

* Passed June 5, 1919. Ratified August 26, 1920.

† Passed March 3, 1932. Ratified January 23, 1933.

AMENDMENT XXI *

SECTION 1. The eighteenth article of amendment to the Constitution of the United States is hereby repealed.

SECTION 2. The transportation or importation into any State, Territory, or possession of the United States for delivery or use therein of intoxicating liquors, in violation of the laws thereof, is hereby prohibited.

SECTION 3. This article shall be inoperative unless it shall have been ratified as an amendment to the Constitution by conventions in the several States, as provided in the Constitution, within seven years from the date of the submission hereof to the States by the Congress.

AMENDMENT XXII †

No person shall be elected to the office of the President more than twice, and no person who has held the office of President, or acted as President, for more than two years of a term to which some other person was elected President shall be elected to the office of the President more than once.

But this Article shall not apply to any person hold-ing the office of President when this Article was proposed by the Congress, and shall not prevent any person who may be holding the office of President, or acting as President, during the term within which this Article becomes operative from holding the office of President or acting as President during the remainder of such term.

AMENDMENT XXIII *

SECTION 1. The District constituting the seat of Government of the United States shall appoint in such manner as the Congress may direct:

A number of electors of President and Vice President equal to the whole number of Senators and Representatives in Congress to which the District would be entitled if it were a State, but in no event more than the least populous State; they shall be in addition to those appointed by the States, but they shall be considered, for the purposes of the election of President and Vice President, to be electors appointed by the State; and they shall meet in the District and perform such duties as provided by the twelfth article of amendment.

SECTION 2. The Congress shall have power to enforce this article by appropriate legislation.

* Passed February 20, 1933. Ratified December 5, 1933.

† Passed March 12, 1947. Ratified March 1, 1951.

* Passed June 16, 1960. Ratified April 3, 1961.

Presidential Elections (1789–1900)

Year	Number of states	Candidates	Parties	Popular vote	Electoral vote	Percentage of popular vote
1789	11	GEORGE WASHINGTON	No party designations		69	
		John Adams			34	
		Minor Candidates			35	
1792	15	GEORGE WASHINGTON	No party designations		132	
		John Adams			77	
		George Clinton			50	
		Minor Candidates			5	
1796	16	JOHN ADAMS	Federalist		71	
		Thomas Jefferson	Democratic-Republican		68	
		Thomas Pinckney	Federalist		59	
		Aaron Burr	Democratic-Republican		30	
		Minor Candidates			48	
1800	16	THOMAS JEFFERSON	Democratic-Republican		73	
		Aaron Burr	Democratic-Republican		73	
		John Adams	Federalist		65	
		Charles C. Pinckney	Federalist		64	
		John Jay	Federalist		1	
1804	17	THOMAS JEFFERSON	Democratic-Republican		162	
		Charles C. Pinckney	Federalist		14	
1808	17	JAMES MADISON	Democratic-Republican		122	
		Charles C. Pinckney	Federalist		47	
		George Clinton	Democratic-Republican		6	
1812	18	JAMES MADISON	Democratic-Republican		128	
		DeWitt Clinton	Federalist		89	
1816	19	JAMES MONROE	Democratic-Republican		183	
		Rufus King	Federalist		34	
1820	24	JAMES MONROE	Democratic-Republican		231	
		John Quincy Adams	Independent Republican		1	
1824	24	JOHN QUINCY ADAMS	Democratic-Republican	108,740	84	30.5
		Andrew Jackson	Democratic-Republican	153,544	99	43.1
		William H. Crawford	Democratic-Republican	46,618	41	13.1
		Henry Clay	Democratic-Republican	47,136	37	13.2
1828	24	ANDREW JACKSON	Democratic	647,286	178	56.0
		John Quincy Adams	National Republican	508,064	83	44.0
1832	24	ANDREW JACKSON	Democratic	687,502	219	55.0
		Henry Clay	National Republican	530,189	49	42.4
		William Wirt	Anti-Masonic	33,108	7	2.6
		John Floyd	National Republican		11	
1836	26	MARTIN VAN BUREN	Democratic	765,483	170	50.9
		William H. Harrison	Whig		73	
		Hugh L. White	Whig	739,795	26	49.1
		Daniel Webster	Whig		14	
		W. P. Mangum	Whig		11	
1840	26	WILLIAM H. HARRISON	Whig	1,274,624	234	53.1
		Martin Van Buren	Democratic	1,127,781	60	46.9

Candidates receiving less than 1 per cent of the popular vote have been omitted. For that reason the percentage of popular vote given for any election year may not total 100 per cent.

Before the passage of the Twelfth Amendment in 1804, the electoral college voted for two presidential candidates; the runner-up became Vice-President. Figures are from *Historical Statistics of the United States, Colonial Times to 1957* (1961), pp. 682–83.

Year	Number of states	Candidates	Parties	Popular vote	Electoral vote	Percentage of popular vote
1844	26	JAMES K. POLK	Democratic	1,338,464	170	49.6
		Henry Clay	Whig	1,300,097	105	48.1
		James G. Birney	Liberty	62,300		2.3
1848	30	ZACHARY TAYLOR	Whig	1,360,967	163	47.4
		Lewis Cass	Democratic	1,222,342	127	42.5
		Martin Van Buren	Free Soil	291,263		10.1
1852	31	FRANKLIN PIERCE	Democratic	1,601,117	254	50.9
		Winfield Scott	Whig	1,385,453	42	44.1
		John P. Hale	Free Soil	155,825		5.0
1856	31	JAMES BUCHANAN	Democratic	1,832,955	174	45.3
		John C. Frémont	Republican	1,339,932	114	33.1
		Millard Fillmore	American	871,731	8	21.6
1860	33	ABRAHAM LINCOLN	Republican	1,865,593	180	39.8
		Stephen A. Douglas	Democratic	1,382,713	12	29.5
		John C. Breckinridge	Democratic	848,356	72	18.1
		John Bell	Constitutional Union	592,906	39	12.6
1864	36	ABRAHAM LINCOLN	Republican	2,206,938	212	55.0
		George B. McClellan	Democratic	1,803,787	21	45.0
1868	37	ULYSSES S. GRANT	Republican	3,013,421	214	52.7
		Horatio Seymour	Democratic	2,706,829	80	47.3
1872	37	ULYSSES S. GRANT	Republican	3,596,745	286	55.6
		Horace Greeley	Democratic	2,843,446	*	43.9
1876	38	RUTHERFORD B. HAYES	Republican	4,036,572	185	48.0
		Samuel J. Tilden	Democratic	4,284,020	184	51.0
1880	38	JAMES A. GARFIELD	Republican	4,453,295	214	48.5
		Winfield S. Hancock	Democratic	4,414,082	155	48.1
		James B. Weaver	Greenback-Labor	308,578		3.4
1884	38	GROVER CLEVELAND	Democratic	4,879,507	219	48.5
		James G. Blaine	Republican	4,850,293	182	48.2
		Benjamin F. Butler	Greenback-Labor	175,370		1.8
		John P. St. John	Prohibition	150,369		1.5
1888	38	BENJAMIN HARRISON	Republican	5,447,129	233	47.9
		Grover Cleveland	Democratic	5,537,857	168	48.6
		Clinton B. Fisk	Prohibition	249,506		2.2
		Anson J. Streeter	Union Labor	146,935		1.3
1892	44	GROVER CLEVELAND	Democratic	5,555,426	277	46.1
		Benjamin Harrison	Republican	5,182,690	145	43.0
		James B. Weaver	People's	1,029,846	22	8.5
		John Bidwell	Prohibition	264,133		2.2
1896	45	WILLIAM MCKINLEY	Republican	7,102,246	271	51.1
		William J. Bryan	Democratic	6,492,559	176	47.7
1900	45	WILLIAM MCKINLEY	Republican	7,218,491	292	51.7
		William J. Bryan	Democratic; Populist	6,356,734	155	45.5
		John C. Woolley	Prohibition	208,914		1.5

* Greeley died shortly after the election; the electors supporting him then divided their votes among minor candidates.

Candidates receiving less than 1 per cent of the popular vote have been omitted. For that reason the percentage of popular vote given for any election year may not total 100 per cent.

Presidential Elections (1904–1960)

Year	Number of states	Candidates	Parties	Popular vote	Electoral vote	Percentage of popular vote
1904	45	THEODORE ROOSEVELT	Republican	7,628,461	336	57.4
		Alton B. Parker	Democratic	5,084,223	140	37.6
		Eugene V. Debs	Socialist	402,283		3.0
		Silas C. Swallow	Prohibition	258,536		1.9
1908	46	WILLIAM H. TAFT	Republican	7,675,320	321	51.6
		William J. Bryan	Democratic	6,412,294	162	43.1
		Eugene V. Debs	Socialist	420,793		2.8
		Eugene W. Chafin	Prohibition	253,840		1.7
1912	48	WOODROW WILSON	Democratic	6,296,547	435	41.9
		Theodore Roosevelt	Progressive	4,118,571	88	27.4
		William H. Taft	Republican	3,486,720	8	23.2
		Eugene V. Debs	Socialist	900,672		6.0
		Eugene W. Chafin	Prohibition	206,275		1.4
1916	48	WOODROW WILSON	Democratic	9,127,695	277	49.4
		Charles E. Hughes	Republican	8,533,507	254	46.2
		A. L. Benson	Socialist	585,113		3.2
		J. Frank Hanly	Prohibition	220,506		1.2
1920	48	WARREN G. HARDING	Republican	16,143,407	404	60.4
		James M. Cox	Democratic	9,130,328	127	34.2
		Eugene V. Debs	Socialist	919,799		3.4
		P. P. Christensen	Farmer-Labor	265,411		1.0
1924	48	CALVIN COOLIDGE	Republican	15,718,211	382	54.0
		John W. Davis	Democratic	8,385,283	136	28.8
		Robert M. La Follette	Progressive	4,831,289	13	16.6
1928	48	HERBERT C. HOOVER	Republican	21,391,993	444	58.2
		Alfred E. Smith	Democratic	15,016,169	87	40.9
1932	48	FRANKLIN D. ROOSEVELT	Democratic	22,809,638	472	57.4
		Herbert C. Hoover	Republican	15,758,901	59	39.7
		Norman Thomas	Socialist	881,951		2.2
1936	48	FRANKLIN D. ROOSEVELT	Democratic	27,752,869	523	60.8
		Alfred M. Landon	Republican	16,674,665	8	36.5
		William Lemke	Union	882,479		1.9
1940	48	FRANKLIN D. ROOSEVELT	Democratic	27,307,819	449	54.8
		Wendell L. Willkie	Republican	22,321,018	82	44.8
1944	48	FRANKLIN D. ROOSEVELT	Democratic	25,606,585	432	53.5
		Thomas E. Dewey	Republican	22,014,745	99	46.0
1948	48	HARRY S. TRUMAN	Democratic	24,105,812	303	49.5
		Thomas E. Dewey	Republican	21,970,065	189	45.1
		J. Strom Thurmond	States' Rights	1,169,063	39	2.4
		Henry A. Wallace	Progressive	1,157,172		2.4
1952	48	DWIGHT D. EISENHOWER	Republican	33,936,234	442	55.1
		Adlai E. Stevenson	Democratic	27,314,992	89	44.4
1956	48	DWIGHT D. EISENHOWER	Republican	35,590,472	457	57.6
		Adlai E. Stevenson	Democratic	26,022,752	73	42.1
1960	50	JOHN F. KENNEDY	Democratic	34,227,096	303	49.9
		Richard M. Nixon	Republican	34,108,546	219	49.6

Candidates receiving less than 1 per cent of the popular vote have been omitted. For that reason the percentage of popular vote given for any election year may not total 100 per cent.

Admission of States

Order of admission	State	Date of admission	Order of admission	State	Date of admission
1	Delaware	December 7, 1787	26	Michigan	January 26, 1837
2	Pennsylvania	December 12, 1787	27	Florida	March 3, 1845
3	New Jersey	December 18, 1787	28	Texas	December 29, 1845
4	Georgia	January 2, 1788	29	Iowa	December 28, 1846
5	Connecticut	January 9, 1788	30	Wisconsin	May 29, 1848
6	Massachusetts	February 6, 1788	31	California	September 9, 1850
7	Maryland	April 28, 1788	32	Minnesota	May 11, 1858
8	South Carolina	May 23, 1788	33	Oregon	February 14, 1859
9	New Hampshire	June 21, 1788	34	Kansas	January 29, 1861
10	Virginia	June 25, 1788	35	West Virginia	June 20, 1863
11	New York	July 26, 1788	36	Nevada	October 31, 1864
12	North Carolina	November 21, 1789	37	Nebraska	March 1, 1867
13	Rhode Island	May 29, 1790	38	Colorado	August 1, 1876
14	Vermont	March 4, 1791	39	North Dakota	November 2, 1889
15	Kentucky	June 1, 1792	40	South Dakota	November 2, 1889
16	Tennessee	June 1, 1796	41	Montana	November 8, 1889
17	Ohio	March 1, 1803	42	Washington	November 11, 1889
18	Louisiana	April 30, 1812	43	Idaho	July 3, 1890
19	Indiana	December 11, 1816	44	Wyoming	July 10, 1890
20	Mississippi	December 10, 1817	45	Utah	January 4, 1896
21	Illinois	December 3, 1818	46	Oklahoma	November 16, 1907
22	Alabama	December 14, 1819	47	New Mexico	January 6, 1912
23	Maine	March 15, 1820	48	Arizona	February 14, 1912
24	Missouri	August 10, 1821	49	Alaska	January 3, 1959
25	Arkansas	June 15, 1836	50	Hawaii	August 21, 1959

Population of the United States (1790-1961)

Year	Total population (in thousands)	Number per square mile of land area (continental United States)	Year	Total population (in thousands)	Number per square mile of land area (continental United States)
1790	3,929	4.5	1833	14,162	
1791	4,056		1834	14,582	
1792	4,194		1835	15,003	
1793	4,332		1836	15,423	
1794	4,469		1837	15,843	
1795	4,607		1838	16,264	
1796	4,745		1839	16,684	
1797	4,883		1840	17,120	9.8
1798	5,021		1841	17,733	
1799	5,159		1842	18,345	
1800	5,297	6.1	1843	18,957	
1801	5,486		1844	19,569	
1802	5,679		1845	20,182	
1803	5,872		1846	20,794	
1804	5,065		1847	21,406	
1805	6,258		1848	22,018	
1806	6,451		1849	22,631	
1807	6,644		1850	23,261	7.9
1808	6,838		1851	24,086	
1809	7,031		1852	24,911	
1810	7,224	4.3	1853	25,736	
1811	7,460		1854	26,561	
1812	7,700		1855	27,386	
1813	7,939		1856	28,212	
1814	8,179		1857	29,037	
1815	8,419		1858	29,862	
1816	8,659		1859	30,687	
1817	8,899		1860	31,513	10.6
1818	9,139		1861	32,351	
1819	9,379		1862	33,188	
1820	9,618	5.6	1863	34,026	
1821	9,939		1864	34,863	
1822	10,268		1865	35,701	
1823	10,596		1866	36,538	
1824	10,924		1867	37,376	
1825	11,252		1868	38,213	
1826	11,580		1869	39,051	
1827	11,909		1870	39,905	13.4
1828	12,237		1871	40,938	
1829	12,565		1872	41,972	
1830	12,901	7.4	1873	43,006	
1831	13,321		1874	44,040	
1832	13,742		1875	45,073	

Figures are from *Historical Statistics of the United States, Colonial Times to 1957* (1961), pp. 7, 8.

Year	Total population (in thousands)	Number per square mile of land area (continental United States)	Year	Total population (in thousands)	Number per square mile of land area (continental United States)
1876	46,107		1919	105,063	
1877	47,141		1920	106,466	35.6
1878	48,174		1921	108,541	
1879	49,208		1922	110,055	
1880	50,262	16.9	1923	111,950	
1881	51,542		1924	114,113	
1882	52,821		1925	115,832	
1883	54,100		1926	117,399	
1884	55,379		1927	119,038	
1885	56,658		1928	120,501	
1886	57,938		1929	121,770	
1887	59,217		1930	123,188	41.2
1888	60,496		1931	124,149	
1889	61,775		1932	124,949	
1890	63,056	21.2	1933	125,690	
1891	64,361		1934	126,485	
1892	65,666		1935	127,362	
1893	66,970		1936	128,181	
1894	68,275		1937	128,961	
1895	69,580		1938	129,969	
1896	70,885		1939	131,028	
1897	72,189		1940	132,122	44.2
1898	73,494		1941	133,402	
1899	74,799		1942	134,860	
1900	76,094	25.6	1943	136,739	
1901	77,585		1944	138,397	
1902	79,160		1945	139,928	
1903	80,632		1946	141,389	
1904	82,165		1947	144,126	
1905	83,820		1948	146,631	
1906	85,437		1949	149,188	
1907	87,000		1950	151,683	50.7
1908	88,709		1951	154,360	
1909	90,492		1952	157,028	
1910	92,407	31.0	1953	159,636	
1911	93,868		1954	162,417	
1912	95,331		1955	165,270	
1913	97,227		1956	168,174	
1914	99,118		1957	171,229	
1915	100,549		1958	174,057	
1916	101,966		1959	177,131	
1917	103,414		1960	179,323	59.9
1918	104,550		1961	182,953	

Presidents, Vice-Presidents, and Cabinet Members (1789–1841)

President	Vice-President	Secretary of State	Secretary of Treasury	Secretary of War
George Washington 1789–97	John Adams 1789–97	Thomas Jefferson 1789–94 Edmund Randolph 1794–95 Timothy Pickering 1795–97	Alexander Hamilton 1789–95 Oliver Wolcott 1795–97	Henry Knox 1789–95 Timothy Pickering 1795–96 James McHenry 1796–97
John Adams 1797–1801	Thomas Jefferson 1797–1801	Timothy Pickering 1797–1800 John Marshall 1800–01	Oliver Wolcott 1797–1801 Samuel Dexter 1801	James McHenry 1797–1800 John Marshall 1800 Samuel Dexter 1800–01 Roger Griswold 1801
Thomas Jefferson 1801–09	Aaron Burr 1801–05 George Clinton 1805–09	James Madison 1801–09	Samuel Dexter 1801 Albert Gallatin 1801–09	Henry Dearborn 1801–09
James Madison 1809–17	George Clinton 1809–13 Elbridge Gerry 1813–17	Robert Smith 1809–11 James Monroe 1811–17	Albert Gallatin 1809–14 George Campbell 1814 Alexander Dallas 1814–16 William Crawford 1816–17	William Eustis 1809–13 John Armstrong 1813–14 James Monroe 1814–15 William Crawford 1815–17
James Monroe 1817–25	Daniel D. Tompkins 1817–25	John Quincy Adams 1817–25	William Crawford 1817–25	Isaac Shelby 1817 George Graham 1817 John C. Calhoun 1817–25
John Quincy Adams 1825–29	John C. Calhoun 1825–29	Henry Clay 1825–29	Richard Rush 1825–29	James Barbour 1825–28 Peter B. Porter 1828–29
Andrew Jackson 1829–37	John C. Calhoun 1829–33 Martin Van Buren 1833–37	Martin Van Buren 1829–31 Edward Livingston 1831–33 Louis McLane 1833–34 John Forsyth 1834–37	Samuel Ingham 1829–31 Louis McLane 1831–33 William Duane 1833 Roger B. Taney 1833–34 Levi Woodbury 1834–37	John H. Eaton 1829–31 Lewis Cass 1831–37 Benjamin Butler 1837
Martin Van Buren 1837–41	Richard M. Johnson 1837–41	John Forsyth 1837–41	Levi Woodbury 1837–41	Joel R. Poinsett 1837–41
William H. Harrison 1841	John Tyler 1841	Daniel Webster 1841	Thomas Ewing 1841	John Bell 1841

Secretary of Navy	Postmaster General	Attorney General
	Samuel Osgood 1789–91 Timothy Pickering 1791–95 Joseph Habersham 1795–97	Edmund Randolph 1789–94 William Bradford 1794–95 Charles Lee 1795–97
Benjamin Stoddert 1798–1801	Joseph Habersham 1797–1801	Charles Lee 1797–1801 Theodore Parsons 1801
Benjamin Stoddert 1801 Robert Smith 1801–05 Jacob Crowninshield 1805–09	Joseph Habersham 1801 Gideon Granger 1801–09	Levi Lincoln 1801–05 Robert Smith 1805 John Breckinridge 1805–07 Caesar Rodney 1807–09
Paul Hamilton 1809–13 William Jones 1813–14 B. Crowninshield 1814–17	Gideon Granger 1809–14 Return Meigs 1814–17	Caesar Rodney 1809–11 William Pinckney 1811–14 Richard Rush 1814–17
B. Crowninshield 1817–18 Smith Thompson 1818–23 Samuel Southard 1823–25	Return Meigs 1817–23 John McLean 1823–25	Richard Rush 1817 William Wirt 1817–25
Samuel Southard 1825–29	John McLean 1825–29	William Wirt 1825–29
John Branch 1829–31 Levi Woodbury 1831–34 Mahlon Dickerson 1834–37	William Barry 1829–35 Amos Kendall 1835–37	John M. Berrien 1829–31 Roger B. Taney 1831–33 Benjamin Butler 1833–37
Mahlon Dickerson 1837–38 James K. Paulding 1838–41	Amos Kendall 1837–40 John M. Niles 1840–41	Benjamin Butler 1837–38 Felix Grundy 1838–40 Henry D. Gilpin 1840–41
George E. Badger 1841	Francis Granger 1841	John J. Crittenden 1841

Presidents, Vice-Presidents, and Cabinet Members (1841–81)

President	Vice-President	Secretary of State	Secretary of Treasury	Secretary of War
John Tyler 1841–45		Daniel Webster 1841–43 Hugh S. Legaré 1843 Abel P. Upshur 1843–44 John C. Calhoun 1844–45	Thomas Ewing 1841 Walter Forward 1841–43 John C. Spencer 1843–44 George M. Bibb 1844–45	John Bell 1841 John McLean 1841 John C. Spencer 1841–43 James M. Porter 1843–44 William Wilkins 1844–45
James K. Polk 1845–49	George M. Dallas 1845–49	James Buchanan 1845–49	Robert J. Walker 1845–49	William L. Marcy 1845–49
Zachary Taylor 1849–50	Millard Fillmore 1849–50	John M. Clayton 1849–50	William M. Meredith 1849–50	George W. Crawford 1849–50
Millard Fillmore 1850–53		Daniel Webster 1850–52 Edward Everett 1852–53	Thomas Corwin 1850–53	Charles M. Conrad 1850–53
Franklin Pierce 1853–57	William R. King 1853–57	William L. Marcy 1853–57	James Guthrie 1853–57	Jefferson Davis 1853–57
James Buchanan 1857–61	John C. Breckinridge 1857–61	Lewis Cass 1857–60 Jeremiah S. Black 1860–61	Howell Cobb 1857–60 Philip F. Thomas 1860–61 John A. Dix 1861	John B. Floyd 1857–61 Joseph Holt 1861
Abraham Lincoln 1861–65	Hannibal Hamlin 1861–65 Andrew Johnson 1865	William H. Seward 1861–65	Salmon P. Chase 1861–64 William P. Fessenden 1864–65 Hugh McCulloch 1865	Simon Cameron 1861–62 Edwin M. Stanton 1862–65
Andrew Johnson 1865–69		William H. Seward 1865–69	Hugh McCulloch 1865–69	Edwin M. Stanton 1865–67 Ulysses S. Grant 1867–68 Lorenzo Thomas 1868 John M. Schofield 1868–69
Ulysses S. Grant 1869–77	Schuyler Colfax 1869–73 Henry Wilson 1873–77	Elihu B. Washburne 1869 Hamilton Fish 1869–77	George S. Boutwell 1869–73 William A. Richardson 1873–74 Benjamin H. Bristow 1874–76 Lot M. Morrill 1876–77	John A. Rawlins 1869 William T. Sherman 1869 William W. Belknap 1869–76 Alphonso Taft 1876 James D. Cameron 1876–77
Rutherford B. Hayes 1877–81	William A. Wheeler 1877–81	William M. Evarts 1877–81	John Sherman 1877–81	George W. McCrary 1877–79 Alexander Ramsey 1879–81

Secretary of Navy	Postmaster General	Attorney General	Secretary of Interior
George E. Badger 1841 Abel P. Upshur 1841–43 David Henshaw 1843–44 Thomas Gilmer 1844 John Y. Mason 1844–45	Francis Granger 1841 Charles A. Wickliffe 1841–45	John J. Crittenden 1841 Hugh S. Legaré 1841–43 John Nelson 1843–45	
George Bancroft 1845–46 John Y. Mason 1845–49	Cave Johnson 1845–49	John Y. Mason 1845–46 Nathan Clifford 1846–48 Isaac Toucey 1848–49	
William B. Preston 1849–50	Jacob Collamer 1849–50	Reverdy Johnson 1849–50	Thomas Ewing 1849–50
William A. Graham 1850–52 John P. Kennedy 1852–53	Nathan K. Hall 1850–52 Sam D. Hubbard 1852–53	John J. Crittenden 1850–53	A. H. H. Stuart 1850–53
James C. Dobbin 1853–57	James Campbell 1853–57	Caleb Cushing 1853–57	R. McClelland 1853–57
Isaac Toucey 1857–61	Aaron V. Brown 1857–59 Joseph Holt 1859–61	Jeremiah S. Black 1857–60 Edwin M. Stanton 1860–61	Jacob Thompson 1857–61
Gideon Welles 1861–65	Horatio King 1861 Montgomery Blair 1861–64 William Dennison 1864–65	Edward Bates 1861–63 Titian J. Coffey 1863–64 James Speed 1864–65	Caleb B. Smith 1861–63 John P. Usher 1863–65
Gideon Welles 1865–69	William Dennison 1865–66 Alexander Randall 1866–69	James Speed 1865–66 Henry Stanbery 1866–68 William M. Evarts 1868–69	John P. Usher 1865 James Harlan 1865–66 O. H. Browning 1866–69
Adolph E. Borie 1869 George M. Robeson 1869–77	John A. J. Creswell 1869–74 James W. Marshall 1874 Marshall Jewell 1874–76 James N. Tyner 1876–77	Ebenezer R. Hoar 1869–70 Amos T. Akerman 1870–71 G. H. Williams 1871–75 Edward Pierrepont 1875–76 Alphonso Taft 1876–77	Jacob D. Cox 1869–70 Columbus Delano 1870–75 Zachary Chandler 1875–77
R. W. Thompson 1877–81 Nathan Goff, Jr. 1881	David M. Key 1877–80 Horace Maynard 1880–81	Charles Devens 1877–81	Carl Schurz 1877–81

Presidents, Vice-Presidents, and Cabinet Members (1881–1933)

President	Vice-President	Secretary of State	Secretary of Treasury	Secretary of War	Secretary of Navy
James A. Garfield 1881	Chester A. Arthur 1881	James G. Blaine 1881	William Windom 1881	Robert T. Lincoln 1881	William H. Hunt 1881
Chester A. Arthur 1881–85		F. T. Frelinghuysen 1881–85	Charles J. Folger 1881–84 Walter Q. Gresham 1884 Hugh McCulloch 1884–85	Robert T. Lincoln 1881–85	William E. Chandler 1881–85
Grover Cleveland 1885–89	T. A. Hendricks 1885–89	Thomas F. Bayard 1885–89	Daniel Manning 1885–87 Charles S. Fairchild 1887–89	William C. Endicott 1885–89	William C. Whitney 1885–89
Benjamin Harrison 1889–93	Levi P. Morton 1889–93	James G. Blaine 1889–92 John W. Foster 1892–93	William Windom 1889–91 Charles Foster 1891–93	Redfield Procter 1889–91 Stephen B. Elkins 1891–93	Benjamin F. Tracy 1889–93
Grover Cleveland 1893–97	Adlai E. Stevenson 1893–97	Walter Q. Gresham 1893–95 Richard Olney 1895–97	John G. Carlisle 1893–97	Daniel S. Lamont 1893–97	Hilary A. Herbert 1893–97
William McKinley 1897–1901	Garret A. Hobart 1897–1901 Theodore Roosevelt 1901	John Sherman 1897–98 William R. Day 1898 John Hay 1898–1901	Lyman J. Gage 1897–1901	Russell A. Alger 1897–99 Elihu Root 1899–1901	John D. Long 1897–1901
Theodore Roosevelt 1901–09	Charles Fairbanks 1905–09	John Hay 1901–05 Elihu Root 1905–09 Robert Bacon 1909	Lyman J. Gage 1901–02 Leslie M. Shaw 1902–07 George B. Cortelyou 1907–09	Elihu Root 1901–04 William H. Taft 1904–08 Luke E. Wright 1908–09	John D. Long 1901–02 William H. Moody 1902–04 Paul Morton 1904–05 Charles J. Bonaparte 1905–07 Victor H. Metcalf 1907–08 T. H. Newberry 1908–09
William H. Taft 1909–13	James S. Sherman 1909–13	Philander C. Knox 1909–13	Franklin MacVeagh 1909–13	Jacob M. Dickinson 1909–11 Henry L. Stimson 1911–13	George von L. Meyer 1909–13
Woodrow Wilson 1913–21	Thomas R. Marshall 1913–21	William J. Bryan 1913–15 Robert Lansing 1915–20 Bainbridge Colby 1920–21	William G. McAdoo 1913–19 Carter Glass 1919–20 David F. Houston 1920–21	Lindley M. Garrison 1913–16 Newton D. Baker 1916–21	Josephus Daniels 1913–21
Warren G. Harding 1921–23	Calvin Coolidge 1921–23	Charles E. Hughes 1921–23	Andrew W. Mellon 1921–23	John W. Weeks 1921–23	Edwin Denby 1921–23
Calvin Coolidge 1923–29	Charles G. Dawes 1925–29	Charles E. Hughes 1923–25 Frank B. Kellogg 1925–29	Andrew W. Mellon 1923–29	John W. Weeks 1923–25 Dwight F. Davis 1925–29	Edwin Denby 1923–24 Curtis D. Wilbur 1924–29
Herbert C. Hoover 1929–33	Charles Curtis 1929–33	Henry L. Stimson 1929–33	Andrew W. Mellon 1929–32 Ogden L. Mills 1932–33	James W. Good 1929 Patrick J. Hurley 1929–33	Charles F. Adams 1929–33

Postmaster General	Attorney General	Secretary of Interior	Secretary of Agriculture	Secretary of Commerce and Labor	
Thomas L. James 1881	Wayne MacVeagh 1881	S. J. Kirkwood 1881			
Timothy O. Howe 1881–83 Walter Q. Gresham 1883–84 Frank Hatton 1884–85	B. H. Brewster 1881–85	Henry M. Teller 1881–85			
William F. Vilar 1885–88 Don M. Dickinson 1888–89	A. H. Garland 1885–89	L. Q. C. Lamar 1885–88 William F. Vilas 1888–89	Norman J. Colman 1889		
John Wanamaker 1889–93	W. H. H. Miller 1889–93	John W. Noble 1889–93	Jeremiah M. Rusk 1889–93		
Wilson S. Bissel 1893–95 William L. Wilson 1895–97	Richard Olney 1893–95 Judson Harmon 1895–97	Hoke Smith 1893–96 David R. Francis 1896–97	J. Sterling Morton 1893–97		
James A. Gary 1897–98 Charles E. Smith 1898–1901	Joseph McKenna 1897 John W. Griggs 1897–1901 Philander C. Knox 1901	Cornelius N. Bliss 1897–99 E. A. Hitchcock 1899–1901	James Wilson 1897–1901		
Charles E. Smith 1901–02 Henry C. Payne 1902–04 Robert J. Wynne 1904–05 G. B. Cortelyou 1905–07 G. von L. Meyer 1907–09	Philander C. Knox 1901–04 William H. Moody 1904–06 C. J. Bonaparte 1906–09	E. A. Hitchcock 1901–07 James R. Garfield 1907–09	James Wilson 1901–09	George B. Cortelyou 1903–04 Victor H. Metcalf 1904–06 Oscar S. Straus 1906–09	
Frank H. Hitchcock 1909–13	G. W. Wickersham 1909–13	R. A. Ballinger 1909–11 Walter L. Fisher 1911–13	James Wilson 1909–13	Charles Nagel 1909–13	

				Secretary of Commerce	Secretary of Labor
Albert S. Burleson 1913–21	J. C. McReynolds 1913–14 T. W. Gregory 1914–19 A. Mitchell Palmer 1919–21	Franklin K. Lane 1913–20 John B. Payne 1920–21	David F. Houston 1913–20 E. T. Meredith 1920–21	W. C. Redfield 1913–19 J. W. Alexander 1919–21	William B. Wilson 1913–21
Will H. Hays 1921–22 Hubert Work 1922–23 Harry S. New 1923	H. M. Daugherty 1921–23	Albert B. Fall 1921–23 Hubert Work 1923	Henry C. Wallace 1921–23	Herbert C. Hoover 1921–23	James J. Davis 1921–23
Harry S. New 1923–29	H. M. Daugherty 1923–24 Harlan F. Stone 1924–25 John D. Sargent 1925–29	Hubert Work 1923–28 Roy O. West 1928–29	Henry C. Wallace 1923–24 Howard M. Gore 1924–25 W. M. Jardine 1925–29	Herbert C. Hoover 1923–25 William F. Whiting 1925–29	James J. Davis 1923–29
Walter F. Brown 1929–33	W. D. Mitchell 1929–33	Ray L. Wilbur 1929–33	Arthur M. Hyde 1929–33	Robert P. Lamont 1929–32 Roy D. Chapin 1932–33	William N. Doak 1930–33

Presidents, Vice-Presidents, and Cabinet Members (1933–)

President	Vice-President	Secretary of State	Secretary of Treasury	Secretary of War	Secretary of Navy
Franklin Delano Roosevelt 1933–45	John Nance Garner 1933–41 Henry A. Wallace 1941–45 Harry S. Truman 1945	Cordell Hull 1933–44 E. R. Stettinius, Jr. 1944–45	William H. Woodin 1933–34 Henry Morgenthau, Jr. 1934–45	George H. Dern 1933–36 Harry H. Woodring 1936–40 Henry L. Stimson 1940–45	Claude A. Swanson 1933–40 Charles Edison 1940 Frank Knox 1940–44 James V. Forrestal 1944–45
Harry S. Truman 1945–53	Alben W. Barkley 1949–53	James F. Byrnes 1945–47 George C. Marshall 1947–49 Dean G. Acheson 1949–53	Fred M. Vinson 1945–46 John W. Snyder 1946–53	Robert H. Patterson 1945–47 Kenneth C. Royall 1947	James V. Forrestal 1945–47
				Secretary of Defense James V. Forrestal 1947–49 Louis A. Johnson 1949–50 George C. Marshall 1950–51 Robert A. Lovett 1951–53	
Dwight D. Eisenhower 1953–61	Richard M. Nixon 1953–61	John Foster Dulles 1953–59 Christian A. Herter 1959–61	George C. Humphrey 1953–57 Robert M. Anderson 1957–61	Charles E. Wilson 1953–57 Neil H. McElroy 1957–61	
John F. Kennedy 1961–	Lyndon B. Johnson 1961–	Dean Rusk 1961–	C. Douglas Dillon 1961–	Robert S. McNamara 1961–	

Postmaster General	Attorney General	Secretary of Interior	Secretary of Agriculture	Secretary of Commerce	Secretary of Labor	Secretary of Health, Education and Welfare
James A. Farley 1933–40 Frank C. Walker 1940–45	H. S. Cummings 1933–39 Frank Murphy 1939–40 Robert Jackson 1940–41 Francis Biddle 1941–45	Harold L. Ickes 1933–45	Henry A. Wallace 1933–40 Claude R. Wickard 1940–45	Daniel C. Roper 1933–39 Harry L. Hopkins 1939–40 Jesse Jones 1940–45 Henry A. Wallace 1945	Frances Perkins 1933–45	
R. E. Hannegan 1945–47 Jesse L. Donaldson 1947–53	Tom C. Clark 1945–49 J. H. McGrath 1949–53	Harold L. Ickes 1945–46 Julius A. Krug 1946–49 Oscar L. Chapman 1949–53	C. P. Anderson 1945–48 C. F. Brannan 1948–53	W. A. Harriman 1946–48 Charles W. Sawyer 1948–53	L. B. Schwellenbach 1945–48 Maurice J. Tobin 1948–53	
A. E. Summerfield 1953–61	H. Brownell, Jr. 1953–57 William P. Rogers 1957–61	Douglas McKay 1953–56 Fred Seaton 1956–61	Ezra T. Benson 1953–61	Sinclair Weeks 1953–58 Lewis L. Strauss 1958–61	Martin P. Durkin 1953 James P. Mitchell 1953–61	Oveta Culp Hobby 1953–55 Marion B. Folsom 1955–58 Arthur S. Flemming 1958–61
J. Edward Day 1961–	Robert F. Kennedy 1961–	Stewart L. Udall 1961–	Orville L. Freeman 1961–	Luther H. Hodges 1961–	Arthur J. Goldberg 1961–62 W. Willard Wirtz 1962–	A. H. Ribicoff 1961–62 Anthony J. Celebrezze 1962–

Source
of Illustrations

Chapter 1

4: Attributed to Ridolfo Ghirlandajo. Museo Navale, Genoa—Pegli. (No painting of Columbus from life is extant.) **13:** Both illustrations, Rare Book Room, The New York Public Library. **15:** William L. Clements Library. **16:** Arents Collection, The New York Public Library. **22:** Houghton Library, Harvard University (Photograph by Cushing).

Chapter 2

31: Radio Times Hulton. **33:** Museum of the City of New York. **38:** The Historical Society of Pennsylvania (Artist: Francis Place). **42:** Collection of the City Art Museum of St. Louis.

Chapter 3

52: Collection of Edgar William and Bernice Chrysler Garbisch. **54:** The New York Public Library. **57:** Bella C. Landauer Collection, The New York Historical Society. **61:** The Henry Francis du Pont Winterthur Museum. **62:** Yale University Art Gallery, Jonathan Edwards College. **66:** Historical Pictures Service, Chicago. **73:** The Henry Francis du Pont Winterthur Museum (Photograph: Gilbert Ask).

Chapter 4

80: Public Archives of Canada. **81:** William L. Clements Library. **91:** Museum of Fine Arts, Boston. **93:** Stokes Collection, The New York Public Library.

Chapter 5

107: Princeton University Library. **109:** The New York Historical Society. **110:** Radio Times Hulton. **114:** Frick Art Reference Library.

Chapter 6

136: The Metropolitan Museum of Art, Bequest of Charles Allen Munn, 1924. **139:** The Metropolitan Museum of Art, Gift of Henry G. Marquand, 1881.

150: The Henry Francis du Pont Winterthur Museum (Photograph: Gilbert Ask). **153:** Museum of Fine Arts, Boston.

Chapter 7

163: Walker Art Museum, Bowdoin College. **172:** Amherst College. **177:** The Henry Francis du Pont Winterthur Museum. **179:** The Henry Francis du Pont Winterthur Museum (Photograph: Gilbert Ask).

Chapter 8

188: New York City Art Commission. **189:** Frick Art Reference Library. **196:** Cincinnati Public Library. **198:** The Metropolitan Museum of Art, Gift of Mrs. John Sylvester, 1936. **199:** The Metropolitan Museum of Art.

Chapter 9

216: The New York Historical Society. **217:** Mellon Collection, National Gallery of Art. **230:** Chicago Historical Society. **233:** Brown Brothers.

Chapter 10

241: Museum of Fine Arts, Boston. **242–43:** (a) George Eastman House; (b) National Archives; (c) Bettmann Archive. **250:** American Philosophical Society. **251:** The Metropolitan Museum of Art, Gift of I. N. Phelps Stokes, Edward S. Hawes, Alice Mary Hawes, and Marion Augusta Hawes, 1937. **255:** The New York Public Library.

Chapter 11

263: George Eastman House. **266:** Henry E. Huntington Library and Art Gallery. **267:** Stokes Collection, The New York Public Library. **281:** (a) Culver; (b) The Metropolitan Museum of Art, Gift of I. N. Phelps Stokes, Edward S. Hawes, Alice Mary Hawes, and Marion Augusta Hawes, 1937.

Chapter 12

292: Harry Shaw Newman, The Old Print Shop. **295:** The Maryland Historical Society. **296:** Collection of the late Frank R. Fraprie, Boston. **300:** George Eastman House.

Chapter 13

311: Library of Congress. **313:** Museum of the City of New York. **314:** Meserve Collection. **316:** Boston Athenaeum. **318:** Chicago Historical Society. **323:** National Archives.

Chapter 14

329: Library of Congress. **330–31:** The Cooper Union Museum. **332:** The Cooper Union Museum. **334:** Chicago Historical Society. **339:** Library of Congress. **349:** Library of Congress. **351:** Ansco Collection.

Chapter 15

358: Library of Congress. **359:** Ewing Galloway. **360:** Library of Congress. **368:** Library of Congress. **370:** Culver.

Chapter 16

378: National Archives. **381:** Library of Congress. **386:** Cook Collection, Valentine Museum. **390:** Steamboat Photo.

Chapter 17

396: National Archives. **399:** Kansas State Historical Society. **404:** Northern Pacific Railroad. **410:** Library of Congress. **414:** Nebraska State Historical Society.

Chapter 18

421: Minnesota Historical Society. **423:** The New York Historical Society. **425:** Edward Steichen, Collection of the Museum of Modern Art. **427:** Brown Brothers.

Chapter 19

446: Culver. **447:** Culver. **448:** Brown Brothers. **450:** Chicago Historical Society. **461:** Culver. **462:** Brown Brothers.

Chapter 20

472: Library of Congress. **475:** Library of Congress. **487:** Culver. **491:** Library of Congress.

Chapter 21

501: Library of Congress. **504:** The New York Public Library. **507:** National Archives. **511:** National Archives.

Chapter 22

518: Brown Brothers. **524:** Underwood & Underwood. **526:** Culver. **535:** Brown Brothers.

Chapter 23

541: Brown Brothers. **546:** State Historical Society, Wisconsin. **548:** Brown Brothers. **557:** Brown Brothers. **559:** Radio Times Hulton.

Chapter 24

568: National Archives. **570:** Imperial War Museum. **574:** Culver. **579:** National Archives.

Chapter 25

593: Brown Brothers. **594:** United Press International. **595:** Library of Congress. **597:** Culver.

Chapter 26

607: Harvard University Library. **612:** Ewing Galloway. **614:** Brown Brothers. **617:** Brown Brothers. **624:** Bettmann Archive.

Chapter 27

631: United Press International. **634:** Ewing Galloway. **639:** Brown Brothers. **644:** National Archives. **645:** Wide World.

Chapter 28

652: Harris & Ewing. **656:** United Press International. **665:** Wide World. **666:** United Press International. **670:** Library of Congress.

Chapter 29

675: European. **683:** Wide World. **686:** Copress. **690:** Kemsley Picture Service. **691:** Radio Times Hulton. **698:** Wide World.

Chapter 30

710: Robert Capa, from Magnum. **715:** United Press International. **719:** United Press International. **723:** Imperial War Museum. **725:** Sovfoto.

Chapter 31

731: National Archives. **733:** European. **736:** Brown Brothers. **742:** Walter Sanders, from *Life*. **749:** Hank Walker, from *Life*. **750–51:** John Dominis, from *Life*.

Chapter 32

762: Eve Arnold, from Magnum. **768:** European. **778:** Burt Glinn, from Magnum. **779:** United Press International. **784:** Sergio Larrain, from Magnum. **790:** Cornell Capa, from Magnum. **792:** Lynn Pelham, from Rapho-Guillumette.

Index

Boldface numbers refer to maps, charts, or illustrations. When an entry is mentioned both in the text and in the artwork of a single page, the page number is set lightface.

Ericsson, Leif, 4
Erie Canal, **197**, 198, 205, 296
Erie Railroad, 297
Erskine, David, 172
Espionage Act (*1917*), 575
"Essex Junto," 169
Estaing, comte d', 111, 112
Estonia, 689
Ethiopia, 498, 682–83, 696
European Advisory Commission
  (EAC), 720, 721, 722
European Common Market, 787,
  790
European Defense Community
  (EDC), 766
Evans, Oliver, 206
Ewing, Oscar, 746
Executive, 136–37. *See also* President, U.S.
Exploration of New World, 4–8,
  10–13. *See also* individual countries
Export-Import Bank, 677, 735, 782

FBI. *See* Federal Bureau of Investigation
FCC (Federal Communications
  Commission), 775
FPC. *See* Federal Power Commission
FTC. *See* Federal Trade Commission
Factory. *See* Industry
Fair Deal, 761, 738, 746–47
Fair Employment Practices Commission, 704, 738, 744, 746
Fair Labor Standards Act, 668
Fairbanks, Charles W., 527
Fall, Albert B., 602
Fallen Timbers, Battle of, 146
Far East, 509, 534, 535, 536, 683–
  84; and Second World War,
  697–99, 705, 712–16, 722–23,
  764
Farley, James, 692
Farm Security Administration, 717
Farmer-Labor party, 615
Farmers' Alliance, 482–83
Farmers' Holiday Association, 643,
  654
Farmers' Union, 643
Farragut, David Glasgow, 339, 352
Farrell, James T., 803
Fascism, 669, 683
Faubus, Orval, 777
Fauchet, Jean, 146
Faulkner, William, 624, 803
Federal Bureau of Investigation,
  591, 753, 774
Federal Communications Commission, 775
Federal Emergency Relief Act, 656
Federal Farm Loan Act (*1916*), 553
Federal Farm Board, 631, 633, 643
Federal Land Banks, 641
Federal Power Commission, 589,
  630, 775
Federal Reserve Act (*1913*), 552,
  641

Federal Reserve Board, 551, 552,
  553, 599, 601, 622, 632, 633,
  775
Federal Trade Commission, 552,
  553, 599
Federalism, 119, 135–59; neo-,
  185–89
Federalist papers, 132, 133, 143, 190
Federalist party: beginnings of,
  132, 147–48; demise of, 180, 188;
  and Louisiana Purchase, 167;
  and Republican challenge, 147–
  59, 161; and War of *1812*, 173,
  179–80. *See also* National Republican party; Whig party
Feiffer, Jules, 801
Ferdinand II, 5, 9
Fetterman, W. J., 397
Field, Cyrus W., 430
Field, James G., 483
Field, Stephen J., 434
Fillmore, Millard, 280, 282; Administration of, 280–82; and
  American party, 295, 310; and
  Japan trade, 291
Finland, 55, 677, 689, 696, 734
Finletter, Thomas K., 754
Finn, William, 450
Finney, Charles G., 245
First World War, 418, 552, 567–76,
  674, 675, 681, 683, 701, 702, 704,
  708, 786; Armistice of, 570, 577–
  78; casualties of, 570–71; debts
  and reparations of, 618–19, 637–
  38; demobilization after, 588–89;
  entrance of U.S. into, 565; home
  front during, 572–76; initial
  U.S. neutrality in, 557–62;
  military operation of, 569–72;
  and mobilization, 562–65, 567,
  572–73; outbreak of, in Europe,
  557, **558, 560;** Paris Conference
  after, 578–84; treaty ending,
  583–87
Fish, Hamilton, 369
Fisher, Irving, 625
Fisk, Jim, 369, 370
Fisker, John, 432, 498
Fitzgerald, F. Scott, 623–24, 803
Fitzhugh, George, 256, 257
Fitzpatrick, Thomas, 264
Five Forks, Battle of, 353
Five-Power Naval Treaty, 596–97,
  620, 684
Flanders, Ralph, 773
Fletcher, 713
Fletcher v. *Peck*, 191
Florida: acquisition of, 183; and
  expansion, 168, 174, 183; statehood of, 260, 270
Florida, 343
Floyd, John, 229
Flynn, Ed, 717
Foch, Ferdinand, 569
Folk, Joseph W., 452
Food Administration, 573
Food and Agricultural Organization, 735
Food for Peace Program, 788
Forbes, Charles R., 602
Forbes, John Murray, 297

Forbes Road, **197**
Force Act (*1870, 1871*), 367
Ford, Henry, 433, 608, 610, 616
Fordney-McCumber tariff Act, 599
Foreign aid, 740, 788; Marshall
  Plan, 740–41, 743, 744; Point
  Four Program, 746–47, 769, 782.
  See also Lend-lease
Foreign policy: containment policy,
  739–41; current, 788–91; and
  "dollar diplomacy," 544, 618,
  637; in federal period, 143–47,
  154–56; "good neighbor policy,"
  636, 676–77; and imperialism,
  507–11; and internationalism,
  533–37, 553–57, 595–97, 619–20,
  675–76; and isolationism, 495–97,
  620, 739; Jeffersonian, 169–71,
  180–83; "liberation" policy of
  Dulles, 762–65, 782; moral principles in, 553–54, 567, 762–63;
  and neutrality, 557–65, 681, 683;
  and U.S. prestige, 782, 785. *See
  also* Good neighbor policy; Imperialism; Internationalism; Isolationism; National defense
Foreign Relations Committee (Senate), 584, 679, 751
Formosa, 498, 714, 715–16, 720,
  765; and Nationalist government, 738; straits of, 763, 765
Forrest, Nathan Bedford, 347
Forrestal, James, 743, 747
Fort Sumter, 321–322
Foster, William T., 625
Foster, William Z., 589
Founding Fathers, 434, 442, 519
Fourier, Charles, 250
Four-Power Treaty, 596–97
Fourteen Points (Wilson), 577–78
France: and American Revolution,
  109–10, 111–12, 113, 114, 115,
  116; and federal period, 154–57;
  in First World War, 557, 565,
  567, 569, 570, 571, 572, 579–84;
  and Indochina, 167–68; and
  Louisiana Purchase, 165–67; in
  New World, 6, 7, 8, 70–72,
  77–81; in Second World War,
  689, 690, 697, 708–11, 722; and
  Suez crisis, 769–71; Vichy government of, 708, 710, 719; and
  Washington Conference, 596–97
Franco, Francisco, 683, 786
Frankfurter, Felix, 573, 593, 615,
  651
Franklin, Battle of, 352
Franklin, Benjamin, 65, 92, 97,
  106, 115, 116, 240; and Albany
  Congress, 76; biography of, 66;
  at Constitutional Convention,
  128, 131, 135; on freedom of
  press, 65; and French alliance,
  109; on social mobility, 66
Frederick II (king of Prussia), 79
Fredericksburg, Battle of, 345,
  346–47
Free enterprise. *See* Capitalism;
  Laissez-faire policy
Freedman's Bureau, 362
Free-Soil party, 277, 282

Hyde, Arthur, 630, 643
Hyde, Edward, 37

ICC. *See* Interstate Commerce Commission
IWW (Industrial Workers of the World), 575
Iceland, 4, 696, 743
Ickes, Harold L., 652, 655, 695, 739
Illinois Central Railroad, 297
Illinois, statehood of, 185, **186, 195**
Immigration, 19, 25, 34, 36, 55, 356, 410, 670–71; and cities, 445–46, 451; and labor, 282, 292–95, 418, 436–37; and nativist reaction, 294–95, 516, 517, 537; restriction of, 592, 610–11. *See also* Colonization; Frontier
Immigration and Nationality Act (*1952*), 754*n.*
Imperialism, American: early expansionist aims of, 287–88; and Far East, 509, 534, 535; and Hawaii, 289, 508; humanitarian elements in, 502–03; jingoist, 499–500; and Latin America, 287–89, 617–18; and Open Door policy, 534, 535; and Philippines, 508–11. *See also* Frontier; Manifest Destiny; Mexican War; Spanish-American War
Imperialism, European: in American colonial period, 41–48, 79, 82–83; in Asia and Africa, 498–99; in Latin America, 532–33; and Second World War, 697–99, 705, 712–16, 722–23
Incas, 7
Income tax, 332, 369, 490, 541, 575, 599, 652; declared unconstitutional, 488–89
Independence, American, 99–101, 116, 126. *See also* Declaration of Independence; Revolutionary War
Independent party, 384
Independent Treasury Act (*1840*), 232, 235
India, 4, 79, 80, 82, 486, 533, 768, 786
Indiana, statehood of, 185, **186, 195**
Indians, American: and Albany Congress plan, 76–77; collapse of confederation of, 182; and colonialist wars, 69–70; and Europeans, 6–8; government and organization of, 3; in Northwest territory, 124; and Proclamation of *1763*, **84, 85,** 94; and removal policy of Jackson, 220–21; in Revolution, 107, 112; in War of *1812*, **178**; wars of, 145, 147, 174, 176. *See also* individual tribes
Indochina, 498, 697, 698, 767–68
Indonesia, 768–69
Industrial League, 478

Industrial Revolution, 300, 405, 776. *See also* Agriculture; Business; Industry; Technology
Industrial Workers of the World (IWW), 575
Industry, 205–09, 299–302, 356–57, 388–92, 417–40; consolidation of, 428–32; and factory system, 205–07, 435–36; and labor, 207–08, 302, 418; mass production techniques in, 418, 608–09; and natural resources, 417–18; regulation of, 422–23, 527–29, 552, 559, 589, 599. *See also* Business; Trusts
Ingersoll, Robert, 802
Inland Waterways Commission, 529
Inquisition, Spanish, 9
Intellectuals: and analysis of society, 804–05; and New Deal, 671; political role of, 509, 546; protest of, 519–20. *See also* Art; Literature
Internal Security Act (*1950*), 754
International Atomic Development Authority, 735
International Bank for Reconstruction and Development, 721, 735
International Conference of American States: 7th, 677; *8*th, 677; *9*th, 687
International Labor Organization, 735
International Military Tribunal, 733
International Monetary Fund, 721, 735
International Red Cross, 720
International Trade Organization, 735
International War Crimes Tribunal, 733
Internationalism, 594–97, 617–21
Interstate Commerce Act, 423–24, 429, 430, 476
Interstate Commerce Commission (ICC), 391, 424, 523, 528, 542, 589, 641, 779
Intolerable Acts (*1774*), 95–96, 97, 98, 100, 109
Iowa, statehood of, 260, **270**
Iran, 736
Ireland, 34, 55, 97
Irish Pioneer Emigration Fund, 293
Iron Curtain, 737, 740
Iroquois Indians, 70, 76–77, 94, 112
Irving, Washington, 286
Isabella (queen of Spain), 5, 9
Ishii, Kikujiro, 583
Isolationism, 495–97, 620, 739; demise of, 695, 696; post-First World War, 674, 676, 678; pre-Second World War, 680–83, 685, 687, 688–89, 691, 695, 696
Israel, 769–71
Italy, 498, 532, 554, 734, 743; in First World War, 557, 572, 579, 583; invasion of Ethiopia, 682–

83, 697; in Second World War, 689, 701, 710–11, 719, 720; and Washington Conference, 596–97

Jackson, Andrew, 525, 552; Administration of, 217–31; and annexation of Texas, 262; and Bank of United States, 226–30; career of, 218; censure of, 229; and civil service, 214, 219; and constitutional interpretation, 220; and Democratic party, 217–18; fiscal policy of, 222, 226–27, 231; and Florida, 183; force bill of, 225–26; Indian policy of, 220–21; and Indian wars, 178; and internal improvements, 221–22; and nullification, 224–26; and tariff, 222–26; and War of *1812*, 174, 178, 180, 182
Jackson, Clairborne, 327
Jackson, Ed, 612
Jackson, Patrick, 206
Jackson, Robert H., 665, 803
Jackson, Thomas J., 341, 345, 347
Jacksonian democracy, 212–14, 218–20, 248, 269, 432
Jamaica, 31, 38
James I (king of England), 12–13, 16, 18, 19, 21, 25
James II (king of England), 30, 31, 35, 44, 47, 87
James, Henry, 461, 462
James, Marquis, 671
James, William, 509, 519
Jamestown, 13–15, 49, 394, 412
Japan, 498, 507, 530, 679, 683–84, 697–98, 782, 786; in First World War, 564, 579; invasion of Manchuria by, 638–40; occupation of Korea by, 533, 535–36; and Russo-Japanese War, 534–35; in Second World War, 699, 701, 705, 712–16, 719, 720, 722, 726–28, 733–34; and U.S. trade, 291, 536–37, 544, 554; and Washington Conference, 596–97
Japanese Peace Treaty, 762
Jay, John, 115, 122, 125–26, 133, 145–47, 157, 469
Jay's Treaty, 146–47, 151, 154, 170
Jefferson, Thomas, 91, 115, 120, 128, 135*n.*, 159, 447, 462, 550; Administration of, 161–71; and American independence, 97, 101; and Deism, 240; and embargo, 171, 206; and French Revolution, 144; and Louisiana Purchase, 165–68; and Missouri Compromise, 204, 205; and Monroe Doctrine, 194; and neutrality, 144–45; on the presidency, 166; on separation of church and state, 116; on society, 116–17, 142; on state rights, 149; and Tripolitan War, 170; Virginia resolutions of, 157, 173
Jeffersonian democracy, 118, 161–64, 432
Jenks, Jeremiah W., 520

Sylvis, William H., 437
Syria, 770

TVA. *See* Tennessee Valley Authority
Taft, Robert A., 691, 743, 755, 761, 762, 774, 806
Taft, William Howard, 523, 535, 554, 578, 594; antitrust policies of, 544–46; election of, 538; foreign policy under, 544, 555; as governor of Philippines, 531; presidency of, 540–46; and T. Roosevelt's reforms, 540–41; and War Labor Board, 573
Taft-Hartley Act, 743–44, 746, 762
Talleyrand, 154, 155, 166, 167
Tallmadge, James, Jr., 204
Talmadge, T. DeWitt, 453
Tammany Hall, 375, 450, 451, 452, 474, 475, 547, 645
Taney, Roger B., 229, 234; and Dred Scott case, 311–12
Tangku Truce (*1933*), 684
Tanner, James, 479
Tappan, Arthur, 245, 251
Tappan, Lewis, 245, 251, 253
Tarbell, Ida M., 519
Tariff, 139, 186–87, 269, 369, 371, 476–78, 488, 502, 528, 541–42, 550–51, 553, 599, 631, 633, 638, 675, 678
"Tariff of abominations" (*1828*), 216
Taxation, 139, 149–50, 332, 488–90, 541, 575–76, 588, 598, 599, 607, 625, 702–03, 746. *See also* Income tax
Taylor, Edward, 63
Taylor, Frederick W., 608
Taylor, John, 168
Taylor, Maxwell D., 767
Taylor, Zachary, 271, 273–74; Administration of, 277–80; career of, 276–77
Taylor Society, 608
Tea Act (*1773*), 95
Teapot Dome Scandal, 602–03
Technical Cooperation Administration, 747
Technology, growth of, 205–07, 797. *See also* Industry
Tecumseh, 173, 176, 177, 182
Teheran Conference, 720–21
Teller, Henry M., 490, 504
Temperance movement, 246–47
Tennent, Gilbert, 61
Tennessee, statehood of, **148,** 164, 203
Tennessee Coal and Iron Company, 529
Tennessee Valley Authority, 657–59, 691, 735, 761, 775, 805
Tenure-of-Office Act (*1867*), 363–64
"Tertium Quids," 169, 188
Texas: annexation of, 262, 269; Republic of, 262; settlement of, 261–62; statehood of, **270**
Texas and Pacific Railroad, 420
Thailand, 768

Thames, Battle of the, **176,** 177
Third International, 590
Thomas, George H., 331, 338, 350, 352
Thoreau, Henry David, 242, 286, 778
Thurman, Allen G., 477
Thurmond, Strom, 744–45
Thomas, Norman, 669, 695
Tilden, William, 616
Tilden, Samuel J., 375, 376, 377, 472
Tillman, Benjamin, 489
Tippecanoe, Battle of, 173
Tito, Josip Broz, 720, 740, 786
Tojo, Hideki, 698
Tolstoy, Leo, 462
Tories. *See* Loyalists, colonial
Townsend, Francis E., 659, 663
Townshend, Charles, 91–92, 93
Townshend Acts, 91–92, 93, 95; repeal of, 93–94
Trade unions. *See* Labor; Unions, labor
Trading-with-the-Enemy Act (*1917*), 575
Transcendental Club, 242
Transcendentalism, 241–43
Transportation, 197–98, 296–98
Transportation Act, 589
Treaty of Aix-la-Chappelle (*1748*), 74, 76
Treaty of Ghent, 180–82
Treaty of Greenville (*1795*), 146–47
Treaty of Guadalupe Hidalgo, 274–75
Treaty of San Ildefonso (*1800*), 165
Treaty of Tordesillas (*1494*), 6
Treaty of Utrecht, 71, 72
Treaty of Versailles (*1919*), 583, 588, 674, 762; U.S. rejection of, 584–87, 595
Treaty of Wanghia, 290
Tripolitan War, 170
Trist, Nicholas P., 274
Trujillo, Rafael, 782, 789
Truman, Harry S., 705, 717, 760, 762, 769, 771; Administration of, 726–28, 730–34, 736–40, 743–55; and atom bomb, 727–28; career, 730–31; and Eighieth Congress, 743–44; Fair Deal of 746–47; foreign policy of, 763, 739–41, 746–47, 782; on the presidency, 760; problems of, 738–39
Trumbull, John, 127
Trusts: and antitrust laws, 429–30, 524–25, 544, 553, 787; growth of, 429; and panic of *1907*, 529; and T. Roosevelt, 524–25, 544–46; Standard Oil, 429–30; State legislation against, 429; and Taft, 544–46. *See also* Business
Tshombe, Moishe, 788
Tugwell, Rexford G., 626, 651, 654
Tumulty, Joseph P., 550
Tunisia, 498, 710

Turkey, 551, 577, 740, 741, 748
Turner, Frederick Jackson, 200, 411–12
Turner, Nat, 201, 203
Turnpikes, 197
Twain, Mark. *See* Clemens, Samuel L.
Tweed Ring, 367, 375
Twiller, Wouter Van, 34
Tydings, Millard, 753, 754
Tyler, John, 232, 262; Administration of, 234–36, 269, 290

UNESCO (United Nations Educational, Scientific, and Cultural Organization), 735
UNRRA (United Nations Relief and Rehabilitation Administration), 721, 735, 740
U-2 incident, 781, 782
Underdeveloped nations: and communism, 765; foreign aid to, 769
Underground railroad, 254, 283
Underwood, Oscar, 547, 548
Underwood-Simmons tariff (*1913*), 550
Unemployment. *See* Depression; Labor
Union, army veterans of, 466, 476, 479; blockade by, 339–40, 343; and border states, 327–28; mobilization of, for war, 331–34; resources of, 331; victory of, 353. *See also* Civil War
Union of Russian Workers, 591
Union Pacific Railroad, 357, 370
Union party, 352
Union Safety Committee, 282
Unions, labor, 437–40, 516, 525–26, 574, 589–90, 591, 600, 665–66, 703, 739, 743–44, 762, 780. *See also* American Federation of Labor; Congress of Industrial Organizations; Labor
Unitarians, 62, 240–41, 242, 243
United Arab Republic, 780
United Mine Workers (UMW), 525, 665–66, 703
United Nations, 732, 781, 785, 788, 790, 799, 802; charter of, 734; General Assembly of, 734–35; and Korean War, 748–52, 763–64; launching of, 734–35; plans for, 721, 723; Security Council of, 734–35, 736
United Nations Atomic Energy Commission, 735
United Nations Educational, Scientific, and Cultural Organization (UNESCO), 735
United Nations Relief and Rehabilitation Administration (UNRRA), 721, 735, 740
United States v. *Cruikshank*, 379
United States Department of Agriculture, 333
United States Department of Commerce, 525

D 4
E 5
F 6
G 7
H 8
I 9
0